DICTIONARY·OF
Jargon

Jonathon Green

DICTIONARY·OF
Jargon

Jonathon Green

Routledge & Kegan Paul

London and New York

First published in 1987 by
Routledge & Kegan Paul Limited
11 New Fetter Lane, London EC4P 4EE

Published in the USA by
Routledge & Kegan Paul Inc.
in association with Methuen Inc.
29 West 35th Street, New York, NY 10001

Set in Linotron Century 11 on 12 point
by Input Typesetting Ltd, London SW19 8DR
and printed in Great Britain
by R. J. Acford, Chichester

Library of Congress Cataloging in Publication Data

Green, Jonathon.
Dictionary of jargon.

Bibliography: p.
1. English language—Jargon—Dictionaries.
2. English language—Business English—Dictionaries.
3. English language—Technical English—Dictionaries.
4. Worlds, New—English—Dictionaries. 5. English
language—Terms and phrases. I. Title.
PE1689.G73 1987 427   87–4960
ISBN 0–7100–9919–3

British Library CIP Data also available

For Coral Toynbee Huxley, Daisy Leitch
and Jake Marcuson

Contents

Introduction   ix

Acknowledgments   xiii

Abbreviations   xv

Dictionary of Jargon   1

Sources   609

Introduction

This Dictionary is a collection of some 21,000 words and phrases, acronyms and abbreviations that have been collected from the jargons, or professional slangs and verbal shorthands, of a wide variety of occupations. It is an expansion of rather than a sequel to my original effort at such a compilation, *Newspeak*, which appeared in October 1983. For all its expanded size it can be, of course, no more definitive than was its predecessor: the very nature of occupational jargon is that for every occupation there is an 'in-house' vocabulary, and I am loathe to call down lexicographical nemesis by claiming that even in those areas with which I have dealt I have amassed every single pertinent word. Nonetheless I hope that this larger dictionary, while quailing at the concept of absolute comprehensiveness, has put together a more representative selection of these specialised vocabularies than has hitherto been achieved or attempted.

The word 'jargon' derives most immediately from the fourteenth century term for the twittering or warbling of birds, which in turn has the root 'garg' from which also stem such throaty words as 'gargle' and 'gurgle'. Etymologists are also inclined to throw in the Middle English for 'creaking like a cart' and the Anglo-Saxon for 'gnashing the teeth'. The fourteenth century also recognised it as denoting unintelligible or meaningless talk or writing. The definition I have used in this Dictionary emerges in the seventeenth century and is listed in the *Oxford English Dictionary*, which cites Hobbes and Swift in evidence, as 'any mode of speech abounding in unfamiliar terms, or peculiar to a particular set of persons, as the language of scholars or philosophers, the terminology of a science or art, or the cant of a class, sect, trade, or profession'. To many of those who use the word in its contemporary context, it stands in addition for deliberate, baffling and possibly mendacious linguistic obfuscation.

It is the categorisation and definition of such vocabularies that I have attempted here. The jargons included fall into a number of groups. There is no doubt that some are created to confound, based, if only unconsciously, on American President Harry S. Truman's dictum 'If you can't convince them, confuse them'. As I put it in the introduction to *Newspeak*: 'Many of these words are aimed to obscure. The calming tones of soldiers and civil servants connive at glossing over the unpalatable facts of our possible nuclear demise. Politicians mask the facts that catch no votes in some fluent polysyllable. Criminals talk in the most genteel of euphemisms to pass off murder and mayhem . . . And so the list goes on.' Slick terminology is vital to the game.

Yet while some jargons undoubtedly do fall into the area of complexity for its own sake, many others are simply professional shorthands, developed out of convenience rather than cunning. The vocabularies of many heavy industries may additionally be rooted in the regional dialects of the environment in which they developed. Those of more recent occupations tend rather to echo the technological developments with which they have to deal. Many jargons offer an innate humour, culled both from the job itself and the way in which the workers play with its language. On top of this, many of those who use this 'trade slang' do so as much out of their desire to make themselves understood (and accepted) by their peers as to confuse the uninitiated or parade their membership of a select group.

The title of my original dictionary, *Newspeak*, published on the eve of 1984, drew unashamedly on the name George Orwell coined for the new language of 'Ingsoc' and 'Airstrip One'. At least one reviewer suggested that this was a little 'naughty', but while acknowledging the point I would contest that though that compilation may have dealt in a world far different from Orwell's nightmare society, offering vocabularies that soothe rather than censor, and straying far from the rigid propagandisms of *1984*, the areas in which it dealt – the media, the military, new therapies, cult religions and so on – succeeded in conveying something of the linguistic tone of the contemporary world. And if Orwell's 'Room 101' was plucked, as is generally accepted, from the sub-sub-basement of Broadcasting House, then surely his 'Newspeak' draws, if only marginally, from the convolutions of the BBC's nomenclature, a portion of which I included.

The aim of this Dictionary is to embrace a far greater range of occupations and pursuits, each of which offers its own vocabulary. It is approximately three times the size of its predecessor, and I have included many more industrial terms, covered a greater variety of sports, and generally spread a wider net. The vocabulary of jargon is inexhaustible, and as one august and academic body, from which I requested aid, told me: yes, we have lists of words, but they have not been finished and we do not think they ever will be. We have no intention of giving them out. And my correspondent closed this lofty dismissal with the remark that such dictionaries as this were merely 'entertainments'.

As a working lexicographer I lack the luxury of compiling my lists so secretively. That this dictionary is, as it were, 'open-ended', is undeniable. Whether in a further four years it will be expanded once again depends on many factors, but not, certainly, on the lack of evolving material. Thus I offer it as what the computer buffs would call 'state of the art' and not the financiers' 'bottom line'. And if it is indeed entertaining as well as informative then I, and I trust its readers too, will regard that as a gratifying bonus.

JONATHON GREEN
Spring 1987

Acknowledgments

Very many people were concerned in the research and compilation of this dictionary. Some gave one word, others offered several, and the replies to my appeals in magazines both in Britain and America were generous and beyond my most optimistic hopes. Some of these replies, and the jargon they offered, were incorporated in my earlier *Newspeak* of 1983. Since this dictionary is a substantially expanded collection, based on the original compilation, I have re-listed those initial contributors, and added to them everyone who has been in any way concerned, as contributors or as sources of encouragement and advice. My sincere thanks to all involved.

Carl Adkins, Rosemary Atkins, J. E. Begley, Estella Boxell-Hutson, Bernard Boys, Celia H. Brackenridge, Philippa Brewster, Richard Burnell, Nigel Burwood, Richard Cassidy, Andrew Cockburn, Lesley Cockburn, Sidney Cohen MD, Nicholas Cole, Angela Coles, J. R. Columbo, M. Cooper, Christopher Corey, George Darby, Peter Davies, Felix Dennis, Tom Doran, Ron Dorfman, Karen Durbin, Pamela Elsom, E. P. Essery, Quentin Falk, Mick Farren, Dr. Rodney Foale, Susan Ford, Leslie Gardner, Gabriel Green, Lucien Green, Col. J. E. Greenwood USMC (retd.), Harriet Griffey, Annie Hansen, Margaret Hill, Philip Hodson, Thomas S. Holman, David Jenkins, Chris Jones, A. M. Jowett, Marjorie O. Kimberley, Ted Klein, Sophia Lambert, Sam Llewellyn, David L. Lockhard, Derek Lovell, Prof. Colin MacCabe, Quentin MacDonald, Donald Macintyre, Rupert Macnee, Denis MacShane, Pearce Marchbank, Alan Marcuson, Jim Mitchell, Wendy Morris, Dr. Guy Nield, Heather Page, Andrew Payne, William Pennington, Barry Phelps, Alison Phillips, Guy L. Playfair, Stephen Porter, Dick Pountain, Norman A. Punt FRCS Ed. DLO, Robert Race, David Rattray, Barry Rolfe, Harold Ruslander, Prof. Gerald J. Schiffhorst Ph.D., Mike Seabrook, Peter B. Shawhan, John Sheppard, Hazel Thompson, W. E. Tucker, Chris Waagen, David Walsh, Nicholas Weaver, David Whyte, Julyan Wickham, Rose Wild, K. Wilson.

Abbreviations

a:	adjective	phr:	phrase
abbr:	abbreviation	RAF:	Royal Air Force
adv:	adverb	RM:	Royal Marines
Aus:	Australia	RN:	Royal Navy
edn:	edition	Rus:	Russian
eg:	for example	Scot:	Scotland
Fr:	French	Sp:	Spanish
Ger:	German	UK:	United Kingdom
ie:	that is	US:	United States
Ital:	Italian	USAF:	United States Air Force
Jap:	Japanese	USMC:	United States Marine
Lat:	Latin		Corps
n:	noun	USN:	United States Navy
NZ:	New Zealand	v:	verb
obs:	obsolescent	v i:	intransitive verb
past		v t:	transitive verb
part:	past participle	Yid:	Yiddish
pres			
part:	present participle		

A

A battery *n* [*Electronics*] a filament battery; a battery used to heat the filaments or cathode heaters of electron tubes. See also **B battery, C battery**.

A check *n* [*Air travel*] a regular 60 hour check on civil airliners. Landing and anti-collision lights, landing gear, doors, oil level and tyre pressure are all checked; the water system and coffee makers are drained and refilled; oxygen masks, escape systems and life-rafts are also checked. See also **B check**.

A licence *n* [*UK*] [*Road transport*] formal permission under the Road Transport Act (1960) for road transport companies to act as general carriers. An A licence covers those who work for others; it does not license them to carry their own goods. See also **B licence, C licence**.

A&P 1. *n* [*US*] [*Medicine*] abbr of **anatomy and physiology. 2.** *n* [*US*] [*Medicine*] abbr of **anterior and posterior**. See also **A & P repair**.

A & P repair *n* [*Medicine*] abbr of **Anterior and Posterior repair** surgical tightening of the muscles between the vagina and the rectum.

A & R man *n* [*Record business*] abbr of **Artistes and Repertory** (US) or **Repertoire** (UK) **man** a company executive who deals with contracted performers and their material.

A ring *n* [*Military*] the circle of complete destruction that surrounds the detonation point of a major nuclear device.

A shares, also **A stock** *n* [*Stock market*] common, rather than preferential stock.

A side *n* [*Pop music*] the more important side of a 45 rpm single; the side that is intended to enter the pop music charts. Thus a 'double A side' is a record which has equally commercial songs on both sides, eg: 'Strawberry Fields Forever' and 'Penny Lane' (The Beatles, 1967).

A staff *n* [*US*] [*Military*] the officers and other ranks who work for the Adjutant-general, the US Army's chief legal officer.

aa *Lat. abbr* [*Medicine*] a prescription notation meaning 'of each'.

AAA *a* [*Stock market*] said of top rating accorded bonds, given by the US financial rating agencies Standard & Poor's and Moody's.

AAs *n pl* [*Publishing*] abbr of **author's alterations** changes made by the author to the typeset proofs of a manuscript. Depending on the contract, the author is sometimes charged for the cost of carrying out these changes. See also **EAs**.

AB *n* [*Market research, Statistics*] a socio-economic label used to designate the upper and professional middle classes. See also **C1, C2, DE**.

abacus *n* [*Architecture*] the top member of a classical capital; usually drawn square on the plan, but it may have concave sides.

abbott *n* nembutal, a sleeping tablet named for its maker Abbott Laboratories.

abc *n pl* [*UK*] [*Security*] abbr of **alarms by carrier** special alarms that ring in police (and fire) stations, carried on the normal telephone lines at special high frequencies.

ABC 1. *n* [*Air travel*] abbr of **Advance Booking Charter** a cheap air fare available to those who book tickets a certain number of days prior to flying and who will be staying at their destination a certain length of time. **2.** *n* [*Medicine*] abbr of **Airway, Breathing, Circulation** major areas of concern in a medical emergency; thus 'Watch your ABCs'.

ABC agreement *n* [*US*] [*Stock market*] an agreement made between a brokerage firm and one of its employees, which sets out the rights of the firm when it purchases a membership of the New York Stock Exchange for that employee.

ABC art *n* [*Art*] See **minimal art**.

ABC warfare *n* [*Military*] abbr of **Atomic, Biological and Chemical Warfare** battlefield strategies dependant on the full range of weaponry available to modern armies: atomic and latterly nuclear armaments; toxins developed from natural substances, including micro-organisms such as anthrax, which can cause disease and death in human, animal and plant life; artificial agents, including nerve gases, which can be used to disable and kill the enemy.

ABD 1. *a* [*US*] [*Education*] abbr of **All But Dissertation** describing a doctoral candidate who has all the necessary academic credits for a PhD but has yet to write the required dissertation. **2.** *n* [*US*] [*Medicine*] abbr of Abdominal Dressing.

A

Aberdeen booster *n* [*UK*] [*Road transport*] a hypothetical gear ratio in which the vehicle is simply coasting along. See also **Scotsman's fifth**.

aberration *n* [*Photography*] blurrings or distortions in an image caused by the imperfect focussing of light rays through the lens.

ability 1. *n* [*Commerce*] the state of having sufficient funds to meet one's debts. **2.** *n* [*Law*] the right or power to act in a given matter. **3.** *n* [*Taxation*] the concept that the weight of taxes should be related to the income of the taxpayer so that each individual should make a proportionate payment.

ability gap *n* [*Sociology*] an allegedly inherent difference in ability between blacks and whites. The term was coined for a survey published in October 1982 by the US National Opinion Research Center, University of Chicago.

ability grouping *n* [*Education*] the teaching of fast or slow learners in separate groups.

abjective *n* [*Journalism*] an apologetic correction published by a newspaper or magazine to correct a previously published inaccuracy or misleading statement. It is however rare for such apologies to achieve the prominence of the original story unless the complainant's lawyers have stipulated this as a requirement.

able *a* [*Education*] clever, or at least clever enough to achieve a satisfactory academic level. Thus 'less able' is used to refer to pupils whose academic ability is below average.

ABM *n* [*Military*] abbr of **Anti-Ballistic Missiles** a variety of nuclear war technology developed as a potential means of destroying in-coming hostile ballistic missiles by using one's own missiles. The **ABM Treaty** which outlawed such weaponry and which was signed at the end of the **SALT I** talks in 1972 has been the most concrete achievement of any attempts at arms control. The SDI or **star wars** concept, with its theories of allegedly defensive, anti-missile systems, will certainly, if it is ever put into practice, negate that achievement.

ABM Treaty *n* [*Military*] abbr of **Anti-Ballistic Missile Treaty** a treaty signed in 1972 by President Nixon and General Secretary Brezhnev which limited severely both sides' deployment of anti-ballistic missiles and as such put a temporary but vital brake on the arms race; it remains the single most concrete achievement of every round of arms talks to date. The repudiation of the treaty, seriously considered by the Reagan administration, is seen by critics as a disastrous move, although the US would allege that Russia has already violated it sufficiently to render any US changes no more than a fair response.

abnormal *n* [*Philately*] one of the stamps of Great Britain, 1862–1880, printed from certain plates or in certain colours from certain plates, which were not usually issued; only five sheets of these stamps were registered at Somerset House.

abnormal indivisible load *n* [*UK*] [*Road transport*] a load which cannot, without undue expense or risk of damage, be divided into smaller loads for the purpose of carriage on roads and which owing to its weight and dimensions cannot be carried on a vehicle which complies with the C&U regulations.

abnormal termination *n* [*Computing*] the termination of a process because the computer has reached a point of operation from which it cannot continue – usually an undefined instruction which it cannot follow.

abort 1. *n* [*Aerospace*] an unsuccessful mission that has to be cut short. **2.** *n* [*Aerospace*] the emergency separation of a spacecraft from its rocket booster. **3.** *v* [*Aerospace*] to cut short a mission at any stage of launch or flight.

abouts *n pl* [*Metallurgy*] lengths of iron or steel with less variation than random lengths: usually amounting to plus/minus 6".

above 1. *a* [*Gambling*] relating to the earnings of any gambling enterprise that are listed for tax or allied legal purposes. **2.** *a* [*Horse-racing*] used to describe an overfed, under-exercised horse, which has not been trained properly for a given race. **3.** *adv* [*Theatre*] a stage direction that implies 'behind', in relation to either a person or an item of stage furniture. See also **below, downstage, upstage**.

above eight-ninety decision *n* [*US*] [*Communications*] a decision made in 1959 by the Federal Communications Commission (FCC) allowing individual firms to build microwave systems for their own use, at frequencies over 890 MHz. This allowed entities other than AT&T and Western Union to establish communications channels for the first time.

above the line 1. *a* [*Advertising*] referring to any form of advertising for which a commission or fee is payable to a recognised agency operating on behalf of a client. See also **below the line 3. 2.** *a* [*Business*] referring to an account that is in credit. See also **below the line 1. 3.** *n* [*TV*] that part of the basic budget of a production which includes both the direct and indirect costs of the programme, other than any unusual expenditure.

above the market *adv* [*Stock market*] at a price in excess of the normal market quotation. See also **below the market**.

abozzo *n* [*Art*] a preliminary sketch, a rough.

abracadabra *n* [*Aerospace, Military*] acro **Abreviations and Related Acronyms Associated with Defence, Astronautics, Business and Radio-electronics** one of the first listings of space age acronyms originally issued in the 1960s by the Raytheon Company, one of the leading contractors to the space-military establishment in the US.

abreaction channels *n pl* [*Industrial relations*] a management technique that allows dissatisfied employees to let off steam either through

A

answering surveys or through conversations with special counsellors. The term comes from the psychiatric word 'abreaction' meaning an emotional response which helps people to rid themselves of a trauma rather than brooding on it.

absent *a* [*Fencing*] said of any situation when the opposing blades are not actually in contact.

absent rider *n* [*UK*] [*Railways*] a man who has not turned up for duty. The term is taken from horse-racing use, where it refers to a jockey who fails to appear for his ride.

absolute address *n* [*Computing*] the specific location within the computer's memory where a given item of information is stored.

absolute architecture *n* [*Architecture*] a hypothetical system of architecture that would be dictated not by utilitarian requirements but by the taste of the individual architect. The antithesis of **functionalism**, these buildings would be 'pure', non-objective and purposeless.

absolute code *n* [*Computing*] program code written in a form suitable for direct execution by the central processor and therefore containing no symbolic references. See also **machine code**.

absolute dud *n* [*Military*] a nuclear weapon that fails to explode on target.

absolute music *n* [*Music*] self-dependant instrumental music without any literary or other external influences; such music is created with the intention of impressing the listener with the ingenuity of its patterns and the beauty of its intrinsic sound rather than with drawing attention to any non-instrumental references. See also **programme music**.

absolute word *n* [*Literary criticism*] a word that is extreme or categorical in meaning and as such cannot be modified; specifically an adjective or adverb that cannot be further qualified by a false comparative.

absorption **1.** *n* [*Commerce*] the assignment of costs, both fixed and variable, to goods and/or services provided, so that the total costs can be recovered in the selling price. **2.** also **overhead absorption** *n* [*Management*] the process or practice of assigning portions of indirect costs to specific activities, products or cost centres on the basis of general principles rather than a detailed analysis of the actual costs incurred.

absorption costing *n* [*Accounting*] an accounting practice whereby factory costs are allocated to each of the products and services making up the total output of the concern.

abstauben *n* [*Military*] used in the French Foreign Legion to denote anything acquired by irregular means. See also **gizzit**.

abstract expressionism *n* [*Art*] a movement in US painting in the late 1940s and early 1950s which gained many adherents. There were a variety of styles but the overall characteristics included large scale, generally abstract subjects

with some figurative/symbolic elements, asymmetrical composition, and dramatic colour or tonal contrasts. See also **action painting, all over paintings, calligraphic painting, drip painting**.

abstract expressionist sculpture *n* [*Art*] work produced by a number of US sculptors in the late 1950s and early 1960s. These sculptors rejected traditional materials in favour of new media intended to reflect the spontaneity and techniques of **abstract expressionism**. See also **assemblage art, junk sculpture**.

abstract illusionism *n* [*Art*] the tendency of American painting in the mid–1960s to return to illusionism, ie. the use of pictorial devices, orthographic drawing, cold/warm colour contrasts, etc.

abstract impressionism *n* [*Art*] paintings created in the US in the 1950s with a uniform pattern of brush-strokes which retained the optical effects of impressionism while dispensing with its representational content. This contrasted with such contemporary schools as **action painting**, etc.

abstract machine *n* [*Computing*] a conceptual machine created simply to prove the properties of programs. This enables a number of unnecessary details to be suppressed for the purpose of the tests, unlike a real machine which would require these details to be retained.

abstract sublime *n* [*Art*] a term coined by Robert Rosenblum in 1961 to describe the work of the abstract expressionists: Jackson Pollock, Barnett Newman, Mark Rothko and Clifford Still.

abstracted empiricism *n* [*Sociology*] the concept of accumulating abstract data simply for its own sake.

abusive dosage *n* [*Medicine*] the amount of a recreational drug required to produce the actions and effects desired by its user; so-called because by the time this amount has been taken, it is usually toxic.

abusive tax shelter *n* [*US*] [*Economics*] a limited partnership, often established for tax benefits, which is deemed to be claiming illegal tax deductions; if such illegalities are proved, the partnership must pay all back taxes, plus interest and heavy penalties.

AC **1.** *adv* [*US*] [*Medicine*] abbr of Lat. 'ante cenum' meaning before dinner; the term refers to treatment or medication to be given before meals. **2.** *a* [*Pop music*] abbr of **Adult Contemporary** referring to music aimed at the grown-up fans of such 1960s rock groups as the Beatles, Rolling Stones, etc.

academic *a* [*Education*] said of the basic subjects of the traditional curriculum: the 'Three Rs' plus science, history and geography.

academic art *n* [*Art*] a term based on the belief that truly 'great' art should not simply copy nature but must improve on the inevitable imperfections to be found there. Universal experiences may thus be portrayed in an heroic, ennobling and uplifting manner. Since the rise of Modern Art in the late 19th century, 'academic' has been generally used in a pejorative sense.

academic socialism *n* [*Politics*] the socialism of words, not deeds, primarily enjoyed and promoted by academics holding forth from their secure and ivory towers; such socialism is neither aggressive nor fast-moving enough for hardliners.

academy leader *n* [*Film*] the length of film numbered from 12 to 3 that is attached to a spool of film so as to ensure perfect cueing during projection.

Acapulco gold, Acapulco red *n* [*Drugs*] brands of Mexican marijuana (gold is the stronger), native to the Acapulco area.

accelerant *n* [*Crime*] any flammable substance used by arsonists to intensify and speed up the work of a fire that they have started, eg: oil, petrol, paraffin, etc. See also **accelerator 3**.

accelerated depreciation *n* [*Taxation*] the practice of the Inland Revenue, or the US IRS, of permitting manufacturers to write off the costs of capital equipment, eg. plant and machinery, by larger amounts in the earlier years of its use than in later years, and over fewer years than it is likely to be used – in order to encourage investment.

accelerated history *n* [*Aerospace*] the testing of an aircraft component by artificially 'ageing' it with machine induced stresses, or 'work' that condenses its potential life-span into a conveniently abbreviated period.

accelerated motion *n* [*Film*] the effect obtained by running the camera slowly: when the film is projected the movement filmed will seem faster since it occupies less frames than it would otherwise do. See also **overcrank**.

acceleration 1. *n* [*Education*] the speed at which a child learns and the progress he or she makes through a school career. 2. *n* [*Law*] the occurrence of an event sooner than expected, or sooner than it might have happened, because of a change in the rights of the parties.

acceleration clause 1. *n* [*Finance*] a condition in a bond to the effect that if a party to the bond fails to make any payment by the due date, then all future payments immediately become due. 2. *n* [*Banking*] a provision in an agreement for the repayment of a loan by instalments which stipulates that if a specified number of the instalments are not paid on time, then all outstanding payments immediately become due.

acceleration principle *n* [*Economics*] the hypothesis that investment in industry varies according to the rate of change, rather than the level of output.

accelerator 1. *n* [*Building*] an additive which when added to concrete during mixing will noticeably quicken hardening and/or setting. 2. *n* [*Commerce*] a relatively small change in

consumer demand for goods which results in a comparatively large change in demand for the capital plant that supplies these goods. 3. *n* [*Crime*] a substance used by arsonists, eg. oil, petrol, paraffin, etc. See also **accelerant**.

acceptable casualties *n pl* [*Military*] the percentage of casualties that can be suffered in combat without forcing a retreat, defeat or similar military reversal; it is a term applicable to all levels of combat up to and including nuclear exchange when such figures would be extended to include the estimated civilian deaths resulting from a first or retaliatory strike.

acceptance *n* [*Banking*] the acceptance by a merchant bank of a bill of exchange drawn on one of a number of specified, reputable export merchants.

acceptance against documents *n* [*Shipping*] a situation where the debtor or drawee is given the shipping documents at the time he accepts the bill.

acceptance by intervention *n* [*Commerce*] the acceptance of an unpaid bill by a person who steps in and promises to pay it.

acceptance for honour *n* [*Commerce*] the act of a person who is not a party to a dishonoured bill, but who as a kindness agrees to pay it off to preserve the honour of the debtor.

acceptance house *n* [*Banking*] a financial house, usually a merchant bank, which lends money on the security of bills of exchange, or adds its name as the endorser of bills drawn by another party. In the UK the leading acceptance houses are those merchant banks incorporated in the Acceptance House Committee.

acceptance market *n* [*Banking*] a section of the money market where accepted bills of exchange are bought and sold by discount houses and bill-brokers. See also **acceptance house**.

acceptance of service *n* [*Law*] the act of a defendant's solicitor in accepting a writ served on his client; once the solicitor has endorsed it, the writ has been served and the defendant need never accept it personally.

acceptance sampling *n* [*Management*] the taking of a random sample from the output of a manufacturing process in order to check for acceptable quality. The assumption is that the mass-production process will ensure that a small sample will be as representative of quality as a large one.

acceptance supra protest *n* [*Commerce*] the acceptance of an unpaid bill in return for which the acceptor receives a commission.

acceptance testing *n* [*Computing*] a series of tests designed to demonstrate the functional capabilities of a new system.

acceptation *n* [*Literary criticism*] the generally accepted meaning of a word, phrase, sentence or concept.

accepted pairing *n* [*Advertising*] the concept of

recognising an advantage possessed by a rival product and using it to boost your own campaign; eg: the 'We Try Harder' slogan used by Avis Cars which played on their undeniable second place to Hertz in the car rentals statistics.

acceptor *n* [*Finance*] an individual who declares him/herself responsible for a bill of exchange by placing a signature on its face.

acceptor for honour *n* [*Finance*] one who takes responsibility for a dishonoured bill of exchange as a favour to the debtor, whose honour he supposedly thus preserves.

Accepting House Committee *n* [*Stock market*] the group of seventeen leading London merchant banks, whose strictly controlled membership is approved by the Bank of England.

access 1. *v* [*Computing*] to retrieve information from a memory store; it is increasingly used for the retrieval of any information, whether or not computer-based. **2.** *n* [*Politics, Business*] a term increasingly used as a synonym for influence: if one is in contact with a given person, one has the influence that stems from that individual's status. **3.** *n* [*UK*] [*TV*] the concept of offering time on the state or independent TV networks to minority or special interest groups to promote their own opinions and cases, usually with some professional guidance; thus: 'access broadcasting', 'access programmes'.

access barred *a* [*Communications*] said of a data facility which permits a terminal to make outgoing, or receive in-coming messages but not both.

access program *n* [*US*] [*TV*] a programme that is shown by a network **affiliate** during specific hours every week; it is often an updated version of a former networked hit show.

access time *n* [*Computing*] the period between the 'request' for information (using a given sequence of keystrokes) and the computer producing it for the user.

accessible television *n* [*US*] [*TV*] programming aimed deliberately at the lowest level of audience appeal. 'Fewer words, more white space, and many more pictures, especially of entertainment figures.' (Michael J. Arlen 'The Camera Age' 1981)

accessorise *v* [*Advertising*] to provide with accessories, especially in the context of fashion.

accident *n* [*Military*] the middle level of problem assailing any form of nuclear device, both military and civilian. An accident ranks more seriously than does an incident, but does not place the nation on whose soil it occurs in danger of 'war readiness'. The events at Three Mile Island and at Chernobyl, as well as the occasional 'losing' of nuclear warheads by US bombers, all rank as accidents.

accidental delivery, also **friendly fire** *n* [*Military*] the shelling of one's own troops, either through poor aiming or through a lack of knowledge of their whereabouts.

accident-repeater *n* [*Law*] someone who is accident prone.

acco collar *n* [*US*] [*Police*] See **accommodation collar**.

accommodation 1. *n* [*Sociology*] the process whereby individuals adapt to situations of racial conflict without actually resolving that conflict or changing the basic inequality. It was originally a term used in experimental psychology showing how individuals modify their actions to fit in with the external social world. **2.** *n* [*Politics*] the process whereby hostile powers establish a modus vivendi under which each can achieve as many as possible of its aims without actually antagonising the other.

accommodation bill *n* [*Banking*] a bill of exchange that has been signed by a person as drawer, acceptor or endorser, without his receiving any value; his purpose is to offer the weight of his name to aid the negotiation of the bill by another person.

accommodation collar *n* [*US*] [*Police*] an arrest made to satisfy the public that the police are on the job and keeping up with the crime statistics. During highly publicised crack-downs on crime, such events may even be pre-arranged between gangsters and police departments, when lowly criminals are sacrificed to satisfy the law and protect the real crime bosses.

accommodation endorsement *n* [*Banking*] similar to an **accommodation bill** but with the added proviso that the endorser not only lends his good name, but undertakes to guarantee that the payment of the bill will take place as promised; such a promise should ensure that the bill is negotiated fast and cheaply.

accommodation party *n* [*Banking*] an individual of excellent reputation whose signature on a negotiable document will facilitate its passage through the market.

accommodation payment, also **kickback** *n* [*Business*] a method of high-level bribery in which a customer is offered a special price, and is then knowingly over-charged – to keep the accounts in order – and is subsequently reimbursed the excess payment.

accord and satisfaction *n* [*Commerce*] an agreement between two consenting parties to alter the original terms of a contract. Both the accord – the change itself – and the satisfaction – the performance of the contract as newly altered – must take place before the old contract is fulfilled, unless both parties agree that the changes mean in themselves that all previous contracts are henceforth cancelled.

according to cocker *adv* [*Navy*] going by the book, following the established methods. See also **cocker**.

according to Hoyle *adv* [*Gambling*] on the

A

highest, most expert authority; it is used both in card games and in more general areas. From 'A Short Treatise on the Game of Whist' by Edmund Hoyle (1742).

accordion fold *n* [*Advertising*] a small, cheaply produced leaflet with alternate folds that can be opened out into one large sheet; usually used as a promotional giveaway or handout.

accordion sentence *n* [*Literary criticism*] a weak, ever-lengthening sentence that is merely a sequence of overlapping subordinate clauses, where each successive one appears to have been added on by the writer/speaker as an afterthought.

account *n* [*Advertising*] the client.

Account, The *n* [*Stock market*] one of the periods of credit, usually of fourteen days, allowed on dealings between members. Shares bought on account during this period must either be paid for at **Settlement**, or carried over or 'continued' to the next **Account Day** when interest, **contango**, must be paid on top of the agreed price.

account conflict *n* [*Advertising*] a situation where an agency is offered a new account by a rival company to an existing client.

Account Day *n* [*Stock market*] the last day of **The Account** and the fifth day of the period's five days known as 'The Settlement' when brokers and their clients must pay accounts due between them, or carry them over, plus interest, to a future date.

account executive *n* [*US*] [*Sex*] a pimp who specialises in high-priced prostitutes.

account for *v* [*Hunting*] to kill the fox or run it to ground.

account sale *n* [*Finance*] a statement of purchase and sale issued by a commodity broker to a customer after a **futures** transaction is **closed out**, itemising the profit or loss, the commission and any other charges applicable.

accountability *n* [*US*] [*Education*] the holding of schools and teachers responsible for the performance of their pupils by allotting school funds and grading teachers' salaries on the basis of student achievement.

accountant's opinion *n* [*Business*] a statement signed by an accountant giving a professional assessment of a given organisation based on an examination of its books and financial statements and records; this is used by potential investors or lenders to assess the viability of the firm in question.

accounting equation *n* [*Accounting*] the premise that the total resources of a business equal the capital (the sum supplied by the owners) plus the liabilities (the amount owed by the business).

accounting package *n* [*Computing*] the computer program that takes care of routine machine operations, particularly in the scheduling and analysis of the workload.

accounting price *n* [*Commerce*] See **shadow price**.

accounts *n* [*Sociology*] the language by which people justify their behaviour when challenged by another individual or group. See also **labelling theory**.

accretion *n* [*Economics*] an increase in the value of an asset by natural growth, eg. the increase of land through alluvial deposits; an increase in money by the addition of interest.

accrual concept *n* [*Accounting*] a basic rule which lays down that when costs are balanced against income to arrive at a profit or loss for a given period, both calculations are 'accrued', ie: services used, whether paid for or not, and payments earned, whether received or not, are included.

acculturation *n* [*Sociology*] the process whereby an individual or group, through direct contact, acquires the cultural characteristics of another and at the same time sacrifices his/their own. This is in contrast to the process of assimilation whereby each 'side' takes on some of the attributes of the other.

accumulation *n* [*Politics*] the socialist equivalent of capitalist 'investment': that part of the national income that is produced but not consumed within the same year.

accumulator *n* [*Gambling*] the carrying forward of money won on one bet to be used as stake money for the next one, and so on as long as possible or desired.

accuracy *n* [*Computing*] the number of **bits** required to define a given number; the more bits required, the greater the accuracy.

accuser *n* [*Religion*] Satan, pictured as accusing men before God; see Revelations 12.10.

ACDA *n* [*Military*] acro **Arms Control and Disarmament Agency** the ACDA was set up in 1961 by the US. It had four aims: 1. 'The conduct, support and co-ordination of research for arms control and disarmament policy formation'; 2. 'The preparations for and management of US participation in international negotiations in the arms and disarmament field'; 3. 'The dissemination and co-ordination of public information concerning arms control and disarmament.'; 4. 'The preparation for, operation of, or, as appropriate, direction of US participation in such control systems as may become part of US arms control and disarmament activities'. Never popular with the right wing, the ACDA has been virtually ignored by the Reagan administration.

AC/DC *n* [*Sex*] bisexuality, 'swinging both ways', from the two forms of electrical current.

ace 1. *n* [*US*] [*Restaurant*] a single, unaccompanied customer; thus a table for one. 2. *n* [*US*] [*Restaurant*] a grilled cheese sandwich. 3. *n* [*Golf*] a hole in one. 4. *n, v* [*Tennis*] an unreturnable shot; or to play such a shot.

ace kicker *n* [*Gambling*] in draw poker, an ace

held with a pair in the hand, with two more cards to be drawn.

acey-deucey *n* [*US*] [*Horse-racing*] a rider who has his stirrups at different lengths.

achieve a solution *v* [*Military*] when a weapons operator – on the ground, in a ship or plane – locks the weapon's sights electronically onto a target, fires and (theoretically) destroys that target.

achievement *n* [*Heraldry*] a person's complete armorial bearings, including shield, **supporters**, helmet, crest and motto.

achievement motivation *n* [*Sociology*] the need to perform well, a major determinant in the individual's effort and/or persistance in a given task, especially when competing against others: its drawback is to accentuate individual success over caring for those who do not achieve.

achievement motive *n* [*Business*] the desired motivation of an executive who should value success for its own sake rather than simply as a path towards acquiring a larger salary; work should thus be seen as 'meaningful' in its own right.

ACI *n* [*US*] [*Prisons*] abbr of **adult correctional institution**.

acid fascism *n* [*Sociology*] a pathological state of mind usually associated with the long-term users of hallucinogenic drugs (specifically 'acid' = LSD25). This is epitomised by the Manson 'Family' murderers of 1969 who based their homicidal crusade on a philosophy fuelled and inspired by psychedelic drugs.

acid test ratio *n* [*Finance*] a test used to determine solvency by relating a firm's most liquid assets – bank balance, cash payments outstanding from customers, easily saleable investments and actual cash – to its liabilities.

acid-test ratio, also **quick ratio** *n* [*Business*] the ratio of a firm's assets to its current liabilities which provides a quick and simple assessment of a firm's ability to pay its debts.

ACK *n* [*Computing*] See **acknowledgement**.

ack *a* [*US*] [*Police*] abbr of 'accidentally killed'.

ackled *a* [*UK*] [*Railways*] used to describe a points relay which has operated as required, or has accelerated; both usages come from standard slang 'ackle' meaning 'to work', from Standard English 'act', especially in RAF use (c1918) 'It won't ackle.'

acknowledgement *n* [*Computing*] a message that describes the status of one or more messages sent in the opposite direction. A positive acknowledgement (ACK) confirms that the previous messages were sent correctly and that more can be sent; a negative acknowledgement (NAK) indicates that the previous messages were not received correctly and should be retransmitted; piggyback acknowledgements are those that are carried in a special field in regular data messages and obviate the need for separate acknowledge-

ments to be sent as long as data is already being transmitted in both directions.

ACL *n* [*Management*] abbr of **Action Centred Leadership** a management training philosophy that believes that leaders can be created, irrespective of their natural abilities or lack of same, and are not simply born; the phrase was coined by Dr John Adair (b. 1934), a former advisor to the British Army in 'Action Centred Leadership' (1979).

a-cockbill *adv* [*Navy*] everything shipshape and in proper order; originally it meant that the anchor was suspended vertically from the hawsehole of the ship, ready for dropping when required.

acol *n* [*Cards*] a system of bidding in bridge, named after the club in Acol Road, Hampstead, London in which it was developed in 1937.

A-copy *n* [*US*] [*Journalism*] lazy, second-rate writing; especially that merely rewritten from a promotional or PR handout.

acorn calf *n* [*US*] [*Cattlemen*] a weakling, a runty calf.

acoustic flat *n* [*Film, Video*] a piece of scenery designed to deaden and absorb sound rather than reflect or bounce it off. Such a **flat** will either have been painted with a special substance or covered in sound-deadening material.

acoustic lens *n* [*Audio*] an arrangement of plates or deflectors that is used to focus, split up or in some way control the leading edge of a sound wave.

acoustic perfume *n* [*Audio*] an overlay of 'background' noise intended to have no specific character of its own, but to drown out a selection of sounds that would otherwise prove irritating.

acoustical excitation *n* [*Military*] sound.

acquiescence *n* [*Law*] assent by remaining silent; such assent removes any right to relief as a plaintiff.

acquisition *n* [*Military*] the meeting of possibly hostile airplanes by a fighter pilot during a patrol.

acquisitive vandalism *n* [*Law*] vandalism accompanied by theft, eg. attacks on vending machines, telephone kiosks, parking meters, etc; it is also the theft of lead from roofs, ornamental plants from parks or buildings, etc.

acquitement *n* [*Magic*] any sleight of hand by which an object is concealed while each hand is revealed as apparently being empty.

acrobat *n* [*Textiles*] in hosiery making, the part of a machine which moves up and down to finish off a stocking.

acrolect *n* [*Literary criticism*] the most prestigious dialect used in a given language. See also **basilect**.

across the board 1. *a* [*Industrial relations*] formerly (1950s) the flat rate; it refers to a wage deal in which a bargain is accepted that embraces all classes and categories of workers without exception within a given union.. **2.** *adv* [*Horse-racing*] referring to the backing of one horse to achieve either first, second or third place in a given race (US: win, place or show).

act in law n [Law] the drawing up of any legal document, eg. a will.

act well v [Theatre] said of a play easy both to produce and to perform; filled with plenty of good lines and 'business' for the actors.

actifan n [Science fiction] science fiction fan who takes part in a number of organisational activities.

acting out n [Sociology] the term comes from the psycho-analytic concept of a subject who, in the grip of unconscious wishes and fantasies, relieves these same feelings without acknowledging their source. It is used by social workers to describe those who cause trouble – especially for social workers – by releasing their own emotional tensions in their dealings with those who probably have little or nothing to do with their cause.

action v [Business] to perform one's job emphatically, purposefully; particularly to act just as one's employer would wish.

action 1. n [Drugs] the availability (and possibly quality) of supplies. 2. n [Entertainment, Business] the commercial potential of any place, be it shop, cinema, club, street, town, area of the country, whole country, etc. 3. n [Gambling] the volume and intensity of betting in a given gambling venue. 4. n [Shooting] that part of a shotgun which contains the mechanism for firing the cartridges and which connects the stock and the barrel of the gun.

action architecture n [Architecture] the concept of creating architecture 'on site' with materials 'as found', using sketches rather than detailed drawings; it also depends on the continuing presence and inspiration of the architect throughout the building process. An optimistic concept, enjoyed by few clients and fewer contractors.

action field n [Photography] the portion of the area in front of the camera that is recorded on the picture taken.

action fish n [Navy] a torpedo fitted with a live warhead.

action house n [Film] a cinema where ultra-popular all-action/drama/romance etc. films are exhibited to mass audiences. Often sited in poor areas and aimed directly at non-discriminating audiences. See also **art house**.

action in rem n [Law, Shipping] an action brought in the Admiralty Court upon the arrest of a ship.

action learning n [Management] a management training activity in which the manager is required to solve an actual problem of an existing organisation.

action level n [US] [Government] the level of concentration in a given food of such poisonous/dangerous substances that public

health authorities are forced to demand a ban on the sale of that food.

action painting n [Art] the loosely painted, highly gestural work of such artists as Jackson 'Jack the Dripper' Pollock. Action stresses the essential act of painting – the process of making being of greater importance than the finished product; it is an extension into oil painting of the Surrealists' technique of automatic writing.

action research n [Business, Sociology, Education] the concept of creating new ideas by combining static 'desk research' with dynamic field work; such ideas are then monitored continuously so that they can be updated further while they are actually in operation.

action stills n [TV] still photographs joined together in sequence by filming under a rostrum camera.

action theory n [Sociology] the analysis of action starting with the individual actor. Analysis takes in the typical actor in typical situations and considers goals, the means of achieving them, expectations and values, the nature of the situation and the actors' knowledge of the situation. It is divided into **hermeneutic** and **positivist** theories: hermeneutic depending on the 'meaningfulness' of the action to the actor, positivist on the social structure and how it determines the goals that are set and the means available to the actors.

actioner n [Film] a type of eternally popular species of escapist film melodrama which contains thrills, spills, sex and violence, all together.

actions n [Art] See **destructive art**.

activated plough n [Coal-mining] see **dynamic plough**.

activated sludge n [Sewage] sludge that has been aerated and subjected to bacterial action in order to accelerate the breakdown of raw sewage during secondary waste treatment.

active balance n [Economics] a favourable economic balance – of trade, of payment, etc.

active bond n [Commerce, Stock market] a bond which bears a fixed rate of interest which is paid from the date when the bond is first put on the market.

active bond crowd n [US] [Stock market] those members of the bond department of the New York Stock Exchange responsible for the heaviest volume of trading. See also **cabinet crowd**.

active box n [US] [Stock market] shares made available as collateral for obtaining brokers' loans or customers' **margin** positions.

active crowd n [Police] an angry or riotous crowd.

active defence n [Military] the use of weapons systems to defeat enemy troops; this is used with the implication that the first hostile attack will have come from the enemy.

active element 1. n [Electronics] any element – a tube, transistor or any complete device – that is in use or 'live'. 2. n [Electronics] any file, routine or record, held in a database and which is currently being used, contacted or referred to.

active list *n* [*Military*] a record of all officers currently employed within any branch of the armed forces.

active listening *n* [*New therapies*] a term used in 'Rogerian' (client-centred) therapy, where the therapist 'reflects back' what he/she hears the client saying, instead of analysing or commenting on it. Unlike the traditional Freudian analyst, the Rogerian presumes the basic goodness and worth of his client.

active money *n* [*Commerce*] money that is in circulation or otherwise being used for business purposes, rather than that which is simply invested or on deposit.

active safety *n* [*Cars*] all those characteristics in a car's design which may help a driver avoid accdients: roadholding (wet and dry), handling, braking, stability over bumps, at speed and in cross winds, and overall predictability of behaviour; the opposite of **passive safety**.

active star *n* [*Computing*] the designing of a network in which the outer nodes connect to a single central node which processes all messages in the network, including those that it forwards from one outer node to another. See also **passive star, star network**.

active title *n* [*Publishing*] a book that is selling well and is thus kept in print for as long as it continues to do so.

activist *n* [*Politics*] high-level political zealots, more concerned with the correct ideology than many of the rank-and-file membership, who at the same time maintain pressure on their fellows to accentuate the political struggle wherever and whenever possible. Similar to **militant** but implying the extent of one's political involvement rather than the depth of one's radical stance.

activity *n* [*Computing*] any read or write operation performed on a file.

activity programme *n* [*Education*] extra-curricular activities: clubs, societies, sports, etc.

activity sampling 1. *n* [*Management*] the recording of on-the-spot observations of the work or other activity being carried out by an employee, or a machine, at specific but randomly chosen points in time. **2.** *n* [*Market research*] a method of observing the frequency of a given activity by using a series of random, but linked tests.

actor proof *a* [*Theatre*] said part-jokingly of a script that should guarantee the management a hit, no matter how grotesque or idiosyncratic the efforts of those entrusted to perform it.

actor's bible *n* [*Theatre*] 'Variety' magazine (US), 'The Stage' (UK).

actual 1. *n* [*US*] [*Military*] radio code for the commander of a force; it is used at all levels of command and is intended to distinguish the officer concerned from the radioman who would actually put through the message. **2.** *n* [*Stock market*] actual price: the price at which a **jobber** is willing to buy or sell a share. **3.** *n* [*TV*] the real, final cost of a programme, calculated at the end of the production; this contrasts with the projected costs, optimistically set out before work begins.

actual money *n* [*Economics*] See **real money**.

actualise *v* [*New therapies*] to fulfil the potential of something or somebody; thus 'actualiser' is someone who makes active and supposedly beneficial decisions for themselves and others.

actualism *n* [*Art*] a term coined by Alain Jouffrey, a French writer, in 1970 to describe the way art in a revolutionary situation is forced to abandon its pretentions to an existence independent of social reality. At this point 'works or art' possess significance only insofar as they are relevant to the current political situation.

actuality 1. *n* [*TV*] a method of reimbursing costs based on the **actual** costs incurred, rather than on some agreed allowance claim settled before production starts. **2.** also **actualities** *n* [*TV*] the on-the-spot reporting of events, especially violent or dramatic ones, but including any live reporting such as a press statement from a government source. Supposedly, in its more dramatic versions, the ideal style of TV news journalism, enhanced particularly by the fact that it is totally unavailable to print media; it comes from Fr. 'actualités'.

actuality programming *n* [*TV*] See **reality programming**.

actually existing socialism *n* [*Politics*] the Soviet and East European description of the socialism that is administered through contemporary government, as opposed to the idealised socialism of propaganda handouts; generally an ironic usage, popular among dissidents who like to underline the distance between government fantasy and popular experience.

actuals *n pl* [*Commerce*] the opposite of **futures**, ie. commodities that are physically available for transfer when deals concerning them have been concluded.

ACU *n* [*Computing*] acro **automatic calling unit** a device that allows a computer or terminal to originate calls over the public telephone network, usually using a **modem**. It is used when the volume of calls is too large for manual operation but not big enough for a **dedicated** connection.

acutance 1. *n* [*Photography*] the ability of a lens or film to reproduce edges sharply. **2.** *n* [*Photography*] the edge sharpness of a particle of film emulsion; the finer the acutance, the sharper the image.

AD *n* [*US*] [*Hotels*] abbr of **additional** a charge that comes through to the accounts department after a guest has checked out.

ad *n* [*Journalism*] abbr of **additional copy** extra material for a story; thus 'ad one' is the first page of such copy, followed by ad two, three, etc.

ad lib 1. *adv* [*US*] [*Medicine*] at liberty, thus, off duty. **2.** *adv* [*Medicine*] Lat. abbr prescription notation meaning 'as desired'.

Ada *n* [*Computing*] a programming language developed for the US Department of Defense for use in **embedded systems** which employ a computer for navigation, guidance, etc. Originally code-named 'Green', the language was renamed in honour of Augusta Ada Lovelace, the assistant to Charles Babbage, the earliest maker of computing machines.

Ada from Decator *n* [*Gambling*] pronounced 'eighter'; in craps dice, the point of eight.

Ada Ross, the stable hoss *n* [*Gambling*] pronounced 'eighter'; in craps dice, the point of eight.

Adam and Eve *n* [*US*] [*Restaurant*] two eggs.

Adam and Eve on a raft *n* [*US*] [*Lunch counter*] two fried/poached eggs on toast.

Adam and Eve on a raft and wreck 'em *n* [*US*] [*Lunch counter*] two scrambled eggs on toast.

adaption-level principle *n* [*Psychology*] a principle which states that one becomes dissatisfied with whatever one grows used to; since self perception is based largely on perceptions of others, one rarely comes up to one's own expectations (even if they once appeared satisfied) if one observes the achievements, or lack of same, of other people, both past and present.

adaptive forecasting *n* [*Business, Marketing*] See **exponential smoothing**.

ADCOM *n* [*Military*] acro **Aerospace Defence Command.** See **NORAD**.

add *n* [*Medicine*] abbr of **average daily dose**.

add *n* [*Pop music*] abbr of **addition** the addition of a new record – album or single – to a radio station's regular playlist.

add time *n* [*Computing*] a means of measuring the performance of a microcomputer: the time required by a given CPU to add two multidigit numbers, not including the time taken to read the numbers or store the result.

added money *n* [*Gambling*] extra money added to the basic stake so increasing the amount won on a race.

adder *n* [*Computing*] a device which produces an output resulting from the sum of two or more numbers presented as inputs.

Addisonian termination *n* [*Literary criticism*] ending a sentence with a preposition, supposedly a grammatical crime; the term was coined by the critic Richard Hurd with reference to Joseph Addison.

additive architecture *n* [*Architecture*] architecture and furniture produced in modular forms which can be added to the original unit as and when needed.

additive mixture *n* [*Weaving*] a colour theory based on adding light rays together to produce colours, the total of which equals white light; the opposite of the **subtractive** mixture.

additus *n* [*US*] [*Law*] the power of the court to increase the amount of money awarded by the jury in certain cases as compensation to a plaintiff.

add-on *n* [*Computing*] anything that can be added to the basic machine which will improve or expand its performance. See also **peripheral**.

add-on sales *n* [*Commerce*] continuing sales to an already satisfied customer.

address **1.** *n* [*Computing*] the location of a specific piece of information within the memory of a computer. **2.** *v* [*Computing*] to indicate or to find the location of a specific piece of information within the memory of a computer.

address bus *n* [*Computing*] the physical connection within a computer between the processor, the computer memory and the rest of the system. See also **bus 1** and **2**.

address commission *n* [*Shipping*] a commission paid to the charterers' agent for his work in arranging the loading of a ship.

address line *n* [*Advertising*] See **base line**.

addressability *n* [*Computing*] in computer graphics, the number of addressable points within a specified display space or image space.

add-to system *n* [*Commerce*] a system whereby a customer gets a number of articles on hire purchase but makes a down-payment only on the first one.

adhocery *n* [*Politics*] decisions, rules, agreements and compromises that are made on the spur of the moment rather than after 'due deliberation'.

adhocism *n* [*Architecture*] the concept of creating a building in which one part is designed by a specialist who takes little or no regard of the overall project. By extension the architect need no longer invent new forms but can select the best available from a suitable catalogue and put or collage the parts together to form the whole construction.

adhocracy *n* [*Government*] a term coined by Alvin Toffler in 'Future Shock' (1970): the concept that in place of monolithic, and thus static institutions for decision-making, there should be temporary organisations which would deal with specific problems and then be dissolved; an 'action group' to fit each new circumstance. Ideally the management system of the future.

adit *n* [*Coal-mining*] a rising road that forms the entrance to a mine, driven from the surface and primarily designed to facilitate dewatering of the workings.

adjective law *n* [*Law*] that part of the law which relates to practice and procedure within the operation of the courts themselves.

adjudicated *a* [*US*] [*Law, Crime*] referring to a juvenile delinquent in criminal or juvenile proceedings.

adjustable peg *n* [*Banking*] a flexible system of fixing exchange rates whereby a rate is allowed to vary within certain narrowly defined limits. See also **crawling peg**.

adjusting the contract *n* [*Film*] . . . 'which

means paying (a writer) a few weeks salary under the threat of keeping his idea until his next option comes up, with everyone knowing that he has no assignment and that no producer on the lot wants him'. ('The Selected Letters of Raymond Chandler' ed. F. MacShane, 1981)

adjustment n [US] [Law] in the US Family Court this is the dismissal of charges by a Probation Officer.

adjustment bond, reorganisation bond n [US, UK] [Commerce, Banking] a bond that results from the reorganisation of a concern which has to be recapitalised rather than go into bankruptcy.

adjustment center 1. n [US] [Prisons] that part of a prison where mentally unstable or dedicatedly rebellious prisoners are kept isolated from the main prison population in solitary confinement. 2. n [US] [Prisons] a segregated area of the prison in which those individuals who cannot survive in the general population can find refuge. See also **Rule 43**.

admass n [Sociology] a term coined by J.B. Priestley in 1955: the economic, social and cultural system that is dominated and controlled by the desire to acquire and consume material goods, an ideology that is expanded and intensified by a barrage of seductive advertising.

administered prices n [Economics] prices which are determined by the policy of some controlling agency, eg. a government or monopoly, rather than by the fluctuations of market forces or some other less authoritative mechanism.

administrative loading n [Military] the loading of a transport vehicle in which priority is given to the volume of material loaded rather than to any tactical need or convenience. See also **tactical loading**.

administrative segregation n [US] [Prisons] solitary confinement. See also **therapeutic segregation**.

administrator ad litem n [Law] an administrator of a deceased person's estate appointed for the purpose of defending the interest of that estate in a legal action.

administrator cum Testamento Annexo n [Law] an administrator of a deceased person's estate appointed when there is a will but no specific executor named.

administrator de Bonis Nonto Annexo n [Law] when the administrator of a deceased person's estate dies before his task is finished, a new administrator 'de bonis non administratis' is appointed to conclude the task.

administrator Durante Absentia n [Law] a substitute administrator appointed to deputise for the main administrator during an absence abroad.

administrator Durante Minore Aetate n [Law] a temporary administrator appointed during the time that the specified administrator remains a minor.

administrator Pendente Lite n [Law] an administrator appointed to administer an estate until such time as a lawsuit concerning that estate is brought.

admiral n [US] [Hotels] a hotel doorman; it comes from the lavishness of his uniform.

admiral of the narrow seas n [Navy] a sailor who vomits on a fellow drinker while himself drunk.

admiral's ham n [Navy] any variety of tinned or potted meat.

admiral's mate n [Navy] an ordinary seaman who likes to give the impression he knows as much as, if not more than, the admiral of the fleet.

admiralty brown n [Navy] service issue toilet paper, made of cheap, brown-tinged paper.

admiralty clown n [Navy] physical training instructor.

admiralty sweep n [Navy] the extravagantly wide sweep of a boat as it approaches a gangplank or jetty.

admissible mark n [Computing] specific rules or conventions used to determine which marks, symbols, numerals and characters are valid in various areas of computing, as regards both hardware and software.

admitted a [Law] used to describe a clerk qualified by admission to the roll of solicitors kept by the Law Society.

adolescent a [Wine-tasting] See **dumb**.

adolescent they n [Literary criticism] a term coined by R. H. Copperud to define the use of the plural pronoun – they or their – with a singular verb; grammatically incorrect, but colloquially sanctioned.

adopted a [Town planning] used when a local authority takes over responsibility – for the upkeep of roads, buildings, etc. – from private owners.

adoption process n [Marketing] the process whereby customers come to accept new products.

ad-pub n [Show business] abbr of **advertising and publicity** usually as a job description: 'He is ad-pub chief', etc.

ADR n [UK] [Stock market] abbr of **American depository receipts** the form in which foreign shares, held physically by the US banks, can be traded in the American markets without local listing.

adrift 1. a [Sailing, Ropework] said of a piece of rigging that has come out of the hole through which it has been threaded. 2. a [Sailing, Ropework] said of a knot which has accidentally come undone.

adshel n [Advertising] a four-sheet poster in a High Street or shopping precinct; it comes from the trade name of a specific poster contractor who specialises in such advertising.

adult 1. a [Sex] euphemism for pornographic; thus adult bookstore, adult cinema, etc. 2. a [TV] reasonably, by the standards of current television, sophisticated; in the UK this implies those programmes shown after 9pm, the cutoff point at which broadcasters optimistically assume that children are in bed.

adult business district *n* [*US*] [*Police, Crime*] any area of a city that has been (tacitly) given over to commercial sex – 'massage parlours', 'book shops', prostitution, etc.

adult contemporary *a* [*Pop music*] See **AC 2**.

adult entertainment center *n* [*US*] [*Police, Crime*] See **adult business district**.

advance 1. *n* [*Journalism*] a story prepared for a future event and filed for suitable use. **2.** *n* [*Politics*] the preparation in advance of a live audience, or the briefing of radio or TV stations to obtain the maximum vote-catching exposure for a political candidate. Such activities are performed by the advance man whose job includes arranging 'spontaneous' banner-waving demonstrations ready for the cameras, writing 'local' inserts for the candidate's speech and generally geeing up the local party activists. Depending on his efforts there can be 'good advance' or 'bad advance'. Such promotions descend from carnival and circus hucksters who would always send a man on ahead of the show to whip up enthusiasm in the next town they were due to play. See also **black advance**. **3.** *v* [*Politics*] to perform the activities described in (2).

advancement *n* [*Law*] an arrangement by which a trustee under a will or settlement advances money in order to better the interests of the beneficiary, eg: to pay for his education, to set him up in business, etc.

adventure 1. *n* [*Commerce*] the taking of a financial or commercial risk. **2.** *n* [*Merchant navy*] cargo entrusted to the captain with the proviso that he is to sell it at the best possible price during the ship's voyage.

adventurism *n* [*Politics*] a derogatory term used both by the US and USSR to imply an aggressive foreign policy, especially as regards the amassing of large nuclear arsenals, the military sabre-rattling that is backed by such 'deterrents', and the involvement (as in Vietnam, Afghanistan) in neo-imperialist military campaigns.

adventurist *n* [*Politics*] a derogatory Marxist term used to condemn those seen as 'right-wing deviationists' who advocate an even more dogmatic revolutionary line.

adverbial dressing gown *n* [*Literary criticism*] a term coined by Ernest Gowers to define the clichéd modification of various verbs or adjectives (especially typical of UK 'society' speech): 'frightfully dull', 'desperately dreary' etc.

adversary journalism *n* [*Journalism*] campaigning journalism that sacrifices any pretence of objectivity for a deliberate, often muck-raking, attack on a given target.

adverse possession 1. *n* [*Banking*] the enjoyment and/or use of property with or without the tacit knowledge of the actual owner; such use becomes absolute if the owner has made no objection during a period of twenty years. **2.** *n* [*Law*] the act of occupying another person's land and claiming it as one's own; if the actual owner fails to counter-claim within a set period – often 10 or 20 years – the ownership duly and legally may change hands.

adverse selection *n* [*Insurance*] the concept of disproportionate risk: those who are poorer and/or more prone to suffer loss or make claims than the average risk.

advertise *v* [*Cards*] in gin rummy the discarding of one card in the hope of luring an opponent into believing that this, in fact your strongest and most desirable suit, is one in which you have no interest and which he, in turn, may therefore safely discard.

advertorial *n* [*Public relations*] advertising by large companies in which editorial copy is used to present them in a self-justifying and favorable light when dealing with areas – eg. pollution, energy saving, environmental matters – in which they are more generally cast as the villains.

advice and consent *n* [*US*] [*Politics*] the Senatorial power, written into the US Constitution as Article II, Section 2, to act as a check on the appointive and treaty-making powers of the President.

advices *n pl* [*Commerce*] formal messages, usually from abroad and from an agent to his principal, giving details and information on current trading conditions.

advisory *n* [*US*] [*Traffic controllers*] a bulletin advising drivers, by radio, as to the current state of the roads.

advocacy *n* [*Sociology*] the action of social workers in representing their clients before tribunals and similar services whose requirements and organisation might otherwise prove too complex for the understanding of the client, thus depriving him/her of their use and possible benefit.

advocacy advertising *n* [*Advertising*] partisan advertising, by both minority groups promoting their own case and major companies defending themselves against adverse publicity.

advocacy journalism, also **campaigning journalism** *n* [*Journalism*] journalism that consciously eschews the traditional objectivity of the reporter and takes a given side on a given issue.

advocacy planning *n* [*Local government*] urban planning by specialists, each of whom attempts to ensure that the group whom they represent – disparate sections of the community for whom the buildings are being created – will have their own interests adequately taken care of in the completed scheme.

adw *n* [*US*] [*Police*] abbr of **assault with a deadly weapon**.

adzine n [Science fiction] a fan magazine containing advertisements.

aerials n pl [Skiing] manoeuvres performed in mid-air in freestyle skiing.

aerobe n [Cheese-making] a micro-organism which can only exist in the presence of oxygen; such aerobes are used in the creation of **bloomy** – rind cheeses and, after suitable preparation, blue cheeses.

aerobics n [Sport] a recently fashionable keep-fit exercise regime which depends on increasing oxygen intake in order to stimulate the activity of the heart and lungs.

aerospace plane n [Aerospace] a space vehicle, eg. the US Space Shuttle, that can be launched beyond the atmosphere, can then re-enter the atmosphere and there be manoeuvred and landed on the Earth's surface like a conventional jet or airliner. Such vehicles are presumed to be manned and to use some form of air-breathing propulsion.

aesthetic surgery n [Medicine] plastic surgery, usually on the face, that is performed purely for cosmetic reasons.

AFAP n [Military] acro **Artillery-Fired Atomic Projectile**.

affectional preference minorities n [Sociology] male or female homosexuals.

affective domain n [Education] the category of instructional objectives relating to attitudes, values and appreciations within human behaviour.

affective fallacy n [Literary criticism] a term coined by Wimsatt & Beardsley in 'The Verbal Icon' (1954) as 'a confusion between the poem and its results (what it says and what it does)'; thus it can mean to judge the merit of a literary work by the emotional effect it produces upon its reader.

affiliates n pl [US] [TV] those local stations that operate independently of the three major US networks, even though they are forced to take much of their programming from them. See also **O & O, wels**.

affine n [Cheese-making] the **washing** of a cheese with a liquid, often a wine or spirit, during curing; it comes from Fr. 'affiner' meaning 'to finish, to refine'.

affirmations n [New therapies] positive self-enhancing statements that accompany the rebirthing process of Theta training seminars. This baptism-like rebirthing takes place complete with snorkel and nose-clips in a bath of water heated to 99°F. – the temperature of the womb's amniotic fluid.

affirmative action n [Politics] the hiring of minority/disadvantaged/poor individuals for jobs (or their enrolling in college/university courses) that might otherwise require higher credentials than those they can offer, on the principle that poverty etc. has made it impossible for them to obtain such credentials. Unfortunately, despite the basic worthiness of such a scheme, those credentials are still missing, and it may be that those so employed still cannot perform the job or academic work as required.

affordable method n [Advertising] the drawing up of an advertising budget on the basis of how much a company can afford, rather than on the effect the company wishes to produce. See also **task method**.

affreight v [Shipping] to hire a ship to carry cargo.

Afghanistanism n [Journalism] a term based on the remoteness of that country from the US; the practice of concentrating investigations on far-off places for problems to which some 'answers' can be put forward, rather than looking at problems nearer to home, for which no such black-and-white solutions will do. The term has naturally suffered somewhat since the US has sought to tackle those difficulties that followed the USSR's invasion of Afghanistan in 1979.

afloat n [Commodity exchange] a price offered for a ship's cargo while that ship is still at sea.

AFSATCOM n [Military] acro **Air Force Satellite Communications System** a USAF communications system which, while it has no satellite of its own, works by mounting its transponders on other satellites. AFSATCOM has been in operation since 1974, as part of the overall US C³I complex, providing the Air Force with communications between command posts and missile launch centres, with its receivers aboard bombers, reconnaissance aircraft and submarines. See also **FLTSATCOM, MILSTAR**.

aft n [US] [TV] the end of a piece of tape that contains a single news item. See also **fore**.

aft through the hawsehole n [Navy] an officer commissioned from the lower deck. Originally the lower deck ranks were accommodated forward in the ship and the officers aft; for the sailor to go aft required him to crawl through the hawsehole.

after hours dealings n [Stock market] deals made between members after the official close at 3.30 pm.

after market 1. v [Computing] to begin buying accessories for a machine after concluding the purchase of the basic equipment. **2.** n [Computing] the second-hand market in personal computers and their accessories. **3.** n [Stock market] the market for a share after its issuer has made the initial sale through the underwriters.

after-acquired property n [Banking] property acquired by a bankrupt after he/she has been formally declared a bankrupt.

afterglow n [Video, TV] See **persistence**.

afternoon bath n [TV] an urgent order for developing film; film is usually developed and put through its chemical 'bath' overnight; if an afternoon bath is required, the film will be developed the same day.

A

AFV *n* [*Military*] abbr of **Armoured Fighting Vehicle**.

against the sun *adv* [*Sailing, Ropework*] counterclockwise. Thus 'with the sun' means clockwise.

agate *n* [*US*] [*Printing*] 5.5 pt. typeface, used for small ads in newspapers.

age, also **ante-man** *n* [*Gambling*] in poker, the player immediately to the left of the dealer, whose task it is to provide the ante payment for the pot, before the deal and the subsequent rounds of betting begin.

age cohorts, age peers *n* [*Education, Sociology*] those in the same age-group, or children of the same age at school.

age the accounts *v* [*Commerce*] to take the various accounts concerning a single firm and arrange them according to the dates on which payments are due, by which payments are owed, etc.

aged fail *n* [*Business*] a contract between two broker-dealers that has not been settled 30 days after the settlement date. After this point the receiving firm can no longer consider the balance of money owed to be an asset and must adjust its capital accordingly.

age-ism *n* [*Politics, Sociology*] one of the various pressure group nouns that emerged after the popularisation of **sexism**; the discrimination against the old on the grounds of their being old. Pressure groups against age-ism include the Grey Panthers (modelled on the Black Panthers of the 1960s). Thus 'ageist', used derogatively as *a* and *n*.

agency *n* [*Law*] the relationship brought about by one person (the principal) who appoints another (the agent) to do business for him.

agency bill *n* [*Banking*] a bill of exchange accepted by the London branch of a foreign bank.

agency comparative *n* [*Advertising*] the posing of a comparison without previously identifying the object, activity, opinion, etc. with which the comparison is being made. When used in advertising, this can be seen as a deliberate evasion for commercial gain.

agency shop *n* [*Management*] a place of employment where all employees doing particular types of work must pay subscriptions to the relevant trade unions, even though they refuse in fact to join those unions.

agency and structure *n* [*Sociology*] a major debate in sociological theory: how do structures determine what individuals do, how are structures created, and what, if any, are the limits on individuals' capabilities to act independently of structural restraints? The main arguments are divided between methodological individualism, ethnomethodology and phenomenological sociology; functionalists and Marxists.

agenda *n* [*Computing*] a set of control language statements used to run a given routine or solve a given problem; the term comes from the standard business or committee use.

agent 1. *n* [*Espionage*] spies who are employed by the CIA on a freelance basis, but are not actually permanent employees. **2.** *n* [*UK*] [*Stock exchange*] a trader who acts on behalf of an investor. **3.** *n* [*Gambling*] a player-cheat who works in collusion with the staff of the casino – the croupiers, pit bosses, etc – but not with its owners.

agent in place *n* [*Espionage*] an espionage agent who has access to a variety of classified information.

agent of influence *n* [*Espionage*] an espionage agent, often working under **deep cover**, who has gained access to the policy-making departments and influential individuals of the country against which he/she is operating. See also **mole**.

agent of necessity *n* [*Law, Commerce*] an agent who takes on his role in conditions of urgency, although he has never been formally appointed by a given principal; eg. when a ship's master has to throw overboard some cargo to save the rest. In such circumstances, the principal is bound to accept any decision made by the agent in his interest.

ager *n* [*US*] [*Textiles*] a box in which fabric is treated with steam or ammonia fumes to fix the colours.

aggie *n* [*Marbles*] a marble made of agate; these are usually used as **shooters**.

aggregate *n* [*Building, Plastering*] sand or similar coarse material used in plastering, concrete and cement mixes.

aggress *v* [*Sport*] to play aggressively; specifically 'to aggress the ball'.

aggressive portfolio *n* [*Stock market*] a portfolio of stocks and shares chosen specifically with the likelihood of their increasing in price.

aggressive pricing *n* [*Commerce*] pricing one's goods cheaper than the equivalent products of one's rivals and thus launching a price war.

aggy *n* [*Navy*] a sailor who is constantly complaining of conditions aboard ship; from 'agony'.

AGI *n* [*Military*] acro **Aliens Gathering Intelligence** the Russian 'trawlers' and similar allegedly peaceable ships which track NATO fleets or anchor near major land-based military bases.

agio *n* this comes from Ital. 'agio' meaning 'ease, convenience'.

agio 1. *n* [*Economics*] the amount by which the value of one metallic currency exceeds that of another; the difference in value between the metallic and paper currency of a country (where this is pertinent). **2.** *n* [*Finance*] a charge, usually a percentage, made by a dealer for changing foreign currency into the local currency. **3.** *n* [*Banking*] the discount on a foreign bill of exchange. See also **agiotage**.

agiotage *n* [*Business*] Speculation: the taking of a business risk in buying and holding foreign currencies or stock exchange securities in the hope of selling later for a profit.

agitator body *n* [*US*] [*Road transport*] a truck body designed to mix concrete while the truck is moving.

agitprop *n* [*Politics*] abbr of **Soviet Department of Agitation and Propaganda** (Odtel Agitatsi i Propagandy) established in 1920 by the Central Committee of the CPSU. The bureaucracy has changed but the concept remains in force: to influence and direct the internal and external propaganda efforts of the USSR in order to promote communist ideology.

agonal *a* [*Medicine*] immediately prior to death.

agony column *n* [*Journalism*] originally the term referred to the personal columns of the daily press, especially those of the London Times, which were often used for illicit assignations, (coded) communications, requests for messages from missing persons, etc. Now it refers to those columns used to deal with the pains and problems of the lovelorn, the sexually perturbed and the generally unhappy; the advisors who run such columns are called agony aunts (and very occasionally agony uncles).

agreed battle *n* [*Military*] a limited conflict, such as is supposed to precede a nuclear war **escalation**.

agribusiness, also **agrobusiness** *n* [*Business*] those wide-ranging enterprises which produce, process and distribute farm products, as well as their ancillary suppliers and allied businesses. The prefix agri– has been extended to such compounds as agribusinessman, agricorporation, agricrime (the stealing of farm machinery), agripower, agriproletariat, etc.

agricultural *n* [*Cricket*] a brutally clumsy swipe of the bat. See also **cow-shot**.

aha! reaction *n* [*Psychology*] the sudden realisation of an ideal insight or similar flash of comprehension which seems to illuminate what had hitherto been a complex and painful problem; the analytical 'Eureka!'.

ahead *adv* [*Gambling*] winning, ahead of the house in one's pile of cash.

ahistorical, also **anhistorical** *a* [*Politics*] said of a theory which treats its subject-matter either as though it has no history, or as though history plays no vital role in its explanation. Such theories are condemned by the ideologically right and left as liberal aberrations which search for universality and deny man's historic development.

AI *n* [*Computing*] abbr of **Artificial Intelligence** the continuing research into creating computers that are less like machines and more like humans in their approach to problems and their solution. The addition of human-type thought, intuition, speech and similar attributes will theoretically lead to the first real androids, the exemplars of AI in action. See also **expert systems**.

AIBD *n* [*UK*] [*Stock market*] abbr of **the Association of International Bond Dealers** an organisation formed in Zurich in 1969; it is the self-regulatory association of dealers in **eurobonds**.

AIDA *n* [*Commerce*] acro **Attention, Interest, Desire, Action** a mnemonic dating from the late 19th century to denote the progressive steps of customer reaction when making a purchase, or the sequence of responses that the successful sales man should evoke from a potential buyer.

aided recall *n* [*Marketing*] an interviewing technique in which subjects are asked for their response to a question and allowed to choose an answer from a pre-selected list.

aids 1. *n pl* [*Fencing*] the last three fingers holding the weapon, other than the thumb and forefinger. 2. *n pl* [*Horse-riding*] the correct and combined use of the hands and legs, in order to make a horse do what is required.

aim point *n* [*Photography*] the point at which colour film is considered to have reached its optimum colour balance; film tends to be sold slightly earlier than the chronological aim point, so that the photographer can choose the ideal moment to use it.

A-I-P *n* [*US*] [*Drugs*] abbr of **Afghanistan, Iran or Pakistan**; heroin that has been manufactured from opium grown in these countries.

air 1. *v* [*Radio*] to broadcast (a programme). 2. *n* [*TV*] space in the framing of a television picture.

air art, also **blow-up art, gonflable art, etc.** *n* [*Art*] a broad category of art which comprises many different structures, all with the common purpose of exploiting the possibilities of compressed air or the natural force of the wind, usually employing inflatables. The artists concerned claim that such works are both public and participatory.

air bell *n* [*Glass-making*] an irregularly shaped bubble generally formed during pressing or moulding operations in the manufacture of optical glass.

air breather *n* [*Aerospace*] a jet engine that requires an intake of air for the combustion of its fuel.

air bridge 1. *n* [*Mining*] a bridge (either natural or constructed) at the crossing of two airways that allows air to ventilate two separate roadways without too great a leakage from one roadway to the other. 2. *n* [*Transport*] a regular public air service between two points.

air burst *n* [*Military*] a nuclear explosion that is detonated sufficiently far above the ground to ensure that none of the ensuing fireball actually touches the ground and that none of the effects of the explosion is in any way diminished or absorbed by the ground. See also **ground burst**.

air dam *n* [*Cars*] a **spoiler** placed across the bottom part of the car's nose to reduce drag and aerodynamic lift by blocking the flow of air beneath the car.

A

air date *n* [*TV*] the date on which any of the various UK television transmission masts went into operation.

air defence warning conditions **1.** *n pl* [*Military*] yellow: attack by hostile aircraft and/or missiles is probable; hostile aircraft and/or missiles are en route; unknown aircraft and/or missiles suspected to be hostile are en route towards or within an air defence division/sector. **2.** *n pl* [*Military*] red: attack by hostile aircraft and/or missiles is imminent/in progress; hostile aircraft and/or missiles are within an air defence division/sector or are in its immediate vicinity with high probability of entering that division/sector.

air defence warning conditions **3.** *n pl* [*Military*] white: attack by hostile aircraft and/or missiles is improbable (this may be issued before or after yellow or red conditions).

air gap *n* [*Audio*] the very narrow gap between the two elements of a magnetic recording or playback head.

air line *n* [*Glass-making*] an elongated bubble found in glass tubing.

air lock *n* [*UK*] [*Prisons*] a metal cage, consisting of two gates with wire mesh across the top; this is intended to control the movement of prisoners between one part of prison and another.

air man *n* [*US*] [*Railways*] air brake repairman.

air miss *n* [*Aerospace*] the official description of a narrow escape from collision by two airplanes flying too close to each other.

air pit *n* [*Mining*] a mine ventilation shaft.

air pocket stock *n* [*Stock market*] stock that falls suddenly and sharply, usually when the market hears bad news – eg. a poor trading return – regarding the company in question; the image is of an aircraft plunging on hitting turbulence.

air ride *n* [*US*] [*Car salesmen*] car equipped with pneumatic shock absorbers.

air slit *n* [*Coal-mining*] See **stenton**.

air that blows cold *n* [*US*] [*Car salesmen*] a functioning air conditioner in a car.

air time *n* [*TV, Advertising*] that percentage of a station's broadcasting schedule that is available to advertisers.

air tucking *n* [*US*] [*Textiles*] the operation of sewing round, puffed tucks into fabric materials in garment making.

air-blind *n* [*Flying*] a pilot who watches the instruments constantly; thus 'air-blindness' is a lack of intuitive flying sense.

airborne alert *n* [*Military*] the policy of maintaining a bomber force on round-the-clock readiness in the air in order to launch an offensive more quickly and to prevent planes from being destroyed on the ground. Such a system was operated by the USAF until 1968, when it was abandoned in the face of a preponderance of ground and sea-launched **ICBMs**, but is activated when the US forces go to any level of crisis warning.

airedale *n* [*US*] [*Marine Corps*] an aviator.

airland battle *n* [*Military*] the integration of planes covering conventional, nuclear, chemical and electronic capabilities in a general style of battlefield fighting that emphasises offensive manoeuvring rather than static defence.

airline nicknames *n* [*Air travel*] Pandemonium Scareways (Pan Am), Try Walking Airways (TWA), Queer and Nice Types of Stewards (QANTAS), Can't Promise Anything (Canadian Pacific Airways), Sweet and Sexy (SAS).

airplane turn *n* [*US*] [*Skiing*] a mid-air turn made after skiing over a **mogul**.

airplay *n* [*Pop music*] the radio broadcasting of a record. See also **needle time**.

airport (art) *n* [*Antiques*] rubbishy, valueless art objects, often of an 'ethnic' type and similar to the sort of things offered to tourists in every international airport.

air-tights *n* [*US*] [*Cattlemen*] canned goods.

aisle sitter *n* [*Theatre*] the critic (who can thus escape quickly to write/phone in his/her review rather than battle the length of a crowded row).

alarm threshold *n* [*Military*] in nuclear research laboratories and nuclear energy plants the level of lost nuclear material (**MUF**) that is considered dangerous: terrorists could have stolen it, other nations might have had it surreptitiously delivered for the manufacture of bombs, etc.

albatross **1.** *n* [*Golf*] a hole played in three strokes under **par**. **2.** *n* [*US*] [*Medicine*] a very sick patient with complex incurable problems; the doctor is stuck with this patient until one of them dies.

Albert *n* [*Printing*] a standard size of writing paper: six inches by four inches.

albino *n* [*Philately*] a stamp that has been mistakenly printed without the correct colour and thus merely shows a colourless impression.

ALBM *n* [*Military*] acro **air-launched ballistic missile** air-to-air, air-to-ground, air-to-sea.

album *n* [*Video*] a single title that, because of its length, has to be packaged on two video discs.

alc *n* [*US*] [*Medicine*] abbr of Sp. **'a la casa'** meaning 'to the house, homeward'; thus it is a patient who is ready to go home.

ALCM *n* [*Military*] acro **Air-Launched Cruise Missile** a subsonic air-to-ground **cruise missile** which is deployed on a variety of US strategic bombers in addition to nuclear bombs and other missiles. Like all cruise missiles it is highly accurate and delivers its 200 kiloton warhead after a 2,500 km. flight to within 30 metres of a target. The Russians also deploy ALCMs, the most accurate and penetrative of which are the AS–4 (Kitchen) and AS–6 (Kingfish). See also **ASALM**.

alderman *n* [*Angling*] the chub, also a large trout.

alert crew **1.** *n* [*US*] [*Air Force*] five-man USAF teams who man the Strategic Air Command (SAC) missile launch facility at Offutt Air Force

Base and the equivalent posts in the **Cover All** flying command post. **2.** n [US] [Air Force] the SAC bomber crews who are ranked second in excellence and skill to the 'select crews'; these categories were originated in 1951 by **SAC** commander General Curtis LeMay.

alert levels n pl [Air travel] regular inspection times laid down for the repair or replacement of defective parts on civil airliners. See also **A check, B check**.

A-level title n [Video] a big budget feature released on cassette by one of the major distributors and backed by some degree of national advertising; it provides a large proportion of the stock of home-video rental stores. See also **B-level title**.

alevin n [Angling] trout or salmon after emerging from the egg.

alfalfa n [US] [Carnival] See **ceazarney**.

ALGOL n [Computing] acro **Algorithmic Language** a computer language intended for programming in higher mathematics and complex technology; it was designed by a committee of European academics and is still more popular in Europe than in the US.

algorithm n [Computing] a set of well-defined rules for solving a problem in a finite number of steps.

alias 1. n [Computing] an alternative **label**. It is possible to use a label and a number of aliases to refer to the same element or point in a program. **2.** n [Photo-typesetting] the faulty inclusion or omission of a **pixel** in the digital record of a typographic character.

alibi copy n [Journalism] a duplicate copy of an original story and the reporter's notes; this is kept in the newspaper **morgue** and filed against any possible challenges, libel suits and similar recriminations.

Alice, also **White Alice** n [Military] acro **Alaska Integrated Communications** the USAF's network of early-warning radar stations in Alaska; this is now obsolete and is being replaced by the **seek frost** system.

alien a [Computing] said of any part of a system – hardware or software – that is non-compatible with the rest.

alien tones n [Audio] any frequencies or harmonics that occur in sound reproduction because of irregularities in the transmission path.

alienation 1. n [Politics] in Marxist doctrine, this means the estrangement of the worker from his true 'social' being – his family, friends and useful work – for the performance of meaningless and unnatural work. It is the feeling of being unable to influence one's own life and environment, thus becoming not a person but a thing. **2.** n [Theatre] from Ger. Verfremdungseffekt, an effect desired by playright Bertolt Brecht (1898–1956) whereby his plays would place the audience at a discernable (and continually stressed) distance from the events related, in direct opposition to the cosy

involvement and identification encouraged by 'bourgeois' theatre.

alienist n [US] [Law] forensic psychiatrist or psycho-analyst who testifies as an expert, either for the prosecution or the defence, in court cases.

alignment n [Role-gaming] a capsule description of a character's behaviour in terms of the basic designations of law, neutrality and chaos.

alimony drone n [Law, Sociology] a divorced woman who deliberately refuses to remarry in order to continue receiving alimony.

all a [UK] [TV] in the independent network a scheduling term that denotes the use of a programme by all IBA companies, without any exception.

all beer and baggy trousers a [Navy] very easy.

all buttoned up a [Merchant navy] completely prepared and ready.

all call n [Education] in an electronic learning laboratory a single control that enables the instructor to talk to all students simultaneously, over-riding the educational programming.

all commodity volume n [Market research] the accumulated turnover of everything sold in a shop, chain or multiple group.

all hands! excl [Merchant navy] all hands to assemble on deck immediately.

all in adv [Printing] a situation where all copy and proofs are available. See also **all up**.

all in hand a [Printing] the state of a job after all copy has been distributed to the typesetters.

all night in with the guts kicked out n [Navy] the middle watch – from midnight to 4.00 am – which 'kicks the guts out' of one's sleep.

all on adv [Hunting] the expression used by the whipper-in to tell the huntsman that every hound in the pack is present.

all or nothing piece n [Clockmakers] a piece of the mechanism of a repeating watch which either allows the striking of the hours and quarters or completely prevents it.

all over the wicket 1. adv [Cricket] used when a batsman is comprehensively and completely beaten by a ball, and is usually bowled or ruled LBW by it. **2.** adv [Cricket] to hit (or to be hit) – : used when a batsman plays havoc with whatever bowling he receives and scores freely and plentifully; thus it is also used when a bowler suffers such treatment.

all published a [Book collecting] despite appearances, or intentions to the contrary, the volume or series so described was not continued.

all standing 1. adv [Navy] used when a ship comes to a sudden stop or a person cuts short an activity. **2.** adv [Navy] fully equipped; thus to sleep all standing means to sleep with one's clothes on.

all things to all men a [Merchant navy] this refers to the captain, who must perform that role during a voyage.

all up *adv* [*Printing*] the state of a print job after all the copy has been set. See also **all in hand**.

all-along 1. *n* [*Book-binding*] the method of hand-sewing the sections of a book on cords or tapes when the thread goes from kettle-stitch to kettle-stitch inside the fold of each section. 2. *n* [*Book-binding*] a machine-sewn book in which each section has the full number of stitches.

Allen charge *n* [*US*] [*Law*] an instruction or charge to a hung jury in which the judge suggests that they reconsider their views in deference to whatever majority already prevails and do their best to reach a verdict; from Allen vs US (1897), in which this 'charge' was first used.

Allende principle *n* [*Politics*] a term named after the late Chilean President Salvador G. Allende (1908–1973) who developed the theory of international compensation for poorer nations; under this theory nations have the right to retain all profits above 10% that would otherwise be owed to the foreign owners of firms that have been nationalised. The principle was first introduced by Allende in 1971 and may well have contributed to the CIA's involvement in his deposition.

alley 1. *n* [*Ice-hockey*] a restricted area of the rink, found at its extreme left and right hand sides. 2. *n* [*US*] [*Journalism*] the floor space between two parallel rows of compositors in a newspaper composing room. 3. *n* [*Prisons*] a corridor between rows of cells in a prison. 4. *n* [*US*] [*Railways*] an empty track in a railway marshalling yard. 5. *n* [*Textiles*] the aisle running between the lines of looms in a mill.

Alliance for Progress *n* [*Politics*] the financial links between the US and certain Latin/South American states through which the US attempts to buy off and undermine revolutionary fervour by strengthening right-wing governments (eg: El Salvador), backing counter-revolutionary guerrillas (the Contras in Nicaragua) or actively destabilising left-wing governments (Allende in Chile).

alligator 1. *n* [*Logging*] a boat that has a windlass and cable for hauling logs. 2. *n* [*Logging*] a sled, often made from the fork of a tree, used in skidding logs. 3. *n* [*Navy*] the ship's navigator.

alligator boots *n* [*UK*] [*Railways*] working boots in which the uppers have parted from the soles, due to constant soaking in diesel fuel; the 'teeth' are the nails so revealed.

alligator spread *n* [*Stock market*] a spread of **put and call options** that generate so many commissions in the market that the actual client for whom they have been arranged is unlikely to make a profit and instead is 'eaten alive' by these commissions.

alligatoring, also **crocodiling** *n* [*Painting*] the cracking and shrinking of paint or varnish caused by contraction; the pattern of cracks thus produced resembles the hide of an alligator.

all-in *n* [*UK*] [*TV*] a special breakfast sandwich provided by TV location caterers for actors and crew; it comprises bacon, egg, sausage and tomato.

all-night money *n* [*Sex*] the fee charged by a prostitute for staying with one client for the whole night.

allonge *n* [*Commerce*] a piece of paper attached to a bill of exchange which provides space for extra endorsements once the space available on the original bill is used up; it comes from Fr. 'allonger' meaning 'to lengthen'.

allonym *n* [*Literary criticism*] a ghost-written work in which the author's real name is used, but the actual writer is anonymous.

allotment note *n* [*Shipping*] a note from a sailor to his employers charging them with the payment of his wages to a specified person or to a bank.

all-over paintings *n* [*Art*] paintings that, in order to create a figure/ground effect, avoid all kinds of central composition or grouping of forms into areas of special interest. They are usually painted in a uniform manner, or with accents distributed evenly across the surface of the canvas, filling it right up to the framing edges.

allowance *n* [*Horse-racing*] a deduction from the weight a horse has to carry in a handicap.

allowed time *n* [*Industrial relations*] the time during which a worker is not actually producing goods, but is resting, eating or maintaining his machine, and during which he is still paid.

all-round price *n* [*Commerce*] an all-inclusive price, taking in everything that might otherwise have been added as an extra.

all-singing, all-dancing version *n* [*Business*] super-glamorised, gimmicky, flashy version of any stock product. There is no guarantee, other than an increase in superficial saleability, that there have been any real improvements to the basic model.

all-up *a* [*Aerospace*] said of the weight of an aeroplane when it is in the air, including the plane itself, its passengers, crew and cargo.

alongside date *n* [*Shipping*] the date on which a given ship is contracted to be alongside a dock for loading/unloading of cargo.

alpha beta technique *n* [*Artificial intelligence*] a technique used in game-playing routines to determine the best set of moves for a given player. The player picks the set of moves to maximise his score and the adversary will attempt to find moves that minimise his losses. The succession of moves is represented as a tree in which the players choose branches at alternate levels. The alpha beta technique eliminates subtrees, thus reducing the effort needed to search for the best moves.

alpha stage *n* [*Finance*] in venture captialism, the initial seed money required to launch a project; thus the beta stage is the making of a financial commitment to a project that has yet to establish a financial track record. The gamma stage is the stage for financial expansion based

A

on the examination of the records of a project over a reasonable period of time.

alpha stocks, also **alpha securities** *n pl* [*UK*] [*Stock exchange*] the sixty most actively traded stocks or securities categorised as such on the London market, with ten or more **market-makers** in each. See also **beta stocks, gamma stocks, delta stocks.**

alphabet fares *n* [*Air travel*] See **ABC 1.**

alphabet soup *n* [*Journalism, Government*] writing which relies heavily on initial acronyms and abbreviations; eg. that which inevitably accompanies writing about politics, bureaucracy, modern warfare, etc.

alpha-beta approach *n* [*US*] [*Stock market*] the mathematical way in which individual stocks differ from the movement of the market as a whole. A beta co-efficient tries to work out in advance what will happen to any one stock or portfolio of stocks when considered against the overall market shift; the alpha measurement accounts for a stock's performance in ways that cannot be attributed to the beta.

also rans *n pl* [*Theatre*] supporting roles, bit parts; it comes from horse-racing terminology referring to the runners-up.

altar service *n* [*Salvation Army*] personal monetary gifts offered annually by SA members during Self-Denial Week.

alternade *n* [*Logology*] the writing of a word or words on two lines – with one letter on top, the succeeding one below, the next one on top and so on – so that the separate lines yield different words.

alternate action *n* [*Swimming*] a swimming style in which either the legs or the arms act in immediate succession and not simultaneously.

alternate demand, also **competing demand 1.** *n* [*Economics*] the demand for two or more products which are each a substitute for the other. **2.** *n* [*Economics*] the demand for factors of production which are interchangeable, and thus can be used in place of each other.

alternates *n pl* [*Air travel*] airports other than the stated destination which are listed on the flight plan of a civil airlines and which are used for emergency landing in the case of engine malfunction, inclement weather, etc.

alum *n* [*Weaving*] abbr of **potassium aluminium sulphate,** a **mordant.**

amateurs *n pl* [*US*] [*Politics*] citizens otherwise successful and powerful who help out in political campaigns – much to the scorn of professional volunteers and party workers. Unlike the stamp-licking, xeroxing volunteer, the amateur uses his/her personal power, status and influence to enhance the candidate's chances. The implication is supposed to be one of honest, open, political work, rather than the harder methods of cynical 'pols'.

A-matter *n* [*Journalism*] the first paragraph of a given newspaper story. See also **stand-first.**

ambidexter *n* [*Law, Crime*] a juror or lawyer who takes bribes from both parties involved in a lawsuit.

ambience *n* [*Audio*] variations on the sound produced by a recording or a live performance due to the characteristics of the room, concert hall, studio, etc. in which the sound is being produced. See also **ambient noise.**

ambient conditions *n pl* [*Technology*] whatever natural conditions are present in a given environment before any synthetic conditions are constructed – for experiments, tests, etc.

ambient light *n* [*Film, TV*] whatever light exists in a given location before the lighting crew begin to add artificial lighting to the set. This can be daylight or, if indoors, the existing electric light sources. See also **ambient noise.**

ambient noise *n* [*Film, TV*] natural sounds – passing cars, ringing telephones, even buzzing insects – that can be picked up by the recording equipment when filming at an outside location. Such sounds must be as far as possible eliminated and replaced on the finished soundtrack – if they are required – by specifically recorded 'natural' **wild tracks.** See also **ambient light.**

ambitty *a* [*Glass-blowing*] said of translucent 'antique' glass which has become devitrified while it is being worked and is used mainly for leaded lights and similar decorative purposes.

ambivalent *a* [*Sex*] bisexual.

ambulance chaser *n* [*Law, Police*] a lawyer who makes a business of persuading accident victims to institute legal actions over personal injuries; he metaphorically pursues the sirens all the way to the emergency room.

ambulance knot *n* [*Needlework*] a reef knot.

American Account countries *n* [*Banking*] certain countries, mainly in Central and South America, where sterling held in accounts with UK banks is freely convertible into dollars.

American baptism *n* [*Navy*] a good bath administred to those joining the ship.

American clause *n* [*Marine insurance*] a clause in some policies whereby the insured party takes out two insurances on the same risk on the same property. The underwriter of the earlier-dated policy is the first to meet any loss and the insured can only claim on the second policy if the first has failed to meet the loss in full.

American sublime *n* [*Art*] See **abstract sublime.**

AMF *n* [*US*] [*Medicine*] abbr of **Adios Mother-Fucker!** a note written on the file of a patient considered to be malingering and who has been taking up the space required for a more deserving case.

amicus curiae *n* [*Law*] a person with special expertise who seeks to advise the court on a given case; a defendant who prefers to dispense with

A

counsel is entitled to use such an expert; it comes from Lat. meaning 'friend of the court'.

ammoniacal a [*Cheese-making*] used to describe a cheese which has passed optimum maturity and has begun to exude the smell of ammonia; usually said of soft or semi-soft cheeses.

ammunition n [*Gambling*] cash with which one bets.

amp n [*Drugs*] abbr of ampoule (of methedrine).

AMT n pl [*Industry*] abbr of **advanced manufacturing techniques**, including various computer-based and robotics applications within factories.

amusement shares n [*Stock market*] a classification of shares, including those dealing with the entertainment and leisure industries.

A.N. Other n [*Sport*] a programme note for a sports event listing a competitor or team member whose name is yet to be announced.

ana n [*Literary criticism*] a collection of sayings, anecdotes, table talk, etc, culled from the lifetime of a given individual.

analog, also **analogue** n [*Photo-typesetting*] a visual image, drawn, painted, engraved or cut from a mask for line characters, or in continuous tone for photographic prints.

analogues n pl [*Catering*] any form of 'meat', 'fish' or other artificial foodstuff created from extruded soyabean.

analytic relationship n [*Technology*] the relationship that exists between concepts and their corresponding terms, as seen in their definition and in the scope of their meaning.

anamorphic art n [*Art*] paintings or drawings containing images that appear distorted or stretched but which become normal when viewed in a mirror with a curved surface, or when seen from a specific vantage point.

anamorphic lens n [*Film*] lens by which an image is 'squeezed', eg. a wide picture on to a standard film. The projector is equipped with a reverse system which 'unsqueezes' the picture back onto a wide screen.

anaphora n [*Literary criticism*] the repetition of a word or phrase in successive clauses, sentences or paragraphs in order to attain a mounting rhetorical effect.

anarchism n [*Politics*] in Marxist terms, a revisionist political movement which, with its blanket condemnation of the organised state, is condemned utterly by orthodox Communist ideologues: 'petty bourgeois, reactionary, social political current, hostile to the proletarian scientific socialism' (Soviet Encyclopedia, 1950).

anarcho-communism n [*Politics*] a movement dedicated to the elimination of the state and the establishment of free collectivism. Society is to be made up of 'associations of working people' and distribution would be according to need rather than as any form of 'reward' for work performed.

anarcho-co-operativism n [*Politics*] a version

of **anarchism** which would base all economic and social life on small co-operative ventures.

anarcho-individualism n [*Politics*] a version of **anarchism** which advocates a return to a free, natural and competitive economy, operated by small, independent owners.

anarcho-syndicalism n [*Politics*] a version of **anarchism** which would take trades unions as the source of all economic and social organisation, management and pursuits.

anarchy of production n [*Politics*] in Marxist terms a description of unrestricted laissez-faire capitalism, cut-throat competition and the in-built destructive instability that such a system must supposedly engender.

anastrophe n [*Literary criticism*] the inversion or withholding of the usual order of words to obtain a rhetorical effect.

anbauhobel n [*Coal-mining*] a coal **plough** in which the independent drive is anchored to an armoured conveyor.

ancestor n [*Computing*] the ancestor of a node: any node in a **tree** on the path from the 'root' of the tree to the node in question.

anchor 1. n [*Athletics*] the runner of the final leg in a relay race. **2.** n [*Athletics*] the end member of a tug-of-war team, who secures the rope around his body. **3.** n [*Building*] a metal fitting that secures a building stone in place on the face of a building. **4.** n [*Mining*] a miner's pick.

anchor cannon n [*Billiards*] a stroke in which the two object balls are kept close to or against the cushion so that a series of cannons can be made without disturbing the basic position of the balls.

anchor cattle n [*US*] [*Cattlemen*] a nucleus of cattle which are used as the basis for rounding up a large herd.

anchor it v [*US*] [*Road transport*] to make an emergency stop; it is slang from anchors meaning brakes.

anchor light n [*Navy*] a white light visible all round the horizon that must be shown fore and aft by all vessels over 150' long when anchored at sea.

anchor man n [*Gambling*] the player in black-jack who sits to the dealer's extreme right, and is thus the last player to play his hand.

anchor man/woman/person n [*TV*] a news-caster who reads the news and co-ordinates the reports of specialists and remote reporters in and out of the studio; the UK usage is 'presenter', but this US neologism is taking over. Two or more anchor persons are co-anchors.

anchor station n [*Coal-mining*] a device – usually hydraulic – which prevents uncontrolled movement of the delivery or return end units of a conveyor.

anchor tenant n [*US*] [*Business, Real estate*] a 'celebrity tenant' – usually a successful, household name business – whose taking up of a lease in a

A

new shopping centre will encourage other firms to follow suit.

anchorage *n* [*US*] [*Building*] a foundation to which one end of a suspension cable is secured.

anchor-and-chain clause *n* [*Marine insurance*] a clause that frees the insurers from the responsibility of retrieving an anchor and chain lost in bad weather.

ancilla *n* [*Bibliography*] an aid or guide to understanding, appreciating or mastering a difficult problem; it comes from Lat. 'ancilla' meaning 'a female servant or helper'.

and cakes *n* [*Theatre*] a supplementary allowance that may be part of the actor's main contract; it means that the management will either supply or pay the bills for board and lodging.

Andrew *n* [*Navy*] The Royal Navy; originally the name for a man o'war or for the government naval authorities in general. Both terms stem from one Lieut. Andrew Millar or Miller who allegedly impressed so many recruits into the Navy that it has borne his name ever since.

Andromeda strain *n* [*Medicine*] any strain of bacteria, viruses or other micro-organisms whose accidental release from a laboratory might have catastrophic effects because of its unknown biochemical makeup; it comes from the book 'The Andromeda Strain' (1969) by Michael Crichton (1942–).

Andy Gump *n* [*US*] [*Medicine*] a patient who has had an operation for cancer of the jaw and whose mandible has been removed; this removal makes it appear that the patient has no chin, and thus resembles 'Andy Gump', a cartoon character.

Andy McNish *n* [*Navy*] rhyming slang meaning any kind of fish served to the crew.

anecdotal *a* [*Education, Sociology*] said of any work that is backed up by example.

anfo *n* [*Military*] a type of home-made explosive used for making terrorist bombs in Ulster.

angel **1.** *n* [*Air Force*] the measurement of height in distances of 1000 vertical feet; thus 'Angels One-Five' = 15,000 feet. **2.** *n* [*Radar*] an otherwise unattributable electronic signal, possibly caused by unusually strong humidity or atmospheric pressure, that causes an 'echo' to be shown up on the screen. **3.** *n* [*Shipping*] an air-sea rescue helicopter that rescues seamen from possible drowning. **4.** *n* [*Theatre*] the backer of a show. **5.** *v* [*Theatre*] to make an investment in a show.

angel of light *n* [*Religion*] Satan as an apparently wonderful but in fact deceitful figure; see II Corinthians 11.14.

angel's share *n* [*Distilling*] in the distilling of cognac, the 3% of the maturing spirit that evaporates while it is still in the cask.

angel's whisper *n* [*Navy*] the bugle call or pipe sounded to summon defaulters before the captain.

angle of attack *n* [*Coal-mining*] the angle which the horizontal axis of a cutting element of a machine makes with the line of a face.

angle station *n* [*Coal-mining*] the place at which the direction of the horizontal movement of a conveyor is changed.

Anglo-American point *n* [*Photo-typesetting*] 0.013833 inch, or 0.35136 mm.

angulation **1.** *n* [*Dog breeding*] the angles created by bones meeting at various joints, especially the shoulder, **stifle** and hock; a dog that exhibits a correct range of angulations for its breed is 'well-turned' or 'well-angulated'. **2.** *n* [*Skiing*] bending the body away from the slope or to the outside of the turn to maintain balance.

animals *n pl* [*Gambling*] professional 'heavies' on the casino payroll; they are used to collect outstanding debts and to ensure that no customers misbehave on the premises.

animatic **1.** *n* [*Advertising*] a rough version of a commercial made from a **storyboard**. **2.** *n* [*Advertising*] any moving, animated element within a TV commercial. See also **photomatic**.

ankle **1.** *n* [*Crime, Police*] ankle holster. **2.** *v* [*Cycling*] to turn the pedal with the foot, using the ankle as an pivot; the optimum way of ensuring smooth cycling. **3.** *v* [*Film*] *vi* to resign: the implication is of instant departure – running away – and leaving the whole production in the lurch. *vt* to dismiss, to fire someone.

annatto *n* [*Cheese-making*] a yellowish-red pulp that surrounds the seeds of the South American annatto tree and which is used to colour cheese such as 'Livarot', 'Maroilles' and 'Munster' prior to **washing**.

Annie Oakley *n* [*Theatre, Film*] a free pass to the theatre; it is named after the markswoman Annie Oakley (Phoebe Ann Mozee Butler, 1860–1926): the holes punched in such tickets supposedly resembled the aces out of which Ms. Oakley would shoot the pips.

annish *n* [*Science fiction*] the edition of a magazine produced on the anniversary of its first issue.

annual **1.** *n* [*Theatre*] the regular Christmas pantomime. **2.** *n* [*Stock market*] the annual report to the stockholders. These days this once basic statement of profit and loss has turned into a massive piece of self-aggrandising promotion and not suprisingly it is often farmed out to a PR company to ensure maximum effect.

annulus *n* [*Oil rigs*] the annular space between the **drill string** and the well bore.

anomalous water, also **orthowater**, **superwater** *n* [*Science*] a type of water that behaves more like a non-crystalline material (eg: glass) than a crystalline one (eg: ice) when at sub-zero temperatures. A variety of opposing views see it either as something totally unknown or alternatively merely water with ionic impurities.

anomaly switch *n* [*Stock market*] in the context of the **gilt-edged** market, an anomaly means that the prices of two stocks have moved out of their normal relationship. When this situation occurs an anomaly switch is carried out: one stock is sold and the other bought with the intention of reversing the process once the price relationship returns to normal.

anomie n [Sociology] literally it means 'without law' (Gr.); it was resurrected from its classical origins by the French sociologist Emile Durkheim in 'Suicide' (1897) to denote a society which had lost its sense of generally accepted social values and standards. The term is increasingly used of an individual who has lost his traditional moorings and is subject to psychic and social maladjustment and disorientation.

anonymous sculpture n [Architecture] a term coined by Bernhard and Hilda Becher in 1970 to describe certain types of industrial building (eg: gasometers) which they feel exhibit sculptural qualities.

another place n [Politics] the formal reference by members of the House of Lords or House of Commons to the other chamber.

another pretty face n [TV] a derogatory putdown by US network **anchor men** of their less celebrated peers who work on the **affiliate** news programmes.

ANSI n [Computing] acro **American National Standards Institution** an industry-supported standards organisation, founded in 1918, that establishes for the US computer industry a variety of **hardware** standards and some software standards.

answer lamp n [Telephony] a switchboard lamp that signifies a connection by lighting up when a plug is inserted into a connecting jack, goes out when the call is answered, then lights up again when the call is over.

answer print n [Film] the first print of a film to contain both the pictures and the sound. Colour values, etc., still have to be added before the release print (the one which is shown in the cinema) can be manufactured.

ant n [Aerospace] abbr of **antenna**, aerial.

antagonistic conditions of distribution n [Politics] Marxist longhand for the fact that some people have more money than others, or in Marxist terms, the inequalities of financial distribution in non-socialist and especially in capitalist countries.

antenna farm n [Telephony, Radio] an area of land on which are sited a number of receiving and/or transmitting antennae.

anti-aliasing n [Photo-typesetting] the avoidance or removal of unwanted elements in a digitised character **mosaic**.

anti-art n [Art] the fundamental concept of the Dada movement, which totally repudiated bourgeois art and culture. Yet, however shocking and destructive of traditional 'art' Dada might have been at its inception, the inevitable historical paradox has caught up with it and now 'anti-art' is as highly priced and collectable as any 'respectable' artefact.

anticipation (US), also **cash discount** (UK) n [Commerce] a deduction from his bill which the customer makes if he pays up before the due date; the UK discount differs in that the bonus is given by the firm rather than taken by the customer – a favour rather than a right.

anticipatory reaction n [Military] a preemptive strike, a surprise attack.

anticipatory retaliation n [Military] a surprise attack.

anticipatory staging n [Computing] a technique in which blocks of data are moved from one storage device to another which has a shorter access time, to prepare for the request for that data by the program.

anti-dive geometry n [Cars] an arrangement of the front suspension to minimise or eliminate nose dipping while braking; this is partly for comfort, partly to maintain adhesion and stability.

anti-dumping measure n [Commerce] a regulation instituted by a government to discourage the importation of cheap goods that undercut the products manufactured by the home country.

anti-economism n [Politics] in Marxist terms the revolutionary belief that politics, not just economic changes, will improve the lot of the workers.

anti-form n [Art] sculptures produced during the late 1960s, that focussed on materials, the force of gravity and the production process; they were a reaction against the geometric, predominantly retangular form of previous abstract sculpture.

anti-godlin n [US] [Cattlemen] a diagonal or roundabout movement.

antigram n [Logology] the transposal of letters in a word to create a new word or words that have a meaning opposite to that of the original word; the term comes from antonym and anagram.

antiloop, also **antispin** n [Table tennis] a type of rubber used on bats to minimise the spin imparted to the ball by one's opponent.

anti-object art n [Art] art that attempts to minimise the art itself in favour of the personality of the artist, his or her ideas, theories and beliefs.

anti-psychiatry n [Medicine] a movement in therapeutic practice, pioneered by R. D. Laing, which rejects traditional concepts of psychiatry – especially such treatments as ECT, leucotomy, major tranquillisers and any form of authoritarian psychiatry – in favour of the properly self-directed resolution of personality disorders. Psychiatrists and mental hospitals were seen as socially repressive and ostensible 'madness' as quite possibly a healthy response to a sick world.

antique n [Printing] a design in which the constituent strokes are of approximately the same thickness, serifs are of a slab formation, with some slight bracketing to the stems.

anti-skating device n [Audio] any mechanism

that provides bias compensation on the pick-up arm of a hi-fi system.

anti-social attitude *n* [*Politics*] among the doctrinaire left, this is the condemnation of any attitudes or beliefs that clash with the current party line.

anti-squat *n* [*Cars*] a modification to the suspension to help reduce the fall of the rear of the car during acceleration.

antonomasia *n* [*Literary criticism*] the substitution of an epithet or nickname for a person's proper name, or of a proper name for a common noun; eg. 'The Big Yin' (Billy Connolly) or 'a Don Juan'.

ao *n* [*US*] [*Police*] abbr of **arresting officer**.

aob *a* [*US*] [*Police*] abbr of **alcohol on breath**.

AOH *n* [*US*] [*Bars*] a corruption of '**out of here**', a customer who does not tip.

AON *n* [*Business*] abbr of **All or None** a lot of goods presented for sale which must be purchased complete and unopened, or not at all.

AOR *n* [*Pop music*] abbr of **Adult Orientated Rock/Album Orientated Rock** music aimed at those who were teenagers in the 1960s and who are now assumed to have adopted 'mature' lifestyles, although still true to the idols of their youth. Such music lacks the gut appeal of rock 'n' roll, retaining only the banality of its lyrics.

AOT *n* [*Journalism*] abbr of **at any time** a story that is not date-tied and which can be used when required.

ap *n* [*Navy*] abbr of **admiralty pattern** used at the RN College, Dartmouth, where it means the right procedure, the correct way to do things.

apa *n* [*Science fiction*] abbr of **amateur press association** a group of science fiction fan-magazine publishers who submit copies of their publications to an official who then combines them for bulk distribution to subscribers.

apartment girl *n* [*Sex*] a prostitute who operates out of her own apartment.

apazine *n* [*Science fiction*] a magazine produced by an individual member of an **apa** for distribution throughout the membership.

APB *n* [*US*] [*Police*] abbr of **All points Bulletin** an emergency call over the police waveband that alerts all officers and vehicles to the identity and description of a wanted suspect.

APC *n* [*Economics*] abbr of the **average propensity to consume** a figure obtained by taking the total domestic expenditure by consumers on goods and services within an economy, and dividing it by the national income of that economy. See also **APS**.

ape *v* [*Theatre*] to steal a line from another actor during a performance.

apecon *n* [*Science fiction*] a science fiction convention and/or film festival featuring stories/films about apes ('King Kong', 'Planet of the Apes' etc.).

aperturismo *n* [*Politics*] the opening out and liberalisation of the former fascist political system

in Spain, after the death of General Franco in 1975. It comes from the Italian word, which was used to refer to new trends in Catholic ecumenism.

APEX *n* [*Air travel*] acro **Advance Purchase Excursion** cheap fare booking for advance purchase of tickets for holidays that are of a declared length, usually 22–45 days. Thus 'back-dated APEX' means cheap tickets issued under the APEX scheme but sold illegally through **bucket shops** and demanding neither the regulation 21 day advance booking nor the minimum stay requirement.

apocope *n* [*Literary criticism*] the loss of a syllable or letter at the end of a word; eg: 'huntin', shootin' and fishin".

apollo suit *n* [*Aerospace*] an integrated suit comprising four layers of garments which insulate and warm an astronaut during space travel, extra-vehicular activity, moon walks, etc.

apologetics *n* [*Politics*] the political development of an originally theological discipline: making doctrine (once religious, now ideological) acceptable to non-believers. Like the Christians before them, today's ideologues put forward sacred texts – Marx, Friedman, etc – on the theory that the public may come to ally their own beliefs with these texts; such alliances are formed through the subtleties and sophistication of the apologetics, the opposite of propaganda's much more simplistic efforts.

apostil *n* [*Literary criticism*] a note or comment made in the margin of a book.

apostrophe *n* [*Literary criticism*] the term for addressing an imaginary or absent person, as in an aside on stage, or a rhetorical digression – 'yet, gentle reader, if we could but . . .'

apparatus criticus *n* [*Bibliography*] additional notes provided in a scholarly edition of a work, eg. variant versions of the text, glossaries, etc.

appeal bond, also **judgement bond** *n* [*Law*] a bond which has to be entered into by an appellant to ensure that all costs and damages will be paid if he loses his appeal.

appear citation *n* [*US*] [*Law*] a written court order demanding that its subject appear at a certain court at a certain time to answer a specific criminal charge.

appearance money *n* [*Athletics*] thinly disguised bribes paid to star athletes in the form of 'expenses', but which are in fact intended to ensure the athletes' appearance at a given venue, thus attracting the paying customers to a stadium. See also **boot money**.

apellation d'origine *n* [*Cheese-making*] as used in France this is a specific definition of a particular cheese; it must indicate the breed of cows, sheep or goats; the area where the milk is produced; manufacturing techniques; composition of the product; its physical characteristics; its specific attributes.

A

appie *n* [*Medicine*] appendectomy patient.

applause line *n* [*Politics*] a line or sentence deliberately inserted into a speech to encourage 'spontaneous' applause from an audience; it is usually found as the answer to a series of rhetorical questions, or similar crowd-pleasing device. See also **pointer phrase**.

apple *n* [*Radio*] a Citizen's Band radio enthusiast.

apple corps *n* [*UK*] [*Railways*] footplatemen based in Yeovil, Somerset, home of cider and its apples.

apple jack *n* [*US*] [*Military*] the lowest level of US military preparedness for war.

applebox *n* [*TV*] a small podium hidden from the camera which raises the height either of short actors or of props.

apples *n pl* [*Wine-tasting*] a fresh, raw smell, indicative of an immature young wine.

appliance computer *n* [*Computing*] a prepackaged microprocessor designed for over the counter sales just like any other home appliance. Take it home, plug it in, and given an adequate manual and an efficient machine, the owner should soon be computing.

application *n* [*Sex*] the first 'interview' by a black pimp of a prospective prostitute, in order to assess her 'qualifications'.

application package *n* [*Computing*] a collection of linked software programs that is directed at a particular application and which can be tailored to a specific instance of that application.

application program *n* [*Computing*] what the computer actually does, rather than the technology that determines how it does it.

application terminal *n* [*Computing*] a combination of input and output devices assembled as a unit to provide a specific service in a particular environment; eg: automatic cash dispensers.

appointment *n* [*US*] [*Crime*] in the US Mafia, this is a business-only meeting between a **capo** and one of his **buttonmen**.

approach 1. *n* [*Golf*] the shot that puts a player's ball on the green. **2.** *n* [*Cards*] a style of bidding in bridge in which the suit rather than the no-trump is to be preferred in a biddable hand.

approach work *n* [*Soccer*] the play that leads towards the vicinity of the goalmouth.

appropriated goods *n pl* [*Shipping*] goods found in a ship's hold after unloading which have no known owner; such goods may be given to an assignee in place of goods delivered short.

approximation of laws *n* [*Economics, Government*] the policy of states, subject to treaties of commerical intent, whereby laws governing or influencing commercial transactions are aligned, thus creating mutual hopes and promoting international trade, eg: the Treaty of Rome, which established the EEC.

appurtenances *n pl* [*Shipping*] everything necessary for the proper functioning of a ship.

april fool torpedo *n* [*Navy*] the phosphorescent wake of a porpoise near the ship.

APRN *phr* [*Medicine*] abbr of **Aspirin When Necessary**.

apron 1. *n* [*Ship-building*] a timber used to strengthen the stem of a vessel. **2.** *n* [*Weaving*] a cloth extension on the **warp** and **cloth beams** of a loom; thus 'apron rod' is the rod in the apron to which the warp ends are tied.

APS *n* [*Economics*] abbr of **the average propensity to save** the proportion of national income not spent on consumption and service goods. See also **APC**.

aptronym *n* [*Literary criticism*] a term coined by the columnist Franklin P. Adams: a name that suits its bearer, eg: Mrs. Doasyouwouldbedoneby; Mr. Wackford Squeers, etc.

APV *n* [*Business*] abbr of **Administrative Point of View** the management or corporate 'party line' which lays down a firm's business orthodoxy.

aquaplaning *n* [*Cars*] a skid in wet weather caused when the wedge of water that builds up where the tyre meets the road is not adequately dispersed by the tread in the tyre; once a car starts to aquaplane the vehicle is uncontrollable until it manages to touch the ground again.

aquit *v* [*Law, Commerce*] to discharge a debt.

ar *n* [*US*] [*Police*] abbr of **armed robbery**.

arabica *n* [*Coffee production*] coffea arabica: the coffee variety native to Abyssinia and Africa but more recently grown throughout the tropics. Arabica coffees are more delicate than the **robusta** varieties and connoisseurs prefer the flavour they produce.

Arakcheyevism *n* [*Politics*] a term named after Arakcheyev (1769–1834), chief of police for Tsars Nicholas I and Alexander I. His regime of arbitrary, crude and militaristic policing left a name that characterises many of his successors. The name now includes any Soviet boss who intimidates his critics with threats and violence.

arbitrage *n* [*Finance*] the simultaneous trading in two markets in order to profit by the difference in prices.

arbitrary *n* [*Printing*] an extra character, supplementary to the normal font of type, used for extra letters, accents, scientific and technical signs, etc.

arbor 1. *n* [*US*] [*Industry*] a spindle or axle of a wheel. **2.** *n* [*US*] [*Industry*] the metal shaft or axis on which a revolving cutting tool, eg. a circular saw, is mounted.

arc *n* [*Film*] a high-powered lamp used for projectors and in studio lights; its illumination consists of an electrical discharge between two carbon rods.

arc light *n* [*Military*] a bomb strike delivered by a B–52 bomber; the flash and explosion of the massive bomb payload provides the bright light that earned this nickname.

arc out *v* [*Film*] used as an order to an actor to

A

cross in front of the camera by walking in a slight arc; on screen this will appear as a straight line, whereas an actual straight line will make it seem as if the actor is approaching and then retreating from the camera.

arch **1.** *n* [*UK*] [*Coal-mining*] a steel skeleton in the shape of an elongated semicircle used to support the roof and sides of a tunnel. This arch comprises three pieces – the bow (sometimes called the crown) and two legs. The bow goes up first, temporarily secured by two iron bars protruding from the last completed arch, the horseheads; once the bow is secure it is covered with corrugated iron sheets, pinned to the bow by wedging them between the bow and roof overhead with wooden wedges; once this is done the legs are bolted to the bow, making a free-standing structure. **2.** *n* [*Glass-making*] the curved roof of a pot furnace. **3.** *n* [*Glass-making*] the opening through which a pot, a small container in which glass is melted, is put into a furnace.

arch it *v* [*Sex*] when a prostitute solicits from alleys or archways.

arch man *n* [*Glass-making*] a worker who controls the heating of refractory material in the roofs of furnaces.

arch tiffy *n* [*Navy*] the warrant engineer in a ship; the name comes from the 'Archangel of Artificers', the Senior Artificer.

archaeopsychic relics *n pl* [*New therapies*] in the terminology of TA (**transactional analysis**) this refers to the child that remains in all human beings; this manifests itself in the adult in the form of his/her excitements and fantasies.

architectural barrier *n* [*Building*] any feature of a building or other construction that prevents or hinders access to use by handicapped persons; such barriers can include awkwardly positioned light-switches, high kerbstones, public toilets positioned down steps, etc.

architectural design *n* [*Computing*] the breaking down of a complete program into a number of interconnected modules. See also **program decomposition**.

architecture *n* [*Computing*] the internal design of a computer in which its components are sited and linked together; like that of buildings, the architecture is a concept lying behind the construction of the computer, and does not refer to the actual chips, boards, wires, etc.

architecture active *n* [*Architecture*] the reciprocal relationship between human beings and architecture, ie: man produces architecture and architecture influences man.

architecture without architects, also **anonymous, exotic, indigenous, non-pedigreed, rude, rural, spontaneous, vernacular architecture** *n* [*Architecture*] shelters and structures, caves, earthworks, tents, tree houses, villages, used or built by people with no professional training in architecture: early

man, ancient and primitive tribes, nomads, peasants.

archivolt *n* [*Building, Plastering*] an architrave around a curved opening.

arcology *n* [*Architecture*] architecture plus ecology: a completely integrated planned city or environment within a singular structure; eg: Paolo Soleri's Arcosanti in the Arizona Desert. The concept is of a vast vertical megastructure housing several million inhabitants and theoretically solving the 20th century's urban problems.

ARCRU *n* [*Banking*] acro **Arab Currency-Related Unit** a basket of currencies linked to the currencies of twelve Arab countries – Algeria, Bahrein, Egypt, Iraq, Kuwait, Lebanon, Libya, Oman, Qatar, Saudi Arabia, Syria and the United Arab Emirates. It was originally devised in 1974 at which time the ARCRU equalled $1.00. The value is calculated by eliminating the two currencies that are strongest against the dollar, and the two that are the weakest, and taking an average of the remaining eight.

arctic smoke *n* [*Aerospace*] surface fog found drifting over arctic regions when very cold air drifts over warmer water.

area defence *n* [*Military*] measures to defend great centres of population by ensuring that fighting is carried out at a great distance from them. Among the theories behind President Reagan's 'Star Wars' plans is that of the area defence of US cities by destroying incoming missiles long before they near their target.

arg *n* [*Computing*] abbr of **argument** the number that a function works on to produce its results.

argent *a* [*Heraldry*] silver, white.

argument *n* [*Computing*] See **arg**.

argument from illusion *n* [*Philosophy*] a philosophical concept which claims that material objects cannot be seen directly but must somehow be perceived from 'sense-data', or impressions, and it is they alone that are directly perceived.

Argyll Robertson *n* [*Medicine*] in ophthalmics, this is the pupil of an eye which fails to contract in response to light, but will contract to deal with seeing objects close at hand.

Arica *n* [*New therapies*] a concept named after a city in N. Chile where the system was first used in the late 1960s by Oscar Ichazo: Arica is intended to raise one's consciousness and 'transform your ability to experience living' through an 'electric' set of mind/body training techniques.

ARIEL *n* [*Banking*] acro **Automated Real-time Investments Exchange Ltd** a company founded in 1974 and jointly owned by the **acceptance houses**; it operates a computer-based block-trading system suitable for use in large-scale dealings in UK securities between institutional investors. The Exchange saves its users certain expenses, but suffers from a government prohibition on its trading in government securities,

A

which normally make 75% of the Stock Exchange's turn-over.

arisings n pl [Military] the various parts created from a large piece of ordnance or material that is broken up for scrap.

ARISTOTLE n [US] [Air Force] acro **Annual Review and Information Symposium on the Technology Of Training and Learning** issued by the USAF.

Arizona trigger n [US] [Cattlemen] a form of cattle trap set near a watering place; it is made up of an adjustable chute into which the cattle can enter but, when suitably arranged, from which they cannot escape.

arm 1. n [Clothing] in a sewing-machine this is the casing which houses and guards all the moving points inside. **2.** n [Printing] a stroke, generally horizontal, and at right angles to the main stem of a Roman letter.

armchair socialism n [Politics] See **academic socialism**.

armed interrupt n [Computing] a break in the normal flow of a program whereby the interruption signal is accepted by the program and held until the flow of the routine is resumed. See also **disabled interrupt**.

armed propaganda n [Politics] terrorist assassinations deliberately intended to gain publicity for a given cause.

armed state n [Computing] the state of an **interrupt** level at which it can intercept and remember an interrupt input signal and thus halt the program as required.

armourers n pl [Military] the ground crew on airbases or on carriers who arm the airplanes for combat.

arms length bargain, also **transaction** n [Management] a bargain between (two or more) persons on terms that have not been affected by any connection between these persons; the bargain is conducted with the same formality as if the persons had no knowledge of or relationship with each other. Such a transaction satisfies the legal necessities in a certain situation to avoid any conflicts of interest. See also **arms length price**.

arms length price n [Commerce] the initial price of a commodity that is stated as a basis for the detailed negotiations and haggling that may follow.

arms stability n [Politics, Diplomacy] a temporary pause in the arms race when neither side feels that it requires new military programmes to ensure that it is not being placed at a strategic disadvantage; the ever-increasing power of the military-industrial complex, with its huge appetite for funding, and its vital role as a major employer – both in the US and USSR – has meant that such periods are now so brief as to be virtually invisible.

armstrong starter n [US] [Road transport] an old-fashioned hand crank starter.

armstrong's patent n [Merchant navy] any equipment that has to be worked by brute strength or 'strong arms'.

Army, the n [Politics] in Catholic areas of N. Ireland, the Irish Republican Army; usually it refers to its Provisional wing. See also **troops**.

army disease n [Drugs] a drug addiction that develops among soldiers who were originally given morphine as a pain-killer.

A.R.O. n [Satellite TV] abbr of **audio receive only** a satellite receive-only earth station that is designed to receive an audio channel transmitted from that satellite.

aromatised a [Cheese-making] said of a cheese whose flavour and smell have been altered by an admixture or coating of aromatic substances.

arome n [Cheese-making] a name used in the Lyons region of France for goat's-milk, part goat's-milk and pure cow's milk cheeses, that have been steeped in marc.

around the world n [Sex] licking and sucking the client's entire body, probably including fellatio and anilingus.

arousal method n [Advertising] the galvanometric method of assessing the response to a given advertisement: the change in skin conductivity due to moisture content (sweat) can be measured on a galvanometer. Such changes may be caused by emotions – both positive and negative – induced by a given advertisement.

arrest v [Medicine] to suffer a heart attack, a cardiac arrest.

arrestment n [Law] a seizure of property by legal authority.

arrière-garde n [Sociology] the opposite of the chic and fashionable avant-garde: those intellectuals who maintain what they regard as the old values and standards in the face of no matter what advances by their more sophisticated peers.

arris n [Building, Plastering] a sharp-edged external angle.

arrival-time n [Audio] the moment at which sound actually reaches the ears; it is particularly relevant to stereophonic systems, where the differences in arrival-time at each ear create the enhanced 'realism' of such recordings.

arrogance of power n [Politics] a term coined in a lecture by Senator J. William Fulbright in 1966, in one of a series of lectures which criticised the involvement of the US abroad, particularly in Vietnam and the Dominican Republic. Fulbright's theory was that the US needed such involvements only to make sure that the world remembered just how powerful a nation she was; the American way of life had to be foisted on the world, whether it wanted it or not, with little concern for the genuine needs of the people of the Third World.

Arrow's theorem n [Economics] a theorem named after the mathematical economist, K. J.

Arrow (1925–), in the theory of social choice which demonstrates that it is impossible to design a 'constitution' that will generate complete and consistent rankings of alternative states of a society according to the preferences of its members, whilst at the same time satisfying certain further conditions.

arse *n* [*Sailing, Ropework*] the hole in a **block** through which a rope is threaded.

art 1. *n* [*Advertising*] all visual material incorporated in an advertisement, as opposed to **copy. 2.** *n* [*Journalism*] illustrations; thus leg art: pictures of scantily clad young girls, focussing on their legs.

art deco *n* [*Art*] a term from 'Exposition Internationale des Arts Décoratifs et Industriels Modernes', held in Paris in 1925; revived sporadically in the late 1960s and early 1970s, deco remains collectable, offering a style that emphasises the ornate, with asymmetrical, geometric shapes and bold colours.

art fabric *n* [*US*] [*Weaving*] a cloth designed specifically to have certain aesthetic characteristics and high art values; such a cloth would not be used in upholstery or garment tailoring.

art house *n* [*Film*] an up-market cinema which concentrates on showing 'intellectual' and 'cult' films, very often made in Europe with or without subtitles. See also **action house.**

art of the possible *n* [*Politics*] this comes from the dictum of German Chancellor Otto von Bismarck (1815–1898), who stated that politics was 'the art of the possible, the attainable . . . the art of the next best.' Adlai Stevenson called President Lyndon B. Johnson 'a master of the art of the possible in politics' and LBJ claimed to accept the necessity of compromise, but only as a step along the road to the complete realisation of one's aims and intentions.

art povera, also **anti-form, concepted art, earth art, matter art, minimal art** *n* [*Art*] this comes from It. meaning 'impoverished art'. Art povera contains a number of trends popularised in the 1960s, all of which stress the 'unworthiness' of the material used, eg. the rejection of the canvas and oils of fine art and the substitution of newspapers, coal and twigs. Art povera is by its nature temporary and is often created far from galleries or even cities and may exist only at second hand in photographs or sketches.

art trouvé *n* [*Art*] this comes from Fr. meaning 'found art': art that has not been created from scratch, but taken by the artist as it is found and adapted as an art object by virtue of its intrinsic qualities.

art wearable *n* [*US*] [*Weaving*] a garment that combines practical wearability with uniqueness of design; it is probably highly priced and aspiring to higher aesthetic status than a mere off-the-peg garment. See also **wearable.**

ARTHUR *n* [*Aerospace*] the automatic flight control system. See also **George 1.**

articulation *n* [*Education*] the process of helping a child move into a new school, and thence through the various groups that the child encounters on its progress through that school.

artificial intelligence *n* [*Computing*] See **AI.**

artificial person *n* [*Law*] a group or association of persons who together are given an imaginary personality – an existence separate from the reality of the individual lives – and are known as corporations and treated for legal purposes as a single person, rather than a group.

artish *n* [*Science fiction*] an issue of a fan magazine that contains mainly artwork/illustrations.

artology *n* [*Art*] the science and theory of art; not aesthetics, since it is not concerned with questions of beauty in nature, but simply with art itself.

artspeak *n* [*Art*] a term devised to describe the tortured, convoluted and obscure jargon of the art critic.

as built drawings *n pl* [*Architecture*] drawings that are made on the completion of a building to show exactly what was built, in contrast to the initial plans which show what was originally meant to be built.

as dug *adv* [*UK*] [*Road transport*] See **loose, in the.** See also **solid, in the.**

as hounds ran *v phr* [*Hunting*] the distance hounds ran during a hunt, including all checks, turns and diversions, rather than the distance in miles between the place at which they find a quarry and the place at which they either kill or lose it.

as usual *a* [*Book collecting*] the admission in a dealer's catalogue that a copy has a fault or imperfection that is generally known to be found in even the finest editions of the book in question.

ASALM *n* [*Military*] acro **advanced strategic air-launched missile** a development of the **ALCM** initiated in the mid–1970s. This bomber-launched missile was designed to skim the ground for long distances at supersonic speed. It had fins like a rocket but because of its speed did not, unlike cruise, require wings to stay in flight. ASALM was intended to destroy hostile aircraft, which were seeking to attack cruise missiles, and to destroy anti-aircraft missile sites as well as attacking strategic targets. ASALM has been abandoned in the face of the current concentration on **stealth** technology.

ASAT *n* [*Military*] acro **Anti-Satellite Weapons** a variety of conventional, nuclear, electronic and laser weaponry designed or intended for the destruction of hostile communications satellites or to defend against hostile ASAT weapons.

ASAT treaty *n* [*Military*] acro **Anti-Satellite Weapons Treaty** the US and USSR started meetings on the possibility of limiting the militarisation of space in 1978. Two further meetings followed, the second being in Vienna in June

A

1979. A fourth was planned for February 1980 but was cancelled after the invasion of Afghanistan in December 1979.

asbestos a [*Wine-tasting*] used to describe a flat alkaline taste, derived from either new filter pads or old, dirty, over-used pads when the wine was bottled.

ascending tops n pl [*US*] [*Stock market*] a graphic representation of the progress of a given share in which each successive peak price of that share can be seen as greater than that which preceded it. See also **descending tops**.

ASCIE n [*Computing*] acro **American Standard Code for Information Exchange** a standard character encoding scheme, introduced in 1963, and used on many computers.

ascots n pl [*Security*] HM Customs term for all members of the Royal Family, other than the Queen and Prince Philip, when they pass through Heathrow Airport.

ascription n [*Sociology*] the theory that certain qualities of an individual – status, occupation, income, etc – are pre-determined by birth or by other circumstances over which they have no control, rather than by achievement.

ash can n [*Navy*] a depth charge; so-called from the shape of the early versions which resembled a large dustbin.

ashcan 1. n [*US*] [*Textiles*] an old hat that has been cleaned, repaired and generally refurbished for subsequent sale. **2.** also **can** n [*Film, Theatre, TV*] a footlight unit in a compartment comprising an open reflector with 2x1KW bulbs fitted with a frosted glass diffuser.

ashcat n [*Navy*] the ship's engineer on board a small vessel.

ashore 1. adv [*US*] [*Marine Corps*] not on the ship. **2.** adv [*US*] [*Marine Corps*] anywhere that is neither US government nor US Marine Corps property. **3.** v [*US*] [*Marine Corps*] go ashore: to go on leave.

asia dollar n [*Economics*] US currency based in Singapore and controlled by the Monetary Authority of Singapore. See also **eurodollar**.

asiatic a [*US*] [*Marine Corps*] slightly mad or eccentric after serving an overlong period on a Far East posting.

ask the question v [*Cricket*] to appeal to the umpire, claiming the dismissal of a batsman.

ASMS n [*US*] [*Air Force*] abbr of **Advanced Strategic Missile Systems** formerly ABRES: Advanced Ballistic Re-entry Systems; an all-service research programme administered by the USAF to develop an advanced precision version of the Manoeuvrable Re-entry Vehicle (**MARV**).

asocial n [*US*] [*Prisons*] an asocial prisoner, often a habitual criminal or a sex offender.

aspect ratio n [*TV, Video, Film*] the ratio of the height to the width of an image.

assault n [*Law*] the threat to inflict physical harm on another person, with the apparent capacity to carry it out. See also **battery 4**.

assemblage art, also **combine painting, emballages, junk sculpture, object art, neo-Dada** n [*Art*] a concept that embraces all forms of composite art – ie. three dimensional structures – created from natural or manufactured articles and materials. There exist no theoretical limits as to what items may be used in such structures.

assemble edit n [*Video*] the re-recording onto blank tape of all the sections of tape chosen from all the sequences that have been shot, in order to create a final programme. See also **insert edit**.

assemble-and-go n [*Computing*] an operation technique which requires no pauses between the assembling, loading and execution of a program.

assembler n [*Computing*] a program that produces a machine language program that the computer can 'understand' and work from.

assemblising imponderables n [*Education*] the actual process of imparting information to pupils.

assembly language, also **assembly code** n [*Computing*] a programming language that is comprehensible to the machine. See also **high-level language, machine code**.

assented bond n [*Commerce, Stock market*] a bond whose owner has agreed to accept a change in its conditions.

assertive a [*Cheese-making*] used to describe a cheese that has a pronounced taste or aroma.

asset n [*Espionage*] any resource – human, technological, environmental, etc – at the disposal of an intelligence agency for use either in an operational or supporting role. In personnel terms it usually means an individual who works with the CIA on a secret mission but is not actually employed by the Agency full-time.

asset management n [*Business*] a style of management that ensures that all the assets of a group or institution – material and otherwise – are managed so as to further the aims and intentions of that group or institution.

asset play n [*US*] [*Stock market*] a stock that is attractive because its current price fails to reflect the full value of its company's assets.

asset-stripping n [*Business*] the process whereby a financier buys up a company or companies with the intention not of expanding or improving them, but simply of selling off such profitable assets as they still possess, and dismissing the employees. The money thus gained is retained either for investment in unconnected enterprises, or possibly for buying more companies for further asset-stripping.

asshole n [*Logging*] a kink in a length of rope.

assist 1. n [*Baseball*] a defensive play that leads to a putout, eg: an infielder's handling of the ball followed by a throw to a baseman. **2.** n [*Lacrosse*] the last pass made before a goal is scored – prob-

A

ably the most important pass in the game. **3.** *n* [*US*] [*Soccer*] a point awarded for passing the ball to the player who actually scores the goal.

associated gas *n* [*Oil rigs*] natural gas found in association with oil, either dissolved in the oil or as a cap of free gas above the oil.

associated liquids *n* [*Oil rigs*] liquid hydrocarbons found in association with natural gas.

association copy *n* [*Book collecting*] a copy of a book that has been annotated by, or belongs to, someone connected with its author; or it may belong to someone interesting in their own right or to someone specifically connected with the content of the book, either by name, circumstance or as the original of a fictional character, etc.

assured destruction *n* [*Military*] the philosophy of nuclear deterrence which means that whatever the aggression one side attempts, the other will be able to inflict 'unacceptable damage' upon his forces, and, more importantly, his human population. It is in essence a form of nuclear blackmail that, for all the fine-tuning of superpower foreign policies, has held the uneasy peace since 1945. See also **MAD**.

assured destruction component *n* [*Military*] the mechanisms built into or carried by a missile – the warhead, the delivery and guidance systems – that ensure that one's weapons will carry out the destructive task for which they are intended.

asterism *n* [*Printing*] a triangular cluster of asterisks, used to draw attention to a particular passage.

astigmatism *n* [*Photography*] a defect in a lens that makes it impossible to focus both horizontal and vertical lines at the same time.

as-told-to *a* [*Journalism*] a euphemism for **ghosted**, a celebrity 'confession', of greater or lesser quality, purportedly written by the star in question with only the help of a professional journalist or writer.

astonisher *n* [*Journalism, Printing*] exclamation mark. See also **dog's cock, screamer 5**.

astragal, also **large torus** *n* [*Building, Plastering*] a common moulding section: half round on a flat back plate.

astringent *a* [*Wine-tasting*] said of a dry taste with a mouth-puckering effect, caused by a high tannin content, and possibly a high degree of acidity.

ASW *n* [*Military*] abbr of **Anti-Submarine Warfare** the single most essential element of NATO sea policy, and the one in which the West has the most commanding lead; it comprises all the active and passive measures to reduce or nullify the effectiveness of hostile submarines. ASW concentrates on detection, precision location, identification and (as yet in theory) destruction. To this end submarines, surface vessels, helicopters, satellites, specially equipped aircraft and underwater listening devices (hydrophones) are all used.

ASW/SOW *n* [*Military*] abbr of **Anti-Submarine Warfare Stand-Off Weapon** a version of the Tomahawk **SLCM**, designed to be fired from a submarine's torpedo tube or from a surface ship's launcher. A lightweight (REGAL) torpedo would be dropped by parachute, plus a sensor array to target a submarine. Once targeted the vessel would be destroyed by the torpedo.

asymmetrical joking relationship *n* [*Sociology*] a joking relationship in which only one of the two individuals involved may joke at the expense of the other.

asyndeton *n* [*Literary criticism*] the omission of conjunctions between clauses, best seen in 'Time' magazine's traditional editorial style, for the sake of brevity or style.

AT *n* [*Technology*] abbr of **Appropriate Technology** alternative forms of technology that rely for fuel not on coal, gas, oil or nuclear power, but on solar energy, wave motion, the wind, etc.

at anchor *adv* [*Merchant navy*] drowned.

at fault *adv* [*Hunting*] referring to hounds which have lost the scent.

at it *adv* [*UK*] [*Crime*] involved in crime; a professional criminal.

at liberty *adv* [*US*] [*Theatre*] out of work, currently unemployed, free to take up a lucrative offer. See also **resting**.

at rise *adv* [*Theatre*] the positions taken by those actors who are on stage for the rise of the curtain at the start of a new act or scene in a play.

at the switch *adv* [*UK*] [*Police*] stealing property by shop-lifting, then taking it back and demanding a cash refund.

at the wash *adv* [*UK*] [*Police*] a pickpocket who specialises in working in the washrooms or public lavatories of hotels, airports, railway stations, concert halls, etc.

at walk *adv* [*Hunting*] foxhound puppies which are boarded out at local farms or with hunt supporters.

at zero *adv* [*Military*] said of a fighter pilot with a hostile fighter on his own tail.

ATM *n* [*UK*] [*Stock exchange*] abbr of **automated teller machine** an unmanned terminal, usually activated by a magnetically coded card, which can be used to dispense cash, take instructions on fund transfers, summarise information on the state of an account, etc.

atmos *n* [*TV, Theatre*] abbr of **atmosphere** the background noises of a scene, barely recognisable when they are present, but glaring in their absence if they are overlooked – cars passing, dogs barking, snatches of radio or TV, etc.

atom 1. *n* [*Computing*] in a programming language, a value that cannot be broken down further. **2.** *n* [*Computing*] the basic building block of a data memory; one atom corresponds to a single record in a paper-based file.

atomic actions *n pl* [*Technology*] actions which are either carried out to completion or not carried out at all; such actions are often those required for operating a database system.

atomic baby *n* [*US*] [*Navy*] a nuclear-powered submarine.

atomic music *n* [*Military*] top secret communications between UK and US concerning mutual control and engineering of nuclear missiles.

atomism *n* [*Sociology*] the concept that societies are entities formed from individual units or 'social atoms' which interact. See also **holism**.

atomistic competition *n* [*Business*] a market in which neither buyers nor sellers have any preference as to whom they do business with, so long as the prices asked are the same.

atomistic evaluation *n* [*Advertising*] the evaluation of specific, individual steps or elements in advertising, often against preset indices of advertising effectiveness. See also **holistic evaluation**.

atoms for peace *n* [*Military*] a program advocated by President Eisenhower in a speech to the UN in 1953; his declared aim was to demilitarise atomic power. Intended as an attempt to maintain the US weapons superiority while scoring a Cold War propaganda coup, the scheme foundered on Russian refusal to be seduced and the US desire, propounded almost simultaneously, to turn the nation's major defences over to nuclear weapons.

atrip *adv* [*Merchant navy*] used to refer to the actual moment when the anchor disengages its grip on the seabed.

attaché-casing *n* [*US*] [*Crime*] handing over bribes that are large enough to necessitate a small case to transport the money. See also **suitcasing**.

attachment 1. *n* [*Law*] the legal process whereby all or part of a person's property is seized and held so that it will be available if needed to satisfy a legal claim or judgement against that person. **2.** *n* [*Law*] the act of detaining in jail a person who is in contempt of court in some way and holding them there until the matter has been sorted out. **3.** *n* [*Law*] in the event that a debtor refuses to pay his creditors despite a judgement against him in the High Court, this procedure lays down that those creditors can have all monies which are owed to the debtor, paid directly to them until the debt is absolved.

attack *n* [*Audio*] the percussive or transient quality of certain musical sounds; it is sometimes used to refer to loudspeakers that have the ability to handle sharp and sudden changes in the sound waves.

attack characterization *n* [*Military*] the picture of an incoming missile attack that can be gleaned from an assessment of material collected at **NORAD**.

attack options *n pl* [*Military*] varieties of methods and targets available to a US President under the **SIOP**; these include MAOs (Major Attack Options): an all-out retaliatory attack; SAOs (Selected Attack Options): on only certain specific targets; LNOs (Limited Nuclear Options): aimed specifically at fixed enemy military or industrial centres; RNOs (Regional Nuclear Options): aimed to destroy the military command of a given area; in addition to these is one special category which covers a US pre-emptive strike (the previous options all assume response rather than initiation), LOW/LUA (Launch On Warning/Launch Under Attack): all out retaliation following a warning or in the event of an attack. LOW assumes a sufficient proportion of US missiles would survive such an attack).

attempting a creep *n* [*US*] [*Police*] See **highway mopery**.

attendance teacher *n* [*US*] [*Education*] euphemism for the truant officer.

attended operation *n* [*Computing*] transmission of data in which human operators are required at both ends of the system to ensure the system works correctly.

attention getter *n* [*Aerospace*] a prominently displayed warning sign in the cockpit, or on the flight deck of a civil or military airplane, that flashes amber or red to denote a malfunction.

attentioner *n* [*Journalism*] a note on a telex message which draws an editor's attention to any dubious language in a story – obscenity, profanity, or possible libel – in case anyone feels it must be cut before the story is run.

attire *n* [*Deer stalking*] the antlers worn by a red deer; divided into brow tine, bay and tray (collectively, the rights); the three tines on top are the cup.

attitude 1. *n* [*Cricket*] a batsman's stance when facing the bowling. **2.** *n* [*Marketing*] a predisposition towards an object or concept; ideally the predisposition in a customer towards buying or the act of buying.

attitude angle *n* [*Cars*] the angle between the longitudinal axis of a car and the actual angle of its direction when taking a corner; this could be as much as 15° at high speeds before the car actually starts to slip.

attitude arrest *n* [*US*] [*Police*] an arrest made not for any specific crime, but because the officer dislikes the attitude of a given individual.

attitude management *n* [*Public relations*] the concept that the individual's supposed 'free choice' can actually be manipulated, and that there exists no hard and fast 'reality', but simply, as in the most persuasive propaganda, what people can be led to believe.

attitude scale *n* [*Sociology*] sets of standardised statements with which people are asked to agree or disagree; the statements are scales in intensity (often on a five-point range from 'strongly agree' to 'strongly disagree') and assessed so as to place an individual on an attitude continuum to a given topic.

attitudinal paradigms *n pl* [*Market research*] market research based tables that offer a general view of a variety of public attitudes to selected topics.

attorn v [Law] to assign, transfer or recognise a new owner.

attrit n [Military] abbr of **attrition** as used in a military sense, death; deaths on the nuclear battlefield are measured in 'attrits per second'.

attrite v [Military] a back-formation from 'attrition': the gradual erosion of resources, both human and material, by the action of various forces encountered in battle.

attrition 1. n [Business] the process whereby the average salaries paid in an organisation decline as new, younger staff are hired to replace older personnel, and can be paid less money to perform the same tasks. 2. n [Market research] the gradual wearing down of an individual's loyalty to one company/brand and its possible switch to a rival; sometimes, but not necessarily, caused by advertising campaigns.

attrition out v [Industrial relations] to reduce the number of jobs or employees by failing to hire replacements for those who have left the firm or have retired.

auctioneering device n [Computing] a device designed to select either the highest or lowest input signal – according to the set-up – from a number of competing signals.

audible n [US] [Football] a play called out by the quarterback to his team at the line of scrimmage and which is thus audible to the opposition; the opposite is a play announced in the isolation of the inter-play huddle.

audience proof n [Theatre] a production that cannot fail to succeed, no matter how obtuse the audience, thanks to excellent acting, script, costumes, etc. See also **actor proof**.

audio n [Radio] a fuzzy, poor-quality interview that has been fed down a telephone wire to a tape recorder at the studio and which is thus of less than ideal quality for broadcasting.

audio active n [Education] in electronic learning laboratories this is a facility whereby the student can hear a master tape, respond into a microphone and hear his/her response.

audio active compare n [Education] in electronic learning laboratories this is a facility whereby the student can hear a master tape, respond into a microphone and have both tracks recorded on separate tape tracks for comparison.

audio quality n [Radio] See **phone quality**. See also **studio quality**.

audio passive n [Education] in electronic learning laboratories this is a facility whereby the student can hear a master tape, usually through headphones. See also **audio active**.

audit n [Aerospace] the comprehensive, detailed overhaul and examination of a plane, especially after one of the same type has been involved in a crash, in order to look for any possible structural faults.

audit trail 1. n [Computing] an inbuilt system which checks automatically on the functions and accuracy of a machine. 2. n [Accounting] a method of double-checking accounts by moving step-by-step through the processes that lead through to the final figures.

Audley it v [UK] [Theatre] to abridge or suddenly cut short a play irrespective of the actual stage of the plot. It comes from the supposed habit of one Shuter, an 18th century travelling showman, who would stretch out each matinée performance until the queue for the next house seemed sufficiently long. At this point he would shout 'Is Audley here?' and the audience would find the play brought to an abrupt conclusion.

auger in v [Aerospace] to crash one's aircraft into the earth; it comes from the idea of boring a hole in the ground.

august n [Entertainment] a type of circus clown notable for his battered bowler hat, tattered clothes and back-to-front jacket; this traditional costume was allegedly created by a German clown some time during the 19th century. The audience, seeing this new variety of clown shouted 'August!' (Ger. meaning 'Crazy!'); the OED Supp. A-G (1972) dismisses this story as 'unsubstantiated'.

Aunt Edna n [Theatre] the slightly derogatory description of the traditional theatre-goer of safely conservative tastes. (Compare the 'New Yorker's 'little old lady from Dubuque').

Aunt Emma n [Croquet] a typically unenterprising player or shot.

Aunt Tabby n [Politics] feminism's version of the black world's Uncle Tom: any woman who refuses to espouse the dogmas of radical feminism. See **Aunt Thomasina**.

Aunt Thomasina n [Politics] in feminist usage, a woman who refuses to accept every excess preached in the name of women's liberation.

Auntie 1. n [Sex] an ageing homosexual client; if rich as well as old, then a 'sugar daddy' (as used similarly by heterosexual prostitutes). 2. n [TV, Radio] the BBC; the term dates back to the Reithian era, and is commonly found today used affectionately, if slightly derogatorily, by the commercial network (IBA) when referring to the state medium.

austere a [Wine-tasting] somewhat tough and severe; simple, uncomplex, possibly underdeveloped taste.

austere cantonment n [Military] a military installation set up by a superpower in a client state, 'prepositioned' there for the purpose of waging a possible **austere war**.

austere war n [Military] the concept (launched in 1983) of winnable nuclear engagements, fought by the client states of the superpowers and as such both geographically distant from those powers and considered to be, despite the use of tactical nuclear weapons, absolutely controllable. See also **austere cantonment**.

A

australian days *n pl* [*UK*] [*Railways*] split shifts which necessitate unsocial hours, ie. night-working; thus the railwayman's 'day' is everyone else's night, except for, on the usual principle of Australia being the reverse of the UK, those living 'down under'.

autarky *n* [*Economics*] a national policy of economic self-sufficiency in food, technology, etc, usually based on stringent import controls. Such policies found their greatest popularity in the depression years of the 1930s and, given more recent fluctuations in the world economy, may once again appeal to the more beleaguered nations.

auteur, auteurism *n* [*Film*] this comes from Fr. meaning 'author'; it is a film term beloved of writers in the 'Cahiers du Cinéma' who preached that the great directors were in fact 'authors' who transformed any scripts they were given into vehicles for their own preoccupations and creative genius. An acceptable theory in moderation, it led too often to the canonisation of the third rate and to the arrogant dismissal of any other contemporary talents who might have contributed to the films under discussion.

authentication *n* [*Data security*] processes which ensure that everything about a given tele-processing transaction is genuine and that there is no invasion of the privacy of either party.

authenticator *n* [*Film*] a studio researcher responsible for establishing the accuracy of all details required by the script, eg: the anonymity of any telephone numbers or addresses used, etc.

authenticity 1. *n* [*Data security*] controls that prevent or detect the interference with and/or accidental destruction of data. If the data is already encrypted, then it should be impossible for a cryptanalyst to alter that code without detection. **2.** *n* [*New therapies*] the concept of honesty, sincerity, and the dismissal of false values, as epitomised by 'bourgeois' traditional hypocrisies and social mores. Thus the authentic individual creates a personality ideally suited to such brandishments of the unfettered ego as **'letting it all hang out'**, **'go with the flow'** and so on. **3.** *n* [*Philosophy*] according to the existentialist philosophies of Heidegger (1889–1976) and Sartre the concept here is that an individual must create himself in and through his own decisions and thus gain freedom by the rejection of any arrangements external to himself. The 'inauthentic' individual abandons this goal and accepts external controls, moral codes, and similar aids that still fail to deal with the central problems of Being which can only be dealt with by reverting to authentic choices.

author language *n* [*Computing*] a programming language used for designing instructional programs for computer assisted instruction (**CAI**) and computer based training systems.

authoring *n* [*Video*] the concentration, when an interactive videodisc is created, on the pre-production tasks of design, flow-charting, story-boarding, script-writing, software design, etc.

authoring system *n* [*Computing*] a computer system capable of executing an **author language**.

authorised state *n* [*Computing*] a situation in which a specific problem-solving program is allowed access to resources that would not otherwise be available.

auto abstract *n* [*Libraries*] an abstract of a document produced by computer analysis; sentences containing a high frequency of particular words are printed out in sequence. See also **evaluative, general, indicative** and **informative abstracts**.

auto pimp *n* [*US*] [*Sex*] a pimp who frequents drive-in movies in order to supply solo males with in-car sex.

autobiographical third *n* [*Literary criticism*] prose written strictly in the third person, but which is obviously an autobiography; it was a term coined by Quentin Crisp which refers specifically to the Norman Mailer 'faction', but extends to any ostentatiously egotistic writing of this sort.

auto-destructive art *n* [*Art*] a term coined by Gustav Metzger in 1961 to describe his own work: instead of canvas and pigment he took sheets of nylon, sprayed them with acid and created rapidly changing shapes until the sheet was completely burnt away. This made for a work that was simultaneously auto-creative and auto-destructive.

autograph book *n* [*Banking*] a book in which a bank records the authorised signatures of its clients.

automatic *n* [*US*] [*Football*] See **audible**.

autoletic *a* [*Art*] referring to a work that creates its own reason for being, rather than acting as a didactic entity.

automatic art, also **automatism** *n* [*Art*] paintings, drawings, or writings produced while their creator is in a distracted state, ie. day-dreaming, or subject to a light trance. An everyday example is doodling. The supposed freedom of such artworks is claimed as a direct key to the artist's subconscious.

automatic programming *n* [*Computing*] the automatic generation of programs by a system which responds to a set of instructions that outline a given task or attribute; eg: the description of the required actions of a robot will cause a program to be generated that fulfils these actions. The description of a system of accounting will generate an accounting program to carry it out. Such systems are still in the early stages of development.

automatic widow adjust *n* [*Printing*] a word processing facility which prevents the first line of a paragraph, title or heading from being the last line on a page; it also prevents the last line of a paragraph, title or heading from being the first line on a page. See also **widow**.

automobile n [US] [Garment trade] a very fast worker.

autopsy n [Aerospace] the detailed examination of the wreckage of a crashed aircraft in the hope of discovering the cause of the disaster.

autoscape architecture n [Architecture] See **electrographic architecture**.

autoscopy n [Medicine] the moment immediately prior to death when a person becomes detached from their own body; it they survive this may be cited as an 'out-of-body experience'.

autumns n pl [Furriers] See **falls**. See also **early-caught**.

aux vaches adv [UK] [Gliding] used to describe landing in a field away from the intended landing site; it comes from Fr. 'vache' meaning cow.

auxiliary chair n [New therapies] the use in psychodrama (developed by Jacob Moreno on the basis of Freud's 'cathartic method') of a chair which can augment the variety of roles which the subject is already taking on; thus it can be a soapbox for the subject to use if he/she feels sentiments of power, or left empty for the subject to use as a 'ghost' with whom he/she can interact, exchange roles, etc.

auxiliary egos n pl [New therapies] in a **psychodrama** this includes the other group members in addition to the subject whose drama is being enacted, ie. the trained assistants of the therapist and 'amateurs' (themselves future clients), all of whom help by playing out assigned roles in the subject's drama.

availability n [Politics] a quality that is ascribed to one who seems to have the potential to become a successfull political candidate, but it can be used derogatively of the over-enthusiastic hopeful who is too keen in putting him/herself forward for selection. The ideal possessor of the quality would offend no interest group, either social or geographical, but instead would offer the widest possible appeal to the greatest spectrum of voters.

available a [Theatre] temporarily out of work and available for new roles. See also **at liberty, resting**.

available light n [Photography] light that has not been intentionally set up by the photographer to take the picture: either daylight or electric light. See also **ambient light**.

avails 1. n pl [Business] the remaining balance of a legacy, an auction sale, etc. after all debts, commissions, expenses and similar outgoings have been accounted for. 2. n pl [Business] the net proceeds of a loan after the discount has been deducted in advance.

aval n [Finance] an endorsement on a bill of exchange that is not made by the drawer.

avalement n [Skiing] a method of bending and then extending the legs to absorb the variations of bumpy terrain; it comes from Fr. 'avaler' meaning 'to lower, to let down'.

avant-garde art n [Art] that art of the current moment in history that is more advanced in concept, more extreme in technique, than all the other art then being produced. The features it generally needs to exhibit are activism, antagonism, nihilism, agonism and futurism.

average n [Shipping] small cash gifts given by the master of a ship to various persons performing services for that ship – eg. a pilot or tug-master – to pay for those services and ensure that special care is taken in their performance. These expenses are either charged direct to the owners of the cargo, or shared between them and the master.

average bond n [Shipping] a formal document prepared and signed by a master, ensuring that he will pay his fair share of any **average** paid out during the voyage.

average clause n [Insurance] a clause in a fire insurance policy stating that the sum payable in the event of a claim shall not be greater than the proportion that the face value of the property bears to its actual value. The intention is to ensure that the policy is taken out for at least the full value of the property.

averager n [Military] a proponent of one of two opposing viewpoints on the hazards of post-nuclear war radiation: the averager looks at statistics for the overall population and works out the average effects on the basis of millions of people affected. See also **hot-spotter**.

averaging n [Stock market] a system whereby a speculator can increase purchases or sales as a result of price movements of stocks in order to average out the purchase or sale prices.

aviary n [Theatre] the chorus-girls' dressing room which is for the 'birds'.

aviator n [US] [Road transport] a speeding driver.

avoidable costs n pl [Business] costs incurred to pay for specific actions, rather than the basic costs that arise from the day-to-day running of a firm, irrespective of any special projects or activities.

AWACS n [Military] acro **airborne warning and control system** an aircraft carried early warning system; by working high over the earth AWACS, operating from converted Boeing 707s, has a far greater range than a static ground-based radar. From January 1979 AWACS replaced the earlier EC–121 radar surveillance planes, deployed by the US to cover the gaps in the **BMEWS** network.

away 1. adv [Crime] serving a sentence in prison. 2. adv [Hunting] referring to a fox that has left a covert. 3. a [Cycling] in the reverse direction from the winning post; thus, in a time trial, the outward half of the race. 4. n [Golf] the first player to start a hole.

away from you adv [Hunting] on the other side of a fence.

AWDREY n [Military] acro **Atomic Weapons Detection Recognition and Estimation of Yield** developed in 1960s to detect nuclear explosions through the heat and electro-magnetic pulses (**EMP**) from the explosion. AWDREY can detect an explosion at least 70m away. The instrument also exists to detect bombs that explode without warning, ie. those that are fired 'the wrong way' and thus avoid radar and other sensors.

AWOL *adv* [*Military*] acro **Absent Without Leave** to 'be AWOL' is to absent oneself from a camp or base in contravention of orders.

axe 1. *n* [*Gambling*] the extraction of a cut from each player's bet by whoever is running a card or dice game. **2.** *n* [*Pop music*] a performer's musical instrument, most often his/her guitar. **3.** *v* [*TV*] to stop before completion; this applies both to

withdrawing a given programme or item from the schedules, and to cutting off a series before all its episodes have been seen.

axel *n* [*Skating*] a jump which entails a leap from an inside back edge to an outside back edge; it was named after Axel Paulsen (1855–1938), a Norwegian skater.

axle tramp *n* [*Cars*] a violent movement of the driven wheels like somebody stamping their feet rapidly on the floor; it is caused by the sudden oscillation of a poorly located axle.

ayjay *n* [*Science fiction*] abbr of **amateur journalism** the activities of those who publish fan magazines.

azure *a* [*Heraldry*] blue.

B

B battery *n* [*Electronics*] a plate battery: an electric battery connected in the plate circuit of an electron tube to cause a flow of electric current in the tube. See also **A battery, C battery**.

B check *n* [*Air travel*] a rigorous overhaul and fullscale examination of every system on a civil airliner, carried out at the end of 400 hours of flying. See also **A check**.

B licence *n* [*UK*] [*Road transport*] formal permission under the Road Transport Act (1960) for road transport companies to act as general carriers; a B licence covers those who carry both their own goods and those of others. See also **A licence, C licence**.

B picture *n* [*Film*] low budget pictures, originally designed as the second feature in a cinema double bill and often of much the same content as their 'literary' peers, the pulp magazines. Now mainly defunct, they have been replaced in studio budgets by 'made for TV' pictures which share similarly low production values and banal plots.

B ring *n* [*Military*] a circle around **ground zero** in which the overpressure registers at between 6–11psi; in this ring there would be an estimated death rate of 40% without adequate shelter protection. See also **A ring**.

B share, also **B stock** *n* [*Stock market*] a

preferred stock, rather than the common or **A stock**.

B side, also **flip side** *n* [*Pop music*] the less featured side, often containing merely filler material, of a 45 rpm single record. Intended simply as a makeweight for the more important A side, some B sides do manage to make the music charts, sometimes even displacing the purported 'hit' song.

B unit *n* [*US*] [*Railways*] a passenger or freight locomotive without a cab.

BA shuffle *n* [*UK*] [*Fire brigade*] an ultracautious style of proceeding through the smoke of a burning building: it involves walking very slowly and continually waving one's hand in front of one's face; the expression comes from the similarity to ballroom dancing.

bab *v* [*Angling*] to fish for eels using worms threaded through wool tied to a line; the eels catch their teeth on the wool and are hauled in gently.

babbing *n* [*Angling*] a technique for catching eels at night; worms are threaded on to coarse wool which catches in the eel's teeth.

babbitt *n* [*US*] [*Industry*] an alloy of tin, antimony, copper and lead, used to coat the contact surfaces between two moving parts of machinery.

babble *n* [*Communications*] the aggregate cross

talk from a number of interfering sources. See also **cross talk**.

babbler *n* [*Hunting*] a noisy, excitable hound; one that gives tongue freely, even when not on a scent.

baboon watch *n* [*Merchant navy*] the skeleton crew left on board a merchant ship while it is in port.

babouvism *n* [*Politics*] extreme egalitarianism as propounded by François 'Gracchus' Babeuf (1760–1797) in 'The Conspiracy of Equals'; the philosophy antedated many 19th century socialist movements.

baby *n* [*TV, Film*] a small spot light, 750W. It is used at a short distance from the subject or object to light up a specific actor or area of the set.

baby bear *n* [*US*] [*Police, Crime*] trainee or junior police officer.

baby beef *n* [*US*] [*Meat trade*] steers or heifers about 15 mths old and no more than 950 lbs in weight.

baby board *n* [*Publishing*] cardboard books produced for the baby market.

baby bond *n* [*US*] [*Stock market*] bonds worth $25–500, rather than the large bonds worth upwards of $1000.

baby catcher *n* [*US*] [*Medicine*] an obstetrician.

Baby Doe guidelines *n pl* [*US*] [*Medicine*] rules governing the post-natal care of seriously deformed or handicapped children in US hospitals. Issued by the Dept. of Health & Human Services, these guidelines made mandatory the saving of all babies, no matter how precarious their health and how small the chance of a 'real life' in the future. Parents' wishes in the matter were overridden and employees were urged to report any physician failing to observe the rules; the term came from the case of Baby Jane Doe, born 9.4.82 with Down's Syndrome.

baby kicker *n* [*Film, TV, Video*] a small key light.

baby legs *n* [*TV, Film*] a low tripod used to support a film camera.

baby split *n* [*Ten-pin bowling*] a split where only the 2 and 7 or 3 and 10 pins are left standing. See also **bedpost, bucket, Cincinnati**.

babykicker *n* [*TV, Film*] a small **key light**.

baby's head *n* [*Navy*] the meat pies served on board ship.

baby-sitter *n* [*US*] [*Navy*] a destroyer that accompanies an aircraft carrier.

baby-sitting *n* [*Espionage*] the controlling of operatives or individuals seen as potential security risks for other, fully secure operatives. (See also **mole**, another term culled from the spy fiction of John Le Carré and popularised within the actual espionage community).

back *adv* [*US*] [*Bars*] on the side, in addition, but not mixed into the drink; thus 'whiskey with soda back'.

back anno *n* [*Radio*] abbr of **back announcement** an extra snippet of information included at the end of a news tape; it is read from the **cue** by the studio producer.

back beam *n* [*Weaving*] the upper horizontal beam at the back of a treadle loom.

back bench *n* [*Journalism*] the senior editorial executives on a newspaper.

back board, also **back stick, back 'un** *n* [*UK*] [*Railways*] a distant signal.

back door *n* [*Golf*] the back or side of the hole into which the ball falls.

back door, go out the *v* [*US*] [*Prisons*] to back away from a dangerous/potentially violent situation.

back door play, also **reverse cut** *n* [*Lacrosse*] when a player makes a fast cut around the back of the defence towards either wing, then heads for goal.

back end 1. *n* [*US*] [*Car salesmen*] the profit made by the dealership from financing a car. See also **front end 3. 2.** *n* [*Commerce*] in mail order selling this is the ultimate response to an offer, especially after a **continuity series**. **3.** *n* [*Film*] the money that is paid after a film has been made and exhibited; often this refers to the percentage **points** that are paid out of the gross profits to certain favoured or powerful individuals. **4.** *n* [*Science*] in nuclear physics this is the part of the fuel cycle of a nuclear reactor in which the used fuel is reprocessed in order to separate usable materials – uranium and plutonium – from radioactive waste.

back of the book 1. *n* [*US*] [*Car salesmen*] below list price; the reference is to the **blue book**. **2.** *n* [*Printing*] general interest material, rather than news, current affairs, etc., which is given low priority treatment at the end of a newspaper, or magazine. **3.** *n* [*TV*] (from **2.**) the division of news programmes into hard news, which takes up the early part of the programme, and less immediate material, possibly including a soft 'joke' item, that follows it.

back of the house *n* [*US*] [*Catering*] those areas of a restaurant where food is stored or prepared and served up, rather than the dining room where the customers sit.

back letter *n* [*Shipping*] a letter sometimes given by the shipper to the shipping company when goods are loaded in substandard condition; the letter agrees to make good all losses suffered by the carrier if any claims arise against possible defects in the goods.

back lot *n* [*Film*] See **lot**.

back man *n* [*Cycling*] the rear rider on a tandem.

back matter *n* [*Publishing*] any material – index, glossary, bibliography, advertisements, etc – that follows the last chapter of the text.

back of an/the envelope *a* [*Science*] said of simple and speedy calculations; the expression comes from the popular image of a genius/absent-minded professor scribbling down great notions on a scrap of paper.

B

back porch *n* [*TV*] a picture signal that lies between the trailing edge of a line sync pulse and the trailing edge of the corresponding blanking pulse. See also **front porch**.

back projection *n* [*Film*] a technique used to save expenditure on backgrounds or **set-ups**: actors perform in front of a translucent screen on to which the required background, often in motion, is projected.

back rise *n* [*Clothing*] the distance, as measured on a garment, from the crotch to the centre back of the waistline.

back scuttle *n* [*Navy*] homosexuality on board ship, with a direct reference to sodomy.

back shift *n* [*Coal-mining*] the afternoon shift at a mine.

back suit *n* [*US*] [*Garment trade*] a loose suit that does not fit the wearer's figure.

back tell *n* [*Military*] the transfer of information from senior to junior levels of command.

back time *n* [*US*] [*Prisons*] the still unserved portion of a prison term that must be served by a parole violator if that person is arrested.

back to back 1. *adv* [*Gambling*] in stud poker this is when a player has two cards of the same denomination dealt in sequence, such as one's hole card (the face-down card) and the first face-up card one receives. **2.** *adv* [*TV, Film*] referring to the making of two or more films where there is an overlap of budget, actors, crew, etc. Such productions may be either consecutive or concurrent. See also **piggyback productions**.

back track *n* [*US*] [*Circus*] one half of the **hippodrome track** in a circus; it is the equivalent of upstage in the theatre. See also **front track**.

back 'un *n* [*UK*] [*Railways*] a distant yellow signal (Midland Region).

back up 1. *v* [*Angling*] to fish a pool from the bottom towards the top by casting across and walking slowly backwards and upstream, a few steps at a time. **2.** *v* [*Lacrosse*] to place a player directly behind the line of a shot at goal in order to ensure immediate repossession in case the shot is blocked or deflected.

back whack *n* [*Navy*] the scale of rations laid down for the Royal Navy by the Ministry of Defence.

backbreakers *n pl* [*Logging*] tree stumps.

back-bye *n* [*Coal-mining*] the underground areas away from the coalface.

backbye work, also **backwork, oncast work** *n* [*Coal-mining*] work done in the direction of the main shaft or surface outlet.

backchannels *n pl* [*Politics*] secret lines of communication within a government, or between two ostensibly rival governments. Such communications which are particularly useful to help balance the formality of summits, arms talks, etc., can often facilitate political decision-making, especially where the public image of a government means that such otherwise sensible moves

cannot be considered. The term comes from the CIA's network of clandestine cable channels which run in parallel to the normal traffic between US embassies and Washington.

back-check *v* [*Ice-hockey*] to check an opponent while skating backwards towards one's own goal.

backcloth star *n* [*Theatre*] a second rank performer who is out of the limelight but who still manages to steal the show from the star by persisting in extraneous 'business' which diverts audience attention.

backdoor entry *n* [*Military*] entering the Army with an officer's commission by any means other than through the Royal Military Academy at Sandhurst.

back-door selling *n* [*Commerce*] making a direct sales approach to the relevant decision-making executive in a firm, rather than being side-tracked through the buying department or similar layers of administrative dawdling.

backed *a* [*Book collecting*] said of a volume whose spine has been covered with a material different to that used on the back and front covers; it usually implies that the spine is of a later date than the covers.

backend 1. *n* [*Video*] the secondary or ancillary rights to a production; thus video tapes and discs provide such rights in respect of celluloid film production. **2.** *n* [*Video*] the later earnings or potential of a given production's useful life, after the first release and accompanying promotion.

back-end load *n* [*Stock market*] the redemption charge, designed to discourage spontaneous withdrawals, paid by an investor when withdrawing money from an investment, especially in mutual funds and annuities. See also **front-end load**.

back-end processor *n* [*Computing*] a processor that is used for a specialised function, eg: database management or a special-purpose arithmetic and logic unit. See also **front-end processor**.

backer 1. *n* [*Shoe-making*] a piece of fabric used to plump out the quarter or to vamp parts of the shoe's upper. **2.** also **bater** *n* [*Hunting*] a deer that has passed maturity and is thus diminishing in size of body and horn.

Backfire *n* [*Military*] the Russian Tupolev TU–22M/TU–26, a large swing-wing supersonic jet bomber; it is currently the Soviets' major strategic bomber. See also **Badger**.

background 1. *n* [*Building, Plastering*] the base to which plastering material is applied. **2.** *n* [*Computing*] less important tasks that can be performed by the machine in the milliseconds that separate the major, **foreground**, tasks.

background program *n* [*Computing*] the program with the lowest priority in a multiprogramming environment.

background region *n* [*Computing*] a region in main memory to which a background job is assigned.

backgrounder *n* [*Journalism, Government*]

press conferences or one-to-one interviews in which lengthy and possibly detailed information is handed out by senior government figures, up to and including Presidents and Prime Ministers; however the information made available may only be attributed to 'a senior White House source', 'a major Whitehall figure', etc.

backgrounding n [Computing] the performing of secondary processing tasks in the millisecond spaces that can be fitted in between the major, foreground processing.

backhanded rope n [Sailing, Ropework] a rope which is made in such a way that the yarns and strands have a right twist and the rope itself a left twist.

backing 1. n [Angling] a light silk line spliced to the **dressed** line to act as a reserve. 2. n [Film] a huge backdrop – representing a city or a landscape – made from a massively blown up photograph. See also **cyc**.

backing support n [Banking] gold or securities that support a country's issue of notes.

backkick n [Electronics] See **kickback 4**.

backlash 1. n [Computing] unwanted play in mechanical systems due to looseness. 2. n [Mining] a blast caused by an explosion which moves in the opposite direction to that in which the force of the explosion is spreading. 3. also **hysteresis** n [Computing] a difference in output value achieved when approaching the same value of input from both directions.

backlist n [Publishing] titles that sell steadily, irrespective of the fluctuations of fashion: literary and modern classics (Dickens, Raymond Chandler, etc), major reference and non-fiction works (dictionaries, certain guide-books) etc.

backloading n [Military] the rearward movement of supplies, troops, casualties, etc. within a given theatre of war.

backorder n [Video] units ordered but not yet shipped by a wholesaler or distributor. When a title sells out of inventory any copies that distributors and retailers have requested are 'backordered' units.

backout n [Aerospace] the reversed numerical sequence that precedes the launch of a missile or rocket, ie: 10, 9, 8, . . .

back-out n [US] [Car salesmen] a customer who refuses to take delivery of a car, even when all the papers have been signed and ancillary arrangements made.

backplane n [Computing] a series of interface sockets wired in parallel and connected to the internal wiring of the computer; it is used for the connection of a variety of **peripherals** to the machine.

back-prime v [US] [Painting] to paint an entire surface of wood – doorframes, windowsills, etc – to seal out moisture, before they are put into place.

backripping n [UK] [Coal-mining] the re-excavation of tunnels behind the coalface which have

collapsed under the weight of earth, and the re-installation of secure roof arches. See also **ripping**.

backs n pl [Coal-mining] Coal still projecting from the line of the face after cutting and/or loading has been completed.

backscatter n [Radar] a radar system that uses the energy reflected from ionised sources to pick up information from over the horizon, an area formerly beyond the reach of conventional radar. See also **OTH, OTH-B radar**.

backselling n [Commerce] an indirect sales promotion which stimulates the conventional manufacturer/wholesaler/retailer chain in reverse; the campaign is aimed at retailers who will then agitate their wholesale suppliers who in turn require more supplies from the manufacturer. Taken one step further the promotion is aimed at the consumer, who will make demands on the retailer, and so on back up the chain.

backshift n [Management] the afternoon shift of a three-shift – morning, evening, night – system. See also **foreshift, nightshift**.

backshop n [Aerospace] the first part of an aircraft manufacturing plant to be shut down as a production programme draws towards its conclusion.

backstamp n [Philately] a postmark applied to the back of a letter for the purpose of recording the time, date and place of arrival and any extra stops en route; it is used mainly on registered mail and (in the UK) on incoming letters from abroad.

backstopping n [Espionage] the provision of a suitable background for a 'cover' story, in case an operative is forced to prove that he is what he claims to be, or enquiries are instituted to discover whether the story has any 'factual' basis.

back-to-back credit n [Commerce] credit provided to a buyer by a finance house which is acting as a contact between foreign buyers and sellers, especially when the seller does not disclose his identity; the terms embodied in the credit reflect those of the original sale.

back-up n [Oil rigs] the process whereby one section of drill pipe is held stationary using **tongs** while another section is screwed out of or into it. Thus a 'back-up line' is a wire rope used to hold one set of tongs in place when two sections of drill pipe are being joined or separated; a 'back-up post' is a fixed post or stanchion to which one end of the back-up line is secured.

backward a [Wine-tasting] retarded, undeveloped for a wine of its age and vintage.

backward channel n [Communications] a channel used for supervisory or error control signals, transmitted in the opposite direction to that in which user information is being transmitted.

backward displacement n [Parapsychology]

the correct naming of a symbol on a card that precedes the target card.

backward integration 1. *n* [*Commerce*] this occurs when a retailer takes over a major supplier or the manufacturers of his most important stock in order to ensure full and continuous supplies. Similarly a manufacturer may take over his sources of raw materials. See also **forward integration. 2.** *n* [*Industry*] See **vertical integration**.

backward price *n* [*UK*] [*Stock market*] a situation in which **market-makers'** two-way quotations are out of line and make it possible for an immediate profit to be made by buying and selling simultaneously and capitalising on the difference; the best bid is higher than the best offer.

backward read *n* [*Computing*] a technique used in magnetic tape drive whereby data can be read when the tape is running backwards.

backwardation *n* [*Commodity exchange*] in the commodity futures market this is a situation whereby future prices become progressively lower as the delivery time recedes.

backwash effect *n* [*Commerce*] this results from the discrepant trade balance between developed and under-developed countries: the manufactured goods of developed countries are more attractive to their under-developed customers than are the products of the latter – low productivity mining and agricultural commodities – to the developed world.

backyard *n* [*US*] [*Circus*] the space behind the big top.

bacover *n* [*Science fiction*] back cover.

bacquote *n* [*Science fiction*] quotes incorporated on the back cover of a fan magazine.

bad actor *n* [*Technology*] any chemical, plant, etc. that has been found to be harmful.

bad bag, also **booster bag** *n* [*US*] [*Crime*] an oversized shopping bag that facilitates shoplifting.

bad delivery *n* [*Stock market*] stocks or shares which, when delivered, are found to have some fault.

bad eggs *n* [*Wine-tasting*] the smell of hydrogen sulphide; it is probably due to bad cellar treatment.

bad laugh *n* [*Theatre*] a moment during a play when the audience choose to laugh at the wrong place, ie. lines that are not deliberately meant to be funny.

bad letter *n* [*Printing*] a letter that does not print or reproduce properly.

bad mender *n* [*Textiles*] an expert mender whose skill means that he/she is given all the worst imperfections to eliminate.

bad order 1. *n* [*US*] [*Railways*] defective material or equipment. **2.** *n* [*US*] [*Railways*] an incompetent employee.

bad paper *n* [*Banking*] bills of exchange which have not been, or are likely not to be, honoured.

bad place *n* [*Textiles*] a flaw in a woven or knitted fabric.

bad secrets *n pl* [*Espionage*] secrets that relate to bureaucratic ineptitude or official misconduct.

bad track *n* [*Computing*] any track on a hard **disk** that is found to be corrupt and which must therefore not be used for the storage of data; hard disks have inbuilt methods for checking such tracks and avoiding them when storing material.

badge *n* [*Heraldry*] a small heraldic device, separate from the coat of arms, but extracted from it, eg: the white rose of York.

badge reader *n* [*Computing*] a device programmed to 'read' information encoded on to a card; this coding is most commonly found in the magnetic strip on a credit or cash-card or on ID cards used to open electrically operated door locks.

Badger *n* [*Military*] the Russian Tupolev TU–16 twin-jet subsonic bomber; the main strategic bomber in the 1960s and 1970s, the Badger is now being phased out and replaced by the superior Backfire.

baff 1. *v* [*Billiards*] to hit the table before hitting the ball. **2.** *v* [*Golf*] to hit the ground immediately behind the ball.

baffle *n* [*Glass-making*] the bottom of a glassware form.

bafflegab *n* [*US*] [*Politics*] confusing, obfuscating political jargon; the term was based perhaps on President Truman's dictum 'If you can't convince them confuse them'. It was coined in 1952 by Milton Smith, then Assistant General Counsel to the US Chamber of Commerce, who had toyed with burobabble and gabbalia, before selecting his own particular synonym for gobbledegook.

baffy *n* [*Golf*] the traditional name for the Number 4 wood.

bag 1. *n* [*Cricket*] the number of wickets taken in an innings or a match by a given bowler; it comes from hunting usage. **2.** *n* [*Drugs*] a measure of drugs which usually comes in a glassine bag, or occasionally a rubber contraceptive (a 'balloon'). Bags can be dime bags ($10) or nickel bags ($5), but given the fluctuating costs of drugs, while the payment remains the same, the amount purchased may differ substantially. The quality, in so small an amount, which will invariably have been adulterated, varies even more. **3.** *n* [*New Therapies*] this term covers one's personal preference, state of mind, way of life, emotional standpoint: '**where you're at**'. One's bag can be qualified variously as one's current feelings: 'a heavy bag', 'a weird bag', etc. It is nearly always preceded by 'in . . .' or 'into . . .'. **4.** also **multiset** *n* [*Computing*] an unordered collection of items where more than one instance of the same item is allowed. **5.** *v* [*Medicine*] to apply an oxygen mask to a patient's nose and mouth. **6.** *v* [*Tyre-making*] to put uncured tyres into the curing machine where they undergo specific chemical processes designed to create the finished tyre.

bag of nuts n [Navy] a signal of congratulations for a job well done which is sent by the Commander-in-Chief. See also **bar of chocolate**.

bag the patient v [Medicine] to attach a clear container to the patient's penis in order to conserve his urine.

bagbiter n [Computing] either hardware or software – the computer itself or the programme it is running – that consistently fails to work; it may also be used as an obscene expletive. See also **bletch, chomp, chomping**.

baggage 1. n [Gambling] one who watches a game but does not participate in it. See also **kibbitzer**. 2. n [Gambling] anyone who gambles but fails to earn sufficient to pay his own way.

baggage (box) boy n [Sex] a homosexual prostitute who offers only active intercourse or fellatio to his clients.

bagged a [Gambling] said of a crook or cheat who has been caught in the act.

baggies n pl [Surfing] loose-fitting 'boxer' shorts worn for surfing, often over a pair of tighter swimming trunks. Also known in Australia as 'board bags'.

bagging out n [Clothing] a method of joining facings and/or linings to the outer material of a garment by sewing them together face to face in the form of a bag and then turning the garment right side out.

baggot, also **bagget, baggit, bagot** n [Angling] salmon still unspawned after the usual spawning time.

baglady n [US] [Gambling] a woman used by numbers racketeers to collect bets and pay off winners.

bagman 1. n [Politics] the intermediary in any form of political payoff or corruption: the person who actually carries the bag of money from A to B. The word is taken directly from criminal use, but always carries the implication that one user of the 'bag' is an allegedly 'honest' politician, policeman, etc. 2. n [Politics] the officer who continually accompanies the President and who is charged with carrying the **football** which holds the nuclear **go-codes**. 3. also **bag-fox** n [Hunting] a fox that is trapped, put into a bag or box, then taken to a covert and released in order to guarantee sport for a hunt. A practice often attributed to landowners who permitted their keepers to shoot such foxes as did appear on their land.

bagpiping n [Sex] coitus in axilla: intercourse between the penis and the armpit, considered to be the province of the homosexual world.

bail out v [Oil rigs] to clean out or clean up any part of the rig; an extension of bailing out the well.

bailer n [Cricket] a full-toss, bowled faster than the bowler's normal pace, and aimed directly at the top of the stumps by a spinner.

bailer n [Cricket] See **trimmer 2**.

bailment n [Law] the legal relationship between the owner of certain personal property who as bailer transfers possession, but not ownership of that property, to the bailee; bailment exists whenever personal property is lent or rent, left for repair or storage, or pledged as security for a debt.

bait 1. n [UK] [Coal-mining] any food taken underground for refreshment. 2. n [Glass-making] a metal piece or bar by which the glass is drawn from the crucible, to start drawing a cylinder or sheet.

bait advertising n [Advertising] a situation in which the vendor touts some item which he is not really interested in selling but which is intended to attract the interest of the potential buyer sufficiently for the vendor to offer something that he genuinely does wish to sell. See also **bait and switch selling, switch selling**.

bait and switch selling (US), **switch selling** (UK) n [Commerce] a scheme wherby a customer is persuaded by the appeal of a low-priced item to enter the store, where he will then be sold a higher-priced item. The 'bait' is heavily advertised, the 'switch' is carefully worked.

bait can n [Logging] a logger's lunch pail.

baits n pl [Marbles] the marbles which a player puts into a game as his ante.

bake v [US] [Cattlemen] to ride in such a way as to overheat the horse.

bake (into) v [Industrial relations] See **consolidate**.

baked a [Wine-tasting] said of the earthy, 'hot' smell produced by burnt and shrivelled grapes, due to excessive sunshine and lack of rainfall; it is typical of the Rhone Valley and wines from California, Australia and South Africa.

baked strength, also **dry strength** n [Metallurgy] in iron founding this is a measure of the degree of cohesion held by grains of sand which have been heated to remove all moisture.

baking n [Fashion] in wig-making and hairdressing, a technique for drying elaborate and fantastic hairpieces.

balance 1. n [Clothing] the relationship between one section of garment and another, especially that of the back and front lengths, where the aim is to harmonise with the natural posture of the figure. 2. n [TV] the concept of offering equal time to opposing opinions that dominates all UK TV current affairs broadcasting. Intended, laudably, to avoid overt propagandising, it often means the dilution of an otherwise powerful statement or investigation, when the balance is inserted simply to satisfy management rulebooks. 3. n [Wine-tasting] the combination and relationship of components in a wine.

balance stripe n [Film] a narrow band of magnetic coating applied to the edge of the film opposite to the magnetic sound track; it makes the film lie flat when passing over magnetic tape heads.

balance of terror n [Military] the current inter-

B

B

national stalemate which is based on the ability of both superpowers to wreak nuclear havoc on the other; the term was probably coined by Canadian PM Lester Pearson in 1955, on the tenth anniversary of the UN Charter, when he said: 'The balance of terror has replaced the balance of power.' See also **MAD**.

balanced ticket n [US] [Politics] a political programme and selection of candidates deliberately designed to appeal to the widest possible diversity of minorities and pressure groups.

balanced weave n [Weaving] a structure in which the **warp** and **weft** are similar in size and spacing.

balcony stalls n pl [UK] [Theatre] seats in the front few rows of the dress circle.

bald-headed row n [Theatre] the first few rows of the orchestra stalls. These were traditionally occupied by ageing roués and sugar daddies who leered up at the chorus girls and leg shows.

bald-tyre bandits n pl [UK] [Police] inter-force nickname for traffic control units.

bale n [Drugs] a measure of marijuana: either one pound (see **weight**) or half a kilo.

balk n [Baseball] the pitcher's act of failing to deliver a pitch promptly after beginning the motion to do so; when there are opponents on base, this is an illegal hesitation which permits the opposing base runner(s) to advance a base.

ball 1. n [Baseball] a pitch that fails to enter the strike zone and which can thus be ignored by the batter; three balls to the same batter cause a **walk**. 2. n [Metallurgy] the spongy mass, weighing about 1.25cwt, produced by aggregating iron particles in the **puddling** furnace.

ball and a beer n [US] [Bars] a measure of spirits, probably whiskey, with a glass of beer to drink between sips of the spirit.

ball bearing creep n [Merchant navy] a cowardly individual, who slides out of challenging situations as smoothly as if on ball bearings.

ball game, not even in the a phr [US] [Medicine] very senile, or confused. See also **program, not in the**.

ball hooter n [Logging] one who rolls logs down a hillside.

ball hooting n [Logging] rolling logs down an incline.

ball park n [Commerce, Politics] a large rough assessment of numbers – based on the cursory glance a commentator might give around an arena before giving his estimate of the crowd attending a sporting occasion. Thus 'ball park figure' is the number estimated to be 'in the ball park'; it is used for people, budget figures, commodities, pricing, etc.

ball point n [Shoe-making] that part of a shoe which lies beneath the ball of the foot.

balloon 1. v [Air travel] when a plane bounces badly on landing because the pilot has failed to master either his controls or the state of the

runway. 2. v [Cricket] to score 0. 3. v [Cricket, Soccer] to hit or kick a ball high into the air. 4. v [Theatre] to forget one's lines. See also **go up in the air, make an ascension**. 5. n [Cycling] a tyre made of extra-lightweight rubber, or having a greater air capacity than the standard makes. 6. n [Finance] the final payment on a debt that has been structured to be substantially larger than the preceding payments. 7. n [UK] [Railways] a foreman who continually begs 'Don't let me down, boys . . .' 8. n [Drugs] a contraceptive sheath part-filled with some form of drug, usually powdered.

balloon freight n [US] [Road transport] light, bulky cargo.

balloon interest n [Finance] in serial bond issues, the higher **coupon** rate that is available on those bonds that have later maturity dates.

balloon maturity n [Finance] when bonds are issued or loans advanced over a period, this refers to the larger issues or payments that fall due in the later years of the arrangement.

balloon note n [Finance] a loan which is to be repaid by a number of small instalments, culminating in a single, large final payment.

ballpark n [Aerospace] the area of predicted impact of a space capsule or missile; the designated ballpark is the focus of recovery ships.

bally stand n [US] [Circus] the platform on which the promoters of sideshows stand to 'ballyhoo' their entertainment.

baloney 1. n [Logging] the large wire rope used in logging. 2. n [US] [Politics] nonsense, rubbish; a reasonably strong alternative, in the opinion of its devotees, to actual obscenity.

Baltic, the n [Commerce] the Baltic Mercantile and Shipping Exchange in the City of London, founded in the 18th century at the Baltic Coffee House. The Exchange specialises in the chartering of ships, and now takes on air freighting; its members are stockbrokers, shipbrokers and general merchants.

Baltimore chop n [Baseball] a batted ball that bounces too high for an infielder to catch it cleanly and thus make an out at first base; the term comes from the Baltimore team of 1890, who perfected the use of such batting.

balun n [Audio] a device which converts a balanced circuit or line to an unbalanced condition, or vice versa; usually a suitably modified transformer.

baluster n [Building, Plastering] a small column/pilaster-like support, generally urn-shaped.

BAMBI n [Military] acro **Ballistic Missile Boost Intercept** an orbiting, armed satellite, designed to target and destroy hostile satellites while still in their initial, or boost, phase of flight, prior to leaving the atmosphere above their launch sites and moving through space towards their targets.

bamboo curtain n [Politics] a term created during the 1950s by US political publicists; the

B

hypothetical barrier between the West and Communist China (much eroded since the death of Mao Zedong) parallels Winston Churchill's 'iron curtain' between the West and the Soviet bloc.

banana 1. *n* [*US*] [*Medicine*] a patient with (yellow) jaundice. **2.** *n* [*Radar*] a line, slightly curving at either end, that appears on high-level radar screens to denote the presence of ships or planes. **3.** *n* [*Wine-tasting*] the bouquet of a wine made from frostbitten grapes; it is a specific smell from old wine in poor condition.

banana belt *n* [*Navy*] an area of calm water, clear skies, etc. found in the tropics.

banana benders *n pl* [*Cricket*] the Queensland, Australia, state cricket team. See also **crow eaters, sand gropers**.

banana legs *n* [*Navy*] a knock-kneed seaman.

banana plug *n* [*Audio*] a connector with a bulging contact surface placed along its shaft.

banana seat *n* [*Cycling*] a bicycle saddle that curves upwards at the back.

banana shot *n* [*Golf*] an extreme slice, which sends the ball on a banana like curve off the required straight line to the green.

bananas *n pl* [*Military*] the Kalashnikov AK–47 rifle, brandished in myriad revolutionary posters, and so named for the shape of its curving ammunition magazine. In Mexico this shape has given the gun the name of 'goat's horns'.

bananas on bananas *n pl* [*Film*] in studio discussions, the description of what is thought to be a complete excess of whatever is the current topic of conversation.

Banbury *n* [*Tyre-making*] a large mixing machine in which the primary mix of rubbers and pigments – the **masterbatch** – is prepared.

banco 1. *n* [*Banking*] bank money on account, as distinguished from actual currency. **2.** *n* [*Gambling*] in chemin-de-fer or baccarat this is a bet against the whole of the bank's stake. See also **va banque**.

band *v* [*UK*] [*Education*] to group pupils, according to their academic ability, in broad bands. These bands can be further divided (by setting or streaming) if a school so wishes.

banded *a* [*Radio*] said of a taped interview where the interview splits into various segments; the engineer indicates the changes in segments by splicing in pieces of yellow leader tape to divide them.

banding 1. *n* [*Industrial relations*] the rationalisation of pay differentials by creating artificial groupings into which all workers, at their various levels, can conveniently be fitted. **2.** *n* [*Video*] an uneven variation in the rotational speed of a video playback head which causes variations in picture colour.

bandits 1. *n pl* [*Computing*] computer criminals who use their knowledge of computer mechanisms, especially in banks or government offices, to extract or transfer money and/or information illicitly. **2.** *n pl* [*Military*] hostile aircraft. **3.** *n pl* [*UK*] [*Police*] a general term for a wrong-doer, but on the whole a slightly ironic description of varieties of lesser criminals which is often qualified as to occupation. Thus 'pisshole bandit' is one who hangs around outside public lavatories; 'gas-meter bandit' is a small time thief who, figuratively, only manages to break into the gas meter, and so on.

bandobast *n* [*Shooting*] Hindustani meaning any preparation or arrangement.

bandsplitting *n* [*Audio*] a scrambling technique whereby each audio channel is split into several sub-bands (usually five), each of which is transposed into a particular frequency.

bandstand *n* [*Navy*] a small, raised, circular platform on which the guns are mounted in small ships.

bandwagon *n* [*Politics*] in propaganda, the device of appealing to people's readiness to jump on a bandwagon, rather than make up their own mind; thus they will join happily in whatever level of patriotic outcry the government chooses to launch.

bandwidth 1. *n* [*Audio*] the spectrum of frequencies that are transmitted in order to reproduce the audio signal (spoken or musical) without distortion. The wider the bandwidth the greater the number of harmonics that can be generated to make a complex signal and thus the finer the quality of that signal. **2.** *n* [*Photo-typesetting*] a term from the audio use, (see **1**); in graphic design a wide bandwidth with frequent sampling enables an **analog** design to be represented in digital form with the least number of errors. **3.** *n* [*Sociology*] the environment or milieu. The term is derived from the elctronics term meaning the difference between the highest and lowest frequencies of a communication channel. Used in such phrases as 'change the bandwidth' in order to attach a spurious technological feel to the simple concept of altering one's physical position.

bang 1. *n* [*Dancing*] in jazz dancing a step equivalent to the 'plié' in classical ballet. **2.** *v* [*Stock market*] to depress prices.

bang box *n* [*Navy*] a gun turret on a warship.

bang out *v* [*Air Force*] to pass out under pressure from gravity when the aircraft performs tight turns at high speed.

bang to rights *adv* [*UK*] [*Police*] caught in the act, no doubt whatsover, absolutely guilty.

bang time *n* [*Military*] the period between sighting the flash of an explosion and actually hearing the 'bang', caused by the discrepancy between the respective speeds of light and sound.

bang up 1. *v* [*Gambling*] to close up a game or a casino voluntarily, rather than be raided by the police. **2.** *v* [*UK*] [*Prisons*] to lock a prisoner in his cell.

bang valley *n* [*Aerospace*] any overland test or training area which supersonic aircraft traverse regularly and which therefore suffers bangs as the aircraft pass through the sound barrier.

banger *n* [*UK*] [*Railways*] a detonator, used for fog warnings, etc. See also **cracker**.

banjo 1. *v* [*UK*] [*Military*] to hit, especially to shell. 2. *n* [*UK*] [*Railways*] a repeating signal; a black band on a circular white disc.

bank 1. *n* [*Coal-mining*] the area immediately surrounding the mouth of a shaft, ie. the surface of the colliery. 2. *n* [*Coal-mining*] the coal face. 3. *n* [*Journalism*] a sub-headline. 4. *n* [*Journalism*] a horizontal division into which a newspaper headline is divided. See also **deck 6**. 5. *n* [*Journalism*] the lower line(s) or section(s) of a headline; usually in a smaller type-face than the line(s) above it. 6. *n* [*Gliding*] See **roll 2**. 7. *n* [*Printing*] a table or stand with a smooth, heavy metal top on which linotype slugs are set up into pages. See also **stone 2**.

bank, in the *adv phr* [*Banking*] said of a discount house which is forced to borrow from the bank of England.

bank bandits *n pl* [*Drugs*] barbiturates, sedatives.

bank off *v* [*US*] [*Prisons*] to put in the punishment cells; a term so used because early cells resembled a bank vault. See also **lay down 4**.

bank shot *n* [*Pool*] a shot which drives the object ball into a cushion before pocketing it.

bank switching *n* [*Computing*] a method of memory management used in microprocessor systems that requires more memory than the microprocessor can directly **address**; data is written to different banks of memory, each of which can be the equivalent size of the whole memory capacity of the microprocessor, and a very large number of such banks can be supported.

bank to bank *n* [*Coal-mining*] the period between the time a miner goes underground and the time he returns to the surface.

bankable *a* [*Film*] this refers to the financial aspect of 'star quality'; the ability of a performer, or possibly a director or cameraman, to guarantee that any film with which he/she is involved will make large profits for its backers; by extension, it can be said of any individual whose name will help the producer of a film gain the necessary investment for making it.

banker 1. *n* [*Angling*] a trout that is lying close to the bank. 2. *n* [*Building, Plastering*] a large receptacle in which plastering material is mixed on site. 3. *n* [*Building, Concrete workers*] a platform on which concrete is mixed by hand. 4. *n* [*Gambling*] generally in gambling a banker implies security, solidity, dependability and (thus) the likelihood of profit. 5. *n* [*Gambling*] in football pools, a result which one forecasts consistently over a series of entries. 6. *n* [*Gambling*] the operator of a **banking game**. 7. *n* [*UK*] [*Railways*] a locomotive which assists at the rear of a train ascending a gradient. 8. *n* [*UK*] [*Taxis*] a regular

route that London drivers can 'bank on' being asked for: Heathrow Airport to the London Hilton, Piccadilly Circus to Harrods, etc.

banker's acceptance *n* [*UK*] [*Stock market*] a note, draft or letter of credit backed by a bank; there has developed a market in letters of credit for traders.

bankers' bank *n* [*Banking*] the Bank of England.

banket *n* [*Gold-mining*] gold-bearing mineral conglomerates; the term originated on the Witwatersrand diggings where Dutch miners named it after a favourite almond sweetmeat.

bankhead *n* [*Coal-mining*] the top of an inclined tracked haulage road, where the gradient changes.

banking game *n* [*Gambling*] any betting scheme that gives the operator or a given player some percentage or odds advantage over his opponents; ie: lotteries, casino games, sporting 'books', etc.

banksman *n* [*Industry*] on a building site, the assistant to a girder crane operator who stays on the ground and uses a short-wave radio to direct the working of the crane.

banner, also **flag** *n* [*Journalism*] a large headline that runs across the full width of a page.

bannickers *n pl* [*UK*] [*Coal-mining*] See **hoggers**.

bannock *v* [*Coal-mining*] to undercut by hand at the top of a seam.

bantams *n pl* [*Philately*] reduced size stamps issued by South Africa to conserve paper during the Second World War.

banter *v* [*UK*] [*Market-traders*] to haggle, to beat down a price.

baptism of the spirit *n* [*Religion*] the indwelling of the Holy Spirit within a person; see Acts 2:17.

bar 1. *n* [*Banking*] a money dealer's term for a transaction on the market of 1,000,000 dollars or pounds; from the slang use of 'bar' = £1.00. See also **buck 6**. 2. *n* [*Coal-mining*] a support set parallel to and in contact with the roof or, occasionally, the floor. 3. *n* [*Heraldry*] a broad horizontal strip across the top of a shield. 4. *n* [*Metallurgy*] a rolled iron or steel product, usually rectangular, circular or hexagonal in section; bars may also be produced by forging. See also **billet, bloom**.

bar hop *v* [*Cycling*] in BMX cycling to move from the seat to the handlebars while the bike is in motion.

bar hustler *n* [*Sex*] any prostitute, male or female, who bases his/her operation in a bar or bars.

bar of chocolate *n* [*Navy*] praise received from a senior officer for work well done. See also **bag of nuts**.

bar weight *n* [*Metallurgy*] the weight of a steel sheet bar per foot length.

barak *n* [*Military*] used in the French Foreign legion to mean luck.

barb *n* [*Printing*] the serif-like formation on a C, S or G.

barber **1.** *n* [*Baseball*] a talkative player, from both the cliché of the verbose barber and the notably vocal commentator 'Red' Barber. **2.** *n* [*Baseball*] a pitcher who fires the ball at the batter's head with the intention of forcing him away from the plate; named after the prime exponent of this tactic, Sal 'The Barber' Maglie.

barber chair *n* [*Logging*] a tree that may collapse because the core is rotting; it is also a stump on which there remains a slab of wood that splintered off the tree as it fell.

barbs *n pl* [*Drugs*] abbr of **barbiturates**.

bare **1.** *v* [*Coal-mining*] to strip or cut coal by the side of a fault or boundary. **2.** *a* [*Commerce*] in insurance, to be without a covering policy; thus to 'go bare' means that a professional or a business(man) is carrying no insurance against claims for malpractice, malfunctioning products, etc.

bare contract *n* [*Law*] See **nude contract**.

bare navy *adv* [*Navy*] said of any activity involving only the absolute minimum outlay; thus living on bare navy would be to eat only the basic service rations.

bareback *n* [*US*] [*Road transport*] a tractor without its **semitrailer**. See also **bobtail 2**.

bare-boat charter *n* [*Shipping*] this is the charter of a vessel for a long period, where the charterer hires the master and crew and pays all expenses.

barefoot **1.** *n* [*US*] [*Cattlemen*] an unshod horse. **2.** *n* [*Radio*] operating a Citizen's Band radio on a legal basis; so-called as a reverse of the CB slang for an illegal transmitter/receiver: **boot**. **3.** *a* [*Radio*] said of a transmitter with no outboard linear power amplifier.

barefoot pilgrim *n* [*US*] [*Car salesman*] a gullible or uninformed customer.

barepole charter, also **barehull charter** *n* [*Shipping*] See **bare-boat charter**.

barf **1.** *v* [*Computing*] to malfunction: when a computer comes up against a process which it cannot deal with; it comes from the US college slang barf meaning vomit. **2.** *excl* [*Computing*] a general term of disgust.

barfucious *a* [*Computing*] said of a computer or its software that consistently fails to work as required. See also **bagbiter**.

bargain *n* [*Stock market*] any deal put through on the Exchange.

bargaining chip *n* [*Politics*] this is derived from gambling chips, of which the more one has, the stronger one's ostensible position; it is the 1970s successor in international relations to 'trade-offs': concessions and compromises that one might use during negotiations. Bargaining chips gained real international currency during the SALT I arms limitations talks of 1969–72 and are generally seen to imply the niceties of nuclear weapons talks. Such 'chips' have taken on increasingly complex forms and often, as the in the case of the yet to be deployed **MX** missile and the yet to be researched '**Star Wars**' project, there are theoretical advantages, realised only on paper, which could be used to extort sacrifices from an opponent, without actually making any material sacrifice – only that of a potential threat – oneself.

bargaining creep *n* [*Industrial relations*] the gradual erosion of a company's bargaining position by the offering of piecemeal concessions to individual shop stewards, rather than making a single, overall offer to the entire workforce, based on full company/union collective bargaining.

barge *n* [*Banking*] a code word used between a cashier and a ledger keeper in a bank; if the ledger keeper used it, the customer's account held sufficient funds for a cheque to be cashed.

barker *n* [*Journalism*] a **kicker** in larger type than the headlines beneath it.

barn *n* [*Science*] in nuclear physics this is the measurement, coined in 1942, of the cross-section of a nucleus of 10 (to the minus 24th power) square centimetres; it comes from the expression 'as big as a barn'.

barn doors *n pl* [*TV, Film*] adjustable flaps fitted to lamps in order to adjust or channel the direction or extent of the beam; thus 'to barn door' means to adjust the flaps on a light.

barnacle *n* [*US*] [*Painting*] a building in poor condition which is difficult to paint.

barnburner *n* [*Politics*] an individual who will further his/her own cause no matter what the cost. It is allegedly derived from the story of a farmer who burnt down a barn full of grain simply to destroy the rats inside it. It is currently used to refer to anti-Establishment radicals.

barnburner wizard *n* [*Commerce*] a variety of 'whizkid' who is so dedicated to his/her goals that they 'burn down the barn' around them with the heat generated by the intensity of their effort. An approving use of **barnburner** as opposed to the political one.

barney **1.** *n* [*TV, Film*] a padded, flexible cover that encloses a film camera and is intended to muffle the noise of its mechanism; thus 'heater barney' is a heated cover that is used to protect the camera against cold in outdoor shooting. **2.** also **bullfrog, donkey** *n* [*Logging*] a small car or truck used to push trucks up a slope or incline.

barnstorm **1.** *v* [*Theatre*] used of a touring company of no great talent that plays the undemanding circuit of rural theatres, sometimes actually situated in empty barns. **2.** *v* [*US*] [*Politics*] as an extension of the theatrical use, this is used of a campaign tour that moves through the rural areas, stopping briefly and often. See also **whistle stop**.

B

barnyard pimp n [US] [Prisons] fried chicken served in the messhall.

barnyardy a [Cheese-making] said of any aroma or flavour in a cheese that is reminiscent of the barnyard; this is not necessarily a condemnation, unless over-pronounced.

barometer stock n [Stock market] a widely held stock of a major corporation, whose ups and downs may be construed as an average indicator of the general market conditions.

baron n [UK] [Prisons] a powerful prisoner inside the prison, usually one who is well supplied with the prison currency of tobacco and possibly drugs, as well as actual money. See also **daddy 1**.

baroque armaments n pl [Military] 'the offspring of a marriage between private enterprise and the state, between the capitalist dynamic of the arms manufacturers and the conservatism that tends to characterise armed forces ... in peacetime'; the technology advances, but only within the limits of far less forward-looking theories of warfare; the concern is with the perfection of current trends, rather than any attempt at genuine revolutionary development. The term was coined by US nuclear physicist Herbert York in 'Race to Oblivion' 1970.

baroud n [Military] used in the French Foreign Legion to mean a fight.

barrack stanchion n [Navy] a sailor who has stayed on shore for a long time without a sea posting and who is thus 'holding up the barracks'.

barratry n [Commerce] the stirring up of unnecessary lawsuits and quarrels; it comes from the naval term for the wilful misdemeanour of a ship's captain against the interests of his owner.

barrel 1. n [Cars] a casting which includes one cylinder, but not the crankcase. **2.** n [Cars] the **venturi** of a carburettor; a single-barrel carburettor has one venturi, a four barrel one has four. **3.** n [Photography] the part of the lens with various adjustable rings controlling focussing, aperture, etc., which is manipulated by the hand. **4.** n [Tobacco] a circular table at which the cigar selectors work. **5.** n [TV, Film] the metal tube that suspends lights from the ceiling of a sound stage or studio.

barricuda n [TV, Film] a telescopic light support, made from lengths of alloy pole.

barrier 1. n [Mining] a strip of coal (or any other mineral) left unworked in a mine either (a) to protect against flooding, fire, flammable or noxious gases or similar dangers; or (b) along the boundary of a mineral royalty, between two mineral fields or two mines. **2.** n [Horse-racing] the starting gate on a race-course.

barrier box n [Communications] an isolation unit that electrically divides the consumer's telephone(s) from the overall telephonic system. See also **demarcation strip**.

barring clause n [Film] part of an exhibitor's contract with a renter which prevents him from showing new films before any other specified cinema in the same area; eg: the exhibition of a film in London may preclude its appearance anywhere within a 50 mile radius until the renter so decides.

barry a [Heraldry] divided into horizontal stripes; the number of stripes is specified as in 'barry of six', etc.

Barth system n [Management] a system of payment by results – named after a US industrial engineer, Carl Barth (1860–1939) – in which (1) a standard time is set for a unit of output, (2) an hourly rate of pay is set, (3) a worker's output for the period is counted. He is paid:- (number of units X standard time per unit X number of hours actually worked) X hourly rate.

basal a [Education] a jargon-emebellished synonym for the traditional word 'basic' as in 'basal reader': the first level of reading material, etc. It comes from the medical use of 'basal metabolism' and allied concepts.

base n [Politics] the term comes from J. Stalin's 'Marxism in Linguistics' (1950): ' ... the base is the economic structure of society at the given stage of its development. The superstructure is the political, religious, artistic, philosophical views of the society and the political, legal and other institutions corresponding to them'.

base camp n [Government] a meeting between the superpowers, eg. at Reykjavik in 1986, which is not a full summit, but at which preliminaries to a subsequent summit meeting may be discussed. See also **sherpa**.

base drift n [Banking] this phenomenon occurs in countries where the money supply is ostensibly controlled by a central bank; the latter sets targets for the limits of the money supply, but the base – the target – always exceeds the figure at which it should hold steady.

base line, also **address line** n [Advertising] that part of an advertisement or promotional material which contains the company's name, address, logo and perhaps slogan; it is usually printed in the house style.

base side n [Photography] the side of the film opposite to that coated with emulsion.

baseline aircraft n [Aerospace] the basic, no-frills design of an aircraft on which all developments and additions are based, and which, in performance, can be used as a yardstick of comparison for later and other models.

baseload n [Commerce] the minimum quantity of goods, services, etc. which are required, or which need to be produced, for a company to stay in business.

bash v [Coal-mining] to fill with rubbish the spaces from which coal has been removed.

basher 1. n [UK] [Military] a covered, makeshift sleeping area, often a shallow depression dug out of the ground and adjacent to a firing trench. **2.** n [US] [Skiing] a notably fast skier; thus it some-

B

times refers to a reckless skier or a fast skier who has lost control. **3.** *n* [*TV, Film*] a small floodlight of 200–500W power.

bashing, also **on the bash** *adv* [*Police, Sex*] working as a street prostitute; the term fell out of use after the Street Offences Act (1959) but is currently returning, as are street prostitutes.

BASIC *n* [*Computing*] acro **Beginners' All-Purpose Symbolic Instruction Code** simple, albeit somewhat lengthy and inelegant (to programmers) computer language for learners. It is the usual starting language for those using microprocessors; thus 'tiny BASIC' is a special form of BASIC geared specifically to micro-computers.

basic encyclopedia *n* [*Military*] a compilation for military use of all local military installations and points of similar importance to be known and considered in the case of an attack.

Basic English *n* [*Literary criticism*] acro **British American Scientific International Commercial** an 850 word basic English vocabulary formulated by C. K. Ogden in 1920s. The language possesses 600 nouns, 150 adjectives and a selection of 'operators' – taking in the other parts of speech – including 16 verbs and 100 'structural' words.

basic English *n* [*UK*] [*Railways*] the jargon of the British Rail rule book, in which the most common word is 'must'. Rule books are treasured, if only because a man may be called upon to produce it at a moment's notice. See also **bible 8.**

basic material *n* [*Film*] the source material for a film: the original play, short story, novel, newspaper piece or whatever. It rarely survives intact or even recognisable in the final shooting script.

basic sediment, also **bottom sludge, settlings** *n* [*Oil rigs*] euphemisms for bullshit (b.s.). They refer to anything unpleasant, in particular the slimy sludge that has to be cleaned out of tanks.

basic swing *n* [*Skiing*] a **snowplough** start to a turn and a **parallel turn** to finish.

basilect *n* [*Literary criticism*] the least prestigious dialect of a language. See also **acrolect.**

basis *n* [*Commerce*] in commodity trading, the difference between the spot (cash) price of a commodity and the future price of the same commodity or of one that is closely related. This difference may represent other time periods, quantities, locations and forms of the product.

basis wine *n* [*Wine trade*] a fermented liquor obtained mainly from raisins or concentrated **must** and which is used as the basic constituent in the manufacture of certain wines.

basket 1. *n* [*Government, Politics*] a group of inter-related issues or topics, especially those that are scheduled for discussion at a national or international conference. **2.** *v* [*Angling*] to catch a fish; thus a 'basketful' means a catch of fish.

basket case *n* [*US*] [*Medicine*] a patient suffering from severe multiple injuries.

baskets are in, the *v phr* [*Theatre*] a full house: the phrase comes from the one-time practise of leaving the prop baskets with the theatre management as security against the income of a touring company; if the size of the house failed to guarantee payment of the theatre's rent, the props were theoretically forfeit.

basket of currencies *n* [*Economics*] a selection of currencies related to the central one under discussion – eg. the pound or dollar – and against which the performance of that particular one can be compared.

bas-offs *n pl* [*Military*] used in the French Foreign Legion to mean the lower ranks.

bass *n* [*Coal-mining*] carbonaceous shale.

bass driver *n* [*Audio*] a low frequency speaker, part of a complete loudspeaker system. See also **woofer.**

basset edge *n* [*Coal-mining*] the outcrop of the coal seam.

bastard 1. *n* [*Journalism*] an unorthodox or irregular headline created to match an exceptional story. **2.** *a* [*Printing*] said of any matter used in printing which is of a non-standard size.

bastard title *n* [*Publishing*] the **half-title** when it precedes the title page.

bastard type *n* [*Printing*] any type cast on a body larger than it actually should be.

bastardisation *n* [*Literary criticism*] See **corruption.**

basting *n* [*Clothing*] temporary stitching, or tacking, either by hand or machine, to hold garment parts in the correct position for subsequent permanent sewing.

bat 1. *n* [*Horse-racing*] a short whip used by a jockey. **2.** *n* [*UK*] [*Market-traders*] price. **3.** *n* [*Music*] a solid electric guitar.

batch, also **charge** *n* [*Glass-making*] the basic mixture of materials used for the making of glass.

batch sheet *n* [*Business*] a daily record held in a financial institution that lists items for collection under the various departments to which they are sent, showing the accumulation of the total debit and credit entries.

bate *n* [*Coal-mining*] the place where material is removed from the floor of a roadway to increase height. See also **dirt.**

bater *n* [*Hunting*] See **backer 2.**

bath *n* [*Film*] the developing tank in which film is processed. See also **afternoon bath.**

bath tub *n* [*Cars*] a combustion chamber that resembles an inverted bath tub.

bathing beauty *n* [*Navy*] blancmange.

bathook *n* [*Mountaineering*] See **sky hook.**

bathtub 1. *n* [*Aerospace*] the heavier armour placed around the cockpit of a fighter plane to protect against ground fire. **2.** *n* [*Aerospace*] in aircraft manufacturing, this refers to a temporary recession: the dip and then the rise of sales figures

B

seem to represent the outline of a bathtub on the graph.

bathtub theorem *n* [*Economics*] the premise that the total stock of goods (the 'bath') is equal to the production (the 'tap flow') less the consumption (the 'drain flow'); ie: the rate of accumulation equals the excess of inflow over outflow.

bating *n* [*Tanning*] the neutralising of hides or skins, after the hair has been loosened by soaking in a lime solution; they are immersed and agitated in a solution of pancrea, ammonia, salts and binder of wood dust; hen or pigeon manure is sometimes used for kid stock.

baton *n* [*Heraldry*] a **bendlet** with the ends cut off.

baton rounds *n pl* [*UK*] [*Military*] the official nomenclature for the plastic bullets used in modern riot control.

baton sinister *n* [*Heraldry*] a **baton** that runs from **sinister** at the top to **dexter** at the bottom; it is used to denote royal bastardy in England.

batonne *a* [*Philately*] said of paper that is watermarked with straight parallel lines some distance apart, originally a handwriting guide; it comes from Fr. 'baton' meaning 'stroke of the pen'.

batphone *n* [*UK*] [*Police*] a policeman's personal walkie-talkie radio, based on an ironic reference to the superheroic Batman.

batsman *n* [*Navy*] the officer on the flight deck of an aircraft carrier who guides in landing aircraft by manipulating two hand-held 'bats'. Gradually disappearing as he is replaced by technological/electronic aids. See also **meatball**.

batt, also **matt, lap, web** *n* [*Weaving*] the mass of **carded** fibres from a carding machine.

batter 1. *v* [*Sex*] to work as a male prostitute. **2.** *n* [*Printing*] a damaged or broken character in print work.

batter the bitch *v* [*Antiques*] to fake an antique by hammering 'age' into the wood.

battered ornaments *n pl* [*Literary criticism*] a term coined by H. W. Fowler; a 'rubbish-heap' which contains 'foreign scraps, old phrases, jocular archaisms,' and similar varieties of facetious formations, such as gallicisms, mannerisms, misquotations and similar efforts to improve the prose style of the second rate.

battery 1. *n* [*Baseball*] the pitcher and the catcher of one team considered as a unit. **2.** *n* [*Farming*] a group of bulls kept for breeding purposes. **3.** *n* [*US*] [*Garment trade*] a group of sewing machines and the bench on which they are all set. **4.** *n* [*Law*] the unlawful inflicting of physical harm on a person. See also **assault**. **5.** *n* [*Management*] a collection of tests which have a similar purpose, or which are to be administered in sequence at a single testing session. **6.** *n* [*Music*] the percussion section of an orchestra.

battery, also **sinkbox 7.** *n* [*Hunting*] a hide used by shooters when waiting for game birds or larger prey such as boar.

battery girl *n* [*US*] [*Sex*] a woman or girl kept under the influence of drugs and held in a barracks, naval ship, or boarding house for the enjoyment of the men there.

batting *n* [*Textiles*] a form of wadding material usually used to stuff soft toys or pillows.

batting track *n* [*Cricket*] See **middle 2**.

Battle of the Roses *n* [*Cricket*] the annual cricket matches between Yorkshire and Lancashire county clubs; it is so called because of the counties' divided allegiances in the Wars of the Roses (1455–1485) when Lancashire chose the red rose as its symbol and Yorkshire the white.

battledore *n* [*Glass-making*] an implement used for shaping the foot of a wineglass.

battleship model *n* [*Aerospace*] a development model made to size but constructed from cheap and speedily assembled materials; it is used in statistical assessment and similar, often repeated, trial runs of experimental aircraft.

batwings *n pl* [*US*] [*Cattlemen*] snap-on chaps made of heavy bullhide with wide flapping wings.

baud *n* [*Computing*] a variable unit of data transmission speed, reckoned at one **bit** per second. Measuring the baud will define the capacity of a communications line.

baulk 1. *v* [*Aerospace*] to pull the aircraft up and away from an intended landing. **2.** *v* [*Aerospace*] to obstruct a runway and thus make landings on it impossible.

bay 1. *n* [*Building, Plastering*] the area of wall/floor/ceiling plastered in any given period of work. **2.** *n* [*Hunting*] a hound's cry when angry or baffled. **3.** *n* [*Deer-stalking*] the second branch of a stag's antler, originally called the 'sur-antlier'. **4.** *v* [*Shooting*] to chase so as to bring the quarry to bay.

Bay Street *n* [*Stock market*] the Toronto Stock Exchange, sited on Bay Street, Toronto; the expression is often extended to denote the whole Toronto financial establishment. See also **Wall Street, Lombard Street**.

Bayes' theorem *n* [*Science*] this is named after Thomas Bayes (1702–1761), a UK clergyman and mathematician; the concept is that hypotheses held before an experiment should be modified in the light of the results.

bayonet *n* [*Photography*] a type of lens mount where the lens is fixed by lining up a spring-mounted pin with a notched piece of metal on the camera.

Bayreuth hush *n* [*Music*] the moment of silence caused by the conductor raising his baton prior to commencing the performance; the term comes from the celebrated German opera centre.

BBA *n* [*Midwifery*] abbr of **Baby Born in Ambulance** it therefore means giving birth in the ambulance on the way to the hospital.

B-bomb *n* [*Drugs*] a benzedrine inhaler.

BBQs *n* [*US*] [*Sociology*] abbr of **Bronx, Brooklyn and Queens** a derisory term for all

New Yorkers who do not live on Manhatten island itself.

B.C. *n* [*Salvation Army*] abbr of **British Commissioner** the head of the SA in the UK and the equivalent to the Archbishop of Canterbury in the Church of England.

B-D *n* [*US*] [*Drugs*] abbr of **Beckton-Dickinson** the makers of a popular brand of hypodermic syringe.

be afraid *excl* [*New therapies*] a command in **primal therapy** that calls upon the patient to surrender to whatever fear and/or pain is being experienced, on the principle that each successive level of anxiety leads on to a deeper one and thence, as intended, to the climactic primal.

be off *v* [*Theatre*] to miss one's entrance.

beach 1. *n* [*Cricket*] a dry, dusty pitch, ideally suited to a spinner. **2.** *a* [*Cricket*] used to refer to the standard of play that one might expect to find among those playing cricket on the seashore.

beach, on the 1. *adv* [*Navy*] ashore and unemployed; especially when retired early. **2.** *adv* [*US*] [*Navy*] on leave.

beach ball, also **personal rescue enclosure** *n* [*Aerospace*] a compact, sealed sphere designed to surround an astronaut in the event of an emergency transfer from an orbiting spacecraft into a rescue vehicle.

beach energy *n* [*Science*] the term was coined by UK mathematician F. J. Dyson, from the film 'On The Beach' which was set in the post-nuclear war environment. It means a unit of fission energy equal to 3x10 (to the power of 6) megatons. The planetary fallout from one Beach would kill 50% of the Earth's population by fallout alone.

beached *a* [*Navy*] an officer retired from the service on reaching the maximum age for his rank; usually such officers have been passed over for further promotion.

bead *n* [*Tyre-making*] a section of rubber-lined wire fabrics which form the outer edge of the sidewall and which press against the metal rim of the car wheel.

bead and reel *n* [*Building, Plastering*] a common form of **enrichment**, whereby three beads alternate with an elongated bead, in **astragal** section.

beak 1. *n* [*Printing*] a serif-like formation at the end of an arm in a letter. **2.** *n* [*Printing*] the end of certain curved lines, especially f and j.

beam 1. *n* [*Deer-stalking*] the circumference of the antler, between the second and third tines, taken at its thinnest part. **2.** *n* [*Hunting*] the main stem of a stag's antlers. **3.** *n* [*Tanning*] a rounded board on which hides are stretched so that all hair, flesh and grease can be removed prior to tanning; thus 'beaming' means the removal of extraneous matter from skins hence 'beaming knife', 'beaming machine' etc.

beam house *n* [*Tanning*] a department within a tannery where flesh, hair and grease are removed from the skins or hides preparatory to tanning; it comes from the **beam**.

beamer, also **skull ball, bouncer** *n* [*Cricket*] any ball bowled fast and aimed deliberately at the batsman, often at the (now helmet-protected) head or other part of the body. The intention is intimidation; an unspoken contract supposedly limits such bowling to attacking recognised batsmen, but it is by no means always honoured.

beaming 1. *n* [*Furriers*] the basic operation of pelt processing: the peltry is put on a circular arm – the beam – with the hair side downward; here fatty or muscle tissue is removed by special knives. **2.** *n* [*Weaving*] the act of winding the **warp** on to the warp beam.

beamy *a* [*Audio*] said of a speaker with a narrowly focussed sound field – a 'beam' – without much dispersion of the treble.

bean bag *n* [*US*] [*Police*] a bag filled with birdshot or sand, which is fired from a shotgun for crowd-control use.

bean counter *n* [*Business*] an accountant.

bean rag *n* [*US*] [*Navy*] a signal hoisted to denote that the ship's company is eating.

beanball *n* [*Baseball*] a fast pitch aimed directly at the batter's head (or 'bean').

beanhauler *n* [*US*] [*Road transport*] a trucker who transports fruit and vegetables.

beanie light *n* [*US*] [*Road transport*] a revolving warning light on top of an emergency vehicle.

beans *n* [*US*] [*Railways*] a meal break.

beanstalk *n* [*TV, Film*] a hydraulically operated extending platform rising to 20' high for use in erecting lights on location.

Bear 1. *n* [*Military*] the general NATO definition of the Soviets and anything pertaining to them. **2.** *n* [*Military*] the NATO description of all Russian bomber planes.

bear 1. *n* [*Metallurgy*] the residual mass of solid metal and slag, often mixed with fuel, which remains in the furnace after a metal melting process has been concluded. **2.** *n* [*Navy*] a large holystone which is drawn across the deck by lanyards attached to it. See also **bible 7**, **prayerbook. 3.** *n* [*Stock market*] one who believes that market prices will fall and operates according to this supposition by selling shares in the hope of repurchasing them when they reach lower levels.

bear campaign, also **bear raid, bear tack** *n* [*Stock market*] the selling of small lots of shares by dealers with the intention of driving overall prices down; the aim is to repurchase these small lots later at a lower price; such manoeuvres are illegal under stock exchange rules. See also **bull campaign**.

bear fighter *n* [*Logging*] the sawmill operator who 'fights the bear', ie. he separates the strips from the boards as they come into the mill.

bear squeeze *n* [*Stock market*] action by buyers of a given share to force **bears** to deliver the shares that they have contracted to deliver at the

B

agreed price on the due date; bears can only achieve this by selling at a loss.

bear tracker n [US] [Police] plain-clothes officer.

bear-cat (UK), **all-in** (US) n [Wrestling] a form of competition which is restricted by a minimum number of rules and throws that are adjudged 'foul'.

bearcats n [Logging] a crew which does particularly hazardous work.

Beard, the n [Espionage] in CIA terminology, this is the hirsute Fidel Castro, President of Cuba.

beard n [Printing] the space extending from the baseline of a typeface to the lower limit of the body copy as it appears on the page.

bearding n [TV, Video] the overflow in a TV or video picture of black tones into the adjacent white areas.

bearer (bonds) n pl [Stock market] securities that can be transferred from one holder to another without the need for registration; one owner simply hands them physically on to the next.

bearer scrip n [Commerce, Finance] a temporary document issued to purchasers of government stocks during that period when some instalments of payment are still outstanding. See also **definitive bond**.

bearers n pl [Clothing] sections fastened to the side seams of trousers to take the weight when the front is opened.

beast 1. n [US] [Painting] a large air compressor used for spray-painting large surfaces, steel work, bridges and similar constructions. 2. n [Religion] the Antichrist; see Revelations 13.15.

beasting n [Marines] the traditional initiation rights forced upon a Marine on his first night of enlistment; these often include being woken at 2am, taken over the camp assault course and then soaked in a water tank.

beat 1. n [Fencing] the sharp striking of the opponent's blade when parrying his blow. 2. n [Journalism] a piece of news discovered and published ahead of one's rivals; this comes from the concept of beating the rest of the press. Beat has almost completely replaced 'scoop' as a description of such a coup.

beat the board v [Athletics] to thrust the propelling foot down hard in jumping events, especially the long-jump.

beat the index v [Stock market] when a portfolio of shares performs better than the average noted by the Index of Prices.

beat the pistol v [Athletics] See **break the start**.

beat the pumpkins v [US] [Road transport] to kick the tyres to check they are hard and in good condition.

beater 1. n [US] [Paper-making] a machine used to reduce four-foot lengths of pulpwood to pulp so that it is ready for making into paper products. 2. n [Textiles] a machine used to flatten cloth by 'beating' it with a set of metal rods or teeth.

beating n [Weaving] packing in the **weft**.

beatout n [Baseball] a play in which a batter achieves a run to first base by outrunning the fielder's throw to stop him.

beatty n [Navy] a special entry cadet at the Royal Naval College; such cadets are named after Admiral Beatty.

beautiful painting, also **lyrical colourism** n [Art] See **new informalists**.

beauty n [Science] in physics, a property of a sub-atomic particle known as a **bottom quark**. See also **quark**, **truth**.

beauty spot n [Advertising] a close up shot (either still or on film) of the product to be advertised, complete with its packaging. See also **pack shot**.

beaux arts n [Architecture] a rigid, highly composed often symmetrical style, based on the criteria encouraged in the Nineteenth Century by the Ecole des Beaux Arts in Paris; it is generally conservative and opposed to any species of the avant garde.

beaver tail n [UK] [Road transport] a lorry or trailer with the rear end of the platform drooping towards the ground; this is used to facilitate loading of engineering plant or other wheeled equipment.

beavering n [Logging] cutting a continuous circle around a tree to make it fall.

beavertail n [UK] [Road transport] a low-loading platform which has a sloping tail beyond the rearmost axle to facilitate loading.

be-back, also **B-back** n [US] [Car salesmen] a customer who does not buy but promises to 'be back'.

becket 1. n [Sailing, Ropework] the rope handle of sea chest. 2. n [Sailing, Ropework] the eye or hook of a block strap.

beckets n pl [Navy] pockets in trousers; this comes from its specific usage as a 'means of holding and securing' loops on ropes, handles on buckets, etc.

becs n pl [Cheese-making] small oblique fissures that form beneath the rind of very old Gruyeres with very few holes; it comes from Fr. meaning 'beaks'.

bed 1. n [Building, Plastering] a recess in a moulding into which an ornament can be placed. 2. n [Clothing] in a sewing-machine, this is the sewing platform which supports the needle plate and the side plate and which contains the lower sewing mechanisms. 3. [US] [Painting] a platform suspended from the top of the building, used to support painters as they work on the exterior.

bed and breakfast deal n [Stock market] a method whereby investors can establish tax losses against possible capital gains by selling shares and then repurchasing them in unconnected deals.

bed bug hauler 1. n [US] [Road transport] a driver of a moving van. 2. n [US] [Road transport] a moving van.

B

bed charge *n* [*Metallurgy*] the first layer of iron which is placed in a **cupola** furnace.

bed, go to *v* [*Cards*] when a player forfeits an opportunity of winning by failing to play a vital card at the correct stage of play.

bed ground, also **herd ground** *n* [*US*] [*Cattlemen*] the area where a herd is bedded down for the night.

bed night *n* [*Travel agents*] the use of one bed for one night in a given hotel.

bedded *a* [*US*] [*Cattlemen*] said of a roped animal that has been thrown with such force that it lies down and does not move.

bedpain *mnem* [*US*] [*Police*] mnemonic used by trainee police to remember items to be reported in a given type of burglary: break, enter, dwelling, person, armed, (with) intent (to kill), (at) night.

bedpan alley 1. *n* [*US*] [*Medicine*] the room where bedpans and similar items are sterilised. **2.** *n* [*US*] [*Medicine*] the hospital ward.

bedpan line *n* [*UK*] [*Railways*] this is the newly (1983) electrified Bedford-St. Pancras line, formerly the 'hot line', because of the unusually large number of fires that broke out on diesel railcar trains running the line.

bedpost *n* [*Ten-pin bowling*] a split where only the 7 and 10 pins are left standing. See also **baby split**, **bucket**, **Cincinnati**.

bedroom *n* [*US*] [*Town planning*] the equivalent to the UK 'dormitory' town.

bedsheet ballot *n* [*US*] [*Politics*] a ballot paper that lists a lengthy selection of candidates and thus confuses the electors. It comes from the practice in the US of using Presidential elections to vote not merely for the Chief Executive but also for a multiplicity of lesser, local officials at the same time.

bee day *n* [*Religion*] a day – presumably of great 'busyness' – spent in work to prepare for a religious convention.

beef 1. *v* [*Aerospace*] to strengthen the structural parts of an aircraft, or to modify current designs and hardware. **2.** *n* [*UK*] [*Prisons*] a chief officer; from rhyming slang for bully beef or corned beef (the latter more common in recent years).

beef book *n* [*US*] [*Cattlemen*] the book in which all records of the ranch's business dealings, herd totals, etc. are maintained.

beef chit *n* [*Navy*] the menu in a Royal Navy wardroom; beef stands for any type of meat served on board ship.

beef screen *n* [*Navy*] the butcher's shop in a warship.

beef (it) up *v* [*Architecture*] to darken up the lines on a drawing.

beefalo *n* [*US*] [*Agriculture*] a hybrid strain of beef cattle developed by inter-breeding domestic cattle and buffaloes: three-eighths buffalo, three-eights Charolais cow and one quarter Hereford. It was first developed by Californian rancher D. C. Basolo, and follows an earlier hybrid, the cattalo,

developed in the 1880s by the Texan Col. Charles Goodnight.

beefsteak 1. *v* [*US*] [*Cattlemen*] to ride so hard that the horse's back becomes sore. **2.** *n* [*Marbles*] any game in which it is agreed that any type of illegal play may be used if a player can perform it undetected.

beer *n* [*Distilling*] the product of fermenting yeasted mash, that will subsequently be distilled into low wines and then high wines, from which whiskey is made.

beery *a* [*Wine-tasting*] said of an unpleasant smell caused by secondary fermentation in the bottle.

beestings *n* [*Cheese-making*] the colostrum, or first milk a cow gives after calving; this is very high in protein and is only used in one cheese: the Spanish 'Armada', a semi-firm, strong cheese.

beet *n* [*Glass-making*] a glass blower who specialises in hollow ware.

beetle crusher *n* [*UK*] [*Railways*] a shunting engine in the Scottish region.

beg *n* [*Crime*] a crime perpetrated by a telephone con-man who will call up his victim and plead with him for a donation to a (perfectly legitimate) charity event that he has actually persuaded the sponsor to let him organise. In the event a proportion of the money thus raised will go to the charity, but a far greater sum will stay with the con-man and vanish with him before anyone can stop it.

beggar-my-neighbour policy *n* [*Economics*] a policy of protectionism at a time of world-wide trade depression; the intention is to encourage home producers to increase output (and thus through increased jobs to improve the home economy). By denying other countries their former export markets through this surge in home manufacturing, it encourages the further economic decline of those countries.

beggar's communism *n* [*Politics*] a term coined by N.S. Khruschev to deride Mao Zedong's ostensible belief in the absolute excellence of subsistance living; a belief which Mao was forced to tout to his people in a pragmatic attempt to make palatable the facts of the Chinese economy.

beginner's luck *n* [*UK*] [*Railways*] an ironic reference to a driver who is derailed on his first day in charge of a locomotive.

behabitive *n* [*Philology*] a term coined by J. L. Austin: everyday phrases, usually no more than automatic politeness, which we use when we meet, converse with and depart from our fellows.

behavioural art *n* [*Art*] an art form based on the principles and techniques of cybernetics and the behavioural social sciences and which assumes that the function of art is to alter behaviour. Its projects involve members of the public and are aimed at increasing participants' awareness of their physical and social environment.

behavioural control units *n* [*Prisons*] solitary confinement cell.

beheadment n [Logology] the eliminating of an initial letter from a word to leave another legitimate word, thus greed/reed, etc.

behind 1. prep [New therapies] in respect of, concerning, about; it is usually used to denote a given experience, eg. 'I could really get off behind space-time conceptualising . . .' **2.** adv [Soccer] any ball that has passed over the goal line but has not actually gone between the posts.

behind motors adv [Cycling] following behind a revolving motor, which is mounted behind a motorcycle and is designed to reduce wind resistance.

behind the wood, also **behind the mahogany, stick** adv [US] [Bars] working as a bar-tender.

belcher n [TV, Radio] one who comes to the microphone or camera without clearing his/her throat adequately.

Belgian block n [US] [Military] a tank testing course designed for the US Army, comprising cobblestones and rainfilled hollows.

belief n [Marketing] an individual's view of the existence of something; in particular the association of one advertised concept with another, ie. the belief that such and such a product possesses such and such a property and that on these grounds it is worthy of purchase.

belker v [UK] [Market-traders] to cry noisily.

bell 1. v [Deer-stalking] See **roar**. **2.** n [Hunting] the **challenge** of a stag during the rutting season. **3.** n [Sport] in any track event – foot or cycling – the bell that is rung to signify the start of the final lap.

bell case, also **bell cast** n [Building, Plastering] the projection over door or window openings which sheds rainwater clear of that opening.

bell, on the adv [UK] [Medicine] working in the emergency ward; it is taken from the bell rung by a working ambulance.

bell-horses n pl [Industrial relations] See **pacers**.

bellows n [Photography] an expandable fixture, similar to an accordion, which can be attached between the camera and the lens to focus in very tightly on the subject.

bellows to mend n [Boxing] a tired and possibly unfit boxer whose heavy, audible breathing betrays his inadequacies.

bells n pl [Navy] in the Royal Navy bells are rung every thirty minutes while at sea to denote the time. The day is divided into four hour watches, each of which comprises one to eight bells, as the half hours proceed. Thus three bells equals one and a half hours into a given watch, eight bells the end of the watch, and so on.

bells and whistles n pl [Marketing] the special features which a given product – especially a computer program – possesses; it is these features that are most heavily advertised and their existence or otherwise is what influences the customer towards making a particular purchase.

belly 1. n [Archery] the convex inner side of the bow. **2.** n [Aerospace] the bottom of the aircraft's fuselage. **3.** n [Metallurgy] the part of a blast furnace, at the top of the **bosh**, where the diameter is greatest.

belly buster n [US] [Cattlemen] a long pole used as a latch for wire gates.

belly cut n [Medicine] abdominal surgery.

belly in v [US] [Painting] when a high ladder bends under the weight of the person who is standing on it to work.

belly lugging n [US] [Road transport] any sort of work that involves the driver in carrying.

belly up v [US] [Painting] to ascend a ladder by hugging the sides and keeping one's body as close to the rungs as possible – a method used by those who hate heights.

below adv [Theatre] a stage direction that implies 'in front of' either a person or an item of stage furniture. See also **above 3**, **downstage**, **upstage**.

below the gangway adv [UK] [Politics] this expression is used when a Member of the House of Commons sits among the general backbench MPs, rather than on the front benches with the Cabinet or Shadow Cabinet (ministers and former ministers of the government or opposition).

below the line 1. adv [Business] an account that is in debt. See also **above the line 2**. **2.** n [TV] the special budget allotted to expenditure on 'extramural' projects, eg. exterior and special set construction, a freelance director, etc. See also **above the line 3**. **3.** also **sales promotion** a [Advertising] used to describe any form of publicity other than direct advertising, eg. give-aways, special offers, store displays, etc.

below the market adv [Stock market] at a price beneath the normal market quotation. See also **above the market**.

below-the-line advertising n [Advertising] advertising activities which do not usually budget for a commission to an agency: direct mail, exhibitions, demonstrations, point-of-sale material, etc. See also **above the line 1**.

belt n [US] [Police, Prisons] a restraining belt, buckled at the back, and fitted with a steel ring through which handcuffs may be locked.

beltman n [UK] [Coal-mining] an operator who installs the conveyor belts which take the coal out of the mine; beltmen patrol in teams throughout the mine making running repairs as required.

B.E.M. n [Science fiction] acro **Bug-Eyed Monster** a genre of notably lurid science fiction depending on encounters with species of bizarre aliens.

bench 1. v [Mining] to work coal or mineral in layers from the top downwards. **2.** v [US] [Football] to retain a player on the **bench** rather than permit him to play; this decision – in effect a

B

suspension on full pay – can keep a player out of the playing team for a single game or any period up to a whole season. **3.** *n* [*Glass-making*] the floor of a pot furnace. **4.** *n* [*Sport*] in soccer, US football, basketball and baseball the shelter or sometimes just an actual bench were the manager, trainer and substitutes can watch the game; it is usually adjacent to the touchline.

bench scientist *n* [*Science*] a scientist or research scientist who works in the laboratory; it is slightly derogatory when used by those scientists who have moved into lucrative and highly publicised careers as government and/or military advisers.

bench tolerance *n* [*Baking*] the property held by dough that allows it to ferment at a rate slow enough to prevent over-fermentation when it is being made up into bread or other products while on the bench.

bench warmer *n* [*Sport*] a sportsman who fails to make the playing team – either through personal incompetence, injury or his/her inability to fit in with the coach's current plans – and thus spends most of the season sitting on the **bench**.

bench worker *n* [*Glass-making*] a worker who forms glassware from tubing or rod by heating it in a flame at a workbench.

benchmark 1. *n* [*Stock market*] a standard of interest paid or offered on investments in a new issue of stock which will serve as a guide to that charged on future issues. **2.** *n* [*Computing*] a standard which serves as a reference and testing point. **3.** *v* [*Computing*] to test a machine against a standardised problem or set of achievements which place it in the context of its peers.

bend 1. *n* [*Heraldry*] a broad diagonal strip running from **dexter** at top to **sinister** at bottom. **2.** *n* [*Motor-racing*] a deliberately understated euphemism for a crash; it comes from the devil-may-care image of the racing driver. See also **shunt. 3.** *n* [*Sailing, Ropework*] a knot which ties the ends of two ropes together. **4.** *v* [*Sailing, Ropework*] to tie two ropes together. **5.** *v* [*Sailing, Ropework*] to tie to an anchor. **6.** *v* [*Sailing, Ropework*] to tie a rope or secure a sail to a spar.

bender 1. *n* [*US*] [*Prisons*] a suspended sentence. **2.** *n* [*Shooting*] a wire snare which is attached to a bent hazel wand and set so that when the animal is caught its struggle frees the wand and the animal is suspended dangling in mid-air.

bendlet *n* [*Heraldry*] a narrow **bend**.

bends *n* [*Diving*] nitrogen narcosis, which afflicts divers working at great depths who fail to observe due precautions as regards returning slowly to the surface and thus allowing the body to adjust itself gradually to the changing pressures.

bendy *a* [*Heraldry*] divided into diagonal strips from **dexter** at the top to **sinister** at bottom.

beneficial owner *n* [*Law*] that person who has the right to live in and exploit a property, even if he does not wholly own it, eg. the leaseholder.

benefit segmentation *n* [*Marketing*] a form of market segmentation which bases its divisions on the differences in benefits required of a product by its potential purchaser.

benevolent capitalism *n* [*Politics*] Marx's alternative description of paternalism: the status quo remains absolutely unaltered – the worker below, the capitalist above – but the sensible capitalist, under the auspices of 'benevolence', papers over the cracks and throws sops to his employees in the form of charity and welfare.

benign testing *n* [*Military*] the testing of a new weapons system in such a way that it will perform in the way that the makers, and the military who commissioned it, desire. Such a satisfactory performance is significantly aided by a variety of underhand means or simple lies, eg. the excellent results ascribed to the AMRAAM, a new US air-to-air missile tested in 1982. These results were helped by the sound-emitting device placed in the target drone, tuned to attract the incoming missile. When this strategem was discovered, USAF explained that they had not wished 'to bore anyone with technical details'.

benny 1. *n* [*Crime*] an overcoat used to conceal the goods that one is engaged in stealing from a shop. **2.** *n* [*Drugs*] abbr of **benzedrine. 3.** *n* [*UK*] [*Military*] a civilian inhabitant of the Falkland Islands; so called by the British forces stationed there as a derogatory reference to 'Benny' the retarded farmboy in the TV serial 'Crossroads'. **4.** *n* [*Tyre-making*] a petrol-based mixture used to clean the surface of the tread and add extra layers of rubber when needed.

benny squad *n* [*US*] [*Football*] the special term used for the most savage and desperate plays which involve the maximum of dangerous physical contact. The name derives from the belief, true or otherwise, that such aggression is fuelled by large pre-match doses of benzedrine (a drug often prescribed for soldiers on the verge of entering combat).

bent 1. *n* [*US*] [*Cattlemen*] a measure of bulk hay: as long, as wide and as high as can be stacked by a derrick on a single setting. **2.** *a* [*UK*] [*Police*] crooked, corrupt; the usual reference is to a 'bent copper', a policeman who has 'gone wrong'.

bent dart *n* [*UK*] [*Railways*] a heavy poker used on steam trains for cleaning the clinker from the fire-box; the 'dart' is an eight foot long steel rod with an arrowhead and bent in the middle. Clinker was shifted through sheer force.

bent spear *n* [*US*] [*Military*] the US emergency code to denote an incident (less potentially dangerous than an **accident**) involving a nuclear device. This code ranks below any accident, as well as below any form of 'war readiness'.

berm *n* [*Cycling*] a banked bend in BMX cycling.

berthage, also **dockage** *n* [*Shipping*] a charge levied on shipowners by a port for the use of its berthing facilities.

B

Bertie, do a *v* [*UK*] [*Crime*] to turn Queen's evidence, to become an informer; named after someone who did this.

besom *n* [*Curling*] the curler's broom with which the ice is swept to vary the speed and direction of the stone.

best boy *n* [*Film*] a film crew member who is the assistant to the **gaffer** or key **grip**.

best case scenario, worst case scenario *n* [*Military, Politics*] planning theories designed to offer models of the most and least favourable outcomes, events, possibilities, results and other generally unknown quantities of the topic under discussion.

best efforts 1. *a* [*Stock market*] of an underwriter: not involving a firm commitment to take up any unsold shares or bonds of any issue being underwritten. 2. *a* [*Stock market*] of an investment banker: an agreement to sell as best he can a new issue to the public. If the shares cannot be sold, the banker simply cancels the authority to sell and forfeits any commission.

bet names *n pl* [*Gambling*] the most popular bets made in horse-racing and dog-racing include: yankee: six horses backed to come first in six different races; nap (napoleon): the horse that a tipster – on course, on TV or in the press – offers his 'customers' as a best bet or a 'certainty'; trixie or treble: half a yankee: three horses backed to win in three races; double: two horses backed to win in two races. See also **across the board 2**.

bet the top *v* [*Gambling*] in poker, to make a bet that equals the number of chips or amount of cash that is already in the pot.

beta factor, also **beta coefficient** (*US*) *n* [*Stock market*] the measure of the performance of a share as regards its risk and the steadiness of its market price. A β of unity is awarded to a share that performs exactly with the market average; thus a β of above unity indicates an above-average performer and one of below unity a below-average share.

beta stocks, also **beta securities** *n pl* [*UK*] [*Stock exchange*] a group of 500 stocks that together comprise the second most popular area of trading on the London stock exchange. See also **alpha stocks, gamma stocks, delta stocks**.

bett, also **bat** *n* [*Coal-mining*] a dirt band interstratified with coal and ironstone.

Betty Martin *n* [*Navy*] corned beef, the consistency and flavour of which supposedly resembles the victim, one Betty Martin, of a once well-known 19th century murderer.

between-lines entry *n* [*Data security*] the use of active wire-tapping by an unauthorised user to gain access to a computer system when the user's terminal is inactive for a short period.

bevels *n pl* [*Gambling*] crooked dice on which one or more sides are slightly rounded instead of cut flat as they should be, thus forcing the die to roll off the rounded face more often than it will off the flat.

bevvy *n* [*UK*] [*Market-traders*] beer; thus 'bevvyken' means beerhouse, public house.

bevvy-merchant *n* [*UK*] [*Market-traders*] a heavy drinker.

BFT *n* [*New therapies*] abbr of **Bio-Feedback Training** see biofeedback.

bheer *n* [*Science fiction*] beer; as in fhate (fate), ghod (god), etc, this superfluous 'h' is a common eccentricity of fan magazine spelling; it is possibly reminiscent of popular words like 'ghost' and 'ghoul'.

BI *n* [*US*] [*Espionage*] abbr of **Background Investigations** interrogations and researches designed to determine whether an individual may be a security risk.

bias compensation *n* [*Audio*] placing a degree of outward force on a pickup-arm to counteract the natural inward bias caused by friction between the stylus and the groove it follows on the record.

bib *n* [*US*] [*Skiing*] the piece of cloth worn front and back to show the number of a competition skier.

bible 1. *n* [*US*] [*Carpenters*] the architect's specifications. 2. *n* [*US*] [*Cattlemen*] a packet of cigarette papers. 3. *n* [*Circus*] a hinged platform of planks on which the reserved seats stand; it is so called because it opens and shuts like a book. 4. *n* [*US*] [*Circus*] the programme. 5. *n* [*Commerce*] See **manifold**. 6. *n* [*Industry, Commerce*] this is used in various employments to denote a book of rules, reference or instructions; a catalogue or price list (specifically the US rural term for the Sears Roebuck mail order catalogue); it is also an employee's tally of bills and receipts which must balance the receipts in the cash register. 7. *n* [*Navy*] a large holystone – a piece of sandstone used to polish the deck. 8. *n* [*UK*] [*Railways*] the railways rule book; it must be carried at all times and produced on request. See also **basic English**. 9. *n* [*US*] [*Road transport*] the driver's rule book.

bible puncher *n* [*Navy*] the ship's chaplain.

bible-thumper *n* [*UK*] [*Market-traders*] a crooked hawker who sells from door to door what he claims is his mother's old bible; the theory is that the purchaser should immediately return the bible, and put the payment down to charity.

bicycle 1. *n* [*Aerospace*] a form of landing gear in which the main wheels and their supports are set one behind the other, like bicycle wheels, along the centre of the aircraft. 2. *n* [*Gambling*] the best possible hand in lowball poker: ace, two, three, four, six; it was originally named after the picture of a bicycle on a popular brand of US manufactured cards. 3. *n* [*US*] [*Garment trade*] a hatter's lathe. 4. *n* [*Logging*] a two-sheaved lead block. 5. *v* [*Horse-riding*] to spur a bucking horse alternately on one side and then the other.

bicycling 1. *n* [*Film*] the involvement of an actor

B

or director in two projects, either concurrently or consecutively. See also **back to back 2. 2.** *n* [*Media*] when TV, print or radio journalists take one source, a programme, feature, or interview, etc., and use it to create extra pieces which are attributed to various numbers of the original production or writing team and then disseminated through fellow media outlets. **3.** *n* [*TV*] in cable TV the showing of a programme on several cable networks. **4.** *n* [*US*] [*TV*] a method of passing syndicating programmes around a chain of affiliate TV stations: each affiliate in an established order will transmit a show one week, and then send it on to the next station in line for transmission the following week; meanwhile it receives in its turn the next segment for that week's schedules. The circuit around which these segments proceed is the 'bicycle route'.

BID *adv* [*Medicine*] acro twice daily.

bid 1. *a* [*US*] [*Police*] brought in dead. **2.** *n* [*US*] [*Railways*] an application for a vacant job. **3.** *v* [*US*] [*Railways*] to submit a sheet listing one's preferences for vacant jobs. **4.** *v n* [*Stock market*] to offer to purchase shares at a specified price, or the offer itself.

bid book *n* [*US*] [*Railways*] a book signed by every employee submitting a **bid** to ensure there are no subsequent arguments.

bidding theory *n* [*Marketing*] the quantification of purchasing determinants and the application of probability theory to arrive at a pricing policy; the numerical expression of relevant factors and their measured likelihood of acceptance at different price levels.

biddy *n* [*US*] [*Medicine*] a gas anaesthetic apparatus.

Bids & Proposals *n pl* [*US*] [*Military*] R. W. Howe 'Weapons' (1980): '... the expenses incurred by defense contractors or would-be contractors in response to official requests for proposals concerning weaponry and weapons technology ...' Such expenses are used as a convenient cover-all to hide additional defence expenditure over and above the regular weapons spending sanctioned by Congress.

big *a* [*Wine-tasting*] said of a substantial wine, well-endowed with the vital elements, and not simply strong in alcohol.

big art *n* [*Art*] artworks of extra-large proportion, specifically poster art.

Big Bang *n* [*UK*] [*Stock market*] the deregulation of the London Stock Market, which took place on October 27, 1986; under the new system, which had been instituted on the New York Stock Exchange in 1975, stockbrokers may make markets in shares as well as deal for their clients, foreign firms may now deal on the UK stock exchange and the old minimum commission rate of deals has been abandoned. See also **dual capacity, market maker**.

big banking *n* [*Commerce*] the financial estab-lishment, often conducting its business on a multinational scale.

big bertha *n* [*Photography*] a large long-range telescopic lens; the name comes from the WWI nickname for the 42cm gun manufactured by Krupp and named after Frau Bertha Krupp (died 1957).

Big Blue *n* [*Business, Computing*] the IBM (International Business Machines) Corporation; the name from the colour of the IBM logo; '... the IBM PC XT–370, which links the Personal Computer to Big Blue's bigger machines.' See also **I've Been Moved**.

Big Blue Cube *n* [*US*] [*Air Force*] the Satellite Test Center, the command headquarters of the USAF Space Division's Satellite Control Facility. A nine-story, windowless, pale-blue block, with administrative buildings and radar and communications installations attached..

Big Board *n* [*Stock market*] the New York Stock Exchange. See also **Lombard Street, Wall Street**.

big bourgeoisie *n* [*Politics*] in Marxist terms this refers to the top strata of the bourgeoisie who own and run the major sources of industrial profit – currently the multinationals and conglomerates – and who control raw materials and allied vital means of production; the super-capitalists.

big brain *n* [*UK*] [*Railways*] the railway control office, responsible for arranging and organising the passage of all trains.

big broadcasting *n* [*US*] [*TV*] the major broadcasting companies – ABC, CBS, NBC – whose interests transcend simple broadcasting and can be seen to blend in with US governmental priorities.

big cat 1. *n* [*Gambling*] a hand recognised in certain poker games; king, queen, jack, ten, eight and containing no pairs; it must include cards from two or more suits and ranks immediately below a flush. See also **little cat. 2.** *n* [*Gambling*] in poker, a hand with king high, eight low and no pair. See also **big dog**.

big character poster *n* [*Politics*] from Chinese 'dazibao' meaning large government-authorised propaganda posters. For a short period following the demise of the **Gang of Four**, the Chinese public were permitted, even encouraged, to write and exhibit such posters themselves. However this freedom was short-lived and ended in a spate of arrests to muzzle the over-enthusiastic.

big con *n* [*US*] [*Crime*] a major confidence trick, often involving a number of people, a large amount of seed money, several months of preparation and resulting, if successful, in very large profits for all. See also **short con**.

big day *n* [*US*] [*Prisons*] visiting day.

big dick *n* [*Gambling*] in craps dice, the point of ten.

big digger n [*Gambling*] in poker, the ace of spades.

big dog n [*Gambling*] in poker, a hand with ace high, nine low and no pair. See also **big cat**.

big dress n [*US*] [*Garment trade*] a garment, not necessarily a dress, that sells well at the asked price.

big education n [*US*] [*Education*] the major universities who are tied by more than just academic excellence to the national establishment.

big eight 1. n [*US*] [*Accounting*] the eight largest US accounting firms, as assessed by total sales audited: (as of mid–1984) Arthur Andersen & Co.; Coopers & Lybrand; Ernst & Whinney; Deloitte Haskins & Sells; Peat, Marwick, Mitchell & Co; Price Waterhouse & Co.; Touche Ross & Co.; Arthur Young & Co. 2. n [*Gambling*] in craps dice, a large area of the table layout where players, who are betting on the likelihood of an eight being thrown before a seven, can place their bets.

big feeling n [*New therapies*] in Theta Rebirthing Seminars, this is the sought after sensation of experiencing one's birth, enhanced, or at least aided, by total immersion in a 99° bath with nose-clips and a snorkel, to approximate the sensation of being back in the womb.

big fish n [*Navy*] large, important targets – aircraft carriers, merchant shipping convoys, etc.

big foot n [*US*] [*Journalism*] a columnist, editor or celebrity journalist who pays temporary visits to the general working press corps, usually those covering a presidential campaign, in order to write a specific piece. See also **little foot**.

Big Four n [*UK*] [*Banking*] Lloyds, Midland, Barclays and National Westminster Banks.

big gee n [*UK*] [*Market-traders*] high praise, flattery, optimum treatment.

big gray dog n [*US*] [*Road transport*] a Greyhound bus.

big hat n [*US*] [*Road transport*] any official – usually a policeman – whose uniform includes a large hat.

big hole v [*US*] [*Railways*] to make a manual emergency application of the brakes; this term comes both from the moving of the brake to its largest notch, and from the noisy release of air into the biggest hole in the brake valve assembly.

big inch n [*Oil rigs*] an oil or natural gas pipeline of at least 20" in diameter.

big iron, also **big sled, rank** n [*US*] [*Car salesmen*] a large car, probably US made.

big jaw, also **lump, lumpy jaw** n [*US*] [*Cattlemen*] actinomycosis: a disease contracted by cattle.

big Joe from Boston n [*Gambling*] in craps dice, the point of 10.

big killer n [*US*] [*Meat trade*] a major meat packing firm.

big lie n [*Politics*] the premise, advocated by, among others, Adolf Hitler in 'Mein Kampf' (1925), that the greater and more audacious the lie, the greater the likelihood of the gullible masses believing it. A popular philosophy of dictators and demagogues and indeed, on a more subtle level, of supposedly 'democratic' governments, who tend to gild the process by explaining that 'what you don't know won't hurt you' when it comes to concealing, or misrepresenting, their activities from those who elected them.

big military n [*US*] [*Military*] a major US military establishment, especially as regards investments in research and weapons projects and the employment of top personnel to staff them.

big nickel n [*Gambling*] the racing and sporting gamblers term for $500.

big noise n [*US*] [*Military*] US government war readiness level six.

big oil, big steel n [*US*] [*Industry*] the leading firms in US oil and steel production, representing the industrial, and thus the national establishment.

big one n [*US*] [*Military*] US strategic intelligence term for a Soviet missile test.

big order n [*Gambling*] a large bet, which may have to be shared around a number of bookmakers to ensure that if the bettor wins, no single bookmaker would be completely bankrupted.

big penny n [*UK*] [*Railways*] overtime payments, mainly on freight-trains, and especially in poor winter conditions.

big rigger 1. n [*US*] [*Road transport*] an arrogant driver. 2. n [*US*] [*Road transport*] a driver who will only drive the 'big rigs': the long trailers.

big science n [*Science*] scientific research that requires massive capital investment but which should yield equally 'big' results.

big six n [*Gambling*] in craps dice, a bet in which a player reckons that a six will be thrown prior to a seven.

big tent n [*US*] [*Politics*] the belief that a political party should shelter many and various arguments and political viewpoints beneath its overall political umbrella, rather than adopt a narrow ideological viewpoint that excludes all but the subscribing zealots.

big ticket n [*Commerce*] a single large sale of goods, services, etc. to a single customer.

Big Ticket leasing n [*Banking*] leasing overseas, or to the oil industry, where the sum involved will probably exceed £1m. Such large-scale operations are carried out by a consortium of leasing companies, the subsidiaries of major banks.

big tiger n [*Gambling*] in poker, a hand with king high, eight low and no pair.

big triangle n [*Commerce*] a merchant navy expression to describe the trade routes between the UK, Australia and South America and back to the UK.

big wheels n pl [*Logging*] a pair of wheels,

usually about 10' in diameter, used for transporting logs.

bighead *n* [*US*] [*Cattlemen*] osteoporosis: a disease contracted by a horse who has eaten poisonous plants; it causes the horse's head to become enlarged.

bight 1. *n* [*Clothing*] the distance between the stitching line and the adjacent edge of the material. **2.** also **bite** *n* [*Sailing, Ropework*] any slack part of a rope between the two ends, especially when curved or looped.

bigot list *n* [*Espionage*] using 'bigot' strictly in the sense of 'narrow', a list of those who have access to particularly restricted and highly classified information. Bigot lists also exists in politics, on the lines of the Nixon Adminstration's 'Enemies List'.

bigwig *n* [*Logging*] the foreman or boss of a logging operation.

bikini head *n* [*US*] [*Journalism*] a headline that highlights a particular aspect of a story.

Bikle's baseball *n* [*US*] [*Gliding*] a glider competition task, formally known as 'distance within a prescribed area'. Pilots attempt to fly around as many as possible of a number of designated turn points; the winner is the one who has covered the greatest distance, estimated by pictures taken with a sealed camera. The task is named after the pilot Paul Bikle and the fact that the course often resembles a baseball diamond.

bilbo *n* [*US*] [*Police, Prisons*] a leg shackle with adjustable fetters.

Bildungsroman *n* [*Literary criticism*] a novel about the upbringing (especially in spiritual and intellectual terms) of a young person, possibly but not inevitably autobiographical, eg: 'Jane Eyre', 'David Copperfield'. It comes from Ger. 'Bildung' meaning 'education' plus 'Roman' meaning 'novel'.

bilge *n* [*Cooperage*] the circumference of a barrel at its widest point.

bilge of stave *n* [*Cooperage*] the arithmetical difference between the width of the end and of the middle of a barrel's stave.

bill *n* [*US*] [*Crime*] $100

bill of health *n* [*Shipping*] a written declaration signed by a consul or port official and given to a ship's master prior to leaving the port, recording the health conditions both on the ship and in the port. Thus a 'clean bill of health' means all persons on ship and shore were healthy; a 'foul bill of health' means recording an infectious disease either on ship or shore; a 'suspected or touched bill of health' means possible infection either in the port or on the ship.

bill from the hill *n* [*Crime*] the police working at the Notting Hill Station, from slang 'old bill' meaning police.

bill of sight *n* [*Commerce*] a document given to the Customs by an importer who cannot complete the necessary forms, since he still lacks a full description of the goods in question. When the goods have landed, he is allowed to examine them and then 'perfects the sight', ie. fills out the papers, making a detailed description as required.

billback *n* [*US*] [*Stock market*] a charge made on members of the exchange when a commodity on which they were advanced money sells for a sum less than that which they were initially advanced.

billboard 1. *n* [*UK*] [*Radio*] an hourly updated list of available news and feature tapes **fed** down the audio line to all subscribing independent local radio stations to show what material is on offer for network use. **2.** *n* [*Radio*] extra large antennae that consist of a series of long poles set up in front of a large vertical metal reflector, they are supposed to resemble an advertising billboard. **3.** *n* [*TV, Radio*] the announcements during a sponsored programme that state 'This programme comes to you thanks to . . .' **4.** *v* [*US*] [*TV*] to announce the names of the **anchor man** and the various specialist 'editors' prior to a news programme or before the individual reports included in it.

billboard pass *n* [*Theatre*] free tickets issued to trades people who allow their shops to be used to exhibit posters for the performance.

billet 1. *n* [*Angling*] a young coal fish. **2.** *n* [*Metallurgy*] a semi-finished rolled steel product intended for re-rolling or forging: it is usually square with chamfered or radiused corners and an average area of 25 sq.ins. maximum. See also **bloom 7**.

billets *n pl* [*Hunting*] fox faeces.

billing *n* [*Advertising*] the total amount of business done by an advertising agency in a given period, usually a working year.

billy board *n* [*Surfing*] a surfboard less than three feet long.

Billy Bunter *n* [*UK*] [*Road transport*] rhyming slang for a shunter.

billy goat *n* [*US*] [*Navy*] lamb.

Billy Williams' Cabbage Patch *n* [*Rugby*] Twickenham Rugby Football Ground, named after William Williams (1860–1951) who established 'the headquarters of Rugby Union' in 1907. In 1970 a local pub was named 'The Cabbage Patch'.

billyboy dolly *n* [*TV, Film*] a heavy duty **dolly** rolling on pneumatic wheels for quietness and ease of movement.

bin 1. *n* [*Aerospace*] for radar surveillance purposes all space is divided into three-dimensional 'chunks' known as 'bins'. Each of these sections should be large enough for a single aircraft to occupy safely at any one time and no one bin should contain – except for a brief moment when one plane enters and another leaves – more than its one designated aircraft. **2.** *n* [*TV, Film*] a container that holds sequences of film during editing. Thus 'binstick' is a stick, usually of metal, which is suspended over the bin; it holds a number of clips from which are hung short sequences of film ready for editing. **3.** *v* [*Military*] to discard a weapons system from the inventories after it has been tried in battle and found inadequate; also, to throw away any useless kit. See also **ditch 4**.

b.i.n. *Lat. abbr* [*Medicine*] a prescription notation meaning 'twice a night'.

binary chop *n* [*Computing*] a binary search algorithm: a searching algorithm that uses a file in which the sortkeys (the information that is to be compared in the search) are in ascending order. In a binary search the midpoint sortkey is compared with the searching algorithm; if the searchkey value is less than the midpoint value, the half of the file above the midpoint is discarded. This process is continued until a single item is selected, all the others having been discarded.

binary weapon *n* [*Military*] a shell or bomb filled with two discrete chemicals, each of which remains stable until they are mixed on impact when they then create a highly toxic substance which is used in chemical/biological warfare.

bind 1. *n* [*Horse-riding*] a bruise on a horse's foot caused by the pressure of a nail on a sensitive part. **2.** also **blaes, blue bind** *n* [*Coal-mining*] shale or mudstone that can be found in coal measures (areas where coal can be discovered). **3.** *v* [*Computing*] to replace the symbolic name used in a system with its machine language form, in which it remains for the lifetime of that program. **4.** *v* [*Fencing*] to push an opponent's weapon from its line.

binder 1. *n* [*Building, Plastering*] the part of the mix that binds the **aggregate** together. **2.** *n* [*Hunting*] the top strand of a cut-and-laid fence; it often causes horses to fall. **3.** *n* [*Law, Insurance*] a temporary form of contract which acts as a record of an agreement until the actual contract is drawn up and signed. **4.** also **binder line** *n* [*Journalism*] a headline that covers a lengthy story or a group of related stories all printed on the same page.

binder head *n* [*Journalism*] See **blanket head**.

binder line *n* [*US*] [*Journalism*] an inside page headline set in large type above a long story or group of stories.

binders *n pl* [*US*] [*Road transport*] brakes.

binder's cloth *n* [*Book collecting*] any cloth binding – old or new – that is only found on the binding of a given copy of a book.

bindicator *n* [*Tyre-making*] See **butterfly**.

bindle *n* [*US*] [*Drugs*] a measure of drugs, usually cocaine or heroin, which is prepared for sale and wrapped in a specially folded square of paper or card; it comes from the slang for a pack carried by a tramp.

Binet, the *n* [*Sociology*] the Binet-Simon personality test; it was named after social scientists A. Binet (1857–1911) and T. Simon (1873–1961).

bing 1. *n* [*Coal-mining*] See **spoil heap**. **2.** *n* [*US*] [*Prisons*] solitary confinement.

bingo *excl* [*Military*] US Dept. of Defense code for:
1. aircraft should proceed to an agreed alternative base other than that from which it took off.
2. aircraft should return to base since fuel has fallen below a prescribed critical level and the mission must therefore be cut short.

bingo calls *n pl* [*Gambling*] doctor's orders (9); legs (11); key of the door (21); all the t(h)rees, Epping Forest (33); droopy drawers (44); the Brighton Line (59); clickety-click (66); two fat ladies (88).

bingo card *n* [*Marketing*] a readers' enquiry card which is bound into a magazine and which contains a set of numbers or letters which relate to similarly labelled advertisements or editorial items within the magazine. It is aimed at facilitating reader enquiries and is usually prepaid for return to the publisher.

binnacle list *n* [*US*] [*Marine Corps*] a list of marines placed on light duties on the orders of the ship's surgeon.

bins *n pl* [*Audio*] large speakers capable of generating a high volume of sound.

bio-energetics *n* [*New therapies*] a therapeutic system that draws on the theories of Wilhelm Reich and uses physical exercises to 'loosen' the body; this in turn should 'loosen' mental blocks.

bioenvironmental integrity *n* [*Aerospace*] the area around an embarking or newly returned astronaut which must be kept free from germs for the safety of both the astronaut and, on his return, those meeting him.

biofeedback *n* [*New therapies*] the use of electronic monitoring and measuring equipment, such as a portable electroencephalograph, to teach people to exercise conscious control over otherwise un-noticed bodily functions, including heartbeat, blood pressure, stomach acidity, mental and physical tension, etc.

biographic leverage *n* [*Espionage*] the use of personal indiscretions, whether voluntary or as the result of falling victim to deliberate entrapment, in order to blackmail a subject for espionage purposes; the intention may be either to recruit them as a spy or simply to nullify the subject's usefulness to their own side.

biographical fallacy *n* [*Literary criticism*] the error of imputing an autobiographical reference to every aspect of an author's work, and judging it purely from what one knows of his/her life.

biopic *n* [*Film*] abbr of **biographical picture**, ie. a film, (loosely) based on a true life-story.

biorhythms *n pl* [*New therapies*] a method of analysing and predicting personal performance on the basis of three body/brain cycles: the 23 day physical cycle, the 28 day emotional cycle and the 33 day intellectual cycle. By charting these cycles one can predict highs, lows, peaks and valleys and plan one's life accordingly for maximum efficiency and benefit.

biosphere overload *n* [*Science*] a population

explosion that threatens to engulf the entire globe.

biotecture n [Architecture] a term coined by Rudolf Doernach in 1966 to describe architecture as an 'artificial super system . . . live, dynamic, mobile, fantastic environment systems.'

bird 1. n [Aerospace] a jocular reference to aircraft, missiles, rockets – anything that flies. 2. n [US] [Hotels] a towel. 3. n [Navy] a sailor who is continually in disciplinary trouble. 4. n [US] [Military] the eagle that on US military insignia denotes senior rank. 5. n [TV] a satellite used for international TV transmissions. 6. n [TV] a programme transmitted by satellite. 7. v [TV] to transmit programmes from country to country via satellite.

bird cage 1. n [UK] [Railways] a wire-trellised road vehicle. 2. n [UK] [Railways] a signal-box built up on girders or mounted on a gantry. 3. n [UK] [Railways] the air pipe compartment on a diesel locomotive; the arrangement of pipes is like a cage.

bird dog 1. n [US] [Car salesmen] a person who sends customers to a salesman, usually for a fee. 2. n [Gambling] a small time or novice gambler who hangs around experienced or professional gamblers to pick up tips. 3. n [US] [Iron workers] a man placed on a job to step up the pace and check on his fellow workers. 4. v [US] [Iron workers] to act as a pusher as in (3). 5. n [Oil rigs] a geologist who 'smells out' oil; a worker who persists in a difficult job; a scout who searches out information concerning the activities of rival companies; the local prospector who points out likely prospects to oil company leasemen. 6. n [US] [Real estate] a salesman or broker who scouts rival real estate listings in order to pick up extra business by cutting into a competitor's sale. 7. v [Oil rigs] to pay close attention to a job or to follow a person closely with intent to learn to help; also to follow up on a job until it is finished. 8. n [Finance] someone who makes it their business to spot rich prospects who are likely to be willing to put up large deposits to back speculative deals.

bird don't fly on one wing v phr [Navy] a phrase pointing out that a warship cannot function properly without the correct equipment.

birdcage 1. n [Glass-making] the domed end of a tank furnace, a large bath-like container which is heated to melt the requisite materials into glass. 2. n [Glass-making] a thread of glass left running across the inside of a bottle. 3. n [Logging] frayed or ragged strands of wire rope that loosely resemble a cage.

birder n [Bird-watching] a bird-watcher.

birdfeed n [TV] programmes that are transmitted internationally by satellite.

birdie n [Golf] a score of one under par for a hole.

birdies n pl [Audio] extraneous whistles and chirps generated when two high frequency tones intermodulate.

bird-roost 1. n [Glass-making] glass with a rough surface. 2. n [Glass-making] a thread of glass that has been accidentally left stretching across the inner surface of hollow glassware. See also **bird cage 2**.

birds 1. n pl [Navy] aircraft based on aircraft carriers. 2. n pl [Navy] lobsters or crayfish, which supposedly have the power of flying over the water.

birds are walking v phr [Flying] the weather is impossible for flying . . . even the birds are walking!

bird's beak n [Building, Plastering] a moulding section: two curves which intersect to form a beak-like **arris**.

bird's beak stop n [Building, Plastering] the feature formed at external angles where a moulded or rounded angle has to be stopped to a square **arris**.

bird's nest 1. n [Angling] a tangle of line or a tangled cast. 2. n [Angling] the resulting tangle after an overrun, while spinning. 3. n [Theatre] the crepe wool used to construct false beards.

birdseye n [Textiles] woollen or worsted fabric.

birdwatcher n [Aerospace] derived from 'bird' meaning 'rocket', someone who makes a habit of watching rockets launched.

birdwatchers n pl [Government, Politics] the derogatory reference by politicians, bureaucrats or businessmen to the more dedicated ecologists and environmentalists whose worries as to the destruction of natural resources stand in the way of vote-catching or money-making schemes.

birdyback n [US] [Road transport] a transportation system in which freight containers can be carried by both road and air. See also **fishyback**, **piggyback 2**.

Birkenhead drill n [Shipping] the traditional call, when a vessel is sinking and the lifeboats are being lowered of 'women and children first'. It is derived from the first use of this order during the sinking of HMS Birkenhead, a troopship bound for South Africa in 1852. The twenty women and children on board were saved, but 445 of the 476 troops drowned, supposedly standing to attention as the ship went down.

birling n [Logging] a game played by loggers: logs are rolled on water.

biro dentistry n [Medicine] illegal boosting of dentists' incomes by claiming payment from the National Health Service for work that has not actually been performed on a patient, merely written down on a bogus form.

birth control engine n [UK] [Railways] a huge steam driven engine which burned up to five tons of coal per shift; it was claimed that firing them left a man impotent for weeks.

birth control hours n pl [UK] [Railways] work which starts between midnight and 5 am. and thus keeps a man from the conjugal bed; it differs

B

from 'night duty' which describes shifts starting between 9pm and midnight.

birthmarks of the old society *n* [*Politics*] in Marxist terms, as propounded in the 'Critique of the Gotha Programme' (1875), these are the surviving features of the capitalist system which might linger on even after the success of the Proletarian Revolution.

biscuit **1.** *n* [*US*] [*Cattlemen*] the saddle horn. **2.** *n* [*Pottery*] earthenware or porcelain that has been fired in the kiln, but has not yet been glazed. **3.** *n* [*UK*] [*Railways*] an electric token, the signalman's authority for a driver to enter a single line. **4.** *n* [*Record business*] a small piece of plastic suitable for the pressing of a single disc record. **5.** *n* [*Rubber*] a small, round cake of crude or synthetic rubber.

biscuit cutter *n* [*Oil rigs*] a short-core barrel which is forced into a rock formation to extract a sample of rock or similarly into sand; the name is borrowed from the kitchen implement.

bishop **1.** *n* [*Art*] a canvas measuring 58" by 94". **2.** *v* [*Horse-racing*] to disguise the age of a horse by tinkering with its teeth; this is supposedly derived from the name of an early practitioner of such fakery.

Bison *n* [*Military*] the Russian Myasischev M–4 subsonic four-jet long-range bomber; it is approximately equivalent to the US B–52 and deployed in diminishing numbers as a strategic bomber since 1956.

bisque *n* [*UK*] [*Politics*] this is when the whips of a party with a substantial majority allow, on a rota basis, some proportion of their backbenchers to be absent from all but the most crucial votes. It comes from tennis usage, when one player gives the other the bonus of scoring one point once during a set at any time he may choose.

bit **1.** *n* [*Computing*] the basic unit of computing, an abbreviation of 'binary digit'. All data can be expressed in binary form – combinations of 0s and 1s – which is clumsy in normal use, but extremely fast and simple for electronic processing, in which it becomes simply an on/off switching action. **2.** *n* [*US*] [*Prisons*] a sentence; thus 'two-year bit', etc.

bit decay *n* [*Computing*] See **software rot**.

bit diddling *n* [*Computing*] trying to pack extra storage into a machine's memory, but taking so much time to work out the method to do this that the time expended makes the relatively small memory gain practically worthless.

bit fiddler *n* [*Computing*] See **bit tweaker**.

bit gatherer *n* [*Glass-making*] the junior member of a team of glassworkers who gathers small quantities of glass which are then worked into decorations on articles being made.

bit of mess *n* [*Police, Sex*] a prostitute's male lover, neither a proper pimp nor a paying customer but simply one half of a relationship that, but for the woman's profession, would be considered 'normal'. See also **tin soldier**.

bit (part) *n* [*Theatre*] a very small speaking role.

bit stuffing **1.** *n* [*Computing*] a means of inserting and deleting **bits** on multiply connected high-speed digital transmission links that are not synchronously clocked. **2.** *n* [*Computing*] in data communications, a technique whereby a 0 is automatically inserted after a pre-determined number of consecutive 1s is present. The receiving unit automatically deletes the surplus 0s before delivering the complete message to the receiving terminal.

bit **tweaker** *n* [*Computing*] a computer programmer who is more interested, if not obsessed, with the machine itself than its potential in practical and useful applications; such a programmer merely tweaks or fiddles with the bits (of information).

bit-breaker *n* [*Oil rigs*] a heavy metal plate which is fitted to the drilling table and holds the drill-bit while it is being unscrewed from the drill collar.

bitch *n* [*Sex*] a black pimp's description of his working woman/women; given the relationship this has all the predictable negative connotations.

bitch chain *n* [*Logging*] a heavy, short chain with a hook and ring, used to fasten a small log to a sled or trailer.

bitches *n pl* [*US*] [*Mining*] a set of supports used to hold up pipes running through a mine.

bite **1.** *n* [*Industry*] the place at which two rollers come together and through which the material they are processing must pass. **2.** *n* [*US*] [*TV*] a short piece of news film inside a **voice wrap**. **3.** *n* [*Wine-tasting*] a notable degree of acidity, acceptable in young wines.

bit-map *n* [*Photo-typesetting*] a mosaic of **pixels** defining an image of a letterform for photo-typesetting. The smoothness of the letter contour will depend on the fineness of the **raster** and the number of pixels to the em. Thus a 12 point em would have approximately 27,556 pixels with a horizontal and vertical resolution of 1,000 lines per inch.

bit-map editing *n* [*Photo-typesetting*] a method of enlarging and then displaying a character or part of a character on a cathode ray tube (CRT) so that the operator can correct any errors by removing or adding individual pixels as required. This editing will create the required effect when the character is finally printed.

bit-slice **architecture** *n* [*Computing*] a computer design used for microprocessors in which the central processing unit (CPU) is constructed from the concatenation of a number of high performance processing units.

bitter almonds *n* [*Wine-tasting*] the smell of almond kernels or bitter almonds comes from a badly fined wine, probably drinkable, but not sound.

bitter end *n* [*Sailing, Ropework*] the inactive end

of an inboard cable abaft the Carrick or windlass **bitts**.

bittersweet talk *n* [*Espionage*] the final element in CIA recruitment: a pep talk that informs the new agent just where he/she stands, stressing primarily that the agent's person is more important than any level of information and that everything will go well as long as all instructions are followed without contradiction. The talk also realigns the relationship: whereas recruitment was effected on grounds of mutual sympathies, the agent now becomes an employee and the principal an employer, however friendly they may still be; meetings, once regular and frequent, are now to be rare and irregular.

bitts *n pl* [*Sailing, Ropework*] upright timbers, usually in pairs, for making fast hawsers and cables.

blabbermouth *n* [*Air travel*] a turret-mounted foam gun used for fire-fighting in airport disasters.

blabbing, also **blebbing**, **blistering** *n* [*Building, Plastering*] the unwanted formation of small swellings on the plastered surface.

blab-off switch *n* [*TV*] a device that enables a viewer to cut out the volume during commercial breaks.

black 1. *adv* [*Banking*] in credit; in the days when bank statements and ledgers were handwritten, credit sums were printed in black and debits in red ink. 2. *v* [*Industrial relations*] to boycott a firm's goods in furtherance of an industrial dispute. 3. *n* [*Printing*] abbr of **black letter** it is also called Gothic, Old English, Church Text. 4. *n* [*Printing, Typesetting*] any very heavy designs. 5. *n* [*Theatre*] the forestage, the apron, which is usually painted black. See also **green**.

black act *n* [*US*] [*Crime*] lock-picking in the dark.

black advance *n* [*Politics*] the deliberate disruption of an opponent's campaign by a series of 'dirty tricks.' An inverted version of the traditional '**advance**' that a candidate sends out ahead of his canvassing to promote his cause; both legal and illegal methods are used to harass and confuse the opponent's supporters and to alienate potential voters.

black agent *n* [*Espionage*] an illegal operative.

black and whites 1. *n pl* [*UK*] [*Police*] official paperwork, warrants, receipts, casenotes, etc. 2. *n pl* [*US*] [*Police*] police vehicles that have black and white paint.

black bag job *n* [*Espionage*] an illegal entry by Federal or intelligence personnel in order to obtain otherwise inviolate information for use against a subject. Generally used as a cover description of all illegal activities by ostensibly law-abiding agencies of the state.

black body *n* [*Science*] a body whose surface absorbs all the electro-magnetic radiation incident upon it.

black book 1. *n* [*Finance*] a privately circulated prospectus used in investment banking to offer special information to favoured clients; such information is never included in a generally circulated public prospectus and includes detailed projections of profits, sales, etc. 2. *n* [*US*] [*Military*] a briefing book of some 75 pages designed to assist the President and his advisors on the various possible courses of action in the event of a Soviet attack. Those familiar with it claim that even this so-called 'assistant' is extremely complex and possibly totally incomprehensible to a President who has probably not had to read it in detail before.

black box 1. *n* [*Business, Technology, Government*] based on technology, where it applies to an instrument or component that can be dealt with as a discrete entity; this term is extended in government or business usage to define a separate area of knowledge within a larger system which can be dealt with as it is, without needing any specialist knowledge of its mechanism or internal structure. 2. *n* [*Cars*] any transistorised form of ignition on racing cars; it is not invariably black. 3. *n* [*Electronics*] a device or system that has accessible inputs and outputs but where the internal functions are unknown. One can gain such knowledge only from the input and output signals. 4. *n* [*Military*] modular components (in aircraft, weapons, etc.) that can be moved or changed with speed and simplicity in case of a breakdown.

black box (recorder) *n* [*Air travel*] a supposedly indestructible flight data recorder which holds on wire a record of everything that happens on a given journey. Most civil airliners have two boxes, one to record the operation of the instruments, the other monitoring the cabin crew's conversations both in the plane and with ground controllers. Such boxes are invaluable in reconstructing events immediately prior to a crash. It is derived from the RAF slang for any navigational aid.

black box syndrome *n* [*Government*] Gerald P. Dineen, US government official, in the New York Times, 1979: '. . . we break systems down into sub-systems, and sub-systems into electronic entities or black boxes. Then we assign to each of these black boxes an obscure name that has at least five words in its title. Finally . . . we refer to them by an unpronounceable acronym.'

black broadcasting *n* [*Espionage*] deliberate broadcasting of misinformation for political or espionage ends.

black cow 1. *n* [*US*] [*Lunch counter*] chocolate milk. 2. *n* [*US*] [*Lunch counter*] root beer.

black crush *n* [*TV*] a method of electronically reducing the black level in TV so as to produce a contrasting white for captions.

black economy *n* [*Economics, Politics*] the parallel economy of those who perform their normal jobs but outside normal working hours

B

and without admitting to such earnings (usually in cash) for tax purposes. See also **moonlight**.

black edge generator n [Video] a device that creates a black edging to the characters in on-screen captions in order to make them stand out properly.

black flag v [Motor-racing] to signal to a driver to leave the course by waving a black flag as he passes the pits.

black Friday n [US] [Stock market] any sharp drop in the overall share market; named after the original Black Friday, 24 Sept. 1869, when efforts by a group of financiers to corner the gold market created a business panic.

black gangsters n pl [Politics] a former Chinese propaganda description of anti-Maoists who operate in the fields of literature and culture.

black hole n [Science] a hypothetical 'hole' in space which acts as an all-powerful, ever 'hungry' vortex into which all matter is sucked. See also **white hole**.

black international n [Politics, Religion] the Communist party description of the Roman Catholic church.

black jack n [Aerospace] a special tool used in the manual forming of sheet metal; it is made of tiny lead shot sealed into a tubular, usually leather, container which resembles the weapon of the same name.

black knot n [Sailing, Ropework] a hard knot or a tangle.

black leg n [Merchant navy] a passage worker: crewmen who join up in a foreign port merely to get a passage home.

black level n [TV] the minimum value of video signal voltage, ie. the darkest spot on the TV display. See also **white level**.

black light v [Navy] to fail to ensure that the light in the signalling lantern is working properly prior to flashing a ship-to-ship message.

black liquor n [Paper-making] an extract composed of alkali and organic matter that results from the digestion of wood pulp and cooking acid during the paper-making process.

black lock n [US] [Prisons] solitary confinement.

black matzo n [Pop music] this comes from the saying that 'if you can't sell them you'd better eat them', referring to the shape of a record album which could be seen to resemble a circular, black matzo, the unleavened bread eaten by Jews at Passover.

black mist n [Politics] the term comes from Japanese 'kuro kiri' meaning 'black fog'; it is a phrase used in Japan to describe scandals and corruption within the government – 'black mist affairs' – and carried the implication that such affairs are discreetly covered up when possible.

black money n [Economics] money not declared for tax purposes; it is often applied specifically to money earned by casino operators and held back from the revenue.

black neb, also **black tail** n [Angling] the sea trout.

black operations n pl [Espionage] activities such as assassination, blackmail, smear campaigns, none of which are admitted by an intelligence agency, but all of which are carried out regularly.

black patch n [Metallurgy] a local patch of scale on steel sheet or strip resulting from imperfect removal of surface defects by **pickling**.

black prince n [UK] [Railways] a locomotive cleaner; in the steam era, men began as engine cleaners and progressed gradually upwards over several years. The cleaners began working underneath the engine, and moved up to the easier jobs, such as the boiler.

black propaganda n [Espionage] See **disinformation, funkspiel**.

black programs n pl [Military] development and research programs carried out by the Pentagon which are so secret that there exists no public and very little military knowledge of them.

black radio n [Military] broadcasts made by one side that are deliberately disguised to seem like those of the enemy radio station; such broadcasts are used to disseminate disinformation and **psyops** distortions.

black rock n [US] [TV] the industry's nickname for the CBS headquarters on 52nd Street and 6th Avenue in New York City.

black run n [Skiing] a difficult run for inexperienced skiers. See also **blue run, red run**.

black sand n [Metallurgy] sand that is used on the bottom of moulds in an iron foundry.

black scour n [Farming] swine dysentery.

black shoe officer n [US] [Navy] an officer who commands strictly by the letter of navy regulations. See also **brown shoe officer**.

black shoes n pl [US] [Navy] the members of the crew of an aircraft carrier who sail and service the ship and its planes but have nothing to do with flying.

black softened n [Metallurgy] stainless steel sheet or strip in the hot or cold rolled and softened condition that has not been descaled by any method.

black spot n [Cars] anywhere – sometimes a street or junction, sometimes a whole town – which should be avoided when planning a rally; this is usually because of prior complaints about dangers, accidents, etc.

black strip n [Metallurgy] steel strip in the hot rolled condition with the rolling scale still intact on the surface.

black wool n [Weaving] in the textile industry, any wool that is not 100% white.

blackboard n [UK] [Railways] an oblong box containing signal lights on a black background, red and white spots of light indicating 'stop' and 'go'.

blackdamp n [Mining] foul air or poisonous

gases that collect in a mine without adequate ventilation.

Blackjack *n* [*Military*] the Russian Tupolev RAM-P (TU-X) variable-geometry supersonic penetration and stand-off bomber. This bomber, still in the development stage, was originally thought to be an improved version of the **Backfire**, but intelligence has pointed to a new and substantially different design.

blackjack *n* [*US*] [*Mining*] sphalerite, a zinc ore composed mainly of zinc sulphide plus some iron, manganese and other elements; it is usually black, brown or yellow in colour.

blackout skit *n* [*Theatre*] a skit or sketch that climaxes with a blackout, the abrupt cutting off of the stage lights.

blacks **1.** *n pl* [*US*] [*Painting*] a painter's white overalls once they have become dirty. **2.** *n pl* [*TV*] any black drapes or black painted flats, etc. **3.** *n* [*TV*] the darkest areas of a TV picture.

blacksmith **1.** *n* [*US*] [*Journalism*] an incompetent reporter who simply 'bashes out' the stories. **2.** *n* [*Printing*] an unskilled compositor.

bladder *n* [*Glass-making*] a poorly made cylinder.

blade **1.** *n* [*Cricket*] the face of the bat that strikes the ball. **2.** *n* [*US*] [*Medicine*] a surgeon. See also **butcher 3, cutting doctor**, etc. **3.** *n* [*Weaving*] the vertical divider in a **reed**.

blaes *n* [*Coal-mining*] See **bind**.

blag *n* [*Police, Crime*] robbery with violence.

blagger *n* [*Police, Crime*] a criminal who specialises in robbery with violence.

blah *n* [*Film*] unsatisfactory sales at the cinema box office.

bland *a* [*Wine-tasting*] weak, characterless, not actually unpleasant, but of no pronounced style.

blank **1.** *n* [*Drugs*] adulterated or fake drugs sold to the gullible. **2.** *n* [*Hunting*] a covert which holds no fox; this is originally from 'draw a blank'. **3.** *a* [*Gambling*] in certain card games, this is said of a card in one's hand which is not supported there by any others of the same suit. **4.** *n* [*Police, Crime*] a rejection, the act of turning down. **5.** *v* [*Police, Crime*] to ignore, to reject, to refuse, to turn down (especially when refusing bail or parole). See also **KB, knockback**.

blank in *v* [*Custom cars*] to fill in any holes or gaps left on the body of a car which one has customised by removing all badges, trim and similar ornamentation.

blanket **1.** *n* [*Dog breeding*] large areas of colour extending over the back and sides, and occasionally up the neck; it is usually used of hounds. **2.** *n* [*Printing*] a sheet of composition (rexine or rubber) used to cover the impression cylinder of a printing machine. **3.** *n* [*Textiles*] a range of cloth patterns in one continuous piece. **4.** *v* [*Oil rigs*] to replace the air or gas around processing equipment with an inert gas, ie. nitrogen, to reduce oxidisation, explosion or fire hazards.

blanket ballot *n* [*US*] [*Politics*] See **bedsheet ballot**.

blanket bond *n* [*Insurance*] an insurance contract that protects an employer in the event of losses resulting from acts of dishonesty or inefficiency by his/her employees.

blanket head *n* [*Journalism*] a headline running across all the columns of a story or the whole of the news section.

blanketing *n* [*Aerospace*] the distortion or suppression of a desired radio signal by an unwanted one, whether or not through deliberate jamming.

blankets *n pl* [*Furriers*] furs of an unusually large size, especially those of the beaver.

blanking **1.** *n* [*Custom cars*] the process of filling in the mounting holes left in a car's body after trim and badges have been removed; this is usually done by dimpling the area, fitting a blind rivet to the hole to block it and then covering the patch with filler. **2.** *n* [*TV*] a period during the transmission of a television picture when the scanning spot (which creates the picture one sees) returns to the top of the screen; the spare lines that are created during this brief period can be used for Teletext, etc.

blast **1.** *n* [*Coal-mining*] compressed air. **2.** *v* [*Computing*] See **blow 10**. **3.** *v* [*Computing*] to program a read-only memory (**ROM**), using a programmable ROM programmer.

blaster *n* [*Golf*] a sand wedge, which 'blasts' the ball out of sand-filled bunkers.

blat *n* [*Politics*] in Russia, the basic currency of influence – the ability to induce the right person to produce the particular privilege, not always legal, that happens to be needed, be it great or small.

blaxploitation, also **blacksploitation** *n* [*Film*] a term derived from sexploitation, ie. films that emphasise their sexual content; a series of films featuring black stereotypes, albeit as heroes and very macho men, dominated the production schedules for a period in the early 1970s. They included the 'Shaft' series, 'Superfly' and many lesser offerings. In the event, for all the money, sex and allied vestiges of white liberal guilt/fear/envy, these films made little advance over the era of Stepin Fetchit.

blaze **1.** *n* [*Dog breeding*] a rather broad and fairly extensive marking starting at the top of the skull and running down to the muzzle; smaller and narrower blazes are known as stars and stripes respectively. **2.** *n* [*Gambling*] in poker, a hand of five court cards, in no particular sequence and of no particular suit, but which is ranked above a hand of two pairs.

blazing *n* [*Gambling*] marking cards with the fingernails or with small pin or needle pricks in the pattern of the backs.

blazon **1.** *n* [*Heraldry*] a shield, a coat of arms; this is the technical description of the coat of arms. **2.**

B

B

v [*Heraldry*] to describe a coat of arms in technical heraldic language.

bleachers *n pl* [*TV*] this term comes from its use in spectator sports to refer to the stadium seats (originally uncovered and in the sun, where those watching would get 'bleached'); here it refers to the audience seating at a live TV recording and thus, by extension, to those who sit in those seats, ie. 'Joe Public', the average viewer.

bled *n* [*Military*] used in the French Foreign Legion to mean the desert, the open country.

bleed 1. *v* [*Building*] to apply a blow lamp to resinous knots to let the resin flow. 2. *v* [*Oil rigs*] to withdraw slowly, from a line or vessel, a small portion of the liquid contained. 3. *v* [*Weaving*] said of a dyed fabric which loses colour during immersion in water. 4. *n* [*Printing, Advertising*] the edge of the page, which would otherwise provide a margin or border around printed material but which is in this case covered over by visual or (occasionally) textual material. 5. *v* [*Printing, Advertising*] to extend the printed area of a page over the normal margins all the way to the limits of the paper area.

bleed space *n* [*Advertising*] an extra charge levied by newspapers and magazines on those advertisers who take up what would normally be white space by running **bleed** advertisements.

bleed the monkey *v* [*Navy*] used to refer to the clandestine practice of tapping a cask of liquor, or swilling out an empty cask with water to retrieve the diluted mixture of such dregs that remain.

bleeding 1. *n* [*Building, Plastering*] water draining from a mix before it has hardened. 2. *a* [*Merchant navy*] very fresh; from the fact that only fresh fish will bleed.

blender *n* [*Theatre*] a wig with a flesh-coloured band at the front which can be covered with the same makeup as is used for the forehead, thus masking the join as naturally as possible.

blending *n* [*Custom cars*] See **frenching**.

bletch! *excl* [*Computing*] an expression of distaste; as an adjective, 'bletcherous' implies anything negative, especially regarding the design and/or function of a machine.

bletting *n* [*Agriculture*] the spotted appearance of very ripe fruit which indicates the start of decomposition.

B-level title *n* [*Video*] a video cassette title that has not secured release by a major distributor but is still better than absolute rubbish; it is usually independently produced on a low budget and initially released on a regional rather than a national basis. See also **A-level title**.

blibe *n* [*Glass-making*] an imperfection caused by undissolved gas in the glass and occurring as a large elongated bubble.

blimp 1. *n* [*US*] [*Medicine*] a grossly obese patient. See also **whale**. 2. *n* [*Navy*] an inflatable rubber life raft. 3. *n* [*TV, Film*] See **barney**.

blind 1. *n* [*Espionage*] a complex security arrange-ment used by secret services for **laundering** money, to hide illicit payments or expenditure, etc. 2. *n* [*Printing*] the impression of letters or symbols without the use of ink, by embossing or raising the surface. 3. *v* [*Civil engineering*] to cover a newly paved road with a coating of sand and gravel so that any joints will be filled up. 4. *v* [*Gambling*] in poker, to bet without looking at the cards. In some schools such a bet forces opponents to double their own bets as long as the blind player continues to bet without looking at his hand, unless they too are willing to play blind. 5. *a* [*Hunting*] said of country in which the leaves are still on trees, hedges and fences – thus making it harder to see the ditches. 6. *a* [*Sex*] uncircum-cised. 7. *adv* [*Marketing*] referring to the testing of a product without revealing the name of the manufacturer to those tested. 8. *adv* [*Theatre*] to work an auditorium 'blind' in either a theatre or nightclub is to start one's act without having previously checked the stage and auditorium for exits, the position of the bar, etc.

blind advertisement *n* [*Advertising*] an adver-tisement in which the name of the advertiser is omitted; it is most commonly found when box numbers are used.

blind attribution *n* [*Journalism*] statements and facts which are included in a story without any specific attribution, particularly as in 'a top Whitehall source'. Such euphemisms are at best hiding the reticent, and at worst existing only in the mind of the writer.

blind auction, also **sealed bid auction** *n* [*Commerce*] an auction in which all parties submit sealed bids by a given date.

blind bidding *n* [*Film*] this is when an exhibitor is forced by a distributor to put in a bid for the rental of a picture without the opportunity even to see a preview. This practice is forbidden in some US states, but remains a quick way of raising some extra funds for a picture that may still be in production.

blind bombing *n* [*Military*] bombing targets that are invisible to those who are dropping the bombs.

blind envelope *n* [*Advertising*] a **mailing shot** which used plain envelopes with no transparent 'window' in them; the principle behind this is that many people associate windowed envelopes with bills and junk mail.

blind figure *n* [*Commerce*] a figure that has been entered by hand into a ledger and written so badly that it is hard to distinguish – a three for an eight, etc. A problem that is declining in the age of office automation.

blind folio *n* [*Publishing*] a page number that is not actually printed on the page, but which is still counted in the numbering sequence.

blind keyboard *n* [*Photo-typesetting*] a keyboard which outputs data to a variety of media for photocomposition, but provides no hard copy or visual display.

blind lead n [Journalism] a lead paragraph in a story that does not name the person who is the subject of the story: 'A leading sportsman . . .' etc. The subject's name will usually appear by paragraph two.

blind man's art n [Art] See **conceptual art**.

blind out v [Building, Painting] to obliterate with paint or distemper.

blind perforation n [Philately] perforations where the holes are not punched out due to blunt or missing perforating pins.

blind pool n [Commerce] a group of speculators who operate in secret, revealing to the market in which they are working only the name of their spokesman.

blind scab n [Metallurgy] a casting defect in iron founding when the sand in the moulds expands and deforms the surface of the metal.

blind stitch n [Weaving] a sewing stitch in which two folded edges are joined together without the stitch showing.

blind trust n [Economics] a trust that manages an individual's assets, usually to ensure that there is no professional conflict of interests between an individual's job as a public official with responsibilities to the voters, and his private business interests.

blind wipe n [Film, Video] a **wipe** effect that resembles the action of a Venetian blind: one picture is replaced by another through the successive replacement of one vertical segment of the screen by a new one, working from side to side.

Blinder n [Military] the Russian Tupolev TU–22 supersonic medium-range twin-jet bomber; the USSR's first supersonic bomber, it was deployed as a strategic bomber in 1962.

blinder 1. n [US] [Cattlemen] a hood that can be placed over a horse's head when it is being saddled or shod. 2. n [Cycling] a race that demands the utmost effort from start to finish. 3. n [Horse-racing] a horse that has been drugged. 4. n [Theatre] a bright light sited next to the proscenium arch and focussed on the audience in order to blind them momentarily during a quick scene change on a blacked out stage.

blindside 1. v [Business, Politics] to surprise an opponent, usually by playing on an area of ignorance, and to use that surprise to overwhelm him or her; it comes from the sporting use of the word. 2. v [US] [Rugby, Football] to tackle a player after approaching from out of his line of sight and thus leaving him no time to prepare himself for the physical shock; such 'surprise' tackles are those most likely to cause serious injury. See also **crackback**.

blind-stamp v [Publishing] to print a design on the cover or some other surface of the book without using ink or foil.

blink 1. n [US] [Fishing] a mackerel of about one year old. 2. v [Shooting] said of a dog which passes by a bird without pointing at it; thus a 'blinker' is a dog that leaves its 'point' through nervousness at the approach of the guns.

blink-fencer n [UK] [Market-traders] one who sells spectacles.

blinks n [UK] [Market-traders] spectacles.

blip 1. n [Radar] the electronic signal on a radar screen that reveals the presence of a ship, aircraft, etc.; thus a 'blip driver' is a radar operator. 2. v [TV] to censor out possibly offensive conversations, libellous references, obscenities, etc. from a TV programme.

blister 1. n [Glass-making] an imperfection in the form of a large bubble in the glass caused by undissolved gas. Thus a 'skin blister' is a blister which occurs on or near the surface; a 'pipe blister' is a large bubble on the inside surface of a glass article, usually caused by dirt or scale on the blow-pipe. 2. n. [Metallurgy] local separation of layers of steel, causing a protuberance on the surface, beneath which is a cavity. 3. n [UK] [Railways] an official request for a driver to explain the late arrival of his train; the first two minutes require no explanation, but anything longer does. 4. n [Textiles] a crimp in the cloth. 5. v [US] [Painting] to remove old paintwork using a blow-torch.

blistered a [UK] [Buses] used in London Transport to mean summoned by the police.

B-lite n [US] [Police] a combination baton and flashlight, manufactured by the Bianchi Corporation.

blitz 1. n [US] [Football] a concerted attack on the passer by the opposing linemen. 2. v [US] [Football] to perform such an attack. 3. v [Military] to concentrate maximum effort on; the original use of blitz, as an abbreviation of 'Blitzkrieg', seems to have no further place in military vocabularies other than historical. 4. v [Tiddleywinks] to pot all six of one colour before a 20–minute time limit has elapsed and thus score an easy victory.

blob 1. n [Aerospace] local atmospheric disturbances. 2. n [Cricket] the score of 0 runs. See also **duck 1**.

blobocracy n [Management] a term coined in 1971 by Professor Albert Shapero: the concept that management, especially in its middle levels, becomes bloated by too many techniques and complex structures when performing what ought otherwise to be relatively simple tasks.

block 1. n [Printing] an illustration, either half-tone or line, which is engraved into metal prior to printing; specifically a single column block refers to a square block the width of one column, usually a head and shoulders portrait. 2. n [UK] [Prisons] the segregation (in solitary confinement) and punishment unit of a prison. 3. n [US] [Railways] an area stretching from one signal to another. In the ABS (automatic block system) no two trains can ever enter a block at the same

B

time. **4.** n [*Sailing, Ropework*] a machine with grooved wheels for diverting the direction of a rope or, when compounded, of increasing the power of a tackle. **5.** n [*Table tennis*] a short stroke played immediately after the bounce of the ball to counter an opponent's aggressive stroke. **6.** v [*US*] [*Theatre*] to plan actors' movements and actions throughout a play.

block booking n [*Film*] the method whereby a distributor forces an exhibitor to purchase a job lot of his products, in which there are a number of third-rate films; these must be shown willy-nilly if the automatic profits, from the one block-buster included in the selection, are to be gained.

block, on the a [*UK*] [*Railways*] this means that the train service is congested.

block out v [*Clothing*] to cut several layers of material simultaneously, thus creating manageable blocks, each of which may include one or more parts of the garment.

blockbusting n [*Politics*] originally, this was a population shift in the inner cities when the black population began moving into formerly white areas, causing the whites to flee and turning such areas into increasingly depressed ghettos. In the last decade the process has begun to be reversed, after thirty years of one-way traffic, as young, reasonably affluent white bourgeoisie move back to ghetto and working class areas. The first middle-class purchaser in a street or block is the 'blockbuster'.

blocker **1.** n [*Shoe-making*] one of a number of leather strips joined together for use as trimming for shoes. **2.** n [*Commerce*] anyone a salesman encounters in a firm who attempts to block his/her access to the actual deal-maker within that firm; these are usually secretaries, receptionists, personal assistants, etc.

blockette n [*Computing*] a subdivision of a group of consecutive machine words transferred as a unit.

blockhead n [*Fashion*] a wooden dummy 'head' used to hold hats or wigs.

blocking **1.** n [*Glass-making*] a method of stirring and fining glass in a pot by immersing a block of wood or other substance capable of giving off gases at the high temperature of the melt. **2.** n [*Weaving*] placing fabric or yarn in a stretched-out position while it is being dried or pressed.

blocks n pl [*Computing*] regular-sized pieces of information that can be transferred as they are from one component of the system to another; this transfer is checked by the interblock gap (IBG) which ensures that the various blocks stay together as units as they move around the system.

blocktime n [*Management*] the mandatory hours that all employees must work in a day – usually three hours in the morning and two hours in the afternoon – under the gliding shift system. See also **flexitime**.

blocky a [*Dog breeding*] solid and squarish, when

describing width in relation to length, as regards the head; blockiness is not desirable.

bloke n [*Navy*] the second in command, the executive officer.

blonde n [*TV, film*] a 2KW quartz iodine lamp.

blood **1.** v [*Hunting*] to daub a novice, often a child, with the blood of a freshly killed fox, as an initiation right to the hunting field. **2.** n [*Merchant navy*] stewards' term for a passenger.

blood and guts n [*Navy*] naval nickname for the red ensign flown by British merchant ships.

blood bank n [*US*] [*Car salesmen*] a bank or finance company. See also **mouse house**.

blood boat **1.** n [*Navy*] boats that deliver supplies of butcher's meat to ships in harbour. **2.** n [*Navy*] small boats used to explode mines brought to the surface by minesweepers; so named from the hazardous nature of the job.

blood chit **1.** n [*Aerospace*] the indemnity form signed by any passenger in a civil or military aircraft who has paid no fare and holds no official rank; once signed, this form means that neither he/she nor their family can make a claim in case of accident or death. **2.** n [*Aerospace*] a military flier's square of plastic or cloth which carries a multi-lingual message offering money to any possible helper or rescuer, in case the pilot crashes in unfriendly territory.

blood knot n [*Angling*] the knot used to join several lengths of differently sized fishing lines.

blood money n [*Gambling*] money that has been hard and painfully earned.

blood, out of a [*Hunting*] said of hounds which have not killed for some time.

blood system n [*Weaving*] a measure of the fitness of wool fibre based on the Merino sheep as 'full blood' and then proceeding in decreasing order of fineness; the 'blood' no longer has any direct reference to actual breeding standards.

bloods n [*US*] [*Medicine*] blood specimens.

bloodwagon n [*Skiing*] a sledge used to move injured skiers off the slopes and into the base station.

bloodworm n [*US*] [*Sex*] an exceptionally ruthless and unpleasant pimp.

bloody shirt n [*US*] [*Politics*] a symbol of reproach flaunted at the opposition party, usually implying their lack of enthusiasm for a supposedly worthy cause, often a war; it is a term that has developed since the US Civil War.

bloom **1.** v [*Cheese-making*] to release a flowery perfume, redolent of the meadows. **2.** n [*Cheese-making*] the growth of penicillium candidum on the surface of **bloomy** rind cheeses. **3.** n [*Dog breeding*] generally admirable outer appearance, with shiny coat, bright eyes, etc. **4.** n [*Glass-making*] a surface film on the glass, caused by weathering. **5.** n [*Glass-making*] a surface film of sulphites and sulphates that forms during the annealing process. **6.** n [*Painting*] a deposit, like the bloom on a grape, which can form on glossy enamel paint or on varnish, causing loss of gloss and dulling of the colour; bloom can sometimes be removed by wiping it with a damp cloth. **7.** *n* [*Metallurgy*] a semi-finished rolled steel product intended for re-rolling or forging, with an area greater than 25 sq.ins. **8.** *n* [*Metallurgy*] a semi-finished mass of steel, usually roughly square in section and not smaller than 6'x6', formed directly from an ingot by hot rolling. **9.** *n* [*Metallurgy*] a mass of iron or steel formed at high temperature by consolidating scrap by hammering or rolling. **10.** *n* [*Manufacturing*] a surface appearance or deposit caused by a particular stage of the manufacturing process; it is found in leather, textiles, newly minted coins, glass, lacquers, etc. **11.** *n* [*Foods*] a surface appearance that reveals freshness in poultry and meat, and on new laid eggs; this comes from Standard English usage for fresh fruit. **12.** *n* [*Foods*] a greyish discolouration on chocolate caused by tiny crystals of fat or sugar. **13.** *n* [*US*] [*Meat trade*] the highly attractive finish showed by well-bred and well-fattened livestock. **14.** *n* [*TV*] the glare caused by an object reflecting an excess of light into a television camera. **15.** *n* [*TV*] excessive luminosity of the **spot** on the screen caused by excessive current generated in the cathode ray electron beam. **16.** *n* [*TV*] a sudden flash on a TV screen that is the result of the sun's reflection on the object, eg. a car windscreen, that is being televised. **17.** *n* [*Wine-tasting*] the characteristic aroma of a wine. See also **bouquet**.

blooming 1. *n* [*Tanning*] the removal of any exudation of tanning solution from leather by rubbing it with a pumice stone or a similar agent. See also **bloom 10**. **2.** *n* [*Weaving*] in natural dyeing, the brightening of colours by the use of additional **mordants** in the dyebath towards the end of the dyeing.

bloomy *a* [*Cheese-making*] a description of the soft, fleecy rind that develops on certain surface-ripened cheeses, such as 'Brie', 'Camembert' and double- and triple-creams. It is formed by spraying the surface of the cheese with spores of the fungus penicillium candidum.

bloop 1. *n* [*Baseball*] to hit the ball in the air, safely but not squarely. **2.** *v* [*TV*] to cover a joint in the sound-track, usually by using thick 'blooping ink' or 'blooping tape'.

blooper *n* [*Politics*] any verbal slip-up made by a politician which can subsequently be used to his/her disadvantage by the opposition.

blooper's syndrome *n* [*US*] [*TV*] the unsophisticated hard-selling of a product on TV commercials.

blossom *n* [*US*] [*Mining*] the weathered outcrop of a seam of coal or mineral ore.

blossom rock *n* [*US*] [*Mining*] quartz stained with metallic oxides which show that mineral deposits are nearby.

blot *v* [*US*] [*Cattlemen*] to deface the brand on an animal.

blot out *v* [*Shooting*] to cover up an oncoming bird with the gun-muzzles.

blotter *n* [*Journalism*] the official police record of arrests.

blouse *n* [*Horse-racing*] the loose colours worn by a jockey. See also **silks**.

blover *n* [*Glass-making*] a thin rim of glass that has to be removed from the neck of a bottle after it has been blown; it comes from the elision of 'blow over'.

blow 1. *n* [*Drugs*] cocaine. **2.** *n* [*Metallurgy*] in the bessemer process this is the product of a single furnace charge tapped into a ladle. **3.** *n* [*US*] [*Paper-making*] See **digester**. **4.** *n* [*US*] [*TV*] the joke or punchline that has to be written into certain types of TV drama or comedy to enable a character to leave the scene. **5.** *v* [*Building*] cement does this when it swells and cracks due to imperfect preparation and curing. **6.** *v* [*Foods*] to become swollen by the products of abnormal fermentation, particularly in the case of cheeses. **7.** *v* [*Paper-making*] to blister, when air is trapped between the wet sheet and the felt, or from too quick drying on the cylinder. **8.** *v* [*Motor trade*] to spray-paint all or a part of a car's body. **9.** *v* [*Sex*] to lose a whore from one's string of girls. **10.** *v* [*Computing*] to record information on a programmable read-only memory. See also **PROM**.

blow and go *v* [*Navy*] when using the Davis Breathing Equipment to ascend to the surface from a sunken submarine, a sailor must blow the air from his lungs as he rises through the water.

blow away *v* [*Hunting*] to encourage hounds by the horn to follow the line of a fox.

blow down *v* [*TV*] to spray a studio set with dark paint in order to create 'shadow' effects or the illusion of decay.

blow hole *n* [*Metallurgy*] a casting defect in iron founding which occurs when gas has been trapped in the metal before it has completely solidified.

blow line *n* [*Angling*] an undressed silk line used for **dapping** which allows the fly to ride realistically on the surface of the water.

blow marks *n pl* [*US*] [*Paper-making*] air pockets that form between the sheets of paper and cause a bulge that forms parallel lines along the length of the sheet. See also **railroading**.

blow out 1. *n* [*UK*] [*Buses*] when due to staff shortages a London Transport bus lacks either driver or conductor and so does not leave the garage; thus the scheduled mileage is completely lost. **2.** *v* [*US*] [*Car salesman*] to use excessive sales pressure and drive a customer off the lot. **3.** *v* [*Hunting*] to encourage hounds to abandon a covert which they have drawn **blank** where they have lost their fox.

blow pit, also **bleacher** *n* [*US*] [*Paper-making*]

a very large tank in which the natural brownish colour of the pulp is removed by chemicals.

blow the grampus v [*Merchant navy*] to awaken the next watch by pouring icy cold water over them; such methods were popular in waking a drowsy grampus or porpoise.

blow the meet v [*Drugs*] when the drug dealer, or possibly the customer, fails to arrive at an arranged meeting to buy/sell drugs.

blow through n [*UK*] [*Railways*] a wagon which does not carry any brakes itself, but which has pipes mounted on it to be connected to the overall braking system of the train.

blow up, also **boil over** v [*US*] [*Cattlemen*] used of a horse that starts bucking.

blowback n [*Espionage*] disinformation and black propaganda spread by one's own agents abroad that sometimes makes its way back to information services at home and then confuses those who are not aware of the original source of such information.

blow-back n [*Shooting*] half-burnt or still burning grains of powder after a shot.

blow-by n [*Cars*] leakage of the products of combustion past the piston rings, owing to wear, faulty fitting or excessive ring gaps.

blowdown n [*Science*] the sudden, explosive rupturing of a cooling pipe, especially one in a nuclear reactor.

blower 1. n [*Cars*] a supercharger or turbocharger – a device which blows air into the engine at increased pressure. 2. n [*Coal-mining*] a discharge of gas, normally firedamp, under pressure from a hole or crack in the strata, which lasts for an appreciable time. 3. n [*Gambling*] the Tannoy system in a bookmaker's shop that broadcasts commentaries on the races, the changing odds, the results, etc. 4. n [*Music*] the pipes in an organ that produce the music. 5. n [*UK*] [*Road transport*] a turbocharger fitted to an engine and giving it more power. 6. n [*UK*] [*Road transport*] a fan fitted to a vehicle that carries materials in bulk; this creates pressure for the discharge of such materials when the distance to the discharge point means that normal gravity discharge cannot be used.

blowin' and goin' a [*US*] [*Painting*] working hard and fast on a job. See also **highballer**.

blow-in card n [*Publishing*] See **lapcard**.

blowing n [*Building, Plastering*] small blow holes in lime plastered surfaces due to expansion of previously unslaked lime particles coming into contact with moisture.

blown away a [*Glass-making*] used to describe a deficiency of glass in the neck of an internal screw neck bottle.

blow-off 1. n [*US*] [*Carnival*] an extra-special attraction offered by a sideshow – the most bizarre, the most attractive or exciting, etc. 2. n [*US*] [*Carnival*] the climax of a performance; or an act following the main event. 3. n [*US*]

[*Carnival*] a pitchman's first customer, who is often ostentatiously given a free gift to encourage further sales. 4. n [*US*] [*Circus*] the climax of a circus clown's routine: a visual punch-line. 5. n [*Gas industry*] a pressure relief station: equipment installed on a pipeline of a distribution system to monitor the gas pressure in that system; it can ventilate gas safely to the atmosphere if the pressure rises above a pre-determined maximum level.

blowout n [*US*] [*Stock market*] the quick sale of all the shares that are offered in the issue of a new security.

blowtorch n [*US*] [*Air Force*] a jet fighter aircraft.

B.L.T. n [*US*] [*Lunch counter*] abbr of **bacon, lettuce and tomato sandwich**.

blubbers n pl [*Textiles*] bags of water which are formed when woven pieces become twisted in dye tubs; these make the fabrics dangerous to handle.

blue 1. n [*Military*] soldier's slang for a sailor; it is an abbreviation of bluejacket, the original uniform of the navy. 2. n [*TV*] the final script, amended and corrected for shooting; it is derived from the colour of the paper on which it is typed. Previous versions are typed on pink or yellow paper. 3. n [*Film*] the earliest drafts of a script; later versions are typed on pink or yellow paper.

blue bag n [*UK*] [*Law*] a barrister's brief-bag, made of blue material; thus, by extension, it refers to the barrister him/herself. See also **red bag**.

blue billy n [*Metallurgy*] the iron oxide residue from the manufacture of sulphuric acid; it is used in the making up of the lining of a **puddling** furnace.

blue blazer n [*US*] [*Medicine*] a member of the administrative staff in a hospital who has no medical duties but deals with complaints, bureaucracy, finances, etc., and who wears a uniform of blue blazer, brass buttons, etc.

blue bloater n [*Medicine*] a fat patient suffering from emphysema whose skin turns blue.

blue book 1. n [*US*] [*Car salesmen*] the list of standard prices for cars. 2. n [*Cars*] the Royal Automobile Club (RAC) British Motor Sports Yearbook; the authoritative manual of British motor sports. 3. n [*UK*] [*Government*] official documents which come before Parliament are bound together as books, with blue covers, when their number reaches sufficient size to make up a volume. Once reasonably candid statements of government policy, their frankness has diminished as the number of the electorate has increased. 4. n [*TV*] a company's weekly production schedule.

blue button n [*UK*] [*Stock market*] an unauthorised clerk, once identified by a circular blue badge worn in the buttonhole, now replaced by a blue badge that bears the name of his firm.

blue chip 1. n [*Advertising*] any client or account considered to be important, big spending, etc. 2.

a [*Stock market*] said of stock considered to be of above-average reliability as an investment, second only to **gilt-edged** issues.

blue collar *a* [*Industrial relations*] referring to manual workers.

blue collar computer *n* [*Computing, Business*] a computer that is used for actual manufacturing operations within a factory, as opposed to a white collar machine that only supplies data to management.

blue day *n* [*UK*] [*Gliding*] a day in which there are no clouds in the blue sky.

blue 'flu *n* [*US*] [*Industrial relations*] the organised absence of policemen or firemen – ostensibly through illness – which can coincide conveniently with wage negotiations.

blue force *n* [*Military*] in NATO military exercises and war games the blue force represents the 'home' or 'friendly' side. See also **orange force**.

blue lib *n* [*US*] [*Police*] a nationwide organisation of US police officers aimed at co-ordinating its legal defences against those who attack them either physically, slanderously or in print.

blue list *n* [*US*] [*Stock market*] a daily financial newsletter that lists those bonds offered for sale by some 700 US dealers in municipal bonds.

blue meat *n* [*Meat trade*] the flesh of an unweaned calf.

blue on blue contact *n* [*Military*] an airborne meeting of two friendly aircraft.

blue one *n* [*UK*] [*Railways*] a green signal light.

blue peter **1.** *n* [*Navy*] a blue flag with a white square in the centre; this indicates that the ship is ready to sail. **2.** *n* [*Navy*] the long service and good conduct medal.

blue pipe *n* [*Medicine*] a vein.

blue, put up a *v* [*Navy*] to make a mistake, to commit a breach of protocol.

blue room *n* [*Air travel*] the lavatory on an airliner.

blue run *n* [*Skiing*] a slope suitable for skiers of intermediate experience. See also **black run, red run**.

blue sky *n* [*US*] [*Stock market*] fake bonds and stocks: one might as well have bought a piece of the wide blue yonder.

blue sky bargaining *n* [*US*] [*Industrial relations*] the opening of wages negotiations by stating completely unrealistic demands – 'the sky's the limit'; these demands will however be succeeded by the eventual compromises.

blue sky laws *n pl* [*US*] [*Stock market*] local laws passed by various US states to control dealing in stocks and shares and which try, where possible, to outlaw the selling of fake bonds.

blue slip *n* [*US*] [*Politics*] each individual senator's personal approval of a Presidential nomination. Blue slips are sent out to each senator by the Majority Leader. A failure to return the slip implies that the senator in question is blackballing the nomination. Sufficient blackballs would result in the cancellation of a nomination, in which case the candidate has been blue-slipped.

blue suits *n pl* [*US*] [*Military*] the military personnel on an airbase, as opposed to the **white suits**, the civilian employees of a defence contractor who work on the aircraft their firm has manufactured.

blue ticket item *n* [*Commerce*] any item that is to be pushed enthusiastically to customers.

blue vitriol, also **bluestone** *n* [*Weaving*] copper sulphate, **a mordant**.

blue water navy *n* [*Navy*] naval forces committed to operating in the open sea, the blue water. See also **brown water ship**.

blue-jay *n* [*Logging*] a worker assigned to keeping the logging road in good condition.

bluenose *n* [*US*] [*Navy*] a sailor who has crossed the Arctic circle; it comes from the general slang for a native of Nova Scotia.

bluer **1.** *n* [*UK*] [*Market-traders*] a spendthrift; one who 'blues in' his money. **2.** *n* [*Gambling*] a racehorse that loses, upon which much cash has been blued.

blue-ribbon program *n* [*Computing*] an independently designed program that has no bugs or errors.

blues **1.** *n pl* [*US*] [*Circus*] general admission seats: they are painted blue. **2.** *n pl* [*US*] [*Marine Corps*] the blue dress or undress uniform worn by enlisted men in the US Marines.

bluffing *n* [*Clothing*] the process of fastening down the front edge of **facings** on to the canvas lining to preserve the shape of edges finished without outside stitching.

blunt *n* [*Tobacco*] a cigar that is the same size at both ends.

blunting mission *n* [*Military*] retaliatory action, presumably employing nuclear weapons, which is designed to destroy enemy troops and material. See also **counter force**.

blurb **1.** *n* [*Journalism*] the announcement, in a suitably titillating form, of forthcoming features and stories in a newspaper or magazine. **2.** *n* [*Publishing*] a brief, invariably laudatory comment about a book. In the UK this is written in-house (at least for the first edition, subsequent editions may include favourable reviewers' comments) and contains facts on the book and its author. In the US the blurb comes from 'celebrity' comments, canvassed prior to first publication. **3.** *n* [*US*] [*TV*] advertising spots on television.

blushing **1.** *a* [*Aerospace*] referring to the surface of an aircraft that has been badly doped or varnished. **2.** *n* [*Painting*] this is a milk opalescence which sometimes develops as a film of lacquer (containing solvent) dries; it is due to chemical interaction between the moisture in the air and the evaporating solvent.

B.M. *n* [*Pop music*] abbr of **beautiful music** banal rearrangements of former hits; like Muzak it is to be found doubling as wallpaper in lifts, waiting

B

rooms, issuing from telephones that have left the caller on 'hold', etc.

BMD *n* [*Military*] abbr of **ballistic missile defence** this was specifically designed as one of the possible ways of protecting the **MX** missile, but was to be deployed against attacks on any US ICBM silos. The drawback to BMD is that under the still-extant **ABM** Treaty of 1972, such 'anti-missile missiles' are banned by the superpowers. Nonetheless on both sides research – split in the US into the Advanced Technology Program and the Systems Technology Program (which turns basic research into usable hardware and guidance systems) – continues. The Strategic Defence Initiative (**Star Wars**) is the ultimate projection of all-encompassing BMD.

BMEWS *n* [*Military*] acro **Ballistic Missile Early Warning System** this is made up of three overlapping radar arcs based on Clear, Alaska, Thule, Greenland and Fylingdales, Yorkshire. These scanners can track anything coming out of the European landmass at a range of 3000 m. Currently BMEWS is restricted to boost phase surveillance, but substantial updating will remedy this deficiency. First missile impact prediction facilities and then improved detection and tracking radars will be added to the system.

bnf *n* [*Science fiction*] abbr of **big name fan** a fan who has made him/herself well-known within the subculture of science fiction fans; thus 'mnf' is a middle name fan and 'lnf' a little name fan.

B.O. **1.** *n* [*Commerce*] abbr of **back out** a customer who promises to buy and then changes his/her mind. **2.** *n* [*Show business*] abbr of **Box Office** the gross income of a theatre, cinema or similar box office, rather than the actual booth that issues tickets.

boa *n* [*Economics*] a proposed system of jointly floated currencies whose rates are allowed to fluctuate against each other but within limits that are wider than those which make up the economic **snake**.

BOA *part. phr* [*US*] [*Medicine*] acro **Born On Arrival**.

board **1.** *n* [*Hosiery*] a special iron, shaped like a human leg, that is heated by steam and then used to press newly manufactured hosiery. **2.** *n* [*UK*] [*Railways*] any signal. **3.** *n* [*US*] [*Railways*] a complete list of all employees and the jobs on which they are working; including those on holiday or on suspension. **4.** *n* [*US*] [*Railways*] a signal bridge. **5.** *v* [*Ice-hockey*] to check an opponent illegally by knocking him heavily into the side boards of the rink.

board of honour *n* [*Politics*] a Soviet internal propaganda technique; a board which features such workers as have exceeded production norms or have similarly covered themselves with socialist glory. It is supposed to be a sufficient substitute for the less altruistic incentives preferred under capitalism.

board one *n* [*Computing*] the thin board of rigid insulating material on which a circuit is constructed.

boarder baby *n* [*Sociology*] a baby or young child who has to be kept in hospital indefinitely either because the parents are unable to take adequate care of it, or because they cannot be allowed to be legally responsible for it, eg. a child born to a heroin-addicted mother and itself addicted from birth.

boarding **1.** *n* [*Tanning*] the process of softening leather and developing its grain by rubbing the surface of two pieces together. **2.** *n* [*Hosiery*] shaping hosiery on heated metal forms that resemble the human leg.

boards *n pl* [*Book collecting*] the 'hard covers', made of wood, pasteboard, straw board, etc. of a book.

boast *v* [*Building*] to dress or shape a stone.

boat nigger *n* [*Sailing*] the single, fully employed and paid member of an offshore yacht crew, as permitted by the Royal Offshore Yachting Club.

boat race *n* [*Gambling*] a crooked horse race, the result of which is known to everybody except the uninitiated long before the start.

boat truck *n* [*TV*] a wheeled platform used for the transport of sets, flats, stage furniture, etc.

boatage *n* [*Shipping*] a charge made to a shipping company by a port for the services provided to that boat, eg. taking ashore the mooring ropes.

boat's left, the *v phr* [*Navy*] to be in trouble; the most serious naval crime is to miss the sailing of one's ship.

bob, also **bob fly** *n* [*Angling*] the top dropper on a wet fly cast; it should bob on the surface. See also **dibble the dropper**.

bob veal *n* [*US*] [*Meat trade*] the unmarketable flesh of the unborn calf of a slaughtered cow.

bobber **1.** *n* [*Fishing*] a worker who loads trawlers. **2.** *n* [*Logging*] a sunken or partly sunken log. See also **sinker 4**.

bobbery pack *n* [*Hunting*] a mixed pack of hounds or dogs, used for hunting any quarry; it is a dismissive term from Anglo-Indian use, meaning 'mixed' or 'mongrel' and only used in this context.

bobbie a rock *v* [*US*] [*Coal-mining*] to blast a rock by placing a dynamite charge on top of it.

bobbing *n* [*Custom cars*] the shortening of body car panels, particularly the wings, when the car has been radically lowered. More popular on older cars which have separate wings and so can be trimmed for a neater appearance.

bobby **1.** *n* [*Meat trade*] an unwanted calf slaughtered soon after birth. **2.** *n* [*UK*] [*Railways*] a signalman who, like the police force original, directs the traffic; early signallers did double as railway police and kept a truncheon in the signal box.

bobtail 1. *n* [*US*] [*Road transport*] See **bareback**. **2.** *n* [*US*] [*Road transport*] a single-unit truck.

bob-tail flush *n* [*Gambling*] See **four flush**.

bobtail straight *n* [*Gambling*] a worthless straight of only three consecutive cards.

bodice-ripper, also **hysterical historicals** *n* [*Publishing*] a traditional 'woman's romance', invariably set in a fantasised 18th or 19th century, but enjoying the added sales potential of a salting of sex and violence, often embodied as rape, whereby once chaste bodices are duly ripped, until, as ever, Mr. Right triumphs once again.

bodied oil *n* [*Painting*] an oil which has had its viscosity increased by a variety of methods.

body 1. *n* [*Cheese-making*] the 'feel' of a cheese on the palate or in the hand; it may be springy, firm, elastic, chewy, grainy, etc. **2.** *n* [*Painting*] the apparent viscosity of paint or varnish as assessed by a user when stirring, pouring, brushing or otherwise employing it in work. Thus it can be 'full-bodied', 'heavy-bodied', 'light-bodied', etc. **3.** *n* [*UK*] [*Police*] a person, especially one who is suspected of and/or charged with a crime. **4.** *n* [*Printing*] the main text of a letter or document. **5.** *n* [*US*] [*Road transport*] a **semitrailer**. **6.** *n* [*Wine-tasting*] the weight of wine in the mouth due to its alcoholic content, **extract** and other physical components. These factors stem from the quality of the vintage and its geographical origin; the hotter the area of cultivation, the greater the body.

body art, also **body sculpture** *n* [*Art*] a vogue popular in the late 1960s which combined aspects of sculpture, performance art and conceptualism and above all elements of narcissism, masochism and sexuality.

body bag *n* [*Military*] a specially made zippered rubber container in which battlefield corpses can be stored and transported prior to burial.

body copy *n* [*Advertising*] the words contained in an advertisement other than the headline(s).

body count *n* [*Military*] the totalling up, after any level of conventional military engagement, of the numbers of enemy dead. Commanders tend to exaggerate their successes, since a good body count, as in Vietnam, proves to those concerned that one's own side is doing well.

body drug *n* [*Drugs*] any physically addictive drug, thus usually a narcotic.

body life *n* [*Religion*] the coming together of born-again Christians for fellowship, teaching and sharing matters.

body shake *n* [*US*] [*Police*] a body search.

body shop *n* [*Business*] a firm that specialises in providing 'bodies' for a variety of occasions; these are people who fill halls, boost numbers at demonstrations and so on. Such individuals are known in the UK as 'rentacrowd'.

body type *n* [*Journalism*] the type face and type size used for the running copy that makes up the individual stories; thus 'body copy' is the matter that makes up those stories, as opposed to headlines, sub-heads, etc.

body work *n* [*New therapies*] certain modern physical therapies – jogging, aerobics, the consumption of herbs – that are seen as an adjunct to psychological ones.

body works, also **corporal art** *n* [*Art*] See **body art**.

bodying *n* [*Painting*] an increase, during a period of storage, in the apparent viscosity of a paint, varnish, resin or lacquer.

body-in-white *n* [*Motor trade*] a newly manufactured car body before paint is applied to the raw steel which is thus, after grinding and other operations, still 'white'.

bodysnatcher *n* [*Navy*] a member of the ship's police; the bodies are usually those snatched from waterfront bars.

bodywash *n* [*TV*] in TV makeup, this is the covering of the entire body with a removable stain to create a darker appearance.

boff 1. also **boffo** *n* [*Entertainment*] anything that succeeds at the box office. **2.** also **boffo** *n* [*Entertainment*] a big laugh, especially in the intensified form 'boffola'. All uses, like the slang meaning of sexual intercourse, stem from the essential idea of a boff, a smack and the idea of action, of stirring things up.

bogey 1. *n* [*Golf*] par for the hole; the maximum number of strokes a good player should require to complete a hole or a full round. **2.** *n* [*US*] [*Navy*] an unidentified aircraft. See also **skunk**.

bogeys *n pl* [*US*] [*Air Force*] hostile aircraft. See also **bandits 2**.

boggy *a* [*US*] [*Meat trade*] soft, flabby – used of a ham.

bogie 1. *n* [*UK*] [*Road transport*] a pair of axles linked by a common, compensating suspension system. **2.** *n* [*Merchant navy*] the ship's stove. **3.** *n* [*Navy*] nickname given to anyone called Knight.

bogie man *n* [*UK*] [*Railways*] worker in the carriage repair shops.

bogie-lift *n* [*UK*] [*Road transport*] a device which enables one axle of a **bogie** to be raised from the ground, usually by a pneumatic system.

bogners *n pl* [*US*] [*Skiing*] popular stretch ski pants, made by the German firm Bogner; the name is used ironically for blue jeans worn for skiing by those who cannot afford/don't like designer clothes.

BOGSAAT *n* [*Management*] acro **Bunch Of Guys Sitting At A Table** a cynical acronym that refers to the realities of what is touted in an organisation as 'high-level decision-making'.

bogus 1. *a* [*Computing*] non-functional, false, incorrect, useless, silly. **2.** *n* [*Philately*] a forged stamp which purports to be genuine, or an actual stamp which bears a fake overprint or surcharge. Such stamps are not forgeries, since they never officially existed.

bogy 1. *n* [*UK*] [*Market-traders*] a difficult

B

customer of a government official (especially the tax inspector). **2.** *n* [*UK*] [*Market-traders*] bad luck, a curse. See also **mockers**.

bohunk *n* [*US*] [*Paper-making*] a spot or blemish on the paper caused by liquid dripping onto it.

boil *n* [*Metallurgy*] the stage of the **puddling** process during which rapid removal of carbon takes place.

boiled beetroot *n* [*Wine-making*] the accepted reference to the aroma of 'pinot' grapes.

boiler *n* [*Hunting*] the kennel man who boils up the hounds' meat.

boiler room 1. *n* [*Crime*] on the model of the stock salesman's **boiler room** this is the action centre for the telephone con-man who has a number of phones installed in his rented or hotel room; he uses this array to defraud as many victims as he can before taking their money and running. **2.** *n* [*Stock market*] the cubicle used by a high-pressure salesman of stocks and bonds who uses a telephone to attempt to talk potential investors into following his advice.

boilerplate 1. *n* [*Business, Law*] standard legal covenants used by large institutions when drawing up the legal papers regarding their investments. **2.** *n* [*Business, Law*] any standard language used for contracts or specifications. **3.** *n* [*US*] [*Journalism*] nationally syndicated wire service material – news stories, features, cartoon strips, pictures, etc. – that are run unchanged in hundreds of newspapers across the US.

boilings *n* [*Metallurgy*] the cinder which overflows from the **puddling** furnace when the **boil** is taking place.

bold *n* [*Pearling*] a shell measuring between 18 and 22 cms. in diameter.

boll weevil 1. *n* [*US*] [*Coal-mining*] a new or inexperienced miner. **2.** *n* [*Oil rigs*] an inexperienced worker on the drilling crew who has to be trained 'on the job' by the regular crew. **3.** *n* [*US*] [*Road transport*] a novice trucker.

bologna *n* [*US*] [*Meat trade*] a low-grade bull, suitable mainly for making into bologna sausage.

boloism *n* [*Politics*] defeatist propaganda aimed at helping the interests of an enemy country; it was named after Bolo Pasha, a German agent, executed in France in 1918.

bolt 1. *v* [*Hunting*] to force a fox out of an earth, usually by using a terrier. **2.** *n* [*Logging*] a short section of tree stem, 2'—5' long, used as the primary raw material in wood turneries, shingle and stave mills. **3.** *n* [*Sailing, Ropework*] See **heaver**.

bolter *n* [*Navy*] an incoming aircraft that fails to hook onto the arrester cables on an aircraft carrier that are intended to slow it down and secure it to the flight deck.

bolt-hole *n* [*Coal-mining*] a short connecting passage used for ventilation purposes.

boltrope *n* [*Sailing, Ropework*] a three-strand rope sewn around the edge of a sail.

B.O.M. *n* [*US*] [*Journalism*] abbr of **Business Office Must** a note attached to a story which the newspaper's business office wishes to be published without question and in a specific position.

bomb 1. *v* [*Computing*] on the model of the US theatrical use (see **3**), a computer bombs when the programmer deliberately writes it a program that will destroy its system. **2.** *v* [*Computing*] when a program halts suddenly and for no specific reason; this is caused by faults in the logic system. **3.** *v* [*US*] [*Theatre*] to flop completely. **4.** *v* [*UK*] [*Theatre*] to do very well. These contrasting meanings can wreak havoc with transatlantic congratulatory telegrams. **5.** *v* [*Tiddleywinks*] to play a wink at a pile of winks with destructive intent. **6.** *n* [*Industry*] a metal cylinder with a screw top, which holds a small, cup-like container filled with coal; the heat content of the coal is measured by running an electric current through the sample and burning it up within its container. **7.** *n* [*US*] [*Football*] a long pass from the quarterback. **8.** *n* [*Basketball*] a long shot that lands in the basket.

bombard *v* [*Technology*] to charge a neon light tube with high-tension electrical current in order to eliminate any gaseous impurities in the tube.

bombproof *a* [*Computing*] **bug** free; a program which cannot be wrecked by any normal circumstances; hence a program which can spot a fault, reject it, and request that the operator correct it, rather than accept the invalid instruction and cause the machine to make an error. See also **crash**.

bomfog *n* [*Politics*] acro the *brotherhood of man under the fatherhood of God*: a term coined by Governor Nelson Rockefeller's stenographer Hy Sheffer who thus abbreviated his boss's oft-repeated phrase. The fortuitious combination of 'bombast' with 'fog' – two essential elements in many political speeches – has given the word a general currency beyond its acronymic derivation.

bomrep *n* [*US*] [*Police*] bombing report.

bon-bon *n* [*Theatre*] a 2KW spotlight that is directed on to a performer's face.

bond 1. *n* [*UK*] [*Stock exchange*] a certificate issued by a borrower giving the holder the right to receive a specified sum on the date upon which the certificate matures, and interest payments on the sum in the meantime. Bonds can be at a fixed or floating rate; maturity is usually for ten years; short-term bonds last for five years or less, medium-term from 6–15 years. **2.** *n* [*Sex*] abbr of **bondage** any pornography that features men or women tied, chained or otherwise restrained for sexual purposes.

bond crowd *n* [*US*] [*Stock market*] members of the stock exchange who transact bond orders on the floor of the exchange and who work in an area separate from the stock traders.

bondard *n* [*Cheese-making*] a family of cheeses from upper Normandy shaped similarly to the bung of a barrel; from Fr. 'bonde' meaning 'bung'. See also **bondon**.

bonded carman *n* [*Customs*] a carrier specially licenced to carry goods which are still in bond.

bonding of salesmen *n* [*Commerce*] the purchasing of an indemnity on behalf of one's salesmen against possible negligence or fraud.

bondon *n* [*Cheese-making*] a group of cheeses from upper Normandy whose shapes suggest the bung of a great tun; it comes from Fr. 'bonde' meaning 'bung'. See also **bondard**.

bond-washing **1.** *n* [*Stock market*] an operation whereby the owner of shares sells them at a price which covers the accrued dividend and then repurchases them **ex** dividend. **2.** *n* [*Stock market*] the conversion of taxable dividend income into tax-free capital gains.

bone **1.** *v* [*Building, Plastering*] to judge by eye the suitability of a line, straight or curved. **2.** *v* [*Navy*] to steal, to pilfer. **3.** *n* [*US*] [*Carpenters*] hard wood. See also **cheese 1**. **4.** *n* [*Hunting*] a measurement of quality in a hound; it depends on the amount beneath the knee or hock of a hound; thus 'good bone', 'plenty of bone' etc. **5.** *n* [*Navy*] the white bow wave formed beneath the prow of a ship; such a wave apparently resembles a dog with a bone in its mouth.

bone out *v* [*UK*] [*Railways*] to survey a stretch of rail, with a view to adjusting the level.

bonedome *n* [*Aerospace*] a padded, rigid protective helmet worn by aircrew.

boneyard **1.** *n* [*Aerospace*] the dumping ground for obsolete, useless, cannibalised aircraft. **2.** *n* [*Aerospace*] a depository for new, unused aircraft that have been made but which, because of a recession, have not found purchasers.

bongs *n pl* [*UK*] [*TV*] the sonorous, portentous chimes, purportedly from Big Ben, that herald the headlines on ITN's News at Ten.

boning rod *n* [*UK*] [*Railways*] a siting or surveying board, used in checking levels of the track.

bonk *n* [*Cycling*] a feeling experienced by cyclists of being devoid of energy; thus 'bonk-bag' means a small satchel that carries emergency rations to stave off bonk.

bonnet **1.** *n* [*Coal-mining*] a protective cover for the flame of a safety lamp. **2.** *n* [*Mining*] a shield or cover for the gauze of a miner's safety lamp. **3.** *n* [*Mining*] a cover over the mine cage that takes miners up and down the shaft.

bony *a* [*Coal-mining*] referring to slaty coal or carbonaceous shale found in coal seams.

boo board *n* [*UK*] [*Surfing*] a surfboard.

boob *n* [*US*] [*Air Force*] acro **bolt out of the blue** a surprise mission for USAF pilots.

boojum *n* [*Science*] a term coined by Professor N. David Mermin to describe a specific vanishing pattern of lines that can sometimes be seen in the flow of superliquid helium; the original boojum exists only in Lewis Carroll's 'Hunting of the Snark'.

book **1.** *n* [*Advertising*] the portfolio of completed advertisements carried by a copywriter or art director when seeking a new job. See also **reel 1**. **2.** *n* [*Advertising*] a magazine. See also **back of the book**. **3.** *n* [*Gambling*] the player who keeps, sells and apportions the supply of chips in a game. See also **banker**. **4.** *n* [*Gambling*] an onlooker or participant in a game who takes sidebets on its contingencies. **5.** *n* [*Gambling*] all the money bet by a number of persons on the outcome of a given event; the aggregate or a portion of that aggregate to be paid to the winner. **6.** *n* [*Cards*] the number of tricks (in bridge or whist) which a player or side must have before any trick has a scoring value. **7.** *n* [*Rubber*] a series of canvas strips secured along one side to a strip of board; rubber sheets in the process of manufacture are placed between the canvas 'pages' to prevent their sticking together. **8.** *n* [*Sex*] the oral tradition of street wisdom handed down from one black pimp to another, containing advice on setting oneself up as a pimp, handling one's women, avoiding police trouble, etc. **9.** *n* [*Sex*] a supply of **tricks**, names and addresses held by one pimp and often traded to another only after the payment of a substantial sum. **10.** *n* [*Sex*] working from a book: when a prostitute conducts her business on the basis of (9) and thus, by working as a call girl, avoids the perils and pitfalls of streetwalking. **11.** *n* [*Stock market*] the operation of a **jobber** in dealing in one specific stock is called 'making a book'. **12.** *n* [*Textiles*] a bundle of skeins of raw silk, usually 30 in number. **13.** *n* [*Theatre*] the script used for prompting during the performance; thus being 'on the book', is to work as the prompter during rehearsals and performances. **14.** *n* [*Theatre*] the story and dialogue of a musical comedy, as opposed to the lyrics. **15.** *n* [*Tobacco*] a stack of half leaves of tobacco from which the stems have been cut. **16.** *v* [*Tyre-making*] to take treads from the conveyor belt and place them into shelved containers for storage. **17.** *v* [*US*] [*Prisons*] to acquire, to obtain.

book of rules *n* [*US*] [*Railways*] The Uniform Code of Operating Rules which contains all the regulations, definitions and rules concerning the conduct of the railroad.

book value *n* [*Commerce, Accounting*] the value of a firm's assets as revealed in its account books. This is not the actual market value, since it is customary to value stock at cost or market value – whichever is lower – and other assets at cost less that written off for depreciation.

bookazine *n* [*Science fiction*] a magazine issue devoted to a single book or series of books by the same author, featuring the same character, etc.

bookends *n pl* [*TV*] the first and last episodes of a TV drama series.

booker *n* [*Rubber*] a worker in a rubber goods

factory who puts strips of rubber or rubberised material between layers of cloth to facilitate handling.

bookie *n* [*Logging*] a timekeeper.

booking spot *n* [*TV*] a one-to-one interview with a celebrity who is in a given day's news; the time for broadcasting such interviews has to be booked in advance.

book-keeping *n* [*Computing*] See **house-keeping**.

books of final entry *n pl* [*Accounting*] those account books/ledgers in which are finally entered the totals of debits and credits initially recorded in the books of first entry. See also **books of first entry**.

books of first entry *n pl* [*Accounting*] day books or journals in which are entered the day-to-day accounts of a firm as they develop; these books provide the rough basis for the full ledgers which are written up later. See also **books of final entry**.

books of prime entry, books of original entry *n pl* [*Accounting*] See **books of first entry**.

book-to-bill *a* [*Commerce*] said of the ratio of materials ordered to those actually purchased and thus ready to be billed.

boom 1. *n* [*Logging*] an enclosed area of a river in which logs are kept together before they are moved to the sawmill. 2. *n* [*TV, Film*] an extension from the camera unit which carries a microphone above the performers and is intended to remain out of shot while it picks up the dialogue. If the boom comes between a light and the shot it may appear on the screen as 'boom shadow'. 3. *v* [*US*] [*Road transport*] to secure the freight by tightening chains around it; a 'boomer' is the device that performs this tightening.

boom box *n* [*Audio*] a speaker with accentuated mid-bass response; this is often a contemptuous term for any badly designed speaker.

boom carpet, also **boom path** *n* [*Aerospace*] the strip of ground over which supersonic jets fly and which therefore suffers the audible booms they make in passing through the sound barrier.

boom corridor *n* [*Aerospace*] a restricted route along which supersonic aircraft must fly in order to minimise the effects of their **boom path** on those living below.

boom man *n* [*Logging*] a worker who poles floating logs down river to a sawmill.

boom ripper *n* [*UK*] [*Coal-mining*] a cutting machine used in the making of roadways.

boomer 1. *n* [*Logging*] an intinerant worker who works for a while before moving on; from slang use meaning 'tramp'. 2. *n* [*US*] [*Painting*] an itinerant, freelance painter, following construction jobs from place to place. 3. *n* [*US*] [*Painting*] a painter, unafraid of heights, who works exclusively on high buildings, bridges and similar jobs. 4. *n* [*US*] [*Painting*] a painter who is always

moving from job to job in search of better pay, conditions, etc. 5. *n* [*US*] [*Road transport*] a lever-operated device for tightening a load of long round objects – logs, lengths of pipe, etc – on a truck. 6. *n* [*Navy*] any strategic submarine, eg: Polaris, Poseidon, Trident I and II.

boomerang 1. *n* [*UK*] [*Railways*] a return ticket. 2. also **boom** 2. *n* [*Theatre*] the mounting for lights placed along the **cyc** and at the sides of the stage.

boondockers *n pl* [*US*] [*Marine Corps*] heavy-weight combat boots, especially worn for trekking through the **boondocks**.

boondocks, also **boonies** *n pl* [*US*] [*Marine Corps*] woods, jungle, marshes, dense and unhospitable undergrowth; it comes from Tagalog 'bundok' meaning 'mountain'.

boondoggle *n* [*US*] [*Politics*] this is derived from a term meaning 'odds and ends', or 'nameless gadgets': originally it described a project deliberately set up to create jobs for the otherwise unemployed. Currently it means any government project on which funds are wasted through inefficiency or corruption.

boonduck *v* [*Tiddleywinks*] to send an opponent's wink as far away – preferably off the table – as possible.

boonducking *n* [*Tiddleywinks*] sending an opponent's wink as far as possible from the cup.

boost *v* [*US*] [*Crime*] to shoplift.

boost phase defence *n* [*US*] [*Military*] a defence against incoming missiles which concentrates on destroying them during the first, boost phase of their flight, at which time the booster engines are emitting a brilliant flame and the multiple warheads have not yet been launched: given the long distances at which such operations must be carried out, such defence is generally ascribed to laser weaponry.

boosted coinage *n* [*Philology*] a term coined by William Safire. It covers newly introduced words or phrases that are modelled on familiar expressions: 'bamboo curtain' from 'iron curtain', 'narrowcasting' from 'broadcasting', etc. It forms the basis of a great deal of modern jargon.

booster 1. *n* [*US*] [*Crime*] a shoplifter. 2. *n* [*Gas industry*] a compressor installation used to raise the pressure in a gas pipeline.

booster bloomers *n pl* [*US*] [*Crime*] special undergarments used by shoplifters and fitted with voluminous pockets to hold shoplifted items.

booster box *n* [*US*] [*Crime*] a specially adapted package, apparently securely wrapped, which has a hinged side into which shoplifters can place their booty as they move through a store.

booster packages *n pl* [*Marketing*] marketing discounts: price concessions given to advertisers who are willing to spend a more than proportional amount in any one or more television areas.

booster pants *n pl* [*US*] [*Crime*] trousers fitted

with special pockets into which shoplifters can slip their booty.

boot **1.** *v* [*Computing*] this comes from **bootstrap** and means to start the machine prior to running a program; the machine can be rebooted while on, which means that programs, utilities, etc. should be reloaded. **2.** *n* [*US*] [*Navy, Marine Corps*] a recruit undergoing training. **3.** *n* [*Radio*] an illegal linear amplifier used by Citizen's Band radio enthusiasts. **4.** *n* [*Stock market*] the common stock that can be sold as a bonus with other corporate securities. **5.** *n* [*Stock market*] either cash or an equivalent consideration paid to make up the difference between two commodities; eg: a large machine that is paid for by a smaller one plus a boot of £1,000.

boot camp *n* [*US*] [*Navy, Marine Corps*] a recruit training camp.

Boot Hill *n* [*Cricket*] the position of 'forward short leg' on a cricket field; its almost suicidally close to the bat (helmets notwithstanding) and is traditionally reserved for the 'junior professional'; the fielder thus selected will, like cowboys of old 'die with his boots on'.

boot money *n* [*UK*] [*Sport*] the payment of bribes, either in cash or in kind, to the ostensibly amateur players of Rugby Union. The money often comes from equipment manufacturers whose trade naturally increases if sports stars can be persuaded to display their wares in major, and thus televised, matches. See also **appearance money**.

boot one *v* [*Baseball*] to make a mistake or an error on the field.

booth *n* [*US*] [*Car salesmen*] the table, office or desk where the final sales transaction is carried out.

boothman *n* [*Film*] a cinema projectionist, who occupies the projection booth.

bootie *n* [*UK*] [*Military*] the basic private soldier; possibly akin to the USMC/USN **boot**, but with no implication of training.

bootlace **1.** *n* [*Sheep-shearing*] a narrow strip of skin cut off by rough shearers, especially when opening up the neck. **2.** *v* [*Sheep-shearing*] to shear in such a way as to create bootlaces.

bootleg **1.** *n* [*US*] [*Mining*] an explosive charge which fails to dislodge any rock. **2.** *n* [*US*] [*Railways*] a protective cover for trackside wires when they are forced to leave the conduit in which they are laid. **3.** [*Pop music*] this comes from the Prohibition era use meaning illegally distilled or imported liquor; here it refers to illegally produced or distributed records, tapes or videotapes of a recording session or a live concert. Invariably expensive, rarely of top quality, they are deplored by the legitimate record business.

bootneck, also **buffalo, bullock, turkey** *n* [*Navy*] British Navy nicknames for the Royal Marines.

boots *n* [*Navy*] the junior ship of a squadron; a role that is allotted to the ship by virtue of the seniority, or lack of it, of its captain.

bootstrap **1.** *n* [*Computing*] a set of inbuilt instructions within the computer's machinery which tell the machine how to load a program. Once loaded, this program takes over the task of operating the machine. **2.** *n* [*Science*] in nuclear physics, this is the theory that all nuclear particles are composed of each other, as opposed to the theory that all particles are built from a limited number of other, elementary particles. The concept suggests that physics can thus 'pull itself up by its bootstraps'.

bootstrap exploration *n* [*Aerospace*] a concept of space exploration whereby the results and gains of each mission are used as the basis for a store of information upon which its successor can be launched.

bootstrapper *n* [*US*] [*Military*] a career military man who is temporarily released from his usual duties to obtain an academic degree.

bootstrapping *n* [*Audio*] coupling between points in a circuit whereby negative feedback (NFB) is used to raise the input impedence of a stage.

borax *n* [*Design*] a US slang term dating from the 1920s (meaning 'gaudy, shoddy knicknacks') that is used to denote the artificial, flashy decorations that characterise design in the 1940s and 1950s: bogus streamlining, blubbery inflations or curves as seen in the period's cars, jukeboxes, etc.

bord *n* [*Coal-mining*] a roadway driven through the solid coal, substantially at right angles to the main cleat of the coal.

bord and pillar, also **pillar and stall** *n* [*Coal-mining*] a system of mining in which roadways are driven through the solid coal, leaving supporting pillars between them; such pillars may be removed at a later stage, or left as permanent supports.

bordereau *n* [*Insurance*] a list, schedule, memorandum or account, especially one joined to a policy or contract.

bordure *n* [*Heraldry*] a solid border running round the edge of a shield.

born again *a* [*Religion*] said of Christians who have been saved, with Christ controlling one's life and Christ living within one; see John 3.3.

borrow **1.** *n* [*Golf*] the compensation in the direction and strength of one's putting that must be made to allow for the slope of the green. **2.** *v* [*Golf*] to alter one's putting to allow for the idiosyncrasies of the green.

borscht belt *n* [*Entertainment*] a show business circuit based on a number of Jewish (hence borscht, the traditional Russian beetroot soup) family hotels in the Catskill mountains in upstate New York.

bosh **1.** *n* [*Glass-making*] a water tank used for cooling glass-making tools or quenching glass. **2.** *n* [*Metal work*] the lower, sloping part of a blast

B

furnace where the diameter increases to a maximum. **3.** [*Metal work*] a trough used in forging and smelting in which ingots and tools are washed. **4.** *n* [*Metal work*] a tank of boiling water in which metal parts are washed.

bosh lines *n pl* [*Theatre*] violin strings used by puppeteers to control their characters.

bosie *n* [*Aus.*] [*Cricket*] this is the same as the **googly**, a ball bowled with an apparent leg break action but which actually breaks in the opposite direction. It is named after the ball's originator, the UK bowler B. J. T. Bosanquet.

boss **1.** *n* [*Building, Plastering*] an **enriched** knob covering the intersection of a moulding, especially on ceilings. **2.** [*Crime*] the capo or head of a Mafia family.

boss player *n* [*Sex*] a star in the world of black pimping; such a star might even choose and achieve the move out of pimping into a more lucrative and 'respectable' racket.

boss word *n* [*UK*] [*Commerce*] a vogue word favoured by management who put a premium on staying fashionable in concepts as well as clothes.

bossism *n* [*US*] [*Politics*] a pejorative description for (usually) big city corruption in which one major figure, through graft, violence, patronage and other dubious tactics, gains control of the party machine he is supposed only to represent. Thus irrespective of the stance or popularity of the actual candidates at the local level, he is able to deliver vast numbers of votes from 'his' city to the national candidate he favours.

Boston arm *n* [*Medicine*] a type of electronically controlled artificial arm, which is operated by the user's willing it to flex, as if it were a real arm. It was developed in Boston, US.

Boston version *n* [*US*] [*Theatre*] a show excised of any potentially offensive lines or business in order to satisfy the puritan censors of a local authority. Boston, the home of puritanism, is used to characterise any such authority.

Bosun of the Yard, Master Attendant *n* [*Aus.*] [*Navy*] the officer responsible for berths, harbour services, pilotage and small craft.

bot **1.** *n* [*US*] [*Prisons*] acro **balance of time** the time that remains to be served by a parolee and which must still be served if parole is violated and the violator arrested. **2.** *n* [*US*] [*Stock market*] p.p. abbr of **bought** a term used by stockbrokers.

botanist *n* [*US*] [*Medicine*] a doctor who considers his patients to have no more intelligence than a plant or tree. See also **geologist**, **veterinarian**.

bott, also **bod** *n* [*Metallurgy*] in iron founding, this is a conical plug of clay inserted in the tapping hole (from which metal will eventually be drawn off) of a furnace to prevent overflow while it is melting.

bottle **1.** *n* [*UK*] [*Market-traders*] the buttocks; from rhyming slang 'bottle and glass' meaning 'arse'. **2.** *v* [*UK*] [*Market-traders*] to stink, to smell. **3.** *v* [*Navy*] to capsize a sailing boat. **4.** *v* [*Navy*]

to reprimand a sailor. **5.** *n* [*Navy*] a reprimand. **6.** *v* [*Table tennis*] abbr of **bottle out**, or to lose one's bottle meaning to lose one's nerve at a crucial point, usually in a close game or match; it comes from general rhyming slang 'bottle and glass', meaning 'arse', therefore bottom, therefore courage, guts. **7.** *n* [*TV repair*] a TV or radio valve.

bottle butted *a* [*Logging*] said of a tree which is greatly enlarged at the base.

bottle dealer *n* [*Drugs*] a large-scale dealer in amphetamines or barbiturates who sells bottles of 1,000 tablets or capsules.

bottle-age *n* [*Wine-tasting*] developmental factors in the wine, hard to describe, but easily recognizable by the expert and vital in assessing the age/maturity of a given wine; on the whole it means a degree of mellowness, and the eradication of possible rawness of flavour.

bottleneck inflation *n* [*Economics*] a term coined in Japan to describe the inflation that results from a rise in prices that is not paralleled by an equivalent rise in the overall demand for goods.

bottler *n* [*Car salesmen*] See **square wheeler**.

bottle-sickness *n* [*Wine-tasting*] temporary oxidation after bottling; this wears off.

bottom **1.** *n* [*Hunting*] a big ditch with a fence on one side. **2.** *n* [*Shipping*] a single ship.

bottom dump *n* [*US*] [*Road transport*] a truck that unloads its cargo through bottom gates.

bottom English *n* [*Pool*] See **draw 6**.

bottom fisher *n* [*US*] [*Stock market*] an investor who specialises in picking up shares that are currently at their lowest ever price, especially those of bankrupt or near bankrupt firms.

bottom fishing **1.** *n* [*Angling*] coarse fishing. **2.** *n* [*Angling*] fishing with a bait on or near the bed of the river.

bottom line *n* [*Economics, Commerce*] the final figure on a balance sheet, the net profit or loss after all expenditure, deductions and tax demands have been taken into account. By extension, both in and out of financial use, this is the ultimate standard for making a judgement, the facts without frills: 'What's the bottom line on . . .'

bottom line syndrome *n* [*Commerce*] the conducting of business in such a way that all decisions, irrespective of more specific needs, are made with regard to the effect they will have on the profit/loss figures of the company.

bottom man *n* [*Glass-making*] a worker in a gas producer plant who removes ash.

bottom out *v* [*Stock market*] when a slump or fall in the market reaches as low a point as possible and prices begin improving once more.

bottom power *n* [*Politics*] this refers to the plump market women of Ghana and the power held in that country by middle-class black marketeers who continue to profit from their own corruption in the face of a declining legitimate economy.

bottom quark *n* [*Science*] See **quark**.

bottom sludge *n* [*Oil rigs*] See **basic sediment**.

bottom woman *n* [*Sex*] that member of a pimp's stable of prostitutes who is considered the most reliable, efficient and profitable.

bottoming 1. *n* [*Audio*] a situation in which the stylus reaches the rounded bottom of the groove on a record; this happens when the stylus is of less than the correct dimensions, since it should not occur. 2. *n* [*Electronics*] a thermionic valve bottoms when its anode can draw no more current and registers at zero. 3. *n* [*Weaving*] in natural dyeing, this means dyeing the cloth a first colour with the intention of **top-dyeing** a second colour.

bottomry *n* [*Shipping*] the mortgage of a ship: when the master borrows cash to pay for repairs and allied expenses necessary to get the ship back to its home port. The ship itself is the security for the loan, but if the ship is lost before the loan is repaid, the lender loses the money advanced.

bottomry bond *n* [*Shipping*] a formal document recording the conditions of the mortgage of a ship. See also **bottomry**.

bottoms 1. *n pl* [*US*] [*Farming*] river bottom land; the richest, most fertile land. 2. *n pl* [*Merchant navy*] the number of ships involved in a particular trade; 'how many bottoms . . . ?' 3. *n pl* [*Oil rigs*] accumulations of mud, sediment and water in a storage tank. 4. *n. pl* [*Oil rigs*] in distilling, that part which does not vapourise during the operation. 5. also **bottom coal** *n pl* [*Coal-mining*] the lowest part of a coal seam, which may or may not be extracted.

bottom-up management *n* [*Management*] the viewing of corporate responsibility and relations as proceeding from the bottom to the top of the management ladder; such responsibility is usually seen as originating at the top.

bottom-up method *n* [*Computing*] a programming technique in which the lowest levels of instructions are combined to form a higher level of operation which in turn forms the basis of yet higher levels and so on. See also **top-down method**.

bought note *n* [*Stock market*] a broker's note to a client, confirming the fulfilment of an order to make a certain purchase of shares.

boulette *n* [*Cheese-making*] a group of cheeses shaped by hand into more or less spherical or conical shapes.

Boulwarism *n* [*Management*] the attitude towards collective bargaining and industrial relations adopted by Lemuel Ricketts Boulware (b. 1895), vice-president for employee, community and union relations of US General Electric Co, 1947–56: management makes a pay offer it regards as genuinely fair (rather than deliberately low, for bargaining's sake) and will only amend this if unions can prove it to be unfair.

The intention was to avoid the usual wage claim game-playing by both sides.

bounce 1. *v* [*Boxing*] to recover very quickly from a knock-down; and thus to 'bounce' back off the canvas. 2. *v* [*Film*] to fire, to dismiss. 3. *v* [*US*] [*Medicine*] when a patient, who has been successfully **turfed** on to another ward or hospital department, is sent back by that ward or department to the doctor who arranged to have him/her moved in the first place. 4. *n* [*Business*] the illegal altering of invoices, order forms, price tags, receipts, etc. by a firm's employees so as to disguise the theft of goods by their accomplices, who are not employed by the firm, but who do the actual stealing. 5. *n* [*Photography*] the light that is created by the flash unit and reflects off the subject; one must make due compensation for this effect. 6. *n* [*Photography*] diffused light with no direction. 7. *n* [*TV*] a variation in the luminance of short duration following a step change in the video signal. 8. *n* [*Printing*] a fault in the keyboard in which a single keystroke causes two or more characters to be transmitted. 9. *n* [*TV repair*] a set that comes back for further attention, even if it has just been repaired.

bounceback 1. *n* [*Advertising*] second thoughts; specifically this refers to the review of a situation and the subsequent changes in attitudes, opinions, plans, etc. 2. *n* [*Medicine*] an habitual patient, who returns constantly to the hospital despite repeated discharges.

bounce-back *n* [*Commerce*] the offering of a new purchasing incentive – sometimes on the same goods, sometimes for a related product – with an initial offer made to a customer in the form of a free gift or a **self-liquidator**.

bouncer 1. *n* [*Archery*] an arrow that rebounds from the target. 2. *n* [*US*] [*Railways*] the caboose on a railway train.

bouncing *n* [*Fireworks*] the insertion of the 'bang' in a firework.

bound *a* [*Computing*] limited in speed of operations by the slowest component in a system.

boundary layer *n* [*Cars*] a very thin layer of air which clings to the surfaces of a car over which the airflow is stable; this makes it very hard to blow the dust off a car, no matter how fast it is going.

boundary maintenance *n* [*Sociology*] a concept from **functionalism**, whereby a social system is defined as boundary maintaining if, in relation to its environment, it preserves certain regularities of pattern. For systems to continue there must also be some exchanges across the boundaries with other systems.

bounded rationality *n* [*Sociology*] a term used in the analysis of administrative and organisational decision-making to demonstrate that there must always be some constraint upon rational or optimizing decisions. Decision-makers can only calculate upon the basis of available

B

information, and their own ability to evaluate is in itself limited.

bouquet 1. *n* [*Espionage*] a selection of cases – usually of internal disaffection – with which a CIA investigator is dealing at any one time. **2.** *n* [*Wine-tasting*] the characteristic aroma of a wine. **3.** *n* [*Shooting*] a number of pheasants crossing the guns in a mass rather than singly as is desired; such a bunch usually stems from inefficient shoot management, especially in the provision of insufficient flushing points.

bouqueté *a* [*Cheese-making*] possessing an agreeable aroma.

bourgeois 1. *a* [*Politics*] this comes from the medieval description of a citizen of a free. city ('bourg') who was thus neither peasant nor lord; the bourgeois is the essential middle-class. Marx praised them in 'The Communist Manifesto' (1848) but the word is currently radical shorthand for reactionary, selfish, culturally, socially and politically conservative. For many radicals the word also means their parents. **2.** *a* [*Wine trade*] a classification of wine that falls between the major classified growths and the basic 'vins ordinaires'.

bourgeois democracy *n* [*Politics*] a Marxist term which condemns contemporary European and American governmental systems; the premise is that however ostensibly democratic the representatives claim to be, power inevitably remains with the bourgeoisie or its agents, safeguarding and promoting the capitalist structure at the expense of the proletariat.

bourgeois economics *n* [*Economics*] a Marxist term condemning any form of economics, currently represented by the monetarist school, since it accepts the laws of the market as the laws of nature. Such acceptance, it is claimed, simply bolsters up the inequalities of the capitalist system which, if Marx is right, will be unnecessary in the ideal socialist world.

bourgeois reactionary line *n* [*Politics*] in Maoist China, this refers to the political opponents of Chairman Mao Zedong.

bourgeois realism *n* [*Art*] the work produced by turn of the century academic painters, and salon artists implacably opposed to all modern movements. Their paintings remain a precise reflection of bourgeois society at the height of its prosperity.

bourgeois revolution 1. *n* [*Politics*] in Marxist terms, the bourgeois/democratic revolution is against the aristocracy, but not in favour of the proletariat. **2.** *n* [*Politics*] in Marxist terms this is the ceaseless drive of capitalism to maximise its profits by research, reorganisation, advancing technology, etc.; such advances also serve to maintain its grasp on society.

bourgeois socialism *n* [*Politics*] weak, utopian socialism propounded by those who would probably not really wish to see it made a fact; socialism

with little bearing on 'real life' as lived by the masses. See also **academic socialism**.

bouse *v* [*Sailing, Ropework*] to move any object around the deck by means of a small tackle.

boutique *n* [*US*] [*Stock market*] a small and specialised brokerage firm that restricts its activities to providing a small clientele with a limited portfolio of stocks.

boutique agency *n* [*Advertising*] a small agency, high on the creative (copy-writing, art direction) side, but lacking the ancillary departments (market research, space buying, etc.) that make up the wider ranging services of the major agencies. See also **hot shop**.

bouzbir *n* [*Military*] used in the French Foreign Legion to mean a brothel.

bovrilise *v* [*Advertising*] the term comes from a vintage advertisement that touted Bovril as 'the best of the meat': hence it means to omit all inessential matter from an advertisement.

bow 1. *v* [*Entertainment*] to launch a new show; it comes from a performer taking a bow. **2.** also **crown** *n* [*UK*] [*Coal-mining*] See **arch 1**.

bow wave *n* [*Navy*] the peak of an officers cap.

bowl 1. *n* [*US*] [*Lunch counter*] the soup of the day. **2.** *n* [*Printing*] the curved, lobed or swelled part of a letter.

bowler hat brigade *n* [*UK*] [*Railways*] railway inspectors, who wear such headgear.

bowler-hat *v* [*UK*] [*Military*] to retire an officer from the British Army before he has reached the statutory age; this early retirement is enhanced by a compensatory financial bonus.

bowling green *n* [*UK*] [*Railways*] the fast line, reserved for expresses. See also **quick, lawn**.

bowwow *n* [*US*] [*Meat trade*] a stunted, aged steer, suitable only for canning. See also **canner, tripe**.

box 1. *n* [*Aerospace*] a tight, diamond-shaped formation of four aeroplanes. **2.** *n* [*Cricket*] a protector, made either of metal or plastic, used to guard the batsman's genital area. **3.** *n* [*Cricket*] a close-fielding position to the off-side of the batsman and slightly behind the stumps. **4.** *n* [*US*] [*Hotels*] a single room. See also **dupe 3**. **5.** *n* [*Journalism*] a small news story, encased in a box to give it prominence; thus 'box head' means a headline enclosed in a box. **6.** *n* [*UK*] [*Railways*] abbr of **signal box**. **7.** *n* [*US*] [*Road transport*] a **semitrailer**. **8.** *n* [*US*] [*Road transport*] the transmission part of the tractor. **9.** *n* [*Sex*] the crotch; thus 'box-lunch' means fellatio. **10.** *n* [*UK*] [*Stock market*] a small room off the floor of the Exchange which is used for dealing by broker firms. **11.** *n* [*UK*] [*Stock market*] a container in the Settlement Room where tickets may be placed for collection. **12.** *n* [*UK*] [*Stock market*] a compartment in the security vaults beneath the Exchange. **13.** *n* [*TV*] the control room overlooking the studio floor from which a show is produced. See also **gallery**. **14.** *n*

[*TV repair*] a television receiver; presumably it comes from general slang use 'goggle box'.

box and cox *v* [*US*] [*Navy*] See **hotbunk**.

box cars *n* [*Gambling*] in craps dice the throw of double six, supposedly from the similarity to the wheels of freight cars.

box Harry *v* [*Commerce*] a commercial travellers' term for avoiding the expensive table d'hôte lunch or dinner and making up with cheaper food served at teatime. It comes from 'boxing a tree' meaning to cut into a tree to draw off the sap; in this case it is the hapless landlady who is 'drained' of her cheap tea.

box out *v* [*US*] [*Medicine*] to die; from the wooden 'box' in which one is placed.

box the paint *v* [*Painting*] to mix paint by pouring it backwards and forwards between two buckets.

box trade *n* [*US*] [*Garment trade*] buyers who purchase only a few garments from the wholesaler and so can take them all away in a box.

box up *v* [*Gambling*] to mix up a set of five or six dice so that the gambler may choose his preferred pair from the selection.

boxed *a* [*US*] [*Medicine*] dead; from the box or coffin in which the corpse is placed.

boxer 1. *n* [*Boxing*] a subtle, intelligent fighter, as opposed to one who depends on brawn rather than brain for success. 2. *n* [*Aus.*] [*Gambling*] in a game of two-up, the player who looks after the apparatus and the stake money.

boxer engine, also **horizontally opposed engine** *n* [*Cars*] an engine with its cylinders arranged opposite each other with a common crankshaft in the middle.

boxman *n* [*Gambling*] the casino employee who runs the craps table.

Boy *n* [*Theatre*] the Principal Boy (invariably an actress) in the annual pantomime season.

boy 1. *n* [*Drugs*] heroin. See also **ghl** 1. 2. *n* [*Military*] any nuclear device that explodes successfully and as required. See also **absolute dud, dwarf dud**.

boylesk *n* [*US*] [*Entertainment*] a variation of burlesk or burlesque; these are third-rate variety shows which are mainly dependent on striptease, but which aim at a homosexual clientele and feature male strippers.

boys *n pl* [*Antiques*] other antique dealers, the trade.

bp *n* [*US*] [*Police*] abbr of **black pimp**.

B-post *n* [*Cars*] the centre post on to which the front door shuts and on which the rear door is hinged; this is made increasingly strong with the need for anti-burst safety locks.

bpv *n* [*US*] [*Police*] abbr of **bullet-proof vest**.

bracket 1. *n* [*Banking*] groups of banks involved in a new share issue. 2. *n* [*Printing*] a curved fillet, used to unite the serif with the stem.

bracket creep *n* [*Economics*] the tendency of inflation to push individuals into higher tax

brackets as their inflation-fuelled income increases – although in real terms they are no better off.

bracketing 1. *n* [*Navy*] See **ladder** 2. 2. *n* [*Photography*] the taking of several shots with exposures around a mean value shown on the light meter. 3. *n* [*Photography*] ensuring that one obtains the correct exposure by trying a number of different f/stops and shutter speeds when photographing the same subject. 4. *n* [*Photography, Film*] a method of gradually bringing a projected image from apparent shadow into full prominence; this is achieved by taking a series of shots of the object, in each of which the lighting is slightly increased until the final effect is reached.

Brady *n* [*US*] [*Medicine*] an abnormally slow heart beat of 60 beats per minute. See also **tachy**.

brady *n* [*US*] [*Theatre*] a seat saved by the management for a personal friend or an important individual; it is named after the late William A. Brady (1863–1950), a US theatrical manager. See also **Annie Oakley**.

brae *n* [*Coal-mining*] a roadway driven on a gradient.

brag rag *n* [*Navy*] a campaign or distinguished service medal worn on a sailor's uniform.

brahmin *n* [*US*] [*Politics*] a term taken from the highest Hindu caste; this is a social and intellectual elite who make up a political aristocracy whose influence pervades the highest levels of the US Government, although no member ever has to suffer the hurly-burly of actual election. They are often futher characterised as Boston Brahmins from their power base among the blue-blood families of Boston, but they are somewhat in abeyance while President Reagan's Californians hold sway, although they will doubtless re-emerge. See also **mandarin**.

braid *n* [*Weaving*] the lowest quality of wool in the blood system of grading.

braiding *n* [*Audio*] the outer conductor of a flexible screened cable which is composed of braided fine bare wires.

brail breasted *a* [*UK*] [*Theatre*] said of a suspended piece of scenery that has been moved to the required position and then fastened in place with rope.

brain candy *n* [*US*] [*TV*] escapist programming – game shows, banal 'thriller' series, etc; it is the equivalent of 'light entertainment' in the UK.

brain stem prep *n* [*US*] [*Medicine*] a deeply comatose patient, a human vegetable. See also **gork 2**.

brain truster *n* [*US*] [*Hotels*] one of the steady workers who has been given a position of responsibility – mail room clerk, etc. – by the management.

brain-damaged *a* [*Computing*] said of a machine and its operator, both of whom are in a useless condition; the operator should have known

B

better than to start work, the machine may well be broken beyond repair.

brains 1. *n pl* [*UK*] [*Police*] an ironic reference by the uniformed branch to their supposedly cleverer colleagues in the CID; this same department is referred to by the villains as 'the filth'. **2.** *n pl* [*UK*] [*Railways*] Traffic Control.

brainstorming *n* [*Business*] intensive group sessions aimed at thrashing out a problem with the help of all those capable of and interested in dealing with it; free association and 'thinking aloud' are encouraged as means of solving the problem. Such sessions were initiated in the US circa 1953.

brake-up *n* [*Aerospace*] a situation in which an aeroplane tips forward onto its nose on landing because the pilot has applied the brakes too harshly and thus the speed of the 'plane forces the tail to flip up.

branch 1. *n* [*UK*] [*Fire brigade*] the metal nozzle at the end of a fireman's hose and thus by extension the whole hose. **2.** *v* [*UK*] [*Computing*] See **jump 1**. **3.** *v* [*Industrial relations*] to bring a union member before a branch union meeting to face disciplinary investigation and possible punishment.

brand awareness 1. *n* [*Commerce, Marketing*] from the consumer's or retailer's point of view, this is the belief in the excellence or value of the product. **2.** *n* [*Commerce, Marketing*] from the manufacturer's point of view, this is in the product that is being made.

brand mapping *n* [*Marketing*] a diagram or 'map', gleaned from market research interviews, of the perceptions that consumers claim to have of a product under survey.

brandering *n* [*Building, Plastering*] the operation of nailing cross-battens to the undersides of joists.

brandling *n* [*Angling*] a type of worm used for fishing.

brand-name author *n* [*Publishing*] a major best-selling author – Harold Robbins, Barbara Cartland – whose work, often of secondary value, sells as much on the name of the author as on its content.

brandstanding *n* [*Advertising*] a pun on grandstanding meaning short term intense brand promotion.

brandstretching *n* [*Commerce, Advertising*] the concept of increasing one's advertising by expanding outside traditional outlets – posters, print and visual media – into sponsorship, usually of sport. It is used especially by tobacco companies whose products cannot be advertised on TV, but who back many of the sports events that are widely and regularly televised; this way they ensure that their logo is indirectly advertised throughout such programmes.

brass 1. *n* [*UK*] [*Police*] a prostitute. **2.** *mnem*

[*Shooting*] a mnemonic used by marksmen: breathe, relax, aim, squeeze, shoot.

brass collar Democrat *n* [*US*] [*Politics*] a voter who slavishly follows the Democratic party line.

brass hat 1. *n* [*Military*] a top ranking officer, from the gold leaves (**scrambled egg**) on his hat; it is often abbreviated to 'the brass'. **2.** *v* [*Military*] to promote an individual into the higher ranks.

brass up *v* [*UK*] [*Military*] to shell; it comes from the brass shell casings that are ejected after firing the projectile.

brassage *n* [*Finance*] the charge made by a government for the manufacture of metal coins; the actual cost of producing the coins.

brassie *n* [*Golf*] the traditional name for a number 2 wood.

brat *n* [*Coal-mining*] a thin bed of coal mixed with pyrites or calcium carbonates.

brattice 1. also **screen** *n* [*Coal-mining*] an airtight partition in a mine which separates intake air from return air. **2.** also **screen** *n* [*Coal-mining*] any form of partition – board, planking, etc. – erected in a mine passage to divert the air into working places.

brattice cloth, also **brattice sheeting** *n* [*Coal-mining*] temporary partitions made of stretched cloth, erected to divert the flow of air into underground working places.

bravo zulu *n* [*Navy*] naval signal: very well done, from code BZ.

breach *v* [*US*] [*Music*] See **jump 6**.

breachy *n* [*US*] [*Cattlemen*] a cow that breaks through or jumps over fences.

bread *n* [*Religion*] inspiring discourse; see Matthew 6.11. See also **crumb 2**.

bread and butter 1. *n* [*US*] [*Carpenters*] a carpenter's tool kit. **2.** *n* [*TV*] long running programmes (eg: **soap operas**) which cost relatively little to produce, require only a modicum of ability to perform or present, and bring in continually high ratings and (in commercial TV) regular advertising income.

bread and butter issue *n* [*US*] [*Politics*] See **pocketbook issue**.

breadboard 1. *n* [*Computing*] an experimental arrangement of circuits set out on a flat surface. **2.** *v* [*Computing*] to set out such an arrangement. **3.** *n* [*Marketing*] an early form of prototype which reproduces the performance of a product but not its associated appearance or other characteristics; the term comes from electronics/engineering usage.

breadcrumbs *n* [*Navy*] an order for junior officers to block their ears, in theory at least, and pretend not to hear, and definitely not repeat, the wardroom conversation of their seniors.

breadth of the market *n* [*US*] [*Stock market*] the percentage of stocks that conform to a given market move; a market achieves a 'good breadth' if more than two-thirds of the shares rise together in a trading session.

break 1. *n* [*Clothing*] the point where the lapel starts to roll over on a coat or jacket, usually at the top buttonhole. **2.** *n* [*Croquet, Snooker, Billiards*] a sequence of shots by the same player; thus to 'set up a break' is to get into a position from which one can initiate a break. **3.** *n* [*Golf*] a sideways slope on a green. **4.** *n* [*Painting*] the separation of slimy, sticky matter that occurs in vegetable oils when they are heated. **5.** *n* [*Lacrosse*] the movement of the defence as soon as a shot at goal has been made by the opposition; the break should move out away from the goal area and offer the goalkeeper a variety of options for the direction of the clearance. **6.** *n* [*Music*] in jazz, a performer's improvised addition to a scored piece of music; it is often specified as horn break, guitar break, etc. **7.** *n* [*UK*] [*Surfing*] an area of water where the waves are good enough to be ridden. **8.** *n* [*US*] [*Paper-making*] a tear in a finished roll of paper. **9.** *n* [*US*] [*Journalism*] the continuation of a story on a following page or pages; thus the 'break page' is the page where that story continues. **10.** *n* [*Horse-racing*] the start of a race. **11.** *v* [*Entertainment, Pop music*] to make an individual, an act or, most commonly, a record successful in the required outlets, media or venues. Thus an act or record that succeeds as desired is a 'breaker' or 'prime mover' (with reference to ascending the pop music charts). **12.** *v* [*Journalism*] to publish or reveal an item of news; a 'breaking story' is one that continues over a number of issues or days with new developments continually being added, as they in turn break. **13.** *v* [*US*] [*Theatre*] to miss a cue, forget one's lines, or break into laughter, often when provoked by a fellow actor. See also **corpse 2, go up in the air** etc. **14.** *v* [*US*] [*Theatre*] to close a show. **15.** *v* [*Gambling*] in cars and dice: to take money from one's opponents. **16.** *n* [*Dog breeding*] the process of colour changes in the growing dog. **17.** *v* [*Dog breeding*] used of a dog when it changes its colour as it grows. **18.** *n* [*Stock market*] the sudden fall in prices of shares on the market. **19.** *v* [*Stock market*] said of shares which decline in price suddenly.

break a leg! *excl* [*Theatre*] a traditional remark wishing good luck to a fellow actor; it is considered very bad luck actually to say 'Good luck!' or even to address an actor prior to his/her first entrance of the night. See also **that play**.

break arch *n* [*Antiques, Horology*] an arched top above the dial which does not reach the full width.

break figure *n* [*Film*] a specified amount of weekly takings; after this figure has been reached the exhibitor, subject to a pre-arranged contract, must start paying a higher percentage to the renter, based on the volume of business.

break in *v* [*Coal-mining*] to advance part of the working face along a narrow front.

break into ship *v* [*Navy*] to board a warship other than by the gangway.

break luck *v* [*Sex*] when a prostitute services the first client of the day.

break one's duck *v* [*Cricket*] when a batsman scores the first run(s) of an innings. See also **open one's account**.

break ship *v* [*Navy*] to leave a warship without permission; to desert.

break soil *v* [*Hunting*] used of a stag when it leaves water. See also **soil**.

break squelch *v* [*US*] [*Marine Corps*] to break radio silence.

break surface *v* [*US*] [*Navy*] to wake up.

break technique *v* [*US*] [*Medicine*] when a nurse or doctor disobeys the rules of sterilisation or neglects the details of sterilisation technique.

break the start, also **jump the gun** *v* [*Athletics*] to make a false start.

break the unit *v* [*US*] [*Road transport*] to uncouple the tractor from the trailer.

break up 1. *v* [*Hunting*] used of hounds when they eat the fox's carcase after the kill. **2.** *v* [*US*] [*Railways*] to separate a portion of a train, or an entire train by using the points.

breakaway, also **breakup** *n* [*UK*] [*Theatre*] a piece of scenery or a costume that has been deliberately designed to alter its shape or to self-destruct on stage.

breakdown clause *n* [*Shipping*] See **off-hire clause**.

breaker 1. *n* [*Book collecting*] a book so imperfect that it has no uses other than to be broken up, especially if its colour plates, suitable for framing, are intact. **2.** *n* [*Building*] See **top man**. **3.** *n* [*Radio*] in Citizen's Band radio usage, a formal request from one broadcaster to others to let him/her use the channel. **4.** *n* [*Tyre-making*] an open weave fabric placed inside a pneumatic tyre to provide extra protection at the point where the revolving tyre touches the road surface.

break-even 1. *n* [*US*] [*Theatre*] the total weekly cost of a production. **2.** *n* [*US*] [*Theatre*] the ability of a touring company to pay the rent of the theatre and any other overheads incurred. See also **get-out 1, nut**.

breaking an account *n* [*Banking*] the ending of operations on a running account, leaving a balance outstanding; such a break occurs when one partner in a firm dies and the partnership account is overdrawn, or when a guarantor dies and the principal debtor so guaranteed has an overdraft, etc.

breaking patter *n* [*US*] [*Cattlemen*] the flow of chatter that a trainer keeps up to the horse which he is in the process of breaking to the saddle.

break-line *n* [*Printing*] See **turnover**.

break-out 1. *n* [*Aerospace*] the first visual references a crew can make after a plane has been flying 'blind' through clouds. **2.** *v* [*Royal Navy*] to leave the ship without permission; the equivalent of the Army's **AWOL**.

breakout 1. *n* [*Military*] the ability of one superpower to escape from the limitations of the threat currently posed by the capability of the other. As seen by pessimistic US officials the theory is that the Soviets are continually searching for loopholes in arms control treaties. **2.** *n* [*Oil rigs*] the process whereby one section of the drill pipe is unscrewed from another. **3.** *n* [*Oil rigs*] any promotion within the hierarchy of the drill team; this is developed from (2). **4.** *n* [*US*] [*Stock market*] when a share rises significantly above its previous maximum price or falls below its previous minimum. **5.** *n* [*Record business*] when a record becomes a hit; the magnitude of this success can be modified in regional terms as a 'national breakout' or a 'regional breakout'.

breakthrough 1. *n* [*Coal-mining*] See **stenton**. **2.** *n* [*Video*] the unintended transference of signals from one piece of electrical machinery to another, when a number of such systems are operating in close physical proximity.

breakup 1. *n* [*TV*] the momentary distortion of a picture. **2.** *n* [*TV*] a makeup process used to enhance the highlights and shadows of an otherwise bland and featureless face.

breast *n* [*Shoe-making*] the forward edge of the heel.

breast high *a* [*Hunting*] said of a scent so good that hounds need not lower their heads to it. See also **heads up**.

breathing 1. *n* [*Audio*] the motion of a speaker cone as it responds to low bass signals that push it to the limits of its mechanical compliance, pulsing visibly in and out. **2.** *n* [*Audio*] a fault whereby background noise appears to change in loudness as dynamics or directions alter; it is caused by poor **logic enhancement** or **compander** action.

breech wool, also **britch wool** *n* [*Weaving*] the short dirty fibres that come from the hindquarters of the sheep.

breed *n* [*Wine-tasting*] a distinctive quality stemming from a fine site, soil, 'cépage' and the skill of the vigneron.

breeder *n* [*Science*] in nuclear physics, this is a nuclear reactor which creates more fissile material than is consumed in the chain reaction; this material is used as a source of power supplies.

breezeway *n* [*TV*] a synchronising waveform used in colour transmission and representing the time interval between the trailing edge of the horizontal sychronising pulse and the start of the colour burst.

breezing *pres part* [*Horse-racing*] moving at a brisk pace, but still one at which the horse is under some restraint from its jockey.

brew up *v* [*Fleet Air Arm*] said of an aircraft which catches fire while landing; originally it comes from a description of a tank hit by enemy fire.

Brezhnev doctrine *n* [*Politics*] a term named after former Russian President Leonid I. Brezhnev (1908–82); as epitomised in the Soviet invasions of Czechoslovakia (1968) and Afghanistan (1979), and the continuing pressure on any liberalising movements – eg: Solidarity in Poland – in its satellite countries, the concept is that if a country is seen as turning against socialism, then this is a problem for all socialist countries to deal with, rather than merely for the government concerned. Thus invasions by the supreme socialist nation can be justified. This was paralleled ironically by Henry Kissinger's justification of the CIA's **destabilisation** of Chile with the words 'We're not going to stand by and let a country go communist just because that's what its people want.'

briar 1. *n* [*US*] [*Crime*] a hacksaw. **2.** *n* [*Logging*] a crosscut saw.

bribe *n* [*Textiles*] a length of cloth cut from a full piece of fabric.

brick 1. *n* [*Banking*] a bundle of brand-new notes. **2.** *n* [*Gambling*] a dice that has been specially cut so that it is no longer a true cube. Dice that have been shaved on one or more sides are known as 'flats'. **3.** *n* [*Navy*] any projectile: a shell, rocket, etc. **4.** *n* [*US*] [*Prisons*] a carton of cigarettes. **5.** *v* [*UK*] [*Market-traders*] to cheat, to defraud.

brick areas *n pl* [*Marketing*] sales areas that have been broken up for research purposes into those which have similar sales potential by virtue of their population, social groupings, amenities, etc.

brick by brick forecasting *n* [*Marketing*] the rough averaging out of views canvassed from a selection of salesmen and consumers.

brickbat *n* [*US*] [*Military*] absolute priority: anything that has been placed on the Pentagon's Master Urgency List of important national defence programmes.

bricks *n pl* [*US*] [*Prisons*] the street, the world of freedom.

bricks and mortar *n* [*Theatre*] a dull, heavy, leaden acting style.

bricks, make *v* [*UK*] [*Buses*] to engage in a variety of methods of defrauding London Transport.

bridal chamber *n* [*US*] [*Mining*] the area at the end of an underground tunnel where the actual mining work is taking place.

bride 1. *n* [*Religion*] the church seen as the 'bride of Christ'. **2.** *n* [*Religion*] the individual believer in evangelism; see Ephesians 5:25. See also **bridegroom**.

bridegroom *n* [*Religion*] Christ himself, for whom the **bride** is waiting; see Mark 2:19–20.

bridge 1. *n* [*Glass-making*] the structure formed by the endwalls of adjacent compartments of a tank furnace and the covers spanning the gaps between the walls. **2.** *n* [*UK*] [*Prisons*] one of the galleries in many of the UK's Victorian prisons that join two of the landings; these run at various levels around the cells in each individual wing. **3.** *n* [*Tiddleywinks*] a wink that covers two of an

B

opponent's winks. **4.** v [*Tiddleywinks*] to cover with one's own wink two of one's opponent's winks.

bridgeware n [*Computing*] any software or hardware that makes it possible to transfer from one computer system to another that is not wholly compatible. Bridgeware is often used to update an older model of a firm's computers to make it compatible with the current model. See also **hardware, software**.

bridging 1. n [*Painting*] the covering of a narrow crack or gap with a film of paint; this results in a weakness in the coating which may lead to cracking in the paint when it has dried. **2.** n [*Theatre*] the insertion by a director of extra explanatory words into the script for use in rehearsals.

bridle 1. n [*Clothing*] a narrow strip of material which is attached to the interlining along the roll of the lapel, to hold and control it. **2.** n [*US*] [*Painting*] a device used in painting steel which comprises a ring placed around the brush to keep the bristles intact and together. **3.** n [*Sailing, Ropework*] a span of rope used to attach halyards, fore-and-aft-sheets, bowlines, etc. **4.** n [*TV*] a rope brace used to help distribute the weight of hanging drapes.

Bridlington n [*Industrial relations*] a term named after the Bridlington Conference (1939); the principles established at this conference set up a TUC disputes committee for the arbitration of inter-union disputes between unions that were competing for the registration of the same workers.

brief 1. n [*UK*] [*Police*] a barrister (who has a criminal's legal brief). **2.** n [*UK*] [*Police*] any form of police identification, especially the official warrant card (the police ID).

brief treatment n [*Sociology*] treatment deliberately planned to have set limits, rather than be on a long-term basis; ie. treatment/inter-relationship between a social worker and a client that lasts, either through design or through the exigencies of the situation, a matter of weeks rather than years.

briefcase buccaneer n [*US*] [*Crime*] a white-collar criminal who specialises in fraud rather than violence; it refers especially to someone who interferes with international trade, alters documents, redirects cargoes, etc.

brig n [*US*] [*Military*] a military gaol, either on shore or, in the Marine Corps, on a ship. Thus 'brig time' is the duration of one's sentence and 'brig rat' is an habitual offender. See also **glasshouse**.

brigadier n [*Politics*] in Soviet use, this is a working foreman or the leader of a Production Brigade; usually a skilled senior worker with an excellent production record.

bright a [*Weaving*] second-to-top classification in the grading of the condition of wool fleece. See also **burry and seedy, choice**.

bright leaves n [*Tobacco*] a medium grade of tobacco leaves, superior to **lugs** and inferior to **good leaves**.

bright work n [*Navy*] any brass or other fittings aboard ship that need polishing.

brighteyes n [*Logging*] payday in a logging camp or sawmill.

brights n pl [*US*] [*Journalism*] small, cheery items, often of marginal hard news value, which are put into a paper to break up the larger stories and amuse the readers.

bring 'em near n [*Navy*] a telescope.

bring forward v [*Painting*] in repainting, to repair local defective areas with suitable paints, so as to make the whole area being painted uniform; then the overall final coat is added.

bring in 1. v [*Theatre*] to switch on a particular stage light or set of lights in response to a given cue. **2.** v [*US*] [*Theatre*] to open a new production in New York, after it has been tried out and revised in the provinces.

brinkmanship n [*Politics*] a term based on the declaration in 1956 by US Secretary of State John Foster Dulles 'if you are scared to go to the brink, you are lost . . . We walked to the brink and we looked it in the face.' A method of conducting international relations (especially between the US and the Soviets) on a level only marginally short of declared war. The Cuban Missile Crisis of 1961 was probably the supreme instance of the art since the word was coined.

brique n [*Cheese-making*] a group of cheeses shaped like a brick.

brisket n [*Dog breeding*] the breastbone or sternum; sometimes also a synonym for the chest or thorax.

briskets n pl [*UK*] [*Market-traders*] female breasts.

bristol v [*Tiddleywinks*] a method of play developed by the Bristol University Tiddleywinks Society: to play a shot with one's own wink, taking with it an underlying opponent's wink that thus remains covered.

britch n [*US*] [*Crime*] a pickpocket term for a pocket; usually defined as left or right britch.

britch wool n [*Weaving*] See **breech wool**.

British Funds n [*Commerce*] fixed interest government stocks; strictly only those which form part of the funded debt of the British Government and which have no fixed date for repayment; however by extension, it can refer to any fixed-interest stocks issued by the Government or by nationalised industries, whether dated or undated. See also **gilt-edged**.

Brixton shuffle n [*UK*] [*Police*] a shuffling gait peculiar to old criminals who had to make their way around the confines of the exercise yard at Brixton Prison, London.

B

broach n [*Manufacturing*] a cutting tool used for cutting holes that are not perfectly circular.

broad n [*TV, film*] a small, box-shaped floodlight.

broad gauge n [*Business, Politics*] the 'big picture', as used by major politicians and businessmen who prefer to talk of 'policy' and broad issues rather than the details that may well interfere with, if not invalidate, their more grandiose schemes.

broad masses n pl [*Politics*] in Marxist terms, those workers who are not actually party members, but who take their orders and their standard of living from the conduct of the party.

broad money n [*Economics*] the overall money supply of a country, reckoned in sterling. See also **M0, M3, narrow money**.

broad tape n [*US*] [*Stock market*] an enlargement of the regular-sized Dow Jones, Reuters, AP or other ticker tapes, which is available to individual brokerage firms; the broad tape is not allowed on the floor of the Exchange, where it might give floor traders an unfair advantage.

broadband n [*Business*] the system of combining several categories of employees under a single title in order to facilitate wider methods of selection and promotion.

broad-based a [*Taxation*] referring to taxes that are levied on all tax-payers, irrespective of whether one receives any indirect benefit from the levy or not.

broad-brush a [*Government*] roughly outlined, lacking detail, incomplete; used when describing policy or planning.

broadening n [*Management*] the process of preparing a middle manager for promotion by rotating him/her through a variety of jobs to gain experience in all of them.

broad-line strategy, also **full-line strategy** n [*Management*] the strategy of offering a wide range of variants within a single product line.

broad-mob n [*UK*] [*Police*] a term from 'broads' meaning 'cards': any kind of cardsharper, especially practitioners of 'the three-card trick' or 'find the lady'.

broads n pl [*UK*] [*Gambling, Police*] originally (c1780) playing cards; it is still occasionally so used, but by extension it now means all forms of 'plastic money': credit cards, cheque cards, cash machine cards and other valuable forms of identification.

broadsheet n [*Journalism*] a newspaper page size equivalent to that of a full-size rotary press plate; it is used in the UK to refer to the Times, Guardian, Daily Telegraph, etc. See also **tabloid**.

broadside n [*Publishing*] a large sheet, folded for mailing purposes.

broadtape n [*Stock market*] financial news and figures carried on the general wire services – AP, UPI, Reuters – as opposed to the exchanges' own price transmission wires which use narrow 'ticker-tape'.

brocket n [*Deer-stalking*] a red deer in its third year.

brod n [*Metallurgy*] in iron founding, a finger-like projection from the grids that are used to reinforce moulds or cores.

broke 1. n [*Paper-making*] paper that is discarded for a variety of defects – dirt spots, wrinkles, tears, etc. – which have developed during the manufacturing process; such paper is usually returned to an earlier stage for reprocessing as new paper. 2. a [*US*] [*Railways*] supplied with insufficient crews to fill vacant jobs.

broken 1. a [*Computing*] of a machine: not working properly. 2. a [*Computing*] of an individual: behaving strangely, exhibiting odd symptoms or extreme depression. 3. a [*Fencing*] not continuous, but kept separate in its constituent parts; said especially of a complex move in a contest.

broken amount n [*Stock market*] an irregular amount of shares, as opposed to the normal sums sold (50 or 100); these are harder to sell and thus require a special price to be made.

broken arrow n [*US*] [*Military*] US Department of defense Nuclear Accident Code, which covers these areas: 1. unauthorised/accidental detonation, no war risk. 2. non-nuclear detonation of a nuclear device. 3. radioactive contamination. 4. seizure, theft or loss (including emergency jettisoning) of the weapon. 5. any public hazard involving nuclear weapons, either actual or implied.

broken head n [*US*] [*Journalism*] a multiple-decker headline in which each line is set to a different width.

broken lot n [*Commerce*] goods that are offered for sale in a quantity that is smaller than usual, often in the form of damaged package goods.

broken mouth n [*US*] [*Cattlemen*] a sheep which has some teeth missing.

broken play n [*US*] [*Football*] improvised offensive play that takes over when the prepared play has broken down.

broken working n [*Coal-mining*] See **second working**.

broken-backed war 1. n [*Military*] nuclear: such fighting as might continue assuming that the **first, second** and **retaliatory strikes** had failed to settle the conflict and the survivors both desired to continue fighting and were capable of so doing. 2. n [*Military*] conventional: the continuing resistance by a guerrilla force after their side's main army has been defeated.

broker n [*US*] [*Road transport*] the owner-operator of a tractor/tractor-trailer who contracts either to carry freight himself or to lease his truck to a carrier by the trip.

Brompton cocktail n [*Medicine*] a pain-relieving mixture of narcotics, usually based on heroin or morphine, and often supplied in an alcoholic drink (hence 'cocktail') administered to alleviate the pain of those suffering from terminal cancer; it is derived from the Brompton Chest Hospital, London, where the dose was first created and used.

broom n [US] [Painting] a large brush used for covering maximum areas quickly on large surfaces.

brooming (off) n [Taxis] the refusal by the cab-driver at the front of a waiting queue of cabs (ie: at a railway station, airport, etc) to take a short, and therefore cheap fare; the driver 'sweeps' the fare back down the line to find some less discriminating cab. Cabbies generally deplore this sharp practice.

broomstick n [Logging] a long pole used to push logs into place in the log pond, and prevent their further movement.

brother n [Computing] See **sibling**. See also **tree**.

brousse n [Cheese-making] a group of Mediterranean cheeses made from milk which has been stirred while being heated; it comes from Provençal 'brousser' meaning 'to stir'.

brow 1. n [Coal-mining] a portion of the roadway floor that has longitudinal convexity. See also **sailly**. 2. n [Deer-stalking] the lowest tine of the horn of a stag and the 'antler' in its original form.

brown 1. v [Military] to bomb a city into destruction; it probably comes from the shooting usage. 2. v [Shooting] to shoot into the centre of a covey of birds, rather than to take a specific target; this usually kills nothing but wounds or harms several birds.

brown bar n [US] [Marine Corps] a second lieutenant, from the single bar that denotes his rank.

brown book n [UK] [Business] the annual report published by the Department of Energy for the government, listing details of the nation's petroleum, oil and gas industries, its current state, future potential and requirements, etc.

brown goods n pl [Commerce] TVs, hi-fi systems; the term dates from the 1950s when such items invariably came clad in boxes of ubiquitous wooden veneer.

brown, into the adv [Shooting] to fire into the brown implies an indiscriminate blast into the heart of a covey of passing birds.

brown job n [Air Force] air force slang for any soldier, from the khaki uniforms.

brown shoe officer n [US] [Navy] an officer who uses the navy regulations as no more than a guide. See also **black shoe officer**.

brown shoes n pl [US] [Navy] sailors' slang for Navy fliers. See also **black shoes**.

brown water n [Navy] coastal waters, as opposed to blue or deepsea water.

brown water navy n [Navy] naval forces which patrol the coastal areas of a nation's sea defence system. See also **blue water navy**.

brown water ship n [Navy] a ship used exclusively for coastal or river work. See also **blue water navy**.

browncoat n [UK] [Police] a junior examiner at London's Police Public Carriage Office, which administers London's black cabs; he tests potential drivers on their **Knowledge**. See also **whitecoat**.

brownie 1. n [US] [Road transport] auxiliary transmission. 2. n [US] [Railways] a demerit given to an employee for a violation of the **book of rules**.

brownie points n pl [Industry] merit marks awarded under an assessment of ranking or job evaluation tables; it mocks the system of awarding points to enthusiastic and well-behaved Brownies, the junior Girl Guides.

browning shot n [Navy] a term from the shooting use of **into the brown**: a shot fired with no specific target into the middle of a group of ships with the hope of hitting one of them.

browsing 1. n [Computing] the searching of files by an unauthorised user. See also **hacker** 2. 2. n [Commerce] a popular method of petty shoplifting: an individual, often a child, picks up something to eat or drink and consumes it, without needing to pay, before they reach the cash register with the goods for which they are willing to pay. See also **shrinkage**.

bruch n [Politics, Industry] a term from Ger., also adopted in Russia since the 1920s; it means a production reject which has to be scrapped.

brue n [Angling] See **grue**.

bruise n [Glass-making] localised surface cracks on glass, caused by impact.

bruised a [Book collecting] said of covers with their corners knocked and bent. See also **bumped**.

brunch word n [Linguistics] any word created by blending two other words into one, eg: infanticipating, workaholic, etc.

brush 1. v [Coal-mining] to disperse an accumulation of firedamp by fanning the air with one's hand. 2. v [Coal-mining] to remove material from the floor of a roadway to increase height. See also **dint**. 3. v [Hunting] used of a fox when it makes its way through thick undergrowth, thus leaving a good scent. 4. n [Logging] those branches, leaves, etc. that have been removed from a tree which has been felled and trimmed.

brush ape n [Logging] a logger who clears roads through virgin forest.

brush contact n [Espionage] a 'chance' encounter between a CIA agent and the person to whom he/she is passing on information. Rather than using a **drop**, the couple meet in public or semi-public places where such encounters should cause no undue interest.

brushback n [Baseball] a pitch that is deliberately thrown straight at the batter's head, in order to force him to retreat off home plate.

brushed a [Cheese-making] said of the rind of an

B

B

uncooked or cooked pressed cheese which has been lightly brushed (from Fr. 'brossé') during the course of its curing or ripening.

brushfire operation n [Military] a skirmish, an improvised conflict on a small scale. See also **brushfire war**.

brushfire war n [Military] a small war which, like a brushfire, flares up and then dies down again quickly. Such wars do not involve the super-powers directly – although the armaments employed will almost certainly have come from one or other of them – but like certain brushfires, they can spread and grow. See also **brushfire operation**.

brushing n [Weaving] See **napping**.

brushwood shrimp n [Catering] in Chinese restaurants this is a grasshopper.

Brussels Nomenclature, also **Brussels Tariff** n [Commerce] as agreed in Brussels in 1950, this is an international system of naming and classifying all goods in international trade for the purpose of standardising customs tariffs.

brutalist a [Architecture] used to describe a movement that emphasised the basic elements of architecture – space, materials and structure – in their most basic, unadorned, and unaltered form. The main practitioners were Le Corbusier and Mies van der Rohe, both of whom offered buildings with rough brickwork, open service ducts, exposed floor beams, etc.

brute n [TV, film] a large, focussing arc lamp of 15–22.5KW strength. Thus 'brute shutters' mean a 'Venetian blind' type of diffuser positioned in front of the lamp; 'brute spud' is a vertical stand for the lamp; 'brute turtle' is a three-legged stand for the lamp.

brute force technique n [Computing] any computing technique which, to solve a problem, substitutes pure power for any elegance of program or operation.

BSCP n [US] [Medicine] abbr of **bedside commode privileges**.

BSI key n [Woodwork] a workbench fitted with a frame on which is mounted a fine saw for cutting marquetry veneers.

BTA n [Advertising] abbr of **Best Time Available** an instruction attached to an advertisement space/time order: no specific date or place is required for the running of the advertisement as long as the newspaper, magazine, radio or TV station places it somewhere.

BTH&H a [Medicine] abbr of **boogying towards health and happiness** referring to a patient who is recovering well and will soon be discharged.

bubaladingi n [UK] [Military] any second-rate third world (usually African) state, considered backward and barely civilised by the British Army.

bubble 1. n [Commerce, Stock market] the over-enthusiastic purchasing of stocks in an otherwise financially weak company, the effect of which is to inflate grossly the market value of the shares. 2. n [Computing] a break in the **pipe-lining** process which halts the flow of relaying instructions. 3. n [TV] any bulb used for TV lighting. 4. n [TV] overtime; thus payments of multiples of the set wage are double bubble, triple bubble, etc.

bubble pack n [Commerce] a bubble of rigid, transparent plastic attached to a product package and which is used to hold and protect some form of sample or free gift.

bubble sort n [Computing] a method of sorting information by exchanging pairs of **sortkeys** beginning with the first pair and then exchanging pairs until the whole file is sorted.

bubble top n [Custom cars] a futuristic plastic top, resembling a bubble, attached to experimental cars during the 1960s; impressive if hardly practical.

bubblegum n [Pop music] extra-banal, easily memorable (and equally easily forgotten) pop music aimed at the pre-teen market, supposedly the prime consumers of bubble-gum.

bubble-gum machine n [US] [Crime, Police] the revolving flashing lights mounted on a police vehicle.

bubblies n pl [Navy] divers.

Bubonicon n [Science fiction] a regional convention held at Albuquerque, N.M.; it has been called this since 'Nightwings', by Robert Silverburg, centred the plague there.

Buchmanites n pl [Politics] followers of Frank Buchman (1878–1961), the founder of the Oxford Group Movement and of Moral Re-Armament (MRA). In Soviet demonology, 'Buchmanites advocate the repudiation of the class struggle and preach racism and other fascist theories ... through the notorious MRA organisation ...' (Tass, 1953)

buck 1. n [Building] a rough supporting frame, placed in an exterior or a partition wall, to which a door or window frame is then nailed. 2. n [US] [Car salesmen] a car in very poor condition. 3. n [Clothing] the lower, static working surface of the pressing machine which may incorporate the shape or contour into which the garment is laid. 4. n [Clothing] the pressing boards of a clothes' pressing machine. 5. n [Tailoring] a tailor's ironing board. 6. n [Film] $1,000,000; a rare understatement from Hollywood, using the usual slang for $1.00. See also **bar** 1. 7. n [Industry] a workstand upon which certain parts are constructed; it is used variously in leather, glass, aircraft construction, etc. 8. v [Logging] to saw logs into smaller, manageable sections; thus a 'bucker' is the worker who does this job. 9. a [US] [Military] used in combination as 'buck private' (the lowest basic rank) and 'buck general' (a brigadier general); in both instances the implication is that the soldier in question is 'bucking' for higher rank.

buck the tiger v [Gambling] in the game of faro, to play against the bank.

buck up v [US] [Iron workers] to support a given object from behind while it is being struck from the front.

bucker, also **cross cutter** n [Logging] a logger who cuts felled trees into shorter, more manageable lengths.

bucket 1. n [Basketball] a field goal. 2. n [Ten-pin bowling] a split where the 2–4–5–8 or 3–5–6–9 are left standing. See also **baby split, bedpost, Cincinnati**. 3. n [Computing] a sector on a disk file. 4. n [Computing] a capacitor whose electric charge is used as a form of dynamic **RAM**. A fully charged bucket/full bucket = a logic 1; an uncharged bucket/empty bucket = a logic 0. When the charge is passed through an array of capacitors and other electronics, they together form the 'bucket brigade'. 5. n [Medicine] a bedpan.

bucket and spade brigade n [Travel agents] passengers booking cheap tours to popular European holiday centres, especially Spain.

bucket and spade mob n [Air travel] passengers who take the charter flights to and from the popular summer holiday resorts such as Spain and Greece; a group generally despised by the air crews.

bucket brigade n [Audio] a variety of analogue delay line circuit in which portions of signals are converted into charges and passed along the circuit from point to point.

bucket broad n [Sex] a prostitute who will allow clients to perform anal intercourse.

bucket gaff, also **bucket job** n [Crime] based on **bucket shop**, this is a confidence trickster's description of any fraudulent company.

bucket shop 1. n [Stock market] an office where illegal, worthless or at best highly speculative stocks are sold by telephone by dealers who in fact own none of the shares on offer but speculate alongside their victims on the performance of the shares in question. 2. n [Air travel] an unlicensed travel agent with no bonds to a trade association (eg: ATOL, ABTA), who buys bulk lots of aircraft seats and sells them, cheap, to the public. Such shops are not de facto criminal, but the public has no redress if they do blunder and naturally, with their increasing popularity, the legitimate operators are campaigning to have them outlawed.

buckle n [Metallurgy] See **blind scab**.

buckra philology n [Linguistics] research into the philology of black American speech by white academics; it comes from 'buckra' meaning 'boss, master, white man', a term used (usually disparagingly) by Southern blacks.

buckwheats n [US] [Crime] in the US Mafia, a description of any individual who is being gradually stripped of his powers within the organisation; it is based on the slang for foolishness.

bucky a [Furriers] said of a skin which is considered tough and rather heavy.

bud 1. n [Cricket] the tie of a county eleven, when, as in Yorkshire, Lancashire, Glamorgan, etc. that county is represented by a flower. 2. n [Military] strategic, long-range nuclear missile.

buddie n [US] [Coal-mining] a small block of wood used to hold a drill trigger in place.

buddy pack n [Aerospace] the refuelling hose and drogue carried on certain planes to facilitate the inflight exchange of fuel between two 'buddies', ie. aircraft of the same type.

buddy system n [Computing] a method of implementing a memory management system whereby available memory is always partitioned into blocks whose sizes are exact powers of two.

budget n [Salvation Army] a weekly newsletter and instruction leaflet sent to all S.A. evangelical centres; it is scheduled for regular arrival each Friday.

budget day value n [Taxation] the value of an asset on April 6 1965; this is used for the calculation of capital gains tax in the UK.

buff 1. n [Film] a specialist or enthusiast who probably does not work within the industry but whose knowledge and involvement exceeds that of the average fan. 'Buff' has been extended to a variety of interests – computers, DIY, etc – with the same meaning. 2. a [Film] for specialists, and enthusiasts only, as in 'The buff National Film Theatre . . .' 3. v [US] [Medicine] this comes from the standard use of 'buff up' meaning 'to polish, to smarten'; it therefore means to check out and smarten up a patient, to run all necessary tests, to put charts in perfect order, prescribe drugs, insert intravenous drips, etc. Such efforts are made both prior to the consultant's ward rounds and as preparation for a **turf** to another ward or department.

buffalo n [Navy] See **bootneck**.

buffer 1. n [UK] [Circus] a performing dog. 2. n [Computing] the temporary storage area, between the various parts of a computer, which helps to cushion differences between the operating speed and efficiency of the components involved and which lets them all work as efficiently as possible. 3. n [Navy] the senior petty officer in a warship and spokesman for the lower deck. 4. n [Navy] the chief bosun's mate. 5. n [TV] a permissable overrun, usually of no more than sixty seconds, which is automatically built into the running time of longer programmes.

buffer stock, also **safety stock** n [Economics] stocks of raw materials, foodstuffs, part-finished products or any other goods which are purchased when supplies are plentiful and cheap and which are stored for subsequent use. Such temporary hoarding, which is used up when supplies are few and dear, helps limit market fluctuations and maintain supply and demand at approximately equal levels.

buffs n pl [Salvation Army] carbon copies of letters sent from the SA International Head-

B

quarters; they are traditionally taken on buff-coloured paper.

buford n [Rodeo] any small, weak animal that is easily thrown and tied.

bug 1. n [Air travel] a white pointer set on the airspeed indicator to mark the required speed limits. **2.** n [Computing] any unwanted and unintended property of a program that has emerged despite the design of that program; it comes from telephone engineers' usage. See **bug 12**. **3.** n [Engineering] a machine for external welding. **4.** n [Gambling] in poker, the joker. **5.** n [Gambling] a steel gimmick placed inside the mechanism of a slot machine to ensure that certain (highly lucrative) combinations of the reels never come up. **6.** n [Gambling] a clip that can be attached to the underside of a table to hold cards that have been secretly removed from the pack. **7.** n [Horseracing] the five-pound weight allowance for apprentice jockeys; it is derived from the * that appears next to their names in the racing newspapers, which is known to printers as a bug. **8.** n [US] [Industrial relations] the official union label affixed to publications which guarantees that legitimate union printing has been carried out. **9.** n [Journalism] the press agency credit line: (AP), (Reuters), (Agencies) etc. **10.** n [Oil industry] an external welder used on oil pipelines. **11.** n [UK] [Printing] an asterisk. **12.** n [Telephony] any interference on the telephone lines for which no apparent source can be traced. **13.** n [Espionage] a clandestine electronic wiretapping or eavesdropping device. **14.** v [Espionage] to use a device as in (13) to gain intelligence.

bug buster n [US] [Medicine] a specialist in infectious diseases who uses antibiotics (**bug juice**).

bug dust 1. n [US] [Coal-mining] fine particles of coal-dust or rocks which come from the use of mining machinery. **2.** n [US] [Farming] ground that has been worked until the soil is the consistency of dust.

bug juice n [US] [Medicine] antibiotics.

bug light n [US] [Coal-mining] an electric lamp worn on a miner's headgear.

bug trap n [Navy] any auxiliary vessel or tramp steamer.

bug whiskers n pl [Navy] a beard that has failed to grow sufficiently to meet the standards laid down by regulations.

buggy n [Clothing] a lining from the neck downwards across the back of an otherwise unlined coat.

buggy rider n [Textiles] a worker employed to sweep the floor around and beneath the looms.

bugle bag n [Air travel] the inflight sick bags provided for the relief of queasy passengers.

build-down n [Military] the deliberate reduction of military (especially nuclear) forces; it is the opposite of the more common 'build-up'.

builder 1. n [Soap-making] used to refer to the mild alkalis, silicates and phosphates which are added to soap to increase its efficiency. **2.** n [Tyre-making] the worker who assembles the various materials that are needed to form the tyre prior to its being cured.

building block system n [Computing] a modular system that permits any assembly of equipment units to be augmented by the addition of further units.

build-up 1. n [Video, Film, TV] a sequence of graphic images appearing on screen, eg: the gradual assembly of a chart or graph or the introduction of a series of words or phrases, etc. See also **pitch, con-act**. **2.** n [Gambling] any performance put on by the proprietor of a gambling game to arouse the betting spirit of the **punters**.

Bukharinites n pl [Politics] these are named after N. I. Bukharin (1888–1938); the original Bukharinites were the supporters of Bukharin's foolish decision to interpret Lenin's qualified permission for some private trade to be carried on under the National Economic Plan (NEP) as a licence for freedom of trade. For this error Bukharin was executed in 1938 as having exposed the Revolution to 'the revival and development of capitalist elements'. Today's Bukharinites are generally 'right-wing deviationists', including the late Josef Broz Tito, President of Yugoslavia.

bulge n [Stock market] a rise in prices.

bulging fish n [Angling] fish not quite breaking the surface when rising.

bulk v [Commerce] to put together for economy and efficiency two or more consignments of goods for different addresses in the same town; they are thus charged for freighting purposes as only one lot.

bulkhead n [US] [Marine Corps] any wall, in accordance with the Marines' use of naval terms on land as at sea.

bulking 1. n [Building, Concrete workers] the increase in the volume of sand, and other granular material, due to moisture. **2.** n [Tobacco] piling the **hands** of tobacco leaves so as to produce uniform moisture between them.

bulky n [Merchant navy] a ship engaged in the bulk transport of minerals and grain.

bull 1. n [US] [Circus] any elephant, male or female. **2.** n [Stock market] a speculator who expects a rise in prices and, thinking on these lines, buys stocks in the hope of selling them again at a higher level. Thus, 'bull market' is a market in which prices are rising. See also **bear 3**.

bull buck n [Logging] the man in charge of those who fell the trees and those who cut them up after felling.

bull campaign n [Stock market] an attempt by dealers to increase prices by buying shares and persuading others to join their efforts. The aim is for demand to exceed supply, thus ensuring that the dealers will make their profits. See also **bear campaign**.

bull chain *n* [*Logging*] the large chain used to hoist logs up the chute from the millpond to the sawmill.

bull copy *n* [*Journalism*] early press copy, usually reduced in status as major stories emerge, when it is downgraded to **filler**. See also **bulldog 4**.

bull gang *n* [*Oil rigs*] labourers who do the heavy, manual work on a pipeline construction job.

bull nose *v* [*Custom cars*] to remove the bonnet emblem on a car and fill in the resulting holes, thus revealing the shape of the bonnet clearly and simply; it may come from the shape of the bull-nosed Morris.

bull of the woods *n* [*Logging*] the head of a logging camp; the overall superintendent.

bull prick **1.** *n* [*Logging*] a pointed bar that is used to pry a hole in a stump prior to filling it with an explosive charge. **2.** *n* [*Logging*] a marlin spike used to splice wire rope. **3.** *n* [*Logging*] a stick used to compensate for slack between the log trailer and the truck that tows it.

bull ring camp *n* [*Sex*] a brothel employing only homosexual prostitutes.

bull week *n* [*Industrial relations*] a week of exceptionally low absenteeism at a factory, and therefore of high productivity. See also **Monday morning model**.

bulldog **1.** *v* [*US*] [*Cattlemen*] to trip and throw a steer, as seen in rodeo competitions. **2.** *n* [*Education*] at Oxford University, these are the bowler-hatted assistants to the Proctors, the officials in charge of undergraduate behaviour. **3.** *n* [*Metallurgy*] roasted cinder, containing approximately 50% iron, that is used for lining a **puddling** furnace. **4.** *n* [*US*] [*Journalism*] the first morning edition of an evening paper or the first night edition of a morning paper. See also **pups**. **5.** *n* [*Theatre*] an iron grip used to fasten one cable securely to another.

bulldog bond *n* [*Commerce, Finance*] a fixed-interest bond issued on the British (bulldog) market by a foreign borrower.

bulldogging *n* [*Rodeo*] the act of leaping off a horse and then wrestling with a steer, the intention being to grasp its horns, twist them and thus force it to the ground.

bulldozer *n* [*UK*] [*Railways*] a locomotive that is used to shunt coaches in a terminus to prepare them for taking on their outgoing engine.

bullet **1.** *n* [*Banking*] a straight debt issue without a sinking fund. **2.** *n* [*Gambling*] in card games, the ace. **3.** *n* [*Gas industry*] a cylindrical storage pressure vessel, usually with hemispherical ends. **4.** *n* [*Publishing*] a small dot (.) used as an ornament, to introduce items in a list, etc. **5.** *n* [*Pop music*] a notation – usually a small black dot – placed next to an entry on the Top 40 record charts which indicates that that song is climbing higher;

thus 'Number Ten with a bullet'. 'Superbullet' is a record that has progressed at least ten places in a week.

bullet points *n* [*Video, Film*] any form of written information, captions, etc. projected onto a screen as a list, where each entry is preceded by a **bullet** or asterisk.

bullet vote *n* [*US*] [*Politics*] this is applicable mainly to those voters who have little grasp of or interest in mainstream politics; the intention is to vote for one candidate, whom one knows and approves, with no interest in any other, either in one's own or in a rival party. The vote is registered direct and fast – like a bullet.

bulletin board **1.** *n* [*Computing*] information placed on a computer-based message system, available to all authorised users. **2.** *n* [*Management*] an outdoor advertisement which consists of a large printed board, sometimes with mechanically operated louvres, which can rotate to display a series of advertisements.

bulletproof **1.** *v* [*Audio*] to design a speaker, amplifier, etc. which is so stable that it is immune to almost any normal accident. **2.** *a* [*US*] [*Law*] free of any legal loopholes.

bullfinch *n* [*Hunting*] a fence or hedge that cannot be jumped; horse and rider must force a way through.

bullfrog *n* [*Logging*] See **barney**.

bull-hook *n* [*US*] [*Circus*] an instrument used by the elephant handler to control and guide his charges.

bullnose **1.** *n* [*Building, Plastering*] profile of plain quarter round, formed at external angles. **2.** *n* [*Custom cars*] the customising of the bonnet of a car by the removal of all badges, trim and similar ornamentation and the filling in of the holes that are left.

bullock *n* [*Navy*] See **bootneck**.

bullpen **1.** *n* [*Baseball*] the warmup enclosure for pitchers and batters, situated just off the **diamond** and near the **dugout**. **2.** *n* [*Advertising*] an extension of the baseball usage (see 1); this is the area in an agency where the **pasteups** and **mechanicals** are assembled for the printer. **3.** *n* [*US*] [*Industry*] any company-operated accommodation or changing rooms used in logging camps, marshalling yards, etc. **4.** *n* [*Motor trade*] a used car parking lot. **5.** *n* [*US*] [*Prisons*] a temporary area used to hold prisoners awaiting transfer or interrogation either in jail or at a court or police station.

bull's eye **1.** *n* [*UK*] [*Railways*] the lighted part of the signal. **2.** *n* [*Sailing, Ropework*] a wooden thimble or block, usually of lignum vitae, with no **shiv**. **3.** *n* [*Marbles*] a ringed **aggie**, rare and valuable.

bullstaller *n* [*US*] [*Carpenters*] a second rate carpenter who covers up his deficiencies by a line of 'bull', ie. smooth talk.

bully beef *n* [*UK*] [*Prisons*] See **corned beef**.

bum 1. *n* [*US*] [*Meat trade*] a worthless animal, of no marketable value. 2. also **bummer** *n* [*US*] [*Cattlemen*] an orphan lamb that lives by robbing others of their mother's milk.

bum-bag *n* [*Skiing*] a banana-shaped bag used for carrying things while skiing, usually worn attached to the belt and positioned above the buttocks.

bumblebee *n* [*US*] [*Road transport*] a two-cycle engine.

bumblepuppy *n* [*Cards*] in bridge, this is a game played at random with neither rhyme, reason nor sensible planning.

bummaree *n* [*UK*] [*Meat trade*] a licensed porter at London's Smithfield meat market.

bummer *n* [*Logging*] a small truck with two low wheels and a long pole, used for skidding logs.

bumming *n* [*US*] [*Crime*] a white-collar crime whereby an individual writes a company cheque to his/her own account and then destroys the cancelled cheque when it returns with the company bank statement.

bump 1. *v* [*Air travel*] when a passenger's flight has been cancelled due to over-booking, the passenger is 'bumped' as soon as possible onto the next available flight. 2. *v* [*US*] [*Car salesmen*] to obtain more payments from a customer than he expected to make. 3. *v* [*US*] [*Music*] See **jump 7**. 4. *v* [*US*] [*Business, Industry*] to exercise one's seniority by taking the job of a younger employee. 5. *v* [*Science*] in chemistry this is to give off vapour intermittently and with almost explosive violence. 6. *n* [*Mining*] a sudden and heavy release of strain energy in the major body of rock surrounding a mine working, resulting in displacement of the strata.

bump steer *n* [*Cars*] a defect in the suspension system which causes the car to be momentarily steered off course when it hits a bump in the road.

bump stops *n pl* [*Cars*] devices which limit the upward movement of the suspension, especially after landing hard from a severe bump; they are usually made out of rubber.

bump-and-run 1. [*US*] [*Crime*] a mugging technique requiring two muggers: one knocks the victim down, the other grabs the bag or wallet and then they run off in opposite directions. 2. [*US*] [*Football*] the legal blocking of a defensive back, consisting of one bodily contact by an eligible pass receiver at the start of that receiver's downfield run.

bumped *a* [*Book collecting*] said of a book with the corners of its covers knocked or bent. See also **bruised**.

bumper *n* [*US*] [*Police*] the stall in a team of pickpockets, who jostles and generally interferes with the victim, but does not actually pick the pocket.

bumping 1. *n* [*Management*] the downgrading of a previously senior employee by giving him the job of a junior who has resigned or been sacked. 2. *n* [*Management*] improving one's own position by using one's seniority to take over the job of a junior and absorbing that job into one's own.

bumping heads *n pl* [*US*] [*Journalism*] two similar headlines side by side. See also **tombstone 2**.

bunce 1. *n* [*UK*] [*Market-traders*] profits. 2. *v* [*UK*] [*Market-traders*] to over-charge.

bunch *n* [*Tobacco*] crushed or shredded filler leaves pressed together to form the inner part of a cigar, around which binder tobacco leaves are rolled.

bunch and crunch *n* [*US*] [*Traffic controllers*] (Detroit use) a danger to vehicles on icy, slippery roads; the image is of cars sliding into each other causing multiple pileups.

bunch grabber *n* [*Tobacco*] the cigar maker who prepares the filler for the cigar before it is finished.

bunch of bastards *n* [*UK*] [*Fire brigade*] a badly tangled hosepipe, twisted and trodden into knots.

bunch of knitting *n* [*Navy*] a group of clumsy individuals.

bunching 1. *n* [*US*] [*Stock market*] the combining of a number of orders for round lots of shares for execution on the floor of an exchange at the same time. 2. *n* [*US*] [*Stock market*] a pattern that occurs on the ticker tape when a series of trades in the same security appear consecutively.

bunching, also **felting**, **matting** 3. *n* [*Furriers*] a situation – caused by high temperatures, pressure or moisture – when the fur fibres become tangled and thus virtually unusable.

bunco *n* [*Police*] fraud, often card-sharping or allied confidence tricks.

bunco-steerer *n* [*Police*] a **shill** who persuades a potential victim to join in a fraudulent scheme or confidence trick.

bundle *n* [*US*] [*Garment trade*] a work assignment; thus 'bundle grabber' is a worker who tries to grab more than a fair share of the available work.

bundle of sticks *n* [*Angling*] the fishing rod.

bundled software *n* [*Computing*] the practice of packaging a variety of free program discs with the computer hardware, in an attempt to make a more appealing 'bargain' product.

bundleman *n* [*Navy*] a married man – distinguished by the number of parcels he carries ashore when arriving on leave.

bundwall *n* [*Oil rigs*] a concrete or earth wall that surrounds crude oil or refined product storage tanks; it is designed to hold the tank contents should a rupture or major leak occur. It is also used for the temporary wall surrounding the building of a rig platform; when the platform is complete the bundwall is broken and the sea enters to let the rig float.

bung 1. *n* [*Angling*] a cork float used for pike fishing. 2. *n* [*Ceramics*] a pile of plates or similar ware. 3. *n* [*Meat trade*] a large sac between the

B

colon and the small intestine of beef viscera. **4.** *n* [*Docks*] a dock-worker who repairs boxes, cases, etc. **5.** *n* [*UK*] [*Police, Crime*] a bribe, given by a criminal to a policeman. **6.** *v* [*UK*] [*Police, Crime*] to bribe someone, often as in 'to bung X' (interestingly, D. Powis – see bibliography – defines this as 'a gratuity of an almost legitimate nature, not quite a bribe').

bung puller *n* [*US*] [*Meat trade*] one who removes the **bung** from the intestines for subsequent use as sausage casing.

bungle *v* [*Angling*] to make a bad cast.

bung-on *n* [*UK*] [*Market-traders*] a gift.

bunk log *n* [*Logging*] the bottom log on a truckload of logs. See also **peaker log**.

bunker *n* [*Politics*] this comes from the name given to the hard-core coalition of ultra-right wing supporters of General Franco (1892–1975); those diehards who wish to see a return of fascism to Spain.

bunnies *n pl* [*UK*] [*Sewers*] rats found in the sewers.

bunny dip *n* [*Sex, Entertainment*] a special method of serving food, drinks, etc. devised for the 'bunny girls' of Hugh Hefner's 'Playboy Clubs', which necessitated passing everything backwards on to the table so as to ensure that the girls' exaggeratedly cantilevered costumes did not spill their breasts on to the customer's table.

bunt 1. *v* [*Baseball*] to hit the ball without swinging the bat. **2.** *n* [*Baseball*] a ball that rolls slowly in the infield after contact with a dead bat as in (1).

bunting tosser *n* [*Navy*] signalman.

buoy jumper *n* [*Navy*] a rating, usually a diver who balances on the buoy and hooks on to the picking up rope as the ship noses into a mooring.

buoyage *n* [*Shipping*] charges paid by a ship's owners to a port as their share of keeping the local buoy system in good repair.

burble *n* [*US*] [*Gliding*] turbulence over the top of an airfoil; known formally as 'separation'.

burden 1. *n* [*Coal-mining*] the distance between the explosive charge and the **free face** that serves as a measure of the 'work' that must be done by the explosive. **2.** *n* [*Management*] See **overheads**.

burelage *n* [*Philately*] a network, usually composed of wavy lines or dots, which forms the background on which a stamp is printed and which is intended to increase the difficulty of making forgeries; it comes from Fr. 'burel' meaning 'spokes of a wheel'.

burger all the way *n* [*US*] [*Lunch counter*] a hamburger with everything available on it.

burger and make it cry *n* [*US*] [*Lunch counter*] a hamburger with onions.

burger D *n* [*US*] [*Lunch counter*] a hamburger with french fries.

burgher *n* [*Sociology*] a locally-based (probably small-town) middle-class person who is content to run a family business or to accept the status of a small professional practice. See also **spiralist**.

burgoo medal *n* [*Navy*] long service and good conduct medal; they were allegedly awarded to those who had eaten the most burgoo (porridge).

burger *n* [*Skateboarding*] a bad bruise or graze.

buried *a* [*US*] [*Car salesmen*] said of a car owner who owes more payments on a car than can be regained by trading it in.

buried in the weeds *a* [*US*] [*Bars*] said of a bartender who is very busy.

buried offer *n* [*Advertising*] an offer to the consumer that is hidden within an advertisement; it is deliberately made to appear as a free offer, but, when disinterred from the surrounding copy, will require financial outlay.

burma road *n* [*UK*] [*Railways*] the Leeds-Carlisle main line, a notoriously difficult and tortuous route, named after the even more unpleasant road constructed for the Japanese by thousands of British prisoners in the Second World War.

burn 1. *n* [*Aerospace*] a means of changing course in midflight by the exact firing, as regards both time and duration of ignition, of the spacecraft's rockets. **2.** *n* [*Sport, Health*] in **aerobics**, the pain barrier through which the cultist devotees must masochistically pass. The accompanying slogan 'Go for the burn!' exhorts participants to greater effort. **3.** *n* [*Video*] the surge of sales that greet the launch and accompanying promotion of a new title. **4.** *v* [*Computing*] See **blow 10**. **5.** *v* [*Drugs*] to sell poor quality, adulterated drugs; thus 'to be burnt' is to be the victim of such a sale. **6.** *v* [*Espionage*] to pressure a victim by exploiting any weaknesses and to use this pressure for gain; to blackmail for intelligence purposes. (Used in fiction by John Le Carré). See also **mole, babysitting**. **7.** *v* [*Espionage*] to expose deliberately the identity and allegiance of an agent who is operating behind a cover story; thus 'to be burned' is to be exposed, to have one's cover blown. **8.** *v* [*Journalism*] to scoop, to embarrass conspicuously the professional opposition. **9.** *v* [*Rowing*] to increase pressure during a race.

burn bag *n* [*Government*] a special bag kept for holding such official documents that must, either routinely or in the case of an invasion, uprising or similar crisis, be burnt.

burn bread *v* [*US*] [*Prisons*] to make any general verbal attack on a fellow prisoner.

burn coal, also **cook chocolate** *v* [*US*] [*Prisons*] to have (homo)sexual relations with an Afro-American.

burn in 1. *v* [*Computing*] to employ a special method in which heat is used to weed out dud electronic components. **2.** *v* [*Computing*] to 'burn' programs into **PROM** chips. **3.** *n* [*Photography*] the prolonged exposure of an image or part of an image to light. **4.** *n* [*TV*] the after-image on a

B

video tube when the camera has been focussed for too long on a bright or contrasting light source.

burn notice n [Espionage] an official statement passed from one intelligence agency to another, either domestic or foreign, indicating that a specific individual or organisation is unreliable for any of a variety of reasons.

burn out 1. n [Government] an occupational ailment of frustrated or exhausted government employees; it is essentially a state of depleted emotions and mental faculties, possibly accompanied by heart attacks, ulcers, high blood pressure, etc. 2. n [Sociology] similar to the government usage, but occasioned here by years of fighting a losing battle against society's ills and often seen as utter disillusion with one's own efforts and with the people one is supposed to help.

burner 1. n [Air travel] a second-rate airliner, so called from its capacity to 'burn' fuel; it is usually restricted to shorthaul flights where economic fuel consumption is less critical. 2. n [Building] in demolition gangs, anyone who uses an oxyacetylene torch for cutting metal.

burning 1. a [Hunting] said of a very strong scent. 2. n [Metallurgy] in iron founding this is the operation of cutting steel scrap with an oxy-acetylene flame. 3. n [Metallurgy] in iron founding this is a method of repairing a defective casting by pouring liquid metal onto the defective area until it fuses with the original casting.

burning and trimming n [US] [Cattlemen] branding, earmarking and castrating calves.

burning the waters n [Angling] a means of poaching salmon by night: the poacher shines a light on the water, the fish rise and are speared.

burn-out n [Cars] preliminary static warm-up of dragsters which involves spinning the wheels in a patch of bleach to burn the rubber to optimum racing consistency.

burnout n [Finance] the end of the benefits available from a given tax shelter; this occurs when the investor begins to receive profits from the investment and tax must henceforth be paid.

burns! excl [Marbles] shouted by a player when his marble hits a stone; this entitles him to a free shot.

burnt a [Furriers] said of pelts that have, either through over-heating or as a result of a chemical reaction, taken on a brittle quality; such furs can usually be restored to their optimum pliable state.

burnt ale n [Distilling] See **pot ale**.

burnt edges n pl [Metallurgy] broken edges which occur during hot rolling, caused by overheating or burning.

burnt wire n [Glass-making] an imperfection in wired glass in which the surface of the glass is badly marred by oxide.

burn-up n [Science] in nuclear physics, the total amount of heat which a nuclear reactor releases per kilogram of fuel employed; it is usually assessed as megawatt days per kilogram.

Burolandschaft n [Architecture] a term from Ger. meaning 'office landscape'; it refers to the sophisticated office planning schemes developed in Germany in the 1950s and 1960s. An open plan office was created, with the various departments and their furnishings disposed according to the flow of paper and the movement of individuals. All this offered maximum flexibility for any necessary re-organisation.

BURP n [Aerospace] acro **Back-Up Rate of Pitch** NASA acronym for a particular type of spacecraft motion.

burr 1. n [Metallurgy] the sharp fringe of metal left at the bottom of a shearing or saw cut. 2. also **coronet** n [Deer-stalking] the swelling at the base of the horns, next to the skull.

burry and seedy a [Weaving] the lowest classification in the grading of the condition of wool fleece. See also **bright, choice**.

burst 1. n [Advertising] the concentration of a number of TV commercials into a short space of time for maximum effect. 2. v [Computing] to separate the sheets of continuous-form paper used for computer print-outs. 3. n [Computing] in data transmission, a sequence of signals counted as a single unit on the basis of a pre-arranged criterion. 4. n [Hunting] the first part of a run when hounds get close to the fox. 5. v [Hunting] to kill a fox during the burst.

burst edges n pl [Metallurgy] edges of steel sheet or strip that have ruptured during hot rolling.

burster n [Computing] a mechanism that separates continuous fan-folded paper into separate sheets; it may also trim off the perforated edges as well as the ragged edge left at the top and bottom of each sheet and sort multicopy carbons.

bursting off n [Glass-making] the breaking off of a blown article from the end of the blowing iron.

bury v [Journalism] to place in an inconspicuous part of the paper; it is often a deliberate device to 'lose' stories that an editor dislikes but is forced to include through various pressures – proprietor's whim, legal apology, etc.

burzhuanost n [Politics] a term from Rus. meaning 'bourgeois-mindedness', a phenomenon much disparaged in the Soviet Union; it is epitomised in the use of 'Mr.' rather than 'Comrade' and similar deviations from egalitarianism.

bus 1. n [Computing] a set of electrical connections between various parts of a computer's hardware. 2. n [Computing] a power line that conveys information to a number of devices. See also **trunk**. 3. n [Military] the stage of a nuclear **MIRV** missile which contains guidance systems and directional jets and delivers the various 'passengers' (the nuclear missiles themselves) to their various targets.

bus bar n [Electronics] a metal conductor forming a common junction between two or more electrical currents.

bus driver *n* [*Computing*] an electronic circuit, often in the form of a logic gate, that is capable of placing signals onto **bus** lines. See also **driver**.

bus stop *n* [*Air travel*] a holiday charter route; the term is based on the economic status of the passengers and relative brevity of the flights.

bushel *v* [*Logging*] to pay piecework rates for felling and sawing up logs.

bushelling *n* [*Metallurgy*] compacting wrought iron turnings, borings and scrap into a solid piece of metal by heating to a welding temperature and then forging.

bushing *n* [*Glass-making*] a small electric unit, made of platinum, with many holes in its base, used for the manufacture of glass fibre.

business **1.** *n* [*Cards*] in bridge this is the act of calling purely for the purpose of gaining a penalty. **2.** *n* [*Theatre*] those movements and gestures, both facial and physical, that contrive to make a role more 'dramatic'. **3.** *n* [*Theatre*] the day's or week's box office takings.

business agents *n pl* [*US*] [*Painting*] skins or settlings formed on old paint which have to be strained off when re-using it.

business art *n* [*Art*] a style and philosophy of art based on Andy Warhol's dictum that 'Business Art is the step that comes after Art. Being good in business is the most fascinating kind of art . . . making money is art and working is art and good business is the best art.'

business double *n* [*Cards*] a double in bridge that is intended to score penalty points; it is the opposite of an **informatory** double.

business entity concept *n* [*Accounting*] the concept that a business has a life of its own, since it is a corporation and entirely separate from the lives of the individuals who own or work within it. Thus all accounts must refer only to that business, and not to the personal finances of any individual.

business house *n* [*Travel agents*] an agency that specialises in the intricacies of business travel rather than in holiday packages; it requires extra knowledge of international ticketing, booking airline changes en route, etc.

Business, the *n* [*TV*] the television industry in all its aspects. See also **Industry**, the.

businessman's risk *n* [*Stock market*] an investment with a moderately high risk factor that is bought with an eye to its growth potential and capital gains or tax advantages rather than simple short-term profit.

business-to-business *n* [*Advertising*] trade advertising, industrial advertising: promotions for products that are bought by companies rather than for individuals.

busk **1.** *n* [*Building, Plastering*] a thin piece of flexible steel used for scraping/cleaning up/finishing fibrous plaster work. **2.** *v* [*Business, TV*] to improvise cleverly and creatively, especially when faced with an unexpected problem; it comes from the activities of street entertainers who work cinema queues, etc.

bust **1.** *v* [*Drugs*] although a general word for making an arrest for any offence, and often found in passive use – 'I've been busted' – it is not a mainstream criminal word (the UK villain or policeman will refer to getting or giving a tug, or a pull) and is used almost invariably by those who are arrested for drug sales or possession. **2.** *n* [*US*] [*Meat trade*] a ruptured hog, usually sold at a cut price. **3.** *v* [*Journalism*] a headline that is too long to fit the available space is said to 'bust' out of a page.

bust caps *v* [*US*] [*Marine Corps*] to fire one's weapon rapidly; thus by extension, it means to make a great fuss over something.

bust off *n* [*Radio*] a notation on the teleprinter printout which is made when an operator has made so many errors that he/she wishes to start again from the beginning of the story. The bust-off marks the point where the entire story starts again.

busted pilot *n* [*TV*] a **pilot** show that has been made and broadcast but has never graduated to the status of a full and continuing series.

buster *excl* [*Aerospace*] a radio command: fly at maximum continuous power.

busters, also **mis-spots** *n pl* [*Gambling*] in craps dice, a pair of dice that are marked with certain numbers only and so will only produce a limited number of combinations.

bust-out man *n* [*Gambling*] a **dice mechanic** whose speciality is the switching of crooked dice, usually **busters** in and out of the game.

bust-outs *n pl* [*Airlines, Travel agents*] ticket fraud: a travel agent sells a ticket to the customer, but does not pay the airline; once the agent's stock has been exhausted and the profits made, the company vanishes into liquidation, thus avoiding the debts to the airline. It is especially popular with organised crime syndicates who use front men to operate these variations on the **long firm**, whereby an agent could make nearly £500,000 on only 200 tickets.

busy **1.** *n* [*UK*] [*Police*] the CID, the detective branch; thus 'The Busies'. **2.** *a* [*TV*] said of a scene or single shot that is too full of action and/or visual distractions to make it either successful as action or easy to view.

busy air *n* [*Police*] police radio frequencies that are jammed with reports of crimes, inter-police communications, etc. See also **quiet air**.

busy hour *n* [*Telephony*] the sixty minute period at which time business traffic is at its maximum.

butch game *n* [*Sex*] from 'butch' meaning 'lesbian': a technique where a lesbian prostitute will persuade a man to hand over money but will not then permit him to have intercourse.

butcher **1.** *n* [*Fashion*] abbr of **butcher blue** a particular shade of blue cloth, as used for butchers' aprons. **2.** *n* [*US*] [*Garment trade*] a

B

retail store that specialises in lavish price reductions. **3.** *n* [*US*] [*Medicine*] a surgeon. See also **cutting doctor**.

butcher boots *n* [*Hunting*] plain black riding boots, without tops.

butchers *n pl* [*US*] [*Meat trade*] trim stock, well-fattened, popular with city butchers.

butcher's bill *n* [*Navy*] the number of casualties suffered by a ship in action.

Butskellism *n* [*Politics*] a term based on a combination of the names of R.A. Butler (1902–81) and Hugh Gaitskell (1906–63): a political situation whereby two parties that are purportedly in opposition achieve some large area of common ground despite the necessities of mutual party antagonisms. It was created from the names of the politicians concerned during their heyday in the 1950s.

butt 1. *n* [*US*] [*Prisons*] the final period of a term in jail; it may cover anything from a few days to a few hours. **2.** *n* [*Tanning*] that part of the hide that lies behind the shoulder and between the belly sides; the most valuable part of the hide.

butter-basher, also **butter-boy** *n* [*Taxis*] a new driver of a taxi-cab who is both an innocent ('butter wouldn't melt . . .') and also 'takes the butter' from his seniors' 'bread'.

butter-boy *n* [*UK*] [*Police*] a fresh, inexperienced young constable – 'butter wouldn't melt in his mouth.'

buttercoat *n* [*Building, Plastering*] the final soft coat of plaster applied to an external wall prior to pebble-dashing.

butterfly 1. also **bindicator** *n* [*Tyre-making*] a four-blade device that controls the pellets of rubber as they move through the machinery. **2.** also **finger hank** *n* [*Weaving*] a small skein of yarn made by winding a figure of eight on the fingers of one hand.

butterfly lighting *n* [*Photography*] in portrait photography the placing of the main light source so close to the subject that it casts a shadow under the nose; this is supposedly ideal for glamourising pictures of women.

butterfly shot *n* [*Shooting*] an incompetent, unskilled, inexperienced shot. See also **tit shooters, foreshore cowboys**.

buttermilk 1. *n* [*US*] [*Cattlemen*] an orphan calf. **2.** *n* [*US*] [*Painting*] poor quality paint.

buttery *a* [*Wine-tasting*] said of a smell and taste, similar to that of butter, which is to be found in some wines.

buttock 1. *n* [*Coal-mining*] in some **longwall** faces, a short step in the line of face, and substantially at right angles to it, from which coal can be more conveniently worked. **2.** also **jib** *n* [*UK*] [*Coal-mining*] a small area of coal cut from the **tailgate** end of the face by a stable machine to give purchase to the main coal-cutting machine.

butt-off *v* [*Logging*] to cut a defective portion from a log, usually from the base or 'butt' end.

button 1. *n* [*Aerospace*] the extreme downwind end of a usable runway. **2.** *n* [*Angling*] a rubber button affixed to the butt end of the rod to stop it chafing the hand or body. **3.** *n* [*Fencing*] the safety plate on the end of a weapon. **4.** *n* [*Sailing, Ropework*] See **knob knot**. **5.** *n* [*Sailing, Ropework*] a leather washer used under the nailheads when securing **stirrups** to the yardarms. **6.** *n* [*US*] [*TV*] See **blow 4**.

button chopper *n* [*US*] [*Commerce*] a laundry, or the proprietor of a laundry.

button her up *v* [*US*] [*Road transport*] to tie down the load.

button layer *n* [*US*] [*Industry*] a worker who lays reflective, ceramic tiles on the surface of roads and parking lots.

button man *n* [*Crime*] in the US Mafia, this is a rank-and-file member of a Mafia **family**, a 'private' in the criminal 'army'.

button mob *n* [*UK*] [*Police*] a large group of uniformed officers deployed in the street, either at a demonstration, riot or similar event.

button on *n* [*Military*] any armament or equipment that can be fitted onto a vehicle subsequent to its being issued to the troops, eg. a machine gun that fits onto a helicopter, etc.

button up *v* [*US*] [*Military*] to seal off, with three-ton anti-blast doors, the **NORAD** Combat Operations Center at Cheyenne Mountain, Colorado. Formerly a secure, **hardened** site, the increased accuracy of modern missiles has made even this site vulnerable.

buttoner *n* [*UK*] [*Crime, Police*] in **three-card monte** this is the assistant who 'steers' victims into the game; in general it is anyone who persuades suckers to put up their money. See also **bunco-steerer**.

buttonhole *n* [*Medicine*] a small, straight opening in an organ or any other part of the body.

buttonhook *n* [*US*] [*Football*] a pass pattern in which an intended receiver runs downfield (away from the passer), then pivots abruptly and faces, or returns a few steps towards, the passer.

buttons 1. *n pl* [*US*] [*Hotels*] tips from the guests. **2.** *n* [*Scientology*] any sensitive material which may be used to condition, control and possibly blackmail a Church member; it comes from slang 'push one's buttons' meaning to work on a person's feelings.

butty *n* [*Coal-mining*] a small contractor who is paid by the mine-owners or managers to undertake a job; those men employed to do this work form the 'butty-gang'; the whole operation is the 'butty system'.

buy *v* [*Gambling*] to lay heavy odds on a favourite horse.

buy a bull *v* [*Stock market*] to buy shares in the hope that they will rise in price.

buy earnings *v* [*Stock market*] to invest money by buying stocks in a company that currently offers a low yield, but which has a good record of growth and which is expected to improve its yield in time.

buy in 1. *v* [*Stock market*] to cover up or **close out** a **short** position; a procedure used in order to obtain the delivery of securities which have not been forthcoming after a reasonable time. 2. *v* [*Business*] used of a new recruit to a firm who accepts unconditionally and enthusiastically a complete commitment to all the tenets and aspirations of that firm's style and operations. 3. *v* [*US*] [*Military*] a contractor 'buys in' to a contract by deliberately making a bid he knows to be too low. Once this bid has been made and accepted it is rarely difficult to persuade the Pentagon to reassess the costs on a realistic, or even grossly profitable level. Thus it is possible for a firm to obtain a contract with a bid for say $1.9bn, and have the final costs paid at $3.9bn.

buy off the page *v* [*Theatre*] to buy a script as such, simply on its own merits, before any **angel**, star or director has shown any interest in the property. Neither on Broadway nor in the West End is this a common occurrence.

buy on close *v* [*Stock market*] to buy at the end of the trading session at a price within the closing range. Thus to 'buy on opening' means exactly the opposite.

buy on the bad news *v* [*US*] [*Stock market*] a buying philosophy that regards the announcement of bad news as a sign that shares will reach a new low, and that they should be bought at this low, since they must soon recover. See also **bottom fisher**.

buy round 1. *v* [*Commerce*] to buy directly from a manufacturer or importer, excluding the middleman. 2. *v* [*Commerce*] to employ any system of obtaining goods more cheaply than the accepted means of supply.

buy the rack *v* [*Gambling*] in horse-race betting, this is to bet on every possible combination of horses that might make up the daily **double**. This goes back to the era when the tickets for each of these combinations were printed up before the race and placed in racks by bookmakers for the bettors to choose. The bettor buying the rack could thus take one of each ticket. It is only used figuratively in the present days of machines.

buyback *n* [*Oil industry*] an oil company's purchase of the oil produced by its own wells; the oil is claimed by the government of the country in which the wells are situated as its share of the total extracted.

buy-back price *n* [*Oil rigs*] the price that an oil company pays to a state for the oil which the company produces but which still belongs to that state.

buybacks *n pl* [*Industrial relations*] reductions in benefits and increases in productivity that are conceded by unions in return for certain financial gains. See also **givebacks, takeaways**.

buyer, also **fence** *n* [*Police*] the receiver of stolen goods.

buyers' inflation *n* [*Economics*] inflation in which the departure from stability originated on the demand side, with buyers demanding more of the nation's output at every level of prices. See also **demand-pull inflation**.

buyers over *n pl* [*Stock market*] a market situation where selling is slow and there are few or no sellers, and so more buyers than can find trade.

buy-off 1. *n* [*Business*] the act of purchasing all rights to a product or a service. It is often performed because the product or service rivals one's own equivalent and it is easier to buy it outright and thus remove a potential rival from the market than risk the public preferring it to one's own offering. 2. *n* [*Entertainment*] a person who has been paid in full: an actor or writer who prefers to accept a flat fee paid immediately, rather than defer the full payment and gain further income from royalties over a longer period.

buy-out *n* [*Business*] the purchase of the entire existing stock of a product.

buzz *n* [*Computing*] a program that runs into very tight loops, endlessly reduplicating itself with no apparent chance of breaking out of the repetition.

buzz group *n* [*Management*] a small group or syndicate formed for the intensive study of a specific problem, which is to be considered within the context of a larger topic.

buzz track *n* [*TV*] 30 seconds of silence recorded on location after an interview is complete; this silence can be used during editing to cover any small gaps with the correct texture of sound.

buzzard *n* [*Golf*] two strokes over par for a hole.

buzzard-head *n* [*US*] [*Cattlemen*] a bad-tempered or seriously ill range horse.

buzzard-wings *n pl* [*US*] [*Cattlemen*] See **batwings**.

by *adv* [*Horse-racing*] Horse B by Horse Y, denotes the horse's sire. See also **out of**.

byework *n* [*Coal-mining*] work that is not directly productive of coal.

by-line *n* [*Journalism*] the name of a story's writer/reporter set above or below the story in the newspaper: 'By X.Y.'

byte *n* [*Computing*] a group of eight consecutive bits which are considered by the computer as a single unit. See also **bit 1, nybble**.

B

C

C *n* [*Government*] abbr of **Commander of the British Empire**. See also **K**.

c. *Lat. abbr* [*Medicine*] prescription notation meaning 'with'.

C battery *n* [*Electronics*] a battery used to maintain the potential of a grid-controlled electron tube at a desired value, constant except for signals imposed upon it. See also **A battery, B battery**.

C licence *n* [*UK*] [*Road transport*] formal permission under the Road Transport Act (1960) for road transport companies to act as general carriers; a C licence is for those who carry only their own goods. See also **A licence, B licence**.

C ring *n* [*Military*] a circular area centred on **ground zero** in which the **overpressure** is measured at 1.5–6psi; in this area blast could cause lethal flying missiles, such as shards of shattered glass. See also **A ring, B ring**.

C$ *n* [*Finance*] See **constant dollars**.

C1, C2 *n* [*Market research, Statistics*] socio-economic labels used to designate the white collar (C1) and skilled working (C2) classes. See also **AB, DE**.

C² *n* [*Military*] abbr of **command and control**.

C³ *n* [*Military*] See **C³I**.

C³CM *n* [*Military*] abbr of **command, control and communications counter-measures** the aspect of electronic warfare which is designed to discover hostile **C³** and take suitable electronic counter-measures – jamming, etc. – and then plan a systematised method of attack and destruction. One's own 'friendly' **C³** is assumed to be capable of defending itself with technology that is superior to anything attacking it.

C³I *n* [*Military*] abbr of **Control, Command and Communications Intelligence** in essence, the ability of commanders to manipulate their forces in battle; 'c-cubed' or 'C³' has, alongside of **'Star Wars'** become the central factor of US nuclear strategy today. The need for a commander to know what is going on and to order his battle accordingly is as old as warfare;. the increasing sophistication of military communications has only added technology to this basic requirement. C³I falls into three areas: early warning sensors, command posts and communications; all three are interdependent, but without the third, the other two are useless. Under Presidents Carter and Reagan the drive towards ever-more sophisticated C³I has been intense and critics point out that soon so great a computer will be required to co-ordinate it that once built it may be beyond human ingenuity to run, let alone to control if it malfunctions.

C⁴I *n* [*Military*] abbr of **command, control, communication, computation and indentification**. See also **C³I**.

cab *n* [*Air travel*] the visual control room overlooking the runways at an airport.

cab freight *n* [*US*] [*Road transport*] a woman passenger.

cab joint *n* [*US*] [*Sex*] a brothel whose customers are supplied by compliant taxi-drivers.

cabbage 1. *n* [*Garment trade*] in fashion, this is the manufacturer's extra on the wholesaler's order: the extra is cut from the same length of cloth as ordered, with great and economic skill, and is then made up by the cutters into extra garments which are sold for pin money to street markets. Originally, around 1660, it denoted tailors' perks, bits of spare cloth, offcuts, etc. **2.** *acro* [*Medicine*] this is formed from **CABG** coronary artery bypass graft, generally known as triple bypass heart surgery.

cabby *n* [*US*] [*Garment trade*] a low grade fur, which is practically valueless.

cabecou *n* [*Cheese-making*] a group of tiny goat's milk cheeses; it comes from Languedoc 'cabre' meaning 'goat', plus the diminutive suffix '–cou'.

cabinet bid *n* [*Stock market*] a means of avoiding unnecessary taxation which is available to investors; instead of allowing an out-of-the-money option to expire, under a cabinet bid the holder may sell off his contract at 1p and gain a contract note for this which can be used for minimising tax returns.

cabinet crowd *n* [*US*] [*Stock market*] on the NY

Stock Exchange, these are the members who deal in rarely traded bonds. See also **active bond crowd**.

cabinet security n [US] [Stock market] any stock or bond that is listed on a major exchange but is not actively traded; it comes from the filing cabinets where the records of such bonds are held.

cable up v [TV] to link a cameraman and his sound recordist for outside broadcast news reporting.

cabo n [Military] used in the French Foreign Legion to mean a corporal.

cabotage 1. n [Air travel] the right granted to any one country to control all air traffic passing over its own territory. **2.** n [Shipping] short voyages made between ports in the same country. It comes from Fr. meaning 'coasting'. **3.** n [Shipping] the action of some countries in forbidding coasting voyages by ships of a foreign country.

cab-over n [US] [Road transport] a vehicle in which a substantial part of the engine is located under the cab.

cab-rank patrol n [Military] a close air support technique: instead of taking off and flying directly to a predestined target which should then be destroyed and abandoned, the planes **loiter** in the air, waiting for **targets of opportunity** which are sent to them by ground control.

cabriole front n [Dog breeding] See **Chippendale front**.

ca'canny n [Industrial relations] this comes from Scottish dialect meaning 'caution, moderation'; it is the deliberate policy of go-slow in furtherance of industrial disputes.

cache memory n [Computing] (pronounced 'cash') a method of speeding up access to the (relatively slow) disk memory. The cache is a **buffer** which attempts to work out whatever material the program requires next and have it ready from the memory for instant use. Cache memory tends to achieve a 70–90% 'hit rate' accuracy.

cachet n [Philately] a printed, embossed or (usually) handstamped inscription or device impressed on a **cover** to denote special circumstances; it is used especially to commemorate or celebrate an achievement or event, and can be either official (when applied by the PO) or private and applied separately.

cackle crate n [US] [Road transport] a truck that hauls live poultry.

cackle the dice v [Gambling] used of a player who pretends to shake the dice – shaking the hand and producing suitable clicking noises – while employing a special grip that prohibits free movement of the dice in the hand prior to throwing them down.

cacklebladder, also **catsup** n [Espionage] a method, usually employing chicken blood which even after exposure to the air still remains red and fresh and resembling human blood, of bloodying up the body of someone whom an opposition target has been forced to shoot. The victim may not actually be dead, but suitably gory pictures of the 'corpse' will convince the target that he is now a murderer and as such ripe for blackmail and possible 'turning' against his own side.

cackler n [Logging] white collar worker, clerk.

cacozelia n [Literary criticism] a studied affectation in diction or style, that is found particularly in absurdly highflown prose writing in which the author's enthusiasms are betrayed by his ignorance.

cadastre n [Law] a detailed register of the ownership of land made for the purposes of assessing taxes on that land; the map made for this purpose is the cadastre; it comes from Lat. 'capistratum' meaning 'the count of the polltax'.

CAD/CAM n [Computing] acro **computer aided design/computer aided manufacture** the marriage of computing technology to design and manufacturing processes, especially in the engineering sector.

caddy n [Video] the plastic housing which protects a **CED** format videodisc.

cadence braking n [Cars] delicately controlled on/off application of the brakes in rhythm with the natural bounce frequency of the front suspension to help stop a car quickly on a slippery surface without locking the wheels and losing control.

cadet n [US] [Sex] junior or apprentice pimp.

cadey n [UK] [Market-traders] hat.

cadre 1. n [Military] a small body of troops assembled for specific instructional purposes. **2.** n [Military] to be cut down to cadre means to be reduced to key personnel only. **3.** n [Politics] 'a man who is able to understand the guiding principles (of communism) and carry them out honestly' (Stalin). **4.** n [Politics] a full-time functionary of the Party of government in China; anyone who exercises leadership in an everyday work or political situation. It is based on the Chinese kan-pu or gan pu (Pinyin).

cad's corner n [Navy] an area of a wardroom used by junior officers.

caesar n [Medicine] the delivery of a child by a Caesarian section.

CAESAR n [US] [Military] US code for the underwater sonar anti-submarine warning system that is positioned at the edge of the US continental shelf.

café coronary n [Medicine] death caused by choking while swallowing and which is often misdiagnosed as a simple heart attack until the autopsy reveals food stuck in the throat.

cafeteria system n [Industrial relations] the opportunity for a firm's executives (and, very rarely, its employees) to choose how they are paid; privileged executives can choose from a 'menu' of methods such as salary with fringe benefits, deferred payments, special insurances, etc.

cage 1. *v* [*Basketball*] to score a goal. **2.** *n* [*Building, Concrete workers*] a rigid assembly of reinforcing rods used to erect concrete pillars, etc. **3.** *n* [*Fashion*] a sheer or lacy outer dress worn over a slip or another dress. **4.** *n* [*Ice-hockey*] the goal area as defined by four uprights with netting stretched over them. **5.** also **chair** *n* [*Mining*] the lift which takes miners from surface to pit bottom and back.

CAI *n* [*Computing*] abbr of **computer-aided instruction** any form of tutorial designed to teach people the use of computers or the programs to run on them. See also **CBL, CMI**.

cake *n* [*Textiles*] an annular package of yarn used in the manufacture of artificial silk.

cake and wine *n* [*US*] [*Navy*] bread and water punishment.

cake course *n* [*US*] [*Education*] an easy course taken at college; it is a 'piece of cake'.

cake-mix solution *n* [*Politics*] a pre-created, ready-made solution to a problem, available to interested parties from government agencies who are keen to standardise aspects of their activities.

Calamity Jane *n* [*Gambling*] the Queen of Spades.

calculator *n* [*Logging*] the head sawyer at a sawmill.

calendar *n* [*US*] [*Stock market*] a list of those securities that are about to be offered for sale. See also **shadow calendar**.

calender 1. *v* [*Textiles*] to produce a flat, shiny, glossy surface on fabrics by pressing between hollow, heated cylinders. **2.** *v* [*Rubber*] to use a similar rolling process to (1) to produce rubber sheeting of uniform thickness. **3.** *v* [*Paper-making*] to produce high-grade printing paper, with a smooth, hard and glossy surface, by rolling the paper between heavy, chilled iron rollers.

calf *n* [*Deer-stalking*] a red deer in its first year.

calf-legs *n* [*US*] [*Cattlemen*] a horse whose legs are disproportionately short in comparison with its body.

California *v* [*US*] [*Cattlemen*] to throw an animal by tripping it.

California buckskin *n* [*US*] [*Cattlemen*] baling wire.

California crossing *n* [*Coal-mining*] an arrangement of plates and ramps, superimposed upon two tracks of rails and which can be slid backwards and forwards to allow tubs to go from one line to another.

California prayer book *n* [*Gambling*] a pack of cards.

California rake, also **California tilt** *n* [*Custom cars*] this is when the front of the car is lowered marginally further than the rear. See also **cowboy rake**.

California seam *n* [*Shoe-making*] a fancy seam, used on certain shoes. A strip of material in a contrasting colour is used to join two pieces of the same colour.

California twist *n* [*US*] [*Cattlemen*] in roping, this is a cast in which the rope is thrown with a single overhand twist, and with no twirling.

calk off *v* [*US*] [*Marine Corps*] to take a nap, to laze about when supposedly performing a task.

call 1. *n* [*Banking*] a demand by a lender for repayment of money that has been advanced on the condition that such a repayment must be made 'on call', ie. whenever the lender wishes, without need of any notice. **2.** *n* [*Stock market*] the right to demand payment of additional money due on partly paid securities **3.** *n* [*Stock market*] the option to buy a security or designated commodity at a specific future date and for a given price. **4.** *n* [*US*] [*Theatre*] a notice for a performer to appear, especially for an audition or a rehearsal. **5.** *n* [*Theatre*] advice to an actor that his/her entrance is coming up. **6.** *n* [*Theatre*] any notice for the whole company to assemble; thus 'treasury call', or 'train call' is when a touring company has to catch the train to the next town on the itinerary. **7.** *n* [*Theatre*] a curtain call is when the assembled company takes a bow at the end of a performance. **8.** *n* [*Undertakers*] the profession of undertaking. See also **job 3**. **9.** *v* [*TV*] used of a producer when he/she gives instructions to the crew through headphones while a show is either being recorded or is being broadcast live.

call a cab *v* [*Horse-racing*] the jockey's action in waving his free arm to keep his balance when he and the horse are taking a fence.

call a taping *v* [*TV*] a director does this when he/she assembles the finished programme by amalgamating on to one master tape live material, videotape, slides, telecine, credits, etc.

call boy *n* [*US*] [*Railways*] the employee who tells freight crews when they are due at the terminal.

call drink *n* [*US*] [*Bars*] a brand-name drink specified by a customer, rather than accepting the bar's own choice of brand.

call for the board *v* [*US*] [*Railways*] to request a proceed signal from the signal tower.

call norm *n* [*Commerce*] the optimum number of visits a salesman would make to a client if the circumstances were perfect; in the event, such an optimum is rarely achieved and both parties accept lower figures. See also **call rate**.

call over 1. *n* [*Gambling*] in a betting shop or during a broadcast of a meeting, this is the reading-through of the current list of available odds on the various horses or dogs. **2.** *n* [*Stock market*] the procedure of fixing the opening and closing prices in those exchanges where auction markets are operated.

call rate *n* [*Commerce*] the number of times a salesman successfully manages to visit his customers; a number of variable circumstances will mean that such visits are not as numerous as he might wish. See also **call norm**.

callable bond *n* [*Commerce, Finance*] a bond which may be repaid whenever a borrower wishes, once he has given notice; thus a 'called bond' is one that has been repaid.

callahan *n* [*US*] [*Police*] the policeman's nightstick.

callback 1. *n* [*Manufacturing*] the temporary recall or total withdrawal of a new model (usually of a car) after the manufacturer has discovered, or angry purchasers have pointed out, that it possesses some potentially dangerous fault. **2.** *n* [*US*] [*Theatre*] a request for a performer to reappear for a further audition.

call-bird *n* [*Commerce*] a lure used by salesmen to promote sales. In a shop this will be an extraordinary bargain displayed in the window with the intention of persuading customers to enter the shop, where they will be faced with more realistic pricing. See also **bait and switch selling**.

called for *adv* [*Book collecting*] used in catalogues to refer to specific details of a book's authenticity as cited by an expert bibliographer.

calligram *n* [*Art*] a visual pun; words drawn or printed in such a way as to form a picture or an image in an attempt to create a verbal/visual effect.

calligraphic painting 1. *n* [*Art*] the products of those Western painters who acknowledged the direct influence of Oriental artists on their own style. **2.** *n* [*Art*] the products of those Western painters who arrived independently at an approach comparable in many ways to the techniques of Oriental calligraphy.

call-off system *n* [*Management*] an arrangement for buying manufactured parts for use in a larger assembly. The purchaser places a firm order for a given quantity of parts to be manufactured over a specific period of time; the goods will then be delivered as and when the manufacturer requires them.

call-outs *n pl* [*Advertising*] small (possibly numbered) paragraphs set around a large illustration and linked by pointers to the various areas/points/aspects of the product which the advertiser wishes to emphasise.

camber, also **bow** *n* [*Metallurgy*] when the edge of the steel sheet or strip departs laterally from a straight line.

Cambridge ring *n* [*Computing*] a local area network (**LAN**) standard developed at Cambridge University which uses a coaxial cable or twisted ring topology and a transmission rate of 10 megabits. It has a message slot protocol.

Cambridge school *n* [*Economics*] a school of economic thought based on Cambridge University which emphasises **macroeconomics** over **microeconomics** in an attempt to create a system suitable for the needs of contemporary government. Its socialist leanings and espousal of the mixed economy have made it popular with various Labour governments and it is a leading promoter of current pessimistic prophecies

regarding the monetarist philosophies of Friedman et al.

camel *v* [*Government*] to act ploddingly, slowly and in a generally bureaucratic manner; it comes from the definition of a camel as a 'horse designed by a committee'.

camel back *n* [*Dog breeding*] a humped back.

camel driver *n* [*US*] [*Medicine*] a derogatory term used by US physicians to describe foreign, especially Middle Eastern, doctors working in their hospital.

camelback *n* [*Tyre-making*] an inferior brand of synthetic rubber used for creating retreads.

camelback body *n* [*US*] [*Road transport*] a truck with a floor curving downward at the rear.

Camelot *n* [*Politics*] an idealisation, especially popular in the mid–1960s subsequent to his assassination, of the brief Presidency of John F. Kennedy. Once the golden boy of American politicians, Kennedy has been increasingly revealed as one more corrupt, self-seeking mortal and this harking back to the mythical days of King Arthur and his Round Table is rarely used in any but an ironic sense.

cameo 1. *n* [*Film*] an important but by no means starring role played by a major film actor. The cameo is probably short, possibly only a single scene, but the performer will be well paid and the company can put another big name on the poster. **2.** *n* [*Printing*] any type face that appears as if it has been hollowed out of a solid background.

camera boom *n* [*TV, Film*] a high moveable platform that can support the entire camera unit.

camera eye *n* [*US*] [*Police*] a witness with a good memory for faces and events.

camp on *v* [*Telephony*] to hold a call for a line that is in use and to signal when it becomes free.

camp dog *n* [*Logging*] the general dogsbody in a logging camp, especially the one who looks after the sleeping quarters.

camp inspector *n* [*Logging*] an itinerant worker who claims to be looking for employment, but really wants only a few meals and a bed for the odd night.

campaign 1. *n* [*Glass-making*] the working life of a tank furnace between repairs, at which times it is necessary to let it cool down. **2.** *n* [*Metallurgy*] the working life of a blast furnace. **3.** *v* [*Horse-racing*] to prepare a horse for a forthcoming race.

campaign basis 1. *n* [*Aerospace*] the solution of an aerospace problem on a campaign basis implies the enlisting of an ultra-intensive all-systems-go community effort, reminiscent of actual war production, to beat the hold-up. **2.** *n* [*Business*] the plunging ahead on a project, and intensifying every effort, but without waiting to see how, or even if, it can be fitted into the overall scheme of things.

campaigning journalism *n* [*Journalism*] See **advocacy journalism**.

C

campus n [US] [Prisons] the grounds surrounding a prison.

can 1. n [Drugs] a measure of approximately 8 oz. of marijuana offered for sale by dealers. See also **Lid 1**. 2. n [Film, Theatre, TV] See **ashcan**. 3. n [Textiles] a large container – approx. 3.5 ft. tall – which receives the cotton fibre as it is produced. 4. n [Golf] the hole. 5. v [Golf] to hole the ball. 6. v [Science] in nuclear physics, this is to cover the fuel element in a nuclear reactor with a portective jacket.

can I speak to you? v phr [UK] [Police] the approach used by a villain, often already in custody, who wishes to suggest offering a bribe to a policeman.

can, in the adv [Film] a completed sequence, scene or entire film is said to be 'in the can'.

can of corn n [Baseball] See **rainmaker 3**.

can opener n [Crime] any tool employed in the opening of a safe.

can openers n [US] [Cattlemen] spurs.

can up v [US] [Skiing] to take a bad fall; it comes from slang 'can' meaning buttocks.

canal n [Glass-making] the part of a tank furnace used for the production of flat glass; it leads from the refining zone to the forming machine.

cancel n [Book collecting] any part of a book that is a substitution for what was originally printed; it may be of any size, from a miniscule scrap of paper pasted over a couple of letters to the replacement of several old sheets by a new set.

cancer n [US] [Car salesmen] rust, corrosion.

canch n [Coal-mining] that part of an underground road which has to be taken down ('top canch') or dug up ('bottom canch') to increase height or to grade the road.

C&F n [Oil rigs] abbr of **cost and freight** a contract in which the seller provides the product and the vessel and delivers the product to a nominated discharge port.

candies n pl [Custom cars] translucent lacquers, pearl paints and metal-flake: the three types of special paints used for the decoration of custom cars.

candle 1. v [Business] to check for quality; it comes from the process of candling eggs to check for freshness. 2. v [Medicine] to treat arthritic hands by bathing them in a bath of liquid paraffin wax.

C&U n [UK] [Road transport] abbr of **Construction and Use** the legal regulations which govern the construction and use of vehicles in British road transport.

candy side n [Logging] the crew in a **high-line** logging camp that has the best equipment.

candy store problem n [Business] a situation which offers a multiple choice of options; the image is one of a child choosing how best to spend its limited pocket money in a lavishly stocked sweet shop where no one sweet/solution suggests itself as noticeably superior to the rest.

candy-striper n [US] [Medicine] a teenage girl volunteer in a US hospital. There volunteers, dressed in red and white striped jumpers, help deliver flowers and newspapers, escort new admissions to their ward, help visitors with directions, etc.

cane n [Glass-making] a drawn glass rod.

cankers n [Textiles] dye spoilage or stains.

canned copy n [Journalism] public relations promotional handouts; these handouts are deliberately tailored for journalistic convenience, and often have only just been written by the reporter before they appear as apparent news or features.

canned presentation n [Commerce, Advertising] any sales or advertising presentation that has been learnt by heart and which can be used repeatedly; it is often the province of junior salesmen, freshly trained, who have yet to develop a spontaneous, personal style which varies according to the circumstances.

cannel coal n [Coal-mining] See **parrot 2**.

canner n [US] [Meat trade] a worthless animal, useful only for canning. See also **bowwow, tripe**.

cannibal n [Angling] a fish that preys on its own species.

cannon 1. n [US] [Crime] a skilled pickpocket or thief. 2. n [Espionage] a professional thief who is used by an intelligence agency for a special job, such as the retrieving by theft of an object (eg. a bribe) used to obtain information from a target, or the obtaining of compromising or revelatory material. Cannons are used when agency funds are low, or when there has been a 'moral' crackdown on in-house criminality.

cannon pot n [Glass-making] See **skittle pot**.

cannons n [Shooting] two birds killed with one barrel; they must therefore be in line.

canoe n [Gambling] in roulette this is one of the thirty-six slots into which the ball may fall to show which number pays off.

canonical schema n [Computing] in a database, this is a model of a data system which represents the inherent structure of that system; this model is independent of the software and hardware mechanisms that operate the database.

canopy 1. n [Coal-mining] a prefabricated roof used temporarily to give protection from falling rock. 2. n [Coal-mining] the roof member of a chock type powered support.

cans n pl [Media] headphones; this term is in general use in TV, film, radio, video, CB, advertising, recording business, etc.

cant n [Logging] a slab of wood cut from a log.

can't walk n [Commerce] merchandise that is ready for delivery.

cantilever n [Audio] the pick-up arm of a record player.

cantilevered verb n [Literary criticism] a term coined by Theodore Bernstein: a verb that would normally require an object or a preposition, but which is often and erroneously used intransitively.

canting n [Skiing] wedges inserted between bindings and skis to ensure that, however bow-legged or knock-kneed the skier may be, the skis lies totally flat on the snow.

canting arms n [Heraldry] a coat of arms that embodies a pun on, or an allusion to, the family name; eg: that of Bowes-Lyon bears bows and lions.

canton n [Heraldry] a square section in the **dexter** top corner of a shield.

canvas n [Clothing] a made-up interlining for a garment.

canvas-making n [Clothing] the sewing together of all the pieces that make up the interlining of a jacket or coat, either by hand or machine.

cap 1. n [Drugs] a capsule, filled with a powdered drug, usually amphetamine or barbiturate; the dealer will cap up his bulk supplies prior to sales and may well have **cut** them to increase quantity. 2. n [Hunting] a money collection made at the meet from those who are not regular hunt subscribers; it also refers to special collections, made for reimbursement of poultry killed by foxes, etc. 3. n [Tyre-making] the external part of the tyre which actual touches the road; the rubber used for this part is of necessity stronger than that used for the side walls.

cap line n [Printing] the normal upper extremity of a face's capital letters.

capability n [Military] the possession of a range of armaments and/or strategic potential by a nation or military force.

capability architecture, also **object architecture** n [Computing] computer design that incorporates both the hardware and operating system software of a machine; its intention is to maximise security and improve multiprocessing.

capability list n [Computing] the list of permitted operations that a user can perform on an object ie. a data structure in memory that may be manipulated by the total – hardware and software – system.

capacity to contract n [Law] the ability of an individual to make himself party to a contract.

capain n [Military] used in the French Foreign Legion to mean a friend; it comes from general Fr. slang 'copain' meaning 'buddy, pal'.

capcom n [Aerospace] abbr of **capsule communicator** the audio link between the ground and the men in space.

cape n [Dog breeding] the profuse, often harsh hair enveloping the shoulder regions of some breeds.

caped a [UK] [Railways] said of a train cancelled through lack of traffic or bad weather conditions; it comes from Ger. 'kaput' meaning 'done for, useless'.

caper n [Film] a genre of film involving a mix of comedy and thriller. It is often sympathetic to the criminals – likeable if villainous bankrobbers, conmen, etc – but no blood is ever shed and no-one, other than the self-righteous or kill-joy, is seen to suffer. And if, by chance, the script leaves our heroes heading for jail, it can be assumed that their wacky adventures will not be arrested for long.

capital fractions n pl [Sociology] in Marxist theory capitalism is divided into various smaller groupings which are both unified by their common economic base, but divided by their sectional rivalries.

capital functions n pl [Sociology] a means of refining the old simple capitalist/proletarian split in the face of modern economic complexity: capital functions are carried out by those who do not own the means of production but perform its duties, such as control and supervision of labour, allocation of capital resources, product design, etc.

capital goods n pl [Industry] goods, usually for industrial or commercial use, which will remain permanent fixtures and find continuous use on site over a long period: plant and machinery, etc. They are the opposite of disposable, short-life consumer goods.

capital logic n [Sociology] those analyses which attempt to explain social phenomena by reference to the needs or requirements of capital (rather than capitalists). Capital requires state aid in certain areas to ensure its survival.

capitalisation 1. n [Stock market] the amount and the structure of the capital held by a company. 2. n [Stock Market] the market value of a company's share capital, ascertained by multiplying the current quoted market price of its shares by the number of shares that have been issued.

capitalism in one country n [Politics] the concept, voiced in 1975 by US writer T. McCarthy, that there was a possibility of the entire world, except for the US, turning socialist. This refers to Stalin's concept of 'socialism in one country' whereby Russia was to perfect socialism at home before attempting to export the Revolution elsewhere. McCarthy suggests that the US should perfect its own system and let the rest of the world fend for itself.

capitalist roader n [Politics] a term coined during the **Cultural Revolution** to vilify those who persisted in maintaining Soviet-style policy and practice: a governmental elite, 'private' elements in industry, bonuses for production, etc. It comes from the Chinese (pinyin) 'Ziben zhuyi daolu'.

capitulationism 1. n [Politics] a derogatory Marxist term that refers to the political philosophy of those regarded as 'left-wing deviationists', ie. those who advocate a revolutionary line that is seen as less than adequately rigid. 2. n [Politics] in China, this is the act of capitulation, ie. weak-

C

ness and falling away from the Party line, which includes negating the basic principles of the Revolution, currying favour with the West, etc.

capo n [Crime] in the US Mafia, this is the head of a Mafia **family**. Thus 'capo-regime' is the second in command and lieutenant to the capo, responsible for the conduct and discipline of 40–60 **button men** or soldiers.

capper n [Gambling] a **shill** or confederate of the gambler or gambling house.

caps n pl [Medicine] abbr of **capsules** a prescription notation.

capsise v [Sailing, Ropework] to change or pervert the shape of a knot.

Captain Armstrong n [Horse-racing] a cheating jockey who deliberately loses a race by using his 'strong arm' to restrain his horse and thus stop him from drawing ahead.

Captain Copperthorne's crew n [Merchant navy] a crew composed of officers with no ordinary seamen.

Captain Hornblower n [UK] [Railways] a driver who uses his engine whistle excessively; it is named after the character created by C. S. Forester.

Captain Queegs, also **pill-rolling** n [Medicine] a term derived from the name of the mad naval captain in 'The Caine Mutiny' (1954 film); it refers to nervous symptoms that feature twitching, twisting hands, playing constantly with imaginary steel ball-bearings.

captain's cloak n [Navy] the metaphorical 'cloak' with which a Royal Navy captain may wrap himself in disciplinary matters; a captain has immensely far-reaching powers while aboard his ship, which date almost unchanged from the Naval Discipline Act, 1866.

captain's mast n [US] [Navy] a daily muster at which the captain deals with defaulters, hands out commendations, answers requests and generally takes care of ship's business.

captain's pigeons n pl [Navy] the Captain's responsibilities to his ship, his officers and men.

captain's protest n [Shipping] a document signed by the captain of a ship which has suffered damage en route and which details that damage and the circumstances of the accident that caused it.

captain's tiger n [Merchant navy] the captain's steward; this comes from the era when such servants were distinguished by a striped coat.

captive n [Technology, Computing] an advanced development of a particular piece of hardware, especially a computer, which has been carried out by a company for its own in-house uses, but has yet to reach the commercial marketplace, if indeed it ever does.

captive audience n [UK] [Railways] a lecture given to railwaymen during working hours.

captive candidate n [US] [Politics] a candidate who is supposedly acting under the domination of others. It is a phrase that is usually brought out when the opposition candidate is too popular for a simple frontal attack to have any effect; one challenges instead his/her immediate entourage.

captive market n [Economics] a market in which one supplier holds a near or total monopoly.

CAPTOR n [Military] acro **Encapsulated Torpedoes** a deep-water anti-submarine 'smart' mine consisting of a Mark–46 torpedo fitted into an 11 ft. long mine casing with accoustic sensors and a miniature computer. CAPTOR is anchored to the ocean floor in areas through which the relatively land-locked Soviet navy must pass when deploying for war and as such is intended to bottle up that navy as far as possible.

capture 1. n [Police] an arrest. 2. v [Computing] to retrieve information from the storage unit of a computer.

capture effect n [Audio] a phenomenon found in FM reception whereby receivers are able to extract the stronger of two overlapping signals without corruption. For this to happen, there must be a difference, albeit very small, between the levels of the two signals: this is the 'capture ratio'.

captured conversation n [US] [Police, Espionage] a tape-recorded conversation that has been recorded by a variety of clandestine surveillance techniques.

car banger, also **car-napper** n [US] [Crime] a car thief.

car card 1. n [US] [Advertising] an advertisement on a card that is displayed in any form of public transport. 2. n [UK] [Advertising] an advertisement on a card that is displayed in buses or London Transport tubes. See also **train spot**.

car knocker n [US] [Railways] an employee who works in the **yard** connecting the air hoses and cables between the locomotives and the coaches.

caramel 1. n [Science] in nuclear power, this is a form of lightweight reactor fuel, developed by French nuclear scientists, which uses only 8% of enriched uranium, well below the 20% that is required for weapons production. It is thus ideal for delivery to countries who genuinely do wish to use plutonium for peaceful purposes only, and not for clandestine military development. 2. n [Wine-tasting] a slightly burnt, toffee-like flavour, often found in madeira and marsala.

carbecue n [Motor trade] a device that uses pressure and heat to destroy an old car.

carbolic soap opera n [TV] a **soap opera** based in a hospital.

carbonzine n [Science fiction] a fan magazine made literally of stapled-up carbon copies.

carcass n [Tyre-making] the foundation structure of a pneumatic tyre, consisting of a number of layers of cord fabric insulated in rubber.

card 1. v [Golf] to record one's score on the score-card after playing a hole or a round; thus 'I carded 69 . . .', etc. 2. n [Logging] a member of a union; it comes from card-carrying. 3. n [Politics] a specific gambit or tactic used either in electioneering or in governmental bargaining, eg: 'human rights card', 'inner city card', etc. **4.** *n* [*Textiles*] an implement for raising a nap on cloth, usually made of metal and consisting of an arrangement of teeth designed to fulfil this task mechanically.

card cage *n* [*Computing*] a framework in which computer circuit boards can be mounted; such a framework incorporates connecting wiring and some form of anchoring for the board.

card, on your *adv* [*UK*] [*Theatre*] referring to free admission to theatres offered to actors who produce their Equity card. See also **courtesy of the profession**.

card worker *n* [*Magic*] a specialist in card tricks; similarly a 'silk worker' uses handkerchiefs, a 'coin worker' uses money, etc. See also **mental worker**.

cardboard bomber *n* [*Air travel*] a detailed, fullscale mockup made of cardboard and drawn up with every dial, level and needle in place. This is used to ensure that those training to be crews of civil airliners are fully 'cockpit familiar' before they even see the inside of an actual simulator, which can be 'flown', let alone a real aircraft.

cardboarding *n* [*Airlines*] flight ticket fraud: a piece of cardboard is slipped between coupons on the ticket. The airline's coupon is written at say 100, while the flight coupons are substantially more, say 4,000. The travel agent then sells the crooked coupons for half the face value, and only needs pass on the first airline coupon, at 100, to the airline. This practice is especially popular in Third World travel agents.

carded *a* [*Weaving*] said of wool fibres that have been combed out, either by hand or with a carding machine in preparation for spinning.

carding *n* [*Weaving*] the process of combing out wool fibres with hand cards or a carding machine in preparation for spinning.

card-stacking *n* [*Politics*] in propaganda, this is the device of loading an argument with strictly one-sided evidence, promoting one's own (war) aims and vilifying the arguments of one's opponent, often by using carefully selected facts and figures.

cardzine *n* [*Science fiction*] a fan magazine created by stapling together series of postcards.

care and control *n* [*Sociology*] a balanced method of dealing with individual cases, using either care to control or control to care, depending on the individual(s) concerned.

career *a* [*Military*] said of any officer who intends to make his/her career in the armed forces and to remain there for the rest of his/her working life.

careerism *n* [*Politics*] in Marxist terms this refers to the negative activities of left-wingers who put themselves before the needs of the whole Party; if convicted of such blatant opportunism, they can be purged from the party.

caret *n* [*Publishing*] the symbol ^ used to indicate

a point at which copy or other matter must be inserted.

caring *a* [*New therapies*] See **loving**.

caring professions *n* *pl* [*Sociology*] those professions that have risen as ancillaries of the welfare state, and particularly of the National Health Service, which are intended to 'care' for those who, it is felt, cannot help themselves. Critics of such professions believe either (from the right) that they are merely molly-coddling those who should be able to look after themselves, or (from the left) that for all the earnest ideology and undeniably sincere efforts behind the whole concept, there has been little advance on the traditionally patronising middle-class 'do-gooders' who help 'the poor' only in an attempt to regiment their individuality.

carl rosa *n* [*UK*] [*Police*] rhyming slang meaning 'poser' (from the eponymous opera star); it is generally used to refer to a fraud, either the con-man himself, or the scheme proposed.

carnovsky *n* [*Tiddleywinks*] the potting of one or more winks from the baseline – a distance of 3 feet. It was first performed by Steve Carnovsky of Harvard University in 1962; after making four baseline pots in succession in his first game he immediately retired.

Caroline nine, also **Carolina niner** *n* [*Gambling*] in craps dice, the point of nine.

carp back *n* [*Dog breeding*] a version of the **roach back**, similar to a **camel back** except that it is less pronounced in its arching.

carpark job *n* [*TV*] a short insert that has to be shot after the main filming is over. To save time and money it is not shot on location but, if possible, somewhere near the company's head office and as such all too often looks like (and may even be) the carpark. Such corner-cutting recalls the traditional Hollywood slogan: 'A tree is a tree, a rock is a rock, shoot it in Griffith Park!'.

carpenter *n* [*US*] [*Medicine*] an orthopaedist.

carpet 1. *n* [*Cricket*] the surface of the pitch and the outfield; hence 'a carpet shot', 'along the carpet', etc. **2.** *n* [*Golf*] the putting green. **3.** *n* [*Golf*] the fairway. **4.** *n* [*Military*] an electronic device used to jam radar reception. **5.** *n* [*UK*] [*Prisons*] a three months sentence; it comes from rhyming slang 'carpet bag' meaning 'drag' meaning a three months sentence.

carpet joint, also **rug joint** *n* [*Gambling*] a well-appointed gambling venue, which boasts, among other luxuries, a carpet on the floor.

carpet, on the *adv* [*Soccer*] referring to a ball that is rolling on the pitch rather than kicked through the air.

carpetbagger *n* [*US*] [*Politics*] the term comes from the influx of victorious Northerners keen to take advantage of the devastated South after the US Civil War ended in 1865, all travelling light – with only a carpetbag – and out for anything they could get. Currently it refers to a politician who

C

moves into a new area to gain power or status at the expense of the local politicians; such a one is often a celebrity who finds his traditional area of operations too crowded but knows his fame will smooth the new path.

carp(s) *n* [*Theatre*] abbr of the stage **carpenter**.

carriage *n* [*Logging*] in a sawmill, this is a wheeled platform that carries a log into the saw and back again.

carriage dog *n* [*Logging*] a steel 'tooth' used to secure logs on the carriage.

carried interest *n* [*Oil rigs*] a term used when a company pays for all or a part of a partner's costs during exploration or development; it is used especially when a company 'carries' a state that retains a participation interest in a field.

carrier *n* [*Audio*] a continuous high frequency (HF) signal used to carry audio information once it has been modulated into some form of storage or transmission medium.

carrot 1. *n* [*Tobacco*] a spindle-shaped bundle of rolled and twisted tobacco. **2.** *v* [*Clothing*] to brush furs with a solution of mercury and nitric acid in order to open the sheaths surrounding each fur fibre and thus facilitate the felting process.

carry 1. *v* [*Hunting*] land 'carries' the scent well or badly, depending on conditions. **2.** *v* [*Hunting*] said of hounds when they use their noses to follow a scent when running. **3.** *v* [*Hunting*] said of ploughed land which sticks to the feet of hounds or fox. **4.** *v* [*Hunting*] a horse or hound 'carries' a well-formed head. **5.** *v* [*Hunting*] when hounds are running well as a pack they 'carry a good head'. **6.** *v* [*Ice-hockey*] to advance the puck down the ice while controlling it with one's stick.

carry the bat *v* [*Cricket*] said of a batsman who remains not out at the end of an innings after the rest of the team have been dismissed. It is said of early or middle-order batsmen, for whom this is an achievement, rather than of the tailenders, who have fewer peers to wait out.

carry-on *n* [*Air travel*] any small piece of luggage that is carried on to the aircraft, where it is placed under the seat or in an overhead container and need not be checked in for carriage in the hold.

carry-through rate *n* [*Advertising*] in radio advertising this is the charging of a higher time segment rate when a broadcast programme covers two segments.

cart 1. *n* [*Merchant navy*] a bunk in a ship. **2.** *n* [*Radio*] abbr of **cartridge** a tape cassette on which commercials, jingles, station identification and signature tunes, etc. are recorded. **3.** *n* [*Video*] abbr of **cartridge** the enclosed container that holds the computer program for a mass-marketed video game.

Cartesian structure *n* [*Computing*] any data structure where the number of elements is fixed and linearly orderd; it is sometimes used as a synonym for 'record'.

cart-napping *n* [*Commerce*] the stealing of supermarket trolleys.

cartoon 1. *n* [*Computing*] a computer printout that forms a visual image or display. **2.** *n* [*Weaving*] a full-scale drawing of a proposed tapestry that is mounted behind the vertical **warp** on a tapestry loom as a guide for weaving the design.

cartouche *n* [*Building, Plastering*] a moulded scroll, frequently containing an emblem/inscription/figure; it is popular in the decoration of theatre box fronts.

cartridges *n pl* [*Salvation Army*] regular weekly monetary contributions offered in individual envelopes from SA members; presumably to 'fight the good fight'.

carve *v* [*Music*] to conduct an orchestra or band.

carve up *v* [*UK*] [*Law*] the defence and the prosecution do this when they sort out the agreed pleas, in a case involving an unusually large number of defendants, with varying degrees of alleged culpability.

carving *n* [*Skiing*] turning and steering using the edges and sidecut of the skis.

cascade *n* [*Audio*] any sequence – of components, circuits or stages – connected one after the other.

case 1. *n* [*Publishing*] the binding of a book. **2.** *v* [*Tobacco*] to put the correct amount of moisture into tobacco.

case goods *n pl* [*Commerce*] wooden furniture, other than occasional or novelty items.

case histories *n pl* [*Public relations*] See **success stories**.

case history *n* [*Advertising*] any files or documents that refer to the history/development of a campaign; it comes from medical use.

case officer *n* [*Espionage*] in an intelligence agency, this is the officer in charge of an operation.

case the deck *v* [*Gambling*] an expert and experienced card player does this when he memorises the deal and play of every card in a game and works out his play and betting on the basis of that recall.

case-ace *n* [*Gambling*] in poker this is the fourth ace to appear, after players have watched the other three dealt out.

cased *a* [*Book collecting*] said of books that have been bound by a machine that uses a mull – a glued strip of canvas – to hold together a number of stitched quires of paper. The bound sheets are then inserted mechanically into ready-made boards and their covering cloth and attached by glueing down the endpapers.

cased-handled *a* [*Furriers*] said of furs that have been removed from the animal by cutting across the undertail portion between the back legs then pulled forward over the head without slitting the belly so that the skin remains in one piece. See also **open-handled**.

casein *n* [*Cheese-making*] an important

constituent of milk, the part which solidifies during coagulation. During the course of ripening, the casein of soft cheeses becomes soluble, that of pressed cheeses soft and that of dry cheeses hard.

case-of-need *n* [*Finance*] a person named by the drawer of a bill of exchange as someone who may be asked for further instructions if the bill is dishonoured.

cash against documents *n* [*Banking*] a means of obtaining payment for export shipments whereby the exporter forwards the shipping documents to a bank in the port of delivery, with instructions to hand them over only when the bill of exchange has been paid. Only by paying this can the importer obtain the bill of loading, and only with this will the master permit the ship to be unloaded.

cash cow *n* [*Business*] any business that generates a continuous flow of cash; shares that offer a dependable income are similarly named.

cash nexus *n* [*Sociology*] this term originated in 'The Communist Manifesto' (1848); it now refers to the conditions of employment in many modern industries whereby the only link between employer and employed is the payment and acceptance of wages and both sides strive continually to gain the advantage regardless of the interests of the other.

cash register *n* [*US*] [*Farming*] a self-feeder for hogs; this is based on the premise that the more weight they put on, the more they will be worth at market.

casing *n* [*Building, Concrete workers*] the concrete that covers the structural steelwork used in erecting buildings.

casing up *n* [*Market traders*] the act of fruit or vegetable wholesalers who disguise damaged produce by rearranging it in its boxes before selling it to retailers.

casket *v* [*US*] [*Undertakers*] to place a corpse in a coffin.

casket-coach *n* [*US*] [*Undertakers*] a hearse.

cast 1. *v* [*Hunting*] used of hounds when they spread out in pursuit of a scent. **2.** *v* [*Sailing, Ropework*] to tie a knot. **3.** *n* [*Metallurgy*] the product of a single furnace charge tapped into a ladle. **4.** *n* [*Angling*] the throw of a fishing line or net.

cast off *v* [*Journalism*] this comes from the calculation of the number of stitches in knitting: it means to assess the space that will be occupied by a given amount of copy when it is set in type.

casting *a* [*Film*] as an estimate of a star's worth, not quite as celebrated as 'bankable', but still a reasonable guarantee of box office returns and thus worth offering a part. See also **bankable, tickets**.

castle *n* [*Cricket*] the stumps and bails; generally an archaic/romantic term, but still used in cricket's more purple passages.

castle beam *n* [*Weaving*] the beam across the top of a treadle loom from which **harnesses** are hung.

castle wheel *n* [*Weaving*] an upright loom of Irish origin in which the wheel is directly over the spindle.

cast-off *n* [*Shooting*] the line of a gun from muzzle to butt is not straight; when the butt is bent to the right, this is the 'cast-off'.

casual *n* [*Magic*] a performance at a lunch, dinner, party etc, rather than on the stage.

casual criminal *n* [*Criminal*] a non-habitual or non-professional criminal who commits perhaps only a single crime to satisfy an urgent or spontaneous need.

casual water *n* [*Golf*] 'Any temporary accumulation of water (whether caused by rainfall or otherwise) which is not one of the ordinary and recognised hazards of the course.' Rules of Golf, 1899.

CAT *n* [*Air travel*] acro **Clear Air Turbulence** a severe hazard to aircraft.

cat *n* [*Noughts and crosses*] a draw.

cat cracking *n* [*Oil rigs*] abbr of **catalytic cracking** a refining process which uses heat and a catalyst to increase the output of lighter products from some of the heavier oil fractions produced in the first stage of refining.

cat film *n* [*Sex, Film*] a pornographic film that features two women fighting.

cat scene *n* [*UK*] [*Theatre*] in pantomime, this is the penultimate scene, preceding the 'happy ending', in which the cavern, prison, etc. in which the characters find themselves is transformed into a fairy grotto or woodland dell.

cat skinner *n* [*Logging*] the driver of the big caterpillar tractor that drags logs out of the woods.

catallactics *n* [*Economics*] the study of the exchange of goods and services; it comes from Gk. 'katallassein' meaning 'to exchange'.

catalogue *n* [*Espionage*] a dossier, first developed by the STB (the Czech equivalent of the KGB), which contains compromising pictures of VIPs using prostitutes, entering and leaving massage parlours, porno 'bookshops', etc. Such pictures are backed up by information supplied by the girls, and the proprietors of the parlours and shops, and the dossier as a whole is useful when planning to **burn** a target.

catalogue raisonné *n* [*Bibliography*] a detailed and systematic classification of books, works of art, etc. which is arranged by subject, and includes critical and informative notes and other pertinent information.

catalytic war *n* [*Military*] a war between two nations caused by the actions of a third which precipitates it by acting as a catalyst.

catastrophe theory *n* [*Social science*] a mathematical system proposed by the French mathematician Réné Thom to describe a discontinuity or phenomenon of sudden change in a continuous

C

process by fitting the attributes of change into a geometric model consisting of dimensional planes that describe the change.

catastrophic failure *n* [*Computing*] any failure – such as a total power blackout – that renders the computing facility null and void.

catatonia *n* [*Computing*] a condition of suspended animation (derived from medical usage) whereby a system is **wedged** and will not work although it is not actually broken.

catch *v* [*UK*] [*Police*] to be assigned to the station complaints desk, where one 'catches it' from the public; it is similar to the US 'catching flak'.

catch a cold *v* [*Theatre*] used of a company which does badly during a provincial tour.

catch flies *v* [*US*] [*Theatre*] to steal scenes by continual facial and/or bodily movement that distracts the audience from the main action. See also **backcloth star**.

catch hand *n* [*Industry*] a casual workman who moves from job to job with the intention of getting the best pay and conditions and with no commitment to any one employer or career.

catch heads *v* [*Distilling*] to regulate the flow of **low wines** into the tanks where they are stored prior to the second distillation which creates drinkable whisky.

catch line *n* [*Advertising*] a note placed at the top of a page or above a piece of type to indicate its place in the overall design of the magazine, newspaper or the advertisement itself.

catch tails *v* [*Distilling*] to control the flow of the third and final part of the distillation process, after the whisky has been diverted into its tanks; this part will, like the first part, be of **low wines**. See also **catch heads**.

catch word *n* [*Printing*] a word placed at the end of a block of text to indicate the first word of the next block of text.

catchpot *n* [*Oil rigs*] a vessel inserted into a pipeline to remove liquid droplets which may be found in a gas stream.

catchword *n* [*Printing*] a word found at the head of the page, in the top margin as in a dictionary or other reference work.

catch-up *n* [*Aerospace*] a steering manoeuvre by which a pilot shortens the distance between his aircraft and the target.

categorically needy *n* [*Social work*] those who fall into one of a variety of set categories that will entitle them to some form of welfare aid.

catenaccio *n* [*Soccer*] a 'sweeper' defence, especially popular in European (specifically Italian) clubs, in which one player is used at the back of the defence to 'sweep up' forward attacks and loose balls.

caterpillars *n pl* [*Air travel*] people who are scared of flying and who refuse to turn into airborne 'butterflies'.

catface **1.** *n* [*Logging*] a fire-scarred tree. **2.** *n* [*US*] [*Painting*] a space on a surface that a painter has

not covered while applying a coat of paint. See also **holiday 2**.

catfoot *v* [*US*] [*Navy*] to carry out one's duties on board a submerged submarine with the least possible noise.

catgut *n* [*US*] [*Cattlemen*] a rope, especially a rawhide rope.

cat-ham *n* [*US*] [*Meat trade*] a ham that lacks the required plumpness.

cathead, also **cateye** *n* [*US*] [*Painting*] See **catface**.

cathedral glass *n* [*Building*] coloured glass, echoing the stained glass of religious buildings, which is used in houses, especially in the panels of the vestibule doors of older houses.

catholic creditor *n* [*Scot.*] [*Law*] a creditor whose debt is a lien or charge on two or more items of the debtor's property.

cats *n pl* [*Pop music*] those contemporary teenagers who enjoy 1950s rock and roll. They wear the US college styles of that era to look like yesterday's high school students, rather than Teddy Boys, who still dress as they, or their parents, did in the 1950s.

cats and dogs *n pl* [*Stock market*] low priced stocks that yield only low returns.

cat's cradle *n* [*US*] [*Gliding*] See **Bikle's baseball**.

cat's ear *n* [*Printing*] See **ear 3**.

cat's eye *n* [*Glass-making*] an imperfection in glass seen as a large crescent-shaped bubble; it is caused by undissolved gas.

cat's hair *n* [*US*] [*Garment trade*] fur felt before it has reached its completed stage.

cat's paw *n* [*Merchant navy*] See **darky**.

catspaw, also **gaul** *n* [*Building, Plastering*] a blemish in a plaster surface due to failure to fill in a small depression when tightening in and trowelling up.

catters *n* [*Tobacco*] a grade of tobacco usually used in cigarettes.

cattle call *n* [*Film*] a mass audition, bearing out Alfred Hitchcock's admonition that 'actors are like cattle'.

cattyman *n* [*Logging*] an expert river driver.

caught in the laundry room *part phr* [*Drug addicts*] a term from the Broadway Lodge Clinic used when a patient expresses lust for a fellow-patient; this is forbidden.

caught in the rain *part phr* [*US*] [*Marine Corps*] used when a member of the Marines Corps is caught in the open air when the colours (the US flag) are being lowered and is thus compelled to stand to attention and salute.

caul *n* [*Wood manufacture*] a heated sheet of metal or other material used in the manufacture of plywood or veneer to equalise the pressure and protect the facings of the material from extraneous glue.

cauliflower *n* [*UK*] [*Railways*] a locomotive with a crested front.

cauliflower head *n* [*Metallurgy*] in iron founding this is a feeder head (containing a reservoir of extra molten metal which can be added to the casting as required) in which the level of the metal rises as gas is created by the solidifying of that metal.

caunchman *n* [*UK*] [*Coal-mining*] See **ripper 1**.

causal explanation *n* [*Sociology*] the theory that one state of affairs brings about another; it is rejected by critics since no control groups can be established in these areas, and human beings are not simply objects and subject to totally dispassionate analysis.

caveat emptor *n* [*Law*] the principle of common law which holds that if purchased goods later turn out to be defective the purchaser has no recourse against the seller unless there exist warranties claiming the goods have no such defects; it comes from Lat. 'let the buyer beware'.

caveman 1. *n* [*Computing*] a machine, program or programmer who is badly behind the times; an antique. **2.** *n* [*Glass-making*] a general labourer, usually working under a glass furnace.

cavetto *n* [*Building, Plastering*] a moulding section: a quarter circle, concave profile.

caviare *n* [*Communications*] a passage of text that has been censored and blocked out by overprinting; the practice originated in the Russian censorship departments. The resulting pattern of white lines and black diamonds vaguely resembles caviare spread on bread and butter.

caving *n* [*Coal-mining*] the controlled collapse of roof strata behind the supports of a working face.

CAVU *part phr* [*Flying*] acro **ceiling and visibility unlimited** excellent weather. See also **ceiling 1**.

C.B. *n* [*Commerce*] abbr of **come back** a customer who looks at merchandise but buys nothing, promising to return later.

CBL *n* [*Computing*] abbr of **computer-based learning**.

CBMs *n pl* [*Military*] abbr of **Confidence Building Measures** mutually agreed measures designed to eliminate the inevitable distrust endemic to arms limitations agreements between the superpowers. CBMs aim to help verify that agreements are actually being maintained by both sides. Methods of achieving this include the establishment of committees and the delivery from one side to the other of inventories of those weapons that are subject to an agreement.

c.b.u. *a* [*Commerce*] abbr of **completely built up** this refers to goods, especially machines, which are fully assembled and offered for sale ready for immediate use by the buyer. See also **c.k.d**.

CC *n* [*Medicine*] abbr of **chief complaint**.

ccw *part phr* [*US*] [*Police*] abbr of **carrying a concealed weapon**.

CD *n* [*UK*] [*Stock market*] abbr of **certificate of deposit** a negotiable, interest-bearing certificate issued by a bank usually for up to 90 days maturity, though sometimes longer.

C'd frame *n* [*Custom cars*] a method of lowering a custom car by cutting the chassis and inserting a C-shaped section above the real axle; this prevents the axle hitting the chassis when **lowering blocks**, or some other means of suspension lowering, are incorporated. See also **Z'd frame**.

cdo *n* [*US*] [*Police*] abbr of **chronic drunkenness offender**.

ceazarney *n* [*US*] [*Carnival*] the language of carnival workers; essentially it is created by phonetic distortion as in Pig Latin.

C.E.D. *n* [*Video*] abbr of **Capitance Electric Discharge** the videodisc format backed by RCA; it is a stylus and groove system which resembles an aural record player and discs.

cedarwood *n* [*Wine-tasting*] the characteristic scent of many fine clarets.

ceiling 1. *n* [*Aerospace*] the maximum height at which an aircraft can maintain horizontal flight, or at which the rate of climb falls beneath 100ft/minute; 'zero ceiling' means clouds or mist at ground level, which preclude safe flying. **2.** *n* [*Commerce*] the highest price a market can reach.

cell *n* [*Film*] a piece of clear, transparent plastic used to create multi-layered on-screen graphic images; it is also an essential ingredient used to build up action in animated cartoons.

cellar *n* [*Oil rigs*] a space directly beneath the rig platform, on a land-based rig, which houses a series of hydraulic rams designed to prevent blowouts.

cement 1. *n* [*Drugs*] wholesale narcotics. **2.** *n* [*Mining*] gold-bearing gravel compacted and hardened into a mass.

cement mixer *n* [*US*] [*Road transport*] a particularly noisy engine or transmission.

cemetery network *n* [*Military*] the main nuclear command link operated by the NATO alliance and based on a high frequency (HF) radio network; it is to be operated in the case of a nuclear war.

cemetery vote *n* [*US*] [*Politics*] electoral corruption carried out by using the vote of someone who has recently died but whose name is still on the voter registration lists.

cendre *n* [*Cheese-making*] any cheese ripened in ashes; it comes from Fr. 'cendres' meaning 'ashes'.

centage *n* [*Theatre*] the percentage of the take paid by a touring company to the local theatres in which it is appearing.

centaur word *n* [*Linguistics*] See **brunch word**.

central war *n* [*Military*] See **general war**.

centre *v* [*New therapies*] to be calm and relaxed, while simultaneously physically energised and psychologically balanced; thus 'to be uncentred' means the opposite.

centre of mass *n* [*US*] [*Police*] a marksman's

term referring to that part of the body, the upper torso, where all the vital organs are situated.

centre point n [*Printing*] a full-stop placed higher than the printer's baseline, often used in dictionaries to separate the syllables of a word.

centring n [*Building, Concrete workers*] See **falsework**.

centrism n [*Politics*] the adopting of a middle way between various extremes.

CEP n [*Military*] acro **Circular Error Probable (or Probability)** the radius of a circle in which it is computed that a single warhead from a missile will arrive; the CEP determines the accuracy of a missile and with the recent advances in such accuracy, the latest weapons can claim to arrive within 30ft of their target, after flights of up to 6,000 miles.

ceremonial opening n [*Printing*] the use of a large ornamental letter to start a chapter in a book.

certainty equivalent n [*Stock market*] an investment that offers a guaranteed return which, though a relatively small sum, does compensate for the uncertainty of more dramatic financial gambles.

certiorari n [*Law*] a writ from a higher court to a lower court, asking for the lower court's records on a given case so that the proceedings can be reviewed as to their legality; it comes from Lat. meaning 'to be informed, to be made more certain'.

cess n [*UK*] [*Railways*] the rails at the extreme edge of the track.

cesser n [*Law*] the ending of a lease or of a mortgage; it comes from Fr. meaning 'to cease, to end'.

chad n [*Computing*] the tiny pieces of paper that are punched out of the holes in a perforated paper tape.

chafed a [*Book collecting*] See **rubbed**.

chafer n [*Tyre-making*] a strip of rubberised fabric that covers the head section of a tyre in order to stop the plies that cover the head from rubbing against the metal rim of the wheel.

chaff n [*Military*] strips of metal foil released from aircraft and missiles to jam radar and/or the guidance systems of missiles, etc; it originated in Germany in World War II. See also **window 5**.

chain gang 1. n [*UK*] [*Buses*] a group of London Transport inspectors who travel round the routes making spot checks on bus crews. 2. n [*US*] [*Railways*] employees who operate non-scheduled freight runs in rotation.

chain of representation n [*Law*] a chain of individuals all of whom are tied into the execution of a given will. While the initial executor is appointed on the grounds of trust and friendship, if he dies, his executor must carry out the execution of the first will as well as the one he has actually been cited to execute; this process extends from will to will through linked individuals.

chaining n [*Computing*] a method of dealing with large programs that might otherwise have exceeded the machine's storage capacity: the task is split into several lesser programs which are then run in sequence.

chains and dogs, also **tensioners** n pl [*UK*] [*Road transport*] screw couplings or friction devices used to secure loads which have too many sharp edges, and which might weaken or cut the ropes that are usually used to tie them on.

chair 1. n [*Glass-making*] a team of three or more glassmakers working by hand. 2. n [*Mining*] See **cage 5**.

chair warmers n pl [*Theatre*] an unresponsive audience.

chairborne division n [*Navy*] the Admiralty, Navy Office or any shore division who do not go to sea.

chairman 1. n [*US*] [*Coal-mining*] the worker who takes tubs or cars in and out of the mine. 2. n [*Glass-making*] the foreman or chief blower of a shop in which glassware is made by hand. See also **chair 1**.

chairs n pl [*Building, Concrete workers*] supports for the metal reinforcing rods built into the concrete.

chalk 1. n [*US*] [*Horse-racing*] the latest odds, especially of a favourite in the betting; they were originally marked in chalk on an odds board. 2. v [*US*] [*Painting*] in a white lead or oil paint this is the process whereby, as the paint ages, it powders and is virtually self-cleaning. A paint that chalks well will permit the easy application of the next coat.

chalk eater n [*Gambling*] a horse-race **punter** who only bets on favourites; it comes from the chalk used by the on-track bookmaker as he marks up the fluctuating odds.

chalk number n [*Military*] a reference number given to a complete load of troops and to the carrier that transports them; hence 'chalk commander', 'chalk troops'.

chalk player n [*Gambling*] See **chalk eater**.

chalk-eye n [*US*] [*Coal-mining*] a coal loader; a general underground labourer.

chalk-talk n [*Education*] a lecture or speech illustrated by chalk sketches made by the speaker.

chalky a [*Cheese-making*] a positive term, referring either to the whitest of colours or to a smooth, fine-grained texture; it is usually said of 'Chèvre'.

challenge 1. v [*Accounting*] to make a careful check for any inconsistencies or possible fraud in a company's accounts. 2. v [*Hunting*] said of a hound when it first gives tongue on finding a scent. 3. n [*Hunting*] the call made by a stag during the rutting season.

challenged a [*Social work*] popular euphemism for 'crippled'.

challenger n [*US*] [*Skiing*] the most difficult run in a ski area.

chamber music n [*US*] [*Law*] off-the-record, out of court meetings between rival attorneys before a judge in chambers for the purpose of arranging some form of plea-bargaining and thus saving the costs and time of a lengthy trial.

Chamber of Horrors n [Antiques] in the London offices of Christie's, the auctioneers, this is a corridor or repository for valueless pictures which are submitted to them for sale.

chamois down v [TV] in TV makeup, to mop a face clean of sweat.

champagne trick n [US] [Sex] prostitute's term for a wealthy, generous client.

champerty n [Law] the offence of interfering in legal actions which do not concern one; specifically it means to encourage a third party to bring a suit, in the hope of sharing in the possible profits that may accrue from that suit. It comes from Fr. 'champart' meaning a certain portion of the produce received by a feudal lord from land held in lease from him.

chance n [UK] [Catering] a customer off the street, one who has not pre-booked; in the case of a hotel restaurant, a non-resident diner.

change n [Horse-racing] the fractions of seconds – measured in fifths of a second – that are used in declaring the time of the winner, second, third and fourth place horses.

change agent n [Business] an individual consultant, or firm of consultants brought in to effect efficient changes in the structure of a corporation. Thus a 'personal change agent' is employed to help the executive shift careers or re-orientate their personal goals.

change coat n [Military] the tweed 'sports' jacket worn by British Army officers when out of uniform.

change-over n [Film] the transition during projection from one reel of film to the next. There are approximately 20–30 minutes per reel and at a set number of seconds prior to the end of a reel a series of cue dots appear at the top right hand of the screen to warn the projectionist.

change-up n [Baseball] the pitcher's disguised ball, which appears to be fast, with a big wind-up, etc, but which is actually delivered slow, thus confusing the batter.

channel 1. n [Clothing] a narrow passage formed between plies of material in a garment, or by the addition of an extra ply of material, usually to form the housing for a drawstring. 2. n [Sailing, Ropework] a broad, thick, plank projecting from the ship's side.

channel conditioning n [Communications] electrical balancing of a transmission channel in order to reduce distortion.

Channel fever n [Merchant navy] the excitement that a crew experiences as they approach their home port after a long voyage, specifically, as they sail up the English Channel.

channel money n [Commerce] interim payments to merchant seamen that are made as they reach various ports and which will be deducted from the total amount of money they are owed when the whole voyage is over.

channel packing n [Communications] the method of maximising one's use of voice frequency transmission channels by combining a number of lower speed data signals on to one higher speed data stream which is then transmitted on a single voice frequency channel.

channelise v [Communications] to subdivide a single channel into several lesser channels of small bandwidth.

channelling n [Custom cars] the lowering of a car body over the chassis by cutting down the body and diminishing the headroom inside the car; this is often teamed with **chopping**.

chaoticism n [Architecture] a term coined by US architect Philip Johnson to describe a confusion of styles.

chap v [Coal-mining] to tap on the surface to ascertain its stability or to estimate the thickness between two separate excavations.

chapel 1. n [Press, Industrial relations] the alternative name for a trade union 'branch' that is used in the UK by all print-related unions, whether of journalists or printers, ie: NUJ, NGA, SLADE, NATSOPA, SOGAT. 2. n [Merchant navy] a longitudinal groove in a made-up or laminated mast.

chaplet n [Metallurgy] in iron founding this is a piece of metal designed to support a core in its correct position.

CHAPS n [Banking] acro **Clearing Hosue Automatic Payments System** a computerised system based in London that offers electronic recording of all major inter-bank transactions between the UK, Europe and the US. See also **CHIPS**.

chapter n [Video] a consecutive sequence of frames in a video disk.

chapter ring n [Antiques, Horology] a round ring on the dial on which are set the numerals; the main chapter will vary in width according to the age of the clock.

character n [Textiles] various factors in a piece of cloth: uniformity of length, strength of fibre, fineness of fibre, **handle**, etc.

character disorder n [Social work] any problem that stems primarily from a person's behaviour but which is neither neurotic nor psychotic; such a condition can best be approached by some form of ego-building. See also **acting out**.

character merchandising n [Advertising] the using of TV/film/entertainment or similar celebrities as the basis for a special offer or competition.

character part n [Theatre] any stock role – wicked uncle, fallen woman, villainous landlord – other than the lead or juvenile lead.

character set 1. n [Computing] the set of characters used by a specific machine. Two of the most widely used sets are the **ASCI** and **EBCDIC** versions, used respectively on many personal computers and on the IBM 360–370 series main-

C

frames. **2.** *n* [*Computing*] the set of characters that is valid within a given programming language.

character stuffing *n* [*Computing*] a means of delimiting frames with a special end of frame character. See also **bit stuffing**.

characteristic *a* [*Wine-tasting*] a vague generalisation on a given wine that excuses the speaker from essaying a more detailed description.

characteristics *n pl* [*Audio*] the characteristic curves that represent the amplifying properties of transistors or valves.

characteristics of easy movement *n pl* [*Management*] a set of basic principles concerning the way in which human movements should be arranged for the easiest methods of working; movement should ideally make the best use of the shape and arrangements of the parts of the body involved. The emphasis is on ease rather than speed of working.

charade *n* [*Logology*] the dividing of a word, without changing the letter order, into other words which are semantically unrelated (not the obvious parts of a compound word); thus 'mendicant' can become 'mend I can't'.

charge 1. *n* [*Glass-making*] See **batch**. **2.** *n* [*Heraldry*] any of the shapes or symbols borne on a shield. **3.** *v* [*Golf*] to approach a round aggressively, playing each hole with maximum energy, force, etc. **4.** *v* [*Ice-hockey*] to take a run at an opponent prior to making an illegal check.

chargeman *n* [*Coal-mining*] a working foreman or team leader who is not an official.

charger *n* [*US*] [*Marine Corps*] this comes from hard-charger; it refers to any member of the Marine Corps who is very highly motivated. See also **gung-ho**.

charitable word *n* [*Logology*] a term coined by US logophile Willard R. Espy; it is a word that, if any of its letters is omitted, still remains a valid word, although with a different meaning.

charity goods *n* [*Sex*] a prostitute who gives his or her services freely.

charley *n* [*Hunting*] the fox; from Charles James Fox (1749–1806), British politician.

charlie *n* [*UK*] [*Market-traders*] a hump, a spinal deformity.

charlie bars *n pl* [*TV*] small flaps that can be fixed in front of a lamp to break up the light.

Charlie Moore *a* [*Navy*] honest, trustworthy; it comes from an advertisement to be found in Malta in 1850, touting a public house: 'Charlie Moore, the fair thing'.

Charlie noble *n* [*Navy*] a galley funnel; it was named after Charles Noble, a merchant navy captain who prided himself on the spotless condition of his ship's galley.

charlie regan *n* [*US*] [*Politics*] a non-existent but highly valuable fictitious personality used by all parties during political campaigns to keep questioners at bay and generally to accept the passed buck. See also **George Spelvin**.

charm *n* [*Science*] See **quark**.

charm price, also **psychological price** *n* [*Management*] the setting of prices at commonly used sums: thus pre-decimal 29s/11d, current £1.99 etc; these prices vary over the years, but are considered to be those most likely to appeal to buyers.

charretting *n* [*Architecture*] in architecture schools, this means working exceptionally hard, often all night; it comes from Fr. 'charrette', the cart used to collect the drawings of students attached to the Ecole des Beaux Arts between 1860 and 1930.

chart 1. *n* [*Pop music*] the ratings of successful records – 45s, LPs – listed weekly as the Top 20/30/40 and subdivided into speciality tastes, eg: Reggae Chart, Soul Chart, etc. **2.** *n* [*Pop music*] in a musical arrangement, the 'chart' is a sheet of music. **3.** *v* [*Pop music*] to appear on one of the record industry charts and thus to become to a certain extent successful: 'This is bound to chart soon . . .'

charter *n* [*Air travel*] essentially this is an aircraft chartered by a group organiser for that group's exclusive use, but latterly the basic charter has been extended to include part charter: blocks of seats on an otherwise scheduled flight that are saved for charter fliers (the agent who buys them receives a large discount from the airline). Half charter refers to flights that are not really charters at all but can be so termed by obtaining the correct official permission.

charter-party *n* [*Oil rigs*] an agreement whereby the shipowner hires his vessel to the charterer subject to certain conditions.

chartist *n* [*Stock market*] an individual who attempts to pinpoint the movements of shares by compiling graphs, tables and similar charts.

charver 1. *n* [*UK*] [*Marker-traders*] a girl, a woman, a person; copulation. **2.** *v* [*UK*] [*Market-traders*] to copulate with (always male activity).

chase 1. *v* [*Gambling*] in stud poker, to play against a better hand which one can already see exposed on the table; such play requires excellent bluffing skill. **2.** *n* [*Music*] a style in jazz where a number of musicians take turns to play solo, during which time each plays several bars of improvisation. **3.** *n* [*Printing*] a rectangular steel or iron frame into which letterpress matter is locked for printing or plating; when all the letterpress and furniture is secured, the whole is tightened by wedges called **quoins**. See also **form 2**. **4.** *n* [*Publishing*] the frame in which letterpress type is positioned firmly – 'locked up' – prior to printing.

Chase doll *n* [*US*] [*Medicine*] a dummy used by nurses in training; it was named after Martha J. Chase (fl. 1880), its inventor.

chase eighths *v* [*US*] [*Stock market*] when a speculator is satisfied with only the smallest profits, one eighth of a dollar.

chaser 1. *n* [*Logging*] a logger who unhooks logs as they are brought in from the wood. **2.** *n* [*US*] [*Marine Corps*] a prisoner's escort. **3.** *n* [*US*] [*Prisons*] a prison officer. **4.** *n* [*US*] [*Theatre*] music played by the orchestra while the audience is leaving the theatre. **5.** *n* [*US*] [*Bars*] a drink of beer that accompanies one of spirits, to 'chase' it down one's throat.

chassis *n* [*Electronics*] the metal base of the machinery, a computer, a circuit board, etc, to which the various parts of the electronic assembly are fixed.

chat *n* [*UK*] [*Market-traders)* a thing, an object.

chat with Susan, a *n* [*Politics*] during the 'Dirty War' in Argentina during the 1970s, this was a phrase used by interrogators to denote a session of torture by the electric shock machine. A descendant, perhaps, of the 15th century British description of the rack as being 'wedded to the Duke of Exeter'; John Holland, Duke of Exeter, introduced the rack into England in 1447.

Chats *n* [*Navy*] abbr of **Chatham** the home of the former Royal Naval Dockyard on the Thames Estuary.

chattamaranta *n* [*UK*] [*Market-traders*] any unspecified object, usually large and not immediately identifiable.

chatter *n* [*Electronics*] the rapid closing and opening of contacts on a relay.

chattering *n* [*Building, Plastering*] the juddering of the stock of a running mould, resulting in a continuous series of flutes or grooves across the work.

chavvy *n* [*UK*] [*Market-traders*] a child.

cheap *a* [*Cricket*] said of a wicket gained after allowing a batsman to score very few runs; thus 'expensive' means the opposite.

cheap money, also **easy money** [*Economics, Banking*] money is 'cheap' when interest rates are low, so loans are relatively easy to obtain and to service. See also **dear money**.

cheap stick *n* [*Logging*] a ruler used by the scaler who can thus work out a sawyer's pay by measuring the amount of wood cut.

cheat 1. *n* [*Film*] the procedure of concealing part of the action necessary for the taking of a shot by excluding it from the camera's field of view. **2.** *v* [*US*] [*Painting*] to do a job carelessly or in the wrong way. **3.** *v* [*TV*] to move something or someone within the frame of a shot when it or they are spoiling the composition, even though such a movement works against **continuity**.

cheat shot *n* [*Advertising*] the use in a commercial of a faked-up picture.

cheat the look *v* [*Film*] the film version of TV's **cheat**.

cheater 1. *n* [*US*] [*Farming*] an iron pipe used to extend the length of a wrench, increasing one's leverage and therefore making it easier to attack stubborn nuts or bolts. **2.** *n* [*Logging*] a length of pipe used to tighten the bindings on truck-load of logs. **3.** *n* [*US*] [*Painting*] a paint-roller which cheats painters out of work and thus money.

cheaters *n pl* [*US*] [*Skiing*] metal skis; so called because their added manoeuvrability when first introduced made traditionalists jealous.

check *n* [*Glass-making*] a surface crack in a glass article or in glass tubing.

check cop *n* [*Gambling*] a light adhesive that a cheat places on the palm of his hand so as to steal chips (checks) from a gambling table. He casually rests his hand on a pile of chips and when he removes it, the top chip sticks to the glue.

check row *n* [*Agriculture*] a row of crops so arranged that the ground between the plants as well as the ground between the rows may be cultivated in addition to the primary crop.

checker *n* [*Gambling*] an employee of a casino or gambling enterprise who checks **luggers** to see how many players they have brought to the game.

checker bricks *n pl* [*Glass-making*] See **stuffing 2**.

checkerboard *v* [*Oil industry*] to lease parcels of oil rights in several scattered patches of land, all of which are sited within an overall defined area.

checkerboard crew *n* [*Logging*] a crew made up of black and white loggers.

checkerboarding *n* [*Photo-typesetting*] removing alternate **pixels** at the edge of an image to obtain the correct effect when the character is printed.

checking 1. *n* [*Stock market*] the agreement between a broker and a **jobber** regarding the details of a business deal, normally on the first business day after that deal has been concluded. **2.** *n* [*Stock market*] checking the market: enquiring of a number of jobbers as to the price and amount of shares in a given security.

checkoff 1. *n* [*Industrial relations*] the system whereby the employer withholds all union dues and other payments from the employee and pays them directly to the union. **2.** *n* [*US*] [*Farming*] a system for livestock producers whereby they contribute an agreed levy to a central body which then uses it for the general promotion of their trading interests. **3.** *n* [*US*] [*Taxation*] a method whereby a taxpayer can indicate to the Revenue whether or not he/she wishes to have a certain percentage of his/her taxes put towards financing an election campaign.

checkout 1. *n* [*Computing*] the activities involved in bringing a new program to the state where it produces some results and so can be tested. **2.** *n* [*US*] [*Garment trade*] a dress that sells well to the retailers.

checks *n pl* [*Logging*] small, lengthwise separations in the wood, caused by the too rapid loss of moisture from the surface.

checks and balances *n pl* [*US*] [*Politics*] the essential fail-safe mechanism of the US government system, built into the US Constitution: the means whereby each of the three branches of the government – legislative, judiciary and administrative – can be limited by mutual interdependence.

checksum n [Computing] a simple error detection method used in data processing and communications that depends on a given set of data items against which the system can be checked.

checky a [Heraldry] divided into small squares of two colours, checked.

cheek 1. n [Glass-making] blocks that form the sidewalls of the **port** that leads into a furnace. 2. n [Mining] the side or wall of a vein. 3. n [Tools] the sidepiece of a piece of equipment by which it is secured to a handle.

cheeper n [Shooting] a young game bird; it comes from the noises it makes.

cheese 1. n [US] [Carpenters] soft wood. See also **bone** 3. 2. n [Clothing] a cylindrical packet of yarn, crosswound on to a flangeless support. 3. n [Oil rigs] paraffin which is saturated with oil from the press of a refinery. 4. n [Skittles] a heavy wooden ball used to knock down the skittles. 5. n [Textiles] a batch of raw fibre stock as it leaves the dyeing kettle. 6. n [Tobacco] a compressed mass of tobacco which will be cut up by machine into chewing or smoking tobacco. 7. n [Textiles] a package on to which yarn is wound. 8. v [Textiles] to wind a length of yarn on to a cheese. 9. v [Sailing, Ropework] to wind a rope's end into a tight, neat coil.

cheese down v [Merchant navy] to coil a rope neatly on the deck.

cheesebox n [Oil rigs] a vertical cylindrical still used in the distillation of kerosene; its name comes from its resemblance to an old fashioned cheesebox.

cheeseburger n [Military] the BLU/82/B11 concussion bomb; the weapon is 11ft long, 4.5ft wide, weighs 7.5 tons and contains over 6 tons of gelled acqueous slurry of ammonium nitrate and aluminium powder. Only a nuclear weapon exceeds the power of this bomb, which sends a mushroom cloud 6000ft into the air and which, if exploded 3ft above the ground, will kill everything (including the worms in the ground) in a surrounding area of 755 acres, as well as most things within 2000 acres.

cheesecake n [Ten-pin bowling] a lane where high scores can be made easily.

cheesecutter n [Navy] an officer's peaked cap. See also **bow wave**.

cheesewinder n [Glass-making] the operator of the machine that winds fibre glass onto spools.

cheesy a [Painting] said of a paint or varnish film that is dry but weak and rather soft.

chef de rang n [UK] [Catering] not a chef, but a senior waiter, usually in charge of two or more junior waiters in a smart restaurant; he is responsible for serving the food and laying the tables.

chemical architecture n [Architecture] a proposed novel form of architecture whereby a variety of chemicals – powders and liquids – could be activated by the addition of catalytic agents to expand into pre-determined shapes.

chemical fog n [Photography] general dimming of the image as a result of chemical contamination.

chemigrams n pl [Art] a form of art based on chemistry and chemical processes, using photographic paper or film.

chequebook journalism n [Journalism] the payment of large sums of money either to celebrities or, more usually, to individuals – mass murderers, royal girlfriends, etc – who are currently notorious and newsworthy. Such payments are intended to sell newspapers and to isolate the recipients from any advances by rival papers.

chequerboard n [TV] in TV film editing, this is the favoured method of cutting negative film, it guarantees no visible joins and is the best way to make **opticals**.

cherries n pl [Gambling] greyhound racing tracks; this comes from rhyming slang 'cherry hogs' meaning 'dogs'.

cherry 1. n [US] [Car salesmen] a car in excellent condition. 2. n [Surfing] a surfboard in perfect condition.

cherry coffee n [Coffee production] coffee beans which have been harvested but not yet dried.

cherry picker 1. n [Aerospace] a mobile crane with a platform that can be placed alongside a free-standing rocket or missile either as a working scaffold or as an emergency escape route for an astronaut trapped during a malfunction on launching. 2. n [Oil rigs] a pointed tool used in **fishing** lost tools from a well. 3. n [US] [Road transport] a high **cab-over** engine tractor, in which the driver sits over the engine.

cherry pie n [US] [Circus] any extra work undertaken by a circus worker to supplement his/her basic income.

cherry soda circuit n [Entertainment] a system whereby US soft drink companies, then selling drinks in bottles rather than cans, would pay touring acts a small fee to accept their bottle caps instead of money for admission to the show. See also **borscht belt**.

cherrypicker n [TV] a hydraulically operated tower used for high lighting or for high-angle camera work.

cherry-picking n [US] [Publishing] the making of trips by publishers for on-the-spot entrepreneurial research into persons or ideas; the findings are then taken back to base (usually New York City) for further consideration and possible action.

chest n [Glass-making] a receptacle in which pieces of excess glass (see **moils**) are allowed to crack off the blowing irons.

Chevaline n [Military] the development during

the 1970s and 1980s of a new 'front-end' for the ageing Polaris A–3 missiles with which the UK strategic submarines are armed until the **Trident** programme replaces them after 1992. The massive over-spending on this project has made Chevaline into a political issue that threatens to obscure any military uses the project may have.

cheville *n* [*Literary criticism*] an unnecessary word added to round off a sentence or complete a line of verse.

chevron *n* [*Heraldry*] a broad strip in the shape of an inverted V in the middle of a shield.

chew the scenery *v* [*Theatre*] used of an actor who overacts, either through a desire to gain disproportionate attention or through an inability to do better; such an actor is a 'scenery-chewer'.

chex *n* [*Commerce*] imperfect but still usable eggs – usually with cracked shells but with the membrane still intact – which are sold at reduced prices.

chib *n* [*Government*] abbr of **child benefit**.

Chicago boys *n pl* [*Economics, Government*] a group of monetarist economists, including the current, if increasingly tarnished, guru Milton Friedman, whose theories stem from their researches at the University of Chicago. These theories have been variously applied to the economies of Israel, Argentina and the UK.

Chicago School *n* [*Sociology*] the domination of American sociology between the world wars by the University of Chicago, best known for developments in urban sociology and the theory of **symbolic interactionism**.

chicane *n* [*Cards*] in bridge, this is when a player holds no trumps in a hand; 'double chicane' is when neither partner holds a trump.

chick *n* [*Logging*] a longitudinal crack in timber, caused by too rapid seasoning.

chicken button, also **chicken switch 1.** *n* [*Military*] a switch or button that can destroy a malfunctioning rocket in mid-flight. **2.** *n* [*Military*] a switch or button that an astronaut or jet pilot can use to eject his capsule from a malfunctioning rocket or his seat from a potentially crashing plane.

chicken feed *n* [*Oil rigs*] small items of miscellaneous expenditure, trivial in relation to the overall budget for the project.

chicken horse *n* [*US*] [*Cattlemen*] a small, ill-made horse, killed for dog and chicken feed.

chicken run *n* [*UK*] [*Buses*] a short journey by a London Transport bus.

chicken soup *n* [*Aerospace*] a solution of amino acids, vitamins, and other nutrients in a 'broth' that is intended to verify the possibility of life on Mars. Any living organism would ingest the nutrients and expel gases that could be picked up by sensors and relayed back to Earth.

chicken stuff *n* [*US*] [*Garment trade*] small sizes.

chicken wire *n* [*Cars*] catch fencing that stops cars which have spun off the track on a racing circuit.

chicks *n pl* [*Military*] friendly fighter aircraft.

chief *n* [*Heraldry*] the top one-third of a shield.

chiefy *n* [*Navy*] the Chief Engineer.

child, also **son, offspring, daughter** *n* [*Computing*] any node in a **tree** except the root.

child-centred *a* [*Education*] this is said of an educational programme which is ostensibly based around the needs, abilities and interests of the child. By extension, it also means the attempt to make lessons as palatable as possible for those who are condemned to endure them.

chili-dip *n* [*US*] [*Golf*] a weak, lofted shot that follows a mishit which has managed to hit more ground than ball. The image is of dipping a taco to scoop up a mouthful of chili.

chill *n* [*Metallurgy*] in iron-founding, this is any material or component of high thermal conductivity which is used in moulds and cores to accelerate the cooling process.

chiller *n* [*Film*] a horror film.

Chiltern Hundreds *n* [*UK*] [*Politics*] the stewardship of the Chiltern Hundreds of Stoke, Desborough and Burnham was established to rid the Chiltern Hills of their many predatory bandits. This requirement fell into disuse, but since 1707 the taking of this stewardship has been used as a legal fiction to permit the resignation of an MP. To hold an office for profit under the Crown – such as the Chiltern Hundreds – automatically disqualifies an MP from sitting in the House of Commons. Thus a member may apply for and will be granted the stewardship, although no such office now exists, nor can it ever be held.

chin *n* [*Aerospace*] the area, logically, directly beneath the aircraft's nose.

china *n* [*US*] [*Undertakers*] the cheapest make of coffin, ostensibly six pieces of redwood nailed together; such coffins were originally used to bury immigrant Chinese.

China syndrome *n* [*Science*] a catastrophe in a nuclear reactor whereby the cooling system fails, causing a resultant **meltdown** and creating a nuclear lava flow of unassailable intensity. It comes from the concept of the flow burning 'all the way through to China'.

chinaman 1. *n* [*Cricket*] the opposite of the **googly**, this is an offbreak bowled out of the back or side of the hand by a left-handed bowler. It is possibly named after Ellis Achong, a Chinese bowler playing for the West Indies around 1940, although he was by no means the first player to use the style. **2.** *n* [*Navy*] a fraction of a knot of speed.

Chinese *a* [*TV, Film*] used of the barn doors on a lamp when they are adjusted to diffuse light through horizontal slits; it comes from the racial cliché of narrow, slitted eyes.

Chinese binary code *n* [*Computing*] a coding system used on punch cards whereby successive

C

bits are represented by the presence or absence of punches in contiguous positions in successive columns as opposed to the more usual rows.

Chinese cut, also **Staffordshire, Surrey, Harrow cut** *n* [*Cricket*] a glancing stroke, quite probably intended to go in another direction, which edges the ball between the stumps and the fielders and earns lucky runs.

Chinese dominoes *n pl* [*UK*] [*Road transport*] a load of bricks.

Chinese gunpowder *n* [*UK*] [*Road transport*] cement.

Chinese landing *n* [*Flying*] a landing in which one wing is lower than the other. It is supposedly from the 'Oriental' sound of the words 'one wing low'; it is also from the racial equation of Chinese as meaning off-angle, unstable. See also **Chinese cut**.

Chinese money *n* [*Stock market*] **paper** rather than cash; a payment made up of a combination of stock certificates and debts.

Chinese six, also **twin-steer** *n* [*UK*] [*Road transport*] a rigid vehicle with three axles, of which the front two are steering axles.

Chinese snooker *n* [*Snooker*] a position in which the white ball is in front of another ball and a shot on the object ball is open, but the white and its adjacent ball are so close together (but not touching) that it is extremely hard for the player to manipulate his cue without fouling on the nearby ball; such a position often necessitates the use of the half-butt.

Chinese wall 1. *n* [*Stock exchange*] a variety of rules and safeguards – a 'Great Wall of China' – designed to prevent price-sensitive information, on which the unscrupulous can make profits, from passing between the dealing, fund management and corporate finance areas of the same financial conglomerate. **2.** also **green baize door** *n* [*Banking*] a type of organisational structure that exists where bankers combine the business of banking with that of investment advice or investment management. To prevent sensitive information passing fron one part of the business to the other, a 'great wall of China' is erected, whereby the various sections are strictly confined to their own limits.

chinger 1. *v* [*UK*] [*Market-traders*] to grumble; to deter a potential customer; thus a 'chingerer' is one who grumbles or puts off trade. **2.** *v* [*UK*] [*Market-traders*] to scold, to tell off.

chip architecture *n* [*Computing*] the arrangement of the chips that make up a microprocessor.

chip one off *v* [*Navy*] to salute a senior officer.

chipped *a* [*Book collecting*] said of small pieces worn or torn from the edge of a dust-wrapper.

Chippendale front, also **fiddle front, cabriole front** *n* [*Dog breeding*] a front assembly which, when looked at from the front, resembles a fiddle or violin shape – the dog's elbows rather wide apart, forearms sloping in towards the centre, with feet turning out.

chipping *n* [*Metallurgy*] removing surface defects by manual or pneumatic chisel.

chippy 1. *n* [*Gambling*] a novice player. **2.** *n* [*Gambling*] a sucker. **3.** *n* [*US*] [*Garment trade*] a dress that can be easily pressed.

CHIPS *n* [*Banking*] acro **Clearing House Inter-Bank Payments System** a computerised system based in New York that offers electronic recording of all major inter-bank transactions between US banks and their European branches. See also **CHAPS**.

chips *n* [*Navy*] the ship's carpenter, joiner or any artificer.

chipspeech *n* [*Computing*] an integrated circuit which stores the sound of speech in digital form for playback.

Chi-square *n* [*US*] [*Journalism*] a professor of journalism or communications whose teaching and/or research concentrates on the statistical determination of normative modes of sending and receiving messages, as defined by the Chi-square test of significance.

chistka *n* [*Politics*] this comes from Rus. meaning 'purification'; hence it refers to periodic purges of the Party.

chitlin curcuit *n* [*Entertainment*] for black entertainers, this is the equivalent of the Jewish **borscht belt**. The food, naturally, caters for a different ethnic group, but the amenities and standards are equally third-rate.

chleuh *n* [*Military*] used in the French Foreign Legion to mean the enemy.

chock *n* [*Coal-mining*] a roof support that is considerably stronger than a prop and supports a proportionately larger area of roof.

chockers *n pl* [*UK*] [*Market-traders*] the feet.

chocking *n* [*UK*] [*Coal-mining*] advancing the **chocks** forward.

chocks *n pl* [*UK*] [*Coal-mining*] the modern system of roof support: a small vehicle with telescopic legs under a metal canopy. The legs can be lowered, the chocks moved forward, then the legs pumped up to hold the roof again.

Choctaw *n* [*Skating*] a step from either edge on one foot to the opposite edge on the other foot, in an opposite direction.

choice 1. *a* [*US*] [*Meat trade*] a grade of meat below **prime** and above good. **2.** *a* [*Weaving*] the highest classification in the grading of the condition of wool fleece. See also **bright, burry and seedy**.

choice, have the *v* [*Stock market*] to have the opportunity if desired of buying and selling shares at the same price with different **jobbers**.

choirboy *n* [*Sex*] See **raw jaws**.

choke 1. *n* [*Audio*] an inductor, especially when used to smooth or filter a given circuit. **2.** *n* [*Cars*] the **venturi** or throat of a carburettor. **3.** *n* [*Oil rigs*] a gauged restriction inserted into a fluid

C

flow line in order to restrict the flow rate. **4.** *n* [*Shooting*] the narrowing of the bore of a tube at one end; usually the left barrel of a shotgun is choked. **5.** *v* [*Music*] to damp down the reverberations of a cymbal soon after it has been struck. **6.** *v* [*Golf, Baseball*] to shorten the swinging length of the club by adopting a lower grip on the shaft. **7.** *v* [*Sport*] to fail to perform at one's best through nervous tension; one's composure is lost and with it goes all skill and chance of success.

choke point *n* [*Government*] an artificially created bottleneck, set up by an incumbent government, whereby all valuable supplies – food, drugs, weapons, fuel, etc. – are controlled and denied to those whom the government wishes to defeat or demoralise.

choker *n* [*Logging*] a piece of wire rope that is tied around a log before dragging or carrying it away.

cholly *n* [*Gambling*] this comes from black slang for $1.00; it is any amount of folding paper money.

chomp **1.** *v* [*Aerospace*] to reset one's co-ordinates on a new direction/communications beacon during flight after reaching the limits of the last one. Airliners navigate by following a line of radio beacons that run along their route, moving from one to the next as they proceed. **2.** *v* [*Computing*] to lose; to chew off something larger than that with which one's teeth can deal efficiently or satisfactorily.

chomping *n* [*Computing*] the act of self-destruction performed by a faulty or badly written program which consistently fails to work and in so doing causes severe problems for its user; the image is of the program 'eating itself up'.

chop **1.** *v* [*Hunting*] used of hounds which kill before the quarry has run. **2.** *n* [*Military*] acro **Change of Operational Control**. **3.** *n* [*Table tennis*] a defensive stroke played with a downward swing of the bat to impart heavy spin in a backward direction on the ball, usually in response to a smash or **loop**.

chop the clock *v* [*Car salesmen*] a method of 'improving' a car's age by turning back the odometer and thus registering a false, lower than actual, mileage.

chop it on *v* [*Cricket*] a batsman does this when he guides the ball on to his own wicket after playing a poor or weak shot.

chopper **1.** *n* [*US*] [*Cattlemen*] a man who cuts out selected cattle from the main herd during a round-up. **2.** *n* [*Electronics*] a device for the intermittent interruption of a beam of light or an electric current. **3.** *n* [*US*] [*Garment trade*] a cutter who neither marks up nor lays out the material, but simply cuts the patterns. **4.** *n* [*Military*] a helicopter. **5.** *n* [*Military*] a machine-gun.

choppers *n pl* [*US*] [*Meat trade*] old ewes in medium flesh, not good enough to grade as fat.

chopping, also **top-chopping** *n* [*Custom cars*] shortening the roof supports on a car to create a stream-lined look with slitted windows; enthusiasts often have trouble cutting the glass to suit their new, slim-line windows.

chopping block, also **punching bag** *n* [*Boxing*] an aging or incompetent boxer who is badly beaten regularly; such fighters are often used for a young hopeful to conquer on his way up.

chops *n* [*Music*] See **lick**.

chop-socky *n* [*Film*] Oriental martial arts films; it comes from a pun on 'chop-suey' and slang 'sock' meaning 'hit'.

chordy *a* [*UK*] [*Market-traders*] stolen; thus 'chordy gear' means stolen goods. See also **chore**.

chore *v* [*UK*] [*Market-traders*] to steal, to thieve; thus 'chorer' means thief.

chose in action *n* [*Law*] the personal right one individual has to bring a legal action against another for payment of debt, for breach of contract or to redress some other harm or personal wrong. See also **chose in possession**.

chose in possession *n* [*Law*] any physical object one possesses, as opposed to 'conceptual right'. See also **chose in action**.

chosen instrument *n* [*Air travel, Government*] the national airline chosen and designated by a government to act as the country's representative in international flying, eg: British Airways, Lufthansa, El Al, etc.

chosisme *n* [*Literary criticism*] this comes from the Fr. meaning 'thingism'; it is the dominant style of such New Wave writers as Alain Robbe-Grillet in which there are minutely detailed descriptions of every item that occurs in a scene.

chouse *v* [*US*] [*Cattlemen*] to treat cattle badly – rounding them up roughly, harassing them, etc.

chow *n* [*US*] [*Military*] food; it is derived either from the allegedly insatiable appetite of chow dogs, or from the era when Chinese cooks dominated railroad camps across the US. Thus 'chow hound' is a greedy eater and 'chow line' a queue for a meal in the mess hall.

christmas tree **1.** *n* [*Aerospace*] an indicator board on an aircraft that shows radar traces; it is so called from its displays of flashing lights. **2.** *n* [*Drag racing*] the arrangement of coloured lights, in horizontal rows attached to a pole sited between the competing cars, which sets off a drag race, signals a false start, etc. **3.** *n* [*Film*] a small cart that transports pieces of lighting equipment; they are strung around it like the lights on a Christmas tree. **4.** *n* [*Military*] a combat uniform belt adorned with grenades, knife, flask, flares and whatever else is required in a battle or assault. **5.** *n* [*Navy*] in a submarine, this is an indicator panel which flashes red and green lights to show that all valves, hatches, etc are locked tight when the submarine dives. **6.** *n* [*Oil rigs*] the valve assembly at the top of a gas or oil well that provides primary pressure reduction, production rate control and shut-in service. **7.** *n* [*Oil rigs*] an assembly of variously sized valves used to control the flow of oil on a rig. See also **nipple**, **sloper**.

christmas tree bill *n* [*US*] [*Politics*] a bill, often aimed at improving the quality of life for special interest or minority groups, that is bedecked with a number of amendments which have been 'hung' on it so as to satisfy those groups. However these amendments are only loosely related to the central issue with which the bill is concerned.

christmas tree effect *n* [*Science*] in astronomy, the theory is that, rather than some quasars actually moving, the 'blinks' that certain scientists feel prove movement are in fact caused by an internal mechanism that causes them to flash 'on and off'.

chrome *n* [*Weaving*] abbr of **potassium dichromate**, a **mordant**.

chuck and chance it *v* [*Angling*] to fish without knowing that a fish is actually lying where the cast is made, or to fish where no rise has been seen.

chuck-up *n* [*Navy*] any kind of vocal support or similar sign of approval.

chuffing *n* [*Military*] a characteristic of some rockets which burn intermittently and with an irregular noise; the image is of an 'old banger' proceeding along the London to Brighton road in the vintage car excursion.

chugging *n* [*Military*] an irregular explosion of exhaust gases from a rocket; this causes the rocket to move with the sound of a steam or electric engine, a sound that is officially termed 'low frequency oscillations'.

chum *v* [*US*] [*Angling*] to lay ground bait; it was originally used in shark-fishing.

chummery *n* [*Fire Brigade*] a small room set aside in a London fire station for chatting, smoking, and relaxing after a major fire, etc.

chumming 1. *n* [*Angling*] strewing the water with ground bait when deep sea angling. 2. *n* [*Military*] a night attack strategy involving two planes. One keeps its lights on and draws fire from the target; once pinpointed, the target is now open for the 'dark' plane to destroy it.

chummy 1. *n* [*Industry*] a chimney sweep. 2. *n* [*UK*] [*Police*] any individual, but particularly a criminal or prisoner.

chump change *n* [*Pop music*] a pittance paid out to an artist; it serves to ensure his survival but little else and he remains a 'chump' to accept what is only marginally more than 'change'.

chunk *v* [*Logging*] to clean up the ground to make clearings or roads, removing all obstructions by hand or machine.

chunking 1. *n* [*Cars*] the deterioration of tyres which occurs when they become hot and chunks of rubber fly off; it usually happens in racing, but can happen at high speed on any road. 2. *n* [*Information*] the process of re-coding information so as to reduce the number of independent symbols while increasing the kinds of symbols. It

is a system that adapts best to the limited number of mental 'slots' human beings seem to possess when dealing with matters that require immediate attention.

Churchill *n* [*Taxis*] a meal break; it comes from the right given by Winston Churchill (as Home Secretary) for cabbies to refuse a fare when stopping to eat.

churn *v* [*Business*] to generate more income by artificially increasing the amount of business carried out, even if, in fact, all such business remains strictly paper- or database-bound and no more deals are made, clients aided, or problems solved, etc.

churn-head *n* [*US*] [*Cattlemen*] a hard-headed, stupid horse.

churning *n* [*Stock market*] by an extension of **churn**, this is a marginally illegal method of pushing up the price of stocks one wishes to sell by making **wash sales** which create the illusion of an 'active' market and so prices duly rise as required.

chute *n* [*US*] [*Horse-racing*] an extension to one of the straights in an oval racecourse, that is used for special races.

chuvvy *n* [*UK*] [*Market-traders*] a flea; thus 'chuvvied up' means 'infested with fleas'.

ci *n* [*US*] [*Police*] abbr of **criminal informant**.

CIF *n* [*Business*] abbr of **cost, insurance and freight**, a contract in which the seller provides the product and the vessel, procures insurance, and delivers the product at a nominated port.

c.i.f. *n* [*Commerce*] abbr of **cost, insurance, freight** costs borne by the seller of exported goods up to the arrival of the ship in the port of destination. If the contract states c.i.f. & landing, the exporter pays for the unloading costs as well.

c.i.f. & c. *n* [*Commerce*] abbr of **cost, insurance, freight and commission** the payment by the seller of export costs and the commission payable to the exporter when acting as a buying agent for the foreign buyer.

c.i.f. & e *n* [*Commerce*] abbr of **cost, insurance, freight and exchange** the payment by the sellers of export costs but here the price includes exchange, ie: either the price stays unchanged, despite future movements of the market or the price includes the banker's commission.

c.i.f. & i. *n* [*Commerce*] abbr of **cost, insurance, freight and interest**, the payment by the seller of shipping costs plus the interest charged by the seller's bank for negotiating a bill of exchange relating to the goods.

cigarette deck *n* [*US*] [*Navy*] the casing of the submarine immediately abaft the conning tower.

cilop *n* [*Aerospace*] the conversion and updating of old aircraft to increase one's armoury, rather than scrapping and destroying the planes with the expenditure of large sums on their replacements.

CIM *a* [*Industry*] acro **computer integrated manufacturing** systems.

Cincinnati *n* [*Ten-pin bowling*] a split where only the 8 and 10 pins are left standing. See also **babysplit, bucket, Woolworth**.

cinching *n* [*Film, Video, Audio*] errors in the mechanical winding process of a spool of tape or reel of film; the spaces thus created within the wound material are 'cinching'.

cinder *n* [*Metallurgy*] the molten by-products of furnaces used for **puddling, bushelling** or reheating; the chemical composition varies but is essentially silicate of iron.

cinderella *n* [*UK*] [*Railways*] an electric train which has lost one of the 'shoes' which picks up the current from the rail and transfers it to the electric motors.

cinderella sale *n* [*Commerce*] an occasional sale that is used to get rid of odds and ends of stock that have 'not gone to the ball' and thus remain unsold.

cinderella liberty *n* [*US*] [*Military*] military leave that must end at midnight.

cinderhead *n* [*Glass-making*] a glass worker; the term originates in the charcoal and coal fuelled furnaces which filled the air, and thus the clothes and hair of the workers, with cinders and ash.

cinematographer *n* [*Film*] the lighting cameraman or the chief photographer.

cinetisation *n* [*Art*] an image of a contorted and distorted building which is produced by the simple device of removing key portions of the original photograph and then remounting them slightly askew – thus utterly shattering the building's 'stability'.

cinniri *n* [*US*] [*Crime*] in the US mafia this is heroin; it comes from Sicilian meaning ashes.

circle of confusion *n* [*Photography*] the circular image of any subject point on a piece of paper.

circuit *n* [*Film*] a chain of cinemas under the same ownership, often playing the same film simultaneously across a state or country.

circuit slugger *n* [*Baseball*] a regular hitter of home runs, who has to run the full circuit of bases every time he hits one.

circular file *n* [*US*] [*Government*] a jocular reference to the waste paper basket.

circular list *n* [*Computing*] a set of items that have been arranged in a memory in such a way that only the earliest and the most recently added are capable of being identified by the program.

circulation *n* [*Lacrosse*] the movement of attack players off the ball as play advances upfield.

circus *n* [*Skiing*] a system of interconnecting lifts linking a number of skiing areas and resorts.

circus job *n* [*US*] [*Theatre*] an extravagant pre-production publicity campaign which increases in magnitude in direct proportion to the management's fears of a flop. It comes from the excesses of circus ballyhoo of earlier eras.

circus makeup *n* [*Journalism*] any bizarre visual effect produced by the use of unfamiliar or oddly combined typefaces and sizes; the whole may resemble a circus poster.

circus wagon *n* [*US*] [*Road transport*] a low-sided trailer with a tarpaulin that rises in a high bow, like a circus tent.

cissing **1.** *n* [*Painting*] the preliminary operation in graining, of moistening the wood with beer and rubbing it over with whiting so that the colour will cover it properly. **2.** *a* [*Painting*] the description of a coat of paint, varnish or water colour which refuses to form a continuous film, recedes from the surface, collects in beads and leaves the surface still partially exposed. The traditional method of countering this was to mix some beer into the paint.

citadel *n* [*Military*] those enclosed areas of a warship without which it can neither sail nor fight; such areas are made safe to the greatest possible extent from gas and nuclear attacks, but are by no means invulnerable, if some less well protected part of the ship is hit and she must still be abandoned.

citronella circuit *n* [*US*] [*Theatre*] a circuit of small, local summer theatres; it is named after a (necessary) brand of insect repellent. See also **borscht belt, chitlin circuit**.

city-busting *n* [*Military*] the targeting and presumed destruction of cities in the case of nuclear exchange. Such **countervalue** targeting is at the heart of the threat of mutual assured destruction (**MAD**) that still maintains the nuclear stalemate, for all the developments since its inception in the 1960s.

civvy *n* [*UK*] [*Prisons*] a proprietory branded cigarette, as opposed to a 'roll-up'; it comes from 'civilian'.

c.k.d. *part phr* [*Commerce*] abbr of **completely knocked down**, this refer to goods, especially machines, which have been taken apart and sold piecemeal, but which must then be assembled by the buyer after purchase. See also **c.b.u.**

claim *v* [*UK*] [*Police*] to arrest.

claimer *n* [*Horse-racing*] a 'claimer' or 'claiming race' is one in which all those horses contesting it (none of which will be of a particularly high or desirable standard) may be purchased or 'claimed' for sums specified before the race.

claims *n pl* [*Religion*] in Christian Science this refers to illnesses, which are only seen as 'claiming' to make the patient ill.

CLAM *n* [*US*] [*Military*] acro **Chemical Low-Altitude Missile**.

clambake *n* [*Audio*] the possibility during a sports or similar broadcast of several commentators all talking over/against each other and thus confusing the listeners.

clamp *n* [*Aerospace*] weather that makes it impossible to fly safely; it 'clamps' planes to the ground.

clamping *n* [*Electronics*] the action of establishing the voltage level of a signal.

C

clamshell n [US] [Building] a large, heavy, steel bucket, divided into two parts, hinged at the top and attached to a derrick or crane for use in digging earth, gravel, etc.

clandestine cache n [Military] secret supplies of fissionable material held within the borders of a nation which is ostensibly party to a disarmament treaty.

clapped a [Shooting] said of game that is frozen in place, squatting to avoid potential danger.

clapperboard n [Film] a hinged board that records the details of each shot. At the start of each 'take' it is held in front of the camera for identification and then clapped to ensure synchronisation of the sound track. Thus 'clapperloader' is an assistant to the cameraman who as well as operating the clapper also loads film into the camera.

clapperloader n [Film, TV] See **clapperboard**.

clash 1. n [TV, Advertising] two commercials in the same or adjacent breaks which employ the same actors, voice over, themes, etc. **2.** n [TV, Advertising] a commercial which seems too similar in style to the programme into which it has been inserted.

class 1. n [Management] a group of members of a registered company (either limited or unlimited) whose joint interests in that company are in some ways different from those of the other members; thus 'class meeting' is a meeting of the members of a particular class of members in a registered company. **2.** n [Politics, Sociology] originally this term was based on the feudal, pre-industrial differences of 'rank' within an intricately ordered world, while modern class, based on differences in material possessions, envolved after the Industrial Revolution. Class has also been described as an endless division between creditors and debtors, based around the 'life chance' (involving skill as well as property ownership) of the individual.

class action n [Law] a legal proceeding enacted to take into account not merely the specific defendant and plaintiff involved, but everyone to whom the case might actively refer.

class As n pl [US] [Drugs] class A drugs: major addictive drugs, opiates, narcotics.

class Bs n pl [US] [Drugs] class B drugs: minor addictive drugs, eg. codeine.

class of channel n [Communications] the medium through which data transmission channels pass: wire, cable, radio, etc.

class enemy n [Politics] in Marxist terms this is the class which stands between the proletariat and its struggle for power: it is usually the bourgeoisie.

class imagery n [Sociology] the perceptions by individuals of their own and other people's social class; these perceptions influence their social attitudes and behaviour.

class 'in itself' and 'for itself' n [Politics] two Hegelian concepts adopted by Marx to describe two stages of proletarian class consciousness. 'Class in itself': the workers become aware as individuals of various grievances against other individuals, ie. their own complaints against their own boss. 'Class for itself': the workers gain a consciousness of class identity and the overall struggle against the whole bourgeoisie – this should culminate in the revolution.

class magazine n [Advertising] a magazine or periodical intended for a group of people who share a common or specialised interest. It is aimed at the consumer market – home computer users, yachtsmen, DIY, etc. – rather than professional groups.

class Ms n [US] [Drugs] class M drugs: non-addictive drugs, soft drugs.

class theoretical n [Sociology] explanations of social phenomena which refer to the existence of social classes; this is the opposite of mode-theoretical explanations which refer back to the mode of production.

class VI [US] [Military] shorthand for alcoholic drinks of any sort.

class Xs n pl [US] [Drugs] class X drugs: medications, such as cough medicines, that contain extremely small amounts of potentially addictive drugs.

classic 1. n [Cars] a car manufactured between 1925 and 1942. **2.** a [Philately] this usually describes certain stamps issued prior to 1875 but is sometimes extended to include more modern rarities.

classical figure n [Military] the amount of special material which provides a critical mass for the production of nuclear bombs: 20 kilograms of highly enriched uranium.

classics n pl [Horse-racing] the five major British horse-races: the 1000 Guineas, the 2000 Guineas, the Oaks, the Derby and the St. Leger.

classification at birth n [Politics] in the classification of certain documents as secret, the concept here is that any ideas developed within overall classified areas – nuclear weapons, espionage, etc – are automatically secret from the moment of their creation and require no specific registration on a secrets file. Thus a lecturer who comes out with a spontaneous idea on such subjects as he talks to his students can be reported for 'thinking classified thoughts'.

classification levels n pl [Government] an ascending ladder of secrecy used to classify data: confidential, secret, top secret and special intelligence. (Special Intelligence covers a range of super-secret classifications hidden from most government and elected officials, let alone from the general public.)

classified a [Government] officially this is used to describe such material that is not of the utmost secrecy, but which can only be circulated amongst a specified group. On the whole all secret material, of whatever level of importance, is termed 'classified'.

classified mode n [US] [Government] any institution thus labelled has been shut to public inspection for an indefinite period.

clastic art n [Art] sculptures consisting of ready-made units, such as bricks, wooden blocks, metal poles, etc, which can be taken to pieces and ressembled, if required. Alternatively the component elements may be returned to their original 'non-art' condition.

clatter v [UK] [Market-traders] to hit, to smack.

clause IV n [Politics] this comes from the Constitution of the British Labour Party: 'to secure for the workers by hand or by brain the full fruits of their industry and the most equitable distribution thereof that may be possible upon the basis of the common ownership of the means of production, distribution and exchange, and the best obtainable system of popular administration and control of each industry or service'; ie nationalisation. The perpetuation of the letter of Clause IV persists in dividing the left (pro) and the right (anti) of the Party. 'Clause IV' is also found as an adjective, eg 'Clause IV socialist'.

clausing n [Banking] a statement on the face of a bill which gives details of the transaction in respect of which the bill is drawn.

claw-back n [Government, Politics] this was originally devised as an attempt by Government to balance increases in social benefits by increasing the the taxation of those with higher incomes, who were less in need of financial assistance. However it is now a method of withdrawing or reducing such benefits either by direct cuts or by raising taxes on everyone, regardless of income.

clean 1. a [Aerospace] said of an aircraft with its landing gear retracted. See also **dirty** 1. 2. a [Aerospace] said of an aircraft carrying no external stores such as extra fuel tanks, above average armaments, etc. 3. a [Audio] free of any audible distortions, having the quality of audio 'clarity'. See also **veiled**. 4. a [Banking] a customer or staff record which shows no undesirable, derogatory features. 5. a [Gliding] said of a glider that has reduced **parasite drag** to the lowest possible value. See also **dirty** 3. 6. a [Horse-racing] said of a horse's leg that is devoid of any injury. 7. a [Journalism] referring to copy that requires little or no subediting before setting up in print; 'dirty' copy requires much attention. 8. a [Military] used to describe a nuclear device that produces maximum blast and thermal effects but keeps radiation fallout to a minimum and thus, in theory, produces most of the deaths immediately, rather than slowly over the succeeding months or years. 9. a [US] [Prisons] said of a well-dressed, neat person. See also **pressed to the max**. 10. a [Sex] a black pimp's description of his whores as smartly turned out and fashionably dressed. 11. a [Shooting] said of deer which have antlers that

are devoid of velvet. 12. a [Stock market] said of the price of a share after the deduction of any fixed interest. 13. adv [Theatre] sold out: thus 'The house went clean.' See also **SRO**. 14. a [Wine-tasting] devoid of unpleasant and alien smells. 15. v [Navy] to change into an appropriate uniform or suit of clothes for a job; thus if the job is dirty, there is no reason why 'cleaning' should actually need clean clothes.

clean acceptance n [Commerce, Banking] the acceptance of a bill of exchange without any special conditions.

clean bed n [Medicine] a bed for a patient who needs surgery, or the setting of a broken limb, or who is to be treated for a non-infectious disease. See also **dirty bed**.

clean bill n [Banking] a bill of exchange that carries no special conditions or documents with it.

clean bond n [Commerce, Finance] a government bond whose price needs no adjustment to allow for accumulated interest, since the interest has just been paid and no more has, as yet, accumulated. See also **dirty bond**.

clean coal 1. n [Coal-mining] coal from which impurities have been eliminated 2. n [Coal-mining] a coal seam free of **dirt**.

clean entrance n [Film] an entrance in which the performer makes sure that neither his/her body nor its shadow is visible prior to moving on to the scene.

clean feed n [TV, Radio] the transmission by one station to another of a programme stripped of all local information – news, advertisements, station identification, etc.

clean fish n [Angling] one that is just up river from the salt water.

clean float n [Economics] money exchange rates which are allowed to adjust themselves to the prevailing market without any government interference.

clean ground n [Hunting] ground on which the scent can be picked up and which has not been obscured by other scents – cattle, etc. See also **foil**.

clean room n [Science] a special room in which precision objects are to be manufactured or assembled. This room will have been completely disinfected and have had all dust removed; its temperature and humidity are kept under static artificial control.

clean wheels n [Police] a car, ideal for robbery and/or getaway driving, which has never had any problems with the law.

cleaned a [Philately] said of stamps which, for the purpose of forgery or allied crime, have had ink, fiscal or other cancellations removed by chemical or other methods.

cleanskin n [US] [Police, Crime] anyone without a criminal record.

cleanup n [Baseball] the place in the batting

C

order of the player who bats fourth; such a player is assumed to be a strong hitter who can drive home previous batters, now on bases, and thus 'clean the bases'.

clean-up *n* [*Mining*] regular, routine separation of valuable minerals from the rock and gravel which have accumulated in the sluices.

clear 1. *n* [*Espionage*] from Fr. 'en clair' referring to a message or audible communication that is neither in cipher nor in code. 2. *a* [*Scientology*] referring to the ultimate state of scientological perfection; the ideal human being. 3. *v* [*US*] [*Railways*] to complete the duties of a given job. 4. *v* [*US*] [*Railways*] to signal a train to advance. 5. *v* [*Sailing, Ropework*] to remove kinks, snarls, etc from a rope.

clear alley *n* [*US*] [*Railways*] an empty track in the **yard**.

clear heart *n* [*Logging*] the best grade of redwood lumber, which is cut from the heart of the centre section of the log.

clear pop *n* [*UK*] [*Railways*] a journey completed without encountering any signals set to stop the train.

clear yourself *excl* [*Film*] an instruction to an actor to make sure that he/she is not masked from the camera by another person or by an object.

clearance 1. *n* [*US*] [*Railways*] train orders delivered at the start of a trip, containing all necessary information for that trip. 2. *n* [*Shipping*] a customs document which permits a master to have his ship unloaded (clearance inwards) or leave the port (clearance outwards). See also **jerque note**. 3. *n* [*Video*] See **window 7**.

clearing *n* [*Stock market*] the settlement department to which brokers and **jobbers** submit a daily list of the transactions in certain stocks. Those securities which are handled by the Settlement Department as known as 'clearing stocks'.

clearing house *n* [*Stock market*] an organisation which provides the stock market with a central body dealing with all settlements, becoming 'buyer' for the seller and vice versa. It was originally established by bankers to adjudicate mutual claims over cheques and bills. Thus 'Clearing member' is any organisation with access to the Clearing House for the purpose of dealing with its customers' business.

clearing the market *part phr* [*Stock market*] the satisfying of all parties – buyers and sellers alike – by moving the price of shares.

clearings *n pl* [*Banking*] cheques, drafts and other **paper** presented by a bank for collection at the clearing house.

cleat *n* [*Coal-mining*] a vertical crack or fissure running through the coal seam.

cleek 1. *n* [*Scot*] [*Angling*] a gaff. 2. *n* [*Golf*] the traditional name for the No. 1 iron or the No. 4 wood.

clem *n* [*Clothing*] a very small dart which is sewn and not cut.

click *n* [*Radio*] local atmospheric disturbances caused by small activity within thunderclouds. See also **grinder 1, tray**.

clicker *n* [*US*] [*Theatre*] a free admission pass.

client 1. *n* [*New therapies*] a description that has taken over from 'patient' for someone who sees a classical therapist. Perhaps this helps all concerned remember the financial basis of the relationship: pay fast, get 'cured' equally fast. 2. *n* [*Politics*] a nation whose economy, armed forces and political stability depend either on one or other of the superpowers, or at least on the patronage of some other far more powerful country.

clift *n* [*Mining*] strong, silty mudstone.

climate for learning *n* [*Education*] the environment in which the child learns, with reference to the personality of the teacher, the architecture of the school, the mental and physical health of the child and other contributory factors.

climb *n* [*UK*] [*Police*] cat burglary; thus 'at the climb' means in the profession of cat burglary and a 'climber' is a cat burglar.

climb the rigging *v* [*Navy*] to lose one's temper; it is the naval equivalent to of 'go up the wall'.

climber *n* [*Horse-racing*] a jockey who sits too upright and too high in the saddle.

climb-out *n* [*Air travel*] the immediate post-takeoff flying phase of the aircraft (the first 50 secs. of flight) during which it must gain full speed, lift its undercarriage and gain sufficient height to allow for local noise regulations.

clinch *v* [*Bird-watching*] to identify a rarity.

Clincher's disease *n* [*Snooker*] the inability of otherwise top class players to clinch a victory at the end of a frame or match; nerves undermine their ability to dispose of otherwise simple pots.

clinching *n* [*Computing*] any wrinkling in the magnetic tape used in cassette memory; this may be the cause of errors in running a program.

clink *n* [*Metallurgy*] a rupture in the metal caused by thermal stress.

clinker *n* [*Shoe-mending*] a shoemaker's nail driven into the sole as a protective stud.

clinquant *n* [*Literary criticism*] showy but value-less writing, literature that is all glitter and no substance; it comes from Fr. meaning 'glittering, clinking'.

cliometrician *n* [*Research*] a historian who pursues research with help from state-of-the-art computer analysis, especially analysis of vast quantities of data which previously would have defeated a human analyst. It comes from 'Clio', the Greek muse of history plus 'meter' meaning 'measure'.

cliometrics *n* [*Research*] a sophisticated form of economic and historical interpretation, based on modern mathematical and statistical evidence, which relies primarily on computer analysis of the data.

clip sheet *n* [*Public relations*] a one-page press

release which combines a number of pictures, short items and small features, all designed for easy use by subscribing newspapers.

clipper 1. *n* [*Electronics*] an electronic circuit in radio and television that clips certain instantaneous signals, thus ensuring that they remain within predetermined amplitudes or frequencies. 2. *n* [*TV*] anyone who makes a hobby of collecting 'Star Trek' film clips.

clippers *n pl* [*US*] [*Meat trade*] short-haired lambs or sheep.

clipping *n* [*Audio*] a form of distortion due to extreme overloading of a circuit: the tips of the sound wave are 'clipped' as the system is rendered incapable of producing an increased output, despite continually increasing input.

clobber 1. *v* [*Antiques*] to re-enamel porcelain and thus increase its saleability if not its actual value. 2. *v* [*Clothing*] to renovate old clothes prior to resale. 3. *n* [*UK*] [*Market-traders*] clothes.

clobbered *a* [*Antiques*] said of porcelain, especially blue and white, that has had enamelled decoration added to it.

clock 1. *n* [*Communications*] equipment that provides a time base used in a transmission system to control the timing of various functions such as the length of signals, **sampling**, etc. See also **clocking**. 2. *n* [*Computing*] an electronic circuit or set of components that generates a set of control signals which govern the overall speed at which a computer functions. 3. *v* [*Navy*] to register a hit with a missile or other projectile. 4. *v* [*Sport*] to record, on a stopwatch, computer or similar timing device, the time of a race or of a competitor within that race.

clock a car *v* [*US*] [*Car salesmen*] to turn back the odometer and thus fraudulently 'rejuvenate' a car. See also **chop the clock**.

clock and a half? *phr* [*Taxis*] a question asked of a naive or ignorant passenger, usually foreign or provincial, who is led to believe that the journey he wants to take carries a 50% surcharge.

clock, on the *adv* [*Taxis*] referring to a cabdriver who hires rather than owns his cab and who pays the owner a percentage of the fares registered on his clock.

clock start *n* [*Radio*] an item that starts exactly to the second – reports, inserts, parliamentary question time, etc – ie anything that dictates its own time to the radio station.

clocking *n* [*Communications*] the use of a **clock** to control the synchronisation of data transmissions in a two-way synchronous system.

clockwork mouse *n* [*Navy*] a submarine used for training ships in anti-submarine warfare.

clod 1. *n* [*Coal-mining*] a thinnish bed of weak rock immediately above a coal seam. 2. *n* [*Coal-mining*] rock that is formed of very fine complex silicates, formed themselves from the decomposition of earlier rock formations.

clod *n* [*UK*] [*Market-traders*] one penny.

clodding, also **clotting** *n* [*Angling*] catching eels by threading a ball of worms on to worsted.

cloddy *a* [*Dog breeding*] said of an inelegant, gross, heavy-set, unattractive, clumsy dog.

clogger *n* [*Soccer*] a deliberately savage player, free with physical fouls and intimidation.

clogging *n* [*Video*] a partial loss of sound or picture that may occur if small particles of loose tape coating interfere between the sound or video heads and the tape that is passing over them.

clone *n* [*Computing*] any form of business computer modelled on the IBM-PC range. Invariably cheaper, often more efficient through capitalising on more modern design and technology, the production of such machines, which is carefully monitored by IBM and its lawyers, is mainly centred on the Far East.

clones *n pl* [*Sex*] gay term for those who dress up as super-masculine sterotypes – truck driver, policeman, construction worker, etc. – which are adopted by many homosexuals.

close 1. *a* [*Cheese-making*] said of a cheese which has a texture that is smooth and dense, with no holes. See also **open 2**. 2. *v* [*Sailing, Ropework*] to twist together three **plain-laid** ropes to form a cable. 3. *v* [*Stock market*] to reverse an **open position** either by buying a security which has been sold **short**, or by selling one that has been purchased earlier. 4. *a* [*Stock market*] a small fraction used in quoting prices for shares; thus 'close to close' is the same fraction either above or below the whole number. 5. *n* [*Futures market*] the end of the day's trading.

close a position *v* [*Stock market*] to eliminate a security from one's portfolio, usually by selling it.

close down *v* [*Soccer*] to deny the opposition players room to manoeuvre.

close out 1. *n* [*UK*] [*Surfing*] a wave that breaks along the whole of its length. 2. *v* [*Aerospace*] to seal a spacecraft prior to its launch. 3. *v* [*Stock market*] See **close a position**. 4. *v* [*Business*] to conclude a successful sale or deal. 5. *n* [*Business*] the conclusion of a successful sale or deal. 6. *n* [*Commerce*] a department store sale of discontinued goods.

close the gates *v* [*US*] [*Road transport*] to close the rear doors of the trailer.

closed bed *n* [*Medicine*] a made-up bed without a patient in it. See also **open bed**.

closed end *n* [*Stock market*] a closed end trust is an investment with a fixed capital, as opposed to an open end trust whose issue of units can expand or contract.

closed out *a* [*Aerospace*] said of a spacecraft that has been finally sealed prior to launch.

closed period *n* [*TV*] the period on Sunday evenings (around 6pm) that is dedicated by law and television charter to paying audio-visual service to 'the Lord's Day'. See also **God slot**.

closed season *n* [*TV*] the summer holiday period which, on the assumption that everyone is on

C

C

holiday, is bad for ratings and for scheduling new programmes. See also **dog days**.

closed shop *n* [*Computing*] a method of running a computing facility whereby only the in-house specialists are allowed to work on problems that have originated elsewhere. See also **open shop**.

closed visit *n* [*UK*] [*Prisons*] a visit permitted to prisoners who are currently undergoing punishment of some sort. Instead of meeting their visitor(s) across a normal table, they are placed in a booth behind glass and no physical contact is permitted.

closer 1. *n* [*US*] [*Car salesmen*] the salesman working in a **system house** who follows up the spadework performed by the **liner** and actually finishes the sale. **2.** *a* [*Stock market*] referring to a situation when the margin between the buying and selling prices of a stock may be narrowed down.

close-up *n* [*Film*] a tight head-and-shoulders shot of a person, or any close shot of an object. The first close-up was apparently of one Fred Ott who sneezed for Edison in an experimental film made in 1900.

close-up worker, also **vest-pocket magician** *n* [*Magic*] a magician who specialises in extracting objects from, or secreting objects in, his or the victim's clothing. See also **mental worker**.

closing *n* [*Clothing*] a sewing operation that seals up the open edge of a garment that has been bagged out.

closing price *n* [*Stock market*] the price recorded during the period of trading designated as the official close.

closing the books *par. phr* [*Stock market*] the procedure carried out by the registrar of a company at the time of a dividend or similar distribution. Only those shareholders registered on the company books at the date they are closed will be eligible for a share of the distribution.

cloth beam, also **cloth roller** *n* [*Weaving*] the roller beam at the lower front of a treadle loom, on to which finished weaving is wound.

cloth cap banking *n* [*Banking*] banking that is aimed at attracting the still relatively untapped potential of the working class customer, a group who persist in preferring cash wages to a salary paid by cheque.

cloth cap pensions *n* [*Industrial relations*] a scheme whereby a worker can choose to take his/her entire future pension in the form of a lump sum payable on retirement. This scheme is usually non-contributory and is aimed at the hourly paid manual worker.

clothesline 1. *n* [*US*] [*Cattlemen*] a rope. **2.** *v* [*US*] [*Football*] a foul move whereby one player jabs his forearm into the throat of an on-rushing opponent, a move that produces a similar effect to that occurring if he had run full tilt onto a taut clothesline and hit it Adam's apple first.

clothespin vote *n* [*US*] [*Politics*] a vote delivered with extreme reluctance, for lack of any option; the image is one of placing a clothespin (clothespeg, UK) over one's nose to banish disgusting smells when one is forced to venture among them.

clothing 1. *n* [*US*] [*Garment trade*] refers to men's clothing only. See also **garment**. **2.** *n* [*Printing*] sheets of paper placed on the cylinder to provide a cushion against which the type prints.

cloture *n* [*US*] [*Politics*] the termination of a debate by a call for an immediate vote on the matter under discussion.

cloud, also **fog** *n* [*US*] [*Police*] a stall in a pickpocket team to whom the wallet or other booty is passed by the actual pickpocket once it has been stolen.

cloud city, also **open field** *n* [*Government*] See **panopolis**.

cloud of title *n* [*US*] [*Real estate*] a defect in the title to a property or a piece of land, thus making it unmarketable.

cloud streets *n* [*Meteorology*] roughly parallel bands of cumulus clouds; their position in the sky indicates the direction of the wind.

cloud watcher *n* [*US*] [*Cattlemen*] a horse that holds it head up too high, and thus fails to concentrate on the cattle.

clout 1. *v* [*US*] [*Crime*] to shoplift. See also **boost**. **2.** *n* [*Politics*] power, influence in politics and government whether or not one stands for election; indeed, sufficient clout makes the process of offering onself for election wasteful of time and (in the US) money, as well as an unnecessary risk. When applied to an elected politician it implies the power to see his programmes carried through; when applied to his fellow citizens, it implies the influence to determine what those programmes shall be. Clout is not restricted to politics, but can be found in any institution/organisation where power struggles go on.

clown alley *n* [*US*] [*Circus*] the area of a circus where clowns prepare for their appearances in the ring.

club money *n* [*Banking*] bank loans made to the discount market by eligible banks; such loans are kept relatively cheap, thus encouraging the discount houses in their turn to invest in a large volume of bills, also competitively priced.

Club, the *n* [*Science*] the organisation of the world's producers of uranium, founded in Paris in 1972.

clubzine *n* [*Science fiction*] a fan magazine produced by a specific science fiction club,.

clump *n* [*UK*] [*Printing*] a single line of cast metal type. See also **slug 9**.

clunch 1. *n* [*Coal-mining*] a fine-grained, often clayey, rock which breaks readily into irregular lumps. **2.** *n* [*Coal-mining*] a bluish, hard clay.

cluster 1. *n* [*Architecture*] a planning term that refers to a type of city which is laid out in a number of small centres, rather than using a nodal point surrounded by concentric rings and a radial road plan. **2.** *n* [*Communications*] a group of terminals or word processing work-stations grouped together and all operating through a central controller. **3.** *n* [*Computing*] a group of magnetic tapes, videos or terminals, usually under the control of one master.

cluster analysis *n* [*Sociology*] a group of statistical techniques used in the analysis of multivariate data to identify internal structure. It is used to identify distinct groupings of individuals, or of responses to attitude surveys.

clustering *n* [*Computing*] the process of grouping together problems with similar characteristics when preparing instructions for a program.

clutch 1. *n* [*US*] [*Marine Corps*] a sudden and serious emergency. **2.** *n* [*Restaurants, Hotels*] a customer who does not tip.

clutch team *n* [*US*] [*Sport*] by extension, from its usage in the USMC, this is a a tough team who can face a very difficult position and keep fighting back until they overcome it.

clutcher *n* [*Oil rigs*] a rotary drill rig driller. See also **rigger, swivelneck**.

clutter 1. *n* [*Advertising*] the great mass/mess of advertising that exists in all media with the resultant problem, for agencies and their clients, of developing messages that will stand out from the rest. **2.** *n* [*Navy*] false echoes on a radar screen caused by high seas and strong winds.

CM *n* [*Science fiction*] abbr of **central mailer** the individual responsible for collating and then distributing the bundles of magazines to members of an **apa**.

CMI *n* [*Computing*] abbr of **computer-managed instruction** the use of computers to create student training programmes based on previous assessments of needs and abilities. See also **CAI, CBL**.

Cmos *n* [*Electronics*] a type of complex semiconductor which features a low power requirement and high 'intelligence'. The Cmos chip is increasingly useful for watches, calculators and other items employing smallscale, portable electronics in which it is convenient not to have the worry or bulk of continual battery changes.

CMT *n* [*Clothing*] abbr of **cut, make and trim** this is a section of the clothing industry in which a contractor is supplied with materials and designs in order to produce garments for a principal.

CO lot *n* [*UK*] [*Police*] Metropolitan policemen's reference to the Special Patrol Group (SPG) who carry CO (Commissioner's Office) on their shoulder straps, where normal officers exhibit a letter identifying their division.

coachwhip *v* [*Sailing, Ropework*] to make a braided cord.

coal head *n* [*Coal-mining*] the working place in a coal heading.

coal mine *n* [*US*] [*Garment trade*] the shipping or stock rooms at a firm; they are often poorly ventilated basements.

coaling *n* [*UK*] [*Theatre*] telling, 'meaningful' lines in one's part; it is possibly derived from 'coal' meaning money, thus implying a meaty part that should attract the paying customers.

coalplex *n* [*Technology*] a theoretical design for an industrial complex in which coal would be used to create a range of secondary fuels and chemical products; these would be used in the various industries sited at the complex and would thus achieve a far higher efficiency than would a plant working on coal power alone.

coarse *a* [*Wine-tasting*] badly made, lacking **breed**; this is not to be confused with **rawness**, which can mature in a developing fine wine.

coarse fish *n* [*Angling*] any fish other than salmon (UK); any fish other than game fish (US).

coarse index *n* [*Education, Libraries*] when two indices are consulted to elicit information, this is the first, less detailed index that is used. See also **fine index**.

coarse stuff *n* [*Building, Plastering*] lime plus sand mortar for use in undercoats.

Coast, the *n* [*Film*] Hollywood, sited on the US West Coast.

coaster *n* [*Mining*] one who searches abandoned mines and attempts to find valuable minerals that may have been missed in the initial mining operation.

coast-to-coaster *n* [*US*] [*Road transport*] an extremely powerful pep-pill.

coating *n* [*UK*] [*Police*] a reprimand; thus 'to give a coating' is to reprimand a fellow officer.

coat-tail *v* [*US*] [*Politics*] to associate oneself closely with the power, influence and probable electability of a strong candidate in the hope of gaining election oneself and using another's strength to mask one's own weaknesses.

coax a strand *v* [*Sailing, Ropework*] to tighten a knot gradually by taking up a little slack at a time and working each strand until all is tight and firm.

COB *n* [*Business*] acro **close of business**.

cobb *n* [*Book-binding*] a paper that comes in a variety which was originally manufactured or used by one Cobb in the 19th century; it is generally used for endpapers.

cobbing *n* [*Navy*] punishments given for small offences.

cobbler 1. *n* [*US*] [*Crime*] a forger of birth certificates, passports, currency notes, etc. **2.** *n* [*Sheepshearing*] the last sheep in a batch to be sheared; this is usually a bad one, with matted, sticky wool, since the easiest sheep tend to be picked first. It is a pun on 'a cobbler's last'.

cobby *a* [*Dog breeding*] compact, strong, thickset, chunky and relatively short; it comes from the similar type of horse.

COBOL *n* [*Computing*] acro **Common Business-**

C

Orientated Language the most popular and widely recognised of the **high-level languages** developed for commercial (rather than technical) computing. Designed in the 1960s, the current version is COBOL–66; an update, COBOL–80 is under development.

cobweb theorem n [*Marketing*] an analysis of a supply and demand situation where supply is a reflection of demand at an earlier time and has therefore minimal relevance to current deamand levels. It is used when short-term production capacity is fixed or dependent on seasonal fluctuations.

cochealed a [*UK*] [*Prisons*] extremely well provided with a given commodity. The spelling and origin of this common prison word are both unknown; possibly it originates in the Gaelic 'cashail' meaning to have something hidden away for a bad time.

cock and hen n [*UK*] [*Market-traders*] this comes from rhyming slang meaning 'ten (pound note)'.

cock fence n [*Hunting*] a thorn fence trimmed very low.

cockade n [*Aerospace*] the national insignia carried as roundels on military aircraft.

cocked pistol n [*Military*] code for the maximum force readiness of US (and NATO) troops, the last step prior to engaging in actual conflict.

cockers n pl [*Navy*] friends, shipmates; thus **according to cocker**.

cocking a fly n [*Angling*] making a fly sit up well on the water when **dry fly fishing**.

cockling n [*Building, Plastering*] the buckling of **firstings** in a fibrous plaster cast.

cocktail 1. n [*US*] [*Medicine*] a barium enema. 2. n [*US*] [*Medicine*] castor oil.

cocktail guard n [*US*] [*Cattlemen*] the last period of watching the herd prior to daylight.

cocktail shaker sort n [*Computing*] a refinement of the **bubble sort** in which alternate passes through the file go in opposite directions, exchanging pairs of elements first from the top of the file and then from the bottom, and so on until the file is sorted.

co-counselling n [*New therapies*] a therapy system whose adherents both offer and receive counselling from each other. No special skills are required other than the ability to listen usefully to another co-counsellor's talk and then to reverse this role within the mutually interdependent framework.

cod 1. n [*Metallurgy*] in iron founding this is a projection in the top or bottom of a mould which forms a pocket or cavity in the casting. 2. also **coddy** n [*Building*] the foreman, who 'cods' his workers along: originally it was a docker's term only.

code four n [*US*] [*Police*] no further assistance required.

code nine n [*US*] [*Medicine*] an emergency code that can be broadcast over a hospital's public address system without alarming patients or visitors: everyone available is to rush to a cardiac arrest emergency. See also **Doctor Blue**.

code seven n [*US*] [*Police*] an officer taking time off from a patrol to eat.

code three n [*US*] [*Police*] an emergency call meaning proceed immediately using siren and/or flashing lights.

code two n [*US*] [*Police*] an urgent call meaning proceed immediately but without siren; flashing lights optional.

codetermination n [*Management*] joint decision-making by the management and the employees in a firm, especially when carried out by formally elected works councils.

coding n [*Sociology*] the translation of raw research data into forms useful for analysis and calculation.

coercivity n [*Electronics*] the force that is required to reverse the polarity of magnetisation.

coey n [*UK*] [*Market-traders*] a thing, an object.

coffee grinder 1. n [*US*] [*Carpenters*] mechanical power drill. 2. n [*Gymnastics*] a manoeuvre done from a squatting position on the floor which involves circling the leg while keeping both hands on the floor. 3. n [*US*] [*Paper-making*] a waterproofing machine.

coffee pot n [*US*] [*Road transport*] a restaurant.

coffee queen n [*Sex*] a homosexual prostitute's derogatory reference to a third-rate rival who will allegedly offer his favours for food and drink, rather than charging a proper fee.

coffee-and pimp n [*Sex*] a third rate pimp whose girls can barely keep him in coffee and doughnuts, never mind the desired pimp accoutrements of Cadillac, cocaine, etc.

coffee-and-cakes n [*US*] [*Theatre*] a part that brings in only a very low salary, barely enough for a subsistence diet.

coffee-housing n [*Hunting*] talking amongst the huntsmen at the covert side, thus disturbing the hounds.

coffee-klatsch campaign n [*US*] [*Politics*] a campaign approach centred on the suburbs through which the candidate moves, giving a number of coffee-klatsch (coffee morning, UK) meetings and addresses.

coffer n [*Building, Plastering*] a deep sunken panel in a **soffit**, dome or ceiling formed by mouldings or beams.

coffin n [*Science*] a specially lead-insulated container used for the transport of radioactive substances.

coffin areas n pl [*Sociology*] those parts of the country in which are situated the collapsing remnants of major 19th century heavy industry, replete with high unemployment, decaying inner cities, and allied forms of deprivation. See also **sunset industry**.

coffin-box *n* [*US*] [*Road transport*] a sleeping compartment independent of the truck's cab.

co-figurative culture *n* [*Anthropology*] a culture in which the young take their role models from within the peer group. See also **post-figurative, pre-figurative culture**.

cogging, also **roughing** *n* [*Metallurgy*] the initial stages of a hot rolling process in which the main aim is to reduce the cross section of the steel.

cognate disciplines *n pl* [*Education*] related or associated disciplines.

cognitive dissonance *n* [*Marketing*] this comes from the psycho-analytic concept of the holding of inconsistent or incompatible ideas which produces tension within an individual. In marketing terms, the feeling that the wonder 'bargain', which the advertisements persuaded one to buy, is infinitely less appealing once it has been unwrapped at home, is followed by a feeling of dissatisfaction with the purchase and the way it has been promoted to the consumer.

cognitive domain *n* [*Education*] the category of instructional objectives relating to knowledge, information and allied intellectual skills within human behaviour.

cogwheel effect *n* [*TV*] a staggered vertical image produced by the relative displacement of alternate electron scan lines.

cohanger *n* [*US*] [*Car salesmen*] See **copilot**.

coherent network *n* [*Communications, Computing*] a network in which all hardware and software is compatible throughout the system; otherwise special conversion systems, affecting both hardware and software, will be necessary.

cohort *n* [*Sociology*] a demographic term to describe a group of people who share the same significant experience at the same period of time.

coin *n* [*Entertainment*] money.

coined titles *n pl* [*Literary criticism*] a term invented by Theodore Bernstein. It refers to identifying words or descriptive nouns which are used to prefix and describe a person, especially in newspaper writing: 'Five-time father and freelance computer programmer Fred Bloggs . . .'

coke 1. *n* [*Tinplating*] tin plate made from iron produced in a cokery. 2. *n* [*Tinplating*] a grade of tin plate more thinly coated than that made over charcoal and which is preferred for canning and general purposes.

cokkies *n* [*Sex*] some unnamed but sought after prize in the cosmos of the black pimp; it is essentially either sexual or economic nirvana.

cokuloris, also **cookie** *n* [*Film*] a light diffuser that has been punched with irregular holes and which can be placed between the light and the camera to give a 'real life' approximation of light and shadow.

COLA *n* [*Economics*] acro **Cost Of Living Adjustment**.

co-lateral constraints *n pl* [*Government*] in arms control talks these are limits on stated types of nuclear weapons, usually new ones developed since a previous agreement, that are not specified in a treaty.

cold *a* [*Electronics*] referring to that part of a circuit which is static at alternating current earth, or at zero potential.

COLD *n* [*Medicine*] acro **chronic obstructive lung disease**.

cold busted *a* [*US*] [*Crime*] arrested for one offence, vagrancy, drunkenness, etc., and then found to be carrying illicit drugs. See also **hot busted**.

cold call *n* [*Marketing*] the appearance of a salesman at a shop or office without a prior appointment; thus the call is 'cold', but the salesman intends, through his own enthusiasm, to 'warm up' the potential for a sale.

cold calling *n* [*Banking*] during a period of low interest rates, US and foreign banks in London – who are not, unlike the clearing banks, penalised by the expenses of collecting money through their branches – can take advantage of this and offer reputable institutions and large companies overdraft facilities at 1% or more below the clearing banks' rate. To offer these overdrafts, the foreign/US bank will approach potential clients on their own initiative – as a salesman makes a 'cold call' on a possible client.

cold canvas *n* [*Marketing*] the term is derived from the blank canvas an artist faces prior to starting a picture; for a businessman this becomes an open situation which he can adapt to his own needs when facing a new problem or a series of decisions. For business consultants the cold canvas implies an assignment which comes with little or no prior outline and offers more than usually wide discretion as to the formation of the task and the methods of approaching it.

cold canvass *n* [*Industrial relations*] a membership drive in which recruiters wait outside a workplace to catch the employees as they change shifts.

cold cut *n* [*Metallurgy*] a hammer-shaped cutting tool designed to cut through cold iron or steel.

cold deck 1. *n* [*Logging*] a pile of logs held for reserve use. 2. also **cooler** *n* [*Gambling*] a specially pre-sorted deck of cards which will be substituted for the legitimate deck at a propitious moment during the play.

cold game *n* [*Gambling*] a game so completely crooked that no honest player will be given a chance to win.

cold launch *n* [*Military*] a system of launching missiles not by igniting fuel, but by using low pressure gas to push the missile out of its silo. Once it has cleared the silo the fuel is then ignited, leaving the silo intact and capable of being used for further launches. This system is incorporated in plans for the **MX** 'Peacekeeper' missile, though still hampered by the indecision over the basing of that missile.

C

C

cold move n [Navy] the movement of a ship without her engines being used.

cold pack n [Cheese-making] two Cheddar cheeses ground or mixed together into a soft spreadable paste without heating or cooking and used for canapés etc; eg: 'Port Wine Cheddar'.

cold player n [Gambling] a player on a losing streak.

cold reduction n [Metallurgy] reducing the thickness of steel sheet or strip to the required finished gauge by working it at room temperature between rolls.

cold ship, also **dead ship** n [Military] a ship without power.

cold shot n [Navy] a catapult failure on an aircraft carrier; the aircraft fails to gain height and crashes into the sea.

cold shut 1. n [Logging] a link that joins two piece of chain. 2. also **cold lap** n [Metallurgy] in iron founding, this is a casting defect caused when two streams of molten metal meet but do not unite.

cold standby n [Computing] the use of a backup system in the event of a failure in the main system. Any data in the main computer at the time, and not in the backing store, will be lost. See also **hot standby, warm standby**.

cold turkey n [US] [Hotels] a guest who does not tip the staff.

cold turkey canvass n [Industrial relations] See **cold canvass**.

cold turkey evangelism n [Religion] door-to-door and street-corner evangelism; the sharing of the gospel of Christ with a total stranger whom one approaches, whether they wish it or not.

cold working n [Metallurgy] permanently altering the dimensions of a piece of steel by rolling it at atmospheric temperatures, rather than by heating it first. Cold working techniques include drawing, pressing, bending, etc.

cold-blood 1. n [US] [Meat trade] an animal that does not fatten easily. 2. n [US] [Meat trade] an animal with mixed ancestry.

cold-blooded 1. a [US] [Cattlemen] referring to horses that are not thoroughbreds. 2. a [Sex] among black pimps, this is a term of approbation; it refers to the ability to control any signs of sexual responsiveness towards one's prostitutes.

collapse 1. n [Cricket] the swift and successive dismissal of several batsmen for minimal scores. 2. v [Cricket] said of a team whose batsmen succumb as in (1.) 3. n [UK] [Theatre] See **breakaway**.

collar 1. v [Coal-mining] to commence digging a hole into which an explosive charge will be placed. 2. v [UK] [Police] to arrest. See also **claim**. 3. n [US] [Coal-mining] the timber in a set which crosses an opening.

collar the bowling v [Cricket] a batsman does this when he knocks the opposition bowling all over the field.

collarette n [Marketing] a card punched with a die-cut hole which fits around the neck of a bottle and carries some advertising copy, announcement of a free gift or competition, or some similar promotional material.

collate v [Bibliography] to compare and examine critically a variety of different texts in order to present readers with a list of all the various editions or versions in which that text has appeared.

collateral damage n [Military] civilian casualties that will inevitably accompany nuclear warfare, no matter to what extent the targeting is supposed to hit military forces and establishments only.

collation 1. n [Bibliography] the detailed breakdown and listing of the pagination and contents of a book. This includes a description of all written and illustratory matter, from the cover and dustjacket to the back endpapers, the edition date, the publishers, the illustrator's name, the chapter headings, the existence of any index, bibliography, etc. 2. n [Book collecting] the bibliographical description of the physical composition of a book, expressed in a more or less standard formula.

collections n pl [Education] interim verbal assessments or examination papers to which Oxford University undergraduates are subjected between matriculation and finals.

collective consumption n [Sociology] those mass needs, usually in the urban environment, such as food, housing and transport, which make it possible for workers to offer their labour for sale day after day.

collective goods n pl [Economics] goods owned by the public as a whole, rather than by an individual, eg: roads, public buildings, hospitals, etc.

collector n [Electronics] that point on a simple amplifying circuit from which the output signal is taken.

college course nicknames n pl [US] [Education] blabs in labs (linguistics), chokes and croaks (first aid and safety education), clapping for credit (music appreciation), darkness at noon (art history slide show), Gods for clods (comparative religion), holes and poles (sex education), jock major (physical education), Monday night at the movies (film studies), monkeys to junkies (anthropology), nudes for dudes (art), number-cruncher (involving complex maths), nuts and sluts (abnormal psychology), physics for poets (basic physics for arts graduates), Plato to NATO (European studies), rocks for jocks (introduction to geology), shocks for jocks (basic engineering), slums and bums (urban sociology), sounds and tunes (campus songs), spick (Spanish), stars for studs (astronomy), stones and bones (pre-history).

college of knowledge, the n [UK] [Railways] the union negotiating committee. See also **syndicate, the**.

collegialism n [Politics] the theory that church or state, or both, are, or ought to be, voluntary associations whose social and political structure can be seen in the model of a college, united in the pursuit of recognised ends, but generating an ethos that transcends simple devotion to these ends.

collision n [Computing] the need to use the same machine for two diverse applications at the same time.

collusive tendering n [Commerce, Industry] the practice of several firms, when offering supposedly rival tenders for a piece of work, in aggreeing to co-operate for their mutual benefit, rather than engage, as the client assumes, in real competition.

colonialism n [Economics] the concept that in any trade between developed and less developed countries, the advantage is always to the advanced countries.

colonise v [US] [Politics] the placing of political supporters in areas where their votes will be of greatest use. It is the opposite of gerrymandering, which is no longer feasible. Under this scheme the people are taken to the electoral areas, rather than attempting to have the ideal electoral boundaries drawn around the concentrations of optimum support.

colour 1. n [Glass-making] a quality of crystal glass: the best glass is of the finest colour, and paradoxically shows no trace of colour whatsoever. 2. n [Journalism] background facts and information, material that lends a degree of 'brightness' to the monochrome relentlessness of basic facts and figures. 3. [Mining] a small particle of gold remaining in a prospector's pan, after most of the waste material has been washed away. 4. n [Paper-making] a coating mixture of pigment and adhesive, whether coloured or not, used in paper manufacture. 5. n [Printing] the overall degree of thickness of, or weight in, a face. 6. n [Science] in nuclear physics, this is used when referring to the three hypothetical quantum states which combine to produce the strong force that binds **quarks**. It comes from the idea of assuming three basic colours – red, yellow and blue – for the basic quarks; then, when they combine, they produce white, representative of the neutralised state of the perfect combined quark. See also **flavour 2**.

colour field painting, also **shaped canvases** n [Art] colour field painters replace tonal contrasts and brushwork by solid areas of colour which usually extend across the canvas from edge to edge and imply that the fields of colour stretch on to infinity, far beyond the confines of the canvas.

colour man, also **colour announcer** n [TV] a broadcaster employed to add **colour** to a commentary, or backup/editorial material to news programmes. It is sometimes used derogatively as 'colour babbler'. See also **colourcaster**.

colour of title n [US] [Real estate] a situation where a title deed appears to be in order, but it hides a defect which then emerges to colour the title and cause problems in the sale.

colouration 1. n [Audio] a visual metaphor for acoustic emphasis, coming from any part of the sound reproduction chain: it refers to the characteristics imparted to recorded sound, usually by the loudspeakers. 2. n [US] [Politics] the ideological identification of a politician based on his/her past record of statements, votes on key bills, etc. The political position thus revealed may have little to do with the individual's actual extra-political point of view, but is based on that vital characteristic of all in his calling: expediency.

colourcaster n [TV] a background commentator, often a retired sports celebrity, who backs up the play-to-play commentators with reminiscence, biographical details, and a general overview of the game that enlivens the basic facts on what is happening.

com v [Medicine] to suffer a coma.

coma n [Optics] a lens aberration resulting in a variation of magnification with aperture; rays through the outer edges of a lens form a larger image than those through the centre.

co-manager n [Banking] a bank that ranks second to the **lead manager** in the marketing of a new share issue.

comb 1. n [Computing] an assembly of seek arms in a magnetic disk unit that holds the read/write heads which move over the appropriate tracks of a disk. 2. v [Navy] a ship does this when it turns into the track of an approaching torpedo in an attempt to avoid being hit.

comb perforation n [Philately] so-called because the perforating pins are arranged in the form of a comb: a long line of pins with a number of shorter lines at right-angles so that the top and sides of one or more rows can be perforated simultaneously.

combat loading n [Military] the loading of a transport vehicle to ensure the best tactical requirements, irrespective of the volume of the load. See also **administrative loading**.

combat radius n [Military] the distance which an aircraft can fly, be of effective use in combat, and then return safely to base.

combi n [Aerospace] abbr of **combination** an aircraft that can be used for either passenger or freight carrying.

combination n [Boxing] a number of punches put together in quick succession.

combination bat n [Table tennis] a bat covered in two types of rubber, one on each side, and which are completely different in character; thus **tacky/long pimples**, fast/**sandwich pimples**, etc.

combination cover n [Philately] a **cover** that bears the stamps of more than one country where the various national stamps pay for sections of the letter's journey.

combine paintings *n pl* [*Art*] Robert Rauschenberg's description of those of his own works that incorporate non-art objects with traditional pigments; such paintings are the logical and extreme extension of Cubist collages, stretching the accepted convention of the easel picture to its breaking point.

combined print *n* [*Film*] a print in which the sound track and picture have been 'married' to produce the standard print which will be shown in the cinemas.

combing *n* [*Weaving*] the process of removing the short fibres and combing parallel all long fibres in the preparation of wool or hair for **worsted** spinning.

combozine *n* [*Science fiction*] a collection of fan magazines bound together for distribution; it is usually created for a convention.

come again *v* [*Angling*] said of a fish when it bites, rises or gives a pull a second time.

come apart 1. *v* [*Religion*] to come together as fellow members of a religious group. 2. *v* [*Religion*] to isolate oneself psychologically from the mass of non-believers; see Mark 6:31.

come back Tuesday *v phr* [*Theatre*] a clichéd piece of pseudo-friendly advice offered by theatrical directors and managers to auditioning hopefuls; it means 'go away'.

come down *v* [*Theatre*] when a performance 'comes down', it ends; the term refers to the coming down of the curtain. This term is also used in business theatre, where a presentation 'comes down' at a certain time. See also **group 3**.

come from *v* [*New therapies*] usually as in 'where are you coming from?' or 'where am I coming from?', etc; the exposition of one's mental attitudes, philosophies, way of life, background to one's stated opinions – all in all an opportunity to sound off at length about the niceties of one's self image.

come in *v* [*Farming*] used of a cow; it means to calve.

come in order *v* [*Tobacco*] used of tobacco which is moist enough to be handled.

come on *n* [*US*] [*Theatre*] a mediocre actor whose attempt at performing is limited to walking on to and possibly around the stage; acting, as such, is not part of his/her repertoire.

come up 1. *v* [*Photography*] said of an image when it appears on photographically sensitive paper. 2. *v* [*Sailing, Ropework*] to slacken a rope or tackle gently.

come up with the rations *v phr* [*UK*] [*Military*] a derogatory description of medals that are so widely distributed that they might as well have been given out at mealtimes, rather than actually and meritoriously earned.

come your cocoa, also **come your fat, lot** *v phr* [*UK*] [*Police*] various references to ejaculation, excretion and vomiting, all of which mean 'to make a full confession'.

come-along 1. *n* [*Industry*] a gripping device used for pulling and stretching wire or metal. 2. *n* [*Logging*] the vehicle which transports men to and from work. See also **crummie**. 3. *n* [*US*] [*Navy*] the fairing which covers a carrier's deck and makes it safe for the storage of aircraft, vehicles and other stores.

come-back money *n* [*Gambling*] money that is placed with off-track bookmakers; these bookies then take it to the track where they bet it again in the hope of changing the odds on a particular horse.

comebacker *n* [*Baseball*] a ball hit directly along the ground from the batter to the pitcher.

come-out *n* [*Gambling*] the first throw of the dice after the shooter has named the point he/she is chasing.

comfort letter 1. *n* [*Finance*] a letter to a bank or other lender of money written to support someone who wishes to borrow money. 2. *n* [*Finance*] a letter written from one party of a contract to the other specifying that certain actions not fully covered in the contract will or will not be taken.

comic cuts *n* [*UK*] [*Diplomacy*] the weekly list of promotions, transfers and similar personnel movements in the UK diplomatic corps.

coming out of hole *n* [*Oil rigs*] the withdrawal of the **drill string** from the well bore.

coming to nature *n* [*Metallurgy*] that stage of the **puddling** process when particles of solid iron clearly form in the molten bath.

coming short *n* [*Angling*] a fish not taking the fly properly.

comint *n* [*Military*] abbr of **communications intelligence** all forms of intelligence derived from satellites, the monitoring of foreign radio and other broadcast media (both public and military), listening in to foreign codes and telephone calls, etc. See also **elint, humint, sigint, telint**.

comma position *n* [*US*] [*Skiing*] a skiing position in which the body is curved to the side and assumes the shape of a comma.

command economy *n* [*Politics, Economics*] an economy that is centrally planned and managed with targets imposed from above. Inflexible, bureaucratic, it was once the norm in socialist states, but recently such economies are looking for a greater degree of flexibility, most notably China. Command economies are imposed on all countries, irrespective of ideology, during a major emergency, eg: war.

commandism *n* [*Politics*] the concentration of power in one strong, central position.

commando selling *n* [*Marketing*] intensive selling – often of a new product – in hitherto virgin markets; a specialised sales force is often trained just for this product.

commensalism *n* [*Sociology*] a term that denotes the relationship which involves both competition and co-operation among those who occupy similarly specialised positions within a division of labour; commensal relations work to maintain the class structure.

comment *n* [*Computing*] a phrase inserted into a program to assist the programmer in debugging operations by pointing out some aspect of the program; comments are ignored by **compilers** and have no effect on the program.

commercial paper 1. *n* [*Finance, Commerce*] a variety of short-term negotiable instruments used by US businesses to make payments, including bills of exchange, promissory notes and trade acceptances. **2.** *n* [*Finance, Commerce*] sums advanced by banks to businesses to facilitate the buying of goods. See also **prime commercial paper**.

commercial set *n* [*Commerce*] the four essential shipping documents needed when exporting goods: bill of exchange, bill of lading, certificate of insurance, and invoice. Two sets of these documents, posted on different days, are sent by the exporter to the buyer.

commercials 1. *n pl* [*Sex*] these are all usages by homosexual prostitutes: various tired old excuses, which no-one believes, to justify this choice of occupation; a personal build-up of one's own charms designed to attract clients; the placing of advertisements in those papers or magazines that will accept the copy in order to increase trade. **2.** *n pl* [*Stock market*] shares in commercial companies, especially those selling consumer goods, as opposed to industrials.

commie *n* [*Marbles*] the target marble in the game. See also **crockie, dib, duck, kimmie, immie, mib**.

commies *n pl* [*Marbles*] glass marbles, especially the creamy ones.

Committee of the Whole House *n* [*UK*] [*Politics*] a situation in the House of Commons in which the Speaker leaves his chair, the mace is placed beneath the table, and the House acts as a Committee under the chairmanship of the Chairman of Ways and Means. This is the only occasion when a Member can speak more than once in a debate.

commodity fetichism *n* [*Politics*] this is Marx's theory that while commodities appear to be simply objects, in fact they contain within them varieties of social relationships: those who produced them, those who will buy them, etc. These make themselves felt once the commodity enters the marketplace, when the essentially social nature of their production is no longer concealed.

commodity paper *n* [*US*] [*Commerce, Finance*] negotiable instruments which are held as security for loans that finance the import of commodities.

commodity trap *n* [*Advertising, Commerce*] the concept that one's product is simply a commodity, no more or less; such a concept limits its advertising potential.

common 1. *a* [*US*] [*Meat trade*] a grade of meat below 'fair', but above **cutters** and **canners**. **2.** *a* [*Weaving*] the second to lowest quality of wool in the blood system of grading. **3.** *a* [*Wine-tasting*] lacking **breed** but perfectly drinkable. **4.** *n* [*Marbles*] the target marble in the game. See also **dib, duck, kimmie, immie, mib**.

common carrier *n* [*Communications*] a telecommunications resource providing facilities to the public, eg: the Post Office through whose cables **LAN** data can be transmitted.

common learnings *n pl* [*Education*] the education which it is considered should be the common experience of all pupils.

common site picketing *n* [*US*] [*Industrial relations*] the picketing of a sub-contractor at a construction site by members of a union whose dispute is essentially with the main contractor.

common stock *n* [*Stock market*] the basic stocks that are made available for those who wish to buy shares in the ownership of a public company. Owners of this stock are entitled to voting rights over the selection of directors and similar important matters, and to receive regular dividends on their holdings. If the company is liquidated, the holders of preferred stock take precedence over those of common stock, but common stock is more likely to yield greater and faster profits.

commonality *n* [*Computing, Communications*] the property of a number of systems, in which each possesses the ability to interchange parts with the others.

communicated authenticity *n* [*New therapies*] longhand for genuineness or sincerity.

communication discrepancy *n* [*Advertising*] the measuring of children's response to an advertisement by comparing their response to the actual object and then to the commercial that features it. Thus one can assess whether a commercial does justice to a product or raises hopes beyond what it can really offer.

communications mix *n* [*Management*] the methods of promotion employed by a company that include the use of a mixed variety of communications media.

communications sink *n* [*Communications*] any device which receives information, control or other signals from a communications source or sources.

community facility *n* [*US*] [*Prisons*] any form of jail – adult and juvenile – in which inmates are allowed to participate in the local community by taking school classes, working at daytime jobs, joining drug or alcohol treatment programmes, etc.

comp 1. *n* [*Advertising*] abbr of **comprehensive** a preliminary version of the artwork, giving the basic look of the advertisement. Thus 'rough comp' is the most basic version and 'tight comp' is a version nearly approximating the finished product. **2.** *n* [*Printing*] abbr of **compositor** the man who sets up the metal type on the **stone**. **3.** *n* [*Theatre*] abbr of **complimentary** a free ticket. See also **orders, paper 3**. **4.** *v* [*Music*] abbr of **accompany** in jazz this is to play an accompaniment, especially when employing irregular rhythmic chords. **5.** *a* [*US*] [*Gambling*] abbr of **complimentary** used when a gambling establishment, usually the large casino-hotels of Las Vegas and Atlantic City in America, offers free board, lodging and other inducements to the 'high-rollers', the big spending gamblers whose overall losses, it may safely be assumed, will far outweigh the bills they may run up in the hotel.

compander *n* [*Audio*] any device or circuit which compresses the dynamics of an audio signal to suit a particular medium or purpose and which reduces any noise that is introduced between the two stages.

companding *n* [*Communications*] abbr of **compressing and expanding** a means of accelerating and simplifying data transmission by compressing the data, transmitting it and then expanding it again into its original form.

companion space *n* [*US*] [*Undertakers*] a grave adjacent to that of a near relative, usually one's husband or wife. When such graves are placed vertically, one creates double depth.

companionate crime *n* [*US*] [*Law*] any crime which is committed by two or more persons against another.

Company *n* [*Espionage*] the Central Intelligence Agency (CIA) of the US.

company doctor *n* [*Management*] on the lines of Broadway's 'play doctors', this is an individual who is brought in to advise businesses, especially those facing severe financial crises. The 'doctor' will usually take a temporary management job until the problem is over.

company union *n* [*Industrial relations*] See **scab union**.

comparability *n* [*Industrial relations*] a theoretical means of working out pay levels by comparing one job with another; easy to propose, it is almost impossible to carry out efficiently.

comparative spot *n* [*Advertising, TV*] a commercial which compares the client's product with that of a rival, invariably to the advantage of the one being touted. See also **accepted pairing**.

comparison shopper *n* [*Marketing*] a researcher, often employed by a retailer, who investigates the merchandising activities of rival retailers.

compartmentalisation *n* [*Government*] the restriction of knowledge (especially of military or scientific developments) to the various 'compartments' in which this knowledge is being developed, giving only a very few people access to the overall picture; a participant should know what is sufficient to perform his/her job, but nothing more. See also **need-to-know**.

compartmentalised *a* [*Espionage*] referring to a method of running agents whereby each is told exactly what he/she needs to know for efficient working, and nothing more. Such a method is intended to restrict the problems that will occur, if the agent is captured or defects.

compash *n* [*US*] [*Crime, Police*] abbr of any **compassionate law officer** eg: prison chaplain, probation worker, social worker.

compatible *a* [*Computing*] used to describe the ability of one computer to deal with material designed for another, including **programs, peripherals, add-ons**, etc.

compensation cafeteria *n* [*Industrial relations*] See **cafeteria system**.

compensation criterion *n* [*Economics*] a criterion for the social desirability of an economic policy, proposed by Lord Kaldor (1908–): if those who gain from a policy could compensate in full those who lose, then the policy is an improvement on one that leaves things as they are.

competence 1. *n* [*Law*] the legal or mental capacity to enter legally into a contract or will. **2.** *n* [*Linguistics*] a term coined by Noam Chomsky (b. 1928) to define an individual's knowledge of the language he/she speaks, its rules, its grammar and its ambiguities. See also **performance 1**.

competent beds *n pl* [*Coal-mining*] beds of rock which have responded to techtonic forces by folding and faulting rather than by crushing and flowing; such beds are relatively strong. See also **incompetent bed**.

competent rock *n* [*Coal-mining*] a strong rock which may not require support during excavation.

competing demand *n* [*Economics*] See **alternate demand**.

competitive parity *n* [*Marketing*] a method of setting the advertising budget by matching it to that of the opposition.

competitive pricing *n* [*Commerce*] See **aggressive pricing**.

compiler *n* [*Computing*] a special program that translates the **source code** into a code that the machine can understand.

compiler-compiler *n* [*Computing*] a program that accepts the syntactic and semantic description of a programming language and generates a **compiler** for that language.

complain *v* [*Education*] at Eton College, to report a boy to the Headmaster as deserving of punishment.

completeness errors *n pl* [*Computing*] errors that are detected after an operator has indicated that the program is complete; such errors are listed sequentially and can be either ignored or corrected as the operator desires, prior to executing the completed program.

completion *n* [*Oil rigs*] the process whereby a finished well is either sealed off or prepared for production by fitting a wellhead.

completist *n* [*Book collecting*] a collector who

concentrates particularly on collecting absolutely everything in his field, sometimes irrespective of quality.

complex *a* [*Wine-tasting*] said of the developing fine wine, offering a many-faceted taste and smell.

complex labour *n* [*Politics*] See **compound labour**.

compliance cost *n* [*Banking*] sums paid to H. M. Customs & Excise in compliance with the provisions of Value Added Tax (VAT).

complimentary play *n* [*Gambling*] a gambling session indulged in by one casino manager in the casino of one of his rivals, or by a professional gambler or racketeer as a gesture of friendship to the casino bosses, since it is assumed that he will lose money.

compo 1. *n* [*Building, Plastering*] sand plus cement or mortar made of lime plus sand plus cement. **2.** *n* [*UK*] [*Military*] abbr of **composite rations** the combat rations issued to members of the British Army on manoeuvres or in battle; they are supposedly of ideal nutritive value. also Sheffield composition. **3.** *n* [*Metallurgy*] in iron founding, this is a moulding material composed of a mixture of crushed and graded firebricks and a refractory clay, used for making heavy steel castings.

compositing the resolution *part phr* [*Trade unions*] a practice popular at TUC and individual union conferences; it is the gathering together of a variety of similar resolutions that have been put to the conference. They are grouped together in one composite resolution to save time for other business.

composition *n* [*Business*] an alternative to bankruptcy in which a firm's or individual's creditors agree to accept a percentage of their claims rather than press for full payment.

compound *v* [*Horse-racing*] used of a racehorse which loses its impetus and blows up during the race.

compound envelope *n* [*Philately*] government postal stationery bearing more than one embossed or printed stamp.

compound labour, also **complex labour** *n* [*Politics*] skilled, especially trained labour. Such skills justify wage differentials on the principle of 'to each according to his work'.

comprehensive physician *n* [*US*] [*Medicine*] a proctologist who sees the 'hole' (rectum) patient.

compressed *a* [*Printing*] used to describe any typeface appreciably narrower than the normal. See also **condensed**.

computer bound, also **computer limited** *a* [*Computing*] said of a limit in the output rate of a program or computing operation due to restrictions on the speed of certain computing functions within that program.

computer cleaner *n* [*US*] [*Crime*] a white-collar criminal, often an employee of the firm he/she defrauds, who specialises in computer fraud, either abstracting or destroying information or using special knowledge to obtain money from the firm's accounts.

comsymp *n* [*Politics*] abbr of **communist sympathiser** the term was coined during the McCarthy era of the early 1950s by ultra-right winger John Birch as a means of branding 'fellow travellers'. It is reasonably rare today, but still popular with the Right.

con 1. *n* [*Crime*] a variety of telephone-based confidence tricks: the con-man rings around, selling tickets in the name of a legitimate sponsor, but pockets the subscriptions for himself. **2.** *n* [*TV*] a convention of science fiction, especially 'Star Trek', fans. **3.** *v* [*Navy*] to direct the course of a ship by giving specific orders to the helmsman who actually controls the wheel; thus 'to have the con' (USN) is to be in control of the ship's course.

con hotel *n* [*Science fiction*] the hotel designated for lodging out-of-town conventioners; it is usually the site of the convention.

concentration *n* [*Mining*] a stage in the separation of valuable minerals from the ore that surrounds them: the ore is washed on a sloped table and the heavier minerals naturally fall towards the bottom of the slope.

concentrations *n pl* [*US*] [*Banking*] measurements used by the Federal Reserve Bank and individual state banking departments to determine the proportion of a bank's assets/liabilities that is related to a single borrower or depositor.

concentrator *n* [*Computing*] a method of combining data from several local phone lines and sending it all down one special high-speed data line, thus saving money when communicating with a distant and otherwise costly computer data bank.

concentric zone theory *n* [*Sociology*] a theory developed by the **Chicago School** which states that cities have five concentric zones: central business and amusement district; transition zone of developing new business, often including rundown and relatively cheap housing; homes of manual workers; middle-class suburbs; and finally the commuter belt. The theory has been heavily criticised (eg: cities fall more into sections, not circles) but it is still useful.

concept art, also **anti-object art, begriff kunst, blind man's art, con art, dematerialised art, documentary art, head art, idea art, impossible art, post-object art, project art** *n* [*Art*] an international idiom of the avant garde, fashionable in the late 1960s/early 1970s which centred on giving low priority to the art work as a physical object – since that merely emphasised the artist's physical ability rather than his mental resources. The aim was for a 'dematerialised art' which would produce works that were physical but not directly available to the human senses, eg: inert gases, detectable only via scientific instruments.

C

C

concept testing n [*Marketing*] the use of a psychological testing panel to decide whether the concept of a product is feasible, prior even to deciding whether or not there exists a potential market for that product.

concept video n [*TV, Pop music*] a promotional video linked to the idea behind an album or single record, rather than simply pictures that record the performer(s) in concert or in the studio. In the last decade such videos have become almost as important as the song and artiste in ensuring the success of a song.

conceptual architecture, also **imaginary architecture, invisible architecture, nowhere architecture** n [*Architecture*] plans for buildings or cities that have never been built; they are considered as legitimate architectural developments which happen not to have been taken beyond the early, conceptual stage. The term was first defined in an essay by Peter D. Eisenman in 1971 in which there was no text, only footnotes.

conceptual art n [*Art*] an art form that, while hard to define exactly, comprises certain basic characteristics: a concern with the concepts that generate art rather than the physical objects that create it; a wide-ranging use of language and art theory which often embraces the functions of the art critic and art theorist; a wide variety of artistic behaviour, which in its most extreme form becomes a philosophical enquiry into the nature of art. Taken to such extremes, conceptual art became excessively introspective and cerebral, but its use is in drawing hitherto understated attention to the role of ideas in art.

conceptual difficulties n [*Social work*] a euphemism for stupidity, both in an individual or, when referring to local government decisions, applicable on an institutional level.

concert party 1. n [*Stock market*] a method of evading the UK law (the Companies Acts 1967, 1976) which states that any single shareholder with 5% or more of a company's shares must inform the company in writing at once. A number of purchasers can, 'acting in concert', each buy less than 5% of the shares, then consolidate their holdings, and thus gradually take over a company. The Companies Act (1981) has attempted to remedy this by declaring such gradual takeovers as illegal and stating that any 'concert party' must by law inform the target company of their joint interest. Concert parties are not exclusively British, but occur both illegally and in secret on many international exchanges. 2. n [*Management*] a term employed by the (UK) City Code on Take-overs and Mergers to refer to 'persons acting in concert' to co-operate in the purchase of shares with a view to gaining control of a company; it is a pun on the traditional show business term.

concerti, also **consigia** n pl [*US*] [*Crime*] intra-family courts held by the US Mafia to sort out differences, punish offences, etc.

concessional exports n pl [*Politics*] exports of grain and similar vital commodities from the developed nations to the less fortunate ones; the recipient countries never pay for such exports and the whole deal is in effect consumer-based propaganda.

concettism n [*Literary criticism*] work that is full of literary artifice and pompous prosing; it comes from Lat. 'conceptus' meaning 'concept'.

concinnity n [*Literary criticism*] elegance and harmony that are notable in the creation of a literary work; it comes from Lat. 'concinnitas' meaning 'skilfully put together'.

conclave n [*Science fiction*] a small or regional convention.

concrete art n [*Art*] a term introduced to replace 'abstract', the latter being regarded as unsatisfactory, since it implied a separation from reality. The concrete artist does not abstract from nature; he/she constructs from elements of natural phenomena, 'the concretion of the creative spirit'.

concrete labour n [*Politics*] work that has actually been performed.

concrete poetry, also **audiovisual tests, constellations, evident poetry, kinetic poetry, machine poetry, objective poetry, optical poetry, poem paintings, poetry of surface, popcrete, process texts, publit, semiotic poetry, visual texts, word art** n [*Literary criticism*] the concrete poet arranges elements freely across a surface, rather than restricting himself to linear syntax.

concurrency n [*Aerospace*] a meeting of a number of scientific, technological, training and allied experts in order to consult each other and if possible accelerate their joint development of a given aerospace programme.

condensed a [*Printing*] used to describe any typeface somewhat narrower than the normal. See also **compressed**.

condition of existence n [*Sociology*] contemporary Marxist theory: a set of conditions that are required for the existence or operation of some social activity; this has replaced strict **economic determinism**.

conditional bond n [*Commerce, Finance*] See **double bond**.

conditionality n [*Government*] rules established by the International Monetary Fund (IMF) to control those countries who need its aid but appear to be moving out of line. Quite simply it is made clear that unless the government in question conducts itself in a way which the IMF finds acceptable, there will be no loan.

condominium n [*Politics*] a term brought into modern usage by Henry Kissinger, apparently trying for a literal Latin translation, to imply the idea of a joint government by the two superpowers; the word is more usually used to describe a large, co-operatively owned block of flats. Its political usage dates at least from the late 19th century Anglo-French Condominium of the New Hebrides, under which the islands, prior to gaining independence as Vanuatu, were governed jointly by the two European powers joined latterly by the New Hebrideans themselves.

conductor casing *n* [*Oil rigs*] a piece of pipe run into the open hole and cemented in to stop the wall from caving in; it also restrains any unwanted fluids from entering the hole from the surrounding rocks.

cone 1. *n* [*Film*] a cone-shaped light that produces soft lighting effects. **2.** *n* [*Weaving*] the conical spool on which yarn is wound.

cone flutter *n* [*Audio*] speaker movements of a lesser intensity than **breathing** which can be caused by a warp in the disc, rather than groove modulation itself.

confab *n* [*Film*] a conference. See also **take a meeting**.

conference *n* [*Politics*] the use of 'conference', bereft of definite or indefinite articles, appears to imply some greater statement of collective force than would the normal grammar. It is much used by British trade union and Labour party annual conference statements.

configuration *n* [*Computing*] the collection of parts that make up a computer system, and the way in which they are arranged.

configuration management *n* [*Aerospace, Management*] the management discipline and the technology required for the building and design of such high-quality, high-precision products as spacecraft. Standards of excellence and customer satisfaction must be far greater than in a normal project and the configuration of the project – the way in which parts are produced and assembled on many and complex levels – must be precise and acceptable.

configure *v* [*Military*] to appear, to resemble, to look like.

confirming house *n* [*Business*] an agent acting in one country for a buyer in another.

conflict model of society *n* [*Sociology*] the theories of history and society which assume that all social behaviour and transformation stem from conflicts between rival interests and forces, at the expense of planning, friendship, peace and creativity; societies exist not through consensus, but by the strong forcing their aims and desires upon the weak.

conflict spectrum *n* [*Military*] all levels of hostility, from the first pre-crisis wrangling and sabre-rattling, through graduating levels of **escalation** to all-out **first-strike** and **second-strike** nuclear exchange. See also **escalation ladder**.

conflict theory *n* [*Sociology*] this is one of the theories regarding competition over the control of

resources or advantages, which stops short of actual violence. Conflicts are settled either by means of mutually accepted rules, or by one of the two sides exerting greater power in the situation.

conflict-generating event *n* [*Sociology*] a controversy; a riot.

conformer *n* [*Industrial relations*] a member of a piece work group who accepts the various fiddles that have been established by the rest of the group. Thus the conformity is to the rules of the group, rather than to those of the employer. See also **job spoiler**.

confrontation *n* [*Sociology*] the action of facing up to someone in order to describe to them their own behaviour and its likely effects in order to evoke a response from them. A particular use of confrontation is to bring home to alcoholics or drug addicts the reality of their situation.

conga *n* [*Air travel*] a chain of snow-clearing vehicles – a line of snow ploughs – led by a high-speed runway clearer.

conglomerate, also **pudding stone** *n* [*Coal-mining*] a rock that consists of rounded pebbles held together by a natural cement.

congo *n* [*Mining*] a variety of commercial diamond incorporated in a bit; thus it also means a variety of bit.

conjugate leaves *n pl* [*Book collecting*] when the sheets that make up a book have been folded, cut and bound, the leaves which, if the book were unfolded, would make up one original single sheet of paper, are the conjugate leaves.

conjuncture 1. *n* [*Economics*] a term used by economists as shorthand for 'the current state and development of the economy', including complex trends in employment, the balance of payments, output, wages, etc. **2.** *n* [*Sociology*] the actual balance of unevenly developed social and political forces in a society at a particular moment.

conk *n* [*Logging*] wood-destroying fungus that grows on trees; thus 'conky' is used of a tree on which this fungus grows.

conkie *n* [*UK*] [*Market-traders*] the nose.

conlog *n* [*Science fiction*] the agenda of activities at a science fiction convention.

connate water *n* [*Coal-mining*] water that exists within a rock formation and is the same age as it, rather than water which has permeated the rock.

connection 1. *n* [*Drugs*] a supplier of narcotics; thus 'to make a connection' is to purchase drugs, and 'connection money' is required for drugs. **2.** *n* [*US*] [*Circus*] the canvas-enclosed corridor that joins the big top and the dressing tent.

connectivity *n* [*Military*] See **strategic connectivity**.

connector conspiracy *n* [*Computing*] the alleged tendency of manufacturers to make sure that none of their current products connect satisfactorily with their new ranges, thus forcing the consumer either to discard his current system and

C

start again from scratch, or to invest in various **interface** devices – both of which decisions will cost money.

conquest sales *n pl* [*Commerce*] sales that capture new customers who had previously bought from a rival.

conscience collective *n* [*Sociology*] those forces of conscience which are promoted externally to motivate an individual, and are separate from his own internal moral attitudes; such forms of conscience coerce members of a group to share moral positions.

conscience money *n* [*Tax*] an anonymous payment of additional tax made by an individual who knows that he has been insufficiently assessed.

consciousness raising *n* [*Politics, Sociology*] essentially this means gaining a greater awareness of one's own position in the world, and with it one's needs and one's potential as a human being. However the phrase was swiftly co-opted by the women's movement to the exclusion of all else. Thus a 'risen consciousness' now means the fulfilment of one's true femininity, and is not open for use by other groups.

consciousness I, II, III *n* [*Sociology*] a term coined in 1970 by Charles A Reich in his best-seller 'The Greening of America'. I: the self-made man with traditional 'American' values; II: the verbal, college educated media man, representing the values of 20th century America; III: what used to be called 'the alternative society' or the 'youth culture'. Reich espoused con. III with all the enthusiasm of an ageing convert. Time has shattered the myth, although one can see certain parallels in the work of another futurologist, Alvin Toffler, whose book, 'The Third Wave' (1980) bears certain similarities, although from a very different standpoint.

consensus gentium fallacy *n* [*Literary criticism*] the fallacy of arguing that merely because a large number of people believe in an idea, or because it has become part of an established ideology, it is necessarily correct; it comes from Lat. meaning 'the consent of the people'. See also **affective fallacy**.

consensus painting *n* [*Art*] a Marxist term that defines the style of painting produced in the UK; it represents the consensus of British bourgeois taste as regards what is 'good art' and thus what is the ideal world which it should represent. It is epitomised in the annual Royal Academy Summer exhibition.

consequentialism *n* [*Philosophy*] the view that the merit of an action is determined by its consequences rather than by the motive from which it springs. Thus the basic concept of morality comes not from obligation but from value, and the rightness of an act is not an intrinsic property but is dependent on the goodness or badness of the consequences, whether actual, predictable or expected. See also **teleology**.

conservatism *n* [*Government, Science*] the philosophy of the US Atomic Energy Commission (AEC) which claimed, in 1971, that although there might be some possible gaps in its understanding of nuclear reactor safety, in practice, the AEC's basic conservatism when designing and building such reactors would automatically ensure that no safety problems would ever arise.

consideration 1. *n* [*Law*] a promise to do something, or to refrain from doing something, in exchange for another person's promise; an essential element of a valid contract. **2.** *n* [*Stock market*] the cost of a purchase of shares before adding on expenses, calculated by multiplying the amount of stock or the number of shares by the cost/unit.

consiglieri *n* [*US*] [*Crime*] the counsellor or advisor to the head of a US Mafia **family**, who advises on overall policy, rather than taking part in any violence.

consist *n* [*US*] [*Railways*] the description of the make up of a train by types and number of cars.

consistency concept *n* [*Accounting*] a fundamental accounting concept calling for consistency of accounting treatment for like items within each period of accounting and from one period to the next.

consolidate *v* [*Industrial relations*] to add the bonus and any other extra payments into the basic rates, so that it is on this large conglomerate sum that calculations of overtime payments (based on multiples of the basic rate) will be made.

consolidation *n* [*Stock market*] the replacement of shares of low nominal value with an equivalent number of a higher nominal value, ie: 20 5p shares replaced by one £1 share.

Consols *n pl* [*Stock market*] abbr of **Consolidated Annuities, Consolidated Stock** interest-bearing securities, issued by the UK Government, which have no repayment date.

conspiracy theory *n* [*Politics*] the theory that whatever benefits a given class only does so because of a prior conspiracy by that class against all others; the usual assumption is that the class in question is the ruling class.

constant *n* [*Computing*] See **literal 2**.

constant dollars, also **C$** *n* [*Finance*] a dollar price of a given year that is established as a base against which the dollar prices of other years can be adjusted to determine relative purchasing prices.

constant mesh *n* [*UK*] [*Road transport*] a design of gearbox in which the gears are always in mesh and, on selection of another gear, a 'dog' on the drive shaft in the gearbox engages an appropriate pair of gears.

constant wear garment *n* [*Aerospace*] a cross between ski pants and long underwear, used by astronauts during their flights to and from the moon, as well as while they are inside the artificial atmosphere of the capsule.

constipation 1. *n* [*Computing*] See **deadly embrace. 2.** *n* [*Computing*] a form of **deadly embrace** in which the computer cannot continue its task through being unable to cope with the demands of an excess of output. See also **starvation**.

constructive dismissal *n* [*Industrial relations*] a form of unfair dismissal which occurs when an employee, who has ostensibly left his job voluntarily, has in fact been forced out by management activity aimed at making his continued employment untenable.

constructive receipt *n* [*Economics*] the date on which a taxpayer received some form of income or dividend; if this income is due to the taxpayer, whether or not he or she chooses to claim it, it is automatically taxable.

constructive sentence *n* [*US*] [*Law*] any sentence in which the terms of the punishment are supposed to fit the crime committed; eg. muggers working in old people's homes, drug users in hospitals, etc.

constructive total loss *n* [*Shipping*] in marine insurance this is a situation where a ship and/or her cargo are so badly damaged that the cost of repair exceeds the market value; in this case the damage is treated as a total loss and the insurers must pay out accordingly.

constructivism 1. *n* [*Theatre*] the concept of using mechanical structures in theatrical settings; it is the theatrical parallel in industrial technique, demanding the exclusion of all useless decoration and the precise functional organisation of the stage. The movement had its heyday in the first flush of the Russian Revolution, the 1920s. **2.** *n* [*Art*] constructivist art echoed the love of industry seen in its theatrical counterpart; it was pioneered in Moscow in 1920 by Naum Gabo and later by the Hungarian Moholy-Nagy.

consul *n* [*Cycling*] a local official of the international Cyclists' Touring Club; it comes from Standard English diplomatic use.

consumer demand analysis *n* [*Economics*] the analysis by a government of what exactly it is that the people want.

consumer need *n* [*Marketing*] any desire or requirement of an individual whether existing and perceptible, or latent and unrecognised; the determination and evaluation of consumer need is said to be at the root of all marketing concepts and subsequent activities. See also **consumer want**.

consumer press *n* [*Pop music*] the specialist publications which deal with pop music and its ancillary interests.

consumer surplus *n* [*Economics*] the amount that a consumer is willing to pay in excess of the current market price to ensure that he secures a particular good or goods.

consumer want *n* [*Marketing*] human physiological and psychological imperatives which, recognised in a tangible form or not, create the desire to possess something, in this case, the marketed product. This is the concrete, active corollary to the theoretical, fantasised 'need'; successful marketing will attempt to promote 'need' into 'want'. See also **consumer need**.

contact 1. *n* [*Aerospace*] the state of flying within visual sight of the surface of the earth. **2.** *n* [*Military*] exchanging fire with hostile forces.

contact magazine *n* [*Sex*] a magazine where those seeking particular sexual pleasures can place advertisements or find others who are putting themselves on offer; it is often used by prostitutes for the legal advertisement of their services.

container premium *n* [*Marketing*] the use of the package itself – a fancy jar, a special re-usable container, etc – as the marketing **premium**, rather than offering something for which the customer must apply, send box-tops, etc.

containment 1. *n* [*Lacrosse*] the object of any defence: each player aims to contain an opponent and hamper opportunities for the creation of an **overlap** or the setting up of attacking play. **2.** *n* [*Politics*] a policy, essentially defensive, of containing the expansion of a hostile power or its ideology within the boundaries which it has already established. At its inception containment implied a degree of positive opposition to such expansion. Today it has declined into a wary maintenance of the status quo and in the end an ineffectual theory when the other side ups the ante and expands willy-nilly.

contaminated runway *n* [*Air travel, Aerospace*] a runway covered by snow, sludge, oil, sand, solid objects or anything else that might threaten a safe landing.

contango *n* [*Stock market*] the percentage which a buyer of stock pays to the seller to postpone the actual transfer of shares either to the next settlement day or to one in the future. Thus 'contango day' is a day on which all transactions of a merely speculative nature are held over for a further fortnight.

contemporary *n* [*Publishing*] romance fiction, wish-fulfilment pulp sold in immense quantities to an almost exclusively female audience. See also **inspirational**.

content analysis *n* [*Sociology*] the analysis of the content of communication which involves classifying the contents in such a way as to bring out their basic structure; it usually refers to documentary or visual material, rather than interviews.

contention *n* [*Computing*] a situation in which two or more devices attempt at the same time to access a common piece of equipment.

contextualistic aesthetics *n* [*Art*] a view of art and aesthetics which is based on maintaining a

C

distinction between intuition and logic. Intuition, since it is gained from individual, empirical experience, is regarded as superior. Logic is considered to be constrained by the fact that it inevitably reflects some rule or ideology.

continental seating n [Theatre] seating that has been arranged without a centre aisle, but with sufficient space between the rows of seats to permit easy movement in and out.

continental shift system n [Management] a rapidly rotating shift system, popular in Europe, under which each group of workers changes from working one type of shift to another three times each week (3 days one type, 2 days a second, 2 days a third) with a 24-hour break at each change. See also **three-two-two system**.

contingency allowance n [Management] when calculating the standard time for a given task, and the payment for its performance, a small allowance (approximately 5%) is added to the basic time to cover matters outside the job itself, answering the 'phone, adjusting tools, consulting superiors, etc.

contingency management n [Business] the ability of an executive to vary his attitudes and methods according to the task, the personalities, the technology and whatever other variables each different task brings with it. In short, it is a capacity for flexibility in handling a variety of situations.

continued bond n [Commerce, Finance] a bond which may be presented for payment by the holder on or later than its official maturity date.

continuing education n [Education] any form of education that continues after the end of compulsory formal education (other than universities, colleges, etc), eg: night school.

continuity 1. n [Advertising, Marketing] the repeated use of a theme, medium, script or allied idea over a given period of time. **2.** n [TV, Film] the careful maintenance of all details from scene to scene – the right clothes, arrangement of furniture, etc – which is made more difficult since scenes are rarely shot in the simple consecutive order of the script. **3.** n [Radio] a series of linking announcements that maintain the flow of a radio broadcast.

continuity series n [Advertising] a promotion in which a number of products are sold and delivered over a period: a set of books, a set of records, etc.

continuous miner n [Coal-mining] a machine used for the continuous cutting and loading of coal in mine entries or similar narrow places.

continuous mining n [Coal-mining] a system whereby the mining process never halts: each shift picks up work at exactly that point at which the previous shift halted.

contour sharpness n [Photography] See **acutance**.

contour-chasing n [Aerospace] flying close to the ground and following the shifting contours of the scenery.

contra-account n [Business] an account kept by a firm that both buys from and sells to the same client so that in effect the transactions cancel one another out and exist only as paper entries.

contraband n [Coal-mining] anything prohibited underground: usually smoking materials and the means of lighting them.

contract 1. n [Police] the hiring of a professional killer to murder a specific target. **2.** n [US] [Politics] an agreement to deliver a particular political favour. Despite the parallel with criminal use, it is felt that political contracts are no longer especially corrupt. **3.** also **cars, lots** n [Commerce] one contract represents a single unit of trading in a specific futures instrument. The use of 'car' dates from an era when (in the US) most commodities were carried by rail and marketed at the major railheads. Exchanges fixed the contract size at whatever amount of a given commodity would fit into a standard size of railway wagon or 'car'.

contract agent n [Espionage] an operative recruited in the field by a regular intelligence agent who runs such operatives himself without their ever having to meet anyone else from the agency. He works as their case officer, issuing orders and paying wages, even though the actual instructions and funds will come from higher ranking, invisible officers. Contract agents are short-term employees and are not listed on any files.

contract in, contract out v [Industrial relations] referring to the decision made by members of trade unions whether or not to pay the political fund levied by their union and paid into Labour Party funds. Essentially a member has contracted in, unless he/she makes a specific commitment out. Current Conservative union legislation requires unions to ballot their members as to their wishes to continue paying the levy: as of late 1985, all those balloted had chosen overwhelmingly to maintain the status quo.

contract month n [Commodity exchange] the month in which futures contracts may be satisfied by making or accepting a delivery of the relevant commodity.

contract presser, also **custom presser** n [Video] a videodisk manufacturer whose activities parallel those of a cassette duplicator, pressing disks to order. He is payed only for units produced and does not receive royalty or licensing income.

contracting for property n [Travel agents] the process of putting together a holiday brochure, based on formulating agreed rates with the hotels concerned.

contraction n [Politics] the procurement by socialist governments of the agricultural products of the state's collective farms and, if they still exist, private farms.

contrarian n [US] [Stock market] any investor who chooses to go against the investing grain of the majority of his peers at any one time.

contraries n [Paper-making] any foreign body or substance which resists the pulping process.

contrast gradient n [Photography] the measure of the extent of contrast in a negative or print.

contribution analysis n [Marketing] the estimation of the difference between product selling prices and their variable costs per unit, thus enabling a calculation to be made of the extent to which each unit contributes to fixed costs and profits.

contribution pricing n [Marketing] a pricing technique which ensures some contribution to profit, even when normal profit margins are not being maintained.

control 1. n [Espionage] a rank below that of **Case Officer** and **Handler** in the chain of command of a clandestine operation. **2.** n [Religion] in spiritualism this is a spirit which controls the words and actions of the medium who is allegedly in a trance.

control car n [US] [Railways] the rear coach on suburban passenger trains which has identical controls to those in the engine, thus permitting the train to be run from either end.

control unit n [Prisons] a solitary confinement cell or block of cells.

controlled counterforce war n [Military] a nuclear attack which will obliterate the enemy's troops but, in theory, leave his cities and the resident civilians unharmed. See also **counterforce**.

controlled play n [Lacrosse] a tactic whereby one player fulfils one position and stays with that position throughout the game.

controller 1. n [Computing] any device or subsystem that controls the functions of attached devices but does not alter the meaning of the data that passes through it. **2.** n [Computing] in data processing this is a device that contains a stored program used to direct the transmission of data over a system.

CONUS n [Military] acro **Continental United States**.

convenience goods 1. n pl [Marketing] goods which are very widely distributed – eg: petrol, cigarettes, etc – and which are brought more for the convenience of their acquisition than for their brand or actual value. See also **shopping goods**. **2.** n pl [Marketing] goods having an element of processing, historically carried out by the customer or user, that gives the product an added value and for which a premium price may be obtained.

conventional n [US] [Road transport] a vehicle with the engine located in front of the cab.

conventional equipment n [Computing] equipment that is generally considered to be part of the computer system but which is not actually built into the computer itself; this is presumably

on the model of conventional and nuclear weaponry.

conventional weapons 1. n pl [Military] weapons that have been sanctioned by agreement or use and which conform to standard agreements on their acceptability. **2.** n pl [Military] all weapons other than nuclear weapons.

convergence n [Government] abbr of **economic convergence** in the Common Market (EEC) this is the allying of all member countries but one against that errant one.

convergence theory n [Social work] the concept that in advanced industrial societies common patterns of behaviour emerge, and that these patterns approve of the existence and pursuit of social welfare.

convergence thesis 1. n [Politics] the middle of the road theory that both capitalism and socialism are losing their more extreme aspects and gradually drawing closer together. Socialists reject this as one more example of the corrupt capitalist attempting to worm his way into the heart of his erstwhile enemies' confidences while his own system, as they have always predicted, starts to collapse in earnest. **2.** n [Sociology] an argument which claims that the process of industrialisation produces common and uniform political, social and cultural characteristics in societies which, prior to industrialisation, may have had very different versions of these characteristics. This occurs because industrialisation forces societies into common styles in order to function effectively.

conversational a [Computing] used of a mode of operation in which the computer responds to each input from the user – vaguely similar to inter-human conversation.

conversational analysis n [Sociology] the analysis of the way in which the ordering of normal language in conversations actually provides order and management of the social settings in which they take place; areas considered include the first five seconds of telephone conversations, courtroom conversations, etc.

conversational processing n [Computing] a form of processing in which the operator's commands to the machine are processed immediately and a reply is sent by the system to the terminal, upon which the operator can act, and so on.

conversion 1. n [Law] the illegal holding of someone else's personal property. **2.** n [Travel agents] the process whereby the despatch of a brochure on request is followed by the customer actually booking a holiday.

convertible 1. n [US] [Road transport] a truck that can be used either as a flatbed truck or as an open top. **2.** n [Stock market] a security issued by one corporation which can be converted into a security of another.

C

conveyor creep n [Coal-mining] the undesirable longitudinal movement of a conveyor.

convict n [US] [Circus] a zebra.

convictional criminal n [Crime] a criminal whose background or philosophy determines his/her choice of profession, rather than any sense of need.

cony, also **coney** n [Furriers] the main industry euphemism for 'rabbit furs' which are very widely used; 'rabbit' is generally disliked by the customers who prefer the verbal illusion; other euphemisms include 'lapin', from Fr. for rabbit, and 'hare'.

conzine n [Science fiction] a science fiction magazine created only for the duration of a convention.

cook 1. n [Paper-making] the digestion of wood pulp in a boiling process. 2. v [Science] to make radioactive.

cook chocolate v [US] [Prisons] See burn coal.

cook off v [US] [Farming] to cook down to a desired consistency, as in apple butter, sorghum, etc.

cooked 1. a [Cheese-making] said of hard cheese whose **curds** have been heated. 2. a [Cheese-making] referring to an accident in the fermentation of Gruyeres which results in an enormous hole. 3. a [Wine-tasting] said of the heavy, possibly sweet smell which is derived from the use of sugar, concentrated grape juice or high temperature during vinification.

cooker n [Oil rigs] a vat in which the original separation of sludge acid (sulphuric acid) is carried out.

cookie 1. n [Deer-stalking] a stag which has abnormal antlers, ie: a fork at the top, **brows**, but no **bay** or **trey**. 2. n [Film] See cokuloris. 3. n [Shoe-making] a piece of leather or metal sewn into a shoe to serve as an arch support.

cookie pusher n [US] [Politics] in diplomacy, this is a smooth young man whose career advances more because of his ability to manipulate the social niceties than because of his expertise in foreign relations; the image is of exquisites sitting around passing cakes and making epigrams.

cookie-book n [US] [Painting] the closed shop agreement and bye-laws of the American painters' union.

cookie-cutter n [Computing] distributors of floppy disks who buy the manufactured, but unfinished disk, then cut and package the finished product under their own brand-name(s).

cooking n [Cheese-making] part of the cheese-making process during which the cheese is heated to help solidify the **curd**.

cook-off n [Military] the spontaneous firing of a round of ordnance when the heat around a gun's breach sets it off.

cool a [Music] in jazz, this means relaxed, unemotional, a state to be desired and attained by those who favour such music.

cool art n [Art] a variety of styles of art which are linked by their exhibition of detachment, rationality and austerity. Cool art is abstract, geometric, with sharply defined forms of contours, comprising repetitive structures or units. There is much emphasis on precision and impeccability of execution.

cool out v [Politics] to kill, in the jargon of Argentina's interrogators during the 'dirty war' era of the 1970s.

cooler 1. n [Gambling] See cold deck. 2. n [Medicine] a hospital morgue.

coolie n [UK] [Railways] the fireman on the steam locomotives.

cooling-off period 1. n [US] [Industrial relations] a period, often 30 days, during which a union is restricted either by law or by a local agreement from striking and an employer from locking out employees. 2. n [US] [Stock market] a period of (usually) 20 days between the filing of a preliminary prospectus for a new security with the Securities & Exchange Commission (SEC) and the offering of the security to the public.

coon v [US] [Painting] to climb around a structure for the purposes of painting it when it is impossible to mount ladders or scaffolds.

coop v [US] [Police] said of an officer who sleeps on duty; such illicit rests are taken in motel rooms, etc.

co-op n [Video] a joint advertising and promotion campaign mounted by manufacturers, distributors and retailers of video material, each of whom pays a proportion of the costs; the manufacturer is the major contributor and reimburses the retailer for a percentage of the expenditure.

co-op mix n [Military] home-made bombs used in Northern Ireland; they are so-called because most of the materials are available in the local supermarket.

cooper up v [Business] this comes from the trade of cooper or barrel-maker, who uses a number of pieces to create the finished product: it means to take all the facets of a proposition and to use one's own skills to make it into a feasible project.

co-operative advertising n [Advertising] advertising that seeks to promote two or more products and their manufacturers in a single campaign.

co-operative measures n pl [Government] in international negotiations these are the steps that each side is willing to take to help the other observe an agreement or treaty.

co-opt v [Politics] to absorb, to persuade into one's own ranks; it tends to be used derogatively of attempts by far-Left activists to take over less virulent, though still essentially socialist parties or individuals.

cop 1. v [Drugs] to purchase drugs, usually as in 'cop for . . .' (name of the drug). 2. v [Horse-racing] used of a bookmaker when he wins on a race; his clerk marks such a race with a 'C'. 3. v [US]

[*Police*] to accept a bribe. **4.** *v* [*Sex*] said of a black pimp who enrolls a fresh woman in his string of prostitutes. **5.** *v* [*Train-spotters*] to see and record the number of a 'wanted' locomotive. **6.** *n* [*Textiles*] a cylindrical, conical or conical-ended mass of thread or yarn wound on to a shuttle.

cop a plea *v* [*Law*] to plead guilty, but with the belief that by so doing one may well gain some form of leniency in court; this is often on the suggestion of the police, who may have promised such a deal.

cop and blow *v* [*Sex*] the exploitation of a woman by a pimp to the greatest extent possible over a short period, once he has decided that she has little useful future as part of his string of prostitutes.

cope *n* [*Metallurgy*] in iron founding, this is the top part of a mould. See also **drag 6**.

co-pilot 1. *n* [*US*] [*Road transport*] a relief driver. **2.** *n* [*US*] [*Road transport*] a pep-pill. **3.** *n* [*Road transport*] an amphetamine drug, the energy of which helps the driver over long distances.

copilot, also **cohanger** *n* [*US*] [*Car salesmen*] a co-signer of a car sales agreement.

cop-out room *n* [*US*] [*Police*] any room where the police can make deals with prisoners or their lawyers, where those lawyers can confer with their clients, and where interrogations often leading to confessions or 'cop-outs' are held.

copper-arse *n* [*UK*] [*Taxis*] a cab-driver who consistently works longer hours than his peers. See also **copper-bottom**.

copper-bottom *n* [*UK*] [*Road transport*] a driver who breaks the law by working an excess of the statutory limit of hours driven per day (currently eight, as of 1982). See also **copper-arse**.

co-prod *n* [*Entertainment*] abbr of **co-production**.

copy 1. *n* [*Advertising*] a carbon copy, or any facsimile. **2.** *n* [*Advertising*] the words of an advertisement, rather than the pictures, the 'art' or the graphics. **3.** *n* [*Advertising*] the manuscript that is sent off to the printer. **4.** *n* [*Advertising*] a complete advertisement (including the artwork) that is sent off to the printer. **5.** *n* [*Journalism*] the written 'story' that a reporter writes, an editor edits and the newspaper prints. **6.** *v* [*Business, Government*] to send out copies; thus one 'copies' one or more recipients when they are sent a communication or memo.

copy platform *n* [*Advertising*] the main copy theme within an advertisement.

copy strategy *n* [*Advertising*] the 'message' of an advertisement, and how best to get it across to the consumer.

copy tests *n pl* [*Advertising*] research carried out to assess and improve the status of one's current campaign – in this case 'copy' includes the entire advertisement.

coral sandwich *n* [*Surfing*] hitting the bottom of the ocean when surfing around coral reefs.

corbel *n* [*Building, Plastering*] a block on a wall made up from a moulding to act as support for a feature such as an arch.

cordage *n* [*Sailing, Ropework*] all twisted rope, regardless of material or size.

cords *n pl* [*Glass-making*] visible streaks in the glass caused by inhomogeneity.

corduroy road *n* [*Transport*] a road built of logs or poles laid side-by-side transversely and used to cross low or swampy places.

core *n* [*Metallurgy*] in iron founding, this is sand which has been pressed into a given shape and then inserted into a mould before it is closed and cast, thus shaping the inside of the casting.

core city *n* [*Sociology, Government*] the (decaying) inner city.

core cream *n* [*Metallurgy*] in iron founding, this is an emulsion of drying oil and water, often mixed with molasses, resin and dextrin.

core curriculum *n* [*Education*] an integrated programme which cuts across the divisions that make up the traditional subjects.

core time *n* [*Industrial relations*] that time in the working day when all employees are present at the factory or office. It is especially relevant to those firms where the working day is staggered.

Corgi and Bess *n* [*TV*] commercial television's nickname for the Queen's annual Christmas afternoon TV broadcast.

coriolis effect *n* [*Aerospace*] named after its discoverer, Gaspard G. de Coriolis (1792–1843), this is the physiological effect upon a person moving in a rotating system, eg the complete loss of orientation caused by the rapid rotation of astronauts during parts of their flight.

corked *a* [*Wine-tasting*] the all-purpose condemnation of a wine that defeats the drinker; it is actually a truly 'off' and oxidised unpleasant smell which has nothing to do with the possible presence of small pieces of cork in one's glass.

corker 1. *n* [*Gambling*] an unusual gambler – either good or bad, but certainly notable. **2.** *n* [*Theatre*] an actor who spoils the overall performance.

corking *n* [*Wine-tasting*] the result of a poor soft or disintegrating cork – the smell of which can transfer to the wine; if the cork collapses completely, the air will be let in, thus causing oxydisation. Wines that have become tainted in this way are known as **corked** or 'corky'.

corks *n pl* [*Logging*] spikes set into logger's shoes that prevent slipping; possibly it comes from 'caulk'.

corkscrew *n* [*Boxing*] a punch that is thrown with the elbow out and which connects with a twisting motion of the wrist.

corky *a* [*Dog breeding*] said of a lively, perky temperament.

corn binder *n* [*US*] [*Road transport*] an International Harvester truck.

C

corned beef, also **bully beef** n [UK] [Prisons] rhyming slang for 'chief' meaning 'chief officer'.

corner 1. v [UK] [Crime] to sell junk under the pretence of its being good, but stolen property. 2. v [UK] [Crime] to sell stolen property to an honest, but gullible tradesman. As soon as the buyer has handed over the cash, in walks a 'policeman' (in fact a confederate) who confiscates the goods and disappears, threatening the worst. Another 'friend' then appears, promising to square the police for yet more money. Sometimes a fake 'solicitor' is introduced, to blind the victim with legal complexities, and to ensure that he never approaches any real policemen; he naturally takes his own fee. 3. v [Stock market] to secure such complete control of a commodity or security as to control its price at will. 4. v [Stock market] to obtain contracts for the delivery of more commodities or securities than in fact exist. 5. v [Stock market] to speculate with the aim of obtaining the whole of a security or commodity so as to force the market to accept one's own dictation of the price.

corner, down in the adv [US] [Road transport] in low gear.

corner-man n [UK] [Police] a confidence trickster, from his use of the **corner**.

cornerstone n [Religion] Christ, the cornerstone of his own religion; see Ephesians 2:20.

cornfield meet n [US] [Railways] a head-on collision between two trains on the same track. See also **Mexican standoff**.

corn-hog ratio n [US] [Agriculture] a method whereby US farmers work out whether it is more profitable that year to sell their hogs or the corn that is used to feed them. This is based on the assumption that 11.5 bushels of corn are needed to put 100 lb weight on a hog. The decision depends on the current price when 100 lb of live hog is divided by 1 bushel of corn.

corona n [Building, Plastering] the outer flat vertical member of a cornice.

coronet 1. n [Deer-stalking] See **burr 2**. 2. n [Horse-riding] the top of the horse's hoof.

corporal art n [Art] See **body art**.

coporate metabolism n [Business] this comes from the 'metabolism': the consumption or 'burning' of food or fuel to replace living cells in the body. In a corporation the metabolism is the overall sum that the employees – of all ranks – contribute to 'fuelling' the organism (the corporation) and maintaining it in its accustomed style, values and professional and personal life.

corporate woodwork n [Business] all the bits and pieces that make a corporation work, its essential fixtures and fittings – policy, procedure, rules and regulations, PR, advertising, etc. Everything, in fact, other than its product and personnel, that combines to create the overall corporate image both internally and in the eyes of customers and competitors.

corporatism n [Politics] the concept of absorbing the business style of a corporation into the running of a state; the major example of this has been Mussolini's Fascist Italy.

corpse 1. n [Navy] tinned beef or mutton. 2. v [Theatre] said of an actor who deliberately reduces another to laughter during a performance – by gestures, grimaces, etc, none of which the audience can see – especially when the lines are not particularly funny. 3. v [UK] [Theatre] to forget one's lines, often after suffering an on-stage fit of the giggles.

corpsman n [US] [Navy] a member of the US Naval Hospital Corps who provide battlefield and peacetime medical assistance to the USN and USMC.

correct v [Politics] referring to the concept of national re-education that tends to follow speedily on successful revolutions as in Vietnam, Iran, etc.

correction n [Finance] the reverse movement, usually downwards, of the price of a stock, bond, commodity, market or index.

correctional custody unit n [US] [Navy] a euphemism for the shipboard jail. See also **brig**.

correctional facility, also **institution** n [US] [Prisons] any form of jail or treatment centre for adult or juvenile prisoners.

correctional restitution n [US] [Law, Prisons] a concept developed in 1958 and applied in various states since then; the idea that once a prisoner has served a jail sentence he or she should then make restitution to their victim(s) through work, thus supposedly making the criminal responsible for the society in which he or she lives.

corrections caseload n [US] [Prisons] the total number of clients registered with a correctional agency or institution at any one time.

correspondence n [UK] [Railways] this is when a set of points is lying in the correct position.

correspondent n [Business] any financial organisation that regularly performs services for another organisation in markets that are inaccessible to the partner.

corridor bashing n [Military] the saturation bombing of hostile airfields, lines of communications and similar vital facilities.

corridor discussion n [Industrial relations] an off-the-record but vital part of wages bargaining when the leaders of both sides of a dispute can talk frankly 'in the corridor', or at least away from the main body of discussion, and admit to the realities of the situation – the actual compromises that can be made, and those that cannot be accepted – thus cutting through much of the rhetoric and bombast that rival supporters require to be included in such talks.

corridor mate n [Chess] a position in which a king can only move along an expected route and can thus simply be trapped by closing the 'corridor'.

corrugate *v* [*US*] [*Agriculture*] to make small irrigation ditches in a field.

corruption, also **bastardisation 1.** *n* [*Literary criticism*] the changing of an unfamiliar or esoteric term to one that is in more popular use. **2.** *n* [*Literary criticism*] a debased or unorthodox word form or wording of a text or document.

corset *n* [*Banking*] the special deposits scheme introduced in the UK from December 1973 to June 1980: it limited the growth of the main categories of bank deposits so that bank lending, based on bank deposits, could be checked at one remove.

corvée *n* [*Military*] used in the French Foreign Legion to mean fatigue duties.

COs *n pl* [*UK*] [*Taxis*] abbr of **Carriage Office** it refers to those policemen who are charged with enforcing the laws as they relate to a cab driver's conduct.

cosche *n* [*Crime*] in the Italian Mafia, this is a cell into which the overall organisation is divided. It comes from Ital. 'cosca' meaning 'artichoke', a plant in which the one tender heart is surrounded by many tough and tightly gathered leaves.

coshes *n* [*UK*] [*Market-traders*] punishment.

cosmetic injury *n* [*Sport*] any injury that requires facial sutures.

cosmic *a* [*Military*] a NATO classification of top secret material.

cosmopolitanism *n* [*Politics*] 'A reactionary unpatriotic, bourgeois outlook on things, hypocritically regarding the whole world as one's fatherland, denying the value of national culture, rejecting the rights of nations to independent existence ... the ideology of US imperialism aspiring to world domination' (Dictionary of the Russian Language). It is used of any manifestation in or out of the Soviet world that might in any way strengthen the US and is a useful theory that permits the Soviets to ally with any ultra-nationalist groups (usually right-wing and reactionary), claiming them as fellow bulwarks against US expansion. Within the USSR cosmopolitanism doubles as a codeword for attacking the Jews, who are deemed to reject the USSR as their unique saviour.

cost centre *n* [*Management*] a location, person, item of equipment or any other division of an enterprise for which costs may be ascertained and which is used for purposes of cost control.

cost-benefit *n* [*Economics*] an analysis which assesses the relationship of the actual cost of a project to the value of social and other benefits accruing or not on its completion.

cost-plus *n* [*Accounting, Management*] the setting of a selling price by adding the actual production costs – or a reasonable estimate of them – to a stated profit figure. It was originally created for wartime manufacturing when it was difficult to put an accurate price on developmental work.

cost-plus contract *n* [*Accounting*] a contract for the performance of specified work under which the firm performing the work is reimbursed the amount of specified costs and is also paid a fee; this fee is either set when the contract is drawn up, (cost-plus-fixed-fee: CPFF) or varies as to the standard of the finished work in terms of the total cost, time of completion, etc. (cost-plus-incentive-fee: CPIF).

cost-plus pricing *n* [*Marketing*] the activity or practice of determining the selling price of a manufactured product by calculating the cost to the manufacturer of making it and adding a standard percentage of the cost to represent profit.

cost-price squeeze *n* [*Management*] a situation in which a firm is forced to pay increased prices for its raw materials, but cannot increase the prices at which it sells the manufactured articles.

cost-push inflation *n* [*Economics*] inflation in which the rising costs of labour and production push up prices, even when demand has not increased. See also **demand-pull inflation**.

costume *a* [*Theatre*] 'costume' dramas imply plays or films set in any era but the present and the costumes, which any production demands by virtue of being acted, actually pertain to 'dressing up', rather than assuming modern dress.

cottle *n* [*Building, Plastering*] a clay fence used in fibrous plaster work.

cotty wool *n* [*Weaving*] an industrial term denoting matted fibres in a wool fleece.

couch *n* [*Hunting*] the lair of an otter, or the hiding places he uses when pursued or driven from his home.

couchant *a* [*Heraldry*] lying down with the head raised.

cough and a spit *n* [*Theatre*] an easy, short part.

counselling *n* [*Public relations*] telling a client what he/she should do that would be best for the optimum personal and corporate image.

count out of the House *v* [*UK*] [*Politics*] used when the House of Commons adjourns because the Speaker cannot find a quorum, a minimum of forty members, present for a vote.

counter 1. *n* [*Computing*] a register for storing a number which is increased or decreased by a fixed amount every time an event occurs. **2.** *n* [*Printing*] the non-printing area within the enclosed or partially enclosed outline of certain letters: A,P,C, etc. **3.** *n* [*Shoe-making*] a piece of stiff material, usually leather or canvas, stitched between the lining and the upper, and used to stiffen the back of the shoe. **4.** *excl* [*Film*] a direction given to an actor telling him/her to put more of themselves in front of the camera, or to allow space for another actor or object to be filmed.

counter trade *n* [*Politics*] a deal whereby the importer forces the exporter to take his payments all or in great part in goods rather than in valuable foreign exchange which he is loathe to sacrifice. It is usually limited to 30% of the whole deal, but can rise to 100% and is often forced on

C

the West when trading with Warsaw Pact countries. To service this flood of unwanted goods a number of brokers, operating from Switzerland, have emerged to sell them off at a discount.

counter-advertising *n* [*Advertising*] advertisements that have been specially written/designed to refute claims made in rival advertisements broadcast or published by groups who disapprove of the original messages put out by those against whom they are campaigning, eg: ecologists vs. General Motors. Such rival campaigns are also becoming an increasing feature of major take-over battles as both sides attempt to woo the shareholders and vilify each other.

counterfactual 1. *n* [*Economics*] a statement concerning a hypothetical event, process or state of affairs that does not exist and runs directly counter to the facts. It is used by econometric historians to posit a variety of 'what if . . . had' or 'what if . . . had not' happened. **2.** *a* [*Sociology*] said of a proposition which states what would have happened if something else not been the case. Many sociologists claim that no proposition is meaningful without a corresponding counterfactual proposition. See also **falsificationism**.

counterfeits *n pl* [*US*] [*Meat trade*] animals that appear to have been well-bred but which in fact have little ability to gain weight.

counterfinality *n* [*Philosophy*] the tendency of an act to thwart its own aim.

counterforce, also **no-city strategy** *a* [*Military*] used to describe a nuclear strike against the enemy's weapons rather than at his centres of population; thus 'counterforce weapons', 'counterforce option', 'counterforce strike', etc. See also **counter value**.

counterforce car *n* [*US*] [*Motor trade*] a specially armoured car designed to provide security for executives who see themselves at risk from attack, kidnapping, etc.

countervailing duty *n* [*Commerce*] an import duty intended to protect a home industry from foreign competition.

countervailing power *n* [*Economics*] a term coined by J. K. Galbraith in 1952 to describe forces such as trade unions, consumer groups, anti-monopoly regulations, etc. that arise to counterbalance the power of the major capitalists and their organisations and which have refined the absolute powers of laissez-faire capitalism.

countervailing strategy *n* [*Military*] the war-fighting strategy initiated by Secretary of Defense James Schlesinger in 1974 and encapsulated in President Carter's **PD–59** (1980). The strategy which promised a retaliatory strike of utter devastation in the face of any form of attack was intended to make sure that no potential adversary of the US or its allies would ever conclude that aggression would be worth the costs that would be incurred, on whatever level of conflict was contemplated. See also **MAD**.

countervalue *a* [*Military*] used to describe a nuclear strike against the enemy's cities and population; thus 'countervalue option', 'countervalue strike', etc. See also **counterforce**.

countervalue targeting *n* [*Military*] the targeting of population centres, rather than of military, scientific or industrial areas. Such deliberate threatening of civilians is at the heart of the nuclear stand-off under which an uneasy peace has been maintained since World War II. See also **city-busting**.

country *n* [*Hunting*] a definite area of countryside in which a hunt may take place.

country club at the top *n* [*Business*] the 'not what you know but who you know' philosophy of corporate management, which is exemplified by continuing to pay a full salary to a member of the board even after his departure from the firm, usually in the guise of using him as a 'consultant'.

country damaged *a* [*Commerce*] damaged in the country of origin, prior to the goods being transported.

country rock *n* [*Coal-mining*] the rock adjacent to a mineral vein or igneous **intrusion**.

country, in the *adv* [*Cricket*] referring to a fielder far from the wicket.

coup-de-bambom *n* [*Military*] used in the French Foreign Legion to mean a sudden physical or mental collapse for which there is no apparent cause.

couped *a* [*Heraldry*] said of a beast's head: cut off cleanly. See also **erased**.

couple *n* [*Hunting*] a pair of hounds; hounds are always counted in pairs, thus a pack is 13+ couple, rather than 27 hounds.

coupling 1. *n* [*Computing*] the use in some form of a co-operative mode of systems that otherwise would be operated separately. Coupling of hardware and processors can be 'loose' or 'tight' according to specific use. **2.** *n* [*Military*] this is usually known as strategic coupling: the linking of low-level conflict – Soviet/Warsaw Pact aggression in Europe – to the threatened use of US nuclear weapons.

coupling up *n* [*Industrial relations*] overlapping shifts which are arranged in order to avoid breaking the flow of productivity in a factory. Those employees involved in such overlaps are eligible for handover pay.

coupon 1. *n* [*Finance*] the promise to pay interest when it falls due. **2.** *n* [*Finance*] a printed form, attached to a bond in coupon form, which is detached and submitted for payment at the correct time.

coupon candidate *n* [*Politics*] a term originated by H. H. Asquith in 1918: any candidate who has been given the personal recommendation of his/her leader.

course 1. *v* [*Coal-mining*] to control the direction of ventilation through the workings. **2.** *v* [*Coal-mining*] to ventilate a number of faces in series.

courtesy announcement *n* [*TV*] the reminder, broadcast a few minutes after a channel has ceased its nightly programmes, that tells viewers to switch off their sets.

courtesy of the profession *adv* [*US*] [*Theatre*] free admission to theatres offered to actors who produce their Equity card. See also **card, on your**.

cousins group *n* [*Management*] in the study of group dynamics (in group training) this is a group that consists of people who work in the same organisation and have similar status, but do not usually work closely together. See also **family group, stranger group**.

co-vary *v* [*Sociology*] a gratuitous amplification of the simple 'vary' with no special or extra meaning, but beloved, like similar intensifiers, by the coiners of jargon who are drawn to sociology.

cover 1. *n* [*Advertising*] the scheduling of a TV commercial in the expectation that the target audience should on average have seen it at least once. **2.** *n* [*Espionage*] a protective disguise assumed by an agent to confuse others and survey or infiltrate a target, and to escape detection by hostile agents or troops. **3.** *n* [*Finance*] the purchase or sale of futures to offset a previously established **long** or **short position**. **4.** *n* [*US*] [*Marine Corps*] any form of headgear worn by a Marine. **5.** *n* [*Philately*] the envelope, wrapper or any other means of covering correspondence. Stamps collected with their envelope, etc, are 'on original cover'. **6.** *n* [*Stock market*] the relationship between a company's net earnings and its dividend payments; such a ratio is the measure of the worth of a company's shares. **7.** *n* [*Stock market*] a deposit of money or shares which a stockbroker makes to protect him against loss in his dealings. **8.** *v* [*Theatre*] to understudy. **9.** *v* [*US*] [*TV*] to replace one picture by another on the screen, eg: to replace a news **anchor man** by a reporter, the reporter by a film clip, etc. **10.** *v* [*TV, film*] said of an actor who obscures another from the camera lens. **11.** also **close** *v* [*Fencing*] to close a line of engagement.

cover a fish *v* [*Angling*] to get the bait or fly over the place where the fish is lying.

Cover All *n* [*Military*] a converted Boeing 707 with a crew of twenty-one which acts as the Strategic Air Command's airborne command post; Cover All planes patrol in three eight-hour shifts twenty-four hours a day, flying at 30,000 ft above the US on constant alert. On board the plane is a Brigadier-General, the lowest rank with authorised access to the nuclear **go-codes**. Despite the constant patrolling of Cover All Planes, and the intentions to 'harden' them against a nuclear attack, it is in fact accepted that the planes would be unlikely to survive, or be of real use after a first-strike attack. See also **Looking Glass, Kneecap**.

cover crop *n* [*Agriculture*] a crop, often clover, that is grown on land not otherwise scheduled for use; it will prevent the spread of weeds or the development of erosion until the land is needed.

coverage 1. *n* [*Espionage*] this is when a representative or representatives of the CIA (up to a whole office full of agents) are put into any area. This area is then said to be 'covered' by the agency. **2.** *n* [*Marketing*] See **reach**.

Coverdale training *n* [*Management*] a form of group training – named after UK behaviourist Ralph Coverdale (1918–1975) – in which subjects are given tasks to perform and then have to analyse their performance. The intention is to develop people's ability to create teams and work within them and to carry out plans originated elsewhere.

covered bear, also **protected bear** *n* [*Stock market*] a **bear** who has enough securities to meet his contracts whether or not the rising market to which he looks materialises or not.

covered wagon *n* [*US*] [*Railways*] the older style of locomotive with the diesel engine fully enclosed.

covert 1. *a* [*Espionage*] said of any form of secret activity, often also illegal (either in the agency's home country or abroad), which is taken for political, economic or social reasons to further the various aims of the agency concerned. The ostensible aim of, and justification for, covert operations and actions is to influence those targeted in favour of the active country's foreign policy. **2.** *n* [*Hunting*] pronounced 'cover'; any stretch of growth where a fox resides.

covert coat *n* [*Hunting*] a riding coat made of lightweight whipcord.

covert hack *n* [*Hunting*] a horse used to ride to hounds.

cow 1. *n* [*Advertising*] the rubber based gum used for sticking paper to paper boards; it is a staple of advertising layout and is not made of cows but by the Cow Proofing Company, of Slough, Bucks. **2.** *n* [*Marketing*] a product which has passed its best performance sales figures, but which can still be 'milked' for profits; these profits often provide the basis for the development of a new product.

cow corner *n* [*Cricket*] a squareish legside boundary over which the successful sweeping **cow-shot** should pass.

cow pasture *n* [*Flying*] an obsolete airport or an emergency landing strip which is neither officially nor technically up to regulation standards.

cow pussy *n* [*US*] [*Metallurgy*] a metal device used in setting forms that are reinforced with iron rods.

cow sociology *n* [*Sociology*] a derogatory assessment by professional sociologists of attempts by industry 'management experts' to bring out the 'human side' of work. As far as the sociologists are concerned, this merely acts to lull the workforce into a state of complacent, cow-like passivity.

C

cowabunga! *excl* [*Surfing*] a cry of exultation shouted by Australian surfers as they surf down a superb wave.

cowbody economy *n* [*Economics*] economic planning based on the concept of limitless resources which in turn created limitless waste; this economy assumed people lived in a careless, rough and even violent way, reminiscent of the Wild West. Such economists rejected the implications and fallacies of the fantasy and concentrated only on infinite growth at all costs. See also **spaceman economy**.

cowboy 1. *n* [*US*] [*Industrial relations*] one who refuses to comply with working at the rate (usually slower than is necessary) set by fellow-workers in a piece-work team, but who chooses to work sufficiently hard to make far more money than they do. See also **job spoiler**. **2.** *n* [*UK*] [*Military*] any member of a sectarian gang. **3** *n* [*Sex*] See **raw jaws**.

cowboy rake *n* [*Custom cars*] the lowering of the rear of the car marginally, but noticeably, further than the front. See also **California rake**.

cowcatcher *n* [*US*] [*Radio*] an advertisement inserted on a sponsor's programme which features one of the sponsor's products that is not being generally featured on that show. See also **hitch-hike**.

cow's mouth *n* [*Logging*] the falling notch in a tree.

cow-shot *n* [*Cricket*] a swipe across the line of a straight ball (or any other ball) that, with more luck than judgment, sends it off towards the legside boundary. See also **agricultural**.

cpa *n* [*US*] [*Police*] abbr of **cattle-prod approach** a method of crowd control that depends on the use of force, specifically on the use of electric-shock batons.

CPM *n* [*Advertising*] abbr of **Cost Per Thousand** (using the Latin notation M = 1000): the estimated cost for the advertiser, using either print or broadcast media, that is entailed in reaching 1000 houses.

C-post *n* [*Cars*] the body pillar that connects the floor pan with the roof and on which the rear door is latched on a four-door car.

CPU *n* [*Computing*] abbr of **Central Processing Unit** the part of the system that actually 'computes' the instructions executed through a program. It contains an arithmetic logic unit (ALU) and a number of special registers and control units. The CPU can decode and execute instructions, perform arithmetical and logical functions, provide timing signals, etc.

CPX *n* [*US*] [*Military*] abbr of **communications, command and control exercises** these are used to check out the US command hierarchy's ability to implement war plans.

crab 1. *n* [*Commerce*] in the retail book trade, this is a book on sale or return that is returned by the bookshop, unsold, to the publisher. **2.** *n* [*Industry*] one of a variety of machines used to raise and/or more heavy weights: overhead cranes, winches, overhead claws. **3.** *n* [*Logging*] a small raft carrying a windlass and anchor that is used to help transport logs upstream or across a lake. **4.** *n* [*US*] [*Air Force*] a computer program used by the USAF for flying the F–16 fighter. This program, a highly sophisticated type of automatic pilot, frees the pilot's hands for weapons control; all other functions regarding direction, locking the plane on target, etc. are 'crabbed' by the computer. **5.** *v* [*TV, film*] to move a camera or microphone sideways. See also **dolly 13**.

crab fat *n* [*Navy*] battleship grey paint.

crabapple *n* [*Commerce*] a fussy customer.

crabbing *n* [*US*] [*Gliding*] pointing up-wind to counteract for wind drift; it is formally known as wind correction. Thus 'crab angle' is the angle required to make this correction.

crabwise movement *n* [*Economics*] a euphemism for any period of economic decline. See also **rolling readjustment**.

crac, also **petto-fuori** *n* [*Military*] used in the French Foreign Legion to mean a brave, devil-may-care fighter; it comes from Ital. for loud fart. See also **gung-ho 1**.

crack 1. *v* [*UK*] [*Market-traders*] to say, to speak. **2.** *v* [*Oil rigs*] to break down hydrocarbon molecules of high molecular weight into lighter molecules.

crack shorts *v* [*US*] [*Crime*] to break into (crack) automobiles (shorts).

crackback *n* [*US*] [*Football*] an outlawed tackle in which a pass-receiver blocks a linebacker or defensive back by smashing into him at knee level. It is a major cause of injuries, some of them permanent. See also **blindside 1**.

cracked squash *n* [*US*] [*Medicine*] skull fracture.

cracked valve *n* [*Oil rigs*] See **flow bean**.

cracker *n* [*UK*] [*Railways*] a detonator. See also **banger**.

crackerjack, also **firecracker, jumping jack** *n* [*UK*] [*Railways*] a lively, enthusiastic, ultra-efficient foreman.

cracking *n* [*Oil industry*] See **cat cracking**.

cradle books *n pl* [*Bibliography*] See **fifteeners**.

cradle-to-grave inspection *n* [*Government*] in nuclear arms treaties this is an agreement whereby one power permits the other to inspect stockpiles of nuclear weapons at the manufacturing stage, in their silo, and immediately prior to their being dismantled as obsolete.

cramping *n* [*TV*] the contraction of either side of the central portion of the TV picture.

cranage *n* [*Shipping*] port fees that cover a vessel's use of its cranes.

crane *n* [*TV, film*] a large, wheeled camera mounting designed to give the maximum variety of movement to a studio camera.

crane shot *n* [*TV, film*] a high-angle shot in

which the camera moves vertically or laterally while mounted on a **crane**.

crap barge n [Navy] a dirty vessel of any sort; it comes from the resemblance to latrine barges used to dump night soil at sea.

crap hat n (UK] [Military] British paratroopers' derisive nickname for any soldier other than wearers of the Paras' red beret.

crap out, also **flake out, fuck off, goof off** v [US] [Marine Corps] to loaf around, to act lazily.

crapper, also **crappereena** n [UK] [Market-traders] a lavatory, a WC.

crapper dick n [US] [Police, Crime] a policeman who frequents public lavatories to survey and arrest individuals who may be committing illegal sexual acts inside them.

crapule n [Military] used in the French Foreign Legion to mean one who eats or drinks to excess.

crash 1. n, v [Computing] any greater or lesser failure in the system. It is an extension of 'head crash' whereby the accumulation of even a tiny amount (a few microns) of dust between the read/write head of the computer and the disk can destroy the information on that disk. It is also used as a verb both intransitively ('The PC just crashed') and transitively ('X crashed the system'). See also **down** 1. 2. n [Hunting] the sound when all the pack give tongue together on finding a fox. 3. n [Publishing] a strip of cloth pasted around the spine of a book to strengthen the binding. 4. n [Theatre] any effect involving a sudden crash: breaking glass, slamming doors, motor accidents, etc. 5. v [UK] [Police] to write off or cancel enquiries into a complaint or crime. 6. v [TV] to work desperately and hurriedly in the face of a deadline; the implication is that the piece in question may well fail to meet that deadline.

crash and dash n [Skiing] in competition skiing, this is a timed run between two given points on a piste.

crash cost n [Management] the cost of fulfilling a task in the fastest possible time.

crash unit n [Espionage] a group of CIA technicians who are required to enter a target building, room, environment, etc., install the eavesdropping **sneakies** and then exit without leaving evidence of their break-in.

crash zoom n [Film, TV, Video] an extremely fast **zoom** into a shot, moving almost immediately from long or middle distance to close-up.

crashworthiness n [Air travel] a plane's ability to withstand a crash and to protect the passengers from impact, fire, smoke, etc.

cratology n [Military, Espionage] the 'science' of obtaining intelligence data by analysing the crates, boxes, containers and similar anonymous packages carried by a target boat, plane, train or truck. Given that these crates tend to be sealed, such information is necessarily highly speculative and must be confirmed by further, more accurate sources. See also **dentology**.

cravate n [Military] used in the French Foreign Legion to mean a braggart.

craven conditional n [Politics, Media] a term coined by William Safire to describe the plenitude of modifying words and phrases – 'far be it from me', 'I would say', 'It would appear', etc – with which politicians and others who are unwilling to move too far off the fence habitually lard their statements.

crawfish 1. v [US] [Coal-mining] to crawl around on one's hands and knees. 2. n [US] [Railways] a bucket-type conveyor system used to unload grain from boxcars.

crawl 1. v [US] [Painting] used of a coat of paint which runs in rivulets when applied over another coat. 2. n [TV] the list of closing titles or credits which 'crawls' across or up the screen. See also **creeping title**.

crawler lane n [Cars] an extra nearside lane on some motorways to leave room for extremely heavy and slow-moving vehicles.

crawler way n [Aerospace] a specially constructed roadway for moving heavy rockets or other heavy equipment from the construction site to the launching pad.

crawling peg n [Economics] an economic system whereby the exchange rate can be frequently and marginally adjusted; it is used in the inter-national money market and is a basic credo of **monetarism**.

crazing n [Building, Plastering] hairline cracks in plaster or cement surface.

crazy n [US] [Cattlemen] a brand in which the image, probably a letter, is upside down.

crazy alley n [US] [Prisons] a cell block reserved for the mentally ill.

creak v [Theatre] used of a play when it starts to appear outdated and stale.

cream v [Commerce] to steal from one's employer in a careful, moderate and, ideally, undiscovered manner.

cream gear n [Crime] the top-class, premier proceeds of a robbery; these are frequently designer-labelled, exclusively brand-named, etc. and are often sold off to fellow criminals.

creamies n pl [Marbles] general term for all glass marbles, irrespective of colour, etc.

creaming n [Marketing] the selling of a product range at a higher than average price in order to improve the quality, or at least the image of the quality, of that product; such products tend to be preferred by the richer consumer.

cream-puff hitter n [Baseball] a weak, ineffective batter.

creamy a [Cheese-making] a description of both the texture – soft, even runny – and the colour of the interior of soft cheeses.

crease n [Ice hockey] the rectangular area in front of the goal that cannot be entered by an offensive player unless he has the puck.

creative a [Advertising] said of someone who is

C

working as either a copywriter or an art director rather than on the business or market research side of an agency; it is a job description, not necessarily a compliment.

creative accounting, also **creative bookkeeping** n [Business] inventive or imaginative accounting procedures, in which figures are manipulated so as to bend, but never actually break, the tax rules in favour of the firm or client.

creative intelligence n [Espionage] common sense; the intelligent interpretation in the CIA of those materials that are available both openly and through intelligence sources.

creative Marxism n [Politics] Marxism that is forward thinking, flexible, constantly changing to suit the times. It is a progressive ideology that refuses to abide religiously by the dogmatic and doctrinaire letter of Karl Marx's 19th century words.

creative punishment n [Law] sentences that attempt to make the punishment fit the crime, often in the form of an allotted period of social work, rather than just custodial sentencing.

creative strategy n [Advertising] the whole style of the advertisement and the campaign on which it forms a part.

credential the relevant competencies v [Education] this phrase was developed in California as a neologism for awarding a certificate of competence because teachers there felt that the use of the word 'certify' had overtones of insanity. It may be extended outside education to any area in which diplomas, certificates, etc. are awarded.

credentialism n [Sociology] the tendency in modern society to allocate status on the basis of academic qualifications; thus the pursuit of the qualifications becomes an end in itself, rather than a search for real skills that may be of use in a job.

credibility n [Military] the concept of making an ally or an enemy believe that you mean what you say, will do what you promise or threaten, and have the weapons to carry it out. See also **capability**.

credibility gap n [Politics, Government] a term coined during the Vietnam War to underline the American public's growing inability to take the statements (as opposed to the actions) of the Johnson Administration at face value, and used since to point up the discrepancies between the actions and words of any government. An internal use of 'credibility', rather than the external, military one.

credible deterrent n [Military] a weapons system (de facto nuclear) which the enemy believes one is willing and ready to use if the situation demands, and which, as such, should ensure that the situation does not arise.

credit squeeze n [Economics] a governmental method of clamping down on inflation by raising the bank rate, thereby making money 'dearer' (loans costing more in interest) and thus causing a cut-back in overdrafts, hire purchase agreements and similar inflationary borrowing and lending.

credits n pl [TV, Film] a list attached to a film or TV programme – in brief at the start and at greater, detailed length at the end – which names the actors, technicians, and, in the case of film, the financiers involved in the creation of the film or programme.

creed n [Marketing] telegraphic printer by which communications are received from news agencies.

creek crawling n [Shooting] stalking through the creeks and channels of the foreshore pursuing game.

Creek Misty n [Military] airborne reconnaissance flights carried out over Europe by NATO forces.

creel n [Weaving] a rack on which spools or **cones** can be set for unwinding.

creep 1. n [Building, Concrete workers] the slow inelastic deformation of concrete that can occur through stress. **2.** n [US] [Coal-mining] the movement of the mine roof, caused by geological strains, which tends to crush or overturn pillars and timbers. **3.** n [Science] the continuous deformation of any material under operational stress, especially at high temperatures. **4.** n [TV] the slight, but gradual decline of any electronic equipment away from its optimum performance standards.

creeper 1. n [Angling] the larvae of the stone fly, used as bait for trout. **2.** n [Cricket] a ball that fails to bounce as expected and simply 'creeps' beneath the bat. **3.** n [Sex] a crooked homosexual **hustler** who 'creeps up' on clients to defraud them of their money. **4.** n [Sex] a pickpocket who works with prostitutes: the girl attracts the victims, the pickpocket robs them. **5.** also **feeder** n [Coal-mining] a slowly moving endless chain that can be locked on to the axles of tubs or cars. **6.** n [Tea-planting] a pupil in the tea-planting trade.

creeper gear n [US] [Road transport] the lowest gear or combination of gears used for extra power.

creepie peepie n [TV] a hand-held TV camera, often used for capturing the action in sports events, political demonstrations, etc.

creeping and weeping n [Navy] searching the seabed for practice torpedoes which have sunk at the end of their run; the torpedoes are recovered by sweeping the seabed and then picking them up in grapples.

creeping crud n [New therapies] in Theta **rebirthing** this is the primal panic that is supposedly experienced due to the recollection of the sensations and memories of life in the womb. It is intensified by the rebirthing process being carried out while immersed in water at a temperature of 99°F (the temperature of the womb) and might just stem from the fear in some people of being drowned.

creeping sync n [*TV*] a technical fault that occasionally occurs in filming when picture and sound, despite being matched at the **clapper-board**, slip out of synchronisation.

creeping title, also **rolling title** n [*Film*] a title which rolls up or across the screen at a reading pace. See also **crawl 2**.

creepy-weepy n [*Publishing*] a genre of popular fiction combining gothic horror with romantic melodrama. See also **bodice-ripper, devotional** etc.

cremains n [*US*] [*Undertakers*] the ashes that remain after a body has been cremated.

cressing n [*Metallurgy*] the reduction of the diameter of the ends of tubes, usually only in fractional measurements.

crest n [*Heraldry*] a beast or object mounted on top of the helmet.

crevice company n [*Business*] a company that aims to exploit the 'niche market', the relatively small areas left between the boundaries of traditional and established markets.

cribble v [*Art*] to decorate wood or metal by making small dots or punctures on its surface.

crifanac n [*Science fiction*] abbr of **critical fan activity** the process of being a highly motivated actifan.

crime v [*US*] [*Military*] to put on the punishment roster.

crime in the suites n [*US*] [*Crime*] white collar crime, corporate embezzlement, computer fraud, etc; it is a pun on 'crime in the streets'.

crime-sheet n [*US*] [*Road transport*] a log-sheet for work performed.

crimp **1.** v [*Gambling*] to bend one or more cards in a deck so that a cheat will be able to cut the deck as he wishes, or know that an innocent player will cut the deck at the desired card. **2.** n [*Weaving*] the serrations in a wool fibre.

crinoline head n [*US*] [*Journalism*] See **deadhead 3**.

cripple n [*UK*] [*Railways*] a wagon needing repair.

crippled leapfrog test n [*Computing*] a variation on the **leapfrog test** in which the tests that are run to check out the machine's internal operations are based on repetitions of a single, rather than a changing, set of storage locations.

crisis communications management n [*Public relations*] a style of PR which is designed to relieve the pressure on a corporation or public individual when a massive blunder has been made which cannot be covered up and which will ruin their image. The PR job is not to undo the blunder but to persuade the public to take a more favourable view of their client's role concerning it. See also **counter-advertising**.

crisis intervention n [*Social work*] the involvement of a social worker with a client who is suffering a breakdown of adequate coping mechanisms, a state that gives rise to great vulnerability and conflict. Early and informed intervention in such a crisis can have long-term beneficial effects.

crisis management n [*Military*] a term coined after the Cuban Missile Crisis (1961) by US Secretary of State Robert MacNamara, who declared that 'there is no longer any such thing as strategy, only crisis management'. Thus it is the concept that foreign relations is in essence a process of keeping such international crises that must occur below the level at which actual conflict would be inevitable.

crisis of capitalism n [*Politics, Economics*] a Marxist term to describe the process whereby capitalism, having harnessed and profited from productive forces, then inevitably progresses to developing those forces beyond its own power to contain them; thus, as these forces reject the restraints of a capitalist society, so capitalism itself precipitates the revolution that destroys it.

crisis theology n [*Religion*] a post-1945 movement that attempted to set Christian dogma against the events of the two world wars, and the period between them; a movement propounded by Karl Barth (1886–1968), which aimed to preserve the otherness of God, while acknowledging that the limitations of human speech prevented these dogmas from being truly satisfactory.

crisis theory **1.** v [*Social work*] to work at speed, dealing with a succession of urgent problems. **2.** n [*Social work*] a comparatively long phase in an individual's psychological development, eg: 'midlife crisis'. **3.** n [*Social work*] See **crisis intervention**.

crisp **1.** n [*Book collecting*] a book in perfect, fresh condition; feeling right, looking clean, etc. **2.** a [*Wine-tasting*] light, refreshing, slightly acidic. **3.** also **up 3.** a [*US*] [*Football*] said of a team that is full of energy, enthusiasm and 'go'. See also **flat 4**.

crispener n [*Video*] an electronic device for increasing the horizontal resolution of a picture.

crit **1.** adv [*Science*] abbr of **critical** in nuclear power this means maintaining a self-sustaining chain reaction. **2.** a [*Military*] abbr of **critical** the minimum mass or size of fissile material required to create a chain reaction in a nuclear weapon.

criteria-cued a [*Sociology*] referring to the state of following critical criteria in such a way that one follows on automatically and deliberately from one criterion to the next. 'Cued' implies preparedness and deliberateness.

critical **1.** adv [*Science*] in nuclear power this means maintaining a self-sustaining chain reaction; thus 'to go critical' is to reach the critical stage. **2.** a [*Military*] the minimum mass or size of fissile (fission) material required to create a chain reaction in a nuclear weapon.

critical area n [*Lacrosse*] the area immediately in front of the goal and on a line from the ball to the goal.

C

critical path analysis n [Management] the analysis of the most important sequence of the individual stages of an operation, thus determining the time required to perform the whole operation.

critical realism n [Literary criticism] a term used by Russian critics to describe works – often produced in the West – which accurately portrayed the evils of bourgeois society. Such works were suited to the pre-revolutionary period; once the revolution had been achieved the correct creative posture would be **socialist realism**.

critical-incident a [Management] of, or relating to, the concentration of attention on a few important occurrences.

criticality one n [Aerospace] the classification of a single part, assembly or system; it is so vital that, like the weakened 'O-rings' that led to the destruction of the space shuttle Challenger in 1986, if it goes wrong, then everything else will fail.

crix n [Entertainment] abbr of 'critics'.

crizzle n [Glass-making] a fine surface fracture on glassware.

croaker n [Logology] a term coined by US logophile Willard R. Espy: it is a sentence that resembles **Tom Swifties** but here the pun is on the verb rather than on the adverb.

crock 1. n [Computing] an awkward feature embodied in the programming technique that should be made clearer. **2.** n [Computing] a programming technique that works acceptably, but which is unstable and prone to failure at the least disturbance. **3.** n [Computing] a tightly woven, almost completely unmodifiable, programming structure. **4.** n [US] [Medicine] a patient who complains long and often of multiple symptoms, many of which stem from simple hypochondria, and all of which are far out of proportion to the actual seriousness of his/her illness.

crock in v [Radio] said of a reporter who sends in the story over the telephone, using 'croc(odile) clips' which can cut into a 'phone line and thus send material on tape through the public lines into another phone, similarly linked into a tape recorder.

crockeries, also **crockies** n pl [Marbles] marbles with a baked glaze finish, usually blue or brown in colour but varying as to hue.

Crockford n [Religion] abbr of Crockford's Clerical Directory – the 'Who's Who' of the Church of England – first issued in 1860 by John Crockford (1823–1865).

crocking n [Textiles] the tendency of excess dye to rub off from a fabric.

crockle n [Marbles] the target marble in the game. See also **common, dib, duck, immie, mib**.

crocodiling n [Painting] See **alligatoring**.

crocus 1. n [UK] [Market-traders] a quack doctor. **2.** n [UK] [Market-traders] a fair-weather stall-holder who, like the eponymous plant, comes out only when the spring weather appears.

cromie n [Deer-stalking] a stag which has an abnormal horn, bending backwards like the horns of an antelope.

cronk 1. n [Aus] [Horse-racing] a horse that is unfit to run, or which runs in some dishonest manner. **2.** n [Aus] [Horse-racing] a race that is in some way dishonest.

crook of the rook n [Navy] the duty messman in a ship.

crop 1. v [Publishing] to cut one or more sides of an illustration or reproduction in print, either to improve its composition, eliminate detail, or simply to fit the space available. **2.** n [Tanning] a rectangular piece of hide from which the belly and leg pieces have been trimmed, and the neck, shoulder and tail pieces retained.

cropper v [Cycling] to fall heavily and possibly painfully off the bicycle; it comes from Standard English slang 'to come a cropper'.

cropping n [Metallurgy] the removal of excess metal from both ends of the rolled or forged product.

crops in n [US] [Farming] the planting of crops; thus 'crops out' is the harvest.

cross 1. v [Stock market] to make purchase or sale transactions in the same amount of the same securities which are matched within the broker's office; this transaction thus obviates the need for **jobbers** or the Settlement Department. **2.** n [Weaving] See **lease**.

cross assembler n [Computing] an **assembler** used on one computer to prepare an **object code** for use on another; eg: using a large sophisticated machine to prepare a program for use on a microcomputer.

cross bordering n [Airlines] ticket fraud: it is used to get money out of a country with tight exchange controls. Tickets are bought in bulk in local currency at face value before taking them in large quantities to the US. A complaisant travel agent is then persuaded to exchange these tickets, either for others or for cash. The effect is to tie up airlines' money but free one's own. The procedure is against IATA rules, but not actually illegal, although it may well be deemed so by the country whose currency one is effectively smuggling.

cross elasticity of demand n [Marketing] a means of determining the sensitivity of demand to competitive price changes by dividing the proportional change in sales 'demand' of the one product by the proportional change in the price of another.

cross head n [Journalism] a centred subhead in the text, used to break up long columns of copy and often created by extracting one sensational word or phrase from the adjacent paragraphs.

cross ownership n [Business] the ownership by a corporation of more than one media outlet – TV or radio station, newspaper, etc.

cross talk 1. *n* [*Computing*] a signal that has 'leaked' from one communications channel on to an adjacent one and which thus interferes with the second channel; it is usually associated with RS232 connections. 2. *n* [*Video*] an unwanted breakthrough between parallel channels of a programme chain. 3. also **cross fire** *n* [*Communications*] an unwanted transfer of energy from one circuit to another.

cross the T *v* [*Navy*] used of a ship or fleet which crosses the enemy's line of advance approximately at right angles and thus secures a tactical advantage in a sea battle.

cross tracks *n* [*Advertising*] railway or underground station poster sites that face waiting passengers from the far side of the tracks.

cross trading *n* [*Commerce*] the business of a shipping line which conveys cargo between a variety of foreign ports.

crossarms *n* [*Logging*] the best grade of timber available: that which is used for crossarms on telephone posts.

cross-check *v* [*Ice-hockey*] to check an opponent illegally by holding one stick with both hands and pushing it across his body.

cross-cut *n* [*Coal-mining*] See **stenton**.

crossed pair *n* [*Audio*] two directional microphones arranged either one above the other or in some way that is very close together, with their axes diverging at approx. 90°; they are used for stereo recording.

crossfire *n* [*Communications*] interference on one telegraph or signalling channel caused by currents in another channel.

cross-firing *n* [*Finance*] the opening of two or (usually) more current accounts at different banks to obtain money fraudulently. The holder of the accounts uses no money, but backs a withdrawal from Bank A with a cheque drawn on Bank B, and so on. The scheme works because of the time-lag in processing the various cheques – before Bank B can complain, a cheque is deposited from Bank A, and so on; the more accounts, the longer the scheme can be made to work.

crossfooting *n* [*Computing*] the addition or subtraction of various factors to processed data to ensure that the processing was carried out accurately; it is used to check input to data bases, accounts, etc.

cross-lining *n* [*Angling*] a means of poaching, carried out by fixing one rod either side of the river, and connecting them with a line carrying many flies or baits.

crossover 1. *n v a* [*Film*] a film that can attract a number of different specialist audiences; thus 'crossover star' is a performer who can attain the same multiple success. 2. *n v a* [*Pop music*] music that crosses over from one specialised area into another; it is often used of black stars who appeal to white audiences, but also of country-and-western material that is enjoyed by pop fans, etc.

crossover vote *n* [*Politics*] the concept that in the US primary elections there will be some voters who, while they will vote for the party of their basic allegiance on national polling day, will for some mischievous reason vote against their party at this earlier stage. In the UK a similar theory applies to the swings between local and general elections. Both concepts are disputed but remain popular with politicians who show up poorly on a local or primary level.

crossroader *n* [*Gambling*] an itinerant card sharp who moves around the country in search of new victims for his cheating skills.

cross-roughing, also **cross-ruffing** *n* [*US*] [*Government*] this comes from the bridge term for 'trumping'; it means to take one idea, 'rub' it against another, possibly opposing, idea, with the aim of refining and possibly redefining the original concept.

cross-slips *n* [*US*] [*Coal-mining*] the cut across the grain of the coal seam.

crosstalk *n* [*Audio*] the breakthrough of a signal between two adjacent stereo channels, or, in cassette recording, of adjacent pairs of channels.

cross-targeting *n* [*Military*] See **spike 6**.

crosstell *n* [*Computing, Military*] the transfer of information or data from one storage system to another.

crotch 1. *n* [*Logging*] a single sled used for dragging logs. 2. *n* [*Printing*] the point where two lines form an angle in a letter: in A,H, etc. 3. *n* [*Sport*] in fives/handball, racquets or squash, this is the intersection of any two playing surfaces on the court.

crow 1. *n* [*US*] [*Military*] See **bird 4**. 2. *n* [*US*] [*Navy*] the eagle that is attached to an officer's cap. See also **eagle**.

crow eaters *n pl* [*Cricket*] the South Australia state cricket team. See also **banana benders, sandgropers**.

crowd *n* [*US*] [*Stock market*] any group of stock exchange members who operate within a defined area of mutual interest.

crowd engineer *n* [*US*] [*Police*] euphemism for a police dog.

crowfoot *n* [*Sailing, Ropework*] radiating lines from a **euphroe block** with which to stretch awnings, nets, etc.

crowie *n* [*UK*] [*Market-traders*] old woman.

crown 1. *n* [*UK*] [*Coal-mining*] See **arch 1**. 2. *n* [*Glass-making*] the roof of a furnace. 3. *n* [*Oil rigs*] the uppermost section of an oil rig derrick.

crown jewels *n pl* [*Business*] the central and most important (and presumably profitable) element in a company; it is this part of the company that is the target of takeover bids and thus a company wishing to fend off such a bid may, in self-defence, sell the 'crown jewels' to a third party.

crown quality *n* [*Metallurgy*] the lowest commercial description of wrought iron; other grades are 'crown best quality', 'crown best best quality' and 'crown best best best quality'.

crows n pl [UK] [Crime] lookout men who are positioned to check the street (for approaching policemen) around the site of a three-card monte game.

crowsfoot n [TV, Film] a three-legged floor brace for a lamp. See also **turtle**.

croy n [Angling] an artificial pier, placed to make lies for fish.

CRT n [Computing] abbr of Cathode Ray Tube.

cru 1. n [Cheese-making] a well-defined region that gives rise to various differing characteristics in its milk and thus its cheeses. 2. n [Finance] an international monetary unit designed to ease the strain on gold and hard-currency reserves in settling accounts between nations.

crud 1. n [US] [Military] a real or imaginary disease. 2. n [Science] in nuclear power, any undesirable residues or impurities that may arise in a system, especially the corrosion that can be deposited on the surfaces of circulating water systems. 3. n [Skiing] bad and broken snow.

crudzine n [TV] a poorly produced, badly written fan magazine for devotees of TV's 'Star Trek' series.

crufanac n [Science fiction] abbr of **crucial fan activity** the cruciality is usually from the viewpoint of those involved in the activity.

crufty 1. a [Computing] poorly built, excessively complex; thus 'cruft' means shoddy construction. 2. a [Computing] unpleasant, especially to the touch; encrusted with some disgusting matter. 3. a [Computing] generally unpleasant and unappealing. 4. a [Computing] 'a crufty thing' is anything that fails to fit satisfactorily into an overall plan or system.

cruise 1. n [Logging] a survey of forest areas to estimate the volume and standard of the timber and the profits that may be obtained from felling it. 2. n [Military] the cruise missile is essentially a small, pilotless airplane that hugs the ground and uses its on-board radar and guidance system to deliver a nuclear (or conventional) warhead over great distances and with sufficient accuracy to threaten hard targets. Cheap to produce, accurate on target, cruise represents in military eyes almost the ideal modern weapon. Cruise missiles include the ALCM ('alkum': Air-Launched Cruise Missile), SLCM ('slickem': Sea-Launched Cruise Missile) and GLCM ('glockem': Ground-Launched Cruise Missile); it is the last of these, deployed in the UK and Europe, that is the focus of current anti-cruise protests. 3. n [US] [Marine Corps] a period of enlistment; 'hitch' is often used in error, but 'cruise', with its naval overtones is the only Marine usage. See also **hitch 1**. 4. v [Sex] used of a homosexual hustler who searches out clients on the street.

cruiser 1. n [Angling] the trout, which can be seen cruising near the surface of the water; its dorsal fin occasionally breaks the surface. 2. n [Logging] an expert appraiser of the quality of lumber that has been obtained from the woods.

cruising n [Angling] when a trout takes a fly here, a fly there, never settling in one place.

crum up 1. v [US] [Marine Corps] to tidy up, to neaten and clean both an individual and his uniform. 2. v [US] [Marine Corps] See **police 2**.

crumb 1. n [US] [Marine Corps] a slovenly, dirty person; thus as an adjective: crummy. 2. n [Religion] an inspiring thought, but voiced more modestly than **bread**.

crumbly a [Cheese-making] both a positive and negative description of texture; old and over-dried out cheeses can become unpleasantly crumbly.

crummie n [Logging] the vehicle, a station wagon or bus, that transports the workers to and from work in the woods.

crummy n, a [UK] [Market-traders] a louse; lice-infested.

crump n [Mining] See **bump 6**.

crunch v [Computing] to process, usually in a time-consuming or complicated way, an essentially trivial but necessary operation that is always painful to perform. See also **file crunching, number-cruncher**.

cruncher n [US] [Marine Air Corps] abbr of gravel cruncher: a term which refers to those troops who are assigned to ground duties.

crunchvid n [Media] highlights on film, TV, video, of sport, public events, etc; the whole event has been 'crunched' together.

crush 1. v [Farming] to hold cattle physically. 2. n [Metallurgy] in iron founding, this is the displacement of sand at mould joints when the two halves fail to fit correctly. 3. n [US] [Paper-making] blemishes in the paper caused by an excess of moisture in the pulp.

crusher n [Navy] a member of a ship's police force; it is used by John Le Carré in his fiction, but there generally extended to imply the Special Branch or a similar clandestine disciplinary group.

crusher's cramp n [Navy] a bribe given to a ship's policemen so that he will overlook some misdemeanour.

crushing n [TV] the foreshortening effect seen on a TV screen which results from the use of a tele-photo lens.

crust n [US] [Police] a criminal who specialises in elaborate confidence tricks, a **big con** operator.

crut n [Coal-mining] a roadway driven through rock rather than through coal.

crutch 1. v [Sailing, Ropework] to marry together the ends of two ropes prior to splicing. 2. n [Sheep-shearing] a mallet-shaped instrument (like a crutch) used to push sheep into a swimming dip; the invention of the spray dip has made the tool largely obsolete.

crutcher n [Soap-making] a machine that mixes liquid soap with perfumes and filler.

crutches n pl [Military] padded and reinforced

supports attached to an aircraft to brace a bomb or missile and prevent any shifting or involuntary dropping of the ordnance during flight.

crutching 1. *n* [*Sheep-shearing*] cutting the wool or hair from the hindquarters of a sheep, a sheep-dog, etc. 2. *n* [*Tanning*] a method of softening heavier grades of leather.

crying room *n* [*Rodeo*] the main office of the rodeo at which the competitors make complaints and the organisers offer excuses.

Cryovac *n* [*Cheese-making*] the vacuum wrapping used to preserve the blocks of mass-produced cheese sold in supermarkets.

crypp *n* [*Espionage*] this comes from cryptology meaning those who work as coding/decoding experts.

CSB [*Military*] abbr of **closely spaced basing**. See **dense pack**.

CSCE *n* [*Military*] abbr of **Conference on Security and Co-Operation in Europe** the so-called 'Helsinki Final Act' signed in August 1975 which aimed at establishing a variety of confidence building measures (**CBMs**) as well as providing for aspects of security and disarmament. These essentially agreed that prior notification would be given of the details and duration of any major troop manoeuvres. It was suggested that 'in a spirit of reciprococity', states participating in this agreement would permit observers from other participant states; there should be a general movement towards the strengthening of European détente and the promotion of disarmament.

CU *n* [*US*] [*Gliding*] abbr of **cumulus** a type of cloud formation formed by condensation due to cooling at or near the top of a rising column or bubble of warm air known as a thermal.

Cuban fork ball *n* [*Baseball*] a suspected spit ball (a type of pitch which is given extra variation in speed and direction by a coating of human saliva and is illegal).

cube *n* [*Shipping*] a fraudulent practice whereby a shipping agent or a manufacturer deliberately underestimates the cubic capacity of a cargo to the shipper, thus paying less, and overestimates it to the exporter, who must pay more.

cuckoo shot *n* [*Coal-mining*] an explosion fired off in the roof of a longwall working, between the face and the waste, or actually in the waste.

cuddy *n* [*Navy*] the captain's cabin aboard a warship.

cues *n pl* [*Radio*] written material – yellow paper for the studio presenter, pink for the control room engineer and the producer – so that those concerned can follow the schedule in the studio.

cuff *v* [*Medicine*] to take the blood pressure by using a blood pressure cuff or sphygmomanometer.

cufferoo *adv* [*Commerce*] on the cuff, ie: on credit.

CUG *n* [*Computing*] acro **Closed User Group** a group of users/terminals that enjoy privacy with respect to a public service.

cull 1. *v* [*Commerce*] in the fruit trade this is to reject inferior produce. 2. *v* [*Military*] used by white troops and mercenaries in Africa, especially during the last, bloodiest days of the fighting in Rhodesia (Zimbabwe) meaning to shoot blacks dead, often on suspicion rather than fact, and essentially for amusement. 3. *n* [*Logging*] a tree of log which in size is suitable for merchandising, but through a variety of defects is rendered useless. 4. *n* [*US*] [*Meat trade*] the lowest grade of animal. 5. *n* [*Tobacco*] a cigar that is not up to standard and must either be resorted at a lower grade or scrapped outright.

cullet *n* [*Glass-making*] broken glass that is added to a mixture of basic materials that are melted to make glass.

culottes *n* [*Dog breeding*] See **trousers**.

cultural art *n* [*Art*] a derogatory term, roughly equivalent to 'fine art' as viewed by the avant garde, that was coined in 1949 by the artist Jean Dubuffet. In cultural art the artist is impotent, his art is tame, exploited and controlled by the bourgeoisie.

cultural capital *n* [*Sociology*] the concept (by P. Bourdieu) that success in school largely depends on the ability of the child to absorb the dominant culture and thus accrue cultural capital.

cultural conservatism *n* [*Sociology*] a variety of conservatism based on the belief that 'high' culture – usually defined by critics as an 'elitist' culture – is both good in itself and a vital component of a society's stability.

cultural deprivation *n* [*Government*] a euphemism for poverty; thus 'culturally deprived environment' means the slums.

cultural domination *n* [*Sociology*] the concept (by P. Bourdieu) that the education system functions purely to reproduce the culture of the dominant classes and thus reinforce this dominance.

cultural lag *n* [*Sociology*] a term coined in 1922 by W. F. Ogburn; it means the stresses that develop between two correlated sections of a single culture which develop at different paces.

cultural relativism 1. *n* [*Politics*] See **relativism**. 2. *n* [*Sociology*] the theory that beliefs are relative to a given society and are not comparable between societies.

Cultural Revolution *n* [*Politics*] the cultural, political, social and concomitantly economic upheaval in China between 1965 and 1969, which was launched by Chairman Mao to regain some of his depleted power, lost through the failure of the **Great Leap Forward**. Intended to crush the bureaucracy and install true egalitarianism, the Cultural Revolution, with its massive purges, its violence and its growing personality cult devoted to Mao, proved a major disaster for China and its people – and one from which the nation has yet fully to recover.

C

C

cultural script *n* [*Sociology*] a pre-established system of rules, roles, codes and assumptions by which we all supposedly live.

culture *n* [*Military*] all names, legends, etc. found on a map; ie. the features of the terrain that are man-made, rather than natural.

culture shock *n* [*Sociology*] the sense of confusion and alienation often experienced by those suddenly exposed to a culture and a society which are totally outside their previous experience. Often it appears that the 'hosts' have no sense or logic in their ways of living and communicating.

culture-fair *a* [*Sociology*] making due allowance (often in examinations/tests/job interviews) for the variety of cultural and ethnic backgrounds of those involved. Culture-fair testing takes all such differences into consideration and attempts to ensure that the non-WASP is not penalised simply for his/her birth. See also **affirmative action**.

cum and ex *adv* [*Stock market*] cum: a word used in connection with dividends, rights, etc. to indicate that the shares so described are entitled to claim such dividends or rights. (It comes from Lat. meaning 'with'). ex: the opposite of cum; 'ex dividend' thus means that such shares are not entitled to the distribution of shares, rights, etc. (It comes from Lat. meaning 'from')

cume *n* [*Advertising*] abbr of **cumulative audience**. See **reach and frequency**.

cumshaw *n* [*US*] [*Marine Corps*] anything free, gratis, buckshee; it comes from Chinese 'kan hsieh' meaning 'with grateful thanks', which became 'a gift' in pidgin.

cumulative penetration *n* [*Marketing*] the build up of customers buying the same brand a number of times over a measured period.

cundy *n* [*Coal-mining*] any small passageway made to improve ventilation or facilitate the movement of materials.

cunt splice *n* [*Logging, Sailing, Ropework*] two ends of rope spliced together, with a gap between the two parts.

cuntlines *n pl* [*Sailing, Ropework*] the surface seams between the strands of a rope.

cunvittu *n* [*Crime*] used in the Italian Mafia to mean a prison; it comes from Sicilian meaning a convent.

cup of coffee *n* [*Baseball*] a short career in the major leagues by a player who then returns to the minors from whence he came.

cup, the *n* [*US*] [*Bars*] the receptacle used by a bartender to retain his/her tips.

cupid's bow operation *n* [*Medicine*] in dentistry, this is an operation which re-adjusts the vermillion border of the upper lip into a perfect 'cupid's bow' shape.

cupid's darts *n pl* [*Gemstones*] long hair-like needles of red or golden-coloured rutile that are found in quartz.

cupola *n* [*Metallurgy*] a vertical shaft furnace in which the metal charge, mixed with fuel (usually coke) is melted by burning in a blast of hot or cold air.

cuppa *n* [*Espionage*] from 'not my cuppa char', ie: not to my taste. An individual who has been targeted for blackmail through the planting of a **sister** (who will create a compromising sexual situation) may well have to be offered a number of such women before he finds one that is sufficiently to his taste – his 'cuppa' – to render the blackmailing a simple task.

cuppers *n* [*Education*] at Oxford University, this is a series of inter-collegiate sports matches played in competition for a cup.

cuppy *a* [*Metallurgy*] said of wire which appears sound but which has a number of noticeable internal defects that will lead to fracture under bending stresses.

curbing *n* [*US*] [*Car salesmen*] an irregular procedure whereby a salesman buys and sells a car independently of the lot for which he works; he is working, as it were, from the kerb outside.

curbstone broker *n* [*Stock market*] a stock-broker who is not a member of any exchange but acts as a middleman between the public, with whom he is allowed to deal, and the exchange brokers.

curd *n* [*Cheese-making*] the solid white mass that coagulates when milk is treated with rennet, an acid-producing enzyme found in the stomachs of calves, and which leaves the **whey**.

cur-dog *n* [*Hunting*] hunt servant's term for any dog other than a hound.

cure 1. *v* [*Agriculture*] to clear land prior to cultivation. 2. *v* [*Industry*] to produce a chemical change in substances – rubber, plastics, concrete, etc – either normally or artificially by a process of heating. 3. *v* [*US*] [*Law*] to make acceptable under legal procedure by the admission of certain evidence giving charges considered under the law to nullify any effect prejudicial to the appellant that any defective evidence or charges might have. 4. *n* [*US*] [*Merchant navy*] the medical care given to a seaman who has been injured or has fallen ill during his duties.

curing 1. *n* [*Building, Plastering*] the process employed to ensure the hardness of cement work by preventing loss of moisture. 2. *n* [*Building, Concrete workers*] a process adopted to guarantee the proper hardening of concrete by ensuring that it is protected from extremes of temperature and from excess evaporation. 3. *n* [*Cheese-making*] the treatment of a cheese that causes it to ripen, generally in suitably arranged underground cellars under regulated conditions of temperature and humidity.

curiosa *n* [*Book collecting*] curiosities, oddities, especially pornography or erotica. See also **facetiae**.

curl 1. *n* [*US*] [*Football*] a pattern of play in which two receivers cross each other. 2. *n* [*Surfing*] a semi-hollow wave which allows the surfer to pick up speed on the top half and then, after it breaks, to move down on to the bottom half and ride free of the white water, protected by the curl of water above. **3.** *n* [*UK*] [*Surfing*] the highest and fastest part of the wave.

curlicism *n* [*Literary criticism*] any form of literary indecency; it is named after Edmund Curll (1683–1747) a bookseller, pamphleteer and publisher, inter alia of 'Venus in the Cloister or, The Nun in Her Smock' (1724) for which he was imprisoned.

curls *n pl* [*US*] [*Painting*] small balls and ridges of paint formed when a coat runs down a surface.

curly *a* [*Printing*] said of any cursive, or script faces, eg: copperplate.

curly cue *n* [*Printing*] a **swash** Q, or its tail.

currant pie *n* [*Social work*] a pun on current/currant and P.I.E. which is short for period of interruption of employment.

currant-jelly **1.** *n* [*Hunting*] the scent of a hare crossing the scent of a fox and thus confusing the hounds. **2.** *n* [*Hunting*] poorly regarded breeds of harriers. dwarf foxhounds or beagle harriers.

currency cocktail *n* [*Finance*] a mix of foreign currencies used in foreign business deals.

current bedding *n* [*Geology*] a form of **false bedding** which has been caused by flowing water or driving wind.

current sheet, also **magnetodisk** *n* [*Science*] a cylindrical region of strong magnetic lines on the boundary of an area dominated by a planet's magnetic field.

curse *n* [*Angling*] the fisherman's curse: minute diptera, on which trout like to feed, but which are very hard to imitate successfully in an artificial manner.

curtailment *n* [*Logology*] apocope, paragoge; the cutting off of the last letter of a word to leave a different word; thus 'noone' becomes 'noon', etc.

curtain **1.** *n* [*Journalism*] a headline which is ruled off on three sides only. **2.** *n* [*Painting*] the effect of using very viscous paint which runs down a surface, rather than covering it smoothly. **3.** *n* [*TV*] from the theatrical 'curtain line' – this is the last line of a play; hence it is also the last line or scene of a **segment** of a thriller series.

curtain sider *n* [*UK*] [*Road transport*] See **tautliner**.

curtains *n pl* [*Clothing*] pieces of material, usually linings, put across the top of the insides of trousers under the waistband from side seam to seat seam.

curtesy *n* [*Law*] a widower's life interest in his wife's **real property**.

curtilage *n* [*Law*] the courtyard or land adjacent to a dwelling house and which is regarded as forming a single enclosure with it; the ground, not otherwise marked off or enclosed, that is regarded as being necessary for the comfortable enjoyment of a house or other building.

curve *n* [*Baseball*] a pitch thrown so that it travels on a curved course towards the batter.

cush *n abbr of* [*US*] [*Crime*] **cushion** the share of the contraband or criminal booty which is divided among those who committed the crime.

cushion **1.** *n* [*Gambling*] a reserve bank roll. **2.** *n* [*Gambling*] money in the bank. **3.** *n* [*Industry*] head of a drilling brace. **4.** *n* [*US*] [*Stock market*] the period of time that elapses between the time a bond is issued and the time it can be called. **5.** *n* [*TV, Radio*] programme material that can be lengthened, shortened or omitted entirely to ensure that a broadcast ends exactly on time. **6.** *n* [*Tyre-making*] a rubber strip built into a pneumatic tyre in order to absorb some of the shocks encountered from the road.

cushty *a* [*UK*] [*Market-traders*] good, enjoyable, of good quality.

cusp *n* [*Ice-skating*] the point in a turn when the skater moves from one edge of the skate to the other; it comes from the astrological point at which one sign moves into the next.

cuspy *n acro* [*Computing*] this comes from **Commonly Used System Program** a utility program used by many operators; thus it describes any program that is well written and functions excellently.

custom and practice *n* [*Industrial relations*] a set of beliefs and understandings, especially among craft workshops and piece-workers, that have developed into hard and fast rules, and are administered as such by shop stewards.

custom presser *n* [*Video*] See **contract presser**.

customary acre *n* [*Law*] the area of land that one man and one horse could plough in one day.

customer engineering *n* [*Computing*] that department of a manufacturer's organisation which deals with customer service, field installations and repairs.

customer service representative *n* [*Air travel*] non-flying airline personnel who work at check-in desks, etc.

cut **1.** *n* [*Coal-mining*] a group of holes fired in a round to provide extra free faces for later explosions. **2.** *n* [*Journalism, Printing*] an illustration. **3.** *n* [*Crime*] a sentence of two to four years. **4.** *n* [*Logging*] the season's output of logs. **5.** *n* [*US*] [*Football*] the regular dismissal during pre-season practice of those players who have been contracted to the team but who are not considered good enough for permanent employment. **6.** *n* [*Golf*] in major tournaments the round by round exclusion of those competitors who have failed to score well enough to rank above an arbitrary figure of shots permitted and who may thus no longer participate in the contest. **7.** *n* [*Textiles*] a length of cloth, usually about 60 yards. **8.** *n* [*Pop music*] a track from an album. **9.** *v* [*Pop music*] to record a song or a piece of music. **10.** *v* [*Meat trade*] to sort out specific animals from the herd.

C

11. *v* [*Pool*] to hit the ball off-centre, causing it to move away at an angle. **12.** *v* [*Railways*] to separate a locomotive or coach from a train. **13.** *v* [*Drugs*] said of a seller of drugs who adulterates his/her wares – oregano or lawn grass into marijuana, mud for hashish, pain-killers for amphetamines or barbiturates, procaine or novocaine into cocaine, milk sugar into heroin, etc. **14.** *v* [*TV, Film*] to make a quick transition from one shot to the next, an effect usually achieved by editing. **15.** *excl* [*TV, Film*] as an interjection meaning 'Stop filming!'. **16.** *v* [*TV, Film*] to edit film or videotape.

cut a log *v* [*Logging*] to move one end of a log backwards and forwards, so that the log will move in the desired direction.

cut a voluntary *v* [*Hunting*] to fall from one's horse when hunting.

cut and hold *excl* [*Film*] an instruction which requests that the cameraman stops filming and the actors hold their current positions so that the director can check lights, angles, positioning, etc.

cut and shut *v* [*Antiques, Rug trade*] to increase the saleability of a worn rug by cutting off the border, slicing away the worn parts and then tightening it all up by sewing it together.

cut back **1.** *v* [*Motor trade*] used of paintwork which cleans up satisfactorily with an abrasive polish. **2.** [*Surfing*] to change direction by 180° whilst on a wave.

cut coils *v* [*Custom cars*] to lower a coil sprung car by the simple removal of one coil of springs; it is a quick and simple method but by altering a basic aspect of the suspension one may create many ancillary problems.

cut 'em down *a* [*Hunting*] excellent, first-rate, superlative.

cut his cong *v* [*Royal Marines*] to break a man's spirit, to make him accept ship's discipline.

cut hogs *v* [*US*] [*Farming*] to castrate hogs.

cut in *v* [*US*] [*Painting*] to paint an edge without touching an adjacent surface.

cut looker *n* [*Textiles*] an inspector in the textile factory.

cut of cars *n* [*US*] [*Railways*] a portion of a train.

cut out *v* [*Boxing*] to dominate a fight and the way in which it is fought.

cut the board *v* [*US*] [*Railways*] to reduce the number of employees at a given location.

cut the cake *v* [*Business*] to work out a deal, to negotiate a contract.

cut up big wins *v* [*Gambling*] to reminisce over nostalgic glories.

cut up the score *v* [*Crime, Gambling*] criminals or gambling partners do this when they divide up their winnings.

cut wheels *v* [*US*] [*Railways*] to remove flat spots from locomotive wheels.

cutability *n* [*Meat trade*] the proportion of saleable meat found on a carcass.

cutback *n* [*Surfing*] to turn one's board back towards the breaking part of the wave.

cut-card *n* [*Silversmiths*] a type of relief decoration of silverware in which a thin sheet of metal is cut ornamentally and then soldered to the flat surface.

cuticle *n* [*Weaving*] the outer layer of scales on a wool fibre.

cut-in *n* [*Film*] a **leader** inserted into a film sequence.

cut-ins *n pl* [*Pop music*] the extra royalties that are paid over, as a reward for the concomitant publicity, to a singer who uses material created by a particular songwriter more than usually often.

cut-me-down *a* [*Hunting*] antique slang for the most fashionable and hard-riding counties.

cut-off **1.** *n* [*Printing*] a full rule across one or more columns. **2.** *n* [*Printing*] the depth of a rotary printed **broadsheet**. **3.** *n* [*TV*] a script that has been delivered, and for which delivery money has been paid, but which has subsequently been rejected and is therefore dropped and 'cut off' from any further payments. **4.** *n* [*TV*] the small frame that surrounds a broadcast picture but which never appears on the home viewer's screen.

cut-off man *n* [*Espionage*] a local intelligence contact man who passes on messages and funds to agents in the field.

cut-out **1.** *n* [*Advertising*] an illustration, often a figure that has been cut out of its background and then printed against white space. **2.** *n* [*Business*] this comes from its usage in espionage: a person or business used as an intermediary between principals in a secret operation. It is used in secret deals and similar operations that a corporation does not wish to be revealed at the time, if ever. **3.** *n* [*Espionage*] a low-level sub-category in the CIA of the **utility operative;** a member of an espionage system with one function only, the passing of messages between an agent and his **principal, case officer** or **station** chief. The use of the cut-out ensures that the agent will have no knowledge of the source of the messages he receives or the destination of the intelligence he passes on. **4.** *n* [*Sheep-shearing*] the finish of a spell of shearing of either a batch of sheep or the whole shed.

cutter **1.** *n* [*Meat trade*] an inferior grade of carcass beef of which only the ribs and loins are marketed as whole cuts; the remainder is processed as sausages and other beef by-products. **2.** *n* [*US*] [*Meat trade*] the third lowest grade of animal, immediately above a **canner**. **3.** *n* [*Tobacco*] a leaf of flue-cured tobacco pulled from the higher portion of the lower half of the stalk. **4.** *n* [*TV, Film*] a film or videotape editor.

cutting doctor *n* [*US*] [*Medicine*] a surgeon. See also **guessing doctor**.

CW *n* [*Military*] abbr of **chemical weapons** Current chemical weapons include: Phosgene (coughing, retching, frothing, asphyxia – lethal);

Prussic Acid (convulsions, asphyxia – lethal); Nitrogen Mustard (blisters, attacks skin tissue – possibly lethal); Sarin (developed by Germany in 1938: attacks nervous system, chronic respiratory problems – incapacitates); Tabun (developed by Germany in 1936: nerve agent causing blurred vision, muscular spasms – incapacitates); Soman (developed by Germany in 1944 to replace Sarin: breathing difficulties, nausea, muscular spasms, involuntary bowel movements – possibly lethal); VX (a 'persistent' version of Sarin, whose oil-like drops evaporate slowly and thus stay lethal for days); BZ (hallucinations, giddiness, slows down mental and physical reactions – incapacitates; BZ was dropped from US CW arsenals since it tended to make its victims act maniacally, rather than collapse conveniently). The main Russian nerve gas is VR–55, a version of Sarin.

CYA *excl* [*US*] [*Government*] abbr of **Cover Your Ass** the first rule of bureaucracy and politics – whatever the blunder and however great its effect, make sure that you are in a position to pass the buck quickly and efficiently, and then, perhaps, think about taking some more altruistic action.

cybercrud *n* [*Computing*] the blinding of gullible people – possibly novice computer purchasers – with a torrent of jargon and esoterica.

cybernetic art *n* [*Art*] the study of control and communication in animal and machine, and especially of messages considered as a means of controlling machinery and society. Feedback (in the form of information for correcting future behaviour of the system) is fundamental. Thus, cybernetic sculpture can respond to such stimuli as the proximity of spectators.

cyc *n* [*Theatre*] abbr of **cyclorama** a large back-cloth, frequently curved, which is stretched around the back of the stage, often representing the sky.

cycle *n* [*Baseball*] a series of a single, double, triple and home runs hit by one player during a game of baseball.

cycle billing *n* [*Business*] a system by which a proportionate fraction of the customers of an organisation are billed on each working day of the month to equalise the work thus involved for the accounts department.

cyclone *n* [*Logging*] a funnel-shaped cone that causes sawdust to circulate under air pressure; this forces the sawdust to the outer edge of the cone, where it slides to the bottom of the cone and onto a conveyor.

cyclone desk *n* [*Logging*] a jumbled collection of logs.

cyclone shot *n* [*Mining*] a very powerful explosive charge.

cyma reversa/recta *n* [*Building, Plastering*] a common moulding section: it is formed by two equilateral segments whose centres are each spun from the centre and one end.

cymatics, also **kymatics** *n* [*Science*] a term coined by Dr. Hans Jenny to describe his research into the structure and dynamics of waves, vibrations and periodic phenomena. Cymatics relates directly to **kinetic art**.

cysto & pyelo, also **C&P** *n* [*US*] [*Medicine*] abbr of **cystoscopy and pyelogram**.

Czech defence *n* [*Chess*] a sequence in which pawn is matched with pawn but the queen's bishop tips the balance.

D

D notice *n* [*UK*] [*Government, Press*] abbr of **defence notice** a voluntary system of self-censorship observed by the British media whereby the government cites a 'sensitive' piece of news – often one that acts against its self-interest – as something best kept out of the public eye, and trusts to individual editors to accept this restriction. This very British variety of state censorship orig-inated in 1912 as the prerogative of the Admiralty, War Office and Press Committee, now renamed the Services, Press and Broadcasting Committee, the secretary of which signs the formal letter referring to the news item in question, which is the actual 'notice'.

D region *n* [*Radio*] that part of the ionosphere, between 50–90 km. that reduces the strength of radio waves in the frequencies between 1–100MHz. See also **E region, F region**.

D sleep *n* [*Medicine*] abbr of **desynchronised sleep** the lightest sleep, taking up 25% of the sleeping cycle. See also **S sleep**.

dab hand *n* [*UK*] [*Railways*] a railway coach painter; a pun on dab (of paint) and dab hand (a skilful craftsman).

dab-dab *n* [*Navy*] a stoker's name for a seaman – much of his peacetime work involves painting the ship.

dabs *n pl* [*UK*] [*Police*] fingerprints.

dadcap *n* [*Military*] acro **Dawn And Dusk Combat Air Patrol**.

daddy 1. *n* [*UK*] [*Prisons*] in Borstals, this is a heavy, powerful inmate who runs the institution, with the tacit acceptance of the warders, through a mixture of fear and threats. See also **baron**. 2. *n* [*Theatre*] stage manager.

daddy tank *n* [*US*] [*Prisons*] a holding cell reserved for lesbians who will otherwise be attacked by other prisoners.

dado *v* [*Logging, Carpentry*] to cut a rectangular hole or slot in wood.

daemon *n* [*Computing*] a program that is never called up implicitly from memory but lies dormant, waiting to respond to the occurrence of certain conditions. The operator who creates such a condition may well be ignorant of the existence of the lurking daemon, although a program may often commit a particular action simply because it is 'aware' that the daemon is waiting to be invoked.

daffies *n* [*UK*] [*Market-traders*] alcohol.

dafia *part phr* [*Science fiction*] acro **drifting away from it all** the gradual disenchantment / lack of intimate involvement with the fan world.

dag *n* [*Sheep-shearing*] wool mixed with dung, dirt or any rubbish, hanging from the sheep. Thus 'to dag' is to cut away this wool.

dagger *n* [*Navy*] this comes from the dagger notation against the names of those officers who have taken one of a variety of advanced specialist courses in a given subject (which will be named after the dagger).

daggers *n pl* [*Sheep-shearing*] handshearers used for clipping off dirty, dung-matted pieces of wool. See also **dag**.

DAGMAR *part phr* [*Advertising*] acro **defining advertising goals for measured advertising response** originally the title of a book suggesting that advertising effectiveness could be better assessed through communications rather than simple sales.

dailies 1. *n pl* [*Film*] the first, rough prints of a day's shooting on a film. These prints are viewed as soon as they have been processed, by those involved or interested in the work done. 2. *n pl* [*Insurance*] reports sent by out-of-town insurance salesmen to inform head office of the daily business accrued.

daily double *n* [*Gambling*] a bet in horse-racing that is based on choosing the winners of the day's first two races.

dairymaid calculation *n* [*Business*] a European business concept based on the activities of the traditional milk-seller who touted her wares from house to house, pouring out the quantities required at each and then totting up her sales at the end. Here it means any elementary calculation.

daisychain 1. *n, v* [*Computing*] the device that connects a number of devices to a single **controller**; hence to connect a number of devices by this means. Usually this is done by connecting the controller to the nearest of the devices, then this device connects to the next, and so on. 2. *n* [*US*] [*Stock market*] fraudulent trading between mutually interested market manipulators who attempt to create an atmosphere of intense market activity in order to seduce legitimate investors into helping to force up the price; they then sell otherwise worthless shares to these investors at inflated prices, leaving their victims with useless, unsellable shares.

daisycutter *n* [*Military*] See **cheeseburger**.

dakota *n* [*Show business*] any prefatory lines spoken before a singer actually starts the song he/she is announcing.

dally *v* [*US*] [*Cattlemen*] to twist the rope around the saddle horn when using it to rope cattle; it comes from Sp. 'dar la vuelta' meaning to take a turn (with the rope).

damage assessment *n* [*Military*] finding out as soon as possible just how much damage – offensive and defensive – has been caused in a nuclear exchange; the theorists of 'winnable' or 'protracted' nuclear wars base much of their planning on obtaining such assessments. See also **damage limitation 2**.

damage limitation 1. *n* [*Business, Government*] any attempt in business, bureaucracy, government, etc. to deal with an unavoidable crisis by minimising its effects to the best extent possible. The damage has been done, and all that the 'survivors' can hope to do is establish what controls are feasible. 2. *n* [*Military*] the concept that judicious planning can limit the damage, and thus the virulence of the conflict and the deaths it must cause, in a nuclear war. The damage that is to be limited is that sustained by one's own side, and such thinking lies behind the current belief in 'winnable' nuclear wars.

damager *n* [*Theatre*] a pun, meaning manager.

dance *v* [*Printing*] to lift or shake a locked **form** to test for rigidity; type that slips when this is done is said to 'dance'.

dancers *n pl* [*UK*] [*Market-traders*] stairs.

dancetty *a* [*Heraldry*] said of a line or shape that is zigzag.

dancing 1. *a* [*UK*] [*Police*] referring to thieves who specialise in robberies on the second and

D

higher floors of houses; it comes from rhyming slang 'Fred Astaires' meaning 'stairs', and thus the 'dancing' image of those who use them. **2.** *n* [*UK*] [*Railways*] the slipping of a locomotive's wheels on the rails.

dancing in the Spirit, also **singing in the Spirit** *part phr* [*Religion*] dancing in a trance-like state, talking 'in tongues' to acknowledge one's joy in the presence of the Holy Spirit.

dandy note *n* [*Shipping*] a delivery order made by an exporter and approved by a customs officer, authorising a shipping agent to remove goods from a bonded warehouse for loading on to a ship.

dandy roll *n* [*Philately*] wire-gauze roller which impresses the paper with its texture as the pulp leaves the vats; wire or metal bits are soldered onto the dandy roll to create a watermark in the paper.

danger line *n* [*Athletics*] the distance a runner must still go before a rival can be overtaken and the race won.

dangerous pairs *n pl* [*Literary criticism*] words that are similar in spelling, and are thus confused when written, although their meanings are quite different; eg: 'jejeune' and 'jejune', etc.

dangerous sense *n* [*Literary criticism*] a term coined by C. S. Lewis: a word's current, popular sense, when this has altered from its original sense and which, therefore, may be misapplied to that word when read by the uninitiated in older works.

dangle *v* [*Medicine*] said of a patient who sits up on the edge of the bed, and dangles his/her legs over the side.

dangle the Dunlops *v* [*Air travel*] to lower the undercarriage on an airliner as it approaches the runway.

dangler 1. *n* [*Linguistics*] this is a word or phrase, usually some form of modifier, which occurs near the start of a sentence without actually standing in some normally expected syntactical relation to the rest of the sentence, and especially without modifying the subject. Such sentences tend, unintentionally, to sound humorous or foolish; eg: 'gazing ahead, the truck slowed to a halt' etc. **2.** *n* [*UK*] [*Road transport*] a trailer. See also **pup 3**.

danny 1. *n* [*Glass-making*] an open crack at the base of the neck of a bottle. **2.** *n* [*UK*] [*Police*] a 'plain-clothes' police car used by the CID for surveillance work. See also **nondescript**.

dapping *n* [*Angling*] fishing with a **blow line**, with live or artificial fly, allowing the wind to carry the line and thus making the fly float or dance realistically on the water.

dapple *n* [*Glass-making*] irregularity of the inside or outside surface of a glass container.

darby *n* [*Building, Plastering*] a light alloy rule about 1.1m long with two handles, used for straightening floating coats.

dark 1. *a* [*Theatre*] referring to a theatre that is closed, especially when the current production has had to be taken off, or there is no money or talent available to mount a new show. **2.** *a* [*TV*] referring to an empty, non-functioning studio.

dark blue *n* [*UK*] [*Military*] British forces' term for a member of the Royal Navy.

dark figure *n* [*Sociology*] in criminal statistics, this is the large proportion of crimes which are not reported to the police – both trivial crimes and major ones, including blackmail, incest and rape.

dark, in the *a* [*Military*] air intercept code for: not visible on my radar scope.

dark money, also **dark time** *n* [*UK*] [*Railways*] bonuses paid for night work.

dark object *n* [*Military*] a satellite which is functioning but which has never emitted traceable signals; these objects may be missile-carrying space weapons, targeted either at earth installations or as anti-satellite satellites (**ASAT**).

dark satellite *n* [*Military*] a special satellite used for military or intelligence purposes, incorporating extra electronic counter-measures to reduce its 'visibility' to hostile sensors, radar, etc.

darks *n pl* [*Commerce*] black or dark blue women's wear.

darky, also **cat's paw** *n* [*Merchant navy*] a ruffled, wind-swept patch on the surface of the sea.

DARPA *n* [*US*] [*Military*] acro **Defense Advanced Research Projects Agency** sited at Kirtland Air Force Base near Albuquerque, New Mexico. The spearhead of US weapons development, currently dedicated to the development of satellites and laser weaponry, and satellite-borne early warning and intelligence sensors, and offering overall 'revolutionary new options for the future defense' of the US, thus 'pulling significantly ahead of . . . adversaries in capabilities for surveillance, target acquisition and homing guidance' (Robert Fossum, head of the agency, 1983).

dart 1. *n* [*Military*] a target towed behind one aircraft and used by others for training in artillery accuracy. **2.** *n* [*Navy*] abbr of Dartmouth, thus an officer trained at the Royal Naval College, Dartmouth.

dash *n* [*Government*] in Nigeria, this is the bribery which is officially condoned and accepted as an integral part of the nation's social/economic/political system.

dashes *n pl* [*UK*] [*Market-traders*] a smacking (given to a child); thus 'to dash' is to chastise, to tell off.

dashpot *n* [*Cars*] the part of some carburettors which is used to damp down certain movements or oscillations.

data *v* [*Espionage*] to compile a dossier of information on a targeted individual or organisation.

data capture *n* [*Computing*] the simultaneous automatic recording and processing of information by means of equipment which connects

D

local terminals with a remote central computer or processing unit.

data collision 1. *n* [*Computing*] in data transmission: a situation that occurs when two or more simultaneous demands are made on equipment that is only capable of handling one at a time. **2.** *n* [*Computing*] a situation in which the same **address** is obtained for two separate data items that are to be stored at that address.

data diddling *n* [*Data security*] the alteration of stored data values for illegal purposes.

data hierarchy *n* [*Computing*] the structuring of data in sets, subsets, etc.

data independence *n* [*Computing*] the removal of the close coupling between the logical and physical structure of a database and the user programs, so that the structure can be altered without affecting the user's view of the data.

data integrity *n* [*Computing*] the preservation of data stored in a computer against errors or loss or corruption.

data migration *n* [*Computing*] the moving of data from an on-line device to an off-line device or to a low-priority on-line device.

data sink *n* [*Computing*] that part of a data communications terminal device that receives data.

data transparency 1. *n* [*Computing*] a property of a network communications system whereby the output data stream delivered is the exact bit sequence presented to the input of the system without any restriction or exception. **2.** *n* [*Computing*] in data communications, a technique whereby any pattern of bits, including those normally reserved for control purposes, may be transmitted as a block.

database *n* [*Computing*] any collection of information kept on an electronic file, though if taken literally, even a file of yellowing press cuttings could comprise a database.

database management system *n* [*Computing*] a feature of the 'electronic office': a **software** package geared to arranging, sorting and retrieving information and generally managing the operation and accumulation of a **database**.

dataframe *n* [*Computing*] a unit of information, typically a page of data, including the margins.

date 1. *n* [*Entertainment*] a theatrical or other entertainment performance, often a single stop on a tour. **2.** *n* [*UK*] [*Market-traders*] buttocks.

dating *n* [*Finance*] the extension of credit in commercial transactions beyond the previously arranged date.

datum *n* [*Building, Plastering*] a fixed point of reference – either datum dot or datum line – from which further measurements are taken when setting out work accurately.

daub *v* [*Metallurgy*] in iron founding, this is to coat or plaster the inside of a cupola furnace or the inside of a ladle with a refractory mixture.

daughter 1. *n* [*Computing*] See **child**. **2.** *n* [*Science*] a nuclide formed by the nuclear disintegration – either spontaneous or induced – of another nuclide. It comes originally from 'daughter atom', which was created from an original nucleus which was the 'parent atom' and the resulting atom is either the 'decay product' or 'daughter atom'.

daughter board *n* [*Computing*] modular elements added to a circuit board to perform specific extra activities such as memory extension or disk control. See also **backplane, motherboard**.

daughter company *n* [*Commerce*] any company that is a subsidiary of a parent or holding company. See also **sister company**.

dawn chorus *n* [*Communications*] a form of atmospherics, audible on radio transmissions, which sounds like the warbling of birds.

dawn raid *n* [*Stock market*] a method of forcing a takeover by the surreptitious purchasing of as many shares as possible of the company in which one is interested at 'dawn' – starting as soon as the Stock Exchange opens for business and completing one's purchases by 10am. One can purchase up to 29% of a company using such methods before legally being forced to announce one's intentions. All purchases over 30% must be declared.

day *n* [*Coal-mining*] the surface of the ground immediately over a mine – where there is, presumably, daylight.

day for night *n* [*Film*] the use of special filters over the lens to obtain the idea of a 'night-time' sequence even though shooting is in broad daylight. The point of this manoeuvre is to avoid the massive overtime payments that are demanded by film unions for actual night-time working.

day order *n* [*Stock market*] an order that is placed for execution, if possible, during only one trading session. If the order cannot be executed that day, then it is automatically cancelled.

day player, also **bit player** *n* [*Film*] an actor who has only a small part and can thus be hired for a single day's work only.

day trading *n* [*Stock market*] the establishing and liquidating of the same **position** or positions on the same day's trading. See also **day order**.

dayglow *n* [*Aerospace*] the visual effect, as seen from a spacecraft, of the contrast between the Earth's atmosphere above a sunlit section of the Earth and the void of space beyond.

daylight *n* [*Engineering*] the distance in a hydraulic press between the faces of the vertical rams in their highest positions and the surface of the work table.

daylight saving *n* [*UK*] [*Railways*] an electrical breakdown in the circuit of a coach.

daylighting 1. *n* [*Architecture*] the provision for and thus the degree of daylight within the design of a given building. **2.** n [US] [Cattlemen] riding so that daylight appears between the saddle and the rider's seat.

daypart n [TV] a subdivision of the broadcasting day created for statistical, ratings and advertising purposes. See also **prime time**.

days of grace n pl [Commerce] additional time – usually a maximum of three days – allowed by customs for the payment of a bill of exchange after the due date.

day-to-day money n [Banking] sums of money lent by banks to **discount houses** or stockbrokers overnight; such loans can be extended by mutual consent.

daze v [Photography] to use lighting which is too strong so that it overwhelms and even temporarily blinds the subject.

dazzle n [Military] the painting of large patches of irregularly shaped colour on warships in order to camouflage them during battles, air attacks, etc.

DB n [US] [TV] abbr of **Delayed Broadcasting** the practice of some **affiliates** in deferring a **network programme** in favour of a programme that deals with events of local importance. The network show is taped for subsequent broadcasting.

db n [US] [Police] abbr of **dead body**.

dbd n [US] [Prisons, Law] abbr of **death by drugs** execution by the administration of a lethal injection, currently legal in certain US states.

DBH n [Logging] abbr of **diameter at breast height** the width of a tree is always calculated by measuring its DBH, including the bark.

D.B.S. n [UK] [Diplomacy] abbr of **distressed British subject** any British national who requires the aid of an embassy or consular official when stranded outside the UK.

D.B.S. n [Satellite TV] abbr of **direct broadcasting by satellite**.

DBs n pl [US] [Police] abbr of **Dirty Books** any allegedly pornographic material.

D-dog n [US] [Police] abbr of **detector dog**, used by police and customs to sniff out illegal drugs.

DE n [Market research, Statistics] socio-economic labels used to designate the unskilled classes and below, including pensioners. See also **AB, C1, C2**.

de facto couple n [Sociology] a couple who live together, possibly have children, and generally act as man and wife without actually being married; thus de facto, if not de jure, they are married.

de-accession, also **de-acquisition** n [Art] the selling off by museums, collections or galleries of various valuable, but still low priority pieces or paintings, often to help fund the remaining collection.

deacon 1. v [Commerce] to pack or display produce with the finest specimens in front, hiding the inferior merchandise. **2.** v [Commerce] to adulterate or doctor an article to be sold. **3.** n [Meat trade] a young calf, especially when too young even for veal; it also means the hide from such a calf.

deacon seat n [Logging] a bench in front of the sleeping bunks in a logging camp.

dead 1. a [Building] having lost the qualities required for workability; hence this refers to plaster that will not set, stone that cannot be worked, etc. **2.** a [Journalism] referring to copy that has been set and used and can now be discarded. **3.** a [Postal services] undeliverable and unreturnable, thus a 'dead letter'. **4.** a [US] [Railways] not running. **5.** a [TV] said of a set that is no longer required and can be dismantled.

dead air n [Coal-mining] air that is not fit to breathe, because it is too heavily contaminated with carbon dioxide.

dead bat n [Cricket] a stroke that **kills** a sharply rising or spinning ball and defuses its potential menace to the batsman.

dead book n [Stock market] a list of defunct companies.

dead coal n [Coal-mining] coal which is difficult to break down from the face, there being no natural force assisting the process. See also **live coal**.

dead drop, also **dead letter box** n [Espionage] a place for the exchange of messages, money, material, etc; one party deposits the 'letter' and, later, the other arrives to collect it.

dead end n [US] [Garment trade] the slack season.

dead end kids n pl [UK] [Railways] men who have declined promotion.

dead fall n [Film] a Western stunt rider; probably so-called from the nature of such riders' most common stunt.

dead fish n [Baseball] a hit that goes fast for a few seconds until it hits the ground and then does not roll any further.

dead freight n [Shipping] freight rate which is paid on empty space in the vessel when the charterer is responsible for the freight rate of a full cargo; it should be paid before sailing.

dead furrow n [US] [Farming] the empty furrow that is left after ploughing.

dead horse work n [US] [Industrial relations] work for which payment has been obtained in advance.

dead log n [Logging] a log that will float.

dead man n [US] [Railways] a control pedal on the floor of a locomotive, in front of the engineer's seat, that must be held down for the engine to operate normally; if released it will automatically operate the train's emergency braking system. See also **dead man's handle**.

dead man's hand n [Gambling] in poker, a full house combining aces and eights; it comes from the hand held by Sheriff 'Wild Bill' Hickok when he was fatally shot in the back in 1876.

dead man's handle n [Transport] in an electric

train (on the London Underground) this is a controlling handle which must be held in position for the motive current to pass. Thus if the handle is released – eg: if the driver actually drops dead or is otherwise taken ill – the current is broken and the train stops.

dead matter n [Publishing] proofs returned by the printer after a book has been printed.

dead money n [Finance] money which is not being used for profit or useful investment.

dead on arrival a [Computing] with an ironic reference to the police/medical use, this is used of an electronic circuit that fails to operate when new equipment is turned on for the first time.

dead, on the adv [Theatre] said of a piece of curtain or a scenery flat that lies properly flush with the stage floor.

dead rod n [Angling] a rod left unattended.

dead room n [Science, Audio] an anechoic chamber, a room made absolutely soundproof by being enclosed in non-sound-reflecting surfaces which 'suck up' all sound and permit no echo or reverberations.

dead security n [Banking] those industries which can be exhausted – mines, quarries, etc – and which thus provide only limited security for long-term loans.

dead ship n [Military] See **cold ship**.

dead stick n [Aerospace] an engine which has lost power and does not respond to the controls; thus 'dead stick landing' is a landing without engine power.

dead stock 1. n [Agriculture] farm machinery, plant, buildings – the opposite of livestock. **2.** n [Management] a stock of goods for which no further demand can be expected.

dead stone n [Printing] a **form** that has been used and will not be required again.

dead time n [Management] unproductive time in a factory, the result of malfunctioning plant or similar problems.

dead wood n [Ten-pin-bowling] pins that have been knocked down and lie around or in front of those remaining.

dead work n [Industry] preliminary work that must be done as preparation for further work, but from which there is no direct return.

dead-bright a [Metal work] so polished that all tool marks are obliterated.

dead-end v [Aerospace] to fly through exceptionally bad weather conditions; it comes from US fliers who refused during World War II to be grounded by even the worst weather and were accordingly nicknamed the 'dead-end kids'.

deadener n [Logging] a form of brake in a log slide: a heavy log, with spikes fixed into it, is set across the slide, so that logs passing down the slide have their speed reduced as they pass under the spikes.

dead-eye n [Sailing, Ropework] See **euphroe block**.

deadhead 1. n [Air travel] a pilot or other member of the crew who is flying as a passenger and is not actually working on that flight. **2.** v [Air travel] to take a free trip by virtue of being employed by an airline. **3.** n [US] [Journalism] an uninteresting, unspecific or abstract headline; thus Claud Cockburn's 'Small Earthquake in Chile, Not Many Dead' which was written for the Times around 1925. **4.** n [US] [Journalism] a newspaper that is given away for free by deliverymen and salesmen, to policemen, etc. **5.** n [US] [Railways] a coach not being used to seat passengers. **6.** n [US] [Railways] a passenger or employee riding on a free pass. **7.** v [US] [Railways] to ride on a pass. **8.** v [US] [Railways] to travel to a distant terminal in order to bring back a train when crews at the other end are not rested.

dead-head v [Theatre] to gain free admission to a performance.

deadhead agency n [Government] a safe job where unenterprising civil servants can while away their careers by simply 'dead heading', or marking time.

deadheading n [Transport] the practice common to the employees of many forms of transport – commercial airlines, railways, truck drivers etc – of taking free rides on their respective conveyances when other pilots, drivers etc, are actually in control of the aircraft, train or vehicle.

deadline 1. n [Military] a vehicle set aside for periodic repair/maintenance. **2.** n [Printing] a guide-line marked on the bed of a printing press.

deadlock, also **constipation** n [Computing] See **deadly embrace** See also **starvation**.

deadly embrace, also **deadlock** n [Computing] a situation where two or more computing processes are unable to proceed further since each is interdependently awaiting the other's performance of a vital action. See also **starvation**.

deadman 1. n [Logging] a felled tree to which the hawser of a boom has been secured. **2.** n [Building] any kind of object buried in or secured to the ground and used for leverage or to anchor another object, eg: a fencepost.

dead-man n [US] [Railways] used to refer to overturned engines or rolling stock.

deadplate n [Glass-making] in the automatic production of glassware, this is a stationary plate between two moving conveyor belts between which the ware is being transferred.

deadweight debt n [Finance] that part of the UK National debt which represents the money borrowed to finance the two world wars and which must now be seen as unproductive, since the things on which it was spent no longer exist.

deadwork n [Coal-mining] work that does not directly produce coal. See also **byework**.

deaf aid n [TV] the small earpiece used by newsreaders and other **anchormen** through which they can hear 'live' instructions from the director.

deaf-smack *n* [*US*] [*Military*] *acro* **Defence Special Missile and Aeronautics Center** the monitoring centre at Fort Meade, Maryland, which operates surveillance and analysis of Soviet electronic intelligence, especially that relating to the telemetry of ICBM tests: 'deaf-smack' has also taken on many of the surveillance activities formerly allotted to **comint** listening posts. See also **elint**.

deal *n* [*Air travel*] a mid-air near-collision between two aircraft.

deal stream *n* [*Business*] a term found in venture capitalism to define those entrepreneurs who have ideas but lack adequate finances and are seeking to obtain these from a venture capitalist. See also **dollar stream**.

dealer *n* [*Drugs*] a seller of drugs, either on a wholesale or retail level. Thus 'dealer's hand' is a method of holding small **bindles** of drugs under a rubber band so as to be able to flick them away immediately if a policeman appears to be approaching with more than friendly interest.

dealer aids *n pl* [*Marketing*] any material supplied to a retailer to facilitate the sales to customers of a product or line of products – samples, dispensers, promotional leaflets, etc.

dealer incentive *n* [*Commercial*] any incentive or **premium** which is aimed at the retailer or wholesaler rather than at the consumer.

dealer leader *n* [*Marketing*] a promotional device that provides incentives to the retailer to stock a given product or line of products in predetermined quantities. See also **dealer incentive**.

dealer loader *n* [*Commerce*] See **dealer incentive**.

dean, also **professor** *n* [*Gambling*] an experienced, successful, professional gambler, notable for his calm, intelligent demeanour and his ability to work out the odds.

deaner *n* [*UK*] [*Market-traders*] a shilling (5p).

dear money *n* [*Economics*] money is 'dear' when interest rates are high and loans become harder to obtain and more expensive to service. See also **cheap money**.

de-architecturisation *n* [*Architecture*] a term coined by SITE Inc. (Sculpture In The Environment, a group of 'surrealist' architects, based in the US) to denote a subversion or inversion of the established post-Bauhaus functional postulates of design, since they regard these ideas as oppressive.

death (at the box office) *n* [*Theatre*] any piece that simply refuses to work in the theatre; but 'murder at the box office' and 'this will slay them' both mean the opposite – a thoroughly successful performance.

death chamber *n* [*UK*] [*Railways*] the high tension cubicle of a diesel locomotive.

death ship *n* [*Commerce*] a ship that has been deliberately wrecked or even scuttled so that the owners can fraudulently collect money from their insurers, irrespective of the loss of life or cargo involved.

death trail *n* [*US*] [*Theatre*] a touring circuit of small, Mid-West towns. See also **borscht belt, chitlin circuit, citronella circuit**.

deathwatch *n* [*Journalism*] a group of reporters waiting for a break or a lead in a major story.

de-bag *v* [*TV*] in TV makeup, this is to remove cosmetically the bags from beneath a performer's or an announcer's eyes.

de-boost *n* [*Military, Aerospace*] the reduction or reversing of the thrust of a spacecraft, rocket or artificial satellite in order to slow down the vehicle prior to altering course or impacting on target.

debouncing *n* [*Computing*] a technique whereby a device is made to pause after the initial detection of the closure of a switch or some other electrical contact to allow the reverberations of the contact – known as contact bounce – to die away. The contact is then sampled again to determine its final state. This ensures that no spurious signals are sent out.

debug **1.** *v* [*Computing*] to isolate and iron out any errors in a program. **2.** *v* [*Computing*] to use a special program to re-configure or re-format one part of the system to make it compatible with the rest. **3.** *v* [*Espionage*] to remove any **bugs** and render a room, building, vehicle, etc. free from electronic surveillance.

debugging *n* [*Photo-typesetting*] the editing of the character's **bit-map** to ensure that the required image is produced when the character is printed.

deburring *n* [*Metallurgy*] the removing of the excess metal (see **overfill**) from the outside of an electrically welded tube.

debutante deviation *n* [*Literary criticism*] an incorrect or excessive use of the word 'so' to mean 'very much' rather than 'in this/that way'.

decade *n* [*Computing*] a group, set or series of ten objects or events.

decapitation **1.** *n* [*Logology*] See **beheadment**. **2.** *n* [*Military*] any attack which might be able to decapitate the US nuclear war effort, ie: by knocking out the massively computerised US World-Wide Military Command and Control System (**WWMCCS**) which operates from thirty ultra-sophisticated centres around the world. If this concept proved true, then the military 'torso' would be rendered powerless once its 'head', containing the C^3I facilities essential to warfighting, was lopped off. US estimates fear that no more than 100 Soviet missiles could achieve satisfactory destruction of command centres, vital government facilities and worldwide communications. It is in the hope of countering this threat that the current development in C^3I is taking place.

decating *n* [*Textiles*] a method of shrinking applied to woollen and worsted fabrics to set the nap and develop lustre; the cloth is shrunk by winding it under tension on a perforated cylinder through which steam passes.

decay 1. *n* [*Gliding*] the stage in the life cycle of a cumulus cloud when lift is changing to sink; the cloud is evaporating and cooling the air, rain showers are likely and the base of the cloud appears ragged. **2.** *n* [*Military, Aerospace*] the date of re-entry of a satellite into the earth's atmosphere, either through natural causes or on human/computer-activated command.

decay time *n* [*Computing*] the time it takes an electronic impulse – usually designated as a character appearing in a cathode ray tube – to fade out.

decentration *n* [*Education*] the gradual progress of a child's view of the world away from a completely egocentric one.

decertification *n* [*US*] [*Business*] the cancellation by a company of its employees' affiliation to a union. The US is currently undergoing a huge, concentrated propaganda campaign to intensify nation-wide decertification.

dechrome *v* [*Custom cars*] to remove all chrome trim from a customised car; the intention is to eliminate all extraneous decoration and let the true shape of the car show through.

decide *v* [*Religion*] to make one's formal acknowledgement of conversion to the faith.

decision matrix *n* [*Military*] a computer program which contains a variety of possible defensive reactions to incoming hostile missiles.

decision tree *n* [*Business*] a flow chart or similar visual aid designed to help in the analysis of complex situations in which various alternative strategies are advanced; it should make available data on the possible outcome, profitability, potential problems and any other information pertinent to such a situation.

deck 1. *n* [*Aerospace*] the ground, specifically the landing runway at an airport or military airfield. **2.** *n* [*Computing*] a number of punched cards that form a related collection; it comes from playing cards. **3.** *n* [*Computing*] a means of storing information for future use, eg: magnetic tape. **4.** *n* [*Computing*] a strip of material on which data can be recorded, eg: magnetic tape, punched paper tape, optically sensitive material. **5.** *n* [*Drugs*] a small folded paper container used for the sales of measured quantities of powdered drugs, notably cocaine and heroin. **6.** *n* [*Journalism*] a separate portion or section of a headline, usually referring to the subsidiary headlines that run after the main one. A headline that comprises a number of decks is a 'double-decker', 'triple-decker', etc. **7.** *n* [*Logging*] the space beside the saw along which the **carriage** runs. **8.** *n* [*Military*] the floor. **9.** *n* [*UK*] [*Surfing*] the upper surface of the board. **10.** *n* [*US*] [*Theatre*] the stage; thus 'deckhand' is a stagehand.

deck head *n* [*US*] [*Journalism*] See **step-head**.

deck job *n* [*Custom cars*] similar to a **bullnose**; the badges, trim, etc. are removed from the bootlid and the holes **blanked** in.

deck, on *adv* [*Baseball*] the next player up at bat is 'on deck'.

deck, on the *adv* [*Aerospace*] flying at a minimally safe altitude, ie as low as possible.

declaration *n* [*Computing*] in programming this is a statement in a language which defines the attributes of data used in the program. See also **statement**.

declare 1. *v* [*Horse-racing*] to withdraw a horse from entry in a race within the permitted period allowed for such withdrawals. **2.** *v* [*Scientology*] to purge a cult member on the grounds of ideological impurity.

decoding *n* [*Satellite TV*] the unscrambling of a satellite-broadcast television picture which has been deliberately scrambled to thwart potential pirates.

decollage *n* [*Art*] the opposite of collage (sticking on): ungluing and taking off. Decollage was very popular in the 1950s and can be seen in its natural state when posters on hoardings start to tear and several layers of previous advertisements begin to show through underneath.

deconstruction *n* [*Literary criticism*] a practice in reading that 'must always aim at a certain relationship, unperceived by the author, between what he commands and does not command of the patterns of language he uses.' (Jacques Derrida 'Dissemination' 1972).

decouple *v* [*Military*] to muffle nuclear weapons tests by arranging for them to take place underground.

decoupling *n* [*Military*] the decision by the US to sacrifice Europe, and the forces it holds there, rather than permit an international conflict to affect the US itself. Such a decision would fly in the face of the 'coupling' theory, which presumes that allowing the US to base missiles in Europe will act as an extra guarantee against Russian incursions. Thus European leaders continue to encourage the deployment of missiles on their national soil. The logical extension of this European fear is that both superpowers might choose to fight a nuclear war outside their own boundaries, pitting NATO against the Warsaw Pact and each preserving their own territory. See also **coupling 2, FBS**.

decruit *v* [*Business*] as whizkid junior employees are recruited, so are tiring seniors decruited: they are placed in a lesser position within the company, prior to being eased into less and less important jobs, or actually passed on, with a flowing testimonial, to an unsuspecting rival.

decrypt *n* [*Espionage*] signals that have been decoded.

ded, also **dead reckoning** *n* [*Aerospace*] abbr of **deductive reckoning** a method of aerial navigation that is based on the recognition of ground landmarks.

dedicated *a* [*Technology*] said of a machine or program or a single part of a machine or system that is completely given over to a specific task; thus 'dedicated word processor', etc.

dedomiciling *n* [*Business*] the moving of a company's parent domicile (its base as cited for tax assessments) to some country where tax incentives and shelters are advantageous and the restrictions on foreign investment are minimal.

de-emphasis *n* [*Audio*] the reduction of high frequency levels in the reproduction of recorded music to compensate for the boosting of that HF when being recorded or broadcast.

deep 1. *n* [*Cricket*] the parts of the cricket pitch furthest from the wicket itself. See also **country, in the. 2.** *a* [*US*] [*Medicine*] in the depths of an anaesthetic or a coma. See also **light 3. 3.** *a* [*Wine-tasting*] usually used in combination – deep bouquet, deep-coloured, etc – and implying richness and layers of flavour.

deep background *n* [*Journalism*] See **not for attribution**.

deep cover *n* [*Espionage*] the assumption by an agent of a cover story and the role it entails with such intensity and over so long a period that he/she almost 'becomes' that cover and genuinely lives in character. It is a more extreme form of disguise than that assumed for a short-term operation and, it is hoped by all concerned, as nearly impenetrable as possible.

deep creep *n* [*Navy*] an attack on a hostile submarine by a friendly vessel while both are at maximum depth below the ocean surface.

deep engagement *n* [*Military*] the strategy of hitting hostile forces well beyond the **FEBA** (the head-on zone of a contact battle), and thus relieving one's own front-line forces and artillery. It is the traditional concept of hitting the enemy behind his lines to create the maximum confusion and diversion of troops.

deep feeling *n* [*New therapies*] in **primal therapy**, that moment of insightful truth that triggers off the primal.

deep going *n* [*Hunting*] soft and holding ground, which is difficult for the horses to cross.

deep six 1. *v* [*US*] [*Navy, Marine Corps*] to get rid of, to lose deliberately, usually by pitching over the side of the ship into the 'deep six', the deep water. The term gained intense, if short-lived, civilian notoriety during the Watergate Hearings of 1974 when it was revealed that John Erlichman instructed John Dean to 'deep-six' some damaging material off the Potomac Bridge in Washington. **2.** *adv* [*UK*] [*Air Force*] behind and beneath one's own plane; on the basis of 'clockface' direction-finding.

deep-basing *n* [*Military*] a concept of nuclear defence strategy whereby a team of tunnellers accompany military personnel into a deep, hard-ened shelter to wait out the initial exchanges in a nuclear war; weeks, or possibly months after these have subsided, the idea is for these tunnellers to drill their way back up to the surface, create a makeshift silo and launch those missiles that have been deliberately kept in reserve. Such a final strike is supposed to destroy the Soviets, assuming they are still putting up a fight, who will hardly expect the ultimate in surprise attacks.

deep-discount bond *n* [*US*] [*Commerce, Finance*] a bond issued by a municipality or in a form that pays only a low rate of interest, but which is sold at a big discount, far below the face value of the bond. The investor thus receives a capital gain when the bond is repaid at face value on maturity.

deepie *n* [*Film*] a nickname for three-dimensional (3–D) films; on this principle, normal, two-dimensional film are 'flatties'.

de-escalation *n* [*Military*] See **escalation control**.

defcon *n* [*Military*] abbr of **defensive condition** these range from 5 (normal readiness) to 1 (maximum force readiness) and are invoked in an international crisis, possibly leading towards nuclear war.

defector in place *n* [*Espionage*] an individual who signals clandestinely to a foreign nation that he/she wishes to defect but, for an indeterminate period, will be willing to stay on in their own country, amassing or passing on valuable information and material.

defence in depth *n* [*Science*] a system of safeguarding against accidents in nuclear reactors which is based on a series of backup systems – redundant safety systems – which provide multiple levels of security.

defender *n* [*Business, Government*] in **game theory**, this is the adversary who attempts to maintain in place the safeguards that he has set up to defeat the incursions of the **diverter**.

defensive industries *n pl* [*Economics*] those industries – food, utilities, insurance, etc. – which provide the ultimate consumer with his/her basic needs and in which business activity is only marginally affected by even large-scale fluctuations in the market.

defensive medicine *n* [*US*] [*Medicine*] the practice by physicians, who, when faced with highly complex and very highly publicised medical problems, order saturation testing of the patient on all levels so as to insure themselves against even the slightest possibility of a malpractice suit. In its most extreme form, some doctors have refused to treat very high risk patients, in case a relation decides to sue if there is no 'cure'.

defensive securities *n pl* [*US*] [*Stock market*] stocks and bonds that are notably stable and thus provide a regular return on invested cash.

deferential *n* [*Philately*] a post-mark designed so

D

that when the stamp was cancelled, the effigy of the monarch upon it was in no way defaced; it was especially popular in Sicily and Spain.

deferential worker *n* [*Sociology*] the conservative member of the working class, deferring to the establishment as the natural rulers of society; they are usually found in small businesses and farms where there is greater personal contact and paternalism.

deferred futures *n pl* [*Finance*] the most distant months listed in a **futures** contract. See also **nearbys**.

definitise *v* [*Business*] this comes from the aerospace term, with the same meaning: to define a function or an action in precise and definite detail. It is a neologism for 'specify'.

definitive *n* [*Philately*] a stamp specifically issued for ordinary postal purposes and placed on sale for an unlimited period, as opposed to commemorative, charity or **provisional** issues; eg: the small, plain 18p first class stamp bearing simply the Queen's head.

definitive bond *n* [*Commerce, Finance*] a permanent document given in exchange for a temporary **bearer scrip** when all the instalments on the purchase of government stock have been paid.

deformed workers' state *n* [*Politics*] a derogatory description of the Soviet Union by the Trotskyite far-left members of the International Socialists.

defund *v* [*Government*] to deprive a government programme or agency of funding and thus, in other words, to close it down.

degafiate *v* [*Science fiction*] to return to fan activities after a period of withdrawal and lack of involvement. See also **dafia, gafia**.

degauss *v* [*Military*] to protect a ship against magnetic mines, or any weapons which rely on magnetism for guidance, by using an electrically charged cable to demagnetise the ship on entering a battle zone. It is named after the German scientist K.F. Gauss (1777–1855). See also **deperm**.

degear *v* [*Finance*] to reduce the amount of a company's fixed-interest debt and replace it with **equity capital**.

degeneracy *n* [*Audio*] a condition in a resonant system whereby two or more modes have the same frequency.

degradation *n* [*Computing*] a situation where a machine is working at a lower than usual level of efficiency because of some form of internal breakdown, although not one so extensive that the system cannot function at all.

degrade gracefully *v* [*Military*] See **graceful degradation**.

degree-day *n* [*Gas industry*] a measure of the coldness of the weather experienced, based on the extent to which the daily mean temperature falls below a reference temperature, usually 60°F (15.5°C).

de-horse *v* [*US*] [*Car salesmen*] to persuade a customer to give up his own car and drive a company car overnight, before he takes delivery of his new car.

deke *v* [*Ice hockey*] to deceive an opponent, thus drawing him out of his defensive position.

dekorier dich, also **démerdez-vous** *expl* [*Military*] used in the French Foreign Legion to mean 'get yourself moving, hurry up!'; literally it means 'get your shit together!'.

del credere agent *n* [*Commerce*] an agent who sells on the risk of his own credit – having purchased the goods himself – rather than on that of a principal.

deliberate abstractor *n* [*Education*] a slow learner; a phrase that mixes euphemism – deliberate meaning slow – with jargon – abstract meaning to take something out of, thus to learn.

delinquency *n* [*Finance*] late payments on contracts, either to credit companies or in a variety of financial uses.

delinquent drift *n* [*Sociology*] the gradual drift into criminality by a delinquent who has defined the norms of law and morals as irrevelant, inapplicable and unimportant in his/her own life.

delivery 1. *n* [*Finance*] in the futures market, this is the actual settlement of a deal, whereby delivery is made to the **Clearing House** and thence to the buyer. 2. *n* [*Stock market*] the transfer of securities between a seller and a buyer, or the documents which are concerned in that transfer. Thus 'good delivery' means the documents concerned are all in good order and the deal can proceed unimpeded; 'bad delivery' means the opposite.

delivery notice *n* [*Finance*] in the futures market, this is the written notice given by a seller of his intention to make delivery against an open, **short futures position** on a particular date.

delivery points *n pl* [*Finance*] in the futures market, these are the specific locations for delivery that suit the commodity – Swiss francs in Zurich, wheat in Kansas, etc.

dell (on to) *v* [*UK*] [*Market-traders*] to chastise.

Delphi technique *n* [*Business*] a method of forecasting, first developed at the RAND Corporation, in which a team of experts are employed. These experts are first polled individually for their opinions, then all are gathered together, their various theories all made public, and during a further discussion these are all modified until a consensus is reached.

delta *n* [*US*] [*Stock market*] the measure of the relationship between an **option** price and the underlying **futures** contract or stock price.

delta stocks, also **delta securities** *n pl* [*UK*] [*Stock exchange*] the least popular of the share groupings listed on the London Stock Exchange; generally unsuccessful shares in which only a few matched bargains are ever traded. See also **alpha stocks, beta stocks, gamma stocks**.

demand driven *a* [*Computing*] said of a

computer **architecture** in which instructions are only selected when the value they produce is required by another, already selected, instruction.

demand reading n [Computing] a process in which data is transferred directly between a processor and a storage device.

demand staging n [Computing] See **anticipatory staging**.

demander n [UK] [Police] an extortionist, a protection racketeer.

demand-pull inflation n [Economics] inflation that is caused when excessive demand for a limited volume of goods and services forces prices up. This demand usually stems from the availability of tax cuts and/or 'cheap' money, ie. easily available loans which are charged relatively low interest. See also **cost-push inflation**.

demand-side economics n [Economics] this was originally 'the new' or 'Keynesian' economics, based on J.M. Keynes' 'The General Theory of Employment, Interest & Money' (1936). The premise is that a lagging economy is cured by creating demand through government spending or tax cuts, and that inflation is removed by depressing demand by cutting spending or raising taxes. See also **demand-pull inflation**.

demarcation strip n [Communications] a terminal board which acts as an interface between a business machine and the common carrier of the communications network.

démarche n [Politics] it comes from Fr. meaning 'trample underfoot', and refers to any political or diplomatic manoeuvre.

de-marketing n [Advertising] the selective and deliberately restrictive provision of scarce goods: instead of actively marketing one's product when it is available in quantity, the seller chooses to ration demand by limiting supply to what is available at the time in question.

demented a [Computing] said of a program which works perfectly well within the limitations of its design, but in which the design itself is bedevilled with technical inadequacies.

demise charter n [Shipping] See **bare-boat charter**.

demit n [Freemasonry] written permission granted to a mason to leave a lodge.

demo n [Pop music] abbr of **demonstration tape** a tape made by a new band or singer or one made of a new song by an established band or artiste; in both cases the tape is used to promote the product to the record companies.

democrat n [Furriers] the pelt of the nutria, a water-rodent native to South America, which has its best fur on the belly rather than as is usual on the back. If a nutria has been inadvertently slit along the belly instead of the back, it is known as a 'democrat'.

democratic centralism n [Politics] the principle by which, in theory, the world's communist parties take policy decisions and carry them out:

after general discussion (democracy) the party line is laid out and everyone (centralism) follows it, irrespective of any personal opinions. Lenin coined the phrase to imply the strengthened power of leadership when backed by such a group decision. In practice it is a useful euphemism for the 'rubber stamp'.

democratic network n [Communications] a data communications network in which no one clock can take precedence over any other. See also **hierarchical network**.

democratism n [Politics] the process of democracy: the gradual assimilation of the exceptional and the eccentric by the mundane and the mediocre.

demographic targeting n [Military] the choosing of population centres as the targets for nuclear attack. See also **countervalue**.

demon n [Computing] a suspended process that waits for a given type of event to occur, then is automatically activated, performs its job and either terminates or suspends itself to wait for the next event of the same sort. See also **daemon**.

DEMON n [Management] acro **decision mapping via optimum networks** a procedure for systematically evaluating whether it will be worthwhile marketing a new product on a national scale, taking account, inter alia, of the results of promotion and test marketing.

demote maximally v [Espionage] to kill by assassination. See also **terminate with extreme prejudice**.

demountable system n [UK] [Road transport] a system of interchangeable bodies on rigid vehicles.

demurrage 1. n [Shipping, Transport] unreasonable delay in keeping a ship or other means of transport beyond the time agreed or allowed. **2.** n [Shipping] a sum of money paid to a shipowner by a charterer if the sailing of the ship is delayed.

den room n [Manufacturing] a room in a fertiliser manufacturing plant where superphosphate – phosphates and sulphuric acid – is temporarily stored.

denaderise v [US] [Business] the term is based on the name of Ralph Nader, the US consumer advocate. His activist 'Nader's Raiders' pursue companies whose products fall below the ideal standards of service and safety. Hence it means to ensure that one's product or process is sufficiently good to keep Nader's criticisms at bay.

dendix n [Skiing] a type of mat used on artificial ski slopes; it is named after its manufacturer.

deniability n [Politics] the ability of any high official to disassociate him/herself from any illegal or improper activity performed by a subordinate. See also **CYA**.

denial 1. n [Communications] a situation that occurs in a network when no circuits are free and the caller hears an engaged tone. **2.** n [Military] any aggressive operations directed at securing a

D

D

military position; thus denial of space would mean the immediate destruction of any hostile attempts to place satellites and/or weapons in what was claimed as 'one's own' space-based areas.

denial of service, also **interdiction** n [Computing] interference with a computer system by a **hacker** which prevents normal access to or service by that system.

denied area n [Espionage] a CIA term for an area in a Communist country, especially Russia or China, to which Westerners have no access and where conventional espionage activities are impossible.

denounce v [US] [Politics] a term used in the US Senate that stands midway between 'censure' (the strongest possible condemnation of a fellow senator) and 'condemnation', and which is used, like them, to show disapproval of allegedly improper conduct.

dense index n [computing] a database that contains an entry for every record to be searched. See also **nondense index**.

dense pack n [Military] a system of basing missiles, suggested in particular for the MX 'Peacekeeper' missile, whereby the weapons are sited in clusters in the belief that even if hostile strikes do penetrate US defences, at least some of the retaliatory missiles will survive to strike back. Dense pack is also designed to promote **fratricide** among incoming missiles – the idea that the explosion of so many nuclear bombs in such proximity must destroy their overall accuracy over the target. In the event dense pack was deemed a failure: the MXs might survive, but the volume of hostile warheads their clusters would attract would mean that little else in the US would.

density n [Computing] a measure of the amount of information in a given dimension of a storage medium.

dent n [Weaving] the space between the **blades** in a **reed**.

dentil block n [Building, Plastering] a rectangular block forming part of a row of such blocks giving a line of **enrichment** in cornices/mantelpieces/pediments etc.

dentology n [Military] the military 'science' of identifying otherwise anonymous, black-painted nuclear submarines by studying dents in a specific hull, the configuration of rivets, and other minor differences.

de-orbit v [Aerospace] to go out of orbit; to cause to go out of orbit.

deperm v [Military] to demagnetise a ship in order to protect it from weapons that use magnetism for guidance on to their targets. See also **degauss**.

depeter n [Building, Plastering] a form of pebbledashing whereby the **aggregate** is pressed rather than thrown on to the **buttercoat**.

deplane v [Air travel] to get off the plane.

depress v [Film, TV] to lower a camera vertically.

depression modern n [Architecture] an architectural style created during the Depression era of the 1930s; it is also seen particularly in the contemporary design of cars, radios, kitchen appliances and domestic furniture.

deprivation 1. n [Sociology] the emotional deprivation of an individual, usually ascribed to the results of inadequate parenting and the unhappiness and social suffering that follows. 2. n [Sociology] urban deprivation, a euphemism for slums, whether created by actual physical decay or by the presence of an excess of the socially deprived.

depth n [Wine-tasting] an apparent interlinking of several layers of flavour, all of which combine to offer richness and subtlety of wine.

depth indexing n [Libraries] See **exhaustivity**.

depth polling n [Politics] voter research questions that go beyond the simple questions as to party allegiance and which make an attempt to ascertain why such allegiances have been formed and whether or not they will be maintained.

deputy, also **examiner, fireman** n [Coalmining] an underground official who has a statutory responsibility for the safe and proper working of a district of the mine.

deque n [Computing] abbr of **double-ended queue** a linear list of items where all insertions, removals and accesses are made at either end of the list.

derate v [Electronics] to use a device or component at a lower power level than it is capable of handling, in order to extend its life or reduce the occurrence of breakdowns due to operational stress.

Derby n [UK] [Railways] The Midland Region of British Rail.

derived demand n [Marketing] this is the term for the situation where demand for one product depends on demand for another one: industrial goods are demanded, in the long run, only insofar as they can satisfy the immediate demand for consumer goods.

derm n [Medicine] abbr of **dermatology** the study of the skin and its related problems.

derrick v [Baseball] to take a pitcher out of the game; the image is of lowering a hook and hauling him directly out of the ballpark.

derrick monkey n [Oil rigs] the member of the drilling crew who works up on the derrick.

descendant n [Computing] of a node, A, in a **tree**: any node, B, which has A as an ancestor. See also **ancestor**.

descending tops n pl [US] [Stock market] a graph of the price of a security which shows that each successive high is lower than the one which immediately preceded it. See also **ascending tops**.

descent group n [Sociology] any social group in which membership depends on common descent from a real or mythical ancestor.

deseaming n [Metallurgy] See **scarfing**.

deselect 1. v [Government] to discharge a trainee

before he/she has completed a training programme. **2.** *v* [*Politics*] under the current (1985) rules of the British Labour Party, this is when the local constituency party decides to withdraw their support from a sitting member and to opt for a replacement who will fight the next by– or general election.

desert dolly *n* [*TV, Film*] a wheeled platform that is used to move the larger lights around a studio or set.

desert principle *n* [*Criminology*] the concept that offenders should receive exactly what is coming to them and should be in no doubt that each particular crime brings with it a specific period of sentence. A simplification of the system already operates in the UK, but is at odds with the US tradition of an indeterminate sentence – 'three to five', 'ten to life' etc. – in which only parole determines how long, between periods of minimum and maximum incarceration, a prisoner serves.

design weight *n* [*UK*] [*Road transport*] the weight for which the manufacturer has designed the vehicle to operate.

designer *a* [*Fashion*] in the clothing trade, this refers to those garments ostensibly created by a major or 'name' couturier. Unlike 'haute couture', in which only a very few, very expensive garments are produced, designer garments are deliberately made for mass production, eg: Gloria Vanderbilt jeans, on the assumption that a pair of trousers or a sweater with a smart name will possess a cachet, and thus a price, above that of a similar garment bereft of the chic label.

desire show *n* [*TV*] any game show that features expensive prizes and requires little knowledge, but merely the ability to choose one box, key, button, etc. fron another: eg: 'The Price Is Right', 'Let's Make a Deal' etc. See also **greed shows**.

desk 1. *n* [*Film, Video, Audio*] a control panel and by extension the area in the studio that surrounds it. **2.** *n* [*Journalism*] the name used on newspapers for the various departments that contribute pages to the paper; thus 'city desk' (US meaning news, UK meaning finance), 'news desk' (UK), 'sports desk' etc. **3.** *n* [*Pop music*] the electronic control board in a recording studio. **4.** *n* [*Pop music*] the control panel of an electronic synthesiser, from which one machine whole orchestras can be created, assuming it is programmed correctly.

desk jockey *n* [*UK*] [*Railways*] any form of railway clerk.

desk man *n* [*US*] [*Car salesmen*] the salesman in a system house who draws up the final papers.

desk research *n* [*Government, Business*] research that is carried out from one's desk, including the necessary use of libraries, **databases**, files, etc. See also **action research**.

Desk, the *n* [*Banking*] the Securities Department at the NY Federal Reserve Bank.

de-skilling *n* [*Sociology*] the concept that management has consciously de-skilled manual and lower-level non-manual jobs, in order to deprive workers of the power – gained through possessing these vital skills – to resist management demands.

desk-man *n* [*Journalism*] a journalist who works mainly from his desk in the office, rather than pursuing stories on the street. See also **desk 2**, **legman**.

desk-top metaphor *n* [*Computing*] **mouse** controlled programs that offer the user an onscreen facsimile of 'layers' of information that are equivalent to the files that might formerly have been found on the average executive desk.

desperado *n* [*Gambling*] an ironic reference to a player who plunges heavily with casinos or bookmakers, but cannot pay if he/she loses.

despotic network *n* [*Communications*] a synchronised network in which one master **clock** controls the operations of all other clocks in the network. See also **democratic network**, **hierarchical network**.

destabilisation *n* [*Politics*] the deliberate interference in a country's government and social structure by the forces, either directly or manipulated at second hand, of a country in whose interest it is to undermine the stability of the target nation. The agents of such destabilisation tend either to be clandestine, eg. the US CIA or the Russian KGB operating abroad, or economic, eg. the funding of indigenous guerrilla groups who are already attempting to topple the ruling authorities.

destabilise *v* [*Espionage*] said of the intelligence services of a major power when they use clandestine methods to undermine and ultimately destroy an incumbent foreign government which is unfriendly to one's policies and then have it replaced by one which is more amenable. This process can include the use of propaganda (both press and radio), the financing and advising of opposition parties, the arming and advising of their military wings, and a variety of black **operations** up to and including the assassination of heads of state.

de-stat *v* [*Commerce*] said of property speculators who use illegal methods to buy or harass statutory tenants out of buildings that they wish to own, rent or sell without interference.

destination marketing *n* [*Marketing*] the process of persuading consumers to patronise specific places: restaurants, hotels, casinos, countries, etc.

destination restaurant *n* [*Catering*] a restaurant of such eminence that its customers are willing to travel great distances to enjoy its amenities. See also **destination marketing**.

destruct *v* [*Aerospace, Military*] to destroy a faulty rocket or missile during its flight. Destruct mechanisms are also installed in the sensitive areas of all large military targets such as ships,

D

D

to ensure that no secret material remains available to an enemy in the case of a military defeat.

destructive art, also **actions** n [Art] a term that encompasses the work of several artists, in all of whose work violence and destruction are used as modes of creation.

destructive cursor n [Computing] a cursor that automatically erases any character through which it passes on a VDU; thus a 'non-destructive cursor' is one that leaves copy in place as it moves over the screen.

destructive read n [Computing] a memory element in which the act of reading the data that it contains automatically erases that data from the files.

destructive readout n [Computing] the readout of data which causes that data to be automatically erased from memory; thus 'non-destructive readout' is a reading action that leaves the data untouched.

detachable front end n [UK] [Road transport] the front end of a **step-frame** or low-loading trailer which may be detached to facilitate trailer loading from the front; both manually and hydraulically operated front ends are available.

detail 1. n [Audio] high levels of information and subtle nuances in both bass and treble. 2. v [US] [Car salesmen] to clean a car, especially the interior, very thoroughly.

detail labour n [Industry] labour that creates only a detail in the production process, rather than a whole commodity; it is exemplified in the succession of individual processes in a production line, which only when combined create the entire manufactured commodity.

detail paper n [Advertising] thin, hard, semi-transparent paper used for sketches and layouts.

detailman n [Commerce] a salesman who visits retail outlets in the hope of persuading them to stock his company's latest products.

detank v [Aerospace] to empty.

détente n [Politics] a policy which encouraged a degree of mutual understanding between the super-powers and even created some short-lived de-escalation of the nuclear arms race; encouraged in particular by Dr. Henry Kissinger, the policy flourished between 1972 and 1973, with its highest achievement being the **ABM Treaty** of 1972. Since then even this little progress has been vilified as 'a sellout' and has been replaced by an increasingly icy cold war, 1980s style. See also **linkage**.

determinism n [Sociology] a sociological pejorative term: theories are deterministic insofar as they emphasise the causal primacy of the social structure to the exclusion of the free will of the individual. Explanations must be sought in the social structure rather than in those who make it up.

deterrence n [Military] literally 'dissuasion by terror', deterrence, 'the highest priority task of the strategic forces' (Kahn), sets out to prevent an enemy from doing something through fear of the inevitable consequences. Deterrence is in effect psychological – and the metaphors surrounding it refer to chess, bridge and poker – but the threat may require a material backup. Nuclear deterrence, planning not for World War III but to ensure that such hostilities never occur, is based on the possession and deployment of ICBMs and SLBMs, the heavyweights of the nuclear armoury. See also **MAD**.

detonation n [Cars] See knocking 2.

deuce n [US] [Theatre] a scenery flat, 2ft wide.

deucer n [Merchant navy] the ship's engineer.

developed a [Wine-tasting] the correct level of maturity; thus 'under-developed' and 'over-developed', are more extreme and less palatable stages of wine.

developing a [Politics, Economics] a euphemism, when referring to nations, which has replaced 'under-developed', which in turn replaced 'backward'; 'developing' is, in its turn, being rivalled by **Third World** and the **South**. It is always assumed that 'developing' countries are gradually creating some form of wealth/stability along Western capitalist lines.

development journalism n [Journalism] a style of journalism practised in the Third World that is based on the concept that since national development depends so heavily on economics, there should be better trained economic specialists who can cover and report, impartially and fully, the situation, with all its economic implications, in developing nations.

developmental a [Education] geared to that with which the child is ready to deal: mentally, physically and emotionally.

deviancy amplification n [Sociology] the concept that much alleged deviance in society stems from police methods, mass media attitudes and popular reaction to deviant stereotypes. Once a group is defined as deviant by society, it is cut off and it therefore withdraws into its own subculture, within which once relatively minor patterns of deviance become amplified. This works well enough with drug abuse, but not so well with murder.

deviation 1. n [Audio] the extent to which the carrier frequency in FM transmission or reception is shifted by audio modulation; maximum modulation corresponds to a deviation factor of 75kHz. 2. n [Politics] the departure or divergence from the over-riding tenets and ideology of a ruling government, especially in Communist countries; it is political heresy, but less heinous and more capable of correction than outright **revisionism**. Those who transgress the ideology are deviationists. 3. n [Politics] straying from party policy in the British Labour Party. 4. n [Politics] post–1980 in the British Labour Party, this is a failure to work towards an agreed tactical objective.

deviator *n* [*Oil rigs*] a well that slants underground to meet a well bored by someone else and then siphons oil from that bore. Thus 'to deviate' is to drill such a well.

devil 1. *n* [*Building, Plastering*] a small tool used to roughen the surface of plaster. **2.** *n* [*US*] [*Coalmining*] a pronged tool that holds down the ties while laying tracks for railways underground. **3.** *n* [*Industry*] one of a variety of machines used for ripping, tearing and shredding. **4.** *n* [*UK*] [*Law*] a junior counsel who does work for his leader, often for free, in order to gain experience, patronage, etc. **5.** *n* [*Painting*] an implement used to burn the paint off large flat surfaces.

devil theory *n* [*Politics, Economics, Government*] when a man, an idea or a piece of legislation has been touted as the cure-all for a particular problem, and that problem is still not solved, then that individual, concept or Act becomes the 'devil' for opponents (and disillusioned supporters) to decry. In effect this is the belief that 'the wrong guys are running the show', at least as far as the 'right guys' see it.

devilling *n* [*Building, Plastering*] scratching the floating surface with a nailed wooden float – the devil float – in order to provide a **key** for the subsequent setting coat.

devil's bedposts *n pl* [*Gambling*] the four of clubs.

devil's pitchfork *n* [*Oil rigs*] a three-pronged implement used for **fishing** lost drilling tools from a well.

devise *v* [*Law*] to give real property by will; the opposite of 'bequeath' which is to give personal property.

devised facility *n* [*Espionage*] a 'business' front behind which clandestine activities are carried out, but which never attempts to perform any actual business, even to maintain a cover.

devotional *n* [*Publishing*] a genre of best-selling pulp fiction aimed firmly at the religious population of the American Bible belt, in which the love of God surpasses its more fleshly manifestations. See also **creepy-weepy, gay gothies**.

DEW line *n* [*Military*] acro **Distant Early Warning line** a system of radar stations on or around the 70th parallel of the N. American continent and at its full extent linking Alaska to Iceland to offer some eight hours warning of approaching nuclear bombers. The system was the most ambitious of those constructed in the 1950s as a defence against surprise Soviet bomber attack. Originally costing $500m and completed in 1962, the system is now well out of date and, under the general plans to modernise the US C³I capability, it is scheduled for substantial improvements and will be replaced by the **seek frost** programme. That such ground-based stations remain extremely vulnerable to swift destruction has not influenced Pentagon planners. See also **BMEWS**.

dexter *n* [*Heraldry*] the right-hand side from the bearer's point of view; for the on-looker it is the left-hand side of a coat of arms. See also **sinister 1**.

D-group *n* [*Management*] a management training group who aim to relate behaviour to the personal work experience of each of the participants. See also **T-group**.

dhobi *n* [*Military/Serviceman's*] a personal laundry; it comes from Anglo-Indian use in the 19th century.

diachronic *a* [*Sociology*] said of the analysis of change.

diadic test *n* [*Marketing*] a paired comparison test involving informants reporting on two products or advertisements, one against the other.

diagonal integration *n* [*Industry*] a form of integration that occurs when a producer buys control of a business which performs services that are useful to the buyer's main enterprises.

diagram *n* [*Transport*] a description of the duties of a shift which is issued to all arriving British Rail engine drivers.

dial back 1. *v* [*US*] [*Government*] to play down, to lower the emphasis on, to have referred back until later: all these stem from the concept of moving the pressure dial back when too great a head of steam builds up in a boiler. **2.** *v* [*Politics, Business*] to diminish, to cut back or go back on.

dial conference *n* [*Telephony*] a PABX facility enabling an extension used to call several parties, all of whom can communicate with each other.

dial your weight *n* [*Aerospace*] a small on-board computer into which is keyed the weight of the crew, the fuel, the weapons payload and any other items that are not normally part of the aircrafts weight; it then calculates and displays the position of the plane's centre of gravity and its maximum permissable takeoff weight.

dialectical materialism *n* [*Politics*] the Marxist concept that explains the way in which events have previously occurred, and therefore will continue to interact and develop: the general 'laws of motion' that cover the evolution both of nature and of society. Every stage of history contains the germ of its own destruction, the thesis produces the antithesis and from the clash between the two a new synthesis arises, formed from the best elements of both; this process then repeats itself. Ideally these repetitions are not infinite, but should lead to the classless, communist society, at which time the process will have achieved perfection and will thus stop. See also **historical materialism**.

dialoger *n* [*US*] [*Radio*] a scriptwriter of daytime series (**soap operas**).

dialoguing *n* [*New therapies*] a Gestalt therapy, a process whereby the subject recreates a conversation with two or more parts of his/her personality; this may be extended to parts of the body, objects in dreams, etc.

D

diamond *n* [*Baseball*] the diamond shaped area within a baseball field which connects the four bases; it is sometimes used to denote the entire playing area.

diamonds *n pl* [*Gliding*] awards for gliding skill, as measured against uniform international standards sanctioned by the FAI (Fédération Aeronautique Internationale); they are given for altitude, cross-country flights to a pre-arranged goal, and distance flights of 500 km or more.

dib *n* [*Marbles*] the target marble in the game. See also **duck, immie, kimmie, peewee, mib**.

dibbing *n* [*Angling*] See **dapping**.

dibble the dropper *v* [*Angling*] to let the fly on the dropper of a wet cast dangle on the surface. See also **cob**.

dibdab *n* [*Navy*] an ordinary seaman, who carried out the menial tasks on board ship.

dice capper *n* [*Gambling*] an individual who makes and uses shaved or loaded dice.

dice mechanic *n* [*Gambling*] a professional cheat who is used to liven up the play, relieve a heavy winner of his gains against the house, etc. It is also used admiringly of a successful player.

dicey *a* [*Coal-mining*] said of a rock that breaks into small pieces resembling dice.

dichotomous question *n* [*Marketing*] a poll question designed to elicit one of two basic replies: yes or no.

dichotomy *n* [*US*] [*Medicine*] the practice of fee-splitting by doctors; it is a gross misuse of the word, which normally means division into two groups, especially mutually exclusive or opposed groups.

dick *n, v* [*UK*] [*Market-traders*] a look, to look.

Dick Whittingtons *n pl* [*Social work*] individuals who arrive in London from the (northern) provincial cities hoping for better work prospects, fail to find them, and join the unemployed homeless, living in hostels or on the street.

dicky bird *n* [*UK*] [*Theatre*] an actor who can sing too.

dictionary 1. *n* [*Computing*] any data structure representing a set of elements that can support the insertion and deletion of elements as well as test for membership. 2. *n* [*Computing*] a list of code words used in a program which also explains their meanings within that program.

didot point *n* [*Photo-typesetting*] a European type size equivalent to 0.0148 inch, or 0.3759 mm.

die *v* [*Theatre, Entertainment*] to fail to amuse the audience; used especially when a stand-up comedian does this.

dier *n* [*US*] [*Meat trade*] an animal that is so nearly dead that its ability to walk to the slaughterhouse is not guaranteed.

diesel *v* [*Engineering*] an internal combustion engine does this when it continues firing after the engine has been shut off.

diesel fuel *n* [*US*] [*Road transport*] strong coffee.

diff *n* [*Stock market*] abbr of **difference** the amount due to a person who has ordered his broker to buy and then sell a given share within the period of a single **Account**.

difference principle *n* [*Sociology*] the principle that there is no justification in securing more attractive prospects for the better-off in the social order unless by so doing the less well-off are the ultimate beneficiaries.

differences *n pl* [*Stock market*] the balances due to clients and other member firms at the end of each **account**.

differential *n* [*UK*] [*Road transport*] a design of rear axle which permits one wheel on the axle to turn faster than the opposite wheel; it is necessary during turning, when the outer wheel must turn faster than the inner one.

differential association *n* [*Sociology*] the theory that crime is learnt within primary groups whose members are already criminally inclined – criminal families, Borstals, prisons, etc.

differential lock *n* [*UK*] [*Road transport*] a device on the **differential** which enables the two wheels on a driving axle to be locked in a solid state to eliminate wheel spin by one wheel when the other has grip. This device should only be used in specific conditions, and not during travel on normal surfaces.

differentiated response *n* [*UK*] [*Police*] this occurs when an enquiry is not top priority: the policeman concerned will make an appointment to call later.

differentiation 1. *n* [*Politics*] a foreign policy theory that prefers to treat each Warsaw Pact country on its own individual merits, rather than lumping them all together as Russian satellites. 2. *n* [*Sociology*] the concept that sets of social activities which used to be performed by one social institution become split up among different institutions; eg. the spread of functions, that were once the province of the family, into various external areas.

diffusion (of innovations) *n* [*Marketing*] the gradual acceptance by the market of a new product.

dig *v* [*Boxing*] to hit heavily, especially with body punches.

dig it in *v* [*Cycling*] to increase speed, ride harder, faster, etc.

digester 1. *n* [*US*] [*Paper-making*] very large tanks in which wood chips are dissolved or 'cooked' into sulphite pulp. 2. *n* [*Sewage*] a tank in which the chemical treatment of sewage sludge is carried out.

digger, also **dockwalloper** *n* [*US*] [*Road transport*] a worker who handles freight on the dock or loads/unloads vehicles.

digitising *n* [*Photo-typesetting*] representing each pixel of a character, diagram or illustration by a separate numerical value, thus creating a medium that can be recognised by a computer.

digitising on the fly *n* [*Photo-typesetting*] the

obtaining by a photo-typsetter of digitised characters as required, by scanning and digitising the typeface from a store master font.

diligence *n* [*Shipping*] in marine insurance this is the duty that falls on the owners of a ship to ensure as far as reasonably possible the safety of the ship, crew and cargo.

dilly *n* [*US*] [*Coal-mining*] an engine used to move coal cars.

dilogy *n* [*Linguistics*] an equivocal expression in which there are two apparent meanings, although only one is ostensibly intended.

dilution **1.** *n* [*Finance*] the reduction in the proportion of a corporation that is still owned by the original share-holders after a new share issue is made. **2.** *n* [*Finance*] a situation in which newly issued shares earn at a lower rate than did the old ones at the point when the new issue was made. **3.** *n* [*Industrial relations*] the infiltration of unskilled labour into a job where previously only skilled workers were employed. **4.** *n* [*Industrial relations*] a situation where skilled union members accept (3) and offer the new workers union membership.

diminishing returns *n pl* [*Economics*] the concept that as an old technology declines, the greater the sums invested in attempts to salvage it and the less the actual improvements that will be created by such investments. See also **increasing returns**.

dimple *n* [*Navy*] a small hole or dent in the side of a warship.

dinette *n* [*US*] [*Navy*] the mess hall in a submarine.

ding **1.** *n* [*Metallurgy*] a kink in the surface of a steel sheet. **2.** *n* [*Motor trade*] an imperfection in the sheet metal used for car bodies; thus 'dingman' is a worker who makes minor repairs on car bodies, especially smoothing out dings. **3.** *n* [*Surfing*] a hole in the bottom of a surfboard. **4.** *v* [*US*] [*Government*] to prod into action.

dingbat *n* [*Printing*] any ornamental piece of type used on a page, eg: an asterisk, a bullet, etc. See also **flubdub**.

dinged **1.** *a* [*US*] [*Football*] suffering from concussion after being hit on the head in a tackle. **2.** *a* [*US*] [*Marine Corps*] hit by a bullet, although not necessarily killed.

dinging *n* [*Building, Plastering*] a cheap one-coat finish of sand-lime-cement, finished with vertical brush-strokes.

dingleberries **1.** *n pl* [*US*] [*Business*] this term comes from US steelworkers' use, referring to an executive's overly vague statement on a given topic, which still manages to leave a number of 'splattered' thoughts lying around which have no relation to the main topic under discussion. Given the US origin of the term, it must be assumed that the coiners were ignorant of the UK slang use: pieces of excrement clinging to a poorly cleansed anus. **2.** *n pl* [*Metallurgy*] splattered

particles of molten metal that accumulate around a weld on a metal pipe or vessel.

dink **1.** *n* [*US*] [*Navy*] a pejorative blanket description of any Orientals, especially the Vietnamese. **2.** *n* [*Tennis*] a drop shot: one which barely clears the net and drops close by it on the other side; 'dink' can also be used as both a transitive and intransitive verb.

dint *n* [*Coal-mining*] the place where material is removed from the floor of a roadway to increase height. Thus as a verb: to remove material in this way.

Dior do *n* [*TV*] any notably lavish and expensive costume; it comes from the name of the haute couture designer.

dip **1.** *n* [*Coal-mining*] See **dook**. **2.** *n* [*Military*] the amount by which a naval mine, moored to the ocean floor and floating above it, is carried beneath its set depth by the current or tidal stream. **3.** *n* [*Mining*] an underground roadway driven downhill, usually following the inclination of the strata. **4.** *n* [*TV*] a metal trap in the floor that covers electrical sockets.

dip face *n* [*Coal-mining*] a coal face that advances downhill.

dip in *v* [*Bird-watching*] to go on a successful trip to see a rare bird. See also **dip out**.

dip one's killick *v* [*Navy*] to be demoted from the rank of leading seaman, and thus to forfeit the killick (anchor) badge of this rank. See also **killick**.

dip out *v* [*Bird-watching*] to fail, on a bird-watching trip, to sight the species desired. See also **dip in**.

dip shop *n* [*US*] [*Car salesmen*] a finance company. See also **blood bank, mouse house**.

dip-locker *n* [*Air travel*] a special secret locked compartment for carrying diplomatic bags on the aircraft. It is often used by air crew for transporting their own small specialities.

diploma disease *n* [*Sociology*] See **credentialism**.

diploma mill *n* [*Education*] an institute of higher education operating without the supervision of a state or federal agency; the diplomas it grants are thus effectively worthless since they are technically fraudulent and lack authorised academic standards.

diploma piece *n* [*Education*] any academic project – thesis, dissertation, etc – which is undertaken purely for the purpose of obtaining a diploma, rather than through any real interest in the subject.

dipper **1.** *n* [*Art*] a small pot that can be fixed to the artist's palette to hold varnish, etc. **2.** *n* [*Building*] the excavating bucket of a power shovel. **3.** *n* [*UK*] [*Market-traders*] a pickpocket.

dipping *n* [*Air travel*] the practice by stewards of funnelling off liquor from the free full-size bottles available to first class passengers and transferring it to empty miniature bottles. Sometimes these bottles are taken home, but more usually they are resold by the stewards to the tourist class, who know nothing about this private enterprise.

dips *n pl* [*UK*] [*Diplomacy*] abbr of **diplomats** those members of an Embassy – from Ambassador to Third Secretary – who have full diplomatic privileges and immunities. See also **non-dips**.

direct access *n* [*Computing*] the ability of a computer to extract the required data immediately; such ability is only available when dealing with floppy or fixed disks which can be scanned. Tape cartridges, which have to run through from end to end, are slower and can offer only 'serial access'.

direct costs *n* [*TV*] see **folding money**.

direct damage *n* [*Law*] damages that arise naturally from a breach of contract.

direct disc *n* [*Audio*] a one-off recording made by feeding amplified and mixed microphone signals directly to the disc cutter, avoiding the usual stages of plating, copying and pressing.

direct placement *n* [*UK*] [*Stock market*] the direct placing of an issue of securities with financial institutions without using underwriters.

direct reduction *n* [*Ecology*] the killing off of counter-productive fauna in a park or nature reserve.

direct response *n* [*Commerce*] high pressure, unsolicited telephone selling.

direct sell *n* [*Travel agents*] a tour operator, often not a member of ABTA (Assoc. of British Travel Agents), who sells directly to the public rather than using the trade.

directed democracy *n* [*Politics*] a concept of Soviet Government under Brezhnev whereby an elite and highly controlled oligarchy ruled in the supposed interests of the disorganised masses. The Communist version of aristocratic rule.

directive management *n* [*Management*] an autocratic management style in which all decisions stem from the leader, who dictates them without any consultation; it is the opposite of a permissive, democratic style.

dirt **1.** *n* [*Coal-mining*] any waste material that has been extracted during mining. **2.** *n* [*Oil rigs*] the debris of rock, earth, etc. that must be displaced from the well bore as the bit end moves downwards.

dirt band *n* [*Coal-mining*] a layer of rock (usually shale or mudstone) found in a coal seam.

dirteater *n* [*Motor trade*] a metal finisher; he is so called from the dustiness of the task.

dirty **1.** *a* [*Aerospace*] used of an aircraft which has its undercarriage down. See also **clean 1. 2.** *a* [*Economics*] said of a floating exchange rate: the manipulation of the market by one country in order to influence the exchange rate in its own favour on the international exchanges. **3.** *a* [*Gliding*] used of the condition of a glider that is hampered to the greatest extent by **parasite**

drag. See also **clean 5. 4.** *a* [*Military*] used of a nuclear explosion that carries the maximum amount of **fallout. 5.** *a* [*UK*] [*Military*] a bomb disposal term describing any device which has yet to be disarmed, defused or exploded. **6.** *a* [*Music*] in jazz music, possessing a slurred or rasping tone.

dirty bed *n* [*US*] [*Medicine*] a bed that is set aside for a patient suffering from an infectious disease; it is usually found in isolation wards. See also **clean bed**.

dirty bill, also **dirty bill of lading**, also **foul bill of lading** *n* [*Shipping*] a document, referring to the state of the cargo, in which the shipowners state that the goods or packing when received were in an unsatisfactory state.

dirty bond *n* [*Finance*] a government bond, the price of which must be adjusted to allow for the fluctuations in interest. See also **clean bond**.

dirty case *n* [*US*] [*Medicine*] an operation which leads to the discovery of an infection in the patient.

dirty colour *n* [*Textiles*] a colour that has lost its true shade.

dirty dishes *n* [*US*] [*Police*] planted evidence, intended to incriminate or to justify an arrest.

dirty dozen *n* [*US*] [*Navy*] an unofficial but widely acknowledged list of the twelve most frequent causes of the unserviceability of naval aircraft.

dirty feed *n* [*UK*] [*TV*] in British commercial feed, this is an input to other stations in the network which includes all the local information – station identifications, local announcements and news, advertisements, etc – that is being transmitted by the originating station. Such transmissions require exact 'outswitching' by the recipient stations for the insertion of their own equivalent programming. See also **clean feed**.

dirty float **1.** *n* [*Banking*] this is when a central bank, which ostensibly should not intervene in the international foreign exchange markets, pushes the home currency, by unobtrusive intervention in those markets, to a level that it would like to see established. **2.** *n* [*Government, Economics*] a currency that has been cut loose from its fixed parity, but which is still kept beneath a fixed ceiling, as determined by the national government or central bank; the term was coined in 1971 by the German finance minister Professor Schiller.

dirty girl *n* [*US*] [*Medicine*] a nurse who works in the operating room to deliver supplies, take messages, etc; she does not wear a sterile gown nor does she help at the operating table.

dirty jacket, also **bad rap sheet, bad snitch sheet** *n* [*US*] [*Police*] a bad police record. See also **jacket 2**.

dirty money, also **abnormal conditions payments, arduous conditions payments, danger money, height money, plus payments** *n* [*Industrial relations*] extra wages that are paid out for particularly difficult or dangerous work.

dirty nurse *n* [*US*] [*Medicine*] a nurse working in an operating room who is assigned to handle unsterilised objects only.

dirty room *n* [*US*] [*Medicine*] an operating room where the surgeon has been dealing with an infection; such an O.R. must be thoroughly cleaned and disinfected prior to commencing the next operation.

dirty towel *n* [*US*] [*Prison*] the prison barbershop.

dirty tricks *n pl* [*Espionage*] illegal activities by a political party or its hirelings (notably the great trickster of the 1960s campaigns – Dick Tuck) which are designed to sabotage the smooth progress of their rival's political campaign. It is derived from the CIA's 'Department of Dirty Tricks', which specialises in covert operations, allegedly restricted to overseas targets. See also **black advance**.

dirtying *n* [*Espionage*] an operation in which agents secretly enter a house to place microphones, **sneakies** and similar surveillance tools; to avoid suspicion they must not tidy up too scrupulously, ensuring that whatever mess existed before their arrival is left in place.

disable 1. *v* [*Computing*] to prevent the machine from recognising and acting upon a function. **2.** *n* [*US*] [*Traffic controllers*] (Texas use) a stalled or disabled vehicle; in Baltimore it is a stall.

disabled 1. *a* [*Computing*] used of a machine which has received a signal from its internal mechanisms that stops it from functioning. **2.** *a* [*Computing*] referring to a situation in which the central processing unit is unable to respond to the occurrence of various **interrupts**. **3.** *a* [*Computing*] in data transmission, referring to a situation in which a transmission control unit cannot accept incoming calls.

disabled interrupt *n* [*Computing*] a signal for a break in the normal flow of a program which is ignored by the program. See also **armed interrupt**.

disadvantaged *a* [*Education, Sociology*] a blanket term, some say euphemism, referring to those suffering from poverty, inadequate parenting, mental inadequacies, environmental deprivation and all the other problems that are considered as detrimental to living the idealised social role.

disaggregated *a* [*Business*] said of a situation in which one sector of a company has been broken down into its component parts for detailed examination.

disappear *v* [*Politics*] the translation of 'desaparecer': used to refer to the arrest and subsequent disappearance of many alleged members of opposition groups in Argentina (prior to the Alfonsin government), El Salvador and other S. American states. Once disappeared, it is assumed that those concerned are dead, imprisoned, suffering torture, etc.

disarm *v* [*Computing*] to put a device into a state where it is still serviceable but it requires a preparatory action before it can be used.

disassociation tableau *n* [*Espionage*] a scene staged to make the opposition believe that an agent of one side has become disenchanted and is looking for new employment with the erstwhile enemy; this is often used to entrap agents of the opposition and break their **cover**.

disaster dump *n* [*Computing*] a printout which occurs in response to a non-recoverable program error.

disbound *a* [*Book collecting*] said of books or pamphlets that have been torn out of composite volumes.

disc *n* [*Ice-hockey*] the puck.

discard 1. *n* [*Metallurgy*] portions of metal at the top and bottom of the ingot which are removed to ensure that the remainder of the material is of the required quality. **2.** *n* [*Metallurgy*] defective material produced in rolling or forging, cut from one or both ends of the product.

discharge *n* [*New therapies*] the joyous outpouring of pent-up emotions gained by verbalising one's opinions of oneself; such outpourings are often heard as laughter.

disclericalisation *n* [*Politics, Religion*] the deliberate destruction by Communist governments of the former role of organised religion as a guiding force in society.

disclosure *n* [*US*] [*Medicine*] the revealing, by means of special vegetable dye preparations, of the existence of plaque on the teeth.

discomfort index *n* [*Economics*] a measure of the fluctuating levels of economic discomfort, represented by the sum of the unemployment rate and the inflation rate.

Discon *n* [*Science fiction*] a science fiction convention held in Washington, DC.

discontinuities *n pl* [*Military*] cracks that occur in the bodies of tanks.

discotetic *n* [*Economics*] a situation which seems inescapably and progressively more appalling and on which no efforts or attempts at change seem to have any useful or positive effect.

discount *n* [*Futures market*] a deduction from face value; it is the opposite of **premium**.

discount house *n* [*Finance*] a firm that specialises in the buying and selling of bills of exchange; such bill brokers act as the channel through which the Bank of England can control the money supply in the financial system.

discount justice *n* [*US*] [*Law*] a form of plea-bargaining whereby the accused pleads guilty to a lesser charge, has the major charge dropped, and thus the cost and time of a jury trial is saved.

discounting the news *n* [*US*] [*Stock market*] the attempt to bid the price of a share up or down

D

in anticipation of an announcement of good or bad news by the firm concerned.

discourse *n* [*Sociology*] a domain of language use, structured as a unity by common assumptions. There may be competing discourses and discourses will change over a period of time; the result, however, of the essential unity is that within an accepted discourse some ideas can be neither said nor even thought.

discovery centred *a* [*Education*] said of teaching that is based on encouraging pupils to find things out for themselves, rather than learning by rote.

discovery method *n* [*Education*] a method of teaching in which students pursue problems on their own and work out their own solutions under the guidance of a teacher. See also **discovery centred**, **open classroom**.

discreet liaison *n* [*Espionage*] relations between the CIA and the security forces in countries – usually of the Third World – whose official policy is ostensibly and noisily anti-American.

discrete element *n* [*Photo-typesetting*] a single pixel of a design; it can be one **bit** of the information contained in a black and white image or one **byte** of the information which codes the grey scale for a tone image, or one element of the **mosaic** of pixels that makes up an entire character.

discretion *n* [*Stock market*] orders 'at discretion' are those in which the broker is supposed to exercise his own judgement in the execution of a transaction.

discretionary account *n* [*Finance*] an account over which any individual or organisation, other than the person in whose name the account is held, exercises trading authority or control.

discriminating monopoly *n* [*Commerce*] a monopoly that exists when a monopolist sells identical commodities at different prices.

discriminating weapon *n* [*Military*] a weapon – especially the newest generations of ICBMs and SBMs – that can attain sufficient accuracy for military planners to choose only those enemy targets they wish to destroy. This belief, the backbone of **counterforce** targeting, and the 'limited' nuclear war it supposes, is presented as a means of sparing the civilian population, and as the final answer to the threats of **assured destruction**. In fact it is an illusion: in the first place, so interwoven are the sites of military installations and urban centres that even pinpoint accuracy will kill millions of civilians. In the second place, launching a counterforce first strike may marginally limit the civilian deaths among one's enemy; it will only increase them at home, as the retaliatory strike, in the knowledge that silos and airbases would now be empty, would be retargeted on cities.

discrimination **1.** *n* [*Audio*] the extraction of the audio signal from an FM transmission. **2.** *n* [*Mili-*

tary] the ability of an anti-missile weapon to differentiate between the missile on which it is targeted and the various electronic and physical decoys with which the missile attempts to confuse it.

diseconomies of scale *n pl* [*Economics*] the increases in average costs as an industrial unit expands.

disgorgement *n* [*Wine trade*] in champagne or 'méthode champenoise' wine-making, this is the temporary removal of the cork from the bottle after secondary fermentation in order to allow the yeasty sediment to be blown out by the escaping gas.

dish *n* [*US*] [*Cattlemen*] the seat of the saddle; this can be shallow-dished or deep-dished.

dished *a* [*Audio*] referring to a faulty record in which the overall shape is saucer-like, rather than correctly flat.

dished face *n* [*Hunting*] the face of a hound which has a concave appearance.

dishonoured bill *n* [*Finance*] a bill of exchange which the debtor on whom it is drawn has refused to pay or which the **acceptor** fails to pay when it falls due.

disideologisation *n* [*Politics*] the decline of both communist and capitalist ideological fervour, which accelerated through the détente era of the late 1960s and early 1970s, but which is currently in abeyance during the new Cold War of the 1980s.

disinformation **1.** *n* [*Business*] the deliberate spreading of inaccurate information about designs, sales, marketing, etc, which is intended to confuse and worry trading rivals. **2.** *n* [*Espionage*] distorted or false information deliberately disseminated either at home to confuse foreign agents operating in one's own country, or in a foreign country to confuse its inhabitants. **3.** *n* [*Politics*] in the view of socialist nations, this refers to any statements that do not wholly support their stance on a given issue; as such these facts are really 'deliberate distortions'.

disintegration *n* [*Economics*] planned action by a group of industrial units to stop producing certain products and to start buying them from outside producers.

disintermediate *v* [*Economics*] to withdraw one's money from intermediate institutions – savings accounts, etc. – for direct investment at potentially higher rates of interest in the stock market.

disintermediation *n* [*Finance*] a method whereby companies can avoid the mediation of banks and deal directly with potential investors.

disk *n* [*Computing*] the basic medium of storing information on modern business micro-computers: data is placed on magnetic disks and is then retrievable through high-speed read/write heads which scan the disk and then extract the required material. Disks fall into two categories: floppy disks, usually holding a maximum of 360,000 bytes of information (although larger capacity floppies are available) and hard disks or fixed disks which can hold infinitely larger quantities running into tens of millions of bytes each. As well as holding far more data, these disks, which cannot be removed from the disk drive as can floppies, provide infinitely faster operations. See also **Winchester**.

diskery 1. *n* [*Record business*] a record producing company. 2. *n* [*Pop music*] a record store.

diskette *n* [*Computing*] See **disk**.

disorderly closedown *n* [*Computing*] the sudden and unscheduled stoppage of the system, usually through some form of equipment error; such an error may well lead to loss of data, messages, etc.

disorderly market *n* [*Stock market*] a market situation in which prices are performing erratically and so buyers or sellers are unwilling to take a chance on trading.

dispatcher *n* [*Computing*] a resident routine that links the computer with its output/input devices; like a taxi firm's dispatcher, the routine maintains a system whereby the computer deals sequentially with the requests it receives for the operation of communications channels, and simultaneously controls a number of other request and operational queues.

dispatchers *n pl* [*Gambling*] any pair of dice that are crooked or in some way loaded.

displaced home-maker *n* [*Sociology*] a married woman who has lost her means of economic support, either through divorce or the death or disability of her husband.

displacement *n* [*Computing*] See **relative address**.

display *n* [*Music*] a piece of music that has been specially selected to display the performer's talents to their greatest advantage.

display outer *n* [*Marketing*] an outer container for protecting goods in transit, which converts into a display unit at the point of sale.

dispo *n* [*US*] [*Medicine*] abbr of **disposition problem** a patient who is admitted to hospital with no actual medical problem other than the inability to take care of him/herself.

disposal centre *n* [*US*] [*Government*] a euphemism for any kind of dumping ground, junkyard or refuse tip.

dissolve *n* [*Film*] a scene that changes as the one that replaces it appears through a process of gradual superimposition. See also **mix 2**.

distance *n* [*Boxing*] to 'go the distance' is to continue fighting through the scheduled length – ten rounds, fifteen rounds, etc – of the fight.

distended *a* [*Printing*] very much wider than standard.

distinguished *a* [*Wine-tasting*] marked by exceptional character and **breed**.

distress *v* [*Antiques*] to fake modern furniture, ornaments, paintings, etc. in order to sell them as 'antiques'; this is usually achieved by some 'ageing' process.

distress borrowing *n* [*Banking, Commerce*] this is the act of a company that, facing liquidation, borrows more money, even at very high interest rates, simply because such loans are the sole alternative to economic collapse.

distress merchandise *n* [*Commerce*] goods that have failed to sell as expected, due to over-ordering, poor quality, etc., and must therefore be disposed of cheaply and fast.

distress pattern *n* [*New therapies*] in **co-counselling** this refers to those inner confusions and miseries which will, in theory, be removed by successful therapy.

distress selling 1. *n* [*Stock market*] the selling of stocks in a recession when the market is worried about the possibility of a sudden crash. 2. *n* [*Stock market*] the selling off of assets when a firm has gone bankrupt.

distressed *a* [*Antiques*] said of furniture, either not of the period claimed or simply reproduction pieces, which has been artificially aged with fake signs of wear and tear.

distressing *n* [*Painting*] the application of a top coat of paint so that the tone of the undercoat shows through.

distrib *n* [*Show business*] abbr of **distributor** thus 'distribbery' means distribution company; hence 'distribbing', 'distribbed', etc.

distribute *v* [*Printing*] to break up composed hot-metal type and melt it down for re-use.

distributed architecture *n* [*Computing*] multiple company facilities, often in various, separate, distant locations, which are tied together in stand-alone systems.

distributed intelligence *n* [*Computing*] the sharing out of a system's intelligence facilities over a number of machines, thus reducing the traffic on communications channels with the main memory and offering flexibility of operation to the individual terminal operator.

distributive education *n* [*Education*] a vocational scheme split between a school and an employer: the pupil mixes classroom lessons with on-the-job training and experience.

district 1. *n* [*Coal-mining*] one of the parts into which mine workings are divided for the purpose of supervision or ventilation. 2. *n* [*UK*] [*Medicine*] 'on the district': a midwife who covers a certain area, which is related geographically to a specified teaching hospital.

distringas notice *n* [*Stock market*] a special notice, served with the approval of a court, forbidding a company to deal in certain of its stocks for a given period without first informing the person serving the notice: it comes from Lat. meaning 'you must distrain'.

DIT *part. phr* [*US*] [*Medicine*] acro **died in transit**.

D

ditch 1. *n* [*US*] [*Bars*] a water or soda **chaser**. 2. *n* [*UK*] [*Navy, Air Force*] the sea; especially those areas of water immediately adjacent to the UK. 3. *v* [*UK*] [*Air Force*] to bring down into the sea either in an emergency or when crashing. 4. *v* [*UK*] [*Navy, Marines*] to throw away useless kit. See also **bin** 3.

ditcher *n* [*Bowls*] a bowl which either runs or is knocked off the green into the surrounding ditch.

dittoanalysis *n* [*Business*] the process whereby consultants manage to arrive at a series of conclusions which were already determined beforehand.

dittogram *n* [*Printing*] a repeated letter caused by a typesetting error.

divergence *n* [*TV*] the failure of the beams on a colour-display tube to land on the same colour cell on the screen.

diverging approach *n* [*US*] [*Railways*] a signal that indicates a section of track where a train can cross from one main line to another.

diversionist *n* [*Politics*] in Communist terms, a saboteur, usually as found in the phrase 'spies and diversionists', where it means foreign espionage agents. On a domestic level, it refers to anyone who is deemed to be conspiring against the state.

diverter *n* [*Government, Military*] in **game theory** this is the adversary who attempts to destabilise the safeguard systems that are established by his opponent, the **defender**.

divide and conquer sorting *n* [*Computing*] a sorting system whereby the file is sorted from the most significant digit of the sortkey through to the least significant. See also **bubble sort, cocktail shaker sort**.

dividend stripping *n* [*Finance*] the taking over of a firm which has large retained earnings (profits that have neither been distributed to the owners nor paid out as interest on shares, nor as taxes, nor set aside for future liabilities) and the declaring of a large dividend to shareholders in such a way that tax is avoided. See also **asset stripping**.

divine passive *n* [*Literary criticism*] a term coined by Richard Mitchell: the stilted use of passive verbs, especially in pompous officialese where such usage is expected to add an air of gravity.

diviner *n* [*US*] [*Bars*] a customer who will not tip.

divisions *n pl* [*Navy*] the parade of a ship's company according to its various divisions; it was once a daily event, but is now more likely to occur only weekly.

divvy *n, a* [*UK*] [*Market-traders*] a fool, foolish.

DJ copy *n* [*Pop music*] a special version of a 45 rpm record in which only the **A side** is pressed for radio play by a disc jockey; the reverse side is left blank.

DLP *a* [*UK*] [*Theatre*] abbr of **Direct Letter Perfect** word perfect in a role.

DMU 1. *n* [*Marketing*] abbr of **Decision Making Unit** that group of people who can most influence purchasing decisions; a DMU can operate in any area of commerce, but as a marketing concept it refers mainly to large scale industrial marketing. 2. *n* [*UK*] [*Railways*] abbr of **Diesel Multiple Unit**.

DNR *v phr* [*Medicine*] abbr of **do not resuscitate**.

do a Brodie, also **take a Brodie** *v* [*US*] [*Theatre*] to fail or flop spectacularly despite, or pehaps because of, an excess of pre-show publicity. It is named after New Yorker Steve Brodie who, in the late 19th century, heavily ballyhooed a forthcoming dive from the Brooklyn Bridge but finally decided that the stunt was far too dangerous to perform.

do a dairy *v* [*Crime*] to keep on the lookout, usually posing as a nonchalant passer-by or window-shopper, etc. Thus 'to take the dairy off' means to divert suspicion.

do a Dutch *v* [*Navy*] to run a submarine aground on submerged rocks or a reef; it comes from the loss of a Dutch submarine in this way during World War II.

do a horse *v* [*Horse-racing*] to work as a stableman.

do a Nelson *v* [*Navy*] to expose oneself to unnecessary risks, emulating Admiral Nelson's legendary bravado.

do bit-and-bit *v* [*Cycling*] said of two cyclists, in the same team or not, who take turns at the front of a race.

do crew *v* [*Parachuting*] said of a freefall team who link their canopies together during the jump.

do nothing instruction *n* [*Computing*] an instruction that causes no action in the program; it is often used to compensate for time adjustments in running the program. See also **no-op instruction**.

do protocol *v* [*Computing*] to perform an 'interaction', as regards a person or a machine, that implies the use of a clearly defined procedure; possibly it comes from the diplomatic 'due protocol'.

do the business *v* [*Greyhound racing*] to win a race, to perform well.

do the crazy dance *v* [*US*] [*TV*] used to describe the frantic efforts of a TV news team to beat the impending deadline with a specific piece. See also **go down in flames**.

dobby *n* [*Fairs*] a wooden horse on a fairground roundabout; it comes from Dobbin, popular name for a horse.

dobby head *n* [*Weaving*] a programming unit, attached to a loom, which automatically controls the lifting of multi-harnesses using only two treadles.

dobson *n* [*TV*] the final rehearsal of a shot during location filming; especially when the shot in question involves complex dialogue and camera-work.

dock 1. *v* [*Aerospace*] the linking together of two vehicles in space; thus 'undocking' is the disen-

D

gagement of two vehicles. **2.** v [*Parachuting*] to link in with the formation of jumpers. **3.** n [*Theatre*] the space behind and at the sides of the stage where scenery is stored. **4.** n [*Theatre*] the theatre basement, which originally, in some theatres, was used as the scenery dock.

dock asthma n [*UK*] [*Police*] the pretended gasps of surprise that are heard from the accused when confronted by incriminating police evidence; by extension it refers to any reaction to an unpleasant surprise by a suspected civilian, in or out of court.

dock brief n [*UK*] [*Law*] a brief handed direct to a barrister in court, when the barrister has been selected on sight by a prisoner in the dock who has not previously arranged for his legal defence.

dock it v [*US*] [*Road transport*] to park one's truck at the loading dock.

dockage n [*Shipping*] dock charges levied on a ship entering/departing a port, based on the tonnage of cargo carried. See also **berthage**.

docket n [*UK*] [*Postal services*] overtime, which is marked down on a docket for weekly assessment.

dockwalloper n [*US*] [*Road transport*] See **digger**.

doctor **1.** n [*US*] [*Paper-making*] a blade built into the paper machine that ensures the surface of the paper is clean and free of foreign bodies. **2.** n [*US*] [*Paper-making*] a mechanism that rewinds narrow rolls of paper to make sure that they are tight.

doctor blade n [*Philately*] the flexible steel blade which removes surplus ink from the printing cylinder on high-speed modern presses; faulty operation of the doctor blade can create non-constant flaws in the printed stamps.

Doctor Blue n [*Medicine*] a radio call that can be put out over a hospital tannoy which will not alarm patients and visitors but signifies 'all available staff to rush to a cardiac arrest emergency'; the 'Doctor' is usually summoned to a given floor or room. See also **code nine, Doctor Green, Doctor Red**.

Doctor Green n [*Medicine*] a radio call that can be put out over a hospital tannoy which will not alarm patients and visitors but signifies the 'all clear' to staff after the termination of an emergency. See also **code nine, Doctor Blue, Doctor Red**.

Doctor Heart n [*US*] [*Medicine*] an emergency code broadcast over a hospital tannoy, indicating a cardiac arrest. See also **code nine, Doctor Blue**.

Doctor Red n [*Medicine*] a radio call that can be put out over a hospital tannoy which will not alarm patients and visitors but signifies to the staff that there is a fire alarm. See also **code nine, Doctor Blue, Doctor Green**.

doctor solution n [*Oil industry*] a chemical solution applied to petrol and oil to detect the presence of decomposable sulphur compounds which can cause an unpleasant smell and will corrode metal parts.

doctor, the n [*Wine trade*] the most popular of Bernkasteller wines.

doctored a [*Book collecting*] said of a book that has in some way been made to appear more valuable and/or collectible than it really is; a fake.

doctored lot n [*US*] [*Garment trade*] a lot of skins sold as the best quality, but which turn out on inspection to be of mixed, even poor quality.

docudrama n [*TV*] a TV dramatisation based on facts – the recreation of an international crisis, a notorious murder, an industrial conflict, etc – which is produced in the style of a factual documentary in order to gain extra authenticity. See also **faction**.

docuterm n [*Computing*] a shorthand description – a word or phrase – referring to a given document or piece of information and useful in retrieving that document or information at later dates.

dodd n [*UK*] [*Railways*] See **dolly 8** and **9**.

doddering dick n [*Navy*] a machine gun.

dodger **1.** n [*Navy*] a sweeper or cleaner aboard ship. **2.** n [*UK*] [*Railways*] a shunting truck (mainly Western Region use).

dodging n [*Photography*] a method used in printing to protect parts of a picture from overexposure.

doer n [*Hunting*] a hound which thrives well is a 'good doer' and badly a 'bad doer'.

doffer n [*Textiles*] a worker who removes the full bobbin and replaces it with an empty one.

doffing n [*Textiles*] the removal of filled boxes, bobbins and cones which have been wound with rayon thread and, often, the replacement of these with empty ones.

dog **1.** n [*Book trade*] an unsaleable book. **2.** n [*Film*] a flop, a failure. **3.** n [*US*] [*Garment trade*] a dress that does not sell well. **4.** n [*Glass-making*] a type of scum that may be found rising to the surface of the glass while melting. **5.** n [*US*] [*Gliding*] a glider achieving only a poor performance. **6.** n [*Horse racing*] a wooden sawhorse placed along the track to keep horses out of muddy patches during training workouts. **7.** n [*Horse racing*] a horse that is slow or difficult to handle. **8.** n [*Logging*] a steel projection on a log carriage or the endless chain that carries logs into a sawmill. **9.** n [*Marketing*] any product retained in production for sentimental/historical reasons as opposed to the possibility – which no longer exists – of its profitability. **10.** n [*Meat trade*] a low grade beef animal. **11.** n [*US*] [*Road transport*] a truck with little power. **12.** n [*TV*] a bad programme. **13.** also **job** n [*Military*] an affectionate nickname for a cavalryman's mount. **14.** n [*TV repair*] a fault in the set which is hard to diagnose. **15.** v [*Sailing, Ropework*] to back the tail of a **block** several turns around a stay, with the twist of the rope. **16.** *v* [*Navy*] said of a sailor who splits a watch with a friend.

dog and maggot *n* [*UK*] [*Military*] throughout the UK forces this means biscuits and cheese.

dog catcher *n* [*US*] [*Railways*] a member of a train crew sent to relieve another who is temporarily prohibited from further train operation because he has worked sixteen hours consecutively.

dog chain *n* [*Logging*] a chain used to hold together the logs in the log pond.

dog days *n pl* [*TV*] the summer season, when viewers are supposedly on holiday and eschewing the TV screen; advertising revenues fall, new scheduling is held back until the autumn and current programmes gain only mediocre ratings. See also **closed season, silly season**.

dog fall *n* [*Wrestling*] a fall in which neither opponent gains a significant advantage.

dog hair *n* [*Glass-making*] a blower of hollow glassware. See also **beet**.

dog heavy *n* [*Film*] the second or third ranked villain in a Western.

dog holes *n pl* [*Logging*] holes that are made in a piece of timber by the spikes that hold the log in position while it is being sawn. See also **dog 8**.

dog house 1. *n* [*Oil rigs*] storage space or a drillers' office on a rig floor; hence it is any small building used thus on an onshore site. **2.** *n* [*US*] [*Road transport*] the portion of the cabover truck that is over the engine.

dog it 1. *v* [*Gambling*] to back down in an argument. **2.** *v* [*Gambling*] to be afraid to bet heavily even when it appears that one is on a winning streak.

dog knot *n* [*US*] [*Coal-mining*] the incrustation of dirt that accumulates on a miner's lamp.

dog leg 1. *n* [*Metallurgy*] strip steel which is bent first in one direction, then in another. **2.** *n* [*Oil rigs*] an abrupt change in the direction of the well bore. **3.** *n* [*Oil rigs*] a deviation in the direction of a pipeline ditch or in the borehole of a well; it is also a sharp bend in the pipeline.

dog licence *n* [*Merchant navy*] a Master's or Mate's certificate.

dog muzzle *n* [*US*] [*Painting*] a mask or respirator which is worn when spraying paint.

dog robber *n* [*Military*] an officer's orderly; someone who would allegedly rob a dog of his bone to please his officer.

dog ship *n* [*US*] [*Air Force*] the trial model of a new aircraft; it comes from the phrase 'try it on the dog'.

dog show *n* [*US*] [*Theatre*] a show that opens in the provinces before coming to New York; it comes from the phrase 'try it on the dog'. See also **dog town**.

dog station *n* [*TV*] a TV station that fails to please the viewers, draw adequate advertising revenue, attract talented people, etc.

dog town *n* [*US*] [*Theatre*] a town used for

theatrical tryouts before the final version is brought to New York or a similar metropolis. See also **dog show**.

dog tracks *n pl* [*US*] [*Road transport*] the movement of a unit or truck which does not go in a straight line but seems to move slightly sideways like a dog.

dogface *n* [*US*] [*Military*] any US soldier, especially an infantryman in the US Army. See also **grunt 1**.

dogger 1. *n* [*Logging*] a worker who attaches logs to the **dog** for movement or subsequent processing. **2.** *n* [*US*] [*Sex*] any military client serviced by a homosexual prostitute; it comes from **dogface**.

doggie 1. *n* [*Navy*] an officer's runner or aide, drawn from the ranks of midshipmen. **2.** *n* [*Navy*] a midshipman who attends either a Captain or a Commander. **3.** *n* [*Military*] an officer's servant or assistant. See also **dog robber**. **4.** *n* [*US*] [*Military*] See **dogface**.

doghole *n* [*Glass-making*] See **throat 3**.

doghouse 1. *n* [*Aerospace*] a cover over the instrumentation, especially that incorporated in rocket design; it comes from World War II slang for a bomber's tail turret. **2.** *n* [*Glass-making*] a small extension of a glass furnace, into which the **batch** of material used in glassmaking is fed. **3.** *n* [*Merchant navy*] a raised structure aft of the main cabin in a vessel. **4.** *n* [*Oil rigs*] a small shelter located on the rig floor for use by the drilling crew. **5.** *n* [*US*] [*Theatre*] the theatre building itself.

doghouse dope *n* [*Oil rigs*] files, records, papers, leases, etc. which are kept in the **doghouse**.

dogleg *n* [*Tobacco*] tobacco of poor quality marketed in twists.

dogman *n* Aus. [*Building*] a man who stays on the ground to give directional signals to a crane operator; dogmen sometimes also ride on the goods which are being moved. See also **banksman**.

dogmatism *n* [*Politics*] a form of **deviation** from the Communist party line that consists in too blind an adherence to the basic tenets of Marxist dogma, irrespective of contrary facts. See also **empiricism**.

dog-robbers *n pl* [*UK*] [*Military*] the mufti (civilian clothes) worn by British officers going on leave.

dog's bollocks *n* [*Printing*] the typographical sign:-. See also **dog's cock 1**.

dog's cock 1. also **dog's prick** *n* [*Printing*] the typographical sign for an exclamation mark! See also **dog's bollocks**. **2.** also **dog's prick** *n* [*Sailing, Ropework*] the crowned and back spliced (with ends turned back and tucked under) end of a rope.

dogtag *n* [*Military*] a stamped metal plate worn around a man's neck to indicate his name, religion and blood group.

dogwarp *n* [*Logging*] a rope with a strong hook

tied to one end, which is used to clear logjams and to move logs from any difficult positions.

dog-watch 1. n [Navy] the watches between 4am and 6am and 6am and 8am (the usual period of four hours on watch is split into two). 2. n [Navy] a very short term of service. 3. n [Printing] the shift on newspapers which runs between 9pm and 12 midnight.

doigt n [Fencing] this comes from Fr. meaning 'finger'; it is the careful manipulation of one's weapon, especially in the use of the foil.

doing the party n [UK] [Crime] in a game of **three-card monte**, a ploy whereby one of the con-man's assistants pretends to have won heavily, thus encouraging the genuine suckers to put down their money – and inevitably lose it.

do-it-yourself kit n [UK] [Railways] diesel drivers' derogatory term for steam engines.

dol n [Medicine] a unit of intensity of pain; the term was coined around 1947.

doll n [Horse-racing] a hurdle that is placed as a barrier to mark the sides of a gallop.

dollar diplomacy n [Politics] the use of US economic power to further her political interests abroad by offering material or financial incentives to allies or potential friends. It was originally used in 1910 to typify the actions of US businessmen who were attempting to open up Latin America; it is now a general term for such economic imperialism wherever it is practised.

dollar drain n [Finance] the amount by which the imports of US goods by a foreign country exceed those goods it exports to the US; the drain is on its dollar reserves, used up to pay its bills in the US.

dollar stream n [Business] **venture capitalists** (see **venture capitalism**) who have adequate funds, but require a suitable area in which to risk investing them. See also **deal stream**.

dollar up v [US] [Agriculture] to fatten up one's cattle so as to get the best price when they are sold.

dollar-an-inch man n [Sex] a homosexual prostitute whose boast is that even were he only to charge clients 'a dollar an inch', he is so well-proportioned that he would still be richer than any rival.

doll's eye n [Aerospace] a warning light in the cockpit that has a white bulb.

doll's head n [Shooting] a small extension of the top rib of a gun which fits into a corresponding aperture in the top of the breech.

dolly 1. n [Motor trade] a shaped metal block used as an 'anvil' for smoothing out imperfections in the metal of the car body. 2. n [Clothing] a strip of fabric rolled up tightly and bound with tape or string at one end; it is used as a brush for applying moisture to the garment during pressing. 3. n. [Cricket] See **sitter**. See also **gapes**. 4. n [Glass-making] a gathering iron with a tip made of refractory material for gathering glass for semi-

automatic machines. 5. n [Logging] a two-wheeled iron support used for moving timber. 6. n [Logging] a type of trailer for a logging truck. 7. n [Mining] a large mortar and pestle used for crushing ore. 8. n [UK] [Railways] a small shunting engine. 9. n [UK] [Railways] an auxiliary engine, used to help pull trains up an incline. 10. n [US] [Road transport] a device that supports a **semi-trailer** when it is not attached to a truck. 11. n [UK] [Road transport] a **bogie** with two or more axles places under the rear end of a long load to support the load and turn a rigid vehicle into an articulated vehicle. 12. n [Textiles] a machine used for scouring certain textiles – woollens and worsteds – during manufacture. 13. n [TV, Film] any wheeled mounting for a camera, usually guided along tracks for backwards/forwards movement. Thus 'tray dolly' is a very low dolly; 'scorpion dolly' is a dolly that is adaptable to various gauges of track; 'crab dolly' is a non-tracked mounting that can move in any direction (see **crabs**); 'dolly grip' is the member of the film crew in charge of moving the dolly. 14. v [TV, Film] to move a camera using a wheeled mounting. See also **dolly** 13. 15. also **dolly bar** n [Industry] a heavy steel bar with a cupped head which is held against the top of a rivet while it is being headed. 16. also **dummy**, **dodd** n [UK] [Railways] a ground shunting signal; a red band on a white disc.

dolly varden n [Angling] a large char.

dolphin n [Merchant navy] timber piles driven into the seabed close to shore to provide a berth for ships.

dolphins n pl [Navy] the submarine branch of the navy; it comes from the dolphin badge of the service.

domain 1. n [Computing] the resources under the control of one or more **host** processors in a network. 2. n [Computing] in programming, the set of values assigned to the independent variables of a function.

domestic replay n [Espionage] See **blowback**.

domesticated word n [Literary criticism] a foreign word that has been borrowed for use in English and has become virtually 'naturalised' into everyday speech.

domestication n [Economics] the re-formation of what had formerly been an overseas branch of an American company, based in the UK, as a separate, non-resident company, operating from the UK.

domestics n pl [Textiles] any articles – sheets, towels, pillow-cases, etc – that are regularly used in the home.

domino 1. a [UK] [Buses] said of a fully occupied London Transport bus. 2. n [Dog breeding] a reverse facial mask pattern on the head of some breeds, eg. Afghan hound. 3. n [UK] [Railways] See **blackboard**. 4. n [TV] the light source that is used to illuminate the cyclorama. See **cyc**.

D

domino theory 1. *n* [*Drugs*] the theory that the use of soft drugs, especially marijuana, will lead automatically to hard drugs, particularly heroin. See also **stepping stone hypothesis**. **2.** *n* [*Politics*] the concept that if one nation in a specific area turned communist, then similarly placed adjacent nations would automatically follow suit, tumbling like a row of dominoes knocking each other down in turn. It was coined in 1954 by President Eisenhower and latterly had been invoked to justify US incursions into Vietnam and more recently Latin America.

Donald Duck effect *n* [*Aerospace*] the distortion of the voice up to a higher pitch which can be encountered during space flight; it comes from the Walt Disney character known, inter alia, for his strangulated vowels.

dongle *n* [*Computing*] a chip that must be present in a microcomputer to enable it to operate proprietary software; such a chip is used to prevent illegal copying of the software.

donkey 1. *n* [*Clothing*] a pressing board in which an upper padded board is supported above the base; it is designed so that individual parts of a garment can be pressed without creasing the garment as a whole. **2.** *n* [*Logging*] an engine on skids that drags logs. **3.** *n* [*Navy*] the chest in which a naval artificer keeps his tools.

donkey doctor *n* [*Logging*] a mechanic who works on any defective machinery in a logging camp or sawmill.

donkey jammer, also **donkey puncher, skinner** *n* [*Logging*] the operator of the donkey engine.

donkey-feet *n* [*Horse-racing*] a description of a horse with especially narrow hooves.

donniker *n* [*US*] [*Circus*] the lavatory.

don't block the key *excl* [*Film*] an instruction from the director to an actor warning him/her not to cast a shadow over another actor; it refers to the **key light**.

don't call us, we'll call you *v phr* [*Theatre*] See **come back Tuesday**.

don't do out like that! *excl* [*US*] [*Prisons*] exhortation to a fellow prisoner not to act in a way that will bring down the derision and contempt of other inmates.

don't fight the tape *v phr* [*US*] [*Stock market*] this is an adage in the US stock market meaning don't attempt to run against overall market trends.

don't know *n* [*US*] [*Stock market*] a questioned trade; any discrepancies that emerge when brokers compare their records of mutual transactions.

don't piss into the cash-register *v phr* [*US*] [*Crime*] a traditional criminal warning against leaving one's fingerprints at the site of a crime.

donut *n* [*US*] [*Road transport*] a truck tyre.

doodlebug 1. *n* [*US*] [*Coal-mining*] a miner's lamp. **2.** *n* [*Oil rigs*] an oil divining device; a twig or branch of a small tree (preferably peach) which when held by an 'expert' as he walks over a given area should indicate the ideal place to drill for oil; more generally it is a term for a variety of geophysical prospecting equipment. **3.** *n* [*US*] [*Road transport*] a small tractor that pulls two-axle **dollies** in the warehouse.

doodlebugger *n* [*Oil rigs*] a member of a crew undertaking a seismic exploration of potentially oil-bearing rock.

doodler *n* [*Logging*] one who cleans out sawdust and scraps of wood.

dook *n* [*Coal-mining*] an underground roadway driven straight downhill, usually along the inclination of the strata.

Doomsday Clock *n* [*Science, Military*] a clock that is printed on the cover of each issue of the Bulletin of the Atomic Scientists (founded in 1954 by a group of physicists at the University of Chicago) which tells the 'time' left before nuclear doomsday. Originally set at 11.52pm, the clock has only been turned back once – when it appeared that Khruschev was 'thawing' out the Cold War – and currently stands at 11.58pm.

doomsday plane *n* [*Military*] See **Looking Glass plane**.

doomsday scenario *n* [*Military*] the 'war games' played by military planners in an attempt to evaluate possible ways in which a nuclear war might start.

doorstep *v* [*Commerce*] used of a salesman who goes from door to door soliciting sales; by extension, anyone – politician, charity organiser, preacher – can doorstep for their own ends.

doorstepping *n* [*Journalism*] this is when reporters wait on a person's doorstep in order to attempt to gain an interview when that person either arrives home or goes out.

doorway state *n* [*Science*] in nuclear physics, this is a theoretical middle state between a simple and a more complex nuclear interaction.

dope 1. *n* [*Motor racing*] racing fuel which is specially designed for racing cars; it is mainly obsolete, since the rules lay down that all racing is performed on ordinary commercial fuel. **2.** *n* [*Cosmetics*] a general name for a variety of cosmetic preparations (usually for dry skin), medicines, lotions and insect repellants. **3.** *n* [*US*] [*Farming*] any chemical used on the farm. **4.** *n* [*Food*] any adulterant added to food in order to create a required flavour, texture, consistency, etc. **5.** *n* [*Glass-making*] colouring used for flint and amber glass. **6.** *n* [*Oil rigs*] a lubricant for the threads on pipe **stands**. **7.** *n* [*Tyre-making*] a soapstone solution that is used to prevent various pieces of rubber from sticking together. **8.** *n* [*US*] [*Marine Corps*] information, which can be either 'good dope' or 'bad dope'. **9.** *v* [*US*] [*Marine Corps*] to sight a rifle, allowing for wind correction and any other pertinent conditions. **10.** *v* [*Electronics*] to add an impurity to a semi-conductor to produce a desired electrical characteristic.

dope sheet 1. *n* [*Horse-racing*] a daily circular for betters listing all runners, riders and up-to-date form. 2. *n* [*TV*] the detailed breakdown of instructions for the shooting of each scene; it is usually prepared in advance by the director.

dope slope *n* [*US*] [*Skiing*] a beginners' slope.

dope story *n* [*US*] [*Politics*] a story deliberately leaked to a reporter and then written up by him as his own investigation; a useful method of quietly assessing public reaction to a new plan or policy.

dopesheet *n* [*Industry*] a circular of up-to-date information, reports, analyses, projections, etc. – such sheets are prepared for a wide variety of professions and their personnel.

doping *n* [*Tanning*] the application of fatty compounds, oils or greases to leather prior to the tanning process.

dormie *adv* [*Golf*] on a match play score, this refers to a player, standing as many holes up as there are holes left to be played, who cannot therefore be defeated.

Dorothy and Toto *n* [*Sex*] a homosexual client and his paid 'escort'.

dorrick *v* [*UK*] [*Market-traders*] to tell fortunes.

DOT *n* [*Medicine*] acro **Death on the Operating Table**.

dot *n* [*Building, Plastering*] a short piece of wood lath which is bedded and then plumbed level, and used as a guide for the formation of a screed.

dote *n* [*Logging*] decay or rot in timber; thus 'doty' means rotten timber.

dotted line responsibility *n* [*Business, Politics*] non-hierarchical relationships: liaisons, exchanges of information, etc; the image is of dotted lines joining nodes of an organisational chart. See also **straight-line responsibility**.

double 1. *n* [*Baseball*] a hit that permits the batter to reach second base easily. 2. *n* [*Cricket*] this is when a batsman scores 100 runs in each innings of a match. 3. *n* [*Cricket*] this is when a player scores 1000 runs and takes 100 wickets in a season. 4. *n* [*Metallurgy*] steel sheet that is folded on itself and then hot rolled. 5. also **dubs** *n* [*US*] [*Road transport*] a unit consisting of truck, semitrailer and trailer. 6. *n* [*Oil rigs*] two sections of drill pipe, casing or tubing joined together. 7. *n* [*Advertising*] an advertisement spanning a double column width, measured according to the relevant journal. 8. *n* [*Hunting*] a fence or bank with a ditch on either side. 9. *v* [*Hunting*] to turn back on one's tracks. 10. *v* [*Espionage*] to give, or to pretend to give information to each of two conflicting parties; thus a double agent works for both sides at once. 11 *v* [*US*] [*Railways*] to split a train into two sections, which are hauled separately up a steep gradient.

double bond, also **conditional bond** *n* [*Commerce, Finance*] a bond that contains a number of specified conditions.

double bottom *n* [*Economics*] a graph of share prices which shows a drop in price, a recovery, a second drop to the previous low, and then a further recovery.

double call *v* [*Commerce*] used of a manager who accompanies a salesman in a visit to a client.

double clangers *n pl* [*Cycling*] double chainwheels.

double dagger, also **double obelisk** *n* [*Printing*] a reference mark used in typesetting, usually indicating the third reference after an asterisk and single dagger.

double digit (inflation), also **double figure** *n* [*Economics*] inflation that exceeds 10% per annum; thus 'triple digit/triple figure' inflation is in excess of 100% per annum.

double dipsies, also **double doodles** *n pl* [*US*] [*Skiing*] a series of short parallel turns close to the **fall line**.

double doodles *n* [*US*] [*Skiing*] See **double dipsies**.

double drive *n* [*UK*] [*Road transport*] when two rear axles on a vehicle are both driven, the drive to the second axle is taken by a secondary propeller shaft from the forward drive axle.

double effect *n* [*Philosophy, Religion*] a Roman Catholic principle which states that an agent is not necessarily responsible for the unwanted side-effects of an intentional action, even if he appreciated that these side-effects would arise and did nothing to forestall them.

double exposure *n* [*Film*] two or more images recorded on the same piece of film; this is often used to denote dreams or fantasies, or for trick shots involving 'twins' who are played by the same actor.

double fleecer *n* [*Sheep-shearing*] a sheep that has been missed at one shearing and comes in at the next.

double float *n* [*Athletics*] that short period, usually in a sprint race, when both of a runner's feet are in mid-air.

double front *n* [*Advertising*] twin poster sites arranged to utilise both panels on the front of a bus or similar commercial vehicle.

double headed print *n* [*Film*] a print in which sound and vision are recorded on separate pieces of film, usually at cutting copy stage (when a print is available for editing), or prior to the final approval being given for making the **combined print** that will be exhibited in the cinemas.

double home turn *n* [*UK*] [*Railways*] a tour of duty when the crew lodge at the terminus overnight, before returning home next day.

double in brass *v* [*Theatre*] to play two parts at one performance; originally it referred to those performers who helped out in the orchestra pit when they were not needed on stage. See also **George Spelvin, Walter Plinge**.

double, on the *adv* [*Clothing*] used of any material which has been folded along the middle

D

of its length, normally with the face side inwards, so that the selvedges are together. Cutting on the double creates two matching pieces of a garment: the left-hand and right-hand sides.

double out v [US] [Railways] to work a second job with less than eight hours rest since the previous one.

double play n [Audio] magnetic recording tape that is half the thickness of standard play tape.

double precision arithmetic n [Computing] See **multiple precision**.

double pricing n [Commerce] the (fraudulent) system of writing price tickets with one (the larger) price crossed out and a second (cheaper) price entered below; the intention is to imply that the goods so ticketed have been reduced.

double strike n [Philately] a double impression of all or part of a stamp's design when printed by the typographical method. See also **double transfer, re-entry**.

double take [US] [Military] US Department of Defense code for the second level of war readiness (out of five).

double team, also **sandwich play** n [Lacrosse] a tackle by two defenders on one attacker.

double top n [Economics] a graph of share prices which shows a rise, then a drop, then a second rise to the original high, and then a return to a lower price.

double transfer n [Philately] a double impression made of all or part of a stamp's design by an inaccuracy in the lithographic printing process. See also **double strike, re-entry**.

double truck n [Advertising, Journalism] a feature or an advertisement that runs across a double-page spread.

double wing n [US] [Football] an offensive backfield formation with two halfbacks stationed close to the line of scrimmage and just outside the ends.

double yolk n [UK] [Railways] two yellow lights on a colour-lot signal.

double-bubble 1. n [Aerospace] a fuselage cross-section consisting of two intersecting arcs with the floor forming their common chord. 2. n [TV] See **bubble 4**.

double-ceiling n [US] [Prisons] placing two prisoners in a cell originally designed for one. See also **twoing-up**.

double-cream n [Cheese-making] the legal definition of a cheese that contains between 60% and 74% butterfat.

double-dabble v [Computing] to convert decimal numbers into their binary equivalents.

double-decker n [Advertising] two outdoor advertising panels, sited one above the other.

double-dip recession n [Economics] a partial recovery in the economy, which follows a recession, and is then followed by a further recession.

double-dipping n [US] [Military, Government] the concept and practice whereby a serving officer in the US military can retire after 20 years with a full pension and then start a new career, often in government, which gives him a new income and, in time, a second pension. It comes from an ice-cream cone with two scoops in it.

double-header 1. n [Espionage] an agent who is working for two employers at the same time; thus 'triple header' is one who works for three employers. These employers are all essentially on the same side, but from different and possibly rival intelligence agencies. 2. n [UK] [Railways] two locomotives pulling the same train.

double-jobbing n [Industry] See **moonlight**.

double-Os n [US] [Prisons] Kool menthol cigarettes.

doublet 1. n [US] [Crime] any fake or imitation item sold as genuine; originally it meant a glass 'jewel' with a thin layer of diamond paste on top so that it would scratch glass properly and thus appear genuine. 2. n [Literary criticism] two words which have come from the same root, but which have developed with quite different meanings, eg: 'urban' and 'urbane', 'person' and 'parson'.

doublet doublet n [Printing] any material that is inadvertently printed twice.

doubleton n [Tiddleywinks] a shot that results in two of the opponent's winks being covered.

doubling 1. n [Audio] distortion in bass reproduction, similar to **ringing**, that is the result of the motion of the speaker after the electrical signal has stopped. 2. n [Metallurgy] bending a pack of 2, 3 or 4 steel sheets back on itself, then hot rolling it.

doublings and grips n pl [Music] the odd, gutteral noises peculiar to the bagpipes.

doubt condition n [Scientology] a state of heresy in which the Church member is less than convinced of the tenets of Scientology.

dough mixer n [Industry] a machine used to mix magnesium dust and solvent to a regular smooth consistency, after which the mixture is rammed into an extrusion machine for further processing.

doughnut 1. n [Cars] a rubber coupling used in applications where only a small angular misalignment between input and output shafts occurs. 2. n [Flying] an extra large, balloon-shaped tyre, requiring very low air pressure for its inflation. 3. n [Air Force] an aircraft tyre. 4. n [Navy] a circular, inflatable life raft. 5. n [Oil rigs] the tubing ring: a steel ring which fits around the top joint of tubing to hold it steady. 6. n [Parachuting] a free-fall formation, with all members of the team forming a hollow circle with their linked arms. See also **star 2, zipper 2**. 7. n [Science] in nuclear physics, this is a toroidal (doughnut shaped) vacuum chamber placed between the magnet poles of a betatron and synchrotron, in which electrons and protons are accelerated.

douse *v* [*Sailing, Ropework*] to lower and stow away a sail in a hurry.

dove *n* [*Politics*] anyone who prefers negotiations to armed conflict in the conduct of international relations; the term was coined by US political writers Stewart Alsop and Charles Bartlett in 1962. See also **hawk 2**.

Dow theory *n* [*US*] [*Stock market*] the theory that any major trend in the stock market will be borne out by a parallel shift in the Dow Jones Industrial Average and the Dow Jones Transporting Average. If both Averages do not perform as expected the shift is only temporary and the market is bound to return to the pattern that Dow Jones does indicate.

dower *n* [*Law*] the widow's interest in her husband's **real property**. See also **curtesy**.

down 1. *a* [*Computing*] said of a computer which is out of action; thus 'take down' or 'bring down' means the temporary turning off of a machine for repair work. See also **crash 1**. 2. *adv* [*Cycling*] leaning well forward as once cycles, to achieve greater momentum. 3. *adv* [*US*] [*Lunch counter*] on toast. 4. *n* [*UK*] [*Market-traders*] this comes from 'low-down' and means inside information. 5. also **downstroke** *n* [*US*] [*Car salesmen*] the down payment on a car.

down below *n* [*US*] [*Police*] in New York City: any area of Manhattan below 42nd Street. See also **up above**.

down quark, also **neutron quark** *n* [*Science*] a type of **quark** with a charge of $-1/3$ and a spin of $+1/2$. See also **up quark**.

down through *n* [*Parapsychology*] the guessing of symbols on a pack of cards, working through from top to bottom. See also **up through**.

down tick *n* [*Stock market*] a drop in the price of a share on the stock market. See also **up tick**.

down time 1. *n* [*Business*] any period when either people or machines are idle due to human or technological error. 2. *n* [*Computing*] any period of time when the computer is not functioning, either because of malfunction or simply because it has been turned off. 3. *n* [*Military*] the time during which an aircraft is out of service and awaiting repair, replacement parts, etc. 4. *n* [*Oil rigs*] any time during which it is impossible to drill, either because of repairs, equipment changes or adverse weather.

down-and-out *n* [*US*] [*Football*] a pass pattern executed by running downfield, then abruptly making a 90° turn and running towards a sideline.

downcomer *n* [*Oil rigs*] a duct which carries the liquid flowing down a distillation tower from one level to another.

downed chicks *n pl* [*Fleet Air Arm*] aircrew who have crash-landed in the sea.

downer 1. *n* [*Film*] a story or film that ends sadly; these are unloved in Hollywood and if possible are always altered for script purposes (other than in unashamed tearjerkers like 'Love Story'). It comes from the hippie slang for a depressing or frightening (drug) experience. 2. *n* [*Industrial relations*] a temporary stoppage of work during which tools are 'downed'; this ranks as the lowest level of strike action. 3. *n* [*US*] [*Meat trade*] an animal that is too weak to stand on its own feet.

downforce *n* [*Cars*] a method of increasing the effective weight of a car (generally used in motor racing) by aerodynamic means, in order to improve roadholding and tyre grip.

downgate *n* [*Metallurgy*] See **sprue**.

downhill *adv* [*Aerospace*] said of a satellite which is descending to the lowest point in its orbit.

downhills *n pl* [*Gambling*] dice that have been loaded to bring up a low or 'down' number. See also **uphills**.

downhole *a* [*Oil rigs*] meaning in a wellbore; thus downhole tools, downhole operations etc.

downlink *n* [*Satellite TV*] a satellite-to-earth link. See also **uplink**.

down-loading *n* [*Photo-typesetting*] the calling up by a user of founts from the stored memory and the using of those founts in photo-typesetting; similarly it can be applied to the calling up and using of stored **logotypes** or **glyphs**.

down-market 1. *a* [*Commerce*] aimed at the lower income consumer. 2. *v* [*Commerce*] to adopt a merchandising/packaging/marketing strategy which is firmly aimed at the poorer end of the market, including the altering of an otherwise 'up market' product so that it will appeal to the lower income groups.

downmouth *v* [*US*] [*Government*] to use a generally negative manner of speech; it is a composite of 'poor mouth', 'down in the mouth', 'down play' and 'downside risk'.

downscale 1. *v* [*Advertising*] to make smaller, to reproduce in a smaller, though still similar version. 2. *a* [*Advertising*] of a lower income; or of a lower income than that previously mentioned, although not necessarily poor.

downside risk *n* [*Finance*] an estimate that a given share will decline in value, as well as an estimate of the extent of that decline, taking into account all the relevant factors.

down-size *v* [*Commerce*] used in the motor-trade, when (possibly less wealthy) car buyers choose smaller cars, a pattern currently dictated by the economic recession.

downstage *adv* [*Theatre*] at the front of the stage, nearest the audience. See also **upstage**.

downstream 1. *n* [*Business*] the flow of business activity from the parent company down to its subsidiaries. 2. *adv* [*Government, Military, Business*] at a later stage in a project or operation; the image comes from the flow of water or oil. Extra costs and expense often appear 'downstream' of a given progress report. 3. *adv* [*Oil industry*] referring to all services relating to processing, refining and distributing the oil; all of these occur down the pipeline from the actual well.

D

dozens offer *n* [*Commerce*] a trade offer where the ordering of a product in sufficient quantity will enable the retailer to obtain some free bonus supplies.

draff *n* [*Distilling*] the spent grain left in the mash-tun after the **wort** has been drawn off; approximately 25% of the malt and unmalted cereals are usually sold off as cattle food.

draft 1. *n* [*Clothing*] the application of body or garment measurements to a flat plane. 2. *n* [*Clothing*] a constructed plan of a garment. 3. *n* [*Metallurgy*] the reduction in the thickness of a tube during the drawing process. 4. *n* [*Mining*] See **leg** 4. 5. *n* [*Weaving*] the graph or code drawn on paper to show the threading sequence through the different **heddles** on the different shafts. 6. *n* [*Weaving*] the code to show which shafts are to be tied to which treadles. 7. *v* [*Hunting*] to sell, transfer or exchange surplus hounds in a pack.

drafting 1. *n* [*Weaving*] drawing out fibres to the right thickness for spinning. 2. also **slip-streaming** *n* [*Motor-racing*] the practice of driving so close to the car in front as to gain added momentum from his slipstream or draft.

drag 1. *v* [*Aus*] [*Gambling*] in a game of two-up, to take out one's winnings from the **guts**. 2. *n* [*Angling*] the situation when the fly is moving at a pace or in a direction different from that of the stream. 3. *n* [*Building, Plastering*] a thin steel plate with an undercut toothed edge used for scraping or levelling fibrous plaster surfaces. 4. *n* [*Cycling*] a noticeable sluggishness in the tyres; it is usually the result of insufficient inflation, thus permitting too much rubber to touch the surface of the road. 5. *n* [*Hunting*] an artificial line or trail, often a sack impregnated with aniseed or a similar strong scent, for hounds to follow. 6. *n* [*Metallurgy*] in iron-founding, this is the bottom half of a mould. 7. *n* [*Logging*] a crew that follows the logging drive to retrieve any wood that has been left stranded. 8. *n* [*UK*] [*Market-traders*] a street. 9. *n* [*Music*] a drum stroke made up of two or more grace-notes preceding a beat. 10. *n* [*US*] [*Railways*] a slow freight train. See also **hotshot**. 11. *n* [*Shooting*] the trail on the ground of a carcass that has been moved.

drag a wing *v* [*Flying*] to fly with one wing lower than the other.

drag down *v* [*US*] [*Road transport*] to shift too slowly to the lower gears.

drag effect *n* [*Commerce*] the commercial benefits that devolve upon the development of one basic item which from the beginning will require a number of add-ons, create ancillary jobs, etc.

drag the field, also **scoop the field** *v* [*Flying*] a pilot does this when he is attempting to land on an emergency airstrip, and checks out that strip prior to making the final landing.

drag the road *v* [*UK*] [*Buses*] to drive slowly on a London Transport route.

dragger 1. *n* [*UK*] [*Police*] a car thief. 2. *n* [*US*] [*Police*] a shoplifter.

dragging over *n* [*Building, Plastering*] the technique, in the formation of floor screeds, of producing a flat surface by ruling out with a straight edge, guided by wood battens. See also **tamping**.

dragon *n* [*Computing*] a hidden, subsidiary programme similar to a **daemon**, but which in this case is never invoked but is used by the machine for the performance of a number of necessary secondary tasks that do not appear in the main program.

dragon's tail *n* [*US*] [*Navy*] a sea thermistor which is towed behind a vessel to measure the temperature of the water.

drain 1. *n* [*Electronics*] the current supplied by a battery or power supply to a cable. 2. *n* [*UK*] [*Railways*] the Waterloo-City line on the London Underground.

drainings *n* [*Merchant Navy*] the ship's cook, for whom the drainings of cooking used to be a perk.

DRAM *n* [*Computing*] acro **dynamic random access memory**.

dramadoc *n* [*TV*] See **docudrama**.

drapes *n pl* [*Theatre, TV*] all studio and stage curtains, fabrics and hanging materials.

draughtsman *n* [*Police*] a criminal specialist who plans the commission of major crimes – usually large-scale robberies – but takes no active part in their execution.

draw 1. *v* [*Boxing*] to move away from one's opponent, after swaying outside and eluding one of his punches. 2. *v* [*Pool*] to put backspin on the cueball to make it move in the reverse direction. 3. *v* [*Sailing, Ropework*] to untie a knot. 4. *n* [*Espionage*] the placing of a variety of lures before a target for potential blackmail so as to put him in a position where the **stable** of **sisters** can commence operations. 5. *n* [*US*] [*Football*] an offensive play that culminates in a delayed run by a back after the quarterback has faked a pass to draw the opposition out of position. 6. *n* [*Metallurgy*] in iron-founding, this is a casting defect that occurs when the loss of metal through contraction while cooling is not made good. 7. also **blow** *n* [*UK*] [*Prisons*] marijuana.

draw dead *v* [*Rodeo*] to draw stock that is so uncontrollable that the rider has no chance of winning a prize.

draw one *v* [*US*] [*Lunch counter*] to order one cup of coffee.

draw pig upon pork, also **pig upon bacon** *v* [*Commerce*] used of a situation in which the drawers and drawees of a bill are the same – eg: a foreign branch of a bank drawing upon its London head office – and there are no documents for goods attached to the bill.

draw stumps *v* [*Cricket*] to end a day's play; the umpires remove the stumps from the pitch and lay them on the ground; this is often abbreviated to 'stumps'.

draw works *n* [*Oil rigs*] the control centre from which the driller operates the drilling machinery.

drawback 1. *n* [*Commerce*] the repayment of customs duty which has been paid on imported goods when those goods are exported again or when they are incorporated in articles which are exported. **2.** *n* [*Commerce*] the repayment of excise duty that has been paid on goods manufactured in the UK when these goods are exported. **3.** *n* [*Commerce*] the document that authorises the repayments made in (1) and (2). **4.** *n* [*Metallurgy*] in iron-founding, this is a section of the mould that can be removed to make it simple to withdraw the **pattern**.

drawbar combination *n* [*UK*] [*Road transport*] a rigid vehicle towing a separate, load-carrying trailer attached by means of a drawbar.

drawbar trailer *n* [*UK*] [*Road transport*] a trailer with axles at both front and rear, the swivelling front axle being connected to the rear of the towing vehicle by means of a solid drawbar; no portion of the weight of the trailer is imposed upon the towing vehicle.

draw-down 1. *n* [*Military*] a reduction or cutback, either in spending, in force numbers or in material. **2.** *n* [*Oil rigs*] the difference between the static and flowing bottom-hole pressures in a well.

drawdown *n* [*Finance*] the total amount that been borrowed under a given loan agreement.

drawers *n* [*UK*] [*Coal-mining*] See **pullers**.

drawing *n* [*Metallurgy*] reducing the cross-sectional area of a product by pulling it at normal temperature through a tool with a hole of desired dimensions for the wire or tube one is creating.

dreadnought *n* [*Cycling*] an exceptionally heavy-weight machine.

dream sheet *n* [*US*] [*Navy*] a form filled in by sailors to indicate their ideal choice of posting.

dreamer *n* [*Gambling*] one who sells lucky numbers, allegedly based on a power of occult prophecy, to policy game betters or horse-race betters.

drench *n* [*Farming*] a special gun used to inject medicines into cattle.

drencher *n* [*US*] [*Theatre*] a sprinkler pipe placed above the safety curtain for protection against fires.

drenching *n* [*Tanning*] the immersing of lime-treated hides in a weak acid bath, or a fermented solution of bran and water, to remove all traces of lime.

drenching the line *n* [*Angling*] See **drowning the line**.

dress 1. *v* [*Coal-mining*] to remove loose material from the coal face. **2.** *v* [*Theatre*] to fill up otherwise empty seats by handing out free tickets. See also **paper 3. 3.** *v* [*Weaving*] to prepare a loom for use. **4.** also **dress the set** *v* [*TV, Film*] to prepare

a set for filming or recording – arranging props, positioning furniture, etc.

dress off *v* [*Film*] an instruction from a director to a performer to use a particular person or object as their **mark** in a given shot; eg. 'X, dress off Y'.

dress out *v* [*Medicine*] to dress a hospital out-patient in a gown, mask, cap, and special shoes before he/she is taken into surgery.

dress ship *v* [*Navy*] to decorate the ship with bunting by day and lights after dark.

dress the house 1. *v* [*Theatre*] See **dress 2. 2.** *v* [*Theatre*] to allot those tickets that have been purchased in such a way as to make an otherwise empty theatre seem more full.

dressed in *adv* [*US*] [*Prisons*] newly admitted to jail, and thus dressed in prison uniform for the first time.

dressed line *n* [*Angling*] a prepared line which has been waterproofed, etc.

dresser *n* [*Theatre*] one who helps an actor or actress put on or remove their costume.

dressing 1. *n* [*Metallurgy*] removing any surface defects by chiselling or burning them off. **2.** *n* [*Tobacco*] fluffing up the shredded tobacco that is used in cigarettes.

dressing the loom *v* [*Weaving*] preparing the loom with the **warp** so that it is ready for spinning.

drift 1. *n* [*Audio*] the variation in the speed of a recording medium that is not greater than one per cent per second. See also **flutter 1, wow 1. 2.** *n* [*Cars*] a controlled slide in which the car drifts bodily outwards on a bend at an **attitude angle**, 20°–30° to the direction of travel, with the tail out and the nose in; it originated in Grand Prix racing in the 1950s but tyre sizes have changed and now it is mainly found in rallying and saloon car racing. **3.** *n* [*Coal-mining*] a roadway driven from the surface; thus used as a verb it means to drive a roadway. **4.** *n* [*Electronics*] the natural tendency of a circuit to alter its characteristics due to changes in time and temperature. In sound recording this can affect the consistency of the signal frequency. **5.** *n* [*Film*] an imperceptible but still disastrous movement out of position by an actor which will ruin a **take**. **6.** *n* [*TV*] the gradually decreasing efficiency of a camera; it is a more serious fault than **creep**.

drift heading *n* [*UK*] [*Coal-mining*] See **drivage 1**.

drifter 1. *n* [*Coal-mining*] a heavy percussive drill that must have some form of rigid mounting. **2.** *n* [*Military*] a parachute instructor who jumps before his pupils in order to ascertain wind speed and direction and similar variables. **3.** *n* [*US*] [*Industry*] one who runs a machine to remove scale from the inside of pipes.

drill *v* [*Surfing*] to be held beneath the water by the pressure of the waves above.

drill string *n* [*Oil rigs*] the pipe with a bit

D

attached to its bottom end that is rotated to drill the hole that will hopefully lead to oil.

drilling n [*Clothing*] marking key positions such as pockets and darts through all the thicknesses of an assembly of materials, which are ready for cutting, by using a drilling machine or some similar machine that has a hollow needle.

drink 1. n [*UK*] [*Police*] a bribe, blackmail payment or payoff for help received (such as the giving of tipoffs and allied information which is given by a villain to a policeman. Thus 'Does X drink?' means is X corrupt? See also **can I speak to you? 2.** v.i. [*Wine trade*] said of a vintage wine that is ready for drinking.

drip 1. n [*Advertising*] a campaign that covers an extensive period of time, usually twelve months. **2.** n [*Building, Plastering*] a hanging member designed to cause water running down the face of a moulding to drip off, thus protecting the wall below. **3.** v [*Navy*] to grumble, quietly but steadily.

drip it up v [*Car salesmen*] to buy a car using hire purchase payments; it comes from slang 'on the drip' meaning hire purchase.

drip painting n [*Art*] a painting technique made famous by Jackson Pollock (1912–56, and nicknamed 'Jack the Dripper') during the late 1940s/early 1950s in which liquid housepaint is flung across or allowed to dribble (by puncturing the can) on to the surface of unstretched canvas. The formal significance of the style is that it compresses the problems of drawing and painting into a single action.

dripping n [*UK*] [*Military*] a condemnation in the British Army of any weakening of morale; it comes from slang 'drip' meaning 'weakling'.

drivage 1. also **scour** n [*UK*] [*Coal-mining*] a tunnel driven through solid rock or stone to get to a new coal seam or to connect one roadway to another. See also **drift heading. 2.** n [*Coal-mining*] a roadway driven through solid coal.

drive 1. n [*Lacrosse*] a fast, hard and direct run for goal. **2.** v [*Logging*] to part-cut trees in such a way that each one, once the first is completely felled, will fall on to the next, thus saving the loggers from cutting down each individual tree. **3.** v [*Sex*] said of a pimp who forces a woman to turn to prostitution.

drive time n [*Advertising*] those periods of the day, morning and early evening, when radio advertisers can expect a captive audience among those driving to and from work. See also **housewife time.**

driven a [*Shooting*] referring to game that has been forced in front of the line of guns.

driver, also **software driver** n [*Computing*] a series of instructions followed by the machine in the process of transferring data to and from a particular **peripheral.**

drivers n pl [*US*] [*Road transport*] the driving wheels or powered axle on a truck.

driving n [*Shooting*] causing game to move forward towards the line of shooters. See also **walk up.**

drogulus n [*Philosophy*] a term coined in 1957 by Sir Alfred (then A.J.) Ayer to represent an entity which one cannot see or touch and which has no physical presence, yet it still exists, even though the lack of such presence puts it beyond verification.

drooling n [*TV, Radio*] unrehearsed talking that fills in unexpected gaps in TV or radio transmissions.

droop snoot, also **droop snoop** n [*Aerospace*] any aircraft with an adjustable nose or with an adjustable flap on the leading edge of a wing.

drop 1. n [*Building, Concrete workers*] a portion of a flat slab, immediately above and surrounding the top of a column, which is thicker than the rest of the flat slab of concrete flooring that that panel is helping to support. **2.** n [*UK*] [*Catering*] a tip, literally sufficient to buy a single drink; it is used in the North of England and Scotland to refer to a measure of whisky. **3.** n [*Communications*] the portion of the telephone system that joins the main distribution cable to the individual subscriber's premises. **4.** n [*Journalism*] a subheadline. **5.** n [*Espionage*] a term used to signify a team's success in a blackmailing operation. **6.** n [*Espionage*] a 'letterbox' where information, money, etc. can be left by one person for another person, who has been informed of its position in advance, so that they can retrieve as required and when convenient. **7.** n, v [*Crime*] a sale of drugs; or to sell drugs. **8.** n, v [*Crime*] a receiver of stolen goods; or to receive stolen goods. See also **fence. 9.** n [*Gambling*] the total amount of money exchanged for chips at a casino in any one night's gambling. **10.** v [*Gambling*] to drop out of a round of betting in a card game. **11.** n, v [*UK*] [*Market-traders*] a bribe; or to bribe.

drop a car n [*US*] [*Railways*] See **flying switch.**

drop a cook v [*Distilling*] to run cooked mash from the grain-cooking boilers into the fermenting vats.

drop a dime v [*US*] [*Prisons*] to denounce a fellow inmate to the authorities. See also **flip 4, turn over 3.**

drop a wad v [*Logging*] to place an explosive charge under a log jam, by inserting it with a long pole.

drop board n [*Building, Plastering*] a clean board laid on the floor to catch any plaster droppings.

drop dead n [*Aerospace*] the last possible moment; the absolute deadline.

drop folio n [*Publishing*] a page number positioned at the foot of the page.

drop in 1. v [*UK*] [*Surfing*] to take off and turn. **2.** v [*Surfing*] to obstruct a fellow surfer by starting to surf directly in his/her path. **3.** [*Surfing*] to slide down the face of a wave directly after take-off.

drop it on the nose *v* [*US*] [*Road transport*] to uncouple a tractor from a **semi-trailer** without lowering the **landing gear** to support the trailer's front end.

drop off *v* [*US*] [*Road transport*] to descend a hill.

drop shadow *n* [*Video, Film*] a shadow that is created either by hand or by computer generation down one or two sides of an object or lettering in order to bring it into sharper relief.

drop ship *v* [*Video*] to distribute large amounts of video products simultaneously to different locations. Such bulk shipments are intended to satisfy all wholesalers that they are starting equal in the launch of a new and popular title.

drop the body *v* [*US*] [*Road transport*] to disconnect a truck from a semi-trailer.

drop the rubber jungle *v* [*Air travel*] to lower oxygen masks into the passenger cabin of an airliner, an action taken in an emergency when the aircraft interior has become depressurised.

drop-a-batch *n* [*Industry*] a term used in the corn products industry to denote the emptying of a definite amount of corn from a storage bin into another vessel for processing purposes.

dropby *n* [*US*] [*Politics*] a brief visit made by a campaigning politician to any potentially vote-catching area: a factory, shopping centre, private home, etc; it is an elision of drop by.

drophead *n* [*US*] [*Journalism*] See **hanger 2**.

drop-in 1. *n* [*Computing*] the presence in a magnetic recording (disk and tape) of one or two **bits** that were not deliberately written to it. Often this is the result of imperfect erasure of previous data on the medium; it is generally only a problem if it falls into the gaps between records, otherwise it is automatically corrected. See also **drop-out**. **2.** *n* [*Video*] any form of graphic information that is superimposed on to an existing visual image.

drop-knee *n* [*Surfing*] a turn that involves bending both knees, with the trail leg crossed behind the lead leg, and kept nearer to the surface of the board.

drop-lock stock *n* [*Stock market*] stock in which the **coupon** value floats in line with short-term interest rates while their general level remains high, but locks into a pre-determined rate once the general level of interest starts to fall below a given line.

drop-out 1. *n* [*Audio*] a momentary drop in the signal from a tape caused by some imperfection in the quality of that tape. **2.** *n* [*Computing*] the loss of one or a sequence of **bits** in magnetic recording on disk or tape due to a fault in the recording medium. Most systems can compensate for this automatically. See also **drop-in 1**. **3.** *n* [*Computing*] in data transmission this is the loss of signals due to noise or attenuation. **4.** *n* [*Video*] the loss of video information caused by irregularities in the oxidised surface of the tape; this appears on the screen as a horizontal streak across the screen during playback. **5.** *n* [*Photo-typeset-*

ting] the loss by error of one or more pixels during the **digitis** process.

dropout *n* [*TV*] small white 'sparkles' on a television picture, the result of impurities in the oxide coating of videotape.

dropper *n* [*UK*] [*Police*] one who passes bad cheques.

drops *n pl* [*US*] [*Painting*] sheets and covers used to keep paint off furniture, etc.

dropsy *n* [*UK*] [*Market-traders*] a bribe; a tip.

drown the fly *v* [*Angling*] in **dry fly fishing** this is when a trout sinks a dry fly without taking it.

drowned *a* [*Gambling*] referring to a player who has lost conspicuously badly.

drowning the line, also **drenching the line** *n* [*Angling*] the situation when the fish turns upstream from below the fisherman and the force of the stream holds the line.

drugstore *n* [*US*] [*Garment trade*] a shop which has a smart external appearance but carries only mediocre stock.

drum 1. *n* [*Glass-making*] the mouth of a **port**, the entrance into the furnace. **2.** *n* [*Aus*] [*Horse-racing*] a tip, a reliable piece of information. **3.** *n* [*UK*] [*Railways*] a tea-can, carried and used everywhere by all railwaymen.

drummer *n* [*Navy*] the ship's bugler; orders were originally passed in ships by a series of drum-rolls, then the bugler took over the task and the title.

drumming 1. *n* [*UK*] [*Police*] the practice of thieves who visit likely houses (slang: drums) to check whether they are empty and thus ideal for breaking and entering. Thus 'drummer' is a housebreaker. **2.** *n* [*Shooting*] the peculiar noise made by a snipe during the breeding season, or that made by a pheasant as part of its spring display. **3.** *n* [*Tanning*] the tumbling of hides or leather in a drum, either in dye or solution, in order to soften or colour the material.

drunk funk *n* [*Air travel*] a pilot alert: a situation in which the cabin crew are forced to ask the Captain to leave the cockpit and sort out a problem among the passengers; it is usually the presence of an obstreperous drunk who, it is assumed, will quieten down when faced by the stripes of authority.

dry 1. *a* [*Gambling*] out of available funds. **2.** *v* [*Theatre*] to forget one's lines. See also **fluff 5**. **3.** *v* [*Theatre*] to make a fellow performer forget their lines. See also **corpse 2**.

dry circuit *n* [*Communications*] a circuit for the transmission of voice signals that carries no direct current.

dry fly fishing *n* [*Angling*] fishing with a floating fly.

dry gas 1. *n* [*Gas industry*] gas whose water content has been reduced by a dehydration process, or, as in North Sea gas, that which naturally has little water content. **2.** *n* [*Gas industry*] gas which contains few higher hydro-

D

carbons which are commercially recoverable as liquid product.

dry hole n [*Oil rigs*] any well drilled without finding oil or gas in commercially useful quantities.

dry joint n [*Computing*] a damaged or badly formed electric connection which prohibits an even and continuous flow of current; it is often used as shorthand for any recurrent and random fault within a computer for which no other definite cause can be found.

dry matter n [*Cheese-making*] all the components of cheese excluding moisture (water); it thus includes proteins, fats, minerals, milk sugars.

dry pan n [*Ceramics*] a large pan holding two milling wheels, used to crush and blend clay and shale. See also **wet pan**.

dry running n [*Computing*] using a flow chart and written instructions to examine the logic and coding of a specific program.

dry ship, also **general ship** n [*Shipping*] a cargo vessel that has not been chartered and is therefore free to carry the goods of any shipper under bills of lading; it is called 'dry' to distinguish it from tankers.

dry single n [*Hunting*] a bank without a ditch.

dry snitch v [*US*] [*Prisons*] to denounce a fellow inmate to the authorities by dropping hints, innuendoes and a variety of indirect accusations; it comes from slang 'dry hump' meaning to simulate intercourse by rubbing against the (clothed) body of a partner.

dry strength n [*Metallurgy*] See **baked strength**.

dry tree n [*Oil rigs*] an undersea wellhead where the equipment is enclosed in a water-tight chamber; it comes from 'christmas tree' meaning a land-based wellhead, the various pipeline connections of which may be compared to 'branches'. See also **wet tree**.

dry weight n [*UK*] [*Road transport*] vehicle weight exclusive of fuel, oil, water and any loose equipment; this exact definition varies from one manufacturer to another.

dry-lining n [*Building, Plastering*] the technique of surfacing walls with plasterboard instead of traditional wet plastering.

dry-suit n [*Diving*] a type of diving suit, usually made from sheet rubber, which uses the principle of air insulation to keep its wearer dry and free from cold; warm clothing is often worn beneath the rubber suit.

dual capacity n [*UK*] [*Stock market*] a dealing situation in which firms can act both as agents and principals. Prior to the **Big Bang** of October 27 1986, members of the London Stock Exchange were not permitted this dual function.

dual phenomenology n [*Military*] the confirmation from more than one US early-warning radar source of the potential threat of a Soviet missile launch.

dual satellitism n [*Politics*] the precarious foreign policy pursued by some small nations who attempt to use neutralism as a guise in which to obtain benefits from both superpowers while still refusing to align with either.

dual track n [*Politics*] the policy that NATO deployment of new weapons would proceed in parallel with the continuous seeking of arms limitation talks with the Russians to reduce, limit or even eliminate the very weapons that were to be deployed. The term originated at a meeting of NATO leaders on Guadeloupe in January 1979. See also **INF talks**

dual-capable a [*Air Force*] said of bombers that are capable of delivering either nuclear or conventional weapons to a target.

duals n pl [*US*] [*Road transport*] two tyres mounted side by side.

dub 1. v [*Film*] to add sound effects to a film's sound track. **2.** v [*Film*] to re-record or replace the original foreign dialogue with the language of the exhibitor country, synchronised as closely as possible to the lip movements of the film's characters. **3.** v [*Film*] to have a professional singer record on to the soundtrack such songs as are ostensibly performed by the stars of the film; this is especially common in India, where all films require songs, but not all stars can sing, and the invisible 'play-back' singers are as well-paid and famous as the stars themselves. **4.** v [*Radio*] to transfer a piece of recorded material on to a new tape where it will be incorporated as part of the whole programme that is assembled on that tape; eg: to put an interview made on cassette tape on to a reel-to-reel tape for transmission. **5.** also **dub plate style** n [*Music*] in West Indian reggae, this is the improvising by a disc jockey against the dub version – using only drums and bass guitar tracks – of a song. See also **toasting**. **6.** also **dubbing** n [*Angling*] hair or other material attached to waxed thread for the purpose of making the body of a fly.

dub up v [*UK*] [*Prisons*] to lock a prisoner in his/her cell.

dubbing mixer n [*TV, Film*] the technician in charge of adding the soundtrack, audio special effects, or any other audio embellishment to a visual recording.

dubbing out n [*Building, Plastering*] the filling in of hollow places on a solid **background** before the rendering or floating coat is applied.

dubbs! excl [*Marbles*] an exclamation which a player must utter to lay claim to two marbles knocked from the ring with a single shot; to claim three, four or five marbles, the cries are 'thribs!' 'fourbs!' or 'fibs!'.

dubok n [*Espionage*] it comes from Russian meaning 'oak tree'; a business or an individual who acts as a front for spying activities and/or as a **drop** for various communications.

dubs *n* [*US*] [*Road transport*] See **double 5**.

ducat *n* [*US*] [*Theatre*] a ticket, whether paid for or issued free.

duck **1.** *n* [*Cricket*] the score of zero, so-called from the resemblance of 0 to a duck's egg. A duck in each innings is a 'pair of spectacles' (the visual 00), which is usally abbreviated to 'a pair', and a duck first ball is a 'golden duck'. **2.** *n* [*US*] [*Medicine*] a urinal used by bed-ridden male patients, shaped like a bird with its long neck. **3.** *n* [*Marbles*] the target marble in the game. See also **dib, kimmie, immie, peewee, mib**. **4.** *n* [*Military*] air intercept code for: hostile forces or ordnance heading towards you.

dude *n* [*Bird-watching*] a serious, staid, experienced bird-watcher. See also **twitch 1**.

dudley, also **cherry nose, flesh nose, putty nose** *n* [*Dog breeding*] unpigmented nose colour in British bulldogs; it also refers to body colouring as a whole. Both forms are undesirable.

duff **1.** *n* [*Coal-mining*] fine coal that is smaller than 10mm in size. **2.** *v* [*Golf*] to top the ball after one's stroke hits the ground immediately behind it.

duff night *n* [*Navy*] guest night in the wardroom; on such nights duff (pudding) is on the menu.

duffel *n* [*Logging*] the personal belongings of a woodman or lumberjack which he takes with him into the woods.

duffel bag *n* [*US*] [*Painting*] the bag or satchel in which a painter's kit is carried.

duggar *n* [*US*] [*Coal-mining*] hard, unmarketable coal of secondary quality.

duggies *n* *pl* [*UK*] [*Market-traders*] female breasts.

dugout *n* [*Baseball*] the enclosed shelter where those members of the batting team who are not actually facing the pitcher or on a base wait for their turn at bat.

dukey *n* [*US*] [*Circus*] a ticket; possibly it comes from **ducat**.

dull *a* [*Wine-tasting*] lacking interest either in appearance or taste.

dull sword [*US*] [*Military*] US Department of Defense Nuclear Accident Code for: any minor, insignificant nuclear incident, rating lower than an accident.

dumb, also **adolescent** *a* [*Wine-tasting*] undeveloped as yet, but promising for the future.

dumb barge *n* [*Shipping*] a barge that has no autonomous power and must be pulled or pushed along.

dumb bomb *n* [*Military*] See **dumb rock**.

dumb device *n* [*Computing*] a peripheral, usually a terminal, which can only transmit or receive data to or from a computer, but which has no independent function. See also **intelligent terminal**.

dumb drift *n* [*Coal-mining*] a passage leading from an airway to a point in a shaft some distance above an inset to allow the ventilating current to bypass a station where skips or cages are loaded.

dumb rock *n* [*Military*] a bomb that is simply dropped from a high-flying aeroplane; without 'smart' or wire-guided directional systems, such a bomb is just a (highly-lethal) lump.

dumb terminal *n* [*Computing*] a remote computer terminal with no intelligence or computing facilities of its own.

dummy **1.** *n* [*US*] [*Coal-mining*] a roll of clay wrapped in paper which resembles a stick of dynamite and which is used as a cushion for tamping down explosives. **2.** *n* [*Commerce*] a person who poses as the principal in a business deal to mask the real operator. **3.** *n* [*Commerce*] a window display that features alluring merchandise which is not actually on sale in the store. **4.** *n* [*Computing*] abbr of **dummy instruction** an instruction that is given to the machine but is not intended for execution. **5.** *n* [*Drugs*] fake or adulterated drugs offered for sale. **6.** *n* [*Glass-making*] a machine which automatically opens, shuts and dips moulds. **7.** *n* [*Journalism*] several sheets of paper, each one the same size as a page of the newspaper, ruled into columns and indicating where stories, pictures, advertisements, headlines, etc. will go on the actual page. **8.** *n* [*Logging*] the operator of a machine that keeps the logs moving against the saw. **9.** *n* [*Publishing*] proofs and other materials pasted up together to give an impression of finished pages. **10.** *n* [*Publishing*] blank pages bound together to give an impression of the size of the whole book. **11.** *n* [*Publishing*] a fully or partially designed and/or written specimen of a magazine, advertisement, etc, which is intended to impress clients, attract investors, etc. **12.** *n* [*US*] [*Railways*] a suburban train with conventional rolling stock. **13.** *n* [*UK*] [*Railways*] See **dolly 16**.

dummy axle *n* [*Coal-mining*] a rigid axle attached to a tub or mine car which can be hooked on to or used as a bumper.

dummy gate *n* [*Coal-mining*] a road which is formed but not maintained behind a longwall face, and is used to provide material for building stone supports. See also **pack 1**.

dummy scissors *n* [*Lacrosse, Rugby*] a **scissors play** in which the ball appears to move from one player to the other as they pass, but does not; it is deliberately used to confuse the defenders.

dummy tendering, also **level tendering** *n* [*Commerce, Industry*] See **collusive tendering**.

dummy week *n* [*Navy*] the odd weeks between the fortnightly pay days.

dump **1.** *v* [*Commerce*] to sell imported foreign goods at prices far below those of the domestic equivalents. **2.** *n, v* [*Computing*] a backup of one's files; to make that backup, usually at regular periods. **3.** *v* [*Computing*] said of a machine which reacts to a problem by printing out all the avail-

D

D

able data that it has on its files with relevance to that problem, much of which may not actually be required. To sort out the problem that caused such a dump will require **debugging**. **4.** *v* [*Computing*] to print out a file or a portion of a file, or simply what appears on the screen at a given moment in an operation, irrespective of whether or not any problem exists, simply for the convenience of the operator. Thus 'screen-dump' is the print-out of a single screen of information. **5.** *n* [*US*] [*Medicine*] a patient whom no department in a hospital wishes to take on. **6.** *v* [*US*] [*Medicine*] to pass on an unwanted patient from one department to another. **7.** *v* [*Surfing*] a wave does this when it knocks the surfer off the board and into the water; the wave that does this is a 'dumper'. **8.** *v* [*US*] [*Theatre*] to return to the Box Office any tickets that have not been sold off by the agencies through which they were distributed. **9.** *v* [*US*] [*Theatre*] to sell off any remaining tickets cheaply in the last minutes before a performance. **10.** *n* [*TV*] any piece that has been prepared for a news programme but which has not been transmitted. Once rejected from the immediate schedule, it becomes a 'takeout'; if judged to be potentially useful at a later date, it is 'put on the shelf'.

dump bin *n* [*Commerce*] a free standing display rack, often holding books, a supermarket's special offers, etc.

dump on *v* [*New therapies*] to lay one's troubles on another person, quite possibly at a time when that person has no real desire to hear them. The speaker's implication is one of apology, but an overriding desire to speak out cancels any feelings regarding possible social errors.

dumper 1. *n* [*Gambling*] a better who exercises neither skill, planning nor restraint, but who plays as if he/she were simply 'dumping' cash on to the table, where it is almost invariably lost. **2.** *n* [*Surfing*] a large wave, just before it breaks. See also **greenie 2, grinder 5**.

dumpers *n pl* [*Scrabble*] the special words that help to clear one's rack when it has accumulated an excess of vowels; eg: oribi, hoopoe, balata, etc.

dumping 1. *n* [*Commerce*] the selling by a firm of surplus production goods to people who are not the firm's regular customers and at very much lower prices than the usual customer would be charged; this term is used especially when such deals are made with foreign clients. **2.** *n* [*Commerce*] severe price-cutting in order to discourage competitors.

dungeon *n* [*US*] [*Garment trade*] See **coal mine**.

dunker *n* [*Navy*] a member of a helicopter crew who is lowered down over the surface of the ocean where he operates a sonar buoy to search for hostile submarines.

dunnage *n* [*Logging*] lumber that ranks below a certain grade, but which can still be used for some purposes. See also **cull 3**.

duopsony *n* [*Commerce*] a form of competition that exists in a market where there are only two buyers. See also **monopsony, oligopsony**.

dupe 1. *n* [*Advertising*] abbr of **duplicate** any copy used in advertising, whether of the whole or part of an advertisement, a book, sheet music, a tape or film, etc. **2.** *v* [*Film*] to carry out the illegal duplication of a film negative for pirate sales, video-taping, etc. It comes from 'duplicate'. **3.** *n* [*US*] [*Hotels*] a double room. See also **box 4**.

duper *n* [*Science fiction*] duplicator, the essential machine used for the creation of fan magazines.

dupey-dupe *n* [*UK*] [*Police*] a singularly stupid member of the CID whose ineptitude will soon see him returned to the uniformed ranks. Usually a detective constable or temporary detective constable.

duplex 1. *n* [*Computing*] the ability to communicate information in two directions down the same line. Thus, 'full duplex' means simultaneous two-way communications; 'half duplex' means two way communications which are restricted to sending/receiving in only one direction at a time. **2.** *n* [*Philately*] abbr of **duplex mark** the first combined two-part cancellation and date-stamp; the heavily barred, oval obliteration which formed the 'cancellation' half is also known as the **killer**.

duress *n* [*Law*] a set of circumstances, involving threatened or actual violence, under which a person is forced to do something against their will. See also **undue influence**.

dust *n* [*Glass-making*] See **spew**.

dust defence *n* [*Military*] a missile defence system based on the theory that exploding missiles create enormous volumes of dust and debris, thus interfering with the guidance electronics of incoming missiles. To protect US missiles, devices could be exploded which would create artificial dust storms and thus interfere with Soviet weapons. This was one of the major schemes investigated for the possible defence of the **MX** missile.

dust devil *n* [*US*] [*Gliding*] a very narrow column of rapidly rising warm air which spins rapidly in a small radius circle, pulling loose dirt and dust up with it; it is visible from a considerable distance, but is of minimal destructive power.

dustbin *n* [*TV repair*] a large capacitor (condenser) used in radio and TV sets.

dustbin check *n* [*Marketing*] a scheme in which selected consumers are asked to keep all empty packages in a special dustbin which can later be analysed to assess patterns of eating, spending, waste, etc. See also **pantry check**.

duster 1. *n* [*Baseball*] a pitch which is deliberately aimed high, and in the direction of the batter. **2.** *n* [*Oil rigs*] a nonproductive oil well.

dusting *n* [*US*] [*Road transport*] driving on the shoulder of the road, causing a cloud of dust.

dusting and cleaning, also **D&C** *n* [*US*] [*Medicine*] dilation and curettage: the scraping and cleaning of the uterus.

dustoff, also **medevac** *n* [*US*] [*Military*] the picking up and ferrying by helicopter to hospitals or aid stations of wounded troops on a battlefield.

dusty *a* [*Wine-tasting*] said of a cellar-like smell, possibly because of its high tannin content.

dusty marty *n* [*US*] [*Bars*] a dry martini cocktail.

dutch bargain *n* [*Commerce*] any bargain in which one party gains all the advantages.

dutch book *n* [*Horse-racing*] a race bookmaker's or price-maker's odds line that totals less than 100%.

dutch lead *n* [*Journalism*] a lead sentence or paragraph in a newspaper story that is utter fantasy – which fact is explained later in the story – but which works to create a spurious and immediate dramatic effect that sucks the reader into the piece.

Dutch oven *n* [*Oil rigs*] the forechamber of a gas-fired boiler that provides an incandescent surface when turned on for the instant lighting of gas.

dutch roll *n* [*Aerospace*] this comes from the supposedly rolling gait of Dutch sailors: the yawing from left to right of an aircraft's nose, which transmits the same effect throughout the length of the entire aircraft. If it becomes bad enough, the plane begins to sideslip and go out of control. Dutch roll is caused either by incorrect application of the rudder, or by a lateral gust of wind.

dutch rose *n* [*US*] [*Painting*] a mark which is left when a carpenter has missed a nail head with his hammer and has made an indentation in the wood.

dutch tilt *n* [*Film*] turning the camera off the horizontal in order to obtain supposedly 'dramatic' or disorientating effects.

dutch turn *n* [*Journalism*] a story that continues in the next column beneath another story that has started at the top of the column and ended short of the bottom.

dutch two hundred *n* [*Bowling*] a score of exactly 200 made by rolling alternate strikes and spares.

dutchman 1. *n* [*Building*] a piece of pipe or duct used as a temporary replacement for a piece of equipment such as a ventilation duct, etc. 2. *n* [*US*] [*Painting*] a patch placed over wallpaper to mask poor work or tears in the paper. 3. *n* [*Industry*] any contrivance used to hide or counteract second-rate work. This includes carpentry: a block or wedge that hides a badly made joint; logging: a stick wedged into a load of logs to prevent any rolling off the truck, etc. 4. *n* [*Logging*] a prop used for a variety of purposes, such as holding logs on a trailer, preventing a saw from becoming stuck when cross-cutting, etc. 5. *n* [*Mining*] See **porcupine** 2. 6. *n* [*Printing*] a toothpick, matchstick or similar sliver of wood used as a makeshift wedge in a **form** when nothing else will produce sufficient rigidity; it is generally the recourse of a poor workman. 7. *n* [*Stonemasons*] in marble cutting, this is the inser-

tion that fills in a flaw in a slab. 8. *n* [*Theatre*] a strip of cloth used to hide the join between two flats. 9. *n* [*Theatre*] a wooden batten or similar support that helps hold up a flat.

dutchman's log *n* [*Sailing*] a means of estimating a ship's speed: a piece of wood is dropped from the bow and the speed is assessed by calculating the time elapsed before the stern passes it.

dwarf 1. *n* [*UK*] [*Railways*] a signal. 2. *n* [*US*] [*Railways*] a signal that is only a couple of feet off the ground. 3. *n* [*Science*] one of the group of smaller stars of greater density, as opposed to the larger, more diffuse stars called **giants**.

dwarf dud *n* [*Military*] a nuclear weapon that explodes as expected but, after doing so, fails to provide the degree of explosive **yield** that might be expected from its size. See also **absolute dud**.

dwell 1. *n* [*Computing*] a programmed time delay of variable duration which is inserted into the running of a routine. 2. *v* [*Horse-racing*] said of a horse that lifts its feet slowly. 3. *v* [*Horse-racing*] said of a horse that hesitates just before a jump.

dwindles *n pl* [*Medicine, Sociology*] a euphemism for those declining years when great old age moves inexorably towards death.

DXing *n* [*Audio*] receiving or attempting to search out transmissions which are beyond their normal reception area.

dymaxion *n* [*Architecture*] a term coined by the Canadian architect R. Buckminster Fuller (1895–1983), who combined 'dynamism', 'maximum' and 'ion' to mean maximum efficiency and performance in the terms of the available technology.

dynamic behaviour *n* [*Computing*] the way in which a control system or individual unit behaves as regards time.

dynamic plough, also **activated plough** *n* [*Coal mining*] a coal-getting **plough** that improves its cutting action by the addition of oscillating or vibrating motion to the cutting blades.

dynamic positioning *n* [*Oil rigs*] the method whereby a vessel is kept on station by computer-controlled thruster propellers rather than by anchors.

dynamic programming *n* [*Management*] mathematical or logical techniques employed to deal with multistage decision processes – problems that involve deciding on an optimum sequence of decisions where each decision in the sequence depends on the ones before it.

dynamic scheduling *n* [*Computing*] the scheduling of jobs for a computer on a minute-by-minute level.

dynamite *n* [*US*] [*Painting*] quick, cheap work.

dynamite the brakes *v* [*US*] [*Road transport*] to make an emergency stop, putting on every brake on the unit.

dysfunction *n* [*Sociology*] a social activity or institution has dysfunctions when some of its consequences impede the workings of another social activity or institution.

D

E

E. & E. *n* [*Espionage*] abbr of **Escape and Evasion** the infiltration of a specialist who will (1) help out or actually evacuate field agents who are either blundering in their tasks or in danger of being arrested, or (2) aid defectors and their families to escape from their own country to the one in which they have chosen to live.

E region *n* [*Radio*] a layer in the ionosphere, between 90–150 km above the earth. See also **D region, F region**.

E.80 *n* [*US*] [*Insurance*] a black man or woman; so-called from the cheap policy such clients supposedly always buy, offering an endowment at age eighty.

eagle 1. *n* [*Golf*] a score that is two strokes below **par** for a hole. **2.** *n* [*US*] [*Military*] the eagle that is attached to an officer's cap.

EAM *n* [*US*] [*Military*] abbr of **emergency action message** the authorised launch codes and signals, issued by the President or, if he is unable to do so, by some member of the chain of command immediately below him, for US nuclear weapons.

ear 1. *n* [*Gambling*] the corner of a playing card that has been bent so as to render it easily identifiable by a cheat. **2.** *n* [*Journalism*] the small advertising space(s) to one or both sides of the front-page title of the newspaper. Thus 'weather ear' (US) is a small box of daily weather information in place of an advertising ear. **3.** also **cat's ear, lug** *n* [*Printing*] the small protruding point at the top right of the letters g and r.

ear loft *n* [*US*] [*Police*] a useful rumour or piece of information.

ear print *n* [*Computing*] a **warmbody device** for user verification which works on a small microphone and sound emitter which are placed next to the user's ear; a series of clicks from the emitter create an audible response through the middle ear which, when relayed through the microphone, can be checked against a table of such clicks derived from all authorised users of the system.

Earl Scheib *n* [*US*] [*Car salesmen*] a quick, cheap paint job; it comes from the Earl Scheib chain of body and paint shops.

early *n* [*Greyhound racing*] a turn of speed in the early part of a race.

early fringe *n* [*TV*] a segment of the TV day that runs from 3.30pm to 6.30pm, directly preceding **prime time**. It is named to facilitate scheduling, ratings assessment, advertising pricing, etc. See also **daypart, late fringe**.

early warning system *n* [*Military*] a variety of the surveillance systems which are devoted to analysing and tracking any possible threat of nuclear war from missiles, submarines or strategic bombers. These systems, all controlled in the US by **NORAD**, are intended to give the US time to prepare its response to a hostile attack.

early-caught *a* [*Furriers*] said of pelts taken before the fur fibre has reached its peak development. See also **firsts 2, late-caught**.

earn out *n* [*Business*] the assessment of a firm's future earnings when a price is being worked out for the takeover of a high-risk enterprise. The purchase price will be a minimum agreed value plus the earn out.

earned for ordinary *n* [*Commerce*] the amount of a company's earnings, after tax, interest on debts and preference dividends have been deducted, that is distributed to the ordinary shareholders.

earnest money *n* [*Business*] money that is paid over at the time of entering into a contract as a deposit against the possibility of a buyer deciding after all to default on the deal – in which case the money is forfeit.

earnings drift *n* [*Business*] a situation in which a firm's salary payments rise above the national average, both for local and corporate reasons.

earrings *n pl* [*Sailing, Ropework*] ropes used to bend the corners of a square sail.

ears 1. *n pl* [*Metallurgy*] the protruding corners of a hot rolled steel sheet, before it is sheared of such excess. **2.** *n pl* [*Radio*] a Citizen's Band radio transceiver. Thus 'ears on' is the state of being tuned into the CB frequency and ready to transmit/receive.

earth art, also **dirt art, earthworks, site art** *n* [*Art*] a mid–1960s movement in which the artists rejected the traditional materials and methods of sculpture in favour of 'actual' materials – earth, rocks, turf, etc. It is utilised both in a gallery and on site (often using bull-dozers and similar plant). As in **conceptual art**, great emphasis is laid on documenting the project.

earth station n [*Satellite TV*] a communications terminal designed to receive TV programmes from a space satellite; it usually includes an antenna, low noise amplifier and a receiver.

earth strap n [*Cars*] an electrical connection from one battery terminal (usually the negative) to the chassis of the car.

earth worm n pl [*UK*] [*Railways*] drivers on London Transport underground trains. See also **sewer rats**.

earthy 1. a [*Wine-tasting*] a characteristic over-tone derived from certain soils. **2.** also **rustic, robust** a [*Cheese-making*] a description of cheeses with hearty flavours, reminiscent of the farmyard.

earwig v [*UK*] [*Market-traders*] to eavesdrop; thus 'earwigger' is an eavesdropper.

EAs n pl [*Publishing*] abbr of **editor's alterations** which are added to the manuscript at galley and page-proof stages. See also **AAs**.

ease v [*Clothing*] in dress-making, this is to join two pieces of material whose edges are of uneven length in such a way that the extra fullness of the larger section is evenly distributed along the join.

easement n [*Law*] the irrevocable right to go over, under or above someone else's property; eg. tunnelling for sewer pipes, erecting power lines, driving through, etc.

east and west mover n [*Dog breeding*] a term used of a Schnauzer whose front feet on extension are thrown out sideways, away from the centre line.

East Coast Sound n [*Audio*] a genre of speaker design, attributed to designers in and around Boston, Mass.; it is usually characterised by low efficiency and uncoloured (see **colouration**) response. See also **West Coast Sound**.

easter egg n [*US*] [*Police*] a conspicuous car that is thus easily identified.

easy excl [*Rowing*] the order to the oarsmen to stop rowing.

easy listening n [*Pop music*] saccharine music, exerting neither intellectual nor emotional demands on the listener; eg. soft rock, disco, **MOR**.

easy money n [*Finance, Banking*] See **cheap money**. See also **dear money**.

eat one's lunch v [*Business*] to humiliate, to overcome completely; it comes from the image of the school playground bully stealing and eating the packed lunch of a weaker child.

EBCDIC n [*Computing*] abbr of **extended binary coded decimal interchange code** a character set used on the IBM 360–370 series mainframe computers.

E.B.G. n [*Coal-mining*] abbr of **Elsewhere below ground** a statistical term which includes all personnel working underground but not at the coal face.

ECC n [*US*] [*TV*] abbr of **Electronic Camera Coverage** a phrase coined and used at CBS-TV.

eccentric 1. a [*Fencing*] said of any grip that is not of an orthodox and symmetrical type. **2.** n [*Technology*] a contrivance designed to change rotatory into backwards and forwards motion.

eccentric abstraction n [*Art*] a label attached to the work of a number of US sculptors in the mid–1960s which was outside the traditional geometric forms and thus 'eccentric'; it favoured ugly/vulgar synthetic materials with the qualities of flexibility and limpness, and evolved into a style that mixed **minimalism** with surrealism.

eccentricity n [*Metallurgy*] this is when the centre of the bore of a tube does not coincide with that of the outer circumference.

ECCM n [*Military*] abbr of **Electronic Counter-Counter-Measures** an area of electronic warfare (EW) that is intended to outsmart hostile EW, while keeping one's own equipment and EW func-tioning usefully and without interference.

echo 1. n [*Audio*] when recording, this is an elec-tronic device that adds a time-delayed signal to the original source. **2.** n [*Radio*] a high-frequency signal received after travelling round the world. **3.** n [*TV*] a second image, slightly to the right of the original, that appears on the screen. **4.** n [*Telephony*] an interference caused by the reflec-tion of the transmitted signal back from the receiving end of the call. **5.** n [*Cards*] in bridge, this is a means of showing one's partner how many cards are held in a specific suit. **6.** n [*Logology*] the repeating of the end of a question or responding with a close rhyme, which serves as an answer: 'What did you do when the King left Parliament?' 'Lament', or 'How did you find the dog?' 'Agog'.

echo box n [*Audio*] a reverberation unit.

echoplex n [*Communications*] a visual means of checking for errors: the signal from the orig-inating device is looped back to that device and displayed on its screen.

echt a [*Literary criticism*] this comes from German meaning 'genuine' or 'true'. It refers to genuine work that epitomises a style or an artist; the essential ingredient that makes that work what it is.

ecological architecture n [*Architecture*] various projects designed to construct self-sufficient, self-servicing houses; they are made as independent as possible of public utilities by using natural energy sources and recycling methods.

ecological art, also **bio-kinetic art, environ-mental art, eco art, force art, systems art** n [*Art*] an art that uses natural physical forces and chemico-biological processes. The artist aims to enhance the spectator's awareness of such natural processes by presenting microcosmic worlds of macrocosmic phenomena.

eco-museum n [*Art*] a French concept of the late 1960s whereby a whole area of the countryside is declared a museum and everything contained therein becomes an exhibit..

economic crimes n pl [Politics] major crimes against property – embezzlement, pilfering, vandalism, bribery, black marketeering – in socialist countries.

economic determinism n [Politics] the Marxist concept that economic factors rule every sector of society: politics, social life, arts, the intellect, etc.

economic man n [Economics] one who manages his private income and expenditure strictly and consistently in accordance with his material interests.

economic normatives n pl [Politics] methods used in socialist economic plans to ensure that the state economy remains focussed on the plan as regards both production and consumption.

economies of scale n pl [Economics, Industry] the advantages gained from large-scale production, especially when lower cost-per-unit enables a firm to offer cheaper pricing, with the potential of taking over a market.

economism 1. n [Economics] a belief in the primacy of economic factors in every area of life. See also **economic determinism. 2.** n [Politics] in Warsaw Pact countries: the concept that the workers must concentrate on the alleviation of their economic position, which will then automatically solve all other problems. **3.** n [Politics] in China: the practice of 'bribing' workers with bonuses and similar incentives to promote productivity.

econuts n pl [Politics, Sociology] those environmentalists who are considered as carrying their worries about the state of the world to an obsessional extent.

edge numbers n pl [Film] the serial numbers that are printed along the edge of film material to assist identification when editing or viewing a given section.

edge work n [Gambling] the marking of certain cards with a slight bevel or 'belly', drawn at crucial points along one edge, which indicates to a cheat the value of the card.

edifice complex n [Architecture] an obsession with large, imposing and costly buildings.

Edison medicine n [US] [Prison] electroconvulsive therapy.

edit n [Computing] one or more instructions to the machine to move data – either to insert, delete or relocate. An edit can be simply a button on the machine that will perform such an operation. Thus 'editor' is a program which makes an edit.

edit pulse n [Video] a magnetic signal placed on the control track of a videotape recording in order to determine where one 'frame' ends and the next begins.

edited American English n [US] [Education] the equivalent of received standard English in the UK: a prescribed standard of American speaking

and writing that rejects the modern obeisance to the adulterations/illiteracies of various minority interest groups.

editio princeps n [Bibliography] the earliest printed edition of a work, especially when it is known to have been circulated previously in manuscript form.

edition-binding n [Book collecting] wholesale quality binding (usually **cased**) to the order of the publisher and distributor, and used for the general edition of a book.

editor n [Computing] a software tool used to help in modifying or **debugging** programs.

EDR n [UK] [Prisons] abbr of **Earliest Date of Release** a date that is given to every prisoner at the beginning of their sentence; it is the earliest date on which they become eligible for parole.

Educanto n [US] [Education] the jargon of the teaching profession; it comes from 'education' plus 'Esperanto'.

educated a [Angling] said of a fish, usually a trout, which has learnt the ways and wiles of fishermen.

educated buyer n [US] [Car salesmen] a knowledgeable customer, not easily fooled.

educated incapacity n [Business] corporate parochialism; the desire to take the easy option in business and to continue doing as one has always done, to perpetuate accepted ideologies and systems – whether or not they actually work or even if they do work, whether or not they are outmoded – and above all to refuse to reassess any of these patterns in the light of 'reality', experience or current needs.

educational visit n [Government] the mandatory visit made to all those registered for Value-Added Tax by the VAT-man who then explains exactly what the tax is about and the ways in which one should best make one's way through its intricacies. This visit is intended less to educate than to make any subsequent prosecution legal, on the basis of 'don't say we didn't tell you'.

educationals n pl [Travel agents] free trips offered by tour operators to the staff of an agency in order that the staff may familiarise themselves with all the details of the tour in question for their presumed customers.

eeph v [Lacrosse] to scoop the ball up from the ground and then pass it.

EEPROM n [Computing] acro **electrically erasable programmable read-only memory**.

effect n [Magic] any magical feat included in a performance.

effective cover n [Advertising] the booking of TV airtime to ensure that members of a target market will have seen a given commercial on average at least four times.

effective demand n [Marketing] the willingness and the resources to purchase a product at the price asked.

effectuate v [Education] an unnecessary amplification of 'effect'/ with no other meaning than its greater appeal to those educators who enjoy such jargon.

efficiency *n* [*US*] [*Real estate*] abbr of **efficiency apartment** any apartment that offers only limited facilities for washing and cooking.

efficient market *n* [*US*] [*Stock market*] a theory that market prices reflect the knowledge and expectations of the investors. Advocates of this theory resist speculation, concentrating simply on the firm's current price and claiming that one cannot beat the market.

Effie *n* [*Advertising*] an award presented for successes in the profession, on the lines of the **Oscar** or **Emmy**; it takes its name from the abbreviation for 'Efficiency'.

effloresence *n* [*Building, Plastering*] the bringing to the surface, as the materials dry out, of white powdry deposits of deliquescent salts.

EFTPOS *n* [*Business*] acro **electronic funds transfer at point of sale** a computerised system which enables customers to have funds from their personal bank accounts transferred automatically to those of the shops at which they are making purchases at the moment when they are actually buying the goods.

EFTS *n* [*Business*] acro **electronic funds transfer system** any computerised system which enables its users to transfer funds by electronic rather than paper means.

egg *n* [*Oil rigs*] a small heavy iron tank used for the process of treating samples of mud; sulphuric acid is blown on to them.

egg and dart *n* [*Building, Plastering*] a common variety of **enrichment**: the bottom half of an egg in a cup alternates with a dart/leaf/tongue carved on an **ovolo** section.

egg beater *n* [*US*] [*Carpenters*] a small, hand-powered drill.

egg position *n* [*US*] [*Skiing*] a skiing position developed by French racers in which the chest is close to the thighs and the whole body is streamlined for speed.

eggbeater 1. *n* [*Aerospace*] a helicopter. 2. *n* [*Sailing*] an outboard motor used by a yacht. 3. *n* [*US*] [*Skiing*] a bad fall during which the skier turns head over skis and whips up a froth of snow.

eggcrate 1. *n* [*TV*] a device placed in front of a soft light source that puts a limit on the diffusion of that light. 2. also **eggshell, egg carton** *n* [*US*] [*Medicine*] a piece of foam rubber, moulded to make it resemble an egg carton, which is put under the back and buttocks to prevent or relieve bedsores.

eggies *n pl* [*Marbles*] borrowed marbles; also the act of borrowing marbles.

ego 1. *n* [*New age*] one's negative, material, ambitious selfish persona; ego is always a bad thing. 2. *n* [*New therapies*] on a Freudian model, the adult part of one's personality, the self; a large

ego, ie. a strong self-image, is de facto a good thing.

ego– *pref* [*New therapies*] the pre-eminence of the ego in a variety of contemporary therapies has lead to various self-explanatory concepts: ego-fulfilment, ego-protective, ego-transcending, ego-enhancing.

ego state *n* [*New therapies*] in transactional analysis (**TA**), this is 'a coherent system of feelings related to a given subject and a set of coherent behaviour patterns'.

egoboo *n* [*Science fiction*] it comes from 'ego' plus 'boost' and means favourable criticism or praise.

Egypt *n* [*Religion*] the state of not being of the faith.

Egyptian night-club effect *n* [*TV*] heavily scratched film; it is sometimes deliberately engineered to give the film an 'archive' look.

eightball *n* [*Aerospace*] a spherical flight-path indicator – the same shape and colour (black) as the eight-ball in pool – which is sited on a space-craft's instrument panel.

eight-ball *n* [*US*] [*Marine Corps*] a useless individual, a loser, one who, from pool imagery, is 'behind the eight-ball'.

eightfold way *n* [*Science*] in nuclear physics, this is a symmetrical pattern among eight different elementary, interacting particles with similar mass, isospin and hypercharge.

eighth card *n* [*US*] [*Military*] a programme established by the US Dept. of Defense for the development of lasers for military use both on the ground and in space. See also **SBL**.

eight-legger *n* [*US*] [*Road transport*] a rigid vehicle having four axles.

eighty per cent communism *n* [*Politics*] See **market communism**.

eighty-six 1. *a* [*US*] [*Lunch counter*] sold out. 2. *v* [*Restaurants*] to refuse to serve a customer; it comes from rhyming slang '86' meaning 'nix' meaning 'no'.

eighty-twenty rule *n* [*Business*] the concept that only a small proportion of all the items used in business – stock, outlets, personnel, etc – are really significant; ie: 20% of these items generate 80% of the total business.

EIS *n* [*US*] [*Government*] acro pronounced 'ice' **Environmental Impact Statement** an assessment of the impact on the environment of a particular advance in technology or science; often this is in connection with major governmental or industrial developments.

either-or fallacy *n* [*Literary criticism*] the mistaken conception that in a given situation there exist only black or white, ie totally contradictory opinions, solutions, etc. The concept of 'grey' tones in one's responses is rejected.

EJ *n* [*TV*] abbr of **Electronic Journalism** news-reporting based on portable electronic cameras shooting in videotape and requiring only a minimum crew to operate them.

ekistics n [Architecture] the science of human settlements: ekistics collates the relevant information from many disciplines, including economics, anthropology, social sciences, urban planning, and a variety of technologies, etc. The term was coined by the Greek architect C. A. Doxiadis, and posits megalopolises of fifty to one hundred million inhabitants, as well as ecumenopolises that stretch from London to Beijing.

elaborated code n [Sociology] a style of speech that depends on explicit, verbal explanations, and a wide vocabulary. See also **restricted code**.

elapsed time n [Computing] the actual time the operator takes to perform a specific computing task. The machine runs on **run time** or mill time, an infinitely shorter period.

elastic power n [Basketball] the right of a referee to make an ad hoc decision in a situation where the rules give no absolute guidance.

elbow 1. n [Horse-racing] a slight deviation in the direction of a race-course. 2. n [Sailing, Ropework] cables that are crossed twice.

elbow, out at a [Hunting] said of a hound, with elbows projecting outwards, who is thus not a straight mover; it is a weakness in the dog.

elective admission n [Medicine] a scheduled, pre-arranged admission to a hospital; it is the opposite of an emergency admission.

electric teeth n [US] [Police] electronically controlled radar speed traps.

electric wellies n pl [UK] [Gas industry] spiked boots used to transmit or receive signals sent through the ground in order to detect buried pipes.

electrographic architecture, also **autoscape architecture** n [Architecture] the building of large-scale neon light advertising signs, ie whole constructions that are intended to be read from passing cars and are designed primarily as pictures or representational sculptures.

electron overload n [Military] a theory that hopes to solve the problems of unexplained malfunctions in highly sophisticated electronics systems (especially in warplanes): the proximity of so many electrical circuits fulfilling different functions and the impossibility of ensuring perfect insulation means that one circuit may be activated by a charge from another.

electronic art n [Art] a variety of **kinetic art** which exploits the abstract patterns to be found on cathode ray tube or oscilloscope screens.

electronic hash n [Electronics] electrical interference that stems from computer pulses or vibrators.

electronic journalism n [TV] See **EJ**.

electronic smog n [Audio] non-ionising radiation – eg: radio or TV waves, or radar – emitted into the air in such amounts as to threaten public health.

electronic sweetening n [TV, Radio] the addition of 'canned' laughter to a TV or radio programme.

elegance n [Wine-tasting] stylish balance and refined quality in a wine.

elegancy n [Literary criticism] 'those words and phrases which the semi-literate and far too many of the literate believe to be more elegant than the terms they displace. Some are genteel; some euphemistic; some plain catachrestic . . .'

elegant a [Wine-tasting] having stylish **balance** and refined quality.

elegant variation n [Literary criticism] the need for second-rate writers, according to H. W. Fowler, to make every effort to avoid using the same word twice in any proximity, and the awkward, ornate and pretentious substitutions they are thus forced to make.

elementary cable section n [Communications] the physical means of connection between the output terminals of one device in the system and the input terminals of the next.

elements n pl [Government] the minutiae of intergovernmental negotiations; small points of discussion upon which agreement may or may not be found and which will, when worked out, go towards assembling the final document, treaty, etc.

elephant n [Weaving] a section of the **warp** that is short and has a length or two tied to it in a bunch, thus making it necessary for the weaver to tie the individual ends on the loom.

elephant cage n [Military] an enormous long range early warning antenna which is shaped to resemble a large cage.

elephant ears n pl [Aerospace] large, heavy metal discs that are added to a rocket or missile body to reinforce it against heat created by in-flight friction and to stabilise the flight orbit.

elevate v [Film, Video] to raise the camera along a vertical line.

elevator n [Wrestling] a move in which one wrestler places his leg behind one of his opponent's legs and raises it to push him off balance.

eleven o'clock number n [Film, Theatre] the finale of a stage or filmed musical: the time for the audience to leave.

ELF n [Military, audio] acro **Extremely Low Frequency** a communication frequency used for reaching strategic submarines, giving out only 2W of radio power and thus making the transmissions – which are also extremely slow – as inaudible as possible to hostile tracking stations.

elhi n [US] [Publishing] the children's market, covering consumers from elementary to high school age.

eligible bank n [Banking] a bank that has been recognised by the Bank of England under the Banking Act (1979) and whose **acceptances** are thus acceptable to the Bank as security for a loan.

eligible liabilities n pl [UK] [Banking] the

liabilities that may be allowed when calculating the reserve/asset ratio of British banks.

eligible paper *n* [*US*] [*Finance*] any form of commercially negotiable document which was acquired by a bank at a discount and which the Federal Reserve Bank will accept for a rediscount.

elint *n* [*Military*] abbr of **Electronic Intelligence** the monitoring, measuring, indentifying and analysing of all varieties of hostile communications and radar activity. Such information, gathered by satellite, airplane, ship and ground installations is referred to the National Security Agency, Forte Meade, Maryland, processed by **Deaf-smack** and used for the analysis of the Soviet 'order of battle', and the development of electronic counter-measures against hostile **CI**; then, based on this overview of Soviet 'intentions and capabilities', the planning of the US 'order of battle' and the selecting of hostile targets can go ahead. See also **comint, humint, sigint, telint**.

eliteness motivation *n* [*Business*] the desire of managers to identify with prestige organisations and their assumption, with this is mind, of a pose of great, if illusory, superiority.

elitism *n* [*Politics, Sociology*] the concept, running in the face of prevailing theories of egalitarianism, that certain individuals, objects, ideas, etc. actually and definitely are superior to others. In politics this means the rule of an aristocracy, whether of merit, power or simply wealth.

Elk River *n* [*Gambling*] three tens in a single hand.

Elmira iron *n* [*US*] [*Gliding*] a glider built by the Schweitzer Aircraft Corp. of Elmira, NY, the dominant US glider manufacturer; built of now obsolete metal, though safe and rugged, they are not regarded as giving the best possible performance.

em quad *n* [*Printing*] See **mutton**.

emanation *n* [*Military*] any form of traceable electronic pulse that is emitted by ships, aircraft, bodies of troops and their equipment, camps and bases, etc.

emancipation *n* [*US*] [*Law*] the right to assume certain legal responsibilities from which one would otherwise have been barred by age, but which, in certain circumstances, eg. the death of both parents at once, may be granted to a minor.

E-mark *n* [*Cars*] a plate on new cars showing with which European safety, emissions or other standards they comply.

emballages *n pl* [*Art*] any art works that are centred on the act of tying, tangling, wrapping, concealing or disclosing, and which use to this end clothes, costumes, bandages, paper, cloth or found objects.

embalm *v* [*Music industry*] to embalm an act – usually a pop group – is to keep them signed to your record label, but not allow them to record or work for anyone else. Any previously recorded

material will be left on the shelf, years later, as a memorial album.

embedded code *n* [*Computing*] sections of **assembler** or **machine code** embedded into a program written in a **high-level language**. Such embedding speeds up operations, reduces storage requirements and possibly provides function unavailable to the high-level language.

embedded system *n* [*Computing*] any system that uses a computer as a prime component, but is not a computer itself; the most obvious examples are advanced weapons systems which use computers for guidance, targeting, etc.

emblem *n* [*US*] [*Marine Corps*] the 'globe and anchor', the emblem of the Marine Corps; the word 'insignia' is absolutely taboo in the Corps.

emblematic art *n* [*Art*] paintings that use common emblems and thus, with a 'given' image that everyone can understand, the painter can concentrate on technique – the application of brushstrokes, colour tones, etc.

embourgeoisement *n* [*Politics*] a derogatory left-wing description of any drift towards the ideals and practices of the bourgeoisie.

emergency action message *n* [*Military*] See **EAM**.

emergent properties *n pl* [*Sociology*] three related notions in the analysis of social systems: (1) social systems have a structure which emerges from the process of social interaction; (2) these emergent properties cannot be reduced to the biological or psychological characteristics of social actors; (3) the meaning of a social act cannot be understood in isolation from the total context of the social system in which it occurs.

emily *n* [*US*] [*Espionage*] a spy who is originally spotted by a KGB Recruiter, also a US citizen, and who is conditioned, recruited and trained according to conventional principles; in the CIA a spy of this type is named after 'Emily', who worked successfully for 14 years relaying information from her job in Washington. See also **willie**.

eminent domain *n* [*Law*] the right of a government to take private property for public use; eg: for the construction of a motorway.

EML *n* [*Building, Plastering*] abbr of **expanded metal lathing** sheets of mild steel meshwork, used to provide a **key** for plastering on hollow surfaces etc. It is available in a variety of perforations to suit various jobs.

Emmy *n* [*TV*] US television's equivalent of the **Oscar** which is awarded annually by the US Academy of Television Arts and Sciences; it comes from 'immy', which is an abbreviation for image orthicon.

emotionality *n* [*Advertising*] advertisements deliberately designed to play on the consumers' emotions – nostalgia, home-sickness, sentimentality, children, pets, etc.

EMP *n* [*Military*] acro **electro-magnetic pulse**

E

the result of a nuclear explosion – the release of intense bursts of energy across the electro-magnetic spectrum. These bursts can temporarily or permanently damage or destroy all kinds of electronic equipment, both on the ground and in space and could be fatal to satellite, as well as earth communication systems. It is quite feasible that the EMP alone that results from a first strike impact would be sufficient, irrespective of the concomitant and devastating heat and blast damage, to wreck the greater proportion of all communications and render further organis-ation – defensive or offensive, civil or military – virtually impossible.

empathy n [Social work] the making of a contact at a deep emotional level and the positive effects on a social work relationship that this can and should bring.

empiricism n [Politics] a form of **deviation** from the Communist party line that consists in showing too great a respect for the facts of a situ-ation, to such an extent that one begins to reject the official Marxist position. See also **dogmatism**.

empty calorie n [Medicine, Health] foods that contain many calories but still have little or no nutritional value, ie: dry breakfast cereals, carbonated soft drinks, etc.

empty medium n [Computing] any medium that is ready to record data: blank **disks**, paper tape with holes punched ready for feeding into the machine, etc.

empty nest syndrome n [Sociology] a form of depression that can assail those whose children have grown up and left home; thus 'empty nester' is one whose children have grown and departed.

emulate v [Computing] a computer does this when it performs the work of another machine without having to have its mechanism or program modified.

en plein 1. a [Gambling] said of a situation in which a single number in roulette or any other banking game is backed by the player's entire bet. See also en clair. 2. a [Espionage] said of messages that are written or broadcast in plain, uncoded speech. See also **plain text**.

enable v [Military] to arm a weapon ready for use; especially to arm missiles with their nuclear warheads.

enallage n [Literary criticism] the substitution of one grammatical form of a word for another – in tense, mood, gender, etc – as in using the noun for a verb, or a singular verb where a plural might be expected.

enarch n [Government] a member of the French Civil Service chosen from the graduates of the Ecole Nationale d'Administration, the nation's elite forcing ground for **high-fliers**.

encierro n [Bullfighting] the driving of the bulls from the corral through the streets to the bullring; it comes from Spanish meaning 'enclosing', and refers to the 'playing' of the running bulls by

many amateurs who like to risk life and limb during this running.

enculturation n [Sociology] those aspects of the learning experience which make a human being different from the other animals; it is a process of conditioning within a regularised and accepted body of custom.

end 1. n [Railways] abbr of **end of steel** the terminal station of a railway line. See also **other end**. 2. n [Weaving] a single **warp** thread.

end around n [US] [Football] an **end run** which uses an offensive end as the ball carrier.

end, on the a [Coal-mining] See **end-on**.

end run n [US] [Football] an offensive play in which a ball carrier attempts to circle either of the flanks of the line of scrimmage.

end throw n [Coal-mining] the distance that the centre of a wagon shifts from the vertical as it travels round the corners of a curved track.

endistancement n [Theatre] a literal trans-lation of German 'Verfremdungseffekt', which was coined by Bertolt Brecht. See **alienation**.

endmark n [Logging] a letter or sign indicating ownership which is stamped on the end of a log.

endo n [Motor-cycling] a crash in which the rider and his/her bike flip end over end.

endogamy n [Sociology] the rules existing in any society that govern those who may be considered as acceptable or unacceptable for marriage within a specific group. See also **exogamy**.

end-on, also **on the end** a [Coal-mining] said of coal that is worked at right angles to the natural plane of the seam.

endorse out v [Politics] in South Africa, this is to send (an African) away from an urban to a rural area as a part of controlling the black popu-lation; it comes from the endorsement of the pass book.

endowments n pl [Finance] the current accounts of bank customers; the bank pays no interest on these funds but they are available to the bank for its own investments.

end-piece n [TV] See **kicker 9**.

end-state n [Sociology] the result, the goals achieved.

endurance n [Military] the ability to fight and control a nuclear war over a period of time. See also **war-fighting**.

end-user n [Government, Politics] those on the receiving end of all the bureaucratically and politically engendered programmes and ideas: the general public. It comes from the industrial use, referring to the customer of a line of goods or consumer durables.

end-user certificate 1. n [Military] a declar-ation that must be made by private arms dealers citing those who will actually be using their wares. This is intended to prevent such arms falling into terrorist hands but in reality is of little use against the many methods of avoiding such restrictions. 2. n [Commerce] a declaration that must be signed by the user of a licensed product – especially computer hardware or software – which is intended to prevent piracy and breach of copyright.

energy bush *n* [*Ecology*] fast-growing trees or other plants grown specifically for the fuelling of adjacent power plants.

energy park *n* [*US*] [*Government*] a concept of taking large tracts of land and installing upon them a number of powerful generating facilities so as to share resources and cut down costs.

enforcer *n* [*Ice-hockey*] a tough player who is used not for his skills, but simply to intimidate the opposition, often to the point of beating up rivals on the ice.

ENG *n* [*TV*] abbr of **Electronic News Gathering** a currently popular style of news reporting which depends on the use of small, portable, cheap, light-weight equipment and minimal crews.

engagé *a* [*Literary criticism*] this term comes from French meaning 'engaged' and is said of a writer of novels or plays who makes his/her political or social stance very clear; ie. writers who are committed, rather than simply producing art for art's or narrative's sake.

engaging force contact *n* [*Technology*] that degree of force necessary to push pins or plugs into sockets.

Engel curve *n* [*Marketing*] a graph of the relationship between the quantity of a good purchased by households over a given period and the incomes of the households; it is named after the German statistician Ernst Engel (1821–1896).

engineman *n* [*US*] [*Railways*] any employee working on a locomotive: an engineer, fireman or **hostler**. See also **trainman**.

english **1.** *n* [*Gambling*] the sliding, spinning action that typifies most throws controlled by the hand of a **dice mechanic**. **2.** *n* [*Snooker, Billiards*] the spin that is imparted to the ball. **3.** *a* [*TV, Film*] said of the **barn doors** when they are adjusted to give vertical slits over a lamp.

english cottage texture *n* [*Building, Plastering*] an external finish, with a texture of projecting daubs.

English inkle *n* [*Weaving*] a large **inkle loom**, which stands on the floor and accommodates long **warps**.

engobe *n* [*Pottery*] a decoration made by applying liquid clay to the body of the object.

engrams *n pl* [*Scientology*] memory traces in which the vicissitudes of pre-natal life are still retained. This is a borrowing of the neurophysiol-ogical term for memory traces, permanent and heritable physical changes in the tissue of the brain, posited as the reason for human memory.

enhanced radiation weapon *n* [*Military*] the neutron bomb: a version of the nuclear bomb in which the notably large quantity of radiation will ensure an exceptionally widespread death toll from **fallout**. While the bomb does not, as was

generally believed, kill people and leave buildings intact, its promotion as a new weapon by the US government managed to convince people of this quality and as such render it somehow a more obnoxious weapon than those in the rest of the nuclear armoury, any of which possess their own horrific but apparently more acceptable effects.

enjoy *v* [*Religion*] to derive spiritual comfort or to be spiritually impressed.

enriched *a* [*Building, Plastering*] ornamented and decorated, usually with carving or moulding.

enrichment **1.** *n* [*Building, Plastering*] a line of decorative embellishment incorporated into fibrous plasterwork: it includes many and various patterns. **2.** *n* [*Education*] the offering to a child of above average abilities the opportunity to learn at a level not generally available to his/her less advanced peers; it means extra knowledge and stimulation for bright children who learn the basic curriculum fast.

ensemble movie *n* [*Film*] a film in which several people star as a group, rather than the **show-casing** of individuals; such playing is often used in films that concentrate more on the concept than on simple action.

entablature *n* [*Building, Plastering*] the main beam, which is carried by columns and moulded to form the cornice/frieze/architrave.

entasis *n* [*Building, Plastering*] the tapering, with a convex curve, of the shaft of a column or pilaster.

enter *v* [*Hunting*] to put young hounds into the pack; thus it means to teach young hounds how to hunt.

enter through the cabin window *v* [*Navy*] to gain a commission in the navy through one's family connections, rather than through pure ability.

entertainment values *n pl* [*TV*] the pre-eminence, even in programmes otherwise devoted to 'education' or 'facts', of an air of 'enjoyment', of amusement for its own sake, so that no-one conditioned to the banalities of TV might possibly find themselves forced to exercise a modicum of intelligence.

entire **1.** *n* [*Dog breeding*] a dog with two normal testes, fully descended into the scrotum. **2.** *a* [*Horse-racing*] said of an uncastrated horse. **3.** *n* [*Philately*] an envelope, postcard or wrapper with stamps affixed or printed on it.

entity *n* [*Computing*] an object or event about which information is stored in a database.

entrenched clauses *n pl* [*Government, Law*] those clauses written into a state constitution which can only be altered or repealed through specific legislation designed for this purpose.

entrepreneurtia *n* [*Business*] a pun on 'entre-preneur' and 'inertia': the problem inherent in large organisations where the powers-that-be have extended to the limit their own abilities just on getting to the top and are thus determined to

E

squash the emergence of any similar efforts and abilities that might unseat them.

entropy *n* [*Science*] the mathematical measure of the amount of organisaiton that is taking place when one form of energy is converted into another; thus 'low entropy' means order; 'high entropy' means chaos.

entry 1. *n* [*Angling*] the entry of a wet fly into the water. 2. *n* [*US*] [*Coal-mining*] a series of **headings** driven in parallel and comprising a haulway and its airways. 3. *n* [*US*] [*Horse-racing*] two or more horses, usually from the same stable, that make up a single betting unit. 4. *n* [*Hunting*] the basic training of young hounds when they are first put into the pack during the cubbing season.

entryism *n* [*Politics*] the infiltration of democratic institutions by those who use this democracy to gain admission, but once in control they ensure that such democracy is no longer available to their opponents.

envelope 1. *n* [*Aerospace*] the limitations of speed, altitude and other technical assets which restrict the performance of an aircraft; thus 'to push out the envelope' is to extend these limits to the fullest extent. 2. *n* [*Architecture*] the shell of a building which gives it its basic shape and support. 3. *n* [*Electronics*] the gas-tight enclosure of a cathode ray or vacuum tube. 4. *n* [*Communications*] a **byte** to which a number of extra **bits** have been added for control and checking purposes. 5. *n* [*Psychology*] the processes by which an individual selects from the environment those aspects of life which he/she can deal with, and rejects the rest.

envelope delay *n* [*Communications*] a distortion caused by the different speeds at which electronic signals are sent out during a transmission due to their difference in frequency.

environment 1. *n* [*Communications*] basically it means place, surroundings or atmosphere, but 'environment' has become a vogue word applied indiscriminately to work, restaurants, education, real estate – in fact any subject in which the writer or speaker feels that the mundane, if accurate, 'place' is insufficiently weighty. See also **situation**. 2. *n* [*Sociology*] the whole world outside a human being's physical/psychic being. 3. *n* [*Sociology*] the physical surrounds, which are deemed to have a major effect on one's growing up and subsequent behaviour. 4. *n* [*Sociology*] 'other people', the rest of the world that influences one's own behaviour.

environmental art *n* [*Art*] structures that totally enclose the spectator, inside which he/she can move around. It is a reflection of the desire felt by many artists to escape the limitations of the single (and often small) 'art object', which is competing for attention with all its peers and rivals.

EOB *n* [*Military*] acro **Electronic Order of Battle** a top secret catalogue of Soviet radar sites along the Soviet coasts and borders and on ships and aircraft, which is complied to create a comprehensive survey of Soviet air defences for use by US bomber crews. See also **elint**.

EPF *n* [*Industrial relations*] acro **Excepted Provident Fund**. See **cloth cap pensions**.

ephemeralisation *n* [*Economics*] a term coined by R. Buckminster Fuller (1895–1983): the increasing of the rate of obsolescence in all goods in order to accelerate the recycling of their elements.

epis *n* [*Midwifery*] abbr of **episiotomy** a cut made in the perineum to facilitate the passage of the child's head and body through the birth canal; it is an operation performed almost automatically in many modern hospital births.

episodic excessive drinker *n* [*Medicine*] an alcohol user who becomes drunk up to four times per year.

epistemology 1. *n* [*Philosophy*] the theory of knowledge; how it is that men have gained knowledge of the external world. 2. *n* [*Sociology*] the methods of scientific procedure which lead to the acquisition of sociological knowledge; thus concepts based on different basic theories will have differing epistemologies.

epsilon 1. *n* [*Science*] the standard mathematical term for a small quantity; it comes from the Gk. letter 'ε' 2. *n* [*Computing*] a small quantity of anything. 3. *a* [*Computing*] very small, barely marginal. 4. *n* [*Computing*] 'within epsilon of . . .' means close enough to be indistinguishable for all normal purposes.

equifinality *n* [*Marketing*] a characteristic of certain systems whereby they always evolve towards the same final state, notwithstanding the initial conditions.

equitable payment *n* [*Industry*] See **felt-fair pay**.

equitable waste *n* [*Law*] the act of a tenant who indulges in wanton or extravagant acts of destruction (the prosecution of which could only, prior to 1873, be settled in a court of equity) unless such acts are allowed in the original lease or contract.

equity 1. *n* [*Finance*] the net worth of a firm or corporation (its total assets less its total debts); this equity belongs to the partners or shareholders. 2. *n* [*Law*] a set of general rules and procedures, based on judicial discretion, that supplement common and statutory law, with the aim of ensuring that those who have suffered some legal injury receive fair treatment and adequate remedies. 3. *n* [*Commodity exchange*] the residual value of a **futures** trading account, assuming its liquidation at the going market price.

equity capital, also **net worth** *n* [*Finance*] the total funds invested in a business by its owners.

equity kicker *n* [*Finance*] an offer of some form of financial benefit to the investor or lender in a deal that primarily involves a loan.

equivalent operational capability n [Military] a euphemism designed to cover a situation where previously ordered or designed material or technology fails to reach its specifications and thus, rather than surpassing the usefulness of the equipment it was supposed to replace, it can only duplicate at far greater (because more recent) cost, the original capabilities.

equivalent orifice n [Coal-mining] a measure of the air resistance in a mine in terms of the area of a circular hole in a thin plate which requires the same pressure difference when passing a certain quantity of air as that required to circulate that quantity throughout the mine.

ER n [Military] acro **Enhanced Radiation** the essential quality of the neutron bomb or **enhanced radiation weapon**.

erased a [Heraldry] said of a beast's head: torn off, leaving ragged or curling pieces. See also **couped**.

ERCS n [Military] **Emergency Rocket Communications System** in the event of all other US land and air-based communications systems being destroyed, a number of Minuteman **ICBMs** are fitted with radio transmitters instead of warheads. Once launched on the orders of the surviving US leadership flying on board the NEACP (**kneecap**) these rockets are programmed to broadcast from many miles high those orders that will command strategic submarines – assumed to have survived a Soviet first strike – to fire their weapons.

erlang n [Communications] a unit of telecommunication traffic intensity calculated by multiplying the number of calls carried by the circuit in one hour by the average duration of the call in hours. Thus 'erlang hour' is a unit of traffic volume equal to an intensity of one erlang maintained for one hour. It is named after Agner Erlang (1878–1979), a Danish mathematician, who created the formula around 1918.

ermine a [Heraldry] white with black spots, or tails.

eroduction, also **sexploiters** n [Film] abbr of **erotic productions** cheap, sex-based films made for Japanese consumers.

erosion n [Politics] the decline, as seen in the opinion polls, of a lead held by one party or individual over the opposition.

error n [Philately] a stamp which, inadvertently, has something abnormal about its production, but which is not to be confused with **flaws** or **varieties** both of which occur during printing due to faulty workmanship. Errors include design error, error of colour, paper error, perforation error, printing error, watermark error, etc. See also **flaw, variety**.

error box n [Science] in astronomy, this is the box-shaped representation of an area in the sky inside which it can be assumed that a particular celestial object can be found or a particular celestial event took place. The aim of astronomers is to shrink these 'boxes' to obtain the greatest possible accuracy in placing the object or timing the event.

error budget n [Military] the factors which together contribute to an assessment of the probable accuracy of a missile; these include variations in the earth's gravitational field, the technical limitations of the guidance system, the imprecision of rocket fuel burn rates, the effects of the atmosphere on re-entering warheads, the exactness of the estimations of the relative locations of launch site and target. See also **CEP**.

error burst n [Communications] a series of consecutive errors.

ersatz architecture n [Architecture] architecture that is based on borrowings from many sources, either as exact copies or in pastiche. Such secondhand creativity is regarded by some as the authentic culture of the masses and it is suggested that a new principle of mediocrity is required to evaluate it properly.

eruption n [Military] See **explosion 2**.

escalated interpersonal altercation n [Sociology] murder.

escalation n [Military] a military coinage as early as 1938, but popularised by nuclear futurologist Herman Kahn (b.1922) in the 1950s and 1960s. It refers to the concept of a build-up of military forces and inter-power conflict that leads from minor crisis through to a series of major crises and thence to nuclear war, which itself develops in intensity from merely 'exemplary' explosions, probably on theatre troops, to full-scale no-holds-barred, no-targets-excluded 'spasm war'.

escalation control n [Military] a concept central to contemporary ideas of 'winnable' and 'limited' nuclear wars: the belief that the escalation of such wars – even after the missiles have been fired – can still be held in check. De-escalation from the lower rungs of Kahn's **escalation ladder** seems feasible – the stepping back from any crisis that threatens the use of nuclear weapons is likely to be greeted with relief, albeit with the proviso that something must be done to make sure that such an event does not recur – and that 'something' need by no means be simply appeasement. De-escalation from the higher rungs, once missiles are actually exploding, seems less likely.

escalation dominance n [Military] the theory that, all things being equal, one side must possess the **capability** to mount the **escalation ladder** one step ahead of the opponent and thus reach the top, or at least the highest rung prior to **de-escalation** in the dominant position. Escalation dominance is 'a function of where one is on the . . . ladder. It depends on the net effect of the competing capabilities on the rung being occupied, the estimate by each side of what would happen if the confrontation moved to other rungs and the means each side has to shift the confrontation to these other rungs.' H. Kahn 'On Escalation' (1965).

escalation ladder n [Military] proposed in Herman Kahn's 'On Escalation' (1965) is 'a generalised or abstract scenario' (for nuclear war); this is an 'escalation ladder', described as 'a linear arrangement of roughly increasing levels of intensity of crisis', divided into 44 'rungs' which are grouped in seven categories, and move through six thresholds. From rung 1 (ostensible crisis) to rung 44 (spasm or insensate war) the progress of a putative third world war runs from Sub-Crisis Manoeuvring (Don't Rock the Boat Threshold) to Traditonal Crises (Nuclear War is Unthinkable Thesheld) to Intense Crises (No Nuclear Use Threshold) to Bizarre Crises (Central Sanctuary Thesheld) to Exemplary Central Attacks (Central War Threshold) to Military Central Wars (City Targeting Threshold) to Civilian Central Wars and thence to Aftermath.

escalator n [Economics] a clause, contract or agreement that provides for an increase (or, rarely, a decrease) in payments, taxes, wages, etc, to meet changing circumstances.

escalator bond n [Commerce, Finance] a dated stock loan on which the interest varies as to the market.

escape codes n pl [Computing] code combinations that prompt a device to recognise all subsequent code combinations as having alternate meanings to their usual ones. Such codes are used to indicate a sequence of control messages.

escapement 1. n [Antiques, Horology] a release mechanism which works with the pendulum to limit the speed at which the hands work. There are generally two types: the anchor (also called the recoil) escapement and the deadbeat escapement. The latter is supposedly the more accurate. The escapement mechanism is what makes the clock go 'tick-tock'. 2. n [Music] on a piano, this is space that is left between the hammer at its full rise and the strings; it is needed so that the strings can vibrate without jarring. 3. n [Printing] on a typewriter, this is the movement of the paper perpendicular to the typing line over a predetermined distance.

escheat n [Law] the transfer of ownership of private property to the state government in the absence of lawful heirs.

escrow n [Law] funds, documents, or property entrusted to a disinterested party and ultimately intended for delivery to someone else, as soon as certain acts are performed or conditions met.

ESI n [Military] acro **Extremely Sensitive Information** a super-secret classification level used specifically for the US **SIOP** war plan.

essay n [Philately] a design which has been submitted for a stamp but not adopted, or a design which has only been accepted after substantial revisions.

essence n [UK] [Market-traders] excessive profits; thus 'put the essence on . . .'

est n [New therapies] acro **Erhard Seminars Training** the creation of Werner Erhard (formerly John Rosenberg): an eclectic package of 'self-realisation' which is on offer to those who desire it during a course comprising three weekends of abuse, sensory deprivation and psychological processing, all geared to creating in the devotee an improved state of mind. This basic course can be followed by more intense immersion, which mixes more conditioning with varieties of game-playing and physical challenges.

establishing shot 1. n [TV, Film] the opening shot of a scene, that shows the location of that scene and the characters involved in it. 2. n [TV, Film] the first appearance of a character and the obvious delineation of that character's role within the overall plot.

establishment expense 1. n [Commerce] an indirect cost which is expended on goods, services or labour but which cannot easily be measured. 2. n [Management] See **overheads**.

esteemed a [Book collecting] said of an author who is well thought of among collectors, whatever may be his/her status among readers and literary critics. When a book is thus marked in a sales catalogue, it may be an attempt to move stock that otherwise has found no takers, by appealing to the less discriminatory buyer.

est-hole n [New therapies] a graduate of **est**.

estoppel n [Law] the insistence by a court that a party to legal proceedings who has in the past misrepresented a state of affairs cannot benefit from the true position but must stand by the original misrepresentation.

ET n [Military] abbr of **emergent technology** the increasingly sophisticated application of laser and chip technology to battlefield weapons, both conventional and nuclear; ET radically enhances accuracy, speed, etc. for weapons used by individual infantrymen. See also **VLSI**.

etching n [Microelectronics] the process of removing excess material left on a chip after the photoresist process is complete.

ethanolic n [US] [Medicine] an alcoholic; it comes from 'ethyl alcohol'.

ether bed n [US] [Medicine] a bed that is specially arranged to receive a patient immediately after undergoing an operation.

ethical relativism n [Politics] See **relativism**.

ethicals n pl [Medicine] medicines which are only available on a doctor's prescription and which are only advertised through the professional medical press.

ethnics n pl [US] [Politics, Sociology] any American who is neither a WASP (White Anglo-Saxon Protestant), a Jew nor a black; such groups tend to hyphenate their nationality, eg: Irish-American, Polish-American, Mexican-American, etc. They are referred to as 'ethnics' by politicians who have to make sure when campaigning not to insult such groups as pander to this internal nationalism.

ethnomethodology n [*Sociology*] a branch of sociology invented by H. Garfinkel (1917–) to analyse the methods used by people in everyday life to describe and make sense of their own activities.

ethology n [*Sociology*] the comparative study of animal behaviour, particularly its non-learned aspects.

ethology and art n [*Art*] ethological theory (the science of function and evolution of animal behaviour patterns), when applied to art, suggests that people have built up species of reactions to certain combinations of colour and form in the same way as animals respond to specific danger signals. Thus it might be possible to create such combinations in art with the intention of triggering the relevant responses in humans.

ETS v [*US*] [*Military*] abbr of **Estimated Time of Separation** to end one's period of enlistment, or to be discharged from a given period of duty.

eunuch rule n [*US*] [*Politics*] a clause in state constitutions that prohibits governors from succeeding themselves in office until they have allowed one further term of office to pass by. The rule was enacted to prevent governors from building self-perpetuating, graft-ridden 'machines'.

euphoric recall n [*Drug addicts*] at Broadway Lodge Clinic this refers to the subjective memories of one's addiction as opposed to actual consideration of the phenomenon.

euphroe block, also **dead-eye** n [*Sailing, Ropework*] a long cylindrical block with a number of holes in it used to secure the lines that comprise the **crowfoot**; it comes from Dutch 'juffrouw' meaning (literally) 'maiden'.

eurobond n [*Economics*] a bond, especially that of a US corporation, sold outside the US on the European markets, but which is denominated and paid for in US$ and which yields interest in dollars. See also **eurocurrency, eurodollar.**

eurocommunism n [*Politics*] the various forms of communism espoused by the parties of Western Europe (especially those of France and Italy): such variations pay lip service to the USSR, but in fact maintain policies of their own, which are fitted to the realities of politics in their own national assemblies, rather than geared to the inflexible ideology of some future international revolution.

eurocrat n [*Government*] one of those bureaucrats, culled from the member states of the Common Market (EEC) who staff the myriad agencies of the EEC headquarters in Brussels; the term carries with it much of the same disdain that attaches to its root 'bureaucrat'.

eurocurrency n [*Economics*] money, particularly US$ and Japanese yen, that is held outside the country of origin and used in the money markets of Europe. See also **eurobond, eurodollar.**

eurodollar n [*Economics*] used to refer to deposits of US$ held with banks outside the US; these overseas banks need not necessarily be sited in Europe. Such currency is barred from being re-imported into the US. See also **eurobond, eurocurrency.**

eurogroup n [*Military*] a group formed within NATO by the defence ministers of the member nations, that is aimed at creating a coherent defence policy for all the states concerned.

eusystolism n [*Literary criticism*] the use of initials as euphemisms: SOB, BF, etc.

evaluated information n [*Espionage*] Western military intelligence agencies use two parallel tables for the evaluation and appraisal of information they receive. These tables consider (1) the reliability of the source and (2) the accuracy of information. They are divided as follows: (1) a: completely reliable; b: usually reliable; c: fairly reliable; d: not usually reliable; e: unreliable; f: cannot be judged. (2) i: confirmed by other sources; ii: probably true; iii: possibly true; iv: doubtful; v: improbable; vi: impossible to judge.

evaluative abstract n [*Libraries*] an abstract of a document which comments on the value of the original. See also **auto, general, indicative, informative, selective, slanted abstracts.**

even working n [*Printing*] a piece of print which is contained in sections of 16, 32, 48 or 64 pages.

evening up n [*Futures market*] buying or selling to offset an existing market situation.

event 1. n [*Military*] a euphemism referring to the site and occasion of a nuclear test. **2.** n [*Military*] an accidental failure or breakdown of any nuclear device, including reactors and power plants.

event chain n [*Technology, Business*] a series of actions that follows the occurrence of an initial event.

event tree n [*Technology, Business*] an analytical diagram with 'branches' labelled to show any possible consequences of the event under consideration, with especial concentration on possible failure or breakdown.

eventuate v [*Sociology*] to happen, to occur, to result, to turn out.

everest syndrome n [*Research*] the tendency of scientific/academic researchers to study a topic because (like Sir Edmund Hillary's alleged reason for scaling Mt. Everest) 'it is there', rather than devoting time and talent to something which has been chosen for its potentially useful outcome.

everts! excl [*Marbles*] the privilege of clearing away obstacles to ensure a better shot.

evoked set n [*Marketing*] a small group of brands which are considered as possible purchases by a consumer.

EW n [*Military*] abbr of **electronic warfare** 'the use of a wide range of electronic systems and subsystems to conduct active or passive measurement of an enemy's offensive or defensive electronic capabilities, attack or defend against those systems, and reach tactical or strategic mission objectives using personnel and/or weapons that include ground forces, ships, submarines, air-craft and missiles.' C. Campbell 'War Facts Now' (1982).

ex *n* [*Stock market*] See **cum and ex.**

ex dividend *n* [*Stock market*] used in sales of stocks to indicate that the next forthcoming dividend is not to be included in that sale. See also **cum and ex.**

exacta *n* [*Gambling*] a horse-racing bet in which one must choose first two horses – in the order in which they finish – in any race. See also **perfecta, trifecta.**

examination-in-chief *n* [*Law*] the questions put by the party calling the witness.

exception *n* [*Computing*] an error or fault condition that renders further execution of a program meaningless.

exception principle system *n* [*Computing*] an information or data processing system that makes reports on situations only when their results diverge from the presumed results. Otherwise results are not reported.

exceptional *a* [*Education*] said of any child of above average intelligence.

exceptions *n* *pl* [*Banking*] the differences between the ledger balances of one bank and those of a correspondent bank.

excess *v* [*Education, Government*] to cancel the assignment of a teacher or a civil servant to a job when that job has been eliminated through over-staffing or re-organisation. The individual concerned remains on the payroll until they are actually dismissed.

exchange *n* [*UK*] [*Coal-mining*] the surface control centre for a mine; it is in touch with all coal faces, runs administration, bureaucracy, etc.

exchange economy *n* [*Economics*] an economy in which there is specialisation of activity and thus social division of labour; such an economy requires an area of exchange, usually provided by the creation of a market.

exchange theory *n* [*Sociology*] the conceptualisation of social interaction, social structure and social order in terms of exchange relations; it falls into (1) individualistic and (2) collective theories. (1) is generally criticised for its emphasis on the self-seeking, calculating elements of personality and only works on a one-to-one scale. (2) implies shared values and trust, the inclusion of at least three individuals and an overall responsibility to the group and to society rather than self-interest.

exchange up, exchange down *v* [*Chess*] said of a player who sacrifices one of his own pieces for one of greater value held by his opponent; and vice versa, giving the opponent the advantage of the move.

exciter *n* [*Electronics*] a small electric generator that supplies the current necessary to produce the magnetic field in another dynamo or motor.

excl *n* [*Computing*] abbr of **exclamation point.**

exclusive *n* [*Media*] an article, of news or feature material, published in one newspaper or magazine or broadcast by a single TV or radio station only, precluding any similar coverage by a rival.

exclusiveness *n* [*Libraries*] a classification principle that holds that it should not be possible to class a specific subject in more than one subject group.

exdis *n* [*US*] [*Government*] abbr of **exclusive distribution** information cited by the US Cabinet for restricted distribution to only a select group, never exceeding more than twelve people; the notation 'exdis' is stamped on special green covers used for such documents.

execute time *n* [*Computing*] the time required for a machine to carry out an instruction or series of instructions. See also **run time.**

execution *n* [*Law*] the seizure by a public official of a person's goods for the purpose of enforcing a judgement or order of the court.

executive *n* [*Computing*] a master program that controls the execution of all other programs.

executive action *n* [*Espionage*] the assassination of a head of state by an intelligence agency.

executive curl *n* [*Navy*] the loop on the topmost ring of an officer's badge of rank as worn on the sleeve.

executive fallout *n* [*Business*] redundancies among those executives whose jobs have been duplicated after a firm has been taken over.

executive privilege *n* [*US*] [*Government*] the right claimed by a US President to withhold certain information from the judiciary and from Congress. Once an alternative phrase for 'presidential privacy', Richard Nixon's brandishing of the concept in order to save himself from impeachment over the Watergate affair has degraded it for the foreseeable future.

executive relief *n* [*Sex*] See **tension relief.**

exerciser *n* [*Computing*] a test program designed to check a program or system under development for possible faults.

exex *n* [*Film*] abbr of **executives.**

exfiltrate *v* [*Military*] to move out from behind enemy lines; to extract oneself stealthily from a dangerous position.

exhaust *v* [*Weaving*] used to describe what happens when the colour in the dyebath is depleted as the dye enters the fibres.

exhaust price *n* [*US*] [*Stock market*] the price at which a broker is forced to liquidate a client's holdings in a stock that was bought on **margin** and has since declined, and for which no further funds have been made available to meet the **margin call.**

exhaustivity *n* [*Libraries*] the extent to which a document is analysed to isolate a required number of areas which can be indexed for search and retrieval purposes. The more areas isolated in a document, the greater the exhaustivity. See also **specificity**.

exhibs *n pl* [*Film*] abbr of **exhibitors** the owners of the cinemas where the films are shown to the public.

exit 1. *v* [*Cards*] in bridge this is to relinquish the lead deliberately. **2.** *v* [*Computing*] to abandon one program or mode of operation and move into another.

exogamy *n* [*Sociology*] those formal rules or social preferences compelling marriage outside the immediate group. See also **endogamy**.

exordium *n* [*Bibliography*] the introductory part of a discourse or treatise.

exotic *a* [*Printing*] said of any face of which the outline fails to conform to the usual Latin outline – it usually refers to foreign faces (Hebrew, Chinese, Cyrillic, etc), but also to some English ones.

expansion *n* [*Military*] a gradual increase in the level of military force employed. See also **escalation**.

expansion club *n* [*US*] [*Sport*] a club that has bought a franchise from a professional league (of football, basketball, etc) and which can now start to recruit players from other, established teams, and from colleges; in a sporting context, 'expansion' essentially means 'new'.

expediters *n pl* [*Politics*] the middlemen, essential to the working of a bureaucratic socialist state, who actually pull the strings that get things done; they are experts in the shortcuts and back alleys of the system. See also **tolkach**.

expendable art *n* [*Art*] works of art made of cheap, easily decaying materials; this includes all art that incorporates expendability as its essential aesthetic and thus reflects the artist's indifference to permanence in his work.

experience *n* [*Advertising*] a redundant amplification used by copywriters who wish to add some extra dimension to the description of a product: 'The XYZ Experience . . .' simply means drinking the drink, eating the food, driving the car, etc. Similarly, the exhortation 'Experience . . .' is merely a weightier way of saying 'Try . . .'

experience curriculum *n* [*Education*] a method of teaching that concentrates on giving practical experience of the ideas that are being taught, rather than keeping them as abstracts.

experience effect *n* [*Business*] the fact that the longer one works at a job, the less each item should cost to manufacture: the cost of industrial tasks declines as the experience accumulates in performing them.

experiential *a* [*New therapies*] a key word in all **new therapies**: only through experience (which differs according to the discipline involved) can the individual grow (a state which also varies according to the demands and rewards of the therapy involved).

experiential referent *n* [*Sociology*] for those who have no knowledge or experience – outside the confines of their own experience – this is a way of using that personal experience as a basis for all one's judgements.

experimental aesthetics *n* [*Art*] a branch of psychology which attempts to evaluate empirical 'truths' about art, its appeal, and its various elements and generally to investigate its cultural values.

expert system *n* [*Computing*] a computer system which reflects the decision-making processes of a human specialist. The system embodies organised knowledge of a defined area of expertise and is intended to work as a skilful, cost-effective consultant. Such a system comprises a knowledge base, the distilled and codified knowledge of the human expert or experts, often the result of years of sophisticated experience; an inference machine, the program which drives the system; an explanation program, which 'queries' the rules laid down by the expert and marks them acceptable to the user; a knowledge refining program which enables the expert to update the knowledge base; and a natural language processor, which enables the user to communicate with the machine in a natural manner. While expert systems are currently limited, the **fifth generation** of artificial intelligence (**AI**) computers should make their deployment and development far greater. See also **fuzzy logic, knowledge engineering**.

expiries *n pl* [*Advertising*] readers who have once subscribed to a magazine but no longer do so.

ex-pit transaction *n* [*US*] [*Stock market*] the purchase of commodities off the floor of an exchange where they would more usually be traded.

explanans/explanandum *n* [*Sociology*] in any explanation, that which is to be explained is the explanandum; what actually makes up the explanation is the explanans.

explication *n* [*Government*] a word particularly popular among EEC bureaucrats: it is a detailed explanation, probably from the French 'explication de texte' which means a detailed examination of a literary work.

exploitation 1. *n* [*Film*] all phases of publicity, advertising and promotion marketing the finished product. **2.** *n* [*Film*] the making of films that depend on a specific topic – aimed directly at a specific audience – which is worked hard for a number of decreasingly successful attempts, and then abandoned, eg: **sexploitation, blaxploitation**. Such films lack any intrinsic value other than the possibility of spectacularly vulgar promotional techniques.

exploitation picture *n* [*Film*] See **exploitation 2**.

explore *v* [*Medicine*] to perform an exploratory operation.

explosion 1. *n* [*Industry*] the analysis of a manufacturing assembly into its component parts. **2.** *n*

E

[*Military*] the sudden transformation of a local war into a central war by the use of nuclear weapons.

explosion shot *n* [*Golf*] a shot that 'explodes' the ball from where it has been lodged in a sand bunker.

explosion wipe *n* [*TV*] a **wipe** that bursts out from the centre of the screen, exploding over the picture it replaces.

explosive fringe *n* [*Coal-mining*] See **flammable fringe**.

exponential smoothing *n* [*Business, Marketing*] a forecasting technique which aims at added accuracy by weighting its results with regard to significant trends within the area under consideration; it is popularly used for inventory and production control, forecasts of margins and other financial data.

exporting unemployment *n* [*Economics*] See **beggar-my-neighbour policy**.

exposure *n* [*Pop music*] the promotion of the **product**; the musical equivalent of a film's **exploitation**.

exposure latitude *n* [*Photography*] the range of the amount of light necessary to produce an acceptable image on film.

exposure weights *n pl* [*Marketing*] the measure of the value of the exposure of one advertisement when carried or broadcast in a variety of different media.

extend *v* [*Military*] to re-enlist for one or two years beyond the original period of one's service.

extended problem solving *n* [*Marketing*] a buying situation in which the buyer has no knowledge or experience of the product category.

extended seasonal slump *n* [*Economics*] a euphemism for any form of economic decline. See also **crabwise movement**.

extender oil *n* [*Oil rigs*] an oil used to alter the physical characteristics of synthetic rubber.

extension 1. *n* [*Ballet*] the stretching of the leg at an angle from the body. 2. *n* [*Horse riding*] the utmost lengthening of a horse's stride at a particular pace. 3. *n* [*Gambling*] the maximum sum of money a bookmaker will take on at his own risk for each event; any sums greater than his own limit will be 'laid off' with fellow bookies.

external, internal upset *n* [*Metallurgy*] See **staving**.

externalisation *n* [*US*] [*Stock market*] the transaction of share deals by transmitting the orders to buy and sell on the floor of the Exchange, rather than through a broker's office.

externalise labour costs *v* [*Economics*] to persuade a customer to perform part of a required job him/herself, usually in the form of 'do-it-yourself'; in the retail trade, this encourages the proliferation of self-service garages, supermarkets, etc.

externalities *n pl* [*Economics*] the direct effect of the actions of one producer or consumer on other products or consumers.

externality *n* [*Government*] anything that occurs for which plans have not been prepared in advance; thus it is a surprise and usually an unpleasant one. The usual method of dealing with an externality is to internalise it, by creating a plan that will deal with it in the case of its reoccurrence. This does not, however, preclude the appearance of other externals.

exteropsychic functioning *n* [*New therapies*] in transactional analysis (**TA**) this is the concept of the **parent**, the judgemental part of one's being.

extra 1. *n* [*Film, Theatre, TV*] a crowd actor who has no dialogue other than, possibly, '**rhubarb**'. 2. *a* [*Printing*] said of any considerable modification from a standard.

extra board *n* [*US*] [*Railways*] a list of firemen who work in rotation, filling vacant jobs in all classes of service.

extra duck *n* [*UK*] [*Catering*] casual waiting staff recruited for special occasions, eg. banquets, weddings, etc.

extracode *n* [*Computing*] a sequence of machine code instructions that are stored within the operating system and which are intended for use in simulating hardware functions.

extract *n* [*Wine-tasting*] soluble solids (usually excluding sugar) which add to **body** and substance.

extrados *n* [*Building, Plastering*] the outer, upper or back curve of an arch.

eye 1. *n* [*Angling*] the metal or gut loop through which the gut is passed to make fast the fly on the cast. 2. *n* [*Coal-mining*] the top or mouth of a shaft. 3. *n* [*Coal-mining*] the central or intake opening of a radial flow fan. 4. *n* [*Farming*] used in the phrase 'the eye' to refer to the ability of a sheepdog to exert control over his sheep simply by the look in his eye. 5. *n* [*Glass-making*] a circular opening in the floor of a melting chamber through which the gas and air enter. 6. *n* [*Printing*] the small blank space enclosed in the curve of a lower-case 'e'. 7. *n* [*Sailing, Ropework*] a spliced, seized (see **seizing**) or knotted loop.

eye dialect *n* [*Literary criticism*] the attempt to write spoken words in the dialect or accent of the person who is supposedly delivering them; this usually relies on pseudophonetic spelling which rarely even approximates to reality.

eyeballs *n pl* [*Aerospace*] the various positions of the eyeballs when travelling in space have created a variety of astronaut shorthand, ie: 'eyeballs down': suffering severe positive acceleration; 'eyeballs up': under negative G-force, downward acceleration; 'eyeballs in': acceleration from behind when upright, from below when prone; 'eyeballs out': deceleration when upright.

eyebrow *n* [*US*] [*Journalism*] See **kicker 3**.

eye-droppin's! *excl* [*Marbles*] a cry that permits

the player to drop his **shooter** vertically from his eye in an attempt to hit his opponent's shooter.

eyes *n pl* [*Cheese-making*] the holes found in some cheese, especially Swiss and Gruyère; they are formed by the release of gases during the curing process.

eyes only *a* [*Government*] a notation on secret or sensitive classified documents that precedes the name of the person(s) for whose eyes and for none other it is destined. See also **need-to-know**.

eye-word *n* [*Literary criticism*] a word that one seldom hears spoken and which is thus likely to be mispronounced.

F

F region *n* [*Radio*] that part of the ionosphere that lies beyond 150km above the earth. See also **D region, E region**.

faan *n* [*Science fiction*] one whose interests lie in fans and their activities rather than in the science fiction they enjoy. See also **fakefan**.

fabulous invalid, the *n* [*US*] [*Theatre*] the stage itself, which survives endless setbacks and gloomy prophesies of imminent demise yet, like an old trouper, invalid or not, keeps coming back.

face 1. *n* [*Coal-mining*] any surface exposed for the excavation of coal; it can be extended to include the supported area in the vicinity of the area where coal is worked. **2.** *n* [*Ice-hockey*] the start of a match: the referee drops the puck between two opposing players who attempt to hit it first; the play is restarted in this way after any stoppages during the game. **3.** *n* [*US*] [*Painting*] the casing that surrounds a window.

face chain *n* [*UK*] [*Coal-mining*] the conveyor belt that runs along the coalface and carries the freshly cut coal to the stage loader chain and then on to the main conveyor out of the mine.

face room *n* [*Coal-mining*] the total length or productive capacity of all faces from which coal can be obtained in a mine.

face washing *n* [*Commerce*] the indication, after a subsidiary company is acquired by a parent company that the financing costs of the operation, plus the possible injection of further development capital, will be approximately matched by the income generated by the subsidiary.

faces 1. *n pl* [*UK*] [*Police*] a general reference to any known criminals. See also **bodies 3. 2.** *n pl* [*UK*] [*Police*] taxi-drivers who refuse any but high-paying fares are known selectively as 'airport faces', 'abortion faces', 'nightclub faces' etc.

facetiae *n pl* [*Book collecting*] exotica, especially erotica and pornography. See also **curiosa**.

facial trauma *n* [*Medicine*] the psychological trauma suffered by anyone enduring a badly deformed facial appearance that may eventually require surgery to put it right.

facilitator *n* [*New therapies*] a member of a Rogerian group who quickly suppresses anyone who attempts to offer a less than completely enthusiastic statement by smothering them with calming embraces and a general expounding of the group philosophy, thus 'facilitating' their acceptance of the therapeutic 'party line'.

facilities house *n* [*Media*] a company which offers all the facilities required to make a programme or a film other than the actual producing, writing, directing, cinematography, and so on, ie: costumes, cameras, editing suites, slide-making equipment, etc.

facility trip *n* [*Politics*] trips, usually on expenses, which are taken by politicians 'to explore local conditions', get a 'hands-on experience of the problem' etc; they are dismissed as 'junkets' by those who either failed to make the party or who genuinely despise such freeloading.

facility visit *n* [*Public relations*] a press visit for the purpose of interviews or picture-taking which is arranged, together with plenty of food and drink, to benefit those individual companies or product promotions that a PR man wishes to push.

facing *n* [*Clothing*] a separate piece of material used as a covering on specific areas of a garment, eg: a lapel.

factage *n* [*Commerce*] the cost of postage on small parcels or packets.

fact-finding *n* [*US*] [*Law*] in the family court, this is a euphemism for the trial in this US version of the UK juvenile court.

facticity *n* [*Sociology*] the way in which the external social and natural world appears to individuals as solid, taken-for-granted and 'thing-like'.

faction *n* [*Publishing*] a work of fiction that derives with only minimal alterations from events that actually happened. It is the printed version of a TV **docudrama**.

factography *n* [*Art*] the method whereby a photographer or artist, operating more as a journalist, presents as 'art' a selection of pictures and information (always bearing a political import) which is reminiscent of the 'dialectical documentary' style of the Novy Lef group in the 1920s.

factoid *n* [*Media*] a published statement that takes on the reality of 'fact' purely by virtue of its having been published and thus assimilated into the public consciousness. It often refers to unsubstantiated events that have developed into modern myth. It was coined in 1973 by Norman Mailer as a defence of such factoids in his heavily criticised 'biography' of Marilyn Monroe.

factor analysis *n* [*Sociology*] a means of looking at survey data to identify any common components or factors underlying a set of items.

factoring *n* [*Data security*] the working out of the two prime numbers that are multiplied together in the Rivest-Shamir-Adelman (RSA) method of public key cryptography. Assuming two 100-digit prime numbers, combined in a 200-digit number, even the fastest of contemporary computers would take several billion years to factor out the two original numbers that have been used.

factory **1.** *n* [*Drugs*] a distribution point for the wholesaling of narcotics. **2.** *n* [*UK*] [*Police*] the police station, especially when it is still housed in one of the gloomy Victorian relics with their implications of dark, satanic imprisonment.

fadding *n* [*Painting*] the application of shellac lacquers using a pad known as the 'fad'.

fade **1.** *n* [*Cars*] partial or even total failure of the brakes due to overheating which is most likely to occur when braking at speed on a long down gradient when the brake pads grow so hot that they lose their coefficient of friction. It comes from 'brake fade'. **2.** *n* [*Golf*] a controlled curve moving from left to right when hit by a right-hander and from right to left when hit by a left-hander. **3.** *n* [*Radio*] the gradual reduction of the volume, using a fader control. **4.** *n* [*TV, Film*] the gradual reduction of the brightness of the picture or the volume of the sound.

fade out [*US*] [*Military*] US Dept. of Defense Level 1 War readiness: every commander is empowered to act for himself in the ultimate state of nuclear combat; first and retaliatory and possibly further strikes have been fired, communications have probably broken down and no central command structure exists.

faded giant [*US*] [*Military*] US Dept. of Defense Nuclear Accident Code for: an accident within a nuclear reactor.

fade-in *n* [*TV*] the slow emergence of a scene from blackness. See also **fade-out 2**.

fade-out **1.** *n* [*Radio*] intermittent, temporary loss of sound through atmospheric disturbance. **2.** *n* [*TV, Film*] the gradual disappearing of a picture into blackness.

fader *n* [*Film, Audio, Video*] any lever or control, operated manually, which is used to modify the level of sound or the visibility or brightness of a picture.

fadge *n* [*Hunting*] a slow pace on horseback, neither a walk nor a trot, which is suitable for accompanying hounds.

FAF *n* [*UK*] [*Military*] acro the **Fuck About Factor** a replacement for what used to be known as 'bull': the tedious, repetitive side of peacetime soldiering – parades, route marches, cleaning kit, etc.

fafia *part. phr* [*Science fiction*] acro **forced away from it all** withdrawal from the activities of science fiction fandom through the pressures of the outside world. See also **dafia, gafia**.

fag **1.** *v* [*Sailing, Ropework*] to fray. **2.** *n* [*Shooting*] red deer: a small stag which accompanies a senior animal. This comes from public school use.

fag end *n* [*Sailing, Ropework*] the unfinished end of a rope, left after manufacture.

faible, also **foible** *n* [*Fencing*] this comes from Fr. meaning weak; it is the 'weak' or lower half of a foil, nearest to the point. See also **forte**.

fail *v* [*Stock market*] said of a stockbroker or his firm that fails to deliver promised stocks at a given time.

fail position *n* [*Stock market*] securities that remain undelivered when the seller fails to deliver them to their broker so that they may be transferred to the buyer; given the large and continuous volume of trading carried out by a given broker, the phrase usually refers to a situation in which there are owed to that broker more securities in outstanding sell transactions than are due in outstanding buy transactions.

fail up *v* [*Religion*] to cease to be a member of the faith.

fail-safe **1.** *n* [*Computing*] a computer system that does not show an error despite the occurrence of a single fault. **2.** *n* [*Aerospace, Industry*] an in-built mechanism that should in theory take over in the case of mechanical breakdown and restore the system to safety. **3.** *n* [*Military*] the US strategic bomber forces have a fail-safe point whereby if alerted they fly only so far towards their targets and then **loiter** there until a code is issued ordering them either to proceed or to return to base. This makes bombers, already the slowest means of weapons delivery, also the safest since, unlike them, ground or submarine launched **ICBMs** cannot be recalled if the emergency turns out not to have lead to war. **4.** n [*International relations*] the concept of establishing a series of precautions, agreed by both sides, that will ensure that a nuclear war cannot be triggered 'by mistake' or by some lone psychotic. See also **two-man rule**.

fail-safe braking n [*UK*] [*Road haulage*] a system that ensures, in the event of brake failure, the automatic application of the vehicle's brakes; it usually involves the use of air pressure to hold the brakes off against a strong spring pressure.

failsoft n [*Computing*] the ensuring that while one part of the computer's mechanism may be faulty, this breakdown does not destroy the overall capacity to work. Full efficiency will obviously be impaired, but it will still be possible to run programs, and no data will be lost, etc.

fair **1.** a [*Book collecting*] the dealer's lowest category which in fact means a book is barely worth purchasing; poor. **2.** v [*Aerospace*] to smooth down the exposed parts of the aircraft to reduce air resistance to a minimum. **3.** v [*Film*] in animation, to make sure that all movements blend together smoothly, so that there are no jumps or jerks in the film. It comes from the traditional use of **fair** in the aerospace industry. **4.** v [*Sailing, Ropework*] to smooth out, to even up a knot, splice or **sinnet**.

fair list (*UK*), **union label** (*US*) n [*Industrial relations*] the opposite of a black list: those individuals and companies with whom union agreements have been made and which are therefore acceptable for trading without any interference from the unions.

fairbank **1.** v [*Gambling*] used of the dealer or bank when they make a cheating move on behalf of a player to encourage him/her to bet more heavily and thus to stay in the game longer; at this point such moves will be directed against the player, who will finally lose even more money. **2.** v [*Gambling*] to let a player win a prize or a bet; the implication being that such fair play is absolutely at the discretion of the game's controller and has nothing to do with the run of play. **3.** n [*Gambling*] a method of cheating at cards whereby the victim is allowed, temporarily, to win.

fair-faced a [*Building, Plastering*] a descriptive term applied to smooth-finished concrete.

fairground n [*US*] [*Cattlemen*] this means the roping of an animal by throwing the rope over its back while it is still running, then throwing it to the ground with sufficient force to keep it from moving before it can be tied.

fair-leaders n pl [*Sailing, Ropework*] boards lashed in the rigging with holes to control the smooth running of the rigging.

fairness doctrine, also **equal time** n [*US*]

[*TV, Radio*] the principle in radio and TV which permits rival points of view to make themselves heard or seen when dealing with controversial issues. See also **balance 2**.

fairweather shot n [*Shooting*] anyone who prefers not to go out in bad weather and as such is considered a weakling by his heartier brethren.

fairy money n [*Advertising*] this comes from the 'money-off' coupons that are attached to such household products as 'Fairy Liquid'; it is the money that manufacturers reimburse to the retailer who accepts such coupons from his customers.

fairyland n [*UK*] [*Railways*] a multiple-aspect colour light signal.

fake **1.** v [*UK*] [*Market-traders*] to take a tip or bribe. **2.** v [*Music*] in jazz, a musician does this when he/she improvises a passage. **3.** v [*Sex*] said of a homosexual prostitute who 'fakes X out' in order to induce the client to pay over more money in the expectation of enjoying some special pleasure: exceptional sexual 'equipment', etc.

fake book n [*Music*] all illegal publication of otherwise copyrighted musical melodies from popular music, which is plagiarised and sold to musicians.

fake the marks v [*Stock market*] used of shares which change hands at fictitious prices which are announced in order to trick a broker's rivals.

fakefan n [*Science fiction*] someone interested in the activities of science fiction fans, but not in the science fiction itself. See also **faan**.

fakems **1.** n pl [*UK*] [*Market-traders*] any form of rubbish or trash on the stall; fake medicines for sale; thus 'to put the fakems on', 'to get the fakems on' means to peddle trashy, fake goods or remedies. **2.** n pl [*UK*] [*Market-traders*] cosmetics, make-up; thus 'to put/get the fakems on' means to apply one's make-up.

Falklands factor n [*UK*] [*Politics*] the phenomenon that followed the Falklands War (1982) when an otherwise unpopular Conservative Government, and in particular the Prime Minister Mrs Thatcher, could for a while do no wrong (despite no apparent alleviation of the catastrophic economic situation) since it was under their/her leadership that the war had been won. This factor is largely historical today, although it may have helped win the Tories the 1983 election.

fall **1.** n [*Sailing, Ropework*] the whole rope of a tackle. **2.** n [*Sailing, Ropework*] the hauling end only of a tackle. **3.** n [*Clothing*] the section of a collar between the crease and the outer edge.

fall away v [*Religion*] to fall from grace, to allow one's fervour to diminish; see I Corinthians 10:12.

fall down v [*Journalism*] said of a reporter who fails to obtain the assigned story.

fall line n [*Skiing*] the line a ball rolling freely downhill would take; thus this is the shortest route down a slope.

fall out of the boat *v* [*Navy*] to become unpopular.

fallacy of accident *n* [*Literary criticism*] the fallacy of using a general truth as the basis of one's argument regarding a specific ('accidental') case.

fallacy of composition *n* [*Literary criticism, Philosophy*] the fallacy of assuming that what may well be true of one or more individuals in a group can by definition be extended to embrace the entire group. See also **fallacy of division**.

fallacy of division *n* [*Literary criticism, Philosophy*] the fallacy of assuming that what applies to an entire group can therefore be extended to each of the individuals or parts that compose it. See also **fallacy of composition**.

fallacy of the beard *n* [*Literary criticism, Philosophy*] the fallacy of arguing by grasping at one aspect or stage of a situation and using that as an attempt to fix statically a role or image of the whole situation when in fact it is still in flux and as such is not susceptible to a final assessment.

fallback 1. *n* [*Industrial relations*] something available in an emergency; something that can be relied on if/when all else fails; it is used especially of a minimum wage that will still be paid even if work is (temporarily) unavailable. 2. *n* [*Military*] the material – earth, remains of buildings, etc. – that is blown into the air by a nuclear explosion and ultimately returns to earth in the form of radioactive fallout.

fallback position *n* [*Politics*] a tacitly accepted position to which a politician or negotiator accepts, from the outset of a new policy or of talks, that he will be willing, if needs be, to retreat.

faller *n* [*Logging*] a logger who actually fells the trees. See also **set 7**.

fallibilism *n* [*Science*] a term coined by the mathematician Charles Pierce (1839–1914): the concept that in science (or in everyday life) there are no beliefs so absolute that they might not in fact be proven fallible.

falling leaf *n* [*Aerospace*] an aerobatic manoeuvre in which an aircraft is deliberately stalled, then allowed to sideslip while losing height until the power is regained. It slips from side to side, like a falling leaf.

fall-off *n* [*Photography*] the lack of a sharp image at the edge of a print, caused by a variety of defects in the lens.

fallout 1. *n* [*Espionage*] See **blowback**. 2. *n* [*Military*] the radioactive refuse of a nuclear bomb explosion and the process of the deposition of such refuse on the surrounding land and human and animal population. The extent of this fallout differs as to the type of explosion – an airburst will be limited as to local effects, but with the greater dispersal into the atmosphere it will have far greater potential as a global pollutant. 3. *n* [*Politics*] by extension from the military use of the term: any unpleasant or unexpected side-effects that follow a political decision, statement or other action.

falls 1. *n pl* [*Painting*] the block and tackle from which are suspended the **stage** or painter's cradle. 2. also **autumns** *n pl* [*Furriers*] furs taken in the autumn, slightly before fur fibre reaches a peak, but sometimes offering a better colour tone than **firsts**. See also **early-caught**.

false bedding *n* [*Geology*] laminations, in a bed of sedimentary rock, which run at an angle to the general layers of stratification.

false comparative *n* [*Linguistics*] See **absolute word**.

false dilemma *n* [*Literary criticism*] See **either-or fallacy**.

false drop *n* [*Computing*] irrelevant material that has been extracted from a database during a search, due to the use of inappropriate search directions. See also **noise 1**.

false friend *n* [*Literary criticism*] a foreign word or phrase which appears in the original to be similar to a familiar English equivalent, but which has a separate meaning; thus any verbal analogy that is semantically deceptive.

false illiteracy *n* [*Literary criticism*] the misspelling of various standard words, when attempting to write 'dialogue or speeches in a pseudo-phonetic manner. This is pointless since it still suggests the same pronunciation as does the original word: 'wimmin', 'duz', etc.

false image *n* [*Photography*] the result of using a defective lens: a secondary image appears on the photographic plate or paper in addition to the desired one. See also **ghost 2**.

false lead *n* [*Journalism*] a misleading opening sentence or paragraph, a topical red herring.

false market *n* [*Commerce*] a market for goods in which either buyers or sellers are acting on false information, eg: buyers pay high prices when they believe in error that a given commodity is scarce when in fact it is plentiful.

false move *n* [*Film*] an unplanned or erroneous action made by an actor during a shot; such a move may confuse a technician into thinking it was a proper cue and he will then compound the error by making his own false move.

false part *n* [*Metallurgy*] in iron founding, this is an additional piece or part constructed on a pattern, possibly to accommodate the removable section of the mould. See also **drawback 4**.

false positive 1. *n* [*Medicine*] a diagnosis that states incorrectly that a patient has a particular disease. Thus 'false negative' is a diagnosis that states incorrectly that a patient is free of a particular disease. 2. *n* [*Criminology*] a prediction by an expert of future criminal activities that turns out to be wrong.

false retrievals *n pl* [*Libraries*] references on a given topic that have been selected – often after a computer search – and are not pertinent to the

F

subject in hand but which, because of the filing system, emerge from the database nonetheless.

false sponsors *n pl* [*Espionage*] false **covers** or **leads** or similar blind alleys designed to confuse the opposition.

false titles *n* [*Literary criticism*] See **coined titles**.

false-flag recruit *n* [*Espionage*] an agent who is led to believe that he/she is working for one country or political group while having in fact been recruited by the other.

falsework, also **formwork** *n* [*Building, Concrete workers*] temporary wood supports that hold the still-wet concrete in place around the reinforcing rods.

falsificationism *n* [*Sociology*] a doctrine which claims that scientific advance can only come through testing and falsifying hypotheses, which are then replaced by new hypotheses to be tested and falsified in their turn; one can only falsify, never ultimately verify.

family 1. *n* [*Cheese-making*] a group of cheeses having the same characteristics or based on the same manufacturing techniques. There are eight major families: drained or undrained fresh cheeses; **bloomy** rind soft cheeses; **washed** rind soft cheeses; natural-rind soft cheeses; internal mold soft cheeses; uncooked pressed cheeses; cooked pressed cheeses; processed or emulsified cheeses. **2.** *n* [*US*] [*Crime*] in the US Mafia, this is a division of the overall organisation, containing 450–600 members who on the whole have neither legal nor blood ties, but are linked by an intense sense of inter-personal loyalty. It is a criminal grouping with its own territory and internal hierarchy. **3.** *n* [*Printing*] a complete range of the design variants of a typeface. **4.** *n* [*Computing*] the full range of a manufacturer's CPUs which can be updated to newer/more powerful versions without forcing the consumer to change the rest of the system or the programs.

family branding *n* [*Marketing*] the use of the same brand name across several product categories.

family ganging *n* [*US*] [*Medicine*] the unethical practice of persuading or requiring a patient who is genuinely in need of personal care to bring along extra members of his/her family so that the programme under which treatment is being given can charge the public funds or insurance company for each of them. See also **ping-ponging**.

family group *n* [*Management*] in group training – the study of group dynamics – this is a group that consists of people who work closely together in the same organisation. See also **cousins group, stranger group**.

family house *n* [*US*] [*TV*] a viewing **daypart** during which it is assumed that children will be watching and from which therefore any hint of sex and/or violence is banned. See also **early fringe, late fringe, prime time**.

family jewels *n pl* [*Espionage*] this comes from slang 'family jewels' meaning male genitals. It is used by the CIA to denote those internal and potentially embarrassing secrets which the agency would prefer were never disclosed in public; they are skeletons in the espionage closet, eg: CIA assassinations and allied illegal forms of **destabilisation**.

family violence *n* [*Social work*] a general term that covers 'baby battering' and 'wife battering' and is being extended to cover a relatively new phenomenon – 'granny bashing': the ill-treatment, often physical but also mental, of elderly relations who either live with or are looked after by members of their family.

famished [*Military*] US Department of Defense radio code for: 'do you have any instructions for me?'

fan 1. *v* [*Baseball*] to dismiss or strike out a batter, who 'fans' his bat ineffectually at the passing ball. **2.** *v* [*UK*] [*Police*] to make a fast superficial body-search in which the officer's hand moves over the subject's clothing, 'fanning' them for any suspicious items.

fan club *n* [*Stock market*] a group of buyers who obtain the same shares but are not acting together as a **concert party**.

fan in *n* [*Computing*] the maximum number of inputs that can be connected to the processing unit without affecting the operation of that unit. See also **fan in**.

fan out *n* [*Computing*] the maximum number of outputs that can be serviced by the processing unit without affecting the operation of that unit. See also **fan out**.

fanac *n* [*TV*] abbr of **fan action** which is carried out by or designed for fans of TV's 'Star Trek' series.

fanarchist *n* [*Science fiction*] a dissenter from organised fan activity.

fancy *n* [*Sport*] a term coined in the 18th century for those, rich and poor, who followed horse-racing, prize-fighting, gambling and kindred excitements. It is still popular with sports writers who wish to evoke a period flavour in their references to such varieties of fans.

faned *n* [*Science fiction*] this comes from 'fan' plus 'editor': an editor of a fan magazine.

fanger *n* [*Medicine*] an oral surgeon.

fanglage *n* [*Science fiction*] the jargon or special language of science fiction fans.

fanning *n* [*UK*] [*Police*] the act of stealing as performed by a pickpocket.

fanny *n* [*Royal Navy*] the mess kettle; 'kettle' here means any small, round, general duty utensil.

Fanny Adams *n* [*Royal Navy*] either tinned meat or the stew that has been made from it; it is a derogatory reference to its provenance, derived from the name of a murder victim of 1867.

fanny belt *n* [*US*] [*Skiing*] the belt that ski patrol

F

men carry to hold their first-aid kit; it is secured on the buttocks, 'fanny' in slang.

fanny-dipper n [*Surfing*] an ordinary swimmer – one who wets his/her behind (fanny) – rather than a surfer.

fanpubbing n [*Science fiction*] the publication of a science fiction fan magazine.

fanquet n [*Science fiction*] this comes from 'fan' plus 'banquet': a formal banquet held at a science fiction fan convention.

fantasy n [*Numismatics*] a coin of questionable origin or purpose, especially one of those issued by countries which mint them specifically for collectors, rather than for use as legal tender.

fantasy fit n [*Sex*] the dressing up by a homosexual **hustler** to satisfy those clients who enjoy 'costume' games; this is usually as a Hell's Angel, Nazi officer, construction worker, policeman or similar 'macho' figure.

fanzine n [*Media*] any magazine produced nonprofessionally by the fans of a particular celebrity, film, book, fictional character, TV series, etc. See also **crudzine**.

farb man n [*Commerce*] a salesman who attempts to sell a customer an article more expensive than the one requested.

fargo n [*Espionage*] a listening device concealed on an agent's body to relay his conversation with a target back to a remote tape recorder or witness; the words thus relayed have 'far to go'.

fari 'n ponciu v [*Crime*] in the Sicilian Mafia this comes from dialect 'to mix a drink' meaning 'to knife'.

farm 1. v [*Cricket*] used of a batsman who plays in such a way that he manages to receive the majority of balls bowled. 2. n [*Espionage*] a CIA training ground, near the headquarters at Langley, Virginia, where novice agents can experience 'real life' simulations of espionage fieldwork. 3. n [*Military*] the launch sites of antiballistic missiles; possibly it comes from their being 'planted' in underground silos.

farm in v [*Oil rigs*] a company does this when it acquires an interest in an exploration or production licence by paying some of the past or future costs of another company which is relinquishing part of its interest. See also **farm out**.

farm out v [*Oil rigs*] a company does this when it gives up part of its interest in an exploration or production licence to another company in return for part-payment of its costs. See also **farm in**.

farm team, also **farm club** n [*Baseball*] a minor league club that is affiliated to a major league club and which is intended for the 'cultivation' of new talent from whose ranks the future stars are recruited.

farmer splice n [*Logging*] a rough splice that forms a temporary loop at the end of a cable.

farmers 1. n pl [*Merchant navy*] two crewmen in a watch who are on standby for emergency or unforeseen tasks. 2. n pl [*Navy*] a derogatory nick-

name used by fighter pilots for those who fly helicopters.

fartlek n [*Athletics*] from Swedish 'speed play', this is a training method for middle- and long-distance runners in which bursts of fast running are alternated with periods of slow speeds.

f.a.s. adv [*Commerce*] abbr of **free alongside ship/steamer** referring to the payment by the seller of all charges and risks up to the point where the goods are placed alongside the ship ready for loading.

fascicle n [*Bibliography*] a single published part of a book that is issued in installments prior to its appearance in a single edition.

fascinoma n [*Medicine*] this is a pun on 'fascinate' and the medical suffix '-oma', meaning illness (as in carcinoma, etc): any particularly interesting disease.

FASGROLIA n [*Journalism*] acro **Fast Growing Language of Initialisms and Acronyms**; coined by 'Time' magazine.

fash, also **flash** n [*Metallurgy*] the sharp fringe of metal left at the bottom of a shearing or saw cut.

fashion goods n [*Commerce*] any goods – not necessarily clothing – that depend for their appeal on shifting tastes and their ability, using fast-altering designs or styles, to take advantage of those shifts.

fast 1. a [*Audio*] said of a circuit that responds quickly to small details in sound waves, coping well with all the fluctuations in the signal and reproducing them accurately. 2. a [*Photography*] said of lenses that have a F-value near 1; films that have a high sensitivity to light. 3. a [*Science*] in nuclear physics, this describes those processes that involve fast neutrons (those neutrons that have not been slowed down by any moderator after being produced by the fission of a nucleus) such as fast-breeder reactors or fast fission. 4. a [*Weaving*] said of dyes that do not fade in water or light. See also **fugitive 2**.

fast break n [*Lacrosse*] the major strategy in the game: a quick move from a **turnover** in defence which brings the ball upfield so fast for a shot on goal at the other end that the defence does not have time to prevent it effectively. See also **break 5**.

fast breeder n [*Science*] See **breeder**.

fast end 1. n [*Coal-mining*] the part of a **rib** adjacent to a coal face. 2. n [*Coal-mining*] the dead end of a roadway.

fast lens n [*Photography*] a lens that can collect a large amount of light: f–2.8 or less. See also **fast 2**.

fast pace [*US*] [*Military*] US Department of Defense War Readiness Code for: the fourth most serious (out of five) level of readiness.

fast rubber n [*Table tennis*] whichever rubber surface is preferred by attacking, aggressive players; such rubber accelerates and helps spin the ball. See also **slow rubber**.

fast side *n* [*Soccer*] from the goalkeeper's point of view, this is the shortest distance the ball has to travel from a player into or towards the net; thus 'slow side' is the longest such distance.

fast track *n, a* [*Business*] upwardly mobile, 'whizz kid', ambitious, go-getting executives travel in the 'fast track' or 'fast lane'; it is the quick way to the top, with all the excitement and risk that such speedy travel can involve. Thus 'fast-tracking' means the pursuit of such a course of self-advancement.

fast track/slow track *n* [*Sex*] this is used by black pimps to describe the differences between East Coast cities (especially New York, hard/fast) and the West Coast (eg: Los Angeles, soft/slow); 'fast track' also refers to the main centre of street-walking and allied vices in any major city.

fast track construction *n* [*US*] [*Business*] a method of building ordinary construction projects that requires all basic decisions to be made at the outset of the scheme and not changed subsequently; thus each segment of the construction can begin as soon as the relevant architectural drawings have been completed. Much time and money can therefore be saved.

fast trotter *n* [*UK*] [*Railways*] any speedy local passenger train.

fast-track procedure *n* [*US*] [*Government*] the act of cutting through bureaucratic red tape and holdups.

fat 1. *n* [*Building, Plastering*] the fine residue formed on the skimming trowel when trowelling up, and used to fill in minor blemishes on the surface. 2. *a* [*Building*] said of mortar which contains a high cement or lime content. 3. *a* [*Building*] said of lime which is nearly or completely pure and which slakes rapidly. 4. *a* [*Building*] said of wood with a high resin content. 5. *a* [*Building*] said of clay or soil that contains a high proportion of minerals which make clay soil hard to work when wet but strong when dry. 6. *a* [*Coal-mining*] having a high content of volatile matter. 7. *a* [*Golf*] used of a ball which has been hit too low – well beneath the centre – to produce the required accuracy and distance in the shot. 8. *a* [*Logging*] referring to wood that is resinous or pitchy. 9. *a* [*Printing*] wide of the standard; it is used especially for pricing a piece of work. 10. *a* [*Printing, Typefaces*] said of heavy or thick strokes. See also **lean** 1. 11. *a* [*Printing*] a printer's description of type-setting which is easy, fast and simple. 12. *a.* [*Theatre*] referring to a meaty, important role which is defined less by its size, which may not be great, but by its dramatic effectiveness. See **meaty** 2. 13. *a* [*Wine-tasting*] fullish body, high in glycol and **extract**. 14. also **loaded** *a* [*Gambling*] referring to any individual with plenty of money.

fat coal *n* [*Coal-mining*] coal with a medium volatile matter content (20–25%). See also **lean coal**.

fat edge *n* [*Painting*] an accumulation of paint in a ridge at the edge of a painted surface.

Fat Man *n* [*Military*] the second atomic bomb, used to destroy Nagasaki at 11.02 am on August 9th 1945. The bomb measured 3 metres, and weighed 4500 kilograms. It was exploded in an air burst 500 metres above the city and had a yield of some 22,000 tons (22 KT) of TNT.

fat paint *n* [*US*] [*Painting*] gummy, heavily oxidised paint.

fat sand *n* [*Metallurgy*] in iron founding, this is sand that has a high clay content.

fat work *n* [*Industrial relations*] any work in which it is relatively easy to obtain productivity bonuses; the opposite is 'lean work'.

fate *n* [*Banking*] the fate of a cheque depends on whether or not it is honoured.

father *n* [*Computing*] used of a node. See **parent** 1.

father confessor *n* [*Espionage*] a senior security official to whom CIA Officers can reveal, in secret and without threat to their career prospects, any minor infringements of security: running up debts, being caught in a police raid, etc.

father file *n* [*Computing*] every time a file is updated, three generations are produced: the father file – the original file immediately preceding the update, the grandfather file – the previous father file, and the son file – the new file, which in turn will 'grow older' as later updates occur.

fattening up 1. *n* [*Building, Plastering*] the increase in plasticity and workability when putty lime, after the slaking process, is allowed to mature. 2. *n* [*Military*] a popular version of the official 'rehabilitation': a system whereby troops just returned from a tough operation are given a variety of 'rewards' including special treatment, extra supplies and similar luxuries calculated to keep them happy, psychologically and physically sound, and ready for the next turn of duty.

fattenings *n pl* [*Painting*] an increase in the consistency of paint while in storage; the paint becomes much thicker but should still be usable.

fault-tree analysis *n* [*Business, Technology*] a system of analysis that starts by positing a possible failure or breakdown and then attempts to trace it back step by step to its source. Fault-trees are feasible in theory, but when used in an attempt to deal with a highly complex machine, rather than the popular but overly simple model of a car that will not start, they can be side-tracked into the literally thousands of possible causes, each of which must be traced and eliminated before considering the next.

faulty internal dialogue *n* [*New therapies*] in assertiveness training, this refers to a means of developing an individual's psychological self-realiance (something on the lines of a 1980s Dale

F

Carnegie course). The idea is that one's self-perception and inner feelings are not adjusted to the correct 'positive' attitude.

favourite fifty n [US] [Stock market] See **nifty fifty**.

favourite son n [US] [Politics] a candidate for a political office, particularly the Presidency, who finds backers mainly among the party organisation and political leadership of his own state. Every convention sees the nomination of a number of favourite sons who stand as less than serious candidates in order to promote the interest of their home state; this is achieved by bartering their support in return for promises of future favours from the real candidate.

FAW n [Military] abbr of **fuel-air weapon**. See **cheeseburger**.

fax n [Journalism] abbr of **facsimile** the transmission by wire or radio of graphic material from one newspaper to another, or from a remote source to a newspaper.

fay v [Sailing, Ropework] to tease, taper and lay flat a strand against a rope, spar or hook prior to securing the two together.

FBS n [Military] abbr of **Forward Based Systems** a term coined by Soviet negotiators to describe those forces – other than **ICBMs** – such as missiles based in NATO countries, allied territory, or on submarines or aircraft carriers, all of which are capable of delivering a nuclear strike against Russia. Given the relative geography of the West and the Warsaw Pact, the USSR has no such forward bases of its own. Thus these systems are seen as giving the US an unfair advantage.

fearnought suit n [Navy] a protective suit made of specially treated strong woollen fibre, which is worn for fighting on-board fires.

feather 1. also **harbour light** n [UK] [Railways] a direction signal – a faint blue colour. 2. n [Glass-making] an imperfection seen as a cluster of fine bubbles in the glass caused by foreign material entering the glass during casting or shaping. 3. n [Glass-making] an imperfection in wired glass seen as the bending of transverse wires. 4. also **fringe, flag, plume** n [Dog breeding] the longish coat on the ears, belly, back of legs and tail of many breeds, including English Setter, Skye Terrier, Papillon, etc. 5. v [Hunting] hounds do this when they wave their tails on an uncertain scent, but have not yet given tongue. 6. v [US] [Painting] in wall-papering, this is to ensure that the seams of the adjacent strips of paper form an invisible join. 7. v [Snooker, Billiards] to run the cue backwards and forwards across the bridge formed by the finger and thumb prior to making a shot.

feather out v [US] [Painting] to smooth out adjacent edges of paint to ensure that no join is visible when the paint is dry.

feather-bedding 1. n [Industrial relations] essentially the obtaining of pay without performing the work: a situation where a lax employer permits the unions to impose such rules as they wish regarding the rate of and pay for production, eg: creating extra jobs where none are needed, etc. 2. n [Industry] the practice by a government of protecting home industries by tariffs or quotas on imports and/or subsidies to those industries.

feathering n [Printing] the smearing of the ink across the paper, causing individual words to be blurred and hard to read.

feature 1. n [Computing] any surprising property of a program which may or may not have been appreciated by its originator. If the feature is not documented it can be termed a **bug**, but likewise the error that is classified first as an apparent bug becomes a feature once it has been documented and can therefore, for all its peculiarity, be expected and thus absorbed into everyday operations. 2. n [Film] a fictional entertainment film of more than 3000' in length or running longer than 34 minutes. The second feature on a double bill is a film that is of less importance than the main film, or a former main feature that suffered poor reviews and has been relegated to an inferior spot. 3. n [Journalism] a non-fiction article, usually longer than a news story and usually illustrated; or it can be a major interview or profile published in a newspaper or magazine.

featured players n pl [Film, TV] leading actors who are ranked below the actual stars but above the 'supporting players'; often, in TV series, these are cited on the credits as 'guest stars', a title that currently applies almost without exception to anyone who manages to get a role in a series.

FEBA n [Military] acro **forward edge of the battle area** that 'line' on a battlefield where the opposing forces are actually fighting and engaging each other in reasonably close combat.

fed a [US] [Meat trade] said of an animal that has been wholly or partially fattened.

Fed funds n pl [Banking] deposits by banks in the US Federal Reserve System.

Fed window n [US] [Banking] abbr of the **Federal Discount Window** a system whereby member banks are able to borrow from the Federal Reserve.

federal revenue enchancement n [US] [Government] a bureaucratic euphemism for the raising of federal (national) taxes.

federalised a [Cars] said of any car that has successfully passed the Federally regulated tests that permit it to be sold in the USA; these tests are especially stringent as regards exhaust emissions and safety.

fee simple n [Law] total ownership of **real property** without any restrictions.

feed 1. v [Religion] to impart knowledge or understanding to another or others; see I Peter 5:2. 2. v [Religion] to inspire, to enlighten spiritually; see I Corinthians 3:1–2. 3. v [Soccer] to pass the

F

ball to another player. **4.** *n* [*Theatre*] the 'straight man' who works alongside the comedian and provides him with the 'feed lines', the cues for his jokes. **5.** *n, v* [*TV, Radio*] a transmission, or to transmit. See also **bird 5, 6** and **7**.

feed dog *n* [*Clothing*] in a sewing-machine, this is a toothed or flat surface acting against the underside of the material being sewn, which operates to move the material rapidly and evenly under the sewing head.

feedback 1. *n* [*Electronics*] the transfer of energy from the output of a circuit back to its input. **2.** *n* [*New therapies*] one person's reaction to another person's action or speech, conveyed by analysing, criticising, rejecting or agreeing, but always in some way modifying the original statement or action by their response. **3.** *n* [*Politics*] the response, from one's peers, supporters, potential voters and opponents, that emerges following a politician's action or statement. Such a response is available both during a campaign and after an election to office, although the candidate's own feedback may well differ according to his/her altering status. **4.** *n* [*Pop music*] any reviews, comments, opinions from media, retailers or consumers concerning a new product.

feeder 1. *n* [*Coal-mining*] See **creeper 5**. **2.** *n* [*Gas industry*] a gas transmission main that emanates from a source of gas such as a coastal terminal. **3.** *n* [*Gas industry*] a main which takes gas from a point on the system which generally has gas available to a point on the system which requires re-inforcement. **4.** *n* [*Gas industry*] a main carrying gas at a pressure greater than the normal pressure of supply and used as a source from which an additional quantity of gas may be introduced into the mains through a governor. **5.** *n* [*Mining*] a small vein that runs into the main one.

feeder head *n* [*Metallurgy*] in iron founding, this is a reservoir of molten metal which is used to supply extra metal to the mould as the original metal starts to contract as it cools.

feeders *n pl* [*US*] [*Cattlemen*] cattle which are being fattened up prior to being sold at market.

feeding 1. *n* [*Metallurgy*] in iron founding, this is the supplying of extra metal to a mould to compensate for the contraction of the metal already in the mould during cooling and solidifying. **2.** *n* [*Radio*] the transmission of live or recorded material from an originating station along specially reserved post office lines either to one other station or to the entire network. Thus 'refeed' means the repeat transmission of material already sent; **clean feed, dirty feed** and line feed mean any feed that is booked on the post office line.

feedstock 1. *n* [*Oil rigs*] the supply of crude oil, natural gas liquids or natural gas to a refinery or petrochemical plant. **2.** *n* [*Oil rigs*] the supply of some refined fraction of intermediate petrochemicals to some other process.

feel a collar *n* [*UK*] [*Police*] to arrest a suspect.

feel for *v* [*US*] [*Police*] to check out a suspect over the police radio.

feeler *n* [*Engineering*] a thin metal strip made to a stated thickness, which is used to measure narrow gaps or thicknesses and is usually one of a graduated set.

feeling talk *n* [*New therapies*] in assertiveness training, this is the voicing of 'meaningful dialogue', rather than idle chatter.

feep 1. *n* [*Computing*] the softly ringing bell of a display terminal. **2.** *v* [*Computing*] to cause the display to make a feep.

feet dry [*Military*] air intercept code for: 'I am over land/the designated contact is over land'.

feet, off its *a* [*Printing*] referring to any letter or word that is not standing right and which makes an incomplete impression.

feet wet [*Military*] air intercept code for: 'I am over water/the designated contact is over water'.

feevee *n* [*US*] [*TV*] pay cable TV, which includes a variety of specialist channels for 24–hour per day news, sport, rock music, porno, first run films, etc.; it is scheduled for the UK in the near future.

feints *n pl* [*Distilling*] the third fraction of the distillate received from the second distillation of the pot still process. They form the undesirable last runnings of the distillation and are returned with the **foreshots** to the spirit still when it is recharged with **low wines**. The feints and foreshots of the last distillation of a season are added to the first low wines of the next season.

felix *n* [*UK*] [*Military*] a British Army nickname for bomb disposal units.

fell *n* [*Weaving*] the top line of the weaving, where the **warp** threads cross in the most recent change of **shed**.

fellow traveller 1. *n* [*Military*] a satellite-conveyed nuclear mine that would be launched to 'shadow' its target – a laser weapon or communications/surveillance satellite – and which can be exploded when desired by ground based computer commands, thus destroying that target. **2.** *n* [*Politics*] this comes from the Russian 'poputchik' (used by Trotsky in 'Literature and Revolution' 1923) meaning one who sympathises with Communism but has never actually joined the Party. By extension it refers to anyone who sympathises with a specific philosophy, but is unwilling to make a firm and public commitment.

felt 1. *n* [*Paper-making*] an endless belt, usually made of textile material, which carries the **web** after it comes from the **wire**. **2.** *v* [*Textiles*] to undergo the process of **felting**.

felt-fair pay, also **equitable payment** *n* [*Industry*] the rate of pay for a job that the employee performing that job feels is fair; the term was coined by UK sociologist Elliott Jacques (1917–).

felting 1. *n* [*Furriers*] See **bunching 2**. **2.** *n* [*Textiles*] the process whereby woollen fabric is shrunk into a more compact, matted whole by dampening and heat. **3.** *n* [*Weaving*] the same as **fulling** but done to such an extent that the fibres actually join together, as in felt.

feminine *a* [*Wine-tasting*] said of a wine of lightness and charm, generally attractive and, for the ideologically impure, redolent of supposedly female characteristics.

fen *n pl* [*TV*] among the devotees of TV's 'Star Trek', this is the recognised plural of the singular 'fan'.

fence 1. *v* [*UK*] [*Market-traders*] to sell (no criminality implied). **2.** *n* [*UK*] [*Crime*] a receiver of stolen goods.

fence mending *n* [*Politics*] the ensuring by a politician that, whatever his/her national responsibilities may be, the voters within his/her own constituency are properly looked after, since they will, after all, be the ones who really matter come the next election.

Fencer *n* [*Military*] the Russian Sukhoi SU–24 large supersonic swing-wing attack aircraft, deployed since 1974.

fender 1. *n* [*Coal-mining*] a very narrow pillar of coal left between adjacent workings. **2.** *n* [*Logging*] a large, heavy pole placed at the side of a skidding trail (along which logs are dragged or slid) to make sure that the moving logs stay on that trail.

ferments *n pl* [*Cheese-making*] various alkalising micro-organisms; the principal ones are **lactic** ferments which neutralise the lactic acid of fresh cheeses; caseic dissolving ferments of soft cheeses; propionic which break down fat in hard cheeses and release the gases that cause internal holes.

fermier *a* [*Cheese-making*] said of a cheese produced on a farm by traditional methods; it comes from Fr. 'fermier' meaning 'farmer'.

fernando's hideaway *n* [*UK*] [*Railways*] an isolated platelayer's cabin.

ferret *n* [*Utilities*] a water-propelled device incorporating a set of cleaning brushes that is used to scour water mains systems.

fertile *a* [*Science*] in nuclear physics this is said of a material, usually uranium 238 or thorium, which is capable of being changed into a fissile isotope by the capture of an neutron.

fertilise the vegetables *v phr* [*US*] [*Medicine*] to order vitamins or tube feedings for comatose patients.

fess *n* [*Heraldry*] a horizontal strip, broader than a **bar**, across the middle of a shield.

fest *n* [*Film*] abbr of **festival**.

Festschrift *n* [*Bibliography*] a collection of writings by a variety of scholars, usually from the same or allied disciplines, which is dedicated to a fellow scholar, often a leader in the field, as a mark of celebration or homage.

fetichism of output *n* [*Politics*] an obsession within socialist countries that centres on reaching pre-set norms of output which have been determined by the current economic plan, irrespective of the quality or quantity of production that is actually required by the current circumstances.

fettle *v* [*Textiles*] to clean the looms; thus a 'fettler' is one who cleans looms.

fettling *n* [*Metallurgy*] in iron-founding, this is the cleaning of castings, and removal of excess metal, either by chipping, grinding or some mechanical process.

feu de joie *n* [*Military*] this comes from Fr. 'fire of joy': a ceremonial firing off of blanks in which a line of troops fire off their weapons one after another, each immediately following his predecessor. The whole line fires three blanks per man.

feuille *n* [*Cheese-making*] a group of cheeses that are wrapped in one or more plane-tree, grape or chestnut leaves. The term comes from Fr. 'feuille' meaning 'leaf'.

feuilleté *a* [*Cheese-making*] said of a cheese that tends to separate into several layers; this results from the use of excessive shrinking **curd** or from too long a wait between successive fillings of the molds. The term comes from Fr: 'feuilleté' meaning 'flaky'.

few *a* [*Military*] said of any total of men or objects that amounts to less than eight. See also **many**.

FGA, also **FMI** *n* [*Marketing*] abbr of **Free Give-Away, Free Mention** premiums that are given away to purchasers of whatever product is currently being promoted.

fi *n* [*US*] [*Police*] abbr of **female impersonator**.

fianchetto *v* [*Chess*] to develop a bishop by moving it one square to put it on a long diagonal of the board; it comes from Ital. 'fianco' meaning 'flank'.

fiat money *n* [*Finance*] money that has no intrinsic value, nor can it be transformed into gold or silver; it gains value as currency through the order of the government which issues it.

fiawol *v phr* [*Science fiction*] acro **fandom is a way of life** the philosophy of pure fandom, putting fan activities before every other consideration. See also **fijagh, gafiate**.

FIBA *past part.* [*Military*] acro **Fighting In Built-up Areas** holding the enemy, fighting room to room, destroying houses, clearing snipers, etc.

fictitious objects *n pl* [*Industry, Business*] various objects for which apprentices, new recruits, etc. are sent by their seniors: bucket of steam, packet of big ends, long stand (railwaymen, UK), stretcher (storemen), anchor watch, key to the starboard watch, key to the compass (sailors), balloon soup (airmen), beaker mender, bottle stretcher (technicians), black whitewash, red, white and blue paint, white lampblack (painters), brass contour (surveyors), bucket of revolutions, bucket of steam (factories), bumblebee feathers, buttonholes (tailors), cable stretcher (telephone linemen), crooked straight-

F

edge, rubber hammer for glass nails, flannel hammer, round square (carpenters), cubic type, half-tone dots, striped ink (printers), left-handed monkey wrench, sky hook, horse-ladder, dime's worth of strapholes, four-foot yardstick, yard-wide packthread (general use), box of cue dots, thousand feet of mixed track (TV).

fictitious person *n* [*Law*] See **artificial person**.

fid *n* [*Sailing, Ropework*] a long, tapering cone, used for rounding out **eyes**, grommets, eyelet holes, etc.; thus 'to fid out' means to round out such a hole, prior to inserting a **thimble**.

fiddle **1.** *v* [*Boxing*] said of a boxer who spars for an opening without aiming or landing a punch. **2.** *n* [*US*] [*Carpenters*] See **coffee grinder 1. 3.** *n* [*Cars*] abbr of 'fiddle brake'; fitted in pairs to any trials car, this brake enables a single driven rear wheel to be stopped, transferring tractive power when required to the opposite wheel. **4.** *n* [*Ordnance survey*] a theodolite.

fiddle front *n* [*Dog breeding*] See **Chippendale front**.

FIDE *n* [*Aerospace*] acro **Flight Dynamics Engineer** an engineer who specialises in the dynamics of space flight – velocity, elevation, variations in height or direction. See also **GUIDO, RETRO**.

fidelity bond **1.** *n* [*Insurance*] See **blanket bond**. **2.** also **fidelity insurance** *n* [*Commerce*] an insurance policy taken out by an employer to protect him against the possible dishonesty or non-performance of an employee.

FIDO **1.** *n* [*Aerospace*] acro **Fog Investigation Dispersal Operation** a method of dispersing fog sited above airports by using the heat from petrol burners. **2.** *n* [*Numismatics*] acro **Freaks, Irregulars, Defects and Oddities** an acronym covering a variety of errors in the minting of coins.

fiduciary bond *n* [*Law*] a surety bond which an individual bringing a lawsuit must take out with an insurance company, ensuring that any costs or damages incurred will be paid.

field **1.** *n* [*Computing*] a subdivision of a record, a single item of information contained by and relating to the rest of that record; thus, if the record were a single quotation, there might be fields for a source, the quoted line, the date, speaker etc. **2.** *n* [*Government*] the 'real world' of want, poverty, violence, deprivation, social inequalities and similar variables which define everyday life for the majority and upon which a government or bureaucracy attempts to impose its solutions or plans. **3.** *n* [*Heraldry*] the surface of the shield, which forms the background to the heraldic symbols. **4.** *n* [*Hunting*] the mounted followers of the hunt, not including the Master, the Hunt servants, the grooms or **second horsemen**. **5.** *n* [*Medicine*] that part of the patient's body on which the operation is actually being performed. **6.** *n* [*TV*] one half of the TV picture of (in the UK) 625 lines: each 'frame' that

the viewer sees is composed of two interlaced fields of 312.5 lines each.

field music **1.** *n* [*US*] [*Marine Corps*] a drummer or a trumpeter. **2.** *n* [*US*] [*Marine Corps*] a small drum and bugle corps created by amalgamating all the various individual field musics on a post into one group.

field painting *n* [*Art*] field painters treat the surface of a picture as one continuous and extended plane with the whole picture regarded as a single unit, so that neither the ground nor the figures are given greater value.

field sweep *n* [*TV*] the movement of the electron beam spot in a vertical direction over the screen.

fiery *a* [*Coal-mining*] used to describe a condition that arises from the presence of flammable gas and/or coal dust.

FIFO **1.** *a* [*Commerce*] acro **First In, First out** a stock inventory method whereby it is assumed that the first item acquired for stock will be the first to be sold. **2.** *a* [*Computing*] acro **First In, First Out** a method of storing data so that the first piece of information stored can be the first one available for retrieval. See also **LIFO 2**.

FIFO list *n* [*Computing*] acro **First In, First Out list**. See **queue**. See also **FIFO**.

fifteen and two *n* [*US*] [*Advertising*] a discount system offered by newspapers to space buyers; fifteen per cent commission plus two per cent discount for prompt payment of invoices.

fifteen minutes *n pl* [*US*] [*Theatre*] a call to remind actors that the performance starts in fifteen minutes. See also **the quarter**.

fifteeners *n pl* [*Bibliography*] incunabula: books written prior to 1501.

fifth column *n* [*Politics*] a clandestine group of one's own supporters operating within an enemy country or within one's own borders, if the country has been occupied; or a hostile enemy group operating in a country which you govern or occupy. The term originated during the siege of Madrid (1936) when the loyalist General Mola claimed that as well as the four columns of his army laying the siege, there was a fifth column of secret supporters working within the city.

fifth generation *n* [*Computing*] the projected computer systems of the 1990s, capable of sustaining artificial intelligence (**AI**) which will make them, in theory, far more like human beings and less like machines. Unlike the previous four generations, which developed the hardware technology substantially, but remained tied to the same basic **architecture**, the fifth has moved away from tradition to exploit four linked areas of research: knowledge-based expert systems, very high-level programming **languages**, decentralised computing and **VLSI** technology. See also **first-fourth generation**.

fifth hand **1.** *n* [*Glass-making*] an extra man put into a team of four men working at glass-making by hand. **2.** *n* [*Glass-making*] an apprentice.

fifth pathway n [US] [Medicine] a means for an individual who has obtained all or the bulk of his/her medicine training outside the US to enter post-graduate training in the US by fulfilling certain criteria.

fifth quarter n [US] [Cattlemen] the hide and entrails of a slaughtered animal.

fifth-wheel coupling n [UK] [Road transport] a connecting device on articulated vehicles consisting of a support plate mounted on the tractive unit with a jaw and locking device to accept and secure the towing kingpin; on the trailer there is a turntable with a kingpin projecting downwards, which locates in the jaw on the tractive unit plate.

fightback n [Cheese-making] the manner in which the cheese presses back against the thumb when the pressure of the thumb is released by the tester; a quality distinct from body or firmness.

fighter alley n [Air travel] civilian pilots' nickname for airspace over the Ruhr in Germany where the air is thick with NATO fighters intermingling with the commercial jets.

fighting for one's corner n [Politics] 'which, freely translated amounts to ensuring that whoever else faces the consequences of expenditure cuts, it is not their department' (L. Chapman 'Waste Away' (1982)); a concept that expands to cover a Minister's efforts to escape the blame for any unpopular measure. See also **CYA**.

figure 1. n [Woodwork] the diagonal markings that are found in wood taken from the point of insertion of large lateral branches into the tree-trunk. 2. n [US] [Car salesmen] the amount a dealer will offer for a car.

figure-eight n [Cycling] a wheel that is very badly buckled and thus resembles this figure.

figure-of-eight n [Audio] a special type of microphone in which the polar response is shaped like a figure-of-eight which makes it particularly responsive to input from front and rear, and insensitive to the sides.

fijagh v phr [Science fiction] acro **fandom is just a goddam hobby** the apostate attitude to science fiction fandom which does not give it undue dominance in one's life. See also **fiawol**.

file v [Journalism] to send in, write or tape a story for a newspaper or radio news programme.

file crunching n [Computing] the reduction of the size of a file by a complex scheme that produces bit configurations which are completely unrelated to the original data; the file ends up as the electronic equivalent of a paper document that has been crumpled into a ball: the data remains intact but the structure is contracted.

file event n [Computing] any access – either reading or writing – that is made to a file.

filibuster n [Politics] a technique which originated in the US and is based on Rule 22 of the US senate; it allows for unlimited debate on any topic before it need be brought to a vote and is used by politicians who wish to defeat a specific measure (usually when they are in a minority and the measure is otherwise popular): they arrange non-stop, lengthy speeches, one after another, to defeat or at least amend the legislation. Filibustering is banned in the UK House of Commons, where the Speaker can deem a speech irrelevant and order the MP to sit down. A similar style of delaying tactics employed in Japan is translated as the 'cow waddle' whereby members of the Diet take infinitely long to progress from their seats to the ballot box.

filk song n [Science fiction] a song, usually anonymous, on a science-fiction theme which is sung at a science-fiction convention; it is a pun on 'folk song'.

fill 1. v [UK] [Coal-mining] to load coal or stone on to a conveyor belt, either by hand or machinery. 2. v [Stock market, Commerce] to execute a customer's order – buying or selling, of securities or commodities. 3. n [Glass-making] the amount of glass-making materials that are required to fill the furnace for a single operation.

fill character n [Computing] See **ignore character**.

fill one's boots v phr [Cricket] to bat well, to take advantage of favourable circumstances.

fill or kill v phr [Stock market] an order to offer a trade to the **pit** three times; if not executed immediately, the order is cancelled.

fill your card v phr [Big-game hunting] the promise made to a hunter that he will be able to kill off whatever number and type of animals he has selected before starting the hunt.

filler 1. n [Journalism] any material, usually of transient or humourous value, that can be used to fill small spaces in the paper. 2. n [TV] a short programme – perhaps 5 minutes long – which is used to fill a gap in the programming schedule. 3. n [TV] a small light used by a cameraman to augment his basic set-up. 4. also **collier, hewer** n [UK] [Coal-mining] a coalface worker who actually cuts out the coal and loads it onto the **face chain**.

filler on n [Glass-making] a worker who fills the tank or pot furnaces with a charge of materials for making glass.

filling n [Weaving] See **weft**.

fillo n [Science fiction] an illustration used to fill up possible blank spaces on a magazine page.

fills 1. n pl [Journalism] extra material inserted in an individual story or into a whole page of news. 2. n pl [Music] in jazz, this is extra and possibly improvised material inserted into a piece to lengthen it, add new interest and generally to appeal to the listener.

film 1. n [Cheese-making] a thin rind that arises spontaneously as the surface of a cheese dries. 2. n [Film] the use of 'film' with neither definite nor indefinite article is ever popular among the cineastes and cognoscenti. The implication is of some great and limitless concept, essentially an art form, that has little relevance to the actual wheeler-dealer commercial world of popular film production and exploitation.

film horse *n* [*Film, TV*] a device used in editing rooms which separates the various picture and sound tracks as and when they are required.

film noir *n* [*Film*] a French coinage, which is now in general use, for the genre of US gangster or crime thrillers, many of them made by Warner Bros. in the 1930s and 1940s.

film tree *n* [*TV, Film*] a wooden stand used in editing rooms; on to it are clipped various lengths of exposed film which will be used for cutting and splicing.

filtering *n* [*Photo-typesetting*] this comes from the audio use – in which high- or low-pass filters are used to eliminate unwanted noise and to enhance accurate reproduction. In image processing low frequencies can be applied to sampling the vertical strokes of a letter while high frequencies sample the detail of curves and serifs.

filth *n* [*UK*] [*Crime*] the CID, the detective branch of the UK police.

fin 1. *n* [*Metallurgy*] See **overfill**. 2. also **flash** *n* [*Glass-making*] a projection of glass caused when a portion of the molten glass has been forced into a badly fitting seam in the mould.

final cut *n* [*Film*] the final stage of editing the film: the version which will be seen in the cinemas. The power to determine the final cut is often the subject of jealous in-fighting between the **front office** which takes a strictly business perspective, and the director, who prefers an artistic one.

final horse *n* [*Rodeo*] one of the most difficult horses to ride, used in the final stages of championships.

final order *n* [*Military*] the last command issued by the US President or his surrogate in a state of **spasm** nuclear war, at which point all military commanders would be empowered to fire at will and let every man act for himself.

final terminal *n* [*US*] [*Railways*] an amount of time after reaching the terminal that is allotted to enginemen to stop the train where it is wanted. See also **initial terminal**.

financial exposure *n* [*Economics, Business*] the outlay of capital ventured on a given project by a firm prior to obtaining any returns on that expenditure.

find a hole *v* [*Flying*] to search for an opening in heavy cloud or fog in order to get one's bearings; this is not usually vital when the radar is functioning.

finding *n* [*US*] [*Law*] in the US Family (Juvenile, UK) Court this is the conviction of the defendant.

finding the balance *n* [*Accounting*] when referring to accounts, this is the process of making sure that all entries in those accounts have been properly completed, ie: balancing the books.

fine 1. *a* [*Angling*] said of lightweight tackle. 2. *a* [*Book collecting*] said of a book with all its leaves present, which is clean, whole and amply margined, sound and undisturbed in its binding, and with the bind, whatever its material, in prime condition. This is the second grade of books, after **mint**, and better than 'very good'. 3. *a* [*Weaving*] the top grade of wool in the blood system of grading; only Merino and Rambouillet wools reach this standard. 4. *a* [*Wine-tasting*] used to describe a wine of superior quality in every respect. 5. *a* [*Philately*] used to describe a stamp of the best quality and in the most perfect condition, given its age, rarity, etc.

fine chemicals *n pl* [*Industry*] chemicals that are handled in small lots and are in a purified state. See also **heavy chemicals**.

fine cut *n* [*TV*] the last stage of editing a TV film or programme when all cutting is over and the material is ready for public transmission.

fine drawing *n* [*Clothing*] a type of invisible mending whereby faults are repaired by hand sewing a garment to fill in areas where threads or yarns are missing.

fine grain print *n* [*Film*] a print which uses high-quality **stock** which has no silver salt deposits (which deteriorate in time) and which is used for making duplicate negatives.

fine index *n* [*Libraries, Education*] when two indices are consulted together to elicit information, this is the secondary detailed and specific index of the pair. See also **coarse index**.

fine paper 1. *a* [*Book collecting*] this refers to the printing of a special edition of a book, using better paper than the general edition; it is for display and collecting rather than reading. 2. also **first-class paper** *n* [*Banking, Finance*] bills of exchange, promissory notes and cheques drawn on or endorsed by financial institutions of absolute respectability and reliability.

fine rate *n* [*Banking*] the most favourable rate of interest or discount, given the circumstances.

fine used *a* [*Philately*] said of a stamp that has been gummed to a cover, then cancelled at the post office, and which retains its quality, as well as bearing a light but readable postmark. See also **fine 5**.

fine writing *n* [*Literary criticism*] any writing that makes too obvious and strained an attempt to improve on plain prose. Such writing is flowery, elaborate and finally precious.

finery *n* [*Metallurgy*] a hearth which may be used for the purifying of pig iron in the manufacture of high quality wrought iron, where the heat is produced by charcoal.

fines 1. *n pl* [*Building, Plastering*] that portion of very finely divided material which is found in sand. 2. *n pl* [*Coal-mining*] very small coal, 4mm size maximum, usually mixed in as fine material with larger sizes of coal.

F

finesse n [*Wine-tasting*] grace, delicacy, **breed**, distinction.

fine-tuning n [*Politics*] the art of excising from a politician's speech any potentially contentious or politically redundant material; this should put the speaker in the best possible light, and minimise the areas on which opponents can attack him or her.

finger 1. n [*Aerospace*] in airport architecture, this is a long, narrow pier which stretches out from the main building to enable a number of aircraft to park around it and embark or disembark their passengers. 2. v [*Police*] to betray, to inform the police about a criminal person or plan.

finger hank n [*Weaving*] See **butterfly 2**.

finger man 1. n [*Gambling*] a middleman who points out a gambler, who is presumed to be well-off, to a hold-up mob. 2. n [*Gambling*] one who informs the police of an illicit gambling game.

finger playing n [*Textiles*] the straightening of needles by hand.

finger trouble n [*Airlines*] human errors that can occur when programming the in-flight navigational computer, thus causing possible course error and even actual crashes.

finger wave n [*US*] [*Medicine*] a rectal examination.

finger-cot n [*US*] [*Medicine*] See **pinky-cheater**.

fingernails n pl [*Journalism*] brackets, parentheses.

finish n [*Wine-tasting*] the end-taste. A good finish is firm, crisp and distinctive, a short finish is watery, with an unsustained flavour. The correct degree of the right sort of acidity is vital.

finish bucket n [*US*] [*Coal-mining*] the end of a shift.

finish fetish n [*Art*] an obsessive concern, shown by several US artists, with giving their artworks the sort of high-gloss, super-smooth surface more usually found on new cars.

finisher n [*Glass-making*] See **chairman 2**.

finite deterrance n [*Military*] a war plan considered by the Eisenhower and Kennedy administrations whereby US nuclear forces would be stripped down to a fleet of (nearly) invulnerable submarines. Political, industrial and military pressures defeated such a move, although it was briefly disinterred by ex-submariner President Carter in the late 1970s.

fink n [*Industrial relations*] a company spy, or a worker who refuses to join a strike. See also **scab 2**.

fins n pl [*Dog breeding*] too profuse an arrangement of hair on the feet of the long-haired Dachshund.

finsburies n pl [*TV, Film*] from rhyming slang 'Finsbury Park' meaning 'arc' meaning 'arc light(s)'.

fire v [*US*] [*Railways*] to carry out the duties of a fireman; originally this was the actual shoveller of coal on steam trains, but is now restricted to the role of assistant engineer on diesels.

fire and forget n [*Military*] any missile that has a self-guiding **smart** internal computer that steers it towards its target with no further help from its launcher and which can thus be 'forgotten' once it has been fired. See also **use them or lose them**.

fire brigade 1. n [*Military*] this comes from the traditional use: a highly-trained, extra-mobile military unit designed to deal speedily with any outbreaks of trouble wherever its commander feels it should be employed around the world – usually in order to preserve its own national interests. 2. also **fireman** n [*US*] [*Garment trade*] a presser.

fire cracking n [*Building, Plastering*] the **crazing** of a skimming coat.

fire damp n [*UK*] [*Coal-mining*] high-explosive methane gas produced by the coal; it is an occupational hazard in mines.

firebreak n [*Military*] this comes from the term in forestry that denotes a bare strip of land between woods, which is intended to suppress spreading fires. It refers to the theoretical gap between **conventional weapons** and their use and the subsequent escalation into a full-scale nuclear war.

firefight n [*Military*] a short-range engagement between opposing forces, usually restricted to the use of light, short-range conventional weapons.

fireman n [*Coal-mining*] See **deputy**.

firing step n [*UK*] [*Theatre*] a platform in the **flies** where spare ropes are coiled away out of sight; it comes from World War I trench teminology.

firm 1. a [*Commerce*] referring to a market in which prices are steady. 2. a [*Commerce*] a 'firm' offer or 'firm' bid is one that carries no conditions, as opposed to a 'subject' bid or offer, which is 'subject' to such conditions. 3. a [*Commerce*] in firm hands: used to describe holders of securities who have a reputable trading pedigree as opposed to short-term operators with less credibility. 4. a [*Wine-tasting*] the opposite of **flabby**: soundly constituted, well-balanced, positive in the mouth. 5. n [*UK*] [*Police*] the ironic use of the normal business term to describe a gang of organised criminals a gang of car thieves, robbers, forgers, etc.

firmware 1. n [*Computing*] **software** and **hardware** so integrated as to make the individual items indistinguishable. 2. n [*Computing*] a hand-wired logic circuit that can perform the functions of a program.

first Australian n [*Government, Sociology*] a euphemism for an Aboriginal. See also **native Americans, new Commonwealth**.

first call n [*TV*] a TV company exchanges the right to make the first call on an actor's services, any time they require him/her, in return for a guarantee to maintain a regular flow of work for the performer.

first change n [Cricket] the third bowler used in an innings after one of the original pair is changed, hence 'second change', 'third change', etc.

first column n [Espionage] this is on the analogy of **fifth column** as a hostile force: it refers to the revival or protection, by one's own agency, of friendly regimes, or the arming and financing of guerrillas whom one wishes to see take power. Given its coinage by the CIA, one may assume that such regimes and guerrillas will always be right-wing and anti-communist.

first customer n [Business] the customer for whom a new product or line of products is actually created and designed; the line is then developed and modified for potential sale to further new clients. It is used especially of armament manufacturing: the home country is the first country, and export sales take on the secondary role.

first degree arson n [US] [Police] the burning of dwellings.

first down, also **first-and-ten 1.** n [US] [Football] the first in a succession of four offensive plays, which must capture a minimum of ten yards territory. **2.** also **first-and-ten** n [US] [Football] the right to begin a succession of offensive plays, resulting from previous gains of ten yards.

first generation 1. n [Computing] the series of computers and calculating machines designed between 1940 and 1955 which are characterised by electronic tube (valve) circuitry and delay line rotating or electrostatic memory. Most had primitive input/output, using punched paper tape, punched card, magnetic wire, magnetic tape and primitive printers. Despite this, such prototype machines performed admirably for their mainly scientific and military users. See also **second-, third-, fourth-** and **fifth-generation. 2.** n [Technology] this is used in all areas of technology – aerospace design, hi-fi equipment, computers, etc – to describe the earliest, and thus relatively simple and/or crude models of a specific machine or piece of equipment.

first half n [UK] [Buses] the mileage completed by a London Transport bus crew before they take their meal break.

first line managers n pl [Industrial relations] the lowest level of management – foreman, supervisors, etc – who actually deal closely and regularly with the workforce.

first man through the door n [Film] the leading villain. See also **dog heavy, heavy 3**.

first notice day n [Finance] the first date, varying as to contract and exchange, on which notices of the intention to deliver actual financial instruments against futures are authorised.

first of exchange n [Commerce] the first of the set of three bills of exchange that are customarily drawn in connection with foreign trade; hence the 'second of exchange' and the 'third of exchange'.

first of May n [US] [Circus] a newcomer to the circus; the annual season begins on May 1st.

first olive out of the bottle n [Business] given that the first olive in the bottle tends to impede the easy extraction of those beneath it, this is a business term for any hindrance or impediment to the free flow of creative ideas, of trading, action or progress. The 'olive' can be a person, a legal restriction, or any other tangle that must be sorted out and disposed of.

first one sharp! excl [Cricket] a batsman's saying to his partner, suggesting that it they run the first, easy run, quickly, they can create a second one before the fielders can react.

first sale doctrine n [Video] a loophole in US copyright law that allows retailers to rent out video-cassettes without giving royalty payments on each individual rental; only on the initial purchase by the retailer does this royalty have to be paid.

first silicon n [Computing] when a new chip has been designed and the designs made up for the first time in the fabrication factory, the first chips to be produced are 'first silicon'; such chips usually have some faults and for first silicon to be work perfect is a major achievement.

first strike n [Military] the first attack in a nuclear war; thus 'first strike capability' is the ability to launch a first strike with the intention of destroying at the outset of war any capacity the enemy may have to retaliate. See also **second strike**.

first team n [Film] those actors – the stars and the support – who are actually filmed, rather than the stand-ins who take their places while the lights, cameras angles and similar time-consuming aspects of the **take** are being worked out.

first use n [Military] the first use in war of a specific intensity or type of military measure: thus if a **first strike** were **conventional**, a nuclear **retaliatory strike** would still represent the first use of such weapons.

first working 1. n [Coal-mining] the driving of **headings** to extract coal and form pillars. **2.** n [Coal-mining] the first extraction of coal from a seam which is worked in more than one layer. See also **second working**.

first-and-ten n [US] [Football] See **first down**.

first-class paper n [Banking, Finance] See **fine paper 2**.

firstings n pl [Building, Plastering] the first coat of plaster applied on to the face of a mould or model.

first run a [Film] referring to a film that is being exhibited for the first time.

firsts 1. n [Industry] any manufactured article considered to be of first class standard. **2.** also **prime peltries, full-furred** n [Furriers] pelts

F

with the best developed fur fibre, taken in midwinter. See also **early-caught**, **late-caught**.

fiscal *n* [*Philately*] a label attached by Customs to a postal package, denoting that it has been examined and passed by them.

fiscal drag *n* [*Economics*] the time that elapses between a government's originating and legislating for an economic policy and its taking effect, either in theory or in practice.

fish 1. *n* [*Scot.*] [*Angling*] the salmon; any other fish is given its actual name. **2.** *n* [*Clothing*] a dart at the waist of a garment, intended to give a closer fit. **3.** *n* [*Navy*] a submarine. **4.** *n* [*Navy*] a torpedo. **5.** *n* [*Oil rigs*] any piece of equipment usually the bit and/or a **stand** of the **drill string** – which has become detached from the drill pipe. **6.** *n* [*Textiles*] pieces of material in the dye tub that are tangled together and require some work to unravel them. **7.** *v* [*Religion, Salvation Army*] to engage in personal evangelism, attempting to convert individuals to Christianity. **8.** *v* [*US*] [*Building*] to draw or pull electric wires – using a hook, line or wire tied to the cable, through a conduit or between the floors or walls of the building on which one is working. **9.** *v* [*Sailing, Ropework*] to mend broken spars by binding wooden splints along the damaged parts. **10.** *v* [*Building*] to pull a wire through a conduit in a building or through the space between the walls and floors, using a stiff looped wire or some similarly hooked object.

fish blind *v* [*Angling*] See **chuck and chance it**.

fish men *n pl* [*Textiles*] efficiency experts.

fish the water 1. *v* [*Angling*] See **chuck and chance it**. **2.** *v* [*Angling*] See **cover a fish**.

fishback *n* [*Gambling*] a marked pack of cards.

Fishbed *n* [*Military*] the Russian MiG–21, probably the most widely used fighter aircraft in the world, since so many were donated to many Third World and other allies by the Soviets.

fish-belly *n* [*US*] [*Railways*] a side or centre horizontal strut, shaped like a fish and used for the construction of trucks and carriages.

fisheye *n* [*Gemstones*] a diamond or any other gemstone cut too thin for proper brilliancy.

fish-head *n* [*Navy*] a naval officer, posted to an aircraft carrier, who does not fly. See also **black shoe**.

fishing *n* [*Oil rigs*] recovering stands of pipe and/or the bit when they become detached from the **drill string**, thus 'fishing tackle' means the specialised tools for picking up and extracting such lost equipment.

fishing expedition 1. *n* [*Banking*] an enquiry made by or of a banker regarding the general business status of a customer. When a banker is asked for such an assessment his answer should only concern a single transaction, which should provide sufficient information. **2.** *n* [*Law*] a legal proceeding carried on for the primary purpose of interrogating an adversary or examining his property, books, papers and records in order to discover information essential to, and to be used as a basis for, a further proceeding or defence. **3.** *n* [*Law*] an investigation that has no clearly defined object and transcends even a stated object in the hope of discovering any form of incriminating or newsworthy evidence, irrespective of its legality or accuracy; it is often seen in apparently 'irrelevant' questioning of witnesses. **4.** *n* [*US*] [*Politics*] an early fact- and theme-finding probe undertaken by a party committee in order to assess good issues and tactics for a forthcoming electoral campaign. It is usually based on an in-depth look at the plans of the opposition party. Such an expedition has no pre-set aims, but will use whatever useful material is 'hooked'.

fishing tackle, also **fishing tools** *n* [*Mining*] a variety of tools and equipment used to retrieve objects lost or stuck in a hole.

fishplate *n* [*Mountaineering*] an expansion bolt which will take a small bracket that will help overcome long expanses of rock without any natural foothold.

fishpole *n* [*TV*] a long, hand-held microphone boom, approximately 2 metres in length.

fish-scale *n* [*Metallurgy*] a defect sometimes found in vitreous enamel coatings which causes the flaking of minute areas of the enamel.

fishtail 1. *v* [*Flying*] to swing the tail in order to reduce airspeed when approaching the landing ground. **2.** *n* [*Archery*] an arrow that wobbles in flight. **3.** *n* [*Metallurgy*] a V-shaped cavity that may develop at the end of the piece during hot-rolling. **4.** *n* [*Logging*] split veneer that is used for filling in the manufacture of plywood. **5.** *n* [*Oil rigs*] a drill bit shaped like an ordinary fish's tail See also **Mother Hubbard**, **water course**.

fishyback *n* [*US*] [*Road transport*] freight that is transported by sea and road. See also **birdyback**, **piggyback 2**.

fission *n* [*Science*] 'the splitting, either spontaneously or under the impact of another particle, of a heavy nucleus into two (very rarely three or more) approximately equal parts, with resulting release of large amounts of energy' (OED Supplement, 1972). This is the basis of the two atomic bombs that were dropped on Hiroshima and Nagasaki in 1945. See also **fission products**, **fission-fusion-fission**, **fusion**.

fission products *n pl* [*Science*] the three hundred or more different isotopes which can be formed when fission takes place.

fission-fusion-fission *n* [*Science*] a three stage thermonuclear bomb with a uranium or fission trigger, a hydrogen or fusion intermediate stage and an outer case of 'natural' uranium.

fist *v* [*Sailing, Ropework*] to grasp a rope or sail and handle it quickly.

fist cods *n* [*Meat trade*] a slaughterhouse worker who removes the hide from the rear legs of lambs and calves and carries calf carcasses; it comes from 'fist' meaning a manual worker plus 'cods' meaning testicles.

fisting n [Building, Plastering] the use of the fingers of one hand to feed material in as a plaster mould is being run.

fit 1. n [Finance] a situation where a portfolio of investments prepared for a client matches exactly the requirements of that client. **2.** n [Photo-type-setting] See **side-bearings**.

fit up v [UK] [Police, Crime] to frame a villain for a crime that he/she may or may not have committed, by 'planting' evidence, bringing in perjured witnesses, etc. It is staunchly denied by the police, but invariably claimed by the villains. It comes from the idea of making a crime 'fit' a criminal.

Fitch sheets n pl [US] [Finance] sheets that indicate the successive prices of securities that are listed on the major stock exchanges; they are published by Fitch Investor's Service of New York.

fitter 1. n [Film] a musical director or a conductor who was given the task of fitting appropriate music to silent films. **2.** n [Logging] a workman who marks the logs for subsequent cutting in sections and cuts limbs and slits the bark on felled trees.

Fitter A n [Military] the Russian Sukhoi SU–7 nuclear-capable strike aircraft; it was first deployed in 1959 and is still in service.

Fitter D/H n [Military] the Russian Sukhoi SU–17 swing-wing ground attack fighter, first deployed in 1974.

fit-up n [UK] [Theatre] a temporary stage that can be taken down, set up and moved from venue to venue according to need; thus, by extension, it refers to the theatrical company who tours with a fit-up stage.

five ahead n [Pool] a method of scoring in which one player wins a match by gaining an advantage five games ahead of his opponent.

five and nine n [Theatre] basic theatrical makeup, based on the numbers of the makeup sticks given by their makers, Leichners.

five biggies n pl [New therapies] a term coined by Leonard Orr for his Theta rebirthing therapy; it refers to the five major areas of personal problems which must be dealt with and overcome if an ideal life is to be achieved: 1. birth trauma, 2. parental disapproval syndrome, 3. specific negatives, 4. unconscious death urge, 5. other life times. Confront and come to terms with all these and all will be well.

five by five adv [Aerospace] said of excellent radio reception which is based on two 1–5 scales covering both volume (loud) and audibility (clear); thus reception can be 4, 2, etc.

five duties n pl [Politics] as prescribed by the Communist Party of Vietnam these are: 1. devotion to communism, 2. the striving for political, ethical and occupational self-improvement

through study and training, 3. close co-operation and rapport with the masses, 4. maintenance of party discipline, 5. the support of the policy of proletarian internationalism.

five good drive n [Politics] a campaign launched in China in 1963 for raising productivity: a five good team excels in 1. implementing party policy, 2. promoting political education, 3. fulfilling the collective production targets, 4. fulfilling these targets in an economical way, 5. doing all tasks in the way ordered and established by the state.

five mile high club n [Air travel] an unofficial 'club' open to anyone – passengers and crew – whose sole membership qualification is to have made love in an aircraft as it cruises, supposedly five miles up in the air. A '125 club' is also supposed to exist, for those who have been similarly occupied on a British Rail Inter-City 125 train.

five percenter n [US] [Politics] on the analogy of 'Mr. Ten Per Cent', the show business agent, this is a self-appointed fixer who claims to know 'the right people' and promises to negotiate a lucrative contract with the Government for a five per cent kickback.

five pure classes n pl [Politics] in China these are: 1. the workers, 2. the poor and lower middle-class peasants, 3. soldiers, 4. good party officials, 5. revolutionary martyrs.

five recommendations n pl [Politics] in China these are: 1. civility, 2. politeness, 3. public hygiene, 4. discipline, 5. morality.

five Ws n pl [Journalism] the five traditional questions a reporter should ask and then include in the perfect lead paragraph of his/her story: who, what, where, why, when?????

five-barred gate n [Hunting] any form of gate encountered in a hunt.

five-blocks n pl [Cycling] five gears; thus 'ten-blocks' means ten gears, etc.

five-pod n [Photography] a particularly rigid form of camera support that uses five legs, rather than the more usual tripod.

fix 1. n [Aerospace] a reliable indication of the position of an aircraft which is obtained by taking a bearing – either visually or by radio – of that aircraft with reference to fixed objects. **2.** n [Drugs] one injection of a narcotic drug; it is the smallest amount of a drug that can be purchased. **3.** n [Espionage] a complex of pressures specially engineered by a sanctifying (see **sanctify**) team to control the target they are blackmailing. Fixes can be 'low intensity', only marginally compromising if it seems that such mildness is sufficient to produce the right response from a easily frightened individual. They escalate to 'high intensity' if the target appears to be brazening things out. The perfect situation is an 'okay fix'.

fix money n [US] [Gambling] payoffs to local police, politicians, etc. that are made by gamblers and casino operators/owners in return for protection. See also **ice 1**.

fixer 1. *n* [*Audio*] an individual who deals with the hiring of musicians, singers and recording facilities for the creation of recorded music. 2. *n* [*Gambling*] a person who has the right political connections to ensure that an illegal gambling enterprise will be – for the right price – fully 'protected'.

fixing *n* [*Finance*] the twice daily determining of the price of gold on the London Gold Market, which is carried out in the offices of N.M. Rothschild by representatives of the four firms of bullion dealers.

fixture *n* [*Shipping*] when chartering ships, this is a firm arrangement to make a ship available in a particular place on a particular date for the loading of cargo.

fizz *n* [*Government*] acro **FIS** Family Income Supplement.

fizzer 1. *n* [*Cricket*] a ball that keeps fast and low and possibly changes direction radically after it has pitched. 2. *n* [*UK*] [*Military*] in the British Army this is a charge sheet; thus 'on a fizzer' means on a charge for some breach of discipline.

flabby *a* [*Wine-tasting*] the opposite of **firm**: lacking crisp acidity, probably without **finish**.

flack 1. *n* [*Entertainment*] a press or publicity agent. 2. *n* [*US*] [*Politics*] this is analogous to the entertainment use (see 1): a government official who propounds the official line, an apologist. Such officials may be high or low in rank.

flag 1. *n* [*Aerospace*] a warning plate that flicks up on an aircraft's control panel either to point out a current malfunction, or to indicate the possibility that a malfunction will occur very soon if no immediate action is taken to pre-empt it. 2. *n* [*Chess*] a device on the chess-clock to denote the end of the time limit allowed to a player. 3. *n* [*Dog breeding*] See **feather**. 4. *n* [*Economics*] a graph on which a concentration of price fluctuations is bounded by sharp rises or falls that occur within a more gradual rise or fall and which may be seen as resembling a flag. 5. *n* [*Film, TV*] a square board or stand that is used to mask a light, or to shade the camera lens. 6. *n* [*Journalism*] See **banner**. 7. *n* [*Journalism*] a statement of the name, ownership, address, etc. of a publication, printed on the front or editorial page. 8. also **fladge** *n* [*Sex*] abbr of **flagellation** magazines or films portraying flagellation in a sexual/pornographic context. 9. *n* [*US*] [*Paper-making*] a piece of paper stuck into a roll to indicate a tear. 10. *n* [*Computing*] any type of indicator that marks a part of the data or program for special attention. 11. *v* [*Computing*] to mark the data or program with a flag. 12. *v* [*Military*] to attach some special indication to a file that announces to any other user that it must not be altered in any way.

flag day *n* [*Computing*] a **software** change which is not compatible with current or future models and which will therefore cost the user a great deal of money in investing in new hardware.

flag list *n* [*Navy*] all active officers of flag rank (equivalent to that of admiral): admiral of the fleet, admiral, vice-admiral, rear-admiral on the General List, plus officers of equivalent rank on the lists of instructors, and medical and dental officers.

flag out *v* [*Business, Shipping*] to run a merchant ship or ships under flags of convenience – usually of Liberia or Panama. Such countries demand less stringent standards in their fleets and thus UK businesses can save money by by-passing domestic regulations.

flag-flying *n* [*Cards*] in bridge this is the making of an overbid that will almost certainly fail, simply to liven up a dull game.

flagging 1. *n* [*Clothing*] the rising and falling of material caused by the action of the sewing machine needle. 2. *n* [*TV*] the vertical breakup at the top of a TV picture which is found on second-rate video recordings. 3. *n* [*Video*] TV picture distortion which is caused by incorrect co-ordination of the playback head timing.

flags 1. *n pl* [*Hunting*] the kennels; it comes from the flags which form the paved flooring of the courtyard. 2. *n* [*Navy*] a flag lieutenant; the admiral's aide-de-camp.

flagship sites *n pl* [*Commerce*] the leading, show-place stores, hotels, garages, etc. on which a retailer concentrates his energies, advertising, promotion and probably greatest pride.

flagwaver *n* [*TV*] an intermittent fault, due to some mechanical malfunction, which is hard to trace and may not, inconveniently, choose to occur when the engineer is attempting to track it down.

flail chest *n* [*Medicine*] a patient with rib fractures and paradoxical breathing.

flak 1. *n* [*Military*] it comes from Ger. 'Fliegerabwehrkanone' meaning 'anti-aircraft gun'; it was coined in World War II and is currently used for any anti-aircraft defences, including missiles. 2. *n* [*Politics*] adverse comment and criticism from the public, the opposition or even fellow party members after a senior politician has made an unpopular decision or statement of policy. Thus 'flak-catcher' is a (usually junior) bureaucrat set up as a buffer between the complaining public and his political masters. See also **negative feedback 2**.

flak jacket *n* [*Military*] a bullet-proof jacket worn by anyone – airman, soldier or sailor – who hopes to gain protection from wounds.

flake 1. *v* [*Merchant Navy*] to coil a rope on deck to ensure that it will run smoothly. 2. *n* [*US*] [*Car salesmen*] See **floater 8**. 3. *n* [*US*] [*Police*] an arrest that has as its main justification the officer's need to meet a specific arrest quota or to satisfy a temporary, but well-publicised drive for increased police efficiency in combating crime. See also **accommodation collar**. 4. *n* [*Sailing, Rope-*

work] a single turn of a coil, or a tier of turns in a coil of rope.

flaking 1. *n* [*Building, Plastering*] the scaling away of patches of the plaster surface due to insufficient adhesion to the previous coat. **2.** *n* [*US*] [*Police*] the planting of incriminating evidence on or around a suspect to facilitate or justify an arrest.

flam *n* [*Music*] a particular beat played on the side-drum.

flame *v* [*Computing*] to speak incessantly and obsessively on a particular topic of little interest to anyone but oneself; or to talk arrant and apparent nonsense about an otherwise interesting subject. Possibly it comes from gay slang 'flame' meaning to act conspicuously.

flammable fringe, also **explosive fringe** *n* [*Coal-mining*] a region where quantities of air (or any other reactant gas) and a flammable gas are present and have mixed to produce a gas which can propagate flames.

flange up *v* [*Oil rigs*] to complete any activity on the ring; it comes from 'flanging up' which means making the last connection in the completion of a well.

Flanker *n* [*Military*] the Russian Sukhoi SU–27; similar to the US F–15, this aircraft came into service in the mid–1980s and is used as an interceptor and possibly a strike aircraft.

flankers *n pl* [*Shooting*] the men who ensure that the **driven** game stays in front of the butts.

flanking in *n* [*Building, Plastering*] the process of filling in the areas between **screeds** with a plastering mix.

flap 1. *n* [*US*] [*Medicine*] an operation to remove the root of a tooth. **2.** *n* [*Military*] any mild state of emergency or general panic.

flap potential *n* [*Espionage*] this comes from the military use of **flap**: any subject which, if brought before the public, would guarantee embarrassment both to the CIA in particular and to the US government in general. See also **family jewels**.

flap shot, also **wide open beaver** *n* [*Sex*] in film or still pictures, this is a close-up shot of the 'open' vagina and labia.

flapping *n* [*UK*] [*Horse-racing*] any racing that is not subject to National Hunt Committee or Jockey Club rules, or, in greyhound racing, those of the National Greyhound Racing Club. Thus 'flappings' are small race meetings of this type; 'flapping track' is a small unlicensed greyhound racing track.

flapping baffle *n* [*Audio*] a type of loudspeaker cabinet in which an extra baffle, speaker cone or drive unit is substituted for the open port that is used in the **reflex** system. See also **reflex**.

flaps and seals *n* [*Espionage*] the standard course given to agents in the interception of mail; thus 'flaps and seals man' is an expert in mail interception.

flaps well down 1. *adv* [*Business*] a more posi-

tive version of the espionage term (see **2.**): referring to an individual who knows exactly what he/she is doing and where they wish to go and would thus rather get on with doing just that with the minimum of interference. **2.** *adv* [*Espionage*] an agent who is attempting to maintain a low profile, usually through fears about current or possible future career problems due to a sense of diminishing efficiency.

flare 1. *v* [*Aerospace*] used of a pilot who pulls up the aircraft's nose immediately prior to landing so that the plane sinks down slowly onto the runway, rather than flying on to it at speed. **2.** *v* [*UK*] [*Theatre*] to place and regulate the lighting and sound equipment. **3.** also **round out** *v* [*Gliding*] when landing, this means to change the final approach flight path from descending to parallel with the landing surface. **4.** *n* [*US*] [*Football*] a pass pattern executed by running a short distance downfield and towards one of the sidelines. **5.** *n* [*US*] [*Football*] a flare pass, made quickly out to a back who is heading towards the sidelines. **6.** *n* [*Photography*] bright patches of light that obscure that printed image; these result from aiming the camera at too intense a light source. **7.** *n* [*Shoe-making*] a piece of leather sewn to the inside of the insole to serve as support for the arch of the foot. **8.** *n* [*TV*] dazzle off reflecting surfaces that shows up in the camera shot.

flare out *v* [*Aerospace*] See **flare 1**.

flaring 1. *n* [*Custom cars*] a variety of methods which adapt wheel arches to cover wider tyres than stock sizes. **2.** *n* [*Oil rigs*] the burning off of the natural gas found in conjunction with oil in oilfields. The current use of this gas on account of its own energy has led to a great diminution in flaring.

flash 1. *v* [*Hunting*] hounds do this when they overrun the scent. **2.** *n* [*UK*] [*Gambling*] the banner or similar name-displaying cloth or board which is erected by a bookmaker to announce his pitch. **3.** *n* [*Journalism*] a brief news report sent over the wire, usually preceding a longer and more detailed story; thus the 'news flash' of TV and radio. **4.** *n, v* [*UK*] [*Market-traders*] a display, a publicity stunt; to show (off). **5.** *n* [*Shooting*] a small pond or pool, often the result of sudden, heavy rainfall or floods; it is attractive to wildfowl and thus popular with their hunters. **6.** *n* [*US*] [*Stock market*] a notation on the ticker tape that trading volume is so heavy that the tape is running five minutes later than actuality; the running tape is interrupted to deliver the 'flash price' of the stock or stocks that are causing such heavy trading. **7.** *n* [*TV*] a very brief shot. **8.** *a* [*TV*] referring to a performer who is very pleased with him/herself and is far too keen to show it.

flash art *n* [*Art*] art that takes as its aesthetic the showy, show-business-orientated extravagant superficialities of the late 1950s and early 1960s;

exponents include Andy Warhol, Richard Hamilton, Allen Jones and Frank Stella.

flash gear *n* [*UK*] [*Market-traders*] showy goods; the value is in the display rather than the quality.

flash nudet [*Military*] US code for **nuclear detonation recorded**.

flash roll *n* [*UK*] [*Police*] a wad of money held by an officer which is never actually used but which is 'flashed' ostentatiously around to convince a criminal, eg: a drug dealer, that one has the money to make a purchase – at which point the arrest will be made.

flash set *n* [*Building, Plastering*] the sudden setting of plaster or cement when mixed with water.

flash the range, also **flash the gallery** *v phr* [*US*] [*Prisons*] to use a mirror or mirror-like surface, pushed through the cell bars, to survey the landing outside one's cell for an approaching guard.

flashback *n* [*Film*] a break in the narrative that permits the insertion of a scene, episode or even the rest of the film, except for a final return to the 'now' of the film's action; it is told as a chronological backtrack, to childhood, another country, etc.

flasher *n* [*UK*] [*Fire brigade*] a sudden gas explosion that a fireman may encounter when he opens a door in a burning building when air mixes with unburnt gas.

flashing 1. *n* [*Film*] the reduction of contrast in a film by exposing it to a weak light before or after camera exposure, but prior to processing. 2. *n* [*Telephony*] a signal sent by the operator to another operator, or by a subscriber to an operator to gain the other's attention. 3. *n* [*Photography*] re-exposing a photographic print to white light while it is still in the developer – this produces a form of solarised image.

flashing blade *n* [*UK*] [*Railways*] the firing shovel used by firemen on steam trains.

flashings *n pl* [*Dog breeding*] the white markings on the chest, neck, face, feet or tail tip of the Cardigan Welsh Corgi.

flashpack *n* [*Commerce*] a package which displays a note touting a 'special reduction' price, '50p off' etc.

flashy *a* [*Angling*] said of a river that rises and falls quickly.

flat 1. *adv* [*Cars*] abbr of **flat out** at top speed. 2. *a* [*Audio*] referring to a properly designed audio system which amplifies all frequencies equally well, with no 'discrimination' over a wide waveband. 3. *a* [*Commerce*] unvarying, fixed, uniform, unmoved by changing external conditions; eg: a flat fare, which works for all journeys, irrespective of the distance travelled, as is found, inter alia, on the New York subway. 4. *a* [*US*] [*Football*] a team that is stale, lacking in energy and 'go'. 5. *a* [*Printing*] said of a serif that is not bracketed to the stem. 6. *a* [*Stock market*]

referring to stock that offers no appeal to the market. 7. *a* [*Wine-tasting*] dull, insipid, lacking acidity; it is also used of a sparkling wine that has lost its bubbles. 8. *n* [*Horse-racing*] those races that are run along a course involving only distance and no jumping; flat racing takes place in spring, summer and autumn. 9. *n* [*Navy*] the open spaces between decks. 10. *n* [*Photography*] a picture that lacks contrast between black and white tones. 11. *n* [*UK*] [*Railways*] the worn flat part of a wheel, due to excess braking; this is London Transport usage. 12. *n* [*TV, Film, Theatre*] a large, moveable section of scenery made of wooden battens and stretched canvas or reinforced hardboard which can be painted to represent a 'wall' or similar large piece of the background.

flat bit *n* [*US*] [*Prisons*] a prison sentence that lasts only a finite and pre-stated period. See also **split bit**.

flat characters/round characters *n pl* [*Literary criticism*] terms coined by E. M. Forster in 'Aspects of the Novel' (1927) to differentiate between characters 'constructed around a single idea or quality' and highly complex characters 'capable of surprising in a convincing way'.

flat engine *n* [*Cars*] See **boxer engine**.

flat face *n* [*US*] [*Road transport*] a truck with the cab over the engine. See also **cab-over**.

flat file *n* [*Computing*] a file comprising a collection of records of the same type which do not contain repeating groups, ie: a group in a record that can occur any number of times and which is thus ineligible for a flat file.

flat head, also **wooden head** *n* [*US*] [*Journalism*] an uninteresting, tedious headline.

flat iron *n* [*Merchant navy*] a collier, with a low superstructure, used for carrying coal and coke.

flat joint, also **flat store** *n* [*Gambling*] any crooked gambling environment.

flat passers *n pl* [*Gambling*] a pair of crooked dice which have had the 6–1 sides shaved on one die, and the 3–4 sides on the other, thus producing an excess of 4,5,9 and 10 throws.

flat spot *n* [*Cars*] a momentary hesitation of the engine when the accelerator pedal is depressed; it is caused by a moment during the increase in the air flow through the carburettor, (when the throttle is opened further or speed increased) when the air-to-fuel ratio becomes so weak as to prevent good acceleration.

flat top *n* [*US*] [*Navy*] an aircraft carrier; thus 'baby flat top' is a smaller aircraft carrier, usually a cargo vessel which has been converted into a carrier for the duration.

flat trading *n* [*Finance*] trading in stocks and shares that have no accrued interest.

flat wheel *n* [*US*] [*Coal-mining*] any injury to the leg or foot.

flat work *n* [*Laundering*] articles that are not to

be starched – sheets, pillowcases, etc – rather than those that must be.

flatbacker *n* [*Sex*] a prostitute who offers quantity to her pimp rather than quality to the clients.

flatfoot *n* [*US*] [*Marine Corps*] a soldier in the US Army.

flathead *n* [*Hot rods*] a side-valve engine with no overhead valves.

flatline *v* [*US*] [*Medicine*] to die; it comes from the flattening of the oscillating line on the monitor screens that are attached to a patient's heart, pulse, etc.

flats 1. *n pl* [*Cycling*] See **straights**. 2. *n pl* [*Publishing*] small, thin, glossy, usually overpriced children's books, that are produced to exploit the indulgent Christmas market.

flat-sour *n* [*Food*] the fermentation of tinned products caused by the action of micro-organisms which attack carbo-hydrates and produce harmful acids which destroy the food. Such organisms do not produce gas, and there is no noticeable distention of the tin.

flat-spotting *n* [*Motor-racing*] a malfunction in driving whereby the tyres spin but the car fails to move; it lasts only fractions of a second, but will rub a bare spot on the tyre and cause massive vibrations inside the car, double-vision for the driver, etc.

flatten *v* [*Skiing*] to make an outward movement of the knees which acts to flatten the skis on the surface.

flatting *n* [*Metallurgy*] the sudden yielding which occurs when normalised or hot rolled steel sheet or strip is distorted.

flatty 1. *n* [*UK*] [*Circus*] a member of the audience. 2. *n* [*UK*] [*Market-traders*] anyone who is not a market-trader. 3. *n* [*Police*] a policeman; it comes from 'flatfoot'.

flatwork *n* [*Textiles*] any fabrics, other than those destined for clothing, such as handkerchiefs, tablecloths, etc; in general, this refers to household linens that will be ironed flat.

flavour 1. *n* [*Computing*] variety, type, kind, style; the addition of new varieties makes a given system or component 'flavourful'. See also **vanilla**. 2. *n* [*Science*] a specific type or variety of **quark**, there have been approximately five flavours discovered so far.

flaw *n* [*Philately*] a fortuitous blemish on the design or perforation of a stamp which has arisen during its manufacture. Flaws may arise from ink crusts or foreign matter on the printing plate, or from a fold in the paper. When a flaw is constant and thus repeats throughout an issue or part of an issue, it becomes a variety. See also **error, variety**.

flea *n* [*US*] [*Medicine*] a medical intern, so called either because they hover about the patient's bed, or because they are continually performing tests that involve the taking of blood samples.

flea box *n* [*UK*] [*Railways*] a cramped guards van on a goods train.

fleck *v* [*Coursing*] used of a greyhound which snatches the hare and then loses hold.

fled *a* [*Pottery*] liable to crack at a late stage of manufacture because of too rapid a change in the temperature during or after a firing.

fleece, put out a *v phr* [*Religion*] to ask God for a tangible sign regarding a specific course of possible action; see Judges 6:36–40.

fleet *v* [*Sailing, Ropework*] to slacken off on a tackle and draw the ropes apart ready for another pull.

fleet the messenger *v* [*Sailing, Ropework*] to rearrange the turns of rope when they have crawled too high on a capstan.

flesher *n* [*Furriers*] a specialist worker who removes the flesh and lower skin membrane; his skills contribute substantially to the creation of a quality product.

fleshing 1. *n* [*US*] [*Meat trade*] fatness, weight. 2. *n* [*Tanning*] the removal of flesh and fat from hides prior to tanning.

fleur de coin *n* [*Numismatics*] a coin in mint or otherwise perfect condition.

flex form *n* [*Journalism*] a style of newspaper design that is based around the advertisements, allowing them to be centred on a page, or otherwise placed so that the copy must flow around them rather than dictating by its own design where the advertisements are sited.

flexibility *n* [*Industrial relations*] the willingness of a union 'shop' to overlook strict demarcation lines in the workplace and/or to accept movement of personnel to other parts of the plant or company.

flexible response, also **gradual deterrence** *n* [*Military*] the concept of meeting aggression with a suitable level of counter-aggression and in the relevant environment; always, unless the initial aggression is a nuclear **first strike**, leaving the options of **escalation** and **de-escalation** available if required or feasible. This was first accepted by NATO forces in Europe in 1967. See also **Countervailing Strategy**.

flexitime, also **flex time, flexible time** *n* [*Industrial relations*] the staggering of working hours in an attempt to improve an employee's working standards by offering a more relaxed 'day' than the traditional 'nine to five'. Research has shown that this choice (within certain limits) of one's working hours has improved both the quality and quantity of productivity, since the workers are using those hours at which they themselves are most alert and efficient.

flicking *n* [*Weaving*] the process of briskly combing out the ends of a lock of raw wool in preparation for spinning. It is performed with a 'flicker': a single card or brush.

fliers *n pl* [*Wine tasting*] solid particles created by the dissolving of yeast cells during the fermentation of champagne; they are rarely found today but were common in the early days of the drink, thus necessitating opaque or coloured champagne glasses to hide them.

flies *n pl* [*Theatre*] the area above the stage where lights, scenery, **drapes**, etc. are suspended and can be raised/lowered as required; such scenery and lights, etc. are thus 'flown'.

flight **1.** *n* [*Shooting*] a number of birds flying together. **2.** *n* [*Shooting*] the birds produced during one season.

flight attendant *n* [*Air travel*] a synonym for the traditional 'stewardess' or 'steward'; this forms part of the contemporary urge to alter facts by 'softening' language, especially that used in job descriptions.

flight capital **1.** *n* [*Finance*] money that has been invested or deposited outside the country of its origin so that its owner may use it in the event of a political reverse at home which necessitates his own immediate departure. **2.** *n* [*Economics*] funds that are transferred from one country to another, often into the anonymity of a numbered account in a Swiss bank, in order to avoid taxes, hide illicit profits, hedge against inflation, etc.

flight envelope *n* [*Aerospace*] a set of limits – of speed, altitude, range, payload, manœuvrability, etc. – that exist in the design and capabilities of any model of aircraft.

flight to quality *n* [*Finance*] the movement of capital to what one sees as the safest investments to protect oneself from instability in the market.

flighty *a* [*Hunting*] said of hounds or scent which are changeable and uncertain.

flim *n* [*UK*] [*Market-traders*] a five-pound note.

flimping *n* [*UK*] [*Market traders*] tinkering with the weights on the stall scales to give the customer short weight.

flimsy *n* [*Navy*] a naval officer's certificate of service.

fling *v* [*Hunting*] to drive on the scent at the least sign of a check.

flinty *a* [*Wine-tasting*] certain white wines grown on certain soils have a hint of gun-flint in the bouquet and flavour. See also **smoky**.

flip **1.** *n* [*Finance*] acro **Flexible Loan Insurance Plan** an insurance scheme in which a down-payment is made into a savings account from which payments can be taken to supplement the interest when the loan falls due. **2.** *v* [*Military*] in gunnery, this is used of the barrel of a heavy gun when it jumps around at the moment of discharge. **3.** *v* [*US*] [*Police*] to turn informer. **4.** *v* [*US*] [*Prisons*] to denounce a fellow inmate to the authorities. See also **drop a dime, turn over 3**.

flip a ruby *v* [*US*] [*Medicine*] to have a haemorrhage.

flip chart *n* [*Advertising*] a campaign presentation prepared on a number of pages which are linked by a ring binder and can be 'flipped

through' from page to page to provide visual backup to the verbal explanations.

flip jump *n* [*Skating*] a jump performed by placing the right toe-point to the right back outside edge at the finish of a left-three.

flip-flop **1.** *n* [*Computing*] the basic memory device employed by computers: an electronic circuit with only two stable states. By placing a pulse on the input to this circuit it can be made to alternate between these two states; one flip-flop stores one **bit** of information. **2.** *n* [*US*] [*Politics*] this comes from its use both as a 'somersault' and in the computing context; it is the ability of a politician to hold two opposing views simultaneously, an essential tool for the aspirant leader, by which first a constituency and later the entire electorate may be baffled.

flip-flop arbitration, also **pendulum arbitration** *n* [*Industrial relations*] a method of arbitration in industrial disputes that is designed to avoid strikes; the arbitrator, in the case of a collapse in negotiations, cannot propose a compromise, but he must come down on one side or another. This supposedly influences both parties towards moderation.

flipper **1.** *n* [*Food processing*] a sealed can of processed food in which the internal pressure has caused the ends to bulge. **2.** *n* [*US*] [*Theatre*] a short, narrow **flat** which is nailed to another, larger flat in order to support it. **3.** *n* [*Tyre-making*] a strip of rubberised fabric used to strengthen the join between the sidewalls and the rubber-and-wire bead that forms the base of the tyre.

flipping *n* [*Finance*] the practice of unscrupulous private loan companies ('loan sharks') who not only charge above average interest on loans, but then charge interest on that interest if payments are not made swiftly enough. See also **vigorish**.

flirt *n* [*Industry*] a device, often a lever, used for causing sudden and intermittent movement, that is used especially in certain clock mechanisms.

flirting *adv* [*Archery*] describing an arrow which wobbles in flight.

flit *v* [*Coal-mining*] to move a coalface machine from a position of use to another when it is not operating as a producing unit.

flitch **1.** *n* [*Building*] one of several elements that are clamped together – as in planks or iron plates – to make a large girder or laminated beam. **2.** *n* [*Woodwork*] a longitudinal section of a log, often one selected for further processing. **3.** *n* [*Woodwork*] a package of thin sheets of veneer cut from a log.

FLK *n* [*Medicine*] abbr of **funny-looking kid** a child with no immediately or easily diagnosable ailment other than something obviously being peculiar; it is generally obsolete today.

float **1.** *n* [*Building*] a flat metal or wooden tool used to smooth fresh concrete surfaces. **2.** *n* [*US*] [*Car salesmen*] the treatment of the customer's deposit by the salesman as a temporary loan. **3.** *n* [*Journalism, Advertising*] a headline – in a newspaper or an advertisement – set inside a large area of white space, in which it 'floats'. **4.** *n* [*Mining*] rock or vein material found at some distance from the main deposit. **5.** *n* [*Table tennis*] a stroke with a disguised swing of the bat which imparts virtually no spin to the ball – despite appearances to the contrary – and is intended to force an error. **6.** *n* [*Video*] the amount of time the manufacturer or distributor will give a customer before demanding payment for a product. **7.** *n* [*Weaving*] a **warp** or **weft** thread that 'floats' over the top of several threads at a time. **8.** *n* [*Commerce*] a customer who leaves the store while the salesman is looking for an item that has been requested from stock. **9.** *n* [*Commerce*] a sale that is lost for any reason. **10.** *v* [*Commerce*] to get rid of a customer whose fussiness transcends their commercial use. **11.** *v* [*Finance*] said of a national currency when it fluctuates as regards its exchange rate in respect of the international currency market. **12.** *v* [*Lacrosse*] used of a defence who moves away from an opponent into the middle of the field; thus it means to make a lateral move. See also **sag 2**.

floated copy *n* [*Book collecting*] a book that was once inlaid, but was subsequently removed from the inlay and rebound in seperate leaves; such books may be recognised by a slight curl at the edges where the glue has left a permanent mark.

floater 1. *n* [*Business*] a bearer bond, especially one that is unlisted but is acceptable as collateral. **2.** *n* [*Glass-making*] a floating refractory shape which holds back scum and impurities in the surface of the glass forming in a pot or tank furnace. **3.** *n* [*Gliding*] a glider with low wing loading, low minimum speed and a low rate of sinking back towards the ground. **4.** *n* [*Industry*] a casual labourer who moves from job to job, looking for the best pay. **5.** *n* [*Police*] a dead body found floating or drowned in water. **6.** *n* [*Politics*] one who votes illegally by using a false registration or by using the name of a voter who has not yet voted or has no intention of voting. **7.** *n* [*US*] [*Road transport*] a driver with no steady job. **8.** *n* [*US*] [*Car salesmen*] a customer who is seen as a bad risk because he moves or changes jobs too often. See also **flake**.

floaters 1. *n pl* [*Banking, Stock market*] government bearer bonds which are given by bill-brokers to a bank as security for money lent to them at **call**. **2.** *n pl* [*Banking, Stock market*] a bearer security: a security for which no title is required, the owner being the person who actually holds it. **3.** *n pl* [*Banking, Stock market*] a local government stock that has a floating rate of interest and changes every six months in response to fluctuations in the general level of interest. **4.** *n pl* [*UK*] [*Prisons*] paperback books which have been sent

in to one inmate and which subsequently circulate through the prison population.

floaters in the snow *n pl* [*Navy*] sausages and mashed potatoes.

floating *n* [*Painting*] the separation of one or more pigments in a coloured paint which can occur while the paint is in storage, but which can be negated by stirring the paint before use. See also **flooding**.

floating accent *n* [*Printing*] an accent which is contained on its own piece of metal and which thus can be positioned over/under the type character to which it belongs.

floating point *n* [*Computing*] the handling of very large numbers in a machine that has only limited computational space by moving the decimal point and performing the calculations with each number expressed as a factor of 10.

floating voltage *n* [*Electronics*] a network or component which has no earth terminal.

floating-rate interest *n* [*Stock market*] an interest rate that changes regularly on a set formula to reflect the fluctuations of the market. It is usually calculated at so many points above the inter-bank rate (**LIBOR**).

floats *n pl* [*Textiles*] small blocks of warp ends that are not properly interlaced with the filling threads and remain on top of the finished cloth.

flodding *n* [*Communications*] in **packet-switching**, this is a routing method in which each node reproduces in-coming packets and sends duplicates to its neighbours; this ensures swift and accurate communications, but uses up a very large amount of transmission capacity.

flog *v* [*Theatre*] to remove the dust from canvas by beating it with a number of canvas strips secured on a wooden handle – the 'flogger'.

flog the clock *v* [*Navy*] the illicit practice of advancing the clock so as to shorten one's time on watch.

flog the water *v* [*Angling*] to keep on fishing indifferently.

flogger *n* [*US*] Painting] a long-bristled brush used in graining wood.

Flogger D/J *n* [*Military*] the Russian MiG–27, a swing-wing supersonic aircraft which has been used both as an interceptor and in a ground attack role.

flong *n* [*Printing*] a sheet of papier maché used to make a mould from a forme; from this mould a metal plate is cast which is used for printing a page of a newspaper.

flood *n* [*TV, Film*] an unfocussed light source.

flood gap, also **flood gate** *n* [*US*] [*Farming*] a gate sited in a place likely to be washed out in heavy rains.

flooding 1. *n* [*Painting*] an extreme case of **floating** when not only do the pigments of coloured paint separate during storage, but they persist in this state despite stirring and so produce a new colour when one attempts to use the paint.

See also **floating**. **2.** *n* [*Psychology*] a method of treating a sufferer from a particular phobia by the gradual and controlled exposure of the patient to the cause of the phobia.

floor 1. *n* [*Business*] a lower limit or base, especially one imposed by governments, beneath which prices, wages, etc. are never permitted to fall; it is the opposite of **ceiling**. **2.** *n* [*Business*] a bottom level imposed by economic factors, and as such more flexible than (1). **3.** *n* [*Coal-mining*] the stratum immediately below a coal seam. **4.** *n* [*Coal-mining*] the base of any excavation. **5.** *n* [*Stock market*] the trading area of the London Stock Exchange. **6.** *n* [*TV*] the ground area of a studio; thus 'on the floor' refers to a programme in production in a studio.

floor, on the *adv* [*Flying*] flying close to the ground. See also **deck, on the**.

floor art also **distributional art, ground art, litter sculpture** *n* [*Art*] a modern style of sculpture that eschews traditional styles in favour of spreading the construction out over the gallery's or the artist's studio floor. This use of the floor parallels the painter's use of a background against which the subjects of a picture are set.

floor broker *n* [*Futures market*] a member of the futures exchange who is paid a fee for executing orders for clearing members or for their customers.

floor planning *n* [*Business*] a system of financed wholesale purchasing of expensive items – cars, machine tools and plant, etc. – whereby the retailer stocks his sales floor with the minimum possible cash outlay.

floor ticket *n* [*US*] [*Stock market*] a document which holds sufficient information to enable a floor broker to perform a securities transaction. See also **ticket 4**.

floor trader *n* [*Futures market*] a member who generally trades only for himself, for an account he controls, or has such a trade made especially for him.

floor whore, also **floor artist** *n* [*US*] [*Car salesmen*] a salesman who works only on the floor, dealing continually with new customers.

floorer *n* [*Skittles*] See **flopper 2**.

floorman 1. *n* [*Business*] any employee who, to some extent, is a representative of his employer to the public; the employer remains within his office, the employee works 'on the floor'. **2.** *n* [*Horse-racing*] the assistant to a tic-tac man (who communicates the shifting odds from the larger bookmakers to the smaller ones by a system of established hand signals); a bookmaker's runner. **3.** *n* [*Oil rigs*] a member of the drilling crew who works on the rig floor.

flop 1. *v* [*Advertising, Printing*] to print a two colour picture with the colours reversed. **2.** *v* [*Advertising, Printing*] to reverse a picture – often the direction in which the subject is looking or moving – for printing purposes: left to right or

vice versa. **3.** *n* [*UK*] [*Police*] any house where a criminal can dump his loot, burglary tools, weapons, etc., so as to be completely 'clean' when the police arrive to question him and search his person and property. See also **slaughter**.

Flop Squad *n* [*US*] [*Police*] New York Transit policemen who act as decoys, pretend to be asleep, and then arrest those who attempt to rob them.

flopper 1. *n* [*Crime, Insurance*] one who specialises in defrauding insurance firms by 'falling down' on apparently 'dangerous' supermarket floors, staircases, escalators, 'collapsing' in front of slowly moving cars, etc. The art of successful flopping is to make sure that it is less trouble for the victim (or his insurance company) to pay up than to fight the claim. **2.** *n* [*Skittles*] a throw which knocks down all nine skittles at once.

floppy *a* [*Stock market*] a floppy market means that prices are unstable.

floppy disk *n* [*Computing*] a flexible storage medium, either 5.25 (the most popular), 8 or 3.5 inches in diameter, on which data can be stored, memorised and retrieved by a computer. The average double-sided, double-density 5.25" floppy can store approximately 360,000 **bytes** of data, making them greatly inferior in capacity, and in operational speed to the larger hard disks or **Winchesters** with storage capacity in the millions of bytes.

flops *n* [*Computing*] acro **floating-point operations per second** the measure of power used for extra-powerful computers; this is always qualified by a statement of the precision to which the operations are carried out.

flopsweat *n* [*Entertainment*] stage fright made manifest: the beads of perspiration that break out on a performer's face when a performance goes wrong, or even if he/she merely fears that it will. It is used especially by stand-up comedians when they 'die' on stage.

Florence Nightingale *n* [*UK*] [*Railways*] a shunter with a headlight, working at night among the wagons; it is named after Florence Nightingale, 'The Lady with the Lamp', (1820–1910).

florilegium *n* [*Bibliography*] an anthology.

flory *a* [*Heraldry*] ornamented with small fleurs-de-lis.

flourish 1. *n* [*Printing*] an extension/addition to a normal letter. **2.** *n* [*Printing*] any ornamental line or shape.

flow bean, also **cracked valve** *n* [*Oil rigs*] the choke valve used to control the flow of oil on a **Christmas tree**.

flow up the bridge *v phr* [*Scientology*] to join the Church and, inter alia, turn over one's bank account to its coffers.

flower bedding *n* [*US*] [*Road transport*] See **dusting**.

flower bond *n* [*US*] [*Economics*] a US Treasury bond that was purchasable at below face value, but redeemable at full face value if the money was to be used in the payment of federal estate taxes (death duties). In this capacity they were known as 'flowers at the funeral'. Since 1976 such bonds are charged some capital gains tax when sold and have thus lost much of their appeal.

flowery *a* [*Wine-tasting*] fragrant, flower-like in odour.

flowline *n* [*Cars*] the car assembly line, pioneered by Henry Ford, and at the heart of modern mass production systems.

flown *a* [*Philately*] said of any envelope or other dispatch which has been posted via air mail.

FLTSATCOM *n* [*US*] [*Navy*] acro **Fleet Satellite Communications** a network of USN communications satellites administered by the Naval Space Command since 1983. It comprises four spacecraft in geosynchronous orbit (an orbit, usually that of a communications satellite, in which the vehicle moves at the same rate as the earth does, fixed at an altitude of 22,000 miles above the equator) that provide global communication for ships, anti-submarine warfare (**ASW**), planes and other mobile forces, including strategic Air Force communications. See also **AFSATCOM**.

flub **1.** *v, n* [*Golf*] to mis-hit the ball; a flub is a mis-hit. **2.** *v* [*Theatre, Film*] to make a mistake in delivering one's lines.

flubdub *n* [*Printing, Journalism*] any ornamental piece of type used on a page, eg: an asterisk, a bullet, etc. See also **dingbat**.

fluctustress *n* [*Printing*] an underlining that is represented by an undulating rather than a straight line.

fluff **1.** *n* [*Motor trade*] a spare part. **2.** *n* [*US*] [*Road transport*] See **balloon freight**. **3.** *v* [*Drugs*] to adulterate such powdered drugs as heroin or cocaine by pulverising them extremely finely and then adding a substance – eg: talcum powder – that has no narcotic content but is of a similar consistency. See also **cut 12**. **4.** *v* [*Golf*] See **flub**. **5.** *v* [*Theatre*] to make a mistake on stage, either in a speech or in one's **business**.

fluffers *n pl* [*UK*] [*Transport*] on the London underground system these are the women whose job it is to spend every night cleaning the tunnels of refuse, in particular the fluffy asbestos dust that accumulates from the passing trains.

fluffing *n* [*UK*] [*Railways*] See **quilling**.

fluffy *a* [*Golf*] said of a ball which is sitting high, and thus easily hittable, on top of the grass.

fluffy link *n* [*Railways*] the best paid duties at a London Transport underground depot.

flugie *n* [*US*] [*Politics*] a rule that benefits only the creator of that rule, and one that can always be changed as required by the creator to ensure that no-one else is ever able to use it to their own advantage.

fluid logic *n* [*Computing*] a means of implementing logic functions not by the usual electronic circuitry, but by the flow of incompress-

ible fluids through tubes that connect intersections and constrictions. This system is very useful in situations where high electro-magnetic interference inhibits the use of electric components.

fluids and electrolytes *n pl* [*US*] [*Medicine*] a nickname for the alcohol that has been put on one side for the medical staff to use for after-work relaxation.

flukey *a* [*Meat trade*] said of liver which still has tubes in it; it is unsuitable for sale.

flukum *n* [*US*] [*Circus*] cotton candy (US), candy floss (UK).

flunkey **1.** *n* [*US*] [*Coal-mining*] the assistant to a blaster or driller. **2.** *n* [*Mining*] a man who works as an assistant cook in mining and lumber camps.

flush **1.** *v* [*Computing*] to scratch out superficially. **2.** *v* [*Computing*] to end work for the day. **3.** *v* [*Computing*] to exclude someone from an activity. **4.** *v* [*Farming*] to prepare sheep for breeding by increasing the feed ration immediately prior to mating rams and ewes. **5.** *v* [*Shooting*] used of a hunter or beater who drives game from cover in order to present the guns with a target. **6.** *a* [*Publishing*] without indentation; type that is set along a given margin is said to be flush left or flush right.

flush bead *n* [*Building, Plastering*] a common moulding section: a segment finishing flush with the surface of an enclosing channel.

flush on warning *n* [*Military*] in the case when a warning is received of incoming missiles, this is an order to all those aircraft threatened by the attack to take off at once so as to avoid being destroyed on the ground or within fatal range of the explosions.

flush production *n* [*Oil industry*] the yield of oil from a spontaneously flowing well.

flusher *n* [*Sewer workers*] a London sewer worker.

flushgate *n* [*Skiing*] a series of three or more slalom gates set vertically on a slope.

flushing **1.** *n* [*Coal-mining*] the displacement of loose material from waste into the supported area. **2.** *n* [*Coal-mining*] the crumbling of the roof or sides around the supports in an excavation.

flute *n* [*Building, Plastering*] a concave groove.

fluther *v* [*Science fiction*] to move around aimlessly.

flutter **1.** *n* [*Audio*] a variety of frequency distortion in sound recording caused by variations of speed in the transport system. See also **wow**. **2.** *v* [*Swimming*] to move the legs alternately up and down in the water, with the body horizontal, face up, on the surface of the water.

fluttering *n* [*Espionage*] giving lie-detector tests to one's own operatives to double-check their loyalty regarding a specific mission or sensitive topic.

fly **1.** *n* [*US*] [*Football*] a pass pattern in which the pass receiver runs straight down the field. **2.** *n* [*UK*] [*Railways*] (Western Region use) a shunting truck. **3.** *n* [*Textiles*] loose lint carried in air

F

currents in a milling room. **4.** *n* [*Textiles*] fabric particles given off by the looms. **5.** *v* [*Hunting*] to jump a fence at a gallop during a hunt; thus 'fly-fence' is any fence which can be jumped in this way. **6.** *v* [*Theatre*] to suspend scenery above the stage in the **flies** from which it can be raised/lowered as required.

fly a kite *v* [*Prisons*] to smuggle a letter out of or into a prison.

fly (ball) *n* [*Baseball*] a ball batted in a high arc, especially to the outfield.

fly blind *v* [*Flying*] to fly without benefit of any instruments.

fly, on the *adv* [*Computing*] said of the examination of data during a program's execution which does not interfere with the execution of that program.

fly on the wall *n* [*TV, Radio*] a style of documentary production in which the camera and/or microphone becomes as far as possible an invisible eavesdropper on the individuals or situation under consideration, in the hope of thus minimising any self-consciousness in those recorded and maximising the 'real life' feel of the production.

fly pitchers *n pl* [*UK*] [*Police*] unlicensed street traders who keep up a running battle to attract custom to their pitches before being moved on or arrested by the police.

fly shunt *v* [*UK*] [*Railways*] to uncouple wagons illegally after the engine has passed over the points.

flyback timing, also **snapback timing** *n* [*Industry*] a method of timing a job using a stop-watch in which the hands of the watch are returned to 0 at the end of each separate element of the job.

flyby *n* [*Aerospace*] a space mission that does not land on a planet, but flies close enough to it for special cameras and other monitoring equipment to send vital information back to Earth.

flyer *n* [*Weaving*] a U-shaped device on the spindle mechanism of certain spinning wheels which flies around the bobbin and winds the yarn on to it simultanously with the spinning process.

flying *a* [*US*] [*Cattlemen*] said of a brand that has 'wings' attached to the basic letter. See also **crazy, lazy**.

flying dutchman *n* [*Logging*] a wire rope with a block on the other end which, attached to a tree, is used to move logs into the required places when piling them up in a **yard**.

flying fences *n pl* [*Hunting*] fences that can be cleared at a gallop.

flying orders *n pl* [*US*] [*Road transport*] trip instructions issued to a driver by a dispatcher.

flying switch, also **drop a car** *n* [*US*] [*Railways*] the decoupling of a car from behind a moving switch engine and then changing the points as soon as the switch engine has passed by them.

flying-carpet salesman *n* [*US*] [*Medicine*] See **camel driver**.

flyings *n pl* [*Tobacco*] the lowest or bottom leaves of the tobacco plant.

FMS *n pl* [*Industry*] acro **flexible manufacturing systems**.

fmz, also **fnz** *n* [*Media*] acro **fan magazine** a magazine produced professionally by a group of fans.

foam *n* [*Glass-making*] a layer of bubbles that forms on the surface of molten glass.

FOB *adv* [*Oil rigs*] abbr of **free on board** used of a contract in which the buyer provides the ship and the seller provides the cargo at the port of loading.

fob *n* [*Soap-making*] the scum or froth that rises to the top of the semi-liquid soap at one stage of its manufacture.

FOBS 1. *n* [*Military*] acro **Fractional Orbit Bombardment System** a strategy of missile attack in which rockets are fired in a low earth orbit (100 metres approximately) and on approaching the target are forced out of the orbit and down to the earth by the firing of retro-rockets. This is intended to keep the missiles beneath radar spotting and allied defensive retaliation until the last available moment. **2.** [*Military*] a missile attack that comes 'the wrong way round' the globe; ie: as far as US planners are concerned, from the South rather than over the North Pole.

focus *n* [*Theatre*] a spotlight that follows only the star of the show.

focus groups *n pl* [*Politics, Advertising*] small, sample groups (eg: twenty people taken on a psychodemographic basis – all types from all areas) that are selected and placed together in one room where they are all asked to air their views on whatever subject is under consideration by the researcher. This session is taped, filmed, and subsequently analysed in depth preparatory to the planning of a campaign, writing questions for an opinion poll, etc.

focus puller *n* [*Film*] an assistant to the cameraman who adjusts the lens to fine tolerances during the filming; the assistant also doubles as a film loader. See also **clapperboard**.

fog 1. *n* [*Photography*] a blurred spot on a photograph which has been caused by exposure to unwanted light, possibly through a leak in the camera itself. **2.** *n* [*US*] [*Police*] See **cloud**. **3.** *n* [*UK*] [*Railways*] a detonator; such detonators act as fog warnings.

fog over *v* [*US*] [*Painting*] to cover a surface badly or inconsistently when using a spray gun.

fogdust *n* [*Angling*] a fine cloud of ground bait which attracts fish but does not provide them with anything substantial to eat.

fogging *n* [*US*] [*Painting*] the action of paint as it spreads out from the nozzle of a spray; caught on a wind, the paint can spread to cover surfaces near the job.

Foggy Bottom *n* [*US*] [*Politics*] shorthand for the US State Department; it is currently used to imply the 'fogginess' of some of those who work there, as well as the obtuseness of some of the decisions that they force on the nation. The nickname originally stemmed from that given to the small, local town of Hamburgh, which was swallowed up into Washington, DC, but was originally celebrated for its swamps and the mists they tended to produce.

FOH 1. *n* [*Theatre*] acro **Front of House** the lobby and the business and box offices in a theatre. 2. *n* [*Theatre*] anything in front of the proscenium arch. 3. *n* [*Theatre*] the audience, who are seated in front of the proscenium arch. 4. [*Theatre*] the staff who work in the lobby, or the business and box offices, ie, the administrators and business staff, rather than actors and technicians.

foil *v* [*Hunting*] to obscure the fox's scent with a variety of other scents; this confuses the hounds. Ground covered by a number of contrasting scents is 'foiled'.

fold *v* [*UK*] [*Law*] used of a defendant who changes the plea from not guilty to guilty; it comes from card use, when in poker one throws away, or 'folds', a useless hand.

fold back *n* [*Audio*] the phenomenon found in recording studios where singers listen to themselves through headphones which produce the sound as the engineer records it, rather than the somewhat abnormal tones of the soundproofed studio. 'Fold-back' describes the movement of the sound from the microphone to the recording equipment and back to the ears via the headphones.

fold up 1. *v* [*Drugs*] used of a drug dealer who abandons his trade and gives up selling drugs. 2. *v* [*Boxing*] to collapse during a fight, though not necessarily to be knocked out.

folding *n* [*Optics*] a method of reducing the actual focal length of a large telescope to a compact package by combining a required number of mirrors to bounce the light around a series of corners and thus create the total required path length.

folding money, also **direct costs** *n* [*TV*] money paid to any organisations that are not already part of the TV company itself. Thus 'indirect costs' refer to all those production costs that are spent on objects or people already possessed, owned or employed by the company.

folio 1. *n* [*Journalism*] a sheet of paper with copy typed on one side, a part of a story. 2. *n* [*Journalism*] the running headline put at the top of a page. 3. *n* [*Journalism*] a **tabloid** sheet. 4. *n* [*Publishing*] a page number.

follow me diversion *n* [*Telephony*] a PABX facility which enables a user to have incoming calls automatically diverted to another extension.

follow slips *v* [*US*] [*Coal-mining*] to cut along the grain of a coal seam.

follow through *v* [*Shooting*] to bring up the gun behind or on a bird, and to continue to swing through and ahead of it.

follow-on theory *n* [*Military*] the concept whereby the completion of work on one **weapons system** is immediately followed by the commencement of work on its successor. This is a concept that lies at the heart of the continuing arms race, based on a mutually convenient, self-sustaining agreement between the army's various units which need the latest generation of weapons to justify their existence and the manufacturers who need orders to stay in profit.

foner *n* [*US*] [*Journalism*] a story that can be covered simply by making sufficient phonecalls.

fonfen *n* [*UK*] [*Crime*] this comes from the Yiddish for 'telling tales'; it is the patter or 'spiel' used by a confidence trickster to entrance and ensnare his victims.

font *v* [*US*] [*TV*] to display letters or figures over a TV picture in order to supply the viewer with extra information to that given in the commentary that already backs up the picture. It comes from the printing use of a 'type font' (an alphabet of letters and set of numbers in a particular typeface) and the use of the vidifont machine to produce such insets.

foolish old man who removed the mountain, the *phr* [*Politics*] this is a dictum of Mao Zedong's which originated in China in 1945 and is used to explain the Maoist approach to the theory of knowledge; ideas must be turned by workers into a material force that will in turn change the world.

foot *n* [*Printing*] the lower part of the printing character; the base of the actual type body.

footage 1. *n* [*Film, TV*] the length of a film calculated in feet and inches; videotape is calculated in minutes and seconds – no convenient time-based measure has ever been evolved for film. 2. *n* [*Retail stores*] the amount of display space – including counters, free-standing displays, dress racks, refrigerated cabinets, etc – that is held in a store; footage is used to calculate both the success of a product and the space that a product or line should be allotted.

football *n* [*US*] [*Military*] the attaché case holding the day's nuclear launch codes that is carried by an officer whose duty it is never to leave the President's side.

footer *n* [*Printing*] a piece of copy placed at the bottom of every page of a book, showing the chapter heading, book title, author's name, etc. See also **header 2**.

footmaker *n* [*Glass-making*] a member of a **chair** of glass-makers who gathers and blows glass and shapes it on a **marver** table.

foot-over-foot *n* [*Ice-hockey*] a method of fast

forward movement when the player is forced to take a direct line along a narrow path.

footprint 1. *n* [*Aerospace*] the area in which it is predicted that the debris from a collapsing satellite or any other space vehicle will land as it returns to earth. **2.** *n* [*Communications*] the area covered by broadcasts from any one TV satellite in the DBS (Direct Broadcasting System) network. **3.** *n* [*Computing*] the space occupied by a machine on the user's desk or table; the trend in office machines is towards the smallest footprint possible. **4.** *n* [*Computing*] the area of a front panel, desk or floorspace occupied by a computer or a peripheral device. **5.** *n* [*Military*] the pattern into which it is calculated that the descending warheads of a **MARV bus** will fall when completing their intercontinental trajectory on target.

foots *n pl* [*Painting*] a settled layer at the bottom of a container of drying oil or varnish when it has been allowed to stand.

foozle *v* [*Golf*] to make a mistake.

for money *adv* [*Stock market*] said of deals that must be paid in cash at once, rather than waiting for the next settling day.

forbidden combination *n* [*Computing*] a combination of **bits** that are not valid according to the criteria established by the designer of the system or the program.

force *v* [*Cricket*] to bat aggressively.

force deficiency *n* [*Military*] failings in either planning or in the amassing of men or material, or in the efficiency of those men or that material.

force in *v* [*Baseball*] used of a pitcher who causes a run to be scored by walking (see **walk**) a batter when all the bases are already occupied by base runners.

force multiplier *n* [*Military*] the premise that what one lacks in quantity, one makes up for in quality; thus in military terms, this is the use of satellites for reconnaissance, navigation, weather forecasting and communications in ways that improve the effectiveness of military forces.

forced coverage *n* [*Film*] the decision made by a director to continue filming a given scene even when it is apparent that an error has been made during the filming; the blunder can be remedied later when the director has extra, correct material shot which can be inserted into the film at the editing stage.

forced-choice question *n* [*Market research*] a question that can be answered only from a limited range of statements supplied with the question.

forceful, also **assertive** *a* [*Wine-tasting*] a marked character, possibly with notable tannin and acidity.

Ford *n* [*US*] [*Garment trade*] a mass-marketed copy of an expensive, model garment; it comes from the automobile of the same name.

fore *n* [*US*] [*TV*] the start of a piece of tape that contains a single news item. See also **aft**.

fore-and-aft cap *n* [*US*] [*Marine Corps*] See **pisscutter**.

fore-end *n* [*Navy*] the forward space in a submarine that is used for storing the torpedoes and as living space for some of the crew.

foreground *n* [*Computing*] the program which takes priority over any other background or secondary program(s) that the machine may be running simultaneously.

foregrounding *n* [*Computing*] processing the priority tasks on the computer, leaving only the milliseconds between the execution of such tasks for the secondary, **background** processing.

foreign *a* [*US*] [*Railways*] said of anything belonging to another railroad – equipment or territory.

foreign crowd *n* [*US*] [*Stock market*] on the New York Stock Exchange this refers to those traders who specialise in foreign bonds.

foreign exchange *n* [*Communications*] a form of private line service which enables a customer to maintain a local call service in another service area.

foreign legion *n* [*UK*] [*Railways*] during busy periods on the railways men from slack depots would be brought in to boost those busy areas requiring extra manpower.

foreign print *n* [*Printing*] a newspaper produced outside London for distribution inside the metropolis; such printing is disliked by the London print unions.

foreigner 1. *n* [*Industrial relations*] a job undertaken by a worker who is ostensibly unemployed and who is thus jeopardising the legal collection of unemployment benefit. **2.** *n* [*Stock market*] an investment house based abroad which has been permitted to buy a Stock Exchange firm.

foreparts *n pl* [*Clothing*] the fronts of jackets, coats and similar garments.

fore-post *n* [*Chess*] See **hole 2**.

foreshift 1. *n* [*Coal-mining*] the first morning shift. See also **back shift**. **2.** *n* [*Management*] the morning shift of a three-shift – morning, evening, night – system. See also **backshift, nightshift**.

foreshore cowboys *n pl* [*Shooting*] novice wildfowlers who lack finesse and skill, but who will shoot enthusiastically at anything, in range or otherwise, in an attempt to imitate their betters. See also **tit-shooters**.

foreshots *n pl* [*Distilling*] the first fraction of the distillate received during the distillation of the **low wines** in the spirit still used in the Pot Still process. They are checked by the stillman and returned, if suitable, to the still.

forest *n* [*Computing*] a collection of **trees**.

forever family *n* [*Religion*] a group of persons who claim they have received eternal life through Jesus Christ.

forfaiting *n* [*Banking*] the purchase by a bank of promissory notes payable by a foreign purchaser of capital goods, over a medium term period (usually 1 to 7 years); such transactions are usually set up by the exporter.

forge pigs *n pl* [*Metallurgy*] pig iron that is suitable for conversion in the **puddling** furnace.

forggy *n, a* [UK] [*Market-traders*] dim-wit, dim-witted.

forging *n* [US] [*Cattlemen*] this is when a moving horse strikes the back of his front shoes with the toes of his hind shoes.

forgiving system *n* [*Computing*] a computer or other system which allows the novice user to make some mistakes without incurring disastrous consequences; confused users may have the option of a 'help' button providing a variety of 'help' screens which will point out on the VDU such suggestions as should aid them to extract themselves from the mess. See also **user-friendly**.

fork 1. *v* [*Chess*] to use a piece, especially a knight, to threaten two pieces simultaneously; if one piece moves, the other will be taken. **2.** *n* [*Weaving*] the (usually) wooden hand beater used to pack in the **weft** in tapestry or rug weaving.

fork quantity *n* [*Clothing*] the allowance of material in a bifurcated garment which is provided for the thickness through the trunk from front to back at the crotch.

fork tail *n* [*Angling*] the grilse, or salmon that has spent one winter in the sea.

form 1. *n* [UK] [*Police*] previous convictions or a criminal record; it comes from the similar use of 'form', meaning earlier performances, as regards racehorses. **2.** *n* [*Printing*] the whole locked up assembly of **chase**, letterpress, **furniture** and **quoins**.

form seven hundred *n* [*Air travel*] a form that must be signed every time a captain takes over an aircraft prior to making a flight; in it he confirms that he is personally satisfied with all pre-flight checks, maintenance and inspection.

formal sociology *n* [*Sociology*] a version of early 20th century German sociology that concentrated on the form of social relationships and studied particularly those relationships which differed in substance but shared a degree of form.

formalism 1. *n* [*Art*] the assignment of priority in art to a work's form, at the expense of any other characteristics, especially the content. **2.** *n* [*Politics*] a situation whereby a communist ostensibly accepts criticism or acknowledges the necessity of an unpopular duty, but does not in any real way alter his/her conduct; it is often expressed as 'formalist perversion'. The charge of formalism is often used to criticise those who fail to toe the line in the literary, artistic or theatrical fields. **3.** *n* [*Theatre*] a movement that started about 1890 in Russia; it began as a reaction to the excessive naturalism of Russian theatre, and then spilled over into its own excesses of symbolism and stylisation.

format *v* [*Business, Advertising*] a word meaning to design in a specific manner, according to the task, item or personality under consideration; it has gained enormous popularity (probably because of its use in the burgeoning world of computing) in the areas of business, the media, education and sociology.

forming 1. *n* [*Electronics*] the coating of battery plates with lead dioxide on the positive plate and spongy lead on the negative to make them ready for use. **2.** *n* [*Photography*] gradually increasing the charge in a new flash capacitor until it reaches maximum power and is ready for general use.

formula investing *n* [*Stock market*] investing in the market according to a plan under which more funds are invested in equity securities when the market is low, and more are put into fixed income securities when the market advances.

formwork *n* [*Building, Concrete workers*] See **falsework**.

forte *n* [*Fencing*] this comes from Fr. meaning 'strong'; it is the 'strong' part of a foil, the half nearest to the guard. See also **foible**.

FORTH *n* [*Computing*] a programming language especially popular in the control of a scientific instrument because of its flexibility and compactness. In contrast to such languages as **BASIC**, the user is not forced to work with pre-set symbols, but can define words as required, and these words can then be used in expressions on equal terms with the system operators. FORTH is written in reverse **Polish notation**. It was created by Charles Moore in the late 1960s as the language for fourth generation computing. The machine on which he worked would accept only five-letter words, thus the misspelt FORTH appeared.

FORTRAN *n* [*Computing*] acro **Formula Translator** the most widely used and generally popular scientific programming language.

Fortress America *n* [*Military, Politics*] the concept, beloved of the American right wing, of a nation so well defended – especially by a nuclear strike-force – that whatever happens elsewhere, it will survive unscathed behind such defences.

fortunate deviates *n pl* [*Education*] above average students, lucky enough to deviate from the less intelligent norm.

forty-eight *n* [*Military*] a two-day or weekend leave pass.

forty-eight sheet *n* [*Advertising*] a billboard poster size: 20' wide by 10' deep.

forty-eight, the *n* [*Music*] the forty-eight preludes and fugues of J.S. Bach.

forty-nine *v* [US] [*Lunch counter*] to request the cook to take special care with an order.

forward *a* [*Wine-tasting*] advanced in maturity considering its actual age or vintage.

forward busying *n* [*Telephony*] in an automatic switching telephone system, this is the process of changing a series of devices from idle to engaged as a call is put through. See also **forward clearing**.

F

F

forward clearing *n* [*Telephony*] in an automatic switching telephone system, this is the process of changing a series of devices from engaged back to idle after a call has been terminated. See also **forward busying**.

forward contract *n* [*Stock market*] a contract for a financial instrument or commodity that is to be settled on a mutually agreed future date. This contrasts with a **futures** contract in that it is not standardised.

forward integration 1. *n* [*Commerce*] the taking over by a manufacturer of his wholesalers' or retailers' companies with the aim of controlling the whole market and thus consolidating his trading position. See also **backward interpretation 1**. 2. *n* [*Industry*] See **vertical integration**.

forward market *n* [*Futures market*] the making of deals concerning commodities which are not currently available for trading, but which will become available at a later date.

forward supervision *n* [*Communications*] the sending of a series of control sequences from node to node to facilitate data transmission.

F.O.S. 1. *a* [*US*] [*Medicine*] abbr of **full of shit** a severely constipated patient. 2. *a* [*US*] [*Medicine*] a patient who lies to doctors with the intention of obtaining medically unnecessary drugs.

fossil word *n* [*Literary criticism*] a word that has no recognised or active meaning by itself, but still survives as part of an accepted and contemporary expression, eg: 'nonce-word', in which 'nonce' (except in slang, meaning 'child-molester') has no modern usage.

foster-mother *n* [*Farming*] in poultry-rearing, this is a device for rearing chickens that have been hatched in an incubator.

foul 1. *v* [*UK*] [*Railways*] to obstruct a track. 2. *a* [*Theatre*] said of ropes, lights, **flats** which have become entangled in the **flies**.

foul bill of lading *n* [*Shipping*] See **dirty bill**.

foul copy *n* [*Publishing*] See **foul proof**.

foul hook *v* [*Angling*] to hook the fish anywhere but in the mouth.

foul one's line *v* [*Angling*] said of a fisherman who becomes mixed up in his own line.

foul proof *n* [*Publishing*] proofs containing corrections that have already been incorporated into a further set of proofs.

foul tip *n* [*Baseball*] a ball, barely touched by a swung bat, that has no forward movement from the home plate and which passes through to the foul territory behind it.

foulard *n* [*Magic*] any large coloured cloth; it comes from Fr. for silk handkerchief, scarf.

found objects *n pl* [*Art*] this comes from Fr. 'objets trouvés'. In Surrealist theory this means the taking of any random object and presenting it as art, worthy of comparison with more 'respectable', traditional art.

four beauties *n pl* [*Politics*] in China these are the beauties of 1. the spirit, 2. the language, 3. behaviour, 4. the environment.

four bigs *n pl* [*Politics*] in China these are the four freedoms of expression: 1. speaking out freely, 2. airing one's personal views fully, 3. holding great debates, 4. writing **big character posters**.

four fingers horizontal *n* [*Navy*] a signal made by coxswain of a boat coming alongside a warship to warn the officer at the gangway that he has a captain aboard.

four firsts *n pl* [*Politics*] in China these are a series of priorities: 1. the human factor over weapons, 2. political work over other work, 3. ideological study over political work, 4. living ideology over book learning.

four flush *n* [*Gambling*] a flush (all cards of the same suit) that contains only four and not five cards and which is thus useless; this is the root of the non-gambling, derogatory use of this term as regards people.

Four Horsemen *n* [*Ten-pin bowling*] a split where the 1–2–4–7 or 1–3–6–10 pins are left standing. See also **baby split, bucket, Cincinnati**.

four modernisations *n pl* [*Politics*] a scheme launched in China in 1975 to modernise 1. agriculture, 2. industry, 3. defence, 4. science and technology.

four olds *n pl* [*Politics*] in China these are 1. ideas, 2. customs, 3. cultures, 4. habits.

four on the floor *n* [*US*] [*Car salesmen, Hot rods*] a four-gear system with the shift on the floor rather than on the steering wheel. See also **three on a post**.

four plus *adv* [*US*] [*Medicine*] to the utmost degree, completely, exceptionally, absolutely, utterly. It comes from the method of reporting the results of laboratory tests as 'negative', 'one plus' and on up to a maximum 'four plus'.

four plus syndrome *n* [*Advertising*] See **effective cover**.

four Ps *n pl* [*Marketing*] abbr of **product, place, price, promotion** the principal factors to be considered when preparing a marketing package. See also **marketing mix**.

four sheet *n* [*Advertising*] a display poster measuring 60" deep by 40" wide.

four wall *a* [*Theatre, Film*] the rental of either a theatre or cinema that is established 'on a four wall basis' implies the rental of the site either to a producer (theatre) or an exhibitor (film) on the understanding that the renter will pay all operating expenses, but instead of adding the usual percentage of the take, will pay only an agreed, fixed sum, irrespective of how many tickets are actually sold.

four waller *n* [*TV, Film*] a fully enclosed set with four actual but adjustable walls, inside which a camera can move, thus facilitating the construction of more complex sets.

four-figure form n [Horse-racing, Gambling] the four-digit code that is found on racing forms and which indicates the horse's performance in the previous four races; thus 0210 means unplaced, second, won, unplaced.

four-in-line n [UK] [Road transport] the rear axle of a trailer which, instead of having two wheels close together at each end of the axle as normal, has four wheels, more or less equally spaced, along the axle.

fourteen (14) n [Journalism] when typed at the bottom of a page of copy this means: more follows.

fourth copy cards n pl [Libraries] in the British Library, these are a set of duplicate General Catalogue entries which are filed by pressmark rather than by author or title.

fourth cover n [Advertising] the back cover (of a magazine or newspaper); thus 'first cover' is the front cover, 'second cover' is the inside front cover, and 'third cover' is the inside back cover.

fourth degree arson n [US] [Law] an attempt to burn buildings or property.

fourth generation n [Computing] the current generation of computer designs, covering those that appeared after 1970 and which feature integrated circuit technology and very large (1 MB+) main memory. Fourth generation machines also offer networking facilities and support a wide variety of languages. See also **first-third, fifth generation**.

fourth generation languages n pl [Computing] a series of programming languages designed for the general rather than the expert user. See also **fourth generation, user-friendly**.

fourth hand 1. n [Glass-making] an extra man in a team or **chair** of three men. 2. n [Glass-making] an apprentice.

fourth market n [Commerce] the direct trading of securities, that are unlisted in the stock market, between investors, thus bypassing traditional trading methods. See also **third market**.

fourth wall n [Theatre] the concept central to the traditional theatre that a stage has three actual walls plus a fourth hypothetical one, running across the proscenium arch, which cuts off the action from the audience.

Fourth World n [Politics] the world's poorest and most backward/underdeveloped countries. See also **Third World**.

four-way entry, also **two-way entry** n [UK] [Road Transport] the alternative ways in which a fork-lift truck can approach and pick up a pallet; the construction of the pallet determines whether the truck can insert its forks on any side or only at either end.

four-wheeler n [UK] [Road transport] a rigid vehicle having two (or three) axles.

fowl n [Navy] See **bird 3**.

fox n [Computing] modifications to a given program that are designed to trace and eliminate the **rabbits** which have been infiltrated into that program and which are disrupting its efficient running. See also **rabbit 3**.

fox message n [Computing] a standard message used to test computers, teletypes and similar electronic communicators; it involves sending the message 'the quick brown fox jumped over the lazy dog 1234567890', which is the classic encapsulation of every letter of the alphabet and every number.

foxed a [Book collecting] said of paper that is discoloured and stained, usually by small brownish-yellow spots which emerge due to chemical action in paper that was badly bleached in manufacture; they are activated by damp or lack of ventilation. The name possibly comes from the colour of the blemishes.

foxhole n [Military] a small hole in the ground in which a soldier fights and sleeps; thus 'foxhole circuit' means appearances by USO/ENSA or similar forces' entertainment teams who travelled to visit the troops in situ. See also **basher 1**.

foxing n [Shoe-making] a piece of leather that forms or covers the lower part of that part of the shoe which extends from the heel to the vamp.

foxmark n [Book collecting] See **foxed**.

foxy a [Wine-tasting] the earthy tang that is a distinctive attribute of wild or 'fox' grapes used in certain native American wines.

fp merchant n [Crime] abbr of **false pretences merchant** anyone committing crimes which involves false pretences.

fraction n [Politics] in Communist use, this originally denoted all the Party members within a larger unit of non-Party members, such as a Trade Union. Since 1940 it has become a derogatory term, similar in use to deviationist (see **deviation**) and it now refers to those Party members within the overall Party itself who repudiate the Party line. Thus 'fractionalism' is the organising of small groups in order to influence or alter Party policy – a forbidden activity.

fractional banking n [Banking] a practice whereby banks keep their cash deposits at a fixed percentage of their deposit liabilities; this is a legal obligation in some countries.

fractionation n [Military] the division of the total **yield** of a MIRVed ballistic missile into the amount carried by each of its warheads.

fraff n [Naturalists] caterpillar droppings.

frag v [US] [Military] this comes from 'fragmentation grenade'; it originated (as a word, though probably not as a practice) during the Vietnam War, and refers to the assassination of one's own (either unpopular or, more important, incompetent and thus personally dangerous to one's survival) officer or NCO by tossing a grenade at him during the chaos of a battle.

fragrant a [Wine-tasting] fresh and naturally scented.

frame 1. n [Film] a single picture on a strip of

film, projected for exhibition at 24 frames/second. Thus 'Film is truth, twenty-four times a second' (Jean-Luc Godard). **2.** *n* [*Gambling*] this comes from the bowling use and means a hand or deal of cards. **3.** *n* [*Sex*] an exceptionally thin prostitute. **4.** *n* [*Entertainment*] a period of time; the limits are usually pre-ordained by the context in which the word is used; it comes from ten-pin bowling. See also **inning**. **5.** *n* [*Telephony*] in an automatic telephone switching system, this is the complete sequence of operation of the devices that is required to generate and terminate a telephone call.

frame height *n* [*UK*] [*Road transport*] the height of the top of the chassis frame from the ground when the vehicle is standing level.

framing 1. *n* [*Computing*] selecting from a continuous stream of **bits** the groupings that represent one or more readable characters. **2.** *n* [*Logging*] the preparation of a telegraph pole – by the cutting and boring of the basic log from which it is made, followed by the insertion of the metal climbing steps etc.

franco *a* [*Commerce*] said of a foreign trade price quotation which includes the cost of the goods and all risks and charges up to a certain point.

frank discussions *n pl* [*Politics*] a popular coded euphemism regarding international talks, where it implies little agreement or even strong arguing between world leaders or their surrogates.

franked income *n* [*Economics*] revenue on which tax has been paid.

Frankenslant *n* [*Advertising*] an advertising approach that creates an illusory need or fantasised crisis to encourage the sales of an unimportant and valueless product.

frankenstein *n* [*Gambling*] the bolting together of four slot machines to which only one handle is attached. Players must insert money in all four machines to stand a chance of a multiple coup on this 'monster'; otherwise only the machine in which money has been deposited will work.

Frankfurt School *n* [*Sociology*] a group of Marxist sociologists working in the Institute of Social Research in the University of Frankfurt, 1923–50. Mainly Jewish, the members were exiled during the Nazi era to Columbia University, NYC. Their main influences on modern Marxism are the critique of orthodox Marxism, the incorporation of Freudianism into Marxism, and the elaboration of an epistemology for advanced capitalism. They are disliked for their essential pessimism regarding the world revolution, their critique of **economic determinism** and their valuing of culture above economics.

frap *v* [*Sailing*] to add strength to cables or lines by tying them together.

frapp *n* [*Sex*] a beating (from the Fr. 'frapper' meaning 'to beat').

frappé *n* [*Sex*] fellatio performed by a prostitute who has placed ice cubes in her mouth (on the lines of 'crème de menthe frappé', etc).

frapping *n* [*Sailing, Ropework*] a number of crossing turns in a lashing or the **leads** of a tackle which serve both to tighten and tackle them.

frasing *n* [*Metallurgy*] the removal of the ragged inside and outside edges at the end of cut tubes.

fraternity *n* [*Social work*] an idealised goal common to all social services which should, in the broad sense, have a linking fellowship of the same values and aims. It is also the concept of 'human fellowship' itself, which claims that 'all men are brothers' and is considered in itself sufficient justification for the establishment of social welfare agencies.

fratricide *n* [*Military*] the theoretical result of the detonation of a number of **MIRV/MARV** warheads when their synchronisation is not absolute or simultaneous – which, given the distance travelled to their targets would most likely be the case. The various massive explosions would tend to destroy other incoming warheads or at least interfere seriously with the accuracy of their guidance systems. See also **dense-pack**.

fraudulent preference *n* [*Commerce*] a payment made by a person, who is incapable of paying his debts as they fall due, to one of his creditors with the intention of preferring that creditor to the others.

FRD *n* [*US*] [*Government*] acro **Formerly Restricted Data** material that has been removed from the status of RD (**restricted data**) and is being trans-classified to that of NSI (**National Security information**). FRD, despite appearances, does not imply that the data involved has now been declassified.

freak off *v* [*Sex*] used of a prostitute who offers sex without charging money for her favours.

freak the rig *v* [*Radio*] to improve one's Citizens Band terminal in order to obtain access to more than forty otherwise restricted broadcasting frequencies.

Freddie [*Military*] air intercept code for the controlling unit of the patrol or force.

Freddie Mac *n* [*US*] [*Economics*] Federal Home Loan Mortgage Company. See also **GinnyMae, Sallie Mae**.

free attention *n* [*New therapies*] See **slack 1**.

free box *n* [*US*] [*Stock market*] any secure storage place for a fully-paid customer's securities, eg: a bank vault.

free face *n* [*Coal-mining*] the surface of a face that is free to move when an explosion is fired beneath it.

free forms *n pl* [*Art*] organic biomorphic shapes – kidney/boomerang/egg shapes – which were produced by hand drawing and which epitomised many popular design motifs in the 1950s.

free good *n* [*Commerce*] a good which, at a given time and place, is either in such plentiful supply

F

that anyone can obtain it without cost (eg: air) or is incapable of being sold (eg: sunshine).

free media *n* [*Public relations*] any media coverage for a product which does not have to be paid for.

free on board *adv* [*Commerce*] referring to the payment by the seller of all charges and risks up to and including the point where the goods are delivered on board the ship. See also **f.a.s.**

free on quay, free at wharf *adv* [*Commerce*] See **f.a.s.**

free on rail *adv* [*Commerce*] the payment by the seller of all charges and risks up to the point where the goods are delivered to a specified railway for onwards transport. See also **f.a.s., free on board, free overside.**

free overside *adv* [*Commerce*] the payment by the seller of all charges and risks up to the point where the goods are unloaded at the port of destination. See also **f.a.s., free on board, free overside**.

free ride **1.** *n* [*Gambling*] the playing of part of a poker hand without betting, usually by 'checking' a round of betting. **2.** *n* [*Politics*] a campaign undertaken by an office-holder who will be able to continue in or return to that office even in the event that he/she fails to win the election; thus little more than personal prestige is at risk. **3.** *n* [*Stock market*] a method whereby a broker can make a deal and turn a profit without actually investing any money: a purchaser buys and sells within the shortest permitted settlement period – five days – and never has to produce any cash, merely move the shares. **4.** *n* [*US*] [*Stock market*] a practice that is forbidden by the Securities & Exchange Commission, whereby an underwriter holds back a proportion of a new issue of securities, hoping to sell it when the price has risen.

free rider *n* [*Industrial relations*] an individual who refuses to join a union but who (where there is no closed shop agreement) is able to benefit from whatever wage agreements are negotiated by that union.

free rocket *n* [*Military*] a missile that is not controlled by a launch computer or by a wire while in flight. See also **fire and forget.**

free wheeling *n* [*Communications*] the most simple level of data transmission, whereby the computer transmitting the data does not know whether or not it has been received, or if received, whether correctly.

freebie *n* [*Gambling, Sex, Drugs*] anything for nothing in these areas of life where such gratis transactions are rare.

freedom *n* [*Lacrosse*] an abstract that determines – given factors of speed, position, and opposition marking – whether a fellow player is well-placed to receive a pass.

free-fire zone *n* [*Military*] an area in which any moving creature – human or animal – is deemed a target for bombs, rockets, artillery or small arms.

freefreighting *n* [*Air travel*] the use of one's own aircraft for the transport home of whatever commodities'items one might wish to have brought back. Some pilots have escalated this into large-scale import businesses dealing in fresh out-of-season fruits or similar exotica, bringing in far more than the permitted 100 kilos per person allowance. It is as popular among military as among civilian fliers.

freelance [*Military*] air intercept code for: 'I am in manual control of the aircraft'.

freelance play *n* [*Lacrosse*] a tactic whereby each player fulfils the position that she happens to find herself in on the field at a given moment. See also **controlled play.**

free-space list *n* [*Computing*] a list of unoccupied areas of memory in a main or backing store.

freeze **1.** *v* [*US*] [*Carpenters*] to glue two pieces of wood together. **2.** *v* [*Film*] an instruction to actors to hold their positions; it is used for 'trick shots' in which objects or people suddenly 'pop up' into the film. **3.** [*Ice-hockey*] to attempt to regain control of the puck by holding it against an area of the boards or by falling on it, thus stopping play. **4.** *n* [*US*] [*Painting*] a muscular spasm that attacks and temporarily paralyses someone high on a ladder who is terrified of heights. **5.** *n* [*Economics*] usually found as 'wage freeze', this is a period during which a government imposes restrictions on the normal increases in wages that employers would otherwise be regularly awarding their employees. This may take the form of an absolute ban on any increase, or the tying of such increases to a very low percentage figure.

freezebank *n* [*US*] [*Medicine*] the hospital refrigerator that is used for storing blood, bone grafts, organs, etc. for use in emergencies and other operations.

freeze-frame *n* [*Film*] a device whereby the action on film appears to freeze into a still; it is accomplished by printing one frame a number of times.

freeze-out *n* [*Gambling*] a variety of poker in which the players continue until all but one – the winner – have lost their entire bankroll.

freeze-out proposition *n* [*Gambling*] a lengthy series of bets arranged between two gamblers which are based on a pre-arranged set of rules and betting conditions, all leading towards a result in which the winner takes all.

freezer *n* [*Meat-trade*] sheep that are reared specifically for freezer packages.

freight-train construction *n* [*Linguistics*] the use of nouns in a string as modifiers of a further noun; it is epitomised by this keyword and is the basis of much modern jargon in sociology and similar disciplines.

french **1.** *n* [*US*] [*Medicine*] abbr of **French catheter** a straight tube, designed in France, for emptying the bladder. **2.** *n* [*Sex*] fellatio.

F

F

French drive n [Cricket] a fortunate snick off the bat through the slips. See also **Chinese cut**.

French fold n [Printing] a printing technique, used especially in greeting cards, in which all the printing is done on one side of the page; this is then folded, leaving the reverse side as the blank back of the folded card.

French front n [Dog breeding] a narrow front with pasterns angled out, supposedly resembling a position assumed by a French dancing master.

frenching 1. n [Tobacco] a disease that causes tobacco leaves to become thick and leathery and arrests the growth of the plant. 2. also **blending** n [Custom cars] the welding and filling up of body seams – like those found between wings and the main body work, etc – with either lead or, more usually, some proprietary plastic filler; this is often confused in UK with **tunnelling**.

frenchman n [Shooting] the red-legged partridge.

French's edition n [UK] [Theatre] the authorised performance edition of a play, used by amateur companies, provincial theatres, etc, which includes prop lists, lighting and sound cues, stage directions, special effects and so on as well as the basic script. It is so called from the publishers Samuel French Ltd.

frequency n [Advertising] the number of times an individual is exposed to a given advertisement.

fresh a [Wine-tasting] retaining its youthful charm and acidity.

freshen v [Sailing, Ropework] to alter the position of the rope so that a new section is moved to an area of possible chafing.

fresher n [UK] [Railways] abbr of **refreshment rooms**.

fret n [Building, Plastering] a variety of **enrichment**: straight lines forming a geometrical pattern.

Freudian aesthetics n [Art] a variety of explanations of the phenomena of art which use as their basis the psycho-analytic theories of the unconscious developed by Sigmund Freud (1856–1939). Such areas of enquiry include the role of the unconscious in the production and appreciation of art, the relations of dream symbolism to art, the value of art as therapy, the relationship between art and neurosis, the relation of creativity to daydreams, etc. See also **Jungian aesthetics**.

Freudian criticism n [Literary criticism] a form of literary criticism based on the Freudian theory that artistic creativity is a form of sublimation and that both art and the artist are pathological phenomena. Critics such as Lionel Trilling and Edmund Wilson (in 'The Wound and the Bow' in 1941) have expounded such beliefs, pointing out the connections in many creators between the circumstances of their upbringing and the work they produce. As Trilling put it in 1947: 'The poet is a poet by reason of his sickness as well as by reason of his power.' Thus Freudian critics concen-

trate on making these biographical connections and elucidating the presence of various symbols in Freudian terms.

friar n [Printing] a light spot on a page. See also **monk**.

frictional unemployment n [Economics] temporary unemployment caused when a mass of workers are changing jobs, or because supply and demand are momentarily out of balance.

fried 1. a [Computing] said of machines, this means burnt out, not working due to **hardware** failure. 2. a [Computing] said of people, this means exhausted, especially referring to those who refuse to stop work no matter how tired they are.

fried egg n [Golf] a ball that lies half-buried in sand.

friend of ours, a n [US] [Crime] in the US Mafia, this refers to any member of one of the US **families**; the use of 'mine' as opposed to 'ours' refers only to a personal friend, who may or may not be a member of a family, but has none of the ties that 'ours' implies.

friendly fire n [Military] See **accidental delivery**.

friendly ice n [Navy] the Polar ice canopy when it is sufficiently fragmented to permit nuclear submarines to surface on those occasions – relatively rare – when they need to do so.

friends n pl [UK] [Government] members of the Secret Intelligence Service (MI6).

friendship evangelism n [Religion] evangelising by lulling the potential convert with apparent friendship prior to introducing the religious hard-sell.

frilling 1. n [Painting] the effect of overly viscous paint which runs down a surface, rather than covering it smoothly. See also **curtain 2, tears**. 2. n [Photography] the pucking and peeling of photographic emulsion from its base during processing.

fringe 1. n [Espionage] in the CIA this refers to that circle of potential agents, most of whom have a greater desire for regular cash than real access to classified information, which includes those members of the local population who gravitate towards the foreign community: academics, journalists, artists, writers, villains, etc. 2. n [TV] those **dayparts** that border on either side of **prime time**.

frisker n [US] [Crime] a pickpocket, who usually works in crowded places, especially on public transport.

frit n [Glass-making] calcined or partly fused materials from which glass is made, after having been fused in a furnace, but before vitrification.

frobnicate v [Computing] to manipulate, to adjust, to make small adjustments; it comes from **frobnitz**. Unlike **tweak** or **twiddle**, the manipulation involved is aimless, and for its own sake rather than for the fine-tuning of the computer.

frobnitz *n* [*Computing*] a widget, a thingummybob, a whatdyoucallit: an unspecified and usually small and fiddly object. It was originally used with the same meaning by model railway enthusiasts.

frock 1. *v* [*US*] [*Marine Corps*] to allow an officer who has been selected for promotion (and so notified) but who has not yet **made his number** to assume the style, title, uniform and authority of the rank he has now attained. 2. *n* [*UK*] [*Theatre*] a costume, for either male or female roles.

FROD *n* [*Military*] acro **functionally related observable differences** developed under the terms of the (unratified) **SALT II** treaty, this is the associating of obvious external features on a given aircraft with its possessing or lacking a nuclear role; this would, in theory, have assisted **verification**.

frog 1. *n* [*Building*] the small depression on one side of a brick into which mortar can be placed. 2. *n* [*Tobacco*] a small bundle of specially prepared tobacco leaves used for filler in cigars. 3. *n* [*Computing*] akin to **crock** as a statement of distaste or, as 'froggy', a derogatory adjective. 4. *n* [*Music*] the nut of a violin bow. 5. *n* [*US*] [*Railways*] a grooved cast-iron implement used for putting derailed equipment back on the track. 6. *n* [*US*] [*Railways*] a device made of rail sections which enables the wheels of a train to pass over the rails of an intersecting track without being derailed. 7. *n* [*Textiles*] a device in a loom that stops the motion when the shuttle is out of position.

frog hair 1. *n* [*Golf*] the well cut grass that divides the fairway from the green itself and which is of a length and smoothness somewhere between the two. 2. *n* [*US*] [*Politics*] money for use in political campaigns.

frog's eyes *n pl* [*Tobacco*] brownish spots that sometimes appear on tobacco leaves shortly before cutting.

from each according to his ability, to each according to his needs *phr* [*Politics*] Marx's policy of the relation of work to personal income as realised in the ideal state of achieved communism. Under the previous, intermediary stage of socialism, Marx allows a remaining trace of inequality, by replacing 'needs' with 'work'.

front 1. *v* [*Drugs*] said of a purchaser who gives the dealer the required price of the drugs before seeing the merchandise; the dealer then vanishes and returns, assuming he/she is honest, with the promised drugs which, for safety's sake, if he/she works on the street, will not be kept on his/her person, but in a secure and nearby hiding place. 2. *n* [*Dog breeding*] the portion of the dog from the elbows to the feet viewed from the front. 3. *n* [*Market-traders*] the show-piece arrangement that is prominent on the front of a stall; in the UK, where traders will not permit customers to touch such produce, the front may well be far superior to what is actually sold from the boxes behind the stall. 4. *n* [*Music*] the first part of the song, prior to the 'bridge'.

front end 1. *n* [*Advertising*] the initial response to a promotion. 2. *n* [*Audio*] a signal source, ie. a turntable, a tuner, etc. 3. *n* [*US*] [*Car salesmen*] the direct profit from the sale of a car, exclusive of financing. See also **backend** 1. 4. *n, v* [*Computing*] simply an amplification of 'at the front' or 'to place in the front'.

front end processor *n* [*Computing*] a secondary unit designed to back up the functioning of the main processor by performing a variety of basic tasks so that the main unit can then take advantage of this spade-work and concentrate on performing major tasks.

front five *n* [*Rugby*] the front row (three men) and the second row (two men) of the rugby scrum when considered as a five-man tactical unit who act as the powerhouse of the scrum and the tactical focal point of the play.

front four *n* [*US*] [*Football*] the guards and tackles on the defensive unit of a football team.

front of the gun, in *adv* [*Drugs*] a dealer who works 'in front of the gun' carries on his trade in the knowledge that he will be offered no protection from his wholesalers if he is arrested; such dealers, often fresh from jail or the hospital, are happy to accept such terms of supply, merely to maintain their own drug habits.

front line *n* [*Sociology, Politics*] this comes from the military definition of a line of confrontation; it refers to certain streets in the UK's West Indian areas (eg: Railton Road, SE24, and All Saints Road, W11, in London) where the black community feel that their rights and freedoms are most heavily under assault, and where, in white/police eyes, such rights and freedoms are paraded most provocatively.

front line manager *n* [*Management*] See **first line manager**.

front loading *n* [*Finance*] a sliding scale charge, usually around 5%, which is added by some finance houses to the principal sum borrowed; this sum, which works as an administration charge, is paid off before the borrower begins to pay off the actual loan.

front matter *n* [*Publishing*] all matter – title, half-title, introduction, copyright page, dedication, etc, – that precedes the text; such material often carries its own numbering, usually in lower case Roman numerals.

front office *n* [*Film*] the business departments of film companies, which are often sited in New York, rather than in Hollywood where the creative side of film-making is centred.

front porch *n* [*TV*] that part of the video signal waveform between the start of the line blanking pulse and the leading edge of the line sync pulse.

front porch campaign *n* [*Politics*] this was

originally a supposedly dignified style of campaigning – whereby the candidate 'held court' from his own front porch, or at least in his own house, and there dealt with the various delegations, power-brokers, interest groups and random individuals as came to visit. It is now used only as an epithet for a lazy candidate who refuses to go out to meet and court the voters.

front rise n [*Clothing*] the distance from the crotch to the centre-front of the waistline. See also **back rise**.

front running n [*US*] [*Stock market*] a situation in which a trader who has advance knowledge of a given transaction will attempt to use this for his own advantage. See also **insider**.

front track n [*US*] [*Circus*] one half of a **hippodrome track** in a circus tent. It is the equivalent of downstage in the theatre. See also **back track**.

front-end n [*Audio*] the input stages of a tuner or a pre-amplifier.

front-end load n [*Stock market*] sales commissions and other expenses paid to a broker which make up part of the initial payments made by an investor under a long-term contract for the purchase of mutual funds shares. It comes from the 'load' (the commission, etc.) being paid at 'the front'.

front-end money n [*Commerce*] money paid over in advance to set up a speculative project.

front-end processing n [*Computing*] the use of subordinate intelligent terminals to perform a large proportion of the processing in a communications network which would otherwise devolve solely upon the central machine. This allows the main computer to devote itself to more purely computational tasks, leaving the smaller machines to deal with peripherals, communications, error checking, device driving, etc.

fronting n [*Lacrosse*] the marking of an attack by standing in front of her, instead of goalside.

frontlash n [*Politics*] the reverse of a backlash; this was coined by President Lyndon B. Johnson in 1964 to explain how the threatened racist backlash against his civil rights legislation would be submerged in the frontlash of its many supporters.

frontline states n [*Politics*] those black African nations which border on South Africa and, formerly, on Rhodesia before it became Zimbabwe.

frontlist n [*Publishing*] the selection of books that have been most recently issued by a publisher; thus the 'spring list' or the 'autumn list'. See also **backlist**.

frontsman n [*UK*] [*Market-traders*] anyone used by a market-trader, especially in mock-auctions, to attract the crowds. See also **gee 2**.

frost n [*TV*] a lighting filter that diffuses light.

front-call n [*US*] [*Marine Corps*] a procedure established within a command whereby under certain emergency conditions all officers and other key personnel may be alerted by special notification.

frosting n [*Dog breeding*] the canine version of greying in humans: the replacement of coloured hair by white, usually spreading from the muzzle area.

frowzy a [*Weaving*] an industrial term for dull-looking wool.

frozen 1. a [*Economics*] said of credits, assets, etc. that can neither be liquidated nor realised in any other way. 2. a [*Oil rigs*] said of a well which has caved in and buried the drilling tools. See also **snakes**.

frozen playlist n [*Pop music, Radio*] a **playlist** that has no changes, no new entries nor any other additions in a given week at a radio station.

frugalise v [*Motor trade*] referring to the drive to retire the old 'gas-guzzlers' and to find a popular series of cars that will consume less petrol and show due respect for the energy crisis.

fruit of the Spirit n [*Religion*] those qualities developed in believers by their belief; see Galatians 5:22.

fruit ranch n [*US*] [*Medicine*] the hospital psychiatric unit.

fruit salad 1. n [*US*] [*Medicine*] a group of stroke patients, unable to care for themselves. See also **vegetable garden**. 2. n [*Military*] a chestful of internationally awarded medal ribbons displayed by a senior officer. See also **scrambled egg**.

fruiting n [*Aerospace*] the refusal by friendly aircraft to respond to radio interrogation by communicators who are considered to be probably hostile.

fruity 1. a [*Cheese-making*] said of the sweet and appealing fragrance or flavour of some cheeses, especially the monastery types (Munster, Port-Salut) or semi-firm mountain cheeses. 2. a [*Wine-tasting*] having the attractive, fleshy quality derived from good, ripe grapes, but not necessarily a grapey aroma.

frustrated cargo n [*Commerce*] any shipment of supplies en route from one port to another which is stopped prior to its arrival and for which further instructions as to its disposition must be obtained.

frying n [*Audio*] when there is no input into a carbon microphone, this is the noise produced by small irregularities in the current.

FTA n [*Industrial relations*] acro **Failure to Agree** shorthand for the breakdown (permanent or temporary) of union-management wage negotiations.

FTL adv [*Science fiction*] abbr of **faster than light**; this is a generalised concept used in science fiction to overcome problems of travel between stars, galaxies, etc.

fuck off excl [*New therapies*] in **primal therapy**, this is an expletive used towards the patient by the therapist in an attempt to curtail any attempts by that patient to raise topics that are not directly related to the object of the therapy: the primal experience.

fudge 1. n [Journalism] the attachment in a rotary press that is used to insert 'stop press' news. **2.** n [Journalism] a piece of 'stop press' news is inserted in the 'fudge box': the small block of white space left available in the newspaper to carry any such news.

fudger n [Marbles] a general term for an unpopular player. It comes from 'fudging': the act of cheating by edging over the line of the ring in which the marbles are shot, because a player lacks sufficient **knuckle**.

fuel fraction n [Military] the amount of fuel an aircraft can carry after other vital weight – the pilot, armaments, machinery and computers, etc. – have been subtracted from the safe flying load.

fuff n [TV] fake snow used for 'wintertime' effects.

fug pants n pl [Navy] heavy underwear worn in very cold temperatures; after lengthy wearing such garments have their own 'fug'.

fugitive 1. n [Textiles] a dye that is not fast; thus this also refers to a garment that is coloured with such a dye. **2.** a [Weaving] said of dyes that may lose colour under light or water. See also **fast**. **3.** a [Painting] used of colours that fade under bright light or extremes of weather.

Fulcrum n [Military] the Russian MiG–29, a multi-role fighter/strike aircraft first developed in 1983 and scheduled to replace the MiG–27 **Flogger D/J**.

fulfilment 1. n [Advertising] filling orders for a product that has been advertised in a mail-order shot. **2.** n [Advertising] inserting the parts of a mail-order promotion into the relevant envelopes prior to addressing and sending them out. **3.** n [Business] the achievement of any set business goal: selling a quota, meeting a production target, serving a given client, etc.

full and plenty n [Navy] food in excess of the official helpings.

full chart n [US] [Car salesmen] the maximum **back end** profit on a car.

full disguise n [Antiques] the highest grade of restoration.

full faith and credit n [US] [Finance] the promise that accompanies the issue of federal and local government bonds: all government revenue collecting powers will be used to ensure that the bonds in question are paid as stated.

full generation n [Military] the most extreme form of nuclear war, employing the complete nuclear arsenals held by both superpowers and their respective allies and satellites. Currently this would mean the explosion of at least 10,000 nuclear weapons.

full gun adv [Flying] full throttle, at full speed.

full O.G. n [Philately] abbr of **full original gum** a stamp as sold to the public, ready for fixing to letters, etc.

full period n [Computing] use of the computer on a seven days per week, twenty-four hours per day basis.

full service agency n [Advertising] a large agency which can supply not only the creative talent – art direction and copywriting – but also those ancillary services such as market research, space buying, campaign strategy and anything else a client might require. See also **boutique agency, hot shop**.

full strip n [Metallurgy] strip steel which has buckled in the centre due to the edges being shorter than the middle.

full-bodied a [Wine-tasting] high in alcoholic content – 13°GL plus – and **extract**.

full-court press n [US] [Politics] this is derived from the basketball term describing an intensive, harassing defensive move; it was absorbed into the political lexicon via the Nixon White House in the early 1970s, when it shed its defensive implications.

full-furred a [Furriers] See **firsts**. See also **early-caught, late-caught**.

fulling 1. n [Textiles] the process of shrinking and thickening wool fabric by the application of moisture, heat, friction and pressure that cause the fibres to **felt**. **2.** n [Weaving] a process that subjects the fabric to hot soapy water and agitation, for the purpose of matting and shrinking it.

full-line forcing n [Business] this is when a salesman persuades a buyer to contract for a number of less popular goods in order to obtain enough of those items which are in high demand and which he really wants; thus he is forced to purchase the 'full line' of a company's goods simply to obtain the few that are really sought after.

full-line strategy n [Management] See **broad-line strategy**.

full-out a [Journalism] referring to a paragraph of typesetting that starts without any indentation.

full-service broker n [US] [Stock market] any broker who provides a full range of services to clients, especially when this involves offering advice rather than simply executing deals.

full-track a [Audio] referring to a tape recorder which uses the full width of its magnetic tape to record.

fully a [Midwifery] said of a woman whose pregnancy has reached full term, or who is otherwise ready to give birth.

fully functioning a [New therapies] referring, in Rogerian therapy, to a body and mind that are working at peak efficiency; it is a modern version of 'mens sana in corpore sano' which will combine mental and physical excellence to create an ideally adjusted individual.

fulminate v [Medicine] said of a disease which takes on sudden, unexpected and severe developments.

functional imperative, also **functional**

F

prerequisite n [Sociology] the concept that the basic needs of a society must be met if it is to survive as a functioning system; this is much criticised on the grounds of it being impossible to state what exactly these 'basic needs' are.

functionalism 1. n [Architecture] the concept that the function and purpose of a building should be the main source of its shape and style; this is embodied in the dictum of US architect Louis Sullivan (1850–1924): 'form follows function'. **2.** n [Sociology] the method of studying the functional interactions and adaptations of particular phenomena within a given structure.

fundamental n [Audio] the lowest frequency component in a complex waveform.

fundamental painting n [Art] a variety of art theory and practice which concentrates on the process of painting, stressing the literal physical character of the materials, and searching for an essential definition of painting. Its critics attack such a search as being no more than 'paintings about paintings'.

funds 1. n pl [Stock market] cash. **2.** n pl [Stock market] a common term for Government securities. **3.** n pl [Stock market] investment portfolios.

fungible a [Business] this comes from the legal term meaning 'taking the place, fulfilling the office of'; in business terms it is the idea of an individual's being moved around as and when he/she is needed. It is often used in the phrase 'the fungibility of technical people' whose skills are used to perform special tasks and then called up again elsewhere.

fungo n [Baseball] a **fly ball** hit in pre-game practice; a coach tosses a ball in the air and bats it towards an outfielder.

funk art n [Art] this comes from the blues/jazz use of 'funk' meaning 'rough' and 'down to earth'; it is a type of **pop** art produced by placing bizarre objects together in eccentric combinations, often with sexual or scatalogical connotations.

funk money n [Banking] money that is quickly, and often surreptitiously, removed from one country to another, usually when the political situation in the first country threatens the security of those who are moving their funds.

funkie-willie n [UK] [Market-traders] anyone known for smelling or stinking.

funkspiel n [Espionage] this comes from Ger. 'radio game'; it was originally a World War II term used by the OSS (fore-runner of the CIA) and is still used to refer to the deliberate broadcasting over the radio of misleading, false information, and using double agents (ostensibly those who are adjudged more favourable to oneself than to the enemy) to support its veracity amongst the general audience. See also **black propaganda disinformation**.

funkum 1. n [UK] [Market-traders] scent, perfume. **2.** n [UK] [Market-traders] a fart.

funky a [UK] [Market-traders] smelly or stinking.

funny n [Espionage] a misleading dossier of false information deliberately assembled to help in the building up of a **cover** story.

funny car 1. n [US] [Car salesmen] a small, foreign car, usually German or Japanese. **2.** n [US] [Drag racing] a dragster which has been disguised with a plastic replica of a normal saloon model body to make it look like a regular production model; unlike such models it reaches speeds of 250 mph in 6 seconds.

funs n pl [Marbles] a game in which, at the end, all marbles are returned to their original owners, irrespective of wins and losses in play. See also **keeps**.

funzine n [Science fiction] a fan magazine devoted to humorous treatment of the topic.

furlough n [US] [Marine Corps] a period of authorised leave allowed to an enlisted man. The term was used earlier in the Indian Army and Civil Service and is still used by overseas missionaries.

furnish n [Paper-making] the mixture of various materials, eg. pulp, sizing, fillers, dyes, from which paper is made.

furnisher n [Textiles] a revolving brush used in printing textiles.

furnishings n pl [Dog breeding] the desirable abundance of coat at the extremities (including head and tail) of certain breeds.

furniture 1. n [Book trade] those leather-bound matching sets of books that are often purchased but rarely read, acting instead as expensive shelf-fillers, ie. basically decoration, in private libraries. **2.** n [Cricket] the bails. **3.** also **reglet** n [Printing] wood blocks that fill out the spaces left within a **chase** when the type has been put in its proper position.

furring n [Building, Plastering] wood or metal battens fixed to **backgrounds**, and to which plasterboard or lathwork can be fixed.

fusher n [Textiles] a sloppy, inexperienced silk worker

fusible fabric n [Textiles] a fabric that can be joined to another fabric for a reasonably permanent period through the application of heat, moisture and pressure.

fusion n [Science] 'the formation of a heavier, more complex nucleus by the coming together of two or more lighter ones, usually accompanied by the release of relatively large amounts of energy' (OED Supplement, 1972); where the fission-based A-bomb depends on the fission of a single nucleus, the H-bomb is created by the fusion of two light nuclei. See also **fission**.

fuss v [US] [Painting] to remedy runs and sags in the paint by painting them out.

future shock n [Sociology] a term coined by Alvin Toffler in his book of that title, published in 1970: a state of stress and disorientation occasioned by an excess of dramatic and continuing changes in society – especially the technological changes that alter the entire social basis and assumptions of that society. 'Future shock arises from the superimposition of a new culture on an old one. It is **culture shock** in one's own society' (A. Toffler).

futures *n pl* [*Finance*] all contracts that cover the sale or purchase of financial instruments or of physical commodities for future delivery on a commodity exchange; they are promises to trade in securities or commodities at a specific date and handled on the **forward market** rather than on the **spot market** which deals only in **actuals**.

futurism *n* [*Art*] a movement based in painting, but touching literature and drama, that concentrated on the violent renunciation of tradition in favour of some imagined law of machine-like perfection. It was founded in the early 20th century by the Italian poet Marinetti.

futuristics *n* [*Sociology*] the study of the future, which can be subdivided into a number of titles, eg: 'stoxology': 'the science of conjecture', 'futurology' and 'mellology': 'the science of the future', 'alleotics': 'the study of change'.

futurity *n* [*US*] [*Horse-racing*] a race, usually for two year-olds, in which horses are entered at birth, or even before.

fuzzball *n* [*UK*] [*Market-traders*] a fart. See also **funkum 2**.

fuzzy logic, also **fuzzy theory** *n* [*Computing*] a form of logic in which the variables may assume a continuum of values between 1 and 0. This branch of logic is especially suitable for the representation of knowledge and human reasoning in terms useful for computer processing. Fuzzy logic is applicable to expert systems, **knowledge engineering** and artificial intelligence (**AI**).

fuzzy theory *n* [*Computing*] See **fuzzy logic**.

FVO *n* [*US*] [*Stock market*] abbr of **for valuation only**. See **FYI**.

FX *n* [*TV, Film*] abbr of a notation on scripts to indicate 'effects'; thus 'SFX' means 'special effects'.

FYI *adv* [*Stock market*] abbr of **for your information** a prefix added to a share price quote that indicates that the quote in question is for information only, and is not a firm offer of trade. Such quotations are given as a courtesy, simply for purposes of valuation.

G

G *n* [*Navy*] the warning note played on the pipe or bugle five minutes before the change of watches.

G, also **gimmick** *n* [*Gambling*] See **gaff 6**.

GaAs *n* [*Technology, Electronics*] abbr of **gallium arsenaide** the material scheduled to replace silicon as the basis of semiconductor chips as used in computers. It has been developed for the past decade, and is very popular with the military for its resistance to radioactivity. GaAs operates several times faster than silicon, is highly resistant to current flow and can withstand a range of temperatures from $-200°$ to $+200°$C. Still rare, and thus expensive, GaAs chips are unlikely, for all their appeal, to overtake silicon until the 1990s.

gable end *n* [*Advertising*] a poster site on the end of a building or terrace.

gabriel *n* [*Computing*] an unnecessary stalling technique, as in 'X is pulling a gabriel . . .'

gadget *n* [*Glass-making*] a tool that holds the foot of a wine glass while the upper part is being finished.

gaff 1. *n* [*Dancing*] a male dancer's belt, the protection under his tights for his genitals. **2.** *n* [*Logging*] the steel point of a spiked pole, that is used to manipulate logs which are floating free in water. **3.** *n* [*UK*] [*Market-traders*] market, fair. **4.** *n* [*UK*] [*Theatre*] a portable, improvised theatre. See also **fit-up**. **5.** *n* [*UK*] [*Theatre*] any cheap, second-rate theatre. **6.** also **G, gimmick** *n* [*Gambling*] any secret device used to aid cheating; thus 'gaffed dice' means crooked dice; to 'gaff a wheel' means to fix a roulette wheel in the house's favour.

gaffer 1. *n* [*Glass-making*] See **chairman 2. 2.** *n*

[*TV, Film*] the chief electrician; thus 'gaffer grip' means a spring-loaded claw used to hold a small lamp; 'gaffer tape' means all-purpose adhesive tape used by electricians.

gaffers *n pl* [*UK*] [*Coal-mining*] National Coal Board managers and their agents.

gaffer's dog *n* [*US*] [*Coal-mining*] the assistant foreman.

gafia *part phr* [*Science fiction*] acro **getting away from it all** withdrawing from science fiction fan activity. See also **dafia, fafia**.

gafiate **1.** *n* [*Science fiction*] one who has withdrawn from science fiction fandom. **2.** *v* [*Science fiction*] to withdraw from science fiction fan activity. See also **gafia**.

gag **1.** *n* [*Film*] a stunt; the stuntman's ironical correlation of his/her dangerous skill with humour. **2.** *n* [*Theatre*] originally an ad-lib; currently a joke.

gag order (*US*), **reporting restrictions** (*UK*) *n* [*Media*] an order issued by the court concerned which prohibits the media from reporting the proceedings in a given lawsuit.

gag rule *n* [*Politics*] any action in Parliament or Congress which can limit their debates; the term originated in the Sedition Acts of the 18th century, which were known as 'gags'.

gagger *n* [*Metallurgy*] in iron founding, this is a piece of metal designed to reinforce or support sand in the deep pockets of a mould.

galactic *n* [*Computing*] said of data held in a database that is accessible from many places and by many applications.

gall **1.** *n* [*Glass-making*] a layer of molten sulphate floating on top of the glass in a furnace. **2.** *n* [*Glass-making*] an imperfection found when sodium sulphate has been included in the glass. **3.** *v* [*Sailing, Ropework*] to chafe or fret; it is used especially of ropes or hawsers.

gallery *n* [*TV*] the production control room that overlooks a TV studio. See also **box 13**.

gallery hit *n* [*Cricket*] a shot that is enjoyed by the crowd; it is on the lines of the theatrical 'playing to the gallery'.

galley **1.** *n* [*US*] [*Marine Corps*] a land or sea mess; a mobile field kitchen (but using the traditional Marine naval terminology, rather than Army use). **2.** *n* [*Publishing*] a long tray in which lines of hand or machine set letterpress type are held.

galley proof *n* [*Publishing*] a copy or impression of the material held in one galley; such material tends to require many corrections by both author and editor. With computerised offset printing, galleys are obtained by numbering and breaking the output of copy. thus producing similar long sheets of un-formatted text.

galloper **1.** *n* [*US*] [*Coal-mining*] an assistant to the mine superintendent, who carries out visits to the entire mine, above and below ground. **2.** *n* [*Fairs*] a wooden horse on a merry-go-round.

galloping goose *n* [*Logging*] a light railroad vehicle which carries a petrol tank.

Galosh *n* [*Military*] the ABM1–B Galosh interceptor is the Soviet nuclear-armed ballistic missile defence system. The Galosh system was first deployed around Moscow subsequent to its introduction in 1964. 64 missiles were in place, in eight batteries of eight missiles each. The Galosh is the only ABM system deployed either by the US or USSR, as permitted by the ABM Treaty of 1972 and the Protocol of 1974. Half the missiles were dismantled by 1980, leaving only four sites. See also **ABM Treaty, PVO strany**.

gambler's fallacy *n* [*Literary criticism, Gambling*] the fallacy of believing that simply because something has not happened in the past, it must be due to happen soon.

game *n* [*Management*] a situation of conflict or competition that can be studied by using **game theory**.

game art *n* [*Art*] essentially this refers to those toys, games and playthings that are made by artists; it also refers to those art works which encourage the involvement of the spectator, and are produced by artists who believe that adults as well as children need the vital cultural functions served by play.

game, on the *adv* [*UK*] [*Sex, Police*] working as a prostitute.

game plan *n, v* [*Business, Politics*] this is derived from the US football term for a strategy prepared for a game; it is taken by politicians (especially the Nixon White House, where the President actually sent in a play to the Washington Redskins – which play resulted in their opponents scoring) and by businessmen to mean a planned strategy aimed at achieving certain goals within defined rules.

game theory *n* [*Business*] a mathematical theory which was developed to describe and analyse competitive situations; it is used by the military and by businessmen to assess a range of possibilities and their concomitant variables when considering both a hypothetical battlefield or its commercial cousin, the marketplace.

games *n pl* [*Sex*] the embellishment of straight homosexual sex by the addition of **toys** such as vibrators, whips, manacles, etc, and as such requested by some clients of gay hustlers. See also **party**.

gamma stocks, also **gamma securities** *n pl* [*UK*] [*Stock market*] the third most popular group of shares traded on the London Stock Exchange; a gamma stock must have at least two **market-makers** registered to its name. See also **alpha stocks, beta stocks, delta stocks**.

gammy *a* [*UK*] [*Market-traders*] second-rate, inferior, said especially of goods on sale.

gamp *n* [*Textiles*] a long piece of metal with a raised centre which is fitted to a sewing machine to produce a round tuck on fabric materials.

gamy a [*Cheese-making*] said of strong cheeses with penetrating aromas.

gandy dancer n [*UK*] [*Railways*] a railway lengthman or platelayer; a maintenance man who keeps the track itself functioning.

gang n [*Sailing, Ropework*] a set of rigging for a mast or yardarm.

Gang of Four, the 1. n [*Politics*] the former Chinese leaders of the **Cultural Revolution** who were immediately pilloried after the death of Mao Zedong in October 1976. 1. Wang Hun-Wen (vice-chairman of the cultural committee of the Party); 2. Chang Ch'un Chiao, (politburo member); 3. Chiang Ch'ing – Jiang Qing (pinyin) – (Mao's widow and cultural supremo); 4. Yao Wen-Yuan. All four were tried between Feb. 1980 and Dec. 1981 for 'counter-revolutionary revisionism' and duly found guilty. Their sentences were (1) life imprisonment, (2) and (3) death, commuted to life imprisonment, (4) 20 years jail. **2.** n [*UK*] [*Politics*] the four leading members of the Labour Party who broke away in 1981 to found the Social Democratic Party (SDP): Roy Jenkins, David Owen, William Rodgers and Shirley Williams: their nickname was modelled facetiously by the British media on their Chinese 'counterparts'.

ganging n [*Technology*] the use of a single knob to accomplish a number of differing functions within a single piece of equipment.

gangue n [*Mining*] material of no apparent value which is associated with valuable minerals found in lodes or veins.

gangway n [*Logging*] an inclined plane up which logs are moved from the water into a sawmill.

ganister n [*Coal-mining*] a compact, highly siliceous, sedimentary rock, often containing plant remains.

gap 1. n [*Audio*] the vertical slit within the metal of a magnetic tape-head over which the magnetising field is created during recording, or a signal is induced during playback. **2.** n [*Audio*] the magnetic gap in a microphone or a moving coil loudspeaker. **3.** n [*US*] [*Stock market*] the difference in a share price that develops between the end of one day's trading and the beginning of the next; the fluctuation occurs after some extraordinary event – usually good or bad news announced by the company – has happened in the interim.

gap analysis n [*Marketing*] the tabulation of all known **consumer wants** with regard to a given product, together with a cross-listing of the features of existing products which attempt to satisfy those wants. Armed with this chart, the researcher can identify such gaps as may exist and plan to exploit/cater for them in a new product.

gap financing n [*Finance*] attempts to obtain extra finance for projects for which the sum of the money so far obtained does not equal all that is required; what is outstanding is the 'gap'.

gap sheet n [*Business*] a personal file which is prepared in respect of a candidate for promotion and which is filled not only with a list of past achievements, but with a list of those skills yet to be obtained – the gaps which are to be filled. Assessment of the candidate is based on both parts of the file.

gap shooter n [*Archery*] one who obtains the range in field archery by working back from widely spaced shots.

gaper n [*Cricket*] a very easy catch; one that would drop into one's open mouth.

gaper's block n [*US*] [*Traffic controllers*] a traffic jam or slow-down caused by travellers who are so fascinated by the scenery that they stop driving fast and carefully (used in Denver, Col.).

garage 1. n [*Military*] a term used by US intelligence to describe the **hardened** defences employed by Soviet rocket forces to shield the SS–20 intermediate range missile (supposedly the equivalent of the US **cruise**). **2.** n [*US*] [*Stock market*] the annex floor on the north side of the main trading floor of the New York Stock Exchange.

garage band n [*Pop music*] a young pop group who have probably yet to find success or even real backing from the business and may well rehearse in a garage or some similar unprofessional environment.

garbage 1. n [*Aerospace*] miscellaneous objects and debris which are orbiting the earth, having been ejected from or possibly broken off a variety of space craft. **2.** n [*Computing*] useless or inaccurate data. **3.** n [*Sports*] this is used in a variety of sports (ice-hockey, basketball, tennis) to imply an easy shot or scoring opportunity. Thus 'garbage collector' is an ice-hockey player who specialises in taking advantage of 'garbage shots'.

garbage collection n [*Computing*] the rewriting of routines in order to eliminate any items in the memory that were only referred to once and which will never be needed again in any subsequent program.

garbage housing n [*Architecture*] buildings made from rubbish and other detritus, but, unlike the makeshift dwellings of slums and shanty towns, this waste has been deliberately designed with this secondary use in mind; eg: the WoBo bottle brick, etc.

garden fly n [*Angling*] a worm.

gardening n [*Cricket*] the exaggerated patting and smoothing of a pitch by a batsman; it usually occurs following the receipt of a ball which he could not play successfully so his intention is to suggest that it was the pitch, not the bowler, that managed to overcome his skills.

garland n [*Skiing*] alternating linked left and right turns across a slope.

garment n [*US*] [*Garment trade*] referring to women's apparel only. See also **clothing 1**.

garnishee order n [*Banking*] an order obtained by a creditor against the person who owes him

G

money (the 'garnishee') that requires that person's employer to pay off the debt directly to the creditor, rather than trusting the debtor to pay it himself; thus a percentage, or all of one's wages/fees/etc can be withheld until a given debt is paid off.

garnishment *n* [*Law*] legal proceedings designed to ensure that a creditor or plaintiff in a legal action will receive payment due from a debtor or defendant. This is often achieved through a garnishee order: one who owes the defendant some money will pay some (or all) of that money direct to the defendant's creditors.

gas! *excl* [*Computing*] an explanation of intense annoyance, implying that whoever caused such anger should be sent swiftly to the nearest gas chamber. It was supposedly coined in 1978 when the killer of George Moscone, Mayor of San Francisco, was scheduled to be executed in that way.

gas *n* [*US*] [*Medicine*] anaesthesiology; thus 'gas passer' is an anaesthetist.

gas meter bandit *n* [*UK*] [*Police*] an ironic reference to any type of petty thief.

gas passer *n* [*US*] [*Medicine*] anaesthetist.

gash *n* [*UK*] [*Military*] waste, possibly from the galley; anything that is no longer wanted.

gash print *n* [*Printing*] a useless piece of paper; a bad photographic print that should be thrown away.

gasification *n* [*Gas industry*] the conversion of another fuel into gas; it is usually 1. conversion of solids or liquids by reaction with a gas such as steam, air or oxygen, and 2. conversion of liquids by thermal or catalytic means.

gasket *n* [*Sailing, Ropework*] a braided cord used to secure sails to yards.

gas-lift well *n* [*Oil rigs*] a well in which the flow of oil is caused by pressure of natural gas beneath it or by the pressure caused when natural gas is pumped into it.

gate 1. *n* [*Computing, Electronics*] a circuit element that can be turned on or off in response to a variety of pre-determined control signals. **2.** *n* [*Cricket*] the gap which may occur between the edge of the bat and the batsman's pads; thus 'through the gate' is when the ball passes through this gap and, often, travels on to hit the stumps. **3.** *n* [*Metallurgy*] in iron founding this is the point at which the molten metal enters the mould and makes its way into the mould cavity. **4.** *n* [*Sport*] the total number of people in a sporting crowd, and the money they have paid to attend an event. **5.** *n* [*TV, Film*] that part of a camera or projector through which the film travels. Each frame is held momentarily, and that image is projected on to the screen at a rate of 24 frames/second. See also **hair in the gate**. **6.** *v* [*Gambling*] to stop the dice moving before they have actually come to rest; this is usually done when either the roll or the dice themselves look suspicious.

gate fever *n* [*Prison*] the unsettled, apprehensive and excited feeling that a prisoner naturally feels as his/her sentence draws to a close. By extension it means any show of impatience shown when waiting for something to happen.

gate guardian *n* [*Military*] the stationary and often vintage aircraft that stands at the entrance gate of many military airfields.

gate happy *a* [*UK*] [*Prisons*] referring to an emotional state prevalent among prisoners whose sentences have only a short time to run. See also **gate fever**.

gate road *n* [*Coal-mining*] a roadway connected with a longwall face.

gatehold *n* [*Air travel*] a delay experienced by passengers who are forced for a variety of reasons to wait at the loading gate prior to entering the aircraft.

gatekeeper **1.** *n* [*Business*] those who control the access of useful/important persons, eg receptionists, secretaries, assistants, etc; they always claim that their employer is 'in conference' etc, and thus bar the way to salesmen or other members of the same company who need that access. **2.** *n* [*Journalism*] largely as in (1), but covering anyone who stops the reporter getting an interview, completing research, eliciting vital facts, etc. **3.** *n* [*Sociology*] a useful middle person who helps to connect needy individuals with social welfare agencies.

gateway *n* [*Communications*] any equipment used to interface networks so that a terminal within one system can communicate with one on another.

gateway status *n* [*Travel agents*] the major airports/seaports that are considered to be the main 'gateways' to a country and through which the bulk of tours/holidays are booked.

gather *n* [*Glass-making*] a mass of molten glass collected on a gathering iron for use in glassblowing.

gather in the stops *v phr* [*US*] [*Stock market*] referring to a stock-trading tactic whereby enough stock is sold to drive the price down to levels at which stop orders (orders to buy/sell at a given price) are known to exist. Once these are reached the orders automatically become market orders (orders to buy/sell at the best available price). This in turn triggers off further stop orders and so on. See also **snowballing**.

gatherer *n* [*Glass-making*] a worker who collects molten glass on the end of a blowing iron preparatory to blowing, pressing or drawing it.

gathering on *n* [*Building, Plastering*] a furry deposit of plaster on the surface of a run moulding, caused by the profile lifting.

gather-write *n* [*Computing*] the ability to take information from several non-adjacent locations in core memory and place it on a single physical record, eg: a tape block. See also **scatter-read**.

gauche de salon, la *n* [*Politics*] the French 'professional socialist'; it is the equivalent of the

G

'limousine liberal' or other adherent of 'radical chic'. See also **academic socialism**.

gauge pot, also **gauge box** *n* [*Building, Plastering*] any suitable receptacle used for measuring out accurate proportions of materials prior to mixing.

gaul *n* [*Building, Plastering*] See **catspaw**.

Gault *a* [*US*] [*Law*] of, relating to, or providing legal rights and protection for minors; it comes from a Supreme Court ruling of 1967 that one Gerald Gault was denied due process under the 14th Amendment of the US Constitution when he was committed to reform school without being informed of his rights.

gay gothics *n pl* [*Publishing*] mass market pulp novels with all the attributes of traditional historical romance except for the fact that all characters are male and the love is homosexual.

gazer *n* [*UK*] [*Market-traders*] a pedlar who stands with a tray of goods in the street.

gazlon *n* [*UK*] [*Police*] this comes from Yiddish meaning 'sneak thief'; it is used by both police and villains as a derogatory description.

gazump **1.** *n, v* [*UK*] [*Market-traders*] the practice of over-charging or swindling; to overcharge, to swindle. A 'gazumper' is one who swindles or overcharges. **2.** also **gazoomph** *v* [*Commerce*] this was originally used in the motor trade for the fraudulent technique whereby the salesman closed a sale with one buyer but then, realising that another buyer would pay more, offered the same vehicle to that buyer before the first one was able to pay and collect the vehicle. When the UK property market was booming in the early 1970s, estate agents and their clients adopted the term (and the practice); as prices calmed down, so did the practice, but it will doubtless continue to parallel their fluctuations.

gcg *n* [*US*] [*Prisons*] abbr of **gas-chamber green** the nickname for the drab green paintwork in many prisons, allegedly an added cause of depression amongst prisoners.

GCW *n* [*UK*] [*Road transport*] abbr of **gross combination weight** the total weight of an articulated vehicle with its load, fuel and driver.

gear *n* [*UK*] [*Market-traders*] clothes, belongings; goods on sale; thus 'geared up' means 'dressed up'.

gear bonger, also **gear jammer** *n* [*US*] [*Road transport*] a driver who grinds the gears when changing.

gearing **1.** *n* [*Finance*] borrowing money at a fixed rate of interest and investing it to produce more than sufficient to pay off the interest on the loan. **2.** *n* [*Stock market*] this is the name for the varieties of relationship between fixed interest capital and **equity**: highly geared shares are those where the fixed capital is high compared with the equity capital; low geared shares present the opposite situation.

gee **1.** *v* [*Dog-sledding*] to direct the dogs to turn right. See also **haw 2**. **2.** *n* [*UK*] [*Market-traders*] an accomplice in the crowd who helps persuade the customers of the excellence of what is on sale; he 'gees up' the buyers. See also **big gee**, **frontsman**.

geedunk *n* [*US*] [*Marine Corps*] the restaurant or bar on board ship. See also **slop chute**.

geisteswissenschaften *n pl* [*Sociology*] the human sciences; with the emphasis that the human sciences employ methods radically different from those of the natural sciences.

gelp *n* [*UK*] [*Market-traders*] money (from gelt?).

gemeinschaft *n* [*Sociology*] translated it means 'community'; it refers to relationships which are based on affectivity, mutuality and naturalness. Such relationships are destroyed by individualism, the division of labour and competitiveness, the gesellschaft or 'association' relationships.

gems, also **seals** *n pl* [*Glass-making*] decorations made by dropping melted glass on to a glass vessel and then using a metal seal to form their shapes.

gen *v* [*UK*] [*Market-traders*] (with hard g) to snap or bicker.

general abstract *n* [*Libraries*] an abstract of a document which covers all the essential points of the article, and is available for readers of varied interests. See also **auto, evaluative, indicative**, and **informative abstracts**.

general orders *n pl* [*US*] [*Railways*] orders governing the movement of trains.

general service *n* [*Military*] the regulation issue of equipment; by extension it means a person who is conscientious, strict, well turned-out and throughly versed in the military regulations. See also **GI**.

general ship *n* [*Shipping*] See **dry ship**.

general war, also **central war** *n* [*Military*] an all-out war in which all forces are engaged and each superpower makes a series of strikes against the other and its allies.

generalisability *n* [*New therapies*] a term freely employed to imply the ability or suitability of a specific concept to fit neatly into any general therapy.

generalised other *n* [*Sociology*] this forms part of the philosophy of G. H. Mead (1863–1931); it is the concept of the social group whose attitudes we internalise in our pursuit of our own lives in society.

generation **1.** *n* [*Art*] a generalisation beloved of art critics to describe groups of artists of roughly similar ages who emerge into the public eye at about the same time. The devout hope that generation will follow generation, each one new, bright and even more innovative that the last, is a modern fantasy encouraged by all those who batten on to culture – businessmen and investors as well as critics – and is hardly restricted to art. **2.** *n* [*Technology*] successive developments of a piece of equipment – a computer, hifi, weapons systems, etc. – in which each new generation can be assumed to be more sophisticated, efficient,

G

capable, etc. See also **state of the art. 3.** *n* [*TV*] the successive reproductions of a videotaped programme: the original is the master, the first copy is 'second generation', a copy of that is 'third generation' and so on. The quality of both picture and sound diminishes as the generations succeed one another.

generic prescribing *n* [*Medicine*] the prescription by doctors of the cheaper 'no-name' drugs, rather than the usual 'brand-name' varieties sold to most patients by chemists.

genesis bean, also **genesis rock, stone** *n* [*Science*] a specimen of lunar or meteoric material believed to retain characteristics of rock formed early on in the development of the solar system, 4 billion-plus years ago.

genetic fallacy *n* [*Literary criticism*] the mistaken belief that the essence of somebody or something can be ascribed to their origins; thus just because an author had a given experience, that experience will thereafter influence his/her writing.

genlock *n* [*TV*] abbr of **generation lock** a device for synchronising video signals generated from different sources.

genny, also **gen** *n* [*TV, Film*] abbr of **generator** a portable generator, usually mounted on a large truck, which provides electricity for the lights used in location filming.

gentle *a* [*Wine-tasting*] mild, pleasant, unassertive.

gentleman *n* [*Deer-stalking*] the amateur deer-stalker, as opposed to the professional forester or stalker who accompanies and if necessary tutors him.

gentles *n pl* [*Angling*] maggots.

gentrification *n* [*Sociology, Real estate*] the taking over – usually by young, upwardly mobile, professional middle-class people – of former slums or similarly run down 'inner city' housing (which may in its earlier days have in fact been smart and bourgeois) and renovating it back towards its former status. See also **block-busting**.

genzine *n* [*Science fiction*] a magazine which is not restricted to one specific type of science fiction material.

GEODSS *n* [*Military*] abbr of **Ground-Based Electro-Optical Deep Space Surveillance** an ultra-fast space-based surveillance system, employed in the surveillance of satellite movements and characteristics, which has substituted an on-board TV camera for the former telescope style film cameras. The two operators at a GEODSS earth station are therefore capable of near-simultaneous spotting and analysis – with computer processing – of the satellite, its origins, its orbit and making a comparison of these factors with previous data.

geologist *n* [*US*] [*Medicine*] a doctor who considers his patients to have no intelligence whatsoever. See also **botanist, veterinarian**.

geometric abstraction *n* [*Art*] a broad category, encompassing both sculpture and painting, which finds in geometric forms the universal symbols for rational, idealist concepts.

geometry of fear *n* [*Art*] a phrase used to characterise UK sculpture in the 1950s: influenced by Giacometti and Richier, often using tortured surface textures and enclosed in cage-like structures, the whole angst-ridden style was supposed to reflect the emotions of the post-war era.

George 1. *n* [*Aerospace*] the automatic pilot used in an aircraft; possibly it comes from the colloquialism 'Let George do it'. **2.** *n* [*UK*] [*Theatre*] the traditional name for any stage-door keeper.

George Spelvin *n* [*US*] [*Theatre*] the regularly used pseudonym – as printed in the programme in addition to his own name and primary role – of any performer who plays more than one part in the same production. The original Spelvin may have been a member of New York's theatrical Lamb's Club. A star of pornographic movies in the 1970s took the name 'Georgina Spelvin', a joke duly noted by the 'profession'. See also **Walter Plinge**.

George Washington *n* [*US*] [*Carpenters*] a hatchet; it comes from the traditional tale of honest young Washington and the cherry tree.

geraniums *n pl* [*Wine-tasting*] a geranium-like odour caused by the presence of a micro-organism derived mainly from esters formed during fermentation.

Geronimo, also **Crazy Horse, Screaming Lord Sutch** *n* [*UK*] [*Railways*] any over-excitable person, especially a foreman 'on the warpath'; it is named after two nineteenth-century American Indian chiefs and a contemporary rock singer.

gerrymander *v* [*Politics*] to organise the division of voting districts or constituencies in such a way that one party will gain unfairly at the expense of its rivals. The practice is named after one Elbridge Gerry (1744–1814), a former Vice-President of the US and a leading practitioner, though not the originator, of redrawing political maps in one's own favour.

gesso *n* [*Building, Plastering*] a mixture used for modelling/casting and made from plaster plus glue plus linseed oil or boiled oil plus glue plus whiting.

gestapo *n* [*US*] [*Road transport*] a state policeman or patrolman.

gestation period *n* [*Marketing*] the time that elapses between the initial enquiry for a product and the placing of an actual order; it is usually applied to **capital goods**.

get 1. *v* [*Coal-mining*] to break coal from the seam preparatory to loading. **2.** *n* [*Horse-racing*] the progeny of a sire; those 'children' he has 'begotten'. **3.** *n* [*Tennis*] the action of returning the ball.

G

get a road on *v phr* [*UK*] [*Buses*] to leave a wide gap between one bus and another along a London Transport route, thus causing heavier than scheduled loading on the second vehicle.

get behind *v* [*New therapies*] to understand, to appreciate; both carry the overriding implication of making offers of approval and support. The image is of standing behind a leader and rejecting all criticism.

get blown up *v* [*Music*] to inflate the bag preparatory to playing the bag pipes.

get centred *v* [*New therapies*] to be true to oneself, to appreciate one's inner being and individuality and to work towards making this the basis of a new and improved life.

get down *v* [*New therapies*] originally this was an exhortation shouted at rock groups, urging them to play with greater intensity; it is currently seen as an abbreviation of 'get down to' (a job or task is assumed) and thus is used with implications of dedicating oneself either to some form of job or to an emotional framework or commitment.

get help, also **get right** *v* [*Religion*] to become converted to the faith.

get home *v* [*Boxing*] to land a punch as and where intended.

get in touch with yourself *v phr* [*New therapies*] a popular incantation offered to those searching for a better life through one or more of the new therapies; the concept is of coming to terms with oneself as an individual by way of concentrating on one's true inner being.

get it on with *v phr* [*New therapies*] to have sex with; it is the equivalent of the UK 'have it off (with)' and as such is possibly more slangy than therapeutic.

get it together *v* [*New therapies*] a popular generality describing the process of trying to realign or integrate one's self in the overall bid for self-awareness, self-improvement or whatever the particular therapy offers as its goal. It comes from the 1960s/70s hippie slang for doing something reasonably efficiently, often as in 'Get it together, man!'

get mud on your boots *v phr* [*Architecture*] said of an architect who leaves the office and visits the site of the building which is being constructed according to his/her plans.

get off it *v* [*New therapies*] in **est**, this is the result of a successful est training; 'the est equivalent to confession' (A. Clare and S. Thompson, 'Let's Talk About Me', BBC 1981) in which the subject comes to appreciate the established patterns in his/her life and starts being able to discard them.

get off on *v* [*New therapies*] this comes from the drug slang meaning 'to enjoy a given drug'; to enjoy, to reach a new and more satisfying emotional state as a result of something. 'Get off on' can also be used to refer to the physical/emotional satisfaction that comes with pleasurable sex.

get one's act together, also **get one's head together** *v phr* [*New therapies*] a phrase that implies pulling onself back from a potential problem, breakdown or similar emotional disability. 'Getting one's head together' stems from the idea of returning to reality after one's 'mind has been blown' by a drug (probably LSD).

get one's buttons *v phr* [*Navy*] to be promoted from leading seaman to petty officer.

get out *v* [*Greyhound racing*] to reach the first bend of a race ahead of rival dogs.

Get Out Of My Emergency Room! *excl* [*US*] [*Medicine*] See GOMER.

get over *v* [*US*] [*Prisons*] to take advantage of someone; to make someone look foolish.

get set *v* [*Cricket*] a batsman does this when he plays himself into his innings and creates a firm base on which to make a large score.

get stories *n pl* [*TV*] amongst the **fen** of TV's 'Star Trek', these are stories which are written by fans who identify over-intensely with the plots and send into fanzines manuscripts that centre invariably on the capture, torture and even murder or execution of one of the main characters (often 'Mr. Spock') who appear unscathed and super-heroic in the actual scripted and transmitted episodes. See also **Mary-Sue Stories**.

get the air *v* [*US*] [*Railways*] to pump air through the hoses running throughout the train in order to get the pressure for braking.

get the breaks clean *v phr* [*Music*] when playing the bagpipes, this is to run one tune into the next one without making any mistakes.

get wet *v* [*Military*] to get blood on one's hands, especially after cutting an enemy's throat. See also **wet work**.

getaway man *n* [*Military*] a specific member of a military formation used in patrols: if the squad is moving in a shallow V-shape, the man at the centre of the V is, logically, the 'point' man; those at either extremity of the V are the 'getaway men', so called from the theory that in the event of an ambush, while the point may be killed or captured, they can disappear.

getaway money *n* [*Rodeo*] money that a regular contestant at rodeos has to live on as he moves to the next rodeo in the tour.

get-in *n* [*UK*] [*Theatre*] the moving of **flats** and other stage equipment, props, etc. which are carried by a touring company into the theatre prior to setting up the stage. Thus a 'good get-in' means a theatre that has a large scene **dock**, easily negotiated entrances, etc; a 'bad get-in' implies the opposite. By extension get-in and get-out apply similarly to any shifting and rigging up and subsequent dismantling and removal of equipment used in presentations, conferences, business theatre, etc.

get-off *n* [*Music*] in jazz this is an improvisation or **break**.

get-out 1. *n* [*Theatre*] the total weekly cost of a

production; it comes from the touring company's reference to the taking of enough money at the box-office to permit them to pay their bills, rent, etc. and leave for the next town on the circuit. See also **nut 1**. **2.** *n* [*TV*] the cleaning and clearing of a studio after a production has been finished.

getting scalps *part phr* [*Religion*] making converts for the sake of their numbers rather than their individual souls.

get-up *n* [*US*] [*Prisons*] See **wake-up**.

GHI *n* [*Advertising*] abbr of **guaranteed home impressions** a guaranteed minimum number of radio or television advertisement impacts – the strength with which a given commercial registers on the audience – for a given sum of money.

ghooming, also **still hunting** *n* [*Shooting*] prowling about silently in the jungle, usually at dawn, on foot or on a pad elephant, in the hope of seeing game; it comes from Hindi 'ghumna' meaning 'to turn'.

ghost 1. *n* [*US*] [*Education, Industrial relations*] in the US this is an absentee either at school or work who is counted as present nonetheless; such cheating was sanctioned at school since funds were allotted to schools on the basis of the total register and an absent pupil meant less cash. Ghosts at the factory were clocked on by friends to ensure they obtained full wages, whether or not they had earned them. **2.** *n* [*Film*] an extra image seen above or below the main image on the screen; it is caused by faulty synchronisation between the shutter and the intermittent mechanisms of the projector. **3.** *n* [*Military*] a spurious signal appearing on a radar screen that does not correspond to any target at the location indicated. **4.** *n* [*Military*] a fake electronic target that has been deliberately projected by a fighter in order to confuse hostile radar scanners either in another plane or on the ground. **5.** *n* [*Navy*] the splash which signifies that a shell has missed its target and landed in the sea. **6.** *n* [*US*] [*Road transport*] an old truck. See also **iron (horse)**. **7.** *n* [*Theatre*] the manager, in his capacity as paymaster to the company; thus the stock question on payday (Friday) is: 'Has the ghost walked?' (intensified by the punning reference to 'Hamlet'.) See also **treasury call**. **8.** *n* [*TV*] a spectral secondary image on the screen; a 'leading ghost' appears to the left of the true image, a 'following ghost' to its right. **9.** also **phosphide streak** *n* [*Metallurgy*] a segregated streak within the steel usually containing a concentration of sulphide, phosphide, oxide, etc, lower in carbon and higher in phosphorus than the surrounding material. **10.** *v* [*Film*] used of a professional singer who **dubs** on to the soundtrack those songs that are supposedly sung on film by the star, who will in fact only be lip-synching (see **lip-sync**) the lyric.

ghost crew *n* [*Film, TV*] a second crew that local trade unions may force a company to hire when

shooting on foreign locations; this crew will not work, but will be paid.

ghosted *a* [*Journalism, Publishing*] said of material supposedly autobiographical (and often with the accent on 'true' and lurid confessions) that has actually been written by a professional writer or journalist on the basis of interviews with the celebrity under whose name the eventual book or article will be published. See also **as-told-to**.

ghoster 1. *n* [*Sailing*] any boat the makes comparatively good way despite the lack of wind. **2.** *n* [*Sailing*] a special sail, similar to a Genoa rig (a large jib that overlaps the mainsail) but made of an especially lightweight material. **3.** *n* [*TV*] a film production that goes on past 1 a.m. and thus incurs all the expensive union-negotiated financial penalties that such late-night working entails.

ghosting 1. *n* [*Marketing*] the providing of an inner view of a package by cutting away part of the exterior. **2.** *n* [*UK*] [*Prisons*] the removal from one prison to another of an inmate who, for whatever reason, is spirited out of one cell and into the new one while the prisoners in both prisons are either asleep or otherwise ignorant of the departure/arrival.

ghosts and fairies *n pl* [*Commerce*] in hairdressing, these are euphemisms adopted by the stylists for fake appointments that are put into the salon diary when they want an extra-long lunchbreak or plan to sleep late the next morning. The management, as in many such fiddles, is tacitly aware, but considers that the expertise so indulged is worth a few hours' occasional freedom.

ghost-train *n* [*UK*] [*Buses*] the last bus on an all-night London Transport route.

ghost-word *n* [*Journalism, Printing*] a spurious word that has originated not in any real etymology, but through a long-dead printer's error; it is usually developed from such mistakes in dictionaries, eg: the verb 'foupe' was found included in Dr. Johnson's Dictionary (1755), when the lexicographer assumed that a long 's', used in a work of William Camden's (1605), was actually an 'f'.

GI *a* [*US*] [*Military*] abbr of **government** or **general issue** referring both to the actual equipment so issued and also to anyone whose bearing, attitude, opinions and so on are strictly military. See also **general service**.

GI series *n* [*US*] [*Medicine*] a full examination of the gastro-intestinal tract involving barium meals, X-rays, etc.

giant *n* [*Science*] in astronomy this is one of the class of large, diffuse stars. See also **dwarf 3**.

gib *v* [*US*] [*Carpenters*] to quit a job.

gibberish total *n* [*Computing*] a total accumulated for control purposes when using addition of the specific fields of various records to handle those records; the total itself has no special sense or meaning and merely uses such numbers as

G

there may be in the fields concerned for its particular needs in context.

gibson girl *n* [*US*] [*Navy*] a portable emergency radio carried amongst the stores on navy life rafts.

Giffen goods *n pl* [*Economics*] goods that do not obey the law that as prices rise, demand for them falls; instead the reverse happens. Thus these are goods for which demand moves in the same direction as price. The term is named after Sir Robert Giffen (1837–1910) who noted the effect in, for instance, the labouring classes' purchase of bread: the dearer it was, the more they bought.

gifted *a* [*Education*] said of a child who is appreciably above the educational attainments of his peers, and as such, like the backward child who needs special remedial care, may well need special treatment far removed from merely praising his achievements.

gig *n, v* [*Pop music*] a performance played by a pop singer or band; thus, to give such a performance.

gig stick *n* [*Building, Plastering*] a radius rod attached to a running mould for forming circular mouldings.

gigabit *n* [*Computing*] one billion **bits**; similar multiples are kilobit (1000 bits), megabit (1,000,000 bits), terabit (one million million bits).

gigantomania *n* [*Politics, Government*] the obsession, prevalent among all ranks and nationalities of leader, with the achievement of huge undertakings simply because of their size, without any consideration of costs, effectiveness, usefulness or similar points.

gigging **1.** *n* [*Textiles*] the raising of a **nap** on cloth by using a gig, a cylinder of varying size which is basically an arrangement of **teasels**. **2.** *n* [*Tobacco*] cutting the tobacco plant from the side and then slitting downwards.

GIGO *phr* [*Computing*] *acro* **Garbage In, Garbage Out** a dictum stating that if one puts worthless data into a computer the machine can only give worthless data back; it possesses no alchemical ability to transmute the 'garbage' into 'gold'.

gilding *n* [*Photography*] a type of reversal effect that can be obtained by pre-exposure and longer than usual development of Polaroid film.

gillaroo *n* [*Angling*] a species of trout which has its teeth in its throat.

Gilligan hitch *n* [*Logging*] any unusual variety of chain hitch.

gills *n pl* [*Furriers*] the sides of the neck in a pelt.

gilly *n* [*UK*] [*Market-traders*] (with hard g) a man.

gilt-edged *a* [*Stock market*] referring to any stocks of high quality and reliability, specifically UK Government stocks, those issued by certain highly ranked corporations and certain public authority issues.

gilts *n pl* [*Stock market*] See **gilt-edged**.

gimmer *n* [*UK*] [*Market-traders*] (with hard g) a gossiping woman.

gimmick *n* [*Magic*] an article secretly brought into play for the successful performance of a trick; it was originally spelt 'gimac', an anagram of magic, but this spelling had been dropped by 1940. Thus a 'gimmicked' deck of cards has been prepared for a given trick.

gimp **1.** *n* [*Angling*] twisted wire and silk. **2.** *n* [*Clothing*] a special thread used to support and raise the stitching around buttonholes. **3.** *n* [*Upholstery*] the upholsterer's braid that provides edging for seat covers, etc. **4.** *n* [*Weaving*] a narrow woven band used to bind edges or seams.

gin *n* [*Logging*] a pole used to load logs.

gin out *v* [*Business*] this comes from the cotton gin, a device used to separate the useful from the waste parts of cotton fibres; it therefore means to analyse a situation or problem and to obtain the required and relevant results and information.

gin pendant *n* [*Navy*] a pendant flown by the officers of one ship to inform officers on others that drinks are on offer in their wardroom; it is usually denoted by a pendant signifying 'starboard'.

ginger *n* [*UK*] [*Police*] a dishonest male prostitute; it comes from general rhyming slang 'ginger beer' meaning 'queer'.

ginger one *n* [*UK*] [*Railways*] a distant signal.

gingerbread **1.** *n* [*Architecture*] fretwork, or any similar small-scale, turned work. **2.** *n* [*Architecture*] showy, tawdry, over-elaborate and tasteless ornamentation or design. **3.** *n* [*US*] [*Painting*] any fussy or ornamental trim or decoration that makes for difficulties in painting.

Ginny Mae *n* [*US*] [*Economics*] *acro* **Government National Mortgage Association** thus 'ginny maes' mean stock certificates issued by this company. See also **Freddie Mac, Sallie Mae**.

giraffe *n* [*Mining*] a truck that is higher at one end than at the other; it is used on inclines.

girdle *v* [*Logging*] to fell a tree by cutting a ring around its trunk.

girl **1.** *n* [*Drugs*] cocaine. See also **boy 1**. **2.** *n* [*Military*] any nuclear device that fails to explode. See also **boy 2**.

give a knee *v* [*Boxing*] to act as a second; it comes from the archaic practice of offering a knee for a fighter to rest on between rounds when stools had not been introduced.

give a pull *v* [*Angling*] said of an angler who feels a sensation as the fish takes a fly or bait.

give a ten *v* [*Rowing*] a rowing eight does this when it makes a spurt in a race and rows flat out for ten strokes.

give a tug *v* [*UK*] [*Police*] to make an arrest; thus a villain talks of 'getting a tug'. See also **feel a collar**.

give and go, also **triangular pass 2**. *n* [*Lacrosse*] said of a ball player who makes a pass to a team-mate then runs on into space to receive an immediate return-pass, usually to bypass a defender.

G

give blade *v* [*Fencing*] to present the blade of the weapon to an opponent. See also **give point**.

give it a haircut *v phr* [*Car salesmen*] See **chop the clock**.

give (one) the bellows *v phr* [*UK*] [*Market-traders*] to get rid of (someone). See also **give the blow-out**.

give point *v* [*Fencing*] to make a direct thrust at an opponent. See also **give blade**.

give quickies *v* [*Sex*] used of a gay **hustler** who fellates a client, probably in some public place and thus necessitating speed.

give slack *v* [*US*] [*Railways*] to push a string of cars together, allowing the brakeman to uncouple the cars.

give the blow-out *v* [*UK*] [*Market-traders*] to get rid of, to send packing. See also **give the bellows**.

give up 1. *n* [*Stock market*] a deal which one broker executes for the client of a second broker, the commission for which must be shared between the two of them. 2. *n* [*Stock market*] that part of the commission earned by a broker from a major client which he is directed to turn over to a fellow broker who provided certain specialised services to the client during the same deal.

giveback 1. *n* [*Industrial relations*] the surrender by a union of previously won fringe benefits in return for wage increases or new concessions from the management. 2. *n* [*Industrial relations*] the acceptance during a recession by trade unions of (temporary) reductions in pay in return for guarantees of continuing employment.

giver *n* [*Stock market*] someone who has purchased shares and wishes to delay delivery until the following **account day**, thus effecting a contango. The giver must give interest to the deliverer of the securities to make up for delaying the payment.

giver aircraft *n* [*Aerospace*] the tanker which brings fuel to another aircraft in a mid-air refuelling operation. See also **receiver aircraft**.

gizzit *n* [*UK*] [*Military*] this comes from a corruption of 'give us it!' and thus means any looted item.

glad hand *n* [*Logging*] an air hose coupling.

glad hands *n pl* [*US*] [*Road transport*] connections for the air brake system between the tractor and the trailer. See also **susie**.

gladiator school *n* [*US*] [*Prisons*] a maximum security prison.

glamour issue *n* [*Stock market*] shares of companies that the market considers, at a certain time, to be fashionable.

glamour word *n* [*Commerce, Government*] See **boss word**.

gland, also **packing gland** *n* [*Oil rigs*] a sleeve which compresses the packing around a shaft or piston.

glass 1. *n* [*Navy*] a telescope; thus 'glasses' are binoculars. 2. *n* [*Shooting*] a telescope. 3. *v*

[*Surfing*] said of the surface of the sea when it becomes smooth and glassy.

glass back *n* [*UK*] [*Railways*] a fireman who did not relish main-line duties, with the intense output of physical effort on long distance trains; his back was too 'delicate' for all the bending.

glass jaw *n* [*Boxing*] a weak jaw, that can be damaged, even broken, with ease.

glass shot *n* [*Film*] a shot that is achieved by the painting on glass of part of the background; this is held carefully in front of the camera so that live action and actual background can be integrated properly with that painted on the glass. This enables extremely elaborate sets to be created at a fraction of the cost that would be incurred by building them or searching for a suitable location.

glasshouse *n* [*UK*] [*Military*] a miliary prison. See also **brig**.

glassies *n pl* [*Marbles*] glass marbles of any kind.

glassy *a* [*UK*] [*Surfing*] said of good clean conditions with little or no wind.

gleithobel *n* [*Coal-mining*] a heavy duty high-speed **plough** which has articulated cutting assemblies at each end and which travels along special ramp plates.

glide path *n* [*Aerospace*] the 'path' down which a landing aircraft flies as it approaches the ground.

glider pilot *n* [*UK*] [*Railways*] the footplateman required to ride a dead locomotive which was being hauled to the depot.

gliding shift, also **gliding work, gliding time** *n* [*Industry*] a variable shift system of work that allows employees to change working hours from day to day, with the proviso that they put in a mandatory period of **blocktime** each day of the five-day week and that the total daily labour amounts to eight hours. See also **flexitime**.

glim, also **glimmer** *n* [*UK*] [*Market-traders*] the eye.

glitch 1. *n* [*Computing*] this comes from Yiddish 'glitchen' meaning 'slide': any form of unexpected electronic interference that involves the computer, either in the power supply or in the program function. It was possibly first used by German scientists working at NASA for the US space programme. 2. *n* [*Politics*] a situation when an unexplained but crucial electronic breakdown or burst of interference results in major problems for a candidate or an office-holder. Faulty transmissions of speeches, especially those in translation, can ruin otherwise satisfactory communications or conferences. Similarly badly printed campaign literature, malfunctioning microphones, etc. all take their toll. 3. *n* [*Science*] in astronomy this is a sudden change in the rotation of any heavenly body, planet or star. 4. *n* [*Technology*] as well as in the computing use (see 1.) this term for a slight and unexpected error is used throughout technology, including TV, radio, radar, motor racing (where the Yiddish 'to slide' is most literally interpreted), space flight and elsewhere.

glitter and sneeze *n* [US] [Prisons] salt and pepper.

glittering generalities *n pl* [Politics] in propaganda this is the dressing up of one's argument as glamorously and grandiloquently as possible, thus appealing to every patriotic emotion; specifics are deliberately left aside.

global *a* [Computing] said of any variable whose value is accessible throughout the whole program. See also **local 1**.

global optimisation *n* [Computing] an attempt to make the running of a program maximally time-efficient through the best possible ordering of the sequences within it. See also **optimisation, peephole optimisation**.

globe and anchor *n* [US] [Marine Corps] the Marine Corps emblem, adopted in 1868.

glockem *n* [Military] acro **Ground-Launched Cruise Missile**: 464 of these **cruise** missiles are deployed in the UK and Europe, after this deployment was agreed by NATO in 1979. The missile has a range of 2,500 km, a speed of 550 mph and delivers a 200 kiloton warhead to an accuracy of 30 metres. It is against the GLCM that anti-cruise campaigners focus their attentions, but its flexibility and devastating accuracy mean that NATO is unlikely to accede to their demands.

glork 1. *n* [Computing] a term of mild surprise, usually tinged with outrage. **2.** *n, v* [Computing] a synonym for **glitch**, especially as a verb when used reflexively, eg: 'The system just glorked itself'. **3.** *n* [Computing] this is used as a convenience description when the correct term has slipped one's memory.

glory hole *n* [Glass-making] a small gas or oil fired furnace used to reheat the ware in hand-working.

glossies *n pl* [UK] [Railways] drivers' Weekly Notices, published each week and distributed to every driver; they specify speed restrictions, signal alterations and similar vital information.

glossing *n* [Sociology] in **ethnomethodology**, this is the method of accepting the impossibility of making a detailed analysis of every experience; one simply takes an instant gloss of what is going on, so that one may respond to it suitably.

glossy 1. *n* [Publishing] a magazine printed on glossy paper (usually a fashion or social publication); the UK Harpers/Queen – which is both – has called itself punningly 'the non-drip glossy'. See also **slick. 2.** *n* [Photography] a photograph with a glossy surface, often used for publicity purposes, eg '8 by 10 glossies'. **3.** *n* [Film] a film depicting supposedly sophisticated, fashionable life – as lived, in naive eyes, within the pages of glossy magazines and portrayed in glossy photos.

glue pot *n* [Cricket] See **sticky wicket**.

Glyndebourne silence *n* [Music] See **Bayreuth hush**.

glyph 1. *n* [Building, Plastering] a vertical channel in a **triglyph**. **2.** *n* [Photo-typesetting] a logotype, graphic symbol or similar character which has been digitised and held in store and which can thus be down-loaded into the typesetter.

GMG *n* [Medicine] abbr of '**gurnisht mit gurnisht**' this comes from Yiddish and means 'nothing with nothing': it is used as a notation on the files of patients whose pains are considered illusory.

gnat's *n* [TV] abbr of **gnat's arse, gnat's prick** the tiniest, barely significant morsel; it is used to describe a movement, an amount, a piece of film to be cut during editing.

gnat's blood *n* [UK] [Railways] tea purchased from railway canteens or refreshment bars; it is generally considered inferior to that which the men brew themselves.

gnat's, within a *a* [Engineering] said of something that fits within a very tiny measurement – perhaps one thousandth of an inch – the space between 'a gnat's piss'ole and its arse'ole'.

go codes *n pl* [Military] the US codes that will be transmitted in the event of launching a nuclear war or in response to a hostile attack: these codes, which change daily, are carried in a briefcase called the **football** by an officer who must never leave the President's side. Only on receiving these codes, which must match with counter codes and similar security devices, can the military begin a nuclear strike.

go down in flames *v phr* [US] [TV] used of a news team who fail, however hard they have tried, in their efforts to put together some item for that night's programme deadline. See also **crash 6**.

go forth *v* [Religion] to enter the ministry.

go for broke *v* [Military] used of an aeroplane which aligns all its aimable weapons simultaneously on one target or part of a target and fires them all.

go green *v* [Military] to transfer a phonecall from an open line to a secure one; it comes from the use of green telephones for secure lines. See also **scramble 1**.

go half-way *v* [Crime] to steal to order: the 'buyer' contracts with a burglar to steal certain objects which have already been selected in a variety of suitable shops; the objects are obtained and paid for at 50% of the actual retail price.

go in hole *v* [Oil rigs] to lower the **drill string** into the well bore.

go in the tank, go in the water *v phr* [Boxing] See **take a dive**.

go into emergency *v phr* [US] [Railways] to make an emergency stop.

go naked *v* [Stock market] on the options trading market this is when traders take option money on stock which they do not own and cannot deliver, in the hope that it can be bought back at a lower level.

G

go negative *v* [*US*] [*Politics*] said of a candidate and his/her staff who launch a campaign geared to exposing an opponent's weaknesses rather than promoting his/her own strengths.

go north about *v* [*Merchant navy*] said of a seaman who dies of any cause other than drowning.

go off-script *v* [*Media*] to ad-lib, to depart from the script in order to make a spontaneous comment; such spontaneity may itself be part of the script – technicians will expect the diversion, even if the specific content is unrehearsed.

go on a drunk *v phr* [*US*] [*Painting*] to paint a bathroom; working in such a confined space may cause the painter to suffer from dizziness caused by paint fumes.

go on the ground 1. *v phr* [*US*] [*Railways*] to become derailed. 2. *v phr* [*US*] [*Railways*] to get off the train.

go out of character *v phr* [*Theatre*] to forget one's accent, business, etc. – either through dozing off, losing concentration or through **corpsing**.

go over *v* [*Military*] See **go green**.

go over the side *v phr* [*UK*] [*Law*] to skip bail and thus vanish before one's trial; it comes from the nautical use.

go round *v* [*Croquet*] to hit one's ball through all the hoops in order.

go round (*UK*), **go behind, go back** (*US*) *v* [*Theatre*] said of a friend, relative, business associate, or any non-actor who visits a performer in his/her dressing room after the performance; one 'goes round' to the back of the stage.

go round the buoy *v phr* [*Navy*] to have a second helping of a meal.

go short *v* [*Horse-racing*] said of a horse which is lame, and whose disability stops it moving at full stride.

go South with 1. *v phr* [*Gambling*] to put money in one's pocket, either legitimately or otherwise. 2. *v phr* [*Gambling*] to remove a card from the deck surreptitiously.

go the route *v* [*Baseball*] to pitch an entire game.

go to bed, also **put to bed** *v* [*Journalism*] to finish writing and editing the newspaper and to consign the finished product to the printing presses.

go to Cain's *v* [*US*] [*Theatre*] to close a show; it comes from Cain's Transfer Co. of New York City, which flourished 1886–1933 and was the main renter of costumes, props and sets to touring companies. Thus a visit to Cain's warehouse implied the return of whatever one had out on loan.

go to the mattresses *v phr* [*US*] [*Crime*] in the US Mafia this is to go to war with another gang or **family**; while the war continues the **soldiers** do not live at home, but in special hideouts where they sleep on mattresses and rarely stay for two consecutive nights at the same address.

go toes up *v phr* [*Commerce*] to go bankrupt, with the implication of a corpse pointing its toes at the sky.

go under the rule *v phr* [*Stock market*] when a member of the London Stock Exchange fails to complete a deal, the Chairman of the Exchange must buy or sell the shares in question and thus complete the deal.

go up 1. *v* [*Education*] undergraduates (rather than students) at Oxford and Cambridge Universities 'go up', rather than 'attend', and 'come down', rather than 'leave'. 2. *v* [*US*] [*Theatre*] to forget one's lines. See also **make an ascension**. 3. *v* [*Theatre*] when a performance begins, the curtain goes up; this has been absorbed into the vocabulary of business theatre, in which a presentation similarly 'goes up' at a given time. See also **come down**.

go up in the air *v phr* [*US*] [*Theatre*] to miss a cue, to forget one's lines.

go up the road *v phr* [*UK*] [*Buses*] to report to the London Transport area manager.

go with the arm *v phr* [*Cricket*] used of a ball which follows the same flight path as the direction of the bowler's arm.

go with the flow *v phr* [*New therapies*] a perfect example of the development of a concept (itself only marginally more demanding) which has turned, through mass popularity into a therapeutic, 'pop philosophical' cliché; the original phrase, which exhorts those concerned to let themselves move in tune with all the different experiences that make up life, rather than fighting against so powerful a current, was 'floating with a complex streaming of experience,' (Carl Rogers 'On Becoming a Person', 1961).

go with the horse *v phr* [*Horse riding*] to lean forward as the horse takes a fence.

goaf *n* [*UK*] [*Coal-mining*] the worked out area which is allowed to collapse, behind the **chocks**.

goat 1. *n* [*US*] [*Cards*] a poor card-player. 2. *n* [*US*] [*Military*] a West Point cadet who has the lowest academic rank in his class. 3. *n* [*Parapsychology*] one who does not believe in parapsychology or its allied phenomena. See also **sheep**. 4. *n* [*US*] [*Railways*] a yard locomotive.

goat'n'shoat man *n* [*US*] [*Road transport*] the driver of a livestock carrier.

goaty *a* [*Wine-tasting*] used to describe a rich, animal-like flavour.

gob 1. *n* [*Coal-mining*] any part of a mine, excluding working places and roads, from which coal has been worked. 2. *n* [*US*] [*Navy*] any enlisted man. 3. *v* [*Coal-mining*] to stow, in the **goaf**, material which has no economic value but which has had to be removed from the face. 4. *v* [*Coal-mining*] to stow or pack a road with waste material.

gob pile *n* [*Coal-mining*] a large accumulation of refuse from a mine, especially slime and silt from washing coal.

gob stink *n* [*Coal-mining*] the odour given off by

the spontaneous heating of coal: this does not necessarily come from the gob.

gobble down *v* [*Computing*] to obtain data.

gobbler *n* [*US*] [*Medicine*] See **turkey 8** and **9**.

gobby, also **gobshite** *n, a* [*UK*] [*Market-traders*] a fool, foolish.

gobby ship *n* [*Navy*] a training ship; a ship that never leaves the harbour.

gobo 1. *n* [*TV, Film*] a portable 'wall', covered in sound-absorbent material. **2.** *n* [*TV, Film*] a small black screen used next to a light to diffuse the light or create some other desired effect.

God slot *n* [*UK*] [*TV*] a period on Sunday evenings, approximately 6pm–7pm, that is set aside by statute (IBA) or constitution (BBC) for the broadcasting of ostensibly religious programmes. In fact, although there is usually some form of hymn-singing (as there is on Sunday mornings) such programmes tend in the pursuit of viewers to bend the rules as far as they can without actually declaring themselves atheist. See also **closed period**.

God squad, also **God committee** *n* [*US*] [*Medicine*] special advisors attached to the hospital staff who deal with such ethical problems as terminal cancer, patients who demand to be allowed to die, parents who might not wish their appallingly damaged new born babies to be kept alive, the switching off of life support systems for human 'vegetables' etc. In other words officials who, in medical terms, are forced to 'play God'.

go-devil 1. *n* [*Oil rigs*] a variety of **pig** with self-adjusting bales, used for cleaning the interior of pipelines. **2.** *n* [*Technology*] the name given to a variety of devices used in drilling, farming, mining, logging, etc: the precise definitions differ accordingly, eg: in farming it is a form of rake, in oil-drilling a cleaner for pipes, in logging a special tool for splitting stubborn logs, etc.

gods *n pl* [*UK*] [*Theatre*] the highest tier of seats in a traditional auditorium, and by extension those who occupy them.

God's medicine *n* [*Drugs*] morphine: a description attributed to Sir William Osler, who observed 'Yes, it is God's medicine, for if it were any better, it would be kept in heaven for the angels to use'.

gofer *n* [*Entertainment*] a corruption of 'go for' and thus identifying anyone around a TV or film studio, theatre or record company, or any similar place, who is employed basically to run errands, make coffee and serve as a general dogsbody. Some gofers, like newspaper copy boys, can rise high, but the description is essentially derogatory, especially when used of executives who would not like to admit that they occupy so lowly a position.

goffer *n* [*Navy*] any non-alcoholic drink, possibly from shandygaff.

go-go fund *n* [*Stock market*] risky, short-term, volatile and above all speculative investment dealing; the implication is of the frenetic atmosphere of a discoteque, the home of 'go-go dancing'.

GOH *n* [*Science fiction*] abbr of **guest of honour** (at a convention).

going *n* [*Building, Plastering*] the distance, measured horizontally, between the flat riser at the foot of a staircase, and the last riser at the top of the staircase.

going away *n* [*US*] [*Stock market*] the speedy selling of the entire volume of shares offered of a new security.

going through the back door *part phr* [*Politics*] in the People's Republic of China this is the near-institutionalised system of bribery that influences officials, by-passes queues, bends the bureaucracy and generally facilitates daily life. See also **tolkach**.

gold *a* [*Record business*] referring to a record – single or album – that has sold one million units; thus to 'go gold' is to sell one million records. See also **platinum**.

gold bond *n* [*Commerce, Finance*] a bond, usually issued by a government, which will be paid in gold.

goldbug *n* [*Finance*] any financial analyst who believes in the value of gold as a safe investment.

golden handcuffs *n pl* [*Business*] a contract that ties an executive to a firm, especially one in which large commissions, bonuses, etc. can be earned by operating under the umbrella of that firm. Under such a contract, the executive who chooses to leave must return a high proportion of all such commissions and thus the company manages to control the movements of an otherwise volatile employee.

golden handshake *n* [*Business*] a large payment given to an employee either on his/her final retirement from the job or as a compensation for his/her dismissal. See also **silver handshake**.

golden hours *n pl* [*TV*] as regarded by the TV unions, these are those lucrative hours worked at weekends, on public holidays, late at night, etc, when normal wages are multiplied several times. See also **bubble 4**.

golden parachute *n* [*US*] [*Commerce*] this is created by executives who fear for their own jobs after a takeover. An executive is put on a massive five-year rolling contract as soon as the news of a takeover attempt is definite; thus if he/she is sacked, the redundancy pay will equal the full total of that contract.

golden shower *n* [*Sex*] urolagnia, a service provided by some prostitutes for some clients.

goldfish *n* [*Opera*] a singer, usually one of the choir or the chorus, who appears to the audience to be singing, but is in fact merely mouthing the lyrics and thus, by opening and shutting this silent mouth, resembles a fish.

goldie [*Military*] US Department of Defense Code for: the aircraft's automatic flight control system and electronic bomb guidance system are engaged and awaiting commands from the ground control computer.

G

goldie lock [*Military*] US Department of Defense Code for: the ground controller has full control of the aircraft.

gold-plating n [*Military*] a habit indulged by the US Pentagon whereby every conceivable piece of arms or avionics gadgetry is attached to aerospace equipment that was initially commissioned in a much more basic form; such embellishments are always cited in the name of combat efficiency, but, even if this proves so, they are rarely connected with any form of economic efficiency.

golf club n [*US*] [*Painting*] a brush that has the bristles set at right angles to the handle.

GOMER 1. v phr [*US*] [*Medicine*] acro **Get Out Of My Emergency Room** a notation on the file of a patient (very often an elderly one) whose less than urgent problems are preventing the offer of real medical aid to someone near death. 2. n [*US*] [*Medicine*] a patient who, while not terminally ill, is apparently too sick to stay at home, so requires long-term care and is keen to take every advantage of the hospital and its staff. The female GOMER is a GOMERe. A further etymology relates GOMER to the Hebrew root G-M-R, and originated as such by Jewish doctors in New York City hospitals.

gondola n [*Commerce*] an island counter used to display merchandise in self-service stores; the typical display unit of the typical supermarket.

gone concern n [*Commerce*] a concept which measures the current worth of a business were it to cease operating as a 'going concern' and be broken up by an official liquidator. Such an assessment is made by a banker who has been asked for credit, and who fears that the firm concerned is likely to collapse.

gonflable art n [*Art*] See **air art**.

gong n, v [*UK*] [*Military, Government, Politics*] a medal; to award a medal.

gonk n [*Sex*] a prostitute's derisory description of the client; it comes from a particularly inane, stuffed doll, briefly popular in the early 1960s.

gonnophta n [*UK*] [*Police*] a skilled woman pickpocket; it comes from Yiddish 'gonnif' meaning a thief.

go/no-go n [*Aerospace*] the step-by-step method of check and countercheck by which space missions are carried out; all decisions are made jointly by the crew and mission control whenever a new step has to be taken and only if all concerned say 'go' is that step taken.

go/no-go gauge n [*Management*] a device used in product inspection to test the size of an article that has been cut from a larger piece of material; it accepts the article if enough has been cut off and rejects it if too much has been cut off. The gauge does not measure the actual size of the article, merely whether it falls within acceptable limits.

good 1. a [*Book collecting*] the second least derogatory category of a dealer's evaluation; such a book

is adequate, but by no means exceptional in a collector's eyes. 2. also **real, television, real radio, etc** n [*Media*] not an assessment of quality in the traditional sense – artistic values, cultural standards, etc. – but an opinion of what, in the critic's view, television or radio ought to be doing, and the extent to which a particular event fulfils this ideal criterion. Thus, for its drama, immediacy and the fact that print could never have achieved such 'live' coverage, the televising in 1981 of the last moments of the siege of the Iranian Embassy in London was 'good television', irrespective of the violence involved and the subsequent near-deification of the SAS. See also **sexy**.

good attack n [*Music*] playing with confidence and élan.

good ball n [*Rugby*] the possession of the ball which sets up a move upon which a potentially try-scoring combination of moves or an individual run can be built.

good box office a [*Theatre*] said of a play that is attracting many paying customers.

good fish n [*Angling*] any fish that is worth catching.

good head n [*Hunting*] hounds 'carry a good head' when they run well together, rather than becoming strung out.

good house 1. n [*Theatre*] See **good box office**. 2. n [*Theatre*] an enthusiastic, interested and responsive audience.

good leaves n pl [*Tobacco*] a superior grade of tobacco.

good meeting n [*Film*] one who is considered to perform well in a movie industry conference; thus the opposite is 'bad meeting'. See also **take a meeting**.

good money n [*US*] [*Banking*] federal funds, which are available on the same day, rather than **clearing house** funds which will take one to three days to clear.

good news n [*Religion*] the basic Christian message: God loves man; man is essentially sinful; man can be reunited with God through the sacrifice of Christ; see Luke 2:10.

good numbers 1. n pl [*TV*] a good showing in the Nielsen audience ratings. 2. n [*Film*] satisfactory **grosses** at the cinema box offices.

good offices n pl [*Law*] in international law this is the intervention in a dispute between two states by a third state, who is party to neither side of the argument, in order to find a solution.

good old England n [*UK*] [*Railways*] a derailment.

good point n [*US*] [*Cattlemen*] cattle in good, well-fed condition.

good samaritan law n [*US*] [*Medicine*] a statute that protects all medical personnel from any legal problems that might arise from their using their skills in an emergency – a car crash in the street – to help injured people who are not their patients and thus who do not fall under the general insurance carried by a hospital.

good secrets *n pl* [*Espionage*] secrets that protect the identities of friendly intelligence sources whose work is vital to one's own national security.

good shop *n* [*Theatre*] a part for which the pay may not be especially good, but which is one in which 'people notice you' and which therefore provides excellent professional exposure.

good spot on the DZ *n* [*Parachuting*] a successful jump in which the team lands as planned on the Dropping Zone.

good theatre *a* [*Theatre*] said of an effective, dramatic play that pleases the audiences and **acts well**.

goodwill 1. *n* [*Finance*] the capital value of an intangible asset. 2. *n* [*Finance*] the amount by which the purchase price of a company exceeds the real value of its assets.

goofer 1. *n* [*Navy*] a hawker in a boat in a foreign port; a bum boat. 2. *n* [*Navy*] a spectator watching aircraft landing and taking off on an aircraft carrier.

goofy *n, a* [*Surfing*] a surfer who stands with the right foot forward on the board; it is the equivalent of boxing's southpaw. See also **natural foot**.

googly *n* [*Cricket*] an off-break bowled to a right-handed batsman with what appears to be a leg-break action. See also **chinaman 1**.

googol 1. *n* [*Mathematics*] ten to the one hundredth power. 2. *n* [*Commerce*] by extension from the mathematical use (see 1) this is the description by a salesman of a deal or commission that has earned him an exceptional sum of money.

googolplex *n* [*Science*] the figure 1 followed by a googol of 0s equal to 10 to the power 10 to the power 100.

goon squad 1. *n* [*Industrial relations*] company thugs who have been hired to break strikes by intimidation. 2. *n* [*Ice-hockey*] specially recruited players whose job is to beat up and generally intimidate the opposition, rather than worry about playing the game itself. See also **enforcer**.

goon stand *n* [*Film*] a large stand used to hold any equipment that is used to light or to modify the lights on a set.

goon suit *n* [*Air Force*] a one-piece coverall rubber suit used for protection when flying in very low temperatures.

goonie boards *n pl* [*US*] [*Skiing*] homemade, primitive, usually short, skis.

goose 1. *v* [*Business*] by extension from the usual, sexual meaning, this is to gee up one's business or its personnel by giving them a sudden shock. 2. *n* [*Distilling*] a partial condenser that cools the mixed vapours in a whisky still.

goose grease *n* [*US*] [*Medicine*] KY jelly, a popularly used lubricant.

goose neck *n* [*UK*] [*Road transport*] See **swan neck**.

goose pen butt *n* [*Logging*] the base of a log which has a hole in it which has been hollowed out by fire.

gooseneck 1. *n* [*US*] [*Coal-mining*] a device which connects cars to an endless chain system. 2. *n* [*Oil rigs*] a curved section of pipe in the shape of an inverted 'U' at the top of the swivel, which is connected to a flexible hose feeding **mud** from a standpipe rising from the rig floor to the top of the **drill string**. 3. *n* [*US*] [*Paper-making*] a roll of paper that has been loosely wound on to its steel core and which thus has an odd, drooping appearance.

goose-walk *n* [*Draughts*] a series of moves whereby one player takes a large number of the opponent's pieces.

GOP *n* [*US*] [*Politics*] acro **the Grand Old Party** the Republicans; it was coined in the 1880s and was influenced by the contemporary naming of the British Prime Minister William Gladstone as the GOM, the 'grand old man'.

gopher 1. *n* [*US*] [*Coal-mining*] a worker who cleans coal from the sides of a passage. 2. *n* [*US*] [*Crime*] a very gullible individual, falling easy prey to confidence tricks.

gopping *a* [*UK*] [*Military*] unpleasant, nasty, distasteful.

go-project *n* [*Film*] a basic project – an idea for a film, or a book or story on which it would be based – which has attracted the interest of a **bankable** star or director; such interest makes it practical rather than merely a theory.

gore *n* [*Clothing*] a wedge-shaped piece of material inserted into a garment part to obtain width at a specific place.

gorge *n* [*Clothing*] the edge of the front part of a jacket, etc, to which the collar or neckband is joined.

gorged *a* [*Heraldry*] wearing a collar, often in the form of a crown.

gorger *n* [*UK*] [*Market-traders*] a man.

gorilla 1. *n* [*Antiques, Auctions*] one thousand (pounds or dollars) 2. *n* [*Business*] a very important person, commanding a great deal of power and influence – a real 'heavyweight'. Thus the 'gorilla scale' is a system of grading the firm's major personnel who are rated as 800 pounders, 400 pounders or simply as The Gorilla. 3. *n* [*Sailing*] in offshore yacht racing, this is any non-specialist member of the crew whose physique, rather than any particular talent, entitles him to his employment; gorillas are differentiated as to their area of operations on the boat, thus 'foredeck gorilla', etc.

gorilla pimp *n* [*Sex*] a pimp who controls his stable of prostitutes through threats, intimidation and actual violence.

gork 1. *n* [*US*] [*Medicine*] a person suffering the after-effects of an anaesthetic – 'spaced out' and disorientated. **2.** *n* [*US*] [*Medicine*] a patient whose brain has ceased functioning above the most basic level and who has thus been rendered, through accident or disease, a 'human vegetable'.

gormalised *a* [*UK*] [*Market-traders*] stupid, foolish.

go-see *n* [*Entertainment*] 'It's like an audition: you go see if they like you . . .' (Andy Warhol, 1982).

gossan *n* [*Mining*] See **iron hat**.

gossen *n* [*Mining*] the weathered upper part of an ore body in which intensive leaching, oxidation and hydration have occurred.

got one's feet muddy *part phr* [*UK*] [*Police*] referring to someone who already possesses a criminal record.

go-team *n* [*US*] [*Football*] a synonym for the offensive team.

Gotham *n* [*Entertainment*] New York City; hometown, inter alia, of superheroes Batman and Robin.

gothic section *n* [*Metallurgy*] a **bar**, **billet** or **bloom** of approximately square section with slightly convex sides and chamfered or radiused corners.

gouch out *v* [*Drug addicts*] at Broadway Lodge Clinic this is to doze off due to the effects of heroin.

gouge *n* [*US*] [*Business*] this comes from current US Navy and obsolete student use for a cribsheet; it is information, which may be 'good gouge' or 'bad gouge'.

goulash *n* [*Cards*] a redeal of cards which are not shuffled but simply pushed together after a round has been dealt and no player (in whist, bridge and similar games) has chosen to bid; it was formerly called 'mayonnaise'.

goulash communism *n* [*Politics*] the term was coined in 1961 by Premier N.S. Khruschev to denounce 'local' mixtures of communism advanced in the name of the Party by various Western European Communism parties. See also **euro communism**, **tutti-frutti communism**.

goulasher *n* [*US*] [*Building*] a worker who puts in the concrete arches or ceilings, supported by steel frames.

gouty end *n* [*Sailing, Ropework*] a weathered and swelled end in running rigging.

government job *n* [*Logging*] any personal job performed in the firm's time.

government relations *n pl* [*Public relations*] a variation of government lobbying – the forwarding of the interests of a specific group of professional lobbyists who work hard and continually to influence Congressmen and bureaucrats to further their ends – whereby a PR company is hired to forward the interests of a particular corporation in its dealings with the Administration. Obviously restricted to the larger, more influential corporations, the PR executive's task is to encourage a feeling of mutual usefulness between the Administration and his/her client, on the lines of the famous slogan 'what's good for General Motors is good for the USA'.

governments *n pl* [*US*] [*Meat trade*] stock that is removed from the market by government buyers.

governor oil *n* [*US*] [*Railways*] the oil that lubricates the engine's governor controls.

goya and kod *phr* [*US*] [*Police*] acro **get off your ass and knock on doors**; a detective dictum that summarises the best way to get results.

gozinto chart *n* [*Industry*] a chart that shows for a given product the sequence in which the individual manufactured parts are integrated into sub-assemblies, which in turn make up the complete assembly; ie: what 'goes into' what.

gozunda *n* [*UK*] [*Railways*] an inspection cradle, lowered by crane, and swung under a bridge to check the state of the brickwork; it 'goes under' when and where required.

GPS *n* [*Military*] abbr of **Global Positioning System** an ultra-sophisticated system, based on an atomic clock, which is accurate to one second in 30,000 years, for the absolutely accurate navigation and positioning of satellites.

grab *n* the company store.

grab baits and run *v phr* [*Marbles*] referring to a despicable act in which one player, usually taking advantage of some instant of panic or commotion, grabs all the marbles, irrespective of ownership, and runs off.

grab one *v* [*US*] [*Road transport*] to shift into a lower gear to gain greater power.

grab (theme) *n* [*Chess*] problems where a single Black piece is captured on two or more squares by a single White piece or by two White pieces of the same kind.

grabber 1. *n* [*Crime*] pickpocket, bag snatcher. **2.** *n* [*Electronics*] a fixture on the end of a lead wire with a spring-activated hook and claw which can make electric contact with a circuit or component. **3.** *n* [*Industrial relations*] a worker who takes advantage of **fat work** to obtain easy production bonuses. **4.** *n* [*TV*] whatever material is put at the start of a programme with the specific intention of getting the viewer's attention. See also **hook 5**.

grace days *n pl* [*Commerce*] three days allowed for the payment of any commercial transaction over and above the time actually stated on a commercial bill.

graceful *a* [*Wine-tasting*] stylish, elegant.

graceful degradation 1. *n* [*Computing*] See **failsoft**. **2.** *n* [*Military*] the concept inherent in positing a possibly 'winnable', 'limited' nuclear war: that one's own command, and control and communications facilities, and the weapons that they administer, will survive longer, or at least collapse less speedily than those of the enemy. They will thus continue (albeit damaged) to work to greater effect than those of the enemy. It is accepted that massive loss and destruction on both

G

sides will accompany this process, so it would seem that such a victory would merely go to the side that was the last to die of its wounds. See also **survivability**.

grade A *n* [*US*] [*Lunch counter*] milk.

grade creep 1. *n* [*Business*] a method of regrading one's employees during a period when the government is demanding a wage **freeze** which makes it possible to raise their pay without actually breaking that freeze. However, in the long run, such ad hoc increases lead to earnings **drift**, which can prove harmful to a company. **2.** *n* [*Military*] the increase in middle-level officers, 'white-collar' military technicians, which has grown up alongside the development of increasingly sophisticated **weapons systems**.

grades *n pl* [*Farming*] cross-bred cattle.

grading 1. *n* [*Clothing*] the process of producing a range of patterns of different sizes from a master pattern. **2.** *n* [*UK*] [*Coal-mining*] the checking of the cutting horizon to ensure a clean cut of the coal, neither cutting into the stone floor, nor leaving coal bottoms behind.

gradual deterrence *n* [*Military*] See **flexible response, countervailing strategy**.

gradualism 1. *n* [*Military*] escalation towards war that is linked to the progress, or more realistically the lack of progress, in a series of gradually disintegrating negotiations. **2.** *n* [*Politics*] a term coined with reference to the abolition of slavery in the British Empire (c. 1835); it is the concept of slow and steady change, rather than violent overturn or the instant adoption of a radically new political ideology or direction.

graduate *n* [*Photography*] a container, with graduated markings for measuring purposes, used to mix chemicals in a darkroom.

grafilm *n* [*Art, Film*] a term defined by J. Byrne-Daniel in 1970 as 'a graphic/poetic approach to film-making rather than a photographic/prosaic one'. Grafilm involves the careful consideration of the elements that make up each shot so that every individual frame is a considered composition.

graft 1. *n, v* [*UK*] [*Market-traders*] work, to work. **2.** *n* [*US*] [*Politics*] the making of money by a politician through the use of dishonest or underhand methods: accepting bribes (though such blatant methods died out to a great extent in the 19th century); taking 'kickbacks' for ensuring that a major public works programme or foreign contract is pointed in the 'right' direction; accepting the many gifts on offer from grateful recipients of political patronage or similar favours.

grafter *n* [*UK*] [*Market-traders*] a worker, a trader; there is no implication of hard work.

grain *n* [*Clothing*] the direction of the warp of a fabric; thus one cuts straight grain (with the grain) or crossgrain (across the grain).

grainy *a* [*Photography*] referring to a style of photographic printing that concentrates on the coarse, rough, indistinctly defined image; it was especially popular in the 1960s.

gralloch *v* [*Deer-stalking*] to disembowel the stag that one has stalked and killed.

grammatical mistake *n* [*Computing*] the violation of the rules of a programming language by the programmer.

Grammy *n* [*Pop music*] the pop music business's annual award, the equivalent of Hollywood's **Oscars** and television's **Emmys**; it comes from the abbreviation of 'gramophone', plus a diminutive '-y' suffix. It is awarded by the US National Academy of Recording Arts and Sciences.

grams *n pl* [*Audio*] sound recording devices; this comes from the dated 'gramophone'.

grand consommation *n* [*Philately*] a type of paper used when regular stocks ran low in France during and after World War 1; this was a low-grade pale grey **granite paper**.

grand rounds *n pl* [*US*] [*Medicine*] the daily rounds of the wards by senior hospital staff, consultants, etc.

grand slam [*US*] [*Military*] US Department of Defense code for: all hostile planes have been successfully shot down.

grand theory *n* [*Sociology*] a term coined by C. Wright Mills (1916–1962) as a condemnation of purely abstract sociology; his own preference was for using the discipline to study the relationship of the individual to society and history.

grand-daddy *n* [*US*] [*Medicine*] an oversized sanitary pad.

grandfather *n* [*US*] [*Government*] this originated in the obsolete 'grandfather clause', which was a provision in the Constitutions of certain Southern states which exempted from suffrage restrictions the descendants of men who had already voted before the US Civil War; now it means either: (*a*) relating to or based upon rights or privileges that date from before the passage of a new law or regulation and thus override that new provision, or (*n*) the exemption of a person, persons or a company from the restrictions of some new law or regulation.

grandfather cycle *n* [*Computing*] the period during which magnetic records are retained, in case any malfunction requires that they be used to replace damaged material held in memory, prior to re-using the medium for new material.

grandfather file *n* [*Computing*] the immediately previous generation of a file which has been updated. See also **father file**.

grandfather rights *n pl* [*US*] [*Air travel*] certificates granted in perpetuity to certain US civil airlines permitting them to fly internal routes; they were signed in July 1940 by representatives of the US Civil Aeronautics Board. Thus 'grandfather routes' are those internal routes flown by those airlines ever since. See also **grandfather**.

grandma *n* [*US*] [*Road transport*] See **creeper gear**.

grandmaster n [Chess] originally this was a player who had won first prize in a major international tournament; latterly it has been expanded to mean an exceptional player (which may well denote the same achievement). See also **master 1**.

grangerise v [Publishing] to illustrate a book by adding one's own prints, pictures and allied material; it is named after James Granger, whose 'Biographical History of England' was the first work thus published.

granite paper n [Philately] paper that has coloured cotton, linen, jute or wool fibres embedded within it (thus looking like the 'veins' in granite) during the pulp stage of manufacture. It is currently common in Swiss and Taiwan stamps. A variety using silk fibres – 'silk paper' – was briefly used by the US for revenue stamps.

grannex n [Estate agents] a 'granny flat' extension to a house in which one's elderly parent(s) can be housed in adjacent privacy.

granny n [UK] [Market-traders] a pretext, an excuse, a false front.

granny bar n [Mining, Logging] an outsize crowbar.

granolithic floor n [Building, Plastering] a floor surface comprised of a mixture of cement and granite chippings.

granularity n [Computing] a measure of the size of the segments into which memory is divided for purposes either of memory protection of virtual-memory management.

grape n [US] [Car salesmen] a customer who is 'ripe for plucking'.

grapes n pl [US] [Navy] aircraft refuellers on US aircraft carriers, who wear distinctive purple jackets.

grapevine 1. n [Journalism] copy that can be used at any time for a **filler** piece. 2. n [Journalism] copy originating from a confidential source.

grapey a [Wine-tasting] used to describe the rich muscatel-like odour produced by certain varieties of grape.

graphics n pl [Computing] anything in representational or pictorial rather than written form that appears on the screen of a **VDU**.

grass 1. n [Aerospace] a fuzzy pattern on a radar screen which indicates the presence of electrical noise. 2. n [UK] [Police] this comes from rhyming slang 'grasshopper' meaning 'shopper' meaning 'informer', one who 'shops' his fellows to the police. 3. also **jade** n [US] [Painting] green paint. 4. v [Angling] to land a fish. 5. v [Boxing] to knock down; it comes from the era of bare-knuckle prize-fights, often sited in the open fields. 6. v [Sport] in contact sports this is to knock an opponent to the ground.

grass hand n [UK] [Printing] a temporary printer who deputises while a regular employee is absent.

grass roots n pl [Politics] a political concept usually advanced by the left that cites a great mass of voters, unsullied by cynicism or sophistication, and swayed only by their instinctively populist aspirations; less idealistically, this refers to the rank and file of any party – left or right – who may want to make their views known, but in the event will need to be given lifts to the polling station and will probably vote for personalities rather than policies.

grass rope, also **grass line** n [US] [Cattlemen] a rope made from any substance other than cotton.

grasseater n [US] [Police] a corrupt policeman who accepts such bribes and similar favours that are on offer, but does not actively solicit them. See also **meateater**.

grasser n [US] [Meat trade] any animal that has been fattened on grass, rather than on corn.

grasshopper n [UK] [Market-traders] a customer who inspects one's goods but doesn't buy.

grass-line n [Logging] a light-weight steel cable used for pulling the main rigging around.

grave n [Shooting] a shallow, camouflaged hide dug on the foreshore in which a shooter can await prey that is flighting (taking off).

gravel grinder n [Navy] the gunner's mate, responsible for marching and drill.

graveyard market n [US] [Stock market] a market in which prices are falling heavily and continually; this is on the analogy of the graveyard where those who are in – the investors – cannot escape and will lose heavily; those who are out prefer to keep their cash liquid and have no desire to get in.

graveyard shift 1. n [Business] the shift that runs from 12 midnight to 4am; it comes originally from naval and merchant shipping use, implying that in the dark, rough hours, there were more disasters than at other times. 2. n [Gambling] the early morning shift worked by the employees of a casino or any other gambling establishment.

gravy 1. n [UK] [Theatre] easy laughs from a friendly audience. 2. n [UK] [Theatre] good lines or **business** that get plenty of response in a farce or comedy.

gravy run n [Rodeo] an animal that makes it easy for the contestant to win prizes.

gray collar n [Industrial relations] repairmen and maintenance service workers. See also **blue collar, white collar workers**.

gray goods n pl [Textiles] knitted goods prior to undergoing the dyeing process.

gray (US), grey (UK) a [Sociology, Politics] an adjective used since the 1960s to denote pensioners or 'senior citizens', usually those formed into pressure groups or advocating some form of **activism**; this is on the analogy of the US Black Panthers who fought and demonstrated for the black cause. Thus the Gray Panthers (founded c. 1972) demand attention for the elderly in the areas of health, housing, protection from crime,

G

finance and utilities. A study on elderly homosexuals published in 1982 was entitled 'Gay and Gray'.

graymail n [US] [Law] a tactic used by a defence lawyer in an espionage trial: he or she threatens the government which is prosecuting the suit that if they persist in the case then he/she will call for a public enquiry which will prove embarrassing to the government and force the discussion of topics otherwise classified.

grayspace n [Science fiction] the brain, the 'gray matter'.

graze v [Military] used of an artillery shell which bursts on impact, rather than in the air.

grazing n [Commerce] a method of low-intensity shop-lifting common to the retail trade whereby the subject picks up some small, edible object, such as a chocolate bar, which is unwrapped, eaten and the wrapper tossed away before the checkout is reached. Other items chosen from the shelves will be paid for without evasion.

grazing fire n [Military] a steady burst of automatic weapons fire that sweeps parallel to the ground and never rises above the height of an average man.

grease 1. v [Military] to kill in a battle. 2. n [Mining] nitroglycerine.

grease, in the [Weaving] spinning or weaving with wool that has not been washed and thus retains the original wool grease within the fibre.

greaser n [Gemstones] a machine for separating diamonds from gravel, which consists of a shaking table made of five shallow galvanised-iron steps, each coated with a thick layer of grease; the diamonds stick to the grease, while the gravel is washed away.

greasing, also **oiling, saucing** n [Tobacco] the oiling of the leaves to produce a darker colour.

greasy a [Logging] See fat 8.

great a [Wine-tasting] over-used description which should in fact be restricted to wines of the highest quality – the top growths of good years, with their 'depth, richness, character, style, complexity, fragrance, length and aftertaste'.

Great Alliance n [Politics] the concept, which flourished in China only for the duration of the Cultural Revolution, that all revolutionary mass organisations had the right to representation on revolutionary committees.

great commission n [Religion] the mission to go out and evangelise the world; see Matthew 28: 19–20.

Great Leap Forward n [Politics] Mao Zedong's effort between 1958 and 1961 to make major steps forward in the Chinese economy and to consolidate the communist revolution in China. A lack of adequate planning, the dearth of modern equipment due to China's deliberate self-isolation from capitalist societies and a series of natural disasters destroyed any chance of success the GLF might have had.

Great Patriotic War n [Politics] the official Soviet term for World War II which for Russia lasted from Hitler's reneging on the Nazi-Soviet Pact in 1941 until 1945.

(great) white hope n [Boxing] the current popularly acclaimed contender for the heavyweight championship; not necessarily, but, given the recent hegemony of black champions, usually a caucasian fighter. It was first created for the various hopefuls who were put up against the first black champion Jack Johnson and who first contended among themselves for the 'White Hope Championship'; this was abandoned when one of them, Jess Willard, finally defeated Johnson in 1915. Since then the title has been used ironically.

Great Yellow Father n [Photography] a nickname for the Kodak Company; it comes from the distinctive yellow packaging of their products.

greats n pl [Education] at Oxford University these form the second, final examination for classics students: Literae Humaniores. See also **mods**.

greed shows n pl [TV] quiz programmes which rely neither on skill nor on knowledge but simply on the cupidity and money-hunger of the audience and contestants alike. Such shows tend to originate in the US, where massive prizes are available, but are toned down by English rules, pretending that the smaller sums on offer somehow reveal a similarly reduced national greed.

greedy method n [Computing] an algorithm that, with a certain goal in mind, will attempt at every stage to do whatever it can, whenever it can, to get nearer to that goal at once. A method that prefers immediate action to the concept of longer-term gains.

greedy pigs n pl [UK] [Police] the policeman's derisory description of the **punters**, the simple public who want something for nothing, then come whining to the police when they discover that not only have they gained nothing, but they have sacrificed a great deal.

greedy shot, also **poacher** n [Shooting] one who shoots at a bird that ought to be left to the next **gun** to the left or right.

Greek 1. n [Advertising] garbled letters used to indicate the size but not the actual words in an advertisement; these are used especially when there is a large amount of body copy. 2. a [Sex] an indication, in an advertisement or contact magazine, that the prostitute so advertised will indulge clients with sodomy – 'the Greek art'.

green 1. a [Cricket] said of an unusually grassy pitch, created either by design or negligence. 2. a [Photography] referring to unexposed colour film that has not yet reached its optimum colour balance. See also **aim point**. 3. a [Wine-tasting] unripe, raw and young. 4. adv [Horse racing, Greyhound racing] a novice horse or dog; thus 'running green' is when such a horse or dog is scared of the crowds, the noise and the general racetrack atmosphere – and so runs below form. **5.** *n* [*UK*] [*Theatre*] the stage; it comes both from rhyming slang 'greengage' meaning 'stage', and from the green carpet that was regularly placed on stage for the performance of tragedies during the 18th and the early 19th centuries.

green baize door *n* [*Banking*] See **Chinese wall**.

green ban *n* [*Aus.*] [*Industrial relations*] the refusal of some trade unions to allow their members to work on environmentally or socially unacceptable projects.

green chain 1. *n* [*Logging*] a long platform on which fresh-cut lumber is sorted and graded as it arrives from the mill. **2.** *n* [*Logging*] an endless chain equipped with hooks which lifts timber from the log pond to the carriage.

green clause *n* [*Shipping*] a clause in shipping contracts which authorises the seller of goods to obtain an advance payment prior to shipping the goods; he may then use this payment both to purchase and to store the goods, prior to loading them on to the ship.

green coffee *n* [*Coffee production*] the dried seeds of the coffee plant, the basic coffee bean.

green concrete *n* [*Building, Concrete workers*] concrete that has set but not yet hardened.

green currency *n* [*Politics, Economics*] any of the artificial **Eurocurrencies** created in 1969 for transactions between the farmers of the member states; the express intention was to ensure that whatever might be the fluctuations of the real economies of those states, the green currency would remain stable and with it the livelihoods of Europe's peasants.

green department *n* [*Film*] a studio department that supervises the supply of all 'garden' equipment – produce, lawns, flowers, trees, ponds, etc. – for filming.

green eyeshade *n* [*Education, Journalism*] journalism students' term for any professor of journalism/communications whose teaching and research concentrate on the practical arts of editing and reporting.

green field handcuffs *n pl* [*Business*] the concept that once an individual has taken a job outside the city, he or she will find it harder to return to urban life. Such unwillingness to be uprooted from the country is apparently a greater restraint on movement than is the idea of simply moving within a city or from city to city.

green film *n* [*TV*] a positive film that has just been returned from the laboratory – it may not even be fully dry.

green light *v* [*Business, Industry*] to give the go-ahead, to agree with a project; it comes from traffic lights.

green man *n* [*Retail stores*] at Harrods this is one of the official commissionaires who work outside the store.

green paper *n* [*UK*] [*Government*] a Government publication that offers 'not a policy already determined, but . . . propositions put before the whole nation for discussion' (Michael Stewart, 1969). See also **blue book 3, orange book, white paper 1**.

green pastures *n pl* [*UK*] [*Railways*] high earnings, bonuses, overtime payments.

green peltries *n* [*Furriers*] freshly skinned furs.

green pound *n* [*Economics*] the British version of the green currency by which agricultural transactions are made through the EEC. Sterling is thus the 'green pound' and there are similarly 'green lire', francs, deutschmarks, etc.

green revolution *n* [*Economics, Sociology*] the increase in production of cereal crops in developing countries after the introduction of high-yield varieties and the application of scientific and planned methods to their cultivation.

green room *n* [*Theatre*] an offstage sitting room in which an actor can rest, relax or entertain friends; thus 'to talk green room' is to indulge in theatrical gossip.

green sand *n* [*Metallurgy*] in iron founding this is sand that still contains moisture, as opposed to sand that has been dried.

green shoe *n* [*US*] [*Stock market*] a clause in an underwriting agreement whereby the issuer of shares agrees, in the case of an exceptional demand from the public for the shares, to make a further issue available to the underwriters for distribution.

green strength *n* [*Metallurgy*] in iron founding this is a measure of the cohesion of grains of a sand that contains free moisture at atmospheric temperature.

green suction *n* [*Building, Plastering*] the early suction of a cement-based backing.

green time *n* [*Transport*] the length of time traffic can flow through a green light at a given location.

green tyre *n* [*Tyre-making*] a tyre that has been assembled but not yet cured. See also **carcass**.

green ware *n* [*Ceramics*] clay that has been shaped into ware and dried prior to firing.

green whisky *n* [*Distilling*] the product of the second distillation of **low wines** which is then diverted into tanks from which drinkable whisky can be barrelled.

greenfield *a* [*Building*] greenfield sites are those rural and undeveloped sites, often near towns or cities, but which are not designated as part of the protected green belts (the strips of land that surround the urban centres and prevent one large town from simply sliding into the outskirts of another through builders' continuing greed for new land).

greenfields 1. *n pl* [*Finance*] land which has never been built on, and which is scheduled for development for the first time. **2.** *n pl* [*Stock market*] new companies that are formed to undertake new ventures carrying high risk and potentially bringing in high returns.

Greenfield's, staying at Mrs. *part phr* [*UK*] [*Road transport*] sleeping in the cab of one's vehicle; it comes from tramps' 'greenfields' meaning sleeping in the fields.

greengoods racket *n* [*US*] [*Crime*] an inter-criminal fraud whereby the victim is tempted into purchasing a machine for counterfeiting money, only to find that the device is useless.

greenhouse 1. *n* [*Aerospace*] a long plastic or glass canopy that covers both the front and rear cockpits of an aircraft. **2.** *n* [*US*] [*Medicine*] a special structure that is placed over an operating table, the patient, the surgeon and the nurses who are assisting at the operation, in order to provide an extra precaution against bacteria.

greenhouse effect 1. *n* [*Military*] a theory of post-nuclear civilisation whereby the effect of multiple explosions would have caused the ozone layer in the atmosphere to be destroyed and would thus permit the harmful rays of the sun to penetrate. The result of this would be akin to living in a superheated greenhouse; water supplies would dry up, plants would 'burn' away and humanity would duly collapse without vital liquids and crops. See also **nuclear winter. 2.** [*Meteorology*] the phenomenon that permits the heat of the sun to pass through the atmosphere and thus warm the Earth, but prevents it from escaping again.

greenie 1. *n* [*US*] [*Car salesmen*] abbr of **green-horn** a novice salesman. **2.** *n* [*Surfing*] abbr of **greenback** a large wave, just before it breaks. See also **dumper 2, grinder 5**.

greenlight *v* [*Film*] to agree to a deal; it comes from traffic lights.

greenlining *n* [*Government, Sociology*] an increasing series of attacks on the socially divisive practice of **red-lining**, by making specific efforts to revive the inner cities and make investing there seem viable and appealing again. See also **blockbusting, gentrification**.

greenmail *n* [*US*] [*Commerce*] this comes from 'green' meaning 'money' plus 'blackmail'; it is a counter against a possible takeover in which the company pays the **raider** to go away but buys back from him the shares he controls at prices far above the market value.

greens *n pl* [*Military*] green service uniform worn by various troops. See also **Blues 2, whites**.

gremlin 1. also **gremmie** *n* [*Surfing*] a young surfer. **2.** also **gremmie** *n* [*Surfing*] someone who frequents surfing beaches not to surf but merely to make trouble.

grey *a* [*Sociology, Politics*] See **gray**.

grey drake *n* [*Angling*] male mayfly spinner; green drake is the female mayfly spinner.

grey economy *n* [*Economics*] unpaid but economically vital activities; the most obvious being housework. See also **black economy**.

grey fish *n* [*Angling*] See **mort 2**.

grey market *n* [*Stock market*] a market in shares that develops in a popular new issue even before it has been properly subscribed and the shares distributed. Dealers promise to trade with each other blocks of shares that they have yet actually to obtain and a 'grey market price', by no means the one that will prevail when the shares exist, is thus established.

grey-hair *v* [*Business*] to use the skills and experience of an older person to further one's own ideas; it is a concept used by consultants and marketing specialists who suggest to firms that such senior figures can be useful as short-term aides working on specific problems.

grey-out *n* [*Aerospace*] a less severe form of a blackout, caused by the action of blood in the head during steep climbs or dives and the loss of consciousness that this causes – this is only partial in a grey-out, but can still cause loss of control of the aircraft during such manoeuvres.

greys *n pl* [*UK*] [*Prisons*] a pair of 'smart' grey trousers required in some prisons for wear either for visits or to Church.

grey-scale *n* [*Photo-typesetting*] a range of greys of different density which can be represented by digitised **pixels** and thus employed to represent a picture that contains various tones of black and white.

grid *n* [*TV, Theatre*] the openwork ceiling above a stage or TV studio from which lights and scenery can be suspended and which contains a catwalk to enable technicians to move around.

grids *n pl* [*Art*] those painters, who opted during the 1960s for art that was completely non-relational and abstract, still needed some form of neutral structure to work with or against; to this end they chose the grid, which painters have always used to square off canvases.

grief stem *n* [*Oil rigs*] See **kelly**.

grief therapy *n* [*Sociology*] supportive therapy for the recently bereaved, often carried out between an 'encounter group' of four or five similarly bereaved individuals, under the direction of a highly motivated counsellor.

griever *n* [*US*] [*Railways*] a union negotiator who deals with disputes between men and management.

grift *n* [*US*] [*Crime*] a word that replaced 'graft' as a description of various confidence tricks when politicians began to use graft (literally and linguistically) as their own. Grift implies non-violent crime, as opposed to **heavy rackets**.

grille *n* [*Philately*] a rectangular pattern of small dots impressed on some issues of stamps; the intention is to make it harder to remove cancellations by helping the cancelling ink penetrate the paper, through the dots, rather than simply staying on the surface.

grimeson *n* [*US*] [*Crime*] in the US Mafia this is

G

a commission made up of the bosses of all the **families**.

grim-gram *n* [*US*] [*Government*] abbr of '**grim telegram**' a term coined around 1980 to deal with the weekly lists of the murdered and the missing that are assembled by embassy personnel in El Salvador and sent back to Washington for analysis.

grimgribber *n* [*Law*] the technical jargon of the law; it comes from the imaginary estate of Grimgribber that is subject to legal wrangles in the play 'The Conscious Lovers' (1722) by Sir Richard Steele (1672–1729).

grimthorpe *v* [*Art*] to do an inferior job of art restoration; it comes from the bungled efforts of the contemporary Lord Grimthorpe to restore St. Albans' abbey at the end of the 19th century.

grin **1.** *v* [*Painting*] said of a coat of paint which shows through the coat painted over it. **2.** *v* [*Textiles*] said of the backing of a cheap carpet which shows through the pile.

grind **1.** *n* [*Gambling*] a low-limit banking game which requires a good number of players to ensure a decent profit for the house; thus 'grind joint' or 'grind store' means a gambling room where such games are played. **2.** *v* [*TV, Film*] to project a film or TV programme.

grinder **1.** *n* [*Audio*] a reasonably lengthy burst of atmospheric disturbance, probably caused by lightning. See also **click**. **2.** *n* [*US*] [*Circus*] the individual who stands in front of the main tent of the circus and attempts to entice the public to come in; the patter he uses is the 'grind'. **3.** *n* [*US*] [*Marine Corps*] a parade ground or drill field. **4.** *n* [*Sailing*] the specialist member of the crew who operates the 'coffee-grinder' winch that hauls in and lets out sails. **5.** *n* [*Surfing*] a large wave, just before it breaks. See also **dumper 2, greenie 2**.

grindhouse *n* [*Film*] a second-rate cinema that shows the standard of films which the studios simply 'grind out'.

grinding in, also **lapping in** *n* [*Cars*] the laborious process of seating the exhaust and inlet valves into a cylinder head to ensure a perfect, gas-tight fit.

grinds *n pl* [*Sailing, Ropework*] kinks in a hempen cable.

grine, also **griny, groiny** *n* [*UK*] [*Market-traders*] a ring (wedding, engagement, etc.).

grinning **1.** *n* [*Building, Plastering*] the appearance on the plaster surface of the pattern of background joints, caused by different **suctions**. **2.** also **seam grin** *n* [*Clothing*] a situation where a seam gapes under stress, usually due to inadequate thread tension when sewing.

grip **1.** *n* [*TV, Film*] any studio employee used to move around heavy equipment, for which job he requires a 'tight grip'; specifically it is the 'dolly grip' who lays the tracks along which the camera **dolly** moves. **2.** *n* [*Wine-tasting*] the opposite of

flabby: a firm and emphatic combination of physical characteristics.

gripe *n* [*Sailing, Ropework*] a rope used to secure a boat on board a ship.

gripped off, to be *v* [*Bird-watching*] to be frustrated, to be annoyed. This is usually used when failing to spot a particular bird, when others have managed to do so.

grips, also **squeezer** *n pl* [*Coal-mining*] a pair of pivoted, converging horizontal beams that grip the sides of a car and act as a brake.

GRIT *n* [*Politics*] acro **Graduated Reciprocated Reduction in Tension** the strategic version of 'turning the other cheek'. It is a version of conflict management that implies not weakness but the desire to avoid all-out conflict and to initiate some process of de-escalation. GRIT was developed in 1962 by US professor of psychology Charles E. Osgood in his book 'An Alternative to War or Surrender'. Under a GRIT scenario, the major problems of international relations – notably the weapons themselves – should be put aside, and nations should concentrate on removing lesser, but more easily accessible, sources of tension. The intention of GRIT is to draw from the opponent a similar degree of restraint, pulling further and faster away from a potential war.

gritty *a* [*Wine-tasting*] coarse-textured in the mouth.

grizzly *n* [*Mining*] a grating that catches the larger stones as they pass down the sluice when ore and the valuable minerals it contains are being washed.

groaner *n* [*Sailing*] a whistling buoy that in fact sounds as if it were in pain.

grody *n* [*Medicine*] used as a term for tramps, vagrants and other 'street people'; it comes from 'Valley Girls slang' meaning disgusting, repellent, and in turn also from Beatles-era 'grotty'.

grog *n* [*Metallurgy*] in iron-founding this is a basic constituent of **compo**: dried fireclays or crushed scrap firebricks.

groin *n* [*Building, Plastering*] the mitre line produced by intersecting vaults.

gronk **1.** *v* [*Computing*] to clear a **wedged** machine of its jammed-up state and to re-start it. **2.** *v* [*Computing*] a machine does his when it breaks down and completely ceases to function. **3.** *v* [*Computing*] when someone is 'gronked' he feels totally exhausted or otherwise ill and sets off home and collapses into bed.

groomers *n pl* [*Air travel*] the team of cleaners who set to work on a commercial aircraft as soon as its passengers have deplaned.

grope *n* [*TV*] any TV documentary that concentrates on investigative journalism.

gross *n* [*Film*] the money that a film earns through the cinema box office before any deductions for tax, salaries, expenses, etc. are made. Thus a 'big grosser' is a successful film. Those involved with a film – the director, stars, possibly

G

the writer(s) – are sometimes offered a percentage of the gross as a bonus to their actual salary, although extracting such sums from the **front office** is a notoriously hard task. See also **points**

gross height examination n [*Aerospace*] a nose dive.

gross index n [*Computing*] See **coarse index**.

gross reach n [*Marketing*] the total number of opportunities for people to see the advertisement contained in a schedule: the sum of the total readership of each publication multiplied by the number of insertions of the advertisement.

gross up v [*Commerce*] to calculate, on the basis of the net amount remaining after making a deduction for tax, the gross amount from which the tax was deducted.

grot n [*UK*] [*Military*] a cabin on board a troopship.

grotzen n [*Furriers*] the back portion of a pelt; it comes from German.

ground animals n pl [*US*] [*Prisons*] hamburgers, hot dogs or sausages.

ground burst n [*Military*] a nuclear explosion which occurs at ground level, or in which the fireball touches the ground. While an air burst maximises heat and blast over a large area, the ground burst creates a fireball that sucks up vast quantities of earth and debris from the crater it has caused and returns them to the earth as radioactive particles. It creates a far 'dirtier' effect with this fallout. See also **air burst**.

ground game n [*Shooting*] hares or rabbits.

ground hog, also **Larry, mule, ram** n [*Logging*] See **barney 2**.

ground resolution n [*Military, Espionage*] the standard of photographic closeness for **remote sensing** taken against the size of the smallest object one can distinguish in the picture. Ground resolution varies according to the wavelength of the light recording the image, the quality of the film used, the quality of the optical system, the focal length of the telescope, the aperture of the telescopic lenses or mirrors, the altitude of the satellite, the haziness of the atmosphere and the contrast between the object and its background.

ground tackle n [*Sailing, Ropework*] all the **cordage** used to anchor, moor and sometimes tow a vessel.

ground zero n [*Military*] the part of the earth that is situated directly beneath an exploding nuclear weapon. See also **hypocentre**.

groundage n [*Shipping*] See **berthage**.

grounded theory n [*Sociology*] a sociological theory based on empirical, systematically researched data, rather than on abstract methods alone.

grounder n [*Baseball*] a batted ball that travels by bouncing or rolling along the ground, rather than flying through the air.

grounding n [*New therapies*] in **bioenergetics** this is the concept that one is, as an entity,

attached to the ground through one's feet; such 'oneness' with the earth is thus supposed to create in the human being qualities of personal strength, stability and confidence that supposedly stem from the immensity of the planet.

group form n [*Architecture*] a term that refers to the sum of relationships between a number of buildings; the form of individual buildings is subordinated to the form of the group as a whole.

group home n [*US*] [*Prisons*] a half-way house designed for young offenders.

group ten n [*Air travel*] a discount fare, initially created for the use of tour operators, which is now widely used by airlines to hide from IATA and similar authorities the large discounts which the airlines offer their passengers. The passengers are consolidated – simply by paperwork – into one group, although none of them ever realises it, and thus the letter, if not the spirit of IATA rules, is still respected.

grouse latitudes n pl [*Merchant navy*] that point in the voyage when, for a variety of reasons, the passengers feel they have been at sea long enough and start to complain.

grouter bit n [*Aus.*] [*Gambling*] in a game of two-up this is a run of good luck.

grovel v [*Computing*] to work interminably and without apparent progress; it is often used as in 'X is grovelling over such and such.' See also **crunch**.

grow 1. v [*Navy*] to stop shaving in order to grow the Navy's regulation full set of beard and moustache. **2.** v [*Sailing, Ropework*] a cable 'grows' in the direction which leads from the hawse hole.

growl n [*Music*] in jazz this is a deep, throaty, rasping sound that can be produced from a wind instrument.

growler 1. n [*Aerospace*] test equipment used to check for short circuits in electronic machinery. **2.** n [*Merchant navy*] a large lump of sea ice (though smaller than an iceberg) which is partly submerged and encountered in high latitudes; when two lumps grind together, they make a 'growling' noise. **3.** n [*Military*] a satellite communications link which is used to provide **secure** communications which cannot be monitored or interfered with by hostile land-based equipment. **4.** n [*Sailing*] a small iceberg or mass of flow ice with the potential to harm shipping.

grown-on n [*Clothing*] a waistband that is cut as part of the skirt or trousers which it is intended to fasten.

growth n [*Metallurgy*] in iron-founding this is the permanent enlargement of an iron casting after graphite has formed within it or it has been subject to internal oxidisation because of heating.

grubber 1. n [*Rugby*] a forward kick of the ball along the ground. **2.** n [*Cricket*] a ball that runs flat along the ground after it has been bowled.

grue, also **brue** n [*Angling*] snow or ice water.

G

gruesome twosome n [UK] [Railways] a derisory description of 'seniority' and 'suitability', seen as the twin paths to promotion within the railways.

grume n [US] [Medicine] a notably filthy **Gomer**.

grunt 1. n [US] [Military] the lowest rank of infantryman in the US Army. The term was popularised in Vietnam, and is allegedly derived from the soldiers' (justified) grumbling as they marched through the hostile, frightening terrain, but it was first used in the 1930s by US electric power workers to describe the lineman's or mechanic's menial helper. **2.** n [Sex] a derisive term used by those who write 'men's magazines' for the frustrated men who buy their product; the grunts are those of unfulfilled lust.

grunter n [Navy] an officer, who tends to grunt in reply to sailors' queries.

grunting n [US] [Coal-mining] the noise made when a mine is about to cave in, hence the warning cry of 'She's grunting!'.

grutsen n [US] [Garment trade] the heavy part of an animal skin best suited for garment manufacturing; it comes from Yiddish.

gryer n [UK] [Market-traders] a horse.

G-spool, also **dub** n [Advertising] a video-taped duplicate copy of a TV commercial which is distributed around TV network stations for their individual use.

G-suit n [Aerospace] this comes from G meaning gravity; it is a specially designed suit which is intended to help jet pilots, astronauts and anyone else who has to encounter g-forces during acceleration to deal better with the physical effects of these forces.

gtt Lat. abbr [Medicine] a prescription notation meaning a drop.

guaranteed week n [Management] a minimum number of hours for which an employer agrees to pay a timeworker (one who is paid per diem) every week, so long as the worker makes him/herself available for work, but irrespective of whether the employer offers any work to be done.

guaranty bond n [Commerce, Finance] a form of surety bond which protects against loss caused by the failure of a named person to perform a specific action.

guard n [Cards] in bridge this is a card which accompanies a higher card of the same suit.

guard a hill v [Logging] to keep a logging road on a hill in condition for use.

guard and steerage n [Navy] extra time in bed for those ratings who stood the middle watch.

guard band n [TV] a buffer of unused frequency space on either side of a TV channel which ensures uninterrupted transmission.

guard book n [Advertising] a file kept in an agency that holds all the advertisements prepared and published for a client over a number of campaigns; such a file doubles as a collection of useful and relevant information on a client's advertising preferences, products, etc.

guard hair n [Dog-breeding] See **master hair**.

guardant a [Heraldry] full-face, staring straight out of the shield.

guarding n [Printing] in book manufacturing this is the attaching of a single leaf to a section of a book or magazine.

guck n [Commerce] in the book trade this is the gilt stamping on a book.

guddling, also **gumping** n [Angling] a means of poaching trout, similar to **tickling**.

guessing doctor n [US] [Medicine] an intern, supposedly lacking the expertise of senior doctors. See also **cutting doctor**.

guffin n [Angling] ground bait (Cornwall).

GUIDO n [Aerospace] acro **Guidance Officer** an engineer in charge of a space flight; the chief navigation officer at Mission Control. See also **FIDE**, **RETRO**.

guilloche n [Building, Plastering] a form of **enrichment**, featuring interlacing circles.

guinea n [US] [Horse-racing] a jockey; undoubtedly racist, and also somewhat archaic, since guinea is slang for Italian and 90% of US jockeys are now black.

gules a [Heraldry] red.

gulliver n [Aerospace] this comes from Lemuel Gulliver, hero of Swift's 'Gulliver's Travels' (1726), who stood out as a monster among the tiny Lilliputians. It is an idea for a device made out of adhesive cords which could be fired from a spacecraft on to the surface of a planet and then hauled up again; the principle being that some microorganisms, if they existed, would have stuck to the ropes and could then be transported back to Earth for proper analysis.

gully n [Cricket] See **box 2** and **3**.

gulp n [Computing] a unit which consists of a number of **bytes** considered as one word.

gum 1. n [Coal-mining] fine coal or dust, especially that which is produced by a coal-cutting machine. **2.** n [Wine trade] the viscous 'threads' that may be found in wine in which a foreign ferment has developed; gum can be precipitated by the addition of a solution of tannin.

gum ball machine n [US] [Road transport] See **beanie light**.

gum flinger n [Coal-mining] a **gummer** which throws cuttings into the **goaf**.

gumbah n [US] [Crime] this comes from the It. 'compare' meaning 'godfather'; the pronunciation has been corrupted, and the word now means a friend, an ally in battle.

gumbo 1. n [US] [Farming] sticking soil found in bottom land. **2.** n [Oil-rigs] sticky shales through which a bit must sometimes move and which hinder the speed of drilling; the term comes from the thick soup of New Orleans.

gum-bucket n [Tobacco] a smoker's tobacco-pipe.

gummer 1. n [Coal-mining] a man who clears the

coal dust or fine pieces of coal (**gum**) from the coal-cutting machine. **2.** *n* [*Coal-mining*] a device attached to a coal-cutter which throws out the coal cut by the machine.

gummings *n pl* [*Coal-mining*] the material produced by undercutting the seam with a coal-cutting machine.

gummy *a* [*Cheese-making*] a negative term for a cheese that has an excessively plastic texture, as well as for overripe rinds that have become sticky.

gumwork *n* [*Medicine*] in dentistry this is the part of the denture which replaces missing natural gum and the alveolar process.

gun **1.** *n* [*US*] [*Hotels*] an elevator. **2.** *n* [*US*] [*Prisons*] the fist; thus 'gun up' is to cock one's fist or grab a weapon. **3.** *n* [*UK*] [*Railways*] a radar speed trap. **4.** *n* [*Sheep-shearing*] an expert shearer. **5.** *n* [*Shooting*] the person carrying and shooting the gun, rather than the weapon itself, although this is also the gun. **6.** *n* [*Surfing*] a heavy surfboard. **7.** *v* [*Stock market*] to gun a stock is to force a rival into letting go a quantity of shares which one wishes to purchase. **8.** *v* [*Logging*] to select the direction in which a tree should fall. **9.** *v* [*Logging*] to sharpen or file new points on a saw.

Gun and Rifle Club *n* [*US*] [*Medicine*] a trauma ward to which patients suffering from gunshot or knife wounds are admitted.

gunbarrel *n* [*Skiing*] a steep, high-walled slope that funnels into a narrow exit.

gunfire *n* [*UK*] [*Military*] a hot drink – tea laced with rum – served at reveille; it comes from the custom of firing a cannon at the start of each day, at which point those officers awakened would be offered some form of drink.

gung ho **1.** *a* [*US*] [*Marine Corps*] this comes from the Chinese 'kung' meaning 'work' and 'ho' meaning 'together' and was adopted as a slogan by the Marines during World War II; it generally means enthusiastic, aggressive, keen on a fight. **2.** *a* [*Politics*] the same sense of enthusiasm and aggressiveness that applies to the military context. In politics, it is often the attribute of young campaign volunteers, or the junior members of a newly appointed White House team (though the attitude is not restricted to the US) who are raring to go, spoiling for a fight and keen to show the world what they are made of.

gunge *n* [*Science*] a soft sticky mass that is created from various gaseous mixtures of chemically abundant compounds; it was officially termed 'tholin' by its discoverers, Carl Sagan and B. N. Khare, but most of their peers prefer the colloquialism.

gunite *n* [*Coal-mining*] mortar applied by a cement gun to the roof and sides of a working.

gun-jumping **1.** *n* [*US*] [*Stock market*] trading securities on information which one has obtained prior to its general release. **2.** *n* [*US*] [*Stock market*] attempting to make orders for a new issue

with an underwriter before the Securities & Exchange Commission registration is complete and such orders can legally be made.

gunning *n* [*Shooting*] the shooting of game with a gun.

gunny *n* [*US*] [*Marine Corps*] abbr of **Gunnery Sergeant**.

gunship *n* [*Military*] a helicopter armed with door-mounted heavy machine guns and air-to-ground missiles.

gunslinger **1.** *n* [*Finance*] a high-risk, high performance investment fund that takes a capital role. **2.** *n* [*Finance*] the manager of such a fund, with, it is assumed, characteristics to match.

gusanos *n pl* [*Espionage*] this comes from Spanish meaning worms; it is US intelligence slang for the highly volatile, but often useful anti-Castro Cubans, many of whom live in Florida while waiting to go home.

gut *n* [*Sheep-shearing*] a flexible shaft which carries the power from an overhead cable to the shearer's handpiece.

gut course *n* [*US*] [*Education*] this comes from the idea of a soft under-belly, or flabby 'beer gut' and refers to those courses in further education that are considered to be the soft options.

gut feeling *n* [*New therapies*] the instinctive spontaneity that comes straight from the viscera and as such is beloved by all new therapies; it is the opposite of **mind-tripping**, ie the thinking out of a problem by employing a degree of intellectual analysis, the result of which might not provide the 'gut' belief in the therapy upon which such groups depend.

gut wrapper *n* [*Logging*] a piece of chain that holds together a group of logs within a whole load.

guts **1.** *n* [*US*] [*Car salesmen*] the interior of a car. **2.** *n* [*Aus.*] [*Gambling*] in a game of two-up this is the money staked by the two principal betters; to lay down a stake is to 'open the guts'.

GUTs *n pl* [*Science*] abbr of **Grand Unified Theories** the current targets of particle physics research, which aims to determine the basic structure of all matter. See also **TOEs**.

gutter *n* [*Journalism, Advertising*] the white space that surrounds the printed material – visual or written – on a page. See also **bleed 4** and **5**.

guttersnipe *n* [*Advertising*] a small poster that is fixed down at street level, almost in the gutter, rather than high up on a building or billboard.

Guzz *n* [*Navy*] the Royal Navy's home base at Devonport, near Plymouth; it is so-called as an abbreviation of 'guzzle' meaning to eat heartily.

GVW *n* [*UK*] [*Road transport*] abbr of **gross vehicle weight** the total weight of a rigid vehicle, including fuel, driver and passenger, if carried.

GWEN *n* [*Military*] acro **Ground Wave Emergency Network** a ground-based radio communications network that will use a system of above- and underground antennae broadcasting on a

G

frequency of 150–190khz (very nearly that of standard AM radio) in order to provide a minimal survivable system which can maintain communications between US command posts and launch sites if the space-based systems are destroyed by hostile action.

GWT *n* [*UK*] [*Road transport*] abbr of **gross train weight** the total weight of a **drawer combination** including load, fuel and driver.

gyppo *n* [*Logging*] a small logging firm that works on a contract basis; it comes either from such companies 'gypping' their employees out of their wages or from their 'gypsy-like' wanderings from job to job.

gypsies *n pl* [*US*] [*Theatre*] a chorus line in a Broadway musical.

gypsy **1.** *n* [*Logging*] a winding drum on a donkey engine. **2.** *n* [*US*] [*Road transport*] See **broker.**

H

H and I *n* [*Military*] abbr of **harassment and interdiction** this was used during the Vietnam war to describe a method of diverting a possible surprise attack by random firing, usually at night; it might or might not hit any enemy but should at least keep him at bay.

habeas corpus *n* [*Law*] a court order requiring that anyone held in prison must be produced in court so that the circumstances of that imprisonment can be determined as legal or otherwise; it is supposedly a pillar of a democratic society. The term comes from Lat. 'that you may have the body'.

habille *n* [*Sex*] the costume worn by a strip-tease artist before she/he begins to remove its various components.

habit hierarchy *n* [*Sociology*] one's personal system of conducting any particular and idiosyncratic rituals: getting dressed, touching or scratching one's body in a certain way, or any other, similar, repetitions.

hacienda *n* [*US*] [*Air Force*] a nickname for the Office of Aerospace Research. See also **Legoland.**

hack **1.** *n* [*Aerospace*] a former combat aircraft, probably captured in hostilities or too old to be used for potential active service, which is working its life out as a general utility or transport plane. **2.** *n* [*UK*] [*Journalism*] this was once a derogatory description of the penny-a-line 'hack of all trades' journalist who wrote anything so long as there was a cheque at the end of it. Such time-servers naturally still exist, but hack is used increasingly as a slightly ironic, somewhat affectionate term for one's fellow journalists, especially in a context such as war reporting, where everyone suffers together in temporary cameraderie. **3.** *a* [*Politics*] a derogatory description of a time– and self-serving graft-ridden politician whose interests lie strictly with himself, and who gained election through influence rather than through putting himself forward as the saviour of the constituency, let alone the country. **4.** *n* [*Computing*] a quick job that produces what is required but lacks standards or quality. **5.** *n* [*Computing*] the result of a hack job. **6.** *n* [*Computing*] 'neat hack' means a clever technique; it is also a stylish practical joke if such a joke is neat, clever, harmless and really surprising. **7.** *n* [*Computing*] a real hack. See **crock. 8.** *v* [*Computing*] hack together, meaning to improve a system quickly but sufficiently smartly to ensure its working. **9.** *v* [*Computing*] to suffer something emotionally or physically. **10.** *v* [*Computing*] to work on something, with the added sense that it is central to one's professional life and justifies one's being involved in that life at all. **11.** *v* [*Computing*] to pull a prank on. See (6). **12.** *v* [*Computing*] to waste time. **13.** *v* [*Computing*] to hack up on. See (4) and (5). **14.** *a* [*Computing*] hack value: the reason for expending effort on what otherwise appears to be a pointless goal, were that goal not simply the pleasure gained from hacking. **15.** [*Computing*] The word is also used in the phrases: 'happy hacking', a joking farewell; 'hack hack', a synonym for bye-bye. **16.** *adv* [*US*] [*Marine Corps*] to be 'under hack' means to be arrested by an officer for a breach of discipline.

hack it **1.** *v* [*Military*] to possess the ability to keep going no matter what the conditions, the weight of one's pack, the intensity of hostile fire and any other negative factors. **2.** *v* [*Politics*] similar to the military use other than that the 'hostile fire' is more likely to be verbal or written than coming from ordnance, and that the 'forced marches' are those taken through a lengthy campaign or against a powerful opposition rather than over treacherous terrain.

hacker 1. *n* [*Computing*] someone who enjoys learning the details of computers and the programs that they run, with the intention of stretching and modifying both hardware and software to their greatest extent. **2.** *n* [*Computing*] computer enthusiasts who devote their energies and undoubted abilities to penetrating major computer networks. In their own eyes they are practitioners of a 'recreational and educational sport'; in those of the institutions with whom they interfere, they are a major and even criminal nuisance. Conquering computer security is often an end in itself, but some hackers actually destroy information, alter programmes, write mysterious messages and generally leave their mark.

hacking 1. *n* [*Building, Plastering*] the roughening, using a bush-hammer or lath-hatchet, of solid **backgrounds** in order to provide sufficient **key** for other coats of plaster. **2.** *n* [*Building, Concrete workers*] using a tool to roughen a concrete surface.

hackle 1. *n* [*Commerce*] a multi-spiked tool which is used in wig-making for separating strands of hair. **2.** *v* [*Commerce*] to draw strands of hair through a **hackle.**

hade *n* [*Mining*] the angle of inclination of a plane to the vertical.

hafia *part phr* [*Science fiction*] acro **hewn away from it all** expelled from one's affiliation to fan activity. See also **dafia, fafia, gafia.**

hags *n pl* [*Religion*] Catholic priests' reference to nuns; it comes from Gk. 'hagiai' meaning holy women.

hagsteeth *n pl* [*Sailing, Ropework*] irregularities in ropework.

hair *n* [*Computing*] the complications which render a problem **hairy**; it is often used in the phrase 'infinite hair' meaning extremely complex.

hair in the gate *n* [*TV, Film*] fine shavings of emulsion that accumulate as the film runs through the camera's **gate** and which, like tiny fibres, will ruin the filming unless they are removed at regular intervals.

haircut 1. *n* [*US*] [*Paper-making*] a blemish in the paper caused by hair dropping from the **felt** on to the **web** of pulp. **2.** *n* [*US*] [*Stock market*] the net capital that can be gained by a broker-dealer on a securities deal; the more certain the transaction, the smaller the haircut.

hairpin *v* [*US*] [*Cattlemen*] to mount a horse.

hairy 1. *a* [*Computing*] when used of machines or programs this means exceptionally and unnecess-

arily complicated; almost totally incomprehensible. **2.** *a* [*Computing*] when used of people this can mean high-powered, or dictatorial; exceptionally skilled and/or incomprehensible. The implication will depend on the speaker's feelings regarding the individual described. He/she does not have to be a programmer but merely someone encountered who might be so categorised.

hairy akin *n* [*US*] [*Garment trade*] fur that has been taken from an immature animal.

hairy mary *n* [*Scot.*] [*Angling*] a variety of salmon fly.

HAL *n* [*Computing*] acro **High-order Assembly Language** a language in which computers can communicate data amongst themselves without requiring a human **interface**. See also **assembly language.**

Haldane principle *n* [*UK*] [*Politics*] a concept named after Prof. J.B.S. Haldane (1892–1964) who stated that ideally all government research agencies should be completely isolated from and external to the influence of those government departments which might eventually benefit from such research.

half 1. *n* [*US*] [*Railways*] the usual length of a pay period: two weeks. **2.** *a* [*Weaving*] the second-to-top category in the blood system of grading wool.

half a bar *n* [*Finance*] in the money market this is a transaction of 500,000 (pounds or dollars).

half a piece *n* [*Drugs*] half an ounce of heroin or cocaine, a quantity usually so expensive as to be restricted to wholesale transactions. Thus 'quarter piece' is a quarter of an ounce. See also **piece 1.**

half a print *n* [*Finance*] one half of one per cent commission on a deal of $1 bn.

half and half *n* [*Sex*] fellatio followed by conventional intercourse, a variation offered by a prostitute to her client for more money than her basic charge.

half breed *n* [*Merchant navy*] a ship registered under a flag of convenience.

half change *n* [*Education*] the tweed 'sports' jacket worn by pupils of Eton when not wearing school uniform.

half curlew *n* [*Shooting*] a whimbrel (Numenius phaeopus).

half dirties *n pl* [*UK*] [*Railways*] drivers working the Broad Street-Richmond 'North London Line' who alternated between steam-driven freight trains and passenger work on electric trains.

half duck *n* [*Shooting*] a teal (Querquedula).

half hard *n* [*Metallurgy*] an intermediate hardness of steel as created by heat treatment and cold rolling.

half seats *n pl* [*Theatre*] seats that are half obscured by their having been sited behind the pillars in the auditorium which support the circle above. This is a problem especially common in older theatres but the seats themselves are not offered at half price.

H

half stick n [*Printing*] a small portrait block measuring half the column width. See also **pork-chop, thumbnail.**

half, the n [*UK*] [*Theatre*] a call to the company reminding them that there are only 30 minutes – actually, by tradition, nearer 35 – before the curtain goes up. See also **quarter, thirty minutes.**

Half Worcester n [*Ten-pin bowling*] a split where the 3 and 9 or 12 and 8 pins are left standing. See also **baby split, bucket, Cincinnati.**

half-a-wheel n [*Cycling*] an extremely narrow victory in a race. See also **wheel.**

half-life n [*Finance*] the point at which half the principal has been repaid on a US government issued mortgage-backed security, usually 12 years.

half-stock n [*US*] [*Stock market*] stock – either common or preferred – that has a par value of $50 rather than the more general $100.

half-title n [*Publishing*] the page, containing only the title of the book, which is included in the page numbering when it immediately precedes the first page of the text. See also **bastard title.**

half-word n [*Computing*] a group of consecutive **bits** which can be dealt with as a single unit and which occupy the storage of half a **word** unit in the machine's memory.

hall show n [*US*] [*Circus*] any form of indoor entertainment, as opposed to an outdoor show.

hall test n [*Marketing*] a test in which a selection of passing consumers are taken at random off a street and brought to a large hall that is acting as a question and answer control centre; here they are subjected to an interview on whatever topic the researchers wish to study.

HALO n [*Military*] acro **High Altitude Large Optics** a programme still in development by **DARPA** to create a space platform carrying an optical structure some 100 ft. across and consisting of approximately 10 million detectors, including mosaics of different frequencies and probably low-light-level TV, phased array radar and laser radar. The infra-red sensors will incorporate integral data processing, thus obviating much of the need for complex linking to a central computer.

halo n [*Advertising*] the knock-on effect that uses the popularity of a best-selling product to enhance sales of another item produced by the same manufacturers and bearing the same brand-name.

halo effect 1. n [*Marketing*] any situation in which assessments/estimates/etc may be coloured by the environment; eg. a buyer's confidence in a product will be helped/hindered by his belief/disbelief in the manufacturer's sincerity and honesty. 2. n [*Marketing*] a statistical term of measurement based on the area of analysis described in (1).

haloing n [*Printing*] an error in printing which appears when each letter is surrounded by a border; this happens when the ink is reproducing the border of the metal on which each letter has been set in relief.

haloir n [*Cheese-making*] a cheese drying room or heated and ventilated area where soft cheeses are placed to drain and eventually to develop surface moulds.

HALT v phr [*Drug addicts*] acro this is used at Broadway Lodge Clinic to mean **don't get hungry, angry, lonely or tired.**

ham 1. n [*UK*] [*Railways*] overtime; thus 'fatty ham' is excessive overtime, the creation of which can be made into a fine art by those who need the money. 2. n [*Theatre*] abbr of **hamfat, hamfatter** an actor who gives an inexpert or more commonly over-melodramatic performance. It comes from those second-rate and thus impoverished actors who, in earlier days, were forced to rub hamfat over their faces, as a base for the powder that was then applied, rather than being able to afford the more sophisticated and sweeter smelling oils.

ham and egg shift n [*Mining*] the shift between 10am and 6pm, reminiscent of an era when the miner would eat his ham before work began and his eggs on its termination.

hamburger queen, also **Hershey queen** n [*Sex*] See **coffee queen.**

hammer 1. n [*Journalism*] a short, teaser headline, above the main headline, which is set in larger type than that below it. 2. v [*Stock market*] to force down a price.

hammer price n [*Stock market*] the price that is realised for the remaining shares held by a member who has just been **hammered.**

hammer the market v [*Stock market*] to sell large quantities of a stock at one time, thus causing a sudden fall in the price.

hammered a [*Stock market*] referring to a member or firm on the Exchange who has failed to meet due liabilities and is then declared a defaulter; this default is made public by the striking of a wooden mallet on a desk to attract the attention of his erstwhile colleagues. Then the head **waiter** of the Exchange hits three strokes and announces the defaulter's name.

hamming code n [*Communications*] a code that is capable of being corrected automatically by the receiving terminal.

hammock v [*US*] [*TV*] to schedule a new TV show between two established successes.

hand 1. n [*Tobacco*] a bunch of five to twenty tobacco leaves tied together by another leaf at the butt end of the bunch. 2. n [*Skittles*] one throw of the allotted number of balls used by each player. 3. v [*Sailing, Ropework*] to gather and secure sails.

hand shank n [*Metallurgy*] in iron founding this is a small ladle that can be carried by two men.

handbanking n [*Logging*] the cutting of railroad ties near a river, so that hauling is made unnecessary.

handbasher *n* [*TV, Film*] a handheld **sun gun** of approximately 800W power.

handbook *n* [*Gambling*] a street bookmaker who accepts bets 'into his hand'.

handcuffed *a* [*Theatre*] an actor's description of an audience who will not applaud; such audiences are also 'sitting on their hands'.

handfilled *a* [*UK*] [*Coal-mining*] said of faces or lips from which the coal or stone is shifted onto the conveyor belt by use of a shovel, without the aid of machinery.

handful **1.** *n* [*UK*] [*Police*] £5.00. **2.** *n* [*UK*] [*Prisons*] a sentence of five years. See also **lagging, stretch 2.**

hand-holding *n* [*Public relations*] the first task a PR man must get done: convincing the client that, come what may, he, the PR man, is doing a wonderful job, despite any fears or even accusations to the contrary. Only then can he devote himself to the client's needs.

handicapper *n* [*Horse-racing*] any horse that is running in a handicap race.

handkerchief buyer *n* [*Commerce*] a customer who only buys cheap items.

handle **1.** *n* [*Cricket*] 'to give (it) the long handle': when a batsman takes control of all the bowlers and scores freely and continually. **2.** *n* [*Gambling*] the total amount of money that changes hands during a day's betting at a racecourse before bookmakers can assess the actual profit or loss. **3.** *n* [*US*] [*Painting*] a worn-out brush which has effectively been reduced to a stump of bristles and a handle. **4.** *n* [*Publishing*] a one-line encapsulation of the theme or content of a book, coined by an editor and used by sales and promotional staff. **5.** also **hand** *n* [*Textiles*] the 'feel' of a piece of cloth: how soft, harsh, smooth, rough, silky, etc. it is to the touch.

handler **1.** *n* [*Computing*] the part of the program which controls the operation of one of the **peripherals. 2.** *n* [*Espionage*] a member of the security services who deals personally with an agent.

handline *v* [*Angling*] to pull a fish from the water without winding in the line.

handling tight *n* [*Metallurgy*] a degree of tightness between screwed joints that ensures that they retain the connection unless it is loosened with a wrench.

handmaiden *n* [*Religion*] a female minister.

hand-mucker, also **hold-out man** *n* [*Gambling*] a cheat whose speciality is palming the cards.

hand-off *n* [*Military*] a method of transmitting instructions to strategic bombers from the **Looking Glass Plane** flying command post. A message is passed slowly from one bomber to another throughout an entire flight en route to the USSR, and is viable as a scheme only while the aircraft are within radio range of each other.

handshake *n* [*Computing*] the communication between any two parts of the system.

handshaking *n* [*Communications*] an exchange of pre-determined signals between two terminal operators to ensure that transmission can proceed without problems.

hands-off *a* [*Computing*] said of a system in which no operator intervention is required for its working. See also **hands-on.**

hands-on **1.** *a* [*Business, Education, Technology*] referring to practical involvement either in learning – where students can obtain real experience of possible future jobs – or in business, where again there is an implication of rolling up one's sleeves and getting involved, rather than simply reading or talking. The involvement can be in a variety of situations where the practical is seen as improving on the merely theoretical. It is usually found as 'hands-on experience'. **2.** *a* [*Computing*] said of any system where the operator is physically in control. See also **hands-off.**

hands-on session *n* [*Politics*] really coming to grips with a political problem, 'getting one's hands dirty' in the same way as in the business use of **hands-on.**

handwriting **1.** *n* [*Design*] the style that indicates to any peer that a particular designer has created the object or image in question, whether it be in fashion, graphics, illustration or in any other visually identifiable medium. The handwriting is, in all cases, that of a 'signature'. **2.** *n* [*Espionage*] the different styles – speed of transmission, pressure of keystroke, etc – that help the expert identify the various users of morse or cypher keys in clandestine communications.

handy billy *n* [*Sailing, Ropework*] a small tackle, kept available for small jobs.

handy weights *n pl* [*US*] [*Meat trade*] beef cattle weighing on average 1000–1200lbs.

handyman special *n* [*US*] [*Real Estate*] a house that requires a good deal of repairs, possibly appealing to the do-it-yourself enthusiast.

hang **1.** *v* [*Horse-racing*] a horse does this when it veers consistently to one side of the course. **2.** *v* [*Metallurgy*] in iron-founding this is when a furnace becomes so choked that the stock can no longer descend. **3.** *v* [*Sport*] in any ball sport, this is when the ball appears to have slowed down in its flight and to 'hang' in the air.

hang a fly *v* [*Angling*] to raise the point of the rod and thus make the fly hang above the fish.

hang a jacket on *v* [*US*] [*Prisons*] to denounce a fellow inmate as an informer.

hang an axe *v* [*Logging*] to fix a handle to an axe-head.

hang five, hang ten *v* [*Surfing*] to ride the surfboard with the toes of either one (five) or both (ten) feet hooked over the front of the board.

hang in there *v* [*New therapies*] to sustain an emotional position whatever the odds; to take a stand and not relinquish it, whatever the pressure. Those who tell another to 'hang in there'

H

tend to imply their backing, if not their actual participation in the problem.

hang loose *v* [*New therapies*] the opposite of being **uptight**: to coast through life taking good or bad as one finds them and letting neither disturb one's equilibrium. See also **go with the flow.**

hang one's beef *v* [*Merchant navy*] to use one's muscles and strength.

hang tough *v* [*Politics*] a variation of 'toughing it out', first coined to encourage heroin addicts who were attempting to withdraw from drugs at the Synanon Foundation in California. It is used by politicians to stress that once they have adopted a position or stance, they intend to stick by it. Politicians also refer to **hanging in there** in much the same way.

hang up *v phr* [*Boxing*] abbr of **to hang up one's gloves** to retire from the ring.

hangar flying *n* [*Gliding*] pilot talk, especially boastful talk, that takes place on the ground.

hangar hooks *n pl* [*Crime*] special devices fitted into the clothes of shoplifters, from which stolen garments can be invisibly hung.

hangar queen *n* [*Aerospace*] an aircraft that is continually laid up in the hangar awaiting repairs. A facetious implication of effeminate homosexuality is given to such a plane.

hangar rash *n* [*US*] [*Gliding*] the bumps and scratches a glider may pick up while on the ground – from hitting the hangar walls and doors, bumping other planes, etc.

hangar rat *n* [*Aerospace*] any non-flying personnel who have a variety of unspecified ground or maintenance jobs on an airbase.

hanger 1. *n* [*US*] [*Garment trade*] an easy work assignment; it comes from billiards use where a hanger is a simple shot. **2.** *n* [*US*] [*Journalism*] the headline that is put immediately below the main headline (see **banner**) and which refers to the same story. **3.** *n* [*Tobacco*] a layer of tobacco leaves hung on sticks in a curing barn. **4.** *n* [*Mountaineering*] See **fishplate.**

hanging gardens *n pl* [*US*] [*Navy*] bunks suspended above the torpedoes in a submarine.

hanging head *n* [*Printing*] a heading that extends beyond the left or right margin of the text material to which it relates.

hanging indentation *n* [*Printing*] an arrangement whereby the first line of a paragraph is printed flush with the left margin and all subsequent lines are indented; it is the reverse of the usual procedure whereby the first line only is indented.

hanging paper *n* [*US*] [*Crime*] the pursuit of passing dud cheques, which is carried out by a 'paperhanger'.

hanging up *adv* [*UK*] [*Police*] the description of a taxi-driver who lingers around theatres, stations or similar places with the intention of driving up and snatching a fare without waiting in the regular rank.

hangnail *n* [*Audio*] a small shred of material drawn up from the top edge of the record groove by the stamping machine when pressing a record.

hangover 1. *n* [*Audio*] a fault in reproduction caused by poor loudspeaker responses to audio **transience** whereby successive sounds, especially at low frequencies, seem to blur into each other. **2.** *n* [*TV*] an effect, due to the camera tube, in which a field image will persist after a scan to contaminate the image produced by the next scan.

hangtag *n* [*Textiles*] a label affixed to a textile – garment, bedding, towel, etc – that describes the material.

hangtime *n* [*US*] [*Football*] the length of time a punted ball stays in the air; the longer it stays up, the longer the defensive team have to tackle the receiver.

happening *n* [*Journalism*] a story.

happenings 1. *n pl* [*Art*] art's action events of the 1960s; 'happenings' were a cross between an art exhibition and a theatrical performance, with great emphasis on shock value and the involvement of the spectator, rather than permitting passive viewing. With artists as their prime movers, such 'performances' stressed the visual and tactile over the literary and verbal. **2.** also **auto-destructive art** *n pl* [*Art*] See **destructive art.**

happy hour *n* [*Military*] a period set aside every evening during which half-price drinks are sold in the NCOs' and officers' messes; this is as in a civilian bar.

happy talk *n* [*US*] [*TV*] a style of news broadcasting in which all topics, no matter how grave or disturbing, are given a jokey, light-hearted veneer and in which, whenever possible, a serious topic is replaced by a humorous one; the over-riding and predictable effect of such broadcasting is to give its consumers – who may well have no other news source – a totally false view of the world.

harbour *v* [*Hunting*] said of a stag when it takes up a resting place in a covert.

harbour light *n* [*UK*] [*Railways*] See **feather 1.**

hard 1. *a* [*Audio, Computing*] referring to materials which still retain their magnetism after the magnetic field has been removed. **2.** *a* [*Military*] said of bases, silos and similar missile installations or military command posts which have extra protection, usually in the form of reinforced concrete defences and the construction of subterranean bunkers, against incoming nuclear weapons. Such hardening must be reinforced to keep pace with advances in the strength and accuracy of new weapons and it is generally accepted that if the hardened silo is to be a useful asset to a weapons system, rather than a static concrete shroud, it cannot realistically be expected to survive a direct hit. **3.** *a* [*Photography*] said of paper that produces a high contrast image. **4.** *a*

[*Wine-tasting*] referring to a wine with an over-prominence of tannin and acidity; it is often the product of a hot vintage or too lengthy a contact with pips and skins during fermentation.

hard arbitrage n [*Finance*] See **round-tripping.**

hard architecture n [*Architecture*] the growth of a sterile and inhuman style of architecture, particularly in the construction of prisons, mental hospitals and similar dumping grounds for 'second-class citizens'. With their windowless, impersonal, rough-textured style, such architecture acts merely to underline the feelings of alienation and isolation that such buildings already contain.

hard bat n [*Table tennis*] the traditional bat, used mainly by older players, covered with **pimpled** rubber, **pimples** out, with no sponge.

hard boot n [*Computing*] a **bootstrap** command performed by the physical pressing of a button or buttons on the keyboard. See also **soft boot.**

hard cases n pl [*Law*] those legal cases which pose fundamental questions regarding the nature of law and legal reasoning; it comes from the maxim 'hard cases make bad law'.

hard coal n [*Coal-mining*] any grade of coal that contains more than 60% of carbon by weight.

hard copy n [*Computing*] copy that has been printed out from the electronic records held in any of the retrieval systems in the machine's memory; it is the opposite of the 'magnetic' records held either on tape or **disk.**

hard crash n [*Computing*] a total breakdown that causes the loss of large amounts of data.

hard currency n [*Economics*] a term without precise meaning, but when used in a British context, it is the currency of any country with which the UK has an adverse balance of payments in currency transactions which has to be settled in dollars or gold. It is a relative rather than specific term, reflecting the relations between one currency and another, and varying as to their strengths and weaknesses around the world.

hard disk n [*Computing*] a rigid storage disk made from aluminium substrate plated or coated, usually on both sides, with a magnetic material; it is used for mass storage of computerised data which may thus be retrieved at faster speeds than similar material stored on **floppy disks.** Hard disks store data in multiples of megabytes (millions of bytes) as opposed to floppies, which usually store 360,000 bytes and at most hold 1.44 megabytes. See also **Winchester.**

hard dollars n pl [*Business*] payments made by a customer for services, including research, that are received from a brokerage house, as opposed to commissions that are paid for actual trading.

hard edge painting, also **stain painting** n [*Art*] See **colour field painting.**

hard error n [*Computing*] a permanent error.

hard funding n [*Government*] a programme which manages to attract a regular supply of government funds from its inception onwards, whether or not the current circumstances or progress of that programme actually merit this continuing government investment. Such programmes may well deserve their money, but may equally well be ill-managed and useless, sustained only because they bolster the image and power base of an individual or a department who cannot afford to have them seen to fail. See also **soft funding.**

hard goods n pl [*Textiles*] worsteds, which have a hard finish, a close weave and little or no nap; they are produced from yarn which is first carded and then combed to eliminate short wool fibres. Typical worsteds are gabardine and serge. See also **soft goods.**

hard hat man n [*UK*] [*Railways*] an inspector.

hard heading n [*Coal-mining*] a roadway driven through rock rather than through coal.

hard hole n [*Metallurgy*] in iron-founding this is a furnace tapping hole that has been blocked by solidified metal or slag.

hard kelly n [*Car-making*] hard hat; it comes from the obsolete name for a straw or derby hat.

hard knot n [*Sailing, Ropework*] any tight knot that is hard to untie.

hard money n [*US*] [*Education*] money appropriated for academic use that has been voted from federal or state funds and which can thus be considered as guaranteed when colleges are preparing their budgets for the forthcoming year. See also **soft money 2.**

hard news n [*Media*] factual, and theoretically important information that leads the TV and radio news bulletins and appears on the front page of a serious newspaper. See also **happy talk, soft news.**

hard paper n [*Photography*] printing paper that produces very high contrast.

hard rock 1. n [*Gambling*] a cautious, 'tight' player who risks little, bets with restraint and rarely bluffs. **2.** n [*Gambling*] a gambler who refuses to lend anyone money. **3.** n [*Gambling*] a player who is hard to beat. **4.** n [*Pop music*] simplistic, noisy 'macho' music that appeals to 'headbanging', denim-clad, badge-bedecked, northerners (UK) or beer-swilling, Midwesterners (US); it is music's equivalent to fantasy writing's 'sword and sorcery' or role-gaming's 'dungeons and dragons'.

hard science n [*Science*] any of the natural, or physical sciences: chemistry, physics, biology, geology, astronomy.

hard target kill potential n [*Military*] the extent to which the **ICBM** can be assumed to destroy a target that has been specifically protected against its war-heads. It has been accepted that ICBMs have this capability, but the introduction of the Trident II D5 missile will extend this threat to submarine launched mis-

H

siles, hitherto only considered capable of destroying soft targets.

hard tasks *n pl* [*Business*] jobs that involve direct assembly of a product at the manufacturing stage, or participation in providing an actual service.

hard ticket *a* [*Film*] said of films exhibited in separate performances (as opposed to continuous programmes); they are booked for long runs in one cinema and offer reservable seats at possibly high prices. Such films tend to be the cinematic version of a successful **legitimate** play.

hard time *n* [*Prisons*] finding one's incarceration in prison hard to bear; often such problems are intensified by a prisoner rebelling against the system and thus getting even 'harder' time by losing remission, spending time in solitary confinement, etc.

hard track/soft track *n* [*Sex*] See **fast track/slow track.**

hard values *n pl* [*Advertising*] as elicited through market research, these are the factors in a product that appeal to hard emotions: masculinity, virility, aggression, etc. See also **soft values.**

hard way *n* [*Gambling*] to make one's **point** in craps dice 'the hard way' is to score the even numbers 4,6,8,10 with pairs of 2s, 3s, 4s or 5s, instead of with combinations of odd numbers – of which there are more on a pair of dice and which should thus be easier to throw.

hard-ass *v* [*US*] [*Police*] to break into a safe by punching, ripping or by using any method other than drilling, pulling the combination or using explosives.

hardball *v* [*US*] [*Politics*] this comes from professional baseball's use of the correct, hard ball, rather than that used in the amateur, if popular, game of softball; it is used in politics to imply a tough, no-nonsense attitude to governmental problems in general and confrontations in particular. It is equally popular in business use, often referring to the refusal to give way easily on a contract or similar deal.

hardbottom *n* [*Glass-making*] a finisher of glassware, especially of the necks on bottles, etc.

hard-edge painting *n* [*Art*] a type of painting that views the entire picture surface as one unit and thus has no division between the 'ground' and 'figures' on it; these paintings are crisp, geometrical and have no apparent interest in personal, emotional statements.

harden *v* [*Military*] to defend one's own weapons systems, particularly **ICBM** sites, and command bases with the intention of making them impervious to hostile missile strikes. The ever-increasing accuracy of new weapons has made such attempts somewhat cosmetic, and it is accepted, at least in the US, that in the event of a nuclear attack, the commanding personnel will have to quit their ground or subterranean bases and hope to ride out the immediate attack in a

variety of specially prepared aircraft. See also **hard 1.**

hardening price *n* [*Commerce*] an increasing price.

hard-laid, also **short-laid** *a* [*Sailing, Ropework*] said of tightly twisted rope. See also **plain-laid.**

hardpack *n* [*Skiing*] compressed, icy snow.

hardrider *n* [*Cycling*] an habitually fast cyclist, usually in a club.

hard-sectoring *n* [*Computing*] a relatively slow means of informing a machine's drive system where a **sector** starts on a **floppy** disk: a hole is punched in the disk to show where each sector begins. See also **soft-sectoring.**

hardship categories *n pl* [*Social work*] a euphemism for the poor.

hardship post *n* [*US*] [*Military*] any posting where US troops must forgo some of the usually very comfortable conditions provided for their service.

hardtops *n pl* [*Film*] cinemas with roofs, ie. the usual buildings designed for projecting and viewing films, rather than open-air drive-ins.

hardware 1. *n* [*Aerospace*] a completed rocket, as opposed to the **software** that comprises its internal engineering, guidance systems, etc. **2.** *n* [*Computing*] the actual machinery – electrical, mechanical, structural – that comprises the working parts of a computer, as opposed to the **software** with which it is programmed and otherwise made to work. **3.** *n* [*US*] [*Medicine*] surgical equipment. **4.** *n* [*Military*] a general term for military **material**, weapons and equipment; in these terms **software** tends to imply the human beings involved in wars. **5.** *n* [*US*] [*Skiing*] trophies won in skiing competitions.

hardwarily *adv* [*Computing*] an adverbial use of **hardware** as in 'Hardwarily, the machine is excellent'. There is no use of 'hardwary'.

hardwire *v* [*Computing*] to wire a circuit directly to a computer. Thus 'hard-wired' implies anything that is firmly and directly attached to something else, not necessarily in the machine, eg: specific expressions that are part of a human face.

hare *n* [*Athletics*] See **rabbit 14.**

hare slap *n* [*Navy*] steaming at high speed, especially at night.

hare's foot *n* [*Dog breeding*] a fault, notably an exceptionally long foot.

hare's fur *n* [*Ceramics*] a brown or black glaze streaked with silvery white or yellow, used on certain varieties of Chinese pottery.

harlequin *n* [*Printing*] a heavy decorative type element.

harling *n* [*Building, Plastering*] an external finish obtained by the systematic throwing of a mixture of sand/lime/cement with pebbles/crushed stone **aggregate** against the wall.

harmonic extraction *n* [*Coal-mining*] the working of one or more coal seams by means of a

H

special layout and a timed sequence of extraction, the aim being to cause a minimum of damange to the surface amenity.

harmonisation *n* [*Industrial relations*] an arrangement whereby all members of a company are seen as having equal status; there are still salary differentials, but socially every one is equal (no directors' dining room, etc) and all groups are expected to have their say in determining company policy.

harmonogram *n* [*Art*] a machine-engraved linear design which features an extremely high level of precision regarding mathematical/geometric patterns, eg: as in the complexities of a British bank note.

harness 1. *n* [*Cars*] See **loom. 2.** *n* [*Weaving*] a set of **heddle** shafts and their roller or pulley system.

harpic *a* [*Navy, Air Force*] unstable, crazy, 'clean around the bend': it comes from the popular lavatory cleaner.

Harriet Lane *n* [*UK*] [*Merchant navy*] the cargo ship's equivalent of the Royal Navy's **Fanny Adams:** canned meat and the stews that are made from it.

Harrow drive, also **Surrey cut** *n* [*Cricket*] a false stroke off the inside edge of the bat which goes in any direction but the one in which the batsman was actually aiming. See also **Chinese cut.**

harrow perforation *n* [*Philately*] a means of perforating whole sheets at a time, the pins being arranged crosswise.

harsh *a* [*Wine-tasting*] unpleasant, due to excess tannin and/or ethyl acetate from acetic acid.

Hart's Rules *n pl* [*Printing*] a set of typesetter's rules codified in 1903 by Horace Hart for use by compositors and print readers.

harvest *n* [*Religion*] the ministry.

has a sign on his back *v phr* [*Gambling*] a phrase that describes a cheat who is so well known that he 'has a sign on his back'.

hash total *n* [*Statistics*] a sum of a set of numbers, each of which refers to a single item of data, which has no significance in itself but is used to check that every item of data has been dealt with.

hasher *n* [*Mining*] a woman employed as an assistant to the cook in a mining or lumber camp. See also **flunkey.**

hashing *n* [*Computing*] a method of allotting storage locations to records of a file which permits rapid searching of the files; it is especially useful for a table to which items are added in an unpredictable manner. An algorithm is used to provide a uniform distribution of locations in the file. All items concerned are given a specific key, which uses its hash function to place the item in the hash table. A further algorithm is used to search the hash table for the required item when selected.

hash-mark 1. *n* [*US*] [*Military*] service stripes

awarded to enlisted men in the US forces; each stripe represents four years service. **2.** *n* [*Computing*] the sign '#'.

hassling *n* [*US*] [*Air Force*] engaging in mock aerial dogfights for training purposes.

hasty breaching *n* [*Military*] the creation of instant pathways through enemy minefields by crude methods such as tossing grenades into them to blow up a number of mines, or by pushing ahead heavy rollers or wrecked vehicles in order to trigger the weapons.

hat 1. *n* [*US*] [*Government*] any corrupt financial dealing: bribery, payoffs, kickbacks, black marketeering, etc. All stem from the phrase 'Go buy yourself a hat' which traditionally accompanies the handing over of the money. **2.** *n* [*US*] [*Police*] a bribe of $5.00; it comes from the phrase 'Go buy yourself a hat'.

hat money *n* [*Shipping*] a small payment – usually 10% of the charges – paid to ensure that shippers take especial care of one's goods. See also **hat.**

hatch *n* [*Frisbee flying*] See **whelm.**

hatched *a* [*US*] [*Government*] dismissed from a post in any federally funded agency for violating the Hatch Act, which specifically outlaws any political activity by federal employees.

hatrack *n* [*US*] [*Meat trade*] a very thin, old cow.

hat-trick *n* [*Sport*] in cricket this is the taking of three wickets with consecutive balls, which is so-called from an earlier tradition of awarding a hat to any bowler who achieved this feat. It is now extended to any sport in which a single player can score three or more goals in a match – hockey, soccer, etc.

haul postholes *v* [*US*] [*Road transport*] to drive an empty truck, or pull an empty trailer.

hauler *n* [*Hot rods*] a notably fast car; possibly it comes from slang 'haul ass' meaning to go very fast.

hauling *n* [*Logging*] the way in which water pressure moves logs together at a boom and piles them up against one another.

Havana riders *n pl* [*Air travel*] any hijackers, although the phrase originated with the destination of many early 1960s hijackers who demanded to be flown to Cuba.

have a bearing *v* [*Sailing, Ropework*] used of a rope when it rests in the proper niche.

have a rush on *v phr* [*Croquet*] to be able to hit another ball with one's own, and thus move it in a required direction.

have lice and fleas *v phr* [*US*] [*Medicine*] to have more than one disease.

have numbers [*Military*] radio code for 'I have received and understood the information on wind speed and direction and my designated runway for my landing'.

Have Quick *n* [*Military*] the code name for a current US development of air-to-air, air-to-

H

ground jamming-resistant UHF communications designed for adoption by the USAF.

have the X v [Gambling] to control the gambling in a given city or state.

haw 1. n [Dog breeding] ectropion: drooping, pouching or sagging of the lower eyelid due to looseness, resulting in the exposure of an abnormally large amount of the conjunctival lining; it is undesirable and leads eventually to eye problems. **2.** v [Dog-sledding] to direct the dogs to turn left. See also **gee 1.**

hawk 1. n [Building, Plastering] a lightweight square platform with a handle below, used to carry the material from the mixing board to the actual face of the work in question. **2.** n [Politics] an advocate of an aggressive posture and policy on foreign relations. The term was coined in 1798 as 'war hawks' by Thomas Jefferson, to describe those who wanted a war with France, and later for those who actually promoted the War of 1812 with England. Revived in 1962 by US writers Stewart Alsop and Charles Bartlett, in a piece on the Cuban Missile Crisis, with its opposite '**dove**', 'hawk' has gained a permanent place in the political/military lexicon ever since.

Hawthorne effect n [Industrial relations] this concept was developed from surveys taken between 1924 and 1936 at the Hawthorne, Illinois, works of the Western Electric Company; the concept is that an initial increase in production tends to follow a newly introduced change – it is interpreted by the workforce not as a specific incentive but as a sign of management interest and goodwill.

hay n [US] [Paper-making] See **broke 1.**

hay in n [US] [Lunch counter] a strawberry soda.

hayrack n [Oil rigs] the portion of the top of a derrick which is used to keep the pipe straight in the derrick; made of metal strips it resembles a farmyard hayrack. See also **swarm.**

haywire a [Logging] the general term for anything second-rate, out of order, disorganised, unpleasant, etc.

hazard 1. n [US] [Coal-mining] a period of six hours following the failure of a dynamite charge to explode and during which the charge may still be dangerous. **2.** n [Computing] a potential or actual malfunction of a logic circuit during changes of state of input variables, ie. at the moment of switching.

hazer n [US] [Cattlemen] an assistant to the horse-breaker or bronco-buster.

HDLC n [Communications] abbr of **High Level Data Link Control** an international standard which detects and corrects errors in data transmission networks as well as controlling the flow of information between the terminals and the exchange.

HDVS, also HDTV n [TV] abbr of **High Definition Video System** (also **High Definition Television**) a proposed new television transmission system operating on 1125 lines (as opposed to the current 625) and using a wide screen display. Given that it requires a bandwidth signal equivalent to four normal channels, it may be restricted to satellite or cable systems.

head 1. v [Coal-mining] to excavate a road or narrow passage. **2.** n [Journalism] abbr of **headline. 3.** n [Printing] the top of the printing character; the upper rear of the actual type shank. **4.** n [Printing] the top edge of a book's pages.

head amp n [Audio] an amplifier circuit intended to boost the low output voltage of a moving coil cartridge.

head and shoulders n [Economics] a graph of market prices in which a small rise and then fall is followed by a higher rise and then fall, and finally by a second small rise and fall equal to the first one, thus providing a 'head and shoulders' outline on the graph.

head and tail rise n [Angling] this is the way in which a fish rises to the surface, with first its head and then its tail breaking the surface.

head art n [Art] See **conceptual art.**

head clog n [Video] malfunctions of the recording or playback heads of a VTR when they become clogged with oxide particles from the running tapes.

head crash n [Computing] the breaking down of a computer which is caused when the read/write head (which 'reads' and 'writes' information that is to be stored on and retrieved from a **disk**) actually touches the surface of the disk it is processing; the result is that, at worst, the data is totally destroyed and, at best, the data is seriously harmed.

head man n [US] [Railways] a brakeman who rides in the locomotive.

head out n [Radio] a tape so wound that the loose end is at the beginning of the interview or feature it contains and is thus available for immediate use without any rewinding; a head out tape is distinguished by its green leader. See also **tail out, top and tail, turn round.**

head rig n [Logging] in a sawmill this is a large saw which makes the initial cut in the process that transforms a log into saleable lumber.

headache n [Oil rigs] any protecting structure which supports weight; it derives from the idea of a driller leaning his aching head against the post when worried, or from its stopping him from receiving a headache were the weight it supports to fall. Thus the cry 'Headache!' is a signal that something has fallen from high on the rig.

headache rack n [US] [Road transport] a heavy bulkhead that extends from the trailer over the cab; it is made from steel pipe and is used for steel haulage.

headbanger n [Politics] a member of the far Left of the British Labour party; it comes from rock music slang for a fan of 'heavy metal' bands.

H

headend *n* [*TV*] the electronic control centre of a cable television network.

header 1. *n* [*Computing*] a piece of coded information that precedes a given collection of data and provides necessary information about it, such as its length, to facilitate processing. **2.** *n* [*Printing*] a piece of copy placed at the top of every page of a book, showing the chapter heading, book title, author's name, etc. See also **footer. 3.** *n* [*US*] [*Road transport*] a protective shield placed at the front end of a flat-bottom trailer to prevent the freight shifting forward. **4.** *n* [*TV*] a short, teasing, pre-credits sequence extracted from a film or programme, which highlights the action to come and is designed to hold the audience through a commercial break, news bulletin, etc.

headhunt *v* [*Business*] to search out and recruit top executives, often with the implication of stealing them from their current employer in order to capitalise on their special abilities, rather than waiting for them to tire of that job and make an approach themselves. Headhunters, who perform such recruitment, may either be regular employees of the headhunting firm, or may operate as consultants, with specific knowledge of the executives in question and hire themselves out to any interested party.

headhunter *n* [*US*] [*Sport*] in contact sports, eg. ice-hockey, these are the players whose task it is to ensure that any of the opposition's stars are speedily removed from the game, or at least intimidated out of their usual prowess; such players are not expected to involve themselves with any of the more skilful aspects of the game in which they play.

heading *n* [*Weaving*] the first few rows of weaving before the actual fabric is started; this serves to equalise the spacing of the **warp** threads where they are tied to the cloth beam rod, and simultaneously keeps the **wefts** from unravelling.

headings *n pl* [*S. Wales*] [*Coal-mining*] tunnels that lead to the coal face.

headland *n* [*Hunting*] the unploughed strip of a cultivated field nearest to the hedgerow.

headline *n* [*Book collecting*] the line of type at the top of every page that gives the author's name and/or the title of the book or the chapter in it.

headphones *n pl* [*US*] [*Medicine*] a stethoscope.

headroom *n* [*Audio*] the extra power output available in an amplifier (above the rated continuous output) in response to dynamic peaks in the signal.

heads 1. *n* [*Navy*] this originated in the Royal Navy, but is currently found mostly in the USN; it is the ship's latrine, from its original position, in the early sailing vessels, in the head, or bows of the ship. In USN and USMC use, 'heads' extends to on-shore lavatories. **2.** *n pl* [*Radio*] abbr of news **headlines** or highlights. **3.** *n pl* [*TV*] the headlines of the BBC's Nine o'Clock and other news programmes; originally an ITN speciality, this tabloid-style listing underlines the new search for populism. See also **bongs.**

heads up 1. *adv* [*Hunting*] referring to hounds when they are running with their heads up. So strong is the scent that they need not bow towards the ground. See also **breast high. 2.** *adv* [*Military*] US radio code for 1. hostile planes have broken through our defences, 2. I am not in a position to engage hostile attackers.

headset *n* [*New therapies*] one's overall attitude to life: the way in which one's head is 'set'.

head-to-foot *n* [*Printing*] printing the reverse side of a sheet of paper so that it can be read by turning the sheet end to end instead of turning it as one would the page of book.

head-to-head *n* [*Printing*] printing the reverse side of a sheet of paper so that it can be read by turning it over as one would the page of a book.

head-tripping *n* [*New therapies*] this is used at the Esalen Institute (California) to mean 'thinking', but more generally it is used as a derivation of the 1960s hippie slang for LSD use – a trip – which was gradually converted by its users to mean any form of activity, good, bad, active or passive, irrespective of whether LSD was used or not.

head-up display *n* [*Technology*] a projection of instrument readings – in a car, aircraft cockpit or any suitably equipped vehicle – that is taken from the actual dials and appears on the windscreen so that drivers, pilots, etc. can read the information without taking their eyes off the road or sky ahead.

headwork *n* [*Cycling*] clever tactical riding, especially at the start of a sprint race.

heapstead *n* [*Coal mining*] the surface works surrounding the mine's shaft.

hear *v* [*New therapies*] to understand and appreciate. 'I hear you' implies a deeper level of listening than merely understanding the superficial statement that is being made; like many allied concepts, it stems from the slightly mystical responses which come from a couple of people enjoying some form of mind-expanding drug and thus claiming a greater comprehension than they might otherwise be able to attain.

heart 1. *n* [*Sailing, Ropework*] a slack-twisted rope or strand used as the core in **shroud-laid rope**, wire rope or **sinnet. 2.** *n* [*Sailing, Ropework*] a form of **deadeye** with a single hole, with three or four grooves to hold the parts of the **lanyard** in place. **3.** *n* [*Theatre*] padding placed in their tights by actors, acrobats and anyone else who might have to take an otherwise painful fall.

heart transplants *n pl* [*Journalism*] newspaper articles concerning the love-affairs and relationships of the famous.

heartbreak corner *n* [*UK*] [*Postal services*] a store-room for post that has been mis-addressed or poorly packaged.

heat 1. *n* [*Metallurgy*] the product of a single

H

furnace charge tapped into a ladle. **2.** *n* [*US*] [*TV*] tension within the script or action of a programme.

heat island *n* [*Science*] a geographical area from which a measurably greater area of heat is radiated than from those areas which surround it; the cause is often a concentration of industrial plant.

heat sink *n* [*Audio*] a metal structure, often part of the circuit board or chassis which is deliberately constructed to conduct heat away from vulnerable transistors and similar delicate elements of the system.

heater *n* [*Baseball*] a fast ball.

heating *n* [*Coal-mining*] the build-up of harmful gases underground.

heave *n* [*Mining*] the horizontal displacement of strata measured at right angles to the **strike** of a fault.

heaver 1. *n* [*Sailing, Ropework*] a sailmaker's tool, also known as a stitch mallet. **2.** *n* [*Sailing, Ropework*] a stick with rope tails used for rope-making, splicing, and **worming**.

heavier *n* [*Deer-stalking*] a stag that cannot reproduce; it comes from Fr. 'hiver' meaning 'winter', meaning that its meat can be eaten in winter.

heavies 1. *n pl* [*Air travel*] the wide-bodied commercial jets: Boeing 747s, Douglas DC–10s. **2.** *n* [*Gas industry*] abbr **heavy fraction** natural gas distillate, that material removed from natural gas at the 'heavy end' portion; aliphatic compounds ranging from C/4 to C/8. **3.** *n pl* [*Journalism*] a description used by journalists on the 'popular' **tabloids** for the 'quality' newspapers such as The Times, Guardian and Daily Telegraph and their Sunday equivalents. **4.** *n pl* [*US*] [*Meat trade*] very heavy beef cattle, over two years old; thus 'mediums', 'lights', 'light-lights', etc. **5.** *n pl* [*UK*] [*Police*] the Special Patrol Group or the Flying Squad. See also **Sweeney**.

heaving line *n* [*Sailing, Ropework*] a light and often weighted line secured to a mooring rope and thrown on to the wharf so that the dockers can haul in the heavier cable which will actually moor the ship.

heavy 1. *v* [*US*] [*Car salesmen*] to have more money invested in a car than it is worth. **2.** *n* [*US*] [*Crime*] a safe-cracker. See also **peterman. 3.** *n* [*Theatre, TV*] as in film use (see **4.**); thus 'first heavy', 'second heavy' etc. **4.** *n* [*Film*] the villain, the antagonist. See also **dog heavy, first man through the door. 5.** *a* [*Film*] 'a heavy producer' etc. It comes from 1960s hippie slang. **6.** *a* [*Glass-making*] said of glass that is still too hot to be handled. **7.** *a* [*Golf*] said of a ball that is lying embedded in a sand bunker. **8.** *a* [*Minerals*] referring to minerals that have a greater specific gravity than the common minerals quartz and feldspar. **9.** *a* [*Cricket*] said of a waterlogged, rain-soaked pitch. **10.** *a* [*New therapies*] meaningful, portentous, intense; aggressive and antagonistic;

important, vital. It comes from 1960s hippie slang. **11.** *a* [*Printing, Typefaces*] bold, with thick strokes. **12.** *a* [*Stock market*] a heavy market is one in which share prices are falling. **13.** *a* [*Wine-tasting*] over-endowed with alcohol and **extract**, although a wine too heavy for one meal may complement another perfectly. It is also the official description for fortified wines.

heavy ball *n* [*Soccer*] a ball which is covered with mud or soaked with rain and thus rendered heavier than normal.

heavy chemicals *n pl* [*Industry*] chemicals that are handled in large lots and are still more or less in a crude state. See also **fine chemicals.**

heavy man 1. *n* [*Industry*] an evaporating tray in which glucose is reduced to the desired consistency for commercial purposes. **2.** *n* [*US*] [*Police*] an individual involved in the transport of narcotics.

heavy market *n* [*Stock market*] any market that is suffering from an excess of offers to sell over those to buy.

heavy metal *n* [*Pop music*] See **hard rock 4.**

heavy mob *n* [*UK*] [*Police*] the Flying Squad. See also **hot lot, Sweeney.**

heavy rackets *n pl* [*US*] [*Crime*] violent crimes – bank robbery, hold-ups, etc, as opposed to **grift.**

heavy roller *n* [*Aerospace*] any influential and extremely important executive, client or contract; it comes from a mix of gambling's 'high roller' and a massive engine or aircraft being 'rolled out' of the hangar.

heavy textiles *n pl* [*UK*] [*Prisons*] official euphemism for the mail-bags which are hand-sewn in British jails as 'employment' for those incarcerated.

heavy user *n* [*Commerce*] any consumer or customer whose purchases of a product exceed the average.

heavy water *n* [*Science*] deuterium oxide (D_2O); it is used in 'heavy water' nuclear reactors.

heddle *n* [*Weaving*] the string, wire, flat steel (or other material) that encircles a **warp** thread, so that it can be pulled up separately from other warp threads.

hedge 1. *v* [*Commerce*] to insure against any losses by setting up whatever **fail-safe** devices are considered necessary for a given situation. Thus 'hedge-selling' refers to deals with an in-built hedge, whereby each purchase is matched with a sale, or each sale with a purchase, ie: a purchase or sale for future delivery is made at the same time to offset and protect an actual merchandising deal. **2.** *n* [*UK*] [*Crime*] the crowd that forms around the periphery of a game of **three-card monte. 3.** *n* [*Government*] a statement, usually from a government/bureaucratic source, so interwoven with conditions and unstated possibilities that no real and useful conclusions can be drawn from / imputed to it.

hedge apple *n* [*US*] [*Farming*] the fruit of the

H

ossage orange; thus 'hedge row' is a line of ossage orange trees; 'hedge post' is a fence post made of ossage orange.

hedge-fund 1. *n* [*Commerce*] an investment group concentrating on capital gains. 2. *n* [*Commerce*] an investment fund established to speculate with capital put up by private investors.

hedgehog 1. *n* [*Military*] the all-round defence of an area, employing anti-tank, anti-aircraft and anti-personnel devices. 2. *n* [*Navy*] a salvo of depth charges fired from a ship with the intention of saturating a hostile submarine with simultaneous explosions. 3. *n* [*Navy*] veal.

hedgehop *v* [*Air Force*] to fly very low, skimming over the ground and 'hopping over the hedges'.

hedging *n* [*Lacrosse*] the forward encroachment by a defender close-marking an attacker; it is a method of harrassing the attacker who is trying to keep the ball away from the defender.

hedonistic *a* [*Wine-tasting*] used to describe a wine that pleases the taster, whatever a more objective assessment may determine.

heel 1. *n* [*Hunting*] the reverse line of a scent to that taken. 2. *n* [*US*] [*Painting*] the place on a brush where the bristles join the handle; when paint hardens on a brush it 'builds up a heel'. 3. also **tail** *n* [*Skiing*] the rear end of a ski.

heel and toe watch *n* [*US*] [*Marine Corps*] men standing watch who take alternate duties, with one succeeding the other for an indefinite period, only taking a rest while the opposite number is on watch.

heels *n* [*Textiles*] the harness on a loom.

hegemony 1. *n* [*Politics*] this term comes from the Greek 'hegemon' meaning leader or ruler and refers to superpower policies, similar to imperialism. In China it was used by Mao Zedong specifically to attack the Soviet Union's neocolonialism regarding parts of China. 2. *n* [*Politics*] bourgeois hegemony: in Marxist terms, this is the aspirations of any one class (especially the bourgeoisie) to rule the others, particularly by conditioning the masses to accept such rule as 'natural' and 'common sense'.

held *a* [*UK*] [*Railways*] said of locked points which prevent one from carrying out a specific operation.

helicopter cadres *n pl* [*Politics*] in the People's Republic of China, these are the party members who rise both fast and straight towards the upper echelons of power.

helix *n* [*Building, Plastering*] one of the spirals found under the abacus of a Corinthian, Ionic or composite column.

helm *v* [*Film*] to direct a film, to 'take the helm'; thus 'helmer' is a director.

helping *a* [*Social work*] See **caring** (professions).

helping the police with their enquiries *part phr* [*UK*] [*Police*] a vintage euphemism that is perpetuated in every British police station to inform the media and the public that an individual or individuals ('a man', 'three women') are under arrest or at least have been picked up for questioning; such 'help' is not usually voluntary.

hemline theory *n* [*Stock market*] the theory – which has more than often, albeit strangely, been proved right – that the fluctuations of the market follow those of the rise and fall of women's hemlines.

herald *n* [*Heraldry*] an officer expert in the technicalities of heraldry. He was originally in charge of tournaments and the ceremonies of warfare; currently he is in charge of royal and state ceremonial, and the granting, recording and inheritance of coats of arms.

herd ground *n* [*US*] [*Cattlemen*] See **bed ground**.

here *adv* [*New therapies*] aware, understanding, appreciative of and sympathetic towards someone else's problems; it is another therapeutic usage originating in 1960s hippie slang, and refers to the attempts of one LSD user to allay the fears of another, lost in the loneliness that LSD can bring out.

heresy of paraphrase *n* [*Literary criticism*] a term coined by Cleanth Brooks in 'The Well-Wrought Urn' (1947): the thesis is that if to paraphrase is to 'say the same thing in other words', then it is impossible to paraphrase a poem, since it means more than simply what it says.

hermeneutics *n* [*Sociology*] the theory and method of interpreting meaningful human action. Its origins go back to the problems of discovering the authentic version of a text at a time when books were still hand-copied and thus filled with many errors; subsequently it was expanded to take in the study of human experience by looking both at the individual and the world-view of which he/she is part.

hermit's box *n* [*Navy*] the Captain's cabin on a warship; the Captain sleeps and eats alone and is only admitted to the wardroom as a guest.

hernia pack *n* [*Commerce*] in the soft drinks trade this is a 2 litre bottle, made of PET (polyethylene terphthalate), an extra-strong, extra-lightweight substance which can contain fizzy drinks in larger sizes than previously, without bursting or breaking; so large are the bottles that to carry a quantity allegedly puts one at risk of a hernia.

herogram *n* [*TV, Journalism*] a message of congratulations sent from the home office to a reporter in the field, who is usually covering a foreign war.

heroic materialism *n* [*Sociology*] the essential spirit of the 19th century as perceived by some historians, critics, etc.

heron head *n* [*Cars*] a bowl-in piston: a combustion chamber contained in the piston instead of in the cylinder-head; it is common in diesel engines.

herring bone *n* [*Skiing*] a method of climbing

H

without kick turns which leaves herring-bone shaped tracks in the snow.

herring gutted *a* [*Hunting*] said of a second-rate hound with a flat-sided weak body and a concavity behind the ribs; it is possibly the result of illness or poor feeding.

hesiflation *n* [*Economics*] a condition of spasmodic, stop-go economic growth accompanied by high inflation. See also **inflation, stagflation.**

hesitation marks *n pl* [*Police, Medicine*] small scars on the wrist of a suicide, who has slashed his/her wrists, that indicate half-hearted preliminary scratchings at the skin, the hesitation before making the actual, fatal cuts.

heterogeneous grouping *n* [*Education*] the opposite of **ability grouping**: taking pupils and arranging them into classes irrespective of ability, using only age as a criterion.

heterosis *n* [*Business*] this comes from the biological term referring to the fact that when two species with differing characteristics are mated, the resulting offspring may well be stronger and larger than the parents. In business use it is the belief that the combination of two projects of differing types may yield exceptional, better-than-expected results.

heuristic **1.** *a* [*Computing*] in essence, trial and error: a situation in which a computer, faced with a set problem, will analyse all the possible solutions before coming up with the ideal one and then, if necessary, moving on to the next stage of its activity. **2.** *a* [*Education*] this is used especially of the teaching of science: the emphasis is that the teaching must centre on practical methods of experimentation and investigation. **3.** *a* [*Sociology*] used to describe the creation of models to facilitate the working out of a solution or a hypothesis.

hex pad *n* [*Computing*] a keypad with sixteen keys numbered 0–9 and A–F, representing all those required for hexadecimal notation.

hiccup **1.** *n* [*Stock market*] a short-lived decline in the market. **2.** *n* [*Film*] the opening of a film with a dramatic scene which precedes the titles and credits.

hickey **1.** *n* [*US*] [*Paper-making*] See **gooseneck 3.** **2.** *n* [*Printing*] any ornament in the type. **3.** *n* [*Printing*] any blemish in the engraving or the printing of an illustration.

hidden agenda *n* [*Management*] those matters that are vitally important to an individual at a meeting but which are neither on the official agenda nor can be placed there since they arise from that individual's emotions rather than the company's business, eg: the personal antagonism between two members of the board/committee/etc.

hidden curriculum *n* [*Sociology*] the values, attitudes and principles which are taught to and assimilated by pupils in an educational system; such curricula are supposed to promote social control, respect for authority and the dominant culture.

hidden decision *n* [*Commerce*] any decisions that are taken automatically and without reassessment or questioning of the status quo.

hide (*UK*), **blind** (*US*) *n* [*Shooting*] a small structure, large enough to conceal one man and his gun.

Hide, the *n* [*UK*] [*Market-traders*] the Caledonian Market, London.

hierarchical network *n* [*Computing*] a network which is synchronised through the use of **clocks** where some clocks exert more control than others. See also **democratic network, despotic network.**

hierarchy of effects *n* [*Marketing*] a marketing model that suggests that consumers move through a set sequence of attitudes as they progress from awareness of a product to actually buying it. It is used frequently in the study of advertising and its effects.

hierarchy of needs *n* [*New therapies*] five main classes of human needs, existing in a high-to-low order of precedence, are posited by US psychologist Abraham Maslow: (1) physiological (food); (2) safety (security, stability, protection); (3) belongingness and love (friendship, a role within a group or family); (4) esteem (constant need for high evaluation of self and the esteem of others); (5) self-actualisation. Maslow presumes that only when the 'lower' needs have been satisfied can the 'higher' ones be considered and achieved.

high abstraction *n* [*Sociology, Business*] the ability to conceive and use abstract ideas; thus 'high abstractors' are the elite individuals in an organisation: the technocrats, decision makers, power and influential figures.

high belly strippers *n pl* [*Gambling*] a deck of cards so doctored that the cheat knows when high cards are being dealt. See also **low belly strippers.**

high burn rate *n* [*Business*] this comes from the aerospace term denoting a rocket that burns the bulk of its fuel early to ensure a fast liftoff; in business use, it refers to an individual or project that involves a great deal of energy or production at an early stage to ensure a successful launch.

high end *a* [*Audio*] said of exotically designed, highly priced audio equipment that is designed for the demanding (and rich) listener.

high end of the conflict spectrum *n* [*Military*] Pentagonese for a state of war.

high explosive *n* [*Logging*] any explosive other than black powder.

high flier *n* [*Stock market*] a fast-moving, high priced speculative stock which moves up and down in the market over a short period.

high fliers **1.** *n pl* [*UK*] [*Government*] the top ranks of the civil service, often selected early in their career, both on the instinct of their superiors as well as on indications of their potential. They are groomed from their early twenties onwards to be future mandarins. **2.** *n pl* [*Stock market*] fashionable issues of stocks that provide an above average return on one's investment. See also **glamour issue.**

High Forest *n* [*Forestry*] a forestry system incorporating trees that have grown from seeds which have been planted naturally or artificially or in combination. The term further indicates that such a forest is of mature, high trees, which have grown up naturally, without any intervention by coppicing or pollarding.

High Frontier *n* [*US*] [*Military*] a system of space-based anti-ballistic missile defences originated by a private study, backed by right-wing funding, and fronted by Lieutenant-General Daniel O. Graham, former director of the Defense Intelligence Agency. Delivered in a report in 1982, High Frontier proposed a three-tiered system of defence including existing technology, nuclear and non-nuclear weapons, chemical and other lasers and particle-beam weapons. Though it was heavily criticised by many experts, President Reagan was highly impressed by the report and took many of his '**Star Wars**' concepts from it.

high hat *n* [*TV, Film*] the smallest type of support available for raising a camera from ground level.

high image *n* [*Business*] See **high profile 1.**

high key *n* [*Advertising, Printing*] an illustration in which the majority of tones in the subject or image lie at the light end of the grey scale.

high net worth individuals *n pl* [*Politics, Government*] the rich.

high percentage shots *n pl* [*Lacrosse*] shots that promise a high success rate; they are usually taken from within the critical **area** and in front of the goal.

high popular *n* [*Sociology*] a synonym for 'very popular' as 'low popular' is one for 'unpopular'; these uses of 'high' or 'low' (found in many areas of the social sciences) rather than more general modifiers, stem from the 'scientific' desire to give a statistical/measurable basis to an evaluation – otherwise considered too abstract for such quantification. Thus, in this context, one should assume some form of invisible 'table' on which popularity is assessed.

high profile **1.** *n* [*Business*] to 'take a high profile' is to act in a noticeable manner, to put oneself forward in the hope of impressing one's superiors with one's enthusiasm or one's inferiors with one's power. **2.** *v* [*Espionage*] to act in an obvious manner, to make no effort to hide oneself or one's occupation – although this apparent openness may in fact be only a way of protecting one's **cover.** **3.** *v* [*Espionage*] to draw attention to an imposter, a member of the opposition whose cover one has managed to blow. **4.** also **high image** *a* [*Entertainment*] well-known, ostentatious, famous, in the public eye; when used as a verb, it

means to aim intentionally to gain such a status. See also **low profile 2.**

high roller *n* [*Gambling*] this was originally used only for those dice gamblers who played for high stakes, but it has long since expanded to include any heavy betters.

high tech *n* [*Architecture, Design*] a design fashion popularised in the mid-late 1970s in which styles more usually found on or around the factory floor – exposed pipes, steel staircases, heavy duty materials for floor and wall-coverings, etc. – were transmuted into the home or office where one would now find various technical artefacts – dentists' trolleys, hospital-style taps, etc, all unearthed from wholesalers' catalogues – in place of the traditional domestic supplies. This factory/workshop style originally used the actual materials employed in the 'tech' environments, but soon degenerated into 'slick tech' when the look was mass-produced for easy purchase.

high wine *n* [*Wine trade*] the distillate from mash containing a high percentage of alcohol; high wine is further distilled to make a variety of spirits.

high-ball *n* [*US*] [*Car salesmen*] an estimate by the salesman of a higher trade-in price for the buyer's trade-in car than will actually be paid. See also **low ball.**

highball **1.** *n* [*Logging*] a signal sent from the woods to the logging-engine operator; it means 'Go ahead'. **2.** *n* [*US*] [*Railways*] a proceed signal; originally it was denoted by hauling a ball into the air. **3.** *v* [*US*] [*Road transport*] to drive a truck at high speeds.

highballer **1.** *n* [*US*] [*Painting*] a painter who works quickly and well. **2.** *n* [*US*] [*Painting*] a contractor or foreman who pushes the workforce hard.

high-boy *n* [*US*] [*Circus*] a clown who performs on stilts.

high-brow car *n* [*US*] [*Car salesmen*] See **cherry 1.**

high-climber *n* [*Logging*] a person who tops and rigs **spar trees** or poles.

high-flagging *n* [*US*] [*Taxis*] the illegal practice of picking up a fare and still keeping one's 'For Hire' flag up, thus keeping the money for oneself and not registering the trip on the meter.

high-hiding *a* [*US*] [*Painting*] referring to the quality of the chemical makeup of a paint which means that it can cover a surface adequately in only one coat.

high-lead *v* [*Logging*] to extract timber by means of an overhead cable attached to a high spar at the hauler end; this ensures that the logs clear any obstructions as they are dragged along.

high-level language *n* [*Computing*] any of the programming languages that are designed for general use, independent of any one machine (although a version compatible with the relevant operating system must be obtained). See also **low-level language.**

highline *n* [*US*] [*Journalism*] See **kicker 3**.

high-line 1. *n* [*Fishing*] the person who, or the boat which, has the best catch on a given day. **2.** *n* [*Logging*] an overhead cable attached to a **spar tree** and used for hauling timber.

high-profile *a* [*Cars*] describing a tyre with a relatively deep side-wall in relation to its width.

high-profile crime *n* [*Crime*] any crime committed in broad daylight and in the view of many witnesses. See also **low-profile crime**.

high-Q *a* [*Film*] a pun on 'IQ' (intelligence quotient) that is used by film executives who are assessing the bankability of the **talent** or **property** as regards the drawing of crowds to the cinemas or providing a film with a good plot.

high-roll *v* [*Pool*] to attempt to intimidate a player by raising the stakes dramatically.

high-sidin' *n* [*Sex*] black pimp usage that describes strutting about, showing off, bragging and generally lording it over one's acquaintances.

high-stick *v* [*Ice hockey*] to make illegal contact with an opponent while holding the stick above shoulder height.

high-stream *n* [*Business*] high stream industries are sophisticated, science-based, often incorporating ecological/sociological standards that their predecessors never considered, other than as hindrances to the pursuit of profit. See also **low-stream, sunrise industry, sunset industry**.

high-toned *a* [*Wine-tasting*] said of a nose of assertive, volatile character.

highway *n* [*Computing*] a major path within the machine along which signals travel from one of several sources to one of several destinations. See also **bus 1** and **2**.

highway mopery *n* [*US*] [*Police*] a fictitious crime which serves as a pretext for the arrest of a suspect who will not otherwise volunteer for interrogation; 'mopery' or 'mopry' is 'a classic jest among criminals: it is supposed to consist of exhibiting oneself in the nude to a blind woman' (Partridge, 'Dictionary of the Underworld' 3rd edn., 1968)

hilites *n pl* [*Radio*] highlights: a short news item representing a succinct summary of the top line of a news story. Hilites are broadcast at regular intervals between the full-length news bulletins – possibly every 15 minutes, using 4 hilites at a time.

Hill *n* [*US*] [*Politics*] Capitol Hill: site of the legislative branch of the US Government, as opposed to the White House which is the executive branch. The Hill is a true geographical description, standing 88' above sea level.

hill and dale *n* [*Record business*] the grooves of a record which contain ups and down which are traced by the path of the stylus as it plays the record.

hill climbing *n* [*Artificial intelligence*] a search technique for finding an optimum value: starting from an arbitrary point the value of the appropriate function is measured at a number of test points in the area and the 'best' direction is chosen from the test values produced. This process is repeated, gradually eliminating directions until all neighbouring test points indicate 'lower' functions than the search point.

hinges *n pl* [*Book collecting*] those parts of the book that fix its cover to its contents.

hinting gear *n* [*UK*] [*Market-traders*] See **hinton-lots**.

hinton-lots, also **hinting gear** *n pl* [*UK*] [*Market-traders*] usually genuine goods offered in a mock-auction to snare those customers who will in fact receive worthless goods.

hip pocket client *n* [*Entertainment*] a phrase used by an agent to refer to any client he/she represents who is not currently under contract and who is metaphorically sitting right there in his/her hip pocket, waiting to pop out and grab some work.

hippodrome *n* [*UK*] [*Circus*] the area within the confines of circus tent.

hippodrome stand *n* [*Rodeo*] a stunt in which the rider stands with his feet in straps and the horse goes at full speed.

hippodrome track *n* [*US*] [*Circus*] the 'ring' in a circus; there is one ring in most European circuses, but three rings in US shows.

hired assassin *n* [*Sailing*] the specialist helmsman, usually of international reputation, who is hired by a captain for major offshore races.

his master's voice *n* [*UK*] [*Railways*] a deputy foreman or assistant echoing the orders retailed down the line by his superior.

histing *n* [*Marbles*] the act of raising one's hand from the ground when shooting the marble.

histogram *n* [*Statistics*] in graphs this is a representation of some kind of distribution in which the frequency percentage is plotted on the ordinate and the varying quantity on the abscissa.

historical cost *n* [*Commerce*] the actual cost that has been incurred in producing or acquiring something.

historical materialism *n* [*Politics*] the essence of the Marxist historical view: 'The mode of production in material life determines the general character of the social, political and spiritual processes of life. It is not the consciousness of men that determines their existence, but . . . it is their social existence which determines their consciousness' (K. Marx 'A Contribution to the Critique of Political Economy', 1859). In other words, the 'relations of production' (the way in which the material production of goods and the relations between the classes are organised) form the **base** of society and this in turn creates the **superstructure** – the whole of society's political, spiritual, intellectual, etc. life.

historical relativism *n* [*Politics*] See **relativism**.

historicism 1. *n* [*Architecture*] the excessive

regard for the institutions and values of the past; a retreat, in the eyes of many critics, to exactly those views that the 19th century 'modern movement' was determined to replace. **2.** *n* [*Sociology*] a philosophical belief that historical development is the most important and fundamental aspect of human existence, and that historical thinking is therefore the most important type of thought. **3.** *n* [*Sociology*] the belief that historical change occurs in accordance with laws, so that the course of history may be predicted but never altered.

historicity *n* [*Politics*] a Marxist term denoting that human institutions and human consciousness gain a part of their significance from the fact that they are also historical phenomena and thus develop at the dictates of processes greater than themselves.

HIT *n* [*Military*] acro **Homing Interceptor Technology** a direct-ascent, non-nuclear, anti-satellite interceptor warhead designed for the destruction of satellites by collision.

hit 1. *n* [*Business*] for a project, a concept or a meeting to 'have a hit' it has to have some impact, some validity; if there is no impact there are no 'hits'. **2.** *n* [*Communications*] a momentary line disturbance, possibly causing corruption of data. **3.** *n* [*Computing*] the successful comparison of two items of data. **4.** *n* [*US*] [*Medicine*] a patient once he/she has been admitted and then assigned to a hospital resident. **5.** *n* [*Sex*] in homosexual hustling (see **hustler**) terms, this is a rich client who is interested in establishing a regular sexual and economic relationship; it comes from US hobo (tramp) slang 'hit' meaning a charitable person (one who can be 'hit on' for cash). **6.** *v* [*US*] [*Papermaking*] to change the shade of colour used in dyeing the paper. **7.** *v* [*Public relations*] See **score 6.** **8.** *v* [*TV, Film*] to turn on a light or the mechanism for some special effect.

hit a century *v* [*Big-game hunting*] to kill one hundred creatures of the same species; it comes from the cricketing term for scoring 100 runs.

hit in *v* [*Croquet*] to hit another ball from a long distance away and thus to start a **break.**

hit list *n* [*Politics, Government, Business*] a list of tasks or projects on which action must be taken.

hit on *v* [*Sex*] said of a pimp who approaches a prostitute in the hope of enlisting her in his **stable.**

hit on the line *n* [*Communications*] a temporary disturbance caused by external interference – man-made, weather-created, etc.

hit on the nose *v phr* [*Merchant navy*] to make an accurate landfall thanks to careful navigation.

hit the bid *v* [*Stock market*] to accept the highest price offered for a stock, even if that is not the asking price.

hit the bricks *v* [*US*] [*Industrial relations*] to go on strike: it comes from the general slang for leaving a place and walking off.

hit the dirt *v* [*UK*] [*Railways*] to become derailed.

hit the line *v* [*Hunting*] used of hounds when they find a scent trail and give tongue.

hit the switches *v* [*US*] [*Railways*] to pass any designated point in the yard at the end of a run.

hit the wall *v* [*Athletics*] to experience a sense of weakness, especially in the legs, when deprived of adequate blood-sugar levels during athletic endeavours.

hit with the tide *v phr* [*Cricket*] used of a batsman who hits the ball in the same direction as it is already moving.

hitch 1. *n* [*US*] [*Military*] a period of enlistment in the army, usually of four years. See also **cruise 3. 2.** *n* [*Sailing, Ropework*] a knot that secures a rope to another object; this can be another rope if it is inert.

hitch-hike *v* [*US*] [*Radio*] said of a radio programme sponsor who advertises on the show a product that is not the one that is being generally featured in that show. See also **cowcatcher.**

hitch-hiking *n* [*Espionage*] the exploitation of an informational channel – activist students, radical labour movements – which the CIA cannot actually control by infiltration; it is also extended to the use of foreign groups that are involved in operations that break the law in their own country but which in no way affect the US, except that their operations may create troubles for anti-US governments.

hits *n pl* [*Gambling*] a pair of crooked, mis-spotted dice that will never throw a 7 and which will continually produce numbers on or against which a cheat can bet.

hive-down *n* [*Commerce*] an operation whereby a receiver buys an off-the-shelf company and sells the assets in his receivership company to the new company in exchange for shares, thus dropping the liabilities.

hive-offs (*UK*), **spin-offs** (*US*) *n pl* [*Business*] the extra stocks that are distributed for the formation of a new or subsidiary company.

hiway culture *n* [*Art*] the ikons, symbols and allied hardware generated by the world of US road transport, which are epitomised by the motifs of traffic signs, petrol stations, truck stops, billboards, etc – and which are found in the work of many **pop** artists.

hobby-bobby *n* [*UK*] [*Police*] a part-time special constable.

hobo *n* [*US*] [*Road transport*] a tractor that is shifted from terminal to terminal.

hobson's *n* [*UK*] [*Theatre*] this comes from rhyming slang 'hobson's choice' meaning 'voice'.

hochwende *n* [*US*] [*Skiing*] this comes from Ger. for a skiing stunt; it is a 180° jump turn.

hockey 1. *n* [*Skittles*] a small raised piece of wood at the skittler's end on which he can rest his heels and get some purchase for the under-arm delivery of the ball. **2.** *n* [*Darts*] a line on the floor, either painted or made of a strip of wood or metal, which determines the length the player must stand from

H

the board; his feet cannot go beyond this, although his arm may be extended across it.

hod *n* [*Horse-racing*] a bookmaker's satchel.

hodad *n* [*Surfing*] a show-off who frequents the surfing beaches, boasting of his exploits and trying to pick up girls, but rarely, if ever, trying to surf.

HOE *n* [*Military*] acro **Homing Overlay Experiment** part of experiments on 'layered' ballistic missile defence, which deals specifically with the exoatmospheric stage of a missile's flight to its target, 300,000' and higher.

hog 1. *n* [*Industry*] a device used in various industries to reduce bulk materials to smaller proportions. 2. *n* [*Logging*] a device used in a sawmill to reduce waste timber to chips which can be used for fuel, etc. 3. *n* [*Motorcycles*] in the outlaw motorcycle gang, the Hells Angels, this is a bike, usually a Harley Davidson, which has been stripped of extraneous gadgetry and embellishments and tuned for use by a member of the Angels. 4. *n* [*Paper-making*] an agitator for mixing and stirring the pulp. 5. *n* [*Sailing*] a frame of timber or a large rough broom which is hauled underneath a boat to clean its bottom.

hogger *n* [*Logging*] the engineer of a logging train.

hoggers, also **bannickers** *n pl* [*UK*] [*Coalmining*] short pants used by working miners, similar to old-fashioned football shorts.

hog-head *n* [*US*] [*Railways*] the engineer.

hoist 1. *v* [*Ice-hockey*] said of two players when they converge on an opponent and sandwich him illegally between them. 2. *v* [*UK*] [*Police*] to shoplift; thus a 'hoister' is a shoplifter. See also **boost, booster** 1. 3. *n* [*Sailing, Ropework*] the perpendicular edge of a sail or flag which lies next to the mast.

hold 1. *n* [*Aerospace*] an area of airspace sited above a commercial airport's control zone where incoming aircraft can be kept safely flying around a radio beacon, separated at regulation distances from each other, until they can be cleared for landing. See also **holding pattern** 1. 2. *v* [*Drugs*] said of a dealer who has a supply of drugs for sale; thus the coded query 'Are you holding?' 3. *v* [*US*] [*Lunch counter*] to eliminate one item of a dish that would usually be added automatically; thus 'BLT hold the mayo' means bacon, lettuce and tomato sandwich, without mayonnaise. 4. *v* [*US*] [*Railways*] to continue on a job by merit of seniority.

hold a conversation *v* [*Fencing*] the highest compliment payable to a fencer, indicating the greatest, most elegant skills in the fencing tradition.

hold harmless provision *n* [*Government*] that part of a government aid programme which spares those people or projects that receive it from further harm or deterioration by allotting sufficient cash to make up for any shortfall in local funding; it comes from the insurance term, describing a clause which prevents the insured party from suffering any extra costs or expenses while making a claim on their policy.

hold the book *v* [*Theatre*] to prompt, to act as prompter – using the prompt book.

hold the rag *v* [*UK*] [*Crime*] said of a confidence trickster or long firm (see **long firm fraud**) proprietor who is left with a quantity of worthless stock when a scheme to defraud the public has failed.

holdback *n* [*Video*] the length of time a title is withheld from other media after it has been introduced to homevideo.

holding *n* [*Mining*] See **take** 6.

holding company *n* [*Commerce*] a trading company which possesses complete or majority control of the share capital of one or more other companies.

holding out *n* [*Commerce*] pretending that a partner who has in fact left the company is still a member of it and using his/her reputation to obtain further credit; the ex-partner who is thus 'held out' is legally responsible for all such debts incurred in his/her name.

holding pattern 1. *n* [*Air travel*] the group of aircraft which are circling a radio beacon sited at a commercial airport and awaiting clearance to land; the pattern describes the way in which the aircraft are arranged in ascending ranks, each circling above the next. See also **hold**. 2. *n* [*Stock market*] an extension of the air travel use (**1**): a situation in which nothing is happening, the market is moving neither up nor down, and trade is static.

hold-out *n* [*Painting, Printing*] the ability of a paint or ink film to dry to its normal finish on a somewhat absorptive surface.

hold-out artist *n* [*Gambling*] a gambler or cheat who lies to his partners or confederates when asked how much money he has made out of a game or an evening's play.

hold-out man *n* [*Gambling*] a card cheat whose speciality is palming cards, then holding them out of the game until such time as it is propitious to reintroduce them. See also **hand-mucker**.

hold-up 1. *n* [*Cards*] in bridge this is the tactical refusal to play a winning card. 2. *n* [*Military*] the amount of material tied up in a separation plant used for the manufacture of nuclear warheads.

Hole *n* [*UK*] [*Railways*] 'the Hole' is the Severn tunnel, taking the main line into Wales.

hole 1. *n* [*Baseball*] the rear area of the infield between the stations of the shortstop and the third baseman; thus 'to go into the hole' is to field a ground ball hit in that direction. 2. *n* [*Chess*] a square on the third or fourth rank, which is not commanded nor liable to be commanded by any friendly pawn. 3. *n* [*Electronics*] in a semiconductor, this is a vacancy for an electron in an atomic structure. 4. *n* [*Oil rigs*] the well bore. 5.

v [*Coal-mining*] to undercut a seam of coal by hand or by machine.

hole, in a *adv* [*US*] [*Railways*] in a siding, waiting for another train to pass on the main line.

hole out 1. *v* [*Cricket*] used of a batsman when he hits the ball straight to a fielder and is caught; it is used especially when the shot is hard and high and the fieldsman is in the deep. **2.** *v* [*Golf*] to sink the ball into a hole, and thus conclude that particular part of the course.

hole-in-the-middle *n* [*Audio*] a fault in stereo reproduction whereby there appears to be an aural 'hole' in the area between the two loudspeakers.

holiday 1. *n* [*Gas industry*] a discontinuity, break or fault in the anti-corrosion protection on pipe or tubing that leaves the bare metal vulnerable to corrosion. Thus a 'holiday detector' is an electric device for locating such faults. **2.** *n* [*Painting*] an area that has been missed by the painter in completing a job. **3.** *n* [*Logging*] an open area in the timber. **4.** *n* [*Navy*] a gap in a row; a part missed when painting the ship. **5.** *n* [*Printing*] a light spot on the page. See also **friar, monk**.

holing *n* [*Mining*] the meeting of two underground roadways which have been driven expressly to intersect each other.

holism *n* [*New therapies*] the term was coined in 1926 by General J. C. Smuts (1870–1950) to define 'the one synthesis which makes the elements or parts act as one or holistically'; it is now favoured by a variety of new therapies, all of which like to emphasise the relationship between biological and psychological well-being which together make up the 'whole' person.

holistic evaluation *n* [*Advertising*] the evaluation of a campaign simply by considering the campaign as a complete entity, rather than breaking down one's evaluation into any of its constituent parts. See also **atomistic evaluation**.

hollow *a* [*Wine-tasting*] used to describe a wine with a foretaste and some **finish** but without a sustaining middle flavour.

hollow tooth *n* [*UK*] [*Police*] an ironic reference to the Metropolitan Police HQ at Scotland Yard, implying the 'rottenness' (corruption) to be found there.

Hollywood numbers *n pl* [*Sex*] the homosexual **hustler's** term for any sex acts – eg: soixante-neuf – that derive their names from numbers.

holmes *n* [*US*] [*Prisons*] a prisoner's friend or ally.

holograph *n* [*Bibliography*] any document – letter, manuscript, etc – written entirely in the handwriting of its author.

holographic will *n* [*Law*] a will written entirely in the handwriting of the person who is making it.

holophrasis *n* [*Literary criticism*] the expression in one word of a whole idea, concept or phrase, eg: 'Ouch!'.

home and colonial *n* [*UK*] [*Police*] this comes from a now defunct chain of grocery stores; it refers to the Regional Crime Squad, which is composed of officers from the Metropolitan (home) and provincial (colonial) forces.

home audit *n* [*Marketing*] See **dustbin check**.

home guard *n* [*Logging*] the local worker, who has worked in the same camp or sawmill for many years. See also **boomer 1**.

home key *n* [*Music*] the basic key in which a piece of music is composed.

home run *n* [*US*] [*Stock market*] a large gain made in a short period of time by an investor.

home show *n* [*UK*] [*TV*] a documentary made within the British Isles.

homebodies *n pl* [*US*] [*Air Force*] USAF long-range bomber crew nickname for the USA-based missile crews, who work from their underground silos.

homebrew *n* [*Can.*] [*Sport*] a player, especially on a football team, who is a native of the town after which the team is named.

homeport *v* [*Navy*] to establish a base in a port that is near a fleet's current area of operations.

homer *n* [*Air Force*] a base that locates aircraft and then guides them in via bearings taken from radio transmissions.

homers *n* [*Navy*] a comfortable shore billet with a family in a strange port.

homevid, also **H.V.** *n* [*Film*] the world of video-tape, discs, cassettes, rented video-films, etc.; all of which are accessible to the home.

homing pigeon *n* [*Flying*] directional antenna on an airplane.

homo fanus *n* [*Science fiction*] the tribe and type of science fiction fans.

homogenised we *n* [*Advertising*] a term coined by William Lamdin: the use of the word 'we' to involve the public in a willing purchase of products that will in fact be of use to only a few people.

homologation *n* [*Cars*] the process whereby complete cars or their components are produced in sufficient numbers to qualify as 'generally available'; it is used mainly in competitions, where officials often demand a certificate of homologation.

honcho 1. *n* [*Politics, Business*] this comes from Japanese 'han cho' meaning squad leader, ie. the boss, the senior figure. **2.** *v* [*Politics, Business*] to honcho something is to take care of it personally and ensure that it is carried out.

honda *n* [*US*] [*Cattlemen*] a knotted or spliced eyelet which forms a loop at one end of a rope.

honest player, also **two-way player** *n* [*Ice-hockey*] a player who has both offensive and defensive skills, eg: a forward who is also a good checker.

honey *n* [*US*] [*Garment trade*] wax used in ironing.

honey barge *n* [*US*] [*Navy*] a garbage **scow**.

honey cart *n* [*Air travel*] the sanitary servicing cart that is attached to the aircraft during a stop-

H

over for the draining, flushing and refilling of the in-flight lavatories.

honey pot *n* [*Navy*] a shore latrine.

honey shot *n* [*TV*] any brief cut to a pretty girl, usually in a sporting crowd, theatre audience, or similar public event.

honey wagons *n pl* [*Film*] portable lavatories used on location by the crew and performers.

honeycomb *n* [*Metallurgy*] a flaw in metal caused by imperfect casting.

hood *n* [*Journalism*] See **curtain 1.**

hood job, also **nose job** *n* [*Custom cars*] See **bull nose.**

hooded *a* [*Custom cars*] said of headlamps which have a shade or hood attached to them; this is usually achieved by building up the headlamp rim with steel tube and sheet metal and blending it into the bodywork.

hoodle *n* [*Marbles*] the target marble in the game. See also **common, dib, duck, immie, mib.**

hoodoo *v* [*US*] [*Car salesmen*] to cheat, especially when the management cheats the salesmen.

hooey *n* [*US*] [*Cattlemen*] a half-hitch knot that is used in tying the legs of a calf.

hoofer *n* [*US*] [*Theatre*] a dancer, especially a tap dancer.

hook 1. *n* [*UK*] [*Crime*] a pickpocket. **2.** *n* [*US*] [*Crime*] abbr of **hooker** a prostitute. **3.** *n* [*Music*] a catchy 'jingle' or phrase in a song that sticks in the brain and keeps the listener humming the tune. **4.** *n* [*US*] [*Railways*] a wrecker train which clears wrecks and repairs tracks. **5.** *n* [*US*] [*TV*] a cliffhanger: any aspect of a script that deliberately sustains the audience's fascination, especially at the end of one segment of a series. It is often caused by a sudden accident or surprise, eg: the 'Who shot JR?' furore implanted in 'Dallas'. **6.** also **crest, shoulder** *n* [*Surfing*] the top portion of a wave.

hook, on the 1. *adv* [*Gambling*] on a losing streak. **2.** *adv* [*Gambling*] losing money in a single game. **3.** *adv* [*UK*] [*Road transport*] on tow.

hooker *n* [*TV*] the first part of a programme, designed to attract viewers into the material/storyline and maintain their interest in what follows. See also **hook.**

hookey 1. *n* [*Navy*] a leading seaman; it comes from the anchor or 'hook' on his arm. **2.** *n* [*Navy*] a nickname traditionally given to sailors with the surname Walker; it comes allegedly from the name of Mr. John Walker, a London merchant, whose hooked nose was very prominent.

hooking 1. *n* [*US*] [*Crime*] engaging in prostitution. **2.** *n* [*UK*] [*Crime*] picking pockets. **3.** *n* [*UK*] [*Crime*] the practice of a dishonest informer who attempts to fob off the police with some fantasy that is being touted strictly in his own interest, possibly to settle an old score or simply to make some money. **4.** *n* [*TV*] picture distortion caused by errors in the head timing co-ordination of a VTR.

hooks 1. *n pl* [*US*] [*Cattlemen*] spurs. **2.** *n pl* [*Cycling*] dropped handlebars; it comes from the visual resemblance. **3.** *n pl* [*US*] [*Meat trade*] the hipbones of a cow.

hooley-ann *n* [*US*] [*Cattlemen*] in roping, this is a throw made from either the ground or from horse-back; the loop is well spread and settles around its object, often the neck of a coralled horse.

hoolihan *v* [*Rodeo*] to bring down a steer by pushing straight down on the horns, rather than twisting and wrestling the animal to the ground. This style of **bulldogging** is barred at most rodeos.

hoop 1. *n* [*Horse-racing*] the horizontal stripes of colour that are used in many owners' 'silks', the shirts that jockeys wear when racing. **2.** *n* [*Aus.*] [*Horse-racing*] a jockey; it is an extension of (1).

hoot owl *n* [*Industrial relations*] the midnight shift at a factory.

hootnanny 1. *n* [*Logging*] the hook on the loading end of a cable. **2.** *n* [*Logging*] a device that holds a crosscut saw in place when sawing a log from the underside.

hoover *v* [*UK*] [*Prisons*] in a Borstal, to steal another inmate's food.

hop 1. *n* [*Computing*] a single journey from one node to the next taken by a piece of information moving through a communication network. See also **store-and-forward. 2.** also **shift** *n* [*Gambling*] a secret move made by a cheat after the cut, which puts the cards back in their original order, and thus negates the anti-cheating provisions of the cut. **3.** *n* [*Radio*] a transmission from one point on the earth to another via the ionosphere.

hopped up 1. *a* [*US*] [*Painting*] used of paint that has had thinners added to speed up the drying process. **2.** *a* [*Horse-racing*] referring to a horse that has been given some kind of drug; it comes from general slang, usually referring to humans.

horizon 1. *n* [*Coal-mining*] a nearly level tunnel driven out from the shaft. **2.** *n* [*Coal-mining*] any system of **cross-cuts** and laterals at any identified level. See also **horizon mining.**

horizon mining *n* [*Coal-mining*] a system of working from nearly level **cross-cuts** and laterals repeated at certain vertical intervals.

horizontal divestiture *n* [*Business*] the disposal of a company's holdings in other companies or organisations that produce similar products to its own.

horizontal escalation *n* [*Military*] a strategy whereby the response to the emergence of a crisis in one area is to initiate one in another area.

horizontal escape *n* [*Espionage*] a situation in which an agent breaks the vertical **need-to-know** chain of information by seeking protection for himself by sharing certain facts with a third party; the latter's knowledge of these facts is designed to give the agent some degree of 'insurance' against betrayal.

horizontal integration n [Business] the expansion of one's business by taking over competitors who are engaged in approximately the same type of enterprise.

horizontal market n [Marketing] a market in which buyers from many different industries purchase a common product or service; eg: typewriters, computers, etc. See also **vertical market.**

horizontal music n [Music] the successive sounds which form melodies, as opposed to 'verticals', the simultaneous sounds that form harmonies.

horizontal proliferation n [Military] an increase in the number of nations who claim to possess nuclear weapons. See also **vertical proliferation.**

horizontal publication n [Publishing] the publishing of books for the widest possible general interest market.

horizontal unions n pl [Industrial relations] craft unions. See also **vertical unions.**

horizontally opposed engine n [Cars] See **boxer engine.**

horns n pl [Building, Plastering] intentional protuberances that are formed on the bulk of a cast.

horns effect n [Management] the opposite of **halo effect**: a negative impression formed regarding the subject of a job performance appraisal when one characteristic creates so great a feeling of antagonism in the appraiser that this colours the grading of the entire test.

hornswoggle v [US] [Cattlemen] an animal does this when it twists and turns in an attempt to throw off the rope.

horrendioma 1. n [Medicine] a patient whose case has many complications. 2. n [Medicine] any collection of problems or disasters that have happened to a patient during hospitalisation. See also **fascinoma.**

horse 1. n [Mining] a mass of barren rock, with no mineral deposits, within an ore body. 2. also **mule** n [US] [Prisons] a guard who has been bribed to smuggle extra supplies – drugs, tobacco, etc – into a jail, and to take letters out. 3. n [US] [Road transport] a tractor. 4. n [US] [Road transport] horsepower. 5. n [Weaving] See **elephant.**

horse and cart n [UK] [Railways] a locomotive and guards brake van.

horse cock n [US] [Marine Corps] either salami or baloney (bologna sausage).

horse dam n [Logging] a temporary dam made by placing large logs in the river, in order to raise the water level behind it and float off any stranded logs.

horse editor n [Journalism] an editor dealing only with relatively unimportant copy. See also **pony editor.**

horse feed n [Oil rigs] expense account items best masked in anonymity for accounting purposes; it dates from the era of horse-drawn transport when such feed was a convenient catch-all for the auditors.

horse logs v [Logging] to drag stranded logs back to the stream, using **peavey** hooks.

horse opera n [TV] this is on the model of **soap opera**: a Western series.

horseback, also **roll** n [Coal-mining] a local thickening of roof or floor strata, accompanied by thinning of a coal seam.

horseheads n [UK] [Coal-mining] See **arch 1.**

horses n pl [US] [Garment trade] employees who push racks of garments throughout the New York garment area.

horse's ear, in the adv [Horse-racing] used of a jockey who leans forward exaggeratedly over the horse's head.

horseshedding, also **sandpapering** n [US] [Law] the process of coaching a witness in preparation for cross-examination in court; it comes from the days when rural courtrooms often stood next to the stables, which were used, for lack of anything better, as a place for lawyers and clients to consult.

horse-thief n [Oil rigs] a Pennsylvania oil rig driller.

horse-trading n [Business, Politics] driving hard bargains.

horsey a [Advertising] used by designers and art directors to dismiss an ugly or badly proportioned layout, especially one that is too large for the space allotted.

horst n [Mining] a block of strata that has been displaced between two fault planes along which strata movement has taken place.

hosepiping n [Film] bad hand-held 8mm camerawork, in which the camera is noticeably shaking; the shots produced end up looking like a hosepipe spraying out water at random.

hospitable word n [Logology] a term coined by US logophile Willard R. Espy: a word that becomes a different word if another letter is added to it.

hospital hobo, also **hospital addict** n [US] [Medicine] a patient suffering from Munchhausen's syndrome: one who tours the hospitals asking for admission and claiming to have a series of imaginary but highly dramatic illnesses

hospitalitis n [US] [Medicine] the crankiness and irritability which follow a lengthy stay in hospital.

hospitality room, also **hospitality suite** 1. n [TV] a reception room at a TV studio set aside for giving guests a drink before and/or after they appear on a programme. 2. n [Business] rooms or suites hired or set up specially when a company wishes to impress favoured customers at a conference or major exhibition, eg: the Motor Show. Major sporting events – test matches, horse races,

H

etc – are also very popular for such company entertaining, especially by the sponsor of the event, and if there are no suites to be hired at the venue, then the company often erects a large marquee.

hospitalised *a* [*US*] [*Medicine*] referring to a patient who has become acclimatised to the niceties and nuances of the hospital system, personalities, etc.

host 1. *n* [*Computing*] a host computer which is attached to a network and provides services other than simply acting as a **store-and-forward** processor or communication switch. Such computers are divided into 'servers', which provide resources within the network, and 'users' which access them. **2.** *n* [*Computing*] in distributed processing, this is the computer that controls a multiple computer installation. **3.** *n* [*Computing*] a computer used to prepare programs to be run on other systems.

hostile ice *n* [*Navy*] the Polar ice canopy when it is so densely frozen that it leaves no areas through which a nuclear submarine may surface.

hostility containment *n* [*Military*] a state of military invulnerability that would guarantee the defeat of any aggressive action against the US; devotees of space-based weaponry consider such arms are the best way to achieve this 'full control of US destiny' and 'long-term security for the earth's population' (from a pamphlet issued by Rockwell Rocketdyne).

hosting 1. *n* [*TV*] the presentation of a programme by a 'frontman' or woman. **2.** *n* [*US*] [*TV*] the engaging of an 'expert' to appear at the start of an imported programme, especially a major series, and explain its niceties to the American audience; thus Alistair Cooke, a token upper-class mid-Atlantic man, was used to explain the TV version of Evelyn Waugh's 'Brideshead Revisited' when it was screened on 'Masterpiece Theatre'.

hostler 1. *n* [*US*] [*Railways*] a fireman who moves engines around and in a **roundhouse**, where they are serviced and repaired. **2.** *n* [*US*] [*Road transport*] a worker in a terminal yard who parks vehicles for their drivers; it comes from 'ostler', whose job was to perform the same duty for horses at inns and taverns.

hot 1. *a* [*Espionage*] any office, room, facility, etc. in the CIA which contains classified material and which is thus subject to extra security measures. **2.** *a* [*Film*] See **bankable**. **3.** *a* [*Film*] an idea or **property** not as yet exposed either to a producer or to the public. **4.** *a* [*Industrial relations*] associated with or affected by an industrial dispute; thus a 'hot cargo' clause is an agreement whereby a lorry owner promises not to handle the goods of a firm with whom his union is in dispute. **5.** *a* [*Media*] in the definition of Marshall McLuhan (1911–1980), a hot medium is one that is full of detail and information and which requires little

or no involvement on the part of the listener or the viewer; radio is a hot medium, TV a cool one. **6.** *a* [*Police*] referring to anything that has been stolen: goods, vehicles, money, etc. **7.** *a* [*Radio*] a notice – saying 'hot' – is placed on a tape machine to indicate that the tape wound on to it is being edited and that it should be left in place, however much the next person wishes to use the machine for their own work. **8.** *a* [*Science*] radio-active.

hot belly *n* [*US*] [*Medicine*] any abdominal problem that requires immediate surgery; eg: appendicitis.

hot bill 1. *n* [*Banking*] a bill of exchange which is due to become payable very soon. **2.** *n* [*Banking*] a Treasury bill which has only just been bought and will therefore not become payable for some time.

hot bills *n pl* [*UK*] [*Government*] newly issued Treasury bills; those bills of exchange that are issued by the Government in large amounts every week and which are redeemable in three months.

hot brass *n* [*Navy*] top senior officers in the service.

hot busted *a* [*US*] [*Crime*] pursued and subsequently arrested on suspicion, which is duly borne out, of possession, sale or similar involvement with drugs. See also **cold busted**.

hot buttons *n pl* [*US*] [*TV*] those special buttons used by a home viewer to 'vote' or otherwise participate in programmes on **interactive** television.

hot cross bun *n* [*Music*] the coda: a section of a movement added at the end to clinch matters there rather than to develop the music any further. It comes from notation in the score.

hot dog 1. *n* [*Surfing*] a particular type of board, somewhere between the usual size and the larger **gun**; thus 'hot dog', also 'hot dogger', is the person who uses such a board to perform stylish, intricate manoeuvres. **2.** *n* [*Skiing*] an exceptional skier, who likes to display his/her abilities; thus one who is a show-off as well as a star.

hot engines *n pl* [*Aerospace*] piston engines; any engine that tends to overheat and break down.

hot frame *n* [*Film*] an overexposed frame, which produces an extremely bright image.

hot issue *n* [*Stock market*] a new issue of stock – usually **common** stock – that is so popular that its premium price immediately rises to several points above **par**.

hot landing 1. *n* [*Flying*] a landing at too great a speed. **2.** *n* [*Air Force*] a landing under enemy fire.

hot line *n* [*Military*] a telex link between the White House and the Kremlin designed for use during any international crisis and specifically during a potential escalation towards nuclear war. It was established by President Kennedy and Premier Khruschev in the 'Hot Line' Agreement, 1963, and the 'Hot Line Moderation' Agreement of 1971 added two additional circuits which use satellite communications systems. Current moves are aimed to update the hot line with modern computer technology, but this decision has not been finalised.

hot load *n* [*US*] [*Road transport*] a rush shipment of cargo.

hot lot *n* [*UK*] [*Police*] the Flying Squad. See also **heavy mob, Sweeney.**

hot money, also **refugee money** 1. [*Banking*] money that has been attracted from abroad, where investors/savers may be threatened by political instability, to a centre where it can be saved/invested in safety. 2. [*Finance*] money owned by investors who move from one investment to another at the slightest shift in the rate of return. 3. [*Finance*] money that is kept moving from currency to currency in a bid to insure against making a loss if any one currency suddenly starts to depreciate noticeably against the others. 4. [*Finance*] all money that has been obtained illicitly, through fraud, theft or other swindle.

hot notcher *n* [*Clothing*] a machine incorporating a heated blade which makes position marks on the edge of cut fabric parts.

hot potato routing *n* [*Communications*] a method of routing in which a **packet** of data is sent onwards from a node as soon as possible, even though this route may not be the optimum choice for transmission.

hot pursuit *n* [*Military*] an internationally accepted manoeuvre whereby a military force is permitted to cross a national border in 'hot pursuit' of enemy (usually terrorist) troops who have made an incursion into that force's home country; such a pursuit is neither hindered nor is it seen as an invasion or a military threat.

hot rock *n* [*Aerospace*] an inexperienced pilot, eager to show off by taking risks.

hot sawing *n* [*Metallurgy*] cutting hot steel to length either during or immediately after rolling, using a circular saw.

hot set *n* [*Film, TV*] a set that has been lit, **dressed** and generally prepared for shooting.

hot sheet *n* [*Police*] a list of stolen cars, outstanding traffic fines, etc. circulated to all policemen concerned – the traffic dept., the beat officers, etc – for their use on a given day.

hot ship *n* [*Merchant navy*] a vessel known to be carrying contraband.

hot shoe *n* [*Photography*] a socket – the 'shoe' – on a camera to which a flashgun can be connected and which serves as an automatic electrical connection for lighting the flashgun.

hot shop *n* [*Advertising*] a small informal, creative agency of a type that flourished particularly in the 1960s and which, although providing fewer in-house services, was successful in pulling away accounts from the major agencies. See also **boutique agency.**

hot shot *n* [*Rodeo*] an electrical shock given to a

horse waiting in the chute, to ensure that it bucks as required in the ring.

hot spot 1. *n* [*Forestry*] a particularly active part of a forest fire; thus 'hot-spotting' is the checking of the spread of a fire by concentrating specifically on hot spots. 2. *n* [*Glass-making*] a thin spot in a refractory structure brought about by wear, usually in side blocks. 3. *n* [*Metallurgy*] in iron-founding this is an area of heat concentration usually found where sections are joined in a casting; it is also formed by the stream of metal that is entering the mould. 4. *n* [*Metallurgy*] those parts of an ingot or casting which are notably porous.

hot standby *n* [*Computing, Communications*] a backup system which is automatically switched on when the primary system breaks down. See also **cold standby, warm standby.**

hot stock 1. *n* [*Stock market*] a newly issued stock that rises quickly in price. See also **hot issue.** 2. *n* [*Stock market*] a stolen stock.

hot stove *n* [*Pop music*] an open bribe offered to a disc jockey to promote a particular record.

hot switch *n* [*TV*] the change of coverage from one event to another without any transitional **voice-over** from the announcer to smooth over the **cut.**

hot tap *n* [*Gas industry*] the connection of branch piping to an operating line and the tapping of the operating line while it is still under pressure ('hot').

hot tear, also **hot crack** *n* [*Metallurgy*] in iron founding this is a casting defect that emerges while the casting is still cooling; it is usually caused when full solid contraction is in some way restricted.

hot zone *n* [*Printing*] in word processing this is an area of adjustable width immediately to the left of the right hand margin in which words may overlap the prescribed line length and may have to be hyphenated or transferred to the next line.

hotbed *n* [*Metallurgy*] a grilled flooring over which iron and steel materials are conveyed by an automatic conveyor for cooling.

hotbox *n* [*US*] [*Railways*] a car with an overheated driving mechanism.

hotbunk *v* [*Navy*] said of ratings on a crowded submarine who share accommodation: those coming off watch take over the sleeping quarters of those who are beginning their turn of duty.

hotchpot *v* [*Banking*] to bring into account sums received by a beneficiary under a will during the lifetime of the testator, so that his share of the total sum available shall not exceed that of the other beneficiaries of equal title under the same will.

hotdog *n* [*US*] [*Medicine*] a patient exhibiting notably eccentric or bizarre behaviour; he/she is usually suffering from psychiatric problems.

hot-dogging *n* [*Skiing*] an obsolete name for free-

H

style skiing; it is sometimes still used to describe **mogul** turns.

hot-pot *n* [*Horse-racing*] a horse that has been very heavily backed.

hot-sheet trade *n* [*Commerce, Sex*] hotels that rent out rooms for short periods, usually to prostitutes or clandestine lovers.

hotshot 1. *n* [*Drugs*] a means of disposing of a customer who is no longer discreet or is trying to cause trouble for the dealer: he/she is sold either absolutely pure heroin – the strength of which will cause an automatic overdose in one who is only used to heavily adulterated drugs, or a substitute for heroin such as some poison (usually strychnine) or battery acid scraped from a car battery; either of these, when injected, will cause death. **2.** *n* [*US*] [*Railways*] a fast freight train. See also **drag 10.**

hot-shot *n* [*Engineering*] a wind-tunnel in which an arc discharge in a pressurised chamber is used to produce a hypersonic pulse of gas in an evacuated chamber; such tunnels are used to test space vehicles.

hot-spot *n* [*Theatre, Film*] any area of a lit set that is notably brighter than the rest of the set.

hot-spotter *n* [*Military*] one of those theorists on the results of a nuclear explosion who believe that the resultant radiation would accumulate in 'hot spots' – areas of concentrated radiation – rather than simply spreading evenly throughout the whole area affected. The hot spots so created would also be the sites of the maximum biological damage. See also **averager.**

hotstuff *v* [*UK*] [*Military*] to steal, to misappropriate.

hotters *n* [*Navy*] Worcestershire sauce.

hot-turn *v* [*Military*] an aircraft does this when it returns to base, refuels, re-arms and takes off for a new sortie without ever turning off its engines, which thus remain 'hot' during the 'turn'.

houlette *n* [*Magic*] any deck of cards used for an **effect** in which a chosen card is made to rise up; it comes from Fr. meaning the 'hook' of an umbrella, a hand-ladle.

hound 1. *n* [*US*] [*Road transport*] See **big gray dog. 2.** *v* [*Shooting*] to hunt with dogs.

hounds teeth *n* [*Printing*] white space created by justification that runs through lines of type.

house 1. *n* [*US*] [*Car salesmen*] a car dealership. **2.** *n* [*Theatre*] the auditorium. **3.** *n* [*Theatre*] the permanent management of a theatre, as opposed to that of the touring company, which is only there temporarily. **4.** *n* [*Theatre*] the audience who, depending on their numbers and their response to the performance, are either a 'good house' or a 'poor house'. **5.** *v* [*UK*] [*Police*] to trail a suspect to their home address and to make sure they are regularly there until such time as it might be desirable to interview or arrest them.

house cheque *n* [*Banking*] a cheque drawn on and presented for payment at the same bank, though possibly at a different branch; such cheques do not move through the clearing house.

house deal *n* [*US*] [*Car salesmen*] a sale concluded by the management without the paying of a commission to a salesman.

house drop *n* [*TV*] the length of coaxial cable that connects each individual house or building to the feeder line of a cable network.

house job *n* [*Journalism*] a piece written by one member of a newspaper's staff in praise of the work of another; or, marginally less venally, a piece which generally criticises that work, and thus gives it some publicity, whether good or bad. See also **log-rolling, market letter.**

house show *n* [*Advertising, Business*] a presentation offered by a production company to a prospective client, featuring the best examples of that company's previous work.

house style *n* [*Business*] the corporate **handwriting** or group identity which finds its visual form in the company logo, letterheads, house magazine, advertising, and similar commonly seen manifestations. All such designs contribute to establishing the company in the public eye.

house, the *n* [*Stock market*] either the premises of the Stock Exchange or its trading floor. See also **floor 5.**

house tic-tac *n* [*Gambling*] a tic-tac man who acts for a small, subscribing group of bookmakers.

house-burn *n* [*Tobacco*] tobacco that has been hung in a barn that lacks adequate ventilation.

households *n pl* [*UK*] [*Postal services*] any items, other than stamped and franked mail, that are distributed by postmen to all relevant households.

house-keeping *n* [*Computing*] those operations performed by a computer which make its work possible, but which have nothing to do with its actual running of programs, calculation of figures and general performance.

housekeeping bill *n* [*US*] [*Politics*] ostensibly a minor bill designed to deal with the alteration or modification of some legal or legislative technicality; however this apparent insignificance can be used by an administration to slip in something infinitely more important which is hidden among the sub-clauses. The bill must therefore be scanned scrupulously by the opposition.

housewife 1. *n* [*Navy*] pronounced 'huzzif', this is a small fabric case that can be rolled up and contains a sailor's all-purpose mending and sewing kit for use at sea. **2.** *n* [*TV*] a broadcasting **daypart** that is assumed for advertising purposes to capitalise on the housewife audience – from 10am to 3pm.

housewife time *n* [*Advertising*] radio advertising slots positioned between the morning and afternoon **drive times.**

how *n* [*Magic*] the secret of how a trick is performed.

how–2 *a* [*Science fiction*] said of an article describing 'how to' do something.

howgozit *n* [*Aerospace*] a dial that shows how much fuel is remaining in the aircraft's tanks thus enabling the pilot to calculate, on the basis of the distance to be travelled, whether it will be possible to complete his journey home safely.

howlback *n* [*Audio*] unwanted positive acoustic feedback that produces absolute or near-continuous oscillation in the signal.

howlround *n* [*Audio*] See **howlback.**

how-to *n* [*Video*] an instructional or educational programme sold on cassette or disc; eg: cooking, keep-fit, etc, often with a large element of entertainment to leaven the tutorial.

HPV *n* [*Business*] abbr of **holocyclatic point of view** pseudo-Greek coinage for an appreciation of the broad view, the 'big picture'.

HSD *n* [*Navy*] abbr of **higher submarine detector** the petty officer operating the asdic on board a destroyer.

huck out, also **hog out** *v* [*Military*] to give something a thorough scrubbing out, a 'spring cleaning'.

huckster room *n* [*Science fiction*] the area at a convention for the sale of science fiction books, magazines, artwork and allied paraphernalia.

huddle 1. *n* [*Cards*] in bridge this is a period of thought in which a player considers his/her next call or play. 2. *n* [*Fleet air arm*] a squadron briefing on an aircraft carrier. 3. also **pow-wow** *n* [*Entertainment*] a meeting, usually for business purposes.

hugger-mugger *n* [*US*] [*Journalism*] a sentence that is (over-) crammed with facts.

hull *n* [*Military*] the chassis of a tank.

hum *n* [*Audio*] a fault in sound reproduction which involves interference from an unwanted low frequency tone.

hum bars *n pl* [*TV*] interference on the screen which is seen as broad horizontal moving or stationary bars; they are caused by a variation in the DC power supply at the AC power supply frequency.

human asset accounting *n* [*Management*] attempts to measure in monetary terms the value of a company's employees to that company.

human ecology *n* [*Sociology*] See **urban ecology.**

human factors engineering *n* [*Industrial relations*] the design of factories, offices, plants, etc. with an emphasis on the position and needs of the human beings employed in them.

human potential movement *n* [*New therapies*] an amalgam of various mental therapies, including the many cults that invariably seem to start in California, and a number of simplified theories that have trimmed classical psychoanalysis of the need for any real dedication by the patient, replacing it with a simple 'cure' available to anyone who is able to pay the fees; this is somewhat removed from Freud's original conception.

human resource administration *n* [*Business*] an amplified title for the corporation's personnel department, dealing with hiring, firing, pensions and allied aspects of employee life.

humanist art *n* [*Art*] a form of art that attempts to struggle against the increasing domination of all areas of life by technology; it is divided into four categories: political, absurdist, existential and metaphysical.

humboldt *n* [*Logging*] a wedge-shaped piece of wood that is cut or sawn from a standing tree.

humbug *n* [*Sex*] a pimp's term for a trumped up, phoney charge levelled by the police. See also **hummer.**

humdinger *n* [*Electronics*] a voltage divider connected across the heater circuit of a valve with the variable tap connected to the source of a fixed potential, so that hum introduced by the heater can be reduced by suitably biasing it with respect to the cathode.

humid *n* [*Cheese-making*] that part of a cheese which is neither **casein** nor fat nor mineral salts, but is a residual amount of **whey** in suspension.

humint *n* [*Military*] abbr of **human intelligence** the traditional intelligence network of spies who collect information themselves, rather than the impersonal surveillance by electronic technology that has become increasingly common. See also **comint, elint, sigint, telint.**

hummels *n pl* [*Deer-stalking*] stags that remain without horns throughout their lives; it comes from Old English 'hamelian' meaning to mutilate.

hummer *n* [*US*] [*Police*] a fake arrest, made on the least pretext, usually in order to allow police to make a search of the suspect. See also **humbug.**

hump master *n* [*US*] [*Railways*] the employee who controls the points in a **hump yard.**

hump speed *n* [*Technology*] the speed of a hovercraft at which the drag of the water is at its maximum.

hump yard *n* [*US*] [*Railways*] a modern **yard** with an incline which uses gravity to switch cars.

humpback *n* [*Logging*] a sawyer.

humped off *a* [*Navy*] reported to the captain for punishment.

humpty-dumpty *n* [*US*] [*Politics*] this comes from the Lewis Carroll and nursery-rhyme character: a loser, anyone who is riding for a fall.

hunching *n* [*Marbles*] moving one's hand forward when shooting.

hundred-and-elevens *n pl* [*US*] [*Cattlemen*] the marks of spurs on the sides of a horse.

hung up *a* [*Stock market*] an investor is said to be 'hung up' if his/her portfolio of stocks has fallen below its purchase price and he/she would, if selling, thus face a loss.

hungry *a* [*Painting*] used of a surface that is particularly porous and which has not been adequately satisfied by such coats of paint as have

H

been applied; a hungry surface will create a patchy finish.

hungry sand n [*Building, Plastering*] sand that will not retain the water when mixed with it.

hung-up a [*New therapies*] depending on the personality of the speaker, the statement 'I'm hung-up' can imply a degree of worry anywhere on a nervous spectrum from mild depression to a full-scale obsession that trembles on the edge of a breakdown and/or hospitalisation.

hungus a [*Computing*] huge, enormous, out-size, barely if at all manageable.

hunt v [*Mechanics*] a machine oscillates alternately either side of a neutral point, or runs alternately fast and slow because of insufficiently stable controls; thus 'hunting' is the activity of a machine in oscillating around an equilibrium speed, position or state.

hunt foil v [*Hunting*] to run over the same track more than once.

hunter-killer n [*Navy*] a naval vessel designed to pursue and then destroy hostile shipping; the target is often a submarine, but hunter-killer submarines also exist, fulfilling a similar role from beneath the sea.

hunting 1. n [*Flying*] the action of a plane in flight which is experiencing periodic lateral instability. 2. n [*Railways*] the swaying from side to side of the carriage or truck. 3. a [*TV*] referring to the malfunction of a camera or videotape machine which will not maintain a constant speed.

hunting licences n pl [*Finance*] official borrowing mandates.

hurdle n [*Coal-mining*] a temporary screen or curtain that deflects the air upwards against the roof to disperse gas.

hurdle rate n [*Management*] the minimum level of earning power, established by the management, that an investment project must guarantee before it is undertaken by a company.

hurricane deck n [*Navy*] the highest deck on a ship.

hurry 1. n [*Mining*] the ore chute. 2. n [*Music*] a tremolo in the strings or a roll on the drums used in the score of a film or TV programme to indicate an exciting situation.

hush puppies n pl [*UK*] [*Railways*] silencing equipment on a diesel rail car.

hustler n [*Sex*] a male prostitute who deals only with homosexuals but who will never admit to being a homosexual himself and who will only take an active, never a passive role in his sexual encounters. Other terms are: ass pro, bird taker, buff boy, bunny, business boy, career boy, cocktail, coin collector, commercial queer, crack salesman, dick peddler, fag boy, flesh peddler, foot soldier, gigolo, he-whore, Hollywood hustler (one who is a little too smooth), party boy, puto (Sp. meaning whore), rent, rent-boy, sport, sporting goods, trabajado (Sp. meaning worked over), working girl, etc.

hustling drawers n pl [*US*] [*Crime*] specially designed underwear, containing large pockets for hiding booty, which are used by shoplifters.

hutch n [*UK*] [*Buses*] an empty London Transport bus. See also **rabbits 1.**

hybrid n [*Computing*] a machine that uses both **analog** and digital methods.

hybridise v [*Business*] in gardening, this is to make a new species by combining two others; thus, in business, it means taking two companies and combining them so as to produce a third, entirely different one. It is also assumed that the hybrid company will be stronger and livelier than its progenitors.

hydroneck n [*UK*] [*Road transport*] a detachable front-end of a semi-trailer, with a built-in hydraulic bed raising and lowering operation.

hygiene factor, also **maintenance factor** n [*Management*] any aspect of a job that may contribute to the dissatisfaction of an employee but not to his/her satisfaction; ie: working conditions, remuneration, inter-employee relations, management style. If these factors fall beneath a certain standard the employee is unhappy, if they achieve that standard, they are merely taken for granted. See also **motivators.**

hygienic management n [*Management*] a management style characterised by high wages, employee benefits, good working conditions and good supervision – all these **hygiene factors** are assumed to create happier, harder-working employees; such a management style is in effect a sophisticated update of traditionally paternalistic management.

hymnbook n [*TV*] a term used by the director for the camera script.

hypallage n [*Literary criticism*] the interchange in syntactic relationship between two terms for the sake of style or brevity; eg: 'a moody forkful', etc.

hype 1. n, v [*Entertainment*] the building up of an act, a record, a film, a performer, etc. by exaggerating its potential appeal and using promotion and advertising to the maximum extent. The implication of hype is always one of slightly fraudulent huckstering, but a hype that succeeds is a merchandising success, even if one that fails is only a hype. 2. also **the sting** n [*US*] [*Crime*] the 'short-change racket': a swindle which involves persuading a sales clerk to give change for $10 instead of $5. One who specialises in this is 'on the hype'.

hyperspace n [*Sociology*] a term to denote a full and exhaustive range of possibilities; (its usage is marginally connected to the more popular concept of hyperspace as the farthest boundaries of the universe, a fictional creation of science fiction authors).

hyperurbanism n [*Linguistics*] the attempt by those who lack the speech patterns and accents that are considered most prestigious to gain them, often at the cost of making gauche errors while so doing.

hyphenates 1. *n pl* [*US*] [*Sociology*] the various racial groups, other than blacks and Jews and WASPs, who make up the US and who tend to hyphenate their names: Mexican-Americans, Irish-Americans, Polish-Americans, etc. See also **ethnics**. 2. *n pl* [*TV, Film*] writer-director, writer-producer, director-cameraman, etc; these are the various two-job permutations worked by individuals in TV and film which are denoted by the linking hyphen.

hypocentre *n* [*Military*] the ground directly beneath a nuclear explosion. See also **ground zero.**

hypocoristic *n* [*Literary criticism*] relating to or characterised by pet names or baby talk; it comes from Gk. 'hypokoristikos' meaning 'diminutive'.

hypoid axle *n* [*UK*] [*Road transport*] a design of rear axle in which the pinion driving the crown wheel is set off-centre to reduce friction and thus wear on the gearing.

hypophora *n* [*Literary criticism*] the rhetorical posing of questions to oneself, and then answering them; thinking aloud.

hypostatise *v* [*Literary criticism*] to reify a concept; to treat a concept or a name as being concrete and real; eg: 'Honesty demands . . .', etc; it comes from Gk. 'hypostatos' meaning 'substantially existing'.

hypotaxis *n* [*Literary criticism*] a sentence style that uses subordinate clauses, carefully choosing the individual words and their connections – a style more common in writing than in speech; it comes from Gk. for 'under arrangement'.

hypothecate *v* [*Commerce*] to put up one's goods as a security for a loan without actually handing over the goods themselves on acceptance of the loan.

hypothetical point *n* [*Air travel*] a means of extending cheap fares by creating a fictional destination which one never actually visits but which must be included in one's itinerary – either before, during or after one's journey; once this destination is included, the maximum permitted milage, against which bargain-fares are calculated, is increased and thus a fare can legitimately be reduced by bending but not breaking any rules.

hypotyposis *n* [*Literary criticism*] a vivid, picturesque description, especially one in which something is represented as if it were present.

H.Y.S. *a* [*US*] [*Medicine*] abbr of **hysterical.**

hysteresis *n* [*Computing*] See **backlash 3.**

hysterical historicals *n pl* [*Publishing*] a genre of best-selling fiction which is based on the traditional historical romance, but which includes greater amounts of violence and sex, usually combined in the form of rape, sanitised only marginally by its 18th century or Regency frills and furbelows. See also **bodice-ripper, gay gothics.**

hysteron proteron *n* [*Literary criticism*] a figure of speech which reverses the logical or chronological order of things; it comes from Gk. for 'latter former'.

I

I am in the room *v phr* [*Auctions*] an indication by the auctioneer that bidding for a given lot has successfully exceeded the **reserve** price.

I formation *n* [*US*] [*Football*] an offensive formation in which the quarterback, standing directly behind the centre, and the other backs form an I-shaped file perpendicular to the line of scrimmage.

I hope it keeps fine for you *excl* [*Theatre*] See **break a leg!**

I statement *n* [*New therapies*] a therapeutic technique that forces the patient to reconsider his/her words by turning every statement that starts off 'You . . .' into one that starts 'I . . .'.

iafd *n* [*US*] [*Police*] abbr of **intentionally administered fatal dose.**

IBBR *n* [*Banking*] abbr of **Inter-Bank Market 'Bid' Rate** the rate of interest which first-class banks are prepared to pay for deposits for a specified period. See also **IBOR.**

IBMable *a* [*Computing*] said of any hard- or

software that can be made compatible with the standards set by the IBM Corporation.

IBOR *n* [*Banking*] acro **Inter-Bank Offered Rate** the rate of interest at which funds are offered on loan for a specified period in the inter-bank market to first-class banks. Offers are subject to availability and may be limited. The LIBOR (London IBOR) is a possible alternative to a bank's base rate as a means of calculating the interest charged on loans. See also **IBBR.**

ICBM *n* [*Military*] abbr of **Inter-Continental Ballistic Missile** a missile that is capable of penetrating targets in either the USA or the USSR after being fired from a site on the territory of the opposite superpower or from a strategic submarine. As defined by both sides in the **SALT II** talks: 'land based launchers of ballistic missiles capable of a range in excess of the shortest distance between the north-east border of the US and the north-west border of the continental part of the USSR, that is, a range in excess of 5,500 kilometres'.

ice 1. *n* [*Gambling*] bribes paid to police and/or politicians to ensure that a casino or other gambling establishment is not raided or otherwise disrupted. **2.** *n* [*US*] [*Theatre*] a tip or premium paid by a ticket agent to the Box Office treasurer or the producer for an extra supply of tickets in addition to those he is usually allotted. **3.** *n* [*US*] [*Theatre*] the premium charged by an agency on ticket sales.

ice cream *n* [*US*] [*Carpenters*] overtime.

ice house *n* [*US*] [*Garment trade*] a cold storage warehouse or department where fur stocks are held.

ice time *n* [*Ice-hockey*] those periods during which a player is on the ice, rather than those when he remains in reserve.

iceberg company *n* [*Business*] a company where two-thirds of the trading is carried on at a lower than break-even point.

iceberg principle *n* [*Marketing*] based on the psychological principle that humanity nurtures many prime desires 'beneath the surface', advertising hopes to trigger such less immediately apparent desires in its campaigns. See also **iceberg theory.**

iceberg theory *n* [*Politics*] the thesis that under normal conditions only approximately 3% of the population are either ideologically or idealistically inclined; Marxists believe that so low a figure can be increased if the political environment is altered through agitation, activism, propaganda, etc.

icebox 1. *n* [*US*] [*Medicine*] the hospital morgue. See also **cooler 2. 2.** *n* [*US*] [*Prisons*] the prison coroner's office and laboratory.

icebreaker *n* [*Theatre*] a fast, snappy song and dance routine for the chorus girls that comes early on in a musical.

iced tea, also **Long Island tea** *n* [*US*] [*Bars*]

any clear liquor – usually gin, vodka, white rum – flavoured and coloured with cola.

icer *n* [*Entertainment*] an ice show, performed on a skating rink.

icing *n* [*Ice-hockey*] an extreme and usually illegal form of clearing that entails sending the puck across an opponent's goal line (but not into the net) in order to keep the opponents from shooting from near one's own goal.

iconics *n* [*Art*] a proposed science that would stand for pictures as linguistics stands for language. Iconics would be concerned with that body of knowledge common to art and aesthetics, cognitive and perceptual psychology, education, learning linguistics, semantics and computer graphics.

I.D. *n* [*Book trade*] abbr of **Independent Distributor.**

ID 1. *v* [*Police*] abbr of **identity** meaning to identify. **2.** *n* [*Radio*] a station's name, theme tune and 'logo', the jingle that goes with the name.

IDB *n* [*Stock exchange*] abbr of **inter-dealer broker** a middleman between two **market-makers** who matches deals between anonymous buyers and sellers.

I.D.B. *n* [*Gemstones*] abbr of **Illicit Diamond Buyer.**

ideal copy *n* [*Book collecting*] this term is used in referring to books published prior to 1800, when corrections were made at the printing rather than at the proof stage. It is a book that ideally shows the final intentions of the author, the printer and the publisher in creating the finished work – so far as this can be established.

ideal format *n* [*Photography*] a negative format of 60x70mm; it is an alternative to the 35mm format of 24x36mm.

ideal point *n* [*Marketing*] consumers' perceptions of the ideal attributes of a product, used in attitude models and perceptual mapping.

ideational 1. *a* [*Sociology*] this was coined in 1937 by P. A. Sorokin to describe the sort of culture that places the spiritual above the material. **2.** *n* [*Education*] a misreading by 'progressive' teachers who use the word to mean only that some of their pupils can use ideas and imagination and grasp some form of theories.

idiolect *n* [*Linguistics*] an individual's unique version of the common language; either during his/her whole life, or during a phase of that life.

idiosyncrasy *n* [*Medicine*] an individual's hypersensitivity to a particular drug or any other substance which can be swallowed, injected or sniffed and which has an adverse effect on that person.

idiot, also **idiot stick** *n* [*Mining*] a shovel.

idiot board, also **idiot card, idiot sheet** *n* [*TV*] a board held up next to the camera, when there is no autocue machine, to provide cues and prompts for an announcer or TV performer; these cues can extend to writing out an entire script for an actor whose memory is failing.

I

idiot box *n* [*TV, Video*] a teleprompter device.

idiot girl *n* [*TV*] a member of the TV crew who has to hold up the successive **idiot boards**.

idiot juice *n* [*US*] [*Prisons*] a mixture of nutmeg and water drunk as an intoxicant.

idiot light *n* [*Technology*] a warning light, usually red, that goes on to indicate a mechanical malfunction on an appliance.

idiot stick **1.** *n* [*Logging*] a peeling stick, used to remove bark. **2.** *n* [*US*] [*Painting*] a felt roller used to apply paint. **3.** *n* [*US*] [*Painting*] an extension that can be added to a roller to extend the painter's reach.

idiot tape *n* [*Computing*] an input tape for a computer typesetting which has been perforated but does not include directions for formatting the copy.

idiothetic *a* [*Sociology*] used to describe methods of study of individuals, unique persons, events or things. See also **nomothetic**.

idle character *n* [*Communications*] a control character transmitted on a telecommunications line when there is no data to be transmitted; this character will not be displayed in any way by the receiving terminal.

idle money *n* [*Finance*] money that is lodged in bank accounts and is not being used for investment or speculation.

idle time **1.** *n* [*Computing*] a situation in which the machine is on and ready, but is not yet performing any job. **2.** *n* [*Computing*] the period during which the operator is preparing various forms of software and allied media for the next computer operation. **3.** *n* [*Transport*] in London Transport bus and underground depots, this is the time when a maintenance man has completed one job and is waiting to be allotted the next.

idler **1.** *n* [*Audio*] a wheel used in a tape recorder or turn-table mechanism to transmit the drive between rotating components, usually plastic or rubber tyred. **2.** *n* [*Coal-mining*] a free running roller that supports a conveyor belt.

idols of the cave *n pl* [*Philosophy*] the second of Francis Bacon's **idols of thought**; these are individual weaknesses from which humanity suffers, due to the selectiveness of learnings, one's own partialities and particularities. See also **idols of the market place, theatre, tribe**.

idols of the marketplace *n pl* [*Philosophy*] the third of Francis Bacon's **idols of thought**; these are the confusions and distortions that arise from human communications and language, specifically the inconsistencies in the meaning of words. See also **idols of the cave, theatre, tribe**.

idols of the theatre *n pl* [*Philosophy*] the fourth of Francis Bacon's **idols of thought**; this refers to the fallibility of humanity in the face of so many varied and confusing, ephemeral and false systems of philosophy, history and theology, which are 'so many stage plays'. See also **idols of the cave, market place, tribe**.

idols of the tribe *n pl* [*Philosophy*] the first of Francis Bacon's **idols of thought**; they are the beliefs, dogmas and ideologies that arise from human nature, human senses and humanity's limited understanding. See also **idols of the cave, market place, theatre**.

idols of thought *n pl* [*Philosophy*] the term was coined by Francis Bacon (1561–1626) in the Novum Organum (1620) to cover the four essential fallacies that govern human behaviour. See **idols of the cave, idols of the marketplace, idols of the theatre, idols of the tribe**.

If God Permits *n* [*Navy*] whisky; it comes from the motto on the label on a bottle of White Horse whisky.

if I could . . . would you . . . ? *a* [*US*] [*Car salesmen*] a description of a sales technique whereby the salesman seeks a commitment from the buyer before committing himself.

IFF *n* [*Aerospace*] acro **Identification of Friend or Foe** transponder equipment installed on military aircraft and used to tell friendly and hostile aircraft apart.

iffy *a* [*UK*] [*Police*] suspect, dubious, dishonest.

igloo **1.** *n* [*Air travel*] the security cover placed over cargo consignments awaiting transportation. **2.** *n* [*Aerospace*] a specially protected area of an air base set aside for storing nuclear weapons. Thus 'igloo space' is an underground storage space, reinforced by concrete and steel, used for the storage of weapons and ammunition.

ignore character, also **fill character** *n* [*Computing*] a character used in transmission to fill an otherwise empty position and whose value is thus ignored.

IKBS *n* [*Computing*] abbr of **Intelligent Knowledge-Based Systems**.

ill *a* [*Espionage*] arrested on suspicion; taken in for questioning; imprisoned.

illegal *a* [*Computing*] referring to a program which has attempted to perform a non-existent or impossible instruction.

illegal character *n* [*Computing*] a character that is not in the **character set** of a given machine or a given programming language.

illegal instruction *n* [*Computing*] any process that a computer is unable to perform; illegal instructions can be inserted in a **debugging** process to provide an artificial break in the running of a program.

illegal operation *n* [*Computing*] any operation which the computer is unable to perform.

illegals *n pl* [*Espionage*] freelance agents who are contracted by the KGB as members of Soviet spy teams operating outside the USSR; such agents are controlled by special officers who, unlike many KGB officers abroad, are based outside the local embassy.

illegitimate **1.** *a* [*Horse-racing*] formerly used to describe steeplechases and jumping races as opposed to flat races. See also **flat, the sticks**. **2.**

I

a [*Theatre*] used of popular productions, with the emphasis on spectacle rather than on literary quality. See also **legitimate 2.**

illeism *n* [*Linguistics*] the use of the third-person singular pronoun to excess, especially when referring to oneself; it comes from Lat. 'ille' meaning 'he'. See also **nosism, tuism.**

illness addict *n* [*US*] [*Medicine*] a patient who claims various problems but reveals no symptoms of any disease. See also **crock 4.**

illo *n* [*Science fiction*] an illustration that is full-page, half-page, etc, rather than mere filler visuals. See also **fillo.**

illusion *n* [*Magic*] specifically, a stage trick, the largest type of magical **effect,** such as 'Sawing a Woman in Half' or Houdiniesque escapology. A development is the 'illusionette': an illusion that can be taken down and packed in a suitcase, but which still seems spectacular when assembled on stage.

image 1. *n* [*Computing*] data from one medium, eg: punch tape, that is recorded on another, eg: magnetic tape. **2.** *n* [*Radio*] interference that occurs in the form of a high-pitched whistle of constantly changing pitch, plus unwanted morse signals. **3.** *v* [*Sociology*] to accept or project an image; it is often used in place of the simpler 'imagine'.

imaginary museum *n* [*Art*] this is the great and ever-increasing body of accurate photographic reproductions of works of art which makes informed criticism and appreciation of such works possible without it ever being necessary to see the actual work; the term was coined by André Malraux in 'La Psychologie de l'art' (1947).

imaginary number *n* [*Mathematics*] any number whose square is negative and which cannot therefore exist in the number system.

imagism *n* [*Literary criticism*] a movement in poetry, launched around 1912 by Ezra Pound, Amy Lowell and others, which was subsequently seen as the turning point in English poetry's transition into modernism.

immediate data *n* [*Computing*] data that is contained in a program instruction rather than held in memory; such data is integral to the operation of the program.

immediate need sale *n* [*US*] [*Undertakers*] the purchase of a grave for a customer who is already dead, paid for by the surviving family and usually arranged by the undertaker. See also **pre-need sale.**

immie *n* [*Marbles*] the target marble in the game. See also **dib, duck, immie, peewee, mib.**

immunity bath *n* [*US*] [*Law*] a grant of immunity that allows a witness to confess to any crime without risking future prosecution.

imp *n* [*Science*] abbr of **indeterminate mass particle** a hypothetical nuclear particle that has no mass.

impact *n, v* [*Politics*] the effect, the result; it is often used verbally as in 'The cutbacks impacted the grass roots negatively'.

impact day *n* [*Stock market*] the day on which a public offer of shares is first announced to the market.

impacted *a* [*US*] [*Sociology*] referring to an urban area which is suffering problems that place an unusual and excessive strain on public resources, especially as a result of a sudden influx of new residents. Thus, 'impact aid' is federal economic aid to those schools where government employees are educated; 'impact area' is a community, eg: a military town, where a lower than average number of taxable properties limit public finances.

impaired physician *n* [*US*] [*Police*] a doctor who is known to suffer from drug or alcohol addiction.

imperatively co-ordinated association *n* [*Sociology*] any group which possesses an authority structure – the state, businesses, etc.

imperfections 1. *n pl* [*Book collecting*] surplus or missing sheets of a given work. **2.** *n pl* [*Printing*] letters that are missing from a font; hence letters that have to be cast to make up deficiencies in a font.

imperialism *n* [*Politics*] a synonym in communist terminology for capitalism: 'the highest form of capitalism' (Lenin). Its essential features are the concentration of capital, and the division of the world into financial and international monopolies. Soviet incursions into Afghanistan, Angola, etc. are criticised by the West as imperialism, as Russia attempts to draw these countries into the communist bloc.

implementation *n* [*Computing*] the installation of a new computer system, or some enhancement of an existing system. Implementation is the last step following a series of specifications, tests, and checks on the hardware and the programs it will run, and possibly the selection of the personnel to run it.

implicit notation *n* [*Art*] See **musical graphics.**

implied agency *n* [*Law*] an agency which is not stated, but which is assumed, eg: that of a wife to act for her husband in buying household goods. See also **agency.**

impossibilism *n* [*Politics*] the belief in, and advocacy of, a variety of Utopian ideals, usually referring to social reform, that can never actually or realistically be put into effect.

impractical, also **impracticable** *n* [*Theatre*] any piece of stage furniture or a prop that appears to be real and usable but in fact is not. See also **practical.**

impression *n* [*Clothing*] surface unevenness after pressing; especially around pockets, seams and similar areas of extra thickness.

impressionism 1. *n* [*Music*] a style of music epitomised by the work of Debussy in the 1880s, which substituted the harmonic system for the themes and structures of the Romantic composers (eg: Beethoven). **2.** *n* [*Art*] the work of a group of French artists – Monet, Degas, Renoir, Cézanne, etc – which stands as the source of the bulk of 20th century art; their movement was launched at a major exhibition in 1874; it concentrated on the movements of light, disregarded sombre colours and outlines, and generally stood for lightness and gaiety.

imprest *n* [*Commerce*] a sum of money given to someone by a firm and which is to be spent by that person for specific purposes defined by the firm.

imprint *v* [*Naturalists*] in animal behaviour, this is to establish a pattern of trust and recognition, usually as regards the young of the same species.

improved *a* [*Building*] said of wood: thin sheets of wood attached to each other by synthetic resin. This is intended to improve their resistance to warping, shrinking, etc.

improved cylinder *n* [*Shooting*] a gun barrel with a slight **choke.**

improved war outcome *n* [*Military*] the strategic aim of limiting war damage to the population and resources of one's own nation and its allies, and of improving, if possible, the military-political outcome of a war. Such a war would entail a **counterforce** rather than **countervalue** strategy.

improver *n* [*Industry*] an employee who is willing to work for low money or no money in order to improve his knowledge of the job.

impulses *n pl* [*Government*] bureaucratic signals which the leaders of two states involved in high-level discussions will send to their respective civil servants and negotiators as a spur to the drawing up of an agreement or treaty.

impulsive noise *n* [*Communications*] short bursts of interference, separated by long periods of satisfactory communication; such impulses can be provided by the ignition system on a car, etc.

imputation *n* [*Economics*] an economic theory of value whereby value is attributed to productive resources in accordance with their contribution to the value of their products.

in *a* [*US*] [*Railways*] off duty at one's home terminal.

in and out *n* [*Hunting*] two fences that are close together, but not close enough to be negotiated in one jump.

in and out trading *n* [*Stock market*] the buying and selling of the same shares within a short period.

in one (*US*), **in a front cloth** (*UK*) *adv* [*Theatre*] referring to a scene that is played in an imaginary area bounded by a 'line' that extends from the farthest downstage left wing to the farthest downstage right wing; thus, 'in two' means the 'line' is drawn from the second left to right wings; 'in three' means the 'line' runs from

left to right three-quarters of the way up the stage; 'in four' means the 'line' runs from left to right upstage.

in run *n* [*US*] [*Skiing*] the distance on a ski jump from the start to the take-off. See also **out run.**

inactive bond crowd *n* [*US*] [*Stock market*] See **cabinet crowd.**

in-and-out trader *n* [*Stock market*] a trader who buys and sells the same security in a single day, hoping to make a quick profit from price fluctuations.

in-basket situation *n* [*Business*] this refers to the 'in' and 'out' trays of the traditional office desk; thus it is a problem that has arrived for consideration but upon which no action has yet been taken.

inbye *a* [*Coal-mining*] describing a direction underground away from the main shaft or surface outlet. See also **backlye.**

incap *n* [*Military*] abbr of **incapacitant** any substance that will render an enemy temporarily out of action but will not permanently damage him.

incendijel, also **incender jell** *n* [*Military*] an inflammable jelly weapon, similar to napalm and having similar effects, which is composed of polystyrene, petrol and benzene.

incentive shares *n pl* [*Commerce*] shares issued to employees of a company to encourage harder work and longer service.

incentives *n pl* [*Travel agents*] the offering of free trips to members of a travel agency by a tour operator; the intention is to promote these tours to the agency's customers.

incestuous dealing *n* [*Stock market*] this is when two companies trade in each other's stocks to create tax or other financial advantage.

incident *n* [*UK*] [*Police*] any event worthy of investigation, from bomb hoaxes to dog bites.

incident process *n* [*Management*] a method of management training in which: (1) the trainer outlines a business situation – the 'incident' – and asks for a decision; there is not yet, however, sufficient information to suggest a useful decision; (2) each trainee is given the chance to discover the necessary extra information by asking the trainer; (3) trainees write down their own decisions; (4) the trainer forms groups, based on the written decision of individual trainees: (5) the groups debate and formulate a group decision and the facts that support it; (6) all groups debate all decisions with the trainer.

incitative planning *n* [*Politics*] in socialist countries, this refers to those incentives created to augment the efficiency of an economic plan.

included *a* [*Linguistics*] said of a linguistic form which occurs as part of a larger form.

inclusions *n pl* [*Metallurgy*] particles of various non-metallic substances – oxides, silicates, sulphides, etc – embedded in the metal.

income elastic *n* [*Economics*] the stretching of

I

any income to take up any possible increases by creating new expenditure, especially when used for previously unaffordable luxuries.

incoming *a* [*Military*] used of shells fired from hostile artillery.

incomparable absolute *n* [*Linguistics*] See **absolute word.**

incompetent bed *n* [*Mining*] a rock bed that is relatively weak in comparison with adjacent beds and which under techtonic stress has crushed or flowed rather than folded and faulted. See also **competent bed.**

incompletions *n pl* [*New therapies*] in **est**, these are the sins or errors one has committed in the past and managed so far to keep hidden. Such sins must now be admitted and atoned for – verbally, economically, emotionally, etc.

incontinent ordnance *n* [*US*] [*Military*] bombs and artillery rounds that fall into areas where they should not have been dropped: friendly villages, on one's own troops, etc.

incorporation *n* [*Sociology*] the process of channelling working-class political and economic activity into existing institutions, rather than letting it remain outside them and thus acting as a potential threat to established order.

increasing returns *n pl* [*Economics*] the concept that as a new technology develops, the more one invests in its progress, the greater will be the returns on that investment and the improvements in the technology See also **diminishing returns.**

independent *n* [*US*] [*Railways*] a brake valve on a locomotive that controls only the engine, and not the coach brakes.

independent business unit *n* [*Business, Technology*] the IBM corporate equivalent of **skunk works.**

indeterminate architecture *n* [*Architecture*] a theory evolved in the early 1960s which claimed that buildings should be designed to incorporate any future alterations or expansion that might occur within the organisation that occupied them; such a design would always be indeterminate from the start, since it would never truly be finished.

index 1. *n* [*Computing*] a sequence or array of items, each of which refers to a record on file. 2. *n* [*Computing*] one of a continuous sequence of numbers each of which specifies one of an ordered sequence of numbers. 3. *n* [*Printing*] the symbol of a hand, with a pointing finger, that draws the reader's attention to a certain part of the text; a visual 'NB'.

index bond *n* [*Stock market*] a bond on which the level of repayment is tied directly to the level of the price.

index crime *n* [*US*] [*Law*] any crime that is included in the Crime Index of the 'Uniform Crime Reports' compiled by the FBI.

index fund *n* [*Stock market*] an investment fund composed of stocks chosen to match, in their values and performance, the performance of the whole market over a period of time.

indexicality *n* [*Sociology*] in **ethnomethodology**, this is the concept that all actions and utterances depend for their meaning on the context in which they occur.

Indian hour *n* [*Navy*] the hour before dawn, when anything unforeseen might happen.

Indian problem *n* [*Chess*] one of those openings in which a player seeks to control the centre of the board with knights, **fianchettoes,** bishops, etc, rather than by moving his centre pawns forward.

Indian system *n* [*Business*] this refers to the low costs of wages in India; in such a system all unskilled jobs are automated, except for those in which it is still cheaper to employ humans rather than to install machines.

indicative abstract *n* [*Libraries*] an abstract which indicates the content of a document rather than its method. See also **auto, evaluative, general, informative, selective** and **slanted abstract.**

indicative planning *n* [*Economics*] economic plans in which targets and tasks are defined in general rather than specific terms or directives; it is commonly used by the bureaucracies of capitalist countries in dealing with nationalised industries.

indie 1. *n* [*Film*] abbr of **independent** any independent production company, and the films which they make; such companies are the opposite of the **majors.** Cinemas, distributors and any other part of the industry not directly connected to a major corporation are also 'indies'. 2. *n* [*Record business*] abbr of **independent record companies** usually small and dependant on the major companies for distribution; although currently in eclipse, they have been responsible for the bulk of the pop industry's innovations in the last decade.

indifference curve 1. *n* [*Economics*] a curve drawn on a graph to represent the various combinations of two commodities that give a consumer equal satisfaction; the use of such curves helps in the prediction of human behaviour when faced by a given set of economic circumstances. 2. *n* [*Management*] a graph, all points on which represent combinations of qualities that are all considered equally valuable by a specified person.

indifferentism *n* [*Politics*] in socialist countries, this is a lack of commitment to social problems and developments as shown by an individual.

indirect *n* [*Management*] abbr of **indirect worker** an employee of a firm whose work does not contribute directly to the manufacture of any of the firm's products.

indirects *n pl* [*TV*] abbr of **indirect costs** the running costs of a company – staff wages, equipment costs – that will always need paying for,

I

whether or not they are actually involved in a production.

indispensable labour n [*Politics*] in Marxist terms, this is the proportion of labour that goes to earn the subsistence, maintenance and **reproduction** of a worker and his family.

individual n [*US*] [*Cattlemen*] the horse that a cowboy actually owns, as opposed to the common stock of horses held by the ranch.

individual action-alternative n [*Sociology*] a person's choice of actions.

individual learning department n [*Education*] a euphemism for the remedial classes in which backward children are taught.

individual working time n [*Industry*] a flexible working system whereby employees may choose each month one of a variety of pre-established working schedules. See also **flexitime.**

individualisation n [*Social work*] the recognition and understanding by the social worker that every new client has a particular problem and personality and must be treated as such, rather than as one more in a mass of similar cases.

indulgency pattern n [*Industrial relations*] a lenient style of management.

industrial n [*Film*] any film about business or industry which is not intended for commercial exhibition but is used by a company for training purposes, etc.

industrial action n [*Industrial relations*] a euphemism for a strike, an event epitomised, in the eyes of its critics, by its industrial inaction.

industrial democracy n [*Sociology*] the participation of workers in industrial decisions that affect their working lives.

industrial inertia n [*Industry*] the refusal of industrialists to relocate their industries, even though the conditions that were originally suitable for the establishment of those industries have long since vanished.

industrial property n [*Commerce*] a collective description of the commercial rights that stem from trade marks, patents, etc.

industry n [*Film, Pop music*] the film or pop businesses, as described by their participants. See also **Profession.**

industry leadership programme n [*Public relations*] a campaign designed to place one's client – either an individual or a corporation – at the head of a profession, brand, industry, etc.

inertia selling n [*Commerce*] a sales technique whereby the merchandise is sent, unsolicited, and is then followed up by a bill.

INF talks n pl [*Military*] **Intermediate-range Nuclear Forces Talks** a series of eventually abortive talks, initiated by the Carter Administration in 1980, which attempted to deal with the problem of intermediate-range nuclear weapons, notably US cruise and Tomahawk missiles, based in Europe and threatening the USSR. Both sides preferred a series of propaganda coups to real initiatives and the talks foundered in late 1981.

inference machine n [*Computing*] in an **expert system**, this is the part that actually drives the system. Its aim is to match the known facts about a problem with one or more of the rules established by the human expert.

infield n [*Baseball*] that area of the playing field within which the home plate, the pitcher's box and the three bases are located; the four infield players.

infimum n [*Mathematics*] the largest number that is less than or equal to each of a given set of real numbers; an analogous quality for a subset of any other ordered set.

infinite baffle n [*Audio*] a type of loudspeaker cabinet in which there is no air path between the front and the rear of the speaker diaphragm.

inflation n [*Economics*] an increase in the supply of money over the quantity of goods available for purchase. This pushes up the cost of those goods that do exist. Thus 'hyperinflation' is a situation where the monetary demand increases too rapidly: people attempt to beat inflation by spending heavily before prices increase even further, and this merely intensifies the whole process. 'Stagflation' is a situation in which both money prices and unemployment are rising to increasingly high levels. 'Reflation', also 'disinflation', is an attempt to manage currencies and thus restore a previous, less inflationary price level.

influentials, also **opinion leaders** n pl [*Public relations*] those individuals, relevant to a given campaign, whom a PR feels must be influenced before all others in the area, given their ability to influence large numbers of other people.

informatics n [*Communications*] the science of collecting, transmitting, storing, processing and displaying data.

information hiding n [*Computing*] the concept, developed by David Parnas, that when developing an overall program structure, each component of the program should encapsulate or hide a single design decision.

information technology n [*Media, Computing*] a popular generality that covers many innovations in the abilities of computers, micro-electronics and telecommunications to produce, store and transmit a wide spectrum of information in ways that will revolutionise modern society.

information theory n [*Computing, Business*] the study of information by mathematical methods. When restricted to communications, the mathematical theory is concerned with the information rate, channel capacity, noise and other factors affecting the transmission of information. When extended to business use, it covers the flow of information in networks.

informational entertainment, also **soft news** n [*TV*] a type of news broadcasting which

I

minimises factual information and its import, and places everything within a context more akin to a purely entertainment programme. It is low on 'importance' but is easily assimilable by those who cannot bear too many demands on their intelligence. See also **happy talk.**

informational programming *n* [*Video*] any video product that is primarily educational rather than purely entertainment orientated, although there will be large elements of the latter to promote sales See also **how-to.**

informative 1. *n* [*Cards*] See **informatory. 2.** *n* [*UK*] [*Fire Brigade*] a message to the fire station that explains the details of the emergency call. See also **shout. 3.** *n* [*Philately*] a type of postmark indicating fees paid or due, censorship, non-delivery and similar information for postal officials and/or the public.

informative abstract *n* [*Libraries*] an abstract which gives detailed information about the original document: its content, conclusions and possibly method. See also **auto, evaluative, general, indicative, selective** and **slanted abstract.**

informatory *n* [*Cards*] in bridge this is a double that is intended to give specific information to one's partner; it is the opposite of a business double. Thus also 'informatory pass'.

infotainment *n* [*TV*] See **informational entertainment.**

infrastructure *n* [*Economics*] the vital services and essential fabric of a nation's life: roads, housing, medical care, educational facilities, transport. Such entities have no direct effect on economic growth, but are indispensable to its continuation.

ingenue *n* [*Theatre*] a female juvenile lead, especially a sweet, naive young girl; known in 19th century melodrama as 'the singing chambermaid'.

ingroup *a* [*Science fiction*] eccentric, esoteric.

inherent vice 1. *n* [*Art*] the process whereby the ageing of paint on old masters tends to make it translucent and thus reveal anything that may have been altered or painted over. **2.** *n* [*Insurance*] the tendency and risk of certain goods – eg: fresh foods – to go bad or spoil during transport. Unless the carrier has been forewarned of that risk, he will not be liable for its occurrence.

inherited audience *n* [*TV*] an audience who have been watching one programme, possible one with high ratings, and who cannot be bothered to switch channels, but will simply settle into whatever programme appears next. The purchase of advertising slots by an agency takes such 'inheritance' into account.

in-house *a* [*Business*] said of anything that is created/designed/built and otherwise originated within a company, rather than being contracted from elsewhere.

initial margin *n* [*Futures market*] the **margin** which is required to cover a new **position.**

initial terminal *n* [*US*] [*Railways*] the amount of time, in addition to that which is allocated, which covers reporting for duty and leaving the yard. See also **final terminal.**

initialise, also **preset** *v* [*Computing*] to reset a system to its starting position in order to ensure that every time the program starts to run everything works in the same way.

injection *n* [*Aerospace*] the process of sending a capsule or manned satellite into orbit.

ink 1. *v* [*Film*] to sign a contract or similar deal. **2.** *n* [*Journalism*] publicity, promotion, especially when written up in a newspaper.

inkhorn word *n* [*Literary criticism*] an erudite neologism, especially a dubious hybrid of Latin and Greek.

inking *n* [*Computing*] in computer graphics this is the creation of a line by 'drawing' with an electronic pointer.

inkle loom *n* [*Weaving*] a small portable loom consisting of a framework with numerous pegs around which the **warp** is wound; it is used mainly for belts and similar narrow bands.

inky *a* [*Wine-tasting*] used to describe an unpleasant tinny, metallic taste, which comes from the presence of tannate of iron (the chief constituent of ink); it is produced by the action of tannin on iron – caused, for instance, by a nail in a cask.

inkydinky *n* [*TV, Film*] See **babykicker.**

inlier *n* [*Mining*] an area of older rocks surrounded by younger rocks. See also **outlies.**

inline *a* [*Printing*] said of a type design incorporating a fine line that appears to be engraved.

inner skiing *n* [*Skiing*] an American psychological approach to conquering one's fears and inhibitions on the slopes.

inning *n* [*Entertainment*] a period of time; it usually comes within the specific limits that are implied by the context within which the word is used. It comes from periods of team play in baseball. See also **frame 4.**

innocent murmurs *n pl* [*US*] [*Medicine*] palpitations of the heart which need not arouse fears of incipient illness.

innovators *n pl* [*Marketing*] the first buyers of a new product, whose action initiates the **adoption process.**

inoculation *n* [*Metallurgy*] in iron-founding this is the process of adding relatively small amounts of alloys or elements to the molten metal in order to improve and strengthen the finished casting.

inoperative *a* [*Politics*] no longer true; a lie. This originated in a statement made by Ronald Ziegler, the White House Press Secretary during the Watergate Affair, who claimed that a number of statements made by President Nixon, and generally known to be untrue, were as of that date 'inoperative'.

in-put *n* [*Computing*] any data or program instructions that are given to the machine; also,

I

the physical medium on which these are represented.

input/output *n* [*Computing*] the equipment used to communicate with a computer, and the data used for this communication.

inquiry station *n* [*Computing*] a terminal from which information can be retrieved from a database.

in-seams *n pl* [*Clothing*] the inside-leg measurement of a pair of trousers.

insecure *a* [*Espionage, Government*] said of any individual who is considered a security risk, or who lacks a sufficiently high security clearance to have access to a given level of classified material.

insert 1. *n* [*Film*] a shot inserted into a dramatic scene which will allow the audience to see it from a screen character's point of view, and thus see more of the headless corpse, the blackmailing letter or whatever is causing the drama. 2. *n* [*Industry*] an integral part, made of metal, that is placed in position during the moulding of an article made of plastic. 3. *n* [*Advertising*] any advertisement or other promotional material that is included inside a product or its packaging. See also **outsert.**

insert edit *n* [*Video*] the creation of a final programme by taking the best possible tape from those already shot and replacing various defective or inferior sections on it by the preferred substitutes extracted piecemeal from other tapes. See also **assemble edit.**

insertion weights *n pl* [*Advertising*] used for weighting expenditures in advertising; they are a means of varying expenditure according to the impression value of alternative publications and they reflect the likelihood of an advertisement being seen.

in-service 1. *v* [*Government*] to train non-professional bureaucrats to improve their performance in government jobs. 2. *n* [*Government*] to hold an in-service is to set up a training programme.

in-service education *n* [*Education*] this is when a teacher continues taking new courses in education to add to the basic qualifications with which he/she began a teaching career.

inset *n* [*Coal-mining*] an opening or entry from a shaft to an underground railway or chamber.

inside *a* [*US*] [*Railways*] working in the **yard.**

insider *n* [*Stock market*] members of the Stock Exchange who can use their special knowledge to make profits on deals that the general public would never have been able to appreciate at the crucial moment; such deals are known as 'insider trading' and are illegal.

insipid *a* [*Wine-tasting*] flat, somewhat tasteless, lacking character.

inspirational *n* [*Publishing*] a list of popular mass-market novels which combine romance and religion; aimed at the US Bible Belt, they combine all the usual themes of such modern pulp, except

for the slightest suggestion of sex; God, rather than the earth, moves. See also **hysterical historicals.**

installation, also **installation show** *n* [*Art*] an exhibition in which the positioning of the artworks depends crucially on their relation to the layout and environment of the gallery.

installed capacity *n* [*Industry*] the highest amount that can be expected to be produced if a factory or plant is at full operation. See also **utilised capacity.**

instantiation *n* [*Computing*] a more defined version of some partially defined object.

institution *n* [*Sociology*] a social practice that is regularly and continuously repeated, is sanctioned and maintained by social norms, and has a major significance in the social structure: family, school, church, etc.

institutional advertising *n* [*Advertising*] advertising that is designed to promote a firm or corporation as an entity, rather than promoting its various products.

institutionalisation of conflict *n* [*Sociology*] the calming of industrial conflict with the development of a division between political and industrial struggles, especially through suffrage and increased citizenship rights for the workers, thus bringing them into the mainstream of society. It is also the creation of specialist negotiating institutions – trade unions – to defuse intense conflict.

instruction *n* [*Computing*] a single step in a program; every program is composed of thousands of separate instructions.

instructional personnel *n* [*Education*] teachers.

instrument *n* [*Banking, Finance*] any formal legal document.

instrumentalism *n* [*Sociology*] the attitude of workers who demand instrumental satisfactions – high pay, job security – from their employment, rather than intrinsic satisfaction deriving from the work itself.

instrumentalities *n pl* [*Politics*] in post-Revolutionary Iran, these are the essential forces – Revolutionary Guards, mullahs (preachers), and hezbollah (militia) – who provide the leadership with its basic support and continue to suppress any opposition; such forces are the 'instruments of Allah'.

instrumentation *n* [*Electronics*] devices used to test, monitor, record and/or control physical properties and movements.

insulate *v* [*Espionage*] in the CIA this is to ensure as completely as possible that an agent does not fall under suspicion.

insult *n* [*Navy*] a sailor's pay, with reference to its insignificance as remuneration for his efforts.

insults *n pl* [*Medicine*] artificially created 'monsters' which are made by injecting the growing foetus with a harmful substance to produce deliberate malformation – they are used by teratologists in their studies of congenital malformations.

insurance *n* [*Sport*] a process whereby a winning team consolidates its lead in the game and ensures that the opposition cannot even attain a tie.

insurance poor *a* [*Business*] used to describe a situation where one holds so much insurance that simply paying the premiums to guard against any possible eventuality leaves insufficient funds to enjoy a normal or sociable life.

intake team *n* [*Social work*] those social workers who deal with the immediate casework – usually referral, decision-making and assessment – that accompanies a new client.

intangible personal property *n* [*Law*] the right to hold property in the form of stocks, shares, bonds, etc. See also **tangible personal property.**

integralism *n* [*Politics*] a political philosophy that suggests that every individual difference should be amalgamated into one, far more useful, whole in which all of society can be linked effectively together in a unit that will benefit all concerned.

integrated battlefield [*Military*] a battlefield in which any combinations of conventional, nuclear, chemical and biological weapons may be employed.

integrity *n* [*Computing*] the resistance within a program to alteration by system errors.

intelligence probe *n* [*Espionage*] a euphemism for breaking and entering into a target's home or office to collect useful information and/or plant **bugs.**

intelligent pig *n* [*Oil & Gas industries*] a piece of equipment which can be sent through an oil or gas pipe and which will relay required information about the condition of that pipe, or about the oil/gas flowing through it, without the pipe having to be taken out of service.

intelligent terminal *n* [*Computing*] a terminal which has some computing ability built into its machinery.

intentional fallacy *n* [*Literary criticism*] the critical error made in judging a literary work on the basis of what the reader assumes, but cannot actually know, was the author's intention in writing it.

intentions model *n* [*Marketing*] a model of consumer attitudes that is designed to predict intentions to buy.

interaction *n* [*Sociology*] the detailed study of behaviour, its biological base and its cultural setting.

interaction matrix *n* [*Business*] a chart used to help solve those problems – such as the layout of a factory – where physical positioning is particularly important.

interactive 1. *n* [*Computing*] See **conversational.** 2. *a* [*Video*] said of any video product that requires some degree of physical involvement

by the user to complete its function; videogames are the obvious example. 3. *a* [*Video*] said of any kind of video hardware (the actual recorder or disc player) that allows a viewer to make decisions as to the course of a programme, as in using the pause button, playing back scenes, slow motion, etc.

interactive video *n* [*TV*] those televisions, available almost wholly in the US, which are linked by a special handset to the studio and which can therefore involve the viewer in the programme, eg: by prompting him/her to use various buttons on the handset to 'vote' in response to a variety of questions put on screen by the programme's host.

intercalation *n* [*Linguistics*] the interspersing within sentences of meaningless words, often implying by such insertion a lack of intelligence or articulateness, eg: 'like', 'you know', 'I mean'.

intercarrier buzz *n* [*TV*] an occasional noise heard on the TV receiver due to variations in the audio signal transmission.

intercept *n* [*Espionage*] any information picked up by the use of a clandestine microphone, telephone tap or similar **bug.**

interdict *v* [*Military*] to make an area unsafe for enemy action or movement.

interdiction *n* [*Computing*] See **denial of service.**

interdiction bombing *n* [*Military*] bombing such targets as will interrupt or even destroy enemy communications and/or transport. See also **corridor-bashing.**

interest inventory *n* [*Education*] a checklist of a pupil's interests, made to reveal his/her relative abilities and strengths. It is used for helping with career choices and is elicited through various standardised multiple choice tests.

interest profiles *n pl* [*Communications*] statements by individuals which explain their specific interests to a central distributive agency who services these interests with a regular output of publications considered pertinent to those interests. See also **SDI.**

interested party *n* [*Scientology*] a Scientology member who is currently under suspicion of heresy and is being interrogated and confined.

interface 1. *n* [*Computing*] anything that serves to connect two separate systems in a machine. 2. *v, n* [*New therapies*] this comes from the computing use (1) and means any relationship between two individuals. Thus A can interface with B at a given interface, ie: A and B can go somewhere to talk.

interfacing *n* [*Textiles*] a layer of fabric placed under the fashion fabric to support it. Interfacing is generally restricted to specific parts of the garment such as collars, cuffs, facings or lapels.

interleaving 1. *n* [*Computing*] a technique of achieving multiprogramming by simultaneously accessing two or more bytes or streams of data

I

from separate storage units and thus making it possible to alternate two or more operations or functions at the same time in the same computer. **2.** *n* [*Computing*] the simultaneous performance of two programs by a computer which can fit the secondary or **background** program into the microspaces left when performing the **instructions** for the primary or **foreground** program.

interliners *n pl* [*Air travel*] those passengers that are transferring from one airline to another at the same airport.

interlock *n* [*Computing*] a hard- or software method of co-ordinating and/or synchronising multiple processes in a computer. This is achieved by ensuring that one process cannot begin until the preceding one has finished.

interlude *n* [*Computing*] a temporary, minor subprogram designed for preliminary computations or data organisation; such a program is discarded and over-written once it has served its purpose.

intermedia, also **mixed media** *n* [*Art*] the use of a large variety of devices and techniques drawn from many artistic areas to produce a complete show or entertainment.

internal colonialism 1. *n* [*Sociology*] a Marxist concept that describes the development within society of under-privileged and unequal groups with fewer political and economic advantages than are held by the dominant group. **2.** *n* [*Sociology*] the exploitation by a nation of the various minority groups and ethnic communities that live within its territory, performing menial jobs that the native population prefers to avoid.

internal haemorrhage *n* [*Computing*] the situation in which a program begins to produce nonsense but continues to run, unaffected by this useless output.

internal orientation *n* [*Business*] a job that is centred in the main office or company headquarters and requires little travel or fieldwork.

internalisation 1. *n* [*Stock market*] a method of transferring stocks between brokerage officers rather than transmitting orders through the floor of an Exchange. **2.** *n* [*Sociology*] the process whereby the individual learns and accepts as binding the social values and norms of the social group and wider society.

International House of Pancakes *n* [*US*] [*Medicine*] a neurology ward holding patients – usually stroke cases – who babble in a variety of unintelligible 'languages'; the phrase comes from the name of a chain of fast-food sellers in the US.

international sound *n* [*TV*] See **clean feed**.

international travel and talk *n* [*Business*] internal corporate slang for ITT, the telecommunications conglomerate. See also **I've Been Moved**.

internationalism *n* [*Politics*] the act of defending the USSR without reservation or conditions, simply because the USSR Is the base of the international revolutionary movement and thus to defend the movement without defending the country is impossible. It is usually prefaced by 'proletarian' and is set against **bourgeois** nationalism.

interpleader *n* [*Law, Banking*] a suit by which the claims of two parties to money or property are determined so that a third party (eg: a banker), on whom the claim is made, can discover to whom payment or delivery is due.

interpositioning *n* [*Stock market*] the involvement of a second broker in a transaction which is already involving two parties; such involvement can be artificially created to gain extra commissions and is closely regulated.

interpreter *n* [*Computing*] software that translates a **high-level language** into **machine code** which responds directly to the computer's operation and which it can 'understand'.

interrabang, also **interrobang** *n* [*Printing*] a punctuation mark that simultaneously expresses a question and an exclamation.

interrogation *n* [*Computing*] the sending of a signal that will initiate a response.

interrupt 1. *n* [*Computing*] the automatic breaking off of the operation of one program, in response to a command, in order to run another one, after which the original program is run to its conclusion. **2.** *n* [*Computing*] a method of detecting errors when 'illegal' (unworkable) instructions are entered into the machine: the program automatically stops functioning and a message is printed out stating that 'illegal' instructions have been used. The program is then terminated.

interrupt mask *n* [*Computing*] a method of selectively suppressing interrupts when they occur to let the system continue running as it is, leaving the interrupts to be acted upon later. See also **interrupt 1.**

interrupter *n* [*UK*] [*Police*] a court interpreter.

interstitial programming *n* [*TV*] the designing and creation of programmes to fit into the short spaces between the 'continuous' scheduling of feature films on pay and cable TV stations.

intersubjectivity *n* [*Sociology*] the way in which individuals relate to each other.

intervention 1. *n* [*Government*] in the Parliament of the EEC, this is any contribution to a debate. **2.** *n* [*Social work*] a synonym for the taking of any form of action by a social worker regarding a particular case; intervention can be strong – as between a married couple – or weak – any purposeful action taken by a social worker.

intervention area *n* [*Military*] the defined limits of operation in a small war, eg: Suez, the Falklands, etc. See also **austere war.**

intervention currency *n* [*Finance*] the action of the International Monetary Fund (IMF) in sustaining the currencies of the 118 member nations by buying their currencies with dollars

I

when any of them seems likely to dip below a set level of control, or selling them in exchange for dollars if any appear to be rising too high.

interventionalism n [*Politics*] in EEC terminology, this is interference in people's lives with the intention of achieving a policy objective.

intimism n [*Art*] a form of **impressionism** applied to the painting of domestic interiors rather than landscapes and usually referring to the work of Bonnard or Vuillard.

into prep [*New therapies*] strongly involved with, interested in, concerned with, fascinated by, etc.

intolerant a [*Ecology*] said of trees and plants that are unable to flourish without adequate sunlight and are therefore unsuitable for deep shade.

intrados n [*Building, Plastering*] the inner curve of an arch.

intraspecific aggression n [*Sociology*] conflict between various members of the same race, culture, religon, etc, as in a civil war.

intra-war period n [*Military*] the period during which actual nuclear exchanges are taking place.

in-tray exercise, also in-basket exercise n [*Business*] a training scheme within a fully simulated office environment, with letters, memos, decisions to be made, etc; in such a scheme the trainee must deal with everything that is in the 'in-tray' within a set time.

introduction n [*Stock market*] the issuing of new shares by a company, not directly to the public, but through the medium of the Stock Exchange.

intrusion 1. n [*Mining*] a mass of igneous rock which, while molten, was forced between other rocks. 2. n [*Coal-mining*] a mass of sedimentary rock found in a coal seam.

intrusions n pl [*Journalism*] the Australian version of **door-stepping.**

inuit art n [*Art*] Eskimo art; it comes from 'inuit', the Eskimo word for the Eskimo people.

inverse segregation, also negative segregation n [*Metallurgy*] **segregation** in which the amount of certain constituents and/or impurities is less than that in the surrounding metal. See also **normal segregation.**

inverted file n [*Computing*] a file structure within a database that facilitates and speeds up searches by providing special extra lists or indices that can be accessed individually rather than searching an entire database.

inverted market n [*Futures market*] a market in which the nearer months are being sold off at a premium to the further off months.

inverted pyramid n [*Journalism*] the traditional style of writing news stories: the major facts (see **five Ws**) are all placed in the lead sentence and paragraph; subsequent lesser detail, interviews with those involved, background and any additional comments are added as space

permits. This system, while repetitive, guarantees that the vital parts of the story will remain even when the demands of space mean that sub-editors start to cut it from the bottom up.

investigative phase n [*Medicine*] a euphemism for investigative surgery, performed when the surgeon is not quite sure what is wrong; the term is used to soothe patients who would prefer to maintain their belief in the surgeon's infallibility.

investment n [*US*] [*Undertakers*] the cost of a funeral.

investment dollar n [*Economics*] See **switch dollar.**

investment dressing n [*Fashion*] the purchase of high-priced clothes and accessories on the principle that such purchases will last longer than would cheaper ones.

invincible ignorance n [*Religion*] this term is used in Roman Catholic theology to denote those who for reasons of heredity, upbringing or environment, are absolutely unable to see religious or moral truth however hard they try and as such are not to be blamed. An apparently intolerant phrase that actually implies a highly tolerant, if patronising, attitude.

invisible exports n pl [*Economics*] non-commodity exports, financial and personal services rendered by a country's native population to foreigners: banking, insurance, the tourist trade, etc.

invisible hand n [*Economics*] an optimistic view of the market economy propounded by Adam Smith in 'The Wealth of Nations' (1776) whereby the pursuit of individual profit leads inevitably to the material advantage of society as a whole as if the merchant was 'led by an invisible hand to promote an end which was no part of his intention'.

invisible painting n [*Art*] any painting whose colour values are so closely attuned that they exist only on the threshold of human perception. At first glance such works appear to have no differences in tone or colour, but the eye gradually becomes attuned to the fine details.

invisible supply 1. n [*Commerce*] unaccounted stocks of a commodity that are held by wholesalers and manufacturers and cannot thus be counted properly in statistics. 2. n [*Commerce*] stocks that exist outside the regular commercial channels but which are still theoretically available to the market.

invisibles n pl [*Economics*] that component of a country's balance of payments that is made up of receipts and payments for services (as opposed to material goods). This includes cash gifts (eg. legacies) and other transfers for which no services are performed, and the two-way flow of the international money markets.

invitation n [*Cards*] in bridge this is a bid which encourages the bidder's partner to continue the game or slam.

invitation to treat 1. *n* [*Commerce*] an invitation, either to an individual or to the world at large, to offer to make a contract. **2.** *n* [*Marketing*] the legal definition of the retailer's practice of placing goods in his/her shop-window, and thus inviting the consumer to make an offer, based on the stated price, if one is stated in the window. Such a definition extends to the invitation carried in advertising, sales catalogues, etc.

I/O *n* [*Computing*] abbr of **input-output.**

IONDS *n* [*Military*] acro **Integrated Operational Nuclear Detection System** a system carried on board the Vela spacecraft to an altitude of 70,000 miles and used to detect atmospheric nuclear tests. When installed on the proposed **NAVSTAR** navigational satellites, IONDS will be integrated with the C³I network to check damage sustained by both the US and the USSR during/after a nuclear attack.

I.P. *n* [*Government*] abbr of **insured person** anyone who is eligible to claim unemployment benefits.

IP *adv* [*UK*] [*Prisons*] acro **in possession** whatever a prisoner has in his/her possession at a given time and which is checked and noted, eg: on his leaving and returning to the cell when he has visitors.

IPO *n* [*US*] [*Stock market*] abbr of **initial public offering** the first offering of a corporation's shares to the public.

ipot *n* [*Electronics*] abbr of **inductive potentiometer.**

IPSE *n* [*Computing*] acro **Integrated Programming Support Environments** the process of ensuring that when there exists a variety of programs used for linked, complex operations, all of these programs should be compatible. The process includes the integration of new programs and the adaption of the existing ones to the new overall system.

IRAN *n* [*US*] [*Military*] acro **Inspection and Repair As Necessary** a NASA acronym that covers the maintenance of certain equipment.

iris *n* [*Film*] a moveable diaphragm on a camera lens – similar to the expanding and contracting iris of the eye – which permits the camera to create an expanding or contracting circle on the screen; thus it can be used as a verb: to 'iris in', 'iris out'.

Irish hurricane, also **Irishman's hurricane** *n* [*Navy*] a flat calm.

Irish mail *n* [*Navy*] sacks of potatoes.

Irish man-o'-war *n* [*Navy*] an unpowered barge.

Irish pennants 1. *n pl* [*Navy*] loose ends of rope left fluttering in a breeze. **2.** *n pl* [*Sailing, Ropework*] frayed rope ends in a variety of **gaskets, seizings, points,** etc.

Irishman's rise *n* [*Navy*] demotion.

iron 1. *n* [*Aerospace*] any magnetic parts in an aircraft's construction, irrespective of the actual metal involved. **2.** *n* [*Angling*] a hook. **3.** *n* [*Cycling*] the bicycle. **4.** *n* [*Military*] any bomb that has no guidance system and is simply dropped vertically from a high-flying aircraft. **5.** *n* [*US*] [*Road transport*] tyre chains. **6.** *n* [*Shoe-making*] a unit of measure used for leather: one forty-eighth of an inch. **7.** *n* [*Theatre*] the safety or fireproof curtain. **8.** *n* [*Weaving*] ferrous sulphate, a **mordant. 9.** *n* [*Wine-tasting*] a faintly metallic, earthy taste, derived from some soils. **10.** also **iron horse** *n* [*US*] [*Road transport*] an old truck. See also **ghost 6.**

iron chink *n* [*Industry*] in salmon canning this is a machine that automatically removes the head and intestines of the fish; it comes from the Chinese ('chinks') manual labourers who originally performed this job.

iron hat, also **gossan** *n* [*Mining*] the outcrop of a lode, usually seen as decomposed rock with a reddish colour gained from oxidised pyrites.

iron law of oligarchy *n* [*Government*] the dictum that in all organisations power is always assumed by a small elite, whatever the constitution of the organisation may lay down; it was postulated by German sociologist Roberto Mischels in 'Political Parties' (1902).

iron lot 1. *n* [*US*] [*Car salesmen*] a junk yard. **2.** *n* [*US*] [*Car salesmen*] a dealership specialising in old, cheap cars.

iron lunger *n* [*US*] [*Road transport*] a conventional 220–250 hp engine.

iron man *n* [*UK*] [*Railways*] an intermediate block post signal.

iron man day *n* [*Commerce*] working a twelve-hour day, for which great stamina is supposedly required.

iron Mike *n* [*Merchant navy*] the gyro compass on a ship.

iron rice bowl *n* [*Politics*] in Chinese terminology this is guaranteed material security, usually a steady job; an iron rice bowl, unlike a porcelain one, will not break.

iron spot *n* [*Building*] an imperfection – a brown spot – in a brick caused by iron ore melting as the brick is fired in a kiln.

ironclad *n* [*Industrial relations*] See **yellow-dog contract.**

ironmongery *n* [*Mountaineering*] picks, crampons, and any other metal equipment used in climbing.

irrational number *n* [*Mathematics*] a number which can be performed but which has a value that cannot be found in finite terms; eg: $\sqrt{2}$.

irredeemables *n pl* [*Stock market*] stocks for which there is no date of repayment, especially UK government bonds.

irredentism *n* [*Politics*] a national yearning to regain territory which was formerly part of that nation but which has long since been taken away by treaty or conquest.

Irving Kaye *n* [*Pool*] a brand of pool table

I

preferred by many good players; its mark is having tight pockets.

is splice *n* [*Advertising*] a term coined by Jacques Barzun: a presumptuous or coy statement designed to link ideas or things, especially commercial companies and their product or image, by the verb 'is', eg: 'General Motors is people', etc.

ISA *n* [*Sociology*] acro **Ideological State Apparatus** this was popularised by L. Althusser (1918–) and refers to the various non-coercive means whereby the dominant capitalist culture keeps control – the media, religion, education, the family, even trade unions and political parties. See also **RSA.**

ish *n* [*Media*] **issue** of any magazines, but especially of fanzines, comics or other publications aimed essentially at the young.

Island *n* [*UK*] [*Prisons*] HM Prison, Parkhurst, on the Isle of Wight.

island copy *adv* [*Advertising*] See **solus.**

island of stability *n* [*Science*] a group of superheavy chemical elements with extremely stable nuclei.

island site *n* [*Advertising*] a space for a newspaper advertisement which is surrounded by at least three sides of editorial matter.

ISO container *n* [*UK*] [*Road transport*] a metal box which meets the requirements of the international standards laid down for the size and construction of such boxes so that they are interchangeable between the different modes of transport – air, boat, road – without unloading/reloading the contents.

isogram *n* [*Logology*] a word that uses no letter more than once; eg: 'lionheart'.

isoquant *n* [*Economics*] a curve that shows the

various possible combinations of inputs required to produce a given output of a given product.

issue management *n* [*Public relations*] the preparation of the public, through a PR campaign, for the reception of an 'issue' in the way that those who have created that issue wish it to be received. This usually occurs when in fact its every aspect, if explained clearly and honestly, would be totally unpalatable to an audience, that had not been softened up by advance propaganda.

iswas *n* [*US*] [*Navy*] any rough and ready calculating device; it was originally a mechanical aid used on World War II submarines.

it 1. *n* [*New therapies*] the essence of **est:** 'what is, is, and what ain't, ain't', or 'It is you experiencing you without any symbology or any concept' (Werner Erhard). **2.** *n* [*New therapies*] a term coined by Georg Grodeck (1866–1934): 'a force that lives in us while we believe we are living'.

Italian gear *n* [*Antiques*] an item that may be in poor condition but which still exhibits some value.

Italian rehearsal *n* [*TV*] the reading through of a script at top speed and with no 'acting' by the cast; it is supposedly a good way of learning the lines.

item *n* [*Computing*] any quantity of data that is treated as one unit, eg: a record or group of records.

I've Been Moved *n* [*Business*] corporate slang for the computer conglomerate IBM; it refers to the constant reposting of its executives.

ivory head *n* [*Philately*] GB Victorian stamps, especially the 1d and 2d issues of 1841, that are of the 'blued' (the addition of prussiate of potash to the ink) variety, which show the Queen's head in white on the back.

J

J curve *n* [*Economics*] a description of the state of a country's balance of trade after a devaluation as displayed on a graph. In the long run this makes the country's exports cheaper, and thus they will increase; and it makes the imports dearer, which thus decrease. Initially, however, there will be an opposite effect. Graphically this

is shown as a short downturn followed by a long upturn – which looks like a 'J'.

jack 1. *v* [*Hunting*] to hunt, usually illegally, at night; the game is trapped by shining a spotlight or torch – the jack – into its eyes, illuminating and momentarily blinding it and thus rendering it an easy victim. **2.** *n* [*Angling*] a pike. **3.** *n*

[*Angling*] a male stonefly. **4.** *n* [*Weaving*] a lever, one end of which raises a **heddle** shaft (the heddle frame and the heddles it contains) by pushing or pulling when the other end is pulled down by a treadle.

jack bricks *n pl* [*Glass-making*] bricks that are placed around a newly set pot.

jack dusty, also **jack of the dust** *n* [*Navy*] the rating or enlisted man in charge of a ship's dry provisions.

jack rabbit *n* [*Oil rigs*] a drill mandrel: the device used to check the size of metal casing and tubing before it is run; the 'rabbit' is put through each joint of casing and tubing to make certain that the inside and outside diameters are those specified for the job.

jack shalloo *n* [*Navy*] a naval officer whose main aim is to be popular with the men.

jack strop *n* [*Navy*] a new recruit who tries to pass himself off as an old hand.

jack trap, also **man trap** *n* [*UK*] [*Railways*] catchpoints which stop unauthorised entry on to a track by a train.

jack up *v* [*Pool*] to hit down on the cueball.

jackaroo *n* [*Aus.*] [*Farming*] a trainee or junior stockman on a sheep-farm.

jackass *n* [*Sailing*] a schooner which has no main topmast.

jacket **1.** *n* [*Oil rigs*] the steel lattice structure used to support an offshore drilling platform; it stands on the sea bed and is secured by steel piling. **2.** [*US*] [*Prisons*] the file which is kept on each prisoner by the authorities.

jacket platform *n* [*Oil rigs*] a platform constructed entirely of steel; such platforms are kept in place by steel piles driven into the sea bed.

jacketing *n* [*US*] [*Cattlemen*] skinning a dead lamb and wrapping an orphan lamb in it so that the mother of the dead lamb will trust the smell and nurse it as her own.

jack-knife *v* [*UK*] [*Road transport*] used when the driving wheels on the tractive unit of an articulated vehicle lock under heavy braking, causing the trailer, which still has forward motion, to push the rear of the tractive unit out of line and into a skid; this eventually results in the tractive unit swinging round and closing on the trailer.

jackknife *n* [*Swimming*] a dive executed headfirst, either forward or backward, in which the diver, beginning usually at the highest point of the dive, bends from the waist and touches or clasps his ankles while holding his knees unflexed before straightening out as he enters the water.

jackleg *n* [*Religion*] an incompetent, unskilled, unscrupulous and dishonest preacher.

jacko *n* [*UK*] [*Railways*] a shunting engine, (Midland, Western Region use).

jackpot **1.** *n* [*Logging*] an ironic reference to any incompetent logging work. **2.** *n* [*US*] [*Meat trade*]

a group of mixed cattle or other stock, usually of **common** quality.

jacks *n pl* [*UK*] [*Police*] detectives.

jackson haines, also **sit spin** *n* [*Skating*] a figure-skating spin executed on the flat of one skate in which the body gradually assumes a low sitting position with the free leg held in front with knee bent and then gradually straightens to an erect position; it is named after US skater Jackson Haines (died 1875).

jack-up **1.** *n* [*Oil rigs*] a mobile offshore drilling platform, essentially a barge that can be elevated off the bottom on tubular or lattice legs; it is used for exploration in shallow waters. **2.** *n* [*Oil rigs*] a type of offshore drilling rig which is towed to an appointed spot, where it lowers its legs until they rest on the seabed.

j'adoube *v* [*Chess*] a statement indicating that a player wishes to touch a piece – to realign it on the board – but not actually move it; it comes from Fr. for 'I adjust'.

j'adoubovitz *n* [*Chess*] a nickname for a player who irritates his/her opponents by constantly moving the pieces; it comes from Fr. **j'adoube** the traditional excuse made for a single adjustment, plus a joke 'Mitteleuropa' suffix.

jaffa *n* [*Cricket*] a fast ball, bowled well up to the wicket.

jagers *n pl* [*Logging*] frayed, ragged strands that break off a wire rope.

jaggies *n pl* [*Photo-typesetting*] sudden jumps in the outline of a character at the point where an extra **raster** line is called; these sudden jumps where the eye expects a smooth curve or straight line can be eliminated electronically by channel-automisation.

jam **1.** *n* [*Merchant navy*] explosives carried on board ship. **2.** *n* [*Photography*] a fault in a camera due either to mechanical failure or a pile up of film. **3.** *v* [*US*] [*Prisons*] to inject drugs intravenously.

jam roll *n* [*UK*] [*Prisons*] rhyming slang for parole.

James the First *n* [*Navy*] See **jimmy the one.**

jammed *a* [*US*] [*Prisons*] used to describe concurrent sentences. See also **running wild.**

jank *v* [*Air Force*] said of an aircraft which simultaneously changes altitude and direction while attempting to avoid anti-aircraft fire.

jankers *n* [*UK*] [*Military*] fatigue duty or confinement to cells. Now mainly obsolete since most punishments are fines.

jannock *adv* [*Navy*] in accordance with naval etiquette.

jar **1.** *n* [*Medicine*] acro **junior assistant resident** in a hospital. See also **sar. 2.** *n* [*Oil rigs*] a tool that uses hydraulic force to displace a **fish** that is resisting all efforts to dislodge it from the bottom of the well.

jargoon *n* [*UK*] [*Police*] a fake or otherwise worthless 'diamond' ring; it comes from the original word for a zircon.

jarhead n [*Oil rigs*] a cable-tool driller. See **rope choker.**

jaunty n [*Navy*] a master-at-arms.

jaw v [*Pool*] said of a ball which rattles between the edges of the pocket but does not fall in.

jawbone n [*Politics*] a policy aimed at urging wage restraints on both unions and management. It was first associated with President Lyndon B. Johnson in 1964, and comes from the slang use of 'jawbone' meaning to talk one's way into something one wants, especially credit or a loan.

jawl v [*UK*] [*Market-traders*] to leave, to depart.

jaws n pl [*Croquet*] the entrance to the hoop.

jazz rail n [*Coal-mining*] a short, abruptly curved section of rail inserted into a track to derail runaway tubs or wagons.

JEEP n [*Military*] acro **Joint Emergency Evacuation Plan** the contingency plans for the evacuation of key personnel from Washington in the event of a nuclear attack. Army and Air Force helicopters take the first 44 of 243 selected personnel – elite scientists, officials, technicians, all holding a JEEP–1 identification – to the Alternate National Military Command Center ('Site R') at Raven Rock and to the civilian government emergency bunker, 'The Special Facility', in Mt. Weather, northern Virginia. All these people have been chosen to run the country during and after a war; in peacetime they remain on permanent standby.

jeep n [*US*] [*Finance*] a graduated payment mortgage: a mortgage in which payments are arranged to start at a low rate, then gradually increase. Such mortgages are designed for young couples whose incomes, it is assumed, will rise as required to meet the heavier payments.

jeer 1. n [*UK*] [*Market-traders*] the buttocks. See also **jeercase.** 2. n [*UK*] [*Market-traders*] the act of defecation.

jeercase n [*UK*] [*Market-traders*] the buttocks. See also **jeer.**

jemmy legs n [*US*] [*Navy*] the master-at-arms; it comes from RN 'jaunty' and Fr. 'gendarme'.

jeopardy assessment n [*Economics*] the power of the US government to make an immediate assessment of an individual's tax liability and to seize money or possessions if the IRS feels that the subject is about to leave the country to avoid payment.

jerk in v [*Car salesmen*] to turn back the mileometer on a second-hand car in order to make it seem 'younger'. See also **chop the clock.**

jerk off n [*Film*] a stunt in which a character is suddenly hauled vertically out of his/her seat on a horse or in a car; they hang suspended in mid-air while their erstwhile conveyance moves on.

jerk over v [*US*] [*Farming*] to plough land.

jerque note n [*Shipping*] a certificate of inward clearance issued by a customs officer – the jerquer

(of possible but unproven origin in Lat. 'cercare' meaning 'to search') – who has checked that all the formalities necessary to discharge cargo have been completed properly.

Jersey hit n [*Bowling*] a hit on the pins which fails to knock them all down, and leaves two disparate pins which cannot both be knocked down on a second throw.

jessie n [*Navy*] custard, which supposedly quivers like the eponymous Jessie's flesh.

jesus factor n [*US*] [*Navy*] an extra margin of safety left for imponderables, those phenomena that exist outside the realms of computers, technology and the finest seamanship.

jet 1. v [*Building*] to remove deposits of sand, dirt, gravel, etc. by using a pressure-driven water-hose. 2. also **jetting** n [*Clothing*] a narrow strip of fabric, usually cut along the line of the warp, which is sewn parallel to the pocket opening and turned over the mouth edge of the pocket.

jet jockey n [*Aerospace*] a pilot or astronaut who has exceptional skills in manoeuvring his craft.

jet shoes n pl [*Aerospace*] special boots which enable astronauts to walk in the weightless conditions on the moon.

jet turn n [*Skiing*] the forward movement of the skis with downward flexing.

jew n [*Navy*] the ship's tailor.

jewelry n [*US*] [*Farming*] the ring in a hog's nose.

Jewish overdrive n [*US*] [*Road transport*] disengaging the gears while a truck is going down a gradient or coasting down a hill.

jib n [*UK*] [*Coal-mining*] See **buttock.**

jig v [*Angling*] said of a fish when it shakes its head in an attempt to dislodge the hook.

jigger 1. v [*Book-binding*] to rub a tool backwards and forwards to polish up a line or other impression in a leather binding. 2. n [*Clothing*] the button on the inside of a double-breasted jacket (usually sewn on a long shank). 3. n [*Electronics*] a device used to create and administer electric shocks. 4. n [*Gemstones*] See **greaser.** 5. n [*Golf*] a short iron club used for approach shots. 6. n [*Logging*] a board inserted into the trunk of a tree so that the axeman can stand on it and thus fell a tree at a point which cannot otherwise be reached from the ground. 7. n [*Mining*] a hook which attaches trucks to an endless belt. 8. n [*Pottery*] a horizontal lathe used in china making. 9. n [*Shoe-making*] a device for polishing the upper leather or the edge of a boot sole. 10. n [*Textiles*] in dyeing this is a machine which dyes cloth by passing it backwards and forwards over a set of rollers in a dye-bath.

jiggerman n [*Glass-making*] a worker who takes containers of glass from the casting ladle to the filling end of the tank furnace.

jiggers n pl [*UK*] [*Market-traders*] the stairs.

jigglers n pl [*UK*] [*Police*] skeleton keys that are used for opening tumbler locks.

jill 1. n [*Logging*] a lazy, inefficient, generally

J

useless logger. **2.** *n* [*Shooting*] a female ferret. **3.** *v* [*Merchant navy*] to manoeuvre a ship in a confined space.

jill poke *n* [*Logging*] a lever used to dump logs from flat cars into a pond.

jim crow law *n* [*US*] [*Politics*] any custom or law that is designed to humiliate the black population; it comes from a song popular in Kentucky c.1840 in which Negroes were identified with the equally black crow.

jim hill *n* [*Logging*] a railroad spike used to hold heavy lines in place while they are being spliced.

jimmie *n* [*US*] [*Road transport*] GMC truck.

jimmie screamer *n* [*US*] [*Road transport*] GMC diesel truck.

jimmies' union *n* [*Navy*] all the first lieutenants in a flotilla. See also **jimmy the one**.

jimmy the one *n* [*Navy*] the First Lieutenant.

jimmying *n* [*UK*] [*Police*] this comes from the instrument – the jimmy/jemmy – which is used to break open doors, safes, etc; hence it means getting into films, dog-tracks or any other entertainment without buying a ticket.

jims *n pl* [*Sex*] inoffensive men who get their satisfaction from hanging around street prostitutes as they go about their business.

jink *v* [*Air Force*] to take evasive action.

jitter 1. *n* [*TV*] small, irregular variations in the signal that cause the picture to shake on the screen; this is due to synchronising defects in the equipment. **2.** *n* [*Video*] a video image that flutters during projection.

jizz *n* [*Naturalists*] the characteristic impression given by an animal or plant; possibly it comes from 'guise', but there is no proof of this connection.

Jo blocks *n pl* [*Engineering*] abbr of **Johansson blocks** standard measuring blocks, accurate to millionths of an inch; they are named after Carl E. Johanssen, a 20th century Swedish armaments inspector who designed them around 1918.

joag *n* [*UK*] [*Market-traders*] 5p, a shilling.

job 1. *n* [*Computing*] the complete description of a unit of work for a computer: a set of programs and the data to be manipulated by these programs. **2.** *n* [*UK*] [*Fire brigade*] an actual fire, rather than merely a call to the station; thus a 'good job' is a large, dangerous fire. See also **shout**. **3.** *n* [*US*] [*Undertakers*] the profession of undertaking. See also **call 8. 4.** *n* [*Military*] a large dangerous fire. **5.** *n* [*Military*] See **dog 13**.

job action *n* [*Industrial relations*] a variation of **industrial action** in which workers stage a go-slow or work-to-rule rather than an all-out strike.

job and finish *n* [*Industrial relations*] an agreement whereby the worker agrees to perform a set of tasks in a day and then to consider his work finished, whether or not it has taken him the usual eight hours.

job backwards *v* [*Stock market*] to remake one's calculations using hindsight, and working out what should have happened if one had only known what was going to occur in the market.

job mix *n* [*Computing*] the set of jobs being executed simultaneously in a multi-programming system. See also **job 1**.

job one *n* [*Motor trade*] the first production car of a new line: the saleable product of years of planning and development.

job spoiler *n* [*Industrial relations*] a member of a piece-work team who refuses to join in the fiddles established as the norm by the rest of the team; he thus spoils the job as performed by that team, although not as required by the employer. See also **conformer**.

job, the *n* [*UK*] [*Police*] the profession of policing; it is also the title of the Metropolitan Police magazine.

jobber 1. *n* [*Taxis*] See **clock, on the. 2.** *n* [*US*] [*Theatre*] originally this was an actor employed for a specific part in a specific production, rather than being one of a permanent company. It is now used for one who has a small role in a touring company. It comes from 'job actor' meaning one who was out of regular work and grateful for a single job.

jobbers *n pl* [*Stock market*] until the deregulation of the London Stock Exchange in October 1986 (**Big Bang**) these were the members and members' firms who maintained the stock market, buying and selling amongst themselves but never dealing with the general public who dealt only with brokers. Subsequent to deregulation, the jobber's role, and title, disappeared.

jobber's turn *n* [*Stock market*] the difference between the prices quoted by a **jobber** for buying and selling shares; if both sides accept these prices, the 'turn' is the jobber's gross profit.

jobble *n* [*Merchant navy*] a short, lumpy sea.

jobsworth *n* [*Pop music*] a time server, a petty official, anyone who refuses a request or prohibits an activity with the stock intonation 'It's more than my job's worth . . .'

jock *n* [*UK*] [*Railways*] food, thus a 'jock tin' is a container for food.

jocket pot *n* [*Glass-making*] a small pot supported in the furnace by two ordinary sized pots.

jockey 1. *v* [*Soccer*] to move backwards, forwards or sideways in order to cover any positional changes made by the opposition players. **2.** *n* [*Finance*] in venture capitalism this is someone who takes control of an investment situation by personally running the management side of the venture. **3.** *n* [*Navy*] any extra – such as cheese – served with a meal. **4.** *n* [*US*] [*Road transport*] See **hostler 2. 5.** also **pilot** *n* [*UK*] [*Road transport*] the truck driver.

Joe Baggs, also **Joe McGee** *n* [*US*] [*Hotels*] any guest who tips poorly if at all.

joe dog *n* [*US*] [*Road transport*] a nonpermanent unpowered set of wheels that can be added to a

J

tractor when it has to take a heavier than usual load.

Joe McGee (it) *v* [*US*] [*Painting*] to use a makeshift item of equipment.

Joe I *n* [*Military*] US intelligence nickname for the first Soviet testing of an atomic weapon, which took place in August 1949; it was named after the then leader Joseph, 'Uncle Joe', Stalin.

Joey *n* [*US*] [*Circus*] a clown, named after Joseph Grimaldi (1779–1837), the leading clown of his era.

joey 1. *n* [*Royal Marines*] a Royal Marine; collectively the Royal Marines are 'jollies'. 2. *n* [*UK*] [*Prisons*] an illicit parcel or any other unofficial consignment from the outer world.

jog 1. *n* [*Video*] the frame by frame movement of the video tape for editing purposes. 2. (*US*), **return piece** (*UK*) *n* [*Theatre*] a narrow **flat** placed at right angles to another flat either to form a corner or to break up a flat wall. Thus 'jogging the set' means varying the wall surfaces.

jogger *n* [*Paper-making*] a device that stacks and jogs sheets of pulp or paper into an even pile.

jogging *n* [*Banking*] a method of storing information.

joggle *n* [*Building, Plastering*] a method of positioning adjoining pieces in a plaster mould by means of an interlocking notch and projection.

joggle roll *n* [*Industry*] a machine with one set of rolls offset vertically in respect of another; it is used to displace the edge of a steel plate so that it will overlap an adjacent plate.

John *n* [*UK*] [*Military*] at the Royal Military College, Sandhurst this is a cadet in his first two years at the college. See also **Reg.**

john *n* [*Sex*] a client; it comes from **John Doe.**

John Doe 1. *n* [*Law*] a general term that is used by lawyers and police to identify any unnamed citizen; the feminine is Jane Doe. 2. *n* [*Law*] a party to a lawsuit whose name is not known or not cited. 3. *n* [*Police*] a person under police investigation, often a murder victim, to whom (as yet) no name has been put.

John O'Groats *n* [*Tiddleywinks*] an attempt at a **bristol** shot which fails and thus loses the opponent's wink.

John Stiles *n* [*Law*] a party to a lawsuit whose name is unknown; usually the third such party, following on John Doe and Richard Roe. See also **John Doe, Richard Roe.**

johnny *n* [*US*] [*Painting*] kerosene which is used to wipe down or 'dust' a varnished or painted surface.

Johnny Armstrong *n* [*Navy*] any hard work that involves hauling or pulling.

Johnny Newcome *n* [*Merchant navy*] a crewman making his first voyage.

Johnson noise *n* [*Electronics*] electrical noise caused by the random thermal movement of conduction electrons; it is named after John B.

Johnson, a US physicist (b. 1887) who first named the phenomenon in 1928.

joint 1. *n* [*Drugs*] a marijuana cigarette. 2. [*Drugs*] the hypodermic syringe used to inject narcotics. 3. [*Fairs*] a stall, tent or concession stand in a fairground. 4. [*US*] [*Horse-racing*] a small battery-operated device that will give a horse an electric shock to stimulate it during a race. 5. [*UK*] [*Market-traders*] a market-stall.

joint and several bond *n* [*Commerce, Finance*] a bond which is supported by two or more guarantors who individually and together assume full responsibility for paying a debt if the actual debtor defaults.

joint mouse *n* [*Medicine*] a small fragment of bone or cartilege floating in the cavity of a joint.

joints 1. *n pl* [*Book collecting*] the sides of the spine. 2. *n pl* [*Mining*] cracks or fissures intersecting a mass of rocks, often found in two sets of parallel planes.

joker 1. *n* [*US*] [*Government*] a clause or amendment inserted into a piece of legislation which does not make its real effect known at first; thus it is any part of a contract that frustrates one of the parties to that contract. 2. *n* [*Textiles*] a size ticket on a garment.

jole *v* [*UK*] [*Market-traders*] to hit, to beat.

jolly 1. *n* [*Clothing*] a machine that sandpapers felt hats. 2. *n* [*Pottery*] See **jigger 8.**

jonah 1. *n* [*Gambling*] a person whose presence is assumed to bring bad luck to other players. 2. *n* [*Gambling*] a superstitious player.

joskin *n* [*UK*] [*Market-traders*] a bumpkin, a simple country yokel.

josser *n* [*UK*] [*Circus*] an outsider, specifically one who works in the circus but who does not come from the old circus families; possibly it comes from 19th century usage 'simpleton', from 'joskin' meaning country bumpkin.

jostler *n* [*US*] [*Crime*] a pickpocket.

journal 1. *n* [*Cars*] that part of a shaft around which a circular plain bearing acts; most often this is applied to the bearing surfaces of the crankshaft. 2. *n* [*Commerce*] a list of financial transactions recorded in the order in which they occur, without the detailed analysis and classification of ledger entries which are compiled from the basic journal material. 3. *n* [*Computing*] the list of all messages sent and received by a data communications terminal. 4. *n* [*Computing*] a chronological list of alterations made to a set of data; it is used for the reconstruction of that data in the event of possible corruption.

journey 1. *n* [*S. Wales*] [*Coal-mining*] the underground train that carries ballast and rubbish underground. 2. *n* [*Glass-making*] a complete cycle of work involved in converting a quantity of material into glass or glass products.

JOVIAL *n* [*Computing*] acro **Jules' Own Version of International Algorithmic Language** a version of the now obsolete IAL (or

J

ALGOL 58) still used on some US military computers.

JR *n* [*UK*] [*Prisons*] abbr of **Judgement Respited** this is usually, and incorrectly, interpreted as 'judge's remand'; in either case it means the imprisonment under full prison regulations, although without benefit of a prison job, of a former remand or bail prisoner who has already pleaded guilty, but who must wait out the trial of those confederates similarly charged who are pleading not guilty.

juck, also **juckle** *n* [*UK*] [*Market-traders*] a dog; it is used as a pejorative description of a man.

juck's lips, also **juckle's lips** *n* [*UK*] [*Market-traders*] a quarrelsome or disagreeable person.

judas *n* [*Meat trade*] an animal that is used to lead the rest of the cattle into the slaughterhouse.

judder *n* [*Cars*] a vibration felt during braking, usually when braking hard from high speed; it is caused by distorted discs, oval drums or worn pads; it comes from 'brake judder'.

Judd's dictum *n* [*Art*] a remark of the US sculptor/writer Don Judd, who answered the perennial question 'But is it art?' by replying 'If someone calls it art, it's art.'

judge-made *a* [*Law*] based on legal interpretations which have been made by a judge.

judgement bond *n* [*Law*] See **appeal bond.**

judge's rules *n pl* [*UK*] [*Law*] a set of rules that are supposed to govern the conduct of police interrogations of suspects held in custody.

judy 1. *n* [*Angling*] See **kelt.** 2. *n* [*UK*] [*Medicine*] a duodenal ulcer; the word comes from the way it is pronounced. 3. *n* [*Military*] air intercept code for: 'I have contact and am taking over the intercept'.

jug, also **jouk, juk** *v* [*Shooting*] used of pheasants or partridges which roost on the ground.

jug hustler *n* [*Oil rigs*] a member of the seismic crew who operates the geophones with which sound-waves from sub-surface strata are detected.

juggles *n pl* [*Logging*] long chips of wood that fly off the tree while it is being felled with axes.

juice 1. *n* [*Politics*] power, influence; it comes from slang for electrical current. See also **clout 2.** 2. *n* [*TV repair*] electrical current; it is also in general slang use outside the trade.

juice joint *n* [*Gambling*] a crooked gambling game in which either dice or a roulette wheel are controlled by 'juice' – hidden electrical magnets – concealed in or under a table or wheel.

juicer *n* [*Film*] an electrician. See also **sparks.**

juke (*US*), **sell a dummy** (*UK*) *v* [*Football, Soccer*] to 'fake' an opponent by pretending to make one move but actually making another and thus 'wrong-footing' the opponent.

julian date *n* [*Computing*] the actual day of the year, eg: 32 instead of February 1st, which is often used in computing.

jumbo 1. *n* [*Coal-mining*] a mobile scaffold that assists drilling in large headings where the higher areas are not easily accessible. 2. *n* [*Coal-mining*] a drill carriage. 3. *n* [*Logging*] a sled used for hauling logs. 4. *n* [*Logging*] a travelling carriage used for transporting drills, saws, etc. 5. *n* [*Tunnelling*] a travelling carriage used to remove excavated material. 6. *n* [*US*] [*Paper-making*] an extremely large roll of paper. 7. *n* [*US*] [*Railways*] a record of carriage movements posted on oversize sheets of paper and kept in a loose-leaf binder.

jumbo-cut *n* [*Film*] an abrupt cut from one scene to another with no form of gradual transition.

jumboise *v* [*Commerce*] to enlarge a cargo ship, especially an oil tanker, by inserting extra sections of deck and hull between the bow and the stern.

jump 1. *n* [*Computing*] in programming this is a departure from the consecutive sequence in which instructions are executed. 2. *v* [*Journalism*] to carry over a story or feature from one part of a newspaper to another. 3. *n* [*US*] [*Journalism*] See **break 9.** 4. *n* [*Theatre*] a one-night stand on a tour, or the distance between two such venues. 5. *v* [*Theatre*] to forget a portion of one's lines and thus jump forward in the script. 6. also **bump, breach** *v* [*US*] [*Music*] to cut into the business of a rival juke box salesman.

jump the bite *v* [*Medicine*] in dentistry this is an operation to correct a faulty bite by bringing forward the mandible.

jump line *n* [*Journalism*] a directional line of print at the end of the first column or page of a piece which makes a **jump** elsewhere; it is usually found as in 'continued col.6', 'continued p.56' etc.; it occurs similarly at the start of the continued piece as in 'continued from p.1' etc.

jump the gun *v* [*Athletics*] See **break the start.**

jump-cut *n* [*Film*] the removal of portions of the narrative to tighten up the action or plot.

jumper 1. *n* [*Basketball*] an attempt to score a field goal in which the player releases the ball at the peak of an upward jump. 2. *n* [*Industry*] an experienced employee who can substitute at random for one or more other workers in a given industry. 3. *n* [*Industry*] on a delivery-round this is the roundsman's helper, who jumps in and out of the van/lorry. 4. *n* [*US*] [*Police*] an actual or potential suicide victim, but not necessarily one who is about to leap from a tall building. 5. *n* [*UK*] [*Railways*] a travelling ticket collector. 6. *n* [*Religion*] a Holy Jumper is a member of a sect who reflect their enjoyment of the Holy Spirit by jumping, clapping, shouting and generally making the spirit physically manifest in their own bodies. 7. *n* [*UK*] [*Buses*] a London Transport inspector, who jumps on and off various buses. 8. *n* [*TV*] a length of cable that provides a variety of different connections for attaching the lights.

jumping jack *n* [*Textiles*] a part of a hosiery machine which jumps up and down to carry out its part of the operation.

J

jumping jinny *n* [*Roadworkers*] a mechanical stamper used to repair the roads.

jump-up, also **van-dragging** *n* [*UK*] [*Police*] the practice of robbing lorries by jumping on to the back and dragging off the goods.

Jungian aesthetics *n* [*Art*] Jungian art theories stress the conscious or unconscious use by an artist of the various archetypes in his/her work, and the semi-conscious awareness of the 'collective unconscious'. See also **Freudian aesthetics.**

jungle rot, also **crotch rot** *n* [*US*] [*Medicine*] a fungus infection in the pubic area that develops as a result of using antibiotics.

junior *n* [*UK*] [*Law*] a barrister who assists the **leader** in a legal case; in general, this is a barrister who is not yet a Queen's Counsel.

junior capital *n* [*Finance*] those shares in a company which represent the **equity** or actual ownership of the company.

junior issue *n* [*Stock market*] an issue of shares that are lower in rank than other shares issued by the same company.

junk 1. *n* [*Aerospace*] a communications satellite which is still in orbit but which is no longer used for transmissions/receptions. 2. *n* [*Oil rigs*] the rock and earth debris in the **mud** that is extracted from the well.

junk basket *n* [*Oil rigs*] an implement used in **fishing** lost tools from a well.

junk bond *n* [*Stock market*] a high-risk, non-corporate bond that is bought at less than its face value.

junk gun *n* [*US*] [*Police*] See **Saturday night special.**

junk pile *n* [*UK*] [*Road transport*] a lorry in very poor condition, fit only for the junk pile.

junk rubber *n* [*Table tennis*] all modern rubber bat coverings produced by technological advances; these include long **pimples, tacky** and **antiloop.**

junk sculpture *n* [*Art*] sculptures that employ miscellaneous street debris either as collages or assemblies. They are sometimes left as 'found objects', sometimes transformed as the artist desires.

junkets *n pl* [*Politics*] expenses-paid trips offered to politicians by a variety of interested parties – pressure groups, lobbyists, business interests, etc. – or trips funded by public money that are arranged allegedly for those concerned to go on 'fact-finding' trips. The term is used in a derogatory sense by the critics of such expenditure. See also **facility trip.**

junksport *n* [*Sport, TV*] such artificial sporting competitions – eg: 'Superstars' – which have been created for TV and in which the stars of one sport take on those of others, none of whom are allowed to compete in the one area in which they are actually expert.

jural relations *n pl* [*Law*] any relations which define the application of the law, eg: right, claim, duty, obligation, privilege, liberty and inability.

jury *n* [*US*] [*Theatre*] the first night audience who 'judge' a play.

jus *n* [*Military*] used in the French Foreign Legion to mean 'coffee'.

justify *v* [*Printing*] to even up the lines in a column of print so that both sides of that column run down the page in a straight line.

juve 1. *n* [*Sex*] abbr of **juvenile** child pornography, whether on film, in magazines or books. 2. *n* [*Theatre*] abbr of **juvenile.**

juvenile 1. *n* [*US*] [*Horse-racing*] a two-year-old horse. 2. *n* [*Theatre*] a youthful role or the starring youth role; thus 'juvenile powder' is makeup that helps approximate a youthful complexion.

juveniles *n pl* [*Book collecting, Book trade*] children's books.

K

K *n* [*UK*] [*Government*] abbr of a **Knighthood.**

K lath *n* [*Building, Plastering*] a variety of metal lathing incorporating a waterproofed building paper laminated into it.

K point *n* [*Skiing*] in ski jumping this is the point that marks the end of the straight landing slope; to land beyond the K point, marked by a red line, can be dangerous for the jumper, since the slopes then begin to dip more drastically. See also **P point**.

K–12 *n* [*Publishing*] kindergarten to 12 years old: the youngest section of the book-buying public, as designated by publishers. See also **elhi**.

Kabuki Sound *n* [*Audio*] a dismissive term for Japanese speaker-design and performance, which, until about 1980, was tailored strictly to specific Oriental demands.

kackling also **keckling** *n* [*Sailing, Ropework*] old rope passed around hawsers and cable to prevent chafing.

kaffir circus *n* [*Stock market*] those brokers who deal in South African gold-mining shares.

kagg *n* [*Navy*] an argument; general talk.

Kahn energy *n* [*Military*] the quantity of fission energy required for the destruction by radio-activity of the total population of one major nation, assuming that there are neither adequate civil defence precautions or air-raid shelters. For the US or USSR this has been estimated at 10,000,000,000 tons. The term is named after Herman Kahn, the nuclear futurologist.

kahuna *n* [*Surfing*] a fictitious 'god' of surfing; it comes from the Hawaiian word for priest, expert or wise man.

kamikaze 1. *n* [*US*] [*Bars*] a cocktail served in a shot glass which is thus to be tossed off in one gulp, rather than in a cocktail glass, from which it is sipped. 2. *n* [*Surfing*] a deliberate **wipe-out** in which the surfer is forced to leave the board and start swimming to the shore.

kamp *n* [*US*] [*Police*] acro **known as a male prostitute** this is used by New York Police Department on reports.

kanga *n* [*Roadworkers*] a road drill; it comes from kangaroo, which is also always jumping up and down.

kangaroo *n* [*Transport*] See **piggyback**.

kangaroo ticket *n* [*US*] [*Politics*] a ticket in which the nominee for vice-president has a greater electoral appeal than does the one standing for president.

kangaroo word *n* [*Logology*] See **marsupial**.

Kansas City Standard *n* [*Computing*] a format standard used in microcomputers for writing and reading data from a tape cassette.

Kapitalistate *n* [*Politics*] a concept based on Marx's 'Das Kapital' and created by the US Marxist James O'Connor: modern capitalism is dominated or at least supplemented by direct or indirect state intervention.

karzy *n* [*UK*] [*Market-traders*] the lavatory.

kata *n* [*Science*] abbr of **katathermometer** an instrument used for measuring the cooling power of ambient air.

katydids *n pl* [*Logging*] See **big wheels**.

kazik *n* [*Antiques, Rug trade*] a bad rug which lacks quality and has probably been over-priced.

KB *n* [*UK*] [*Prisons*] abbr of **knockback** a disap-

pointment or rejection, referring specifically to an appeal against sentence or for parole.

KBS *n* [*TV*] abbr of **kick, bollock and scramble** a period of intensive work which may last from a few hours to a number of weeks.

keel the goods *v* [*UK*] [*Railways*] to code goods for consignment on a given train.

keelage *n* [*Shipping*] the charges paid by a ship while it occupies a berth in port.

keep-alive *a* [*Electronics*] said of devices and phenomena in certain kinds of discharge tubes which operate or occur continuously and serve to initiate an intermittent main discharge or facilitate its establishment.

keeper 1. *n* [*US*] [*Football*] an offensive play in which the quarterback attempts to run with the ball, rather than passing it or handing it off to a teammate. See also **quarterback sneak**. 2. *n* [*US*] [*Journalism*] a news story that is reserved for later publication, at which time it will have a greater impact and effect on the readers than it will at the earlier date. 3. *n* [*US*] [*Medicine*] the appendix: 'You go in there with a steel blade, and you find 'er, and you keep 'er'. (S. Shem, 'The House of God', 1978)

keeping house *part phr* [*Commerce*] the action of a debtor facing bankruptcy, when he makes it hard for creditors to see him. Since a writ must be served in person, if the debtor refuses to open his door and never leaves his home, it is exceptionally hard to serve it.

keeping one's belt on *part phr* [*Sex*] referring to a **hustler** who rigorously preserves his cherished self-image of absolute masculinity by refusing ever to take a passive role in a paid homosexual encounter.

keeps *n* [*Marbles*] a game in which the winners keep the marbles they have won. See also **funs**.

keeps and fastenings *n pl* [*Merchant navy*] the stopping of one engine for repairs and adjustments after the ship has been at sea for a week.

keester plant *n* [*US*] [*Crime*] any form of container or suppository which can be used to hide contraband by inserting it into the anus.

kegler *n* [*Ten-pin bowling*] anyone who plays ten-pin bowling, skittles or allied sports.

keister 1. *n* [*US*] [*Crime*] a burglar's tool-box or satchel. 2. *n* [*US*] [*Crime*] a safe. 3. *n* [*US*] [*Painting*] the bag which carries a painter's working clothes.

Kelly *n* [*US*] [*Medicine*] a tubular speculum for rectal examination; it describes both the speculum, which extends the orifice, and the clamp which closes it up.

kelly *n* [*Oil rigs*] a square or hexagonal hollow shaft about 40ft. long which engages at one end with the drilling table and at the other with the drill pipe and transmits the rotating torque from the drill table to the drill string. Thus 'kelly joint' is the stand of pipe that carries the kelly; 'kelly drive' is a collar carrying the kelly.

K

kelt, also **kipper** n [*Angling*] an unclean fish, which has not yet recovered from spawning.

kemp n [*Weaving*] a coarse fibre that occasionally grows on malnourished sheep; it resembles vegetable fibre and tends to resist dye; thus 'kempy wool' is wool which has kemp in it.

ken n [*UK*] [*Market-traders*] a house.

kensington gore n [*Film, TV*] fake blood used for deaths and disasters on the screen; it is a pun on the road that runs along the southern boundary of Hyde Park, London.

Kent n [*UK*] [*Building, Plastering*] plaster with a grey finish. See also **Nottingham**.

keps n pl [*UK*] [*Coal-mining*] four iron bars which drop down from the side of the shaft, on which the **cage** comes to rest.

kerb trading n [*Stock market*] trading that takes place after the **closure** of the official market.

kerb weight 1. n [*Motor trade*] the weight of a vehicle without the occupants or their luggage, but with oil, water and some petrol. **2.** [*UK*] [*Road transport*] the weight of the vehicle in road-going condition, excluding the weight of the driver and a possible passenger, prior to loading. See also **tare weight.**

kerbside conference n [*Commerce*] a post-interview conversation between a salesman and his sales supervisor to analyse selling method, performance and achievement.

kerf n [*Coal-mining*] **holing** made by hand by a coalcutter.

kerfing n [*Building, Plastering*] the bruising of reinforcement laths to make them assume curved shapes in fibrous plaster casts.

kermesse n [*Cycling*] a circuit race; it comes from Fr. for a feast or fair day (originally held on the anniversary of the consecration of a church).

kern n [*Printing*] that part of a printed character which overhangs its own body and thus overlaps onto an adjacent piece.

kernel 1. n [*Computing*] the part of an operating system that must always be in main memory, once loaded; it comprises the basic loading and supervisory functions. **2.** n [*Computing*] the part of a segmented program that must always be kept in main storage when any other segment is loaded. If a system is divided into a series of levels, each dealing with some part of the system hardware, the kernel is the lowest; it is the only part of the operating system that must be checked out by strict program verification.

kettle 1. n [*Angling*] a receptacle for holding live fish which will be used as bait. **2.** n [*Glass-making*] a hemispherical vessel, 3ft–4ft. in diameter, into which molten glass is ladled. **3.** n [*UK*] [*Market-traders*] a watch. **4.** n [*Metallurgy*] a wide, shallow saucer-shaped vessel in which operations are carried out on metal in the liquid state. It is also applicable to plastics. **5.** n [*Navy*] a ship's boilers. **6.** n [*US*] [*Paper-making*] a rotary form of **digester.**

kettle stuffer n [*Logging*] a sawmill camp foreman.

key 1. v [*Advertising*] to distinguish an advertisement by including some special feature that will have an immediate appeal to the consumer. **2.** v [*US*] [*Football*] said of a defensive player who concentrates on a particular member of the opposition, often a running back, in an attempt to constrain that player; it comes from movie use: **key light. 3.** n [*Chess*] the first move towards the solution of a problem; it is a move which sets the whole style of solving that problem. **4.** n [*Computing*] one or more characters used for identifying data. **5.** n [*Plastering*] the irregular lines scratched into the first coat of plaster to provide the best surface to which the smooth top coat will adhere. **6.** n [*Drugs*] one kilogram. See also **weight.**

key book n [*Public relations*] any publication in which the PR's client is very keen to appear.

key click n [*Communications*] See **impulsive noise.**

key light n [*TV, Film*] the main light used to illuminate a particular person or object in the scene; it refers especially to the light focussed on the star.

key travel n [*Computing*] the movement of the key from its rest position to being fully depressed.

key up v [*Building, Plastering*] to prepare a surface so as to provide an adequate base for a successful bond with the material applied to it.

keyboard phobia n [*Business, Computing*] the antagonism many managers/executives feel towards using a keyboard for inputting data into the office computer; this stems either from an actual inability to use the machine or the snobbish belief, endemic to management, that typing is a lowly task that threatens their own status.

keyed advertisement n [*Advertising*] an advertisement designed to cause an enquirer to indicate the source of his information, for instance by including a code number or a particular – if fictitious – 'department' with the return address.

keyhole n [*Aerospace*] the area through which a spacecraft must pass in order to reach a particular objective.

keyhole wound n [*Medicine, Police*] the wound a victim sustains after being shot with a worn gun: since the barrel is no longer perfectly smooth, the bullet tumbles rather than rotates and thus tears a ragged entry wound, causing serious internal damage to the victim. Such wounds are harder to treat than those inflicted by new weapons.

keynoter, also **keynote speech** n [*US*] [*Politics*] the opening address at a political convention or similar meeting that sets the tone, outlines the topics on the agenda and generally attempts to promote a feeling of unity.

keystone n [*Advertising, Business*] the correct angle for projecting slides, film, etc. when making

K

a presentation; optimally this is at 180° to the screen, but the positioning is rendered more complex when several projectors are being used.

keystone approach *n* [*US*] [*Undertakers*] a sales method coined by W. M. Krieger of the U.S. National Selected Morticians Assoc.: the customer is shown first the dearest and then the cheapest coffin in a range, thus playing on the general human psychology that will usually cause one to buy a coffin of intermediate price, even if the cheapest was really desired.

keystoning 1. *n* [*Optics*] a geometrical image distortion arising when a plane surface is photographed at an angle other than perpendicular to the lens axis. **2.** *n* [*Optics*] when showing slides, this is the distortion of a projected image, usually with a wide top and narrow bottom effect. To avoid this, the screen must be place at 90° to the projection axis.

keystroke *v* [*Computing*] to type a single character into a computer.

keyter *n* [*TV*] a vision mixer which 'cuts holes' in the main picture and allows captions or other material to be inserted on-screen.

khaltura *n* [*Politics*] in Russia these are those black market operations deemed necessary for the functioning of the economy and which are thus unofficially connived at by the authorities. Factories that produce consumer goods will siphon off a percentage for this black market, where the producers of such goods can sell them and thus augment their incomes.

ki *n* [*Navy*] cocoa.

kibbitzer *n* [*Gambling*] a non-player who nonetheless likes to comment and advise the players on the progress of the game.

kibosh *v* [*Art*] to add cement or plaster to a sculptured wooden form.

kick 1. *v* [*Athletics*] said of a runner who accelerates during the final phase of a race. **2.** *v* [*Cricket*] used of a ball which rises sharply off the pitch or in the outfield when it hits a deviation in the surface. **3.** *n* [*Oil rigs*] the entry of formation fluid into a well bore when the formation pressure exceeds the hydrostatic head of the **mud** column.

kick and shove *v* [*US*] [*Railways*] to operate the points to switch cars in a yard.

kick off *v* [*Computing*] to deprive a job or task of access to the computing system.

kick the bucket over *v* [*Navy*] to involve oneself in serious trouble; kicking a bucket over was a serious naval crime.

kickback 1. *n* [*Oil rigs*] the sight of mud bubbling up through a bore-hole that can be a warning of a possible blow-out. **2.** *n* [*Railways*] a gravity-operated device which reverses the direction of a wagon or wagons in a marshalling yard. **3.** *n* [*Wood work*] in wood preservation this is the amount of liquid that is forced out of the wood when pressure is released. **4.** also **backkick** *n* [*Electronics*] high voltage produced (as in a radio

transmitting set) by the sudden interruption of current in a low-voltage circuit.

kickbacks *n pl* [*US*] [*Meat trade*] animals that are rejected by the buyer for any reason.

kickdown *n* [*Cars*] an accelerator-linked device on a car with automatic transmission that enables a driver to select and get full performance from a lower gear.

kicker 1. *n* [*Finance*] See **sweetener**. **2.** *n* [*Gambling*] a high third card which is retained in the hand, alongside a pair, when changing one's first-round discards in draw poker. **3.** *n* [*Journalism*] a line of type set above a headline, usually in a different typeface, which is intended to provoke interest in and amplify the impact and meaning of that headline. **4.** *n* [*Merchant navy*] an outboard motor. **5.** *n* [*US*] [*Air Force*] an aircrew member who pushes out of the aircraft the packages, crates, etc. that are to be parachuted on to a given target or drop zone. **6.** *n* [*Printing*] a metal arm attached to the press that is used to divide the flow of newly printed newspapers by pushing every 25th, 50th or 100th out of line, to facilitate the composition of bundles. **7.** *n* [*Journalism*] a story that runs down the left-hand column of the page, and thus 'kicks it off'. **8.** *n* [*Sailing*] an outboard motor, or the boat which uses one. **9.** *n* [*TV*] a light, possibly humorous story that comes at the end of an otherwise serious news programme; it originated in the US and is being increasingly adopted in the UK.

kick-off room *n* [*US*] [*Medicine*] a ward or room in which terminally ill patients are placed when hope has been abandoned and they are about to die.

kick-out *n* [*Surfing*] the pressing down of the rear of a surfboard to turn it, and thus mount a wave.

kicksorter *n* [*Technology*] an electronic device that classifies electrical pulses according to their amplitude.

kickturn *n* [*Skiing*] a change of direction while standing on a slope, by moving each ski in turn through 180°.

kick-up *n* [*Custom cars*] a chassis modification whereby the rear section is raised by means of cutting and inserting a new piece of side rail; the effect is to lower the back of the car, since the axle now sits higher up in the chassis.

kid show *n* [*US*] [*Carnivals*] the freak show: because human freaks are seen as another variety of children. So these are shows by children, although not necessarily for them.

kideo *n* [*Film*] any video programming aimed specifically at the child market. See also **kidvid**.

kidney buster *n* [*US*] [*Road transport*] a truck that gives the driver an uncomfortable ride.

kidvid *n* [*TV*] television shows designed for children.

kilburn *n* [*UK*] [*Police*] this comes from rhyming slang 'Kilburn priory' meaning 'diary', the official police notebook that backs up police evidence in court.

kilhig, also **killig** n [*Logging*] See **samson**.

kill 1. v [*Building, Plastering*] to destroy the set of semi-hydrate plasters by continuing the mixing after the normal setting time has elapsed. 2. v [*Cricket*] to drop a **dead bat** on the ball and thus render harmless any speed or spin that it may threaten. 3. v [*Journalism*] to stop a story before it is set or printed. 4. v [*Publishing*] to delete material, to remove standing type or stored text. 5. v [*TV, Radio*] to stop a story from being completed or if completed from being broadcast, because of inaccuracies, fear of libel suits or simply because it is already out of date. 6. also **save** v [*Theatre, TV, Film*] to extinguish a light or a sound effect. 7. n [*Shooting*] any animal that has been killed by a carnivore; either killed naturally or after being tied up as bait. 8. n [*Tennis*] a stroke that the opponent cannot play. See also **ace 4**. 9. also **smash** n [*Table tennis*] a winning stroke played with maximum power against a ball which was returned high by one's opponent.

kill a well v [*Oil rigs*] to overcome the natural flow of a well by controlling it with high density **mud** flow.

kill fee n [*Journalism*] the money paid to a free-lance writer who has submitted a commissioned piece which is then not printed; it is usually 75% of the original fee.

kill line n [*Military*] that theoretical point in space where it is calculated that an anti-ballistic missile (**ABM**) would intercept and destroy an incoming hostile missile.

kill ratio n [*Military*] the difference between the number of hostile troops and the number of one's own forces killed in an engagement. See also **body count**.

kill the number v [*US*] [*Garment trade*] to undercut the price of an expensive dress by promoting one's own, cheaper version.

killer 1. n [*US*] [*Meat trade*] any animal suitable for killing and packing. 2. n [*Philately*] an early form of obliteration, using heavy bars, cork impressions and similarly crude devices. 3. n [*UK*] [*Railways*] a diesel engine; this comes from its relatively (to steam engines) silent approach along the track.

killer bees n pl [*Business*] individuals who help a company fend off takeover bids; often they are investment bankers who devise the best means of making the target company less appealing to predators.

killick n [*Navy*] a leading seaman; it comes from his badge, which bears the symbol of an anchor ('killick' in dialect).

killing n [*Metallurgy*] a means of preventing any further strains or possible defects by applying a certain amount of cold work (see **cold working**)

to narrow strip steel which has already been heat treated to reach its current dimensions.

killing bait, also **killing fly** n [*Angling*] a successful bait or fly.

kilo n [*Computing*] normally the number 1000, but in computer terms the number 1024, because it corresponds to the binary number 10 000 000 000.

kilroy n [*TV*] a shot in which the announcer's or performer's chin is missing; it comes from the slogan 'Kilroy was here'.

kilter n [*Gambling*] a hand that consists of cards of little or no use to the player.

kimmie n [*Marbles*] the target marble in the game. See also **dib, duck, immie, peewee, mib**.

kindly tenant n [*Scots.*] [*Law*] a tenant favoured with a low rent because the landlord either likes him or believes him to be a descendant of the original owner of the land on which he lives.

kinetic architecture n [*Architecture*] the theories of a school of architects who claim that traditional architecture is too static to respond adequately to modern social pressures and who posit a 'kinetic' style that incorporates adaptable buildings that can respond, with moving walls, foundations on rafts, etc.

kinetic art n [*Art*] any artwork that requires and incorporates a degree of movement: of the work itself, of the spectator in front of it, of a part of the work by the spectator. Thus 'kinetic sculpture' is a form of sculpture which requires the same movement/involvement as kinetic art.

king and queen n [*US*] [*Bars*] a double measure of a drink.

king kong n [*US*] [*Prisons*] prison distilled liquor, often fake gin.

king pair n [*Cricket*] a batsman gets this if he is dismissed with the first ball of both his innings in a match.

king snipe n [*Logging*] the foreman in charge of maintaining the logging railroad.

kinger n [*UK*] [*Market-traders*] a good customer, especially after a hard day with few profits; it comes from King.

king-of-arms n [*Heraldry*] a chief **herald**; Garter King-of-Arms is chief herald of England, Lyon King-of-Arms of Scotland.

kingpin n [*UK*] [*Road transport*] the connecting pin on a semi-trailer which locates with the fifth-wheel plate on an articulated tractive unit.

King's eye n [*US*] [*Carpenters*] a plumb rule, a spirit level.

King's gambit n [*Chess*] a series of opening moves in which one sacrifices one's pawns.

kinker n [*Circus*] an acrobat or contortionist.

kinking n [*Metallurgy*] See **flatting**.

kip 1. n [*Angling*] the male salmon's nose at spawning time. 2. n [*Gymnastics*] a vigorous and rapid extension of the hip joint in order to raise the body's centre of gravity.

kipper 1. n [*Angling*] the male salmon during the

K

spawning season; it is so called from its dull gold colour, reminiscent of the smoked fish. **2.** also **tinfish** *n* [*Navy*] a torpedo. **3.** *n* [*Aus.*] [*Navy*] a British sailor.

kipper trip *n* [*UK*] [*Railways*] an angler's special.

KIPS *n* [*Computing*] acro **Kilo Instructions Per second** a measure of the speed of computer operation – 1024 operations per second. See also **flops, LIPS, MIPS.**

kirvings *n pl* [*Coal-mining*] See **gummings.**

kish *n* [*Metallurgy*] in iron-founding this is graphite which is thrown out very easily by liquid cast iron on cooling.

kiss marks *n pl* [*Dog breeding*] tan spots on the cheeks of black and tan, and black and tan and white, coloured dogs.

kiss spot *n* [*Tanning*] a mark that appears on a vegetable dyed hide when it has been in contact with another hide during the tanning process.

kiss the mistress *v* [*Bowls*] used of a bowl which barely grazes the jack (originally 'the mistress').

kisser **1.** *n* [*Archery*] a protuberance of limited diameter on a bow string designed to aid a constant draw length. **2.** *n* [*Metallurgy*] a local patch of scale that results from two steel sheets remaining in close contact during **pickling.**

kissing spot *n* [*Dog breeding*] the name occasionally given to the lozenge-shaped mark on the head of the Cavalier King Charles spaniel.

kissing-crust *n* [*Baking*] the crust which forms at the point where one loaf touches another in the oven.

kit *n* [*Air Force*] computerised guidance systems, installed in a series of black boxes, that control the flight path and performance of modern fighter aircraft.

kitchen **1.** *n* [*Gambling*] a part of the casino at Monte Carlo where gamblers can place smaller bets than those wagered in the prestigious 'salle privée'. **2.** *n* [*Shuffle board*] the minus – 10 section of the scoring area. **3.** *n* [*Textiles*] the room where dyes are prepared and mixed preparatory to use.

kitchen junk school *n* [*Art*] the realist paintings of four UK artists – Bratby, Greaves, Smith, Middleditch – working in the mid–1950s. They specialised in squalid scenes, often actual kitchens, and anticipated much of the content of **pop** art, even if their style remained basically academic.

kite **1.** *n* [*Gemstones*] a step cut for a gem having a diamond shape and eight quadrilateral facets. **2.** *n* [*UK*] [*Law*] a **junior** barrister who is allotted a case at an assize court when the plaintiff can find no other defender. **3.** *n* [*US*] [*Prisons*] a letter or any form of written message.

kite-flying *n* [*Banking*] the illegal drawing of an accommodation bill on a person; this bill is quickly discounted at the bank when it is then found that the person on whom the bill is drawn

fails to honour it since he has received no goods or money in return.

kiting **1.** *n* [*Stock market*] any manipulation that results in the artificial boosting of prices. **2.** *n* [*Finance*] See **kite-flying.** **3.** *n* [*Medicine*] on the model of the criminal use (see **4**) this is the illegal altering of a prescription to increase the number of pills or other drugs actually prescribed by the doctor. **4.** *n* [*UK*] [*Police*] the passing of 'kites' – dud cheques.

kittens, also **kitts** *n pl* [*Furriers*] a group designation for a miscellany of furs belonging to branches of feline or rodent animal groups.

Kitty Hawk *n* [*Air travel*] HM Customs code for the Queen when she is flying via Heathrow Airport. See also **Kitty Rainbow.**

Kitty Rainbow *n* [*Air travel*] HM Customs code for the Duke of Edinburgh when he is flying via Heathrow Airport. See also **Kitty Hawk.**

kiwi **1.** *n* [*Aerospace*] a ground test reactor which, like the kiwi bird, is never intended to fly. **2.** *n* [*Air Force*] an RAF crew member who does not fly but remains on the ground to service the aircraft.

klang association *n* [*Linguistics*] the phenomenon whereby the association of a word, by those who hear it, is affected, and somewhat misconstrued, because of a familiar sound or word within that word.

klavern *n* [*Ku Klux Klan*] 'Klan' plus 'cavern' meaning a local Klan organisation.

kleagle *n* [*Ku Klux Klan*] 'Klan' plus 'eagle' meaning the head of the Klan organisations in a US state.

klinefelter *n* [*Medicine*] a syndrome that causes hermaphroditism in humans, and is found in people with an extra X sex chromosome, eg: XXY, XXXY and XXYY; it was named after Harry Klinefelter Jr. (born 1912). See also **Turners.**

klong *n* [*US*] [*Politics*] a term coined in 1972 by Frank Mankiewicz (working for Senator George McGovern's presidential campaign): 'a sudden rush of shit to the heart', ie: a reaction of horror on realising that one's own apparently minor mistake has led, or will lead, to a far more serious problem.

kloran *n* [*Ku Klux Klan*] 'Klan' plus 'Koran' meaning a Klan's book of rules, including passwords, prayers, duties and obligations.

kloxology *n* [*Ku Klux Klan*] 'Klan' plus 'doxology' meaning the ethos and philosophy of the Klan, encapsulating their bigotry and racism.

kludge **1.** *n* [*Computing*] an improvised, do-it-yourself **'lash-up'** which may well work. **2.** *n* [*Computing*] a factory assembled machine which still offers some (endearingly) eccentric characteristics.

kneecap *n* [*Military*] acro **the National Emergency Airborne Command Post** a converted Boeing 707 that will be used as an alternative Presidential command post in the event of a nuclear war, and will carry the President, the

K

Secretary of Defense and the Joint Chief of Staff. From here the nuclear exchanges can be carried out and the **SIOP** executed. The 707, which will thus be the central pivot of all US **C³I**, can stay in the air for ten hours before taking on midair refuelling and is equipped with computers, duplicate **go codes** and other command needs; aside from the President and his advisers it carries 15 staff officers and 27 crew.

knees *n pl* [*Logging*] devices for moving a log into place on a sawmill **carriage.**

Knife and Fork, the *n* [*UK*] [*Railways*] 'The Master Cutler', the London-Sheffield express.

knife happy *a* [*US*] [*Medicine*] used to describe any surgeon who is considered over-eager to operate without considering possible alternatives.

knife-fighting *n* [*Military*] a short-range aerial dogfight that resembles the close-in fighting of two adversaries using knives.

knife-rest *n* [*Military*] a barrier or obstruction composed of barbed wire coiled around a timber frame, resembling a knife-rest.

knitting *n* [*Navy*] girls, either in general or referring to a man's specific girlfriend.

knittles, also **knettles** *n pl* [*Sailing, Ropework*] See **nettles.** See also **small stuff.**

knob *n* [*UK*] [*Railways*] the switching handle of a set of points.

knob knot *n* [*Sailing, Ropework*] a bunch in a rope to prevent it slipping or coming unthreaded from the block.

knob up *v* [*UK*] [*Railways*] to alter the points, using the **knob.**

knobber, also **knobbler, pricket** *n* [*Deerstalking*] a red deer in its second year.

knobber up *n* [*UK*] [*Railways*] a points operator in the marshalling yard.

knobblies *n pl* [*Cars*] the chunky treaded tyre surfaces used in rallying for loose surface work.

knock 1. *n* [*Cricket*] a batsman's innings, during which he supposedly hits the ball with the bat. **2.** *n* [*Cycling*] any regular but unusual noise that may indicate any one of a variety of malfunctions in the machine. **3.** *v* [*Pool*] to recognise a pool hustler (who makes a living by playing pool, often pretending to have less skill than he really does) and to spread the word around; an act considered despicable by professional players.

knock back, also **retemper** *v* [*Building, Plastering*] to remix a stiffening mix.

knock knock *n* [*Navy*] an acoustic mine which is triggered by the sound of a ship's engines.

knockback *n* [*UK*] [*Crime, Police*] a rejection or dismissal, especially of an appeal for parole or bail, or against one's sentence.

knockdown *n* [*Film, TV*] a temporary, collapsible, portable dressing room for use on location.

knock-down path *n* [*Aerospace*] the route taken by airport firefighters when approaching a crashed and burning aircraft, when the flames have to be 'knocked down', ie: blown aside.

knocker 1. *n* [*Commerce*] a door-to-door salesman who knocks, or rings at every potential customer's home. **2.** *n* [*UK*] [*Railways*] a person who fails to tip a porter for carrying heavy luggage. **3.** also **tomahawk** *n* [*US*] [*Carpenters*] a hand axe, a hammer.

knocker, on the *adv* [*UK*] [*Police*] this comes from the legitimate **knocker;** it refers to a confidence trickster who tours houses, buying or selling goods, and who specialises in persuading or bullying the old or gullible to sell off their treasures cheaply.

knock-for-knock *n* [*Business*] an agreement between two insurers that each will pay his own policy holder in a dispute, regardless of actual liability.

knocking 1. *n* [*Antiques*] persuading the owners of valuables to part company with their possessions in order that a dealer may then sell them for his/her own profit; this sophisticated technique often employs two 'persuaders', one playing the 'hard' and one the 'soft' role. **2.** also **detonation** *n* [*Cars*] the combustion of fuel with explosive, damaging violence, sometimes caused by using fuel of too low an octane; in extreme cases it can break through the piston crown.

knocking copy *n* [*Advertising*] an advertisement that bases its appeal on a claim that a rival product is inferior to that which is being promoted.

knocking on the grass *n* [*UK*] [*Journalism*] a situation in which a reporter is sent on a difficult story and cannot face actually approaching the bereaved parents, raped girl, etc; to save face he tells the office that they were not at home and instead of knocking on the front door, knocks on the metaphorical front lawn.

knocking out, also **shaking out** *n* [*Metallurgy*] in iron-founding this is the separating of sand and casting.

knockoff *n* [*Engineering*] any part of a machine which can be removed or disengaged by knocking it.

knock-offs 1. *n pl* [*UK*] [*Catering*] pilferable items which are usually seen as part of the normal and expected earnings in many restaurants; thus 'knock-off bag' is a large bag used to carry such items. **2.** *n pl.* [*Antiques*] reproductions of an antique original. **3.** *n pl.* [*Fashion*] cheap copies of best-selling lines and models (eg: a royal wedding dress) which are aimed at the mass market. **4.** *n pl.* [*Publishing*] quick hack productions that either echo a current fiction best-seller, or, as nonfiction, are tied into a major event, eg: the Falklands War, and attempt to cash in on the public's appetite for all material related to it.

knock-out, also **knock** *n* [*Auctions*] an illegal private auction held by a 'ring' of mutually supportive dealers who have worked in concert to freeze out any public bids at the genuine auction

K

and who now will bid against each other in earnest until the knockout is over.

knockout axle *n* [*UK*] [*Road transport*] a system which enables the in-line axle at the rear of a low-loading trailer to be detached from the trailer. Wheels and axle must be detached from the trailer complete with suspension units to allow the loading bed to be lowered to the floor for ease of loading.

knock-out price *n* [*Commerce*] the lowest possible price.

knot *n* [*Glass-making*] an imperfection occurring as a localised glassy inclusion in glass.

knot-hole *n* [*Ceramics*] the hole formed by the excavation of china-clay.

knots *n pl* [*Surfing*] the surfer's badge of status: the bruises and cuts gained from battling the waves and the board.

know your customer *v phr* [*US*] [*Stock market*] a basic tenet of the US securities industry: one should have reasonable grounds for trusting the ethics and financial probity of those with and for whom one deals.

know-how agreement *n* [*Management*] an agreement whereby the possessor of a given area of expertise – the know-how – promises to disclose it to someone else. If the knowledge is then to be used for commercial exploitation, the agreement is called a 'know-how licence'. If the disclosure is merely for further evaluation of the technology or for the extension of either party's research, it is a 'secrecy agreement'.

knowledge base **1.** *n* [*Computing*] the database used within an **expert system** to encode the knowledge, experience and rules that are formulated for the system by the expert or experts who create it. **2.** *n* [*Social work*] psychological and sociological theories which provide the background for practical social work.

knowledge engineering *n* [*Computing*] the process of building an **expert system.**

Knowledge, the *n* [*UK*] [*Taxis*] the compulsory learning up of the streets of Greater London – specifically a number of basic routes, which are compiled by the Police Public Carriage Office and set down in the 'Blue Book' – which must be undertaken by any driver who wishes to obtain a licence to drive a London black cab.

knuckle *n* [*Marbles*] the power to shoot a marble effectively.

knuckle down *n* [*Marbles*] a penalty when one's **shooter** is stuck within the ring: the player is

forced to twist his wrist and thus shoot downwards and lose any chance of a good shot.

knucklebuster **1.** *n* [*US*] [*Painting*] a wrench, used to adjust spray guns, airhose connections, etc. **2.** *n* [*US*] [*Painting*] a hammer; it comes from carpenters' usage.

knuckler *n* [*Baseball*] a breaking pitch, known for its unpredictability of course, which is thrown by gripping the ball with the knuckles or fingernails.

kodak *adv* [*TV*] a codeword among film crews: if a sequence is, on the director's word, shot 'kodak', the crew mime filming but do not operate the camera or sound equipment.

kop *n* [*Soccer*] a bank of terracing for the supporters of the home team, most famously the one at Liverpool FC; it comes from the battle of Spion Kop which took place on a hill near Ladysmith during the Boer War (1899–1902).

Kremlin **1.** *n* [*UK*] [*Police*] an ironic description of New Scotland Yard. **2.** *n* [*UK*] [*Railways*] the headquarters of British Rail, Marylebone, W1.

Kresge *n* [*Ten-pin bowling*] a split where the 5 and 7 pins are left standing. See also **baby split, bucket, cincinnati.**

Kunstkompass *n* [*Art*] a listing of the 100 supposedly best Western artists, first devised in 1969. Like all such lists, the criteria which make it up are subject to many criticisms and to the subjective opinions of those who are asked to help compile it.

Kunstlerroman *n* [*Literary criticism*] this comes from Ger. 'Kunstler' meaning 'artist' plus 'Roman' meaning 'novel'; it is a novel that takes as its theme the making of a novelist; eg: James Joyce 'The Portrait of an Artist as a Young Man' (1916).

kurumaku *n* [*Business*] in Japan this is a business fixer, literally a 'wire-puller'; it comes from the Kabuki theatre where the word means 'black curtain', thus implying the essentially 'off stage' activities of such a figure.

kurve *n* [*US*] [*Garment trade*] a garment worker who has completed a probationary period (of a week) in a factory; it comes from Yiddish 'kurve' meaning 'whore'.

K.W. *n* [*Commerce*] abbr of **kept woman** a woman, kept or otherwise, who buys the most expensive items for which her male escort pays.

KW *n* [*US*] [*Road transport*] a Kenworth truck.

kye **1.** *a* [*Navy*] dirty. **2.** *n* [*Navy*] See **ki.**

kymatics *n* [*Science*] See **cymatics.**

K

L

L *n* [*US*] [*Economics*] abbr of **liquid** the part of the money supply that covers liquid assets such as treasury bonds, savings bonds, commercial paper, bankers' acceptances, etc. See also **M1**.

l and w *a* [*US*] [*Medicine*] abbr of **living and well** a file notation to describe a patient who has returned to ideal health.

laager *n* [*Military*] a close defensive formation adopted at night by tanks which form a circle inside which unarmoured vehicles may be parked.

label **1.** *n* [*Computing*] a character or set of characters chosen to identify a statement in a program so that it may be identified for use elsewhere in that program. **2.** *n* [*Journalism*] the first paragraph of a news story. See also **lede**. **3.** *n* [*Record business*] a record company, whose label is affixed to its products.

labelling theory *n* [*Sociology*] the concept in deviance theory that sociological explanations of deviance treat it as a product of social control rather than of individual psychology or genetic inheritance. Deviance exists not in the act, but in the labelling of that act by society which then amplifies and produces deviance; the deviant accepts his/her label and thus procedes to further deviance and acceptance of the permanent deviant role.

labor skate *n* [*US*] [*Industrial relations*] a veteran union member, an old-timer.

laboratory experience *n* [*Education*] any situation in which pupils are present for the purpose of instruction or observation. In the context of teacher training, the student teacher is the researcher and the pupils become his/her raw material or guinea-pigs.

laboratory techniques *n pl* [*Marketing*] originally restricted to the use of psychological models for market research, these techniques now include such general studies as simulated shopping for research into pricing.

laboratory training *n* [*Management*] this is a synonym for group dynamics training: the study by various combinations of individuals of the structure and mechanics of a variety of groupings. See also **cousins group, family group, stranger group.**

labour power *n* [*Sociology*] the worker's capacity to work, rather than the work itself; it is this power that is purchased by capitalism.

labour process *n* [*Sociology*] the process of production in which **labour power** is applied to raw materials and machinery to produce commodities.

labour shed *n* [*Economics*] the area from which the labour supply is drawn.

labour statesman *n* [*Industrial relations*] See **tuxedo unionism.**

labyrinth *n* [*Audio*] a type of loudspeaker cabinet incorporating partitions, which have been lined with sound-damping material, to produce a long, convoluted path between the rear of the drive unit and the outlet point and to confine resonance to low frequencies.

lace *v* [*Book-binding*] to attach the covers to a volume sewn on boards by passing the slips through holes pierced in the covers.

lace up *v* [*TV, Film*] to thread a film into a projector for viewing or transmission.

laches **1.** *n* [*Commerce*] negligent or unreasonable delay by a person in claiming what is due to him; eg: taking an excessive time to deposit a cheque in the bank; it comes from Old Fr. 'lachesse' and originally from Lat. 'laxus' meaning loose. **2.** *n* [*Law*] neglect or unreasonable delay in claiming the remedy of a legal wrong; it comes from Old Fr. 'lachesse' meaning loose.

lacing **1.** *n* [*Coal-mining*] the arrangement of picks in the cutting unit of a coal cutting machine. **2.** *n* [*Navy*] a reprimand for careless work by a sailor.

lackey *n* [*Politics*] a popular left-wing term of abuse denoting a lick-spittle follower of the ruling class, invariably the bourgeoisie; it comes from the original meaning of footman or servant. See also **capitalist roader running dog.**

lactic *a* [*Cheese-making*] said of cheeses with a clean, wholesome, milky flavour.

ladder **1.** *n* [*US*] [*Marine Corps*] a stairway, on a ship or on shore. **2.** also **bracketing** *n* [*Navy*] a method of establishing an accurate firing range by increasing and decreasing the range of successive salvos until the enemy is pinpointed.

ladder man n [Gambling] a casino employee who sits on a high chair from which he can watch both croupiers and players to spot mistakes or foul play.

ladder of participation n [Government] a term used in urban planning to rank the varying degrees of public participation in the process: (from the least influential) manipulation; therapy; informing, consultation; placation; partnership, delegated power; citizen control.

ladders n pl [Glass-making] See **washboard.**

ladies 1. n pl [Sex] a black pimp's reference to prostitutes. 2. also **sisters** n pl [Espionage] an ironic reference to amateur or professional women who are involved in blackmail operations. Ladies tend to set the operation in motion, but it is the sisters who actually sleep with the target (and may well be thus taped or photographed).

ladies' sea n [Merchant navy] a calm sea.

lady n [US] [Painting] an area of a surface that has been missed by the painter when applying a coat of paint. See also **catface, holiday 2.**

lag 1. v [Marbles] to roll a marble as near as possible to those in a pixie; it is used to determine the order of shooting – the nearest starts, etc. 2. v [UK] [Market-traders] urination. See also **lagger.**

lagan, also **lagin, ligan** n [Shipping] goods lost or thrown overboard – such goods have sunk to the bottom but are marked; possibly it comes from Old Norse 'legn' meaning a net laid in the sea.

laggard n [Stock market] a share that has for no apparent reason lagged behind the average price of its peers or of the market in general.

laggareena n [UK] [Market-traders] a lavatory, WC. See also **crapper, lag, lagger.**

lagger 1. n [Economics] an economic indicator that maintains an existent trend for some time after the state of the general economy has moved on in a different direction. 2. n [UK] [Market-traders] chamber-pot, lavatory. See also **lag, laggareena.** 3. n [Hopscotch] the stone or twig tossed into the numbered squares.

lagging n [UK] [Prisons] a sentence of three years or more.

lagoon 1. n [Coal-mining] a deposit of waste on the surface of a mine which consists of refuse that is wholly or mainly in solution or suspension. 2. n [Sewage] an artificial, shallow pool used for the treatment and concentration of sewage and slurry.

laitier 1. n [Cheese-making] a dairyman. 2. n [Cheese-making] a product made entirely from milk. 3. n [Cheese-making] a product made in a commercial establishment.

lake pipes n pl [Custom cars] unsilenced exhaust pipes that run along the side of a car. Such exhausts can be purely decorative or the driver can rig up a system which diverts the exhaust gases through a regular silenced pipe for road use while using the lake pipes for competitions, etc.

The term comes from the salt lakes on which early custom competitions were held.

lakes a [UK] [Market-traders] stupid, foolish.

lakeside cart n [US] [Medicine] a surgical dressing trolley.

lambs n pl [Stock market] ignorant or inexperienced speculators on an Exchange.

lame duck 1. n [Business] any business, industry or other enterprise which cannot survive without government intervention. 2. [US] [Politics] any office-holder who cannot be re-elected. It is used particularly of a lame duck President: the President who has suffered a defeat in the November elections, but cannot, according to the US Constitution, relinquish office until his successor is inaugurated the following January. 3. n [Stock market] any member of the London Stock Exchange who has defaulted on his dealings and been **hammered**; the Court of the Stock Exchange was formerly known as the 'Duckery'.

lammy n [Navy] a duffel coat.

lamp post navigation n [Navy] steering a course from buoy to buoy.

lamping station n [S. Wales] [Coal-mining] the place, situated about half way long the **mains** (about one mile from the entrance), where miners collect oil lamps which they check for gas.

lampshade n [Military] radiation lampshade: a device for determining the height of an atomic **air burst**; it is about one ft. wide and shaped like a lampshade.

lams n pl [Weaving] the horizontal bars on a treadle loom that provide the intermediary action between the treadles and the **heddle** shafts.

LAN n [Computing] acro **Local Area Network** a communications network linking a number of stations in the same local area, which may be a single office building, factory or actual local area.

lance-jack n [UK] [Military] a lance corporal or lance bombadier in the British Army.

land n [Technology] an area between adjacent grooves, eg: those on a gramophone record.

land art n [Art] the use of the land to create artworks; such projects always need aerial documentation to make them accessible to the general public. See also **earth art.**

land Crabs n pl [UK] [Police] a term used by members of the London River Police to describe all earth-bound members of the Metropolitan Police. See also **Matelots.**

land of plenty n [UK] [Railways] overtime.

landed price n [Oil rigs] the actual cost of oil to a refiner, taking into account all costs from the well to the refinery.

landing n [Coal-mining] a shaft inset, at which skips or trucks are loaded.

landing account n [Commerce] a document issued by a warehouse, giving details of goods held and charges incurred for their storage.

landing gear n [UK] [Road transport] legs

L

supporting a semi-trailer when it has been uncoupled from a tractive unit.

landscape 1. *n* [*Advertising*] a booklet or illustration in which the horizontal dimensions are greater than the vertical ones. 2. *v* [*Business*] to create an open-plan office where all employees, regardless of status, are contained within the same area, divided only by low partitions.

lane *n* [*Lacrosse*] a channel of space down the field from goal to goal; the centre lane is the highest priority area for defensive cover.

language 1. *n* [*Art, Advertising*] the overall visual tone or style of a design or layout; thus to 'break the language' is to alter that style by including an incongruous or unlikely typeface, visual, etc. 2. *n* [*Computing*] any of the many systems and rules that have been created for the operation of a computer. See also **BASIC, COBOL, FORTH, FORTRAN, high-level language, machine code.**

language arts *n pl* [*Education*] reading, writing, speaking, listening.

langue *n* [*Linguistics*] a term introduced by Ferdinand de Saussure (1857–1913) to denote language viewed as a complete system of forms and contrasts held intact in the brain of the user of that language. See also **parole.**

lantern 1. *n* [*UK*] [*Theatre*] the skylight over the stage that acts as an extra protection against fire. 2. *n* [*UK*] [*Theatre*] a light or lighting unit.

lanyard 1. *n* [*Sailing, Ropework*] a small rope used for making fast the end of a stay, etc. 2. *n* [*Sailing, Ropework*] a handle for a bag, knife, whistle, etc.

lap 1. *n* [*Glass-making*] a fold in the surface of a glass article. 2. *n* [*Painting*] this is where the current coat extends over the edge of a recently painted coat; the painter's intention is to mask these laps in invisible joins to produce a seamless surface. 3. *n* [*Logging*] tops left in the woods after logging. 4. n [*Medicine*] abbr of **laparotomy** surgery performed on the abdomen. Thus 'lap sheets' are sheets slit down the centre which are used specifically to cover the patient during operations on the abdomen. 5. *n* [*Navy*] in naval mine warfare this is the area assigned to a minesweeper or section of sweepers for clearing; this 'lap track' is the track to be followed by a sweeper; 'lap turn' is a turn made by a sweeper between two runs over a disignated lap; 'lap width' is the path taken by a sweeper as it clears the mines. 6. *n* [*Printing*] a small overlap between two colours to ensure that there is no white space left due to a potentially incorrect register. 7. *n* [*Textiles*] a continuous sheet of combed fibres ready to be spun into yarn. 8. *n* [*Weaving*] See **batt.** 9. also **overlap** *n* [*Metallurgy*] a surface defect in steel caused by the folding of a metal surface against itself. 10. *v* [*Shooting*] to bore out the barrels of a shotgun when they have developed pitting, the small pits

that are caused by corrosion and general lack of care.

lap card *n* [*Publishing*] small cards which carry advertising material, usually soliciting magazine subscriptions, that are inserted into newspapers and magazines.

lapping *n* [*Commerce*] an accounting fraud in which shortages are concealed by a series of entries that keep postponing the writing down of the receipt of money or of an asset from one accounting period to the next.

lapping in [*Cars*] See **grinding in.**

laps *n pl* [*Building, Plastering*] small pieces of canvas used in the process of casting.

large calorie *n* [*Science*] 1000 calories, a kilocalorie.

large numbers, the law of *n* [*Statistics*] 'if a series of independent trials or observations is made, in each of which there is the same probability of a particular outcome, then, as the number of trials is made larger, the chance that the observed proportion of such outcomes differs from the probability by less than any given number, however small, approaches a certainty (or, in stronger terms, the observed proportion approaches the probability.' (OED Supp H-N, 1976).

large torus *n* [*Building, Plastering*] See **astragal.**

lark *v* [*Hunting*] to jump fences on one's way home from hunting, or when the hounds are not running.

larry *n* [*Building, Plastering*] a rake-like implement used, in conjuction with a trough, in the manual mixing of lightweight plasters.

l'art brut *n* [*Art*] this comes from Fr. meaning 'raw art'. It was coined in 1949 by French artist Jean Dubuffet to describe any crude, unsophisticated work by non-professional artists, especially that of children or primitives. Dubuffet admired this work for its innocent vision, directness of technique and use of unconventional materials and tried to emulate these qualities in his own work. In turn his own work came to be termed 'l'art brut'.

laser art *n* [*Art*] the use of lasers (light amplification by stimulated emission of radiation) either as tools for artists or in the production of holograms or forms of **light art.**

lash on *v* [*Coal-mining*] to attach tubs or cars to an endless belt.

lash out *v* [*Navy*] to pretend to work hard for the benefit of the supervising officer.

lashing *n* [*Clothing*] the fastening of the inside seams of coat edgings or **facings** to the outer material or interlining, to hold them in position.

lash-up *n* [*Science, Computing*] any form of makeshift or home-made gadget. See also **kludge.**

last resort theory *n* [*Politics*] a concept used to justify the UK's continuing possession of an independent nuclear force: if Britain had to stand

L

alone with no allies, its nuclear weapons, while they could not guarantee the nation's defence, could at least deter by the threat of massive retaliation against a potential aggressor.

last time seller *n* [*Commerce*] someone who is selling a house either for a smaller replacement or for no new house at all.

last trading day *n* [*Futures market*] the final day, as cited under an Exchange's rules, during which trading may take place in a given delivery month.

last year's bronc *n* [*US*] [*Cattlemen*] a horse in its second year of work.

lastage *n* [*Shipping*] the cargo-space in a ship; originally it was the ballast.

last-bag system, also **two-bin system** *n* [*Management*] a system of stock control in which stock is divided into two parts; the first part is for normal use, the second is only made available when the first is exhausted. Exhaustion of the 'first bag' is the signal to reorder the stock and refill that bag.

lastish *n* [*Science fiction*] the immediately previous issue of a fan magazine; occasionally, it is the last issue published.

latch *n* [*Computing*] a circuit which, when triggered, stores whatever appears on its inputs and saves it for subsequent use.

latch lifter *n* [*UK*] [*Railways*] the first drink of the evening.

latching *n* [*Audio*] an extreme form of **clipping**.

late blooming *n* [*Psychology*] the concept that an individual who has shown no apparent benefit from a period of therapy, may well show it in his/her life some months after concluding that therapy.

late capitalism *n* [*Politics, Economics*] a Marxist term for the type of capitalism that has developed since the industrial revolution and which, in various modified forms, is that which dominates Western society. The use of 'late' implies the Marxist belief that its demise is already in progress and soon will be complete.

late fringe *n* [*TV*] a statistical **daypart** that follows prime time and lasts from 11.00 pm to closedown; it is used for calculating ratings, advertising charges, etc. See also **early fringe, housewife, prime time.**

late night *n* [*TV*] a statistical **daypart** that is reckoned to run from 10.30pm to 12.00 midnight. See also **early fringe, housewife, late fringe, prime time.**

late relief *n* [*UK*] [*Buses*] a London Transport bus that has arrived late at its destination and which will therefore arrive so late back at its point of departure, when the new crew take over, that a whole journey out and back will have been lost.

late-caught *a* [*Furriers*] said of furs taken after the midwinter peak development; such pelts tend to be thin or shedding and of inferior quality. See also **early-caught, firsts 2.**

latency *n* [*Computing*] the time that elapses between giving the instruction to perform an action and the actual performance of that action.

latent *a* [*Police*] used of fingerprints which are invisible to the naked eye.

latent function *n* [*Sociology*] the unintended and unrecognised consequences of social action upon other social actors or **institutions**; such consequences can be harmful or otherwise.

latent period *n* [*Military*] the time that elapses between the exposure of an individual to radioactive fallout and the onset of the effects of that fallout.

lateral diversification *n* [*Commerce*] the entry of a company into an area of marketing that has no connections with its previous field of activity.

lath tank *n* [*Building Plastering*] a narrow, shallow, trough containing water in which long laths are soaked prior to casting.

latitude *n* [*Photography*] the built-in margin of exposure error that the manufacturer automatically puts into any film.

lattens *n pl* [*Metallurgy*] hot rolled steel sheets of 0.0220" to 0.016" thickness inclusive. Thus 'extra lattens' are sheets of less than 0.016" thickness.

laugh-track *n* [*Radio, TV*] a tape of pre-recorded laughter which is **dubbed** on to radio or TV shows in order to create the effect of a live audience.

launch a caterpillar *v* [*Parachuting*] said of a jumping team which leaves an aircraft with each member holding on to the legs of the one in front.

launch on warning *n* [*Military*] the firing of one's own missiles during the period between receiving a warning that hostile missiles have been launched and the arrival and impact of those missiles.

launch window *n* [*Aerospace*] that period when the Earth and a target are in a mutually favourable position for the launching of a rocket and/or capsule.

launching pad *n* [*UK*] [*Railways*] the turntable in a roundhouse engine shed.

launder 1. *v* [*Airlines*] used of ticket fraud involving the exchanging, sometimes up to sixteen times, of stolen tickets for legal ones by simply putting them across an airline or travel agent's booking office with some excuse for altering one's flight. **2.** *v* [*Finance*] to transfer any funds that have been obtained illegally to a bank, usually in a foreign country, and then to withdraw those funds through legitimate means.

laundry list *n* [*US*] [*Politics*] a detailed and often lengthy list of plans, priorities and other political intentions, that is often included in a speech.

Laura Ashley *a* [*Music*] replacing 'schmaltz' as a word indicating excessively flowery, sugary or weedy music.

lavender *n* [*Film*] positive film stock used for producing duplicate negatives; it is also a print made from such stock.

law *n* [*Coursing*] the amount of space a hare is

allowed to cover before the hounds are slipped; it is usually 60–80 yards.

law label *n* [*Textiles*] a label attached to various US products using textiles that declares 'Do not remove this label on pain of law.'

law of diminishing returns *n* [*Commerce*] the phenomenon that when output depends on several inputs (eg: labour, materials, machines) and some of these inputs are constant, then, beyond a certain limit, increases in the other inputs result in smaller and smaller increases in output.

law of the situation *n* [*Management*] a concept of US business philosopher Mary Parker Follett (1868–1939): some actions must be taken simply as the correct response to a situation, and not just because they are ordered by a superior. Employees who accept her principle ought to feel themselves less subordinated to the hierarchy in their firm.

law of uneven development *n* [*Politics*] a concept developed by Marx and expounded by his heirs to explain why the revolution when encountered in under-developed countries often fails to proceed along the correct dogmatic lines; the intent is to reconcile the discrepancies with Marxist theory.

law twenty-nine *n* [*Rugby*] a non-existent law that is otherwise referred to as the 'common-sense' law, regarding one's on-field conduct.

lawing *n* [*UK*] [*Crime*] See **corner 2.**

lawn *n* [*UK*] [*Railways*] the fast line, kept for express trains. See **bowling green, quick.**

lawn meet *n* [*Hunting*] any meet held by a pack of hounds at a house, by invitation of the owner.

lawyer *n* [*Commerce*] the customer's friend who advises on purchases, styles and may either help or hinder the sale by their opinions.

lay 1. *v* [*Politics*] said of a minister or MP who places documents before the UK House of Commons for the information of the members. 2. *v* [*Sailing, Ropework*] to form a rope in a ropewalk by twisting the strands together. 3. *n* [*Sailing, Ropework*] the direction of twist in a rope. 4. *n* [*Clothing*] an assembly of materials placed on top of each other in preparation for cutting. 5. *n* [*Textiles*] the number of suits marked and cut at the same time after the cutter has drawn the pattern on to the fabric; this can be as many as 40 layers of cloth deep for each cut.

lay away *n* [*US*] [*Car salesmen*] a high-gross sale in which the customer is overchanged.

lay back *v* [*Video, Audio*] to finalise all the various sound tracks for mixing into the final **master** tape.

lay days *n pl* [*Oil rigs*] the days allowed by charter for loading or discharging cargo, at which time the vessel is lying alongside a port.

lay down 1. *n* [*US*] [*Car salesmen*] a customer who is prepared to 'lay down' the entire cost of the car in cash. 2. *v* [*Gambling*] said of a player who lays down a hand of cards before the betting has finished in order to show that his hand cannot

be bettered by any player. 3. *v* [*Music*] to play any piece of music. 4. *v* [*US*] [*Prisons*] to put in the punishment cells; it is so used because early cells were so small that men were forced to lay down to gain any space. See also **bank off.**

lay member *n* [*New therapies*] a term used at the Synanon drug addiction centre in California to describe those individuals who have not actually been addicts but who wish to undergo the centre's style of encounter therapy that is essentially designed to keep ex-addicts off drugs.

lay off 1. *v* [*US*] [*Railways*] See **mark off.** 2. *v* [*Gambling*] a bookmaker does this when he places a bet with a fellow bookmaker in order to insure himself against a heavy loss when one or more horses have been backed very strongly. 3. *v* [*Painting*] to brush paint on to wood in the same direction as the grain of the wood or, in painting metal, to paint in the longest direction.

lay off a course *v* [*Navy, Air Force*] to work out a course on a chart.

lay official *n* [*Industrial relations*] a union member who is the unpaid holder of some office in that union, eg: a shop steward.

lay on *v* [*Drugs*] said of a dealer (or other drugs user) who gives a small, free, sample of drugs to a potential customer. See also **taste 2.**

lay on the air *v* [*US*] [*Road transport*] See **anchor it.**

lay pipe *v* [*US*] [*TV*] to make sure by the script-writing that the audience for a series gets to know the life history and background of all the major characters.

lay the note *v* [*Crime*] See **hype 2.**

lay tracks *v* [*TV*] to arrange a number of film sound-tracks in exact relation to each other and to the film's pictures.

lay up *v* [*Croquet*] to end one's turn leaving the balls in a position that favours oneself but puts one's opponent at a disadvantage.

layboy *n* [*Printing, Paper-making*] See **jogger.**

laying off *n* [*Painting*] the final, light, brush-strokes, which are aimed at smoothing away any final imperfections in the coat.

layup *n* [*Basketball*] an attempt made to score a field goal with a shot made from a jumping position alongside or under the basket, with the backboard serving as a rebounding surface.

lazaret 1. *n* [*Shipping*] a building in a port reserved for the fumigation of such goods as may need it. 2. *n* [*Shipping*] a space in a ship set aside for anyone who has to be kept in quarantine. Both (1) and (2) come from the Biblical Lazarus, and thence to Ital./Fr. meaning 'diseased person'.

lazarus layers *n pl* [*Politics*] left-wing description of the poorest sectors of society.

lazy 1. *n* [*US*] [*Cattlemen*] a brand in which the image, probably a letter, is on its side. 2. *n* [*Military*] air intercept code for equipment indicated at standby.

lazy eight *n* [*Gliding*] a mild aerobatic

L

manoeuvre developed from a pair of 180° turns in opposite directions. Climbs and dives alternate.

lazy kate *n* [*Weaving*] a rack on which bobbins of yarn can be put for unwinding.

lazy line *n* [*Merchant navy*] a messenger line between a tug and the vessel it is towing; if the tow line breaks, the lazy line is used to pass a new one.

LCD *n* [*Computing*] abbr of **Liquid Crystal Display** the device used in digital watches, computer games, etc. to display numbers and letters. A display uses groups of segments which can be combined to form individual characters; application of an electric field across the segments – each a normally transparent anisotropic liquid to change and the segment to become opaque. Individual segments can thus be manipulated to form characters.

LD–50 *n* [*Military*] abbr of **lethal dose for fifty** the amount of post-nuclear attack radiation required to kill fifty percent of a given population within a specified time.

leaching **1.** *n* [*Tanning*] the process of extracting tannin from bark by boiling it in water; this solution is the main constituent of a vegetable tanning solution. **2.** *n* [*Mining*] the natural or artificial separation of valuable minerals from the ore that surrounds them either by the seepage of water or by washing in solutions of sulphuric acid and various sulphates.

lead **1.** *n* [*Commerce*] the first contact that a salesman makes with a potential customer; it is usually a phonecall to arrange a **sit.** **2.** *n* [*Espionage*] any form of trickery designed to confuse an enemy or a target of one's espionage plans. **3.** *n* [*US*] [*Real estate*] any customer who is looking for a property. **4.** *n* [*Journalism*] the main news story in the paper, or the first paragraph of any story or feature See also **lede.** **5.** *n* [*Printing*] slugs of lead that can be inserted into the makeup of a page as required by the compositor to increase margins, line spacing and other areas of white space. **6.** *n* [*Sailing, Ropework*] the direction of a rope; the direction of a strand in a knot. **7.** *n* [*Weaving*] the difference in speed between the rotating spindle and the bobbin on a **flyer** wheel, which results in the yarn being wound on to the bobbin. **8.** also **lead down** *v* [*Military*] to shoot, to shoot at, using leaden bullets.

lead manager *n* [*Stock market, Banking*] the principal bank in a syndicate handling a new share issue, which co-ordinates and directs the efforts of the syndicate handling the issue. See also **co-manager.**

lead out *v* [*Printing*] to add blank spaces to a page or a column of copy by inserting slugs of lead where necessary, thus lengthening the material to fit the required design of the page.

lead sled **1.** *n* [*Custom cars*] a car which, in order to minimise all extraneous trim that would slow it down, has had the gaps between the body panels

filled with lead. **2.** *n* [*Gliding*] a high performance glider with high wing loading, resulting in a fast, flat glide at some sacrifice when using thermals to gain altitude.

lead through *v* [*Mountaineering*] two climbers do this when they take it in turns to act as the leader of a team.

lead time **1.** *n* [*Business*] the time that elapses between the origination of a new concept and its final creation and/or delivery. **2.** *n* [*Commerce*] the time taken to manufacture a given product. **3.** *n* [*Publishing, Journalism*] the gap between the production deadlines for a magazine or book and the actual publication date.

lead with the chin *v* [*Boxing*] to have a poor stance – one ought to lead with one's fists – and thus to make it simpler for an opponent to land punches.

leader **1.** *n* [*Economics*] any economic indicator that sets off in a new direction before the bulk of the market has started to follow this new trend, eg: the level of one particular company's share prices. See also **lagger.** **2.** *n* [*UK*] [*Law*] a senior barrister, often a Queen's Counsel, who leads the prosecution or the defence in court. See also **junior.** **3.** *n* [*Printing*] a line of dots – thus:. . . . . – used to direct the eye along the printed page. **4.** *n* [*Radio, TV, Film*] a length of blank film or tape, possibly in an identifying colour, that is attached to a film or tape to facilitate threading into a tape recorder or film projector. See also **academy leader.** **5.** *n* [*Textiles*] a length of fabric or other material attached to a bolt or reel of cloth that is used to guide the roll through a machine at the beginning of an operation. **6.** *n* [*Weaving*] a short length of yarn tied to a spindle to which the first fibres for spinning can be joined. **7.** also **cast** *n* [*Angling*] two or three yards of transparent line made of gut or gut substitute, attached to the running line. **8.** *v* [*Paper-making*] to build up the roll of paper, making sure that no wrinkles develop.

leaders **1.** *n pl* [*Commerce*] goods advertised and sold below the actual cost of production. **2.** *n pl* [*Journalism*] a row of dots inserted at the end of a story.

leading *n* [*Printing*] extra space between lines of type; in letterpress metal-setting, this is achieved by the insertion of extra lead strips between the lines.

leads *n pl* [*Sailing, Ropework*] that part of the tackle between the two **blocks** as opposed to the inactive 'standing' part and the **fall.**

leads and lags *n pl* [*Finance*] in international finance this is the hastening to pay, or the delay in paying, sums in various different currencies, in the hope of thus gaining from any possible fluctuations in their relative exchange rates.

leaf **1.** *n* [*Advertising*] two pages. **2.** *n* [*Computing*] abbr of **leaf node** any node on a tree that has no descendants and which is thus at the end of a

L

'branch'. See also **tree. 3.** n [Publishing] one sheet of paper in a publication, consisting of both its sides.

leaf edge n [Clothing] the outer or fall edge of the collar.

leak n, v [Politics] the discovery by the press and thus the public of facts that the politicians would rather not see revealed, or the act of making such revelations. Many leaks, however, are deliberate, and can be planted on eager journalists with the intention of confusing, rather than informing. The leak is also a weapon used by one party or politician against another, or in the furtherance of his/her own interest.

leakage 1. n [Coal-mining] an unintentional diversion of ventilation air from its designated path. **2.** n [Military] any degree of penetration by missiles on to an assigned target which will thus be destroyed despite the best efforts of anti-ballistic missile defences.

leaky 1. a [Genetics] used of a mutant: producing the protein specified by the mutated gene in a form with reduced activity compared with the wild type. **2.** a [Military] referring to a reactor on board a nuclear powered submarine that has been inadequately sealed against leaks of radio-activity. Soviet strategic submarines are notoriously leaky.

lean 1. a [Printing] narrower than standard width. See also **fat 9. 2.** a [Technology] used of a variety of products and equipment to indicate sub-standard performance, quality or content.

lean burn n [Cars] an approach to pollutant control which uses a very weak mixture – 18:1 – of air to fuel; this creates minimum levels of petrol-borne pollution.

lean coal n [Coal-mining] coal with a low volatile matter content (less than 19%). See also **fat coal.**

lean concrete n [Building, Concrete mixing] concrete that has a high ratio of aggregate to concrete.

lean mixture n [Gas industry] a gas-air mixture in which the air content is more than adequate for complete combustion and so the resultant combustion gases contain an excess of oxygen. See also **rich mixture.**

lean sand n [Metallurgy] in iron-founding this is sand that has a low clay content. See also **fat sand.**

leaning to all sides n [Politics] this refers to the diversification of Chinese trade since 1960; prior to 1960 China traded almost exclusively with socialist nations, a process known as 'leaning to one side'.

leaper n [Police] anyone who is threatening to jump, is in the process of jumping or who has completed jumping from a building in order to commit suicide. See also **floater 5.**

leap-frog v [Industrial relations] used of a method of gaining higher wages. In order to further their own claim one group of workers makes use of the fact that a similar group has already gained a desired increase, or points out where a lesser group has so profited, and demands that their own differential status be maintained.

leapfrog test n [Computing] a routine designed to test the internal operations of a computer that involves the repetition of a prescribed series of arithmetic or logical operations.

leapfrogging n [TV] a method of obtaining greater program diversity for a community antenna TV network by skipping one or more of the nearest TV stations in order to pick up new material from a distant station.

learn cold v [US] [Navy] to learn from a book.

lease, also **cross** n [Weaving] the cross formed by winding **warp** threads in a figure-eight to keep them in sequence.

leash 1. n [Angling] three fish. **2.** n [UK] [Surfing] an elasticated cord attached to the ankle from the rear of the surfboard.

least significant bit n [Mathematics] in a binary number this is the figure that is on the furthest right of the number, having least influence on the value of that number. See also **most significant bit.**

leather n [Dog breeding] the lobe of the outer ear; it is usually used of gundogs. Thus 'leather ends' are short-coated or partially hairless ear tips on otherwise well-coated ears.

leatherneck n [US] [Military] a Marine: it comes from the leather neckband attached to early 19th century marine uniforms.

leave n [Billiards] the position of the balls at the end of one player's stroke or break.

leaving here part phr [US] [TV] 'it looked good leaving here' (NBC), or 'it left here all right' (ABC/CBS): the major networks' stock rejoinders to any public complaints about bad reception or any other interference with their transmissions.

lection n [Bibliography] a variant reading of a copy or of an edition of a text.

LED display n [Computing] abbr of **Light Emitting Diode display** a device used in some digital watches, calculators, etc. to display individual characters. LEDs are semi-conductor diodes which can be manipulated to create numbers and/or letters. See also **LCD.**

lede n [US] [Journalism] a spelling differential which describes the lead story in a paper or lead paragraph in a story and thus avoids confusion with lead, the spaces between the lines of that story. See also **lead, lead out.**

ledge n [Meteorology] a layer in the ionosphere in which the ionisation increases less rapidly with height than in the regions immediately above and below it.

ledger 1. n [Angling] bottom fishing with the weight above the hook; the weight rests on the bottom. **2.** n [Building] in scaffolding systems this is the scaffold tube which runs horizontally along the face of the scaffold at each lift.

L

left hanging Judas n [Navy] a line left hanging over the side of a warship.

left-footer n [Sociology] this is used in N. Ireland to denote a Roman Catholic. It originated in the different styles of turf cutting prevalent in Ulster; Catholics used spades with a lug on the left side, while Protestants used those with the lug to the right.

left-handed course n [Horse-racing] a racetrack on which the horses race in an anti-clockwise direction; most courses are right-handed.

left-handed knot n [Sailing, Ropework] a knot tied in any way contrary to prevailing tradition.

leftism n [Politics] in socialist terms this is the refusal to make such necessary compromises with the right as are sensible and useful.

leg 1. n [Journalism] the length of a story as it appears on the printed page: thus one that runs over three columns has three legs, and so on. 2. n [US] [Military] a paratrooper term for those trainees who have not gained their certificates of jumping proficiency. 3. n [Sailing, Ropework] when a rope branches into more than one part, this is the name of each part; also the name of single strands separated out for splicing purposes. 4. also **draft** n [Mining] a survey line in a traverse. 5. v [Shooting] to slit one hind leg of a dead hare or rabbit above the hock and then slide the other through it to facilitate carrying; sometimes a pole is thrust between the linked legs of a number of such corpses.

leg art, also **cheesecake** n [Journalism] any pictures, eg: the 'Sun' Page Three Girls, of pretty, scantily clad girls that are used in newspapers or magazines; the male versions, when they are found, are 'beefcake'.

leg line, also **stage line** n [Athletics] the line that marks the end of a stage in a relay race.

leg theory, also **bodyline** n [Cricket] a form of aggressive bowling whereby the bowler pitched the ball short on the leg stump in the hope of forcing the batsman to offer a catch to one of a ring of specially positioned fieldsmen. Such bowling, during the England tour of Australia in 1932–33, very nearly brought the two countries to diplomatic blows.

legal day n [Law] a day up until midnight, calculated as such for the payment of debts by a given date, etc.

legal person n [Law] See **artificial person**.

legend 1. n [Aerospace] any fixed, printed notice in an aircraft's cockpit. 2. n [Espionage] an operational plan used while working under **cover**. 3. n [Espionage] a false biography prepared for an agent operating under cover. 4. n [Navy] the estimated or planned dimensions or performance of a ship before construction or testing. 5. n [Journalism, Advertising] a caption used for a photograph or illustration.

legger n [Meat trade] a butcher or packer who works only on the legs of carcases in a slaughterhouse.

legislative advocacy leadership n [Government] lobbying for and by special interest groups.

legislative veto n [US] [Politics] See **one house veto**.

legitimate 1. a [Music] referring to serious, classical music as opposed to jazz, rock, pop, etc. 2. a [Theatre] this is often abbreviated to 'legit' and refers to literary plays, eg: Shakespeare, as opposed to musicals, comedies, farces, etc.

legitimation n [Politics, Government] the process whereby power gains acceptance in the eyes of those who have to accept it, however dubious may have been its initial claims over them. In Marxist societies, it is the function of ideology to establish and maintain such legitimation.

legman n [Journalism] a reporter who works mainly out of the office, tracking down stories and the individuals or events that create them. See also **desk man**.

Legoland n [Navy] the British Fleet Headquarters at Northwood, Middlesex; it comes from a make of plastic building bricks used by children and thus refers both to the architectural style and possibly to the military fantasies created inside.

legs 1. n pl [Film, TV] this refers to any film that shows staying power at the box office or a TV series that continues to attract high ratings; 'this one will run and run'. Such films and programmes are 'leggy', and if they fail, are condemned as 'legless' meaning a flop. 2. n pl [Wine-tasting] the globules that fall down the sides of a glass after the wine has been swirled; they are usually indicative of a rich wine. 3. also **page-turners** n pl [Publishing] best-selling books whose staying power has the same connotations as the film and TV use (see 1).

Lehr n [Glass-making] proprietory name for the continuous annealing oven, with conveyor facilities to move on the glassware.

leisure development n [Commerce] a specially designed retirement ghetto for old age pensioners.

lek n [Shooting] dial: the ground on which black game (the black grouse) carries out its elaborate mating dance.

lell v [UK] [Market-traders] to prosecute, to summons.

lemon juice n [Military] US Dept. of Defense code for the second lowest state of war readiness.

lemon socialism 1. n [Politics] the sort of half-hearted socialism epitomised by the UK welfare state where state intervention under capitalism takes the place of real socialism. 2. n [Politics] the propping up by the state of declining industries, rather than imposing on them a proper economic plan for a fully socialist future, and the opting for an illusory, capitalist 'sound' economy.

lemon time n [UK] [Railways] the regulation thirty minutes refreshment time allowed to the

L

driver and fireman after four hours continuous shunting.

lemonade *n* [*Drugs*] a weak sample of heroin.

lender of the last resort *n* [*Banking*] the central bank in a country which controls the national banking system.

length 1. *n* [*Theatre*] a unit of 42 lines by which parts can be measured and compared. **2.** *n* [*Theatre*] a row of lights suspended from the same unit.

lennie 1. *n* [*US*] [*Gliding*] abbr of **lenticular cloud** which is formed by condensation at the peak of a **wave. 2.** *n* [*US*] [*Gliding*] a pin awarded to a pilot who has flown a glider at a height in excess of 30,000 ft. or 40,000 ft. in a wave.

lens louse, also **angler** *n* [*Press*] any member of the public who cannot resist posing for any camera, despite the fact that the cameraman is rarely pointing it at them. An 'angler' is anyone who is always trying to present their 'best angle' to the lens.

lenser *n* [*Film*] the director of photography.

lenses *n pl* [*Mining*] well-defined deposits of minerals which occur not in an extended vein, but in discrete, lens-shaped forms.

lensing *n* [*Film*] the shooting of the film.

lenures *n pl* [*Cheese-making*] small horizontal fissures that develop in very fatty Gruyeres with few or no holes; they are preferred by connoisseurs.

lepper *n* [*Horse-racing, Hunting*] a good jumper, often used in hunting terminology.

less developed countries *n pl* [*Politics*] the current variation on 'under-developed countries' or the **Third World.**

let out *v* [*US*] [*Car salesmen*] to allow a customer to leave a dealership without buying a car.

let out figure *n* [*US*] [*Car salesmen*] an inflated estimate on a trade-in, to induce a potential customer to return and make a purchase.

let the pressure down *v* [*Music*] to stop blowing too early when playing a tune on the bagpipes and thus losing some notes.

let-down *n* [*Farming*] the action of a cow yielding milk.

lethality *n* [*Military*] the ability of a weapon – conventional or nuclear – and the platform which launches it, to destroy its target.

letter of regret *n* [*Stock market*] a formal letter sent out after a new share issue has been subscribed to those investors whose applications were unsuccessful.

letter of set-off, also **lien letter** *n* [*Banking*] a document signed by a customer whose credit balance is held as security for a loan on another account guaranteeing that the sum of money in credit will never fall beneath 50% of the loan, and accepting that the banker who lends the money can combine the accounts without giving notice.

letter stock *n* [*Stock market*] unregistered stock which a company will not offer on the open market

for fear of driving down the price of its officially registered stock; instead it is sold well below market value, but has the advantage of avoiding time-consuming and expensive bureaucracy.

letterbox 1. *n* [*Espionage*] a place or person that acts as a **drop** for information that must be channelled between members of an espionage team. **2.** *n* [*Mountaineering*] a rectangular hole in a narrow ridge of rock. **3.** *n* [*TV*] an oblong 'hole' which is projected electronically into the bottom third of the picture and into which extra information – subtitles, football scores, elections results, etc. – can be projected.

letterbox company *n* [*Commerce*] a company that has been set up in one of the international tax havens and which exists in that country as no more than a letterbox and an address. The real business is still carried out in the executives' home country, except for the paying of that country's taxes.

letterhack *n* [*TV*] among fans of the TV series 'Star Trek' this is one who corresponds with other **fen.**

letting it all hang out *part phr* [*New therapies*] the concept that the absolute, unrestrained declaration of one's feelings and emotions, irrespective of potential offence to others, will guarantee a beneficial effect on one's personality and on the conduct of one's life. In the event, such 'open-ness' tends to be little more than the insensitive flailing around of the subject's ego. See also **authenticity, go with the flow.**

lettrism *n* [*Art*] an international avant-guarde movement established around 1950 with the intention of replacing both figuration and abstraction in painting and sculpture with a new formal structure based on letters and signs.

lettuce *n* [*Finance*] paper money.

level *n* [*Weaving*] the even penetration of dye into a material.

level four 1. *n* [*US*] [*Law*] a lethal injection or dose of barbital or similar drug. **2.** *n* [*Video*] a video disk player with sophisticated facilities, including an extensive memory, control and processing capability.

level money *n* [*Motor trade*] in the second-hand motor trade this is the most appropriate multiple of £100 for a deal.

level one *n* [*Video*] a player with freeze frame, picture stop, chapter stop, frame accessibility and dual channel but with limited memory and virtually no processor power.

level tendering *n* [*Commerce, Industry*] See **collusive tendering.**

level three *n* [*Video*] a video disk player of **level one** or **two** status which is interfaced with a computer.

level two *n* [*Video*] a video disk with **level one** facilities plus on board programmable memory and faster access times.

levels on the splonk *n pl* [*Gambling*] a term

used by bookmakers for evens, in stating betting odds.

leverage 1. *v* [*Business*] to use as a lever, to gain impetus from; thus 'I leveraged off their promotion', etc. 2. *n* [*Finance*] borrowing money at a fixed rate of interest and then investing it to yield enough money to deal with that interest and still leave a profit. 3. *n* [*Finance*] when used of a company's capital, this refers to the relationship of the amount of its loan capital (money borrowed at a fixed rate of interest) to its ordinary-share capital. See also **gearing**. 4. *n* [*Politics*] the indirect pressure that can be brought to bear on a politician by his/her influential supporters or other interested parties.

leveraged buyout *n* [*Business*] the takeover of a company by using borrowed funds, for which collateral is provided by the assets of the company one intends to take over.

L.F. gear *n* [*UK*] [*Police, Crime*] abbr of **long firm gear** often quite legitimate goods that are offered by criminals as the ostensible proceeds of a **long firm fraud** in order to attract the sort of customer who enjoys such flirtations with crime.

LGM *n pl* [*Science*] abbr of **Little Green Men** pulsars; this was originally applied to them by their discoverer Anthony Hewish (b.1924), with a conscious reference to science fiction fantasies of extra-terrestrials.

LHD vehicle *n* [*Coal-mining*] abbr of **Loading, Haulage and Dumping vehicle** a rubber-tyred articulated vehicle capable of all these functions.

liberation theology *n* [*Religion*] a primarily South American theological standpoint whereby left-wing Catholic priests ally themselves with the aspirations (and sometimes actions) of the oppressed masses, despite the official denunciation of such support from both the Pope and the various national authorities.

liberty *n* [*Navy*] short periods of leave: 24 hours (RN), 48 hours (USN).

LIBOR *n* [*UK*] [*Banking*] acro **London Inter-Bank Offered Rate** the rate of interest that London banks offer for loans between themselves. This rate is used to calculate interest charged to the public.

librarian *n* [*Computing*] a program that creates, maintains and makes available those programs, routines and data that make up a given operating system.

library 1. *n* [*Computing*] an organised collection of routines, especially those designed for operation by one specific machine. Such routines are often referred to by the machine to enable it to function, but are not actually part of its memory. 2. *n* [*UK*] [*Railways*] See **shanty** 2. 3. *n* [*Theatre*] a ticket agency. 4. *n* [*Video*] a manufacturer or retailer's catalogue of video cassettes and disks. 5. *n* [*Video*] the amount of titles to which a manufacturer has the rights, released or unreleased.

library music *n* [*Media*] as in **library shots**, this is 'off-the-peg' music that can be rented from specialist suppliers for use in advertisements, presentations, films, TV programmes, etc. Such music has been recorded in carefully timed segments to facilitate editing.

library shot 1. *n* [*Film*] any hired or archive film of useful material that would otherwise cost time and money to shoot and which does not need to be originated for a specific film, eg: a plane taking off/landing, a train leaving, etc. See also **stock shot**. 2. *n* [*TV*] any archive footage – film or video – which can be used both as in (1) and, especially, inserted into news programmes when an event has to be covered for which there are as yet no immediate pictures.

lick *n* [*Music*] in rock or jazz this is a short musical phrase, particularly runs of notes on the lead or bass guitar.

lick-a-take *v* [*UK*] [*Crime*] in West Indian terminology this means to pull off the successful robbery of a bank, shop, post office, etc.

lid 1. *n* [*Drugs*] approximately 1 oz. or 22 gms. of marijuana; it originated in the US from the quantity of the drug that would fill a widely used tobacco tin lid. 2. *n* [*US*] [*Politics*] the suspension of activity regarding a given topic, during which time politicians and political journalists can turn to other things. 3. *n* [*UK*] [*Coal-mining*] a wooden block about 6 in. square used to tighten wooden or hydraulic props.

lie sheet (*US*), **swindle sheet** (*UK*) *n* [*Road transport*] a driver's official log book which is required by state or national authorities to ensure the driver is taking sufficient rest, not overloading his truck, etc.

lien letter *n* [*Banking*] See **letter of set-off**.

life *n* [*Cricket*] a second chance given to a batsman – after a catch has been dropped, an appeal turned down, etc; it comes from chances offered in children's games.

life bond *n* [*Commerce, Finance*] a document which shows proof of the existence of an annuity contract.

Life, the *n* [*US*] [*Crime*] the world of pimps, drug dealers and the allied underworld sub-culture of successful and lucrative criminality.

life-actor *n* [*Business*] one whose position as an executive is underlined by complete and total commitment to, and identification with, the job.

life-belt *n* [*Banking*] the security put forward for a loan.

lifeboat ethics *n pl* [*Government*] a style of foreign and domestic policy in which decisions are made strictly on grounds of expediency and political priority and not on humanitarian grounds; thus the weakest are usually abandoned to their own inadequate devices.

life-chances *n pl* [*Sociology*] according to Max Weber (1864–1920) these are the chances that an individual has of enjoying a share of the economic

L

and cultural goods of a society; such opportunities are almost always unequal.

life-cycle analysis n [Marketing] a method of forecasting the sales of a new product by analysing its life-cycle, ie: the growth of its acceptance among the various levels of purchaser from the early adapters, the early majority, the late majority and the laggards.

lifed a [Aerospace] referring to an older aircraft which has undergone a variety of maintenance programmes designed to check all items that have a specific 'life' and to replace them when necessary.

lifer n [US] [Military] a career soldier, sailor, airman or marine in any of the US forces.

lifestyle n [Media, Sociology] the way individuals or groups choose to live, and the commodities and attitudes that epitomise each of the various ways chosen.

lifestyle concept n [Advertising] the market philosophy that notes the extent to which individual or family lifestyles influence comsumption.

lifestyle merchandising n [Commerce] any sales outlet, especially in the fashion trade, that attempts to arrange its areas or departments according to the customers' life styles rather than in the usual divisions according to product group.

lifestyle segmentation n [Marketing] the subdivision of a market based on lifestyle – interests, activities, opinions and values.

life-world n [Sociology] the every-day world as experienced by ordinary people, and as such the prime target of sociological investigation.

LIFO 1. a [Business] acro **last in first out** a method of compiling accounts for inventory that relates the cost of goods sold to the price of the most recent purchases; in a period when overall prices are rising this can be used to give lower profits and thus less taxable income. 2. a [Computing] acro **Last In First Out** a system in which the next item to be selected is the one most recently added to the list. See also **stack 3**. 3. a [Industrial relations] acro **Last In First Out** a practice whereby if redundancies are needed, the last worker to have been employed is the first to be dismissed.

lift 1. v [Coal-mining] See **bench**. 2. v [Farming] said of a sheep-dog that establishes control over a flock of sheep. 3. v [Hunting] to take hounds to where the fox was seen, or is thought to have been, without trying to find a scent on the ground on the way there. 4. v [UK] [Police] to arrest; it is also used by the British Army in N. Ireland with the same meaning. 5. v [Printing] to raise lines of type from a composing stick on to a galley, or to prepare them for the distribution of type. 6. v [Metallurgy] to increase the bore of a drilled **billet** prior to manufacturing an extruded tube, by forcing a tool of suitable diameter through it when the metal is still hot. 7. n [Coal-mining] to take a slice off a **pillar** during pillar extraction. 8. n

[Gas industry] one of the moveable sections of a liquid-sealed or telescopic gasholder. 9. n [Gas industry] the vertical distance a liquid is pumped. 10. n [Mining] the space that separates one level of the mine from another.

lift engrams v [Scientology] the bringing out of prenatal memories (**engrams**) for the purposes of therapy and the destruction of the 'aberrant content' in the patient's life.

lifter n [Metallurgy] See **gagger**.

lifters n pl [Coal-mining] holes drilled at floor level, into which explosive charges are placed.

lifting n [Painting] a wrinkled appearance in paint which occurs when the coat which has been over-painted reacts to the new paint by swelling up under it.

lift-off 1. n [Aerospace] the launching of a rocket. 2. n [Parachuting] opening the parachute while standing on a wing, which causes the parachutist to be lifted off the plane by the moving air.

ligature n [Printing] two or more letters joined together, forming a single character, or the stroke which connects two letters.

ligger 1. n [Angling] See **kelt**. 2. n [Building, Plastering] See **drop board**. 3. n [Pop music] hanger-on, free-loader; a general term for the good-for-nothings who besiege rock stars, concerts and journalists; it comes possibly from 'lingering' around or from the acronym 'LIG' meaning 'least important guest'.

light 1. n [Crosswords] the answer to a clue in a crossword puzzle. 2. a [US] [Car salesmen] See **right, in it 3**. a [US] [Medicine] emerging from an anaesthetic, or a coma, but not fully conscious. See also **deep 2**. 4. a [Printing] said of a fine/delicate version of a face. 5. a [Wine-tasting] low in alcohol – under 12°GL; it is also the official designation for unfortified, table wines. 6. v [Sailing, Ropework] to move a heavy cable in short bursts, by hand.

light and shade n [Theatre] the variations and graduations of delivery, dramatics, plot and the like in a play or a single performance.

light art n [Art] the use of light in art: colour organs, fireworks, projected light, lasers and neon tube sculpture.

light box n [Video] a display unit sold or given to a retailer to promote a particular product; it consists of a backlit plastic shell which has been covered with the appropriate artwork.

light bucket n [Science] in astronomy this is a telescope which collects and focuses a large quantity of low-intensity radiation in its lens – the bucket.

light engines v [US] [Railways] to move engines, without cars, from one location to another.

light water n [Science] water that contains less than the normal proportion (approx. 0.02%) of deuterium oxide. See also **heavy water**.

light work n [Gambling] cards that have been marked with very fine lines for the use of cheats;

L

thus 'strong work' means marking with heavy lines.

lighthouse tube *n* [*Computing*] an ultra-high frequency triode that resembles a minature lighthouse.

lightning conductors *n pl* [*Navy*] the trousers of an officer's dress uniform which have gold stripes down the sides.

lights *n* [*Theatre*] an electrician. See also **sparks**.

Lilian Baylis' leg *n* [*Theatre*] the stew served to actors in the canteen of the National Theatre; it is named after Lilian Baylis, CH (1874–1937), theatrical manager and founder of the Old Vic and Sadler's Wells theatres.

lily *n, v* [*UK*] [*Market-traders*] ear-trumpet; thus 'to lily' means to eavesdrop.

limb *n* [*Aerospace*] the edge of a star or planet, especially the sun, which is visible to a spacecraft.

limbo *n* [*Film, TV*] an area or set that has no specific visual identification and which is thus useful as a background for **close-ups** and **inserts**.

limdis *n* [*Espionage*] abbr of **Limited Distribution** a notation placed on classified information to limit its distribution to a maximum of fifty people. See also **exdis**.

lime *n* [*UK*] [*Theatre*] any light, especially a spotlight.

lime bloom *n* [*Building, Plastering*] a film of hardened lime on the surface of plasterwork, produced by hydrated lime being brought out and deposited by water in the course of drying out.

limehouse *n* [*Politics*] abuse of one's political opponents; it comes from a vituperative speech delivered by Lloyd George in Limehouse, London, 30 July 1909.

limit price *n* [*Futures market*] See **maximum price fluctuation**.

limited company *n* [*UK*] [*Railways*] a trade union meeting that only attracts a low turnout of members.

limited enquiries *n pl* [*UK*] [*Police*] a euphemism for the admission that there is very little that the police can do to help with a given enquiry or complaint.

limited order *n* [*Futures market*] an order given by a customer to a broker which has certain in-built restrictions as to the price and the time of its execution.

limited problem solving *n* [*Marketing*] a buying situation in which the buyer has some knowledge and experience of the product category.

limited slip differential *n* [*UK*] [*Road transport*] a design of **differential** which limits the extent to which one driving wheel on an axle is allowed to spin in relation to the opposing wheel when it cannot obtain a grip on a slippery surface.

limousine liberal *n* [*Politics*] the type of wealthy liberal whose affection for the masses and concern for their plight is modified (and possibly only sustained) by his/her never actually having to meet them except, probably, as employees.

limpid *a* [*Wine-tasting*] with a clear colour; thus 'limpidity' is colour that apparently has an extra sheen, or outstanding brightness.

linage 1. *n* [*Press*] the charge made by a newspaper for each line of a classified advertisement. 2. *n* [*Journalism*] the rate paid to freelance journalists on a basis of so much per line printed.

line 1. *n* [*Advertising*] a unit of space used in buying print advertisements: one fourteenth of an inch high by one column wide. 2. *n* [*Music*] an instrumental or vocal melody or any structured sequence of notes or tones. 3. *n* [*Ballet*] the physical outline of a dancer, particularly the way in which the dancer's limbs and body are placed, either in movement or repose; it comes from the naval use, referring to the shape of a ship. 4. *n* [*Economics, Commerce*] See **bottom line**. 5. *n* [*Communications*] a string of characters accepted by a computer as single block of input. 6. *n* [*Flying*] a concrete apron positioned just outside a hangar on which aircraft stand awaiting takeoff, maintenance, etc. 7. *n* [*Hunting*] the scent left by a fox. 8. *n* [*Ice-hockey*] three forwards (a centre and two wings) considered as a performing unit. 9. *n* [*Publishing*] a series of books that are similar or inter-related – science fiction, historical romances, detective fiction, etc. 10. *n* [*Bowls*] a complete game of ten frames. See also **string 5**. 11. *n* [*Gambling*] the pass line on a craps table, a strip on which are placed side bets to the effect that the **shooter** will **pass**. 12. *n* [*Cards*] a hand won in gin rummy, and the points gained by winning. 13. *n* [*US*] [*Football*] the 7 offensive players who line up within 1 ft. of the line of scrimmage; the defensive players who line up within 1 yd. of the line of scrimmage. 14. *v* [*Baseball*] to hit a line drive, a shot that travels fast and low. 15. *v* [*Stock market*] any large amount; specifically it means a line of shares.

line contact *n* [*Audio*] an extended ellipse shape used in cartridge stylus design.

line discipline *n* [*Computing*] See **line protocol**.

line, down the 1. *adv* [*TV*] the transmission of a programme or part of a programme for internal assessment only, prior to its being broadcast to home screens. 2. *adv* [*Radio*] an interview 'down the line' is carried out when the interviewer, either live or at a recording console, sits in a studio in one town, while the interviewee talks to him/her through a radio link while sitting in another.

line haul *n* [*Road transport*] a scheduled route between cities that is followed by trucks.

line hunter *n* [*Hunting*] a hound which keeps close to the scent.

line out 1. *v* [*US*] [*Painting*] to unload from the truck the materials required for a job. 2. *v* [*US*] [*Painting*] to assess a job before starting work.

line protocol *n* [*Computing*] a formally specified set of bit sequences that ensures that the two ends of a communication link will be able to pass

L

information between them in an understandable way. A number of standards have been developed to implement these protocols.

line up n [TV] a period immediately prior to recording when electronic cameras are aligned for colour balance, brightness and contrast, etc. As studio equipment becomes more technically sophisticated, the line-up period has correspondingly diminished.

line work n [Gambling] the embellishment of the patterns found on the backs of some playing cards so that they can be identified by cheats.

lineback n [US] [Cattlemen] a cow that has a distinctive stripe, of a colour different to that on the rest of its body, running down its back; it occurs specially in Hereford cattle.

linepack 1. n [Gas industry] the storage of gas in a pipe system by raising the pressure above that of normal operation. 2. n [Gas industry] the inventory of gas in a pipeline.

liner 1. n [US] [Car salesmen] a salesman in a **system house** who precedes the **closer** by getting the customer initially interested in a given car. 2. also **line drive** n [Baseball] a ball batted sharply in the air, on a low course that approximates a straight line rather than in an arc.

line-up 1. n [Billiards] this is when the three balls are in a direct line, with the opponent's ball standing exactly between the cue ball and the red. See also **three-masted schooner**. 2. n [UK] [Surfing] this is where the waves break regularly, normally a reef.

lining figures, also **modern or newspaper figures** n pl [Printing] figures of a common height, aligned at both head and foot.

link 1. v [UK] [Government] to claim for unemployment benefit within eight weeks of the last such claim for sickness or unemployment benefit. 2. n [Radio] See **cues**. 3. n [UK] [Railways] a group of porters working under a foreman.

linkade n [Logology] the pairing of two words whereby a one letter overlap will yield a different word; thus 'for' plus 'reign' makes 'foreign', etc.

linkage n [Politics] the linking within superpower relations, especially in the field of arms negotiations, of progress in military and diplomatic accords with that in 'humanitarian' and social issues, especially as regards Soviet interests in the Third World. This was particularly espoused by the Carter Administration (1976–80) during which Congress refused to ratify **SALT II** until Russia showed itself willing to take real steps to improve domestic policies on dissidents and 'human rights', to set up a grain deal with the US, to moderate 'imperialistic' ambitions in Africa, etc..

linkage politics n [Politics] a means of analysing international relations based on the use of this term in systems analysis to describe any recurrent system of behaviour that originates in one system and produces a reaction in another.

Such reactions can be penetrative (often as a result of a post-war occupation of one country by another); emulative (the spread of a general political ethos, eg. social welfare, through a number of adjacent or similar states), or reactive (eg: the arms race East and West).

linking n [Clothing] the process of using a linking machine to join up the various parts of a knitted garment.

linkman n [TV, Radio] anyone who acts as the 'host' of a programme containing a number of items and who provides the verbal links between them.

linter n [Textiles] in cotton mills this refers to the short downy hairs that stick to the cotton seeds and are unsuitable for spinning into yarn but are used as a source of cellulose, etc.

lion tamer n [Espionage] in a blackmail operation this is a strong-arm man who makes sure that the target, once he/she has been informed of the blackmail evidence, does not make an embarrassing and potentially destructive fuss which could thus ruin the operation.

lip 1. n [Cycling] the edge of a special BMX freestyle cycling area, often a former skateboard track. 2. n [Coal-mining] the face and edge of an area where the roof has been brought down to create more height in a roadway. 3. n [Coal-mining] any step in the floor or roof of a working.

lip flap n [TV] a malfunction in transmission which permits viewers to see but not hear a speaker on the screen.

lipogram n [Logology] a composition or book which is deliberately written to exclude a single letter from all its words; thus the 'Odyssey' of Tryphiodorus, which has no alpha in book one, no beta in book two and so on.

lippy 1. n [Theatre, TV, Film] abbr of **lipstick**. 2. also **overhung** a [Dog breeding] used to describe excessively pendulous lips.

LIPS n [Computing] acro **Logical Interferences Per Second** a measure of the power of an inference machine by denoting the number of syllogistic inferences per second that can be performed. One syllogistic inference is the equivalent of 100–1000 conventional computer instructions. See also **flops, KIPS, MIPS**.

lip-sync n [TV, Film] abbr of **lip-synchronisation** sound that is recorded at exactly the same time as the pictures and which can be exactly synchronised with the lip movements of each character. See also **dub 1–3**.

liquid cosh n [UK] [Prisons] any heavy tranquilliser, eg. largactyl, which is used to control otherwise unruly prisoners.

liquidisation n [Futures market] any transaction that **closes out** or **offsets short positions**.

liquidity n [Finance] the interchangeability of assets and money.

liquidity crisis n [Economics] a situation where

L

the banks lack sufficient ready cash to make loans as required by companies.

liquor *n* [*Paper-making*] a chemical liquid used to reduce wood chips to pulp and to remove chemical impurities.

LISP *n* [*Computing*] acro **List Processing** a language designed for the manipulation of non-numeric lists and symbolic strings. LISP is very widely used in artificial intelligence research.

lissee *a* [*Cheese-making*] used to describe a fresh cheese that has been processed in a lissoir (a mashing apparatus) as part of its manufacture; it comes from Fr. 'lisser' meaning 'to smooth'.

list-broker *n* [*Commerce*] anyone who trades in mailing lists, which are used by charities, companies, **inertia** salesmen, etc.

listening post *n* [*Journalism*] towns, cities, or places in them which are used by journalists to catch up on local or national gossip, to obtain stories and to cultivate contacts.

lister *n* [*Bird-watching*] an excitable, over-enthusiastic bird-watcher, religiously listing every species he sees for future reference. See also **tick-hunter, twitcher 2.**

listing *n* [*Real estate*] a property offered by its owner for sale, lease or rent.

literal 1. *n* [*Printing*] See **typo 1. 2.** also **constant** *n* [*Computing*] a program instruction which tells the machine how to operate that program, rather than acting as either an **address** or **label;** any symbol that means nothing more than itself.

Literaturwissenschaft *n* [*Bibliography*] literature considered as a scholarly study based on historical and philological principles.

little *a* [*Wine-tasting*] used to describe a wine with scarcely any bouquet or aroma; a wine of no character.

Little Bang *n* [*Stock market*] the first level of deregulation in the UK stock market, permitting brokers dealing in overseas markets to act both as principal and agent. See also **Big Bang, dual capacity.**

Little Boy *n* [*Military*] the first atomic bomb, dropped on Hiroshima at 8.15 am on August 6, 1945. The bomb, 3 metres long, weighing 4000 kilograms, was exploded in an air burst 510 metres above the city, with an explosive yield of a minimum of 12,000 tons (12 KT) of TNT. See also **Fat Man.**

little cat *n* [*Gambling*] a hand recognised in certain poker games: eight, seven, six, five, three; it contains no pairs, and is composed of two or more suits; it ranks next below a **big cat.**

little dick *n* [*Gambling*] in craps dice, the point of four. See also **little Joe.**

little dog *n* [*Gambling*] in poker, a hand with seven high, deuce low and no pair.

little F *n* [*Fleet air arm*] the Lieutenant Commander (Flying) who is assistant to the commander (Air) on an aircraft carrier.

little foot *n* [*US*] [*Journalism*] a member of the general working press corps, a junior reporter; the term is usually used to refer to those who cover a presidential or similar campaign. See also **big foot.**

little Jimmy *n* [*Gambling*] in bingo, the number 4,

little Joe (from Kokomo) *n* [*Gambling*] in craps dice, the point of 4.

little old ladies *n pl* [*Journalism*] eccentric, complaining letter writers of either sex who constantly bedevil anyone whose opinions are printed or broadcast for mass circulation.

little phoebe *n* [*Gambling*] in craps dice, the point of five.

little science *n* [*Science*] research or technology that requires few or inexpensive resources. See also **big science.**

little steel *n* [*US*] [*Business*] a group of secondary steel producers, smaller than the major US steel corporations.

little 'un *n* [*UK*] [*Railways*] a 'shunt ahead' signal mounted on a signal gantry.

livarisi la petra di la scarpa *v* [*Crime*] in the Italian Mafia, literally this means 'to take the stone from one's shoe' ie. to take revenge.

live 1. *a* [*Audio*] used of any room or enclosed area that has a relatively long reverberation time and which produces a degree of echo. **2.** *a* [*Theatre*] used of any set that will be required again later in the performance.

live card *n* [*Cards*] a card that has not yet been played; it is either still hidden in the pack or held by an opponent.

live coal *n* [*Coal-mining*] coal that can easily be extracted from the face because of a distribution of rock stresses within the strata caused by mining operations, or because of gas emissions from the seam. See also **dead coal.**

live customers *n pl* [*Commerce*] customers who are currently trading with and may be assumed to be continuing to trade with a given company.

live food *n* [*Commerce*] in the health food business, this is food that is 'still growing', ie: fresh rather than packaged products.

live labour *n* [*Politics*] in Marxist terms, this is an indispensable element in the mode of production: the purposeful expenditure of physical or mental energy during production. As this expenditure attaches itself to the product as one of its actual values, it becomes 'materialised labour'.

live oil *n* [*Gas industry*] oil that contains dissolved gas.

live one *n* [*US*] [*Hotels*] a guest who tips well.

live wires *n pl* [*UK*] [*Railways*] in London Transport these are underground train maintenance electricians.

lively 1. *a* [*Cycling*] said of tyres that respond fast to effort and/or to overcome the surface resistance of the road. **2.** *a* [*Wine-tasting*] used to describe either a fresh, young wine or an older wine with youthful characteristics.

L

liven up v [US] [Painting] to create a paint colour that does not come from the usual selection; to create a new colour by adding an extra tint to the basic colour.

liveware n [Computing] the human beings – programmers, engineers, users – who are involved with computers. See also **firmware 1, hardware 2, software 1.**

living buoys n pl [Navy] See **mark boat.**

living dead n [Stock market] such financial situations that neither prosper nor fail to any great extent, but seem merely to exist interminably without any hope of a positive or negative resolution.

living debt, also **productive debt** n [Finance] that part of the UK National Debt which is used to finance useful national assets, eg: roads, hospitals, schools, etc.

living in place n [New therapies] the idea of one's being continually aware of the effect that everything has upon one: breathing, walking, drinking coffee, etc.

living room group n [New therapies] a small encounter group, the opposite of the larger 'growth centre'.

living sculpture n [Art] the use by an artist of his/her own body, its processes and products as the actual artwork, often as a 'tableau vivant'. This concept can be extended to include plants and living animals. See also **performance art.**

lizard 1. n [Aus., NZ] [Farming] general musterer of sheep. 2. n [Aus., NZ] [Farming] a farm worker who maintains boundary fences. 3. n [US] [Medicine] a patient who is both dirty and has a noticeable skin complaint. 4. n [Sailing, Ropework] a short pennant with a **bulls eye** or **thimble** spliced in one end.

Lloyd Morgan's canon n [Psychology] the concept that no action must be interpreted as a higher psychological process if it can be interpreted as one lower down the scale; it is named after Conwy Lloyd Morgan (1852–1936), a British psychologist.

LMD n [Medicine] abbr of **local M.D.** a general practitioner as opposed to a hospital doctor. See also **real doctor.**

load 1. n [Industry] the use that is to be assigned to a production facility – a worker, a machine, etc – over a period of time. 2. n [Navy] venereal disease.

load and go n [Computing] an operating technique in which the operator is powerless to interfere between the loading of the program and its immediate execution.

load of wind n [UK] [Road transport] a very light load.

load on the high side v [US] [Road transport] to load the freight with a bias towards the side of the truck nearest the centre of the road.

load out v [US] [Painting] to load up one's equipment prior to leaving a job site.

load transfer n [UK] [Road transport] a system by which the weight on an individual axle of a two-axle **bogie** under braking, heavy loading or on an uneven ground, is transferable so as to retain an even distribution of load.

loadability n [Commerce] in either private or commercial transport this is the facility with which a vehicle can be loaded.

loaded 1. a [Baseball] used of the situation when there are base runners on each of the three bases. 2. a [Magic] said of a magician who has prepared his equipment for a performance.

loader n [Shipping] a ship that is loading passengers or cargo preparatory to sailing.

loading 1. n [Paper-making] the adding of a substance – usually china clay – to pulp in order to produce a high-class finish. 2. n [Telephony] the introduction, at intervals along the line, of inductances (creating changes in current) which will improve the quality of transmission/reception. 3. n [Psychology] the extent to which any one factor influences an overall situation, which can often be expressed in statistical form. Such factors can be increased or decreased in the final analysis in accordance with their relative importance to the situation.

LoADS n [Military] acro **Low-Altitude Defence System** a ballistic missile defence system designed specifically to eliminate those 4% of hostile missiles that can be presumed to elude all **BMD** systems which would be targeted on incoming missiles and presumably successful in destroying most of them at earlier stages of their flight. Ground-based radar would calculate the intercept trajectory and the missiles would be attacked by a gun-launched hypervelocity interceptor. LoADS would destroy missiles below 50,000' – possibly as low as 6,000–8,000' – with its own small nuclear bombs of about 2KT yield.

load's walking v phr [Merchant navy] the cargo is shifting.

loan crowd n [US] [Stock market] those members of the exchange who lend or borrow securities needed to cover the positions of customers who sell **short.**

loaver n [UK] [Market-traders] money.

lob, also **jerk** n [Gambling] a hanger-on at a gambling establishment who runs errands for the players. See also **gofer.**

lobby n, v [Politics] the use of special pleading by a variety of interest groups – both ostensibly powerful commercial interests and otherwise under-represented minorities – to ensure that their requirements and aims are catered for by the incumbent government; thus the 'farm lobby', the 'small business lobby', 'the environment lobby' etc. It originated in the 18th century use of an ante-chamber in the House of Commons in which interested parties could meet and entreat their MP.

lobby banking n [Banking] out-of-hours

banking facilities provided by 'cash cards' which can be used in computer operated automatic tellers to obtain cash, request statements, order cheque-books, etc.

lobby terms, on *a* [*Politics*] the relationship fostered between politicians and the select band of lobby correspondents, whereby both accept the situation in which the politician can say what he wants and the journalist duly write it up (unless asked not to) but at no time will the story every be attributed to the actual source.

lobby-fodder *n* [*UK*] [*Politics*] members of the House of Commons who have little influence on Parliamentary affairs, but who still count when it is time to register a vote by walking into either the 'Yes' or 'No' lobby as required by their party.

lobby-shopper *n* [*Sex*] a prostitute who specialises in picking up clients in hotel lobbies.

lobster *n* [*Navy*] a Royal Marine; it comes from the colour of the original marine uniforms.

lobster shift 1. *n* [*Journalism*] a tour of duty that covers late evening or early morning hours. See also **dog-watch 3, graveyard shift 1**. 2. *n* [*Journalism*] the skeleton staff who cover the period between one edition going to press and work beginning on the next.

lobsterscope (*US*), **flickerwheel** (*UK*) *n* [*Theatre*] a slotted disc that can be rotated in front of a light to simulate slow motion effects.

loc *n* [*Science fiction*] acro **letter of comment** the bulk of contributors to the 'lettercols' of fan magazines are commenting on the fiction or on other fan letters.

local 1. *n* [*Computing*] a variable which is defined and used only in one part of the program. See also **global**. 2. *n* [*Computing*] equipment that is installed in an office or home and can function alone and independently, rather than being simply a terminal. See also **stand-alone**. 3. *n* [*Commodity exchange*] See **floor trader**. 4. *n* [*Futures market*] one who has bought a futures contract to establish a market position and who has not yet **closed out** that position through an **offsetting sale**; it is the opposite of **short**.

local networking *n* [*Computing*] the interconnection of a number of computers situated within the same building; it is usually found in offices for interdepartmental communication.

local optimisation *n* [*Computing*] See **peephole optimisation**. See also **global optimisation, optimisation**.

local time *n* [*US*] [*TV*] See **station time**.

localitis 1. *n* [*Military*] a military quirk whereby each commander tends to see his own position or area of operations as central to the overall situation, and therefore urges actions which may not usefully bear on that situation; it is especially noticeable among those commanders in the most remote and marginal positions. 2. *n* [*Diplomacy*] an extension of (1), whereby diplomats in minor postings attempt excessively to forward 'their'

nation's interests without looking fully at the world situation.

locals *n pl* [*US*] [*Meat trade*] animals brought to market from nearby areas.

location 1. *n* [*TV, Film*] any shooting of a film or TV programme that is done away from the home studio 'on location'. 2. also **situation** *n* [*Film*] a film theatre; the place where a film is shown.

loccol, also **locol** *n* [*Science fiction*] abbr of **letter of comment column** See **loc**.

lock *n* [*Computing*] a mechanism that controls multiple access to a common device and ensures that a given process has access to a particular resource.

lockaway *n* [*Stock market*] a long-term security that can be 'locked away' as an investment for the distant future.

lock down sequence *n* [*Photography*] a method of taking a series of slides whereby a camera with a zoom lens is locked into position on a tripod, aiming at the object of interest. A sequence of shots is taken, each one with the zoom slightly advancing, thus creating a series of shots that gradually 'approach' their subject.

lock on *v* [*Aerospace*] said of any radar, guidance or weapons system that traces a target, beacon, radio mast, etc, electronically, and then 'follows' it for as long as necessary.

lock up 1. *v* [*Pool*] to beat an opponent speedily and conclusively. 2. *n* [*Printing*] the final stage of paste-up for the pages in computer-generated newspaper design; it is the same term as in traditional hot-metal setting. 3. *n* [*Stock market*] any long-term investment, especially one that will produce a regular income rather than a spectacular gain.

lockable third differential *n* [*UK*] [*Road transport*] an additional **differential** interposed between the two driving axles to compensate for different turning speeds on the two axles (due to discrepancies in tyre diameters, etc) and which can be locked to ensure equal driving speed on all wheels on the axles.

locked in *a* [*Stock market*] referring to an investor who resists taking the profits on investments so as to avoid paying the capital gains tax that such a move would involve.

locker *n* [*Coal-mining*] See **sprag 2**.

lockout *n* [*Computing*] a technique used to prevent access to critical data by two separate programs in a multiprogramming environment. See also **lock**.

locks and keys *n pl* [*Computing*] a system of memory protection in which segments of memory are assigned identification numbers (the locks) and authorised users are provided with the numbers (the keys) by the operating system. This provision is performed by a **privileged** (see **privilege**) process in some location in the operating system, not accessible to the user.

L

lock-up n [*Printing*] a device for securing in place all the components of a page of metal-set type.

lockwasher n [*Science*] in cell biology this is a helical form occurring in the structure of protein as a result of some dislocation.

loco n [*Commerce*] in foreign trade this is a price quoted regarding goods that are in a certain place at a certain time; in accepting this price, the buyer must accept all costs incurred in moving the goods to another place; it comes from Lat. 'in place'.

locus classicus n [*Literary criticism*] an authoritative source; the example of a style, linguistic usage, aphoristic or proverbial statement, etc. that is generally considered to be the classic, ideal version.

lodge n [*Shoe-making*] a thin flap of leather cemented to the forward face of a shoe's heel.

lodging rooms n pl [*Hunting*] hounds' sleeping quarters with benches round three sides of the wall covering the bulk of the floor space

lodging turn n [*UK*] [*Railways*] any period when a railway employee has to spend time in a lodging away from home before returning to his home station.

loft n [*Theatre*] the part of the stage area above the **grid**.

loft-bombing n [*Military*] the use of an aircraft's speed to project its bombs as if they were artillery shells; it is used to save a bomber from the fireball that the exploding bombs will create beneath it.

lofting n [*Aerospace*] the reproduction of the original plans for an aircraft at full size, so that any possible errors in the design of these plans can be ironed out. Those who perform this are 'loftsmen' and their workplace is the 'mould loft'.

log n [*Surfing*] a large, cumbersome, surfboard, resembling an unwieldly treetrunk.

log boy n [*US*] [*Road transport*] a low trailer for hauling heavy machinery.

log in, also **log on** v [*Computing*] to gain access to a computer by using a **password** or simply calling up a given program; thus 'log off/out' is to relinquish that access by using a further password or abandoning that program.

logger v [*US*] [*Military*] to build a hastily assembled, makeshift camp; it comes from the Afrikaans 'laager' meaning camp.

loggerhead n [*Angling*] the chub. See also **alderman.**

logic 1. n [*Computing*] the operations performed by a computer for the purposes of sorting, collecting and analysing data. 2. n [*Computing*] the system and the principles that are the basis of the operation of a computer, of representing operation and variables by electronic and other signals. See **flipflop 1.**

logic bomb n [*Data security*] a part of a program specially written so as to trigger off a warning of a fraud if activated by a succession of pre-determined events.

logic enhancement n [*Audio*] a method of increasing the separation and directional accuracy of quadrophonic reproduction: all the signals are continually monitored and adjusted by dedicated electronic circuitry to achieve optimum standards.

logic family n [*Computing*] a range of electronic devices made by the same manufacturing technique and providing a number of logic functions. The range includes logic gates, **flip-flops** and **counters.**

logic time bomb n [*Computing*] a fault which can be deliberately programmed into a system, usually by an employee who operates or programmes that system, with the deliberate intent of wrecking its proper functioning. Such bombs are often placed by a dissatisfied or soon to be made redundant employee. See also **virus.**

logical n [*Computing*] abbr of **logical device** the use of an arbitrary name to refer to a physical device; thus in this context 'logical' implies a meaning that does not necessarily correspond to reality.

logical atom n [*Philosophy*] one of the essential and indivisible elements into which some philosophers maintain that statements can be analysed.

logology n [*Linguistics*] the science of words, especially in the field of orthographic and homophonic word games.

logoptics n [*Art*] the trademark, registered in 1974, of a pictorial sign system designed to replace verbal language (eg: the instructions on medicine bottles) by a simpler, universally comprehensible system.

logotype 1. n [*Printing*] in traditional metal-setting this is two or more characters cast on one shank to assist hand-setting of common words or syllables, eg. 'and', 'ment'. 2. n [*Printing*] See **ligature. 3.** n [*Printing*] a trademark, newspaper or magazine title, etc.

log-rolling n [*Politics, Media*] this comes from the US frontier-era practice of everyone helping everyone else when heavy logs had to be shifted; it refers to the mutual aid systems established by politicians whereby A will ensure the B grants his support on a given issue, so long as, when required, he will be willing to repay the favour. It is similarly found throughout the media, especially when critics are also creators and, within their own small but influential circle, write each other congratulatory reviews.

loid n [*UK*] [*Crime*] this comes from rhyming slang 'Harold Lloyd' meaning 'celluloid'; it is a picklock made from a celluloid strip (often simply a plastic credit or bank card) that works on spring ('Yale') locks.

loiter v [*Military*] said of a fighter plane when it stays near the battle area, awaiting instructions from the ground or base commander prior to making swift strikes into assigned targets in that area.

loiter time n [*Military*] that period of time during

L

which a fighter aircraft can **loiter** over a target and still make a safe journey home. Such a capability is vital to modern specifications, eg: 'Range 300m radius, plus 2 hours loiter time'.

LOL In NAD *n* [US] [Medicine] acro **Little Old Lady in No Apparent Distress** any patients of either sex who enjoy the care and comforts found in a hospital, but have no immediate or critical physical problems. See also **GOMER.**

lollipop *n* [UK] [Railways] a shafted tool, with an iron ball, resembling the sweet, which is used for testing sleepers.

lollipop flight *n* [Air travel] flights that are more than usually filled with child passengers – at the start and finish of school terms and holidays when expatriate children rejoin or leave their parents.

lollypop *n* [Skiing] piste marker.

lo-lo-high mission *n* [Military] an airborne mission in which the out journey is flown low to avoid hostile radar and the return flown high to avoid anti-aircraft fire.

Lombard Street *n* [UK] [Finance] shorthand for the financial centre of the City of London; it is the equivalent of New York's **Wall Street.**

London weighting *n* [UK] [Business] the payment of extra wages to those employed in London to compensate for the higher cost of living in the capital.

long 1. *a* [Cycling] when assessing a time-trial this refers to a time marginally over the figure stated; thus 'long fifty-eight' is a time fractionally over 58 minutes. See also **short** 1. 2. *a* [Stock market] referring to a **jobber** who has bought more stock than he has sold and is therefore hoping that prices will rise so that it will be worth having; it is a synonym for a **bull** position. 3. *a* [Stock market] when used of UK government stocks this means having a life of more than fifteen years. 4. *a* [Wine-tasting] used to describe a lingering flavour that is a sign of quality.

long blow *n* [Sheep-shearing] a single stroke of the shears which cuts away the fleece from rump to neck.

long bomb 1. *n* [US] [Football] a move in which a quarterback throws a long ball to a receiver positioned in or near the end-zone to score a touchdown: it is the favourite spectacular move for spectators and TV audiences. 2. *n* [Public relations] from the sporting use (see **1**) this is any exceptional piece of PR work, exposing the client just as required, or even better. See also **keybook.**

long cards *n pl* [Cards] in bridge, the holding of five cards in a trump suit or four in a side suit makes those cards 'long'.

long dogs *n pl* [Hunting] greyhounds.

long dozen *n* [Commerce] thirteen, a baker's dozen.

long exchange *n* [Banking] foreign bills of exchange that will not mature for 60–90 days.

long filler *n* [Tobacco] a grade of tobacco used for the best cigars.

long firm fraud *n* [UK] [Crime, Police] a fraud in which a large amount of goods are purchased on credit and then sold cheaply and quickly; the 'firm' which has run up the credit then vanishes and the bills incurred are never paid to the wholesalers.

long haul network *n* [Communications] geographically disparate networks, using several host computers in a variety of cities, which are linked by the public telephone system, satellite communications, etc.

long hedge *n* [Futures market] a **hedge** against a fall interest rates. See also **short hedge.**

long hundred *n* [Commerce] one hundred and twenty.

Long Island tea *n* [US] [Bars] See **iced tea.**

long legs *n pl* [Military] the distance an ICBM can travel towards a target.

long letters *n pl* [Printing] figures that extend over the whole shoulder, from the back to the front of the type stem.

long pimples *n pl* [Table tennis] a type of rubber used on bats which features outward projecting long pimples which flex on impact and give an unpredictable spin to the ball.

long rabbits *n pl* [UK] [Postal services] items eligible for large rebates – third-class mail.

long run 1. *n* [Economics] the time taken for a change in demand to be balanced by a change in supply. 2. *n* [Economics] the time taken for all the economic factors in a situation to reach a new equilibrium at which point the rate of change levels out.

long tap *n* [Stock market] government securities that are issued in unlimited quantities and have a long-term maturity date, at least fifteen years.

long term team *n* [Social work] a group of social workers who deal with cases that are assessed as being likely to continue for some time, ie: over a minimum of three months.

long Tom *n* [Photography] an especially high-powered lens used on still, TV or film cameras; it is often used for long-distance work, for surveillance in espionage operations or for 'candid' shots taken by newspapermen or paparazzi.

long ton *n* [Commerce] the imperial ton of 2,240 ob. See also **short ton.**

long twos *n pl* [US] [Cattlemen] cattle that are nearly three years old.

long yearling *n* [US] [Cattlemen] a cow that is between eighteen months and two years old.

longer, go *v* [Stock market] in the fixed interest security market this is to sell short-dated stocks and use the money to buy medium- or long-dated stocks.

long-fed *a* [Farming] said of cattle that have been fed finishing rations for eight to ten months.

longform *n* [US] [Radio] a programme which concentrates on lengthy, in-depth news and features and analysis, rather than a collection of brief headlines and newsflashes.

L

long-haul *a* [*Travel agents*] used to describe journeys outside Europe and the UK, thus the US, Africa, India, the Far East, Australasia etc. See also **short-haul**.

longitude roulette *n* [*Merchant navy*] sailing a hypothetical course, especially in polar areas where it is not possible to establish a true longitude.

long-jawed *a* [*Sailing, Ropework*] said of old rope that has stretched and lost most of its twist.

long-legged *a* [*Sailing*] referring to any vessel that draws a good deal of water.

longliner *n* [*Fishing*] a fishing vessel that used long lines, each of which holds many baited hooks.

longs *n pl* [*Stock market*] long term stocks which are repayable in fifteen years or longer.

long-stroke, also **under-square** *n* [*Cars*] abbr of **long-stroke engine, under-square engine** one in which the length of the stroke is greater than the bore diameter.

longwall *n* [*Coal-mining*] a system of working coal in which it is extracted from the seam on a broad front or a long face.

look down/shoot down capability *n* [*Military*] an airborne radar system, under development by the Soviets as a counter to the US **AWACS**, that is particularly geared to spotting aircraft and cruise missiles which are attempting to elude conventional ground-based radar observation nets. The result of such a capability might well negate the usefulness of **cruise** and as such render any use of these missiles as a positive bargaining chip pointless.

look for runs *v* [*Cricket*] said of a batsman who takes every available opportunity to score a run.

looker *n* [*Real estate*] one who expresses interest in looking over a number of properties, but who obviously has no interest in buying one.

lookie Lou *n* [*US*] [*Real estate*] an individual who asks to inspect many properties but never finds one to his/her taste.

look-in *n* [*US*] [*Football*] a pass pattern executed by a receiver who runs a short distance beyond the line of scrimmage on a diagonal course towards the centre of the field.

looking at you *part phr* [*US*] [*Lunch counter*] fried eggs with the yolks still soft, the equivalent of 'sunny side up'.

Looking Glass plane *n* [*Military*] the flying command post which preceded **Cover All**; it was so called because its capabilities reflected in the air (like a mirror) the same command and control functions as existed at land-based command posts.

look-out book *n* [*Government*] a list of prohibited or suspected aliens used by H.M. Customs to check immigrants to the UK. Twenty different codes list some 20,000 individuals suspected of political subversion, immorality, criminal offences, lacking a work permit, etc; not everyone listed is barred, but the 'book' aims to ensure that all are recognised.

look-see *n* [*Fashion*] an audition taken by a model who visits photographers, magazines, etc, looking for work.

lookthrough *n* [*Paper-making*] the appearance of a sheet of paper when held up to the light to reveal its texture of formation.

loom, also **harness** *n* [*Cars*] the collection of wires, coded and cut to correct lengths, which complete the wiring circuits in any car.

loop 1. *n* [*Computing*] a sequence of instructions that are repeated over and over by the computer until such time as a given criterion has been fulfilled. **2.** *n* [*Cycling*] the curved tube of a lady's bicycle that differentiates it from a man's model. **3.** *n* [*US*] [*Government*] in the Reagan Administration this is the inner circle of advisers who receive top-level restricted information. **4.** *n* [*Table tennis*] an attacking stroke played with an upward swing of the bat to impart heavy topspin on the ball in an attempt to force the opponent to return the ball high in the air or off the end of the table.

looped *a* [*Navy*] to be hit by one's own torpedo which has malfunctioned and run a looped course back to the ship that fired it.

looping *n* [*Gas industry*] this is when another line is run parallel to an existing pipeline, over all or part of its length, to increase capacity.

loo-roll *n* [*TV*] the continuous roll of paper onto which a script is typed for use with a teleprompter machine.

loose *a* [*Book collecting*] See **shaken**.

loose change *n* [*Politics*] minor concessions or demands that determine the progress or lack of it in diplomatic negotiations. See also **bargaining chips**.

loose end *n* [*Coal-mining*] that end of a longwall face that abuts previous workings.

loose, in the, also **as dug** *adv* [*UK*] [*Road transport*] used of material to be carted away from a site and which has already been dug up; quotations for such jobs are based on the volume of material to be removed. Material which has already been dug out will have less volume than material still to be excavated. See also **solid, in the**.

loose sentence *n* [*Literary criticism*] a sentence that contains a complete thought before it reaches its end, and then attaches a number of subordinate clauses after this thought has been completed in the main clause. See also **periodic sentence**.

loran *n* [*Military*] abbr of **long range navigation** the use of radio signals from special ground stations for military (and civilian) navigation; such stations can only be based in friendly countries, and thus loran systems have strictly definable geographical limits.

lose *v* [*Media*] See **kill 3–5**.

lose tempo *v* [*Chess*] used of a player when he

L

requires two or more moves to achieve a position that should have been reached in one.

loss leader *n* [*Commerce*] a product which is offered at an exceptionally low price in order to tempt buyers towards other, more expensive, products.

loss-pricing *n* [*Commerce*] the holding down of prices despite the possible losses this may entail, in the hope of luring new customers away from one's (temporarily) more expensive rivals.

lost *a* [*Military*] referring to any shell or mortar round that has not been seen to explode by a spotter.

lost positives *n pl* [*Literary criticism*] archaisms or humorous coinages that offer positive versions of words for which contemporary usage only had the negative, eg: 'ane' from 'inane', 'couth' from 'uncouth', 'gorm' from 'gormless', etc.

lost sculptures *n pl* [*Art*] 'lost' stands as the opposite of 'found' as in **'found objects'**; they refer to sculptures with so sparse a visual appeal that they may be seen simply as nondescript objects of the everyday world; thus 'invisible sculpture' is a structure whose existence the spectator must take on trust.

lot *n* [*Film*] the land around a film studio which is owned by that studio and used sometimes for exterior filming.

Lot's wife *n* [*Navy*] the salt cellar in a ship's mess.

lounge *n* [*Entertainment*] the auditorium, usually a night club, in which a singer or comedian performs. See also **room 2**.

love *n* [*Fishing*] in herring-curing this is a beam set across a smoke-house, from which the herrings are suspended.

love-bombing *n* [*Sociology*] the softening up process which is aimed at a potential convert to a 'cult' religion, eg: Moonies, Hare Krishna. Its members saturate the neophyte with affection, optimism, Utopian theories, etc. and thus, usually, manage to effect the seduction into the cult. At this point the affection is replaced by less appealing but equally intense conditioning processes, from which escape is far less simple than from the initial induction.

loving *a* [*New therapies*] usually found as in 'loving relationship' or 'caring relationship'; the emphasis is on emotional rather than physical love or care, although the inference is a fully integrated relationship (hetero- or homosexual) in which the needs, feelings and any other desires of both individuals are accepted and nurtured by the other.

low *a* [*Antiques, Rug trade*] said of a rug with insufficiently long pile; a worn rug.

low abstraction *n* [*Business*] an inability to conceive of or manipulate abstract concepts; thus the low abstractors in a firm are essentially a white collar proletariat, the lower echelons of a corporation, reduced by their inadequacies to such

routine and spiritually unrewarding occupations as filing and copy-typing. See also **high abstraction**.

low ball *n* [*US*] [*Car salesmen*] an estimate by the salesman of a lower price for a new car than it will actually cost. See also **high-ball**.

low belly strippers *n pl* [*Gambling*] a pack of cards used for cheating in which the edges of the high cards have been made slightly concave – after being 'stripped' with a scapel – and are thus easily identifiable. See also **high belly strippers**.

low colour *n* [*Glass-making*] a green tinge to glass which is produced by the inclusion, deliberate or not, of iron in the **batch**.

low key *n* [*TV, Film, Photography*] any image in which the majority of tones are dark or grey.

low level language *n* [*Computing*] a programming language that is closely related to the machine code language within the architecture of the computer. Such languages are, because of this relation, more efficient to operate – faster, requiring less memory, etc. – but they are hard to write and their application is restricted to specific hardware configurations. See also **high-level language**.

low loader *n* [*TV*] a low, wheeled, flatbed platform that is towed behind a moving vehicle and carries a cameraman who can thus shoot interiors of that vehicle, chase sequences, etc. without having to resort to back projection.

low pressure selling *n* [*Commerce*] See **soft selling**.

low profile **1.** *a* [*Cars*] used to describe a tyre with a relatively shallow sidewall in relation to its width. See also **high-profile**. **2.** *n* [*Military, Government, Business*] originally this was a military term for ensuring that troops, vehicles and weapons all offered the least possible target to the enemy by keeping low or under cover; in the various civilian senses, it means acting quietly and discreetly, maintaining anonymity, and staying as far as possible, whatever one's plans, indistinguishable from the grey mass.

low quarter *n* [*Weaving*] third-to-lowest category in the **blood system** of grading wool.

low wines *n* [*Distilling*] the product of the first distillation in the Pot Still process, containing alcohol, secondary constituents and some water; it provides the raw material for the second distillation in the second still.

lowball *v* [*Commerce*] said of a salesman who lures customers by offering an estimate for a contract that is so low that there is no possibility that, once the contract has been signed, it can ever be honoured.

lowballer *n* [*Stock market*] an investment manager who deliberately underestimates any future predictions of expected financial results.

lower the boom (on) *v* [*US*] [*Navy*] to punish or reprimand severely.

L

lowering *n* [*Custom cars*] dropping the suspension on a car to facilitate its handling.

lowering blocks *n pl* [*Custom cars*] a method of lowering the rear suspension of a leaf-sprung car; steel blocks are inserted between the rear axle and the springs, raising the axle and thus lowering the rear of the car.

low-loader *n* [*UK*] [*Road transport*] any trailer designed to provide a low-loading facility for heavy plant and equipment; such trailers are usually fitted with a **swan-neck**.

low-profile crime *n* [*Crime*] any crime committed as secretively as possible, usually at night, and without the presence of any witnesses. See also **high-profile crime**.

lowse *n* [*UK*] [*Coal-mining*] the end of a shift underground; it comes from dialect 'lowse' meaning 'loose' and refers to the 18th/19th century use of hempen ropes and a chaldron – a wooden or woven 'tub' – in the shaft. At the shift's end the chaldron would be loosed off to allow miners to ride up the shaft on 'arse loops' attached to the rope.

low-stream industry *n* [*Business*] a small industry in which individual or local aspects are stressed over any allegiance to or imitation of a giant conglomerate; almost a cottage industry. See also **high-stream, sunrise industry, sunset industry**.

lox *n* [*Aerospace*] abbr of **liquid oxygen** the main propellant for rockets.

loxed *a* [*US*] [*Medicine*] **lack of oxygen** the decreased state of consciousness in a patient who has suffered a heart attack.

lozenge 1. *n* [*Heraldry*] a shape similar to that of the diamond in playing cards. **2.** *n* [*Heraldry*] a diamond-shaped shield borne by an unmarried lady or widow.

LPC *n* [*UK*] [*Military*] abb of 'leather personnel carrier' a boot.

LPT *n* [*Computing*] abbr of **line printer**.

L.S. *n* [*Law*] abbr of **locus sigilli** it comes from Lat. meaning the place of the seal; it is used on many modern contracts as a substitute for a real seal.

L-Sat *n* [*Satellite TV*] abbr of **large satellite**.

LSI *n* [*Computing*] abbr of **Large Scale Integration** an integrated curcuit fabrication technology that allows between 10,000 and 100,000 transistors to be integrated on a single chip. See also **MSI, SLSI, SSI, VLSI**.

LTP *n* [*US*] [*TV*] abbr of **living telops** pictures on the screen that show a story for which the commentary is provided not by an on-the-spot reporter but by the newscaster reading over them.

lucky dip *n* [*Air travel*] the practice among aircraft loaders of snatching suitcases, bags and packages at random, on the off-chance that they might contain something worth stealing.

lucrative target *n* [*Military*] any target considered worthy of destruction.

lucy, also **grant** *n* [*Advertising*] the proprietory names of the two photographic processors most generally used by graphic designers.

luetic *a* [*US*] [*Medicine*] syphilitic; a term used deliberately to confuse patients who generally will not understand it.

lug *n* [*Printing*] See **ear 3**.

lug box *n* [*Agriculture*] a wooden box used to transport fruit from the fields to the cannery; it contains approximately 40lbs.

lugger *n* [*Gambling*] anyone who transports players to a game of cards, dice, roulette, etc.

lugs *n* [*Tobacco*] the lowest grade of tobacco.

lulu *n* [*US*] [*Government*] this comes from 'in lieu of'; it is a flat payment made to legislators to cover their expenses in lieu of dealing with a detailed claim. Such a lump sum removes their need to itemise such expenses for greater scrutiny by the US Treasury.

lumber 1. *n* [*Dog breeding*] excessive muscular and/or bony development, to the extent that the dog's movement becomes heavy and **cloddy. 2.** *n* [*Gambling*] players who have run out of money, ie: 'dead wood'. **3.** *n* [*Gambling*] non-playing spectators at a casino, of no use to its operators.

lumber boy *n* [*US*] [*Road transport*] a truck or trailer designed for carrying sawed timber.

luminal art, also **luminist art** *n* [*Art*] any form of art which is based on light or lighting effects.

lump 1. *n* [*Building*] those self-employed building labourers who move at random from job to job and take a 'lump sum' as pay, rather than contract for a job and have tax and insurance deducted at source. **2.** *n* [*Glass-making*] piles of unmelted materials floating in the molten glass in a tank furnace.

lumper 1. *n* [*Taxonomy*] one who is unwilling to use minute variations in assembling the classification of different species but who simply 'lumps' similar varieties together. See also **splitter. 2.** *n* [*Textiles*] a general odd job man in a textile factory.

lunar armour *n* [*Aerospace*] a specially hardened aluminium space suit used by astronauts on the moon.

lunar light *n* [*UK*] [*Railways*] See **feather 1**.

lunar window *n* [*Aerospace*] the specific **launch window** through which a spacecraft must pass to achieve a successful moon landing.

lunchtime abortion *n* [*Medicine*] any quick abortion – as easily performed in a lunchbreak as at any other time – which is performed by the use of vacuum aspiration.

lunette *n* [*Building, Plastering*] a barrel vault in a domed or vaulted ceiling which admits light.

lunge *n* [*Horse-racing*] a long rope used for exercising and training a horse; thus 'lungeing' means training with such a rope.

lunger 1. *n* [*US*] [*Meat trade*] an old, wheezy sheep that has lost one lung. **2.** *n* [*US*] [*Medicine*] a patient with a chronic lung problem.

L

lurching n [*Coursing*] a greyhound's act of running cunning, or leaving the bulk of the work to its opponent.

lurk v [*Navy*] to be ordered to perform a distasteful job without any chance of escaping the duty.

lush worker n [*US*] [*Crime*] one who specialises in robbing victims who are either too drunk or too drugged to defend themselves.

lutz n [*Ice-skating*] a jump in which a skater takes off from the outside back edge of one skate and lands, after a complete rotation in the air, on the outside back edge of the opposite skate. It is probably named after the Swiss figure skater, Gustave Lussi (1898–), the inventor of the jump.

lyrical colourism n [*Art*] See **new informalists**.

M

M 1. n [*Book collecting*] abbr of **mint** a book in perfect condition; the ultimate accolade from a dealer. 2. n [*UK*] [*Government*] abbr of MBE. See also **K**.

m and e track n [*Film*] abbr of **music and effects track** a tape-recording of the music and special effects in a film which is used at the editing and dubbing (see **dub**) stage of assembling a film.

M and M n [*US*] [*Medicine*] abbr of **morbidity and mortality** a list of who in the hospital/ward is still sick and who has actually died; these are the basic statistics used for discussion at the regularly scheduled conference of a hospital's medical hierarchy.

M1, M2, M3, M4, M0 n [*Economics*] abbr of **Money 1, 2, 3, 4, 0** M1 is the basic money supply, consisting of currency in circulation, plus demand deposits held in current (cheque) accounts; M2 is the money supply of a country, including M1, as well as commercial bank time deposits, but not certificates of deposit; M3 is the overall money supply of a country, including M2, plus deposits in savings and loan associations (including building societies) and certificates of deposit; M4 (not usually used by economists) is savings bonds and credit union shares; M0 is a money aggregate consisting of notes and coins, both in circulation with the public and held in banks' tills and banks' operational balances with the Bank of England.

ma n [*UK*] [*Theatre*] a theatrical landlady.

MAAG n [*Military*] acro **Military Assistance Advisory Group** teams of American advisors working with a host nation to create and train an army; such armies would naturally be biased towards US alliances. Since the US International Security Assistance & Arms Export Control Act (1976), the use of MAAGs has declined, but many such programmes are now carried out by private companies.

MAC 1. n [*Computing*] **Machine Aided Cognition/Multiple Access Computer** a project at the Massachusetts Institute of Technology (MIT) for the development of a practical multi-access system which will enable a number of users to work on the computer simultaneously. 2. n [*Gas industry*] acro **Marketing Account Control** a very large computer database used as a management tool to run the industry at maximum efficiency and profitability.

macaroni n [*Logging*] sawdust.

macaroon n [*Navy*] a new recruit.

Macbeth trap n [*US*] [*Theatre*] a trap door set into the stage which covers a lift on which sundry surprise entrances, such as that of Hamlet's father, various ghosts, etc. can be made.

mace 1. v [*UK*] [*Market-traders*] to owe (money). 2. v [*UK*] [*Market-traders*] to cheat, to swindle.

mace, on the adv [*UK*] [*Market-traders*] practising confidence tricks; obtaining goods without paying, under false pretences.

macer 1. n [*UK*] [*Market-traders*] confidence trickster, swindler, cheat. 2. n [*UK*] [*Police*] a thief or cheat, specifically a practitioner of the 'three-card trick'.

Macguffin n [*Film*] a plot device created by Alfred Hitchcock (1899–1981) as a 'demented red herring' which was pursued by the characters in his films but which in the end had absolutely no relevance to the plot or its outcome.

M

machan n [*Shooting*] a platform, from Hindi.

machinable a [*Computing, Technology*] capable of being read, sensed or otherwise operated by a machine that is programmed to perform such functions.

machine art n [*Art*] any artwork created from mechanical or electronic devices; similarly 'machine sculpture'.

machine code, also **machine language** n [*Computing*] the translation into binary notation of any other language (BASIC, FORTH, etc) which can then be 'understood' by the machine, and which it needs if it is to perform the tasks required. See also **high-level language**.

machine independent n [*Computing*] a program written with no consideration as to the machine it may run on.

machine language n [*Computing*] See **machine code**. See also **high-level language**.

machine time n [*Computing*] the time the computer, rather than its operator, takes to perform a given task. See also **user time**.

machtpolitik n [*Politics*] this comes from Ger. for 'power politics'; it is the use of strength rather than diplomacy to achieve a required result. See also **real politik**.

mack man n [*Sex*] a pimp; it probably comes from Fr. slang 'maquereau' meaning pimp; thus 'hard mack' is a tough, sadistic, mean pimp; 'sweet mack', 'sugar mack' is a generous, tolerant pimp.

Mack the knife n [*US*] [*Medicine*] a surgeon. See also **blade 2, butcher 3**.

Mackenzie! excl [*Commerce*] in US shoe stores this is the warning cry that alerts assistants to the presence of a possible shoplifter; it comes from Yiddish 'm'ken zie' meaning 'we know her'.

macker n [*Navy*] an ordinary seaman.

mackle n [*Printing*] a spot or blemish on the printed sheet caused by wrinkling, double impressions, etc.

macky n [*TV, Theatre*] this comes from French 'maquillage' and means make-up.

MacNab n [*Shooting*] a term used by Scottish huntsmen to describe the shooting of a stag, the killing of a salmon and the shooting of a brace of grouse between dawn and dusk on the same day.

Macready pause n [*Theatre*] a marked pause, or noticeable catching of the breath, before delivering certain lines; it is named after William Charles Macready (1793–1873) whose delivery epitomised such melodramatics.

macroeconomics n [*Economics, Government*] the study of the economy as a whole, dealing with what determines the overall level of activity and other aspects of the economy. See also **Cambridge School, microeconomics**.

macrofount n [*Photo-typesetting*] a digitised character image of every sort in a fount retained as a master by the designers, usually to a much finer resolution than that required by the typesetters. These images are capable of being repro-duced in a range of digital resolutions which can be modified to suit each **raster**. The macrofount can also be used to generate a 'family' of related type designs: roman, bold, condensed, expanded and sloped or italic.

macromarketing n [*Marketing*] the investigation of marketing behaviour by analysing an entire marketing system. See also **micro marketing**.

MAD n [*Military*] acro **Mutual Assured Destruction** the basis of the continuing nuclear standoff between the US and the Soviet Union: the belief, backed by massive nuclear arsenals, that any nuclear exchange must inevitably lead to the destruction of the civilian populations of both superpowers and, most likely, of the entire planet. For all the fine-tuning of nuclear foreign policy, MAD remains the lynchpin of peace.

Madame Misharty n [*UK*] [*Market-traders*] the personification of extreme sales-talk with exaggerated claims, inflated descriptions, etc.

made 1. a [*US*] [*Farming*] said of the stage at which a crop is fully developed, and thus unlikely to be harmed by adverse conditions. **2.** a [*Hunting*] used of a horse which has been trained for safe cross-country work and is accustomed to hounds and hunting.

made bills n pl [*Finance*] bills of exchange that are drawn abroad and payable abroad, but which are negotiable in the UK.

made dirt n [*US*] [*Farming*] deposits of silt; dirt that has been 'manufactured'.

made up/made down part phr [*Stock market*] the process of setting those deals left unresolved by a member of the Exchange who has been **hammered**.

made-for n [*Video*] any production designed and created specifically for the video market.

maderised a [*Wine-tasting*] used to describe the heavy, flat smell of an over-mature, somewhat oxydised white wine.

made-up a [*Book collecting*] said of a book that has had missing pages or illustrations made good by insertions from another copy of the same edition.

Madison race n [*Cycling*] a track point-to-point cycle race competed for by teams of two riders, who ride singly and relieve each other in turn.

madman theory n [*Military*] according to his former aide H. R. Haldeman, this is a theory developed by President Nixon whereby an implied threat of nuclear immolation would bring the North Vietnamese to the conference table. To quote Haldeman's memoirs 'The Ends of Power' (1978), Nixon explained 'I want the North Vietnamese to believe I've reached the point where I might do *anything* to stop the war. We'll just slip the word to them that "for God's sake, you know Nixon is obsessed about Communism. We can't restrain him when he's angry – *and he has his hand on the nuclear button!*" – and Ho Cho Minh

M

himself will be in Paris in two days begging for peace.'

mag *v* [*UK*] [*Market-traders*] to talk.

magazine *n* [*TV*] in the Teletext information system this is a group of 100 visual 'pages', indexed together for coding purposes.

magged *a* [*Sailing, Ropework*] said of worn or fretted rope.

maggie miller *n* [*Navy*] the practice of washing clothes by trailing them on a line astern of the ship.

magi *n* [*Magic*] any kind of magician; fellow magicians use compeer which comes from Fr. compère, to distinguish the magical fraternity.

magic 1. *a* [*Computing*] as yet unexplained; too complicated to explain. 2. *a* [*Computing*] referring to a feature of the machine's operation which is not generally publicised, but which allows for operations that would otherwise be considered impossible.

magic acid *n* [*Science*] in chemistry this is fluoro-sulphonic acid (FSO_3H) into which antimony pentafluoride is dissolved, thus giving it exceptional qualities as a reagent.

magic ball *n* [*Cricket*] an unplayable ball which will invariably dismiss the batsman, despite any defensive measures.

magic bullet *n* [*Medicine*] a drug or other medicinal agent which can destroy disease-carrying bacteria, viruses, cancers, etc. without harming the host.

magic moment *n* [*TV, Film*] a time, just after sunset, when there is still enough light for shooting; it is especially useful for 'romantic' scenes.

magic number *n* [*Gambling*] any number that represents a combination of wins for a leader (as in a football league) and losses for the rivals which automatically guarantees the leader's ultimate victory.

magic numbers *n pl* [*Science*] those numbers that indicate particular stability in a proton or neutron count: 2, 8, 20, 28, 50, 82, 126 (and possibly 184).

magic paper *n* [*Computing*] an on-line system designed for the manipulation of symbolic mathematics.

magic shop *n* [*New therapies*] in psychodramatic therapy this is the concept of creating for a patient a 'magic shop' in which he/she can ask for anything they want, but which must be 'paid for' with something that they value. The therapist is the 'shopkeeper', and the intention is for the patient, through this interaction, to appreciate the conflicts within him/herself.

magic spot *n* [*Medicine*] guanosine tetraphosphate (ppGpp), the appearance of which in cells is supposed to inhibit the synthesis of ribosomal RNA; it is thus named from the unexpected spots that show up in cells so affected.

magnetic bottle *n* [*Science*] a magnetic field that confines a plasma in a thermo-nuclear reaction.

magnetic bubble memory *n* [*Computing*] a type of digital memory in which data is represented by magnetic bubbles, made inside an aluminium garnet substrate. The bubbles (or domains) are circulated within the substrate and directed to the output by magnetic fields. Bubble memory is the opposite of the currently standard magnetic disk or tape recording methods in which the medium moves, but the data bits remain stationary. The sytem has the advantage of being non-volatile and devoid of moving mechanical parts but compared with floppy disks it is expensive, and there are as yet no methods of removing one set of data – as in taking a floppy and putting it in a drawer or cabinet – and replacing it with another.

magnetic media *n* [*Computing*] the various types of media upon which data can be stored by writing a magnetic pattern onto the magnetic surface of the medium. Such media include floppy and hard disks and tape cassettes. Non-magnetic media are optical disks, punched cards and paper tape.

magnetic mirror 1. *n* [*Science*] a magnetised surface that reflects light. 2. *n* [*Science*] a magnetically charged field that causes advancing particles to be repelled.

magnificent seven *n pl* [*UK*] [*Railways*] dining car attendants.

magnolia *n* [*US*] [*Politics*] shorthand for a reference to anyone or anything from the American South.

mags *n pl* [*Custom cars*] abbr of **magnesium alloy** special lightweight road wheels.

mahogany bomber *n* [*Royal Air Force*] the desk which is all that an office-bound pilot can 'fly'.

mahogany, on the *adv* [*UK*] [*Railways*] See **ride on the cushions**.

mahogany tops *n pl* [*Hunting*] brown leather tops to black hunting boots, only ever worn with a red coat.

maid Marian principle *n* [*Navy*] refuelling ships at sea; the fuel line is 'fired' from one ship to another to initiate the process.

maiden 1. *n* [*Angling*] a fish that has never spawned. 2. *n* [*Bell-founding*] a bell that requires no tuning after it comes from the mould. 3. *n* [*Horticulture*] a strawberry plant bearing its first crop. 4. *n* [*Horse-racing*] a horse that has yet to win its first race; thus to 'break one's maiden' is to achieve a first victory; both terms also apply to jockeys. 5. *n* [*Cricket*] an over in which no runs are scored. 6. *a* [*Cricket*] a maiden test is the first test match for which a player is chosen. 7. *a* [*Cricket*] a maiden century is the first score of 100+ runs that a batsman achieves in his career.

maidens *n pl* [*Weaving*] the vertical members that hold the **flyer** assembly on a flyer wheel.

M

mail art *n* [*Art*] any art in which the use of the postal system plays a major part; by its nature, this art is often collaborative, as in a 'chain-letter' collage.

mail box *n* [*Computing*] a set of locations within the machine's **RAM** storage area which are reserved specifically for those instructions addressed either to a **peripheral** or to another microprocessor.

mail cover *n* [*Espionage*] the illegal opening of mail as practised by the CIA; when carried out by the FBI, the operation is called the 'mail run'.

mailing shot *n* [*Advertising*] the sending out of material to potential customers as part of a campaign.

main gate *n* [*UK*] [*Coal-mining*] the main tunnel underground. See also **mains, ripper 1**.

main plane *n* [*Aerospace*] the principal supporting surface of an aircraft.

main storage *n* [*Computing*] the part of a computer in which the data and programs for random access (**RAM**) by the **CPU** are held. Main storage has a fast access time, but its cost means that such bases are usually small – 64K bytes on an 8-bit machine.

mainframe *n* [*Computing*] the largest type of computer installations, with great capacity, and large and static equipment; they require installation in air-conditioned, ultra-clean rooms and a variety of other special criteria for their use. Originally it was used to describe the main framework of the central processing unit within a large computer but now, with the development of mini- and micro-computers, it means the whole large, central machine.

mains *n* [*S. Wales*] [*Coal-mining*] the main driveway from the pit bottom to the coalface.

mainstream **1.** *v* [*Pop music*] to adapt one's music to a generally more popular, if less demanding, style. See also **AOR, MOR**. **2.** *v* [*Social work*] a social worker does this when he/she gains government recognition and funds for, and commitment to, a pet project by taking it off the sidelines of concern and forcing the relevant authorities to take notice.

mainstream economics *n* [*Economics*] in Marxist terms this is the type of Western, capitalist economics that is based upon market forces and analysis at the expense of any social or political factors.

mainstreaming *n* [*Education*] the placing of the exceptional child – whether more or less intelligent than his/her peers – back in the normal classroom world of 'average' children.

maintainability *n* [*Computing*] the ease and effectiveness with which a system can be kept in good operating condition.

maintenance factor *n* [*Management*] See **hygiene factor**. See also **motivator**.

maintenance margin *n* [*Futures market*] a sum, usually smaller than the initial margin, but still a part of it, that must be held on deposit at all times against the possibility of a customer's **equity** dropping down to or below the level of this deposit, at which point it can be used to bolster the equity.

major 1. *n* [*Commerce*] any major company, usually implying on a general level all multinational conglomerates, and when referring to a specific industry, the various field leaders. **2.** *n* [*Video*] a home-video company that is a division, subsidiary, or part of a joint venture with the eight Hollywood **majors** that make up the Motion Picture (Export) Assoc. of America.

majors *n pl* [*Film*] the large film companies – MGM, Paramount, Columbia, etc – as opposed to the independents.

majuscule *n* [*Printing*] a capital letter. See also **minuscule**.

make 1. *v* [*Hunting*] to count the number of hounds in a pack. **2.** *n* [*Merchant navy*] tips received by stewards on passenger ships.

make a hose *v* [*US*] [*Railways*] to connect up the air hoses between cars.

make a number 1. *v* [*US*] [*Marine Corps*] to gain a promotion when a vacancy occurs. **2.** *v* [*US*] [*Military*] to pay one's respects to a senior officer or any influential superior.

make a trip *v* [*Oil rigs*] to replace a drill bit by taking out the entire drill pipe, exchanging the old and new bits, and returning it to the bore.

make an ascension *v* [*Theatre*] to forget one's lines, which 'fly up' out of one's head.

make and mend *n* [*Navy*] time off for mending clothes and pursuing hobbies on board ship; recently it has tended to be time off for sports.

make good *v* [*Gambling*] players do this when everyone in a round of betting places a stake in the pot equal to that bet by the first player in the round.

make one's numbers *v* [*Industry*] the task of junior executives in a large company; they have to achieve the goals and quotas established by the demands of profitability and set by senior managers.

make runs *v* [*US*] [*Navy*] to make derogatory criticisms.

make the wheel *v* [*Dog breeding*] when a Pyrenean Mountain Dog is excited, its tail, normally carried low, with the tip slightly to one side, is raised and curls high above the back in a circle – 'the wheel'.

make up *v* [*US*] [*Railways*] to switch cars in the **yard** until a freight train is assembled as required.

make-good *n* [*Advertising*] a free repeat of an advertisement which has in some way been subject to an error in printing, broadcasting, etc.

make-off 1. *n* [*UK*] [*Theatre*] one of the two **flats** furthest downstage on either the left or right of stage. **2.** *v* [*UK*] [*Theatre*] to tie up a rope.

make-over *n* [*Journalism*] fresh or revised news

M

material that replaces the copy of one edition when the next one is made up and printed.

make-ready n [Industry] the preparation stage of any process, eg: setting a die prior to cutting, preparing a press for printing, etc.

make-up n [Finance] the balancing of accounts carried at at a set date.

make-up editor, also **production editor** n [Journalism] the editor who supervises the setting up of the individual typeset pages of the newspaper.

making hole n [Oil rigs] the act of rotating the **drill string** to excavate the basic hole in a search for oil.

male v [Chess] this comes from Old Fr. meaning to overcome, to overpower, to conquer.

malhini n [Surfing] a novice or beginner; it comes from the Hawaian for stranger.

Mallaby-Deeley n [Navy] a suit worn by officers and men on shore leave; it comes from a variety of cheap, mass-produced suiting produced in 1920s by one Mallaby-Deeley, MP.

mallet v [UK] [Military] to shell.

mama-house n [US] [Garment trade] a shop that specialises in catering for the needs of 'the fuller figure', ie: fat customers.

man 1. n [Drugs] the dealer or connection. 2. n [Drugs] the police.

man made noise n [Communications] interference caused by human activity – using non-suppressed household appliances, turning on a car's ignition, etc.

man profile n [Marketing] the specification of those characteristics – training, experience, personality, etc. – required for the optimum performance of a given job; it is usually formulated to match a job specification.

man trap n [UK] [Railways] See **jack trap**.

managed bond n [Economics] a special bond fund into which an investor buys and whose managers then invest on the basis of their own expertise in whatever areas will produce the optimum returns.

managed currency n [Finance] a currency system that is managed by the government of the country that uses it.

managed news n [Politics] the information supplied by government sources and press officers which sets government interests over public ones, particularly when it comes to hiding 'sensitive' and controversial facts. See also **word-engineering**.

managed text n [Publishing] a book, usually on an academic subject, for which the 'author' – usually a well-known expert in the field – acts merely as an overseer and the actual content is prepared and written either by free-lancers, researchers and/or graduate students.

management buy-out n [Industry] a situation whereby the management of a liquidated

company use their own cash to buy up the firm and start it working again.

management by exception. n [Business] a term coined by US engineer F. W. Taylor (1856–1915): the reduction of extraneous material in management decision-taking by the elimination from reports of all information other than that which details a significant deviation from a plan, budget or similar established procedure.

management by objectives n [Management] a management procedure created by US consultant Peter Drucker (1909–). It is characterised by the collaboration between each manager and his superior in analysing the manager's tasks and establishing quantified objectives for a manager to achieve within set periods of time. Emphasis is placed on integrating the objectives of individual managers with those of the whole organisation; procedures are established to monitor and assess progress towards the achievement of the objectives.

manchesterise v [Industrial relations] in the cotton industry this refers to the unrestricted importation of low-cost textiles from abroad, which tends to undermine the home industry. It was originally used by Manchester's 19th century European rivals, but latterly has been used in a declining Manchester cotton industry itself, referring to the Far East.

mandamus n [Law] a court order that demands the performance of a given public act or duty by a public official.

mandarin n [Government] a senior British civil servant, supposedly a possessor of the intellect, deviousness and subtle powers of his Chinese predecessor. See also **brahmin**.

mandated programme n [TV] a programme that the IBA (the British independent television authority) compels all its affiliated stations to broadcast.

manfredi n [Film] a film stunt in which cars are spun at high speeds to simulate crashes.

mangle n [UK] [Printing] the mat roller of a cylinder press.

mangling n [Metallurgy] a method of flattening steel plates, when hot or cold, by passing them through a multi-roll straightening machine.

maniac n [US] [Road transport] a workshop mechanic.

manifest function n [Sociology] the intended and recognized consequences of social action upon other social actors or institutions.

manifold, also **bible** n [Meat trade] a hard, round portion of the cow's stomach which is generally consigned to the pet food industry.

manipulated democracy n [Politics] in Marxist terms, this is the concept that the alleged 'choices' between left and right in a capitalist state offer in fact no choice at all, and that all such elections are merely cypher votes for hand-picked and non-representative candidates.

M

manipulative *a* [*Sociology*] a popular feminist buzzword used to condemn whatever particular male excess is deemed worthy of attack within the relevant context.

manly, also **muscular** *a* [*Wine-tasting*] used to describe a positive, even assertive and aggressive, **big** wine.

mannigant *n* [*UK*] [*Market-traders*] a conceited person, a braggart.

manor, also **patch** *n* [*UK*] [*Police*] any police district or unit or police administration.

man-rate *v* [*Aerospace*] to certify a rocket or other space vehicle as safe for manned flight and operation.

manway *n* [*Oil rigs*] a port in the wall or cover of a tank or reactor, for inspection purposes or for charging the container with additives or raw materials.

many *a* [*Military*] eight or more, referring to troops, planes, ranks, etc.

map 1. *v* [*Computing*] to transfer information from one form to another. 2. *n* [*Computing*] See **memory map**. 3. *n* [*US*] [*Painting*] a large brush, used for quick covering of substantial areas. See also **Broom**.

MAP 1. *n* [*Military*] acro **Multiple Aim Point** system – one of the systems proposed for the protection of the **MX** missile. It is a concept whereby the vulnerability of a static silo-based missile can be reduced by shuttling it around between a variety of identical under-ground silos; such shuttling would theoretically confuse hostile targeting. 2. *n* [*Air travel*] acro **Modified American Plan** a variety of ticket pricing used for passengers making internal flights on American airlines.

map of Ireland *n* [*Hotels*] the chambermaid's description of semen stains left on bedsheets.

marage *n* [*Aerospace*] abbr of **martensite ageing** the use in construction work of a superhard steel, high in nickel but very low in carbon content; it can be rolled to a very thin gauge and will withstand extremes of heat distortion.

Marathon *n* [*Sex*] a prostitute's assignation which lasts a whole evening – wining, dining and visiting night-clubs and casinos – before she actually goes to bed with the client.

marathon *n* [*New therapies*] an extra-lengthy session of group therapy.

marbling *n* [*Meat trade*] the thin layer of fat which streaks the best varieties of lean meat and which, when the meat is being cooked, will help to keep it moist.

marche *n* [*Weaving*] the UK and Scandinavian equivalent of **lam**.

marching display *n* [*Photo-typesetting*] a display device which shows the last 30–40 characters keyed. See also **thin window display**.

Mareva injunction *n* [*Law*] an interlocutory injunction barring a party to proceedings from removing his/her property from England or Wales because the final judgement in the proceedings might well involve costs or payments for damages which would have to be met by the sale of that property; this comes from a case in which such an injunction was granted to the owners of a vessel, the Mareva.

margin 1. *n* [*Futures market*] an amount of funds, in cash, which must be deposited with a broker or a leading member of the Exchange, as a guarantee of the fulfilment of a futures contract. 2. *n* [*Stock market*] an amount payable on a speculative order by a client, the balance of which is financed by the broker. If the price of a share bought 'on the margin' falls so far as to require the use of that margin payment, the broker may close the transaction, rather than put his own capital at risk.

margin call *n* [*Stock market, Futures market*] a demand for extra funds to guarantee the **margin** or the overall investment, after a fall in share prices or problems in delivery of a futures contract.

margin men *n pl* [*Drugs*] drug runners or smugglers who act as middlemen between the wholesalers and the bulk importers; margin men often manage to resist the lure of their wares and work simply for the profit.

margin of safety *n* [*Military, Politics*] a euphemism for military superiority, coined in 1983 by US bureaucrat Richard V. Allen as the 'margin of safety, that vital margin that has kept us free over the past 35 years'. The term was used by Ronald Reagan in an attempt to deflect criticisms of the more bellicose 'superiority'.

marginal 1. *a* [*Computing*] with an extremely low probability of succeeding. 2. *a* [*Computing*] of minimal worth or merit. 3. *a* [*Computing*] extremely small. 4. *a* [*Politics*] a Parliamentary constituency in which the vote may go unpredictably to any of the main contenders in an election.

marginal land *n* [*Economics*] land that is barely worth cultivating at current prices, but which will be used when prices improve or discarded if they fall heavily.

marginal weather *n* [*Aerospace*] weather conditions that are barely acceptable for either safe or legal flying.

marginalism *n* [*Economics*] an economic system which lays stress on any marginal factors in the economy.

mark 1. *n* [*Computing*] a punched hole in the paper tape used by older and larger computers. 2. *n* [*Film, TV*] the position on the studio floor, marked with tape or chalk, on which actors should stand at the start of a sequence or on which they should come to a halt after an entrance, a movement, etc. 3. *n* [*Espionage*] any accidental victim of either blackmail or a similar confidence trick who can be conveniently manipulated as a result of this weakness, although he/she was not the original target and there had been no intentional plan to trap him/her. 4. *n* [*Military*] general mili-

M

tary code for: the weapon is to be fired. **5.** *n* [*Crime*] the intended victim of a confidence trick, pick-pocket gang, etc. **6.** *n* [*Stock market*] the price at which a bargain has been executed and which is thus recorded in the Official List. **7.** *v* [*Hunting*] hounds 'mark' when they bay at the mouth of an earth or a drain after a fox has entered it.

mark boat, also **living buoys** *n* [*Navy*] small boats or submarines used to mark a given course.

mark it! *excl* [*TV, Film*] an instruction to the **clapper-loader** to operate his clapper-board prior to the start of a new **take**.

mark mark *n* [*Military*] a command from a ground controller ordering an airborne pilot to release his bombs.

mark of the beast *n* [*Navy*] the colourful flashes worn on the lapels of a midshipman's jacket.

mark off, also **lay off** *v* [*US*] [*Railways*] to take time off.

mark to market 1. *n* [*UK*] [*Stock market*] the process whereby all the profits and losses of a day's trading are paid in and out of the **Clearing House**. **2.** *n* [*US*] [*Stock market*] the assessment of the value of a securities portfolio to ensure that it is being maintained according to market regulations.

marked out *a* [*US*] [*Coal-mining*] said of an area which has been designated as unsafe or as the starting point for a new heading.

marker *n* [*Clothing*] a master plan, for the cutting out of the various parts of a garment, that aims to use the material available in the most economic way. The marker is laid on top of the material before cutting starts.

marker out *v* [*US*] [*Skiing*] when the boot escapes the release binding during a run; this comes from the name of one Marker, a German manufacturer of bindings.

market *n* [*Stock market*] the actual dealing floor of the London Stock Exchange.

market aggregation *n* [*Marketing*] a concept which assumes that all consumers in the market have similar requirements and as such can be reached and persuaded in the same way.

market communism, also **80% communism** *n* [*Politics*] a rare concept that postulates a Communism which places 20% of its economy within free markets, primarily those dealing in luxury consumer items.

market letter *n* [*US*] [*Journalism*] a directive from the proprietor or editor indicating that a specific story is to be covered and that it is to be written in a certain way (possibly to praise or condemn according to the proprietor's special interest or bugbear).

market maker *n* [*Stock market*] a stock exchange firm which commits itself to being ready at any time to deal in the range of stocks in which it is registered. It is the post-**Big Bang** name for **jobbers**.

market order *n* [*Futures market*] an order to a broker telling him to buy or sell at the best possible price.

market overt *n* [*Commerce*] any public market where goods are openly on offer; stolen goods that reach such markets become the property of the buyer, no matter what their origin, but only if the sale has taken place between sunrise and sunset, and if the original thief is not brought to trial; if he is, the title in the property reverts to the original owner.

market penetration *n* [*Marketing*] a strategy for obtaining extra sales with the same product and the same target market by concentrating on gaining a greater share of that market.

market potential *n* [*Marketing*] the maximum amount of a product that can be bought from suppliers within a certain period, given an intense promotional effort throughout the market.

market research *n* [*Marketing*] the study of a market for a product.

market segmentation *n* [*Marketing*] the subdivision of a market into relatively homogeneous parts, so that plans can be developed to cover each of the segments so created; it is a popular way of defining the various target markets.

market Socialism *n* [*Politics*] a term coined in the 1930s by Otto Lange; it refers to a strong market economy with only a minimum of discreet planning and state interference, but with a predominantly social ownership of the means of production.

market weight *n* [*Marketing*] the weighting of advertising expenditure according to the pattern of consumption by different target groups.

marketing concept *n* [*Marketing*] the concept that an organisation must attempt to understand and anticipate consumer needs as a basis for all decisions affecting its own market.

marketing mix *n* [*Marketing*] the composite of plans created by an organisation to cover promotion, pricing, research, distribution and so on, and then the finding of the correct balance between the various areas so developed.

marketing research *n* [*Marketing*] the study of the marketing of a product.

markup *n* [*US*] [*Government*] the process of putting a legislative bill into its final form.

mark-up *n* [*Commerce*] the amount a retailer adds to the wholesale price of goods to pay for his overheads and to make a profit.

mark-up, at the *adv* [*UK*] [*Crime, Police*] said of a villain (or corrupt policeman) who takes more than his fair share of a bribe, blackmail payment or proceeds of a robbery.

marra *n* [*UK*] [*Coal-mining*] workmate; it comes originally from Geordie dialect, but has drifted through the industry as the Northern miners have done.

marriage 1. *n* [*Antiques*] an item sold as perfect, but which is in fact composed of various parts which do not really belong together; thus, a fake.

M

2. n [*Antiques, Horology*] the practice of putting a clock in a case not originally built for it; a fraudulent attempt to trap the unwary.

married failure n [*Military*] a mine that has failed to detach itself from the seabed, despite being electronically triggered.

married print n [*TV, Film*] a film in which the sound and pictures have been correctly synchronised.

marrow spoon n [*Angling*] a spoon that is put down a fish's throat to see what it has been eating.

marry v [*Stock market*] to set one transaction against another, such as a buying order against a selling one.

marry Mistress Roper v [*Royal Marines*] to enlist in the Royal Marines; it comes from the Royal Navy nickname for the Marines, whose naval, as opposed to military, skills were considered to be no more than those of a woman, particularly the cack-handed, mythical 'Mistress Roper'.

marry up v [*Commerce*] said of an auctioneer who puts two lots together, since one lot is obviously less likely to sell if offered alone, due to damage, worthlessness or some allied defect.

marsupial n [*Logology*] a word that carries within its letters, without any transposition of those letters, a synonym for itself: 'encourage' holds 'urge', 'evacuate' has 'vacate', etc.

martians n pl [*Fleet air arm*] the emergency fire rescue crew on an aircraft carrier; the name comes from the heat-resistant 'space suit' they wear.

Martini norm n [*Business*] the concept that one supplier in an industry is, as far as consumers are concerned, much the same as another. This assumption, disastrous for those attempting to market their own variety of a given product, is ostensibly overcome by the provision of drunken lunches and similar inducements to salesmen and retailers.

MARV n [*Military*] acro **Manoeuvrable Re-entry Vehicle** any missile of which the warhead can be steered electronically, usually by internal inertial navigation guidance systems. MARVed weapons can rely on mid-course and terminal guidance options that include television, imaging infra-red laser and distance-measuring equipment (DME). Such weapons are also able to take evasive action if targeted by another missile. MARVing has added appreciably to the accuracy of **MIRV**ed missiles which would otherwise be susceptible to atmospheric conditions.

marver n [*Glass-making*] a flat slab – of wood, stone or metal – on which a gather of glass is rolled, shaped, and cooled.

marverer n [*Glass-making*] a worker who uses the **marver** to shape and position a gather of hot glass on the blowing iron before blowing it.

marxising n [*Politics*] the permeating of one's speech and writings with a variety of Marxian thoughts and jargon in order to establish one's credentials as a serious member of the ideological left.

Mary Ann 1. n [*US*] [*Navy*] a floating salvage crane used to pick up aircraft that have fallen off or overshot carriers. **2.** n [*Taxis*] a taximeter.

Mary Sue stories n pl [*TV*] amateur storylines written by fans of TV's 'Star Trek'; such stories invariably centre on the author's self-projection as 'Mary Sue', a hitherto unknown who emerges to save the regular heroes, seduces her favourite star, and generally takes over.

maryanning n [*UK*] [*Railways*] cleaning, sweeping and polishing duties.

marzipan n [*Motor trade*] in the second-hand car trade this is the filler used to make good the body-work of a crashed or ageing car.

marzipan generation n [*Business*] the younger members of a stockbroking company – the 'layer' immediately junior to the firm's partners: above the 'cake' but below the 'icing'.

MAS n [*Military*] acro **Mutually Assured Survival** a term coined by Max M. Kampelman, a leading negotiator in the 1985 arms control talks in Geneva; it is the favoured gospel of the originators of the **High Frontier** study, the foremost supporters of 'star wars' development. While deterrence by **MAD** is 'a time worn and morally bankrupt doctrine' (Gen. Daniel O. Graham, 1985), the **SDI** with its space-based super-defences would ensure that under the stern but necessary umbrella of US omnipotence, neither side would need to launch an attack and thus both would be assured survival – an extreme example of the Orwellian 'war is peace' philosophy.

mashie n [*Golf*] the traditional name for the Number 5 iron.

mashie-niblick n [*Golf*] the traditional name for the Number 6 or Number 7 iron.

mask 1. n [*Advertising*] the blocking out of unwanted areas of a picture needed for an advertisement by covering them with card or paper. **2.** n [*Electronics*] in microcircuits this is a thin surface layer that is removed in parts so as to permit modification of the underlying material. **3.** n [*Film*] a technical device used to block out part of the filmed image.

masking n [*Audio*] a hearing effect whereby a normally audible sound is pushed beneath the threshold of hearing by another sound.

masquerading n [*Data security*] unauthorised access to a system by using the password of a legitimate user; it is in the province of **hackers**.

mass society n [*Sociology*] the concept that most contemporary individuals are similar, undifferentiated, and equal, showing no individuality; work is routine and alienating; religion has lost its influence, there are no deeply held and important moral standards, although the masses are prone to ideological fanaticism; relationships between individuals are weak and secondary and ties of kinship are not important; the masses are politi-

M

cally apathetic and open to manipulation and mass culture abandons all but the lowest standards of taste.

massaging *n* [*Printing*] the manipulation of input copy on a VDU in order to create the desired visual layout.

massive retaliation *n* [*Military*] the US nuclear policy as put forward during the Eisenhower administration: the concept that since the US possessed over-whelming superiority in the arms race, the Soviets should appreciate that whatever military schemes they envisaged, great or small, localised or inter-continental, the US strategic bomber fleet would obliterate their country with nuclear weapons. This policy faltered after 1957 when the Soviets produced the SS–6 rocket, capable of reaching the continental US.

MAST *n* [*Military*] acro **Military Anti-Shock Trousers** special pressurised trousers worn by astronauts.

master 1. *n* [*Chess*] a player whose abilities fall marginally short of excellence. See also **grandmaster**. **2.** *n* [*Pop music*] the tape of a record after the mixing (see **mix**) process has been completed. **3.** *n* [*Pop business*] a vinyl record which is used as the basis for the mass production of a particular record. **4.** *v* [*Pop business*] to complete the final stages of making a record, ie. using (**2**) to create (**3**).

master hair, also **guard hair** *n* [*Dog breeding*] the longer, stiffer hairs that make up the dog's outer 'jacket' and which protect the softer, dense undercoat.

master shot 1. *n* [*Film*] a shot in which the camera is so placed as to encompass all the action that takes place. **2.** *n* [*Film*] a single shot of an entire piece of dramatic action into which detail – closeups, reaction shots, effects, etc. – can be inserted at the editing stage.

masterbatch *n* [*Tyre-making*] the mix of all rubbers and pigments except for the curing agents.

master-slave system *n* [*Computing*] a system which incorporates more than one processor, with the proviso that one processor is nominated the 'master' and the others the 'slaves'. The master is capable of actions that the slaves cannot perform, usually regarding resource scheduling and the initiation of peripheral transfers.

masthead 1. *n* [*Advertising*] the specific style of the name or title of a newspaper or magazine. **2.** *n* [*Journalism*] the title of a newspaper or magazine, plus a list of its major personnel, printed in a box and placed in a conspicuous position somewhere in the newspaper or magazine. **3.** *n* [*TV*] by extension from the journalistic use (see **2**) this is the symbol, of a station or production company, that precedes or follows a programme.

mat 1. *n* [*US*] [*Building, Concrete workers*] a grill of reinforcing rods used to strengthen concrete. **2.** *n* [*Printing*] abbr of **matrix** the sterotypers' **flong**

after a mould has been made. **3.** *n* [*Printing*] abbr of **matrix** the individual brass letter moulds on a linotype composing machine.

match boxes *n* [*Navy*] an order to midshipmen to maintain absolute silence.

match dissolve *n* [*Film*] a (clichéd) dissolve from one scene to another whereby an object in the first scene – eg. a church clock – turns into a similar object – eg. a watch face – in another.

matched orders 1. *n pl* [*Stock market*] the illegal manipulation of a price by the simultaneous orders given by one person to different brokers to sell and buy the same stock. **2.** *n pl* [*Stock market*] a legitimate matching of buy and sell orders by a specialist in a stock who aims to arrange an opening price that matches as nearly as possible the previous closing price.

matcher *n* [*Wood working*] a machine that planes and shapes boards to form tongue-and-groove joints.

Matelots *n pl* [*UK*] [*Police*] the Metropolitan Police nickname for the London River Police. See also **Land Crabs**.

material fallacy *n* [*Philosophy*] reasoning that is unsound because of an error concerning the subject matter of the argument.

materialism *n* [*Politics*] the philosophy that the universe consists only of matter and that any concepts that are based on giving that universe or the minds of the humans that inhabit it a spiritual basis is irrelevant. See also **dialectical materialism, historical materialism**.

materiel *n* [*Military*] this comes from Fr. meaning 'material'; it refers to all the non-human resources of an army – guns, ammunitions, planes, missiles, electronic surveillance equipment, etc.

mateys *n pl* [*Navy*] dockyard workers.

matrilocality *n* [*Sociology*] a principle of residence whereby the couple live near the wife's mother.

matrix *n* [*Government*] originally this was a place of origin or growth, or the mould from which copies could be taken, but now matrix (like **parameter**) has taken on many and flexible meanings for bureaucrats. Used in government, it can mean 1. context, 2. one variety of many, 3. the totality of an event or concept.

matt 1. *n* [*Weaving*] See **batt**. **2.** also **matte** *n* [*Film*] a device that blends actors who have been filmed in a studio with backgrounds either shot on location or created by special effects; the actor is shot against a non-reflective background, eg: black velvet, and a high contrast negative is then combined with the desired background; thus 'ghosts' or 'monsters' can appear in the same scene as humans, all equally 'alive'.

matt down *v* [*Music*] to perfect one's playing or singing; it comes from the image of a painter putting a smooth finish on his work.

matter *n* [*Printing*] any manuscript or **copy** that has to be printed, or type that has been composed

M

or set. Thus 'live matter' is work that is awaiting printing; 'dead matter' is work that has been printed.

matter art *n* [*Art*] a genre of the 1950s in which the artist used such 'unworthy' materials as sand, cinders, sacking, etc. in place of or in addition to traditional oil paint; the intention was to add an extra 'reality' to the work.

matting *n* [*Furriers*] See **bunching 2**.

mature *a* [*TV*] a euphemism for the inclusion of sex or violence in a TV programme.

mature economy *n* [*Economics*] a declining economy in a country which was previously strong, eg. many of those in Western Europe.

maturing *n* [*Building, Concrete workers*] the correct and required hardening of concrete.

maturity 1. *n* [*Banking, Finance*] the date upon which a given financial instrument becomes due for payment. **2.** *n* [*Finance*] the time when a debt becomes repayable. **3.** *n* [*Finance*] the period for which money is loaned.

maturity ladder *n* [*Banking*] a system for categorizing the deposits in a bank and simultaneously evaluating its ability to turn assets into ready cash: the creation of such a system makes it possible to assess a bank's overall liquidity.

maturity transformation *n* [*Banking*] the use of short-term deposits to finance long-term loans.

maul *n* [*Art*] a stick used as a steady rest for the hand during delicate painting or lettering operations.

mauve economy *n* [*Economics*] jobs which can be run from home – consultancies, singing telegram service, etc. – and which can be carried on outside the tax economy. See also **black economy**.

mawkish *a* [*Wine-tasting*] somewhat **flat**, drab-flavoured, sickly.

max out *v* [*US*] [*Prisons*] to complete a maximum sentence, without previously earning parole.

maximax *n* [*Business*] a strategy that concentrates on making decisions that will maximise potential profits, however much such decisions may also intensify potential risks. See also **maximin, minimax**.

maximin 1. *n* [*Business*] a strategy that concentrates on making decisions that will maximise the chance of incurring the minimum potential loss, however much this may simultaneously minimise potential profits. See also **maximax, minimax**. **2.** *n* [*Sociology*] a principle of social justice which states that the optimum distribution of goods among a class of recipients is one in which the worst off receives the best possible amount given his position in the hierarchy.

maximum cross artic *n* [*UK*] [*Road transport*] an articulated vehicle which is operating at the maximum permitted weight for that vehicle in the UK; this includes the weight of the vehicle, its accessories, equipment and the load.

maximum price fluctuation *n* [*Futures market*] the maximum amount within which the contract price can fluctuate up or down within one trading session.

maximum security dormitory *n* [*US*] [*Prisons*] a cellblock.

maximum working area *n* [*Industry*] the space within which a seated or standing worker can reach and use tools, materials and equipment by moving his/her arms but not the rest of the body. See also **normal working area**.

maxi-series *n* [*TV*] a multi-part adaptation for the TV audience of a block-busting, best-seller novel; it uses a more traditional format than the two-or three-episode mini-series of recent years. See also **mini-series**.

mayday! *excl* [*Military, Radio*] this comes from Fr. 'm'aidez!' meaning 'help me!'; it is an international radio callsign requesting emergency assistance and is usually broadcast over 121.5 mHz.

maze *n* [*UK*] [*Railways*] Clapham Junction, the most intensive railway junction in the world.

mazut *n* [*Oil industry*] a viscous liquid residue left after the distillation of Russian petrol, that is used as fuel-oil or low-grade lubricant.

MBFR *n* [*Politics*] abbr of **Mutual and Balanced Force Reduction talks** begun in Vienna in 1973, these talks aimed to set up controls for non-nuclear forces based in Europe. Direct participants are Benelux, W. Germany, the UK and the US; Czechoslovakia, E. Germany, Poland and the USSR. While both sides of negotiators have put forward a massive variety of possible re-structuring of the balance of forces, none have yet appeared realistic to both parties. The talks were suspended shortly after the Russian walk-out from the nuclear **START** and **INF** talks, in January 1984.

MBO *n* [*Industrial relations*] acro **Management By Objective** a management style in which the manager and his assistants decide on the firm's objectives and the workforce agrees to work towards them. This style of consultative management is intended to alleviate stress in industrial relations as well as boost wages and productivity, since the workers should now feel that they have a personal interest in the firm's prosperity.

MD *n* [*US*] [*Lunch counter*] a Doctor Pepper soft drink.

MDLs *n pl* [*Banking*] **Manager's Discretionary Limits** the limits to which a bank's branch manager may lend money without reference to higher authority.

mean busy hour *n* [*US*] [*Telephony*] an uninterrupted period of one hour starting at the same time on each of a number of weekdays during which telephone traffic is at its peak.

mean line *n* [*Printing*] the height to which all X-height characters seem to rise.

meaningful *a* [*Sociology*] usually used as a prefix to 'relationship' or 'experience', and implying

M

something out of the ordinary and exceptional, with a deeper spiritual appreciation of the experience/relationship than might otherwise be expected. See also **caring, loving**.

meaningful action n [Sociology] an action invested with meaning, deriving from a definite motive and intention, rather than simple habit of instinct.

means/ends analysis n [Computing] a technique used in artificial intelligence (**AI**) for forming plans to achieve goals. If a plan consists of a sequence of actions, then it can be formulated by comparing the means (the goals that each action achieves) with the ends (the goals that must be achieved).

measles n [Espionage] used by the CIA to refer to a death that appears to have been caused by natural causes, although it has not been.

measure of central tendency n [Marketing] in statistical method this is the description of various forms of average, based on the tendency of quantitative data to cluster around some middle value or values in sets of variable values.

measurement goods n pl [Shipping] goods that are light but bulky and are thus charged by their volume rather than their weight, calculated at 40 cu.ft. to the ton.

meat cutter n [US] [Medicine] See **butcher** 3. See also **cutting doctor**.

meat hand n [Baseball] the hand which is not covered by a glove.

meat rack n [Sex] a gathering place, found in most cities, for young homosexual prostitutes.

meat shot n [Sex] in pornographic films or pictures this is a close-up of the erect penis, the 'open' vagina, or actual penetration during intercourse. See also **flap shot**.

meat wagon 1. n [US] [Medicine] an ambulance. 2. n [UK] [Prisons] a specially equipped van which contains separate compartments in which prisoners can be transported to and from the courts or between various prisons. 3. also **Black Maria** n [UK] [Police] any police van – originally all-black but now often white with police markings – used for transporting officers, taking away those arrested, ferrying prisoners to court or jail, etc.

meatball [US] [Navy] the arrangement of coloured lights on the deck of a carrier by which a pilot can correct the speed and direction of his approach at night and land accordingly. In the daytime the lights are replaced by a mirror into which a light is shone at 3°, and similar course corrections can be made against this reflected light.

meateater n [US] [Police] a corrupt policeman who is not satisfied with the bribes he is offered, and actually solicits larger payments from those concerned. See also **grasseater**.

meaty 1. a [Wine-tasting] said of a rich, almost 'chewable' wine. 2. also **fat** a [Theatre] a good,

showy role, with plenty of lines, emotion and **business**.

mec n [Military] used in the French Foreign Legion to mean a well-dressed legionaire; it probably comes from Fr. 'maquereau' meaning pimp.

mec art n [Art] abbr of **mechanical art** 'paintings' that have been produced entirely by the creative manipulation of photo-mechanical reproduction processes, epitomised in the work of Robert Rauschenburg and Andy Warhol.

mechanic 1. n [US] [Bars] an extremely efficient bar-tender. 2. n [Gambling] a skilful cardsharp or dice manipulator who uses sleight of hand to gain his successes.

mechanical 1. n [UK] [Buses] a London Transport bus which has developed some form of mechanical fault that involves it being withdrawn from service. 2. n [Printing, Advertising] the art work and the copy that accompanies it assembled and ready for printing.

mechanical boy n [Glass-making] a mechanical device, operated by the blower's feet, which wets, raises, opens and closes the mould while mouth-blowing is in process.

mechanical games n pl [Gambling] any games of chance that lack the element of skill, eg: craps and roulette rather than poker.

mechanical key n [Building, Plastering] openings or grooves in the surface of an undercoat or background, into or through which plastering material may pass and to which, when set, it will be bonded mechanically.

mechanic's grip n [Gambling] a method of holding a deck of cards which facilitates dealing from the bottom of the pack and similar tricks: three fingers are curled around the long edge of the deck, while the index finger is held at the narrow upper edge, away from the body.

Med n [Bird-watching] a Mediterranean bird.

media behaviour n [Sociology] an assessment of an individual's attention to the various forms of printed and broadcast media as sources of news and information.

media buzz n [Pop music] the growing interest in a new record or performer(s) that develops in the press, TV, radio and specialist publications, all of which aid direct promotion and sales.

media event n [Public relations, Politics] any event of supposed importance that is staged less for any real effect than for its potential impact on the TV, radio, and print journalists who have been carefully mustered to record it.

media fragmentation n [Marketing] the concept that there are too many outlets for the concentration of a successful campaign; the customers are assailed by too many appeals to their pockets for any one to be guaranteed the desired impact.

media vehicle n [Marketing] any specific medium of communication in TV, radio, or print.

media weight 1. n [Marketing] the measure of

M

various qualitative factors to be taken into account when planning where to place one's advertising. **2.** *n* [*Marketing*] the quantity of advertising used in a promotion.

media-weight *n* [*Advertising*] the weighting of advertising expenditure based on criteria which depend on the relative values – usually qualitative – of the media outlets under consideration; such weighting should reflect the effectiveness of a given campaign in a given medium.

Medicaid mill *n* [*US*] [*Medicine*] a private clinic where the doctors indulge in malpractice by charging the Medicaid health insurance scheme for services that are either unnecessary or were never even performed for a patient.

medicalisation *n* [*Sociology*] the increasing practice of attaching medical labels to behaviour considered as socially or morally undesirable; this gives rise to the concept that once a phenomenon is identified as a 'disease' it can automatically be 'cured'.

medium *a* [*Wine-tasting*] used to describe wines that are between **light** and **heavy**; between 12–13° GL.

medium dated *a* [*Stock market*] referring to **gilt-edged** stock that has more than five but less than ten years to run before its final redemption date.

mediums *n pl* [*Stock market*] See **medium dated**.

MEECN *n* [*Military*] abbr of **Minimum Essential Emergency Communications Network** the US last-ditch radio network carried on aircraft and satellites and intended to guarantee that US forces could carry on a nuclear war even if major command and control installations were destroyed. All use VLF transmitters and would be activated to substitute for more sophisticated systems.

meet *n* [*UK*] [*Police*] an appointment, 'one to meet', usually with the implication that a policeman is meeting a contact, an informer, or a villain.

meet'em and street'em *v* [*US*] [*Medicine*] the process of evaluating admissions to a hospital Emergency Room, whereby those considered insufficiently hurt to qualify as genuine emergencies are sent smartly back on to the street.

meet me conference *n* [*Communications*] in teleconferencing this is a switchboard facility that makes it possible for a conference call to be established at some future time by each participating extension user using a designated conference code.

meg 1. *v* [*Film*] abbr of **megaphone** thus it means to direct a film; it comes from the megaphone used by directors in the silent film era; thus 'megger' is a director. **2.** *n* [*Finance*] $1,000,000. **3.** also **meggie** *n* [*UK*] [*Market-traders*] a halfpenny. See also **megs**.

megadeath *n* [*Military*] one million deaths; it is the basic figure for calculations of casualties in a nuclear exchange.

megaflops *n* [*Computing*] acro a measure of **one million floating point operations per second** multiples of one megaflops are used to measure the power of a very powerful computers. See also **flops**.

megaphone *n* [*Cars*] an exhaust pipe with the open end flared in the shape of a cone; it is used in racing to improve power output.

megastructures *n pl* [*Architecture*] the concept of erecting vast, new structures which would replace existing cities, submerge individual styles in a 'total environment', and facilitate the parallel demand for 'total mobility'.

MEGO *n* [*Journalism*] acro **My Eyes Glaze Over** any topic that combines maximum importance with massive tedium if one is forced to report on or write about it.

megs *n pl* [*UK*] [*Market-traders*] spectacles (possibly from the shape of each lens). See also **meg**.

meller *n* [*Film*] abbr of **melodrama** it is usually used of a general-interest, action and adventure film.

melon-cutting 1. *n* [*Horse-racing*] the sharing out, often by a syndicate of bettors, of heavy winnings. **2.** *n* [*Stock market*] the dividing up and sharing out of large and generous profits.

melt *n* [*Metallurgy*] in iron-founding, this is the product of a single furnace charge tapped into a ladle.

meltdown *n* [*Technology*] the collapse of the core of the reactor at a nuclear power station, possibly through the malfunction of its cooling system, when it has become heated above its melting point. Such a meltdown may cause a major disaster if it develops a critical mass of fissile fuel which can sustain a chain reaction and thus cause a nuclear explosion.

memorial counsellor *n* [*US*] [*Undertakers*] a grave salesman.

memorial release *n* [*Pop music, Film*] the speedy re-release of the most popular records or films of a recently dead star in order to cash in on the surge of popular nostalgia.

memory *n* [*Computing*] that part of a computer in which data and programs can be stored and from which they can be retrieved when required.

memory bank *n* [*Computing*] the memory unit of a computer, plus the data it contains.

memory map *n* [*Computing*] a drawing or table showing how the main memory has been allocated to output devices and programs.

mend a line *v* [*Angling*] to raise the top of the rod and to reverse the belly of the line in order to prevent drag on the fly.

mended kelt *n* [*Angling*] a **kelt** that is getting into better condition in the river.

mental handicap *n* [*Social work*] a euphemism for 'sub-average intellectual functioning and impaired adaptive behaviour'.

mental worker *n* [*Magic*] a magician who

M

specialises in mind reading. See also **close-up worker**.

menu 1. n [Computing] a list of instructions and service options which appears at the start of a program, and which shows the user the particular tasks that this program can be expected to accomplish. **2.** n [TV] the preliminary 'trailer' which lists the items that will be featured in a news review programme.

merge and purge v [Advertising] See **purge and merge**.

merry-go-round n [Rodeo] trick roping in which one spins the noose around one's own body, using first one hand and then the other.

mesh n [Computing] a configuration in a network where there are two or more paths running between any two nodes.

mess traps n pl [Navy] food containers in a warship.

message unit n [Advertising] the preferred designation of advertising slots on radio or TV.

messaging n [Computing] the using of office **networks** for external and internal communications between two users.

messenger 1. n [Sailing, Ropework] a rope belt passing around two capstans, by means of which a cable is hauled in. **2.** also **worker** n [Religion] a minister; thus head messenger is the chief minister in a state, province or country.

messer n [UK] [Market-traders] anyone who puts the stall-holder to a great deal of trouble, but buys nothing.

meta-art 1. n [Art] any artwork that takes as its basis another work. **2.** n [Art] any artwork that takes as its subject the whole concept of 'Art'. **3.** n [Art] anything that has no aesthetic significance in itself but which takes on such significance when placed in certain contexts; eg: Carl André's piles of bricks which were placed in the Tate Gallery and labelled 'sculpture'.

metal Mike n [Sailing] the automatic helmsman. See also **George**.

metalanguage 1. n [Computing] a language used to describe a programming language. **2.** n [Linguistics] a language used to describe another language (the object language), eg: the text of a book on semantics or linguistics.

metalinguistics n [Linguistics] a branch of linguistics that deal with the relation of language to other areas of culturally determined behaviour.

metallege n [Logology] a pair of words differing only in the transposition of two letters.

metallic a [Wine-tasting] used to describe a tinny, unpleasant quality, due to some metallic contamination during making, storage in cask, or bottling.

metamarketing 1. n [Marketing] a method of studying marketing and its relationship to every aspect of human life, thus creating a wide body of knowledge based on experience of human personalities and lifestyles, in all their variations. **2.** n [Marketing] the application of the principles and practices of marketing to the tasks of increasing public acceptance of ideas, giving to charities, voting for political parties, etc – all matters which are not directly concerned with the promotion and purchase of goods and services.

metamatics n [Art] a series of combination sculptures and painting machines created and built by the French artist Jean Tinguely between 1955–59.

metaphrase n [Linguistics] a word-for-word translation, as opposed to a paraphrase.

metaphysical pathos n [Sociology] the underlying mood of pessimism that informs analyses of bureaucracy; it is the feeling that loss of freedom always runs hand in hand with large-scale social activity.

metapolicymaking n [Business] the making of policy on how to make policy, which involves three main elements: identifying problems, values, and resources and allotting them to various policy-making units; designing, evaluating, and redesigning the policy-making system; determining major policy-making strategies.

meta-theory n [Sociology] the general background of philosophical assumptions which provide rules for the construction of particular sociological theories and methods, eg: **hermeneutics**.

meteor bumper n [Aerospace] a protective structure built on to the exterior of a spacecraft to make it secure against damage from a shower of meteors.

metes and bounds n pl [Law] the measurements that determine the dimensions of a piece of **real property**.

method n [Theatre] a system for the training of actors that emphasises inner emotional experience, discovered through improvisation, rather than technical expertise. It is based on the theories and practice of Konstantin Stanislavsky (1863–1938), and is elaborated and continued at the Actor's Studio in New York, which was founded in 1947 by Lee Strasberg, Cheryl Crawford and Elia Kazan.

methodological individualism n [Sociology] the doctrine that all sociological explanations can be reduced to the characteristics of individuals.

Methods and Standards n pl [US] [Industry] a euphemism for Time and Motion studies and the individuals who carry them out.

metope n [Building, Plastering] the space between two **triglyphs** in a Doric frieze.

metric prose n [Literary criticism] prose that has an unintentional poetic rhythm.

metro gnome n [UK] [Railways] a driver on the London Transport Metropolitan line; it is a pun on the musical time keeper.

mexican drag-line n [US] [Iron workers] a shovel; the racial slur assumes the Mexican's

M

weakness/incompetence. See also **mexican dump-truck**.

mexican dump truck n [US] [Iron workers] a wheelbarrow; the racial slur assumes tha laziness/weakness of the Mexican. See also **mexican drag-line**.

Mexican overdrive n [US] [Road transport] See **Jewish overdrive**.

Mexican stand-off n [Gambling] the quitting of a gambling game, when one has lost or won only a small amount; it comes from general slang referring to an encounter in which neither party has an advantage and both are most likely to give up and walk away.

Mexican standoff n [US] [Railways] a head-on collision between two trains running on the same line See also **cornfield meet**.

mezzanine financing n [Finance] on the principle of 'getting in on the ground floor', this refers to the practice of those investors who do not put their money in at the very start of a project, but wait until after its originators have made it work, and just before it is opened up to the public.

mezzanine level n [Finance] a company which is at the stage immediately prior to going public.

MFC v phr [Medicine] abbr of **Measure for coffin** ie: dead.

MHIV n [Military] abbr of **Miniature Homing Intercept Vehicle** the destructive payload of the US **PMALS ASAT** system which is designed to ram a target satellite at high speed and destroy it conclusively as its own velocity of 7200mph smashes into a target travelling at 10,000 mph.

miaow n [US] [Subways] a term used by volunteer subway patrols – the Guardian Angels – to describe hooligans, troublemakers.

mib n [Marbles] the target marble in the game. See also **commie, dib, duck, kimmie, immie, migg**.

mice n pl [Audio] small microphones which can be placed on stage near the footlights.

Michigan bankroll, also **California bankroll** n [Gambling] a large and ostentatious bankroll which actually consists of a few large denomination notes wrapped around a majority of very small ones.

mick course n [US] [Education] an easy course; it comes from general slang 'Mickey Mouse' meaning easy, inconsequential. See also **cake course, gut course**.

mickey 1. n [Espionage] in the CIA this is a spy who offers his services to a foreign country simply by 'walking in' to the embassy or contacting its intelligence service and offering his services. The name comes from a spy who successfully offered information taken from his job high in the CIA from 1952–64. The original 'Mickey' died 'of heart failure' during his interrogation by his own agency. See also **emily, willie**. 2. n [Textiles] a bobbin on which the finished thread is wound.

Mickey Mouse 1. n [Film] a sound track style in which the music that accompanies a film relates directly to and even mimics the action on that film; initially it was a cartoon technique, but has been extended into more general use. 2. a [Military] said of anything petty, unnecessary, outdated and obstructive; regulations that exist only for the sake of having regulations.

mickey party, also **scratch party** n [US] [Hotels] an unmarried couple sharing a room and registering as 'Mr. & Mrs. X'.

microcode n [Computing] **microinstructions** which are used in a product as an alternative to **hardwired** circuitry to implement certain functions of parts of the system or of the processor. See also **middleware**.

microeconomics n [Economics, Government] the study of the economy as a complex of individual entities – companies and firms, individual households, wages, prices and incomes. See also **Cambridge School, macroeconomics**.

microflora n [Cheese-making] molds that develop on or inside cheeses.

microinstruction 1. n [Computing] a small, single, short instruction, eg: shift, delete, add, etc. 2. n [Computing] a bit pattern that is stored in a microprogram memory word and is used to specify the actions to be performed by a given component of the system. See also **microcode, middle ware**.

micromarketing n [Marketing] a method of analysing a marketing situation by looking at just a single, individual, firm or consumer. See also **macromarketing**.

micro-teaching n [Education] a teacher-training technique developed at Stanford University, California, in 1960: a teacher takes a small class (5–10 pupils) for a specially contructed lesson of 10–30 minutes; an observer assesses this lesson, and the observer and the teacher, possibly with the aid of videotape, analyse it together afterwards.

MICU n [US] [Medicine] acro **Medical Intensive Care Unit**.

mid user n [Computing] an operator who has an intimate knowledge of a database and who can use this to perform searches for an unskilled end-user who cannot access the database.

midair n [US] [Gliding] a midair collision between two gliders; unless the pilots are wearing parachutes, the results are almost invariably fatal.

MIDAS n [Military] acro **Missile Detection Alarm System** an originally top secret military satellite programme initiated in the late 1950s; it is intended to detect missile launches by recognising the infra-red emissions from the heat of the missile's rocket engines.

middle 1. n [Meat trade] the colon or large intestine of an animal. 2. also **batting track** n [Cricket] the actual wicket in the middle of the cricket pitch, at either end of which the stumps are pitched, the bowler and batsman face each other,

M

etc. **3.** *v* [*Sailing, Ropework*] to determine the centre of a piece of rope by putting the two ends together.

middle eight *n* [*Music*] the eight bars, in the middle of a conventionally structured tune, that are often structured differently from the rest of the tune.

middle novel *n* [*Literary criticism*] the second or third novel written by an author whose original work shows potential, but who has yet to achieve a massive paperback advance or film sale. In the current literary marketplace, such novelists find fewer and fewer buyers for their worthy but unfortunately uncommercial efforts.

middleware 1. *n* [*Computing*] computer **software** designed to perform tasks that stand midway between control programs and applications programs. **2.** *n* [*Computing*] software that has been designed to cater for the specific needs of a particular institution.

middling *n* [*Metallurgy*] cutting of steel tubes into two or more lengths during the manufacturing process, when they have become too long to work in a single length.

midfeather *n* [*Glass-making*] See **tongue**.

Midgetman *n* [*Military*] the growing disenchantment by 1982 with **MIRV**ed weapons, and the apparent inability of the Pentagon to decide once and for all on a basing system for the **MX**, led some US strategists to turn to a new weapons system: a small, single-warhead, mobile missile which, theoretically should neither threaten nor provoke a first strike. Such missiles had been termed by negotiator Paul Nitze the 'little guys' (as opposed to Titan and Minuteman) and became generally known as Midgetman. Unlike those ICBMs currently in position, Midgetman would eschew hardened silos and would move around the country as and when required. Midgetman remains, until cost and technical problems are solved, more theory than actual weapon. See also **SICBM**.

midrash *n* [*Military*] abbr of **midnight rations** the late night meal on a nuclear submarine.

migg *n* [*Marbles*] the target marble in the game. See also **commie, dib, duck, kimmie, immie, mib**.

miggles *n pl* [*Marbles*] general term for marbles.

migration *n* [*Computing*] in a database, this is a technique whereby the use of the fast access store is optimised by removing the less frequently accessed items to a slower storage device.

mike 1. *v* [*TV, Radio, Film*] to place a microphone near someone, or to attach one to the throat or clothing, for the purposes of recording. **2.** also **mic** *n* [*Drugs*] abbr of **microgram** the basic unit of measurement for LSD. **3.** *v* [*Engineering*] to use a micrometer screw gauge.

mike stew *n* [*TV*] unwanted background noise picked up by a microphone.

miker *n* [*Navy*] a lazy, workshy sailor.

milage *n* [*TV*] the potentially long run of a TV series format designed for a **situation comedy** or **soap opera**. See also **legs 1**.

milieu therapy 1. *n* [*New therapies*] a form of group psychotherapy that relies mainly on the environment created by the patients involved and the staff and unit who deal with them. **2.** *n* [*Prisons*] treatment given to prisoners who have served lengthy sentences and must therefore be slowly reintroduced into society.

military advisors *n pl* [*Military*] unofficial troops sent by the superpowers into those countries where they wish to advance their causes or bolster up their supporters; the theory is that such advisors have no real involvement, but in reality most train up local troops, service the weapons their governments have supplied, and even fight alongside those troops. Military advisors can often act as the first echelon of far larger troop involvements, eg: as in Vietnam or Afghanistan.

military medium *n* [*Cricket*] straight, regularly paced, up and down bowling which makes up in accuracy what it lacks in speed or penetration but on neither account worries a competent batsman.

milk *v* [*Theatre*] to obtain the maximum audience reaction, whether for a joke, a dramatic incident, a piece of **business**, etc.

milk round *n* [*Industry*] the annual recruitment tour of universities by major firms, usually undertaken in February.

milk run 1. *n* [*Air travel, Military*] this was originally used by USAF/RAF pilots in World War II to describe bombing raids which encountered minimal anti-aircraft fire; it is now used by commercial airlines to describe routine flights to and from the major European capitals. **2.** *n* [*US*] [*Skiing*] the first run of the lift; thus it is the first morning run down a slope.

milker *n* [*Banking, Crime*] a thief who specialises in frauds on travellers' cheques: he steals a book of cheques, tears out a number of cheques from the middle of the book, then replaces it. The odds are that the owner will not notice the theft until far too late.

milkey, also **milchy** *a* [*Furriers*] used of female furs which have encased fatty deposits of the mammary glands for nursing young.

mill 1. *n* [*Hot rods*] an engine which has been tuned to its best potential. **2.** *n* [*Journalism*] a typewriter.

mill coil *n* [*Metallurgy*] the product of a single steel **billet** or slab which has been hot-rolled into a narrow strip.

mill time *n* [*Computing*] See **run time**.

mille trous *n* [*Cheese-making*] a defective Gruyere riddled with small, close-set holes; it comes from Fr. meaning 'a thousand holes'.

Millerandism *n* [*Politics*] a derogatory left-wing term used to describe those socialist MPs in any country who are elected on a radical platform but who drift inexorably to the right; the term comes

M

from the career of A. Millerand (1859–1943), who was elected to the French parliament in 1885 as a radical, and who moved so far to the right that he became President of the Republic between 1920–24.

milliard *n* [*Banking*] one thousand million, one billion.

milline rate *n* [*Marketing*] a unit used for comparing newspaper advertising rates in relation to circulation.

milly *n* [*UK*] [*Market-traders*] a shirt.

MILSTAR *n* [*Military*] acro **Military Strategic-Tactical and Relay** a satellite system currently under development that is designed to maximise communications technology in one vehicle for inter-military use during a nuclear war. According to Major-General Gerald Hendricks of the USAF Space Division, MILSTAR is 'designed to be a war-fighting system' which will work 'during all levels of conflict, have worldwide two-way communications, and be survivable and enduring.'

mimmies *n* [*UK*] [*Market-traders*] alcoholic liquor.

minac 1. *n* [*Science fiction*] the minimum space allowed for a participant in an **apa** publication. **2.** *v* [*Science fiction*] to participate only at the lowest possible level in the creation of a magazine.

minder 1. *n* [*Journalism*] one of the Ministry of Defence press censors who accompanied war correspondants during the Falklands War (April–June 1982); they were much resented for their interference and inconsistencies. **2.** *n* [*UK*] [*Police*] a strong-arm man deputed to take care of a criminal; he collects protection money and similar payments, works as a bodyguard, and generally stands in as 'muscle'.

mind-fucking *n* [*New therapies*] in the terminology of **est**: thinking.

mind-set *n* [*New therapies*] one's mental attitudes and opinions; by inference it means those which are firmly set and which one is unwilling to alter without a struggle.

mind-tripping *n* [*New therapies*] thinking out a problem by employing a degree of intellectual analysis, a process which will create the opposite effect to the **gut feeling** which is the basis of many new therapies.

mingling *n* [*US*] [*Real estate*] the occupation of a single dwelling place by a number of single people, couples or families.

mingra *n* [*UK*] [*Market-traders*] a policeman.

mini 1. *n* [*Audio*] a small (under 12 in. tall) speaker; such speakers have certain common characteristics, including two-way systems, 3–5 in. **woofer** etc. **2.** *n* [*Computing*] abbr of **mini-computer** originally this was any computer which could be fitted into a single equipment cabinet. Today the mini stands between the microcomputer (to which it is superior) and the **mainframe**, although the line between the more so-

phisticated micros and the minis is growing increasingly blurred.

mini-majors *n pl* [*Film*] film production companies that rank between the **majors** and the independents: Orion, Tri-Star, Embassy. See also **indie 1, majors**.

minimal art also **ABC art, anti-illusionism, barebones art, cool art, know-nothing nihilism, literalist art, idiot art, object art, primary structures, reducative art, rejective art** *n* [*Art*] almost always found in the form of sculpture, such art rejects any elements of illusion or expressiveness in favour of clarity and simplicity, eg: Carl André's controversial pile of bricks at the Tate gallery.

minimalism *n* [*Art*] See **minimal art**.

minimax 1. *n* [*Business*] a business strategy which concentrates on minimising the possibility of a maximum loss. See also **maximax, maximin**. **2.** *n* [*Computing*] in artificial intelligence (**AI**) this is any state which is a minimum when considered from one point of view and a maximum when viewed from another.

minimil *n* [*Marketing*] the lowest **milling rate** or an average of the lowest milling rates.

minimum deterrence *n* [*Military*] the smallest quantity of nuclear weapons required to assure a potential attacker that they would suffer unacceptable national damage in a retaliatory strike. Such a form of deterrence, in effect the policy of **assured destruction** cut back to the barest necessary arsenals, would dispense with all but the vital warheads, thus making obsolete any 'war-fighting' or 'limited' capabilities, especially the short-range 'battlefield' nuclear weapons.

minimum price fluctuation *n* [*Futures market*] the smallest amount of price movement possible in the trading of a given contract.

mini-page *n* [*Advertising*] an advertising space on the page of a newspaper or magazine that is approximately 75% of the width of the page by 75% of its depth; it is completely surrounded by editorial matter.

minipod *n* [*Photography*] a small tripod used to keep the camera steady in spaces where a normal tripod would be too bulky.

mini-series *n* [*TV*] the television version of a best-selling novel, or possibly the remake of a classic film, which is divided up, to garner maximum audience ratings and advertising revenue, over two, three, or even more nights.

minnie *n* [*US*] [*Road transport*] abbr of **minimum** a load of less than 100lb.

mint *n* [*Book collecting*] the perfect specimen of a collectible book: with all the features that it contained when it left the publisher's warehouse. Some collectors and dealers dispute such a category, claiming that **fine** is an adequate description for such volumes.

minus advantage 1. *n* [*Espionage*] an operation which not only failed, but also resulted in those

M

involved being left in a worse position than they were prior to its inception. **2.** *n* [*Business*] by extension from the espionage use (see **1**) this is a new venture which has failed and has left the company who launched it in a worse financial position than previously.

minus tick *n* [*US*] [*Stock market*] See **down tick**.

minuscule *n* [*Printing*] a lower case letter. See also **majuscule**.

minutemen *n pl* [*UK*] [*Railways*] work study engineers, time and motion inspectors who may only enter a yard by permission of the union officials involved.

MIPS *n* [*Computing*] acro **million instructions per second** a measure of computing power. See also **flops, KIPS, LIPS**.

Miranda *n* [*US*] [*Law, Police*] abbr of **Miranda decision** this was based on the case of Ernesto A. Miranda vs. the State of Arizona (1966). It consists of a set of rules established by the US Supreme Court whereby the US police, on arresting a suspect, must inform him/her of all due rights and privileges before beginning any subsequent interrogation – the equivalent of the 'caution' in the UK. Thus 'Miranda card' is a card with the suspect's rights written down on it; hence 'Miranda rights', 'Miranda warning', 'Miranda rule'.

mirt *part phr* [*Oil rigs*] acro **moving in rotary tools**.

MIRV *n* [*Military*] acro **Multiple Independently Targeted Re-Entry Vehicle** separate warheads ('passengers') are carried by the same launch vehicle (the 'bus') and delivered by computerised internal and stellar inertial guidance (SIG) to multiple targets over an area of up to 20,000 sq.miles. The MIRV system in the final stage of the missile has its own set of directional jets – like a space capsule – and can thus manoeuvre from target to target.

MIS *n* [*Computing*] acro **Management Information System** an information system whose prime purpose is to supply information to managers. Such systems are either created by systems analysts to fulfil management requirements, or exist as decision support systems, designed to give managers the maximum independence in using computers for their planning and decision making. Such systems involve managers in creating their own databases as well as using the corporate databases, with both functions being performed independently of specialist intermediaries.

mischsprache *n* [*Linguistics*] a language that is supposed to have been made up of a mixture of two or more established languages.

mise en place *n* [*UK*] [*Catering*] one who prepares the **station** for the next sitting, ensures that food from the kitchen is ready for serving and generally assists the **chef de rang** in such tasks as laying the table and replacing any materials that a waiter might need.

miser rate *n* [*UK*] [*Railways*] a minimum bonus payment.

misfeature *n* [*Computing*] a feature in a computer that is not capable of dealing with certain new situations that arise in the operation of that machine.

misfeed *n* [*Computing*] any form of data that fails to pass correctly through a device.

mismatching *n* [*Banking*] See **maturity tranformation**.

misrun *n* [*Metallurgy*] in iron founding this is a casting defect that is manifested by the casting not being completely formed.

miss *n* [*US*] [*Painting*] See **catface**.

Miss Jones *n* [*Commerce*] a name given by a supervisor or fellow salesperson to any female salesperson who is free to help a customer. See also **Mr. Franklin**.

miss out *v* [*US*] [*Railways*] to fail to report for duty despite receiving a call.

misses *n pl* [*Gambling*] crooked dice that have been fixed so that more 7s than point numbers are thrown.

missile envelope *n* [*Military*] the area of the sky that can be saturated by a salvo of hostile missiles and which therefore will inevitably prove fatal for any target airplanes.

missile gap *n* [*Military*] a descendant of the 'bomber gap' of the early 1950s which was created as a spurious but effective plank in John F. Kennedy's Presidential campaign of 1960: it was alleged that the USSR had created a 'missile gap' by investing heavily in nuclear weapons, while the US under President Eisenhower had not bothered. Statistics prove that this was nonsense – the superpowers had 22 missiles between them in 1960, and the US had 18 of those, rather than the 100–30 USSR-US imbalance touted by Kennedy – but the ploy worked. As a means of forcing through military expenditure it has remained popular ever since.

missionary salesman *n* [*Marketing*] a salesman specialising in visiting not the actual purchaser, but a third party who will influence that purchaser and whose goodwill should be sought; eg: a doctor, who can write prescriptions for the salesman's product which will actually be purchased by the patient.

mis-spots *n pl* [*Gambling*] See **busters**.

Mister Prospect *n* [*Commerce*] a salesman's term for the person in a company who might actually make a deal, and who has the real responsibility for useful decisions on purchasing.

Mister Wood *n* [*UK*] [*Police*] a truncheon.

mistletoe men *n pl* [*UK*] [*Railways*] railwaymen who do not belong to a rail union; like the plant in question, they are stigmatised as parasites on the body of their fellow-workers. See also **outriders**.

M

MIT *v phr* [*Futures market*] acro **Market If Touched** a price order that automatically becomes a market order if the price is reached.

Mivtzam Elohim *n* [*Espionage*] this comes from the Hebrew 'the wrath of God'; it refers to covert Israeli assassination squads, organised primarily to avenge the massacre of Israeli athletes at the Munich Olympics (1972) by members of 'Black September'.

mix 1. *n, v* [*Film, Audio, TV*] the mixing of a number of pictures or tapes to create a finished programme, film or record; thus 'mixer' (broadcasting) is the person who actually operates the machine that mixes and balances the sound transmission. **2.** *v* [*TV, Film, Video*] to **dissolve** from one picture to another; mixing tends to change the images somewhat faster than does the relatively gentle dissolve.

mixed manning *n* [*Military*] a military unit composed of troops from a variety of nations; eg: a UN peace-keeping force.

mixer *n* [*US*] [*Bars*] a woman who is paid to mix with the male customers and encourage them to drink heavily.

mixing *n* [*Printing*] the use of more than one typeface in the printing of a single word or line of text.

mixologist *n* [*Pop music*] a disc jockey, especially one who specialises in remixing the original tapes of a song, or in **scratching**.

mizzle one's dick *v phr* [*Merchant navy*] to miss the sailing of one's ship.

MK *n* [*Religion*] abbr of **missionary's kid**.

MMI *n* [*Computing*] abbr of **Man-Machine Interface** the relationship between the operator and the computer.

M'Naghten Rules *n pl* [*UK*] [*Law*] those criteria which must be answered by any defendant who intends to plead insanity as a defence against criminal actions; the term comes from the trial in 1843 of Daniel M'Naghten, murderer of Sir Robert Peel's secretary Edward Drummond, who was acquitted on the grounds of insanity.

Mob *n* [*US*] [*Crime*] one of the various euphemisms for the families of the US Mafia; others include 'Cosa Nostra', 'the Syndicate' and 'organised crime'.

mob 1. *v* [*Hunting*] to kill a fox without giving it any chance of escape, by surrounding it in a covert, or in some similar manner. **2.** *n* [*Military*] a battalion, regiment, company or any other military grouping.

mobicentric manager *n* [*Business*] a flexible manager, possibly the blueprint of the business executive of the future, who has no particular loyalty and no long-term company position, but who shifts quickly and efficiently from task to task and company to company. As well as the gains he can make, the mere fact of continual movement is reward in itself.

mobilisation *n* [*Sociology*] in **modernisation theory**, this is the process by which the peasants or workers are brought together to achieve collective goals. Political mobilisation is the process whereby the population is brought into the political arena by the formation of new parties and similar institutions supposedly to represent their interests.

Mobius mot *n* [*Literary criticism*] a term coined by Donald Westlake: 'a sentence that turns back on itself with a useless and irrelevant self reference . . . a sentence with a short circuit in it'; eg: 'I was ripped off buying that lavatory paper'. It is named after F. Mobius (d.1868), a German mathematician who invented the Mobius band: a one-sided surface formed by holding one end of a rectangle fixed, rotating the opposite end through 180°, and applying it to the first end.

moby *a* [*Computing*] large, immense, complex; possibly it comes from Herman Melville's 'Moby Dick' (1851).

mockers *n* [*UK*] [*Market-traders*] a curse, bad luck, as in 'put the mockers on'. See also **bogy 2**.

modalities *n pl* [*Diplomacy*] techniques and methods which are fundamental to the negotiations but which are the responsibility not of the primary negotiators but of their underlings; ie. they are the nuts and bolts of the meeting, treaty, etc.

modality *n* [*Politics*] a popular diplomatic word that denotes the method one uses for attaining the ends that one desires.

mode 1. *n* [*Communications*] an all-purpose jargon word, a synonym in many cases for situation. **2.** *n* [*Computing*] the general state of being; used most commonly, despite its technological background, to refer to humans.

model *n* [*Sex*] a euphemism for a prostitute of either sex, particularly those who work by telephone – call-girls and call-boys – and who advertise themselves as 'models' in shops windows and contact magazines.

modem *n* [*Computing*] acro **Modulator and Demodulator** a device that makes it possible to transmit messages between computers through a suitable communication channel, often the public telephone system. The modem modulates the transmitted digital bit stream into an analog signal that can be transmitted, and then demodulates back to the digital state at the receiving station.

moderate *v* [*Science*] in nuclear physics, to slow down a neutron; to provide a reactor with a 'modifier', a device which slows down neutrons in order that they may cause fissions more readily.

modern figures, also **newspaper figures** *n pl* [*Printing*] See **lining figures**.

modernism 1. *n* [*Art*] an international movement throughout the arts that developed towards the end of the 19th century and, in its turning away from, and progressing beyond, the previous values and styles, paved the way for many developments in 20th century art. **2.** *n* [*Religion*] a 20th century tendency, especially in Roman Catholicism, to modify traditional dogma according to the developing tenets of modern criticism and research.

modernisation theory *n* [*Sociology*] the paradigm in American sociology whereby traditional societies achieved modernity. Including political, cultural, social and economic facets, it has been criticised because all premises are based on a Western model and because it does not contain guarantees of development towards industrial growth and equal distribution of social benefits.

modesty shield *n* [*Military*] a 140,000lb reinforced steel shield that covers the transporters of the MX missile and prevents observation from spy satellites.

modified re-buy *n* [*Marketing*] See **limited problem solving**.

modoc *n* [*US*] [*Air Force*] anyone who joins the Air Force for the glamour, the social life, or the fulfilment of some other fantasy unrelated to the realities of military life.

mods *n* [*Education*] at Oxford University this is the first examination for classics students: Honour Moderations. See also **greats**.

modular art *n* [*Art*] any painting or sculpture that is based on a unit of size and measurement that is repeated throughout the work.

module *n* [*Oil rigs*] a package of plant, equipment, living quarters, etc., installed on (or for installation on) an offshore structure, such as a production platform.

modulo *prep* [*Computing*] except for.

moey *n* [*UK*] [*Market-traders*] the human face.

moggie *n* [*Motor trade*] a Morris 1000 motor car.

mogul *n* [*Skiing*] a bump in the snow formed by skiers continually turning at the same place; it comes from Ger. mugl meaning hill, bump.

MOHLL *n* [*Computing*] acro **Machine-Orientated High-Level Language** generally known as machine-orientated language, this is a programming language with the control structures of a typical **high-level language** whose data types and structures map on to the underlying machine **architecture**. These languages can offer an alternative to **assembly language** for systems programming at hardware-interface level.

moil 1. *n* [*Glass-making*] excess glass left at the end of an article which is in contact with the blowing mechanism during the manufacture of blown glass and which is removed during the finishing process for the article. **2.** *n* [*Glass-making*] a coating of glass on the gathering iron to prevent it from scaling off into the molten glass.

moire *n* [*Furriers*] a pelt which has hair growing out of it in different directions, producing a visual effect many customers appreciate.

moke *n* [*UK*] [*Surfing*] a car or van used by surfers.

moko *n* [*UK*] [*Theatre*] paint distempered with oil

so as to give a glossy surface to scenic pieces and flats.

mole *n* [*Espionage*] a deep cover agent who is put in place many years before he/she can be of use, but on the assumption that such an agent will gradually gain greater access to the centres of power, and become increasingly useful and damaging as time passes. 'Mole' stands as the perfect example of the blurring of fact and fiction: while Sir Francis Bacon used it first in his 'History of the Reign of King Henry VII' (1622), it has otherwise been found in the works of John Le Carré, notably 'Tinker, Tailor, Soldier, Spy' (1974). In a BBC-TV interview Le Carré claimed that 'mole' was a genuine KGB term, but it was the televising of 'Tinker, Tailor...' plus the revelations of the 'Fourth Man' (Anthony Blunt) in October 1979 that took the word out of fiction and into the headlines for good.

Molly Hogan *n* [*Logging*] an improvised eye on the end of a logging cable.

mom and pop *n* [*Video*] a small, somewhat amateurishly run video store which may actually be the property of a husband and wife.

MON *n* [*Economics*] abbr of **money narrow** a narrow-definition national money base: the notes and coin held by the public. See also **M1, M2, M3**, etc.

monastery *a* [*Cheese-making*] used of cheeses developed by Trappist monks since the Middle Ages; they include Munster, Tête de Moine, Port-Salut, plus derivations such as Tilsit, Saint-Paulin, Esrom, etc.

Monday *n* [*Building*] a 14–lb sledge hammer; it is so-called because only those who are not too hungover after a weekend's drinking are still able to wield it on Monday morning.

Monday Morning model *n* [*Commerce, Industrial relations*] damaged or defective goods from a production line; the workers responsible are either off sick, tired, or hungover after the weekend, or simply depressed by the prospect of another week on the line.

Monday morning quarterback *n* [*Sport*] one who is particularly conspicuous in relation to US football, in which many big games are played on a Sunday; it is the name for an armchair critic who offers his own erroneous opinions on the results of the previous day's games, written up in the newspapers.

Monday's newcomers *n pl* [*TV, Advertising*] a closed circuit showing for those concerned of the latest commercials to be used by the independent TV networks, which start their transmission life on a Monday.

mondegreen *n* [*Linguistics*] a term coined by Sylvia Wright; it is a linguistic analogue of the children's game 'Chinese Whispers', when heard speech is misinterpreted by the hearer because of sound-alike words within that speech. It was developed from Wright's own childhood interpret-

M

ation of the line 'They hae slain the Earl a' Murray/And laid him on the green' as . . . 'and Lady Mondegreen'.

monetarism *n* [*Economics*] an economic theory, epitomised by the teachings of Milton Friedman and his fellow-members of the 'Chicago school' of economists, that is based on the belief that increases in inflation can be traced directly to those in the money supply; thus if the money supply is cut, inflation will fall as well.

monetary correction *n* [*Economics*] index-linking, to the fluctuations of inflation, of prices, wages, mortgages, loans, government securities, etc.

money, in the *adv* [*Horse-racing*] a horse that runs 'in the money' has been placed first, second or third in the race and the bettor who is 'in the money' has bet on one of those three horses; thus the opposite for both horses and humans is 'out of the money'.

money illusion *n* [*Economics*] the illusion that an increase in the amount of one's wages automatically equals an increase in their value; in a period of high inflation one might actually be fortunate to remain even as well off as previously, and it is possible, due to higher taxes, that one might become noticeably poorer. The term was coined by US economist Irving Fisher in 1937.

mongolian *a* [*TV, Film*] referring to the setting of the **barn doors** at a slanting angle.

mongrels *n pl* [*US*] [*Meat trade*] animals with unknown or mixed pedigree.

monitor *n* [*Computing*] See **operating system**.

monk *n* [*Printing*] a smudge or blot of ink on the printed page.

monkey 1. *a* [*Navy*] small. **2.** *a* [*Sailing*] anything either particularly small or peculiar in location or arrangement on a ship. **3.** *a* [*Coal-mining*] used of anything notably small in size. **4.** *n* [*Coal-mining*] a pivoted axle catch on a haulage track that stops any tubs from running away down a slope. **5.** *n* [*Boxing*] the left hand. **6.** *n* [*Gambling*] £500. **7.** *n* [*Industry*] a falling weight used when driving something by percussion; ie: a pile driver or drop hammer. **8.** *n* [*Metallurgy*] a heavy weight slung from the roof of an ironworks and used in upsetting the end of a piece too long to be treated by the forging hammer. **9.** *n* [*Mining*] a casing drive hammer: a weight used to push the casing – the pipe that holds the sides of a borehole in place – down into a borehole. **10.** *n* [*UK*] [*Road transport*] a two-wheeled trailer used for carrying very long loads.

monkey board *n* [*Oil rigs*] a high-level platform in the derrick on which a derrick man works.

monkey bridge *n* [*Navy*] the after end or the stern of a vessel.

monkey fist, also **monkey paw** *n* [*Film*] a piece of rope work which is dangled from a sound or camera boom in order to stop anyone from walking into the boom and thus ruining a shot.

monkey forecastle *n* [*Navy*] a short, low fore-castle, used to stow anchor gear.

monkey house *n* [*Sailing*] the top of the pilot-house; thus 'monkey ladder' is the light ladder leading up to the pilothouse roof.

monkey jacket *n* [*US*] [*Medicine*] a hospital gown.

monkey pole *n* [*UK*] [*Theatre*] a special pole with a hole in it, through which lines can be threaded and then guided when lashing **flats** together.

monkey rope *n* [*Sailing*] a safety rope attached to a sailor when he is working over the side.

monkey vein *n* [*US*] [*Coal-mining*] a bed in which there are thin alternating layers of rock and coal.

monkeys *n pl* [*Printing*] See **muttons**. See also **nuts**.

monkey's fist *n* [*Navy*] the weighted knot at the end of a heaving line.

monks *n pl* [*Logging*] yardmen who store the lumber or prepare it as required for shipment.

monnicker *n* [*UK*] [*Market-traders*] a person's name.

monnisher *n* [*UK*] [*Market-traders*] a young woman.

mono *n* [*Skiing*] skiing on one ski only, with boots that are specially fixed side by side.

monochromatic painting, also **monotone painting** *n* [*Art*] paintings produced in a single colour or a single tone.

monocoque *n* [*Cars*] a type of chassis construction used for current Grand Prix racing cars; sheet metal, usually in the form of body pressings, is formed into an integral body/chassis unit, offering great lightness and rigidity.

monoline *a* [*Printing*] See **monotone**.

monolithic *a* [*Politics*] that condition of communist perfection sought in both ideology and organisation; the Communist Party is monolithic when it is 'carved from a single block, having one single will, and uniting all shades of thought in one stream of political activity' (Moscow Radio, April 1953).

monolithic arrays *n pl* [*Electronics*] single printed chips, without wires between the elements; such arrays can incorporate a number of 'charged-coupled devices', detectors that are used in bulk in space-based reconnaissance and early-warning systems to scan large areas of the earth's surface for the transmission of intelligence pictures.

monolithic floor *n* [*Building, Plastering*] a floor screed placed within 3 hours of the concrete base being laid.

monomorphic station *n* [*Radio, TV*] a radio or TV station that concentrates absolutely on a single area of interest: the news, the weather, rock'n roll, etc.

monopsony *n* [*Commerce*] a market situation in which there is only one single buyer for a given commodity.

M

monotone, also **monoline** *a* [*Printing*] a characteristic of types that show an evenness of stroke.

monsooned coffee *n* [*Coffee production*] the green beans that have been obtained from unwashed coffee, which have then been exposed to a humid atmosphere in which they have turned a light brown or gold colour.

montage 1. *n* [*Film, TV*] the whole art of editing and assembling the various shots, takes, close-ups, effects, etc. into the final programme or film. 2. *n* [*Film, TV*] specifically this is an impression-istic sequence of short **dissolves** used to bridge a time gap, set a situation or establish a background for the main story.

monte *n* [*UK*] [*Police*] abbr. See **three-card monte**.

Monte Carlo Method *n* [*Computing*] a trial and error system of calculation, used to discover what is the best solution to a problem; it is ideally suited to a machine which is able to perform the infinity of calculations required with speed and accuracy. The name comes from the random numbers of the roulette tables of Monte Carlo.

monty hall *n* [*Role gaming*] in the game of 'Dungeons and Dragons' this is a type of dungeon or campaign in which the rewards are dispro-portionately large in comparison to the dangers faced in gaining them. The term comes from the name of Monty Hall, host of US TV's 'Let's Make a Deal', a game show with similar characteristics.

mooch 1. *n* [*US*] [*Car salesmen*] a customer who thinks he can outsmart the salesman. 2. *n* [*Commerce*] a customer to whom it is easy to sell.

moody 1. *v* [*UK*] [*Market-traders*] to put into a good humour by flattery, charm, wheedling talk. See also **moody-merchant**. 2. *n* [*UK*] [*Police*] lies, deceit, anything that goes wrong and prevents one from achieving a desired and expected result.

moody-merchant *n* [*UK*] [*Market-traders*] one who can flatter or charm skilfully and usefully. See also **moody**.

moondoggle *n* [*Aerospace*] useless exploration of the moon that wastes time, energy and money. See also **boondoggle**.

moonlight *v* [*Industrial relations*] to take a second job in addition to one's main employment; usually at night, or at least after work.

moonpool *n* [*Mining*] a shaft in the centre of a deep-sea mining ship, through which equipment is raised and lowered.

MOOSE *n* [*Aerospace*] acro **Manual Orbital Operations Safety Equipment** a device used to protect an astronaut who is working in outer space; it is a space-based life-raft.

moose *n* [*US*] [*Military*] this comes from Jap. 'musume' meaning 'girl'; it is a term, used by the US forces based in Korea or Japan, for girls.

mooz *n* [*TV, Film*] the reverse of **zoom**: a fast zoom-out shot.

mope *n* [*Medicine*] acro **medical officer par excellence**.

mopping up *n* [*Finance*] the process whereby the Bank of England will automatically purchase any spare montary funds from the banks of the **Discount Houses** by selling them Treasury Bonds and thus absorbing the excess cash.

MOR *a* [*Pop music*] acro **Middle Of the Road** simple popular music of little lyrical or musical merit, but adequate and saleable fodder for the pop charts and radio stations. See also **AOR**.

moral panic *n* [*Sociology*] the over-reaction by the mass media, the police and 'community leaders' to relatively trivial acts of delinquency.

morbs *n* [*US*] [*Medicine*] abbr of **morbidity** burst of temporary depression.

mordant *n* [*Weaving*] chemicals, usually acids or metallic salts, which combine with dyes on fibres to make more or less insoluble compounds.

morgue *n* [*Journalism*] newspaper cuttings libraries, where 'dead' stories from yesterday's papers are laid to rest.

morkrumbo *n* [*US*] [*Journalism*] journalese; it comes from the Morkrum machine which trans-mits wire service reports to US newspaper offices.

morning drive *n* [*US*] [*Radio*] a **daypart** created for advertising and statistical purposes; it is the early morning period up to 10am, during which commuters are driving to work.

morning line *n* [*Gambling*] the list of probable betting odds on the day's horses which appears in the morning papers; such odds may well change as the races in question approach. These are also the odds printed on the daily racecards available at the course.

morning prayers *n pl* [*UK*] [*Military*] the daily briefing given to staff officers by the commander during a war or on a battlefront.

morphidite *n* [*Logging*] any vehicle that differs from a standard truck – a lift truck, straddle truck, etc.

mort 1. *n* [*UK*] [*Market-traders*] an old woman. 2. also **grey fish** *n* [*Angling*] the sea trout. 3. *part phr* [*Oil rigs*] acro **moving out rotary tools**.

MOS 1. *adv* [*Film*] acro '**Mit Out Sound**' (alleg-edly a German director's command); a script direc-tion indicating that a scene should be shot without its dialogue. 2. *n* [*US*] [*Marine Corps*] acro **Mili-tary Operational Speciality** the special area of activity in which every Marine, over and above simply serving in the Corps, works; it is denoted on his record by a special four-digit number, coded as to the speciality.

mosaic *n* [*Photo-typesetting*] the design elements in the form of individual **pixels** or **pels** which make up the complete letter shape. See also **bit-map**.

Moscow criterion *n* [*Military*] the belief among UK strategic planners that any UK weapon should be able to attack Moscow. This belief influenced the decision in 1973 to adopt the

M

Chevaline modification of the Polaris A–3 missile, rather than opting to replace the Polaris by the Poseidon missile.

moses n [Merchant navy] the youngest member of the ship's crew; it comes from the biblical story of Moses floating in the bulrushes.

mossback n [US] [Politics] a dedicated reactionary, one who resists all change at any time; it comes from the image of a creature which moves so slowly as to permit moss to grow on its back.

most significant bit n [Mathematics] in a binary number this is the leftmost figure of the number which has the greatest impact on the value of the whole number See also **least significant bit**.

mothball v [Military] to take out of service and store disused, obsolete or excess equipment and **materiel;** thus 'demothball' is to remove from storage, refit and restore such items to service.

mother 1. n [Food processing] a slime of yeast and bacteria that forms on fermenting liquids and is used to make cider turn into vinegar. 2. n [Food processing] sediment that forms in vinegar. 3. n [Audio] a grooved disc which is made from the plating of an electrotyped master matrix and which is used as a stamper in the mass production of vinyl records.

mother and children n [Fleet air arm] an aircraft carrier and the aircraft based on her.

mother coal n [US] [Coal-mining] fusain: a charcoal-like constituent of banded, bituminous coals; it is the cause of much of the dust in a mine.

mother culture n [Science] the original culture of a bacteria from which small portions may be removed to start other cultures.

Mother Hubbard n [Oil rigs] a drill bit which is almost as wide at the top as it as the cutting point; it is named after the baggy, shapeless garment with this name. See also **fish tail 5, water course**.

motherboard n [Computing] a circuitboard with space for all the printed circuits required by a system – the interfaces, memory, etc.

mother-bombs n pl [Military] canisters that are dropped on to a target and which, as they disintegrate, shower shrapnel grenades over the target zone.

mothergate, also **main gate, mullergate** n [Coal-mining] the principal road from a **longwall** face along which coal is usually transported.

mother-in-law research n [Business] research that draws its conclusions from the sampling of only a small group, usually relatives, friends or neighbours. It is often used both to underline a decision that is already desired, or to kill off an unpopular plan which wider research might still support.

mother-of-all n [Weaving] the horizontal member into which the **maidens** are set.

motion discomfort n [Air travel] a euphemism for air sickness.

motivate v [Sex] in black pimp terminology this is to force oneself to do something, eg: when a girl starts her night's work.

motivation-hygiene theory n [Management] a theory of job satisfaction developed by US psychologist Frederick Herzberg (1923–) whereby an employee derives satisfaction from two separate sources: **hygiene factors** and motivators. A combination of the two, dealing respectively with the factors ancillary to the task and the task itself, will ideally create the optimum work environment and the fully satisfied employee.

motivators n pl [Management] in Herzberg's motivation-hygiene theory, motivators concern the actual tasks that are performed by employees: these include the nature of the task, its potential for career advancement, and the satisfaction one may gain from performing the task. If these factors are present, then the employee will be satisfied, but if they are absent, there is no reason for the employee to be especially dissatisfied. See also **hygiene factor**.

motorboat look n [Custom cars] See **cowboy rake**.

motor-boating n [Audio] this comes from the sound – like a put-putting motor – that it creates; it is a type of instability in the amplifier caused by inadequate high tension voltage smoothing or positive feedback at sub-sonic frequencies.

motorised shoulders n pl [TV] a cameraman whose hand-held work is conspicuously steady is said to possess these.

motty n [Coal-mining] See **tally**.

mouldies n pl [Navy] torpedoes.

mount v [Angling] to mount a **cast** is to put a fly on it, and to tie droppers to it when fishing with more than one fly.

mount money n [Rodeo] payments made to exhibition, rather than competition, riders.

mouse n [Computing] a small, wheeled, box, attached to a computer and equipped with certain electronic controllers, which, when teamed with suitable **software** and graphics can improve on the performance of keyboard-only computers in the field of high-resolution graphics. Developed by Xerox in 1960, but not widely recognised until the last few years, the mouse is most commonly touted as the best way for non-typists to operate their machine.

mouse for a down v phr [US] [Car salesmen] to send a customer off to a bank or finance company to obtain the down-payment and subsequent financing.

mouse house n [US] [Car salesmen] a bank or finance company. See also **blood bank**.

mousehole, also **rat hole** n [Oil rigs] a shallow hole in the drilling floor near the drilling table in which the **kelly** and other **stands** of pipe are stored while the **drill string** is being lengthened.

mousehole connection n [Oil rigs] the addition of a length of pipe to the active **drill**

M

string. The length to be added is placed in the **mousehole**, made up to the **kelly**, pulled out of the mousehole, and then added to the string.

mousetrap 1. *n* [*US*] [*Football*] a play in which a defensive player is allowed to cross the line of scrimmage and is unexpected blocked from the side while the ball carrier advances through the hole he has vacated. 2. *n* [*Fleet air arm*] a submarine. 3. *n* [*US*] [*Navy*] an anti-submarine (**ASW**) warfare device that throws depth charges ahead of small ships as they move through the sea. 4. *n* [*Oil industry*] a specific type of instrument for **fishing** small objects dropped into an oil-well. 5. *n* [*US*] [*Painting*] a rickety, unsafe rigging on which a cradle in suspended.

mousey *a* [*Wine-tasting*] flat yet acetic; the specific smell and taste of wine suffering a bacteriological disease – 'tourne' – that only occurs in cask.

mousing *n* [*Sailing*] a turn or lashing of rope used by seamen across the open end of a hook, to ensure that the load carried on that hook does not slip off.

mousse *n* [*Cheese-making*] a cheese whose surface has just started to be invaded by the white mold penicillium candidum; at this stage cheeses are moved from the drying room to the ageing cellars.

mouth gag *n* [*US*] [*Medicine*] See **seizure stick**.

mouthing *n* [*Horse riding*] the process, usually started on the third day of breaking in, of accustoming a horse to a bit and bridle.

Mouton d'Or *n* [*TV*] an imaginary prize, modelled on the various Golden Roses, etc., awarded to programmes of great length, painstaking attention to detail, utter humourlessness and relentless tedium.

move 1. *v* [*Angling*] to make a fish take notice of the fly or bait. 2. *n* [*Glass-making*] a fixed number of glass articles which are to be made for a fixed amount of pay by a team of glassworkers; it is the basis of establishing rates of pay in a glass works.

Movement *n* [*Literary criticism*] a genre of English poets that flourished in the 1950s and included Philip Larkin, Kingsley Amis and John Wain.

Movement movement *n* [*Art*] See **kinetic art**.

moves *n pl* [*Pop music*] the various positions that a record may take as it moves up and down the charts as listed in the pop press or as used on radio playlists.

mow *v* [*Cricket*] to make a sweeping shot that resembles someone cutting grass with a scythe.

MOW *n* [*Economics*] abbr of **money wide** a wide-definition national money base: the notes and coin held by the public, plus the money held in bank tills and the deposits the banks hold at the Bank of England. See also **M1, M2, M3, M4**.

Mr. Franklin *n* [*Commerce*] a name given by a supervisor or fellow salesperson to any male salesperson who is free to help a customer. See also **Miss Jones**.

Mr. Gillpots *n* [*UK*] [*Market-traders*] a drunkard.

Mr. Wood *n* [*UK*] [*Circus*] empty seats in the big top.

MRBM *n* [*Military*] abbr of **Medium Range Ballistic Missile** a type of land-based ballistic missile with a range between 900km and 2400km; the US deploys Pershing II and Tomahawk (**cruise**) and the USSR has the near-obsolete SS–4 and the new SS–20. The status of these medium-range missiles, designed essentially for the European theatre, remains central to inter-power arms talks. See also **INF talks, theatre nuclear forces**.

Mrs. Chase *n* [*Medicine*] See **Chase doll**.

MRV *n* [*Military*] abbr of **Multiple Re-entry Vehicle** one of a number of warheads which can be carried on a single booster rocket; unlike the more sophisticated **MIRVs** and **MARVs** which have replaced them, these warheads simply increase the on-target throw weight of a given booster; they cannot be independently guided to a variety of targets.

MSI *n* [*Computing*] abbr of **Medium-Scale Integration** integration technology which will allow the placing of 100–10,000 transistors on a single chip. See also **SLI, SLSI, VLSI**.

MST *n* [*Coal-mining*] abbr of **Man-Shifts per Thousand tonnes**.

MTBF *n* [*Computing*] abbr of **Mean Time Between Failures** a figure that represents the period in the life of a piece of machinery, bracketed by two breakdowns, when it has functioned perfectly; it is a means of estimating the excellence of the machine.

muck *n* [*Mining*] waste material that is removed during mining or civil engineering operations.

muck and bullets *n* [*TV*] in makeup this is the deliberate 'dirtying down' of a group of extras who are due to appear as soldiers, beggars, or some similar group who must not appear too elegant and clean.

muck bar *n* [*Metallurgy*] a semi-finished bar produced in the forge.

muck rolls *n pl* [*Metallurgy*] the first pair of a train of rolls for rolling wrought iron.

muckbird *n* [*UK*] [*Railways*] dirty oil waste.

mucker 1. *n* [*Coal-mining*] a machine which loads waste products on to the conveyor or into tubs. 2. *n* [*US*] [*Coal-mining*] in open-cast mining this is a very large shovel used to clear earth and dirt from the top of the coal. 3. *n* [*Textiles*] a wool sorter.

muckey-muck *n* [*US*] [*Politics*] this is usually 'high muckey-muck'; it probably comes from Chinook 'hiu' (plenty) and 'muckamuck' (food), denoting a powerful man in the tribe: thus any political bigwig. It is often used by lower echelons to attack the party leaders.

mucking out *n* [*Coal-mining*] the operation of loading out the excavated pillars in roadways, shafts, etc.

M

mud 1. *n* [US] [Circus] greasepaint. See also **slap**. **2.** *n* [US] [Painting] a plaster mixture that cements paper or fabric tape to the seams between sheets of plasterboard. **3.** also **drilling mud** *n* [Oil rigs] a mixture of clays, water, and chemicals pumped down the **drill string** and up the **annulus** during drilling, in order to lubricate the system, carry away rock cuttings, maintain the required pressure at the bit end, provide an aid to formation evaluation, etc.

mud hen *n* [US] [Logging] a logger who works in swampy areas.

mud hog *n* [Oil rigs] a pump which circulates drilling **mud** in rotary drilling; a **slush pump**.

mud man *n* [Oil rigs] the service engineer who maintains the **mud** systems on a drilling rig.

mud pump *n* [Oil rigs] See **slush pump**.

mudder, also **mudlark** *n* [Horse-racing] a horse which runs at its best on a muddy course.

MUF *n* [Technology] acro **Material Unaccounted For** in nuclear energy and weapons development, this refers to those amounts of nuclear material – plutonium or enriched uranium – which have vanished without trace from government stockpiles and are marked thus on the annual inventory.

muff *v* [Journalism] See **fall down**.

muffle *n* [Building, Plastering] a thickness piece placed beyond the profile of a mould when coring out.

MUFTI *n* [UK] [Prisons] acro **Minimum of Force Tactical Invervention squad** a specially trained prison riot squad, composed of prison officers who are supposed to use tactics rather than brute force in dealing with disturbances in the prison.

mug *v* [Theatre] to make exaggerated facial expressions.

muggo *n* [Dockers] abbr of '**mug o' tea**' a cup of tea.

mugs *n pl* [UK] [Crime] to the confidence trickster of any persuasion: the foolish, gullible public at large.

mugshot *n* [Police] the head and shoulders, front and profile shots of criminals that are placed on file, with their fingerprints, for future identification purposes.

mugsnatcher *n* [UK] [Market-traders] a photographer who works the street, the fairs or the markets.

mule 1. *n* [Drugs] a smuggler of contraband drugs, not an organiser of the deal but a temporary 'employee' who is paid a flat fee to take drugs from A to B, and risk discovery by the customs. **2.** *n* [Glass-making] a common wine glass. **3.** *n* [Industry] an unskilled labourer who performs heavy, dirty work. **4.** *n* [US] [Prisons] See **horse 2**. **5.** *n* [US] [Railways] a small locomotive used in shunting yards. **6.** *n* [US] [Railways] a large wooden board used to unload grain from railroad cars. **7.** *n* [US] [Road transport] a small tractor used in the warehouse or terminal yard. **8.** *n* [Textiles] a spool of wool yarn. **9.** *n* [Yachting] a large triangular sail, sometimes used on a ketch.

mule shoe *n* [Oil rigs] a small attachment to the end of a pipe which eases the re-entry of tools.

mullahed *a* [UK] [Prisons] beaten up severely.

muller *n* [Metallurgy] in iron founding this is a sand mill in which sand is kneaded and squeezed as part of the preparation for its use in a mould.

mullergate *n* [UK] [Coal-mining] See **mothergate**.

mullier *n* [UK] [Market-traders] a murderer.

mulligan *n* [Golf] a free shot awarded to a player who has just made a bad one – it is not counted on the score-card.

mully *n, v* [UK] [Market-traders] murder; to murder.

multi *n* [Midwifery] a woman with a number of children in addition to the one with which she is pregnant.

multicam *a* [Film] abbr of **multicamera** the making of a film in which the director uses more than one camera to record a scene or scenes; it is often used for action sequences or for chases when the various angles recorded can be intercut for maximum effect.

multidrop circuit, also **multipoint circuit** *n* [Communications] a circuit used to communicate between a number of terminals and a central computer. In such a network two-way transmission is possible between the terminals and the control computer, but not between the individual terminals.

multilateral *a* [Politics] referring to any agreement, treaty, trade negotiation, arms talks, etc. that concerns three or more nations or interests.

multip *n* [US] [Medicine] the second born, or any further child after the first born.

multiplane *n* [Film] an animation technique pioneered by Walt Disney in 'Fantasia' (1941): instead of building up drawings by laying the 'cells' directly over each other, the illusion of depth could be created by leaving a slight space between the celluloid images of the foreground, the main figure, the background, secondary figures, etc.

multiple *n* [Travel agents] an agency with a large number of branch offices.

multiple branding *n* [Marketing] the selling by a manufacturer of a number of similar products, or even the same product in a variety of different packagings, brand-names, etc.

multiple kill capability *n* [Military] a weapons platform – aircraft, tank, ship – that carries more than a single type of weapon, eg: guns and bombs, bombs and missiles, several types of missile, etc.

multiple precision *n* [Computing] the use of two or more computer **words** to represent a number and thus increase its precision.

multiple protective structure (or shelter) *n* [Military] See **racetrack**.

multiple track plan *n* [Education] a method of

dividing children up into classes. See also **ability grouping**.

multiples 1. *n pl* [*Art*] an extension of the traditional 'limited edition' concept, whereby one produces artworks which can be repeated in production, theoretically in as great a supply as there exists demand, on the basis of a single original matrix. 2. *n pl* [*Science*] the principle that all scientific 'discoveries' are in fact progressive developments and that the 'star' to whose name is attached the glory of the important conclusion is merely bringing to a close the work of many unsung predecessors.

multiplex *v* [*Film*] to convert a large old cinema that is no longer proving economic into a number of smaller, refurbished auditoria which can offer a selection of films at the same time.

multiplexing *n* [*Computing*] the process of combining a number of signals to share a common means of transmission.

multipoint circuit *n* [*Communications*] See **multidrop circuit**.

multiprogramming *n* [*Computing*] the maximising of a machine's output by doubling the load in the operating system and having it switch at high speed between the programs, thus working on them both almost simultaneously.

multiseries *n* [*TV*] one of several television series, with fewer segments than a regular series, that are scheduled to be televised in rotation in the same weekly or daily time slot. See also **maxiseries, mini-series**.

multiset *n* [*Computing*] See **bag 4**.

multistable deterrence *n* [*Military*] a three-way theory of nuclear stability: 1. a devastating capability for retaliation after a first strike; 2. the holding by both sides of so credible a first strike capability that neither would be advised to start a war; 3. the balance of terror epitomised by (2) should lead to the reduction of potential tension flashpoints across the world.

multitasking *n* [*Computing*] the concurrent execution of a number of tasks – jobs or processes – by the same machine.

multum in parvo *a* [*Dog breeding*] said of a pug, it indicates stamina, compactness and strength out of proportion to its relatively small frame; it comes from Lat. and means much within little.

mum *n* [*Sociology*] a specific use of the word to denote the type of working-class mother who remains a major influence on her children, even after they have left home and married.

mumblage *n* [*Computing*] the topic of one's **mumble**.

mumble *n* [*Computing*] the answer made to a question when the correct response is either too complicated to explain briefly or the speaker has not thought it out properly; it is a general sign that the speaker is too busy to start a long conversation.

mummerset *n* [*UK*] [*Theatre*] fake peasant accents adopted by actors to denote a supposedly rural accent; it comes from 'Somerset' plus 'mummer'

mumpsimus *n* [*Linguistics*] an incorrectly spelt word that has become incorporated into the language after many years of usage. Thus it means one who refuses to alter an incorrect usage, or a scholar who refuses to reject an incorrect reading of a manuscript. It comes supposedly from an illiterate priest who refused to reject his own pronunciation of 'sumpsimus' in the Mass as 'mumpsimus'.

Munchausen syndrome *n* [*Medicine*] a form of 'hospital addiction', whereby patients either refuse to leave hospital or try by infinite subterfuges to be readmitted for as long a stay as they can achieve.

Munchausen syndrome by proxy *n* [*Medicine*] a form of child abuse, whereby parents will claim that their children are ill when they are actually healthy, and in many cases may make the child ill in order to gain their ends. This was first noted in 1977 by Prof. Roy Meadow of St. James' University Hospital, Leeds.

munchers *n pl* [*Military*] Nimrod submarine reconnaissance aircraft, so nicknamed for the allegedly lavish meals the crews take with them for their ten hour missions.

mundane 1. *a* [*Science fiction*] not connected with science fiction activities. 2. *n* [*Science fiction*] the opposite of a scifi fan or enthusiast; an unimaginative person who does not appreciate the delights of science fiction.

mung 1. *v* [*Computing*] to make major alterations in a file, usually irrevocable ones. 2. *v* [*Computing*] to destroy data accidentally. 3. *v* [*UK*] [*Market-traders*] to ask, to request. 4. *v* [*UK*] [*Market-traders*] to ask for a loan.

murder one *n* [*US*] [*Law, Police*] a charge of first degree – pre-meditated – murder.

murgatroyd *n* [*Tiddleywinks*] a badly manufactured wink which is flat on both sides.

Murphy game *n* [*Crime, Police*] a prostitute's fraud, whereby a client is lured into an alley or a bedroom, at which point, bereft of trousers and dignity, he is faced by a supposedly 'outraged brother' or 'husband' who takes his money, and possibly also his trousers, and departs with the girl.

muscle-car *n* [*US*] [*Motor trade*] a souped-up hot rod, as defined by the mainstream Detroit motor manufacturers.

muscular *a* [*Wine-tasting*] See **manly**.

musette *n* [*Cycling*] a shoulder bag for carrying food during touring or racing; it comes from Fr. meaning a school satchel, a horse's nosebag.

museum piece, also **relic** *n* [*US*] [*Road transport*] See **ghost 6**.

museum restoration *n* [*Ceramics*] a standard of restoration that lets the cracks show more obviously than in **perfect** restoration.

M

mush 1. *n* [*UK*] [*Market-traders*] a man. **2.** *n* [*UK*] [*Market-traders*] the mouth. **3.** *n* [*Surfing*] the foam produced when the wave breaks – the surf itself.

mush log *n* [*Logging*] the outside log of a load.

musher, also **mushie** *n* [*Taxis*] a self-employed cabbie who owns his own cab; such drivers have to be up early enough to pick mushrooms if they want to make a day's wage.

mushroom *n* [*Architecture*] a reinforced concrete pillar that broadens out towards the top, with its reinforcing rods passing up through the pillar into a concrete slab that forms part of the floor above.

mushroom job *n* [*TV*] a derogatory reference to any distasteful work; it comes from the popular reference to mushroom cultivation: 'They keep you in the dark and feed you on shit'.

mushroom theory *n* [*Management*] a theory of management which tacitly considers that the best way of treating employees is to 'put them in the dark, feed them shit and watch them grow.'

mushroomy *a* [*Wine-tasting*] used of the specific smell of some very old wines.

music 1. *n* [*Hunting*] the sound of the pack during a hunt. **2.** *n* [*Military*] electronic jamming.

Music Row *n* [*Music*] the centre of the US country music industry, in Nashville, Tennessee.

musical graphics *n pl* [*Art*] drawings and designs created with the purpose of stimulating a musician to produce sounds that can in some way be related to those designs.

musicality *n* [*Audio*] the ability of a hi-fi system to reproduce recorded music in a satisfactory manner.

musique concrète *n* [*Music*] this comes from French 'concrete music'; developed by Pierre Schaeffer in 1948, it is a style of music that involves sounds of all sorts – human, animal, mechanical, natural – which are combined on one tape which is then played as a performance.

muskra *n* [*UK*] [*Market-traders*] a policeman.

mussels *n pl* [*Mining*] a general term covering all non-marine fossilised shells.

must *n* [*Wine-tasting*] unfermented grape juice.

mustang *n* [*US*] [*Military*] an officer who has been promoted from the ranks.

muster *n* [*Journalism*] a news story considered important enough for an editor to scrap other stories in order to give it more space.

musty *a* [*Wine-tasting*] said of an unpleasant smell which is due to poor casks or a cork fault; if the latter, it should wear off if the wine is allowed to stand after pouring.

mutate *v* [*Chess*] said of a player who is forced to abandon completely a set of moves towards a mate and substitute a new reply to his opponent's defences.

mute *n* [*Film*] any film print – positive or negative – which has no synchronous sound track.

mutton *n* [*Printing*] an 'em quad': a space the square of the type body. See also **Nuts**.

mutual interdependent fixation *n* [*New therapies*] obscurantism meaning 'marriage'.

mutuality *n* [*Industrial relations*] the agreement which is made between employers and workers on the going rates for each part of a production process prior to any introduction of major changes in company policy or practice.

mutule *n* [*Building, Plastering*] a projecting inclined block in a Doric cornice.

muzzler *n* [*US*] [*Police*] a minor criminal, specifically a frotteur.

MVP 1. *n* [*US*] [*Sport*] abbr of **Most Valuable Player** an equivalent, in context, of the UK 'Man of the Match', 'Man of the Series', etc. **2.** *n* [*US*] [*Law*] abbr of **Most Valuable Player** it comes from the sporting use and is a nickname awarded to FBI agents who have been assigned particularly challenging duties.

MX *n* [*Military*] abbr of **Missile-Experimental** a four-stage ICBM, combining 3 stages of solid and one of liquid fuel. It is 72ft long, with a diameter of 92in. and it weighs 190,000 lb (7.5 tons, three times heavier than the Minuteman III). It will use the highly accurate Advanced Interial Reference Sphere (AIRS) guidance system to deliver 10 **MIRV**s, each armed with the 300KT Mk.21 warhead, at a minimum range of 7,000 nautical miles. AIRS will guarantee a basic CEP of 400–600ft; using the **NAVSTAR** global positioning system this can be reduced to 300ft; adding **MARV** technology cuts it to 100ft. MX has been designed to combine two important factors necessary in an ICBM: pinpoint accuracy on target and, when a suitable basing system is developed, survivability. Ostensibly it is a second-strike counterforce weapon which will ride out a hostile attack, then act as the spearhead of a counter-attack, but its very accuracy makes critics in the US and USSR suspect that its real destiny is as a **first-strike** weapon. See also **deep basing, dense pack, fratricide, racetrack**.

mystery shopper *n* [*Advertising*] a manufacturer's representative who tours shops asking for a specific product; if the retailer offers or demonstrates the manufacturer's version of this product he/she will be rewarded. Such 'shoppers' are also used to motivate normal customers who are in the store at the same time.

M

N

N 1. *a* [*Computing*] a large and indeterminate number. **2.** *n, a* [*Computing*] an arbitrarily large and perhaps infinite number. **3.** *n, a* [*Computing*] a variable whose value is specified by the current context, eg: 'We want N soups and fish for N minus 1'. **4.** *a* [*Computing*] used of a large and indeterminate number of objects, eg: 'there were N bugs in that crock'. **5.** *a* [*Computing*] as in Nth which is the ordinal counterpart of N, eg: 'for the Nth and last time . . .'

nabes *n pl* [*Film*] abbr of **neighbourhoods** local cinemas, rather than the major first-run houses.

nadgers *n* [*UK*] [*TV*] a small technical problem occuring in equipment.

naff *a* [*TV*] useless, unpleasant, vulgar; originally, it is claimed, this was a TV coinage, but it has recently been extended into far more common usage. See also **OTT**.

nailing *n* [*UK*] [*Market-traders*] in a mock-auction this is the successful persuading of customers to bid in the auction.

Naisimith's formula *n* [*Hiking*] a method of estimating the length of the hike: allow one hour for every three miles to be covered plus an extra hour for every 2000ft to be climbed.

naive *a* [*Art*] referring to any painter who has not been trained in a formal manner.

naive user *n* [*Computing*] someone who wishes to use a machine but knows little about its operation, and is not particularly keen to learn properly.

naives *n pl* [*UK*] [*Politics*] the original recruits to the Social Democratic Party (SDP): those people who were previously apolitical – at least insofar as they had joined no party before – and were usually leftish, educated, and middle-class.

naked call *n* [*Stock market*] an option to buy stock or any other security that is not actually owned by the seller who is offering it.

naked debenture *n* [*Banking*] an acknowledgement of indebtedness, without any security.

naked option *n* [*Stock market*] an option for which the buyer or seller has no underlying security position; it is the very risky but potentially very profitable speculation on shares which one does not own and which, if prices fail to move as one wishes, can cause the speculator major losses.

naked trustee *n* [*Law*] a trustee who is holding property for the absolute benefit of beneficiaries who are not yet of full age; the trustee has no interest in the property other than its transfer to the beneficiaries at the due date.

name 1. *n* [*Commerce*] an underwriter at Lloyds of London. **2.** *n* [*Stock market*] a ticket labelled with the name of the purchaser, handed over to the selling broker on 'ticket day' or '**name day**'.

name day *n* [*Stock market*] the day on which a seller of registered securities receives from their buyer a ticket – the **name** – with the name and details of the person to whom the securities are to be transferred.

name ID *n* [*Politics*] abbr of **name identification** the recognition of a candidate's name by those whom he/she hopes will be supporters at the forthcoming election.

name-calling *n* [*Politics*] in propaganda this is the vilifying of one's opponent in general and specific terms, often literally at the level of childish abuse, avoiding any reference to one's own case, or to the detail of his.

nanniking *n* [*UK*] [*Market-traders*] fooling about, larking about; showing off.

nanny nine holes *n* [*Angling*] the lamprey.

nano-second *n* [*Computing*] one thousand millionth of a second.

nanty, also **nunty 1.** *excl* [*UK*] [*Market-traders*] be quiet, say nothing, look out, etc. **2.** *a* [*UK*] [*Market-traders*] reticent, silent, quiet.

nap 1. *n* [*Textiles*] the soft, fuzzy, fibrous surface of cloth, created by brushing it against a rough surface – a cylinder covered with wires – to raise some fibres from the body of the cloth. **2.** *n* [*Weaving*] the surface of a fabric formed by fibres standing at an angle to the plane of a fabric.

nape *v* [*Military*] to bomb with napalm.

napping, also **brushing** *n* [*Weaving*] raising a fuzzy surface or nap on a fabric by brushing with fine wire brushes or hand cards.

nark *n* [*UK*] [*Market-traders*] a difficult customer, one who has no intention of buying.

N

nark it! *excl* [*UK*] [*Market-traders*] shut up! be quiet! look out!

narrative figuration *n* [*Art*] narrative art that represents events in time (with or without a story-line) on a single canvas; frequently its imagery is distorted and its subject matter fragmented, and several sequences may be compressed into one painting.

narrow **1.** *a* [*Printing*] said of a typeface which is less than standard width. **2.** *a* [*Stock market*] a narrow market can offer quotations on only a very small number of stocks; a dull market.

narrow money *n* [*Economics*] the current supply of coin and notes held by both the public and the banks. See also **broad money, M3, M0**.

narrowcasting *n* [*Radio, TV*] the transmission of programmes that are aimed specifically at a small, tightly defined audience.

nart *n* [*Art*] this comes from 'nothing' plus 'art'; it is a term coined by art critic Mario Amaya in 1966 to mean, essentially, that in the world of art, less equals more. Nart is characterised by impersonality and the boredom of repetition.

Nassau *n* [*Golf*] a three-part bet, with equal money on the first half, the second half and the whole round.

nasties *n pl* [*Video*] videotapes featuring ultra-horrific sadistic films of mutilation, cannibalism and similar painful, blood-soaked excesses. Cheaply produced abroad, they are vociferously decried by the puritan lobby and hugely popular in the video rental market.

National Military Establishment *n* [*Military*] the US military machine.

nationalism *n* [*Politics*] in Marxist terms, when describing a non-aligned country, this is used as an admirable example of a nation that is standing as a bulwark against US imperialism. However when referring to a nation that is attempting to escape its ties to the USSR, 'bourgeois nationalism (is) a dangerous enemy, and a criminal associate of international reaction'.

nationals *n pl* [*US*] [*TV*] a weekly breakdown provided by the Nielsen TV Index company of the programme ratings throughout the US.

native Americans *n pl* [*Sociology*] a belated recognition, if only in bureaucratic and liberal vocabularies, of the American Indians. See also **first Australians, new Commonwealth**.

natives **1.** *n pl* [*US*] [*Meat trade*] common bred cattle, without the characteristics of any particular breed. **2.** *n pl* [*US*] [*Meat trade*] cattle or sheep coming from nearby farms.

NATO phonetics *n* [*Military*] the internationally agreed phonetic code for use in military and civil radio communications: A Alpha, B Bravo, C Charlie, D Delta, E Echo, F Foxtrot, G Golf, H Hotel, I India, J Juliet, K Kilo, L Lima, M Mike, N November, O Oscar, P Papa, Q Quebec, R Romeo, S Sierra, T Tango, U Uncle, V Victor, W Whiskey, X X-ray, Y Yankee, Z Zulu.

natural *a* [*Cheese-making*] used to describe a cheese whose rind has not been seeded with selected strains of mold and has not been **washed** during ageing.

natural area *n* [*Sociology*] the area of a city that is inhabited by a population of a given type, eg: suburbs, ghetto.

natural coffee *n* [*Coffee production*] unwashed or dry-processed coffee.

natural foot *n* [*UK*] [*Surfing*] when riding a wave with the right foot to the rear; this is the usual surfers' stance. See also **goofy**.

natural language *n* [*Computing*] a language – human speech – in which a user speaks normally, as opposed to the circumscribed languages necessary for communication with machines, indexing documents, etc.

natural person *n* [*Law*] any single human being, man, woman or child. See also **artificial person**.

natural shoulder *n* [*Fashion*] a straight-hanging jacket with medium width, lightly padded shoulders and a central vent.

naturalism **1.** *n* [*Art*] See **socialist realism**. **2.** *n* [*Sociology*] the concept that the methods of sociology are in fact the same as those used in the natural sciences.

naturals *n pl* [*Weaving*] colours of fibres that are in their natural undyed state.

Nav. House *n* [*Navy*] abbr of **Navigation School**, sited at H.M. Dockyard, Portsmouth.

navaglide *n* [*Air travel*] an airport instrument approach system with the ability to indicate distance by utilising a single frequency.

navaglobe *n* [*Air travel*] a long distance navigation system that automatically indicates bearing by using low-frequency broadcasts.

NAVAR *n* [*Air travel*] abbr of **navigation and ranging** a navigation and traffic control system for aircraft.

NAVSTAR *n* [*Military*] abbr of **navigation system using timing and ranging** a sophisticated, navigational system based on ultra-accurate time-clocks which will provide US forces with sophisticated global positioning from a network of 18 (eventually 24) satellites. As 'one of the most important and far-reaching programmes in the Department of Defense' it will facilitate blind bombing, en-route navigation, artillery ranging, troop movements and rendezvous. It will have particular effect on missile delivery, giving navigational accuracy to a **CEP** of 300ft, enhanced with **MARV**ing to only 30ft. See also **IONDS**.

navvy's wedding cake *n* [*UK*] [*Railways*] bread pudding.

navy blues *n* [*Navy*] the psychological effects of a long voyage: depression and the craving for shore leave.

NBC *n* [*Military*] abbr of **nuclear, biological and chemical** warfare. See also **ABC warfare**.

'ncarugnutu *n* [*Crime*] this comes from Sicilian meaning 'carrion'; thus in the Italian Mafia it refers to any Mafioso who breaks the oath of silence, 'omerta'.

NCD *n* [*Navy*] abbr of **no-can-do** a signal refusing a ship-to-ship invitation.

NEACP *n* [*Military*] See **kneecap**.

near beef *n* [*US*] [*Meat trade*] cattle that have been partly fattened.

near cash, also **near money** *n* [*Stock market*] short term investments that can easily be transferred back into cash.

near money *n* [*Banking*] an asset that is not money but which can be used as if it were, eg: a bill of exchange.

near space *n* [*Aerospace*] an orbit just outside the earth's atmosphere.

nearbys *n pl* [*Futures market*] the nearest active trading months of a financial futures market.

neatlines, also **sheetlines** *n pl* [*Military*] those lines on a military map that immediately border the main body of that map.

nebe *n* [*Textiles*] a tiny portion of the sheep's flesh that clings to the wool throughout all the production processes.

necessaries *n pl* [*Law*] the basics without which one cannot live: food, adequate clothing, lodging, etc.

necessary labour *n* [*Politics*] See **indispensable labour**.

neck 1. *n* [*Angling*] the upstream end of a pool. See also **tail 1. 2.** *n* [*US*] [*Coal-mining*] a narrow opening of the coalface, where it leaves the main heading. **3.** *n* [*Glass-making*] the section of a **port** between the gas uptake and the furnace wall.

neck/head/nose *n* [*Horse-racing*] the distances under a whole length by which horses are deemed to have been separated: 4 noses = 1 head; 2 heads = 1 neck; 2 necks = half a length.

neck lock *n* [*UK*] [*Law*] the vertical curl sited at the base of a barrister's wig.

necking *n* [*Building, Plastering*] the area between the **astragal** of the shaft and the shape of the capital proper.

necktie *n* [*Logging*] See **choker**.

need another neuron *v* [*US*] [*Medicine*] to be very stupid; two neurons are required for a synapse to take place, to be able to think or act.

needle 1. *n* [*Gemstones*] any foreign body found in quartz crystal. **2.** *n* [*UK*] [*Market-traders*] an awkward customer who causes trouble but does not buy. **3.** *n* [*Sport*] this is in general use in all competitions for mutual antagonisms, tensions, even overt violence, especially between old or traditional rivals; thus needle match is a competition involving such tensions and intensities.

needle noses *n pl* [*UK*] [*Railways*] railway auditors who check drivers' and guards' work sheets and waybills to discover any potentially unproductive time. See also **razor gang**.

needle time *n* [*UK*] [*Radio*] the proportion of broadcasting time that is, by arrangement with the unions, devoted to recorded music.

needled lead *n* [*Journalism*] a lead sentence or paragraph that is deliberately written in a more sensational style than the facts and story warrant; it comes from the adulterated 'needled beer' of the Prohibition era.

needs sensing *n* [*Government, Politics*] the discovery by bureaucrats and social agencies of what exactly it is that the people want, or claim to want; those who undertake this research are 'needs sensors' and 'needs assessors'. It also denotes the effort made by politicians to find out what it is that the voters want.

need-to-know *a* [*Government*] referring to the concept that no information need be passed on to anyone who does not genuinely 'need to know'; this is a classification that in the event is arbitrary and almost invariably those who use it automatically exclude the media and general public from such a need. See also **eyes only**.

negative carry *n* [*US*] [*Stock market*] a situation where the cost of money borrowed to finance the purchase of shares is greater than the profits yielded by those shares.

negative cost *n* [*Film*] the sum of the costs both **above the line** and **below the line;** it is the cost of producing the finished version of the film, of paying all the bills other than those for advertising, publicity, and printing copies of the film.

negative deficits *n pl* [*Politics*] in governmental economic statements this is an obscurantism for profits.

negative feedback 1. *n* [*Audio*] a signal from the output of an amplifier or electronic network which is applied to an input in a directly opposing phase in order to reduce any distortion and noise present in that input. **2.** *n* [*Government*] feedback that maintains stability by monitoring change and suppressing it when it threatens to alter the status quo.

negative interest *n* [*Economics*] money deducted from or paid out of interest.

negative option *n* [*Business*] the choice that is offered to the consumer in accepting or returning unsolicited goods sent through the post; since no positive option has been taken in ordering the goods, the only ones open have to be negative. See also **inertia selling**.

negative pledge *n* [*Banking*] a clause in an agreement whereby a company who is borrowing from a bank promises not to pledge its assets elsewhere without the bank's consent.

negative segregation *n* [*Metallurgy*] See **inverse segregation**. See also **normal segregation**.

negative sum game *n* [*Business, Economics*] a 'game' played by managers and economists in which the amount that the losers lose exceeds the amount that the winners win.

negative targeting *n* [*Politics*] the concept of

designing one's political campaign not to maximise one's own image and appeal, but to minimise, undermine, and disrupt the efforts made by one's opponent(s), by harping on past errors, assassinating his/her character, using **black propaganda** etc.

negatively privileged *a* [*Sociology*] a euphemism for 'poor'.

negotiated *a* [*Military*] used by the SAS (Special Air Service) commandos to denote the execution of the targets during a mission.

negotiated order *n* [*Sociology*] the concept that social phenomena, especially organisational arrangements, emerge from the continuing process of interaction between people, and the constant negotiation and renegotiation of the terms of social action that this involves.

neighbourhood connection *n* [*US*] [*Crime*] a small-time receiver and re-seller of stolen goods who operates strictly within a limited, local area.

Neil Robinsons *n pl* [*Navy*] stretchers for transferring patients between ships at sea.

nelly *n* [*US*] [*Meat trade*] an old, thin cow suitable only for canning.

Nelson *n* [*Cricket*] the score, by a team or an individual, of 111 runs; originally it was a banking term meaning 1.1.1 and was allegedly derived from Lord Nelson's 'one arm, one eye and one anus'; the score is traditionally considered unlucky for England teams.

Nelson huntaway *n* [*NZ*] [*Farming*] the use of a large stone, deliberately pushed down a slope, to move stock, rather than using a dog to herd them.

NEMO *part phr* [*Radio, TV*] *acro* **Not Emanating from Main Office** referring to any remote, outside broadcast transmitted on TV or radio.

neo *n* [*Science fiction*] a newcomer to science fiction.

neo-conservatism *n* [*Politics*] a style of conservatism that rejects the extremes of liberal/socialist utopianism and continues to believe that democratic capitalism is the ideal method of government, while still allowing for a degree of welfare state interference – payments to the needy, health insurance, etc.

neocorporatism *n* [*Economics*] the close co-operation in public policy between the state and organised economic interests.

neon *n* [*Advertising, Business*] particularly brightly coloured artwork that is used for emphasis and excitement in a presentation.

neopsychic functioning *n* [*New therapies*] in transactional analysis (**TA**) this is the concept of the 'adult', the grown-up life that we have to lead in society in order to survive.

nep *n* [*Weaving*] a bunch of tangled fibres that sometimes forms during the **carding** process.

nephron *n* [*Medicine*] an intern specialising in kidney problems.

nerf *v* [*Hot rods*] to bump another car out of one's

way; thus 'nerfing-bar' is the small, lightweight bumper fixed to a hot rod.

nerf bar *n* [*Custom cars*] a chromed tube that replaces the conventional bumper. See also **nudge bar**.

nerve centre *n* [*UK*] [*Railways*] the yard foreman's office.

nest 1. *v* [*Computing*] to embed a subroutine within a larger routine. **2.** *n* [*Industry*] any compact group of devices working together within a larger set-up.

nesting *n* [*Computing*] the inclusion of a small block of data within a larger routine or block of data.

net net *adv* [*Book trade*] a term denoting that a book will not be sold by publishers to the trade at any discount at all.

net worth *n* [*Finance*] See **equity capital**.

net-net *a* [*Business*] absolutely final; the synthesis of a number of previously determined **bottom lines**.

nettles, also **knittles, knettles** *n* [*Sailing, Ropework*] rope under 1 in. in circumference. See also **small stuff**.

network 1. *v* [*Computing*] to link together a number of machines – often as terminals operating from a large central computer – in order to pool data, speed up operation and to enable many operators to gain a degree of access and computing power that they could not obtain working alone on a single machine. See also **LAN**. **2.** *v* [*Government*] to link a bureaucratic department to the area it is supposed to be serving by forming miniature bureaucracies that link those in the **field** with those in the office. **3.** *n* [*Management*] a diagram used in project network techniques for the evaluation and analysis of the component activities and events in a particular project and the definition of their various inter-relationships. A network consists of lines – arrows – and points (or circles or rectangles) – nodes. In effect the network is a graph, but its techniques are almost always different from those employed in normal mathematical graph theory. **4.** *n* [*Sociology*] in family and urban sociology, the network describes the system of personal relationships in which an individual is involved.

network architecture *n* [*Computing*] the design and construction of a communications network with regard to the communication it performs and the physical connections of its components. Such architecture deals directly with encoding and transmitting of information, control of the data flow and of any errors within it, techniques for addressing the various subscribers to the network and analysis of the network's overall performance. See also **architecture, network 1**.

network front end *n* [*Computing*] an extra processor or other system which is used specifically to connect a computer into a network which already has a central computer. The intention of the extra machine is to improve overall network performance. See also **network 1**.

network programme *n* [*TV*] any programme that is transmitted by all the companies of a television network; such programmes may be assumed to attract larger audiences and have greater importance in scheduling than items of more local interest.

networking *n* [*Sociology*] the conscious and deliberate cultivation of a peer group for the benefits that will derive from these extended relationships; usually in a professional, working context.

neuks *n pl* [*UK*] [*Coal-mining*] the corners or ends of the coalface.

neutral *a* [*Wine-tasting*] with no positive flavour or marked physical characteristics; a common feature of many blended wines.

neutron bomb *n* [*Military*] See **enhanced radiation weapon**.

neutron quark *n* [*Science*] See **down quark**. See also **up quark**.

never *n* [*Navy*] a sailor who regularly manages to avoid work and other onerous duties.

never, do a *v* [*Navy*] to shirk one's duties.

never enough *phr* [*New therapies*] in **primal** therapy this is a stock phrase used to explain how as a child in a 'non-giving' world, one could never get what it was one actually wanted.

new *n* [*Navy*] a naval cadet in his first term on a training ship; the naval equivalent of a public school fag.

New Age *n* [*Sociology*] the new spirituality that emerged from the 'counter-culture' and the 'alternative society' of the 1960s and which developed into a number of cult religions, variations on traditional Oriental themes and a general move into the mystic. See also **new therapies**.

New Brutalism *n* [*Architecture*] an 'ethical' movement in British architecture of the 1950s which sought to replace the diluted styles of the period with a specific dedication towards the original strength and integrity of modern architecture, using structures and materials 'honestly' and 'truthfully' in the style of Le Corbusier.

new class *n* [*Politics*] a term coined in 1957 in Milovan Djilas' 'The New Class'; it refers to the emergent elite of the various Communist bloc states, officials and bureaucrats who were strengthening their own position and, just like the bourgeoisie, enjoying privilege, corruption, bribery and consumer luxuries far beyond the dreams of their alleged peers, the masses.

new Commonwealth *n* [*Government*] an identifying catch-all used by UK bureaucrats and politicians for those immigrants arriving from states other than Canada, Australia and New Zealand, ie: coloured immigrants. This euphemism is made doubly otiose, since apart from its essential racism, it is not even chronologically accurate since India was hardly a 'new' member of the

Empire on which the Commonwealth was based. See also **first Australians, native Americans**.

new Communist man, also **Soviet man** *n* [*Politics*] Marx's model citizen, a character based on ten essential criteria: 1. ideologically pure, 2. honest and brave, 3. law-abiding, 4. no acquisitive instincts, 5. he subordinates his individual needs and desires to those of the common good, 6. he respects and protects social property, 7. he is socially co-operative, 8. he enjoys all-round occupations and recreational activities, 9. he is wholeheartedly Marxist, 10. he is a committed internationalist.

new frontier *n* [*US*] [*Politics*] a slogan and a concept initially coined in the 1930s, but brought to prominence by President John F. Kennedy when he accepted the Democratic Party nomination in 1960: 'We stand together on the edge of a new frontier – the frontier of the 1960s, a frontier of unknown opportunities and paths, a frontier of unfulfilled hopes and threats. . . . (it) is not a set of promises, it is a set of challenges'.

new informalists, also **new colourists** *n pl* [*Art*] the general description of a number of contemporary US painters who produce large-scale abstract pictures of a highly decorative nature and who pursue 'the natural way of forming matter' in opposition to the 'formalism' of US painting in the 1960s.

new journalism *n* [*Journalism*] a genre of involved and concerned (although not especially campaigning or 'investigative') journalism that emerged in the mid–1960s from such writers as Tom Wolfe, Gay Talese, Jimmy Breslin, Hunter S. Thompson, et al. Aiming to resurrect the 'social realism' of the 19th century, the new journalists rejected the traditional objective style of reporting in favour of a trumpeted personal viewpoint, unrestrained speculation on almost any aspect of the story, and a lack of worry as to the absolute facts and other 'straight' aspects of writing.

New Left *n* [*Politics*] this term was coined as a description by US sociologist C. Wright Mills (1916–1962); the New Left were youthful radicals who rejected the traditions of the **Old Left** and attempted to inject novelty and energy into what was, in the wake of McCarthy, Hungary, and similar attacks and disillusions, more a name than an active, radical movement. At its height during the protests against the Vietnam War, the New Left barely survived the end of US involvement, which was the source, undoubtedly, of its main rallying point.

New Look *n* [*Fashion*] the style of women's clothing introduced in Paris by Christian Dior in 1947; skirts were longer and fuller and the whole ethos demonstrated a rejection of the austerity of the war years.

new look *n* [*Politics*] the alteration in US defence policy that developed during the Korean War and which started the trend towards de-emphasising conventional forces in favour of almost total dependence on nuclear strategic planning.

new materialism *n* [*Art*] a broad category that embraces any artist who works in 'unworthy' materials in order to produce an amalgam of painting, sculpture and stage props.

new psychology *n* [*Psychology*] varieties of recent psychology that concentrate on studying the irrational and unconscious motivations for human behaviour.

new Puritanism *n* [*Sociology*] a derogatory description used by supporters of nuclear power in the US to attack those who are attempting to control the further spread of nuclear power in the overall US energy programme.

new sensualism *n* [*Architecture*] a movement in modern architectural design whereby buildings are sculptural and possess a sensuous plasticity of form in contrast to the hard-edged rectilinearity that is usually equated with 'modern architecture'.

new task *n* [*Marketing*] See **extended problem solving**.

new therapies *n pl* [*Sociology*] a variety of modern quasi-psychiatric therapies, including **est**, transactional analysis (**TA**), **rebirthing, co-counselling, primal therapy**, etc, which have become popular in the past decade. Most of them can be traced back to easy simplifications of Freudian theory and practice and, unlike Freud himself, they aim to eliminate the lengthy learning processes of classical analysis, promising instead to provide all who can pay their fees with a speedy and almost miraculous 'cure'. See **New Age**.

new thing *n* [*Arts*] a development in jazz and black writing in the 1970s which emphasised original and aggressive playing and writing, and reflected the developments in black consciousness of the time.

new time **1.** *n* [*Stock market*] when used in connection with dealings this means having the settlement postponed to the next settling day. **2.** *n* [*Stock market*] when used in connection with prices, this means having prices quoted for the next settling day before the previous settlement is completed.

new wave **1.** *n* [*Film*] a trend in film-making that developed in France during the 1950s, epitomised in the work of such directors as François Truffaut and Jean-Luc Godard; it comes from the Fr. 'nouvelle vague'. **2.** *n* [*Pop music*] the 'punk' music of 1976–77, epitomised in the work of such bands as the Sex Pistols, the Damned, the Clash and the Jam.

newbuilding *n* [*Ship-building*] a newly constructed ship.

news **1.** *n* [*Advertising*] a copyline in an advertisement that points out to the consumer some aspect of its specific novelty; this may not in fact be new, but simply a new way of looking at the product,

or using it afresh, etc. **2.** *n* [*Espionage*] the conveying to a blackmail target that he/she has in fact been usefully entrapped and that it might be wise to start paying off in information, etc., unless embarrassing exposure is preferable – which targets rarely feel is the case.

news advisory *n* [*Public relations*] a brief announcement of a forthcoming event, designed to alert the media to the event, without actually informing them as yet of any details as to its content.

news break **1.** *n* [*Media*] any newsworthy item of information. **2.** *n* [*Publishing*] specifically in the 'New Yorker', these are small amusing items culled from US magazines and newspapers, given an amusing headline and printed at the bottom of columns in the magazine.

news hole *n* [*Journalism*] the space on a newspaper page which is reserved for news, as opposed to advertisements.

news peg *n* [*Media*] a news story that forms the basis of an editorial, feature, cartoon, etc.

newsies *n pl* [*US*] [*Politics*] shorthand for the media in general; it is further subdivided into 'wires' (wire services), 'reels' (TV), and 'stills' (print journalism).

newspaper *n* [*UK*] [*Prisons*] a thirty-day jail sentence; allegedly it comes from the time it was considered an illiterate would take to read one.

Newsthink *n* [*Journalism*] a term coined by Arthur Herzog; it is the ethos of modern journalism – the vested interest of the news media in creating the news on which they thrive, and the attitude that accompanies this, justifying among other excesses exaggeration, misquotation, invasion of privacy and 'tagging, trending and countertrending'.

newszine **1.** *n* [*Science fiction*] a magazine containing only news and information; it is published every two weeks, or at least monthly. **2.** *n* [*TV*] any fan magazine that contains only facts and information and rejects any amateur fiction.

next friend *n* [*Law*] a person who acts on behalf of someone who, either from infirmity or legal incapacity, is unable to act for him/herself.

nextish *n* [*Science fiction*] the following issue of a science fiction magazine.

nib **1.** *n* [*Building*] a small projection on the underside of a tile, by which it is hung on the battens of the roof. **2.** *n* [*Glass-making*] a small protrusion found at the corner of a piece of glass, due to faulty cutting. **3.** *n* [*Painting*] a speck of solid matter in a coat of paint or varnish.

niblick *n* [*Golf*] the traditional name for the Number 9 iron.

nibs *n pl* [*Painting*] small pieces of foreign matter which are seen projecting above the surface of paint or varnish.

NIC *n* [*Economics*] acro **newly industrialising**

N

country this refers to **Third World** countries that are beginning to export manufactures.

nickelling n [Military] the fouling of a gun's bore by small pieces of the cupro-nickel casing of the bullet.

nicker n [UK] [Market-traders] a pound note.

niddy-noddy n [Weaving] a two-ended T-frame with top and bottom Ts at right angles to each other, on which yarn is wound from a spinning wheel or spindle to make a skein.

NIE n [Military, Espionage] acro **National Intelligence Estimate** the CIA's regular assessments of the current strength of the USSR's nuclear capability, and the current and future structure of its nuclear forces.

nifty fifty n [US] [Business] the fifty stocks preferred by major financial institutions.

nigger, also **steam nigger** n [Logging] a long-toothed power-propelled lever arm used to position logs on a carriage, as in a sawmill.

nigger brand n [US] [Cattlemen] a galled sore on the horse's back, caused by careless riding.

nigger local n [US] [Railways] a slow freight train.

niggerhead 1. n [Industry] a spool attached to a hoisting drum; it is used to move loads by tightening or loosening a rope wound around the spool. 2. n [Printing] a nail fixed into the form of a cylinder press to produce a regular mark on the edge of the printed sheet as a guide to folding and trimming. 3. n [Shoe-making] a machine that secures the last to the upper by driving in a series of tacks along the upper edge of the shoe.

niggerheads n pl [Navy] a row of bollards along the edge of a dock.

nightcap 1. n [Baseball, Horse-racing] the final game of a night-time double-header; it is also used for the last horse race on a day's card. 2. n [Military] acro **Night Combat Air Patrol**. See also **dadcap**.

night-cap n [Horse-racing] a hood that fits closely over the horse's head and halfway down its neck.

nightingale ward n [Medicine] a type of hospital ward in which several patients can be accommodated together.

nightshift n [Management] the night shift of a three-shift – morning, evening, night – system. See also **backshift, foreshift**.

nightwatch n [Military] See **kneecap**.

nightwatchman n [Cricket] a batsman from the lower order of the team who is sent in to defend when a wicket has fallen within a few minutes of the close of the day's play and the captain does not wish to expose a recognised batsman.

NIH syndrome n [Advertising] abbr of **Not Invented Here syndrome** the term was coined by Prof. Levitt of Harvard University to describe any campaign which originates outside the country in which it is to be run and which is thus very likely to be opposed by indigenous producers.

Nina from Carolina n [Gambling] in craps dice, the point of nine.

nine and nine a [Midwifery] referring to a baby in perfect condition, with no problems.

nine, ten, jack n [Cricket] the tailenders of the batting side, coming in at numbers 9, 10 and 11.

nineteenth hole n [Golf] the clubhouse, and in particular its bar.

ninety n [TV] a 'made-for-TV' film that last for ninety minutes.

ninety day wonder n [Military] the graduate of a ninety day officer's training course and thus an inexperienced, possibly incompetent, soldier in the field.

ninety days n [Gambling] in craps, the point of 9.

nip 1. n [Tobacco] the end of the cigar which is held in the mouth. 2. n [Sailing, Ropework] the spot within a knot where the end is gripped and thus kept secure; thus to nip means to become secure.

nip out, also **pinch out** n [Coal-mining] the local thinning or disappearance of a coal seam due to tectonic movement.

nipper 1. n [Book-binding] a power press that compresses the leaves of books during the binding process. 2. n [Fishing] a pair of heavy gloves or mittens worn by deep-sea fishermen for safer handling of the nets. 3. n [UK] [Railways] the junior member of any gang working on the railways. 4. n [Sailing] a piece of braided cord used to prevent cables, to which they are attached, from slipping. 5. n [Textiles] the cushion plate, part of a cotton spinning machine.

nippers 1. n pl [US] [Police] chain-grip activated handcuffs. 2. n pl [Sailing, Ropework] small ropes which secure the **messenger** to the cable.

nipple 1. n [Industry] a variety of joint which is used between rubber, leather, metal or other tubes and pipes. 2. n [Oil rigs] a variety of valve used on an oil-rig. See also **sloper**.

nipple chaser n [Oil rigs] an oil field worker responsible for the valves on the pipe. See also **nipple**.

nit n [Pool] a player who will not gamble; it is the ultimate insult in pool.

nitro 1. n [Cars] abbr of **nitromethane** the specialist fuel used by drag racers, consisting of 90% nitromethane, plus small quantities of methanol, propylene oxide, acetone and castor oil. See also **dope**. 2. n [Hot rods] abbr of **nitromethane** (see 1) or a similar nitrated compound used for racing fuel mixtures.

nitrogen narcosis n [Diving] See **rapture of the deep**.

nix n [UK] [Market-traders] nothing, zero.

nixie n [US] [Postal services] misaddressed mail; hence it means the clerk who has to sort it out.

nixy n, excl [UK] [Market-traders] nothing; as an exclamation it means: 'it's not worth the bother', 'it's rubbish', etc. See also **nix**.

N

NMCC *n* [*Military*] abbr of **National Military Command Centre** the 'War Room' of the Pentagon, one of the four US military command centres which comprise the US National Military Command System and which would conduct a nuclear war. The oldest of the NMCS posts, the NMCC was orginally known as the 'Joint War Room Annexe' and was set up in 1959 after the panic engendered by the launch of Sputnik 1. See also **NMCS**.

NMCS *n* [*Military*] abbr of **National Military Command System** the command system of all US nuclear forces, established in the late 1950s to co-ordinate the previously disparate branches of US defence. The consolidation followed the US military reaction to the launch of Sputnik 1, the implication of which was that the Soviets had developed a rocket powerful enough to challenge US ICBM superiority. See also **NMCC, NORAD, SAC**.

no day *n* [*Merchant navy*] the day lost when a ship crosses the International Date Line.

no go *v* [*Film*] to turn down a potential film-making deal.

no heroics *n* [*US*] [*Medicine*] a notation on the chart of a terminally ill patient to stop medical staff from taking any remedial action if the patient suffers a heart attack, since both the patient and his/her family would prefer not to postpone the inevitable death any further.

no joy [*Military*] air intercept code for: I have been unsuccessful; I have no interception.

no Mayday *n* [*US*] [*Medicine*] a code issued to the relevant staff advising them not to attempt further resuscitation of a given patient should that patient's condition decline severely. See also **no heroics**.

no show *n* [*US*] [*Industrial relations*] any worker, especially one on a government payroll, who collects a salary but fails to turn up to perform the job; by extension it also means a 'fake' worker who does not exist, but whose name is put on the payroll and whose wages are collected by the corrupt official who has arranged the paperwork.

no side *n* [*Rugby*] the signal for the end of the game, the final whistle; possibly it comes from the idealised sporting concept of their being no hard feelings – 'side' – once the rough and tumble of a match is over.

no sky line *n* [*Architecture*] a line in a room from behind which no sky is visible to those looking out of a window from table height.

no squash *adv* [*US*] [*Medicine*] referring to irreparable brain damage; it is caused by trauma, drug/alcohol abuse, inter-cranial haemorrhage, etc.

noa word *n* [*Linguistics*] the use of a euphemism or, generally, a milder word in place of an obscenity, blasphemy, etc; eg: 'Gosh' for 'God', 'sugar!' for 'shit!', etc.

Noah's Ark *n* [*UK*] [*Market-traders*] one who accompanies a **nark** and puts him/her off buying; possibly it comes from rhyming slang.

Noah's syndrome *n* [*Business*] a management situation in which a scheme is prepared to cope with possibly adverse circumstances and the proponent of that scheme refuses to relinquish any vestige of it, even though the reality has no bearing on the pessimistic theories embodied in his/her plan.

nobbings *n pl* [*UK*] [*Circus*] the takings at the box office.

noble *a* [*Wine-tasting*] used to describe marked stature and **breed**, very great **elegance**.

noble gases *n pl* [*Science*] the elements helium, neon, argon, krypton, xenon and radon, all of which are gaseous at room temperature.

noble rot *n* [*Wine-tasting*] from Fr. 'pourriture noble': a common grey mould – Botrytis civierea – which affects grapes and which is deliberately cultivated to enhance certain French and German sweet wines and the Hungarian Tokay.

no-brainer *n* [*US*] [*Stock market*] a market in which the direction of prices is obvious and thus requires no in-depth analysis.

no-city strategy *n* [*Military*] See **counterforce**. See also **countervalue**.

no-cut contract *n* [*US*] [*Sport*] a contract offered to a professional sportsman which guarantees that he will not be **cut** from the team at any time during the pre-season practice period or during the season that follows.

nod *v* [*Theatre*] to take the traditional bow at the end of the performance.

noddies, also **nodders, nods and winks** *n pl* [*TV*] the interviewer's reaction shots, which are often no more than ritualistic nodding at the answers to his/her questions; these shots are usually filmed after the actual interview and edited into the tape prior to transmission.

nodding donkey *n* [*Oil industry*] the device which continues pumping oil from the well when the oil stocks cannot rise naturally at the required production rate; the device can be compared with a perpetually nodding donkey's head.

noddle *v* [*Music*] to improvise on a musical instrument, or to play a particularly decorative series of notes.

noddy cap *n* [*Military*] the protective cap that covers the sensitive nose of a missile; it comes from the pointed cap worn by a popular children's comic character.

node *n* [*Computing*] See **atom**.

nodis *n* [*Government*] abbr of **no distribution** a classification level affixed to sensitive documents; such material is meant only for the individual to whom it is sent on a strictly **eyes-only** basis. See also **exdis, limdis**.

noforn *n* [*US*] [*Government*] abbr of **no foreigners** a notation on classified documents that prohibits anyone but a US citizen from reading them. See also **exdis, limdis, nodis**.

nog *n* [*Coal-mining*] a steel or wooden wedge inserted in a cut in the coal-face to delay or prevent convergence and to stop the coal spilling from the face.

noggin *n* [*Building, Plastering*] a timber cross-member between the main members of a timber-framed construction.

no-hitter *n* [*Baseball*] a game in which one team achieves no hits.

noils *n pl* [*Weaving*] the short fibres which are removed from the long fibres in the combing of wool for worsted spinning.

noise 1. *n* [*Computing*] any changes to the electronic signal that ought not to be there; any interference. See also **false drop, glitch 1. 2.** *n* [*Electronics, Communications*] any signal disturbance that interferes with normal operations. **3.** *n* [*Electronics, Communications*] any random, undesired signal. **4.** *n* [*Libraries*] the percentage of irrelevant material that may be produced by a search, usually through applying insufficiently stringent search methods. **5.** *n* [*Photo-typesetting*] unwanted **pixels** or **aliases** which occur in the mosaic or image of the character; such unnecessary elements can be removed electronically.

noise bar *n* [*Video*] the bar of white flashes that appears during freeze frame or slow motion operations.

noise immunity *n* [*Computing*] the extent of external disturbances that a digital circuit can over-ride without suffering errors in its performance. See also **noise 1.**

noise level *n* [*Government, Business, Science*] the general level of activity in any organisation, the existence of which may well serve to defeat even the most scrupulous researcher, since he/she will lose sight of a specific objective, eg. a particular aspect of that organisation, among the continual mass of comings and goings.

noise the edge *v* [*UK*] [*Market-traders*] to avoid any trouble.

noise word *n* [*Computing*] a word included in a program to improve its readability but which is not necessarily employed in running that program and as such is ignored by the machine.

noisy *a* [*Hunting*] said of a hound which **speaks** without having actually found the **line**.

no-knock *n* [*US*] [*Police*] a raid by the police on a private home that comes without permission or warning; the provisions of a legitimate search warrant specifically provide for the entering officers to identify themselves and ask permission to enter.

nolified, also **noly** *a* [*UK*] [*Market-traders*] simple-minded, foolish.

nolle pross *v phr* [*Law*] abbr of **nolle prosequi** this comes from Lat. meaning 'I am unwilling to pursue'; it is used when the prosecution abandons its case against the defendant.

nolo contendere *v phr* [*Law*] this comes from Lat. meaning 'I do no wish to plead'; it is a plea by a defendant that does not actually admit to guilt per se, but which does lay him/her open to judgement and sentence without a defence, although the truth of the charge can still be defended in a collateral proceeding.

no-load fund *n* [*Stock market*] a mutual fund which charges little or no commission to buyers and involves no sales organisation.

no-loads *n pl* [*Stock market*] shares which are sold at their net asset value without any commission being added.

nomadic furniture *n* [*Design*] on the principle that the average American moves house every three to four years, this is a style of furniture designed for easy shipment, stacking, assembly, etc.

nomenklatura *n* [*Government*] used in the USSR to mean the Party elite.

nominal price *n* [*Futures market*] price quotations on futures for a period in which no actual trading took place.

nominal yield weapon *n* [*Military*] a nuclear bomb with an explosive **yield** of approximately 20,000 tons.

nommus! *n* [*UK*] [*Crime*] backslang meaning 'someone!' It is a warning shout at the approach of police and is used by market traders, illegal street traders, con-men, pitch and toss players, etc.

nomothetic [*Sociology*] methods of study which seek to find general laws which subsume individual cases. See also **idiothetic.**

non bonko *adv* [*TV*] out of sync; it was allegedly coined by a monoglot Italian director at a loss for the correct English.

non sync *n* [*TV, Film*] See **wild track.**

nonce *n* [*UK*] [*Prisons*] any sexual offender.

nondense index *n* [*Libraries*] a database index that provides information on the location of a group of records; once the location is established, the records must be scanned sequentially to find the correct one. See also **dense index.**

nondescript *n* [*UK*] [*Police*] any unmarked police car used for surveillance purposes. See also **danny 2.**

non-dips *n pl* [*UK*] [*Diplomacy*] abbr of **non-diplomats** those members of an Embassy staff – secretaries, clerks, drivers, etc. – who are not accorded diplomatic status with the relevant privileges and immunities. See also **dips.**

non-judgmental attitude *n* [*Social work*] the belief, considered fundamental to effective casework, that concepts of guilt or innocence are irrelevant to the assessment of a situation, although some evaluation must be made as to the client's attitudes, standards and actions.

non-procedural language *n* [*Computing*] a language, designed for fifth generation computers, which permits the user simply to specify the desired end result rather than the means required to arrive there. See also **procedural language.**

N

non-relational art *n* [*Art*] while 'relational' paintings depend for their effect on the idea of 'figures in a field', non-relational paintings have a single uniform space, avoid depth effects, and stretch from edge to edge across the canvas, thus giving greater importance to the shape of that canvas.

non-secrets *n pl* [*Espionage*] de-classified information, now in the public domain.

non-specific inflammatory bowel syndrome *n* [*UK*] [*Medicine*] this means 'the patient has a stomach ache, and the doctor cannot diagnose it'.

non-theatrical 1. *a* [*Film*] an exhibitor's term which embraces any show for which no paid admission is charged: charities, school outings, etc. **2.** *a* [*Film*] used of all showings of 16mm films.

non-volatile memory *n* [*Computing*] a memory system which will retain its content even if the machine's power supply is switched off; ie: **disks**, tapes and the internal **ROM**.

Noo *n* [*Navy*] Scotland.

noodle 1. *n* [*Art*] a work that lacks artistic vigour. **2.** *v* [*Art*] to over-ornament a work of art by adding an excess of detail, redefinitions and 'corrections'.

noodles, also **spaghetti** *n pl* [*Tyre-making*] long strings of rubber that are created when the knives of the pelletizer machine fail to cut the rubber properly as it moves through the holes in the machine.

noodling 1. *n* [*Aus.*] [*Mining*] sifting carefully through the refuse dumps of old mines, looking for any gold or gemstones that might have been overlooked. **2.** *n* [*Film, TV*] music that is played while the final titles or credits are rolled. **3.** *n* [*Music*] tuning up with a variety of practice runs, trills, etc; thus in jazz it means playing a variety of improvised and elaborate series of notes.

noojaks *n pl* [*Navy*] new entry, inexperienced seamen.

Nooky-poo *n* [*US*] [*Navy*] USN Advanced School of Nuclear Power.

noon balloon *n* [*Air travel*] the 'rush hour' in air traffic control at Miami Airport when from 11.30am to 2.00pm a plane lands or takes off every 45 seconds.

no-op instruction *n* [*Computing*] an instruction that causes no action in the program; it is often used to compensate for time adjustments in running the program. See also **do nothing instruction**.

NORAD *n* [*Military*] acro **North American Aerospace Defense Command** an elaborate network of complementary and overlapping surveillance systems designed to warn of imminent nuclear attack. NORAD – buried one third of a mile beneath Cheyenne Mt, Colorado – was opened in 1966 as one of the three hardened US command posts (the others are **SAC HQ** at Ofutt Air Force Base and the War Room in the Pentagon). Originally established in the 1950s to locate and intercept Soviet bomber strikes, NORAD today, plugged into 19 radars and 9 special telescopic cameras across the world, is simply charged with spotting the incoming missiles and reporting their launch, progress and supposed targets, to the President, the Pentagon and SAC. The NORAD complex also includes the Aerospace Defense Command (ADCOM) which in turn controls the Space Defense Operations Centre (SPADOC).

norfolks *n pl* [*Music*] this comes from rhyming slang: 'norfolk broads' meaning 'chords'. See also **norwegians**.

normal segregation *n* [*Metallurgy*] segregation in which the amount of certain constituents and/or impurities is greater than that in the surrounding metal. See also **inverse segregation**.

normal working area *n* [*Industry*] the space within which a seated or standing worker can reach and use tools, materials and equipment when his/her elbows fall naturally by the side of the body. See also **maximum working area**.

normalisation *n* [*Politics*] the return of a socialist country to the status quo after a period of liberalisation, eg: Czechoslovakia after the 'Prague Spring' of 1968 and Poland after the imposition of martial law in 1981.

norman *n* [*Sailing, Ropework*] the horizontal iron pin in a **bitt**.

normative *a* [*Education*] referring to a pupil who achieves the normal standards, ie: an average child.

normative forecasting *n* [*Business*] a system of forecasting that posits a future demand, mission or goal, and then attempts to plot backwards in time from the achievement of that goal through the steps that would have to be made to take a company from 'today' – starting from scratch – all the way up to that achievement. Rather than predicting some idealised future, normative forecasting is designed to take into account a variety of obstacles, problems and setbacks, focusing not on what might but on what should happen.

norm-referenced *a* [*Education*] referring to examination results that are judged against the performance of all the children taking the papers, rather than against an absolute standard that is established without considering the children concerned.

North *n* [*Economics*] the industrially advanced and technologically sophisticated countries of the world, the bulk of which lie North of the Equator.

north-easter *n* [*Navy*] non-entitlement for pay which applies to those sailors who are deprived in this way as a form of punishment; it comes from the abbreviation 'NE'.

northpaw *n* [*Baseball*] a right-handed player.

norwegians *n pl* [*Music*] from rhyming slang:

N

'norwegian fjords' meaning 'chords'. See also **norfolks**.

nose 1. *n* [*Glass-making*] the tip of a blowing iron. 2. *n* [*Horse-racing*] See **neck**. 3. *n* [*UK*] [*Radio*] the 'top' of a story, the single line that sums up everything that follows; it is the equivalent of print journalism's **lead**. 4. *n* [*US*] [*Road transport*] the front end of a **semi-trailer**. 5. *n* [*UK*] [*Surfing*] the front 12 in. of a surfboard.

nose and deck *v* [*Custom cars*] to remove all extraneous ornamentation from the front of a car and from the boot lid; ie. hood ornaments, the maker's logo, handles, etc.

nose, on the *adv* [*Photography*] estimating the exposure by using a light meter.

nose-in *n* [*Air travel*] the position of a commercial aircraft that is waiting on its stand for passengers to complete boarding.

nose-picker *n* [*Commerce*] a salesman's derogatory description of a potential client who cannot make up his/her mind and who in fact has no real power of decision-making within the firm.

nosepicker *n* [*Journalism*] See **wart**.

nose-riding *n* [*Surfing*] See **hang five**.

no-show *n* [*Air travel*] any passenger who fails to take the seat booked in his/her name.

nosism *n* [*Linguistics*] the pretentious use of the first person plural when referring only to the first person singular; the 'royal we' as extended to egocentric commoners; it comes from Lat. nos meaning we. See also **illeism, tuism**.

nostril shot *n* [*TV, Film*] an extreme close-up.

nostro accounts *n pl* [*Banking*] accounts maintained by home banks with banks abroad.

not a fin! *n* [*Angling*] nothing doing for the fisherman.

not doing well *adv* [*Medicine*] a euphemism for dying.

not for attribution *a* [*Journalism*] this refers to the release of information to a journalist on the understanding that its source will not be mentioned nor even hinted at within the written story; in the case of any difficulties arising with the publication of such a story, the journalist is honour bound to deal with any such problems without incriminating the source. See also **lobby terms, on**.

notams *n pl* [*Air travel*] regular notices issued to all aircrew, containing detailed information about the flights.

notching *n* [*Photo-typesetting*] the removal of **pixels** from the **bit-map** of a character in order to avoid distortion when the character is generated on to the screen of a photo-typesetter.

note *n* [*Perfumery*] one of the basic components of a perfume, and thus one that gives it its essential character.

note verbale *n* [*Politics*] in diplomatic use this is an unsigned note, written in the third person, which acts as a type of memorandum between nations.

notice *n* [*Theatre*] a review in the press.

notice day *n* [*Futures market*] a day on which notices of intent to deliver pertaining to a specified delivery month may be issued.

notice of dishonour *n* [*Banking, Commerce*] a notice that must be given to the drawer and each endorser of a bill of exchange by the holder when the bill has been dishonoured.

notice paper *n* [*UK*] [*Government*] a paper supplied to members of the House of Commons that gives details of the day's proceedings.

notice up *n* [*Theatre*] the show is due to close.

noting *n* [*Law, Banking*] the action by a notary in proving the non-acceptance or non-payment of a bill of exchange when it becomes due.

noting score *n* [*Advertising*] the number of readers/viewers who have been found to have noted – registered, rather than understood or acted upon – a given advertisement.

notional weekend *n* [*TV, Industrial relations*] days other than Saturday or Sunday that are counted as the weekend for the purpose of fulfilling union agreements which state that members must have two days off per week, even if they work over the real weekend.

notionals *n pl* [*Espionage*] fake businesses which exist only on their headed notepaper and which serve as the cover employer of members of an intelligence agency or as the sponsor of various activities which are simply fronts for subversive, **black operations**.

no-touch *n* [*Medicine*] a method of dressing wounds in which no-one may touch either the wound or its dressings.

Nottingham *n* [*UK*] [*Building, Plastering*] plaster with a pink finish. See also **Kent**.

Nottingham style *adv* [*Angling*] in coarse fishing this is a method of casting involving a loop of line drawn off in the left hand, ready to be shot at the required moment in the cast.

noun-banging *n* [*Linguistics*] the clustering together of a number of successive nouns to promote an important-sounding portmanteau description, often a bureaucratic, military or sociological obfuscation. It is the essence of much modern jargon; eg: 'hard target capable first strike survivability'.

nouveau roman *n* [*Literary criticism*] a term coined by Alain Robbe-Grillet around 1955 and further expanded in a book of essays 'Pour un nouveau roman' (1963). In essence, Robbe-Grillet rejected such traditional trappings of the novel as plot, narrative, character delineation and analysis; he replaced them with a novel concentrating on things, a systematised, analytical and highly detailed record of objects – rooms, adorning people, etc. It was through such infinite accumulations of detail that the reader was to appreciate the mental state of those who in the book were experiencing or seeing these objects.

nouvelle vague *n* [*Film*] See **new wave 1**.

N

novation 1. *n* [*Law*] the agreement to replace one party to a contract with a new party; the new party automatically assumes the right and obligations of its predecessor. 2. *n* [*Law*] the replacement of an older debt or obligation with a newer one.

novelist *n* [*USSR*] [*Prisons*] a prisoner who makes a confession, voluntary or otherwise.

novelty *n* [*Fashion*] a type of fabric that is made from more than one basic fibre and which may be found in an exotic or unusual weave.

novocain *n* [*Espionage*] built in 'suspicion deadeners' that a **principal** in the CIA ties into the preliminary offers which initiate the recruitment of a full-time agent so as to regulate the pace of 'conscience expansion' that will eventually create a working operative.

no-win *a* [*Business, Politics*] often found as in 'no-win situation' or 'no-win contest'; it means any conflict or situation from which the protagonist(s) is/are unable to extract himself/themselves without suffering some form of defeat or loss.

NPC speciality *n* [*US*] [*Medicine*] abbr of **No Patient Care speciality** after an initial year as an intern, all junior doctors must opt for a speciality in which they will make their career; NPC specialities include anaesthesiology, dermatology, opthalmology, pathology and psychiatry. See also **Derm, Gas, Path, Rays**.

NPO *n* [*US*] [*Medicine*] abbr of **nil per oram** a Lat phrase meaning nothing by mouth; it is a notice placed on a patient's bed, usually prior to an operation.

N.S.B., also **N.A.B., N.B.A.** *n* [*UK*] [*Buses*] abbr of **No Service Bus, No Available Bus, No Bus Available** when a London Transport bus, scheduled for a conductor and driver, is off the road for repairs, such a bus is unavailable for that crew to work.

NSI *n* [*US*] [*Government*] acro **National Security Information** any information the disclosure of which could be expected to cause at least identifiable damage to the national security; it touches many related areas including military, nuclear, scientific, diplomatic and technological intelligence among others.

'ntasciatu *a* [*Crime*] this comes from Sicilian 'dried out' and in the Italian Mafia it is a description of the victim of an assassination (with a sawn-off shotgun) from whom the blood has drained.

NTP *v* [*Stock market*] abbr of **Not To Press** when a security has only a limited market, a jobber may well sell shares that he does not actually own on the understanding that the buying broker will not immediately press for delivery.

nuance *v* [*Politics*] to approach any topic with extremes of subtlety, always emphasising the 'grey shades' rather than harsh blacks and whites.

nubbins *n pl* [*US*] [*Farming*] undeveloped ears of corn, often a second ear.

nucflash [*Military*] US Department of Defense Nuclear Accident Code for: 1. an accident involving nuclear material which has the potential of sparking off an actual war with the USSR; 2. the appearance of an (as yet) unidentified object on missile early-warning radar.

nuclear art *n* [*Art*] a short lived movement, popular in Italy around 1957, which opposed all fixed forms of art, particularly any type of geometric, abstract creations; in their place it proposed experimentation with a variety of automatic techniques.

nuclear cinc *n* [*Military*] abbr of **nuclear commander-in-chief** the overall C-in-C – the President – plus C-in-C Atlantic, Pacific and Europe; all nuclear cincs work from an airborne command post which would be launched as soon as a positive indication of incoming hostile missiles was received. See also **kneecap, Looking Glass plane**.

nuclear freeze *n* [*Military*] a nuclear freeze does not seek to reduce weapons or to promote disarmament, but simply to ban any further production of weapons, either in their current forms or as new systems. A freeze would demand an end to the production of the fissionable material used in nuclear weapons of the manufacture and testing of warheads, the production and deployment of missiles and the testing of any new strategic bombers.

nuclear thimbles *n pl* [*Science*] special containers which hold radio-active waste and are designed by the Atomic Energy Commission to hold some 103 million gallons of waste each.

nuclear threshold *n* [*Military, Politics*] the time when nuclear weapons are finally used for the first time.

nuclear umbrella *n* [*Military*] the concept that US nuclear weapons are to be used in the defence of European countries as well as of the continental US. Such a concept, given the relative paucity of European arsenals and the proximity of the Soviet threat, gives the US a certain degree of leverage over its ostensible allies.

nuclear winter *n* [*Military*] the concept, currently popular amongst nuclear theorists, that the result of a prolonged nuclear interchange would be the destruction of the climate as we know it; instead, beneath perpetual clouds of radioactive debris, would be increasingly colder temperatures, which would ruin crops, human and animal life and condemn the survivors of the war to a minimal existence in an endless 'winter'. See also **greenhouse effect 1**.

nucleus *n* [*Computing*] See **kernel**.

nude contract, also **bare, naked contract** *n* [*Law*] an agreement which provides no consideration – mutual gain for each party – and which has no binding force unless it is a contract under seal.

NUDETS *n* [*Military*] acro **Nuclear Detection**

System a computerised analysis of the progress and results of a nuclear attack, counting the missiles, checking their launch sites (for retargeting of friendly missiles in a retaliatory attack), registering impact and destruction, and assessing the overall position following the strike. This enables the President or surviving authority to make – in theory – a suitable decision as to the next step in the conflict.

nudge bar n [Cars] a length of tubing fitted in the gap between the exposed wheels of dirt track race cars to discourage interlocking of wheels and the accidents that this would cause. See also **nerf bar**.

nuisance n [Law] the use of one's own property, or that of someone else, that interferes with the rights of others. 'Private nuisance': affects only one's immediate neighbours, eg: loud music; 'public nuisance': affects large sections of the public, eg: factory pollution; 'attractive nuisance': a potentially dangerous situation which attracts children or others who might suffer injury, for which the owner of the nuisance is responsible.

nuke 1. n [Military] a nuclear weapon. 2. v [Military] to attack with a nuclear weapon.

null n [Navy] the lowest sound emitted by a radio beacon.

nullah n [Shooting] a watercourse, usually dry.

number n [Sex] a client for a homosexual prostitute. See also **john**.

number cruncher n [Computing] a computer which is specially designed to perform lengthy and complex mathematical calculations at speeds of several million operations per second, thus dealing with problems that would take humans whole lifetimes to attempt.

number facts n pl [Education] the basic mathematical abilities: adding, subtraction, multiplication and division.

number fives n [Navy] a sailor's white tropical uniform. See also **number twos** etc.

number fours n [Navy] the uniform worn at night on a ship. See also **number ones** etc.

number one n [Navy] a first lieutenant, especially when he is second in command to the captain.

number one man n [US] [Painting] a contractor for whom it is good to work.

number ones n [Navy] a sailor's best uniform. See also **number twos, number threes**.

number sevens n [Navy] a sailor's white going ashore uniform, the equivalent of **number ones**. See also **number ones** etc.

number sixes n [Navy] a drill uniform with denim collar and cuffs. See also **number ones** etc.

number snatcher n [UK] [Railways] a checker of goods wagons.

number taker n [US] [Garment trade] a buyer who comes only to look, and check out comparative prices in various shops, rather than to buy.

number threes n [Navy] a sailor's working dress. See also **number ones, number twos**.

number two n [UK] [Theatre] a provincial town that is not especially famed for its theatre or the interest of its audiences, as opposed to the large, popular touring theatres, and the towns in which they are found.

number twos n [Navy] a sailor's second best uniform, worn during wartime. See also **number ones, number threes**.

numbers 1. n pl [Advertising] statistics, sales figures for a given product or campaign. 2. n pl [US] [TV] the weekly Nielson Television Index statistics which tell the industry how programmes are being rated throughout the US.

numbers cruncher n [Politics, Finance] a financial analyst or pollster who bends statistics to fit theories.

nuplex n [Business] a complex of manufacturers all of whom use nuclear power within their factories or plants.

nurdle v [Tiddleywinks] to play a wink into a position so near the pot that it cannot be potted.

nurry n [UK] [Market-traders] the head.

nurse 1. v [Stock market] to keep stocks unsold in the hope of a price rise. 2. v [Banking] to 'nurse an account' is to help a customer whose account is overdue by giving him time to make the necessary payment, especially when the market value of the security given will not cover the amount of the debt. 3. v [Cycling] to make the pace, during a long road-race, for a team-mate who is going through a temporarily difficult patch.

nursed account n [Commerce] a supplier whose invoices are always paid immediately by a firm which is generally slow in paying its other creditors. This nursed account is kept sweet – it is useful for providing vital references when the firm needs to expand its lines of credit.

nursemaid n [US] [Cattlemen] the man who looks after the sheep and their offspring during the lambing season.

nursery n [Cricket] any club or part of a club that is set aside for the training and promotion of the talents of young players.

nursery finance n [Finance] the loaning of funds by stockjobbers or merchant and investment banks to those successful private companies which are scheduled to become public companies within 36 months. To ensure that their investment is looked after properly, the investor usually places its own nominee as a director on the board of the borrowing company.

nursery slope n [Skiing] a gentle slope suitable for novice skiers.

nurse's goals n [Medicine] specific indications of illness in a patient, and the treatment which is therefore required to bring that particular patient back to good health.

nut 1. n [Theatre, Film] the total of all overheads in a theatre, cinema or any public auditorium which must be paid off before the owner can start making a profit; thus 'off the nut' means in profit; 'on the nut' means in deficit. **2.** *n* [*Gambling*] the living expenses and other overheads that a gambler must meet from his/her winnings; it comes from the entertainment use (see **1**). **3.** *n* [*US*] [*Police*] a bribe offered to and taken by a corrupt policeman. See also **bung, drink, grass-eater, meateater**. **4.** *n* [*Printing*] one en: a type measure of half an em.

Nutcracker Man *n* [*Anthropology*] Australopithecus robustus, the maker of the oldest stone tools known, specifically the specimens discovered in the Olduvai Gorge, Tanzania in 1959 by LSB & MD Leakey. He was so called from the powerful premolar teeth.

nut-cutting *n* [*Politics*] this comes from general slang for 'castration'. It is the dirty work of politics, especially as regards the giving and with-

holding of political patronage and favours in return for loyalty, betrayal and all the gradations between.

nutmeg *v* [*Soccer*] a player does this when he deliberately kicks the ball between an opponent's legs, rather than trying to dribble it round him.

nuts *n pl* [*Printing*] an 'en quad': a space one half the thickness of the type body. See also **muttons**.

nuts and bolts *n* [*Film*] a basic-level, unsophisticated training film.

nutter *n* [*US*] [*Cattlemen*] the man who castrates the young males of the new lambs.

nutty 1. *a* [*Cheese-making*] used to describe the taste of cheese, especially goat's-milk cheese, which suggests fresh hazelnuts. **2.** *a* [*Wine-tasting*] said of a crisp rounded flavour, usually associated with **full-bodied** dry white wines.

nybble *n* [*Computing*] four **bits** or half a **byte**.

O

O 1. *a* [*Film*] abbr of **morally offensive** a rating for films that was established by the US Catholic Conference. **2.** *n* [*UK*] [*Government*] abbr of **OBE** Order of the British Empire.

O and M *n* [*Industrial relations*] abbr of **organisation and methods studies** special studies designed to research and improve the running and efficiency of a company's management or of a department of local or national government.

O & O *a* [*US*] [*TV*] abbr of **owned and operated** the five VHF stations that a major TV network is allowed to own under Federal law, rather than those **affiliates** which are merely allied to the network; O&O stations are invariably in the major cities.

oakie blower *n* [*US*] [*Road transport*] an air scoop on the air intake that increases power.

oao *n* [*US*] [*Navy*] abbr of **one and only** used at the US Naval Academy as a synonym for girlfriend.

oater, also **horse opera** *n* [*Film*] a Western film with cowboys and Indians, ranchers and farmers, etc.

obbo *n* [*UK*] [*Police*] **observation**. See also **obs**.

obc *n* [*US*] [*Prisons*] abbr of **old brutal convict** one who controls his fellow inmates through violence and intimidation.

OBE *n* [*Economics*] acro **One Big Explanation** a term coined by Professor Jim Ball of the London Business School: the idea that there is one all-embracing explanation for the economic malaise that the UK (and the world) is suffering and that, concomitantly, there is one simple solution.

obie *n* [*US*] [*Theatre*] an award for Off-Broadway productions; it comes from the initials O.B. See also **Emmy, Oscar**.

object *n* [*Computing*] any data structure within the computer's memory which can be manipulated by the total system — both **hardware** and **software**.

object architecture *n* [*Computing*] See **capability architecture**.

object art *n* [*Art*] this was originally used to describe the paintings and constructions of the Futurist, Dadaist and Surrealist schools which incorporated otherwise 'non-art' objects; it was later used in the 1960s as an alternative to

minimal art, in that minimalists emphasise the 'real' materials from which 'art' is made.

object code, also **object program** *n* [*Computing*] the 'language' which is coded so that the machine can 'understand' it and thus perform the operations required. See also **high-level language**.

object language *n* [*Linguistics*] a language which refers to subjects other than that of itself; it is the language that is used in speech to refer to anything other than semantics, linguistics, etc. See also **metalanguage 2**.

objecthood *n* [*Art*] a term of Formalist criticism which contends that there is a conflict between our reading of physical works of art as art, and as objects; thus, when we view a painting as an object we are no longer regarding it as art. The task of modernist painting is to defeat or suspend this objecthood without resorting to the illusionist pictorial devices of the past.

objectification *n* [*Politics*] in Marxist terms, this is the process of transmitting labour – ie: value – into the objects of that labour; by extension it is the struggle by man for the mastery of nature and of his social destiny.

objectivism *n* [*Politics*] in Marxist terms, this is what the West might call 'impartiality', and as such is a pejorative; it is a rightist disease which sees problems even when the Party has stated that there are none, by attaching too much importance to 'facts' and 'reality' when the Party line quite clearly negates such facts, however accurate they may be.

object-speak *n* [*Linguistics*] an impersonal language that anthropomorphises objects for the purpose of jargon, officialese, etc; eg: 'From The Desk Of', 'Scotland Yard admits'.

obs *n* [*UK*] [*Police*] abbr of **observation**. See also **obbo**.

obscurate *v* [*Government*] to preserve bureaucratic obscurity in the face of all investigations and enquiries.

observer *n* [*Military*] the second crew member in a two-seater military plane; it originated in World War I, when the observer simply observed, but the term now covers various tasks including electronic warfare, command and guidance of weapons, navigation and anything other than the actual flying of the aircraft.

OC *n* [*Industrial relations*] acro **organisational climate** the overall atmosphere of an office or factory; positive OC is required for maximum productivity and ideal industrial relations.

occasion dressing *n* [*Fashion*] the purchasing of 'Sunday best' or 'party' clothes.

occurrences *n pl* [*UK*] [*Police*] a variety of events that includes sudden death, suicides, injury to policeman, etc.

ockier *n* [*UK*] [*Market-traders*] a liar.

ocky *n* [*UK*] [*Market-traders*] a lie.

OCR *n* [*Computing*] acro **Optical Character Recognition** a process whereby a machine 'reads' into its own memory (by scanning, recognising and encoding it) information printed or typed in alpha-numeric characters. In its simplest form, light is beamed on to the character and the reflected light is projected on to a matrix of photo-cells; the output of the matrix is scanned and the received signal is read into a storage cell where it is compared with a set of stored character patterns. The original OCR devices, marketed around 1955, were strictly limited as to the characters they could recognise; more recent developments can read and encode copy that appears in any of the seven most popular type-writer faces.

octave *n* [*Computing*] a specific area or portion of data isolated from the other areas.

octopus *n* [*Cars*] a semi-automatic gauging machine for the alignment of the front-end of a motorcar.

o.d. *Lat abbr* [*Medicine*] a prescription notation meaning 'every day'.

odd-even 1. *a* [*Science*] in nuclear physics, of, or pertaining to, the nuclei of an odd mass number and those of an even mass number. **2.** *n* [*Science*] in nuclear physics, this is a nucleus which contains an odd number of protons and an even number of neutrons. See also **odd-odd**.

odd-lot *a* [*Stock market*] said of any transaction involving a smaller number of shares than it is usual to deal in; thus 'odd-lotter' is a small investor, a speculator who buys stock in less than round lots.

odd-odd 1. *a* [*Science*] in nuclear physics, of, or pertaining to, the nuclei of an odd mass number only. **2.** *n* [*Science*] in nuclear physics, this is a nucleus which contains an odd number of protons and an odd number of neutrons. See also **odd-even**.

OE *n* [*Science fiction*] abbr of the **official editor** the chief of an **apa**.

O.E.M. *n* [*Satellite TV*] abbr of **original equipment manufacturer**.

O.E. tyres *n pl* [*Tyre-making*] abbr of **original equipment tyres** those tyres scheduled for use on new vehicles, tractors, etc.

off 1. *a* [*Angling*] when used of a fish this means lost. **2.** *a* [*Stock market*] said of shares which are lower in value, by a stated number of points or a specific value, than at a previous quotation. **3.** *v* [*Military, Politics*] used by both soldiers and radicals to mean kill or assassinate. **4.** *adv* [*Theatre*] abbr of **off stage** referring either to people or to effects and music.

off brand *n* [*Commerce*] merchandise which is not up its usual standard.

off Broadway *n* [*US*] [*Theatre*] that part of the New York professional theatre which works outside the mainstream of popular musicals and 'straight' plays and is geographically and ideologically outside the Broadway style, especially in its espousal of experimental works. See also **off-off Broadway**.

off-year *n* [*US*] [*Politics*] those years in which there are Congressional elections but no Presidential election.

off-balance sheet *n* [*Banking*] a form of borrowing that does not need to appear on a company's balance sheet.

off-board *n* [*US*] [*Stock market*] **over the counter** trading at the New York Stock Exchange, known as the Big Board.

off-brand 1. *a* [*US*] [*Painting*] said of inferior, second-rate materials. **2.** *a* [*US*] [*Painting*] said of paint made by a strange manufacturer, or a paint which the painter has never seen or used before.

offer *n* [*Futures market*] the indication of a willingness to sell a futures contract at a price. See also **bid 4**.

off-fall *n* [*Distilling*] waste created during the distillation from 'beer' to high wines.

off-gauge *n* [*Metallurgy*] steel sheet or strip which differs from the specified thickness by more than the permitted limit.

off-handed *a* [*Coal-mining*] referring to men who are not actively engaged in cutting coal.

off-hire clause, also **breakdown clause** *n* [*Shipping*] a condition in a charter contract that the hirers of a ship will not be charged for any time during which the ship has broken down.

office 1. *n* [*Air travel*] the cockpit or flight deck of a commercial airliner. **2.** *n* [*Sex*] the area, usually some part of a street, where the homosexual hustler establishes his pitch and meets his clients. **3.** *n* [*Stock market*] general office: those departments of a stockbroking firm which deal with the accounts and the transfer of securities. **4.** *n* [*Stock market*] in the office: a phrase which indicates that an initiating order has been given by a broker's own clients, rather than coming from the market.

office hours *n pl* [*US*] [*Marine Corps*] a regular daily occasion at which the Commanding Officer can see marines for discipline, commendation, the answering of requests and similar business.

office manager *n* [*Rallying*] the co-driver of a rallying team, who takes care of nagivation, registering at checkpoints, producing documents and any similar tasks other than actually driving the car.

officer *n* [*Espionage*] any member of the CIA, as opposed to an **agent**.

officers' country *n* [*US*] [*Navy*] the forward areas of a warship, allocated to officers.

official quotations *n pl* [*Stock market*] the price quoted on the Stock Exchange's daily list of shares.

off-line *a* [*Computing*] said of any computer which is neither part of, nor under the control of, a central machine.

off-off Broadway *n* [*US*] [*Theatre*] the most radical and experimental of New York theatre

which exists outside the 'real' theatre and concentrates on the impromptu, the improvised and the extreme; it is often only marginally definable as 'theatre'. See also **off Broadway**.

offset 1. *n* [*Economics*] a purchase whereby the revenue spent is balanced by that which is earned. **2.** *n* [*Futures market*] See **evening up**.

offsetting sale 1. *n* [*Stock market*] a closing transaction that involves the purchase or sale of an **option** which has the same features as one which one already holds. **2.** *n* [*Stock market*] See **hedge 1**.

off-shore *n* [*UK*] [*Surfing*] wind blowing off the land.

off-shore funds *n pl* [*Finance*] investments which are registered outside an individual's or a company's home country and which are therefore liable to more advantageous tax positions than those registered at home, due to the deliberate choice of a country of registration with less stringent demands than the US or UK.

offspring *n* [*Computing*] See **child**.

offtake *n* [*Gas industry*] the main taking gas into a regional distribution system from the high-pressure transmission system.

ogee *n* [*Building, Plastering*] a moulding section. See **cyma reversa**.

ogg *n* [*UK*] [*Market-traders*] 5p, a shilling.

oggin *n* [*Navy*] the sea; it comes from '(h)og-wash'.

oh-one *n* [*US*] [*Marine Corps*] a clerk; this comes from the number 0100, the four-digit number which is appended to Marine service numbers and which shows his **MOS**.

oids *n pl* [*Medicine*] abbr of **steroids**.

oil burner routes *n pl* [*Military*] published military routes across the US, over which the armed forces are permitted to carry out low-level, high-speed training flights. See also **olive-branch routes**.

oil canning *n* [*Gliding*] the bulging in and out of the aircraft skin during flights; it is not normally dangerous.

oil in place *n* [*Oil rigs*] an estimated measure of the total amount of oil contained in a reservoir, and, as such, a higher figure than the 'estimated recoverable reserves'.

oil spot *n* [*Military*] in a war of occupation this is the first town or village to be captured and used as a base for spreading one's influence further; it is the first part of the 'troubled waters' to receive the pacifying oil.

oilberg *n* [*Oil industry*] a massive oil tanker with a capacity of 300,000 tons or more; it is so called because the bulk of a full ship, like that of an iceberg, remains hidden beneath the water.

oilcan operation *n* [*Government*] any variety of cosmetic change that is supposedly tackling a problem within the bureaucracy; in fact rusty parts are merely being oiled, when they ought to be replaced.

oiler, also **flame lamp** *n* [*UK*] [*Coal-mining*] the traditional 'Davy' lamp, designed to burn without igniting the methane in the air; originally it was used as a safe underground illumination, now it is only used for testing for gas; the battery driven cap lamp is now used for actual lighting.

oiling *n* [*Tobacco*] See **greasing**.

oily *n* [*UK*] [*Prisons*] referring to any legal visitor, often a solicitor's clerk or his assistant; the main solicitor can also be ranked as the 'oily', since in effect he is an assistant to the barrister.

oilywad *n* [*Navy*] a seaman with no particular skills and no particular ambitions.

OK *n* [*Salvation Army*] abbr of **Officer's Kid** the child of a serving Salvation Army officer.

old **1.** *adv* [*US*] [*Railways*] at work for a specified amount of time. **2.** *a* [*Social work*] used to describe a man aged between 65 and 75 and a woman aged between 60 and 75. **3.** *a* [*Wine-tasting*] this is used when the bouquet and taste are adversely affected by over-maturity; it is also simply an old wine.

old bill *n* [*Gambling*] a word or hand signal (an open palm) which asks the initiated 'Is there another card cheat in this game?'

old friends *n pl* [*Antiques*] old stock, which has been around for a while and which other dealers will know one has been unable to offload.

Old Left *n* [*Politics*] the traditional restrained, socialist Left which preceded the more radical melodramatic New Left of the 1960s; on the whole its members accepted traditional Marxism and the Party's values and directives as sent from Moscow, but rarely considered the guerilla tactics of their youthful successors. See also **New Left**.

old man **1.** *n* [*Military*] the commanding officer. **2.** *n* [*Religion*] man without the spirit of God; thus the natural, sensual man; see Romans 6.6.

old man's entrails *n* [*Navy*] a poorly executed knot.

old salt *n* [*US*] [*Marine Corps*] any veteran or long-serving member of the Marines.

old soldier *n* [*Angling*] a male salmon after spawning.

old woman *n* [*Logging*] any small container in which loggers keep needles and thread, buttons, glue, ointment, etc. See also **housewife 1**.

old-old *a* [*Social work*] referring to a member of either sex aged 75 or over.

oligopoly *n* [*Marketing*] the influence exerted over a market supply by a small number of independent companies, although the group may not act in collusion.

oligopsony *n* [*Economics*] the economic state which occurs when there are only a limited number of buyers for products because there are no real alternatives. See also **monopsony**.

oliopoly *n* [*Economics*] a market in which there are only a few sellers.

olive-branch routes *n pl* [*Military*] low level training routes which cross the US and which are used for B–52 bomber crews; the name comes from the motto of the Strategic Air Command (SAC):

'Peace Is Our Profession'. See also **oil-burner routes**.

oliver *n* [*US*] [*Paper-making*] a machine in the bleach room that removes part of the liquid from the pulp.

O.M. *Lat. abbr* [*Medicine*] a prescription notation meaning 'every morning'.

omee *n* [*UK*] [*Theatre*] a man, especially a landlord or an itinerant actor; it comes from the Ital. 'uomo' meaning man, and Parlyaree, a theatrical jargon.

omerta *n* [*Crime*] this comes from Ital. 'umilita'; it is the code prevalent in the Italian Mafia that demands submission to the leader and the group as well as absolute silence as regards their activities.

omission factor *n* [*Libraries*] the number of documents which are in fact relevant to a search but, through inadequate or mis-directed search methods, are not retrieved by the user.

omnibuildings *n* *pl* [*Architecture*] See **megastructures**.

omnium *n* [*Cycling*] a series of matches in which competitors are awarded points on the basis of their performance in each one; the winner is the rider who has amassed the most points at the end of the series.

OMS *n* [*Coal-mining*] acro **Output per Man-Shift**.

OMY *n* [*Coal-mining*] acro **Output per Man-Year**.

on **1.** *adv* [*Baseball*] abbr of **on base** when a batter has reached a base safely. **2.** *adv* [*Stock market*] used of prices to mean higher, rising, moving up.

on all fours *adv* [*Law*] referring to the existence of direct legal procedure for the case currently under consideration.

on top *n* [*Gambling*] any bet that is announced to a bookmaker with the addition of the phrase 'on top' is a spurious bet, made by an accomplice to egg on other punters who have yet to make up their minds; it will not be recorded in the ledger and no money will change hands, whatever the result. See also **rick 1**.

on-call target *n* [*Military*] a specific nuclear target which will only be attacked on a direct command, rather than automatically at a given time.

oncast work *n* [*Coal-mining*] See **backbye work**.

one *n* [*Cycling*] the most distinguished rider present at a track meet.

one armed bandit *n* [*UK*] [*Railways*] cab equipment on a diesel for the automatic warning system.

one badge man *n* [*Navy*] a sailor with one good conduct badge representing four years' satisfactory service.

one big one *n* [*Gambling*] $1,000.

one chain *n* [*Advertising*] See **tailor made 1**.

one for the shelf *n* [*Stock market*] any share

that is expected to stand as a secure, long-term investment.

one glass of water doctrine *n* [*Politics*] originated by Lenin, then abandoned by him, but still maintained as 'pei-shui-ch-i' by Chinese Communists, this is the concept that sexual desire should be no more vital to a revolutionary than a single glass of water.

one gun salute *n* [*Navy*] the salute fired to signal a court martial. See also **rogue's salute**.

one house bill *n* [*US*] [*Politics*] legislation that is never intended to pass into law – or through either part of Congress – but is used by its sponsoring politician purely for publicity purposes.

one house veto, also **legislative veto** *n* [*US*] [*Politics*] the power provided under the US Constitution that enables either the Senate or the House of Representatives to veto any Presidential initiative.

one in *n* [*US*] [*Lunch counter*] a chocolate ice-cream soda.

one of a kind *a* [*US*] [*Weaving*] used to describe a weaver who does not replicate designs, but aspires to high creative control of his/her work; function is secondary to aesthetic impact, but such designs can be incorporated in one-off, unique **wearables**, which are garments and virtual art objects in one.

one on/one off *phr* [*UK*] [*Prisons*] when an inmate is moved around the prison, passing from the control of one set of officers to another, the officer bringing the prisoner announces 'One off' as he hands him on to the new escort, who similarly announces 'One on'.

one per cent out look *n* [*Fashion*] a dressing style that involves the wearing of certain traditional costumes – dinner jackets, etc. – with the addition or substitution of a single discordant item.

one plus one *n* [*TV*] a specially small camera crew – one cameraman, one reporter, one soundman and one electrician – that is used for reporting in war zones, or for clandestine surveillance for investigative programmes.

one sheet *v* [*Theatre, Film*] to give a show or film the lowest possible billing; it refers to the smallest size of poster which would be used to advertise it.

one way street *n* [*US*] [*Prisons*] any sexual activity in which one partner remains passive, the other being active.

one with *n* [*US*] [*Lunch counter*] a toasted sandwich with mayonnaise.

one-arm Johnny *n* [*US*] [*Coal-mining*] a small pump worked by hand.

one-legged *a* [*TV*] referring to a poor quality of sound in the transmission.

one-lunger *n* [*Yachting*] any boat driven by a single-cylinder engine.

one-man company *n* [*Commerce*] a company in which nearly all the shares are held by a single individual, with a few others allotted only to make up the statutory number of people required to make that company legal.

one-name paper *n* [*Finance*] a promissory note which carries only the name of the borrower; such notes have less security than a commercial bill of exchange – two-name paper – which also has the guarantee of the signature of a merchant bank.

one-pipper *n* [*UK*] [*Military*] a second lieutenant.

one-pocket *n* [*Pool*] the toughest game in pool; it is played with a full rack of 15 balls, each of which must be potted in a designated pocket. A game of strategy, shotmaking and defence, it pleases only the connoisseur.

ones *n pl* [*UK*] [*Prisons*] the first floor of cells in the traditional Victorian designed British prison wing; thus the ascending floors are the 'twos', 'threes' and 'fours'.

one's card, on *adv* [*Theatre*] to gain free admission to a variety of entertainments by producing one's Equity (actor's union) card at the box office.

one-shot 1. *n* [*Computing*] a digital circuit which has only one stable output state. 2. *n* [*Publishing*] a publishing idea – often a small magazine which is linked to the publicity for a specific event or fad – this is produced only once, without any hope or intention of any sequel. 3. *n* [*TV, Film, Video*] any shot or sequence in which there is only a single performer in view. Thus 'two-shot', 'three-shot', etc.

one-stop *n* [*Pop music*] music industry wholesalers who are only 'one stop' away from the manufacturers; these middlemen sell records to retailers, juke boxes, etc.

one-tailed test *n* [*Parapsychology*] a test of statistical significance is known as 'one-tailed' if the direction of the statistic being tested has been specified in advance as being either definitely positive or definitely negative. Any result that contradicts this prediction should be automatically ignored. See also **two-tailed test**.

one-time pad *n* [*Espionage*] in cryptography this is a secret message which is encoded in a cypher that has been devised for that occasion and subsequently destroyed or abandoned.

one-twenty *n* [*TV*] a 'made-for-TV' film lasting one hundred and twenty minutes. See also **ninety**.

one-two-three bank *n* [*Banking*] a bank that is superior to a mere moneylender, but which, while it offers certain services and has something of the prestige of a large bank, is not a fully accredited clearing, commercial or merchant bank; it is a fringe bank.

on-going *a* [*Communications*] happening now, continuing, in action; it is a redundant and overused phrase, often found as in 'on-going situation' and fortunately, as with many such phrases, it is gradually vanishing beneath the weight of its own absurdity.

onion *n* [*Navy*] in the calculation of a ship's speed this is a fraction of a knot (one nautical mph).

O

onion skin concept n [Government] the concept of developing any initiative – eg: international aid – gradually, through a number of multilayered – onion-skinlike – stages, so that one proceeds eventually to the heart of the matter. In many ways, it is a justification for the leisurely, paper-laden processes of bureaucracies.

on-lending n [Finance] the further lending of money that one has borrowed.

on-line 1. a [Air travel] in commercial airlines this means pertaining to or on the regular routes allotted to and flown by these airlines. 2. a [Computing] any system in which a central processing unit controls the operations and the **peripherals**. See also **off-line**.

onsetters n pl [UK] [Coal-mining] men in charge of the **cage** at the bottom of the shaft; they signal for men or material to go up the pit.

on-shore n [UK] [Surfing] a wind blowing off the sea.

o-o v [Entertainment] abbr of **once-over** thus, to look at, assess, check out, etc.

oojiboo n [UK] [Military] a thingummibob, a whatchamacallit, etc.

OP adv [Publishing] abbr of **out of print**.

op art n [Art] an art movement of the 1960s which specialised in producing dramatic effects on the viewer's optical system by creating sharply painted abstract patterns whose colour and contrasts forced the eyes to deal with fluctuating images, a 'shimmer' and other visual illusions.

op-ed n [Journalism] abbr of **opposite the editorial** a page of opinionated or feature material, usually related to current news, topics, that appears in US papers opposite the page on which editorials appear, it is often the home of the paper's regular columnists.

open 1. a [Audio] an impression of 'spacious' sound, as regards width, height and depth. See also **recessed**. 2. a [Cheese-making] used to describe cheese with an open texture or one which contains holes; these can be either close and regularly patterned or variously scattered. See also **close** 1. 3. a [New therapies] the opposite of **uptight**: vulnerable, willing to accept new ideas and concepts, offering accessible emotion, parading one's feelings. 4. a [Printing] said of a face that is wider and rounder set than is usual. 5. v [Sailing, Ropework] to untie a knot. 6. v [Hunting] the action of the first hound to **speak** on sighting a fox. 7. v [Hunting] See **challenge**.

open a crossing v [Banking] said of the drawer of a cheque who cancels its 'crossing', by writing 'Pay Cash' across it, and adding a signature.

open a vein v [Mining] to start mining ore from a vein.

open admissions, also **open enrolment** n [Education] the policy of enrolling all and every student in the college of their choice, irrespective of their being able to fulfil the admissions criteria of that college; the intent is to eradicate the advantages that the more privileged (white, middle-class) child possesses in such competitions, even if such a policy may well sacrifice the academic standards of the colleges so affected.

open bed n [Medicine] a bed that has had its sheets turned down for the night. See also **closed bed**.

open broad v [Film] to launch a new film simultaneously at a number of major cinemas right across a market or a whole country. See also **roll-out**.

open classroom, also **open corridor** n [Education] a style of education, especially at primary school level, where children are not forced to stay at their desks, but enjoy unstructured education, centred on investigation and discussion, rather than on traditional, formal instruction.

open cold v [US] [Theatre] to open a play in New York, without the benefit of the usual round of out-of-town try-outs.

open contracts n pl [Futures market] contracts which have been bought or sold without the transaction having been completed by a subsequent sale or purchase, or by making or taking delivery of a financial instrument.

open convention n [US] [Politics] a political convention which starts off with no single possible candidate holding a safe majority; such a majority, it is assumed, will emerge as the convention proceeds.

open door n [TV] **access** television designed for minority groups: they put together the content and the presentation and a studio expert helps out with the necessary technical details.

open field n [Government] See **panopolis**.

open heifer n [US] [Cattlemen] a heifer that has not been spayed.

open housing n [US] [Government] the official prohibition of any racial or religious conditions being attached to the sale of a house. Thus, by extension this is a policy aimed at ending the perpetuation and creation of ghetto areas, inner city slums and the general divisiveness that exists within urban populations.

open interest n [Futures market] a number of open futures contracts; the term refers to unliquidated purchases or sales.

open light n [Coal-mining] a naked light; any light which is not protected and enclosed in order to avoid the ignition of firedamp.

open (one's) account v [Cricket] a batsman does this when he begins scoring runs or a bowler when he takes his first wicket.

open order n [Stock market] an order to a broker that remains good until it is either cancelled or fulfilled.

open shop n [Computing] a method of running a computer facility so that the design, development, writing and testing of new programs is carried

O

out by the originator of a program rather than by in-house specialists. See also **closed shop**.

open skies *n pl* [*Politics*] a scheme proposed by President Eisenhower at the Geneva Summit Conference of June 21st, 1955: the superpowers would exchange military blueprints and allow aircraft flights over each other's territory. Given that the US then possessed a 5:1 superiority in nuclear warheads, the Russians rejected the policy out of hand. Despite this, the US commenced a programme of secret spying overflights by U–2 aircraft, a clandestine practice that collapsed after the plane piloted by Gary Powers was shot down in 1960, concomitantly wrecking the current summit talks.

open sky policy *n* [*Military*] See **open skies**.

open stance *n* [*Skiing*] skiing with the feet and skis apart.

open the kimono *v* [*Business*] this refers to a means of countering possible business opposition by taking potential buyers into one's confidence and revealing otherwise secret details of future products or similar information. These disclosures should impress the client sufficiently enough to ensure his signing of a lucrative purchasing contract.

open up 1. *v* [*Theatre*] to turn the body fully towards the front of the stage to increase the emphasis of a line or gesture. **2.** *v* [*Theatre*] to make any form of on-stage emphasis, such as picking up a prop or similar **business**. **3.** *v* [*Sheep-shearing*] to shear wool from a particular area, especially the neck of a sheep.

open-door policy *n* [*Industrial relations*] the policy whereby union officials and/or shop stewards have the right of access to senior managers.

open-handled *a* [*Furriers*] used of furs which come from animals that have been opened along the belly and stretched out flat for skinning. See also **cased-handled**.

opening 1. *n* [*Futures market*] the period at the start of a trading session officially designated by the Exchange during which all transactions are considered to have been made 'at the opening'. See also **close 4. 2.** *n* [*Metallurgy*] separating the steel sheets of a mill pack, when a number of sheets have been rolled together.

opening price, also **opening range** *n* [*Futures market*] the price or range recorded during that period which is officially designated the **Opening**.

open-jaw ticket *n* [*Air travel*] an airline booking that takes one route out and another one back; it is also a trip which comes back along the same route, except that it terminates at a different destination.

open-list *v* [*Commerce*] said of a retailer who sets prices between two limits, neither of which is particularly higher or lower than the recommended full price.

openness *n* [*Clothing*] the provision for leg stance in the angle of the seams.

opera house *n* [*US*] [*Cattlemen*] the top rail of the corral fence, popularly used as a meeting place and gossip centre by cowboys.

operant conditioning *n* [*Industrial relations*] the persuading of one's workforce to do what you want them to do – often by offering productivity bonuses, incentive schemes, etc.

operating *n* [*Tobacco*] cutting off cigars so that they taper off at the end which is to be lit.

operating in reverse *n* [*Finance*] See **mopping up**.

operating system, also **executive** *n* [*Computing*] the **software** required to manage a system's **hardware** and logical resources, including scheduling and file management.

Operating Thetan *n* [*Scientology*] a leader of the Church.

operational analysis *n* [*Industrial relations*] a branch of applied psychology that is designed to achieve ideal relations between a machine and its operator; the main intention is to eliminate the human errors which can mar effective joint productivity.

operationalise *v* [*Government*] to put into operation.

operationalisation *n* [*Sociology*] the measuring and quantifying of a concept so that it may be tested.

operations research *n* [*Business*] any form of research that attempts to find the solutions to problems which occur in the management of a complex organisation.

operator *n* [*Computing*] any symbol within a program which indicates that an operation is about to be performed: +, –, *, @, etc.

opinion leaders *n pl* [*Public relations*] See **influentials**.

opinionaire *n* [*Sociology*] a questionnaire that is designed to obtain the opinions of a respondent; 'A word of doubtful usefulness' (R.W. Burchfield, OED Supp. Vol.III).

OPM *n* [*Finance*] acro **Other People's Money** the ideal financing for a speculator: one obtains money from another person and uses it as one sees fit; if the speculator profits, then so does the other person, if the speculator loses, then only the other person need suffer the loss.

OP/OS *adv* [*Publishing*] abbr of **out of print/out of stock** permanently out of print once current stock is exhausted.

opportunists *n pl* [*Politics*] in Marxist terms, these are the proletarian leaders who use their own positions to subordinate the class struggle and the demands of ideological purity to their own selfish ends, most notably in collaborating with the bourgeoisie and enjoying the trappings of their lifestyle.

opportunity class, also **opportunity room** *n* [*Education*] a euphemism for those special classes in which backward pupils are given 'an opportunity to learn'; such pupils are 'not quite bright enough to be classed as slow', (J. LeSure, 'Guide to Pedaguese', 1965).

opportunity cost *n* [*Economics*] the cost of something that one has decided not to take the opportunity of buying; since the supply of goods is limited, the buyer is continually making a choice between purchases. Thus if one buys one object and not another, the real or opportunity cost of the object bought is that of the object left unbought; similarly a manufacturer, in choosing to produce one form of goods over another, creates an opportunity cost of the article he does produce in terms of the one which has not been produced.

opportunity servicing *n* [*Aerospace*] servicing of an aircraft that can be carried out at any convenient time, although such times must fall within the broad limits set down for the checking of the components involved. See also **A check, B check**.

Oprep *n* [*Military*] abbr of **operations report** any report which covers the multitude of worldwide events – great and small – in which US forces are involved.

opt out *v* [*Radio*] a local station does this when it takes advantage of the opt-out or opt out point – that moment during a networked transmission, eg: a news bulletin, when the local stations can cease receiving that transmission – and returns to its own programming. The opt-out point is forewarned by a time check or similar notification.

optical wand *n* [*Computing*] an electronic device which is used in supermarkets to 'read' the pricing bar-codes that are increasingly found on products.

opticals *n pl* [*TV*] all visual tricks, special effects and other techniques that involve special laboratory work on the basic print.

optimise the objective function *v* [*Business*] to find a plan that allocates the resources available in the best possible way for achieving the desired goal.

optimisation *n* [*Computing*] the process of finding the best solution to a problem, where 'best' must conform with a series of pre-stated criteria. In computer programming, the word refers to the production of an object code which attains the optimal state by making the best use of the resources of the target machine either in the field of putting the maximum memory into the minimum storage space or that of making the program as efficient as possible; the latter field is the more common. See also **global optimisation, peep-hole optimisation**.

optimum mix *n* [*Military*] See **massive retaliation**.

option *n* [*Stock market*] the right to deal in a security at a fixed price over a specified period. Thus 'call option' is the right to purchase a share at the 'striking price' (the exercise price at which a holder can call for stock) over a period of up to 90

days; 'put option' is a similar right, when selling rather than buying shares; 'double option' is a mix of the call and put options, conferring rights in either buying or selling over the 90 day period.

option art *n* [*Art*] works which allow the artist and the spectators a number of choices in the arrangement of the elements which make them up.

option play *n* [*US*] [*Football*] an offensive play for advancing the ball that gives a back the choice of either rushing or throwing a forward pass.

opt-out *n* [*TV, Radio*] a programme broadcast by a regional or local TV or radio station for local consumption only, and from which the other network stations can choose to **opt out**.

or *a* [*Heraldry*] gold, yellow.

oral note *n* [*Politics*] a written but unsigned diplomatic communication which is given the status of the spoken word and which is thus useful to but not binding on those parties who use it during a negotiation.

orange *n* [*UK*] [*Telephony*] a long distance line; thus 'put me on to an orange' means give me a long-distance exchange.

orange book *n* [*Government*] a report, published between yellow covers, that deals with the marketing of foodstuffs and other commodities.

orange fin *n* [*Angling*] a young sea trout.

orange force *n* [*Military*] the 'hostile' force during NATO simulated wargames and other exercises; it must be assumed that orange has replaced 'red' out of some sense of tact towards the Soviet bloc. See also **blue force**.

orange goods *n pl* [*Commerce*] those products which are rated at a medium level of consumption, servicing and markup, eg: clothing.

orange peel **1.** *n* [*Building*] a heavy, split steel bucket made up of three or more sections that are hinged together at the top of adjacent sections; it is attached to the boom of a crane or derrick and is used to dig and lift earth, gravel, etc. **2.** *n* [*Glassmaking*] surface irregularities on glass that resemble the pitted surface of an orange. **3.** *n* [*Painting*] a pock-marked look that can mar an area of paint which has not been spread properly; it is especially prevalent when a paint sprayer has been used. **4.** *n* [*Metallurgy*] a roughening of the surface of steel sheet or strip which develops when the metal has cooled if the grain size is too course. **5.** *n* [*UK*] [*Railways*] the bright orange day-glo jackets worn by plate-layers.

oranges sour *n* [*Military*] US Dept. of Defense code for: weather unsuitable for flying.

oranges sweet *n* [*Military*] US Dept. of Defense code for: weather suitable for flying.

orbital elements *n pl* [*Military, Aerospace*] the measurable characteristics of a satellite orbit, including the apogee and perigee (the points at which the satellite is farthest from and nearest to the earth); the period (the time it takes for the satellite to make one orbit of the earth); the incli-

O

nation (the angle it makes with the equator on its northerly pass); the right ascension (a measure that locates the plane of the orbit with respect to the stars and the length of time between launch and final **decay**.

orbiter *n* [*TV*] a TV communications satellite which orbits the earth.

orchard *n* [*UK*] [*Railways*] a marshalling yard at Cricklewood Junction, so called because it was built on the site of an old orchard.

orchestra *n* [*Espionage*] a term coined by Lenin and subsequently adopted by major intelligence agencies, to refer to those tame 'targets', suitably primed by threats and/or blackmail, who can be used when necessary but are generally left to await such a summons until a suitable occasion arises.

orchestra stall *n* [*Theatre*] the very front rows of the stalls, next to the orchestra pit. See also **bald-headed row**.

ordering *n* [*Tobacco*] conditioning of leaf tobacco for handling by subjecting it to steam or water, or by removing excess moisture in a humidity-controlled machine.

orderly buff *n* [*Military*] a sergeant who attends to the domestic needs of the troops. See also **orderly dog, orderly pig**.

orderly dog *n* [*Military*] an officer who attends to the domestic life of the troops. See also **orderly buff, orderly pig**.

orderly market *n* [*Stock market*] a steady market with a good supply of buyers and sellers as required. See also **disorderly market**.

orderly pig *n* [*Military*] a corporal who attends to the domestic needs of the troops. See also **orderly buff, orderly dog**.

ordes *n pl* [*Theatre*] free, complimentary tickets. See also **comp 3, paper 3**.

ordinary 1. *n* [*Stock market*] common stock without any preference; thus 'ordinaries' are those shareholders who possess such stock. **2.** *a* [*Wine-tasting*] used to describe a wine of no pretensions and no merit.

oreo *n* [*US*] [*Military*] a derogatory description used by black troops to describe those of their fellows who seem to be toadying to the authorities; it comes from Oreo cookies, which are made of two chocolate wafers surrounding a white sugar cream filling. Oreo has replaced the earlier 'Uncle Tom' with much the same meaning.

org *n* [*Entertainment*] abbr of **organisation** any show business corporation, agency, chain, etc.

organ recital patients *n pl* [*US*] [*Medicine*] patients with 'a positive review of systems' who apparently have something the matter with every part of their bodies.

organic analogy *n* [*Sociology*] the attempt to understand the function and structure of society by analogy with the nature of living organisms.

organicism *n* [*Sociology*] See **organic analogy**.

organicity *n* [*Business*] the degree of partici-

pation by subordinates in the establishment of goalsetting and in decision-making within a company; it is also the maintenance of open lines of communication between all levels of an organisation.

organise *v* [*UK*] [*Military*] to scrounge, to obtain unofficially, to steal.

organised market *n* [*Commerce*] an institution – such as a stock exchange – that provides facilities for approved people to buy and sell particular goods (often intangible property such as shares, futures contracts, etc); transactions are usually agreed verbally and at great speed; the public can trade in the market, but only when represented on the trading floor by brokers with specialised knowledge and membership of the institution.

organismic sensing *n* [*New therapies*] a concept developed by Carl Rogers, pioneer of encounter therapy, to infer the use of one's entire being, its mental and physical attributes, in experiencing a particular situation or person.

organisation theory *n* [*Sociology*] a set of empirical and conceptual observations about the social behaviour of people in enterprises and the factors that affect organisational structure. It deals mainly with the administrative level of an enterprise which comprises clerical and managerial positions; it deals with the actual bureaucracy involved as well as the behaviour of the managers both as individuals and within groups.

orifice *n* [*Oil rigs*] a device which will partially restrict the flow through a pipe; the flow rate can be measured by comparing the pressure on the two sides of the orifice.

original 1. *n* [*US*] [*Cattlemen*] a horse which has not been castrated correctly. **2.** *n* [*Fashion*] a garment which has been especially designed as part of a designer's new collection of clothes and which is first revealed when that collection is officially displayed to clients and journalists.

original classification authority *n* [*Government*] the power to classify information which has not been classified previously, thus withdrawing it from circulation.

originals 1. *n pl* [*Motor cycles*] among the outlaw motor-cycle gangs, especially the Hells Angels, these are the set of denim jacket and jeans which are worn for one's (inevitably very dirty) initiation into the club. These garments, no matter how foul and tattered they become, are worn (often over less dilapidated ones) as one of the badges of membership. **2.** *n pl* [*TV*] the standard costumes worn by characters in a long-running series or **soap opera**.

origine *a* [*Cheese-making*] said of cheese that is made in the same place from which its raw materials originate.

ormolu *a* [*Navy*] used of anything ornate or expensive looking; it is a wardroom term.

ornamentation *n* [*Music*] the use of grace notes to embellish melodies.

orphan *n* [*Motor trade*] in the second-hand motor trade, this is any discontinued model of car.

orphan drug *n* [*Pharmaceuticals*] a drug which has been synthesised and which is known to exist, but for which the demand is only minimal; thus the makers maintain its production at a minimal, technically experimental-only level.

orraman *n* [*Scot.*] [*Farming*] a day labourer, an odd-job man.

orsle *n* [*Fishing*] a short piece of line which carries a bait.

ortho *n* [*Medicine*] abbr of **orthopedics** a surgical speciality which concentrates on dealing with bones.

orthopad *n* [*Medicine*] an orthopaedic surgeon.

orthowater *n* [*Science*] See **anomalous water**.

OS *adv* [*Publishing*] abbr of **out of stock** temporarily unavailable.

Oscar *n* [*Film*] the annual award for excellence in the various branches of film-making that is made by the Hollywood Academy of Motion Picture Arts and Sciences. The award was allegedly named after one Oscar Pierce, a US wheat and fruit grower, whose niece worked in pictures and who remarked on seeing the prototype statuette in 1931 how greatly it resembled her uncle.

oscar 1. *n* [*Mining*] a large shovel; the reference is to the Hollywood award. **2.** *n* [*TV*] a light diffuser, split into adjustable quarters, which varies the power and/or direction of that light. Thus 'female oscar' means 75% of the illumination is blacked out; 'male oscar' means 25% of the illumination is blacked out.

O.S.P. *n* [*Ice dancing*] abbr of **Original Set Pattern** a couple's personalised routine, as opposed to the compulsory dances that all competitors must perform.

OSS *n* [*Publishing*] acro **Obligatory Sex Scene** a piece of soft-core pornography inserted into a novel to satisfy the author's market.

OTH *n* [*Advertising*] acro **Opportunities To Hear** a stastical reference to the number of times a member of a target audience is exposed to a TV or radio station that is running a particular advertisement. The 'weight' (or impact) or a campaign can be judged by the average OTH for all members of the target audience.

OTH radar *n* [*Military*] acro **over-the-horizon radar** radar signals that follow the earth's curvature and are thus able to capture objects far out of the line of sight; these signals hit their target, then bounce up to the ionosphere before they return to the monitor.

OTH-B radar *n* [*Military*] acro **over-the-horizon backscatter radar** radar that can transmit signals from out of the line of sight by following the curvature of the earth; 'backscatter', means that unlike basic **OTH radar**, which bounces its signals off the ionosphere, the signals return to the monitor along the same track as

that on which they were sent out; the range is approximately 1800 metres.

other body *n* [*US*] [*Politics*] the official term used by members of the US Senate or House of Representatives to refer to their opposite numbers in the US Congress. See also **another place**.

other end *n* [*US*] [*Railways*] the destination point of a journey from the home terminal.

other ranks *n pl* [*Military, Navy, etc*] members of the armed forces other than commissioned officers.

other shoe syndrome *n* [*Business*] in the case of a number of executives in a firm being made redundant, the survivors, rather than feeling relieved, find their own morale sabotaged as they wait for the 'other shoe' to come down in turn on them. Thus the cost-cutting plans that initiated the first dismissals can backfire to such an extent that the survival of the company may be threatened by this low morale, despite its new economic stability.

other than honourable discharge *n* [*US*] [*Military*] the equivalent of the enlisted man's 'dishonourable discharge', but sanitised for the supposedly more sensitive (since middle/upper class) officer.

other-directedness *n* [*Sociology*] the other-directed individual depends completely on the constant support of and approval from others as the confirmation of his/her self-image; such a personality – the ultimate conformist – is seen as the product of a consumer society.

OTS *n* [*Advertising*] acro **Opportunities To See** the TV version of radio's opportunities to hear; the total exposure of an advertisement to a potential target viewer. See also **OTH**.

OTSOG *phr* [*Sociology*] acro **On The Shoulders Of Giants** a concept of the development of learning through the continual transfer of one innovator's discoveries to his successors and then to the next generation and so on. See also **multiples 2**.

OTT *adv* [*TV, Film*] acro **Over The Top** an expression of disgust, amazement, shock, delight, amusement, etc; it originated in TV crews, but has long since spread into general use.

otter *n* [*Angling*] a method of poaching: a line is used to which many flies and a leaded board are attached; it can be made to go out by pulling the line.

out 1. *n* [*Audio*] a signal in radio communications – military and civilian – that the speaker has finished his conversation and wishes to break the connection. **2.** *n* [*Radio*] the last few words of a tape that are written on the **cue** sheet, on the label and on the box that holds the tape; using the out and a timed length, the engineer, producer or presenter can plan accurately timed programmes which feature tapes and live material. **3.** *adv* [*US*] [*Railways*] away from the home terminal.

O

out grass *v* [*Merchant Navy*] to pay out the sisal line used for towing.

out of *prep* [*Horse-racing*] Horse X 'out of' Horse Y, refers to the horse's dam. See also **by**.

out run *n* [*US*] [*Skiing*] in ski-jumping this is the distance between the take-off and the landing point. See also **in run**.

out 2Ds *n pl* [*Scientology*] sex crimes: especially and usually adultery.

outage *n* [*Communications*] a period during which a system is unable to function, due to malfunction, breakdown or a power shortage.

outbye *n* [*Coal-mining*] a direction underground towards the main shaft or surface outlet.

outcue *n* [*Radio, TV*] a cue which indicates that a broadcast or transmission is about to end.

outfit 1. *n* [*Commerce*] in the terminology of the Canadian Hudson Bay Company this is one fiscal year, dating from June 1 to May 31; at the end of the outfit a full inventory was taken of the Company's stocks. 2. *n* [*Military*] any group of servicemen, small or large. 3. also **works** *n* [*Drugs*] the syringe and other implements required by a drug addict to administer injections.

outgribings *n pl* [*Science fiction*] fan-magazine contributions; (the word comes from Lewis Carroll's 'Jabberwocky': 'the mome raths outgrabe').

outing *n* [*Horse-racing*] a race for which a horse is entered.

outlaw *n* [*Sex*] in pimp terminology this is any prostitute who does not work for a pimp.

outlay creep *n* [*Business, Politics*] the gradual increase in governmental or corporate expenditure that inevitably occurs, irrespective of actual plans providing for some approved increases in budgeting.

outlier *n* [*Mining*] an area of younger rocks surrounded by older rocks. See also **inlier**.

output 1. *n* [*Computing*] the results one receives from operating the machine. 2. *v* [*Computing*] to transfer information from the machine to an external peripheral, eg: a screen or printer.

outreach 1. *n* [*Religion*] anything directed primarily at the non-believer. 2. *n* [*Social work, Government*] the extending of government or social services beyond their current or conventional limits; this occurs particularly in a situation where the people at whom these services are aimed are seen to be uninterested in using them and it is deemed necessary to bring those services to them, whether they desire such aid or not.

outrider *n* [*Education*] at New College, Oxford, this is a fellow who is appointed to accompany the Warden on his annual progress around the estates owned by the college every summer.

outriders *n pl* [*UK*] [*Railways*] non-union members. See also **mistletoe men**.

outro *n* [*Media*] the opposite of intro – the introduction – and thus the final few minutes or seconds of a broadcast, film, tape, etc.

outs *n pl* [*US*] [*Meat trade*] any individuals in a bunch of cattle which are sold at a lower price than all the rest.

outseg *v* [*US*] [*Politics*] abbr of **outsegregate** to offer policies that are more racist and segregationist than those of one's already openly right-wing opponents.

outsert *n* [*Advertising*] the opposite of **insert**: thus any advertisement or other promotional material that is attached to the outside of a product or its packaging.

outside 1. *n* [*US*] [*Marine Corps*] the civilian world outside the Marine Corps. 2. *n* [*Shoemaking*] any material used in the manufacture of the outside parts of a shoe. 3. *n* [*Surfing*] that part of the sea out beyond the breakers. 4. *excl* [*Surfing*] a call that points out to other surfers that a set of large, surfable breakers is starting to roll in.

outside broker *n* [*Stock market*] See **curbstone broker**.

outside man *n* [*UK*] [*Police*] an individual who may take on one of several specialist roles in the carrying out of elaborate confidence tricks.

outside, on the *adv* [*Espionage*] referring to an agent who works in the field; it is the opposite of 'on the inside': the case officer who runs that agent from his office.

outside work *n* [*Gambling*] any tampering with dice that concerns their external surfaces.

outside world *n* [*US*] [*Politics*] those voters or parties that exist beyond the horizons or allegiances of the party which is using the phrase; non-aligned voters who have yet to be accounted for on the pollsters' lists.

outsider art *n* [*Art*] the art produced by artists who stand outside 'normal' society and its conditioning; their highly original works are designed to satisfy their own psychic needs rather than those of the public and the art market. Many such artists are schizophrenics or hermits, but they do not include **naive**, folk, prison, tribal or children's artists.

outstanding *a* [*US*] [*Military*] the foremost of the US Army's ratings of an individual's performance, ie: 1. outstanding, 2. superior, 3. excellent, 4. effective, 5. marginal, 6. inadequate. These ratings are applied only to officers and appear on their 'efficiency reports'.

out-takes 1. *n pl* [*TV, Film*] those sequences or scenes which are rejected by the editor or director at the cutting stage and are not included in the final film; out-takes often involve unscheduled moments of humour, actors forgetting their lines, effects failing to work, etc. 2. *n* [*Business*] by extension from the entertainment use (see 1) these are the parts of a commercial presentation that are deliberately dropped prior to making that presentation to a client.

out-turn *n* [*Economics*] actual, practical results,

predictions that did turn out as planned, as opposed to random, if detailed, estimates.

outyear n [*Economics*] future spending estimates, referring to provisions that will not take effect for one or more years.

oven n [*Technology*] an enclosure, with its associated sensors and heaters, which is designed to keep components at a constant, controlled temperature.

over n [*Printing*] those copies in excess of the print-run which are deliberately printed up to allow for wastage.

over and under n [*Shooting*] a shotgun in which the barrels are positioned one on top of the other, rather than in parallel.

over-achiever n [*Education*] a pupil who attains higher standards than his/her IQ had indicated should be expected; rather than praise such efforts, teachers tend to attribute them to neurosis, parental pressure and other deviations from a preferred norm.

overages n pl [*Video*] the money earned by a title above and beyond any advance paid by a rights purchaser to secure video rights to the title.

overalls n pl [*UK*] [*Military*] close fitting trousers worn as part of the uniform, especially by cavalrymen.

overbought a [*Stock market*] said of any individual stock or whole market that has recently experienced a sharp price rise and may thus be vulnerable to an equally sharp fall. See also **oversold**.

overbreadth n [*US*] [*Law*] the invalidation of a legal statute because it has been framed in too vague a manner for the courts to use it sufficiently precisely when dealing with the situations it ought to cover.

overburden n [*Mining*] material which has to be removed before a mineral can be worked.

overcharge v [*Law*] to charge a defendant deliberately with every conceivable crime relating to his or her actual offence and thus gain an automatic advantage when such charges are whittled away during the plea-bargaining process.

overcrank v [*TV, Film*] to operate a camera or projector at a faster speed than is correct and thus create 'slow motion' on the screen; thus 'undercrank' is to operate the camera or projector more slowly than is correct, producing 'fast motion' on the screen. Both varieties of 'cranking' came from the early cameras which had to be hand-cranked and so were more susceptible than modern machinery to variations in operating speed.

overdetermine v [*Sociology*] a contemporary Marxist concept whereby the most important element of the social structure not only determines other elements but is also affected by them.

overdevelopment n [*Gliding*] an increase in the extent of cumulus cloud cover which reduces the sun's ability to heat the earth and thus slows thermal activity and hampers successful soaring.

overdub v [*Pop music*] to add extra sound tracks to a basic recording – more instruments, vocals, special effects or whatever is desired.

overfill n [*Metallurgy*] a protruding rib of metal which runs the length of a rolled product; it results from overfilling a **pass**.

overflow v [*Computing*] a computer does this when it generates, as a result of its calculations, a number that is too great for its screen to display or for the program to use for further calculations.

overhang n [*Stock market*] a large block of securities which, if placed on the market, would push prices down.

overhead 1. n [*Computing*] the time that a computer reserves purely for the maintenance of its own systems, rather than that used for running programs for the user. Such an overhead can detract marginally from the efficient and speedy running of those programs. 2. n [*US*] [*Journalism*] a wireservice bulletin which carries local news only and thus goes on 'over' the major newspapers towards its various local destinations. 3. n [*US*] [*Marine Corps*] the ceiling.

overhead absorption n [*Management*] See **absorption** 2.

overheads, also **burden, establishment expense** 1. n [*Management*] any expenditure on goods, services or labour which benefits a number of activities, products or **cost centres** but which cannot easily be measured. 2. n [*Management*] a portion of (1) that can be associated with a specific activity, process or cost centre by **absorption**. 3. n [*Management*] the total amount of overhead costs that are associated with a particular activity, product or cost centre.

overheating n [*Economics*] inflation which is caused by excessive pressure on resources during a period of expansion in demand.

overhung a [*Dog breeding*] See **lippy** 2.

overkill n [*Military*] the concept of being able to destroy a target more than once; it is a requirement which justifies the building of massive arsenals and the firing of many missiles, but which has no useful military application. See also **underkill**.

overlanded a [*UK*] [*Railways*] said of goods that arrive at a depot without a covering invoice.

overlap 1. n [*Lacrosse*] a numerical superiority achieved by the offensive team, by getting one player further ahead of the ball than the defence. 2. n [*Printing*] material added to the packing on a printing press to make a stronger impression on the medium. 3. n [*US*] [*Railways*] a section of the line controlled by one signal, that extends into a zone that falls under the responsibility of a separate signal. 4. n [*TV*] those areas of the country which can receive more than one independent television transmission.

overline n [*Journalism*] a caption set above an illustration or photo. See also **underline**.

overlines n pl [*US*] [*Banking*] credits available to

borrowers who have reached the limit of their borrowing from a small local bank – whose own limits are necessarily small – but who can obtain extra funds from a larger bank which will take on part of the commitment.

overman n [Coal-mining] an official of the mine who ranks between an undermanager and a **deputy**.

overmatter n [Printing] **matter** that has been typeset but is superfluous to the needs of an issue or edition.

overnight money n [Finance] ultra-short-term loans that are offered for the duration of one night only.

overnight multiple n [Finance] the dramatic results of a public offering of shares usually only held by **insiders**; such an offer usually multiplies the value of insider holdings 'overnight'.

overnights 1. n pl [UK] [TV] expenses paid to employees who are forced to stay away from their homes overnight while working on location or on any programme that is filmed away from the company studios. 2. n [US] [TV] the most immediate version of the ratings produced by the Nielsen TV Index, which are available to the networks on the morning after transmission.

overplay v [Lacrosse] to force an attacker to one side by blocking the direct path towards goal.

overpressure n [Military] nuclear blasts that are strong enough to destroy hardened silos or command bunkers; it is the amount of pressure generated by a nuclear explosion that exceeds the normal atmospheric pressure of 14.7 psi. Buildings collapse at 6 psi overpressure; humans can withstand levels of up to 30 psi but anything over 5 psi overpressure can cause burst eardrums and haemorrhaging.

overs n pl [UK] [Police] that surplus of property or money which has been taken in a robbery and not yet sold off, and which might now be stolen itself by other thieves unless it can be hidden securely.

overscan n [TV] the portion of the **raster** which extends beyond the visible area of the screen.

overshot 1. n [Oil rigs] a tool which retrieves lost **fish** from a well bore or formation. 2. n [Weaving] a weave structure in which the **weft** shoots over several **warp** threads at a time to make decorative areas.

oversold n [Stock market] an individual stock or a whole market which has experienced a sharp decline in price and which is thus considered ripe for an equally sharp rise. See also **overbought**.

oversquare n [Cars] when the bore (the diameter of the cylinder) exceeds the stroke of a piston.

overstretch v [Military] to overextend one's forces.

over-the-roof head n [US] [Journalism] See **skyline**.

overtrading n [Commerce] transacting more business than working capital permits and thus exerting a serious strain on cash flow due to the gaps between the manufacture of orders and the payment for them.

overture and beginners! excl [Theatre] the call to those actors who are to be 'discovered' on stage at the start of a play's first act, warning them to take up their positions.

overview n [Media, Government] a general, wide-ranging view; it comes from the concept of making an 'aerial surveillance' of an abstract or concrete problem.

ovolo n [Building, Plastering] a moulding section: convex quarter-round in profile.

owe are n [Government] **O.R.** which is an abbreviation of overall requirements; it is a payment which includes supplementary benefit to meet an insured person's expenses.

owls n pl [UK] [Railways] men working regular night shifts; they wear a badge consisting of two owls on a dark blue background.

own v [Hunting] said of hounds when they 'announce' that they have found a scent.

own goal n [Politics] this is when a terrorist blows him/herself up with a bomb designed to kill an opponent; the term was originally used of the IRA, but is now in more general use.

own the line v [Hunting] a hound which gives tongue on a **line** is said to 'own the line'.

oxidised a [Wine-tasting] said of a flat, stale, off-taste, due to exposure to air while in the bottle.

o.z. n [Drugs] pronounced Oh Zee, this means one ounce, a common measure for hashish or marijuana.

ozoners n pl [Film] drive in cinemas, where one can theoretically enjoy the fresh air and 'ozone'.

P

p and q *n* [*Prison*] peace and quiet meaning solitary confinement.

P and S *n* [*Futures market*] abbr of **Purchase and Sale statement** a statement provided by a broker which shows changes in the customer's net balance after the **offset** of a previously established **position**.

P, p *n* [*Basketball*] abbr of **personal** 'P' is a personal foul for which several free throws can be given; 'p' is a personal foul for which only one free throw is given. See also **T**.

P point *n* [*Skiing*] in ski-jumping this is the point that marks the start of the straight section of the landing slope; marked by a blue line, it is the optimum point for making a safe landing. See also **K point**.

PA 1. *n* [*Audio, Pop music*] abbr of **public address system** in pop performances this is the public equipment as opposed to the equipment that the band brings for its own use. **2.** *n* [*Business*] abbr of **personal assistant**. **3.** *n* [*Film*] abbr of **Personal Appearances** the promotional tours made by film stars to boost the release of their latest film.

pacers, also **speeders** *n pl* [*Industrial relations*] fast workers who are used by the management to accelerate production or to establish a high rate for the setting of piecework norms.

pacification *n* [*Military*] the removal of hostile guerrilla opposition from an area, often by such measures as destroying potentially friendly towns and villages – rather than let them provide bases for the guerrillas – as well as crops, cattle, wells, etc. which might provide them with supplies. Such efforts, rather than securing the loyalty of the local population – whose towns, crops and cattle are being destroyed – tend mainly to send more of them into the guerrilla ranks.

pacing *n* [*Communications*] a method of controlling the rate of transmission of data used by a receiving station to prevent the loss of information.

pack 1. *n* [*Coal-mining*] a stone support built to resist strata movement and sited at the roadside or in the **goaf**. **2.** also **scene pack** *n* [*Theatre*] a group of **flats**, all used in the same scene, which are stored together in the scenery **dock**. **3.** *n* [*Metallurgy*] a pile of steel sheets one on top of another; they are thus arranged for a variety of processes. **4.** *v* [*Computing*] to save space within a computer's memory by using electronic 'shorthand' to represent various data while it is being stored; the shorthand can be 'unpacked' when the data is actually required for retrieval and use. **5.** *v* [*Cycling*] to grease a bearing cup to ensure the proper lubrication of ball-bearings.

pack hunting *n* [*Business*] the recruiting en masse of a complete section or department of skilled staff who have already been working as a team for another firm.

pack rolling *n* [*Metallurgy*] the rolling of a number of steel sheets together; the result of this operation is a 'mill pack'.

pack shot *n* [*Advertising*] a close-up shot of the product for which the advertisement is being made; it is usually the final, climactic shot of the film.

package 1. *n* [*US*] [*Crime*] the victim of a kidnapping or gangland assassination. **2.** *n* [*Education*] any unit of educational material which is developed by someone other than the teacher and which can then be used by any teacher as and when required; it often refers to varieties of audiovisual teaching aids. **3.** also **wrap** *n* [*Radio*] a newsreader's script which sums up one or a number of stories; it is made from his/her comments, interviews, pieces of **actuality** and any other useful ingredients.

packaging *n* [*Art*] this was originated by the Surrealist Man Ray, with a one-off mysteriously wrapped package; the wrapping and bagging of objects large and small has been developed greatly by artists in recent years. The most notable packager is Christo, who wraps sections of Australian cliffs and similar massive natural structures.

packet *n* [*Computing*] a segment of data which is processed as a single unit in a communications system; thus 'to packet' is to sort out and segment suitable pieces of data for processing as a unit.

packet radio *n* [*Communications*] a packet-switching network which uses radio links to send packets to more than one station.

P

packet-switching *n* [*Communications*] the transfer of **packets** of data over a communications system, with each unit of data restricted as to size and bearing a specific **address**.

packhole *n* [*UK*] [*Coal-mining*] solid pillars of stone built at the face ends to hold up the tunnel.

packing *n* [*Computing*] the process of making the best use of available storage by fitting the data elements as closely together as possible within the memory.

Pac-Man strategy *n* [*Business*] a method of fighting off a takeover bid whereby the target company begins buying up shares of the predator company, thus threatening a counter-takeover; it is named after the popular arcade video game.

pact *v* [*Film*] to sign a contract. See also **ink**.

pad 1. *n* [*Aerospace*] a small section of an airfield where planes can warm up their engines prior to takeoff. 2. *n* [*Aerospace*] that section of the runway which the plane touches last or hits first when taking off or landing. 3. *n* [*Music*] sheet music. 4. *n* [*Opticians*] a small section of the spectacle frame that is attached to the inner side of a lens in front of the eye, to prevent the lens chafing against the sides of the nose.

pad, on the *adv* [*US*] [*Police*] referring to a policeman who shares in the receipt of bribes and payments made by members of the public to a corrupt police force.

pad room *n* [*US*] [*Circus*] the dressing tent for circus performers.

pad up *v* [*Cricket*] a batsman does this when he takes the ball deliberately on his pads rather than attempting to play it with his bat; it is a useful move, if sometimes risky given the vagaries of the LBW rule.

padding 1. *n* [*Dog breeding*] a reference to the lip thickness of certain breeds – Boxer, British Bulldog, etc.; such padding is vital for the correct appearance. 2. *n* [*Metallurgy*] in iron-founding this is the adding of extra metal to a casting to ensure solidity and uniformity.

paddle *n* [*Glass-making*] a device on which moulds are transported to the lehr oven.

paddlefoot *n* [*US*] [*Air Force*] an infantryman; or a member of a ground crew who helps maintain the aircraft but never flies.

Paddy *v* [*Navy*] abbr of **to do Paddy Doyle** to serve a period of detention in punishment cells.

paddy 1. *n* [*UK*] [*Coal-mining*] a general name for a variety of man-riding equipment used underground. Two sorts are used: a train drawn by a locomotive or a set of coaches attached to a rope which winds on and off a drum. Possibly it comes from the large number of Irish originally employed in mines. 2. *n* [*UK*] [*Railways*] a coal train that runs from the mine to the railhead.

Paddy Doyle *n* [*Navy*] a Royal Navy detention barracks or military prison. See also **brig**.

paganini *n* [*Film*] in Italian film crews this is a system of graded blocks used to raise or lower the height of the camera with great speed and accuracy. See also **two-four-six**.

page 1. *n* [*Computing*] a block of information which fills the display screen of the computer and which can be read as one might a page of a book or a file. 2. *n* [*Computing*] a set of 4096 consecutive bytes. 3. *n* [*Computing*] a subdivision of a program which can be moved in and out of main memory by the program operating system as and when required.

page traffic *n* [*Advertising*] an estimate of the number of readers per page of a publication.

page-turner *n* [*Publishing*] a best selling book which keeps its readers fascinated until the end. See also **legs 1**.

pagger *v* [*UK*] [*Market-traders*] to smash, to break, to ruin.

paid off in gold *part phr* [*Drugs*] this is when a dealer makes an arrangement to sell drugs to an undercover policeman who offers his gold badge rather than the money which the dealer is expecting.

pail hands *n pl* [*UK*] [*Railways*] carriage cleaners; it is a pun on 'Pale hands I loved beside the Shalimar' by Laurence Hope (1865–1904).

paint 1. *n* [*US*] [*Farming*] the brand of an implement, taken from its predominant colour; thus John Deere is 'green paint'. 2. *n* [*Gambling*] any picture cards. 3. *v* [*Computing*] in computer graphics this is to fill in an area with a colour, or with an identifying pattern, etc. 4. *v* [*Medicine*] to appear on the screen of a cathode ray tube. 5. *v* [*Military*] said of an object when it creates a **blip** on a radar screen, especially one that reveals itself as the position of an aircraft.

paint down *v* [*TV, Film*] to create fake 'Negroes' by making up white actors in blackface.

paintbox *n* [*Computing, TV, Video*] this is the tradename of a computer generated graphics system, made by Quantel, which can use its highly sophisticated hardware and software to create in a few minutes images which would take a studio or film laboratory days to achieve. The high cost to date of such machines means that they tend to be few in number and are rented for short periods at heavy costs.

painter *n* [*US*] [*Garment trade*] a worker who tends to soil white materials.

painterly painting *n* [*Art*] a term used to translate the German 'malerisch'; it is an attempt to represent in the artist's technique the vague and shifting essence of a subject. This style of painting is characterised by colour, texture and stroke, rather than by contours or by line.

painter's brush *n* [*Navy*] high, thin cirrus clouds that indicate potential bad weather.

painting the bus *n* [*Business*] the cosmetic, artificial alteration of a plan, proposal or request which still leaves the essence of that plan or proposal unchanged; it is expedient window-dressing with no really substantial modification.

painting the tape 1. *n* [*US*] [*Stock market*] illegal share price manipulation whereby a number of dealers trade together to create an artificial price rise, thus luring foolhardy investors who watch the fluctuations on the ticker tape. **2.** *n* [*US*] [*Stock market*] heavy trading in a given share which causes its repeated appearance on the ticker tape.

paintpot *n* [*TV*] a highly sophisticated version of telecine machine with which a producer can make electronic alterations in the colour ranges of a transmission.

pair *v* [*Politics*] when members of rival parties in the House of Commons or US Congress and other parliamentary bodies agree to abstain together from voting at such times as one of the pair is unable to attend the legislative assembly.

pair of spectacles *n* [*Cricket*] the score by a batsman of 0 in both innings; the 00 thus achieved supposedly resembles a pair of glasses.

pajama wagon *n* [*US*] [*Road transport*] a tractor equipped with sleeping quarters.

PAL 1. *n* [*US*] [*Marine Corps*] acro **Prisoner At Large** an individual who is being punished by being confined to the limits of the camp. **2.** *n* [*Military*] acro **Permissive Action Link** a remote digital code lock system on nuclear weapons which ensures that a bomb or warhead accidentally dropped does not detonate – although some release of radiation is generally seen to be inevitable. PAL equipment works with a code that is frequently changed and may also destroy the weapon if unauthorised arming or detonation is attempted.

palace guard *n* [*US*] [*Politics*] those in any US Administration considered to have the greatest (and most influential) access to a President.

pale *n* [*Heraldry*] a broad vertical strip through the middle of a shield.

palimony *n* [*US*] [*Law*] this comes from 'pal' plus 'alimony'; it is the payments that a growing number of former lovers, of no especial ability in themselves, are managing to extract from the celebrities with whom they once happened to live.

pallet-bombing *n* [*Military*] a means of bombing targets by placing bombs on flat pallets and then dropping both the bomb and its pallet from the doors of the plane.

pallet-track *n* [*UK*] [*Road transport*] runners incorporated in the vehicle floor, in which hydraulically raised arms run from front to rear to enable heavy pallets to be lifted off the floor to facilitate easy movement.

palm *n* [*Sailing, Ropework*] a small mitt with a thumb hole and a piece of chequered metal at the palm for pushing sail needles through tough canvas.

palm tree *n* [*Car salesmen*] See **square wheeler**.

paly *a* [*Heraldry*] divided into vertical strips.

pan 1. *n* [*Building*] a large, shallow metal container used as a mould for pouring concrete floors. **2.** *n* [*Film*] abbr of **panoramic shot** the action of rotating the camera horizontally to create a long, flat shot. **3.** *n* [*Shipping*] a shipping code; the calling station has an urgent message concerning the safety of a ship, aircraft or other vehicle or person on board or in sight of the plane or ship. **4.** *n* [*Music*] in West Indian steel bands this is a drum made from the top of a 44–gallon barrel; by extension, pan represents the whole lifestyle that surrounds steel-band music. **5.** *n* [*Theatre*] abbr of **panorama**.

pan, down the *adv* [*Motor-racing*] said of a competitor who is too far behind the other drivers to remain in any real contention.

pan the patients *v* [*US*] [*Medicine*] to distribute bedpans around a ward.

pancake 1. *n* [*Air travel*] a specially designed bullet for use by airline security guards who have to fire pistols inside the pressurised cabin of an aircraft; the bullet is in fact a canvas bag filled with lead shot which will make a killing wound at close range but will have slowed down so much by the time it reaches the far end of the aircraft that it will not penetrate the hull. **2.** *n* [*US*] [*Cattlemen*] a small riding saddle, as used in England. **3.** *n* [*Custom cars*] a hood modification, especially for cars with rounded, bulbous bonnets; the actual bonnet would be welded to the wings and front panel and a new, smaller bonnet would be cut out from the very top of the old one. **4.** *n* [*Electronics*] a flat or very short inductance coil. **5.** *n* [*TV, Film*] a small chunk of wood, hidden from the camera, on which short actors can stand to bring them up to the correct height demanded by their image and their role. **6.** *v* [*Air Force*] an aircraft does this when it descends rapidly in a level position in stalled flight, especially when it lands in this way, with the undercarriage still retracted. **7.** *n* [*Military*] US Dept of Defense code for: I wish to land.

pane 1. *n* [*Philately*] the sub-section or part of a sheet of stamps, usually separated by **gutter** margins. **2.** *n* [*Philately*] a leaf of 2,3,4,6 or more stamps in a booklet.

panel 1. *n* [*Coal-mining*] an area of coal worked within specific boundaries. **2.** *n* [*Journalism*] a short item, indented on either side, which is usually in bold face or italic type, with a rule or border at top and bottom.

panelling *n* [*Custom cars*] the filling of openings – windows, etc – with sheet metal, or covering a tube framework with steel.

pangram *n* [*Logology*] a word or sentence that contains every letter of the alphabet, eg: 'Quixotic knights' wives are found on jumpy old zebras', etc.

panhandle *n* [*Aerospace*] the firing handle of an ejector seat.

Panhonlib *n* [*Commerce*] acro **Panama, Honduras, Liberia** a merchant ship registered in one of these countries and flying a flag of convenience. See also **Panlibhonco**.

P

Panlibhonco n [Commerce] acro **Panama, Liberia, Honduras and Costa Rica** a merchant ship registered in one of these countries and flying a flag of convenience. See also **Panhonlib**.

pannikin-boss n [Aus. NZ] [Farming, Building] the foreman of a building site; the manager of a sheep station.

panopolis n [Government] in urban planning this is the gradual movement of population away from dependence on one centre towards the establishment of a number of separate centres and hierarchies as that population increases and becomes more dispersed.

panpot n [Audio] abbr of **panoramic potentiometer** an instrument which can vary the apparent position of a sound by altering the strengths of the signals to a number of speakers without altering the strength of the overall signal.

panther tracks n pl [US] [Cattlemen] spur marks across a saddle.

panting n [Ship-building] the movement of the plates of a ship's hull under stress, especially at the fore and aft of the ship; thus structures are designed to prevent such movements.

pantouflage n [Government] this comes from Fr. 'pantoufle' meaning 'slipper'; it is the tradition in the French civil service for its senior members to move smoothly and automatically into equally senior and influential positions within the nation's industries.

pantry check n [Marketing] a check into what is on the subject's kitchen or larder shelves; when combined with a **dustbin** check, the market researcher can provide his client with a full 'home audit'.

pants 1. n pl [Dog breeding] See **trousers**. 2. n [UK] [Prisons] a scrounger: 'he's always on the bum'. 3. n pl [Textiles] tangled loose threads. 4. also **spats, trouser** n [Aerospace] the fixed fairing that covers an aircraft's wheels and landing gear.

panzer n [Coal-mining] the armoured flexible conveyor (AFC); this is a heavy-duty chain conveyor which carries a coal-cutter or power loader and which can be moved forward as the face advances.

papavero n [Crime] in the Italian Mafia this means 'a real daddy', a senior Mafioso, a big shot.

paper 1. n [Finance] any form of money that is not in currency or specie: stocks, bonds, loan certificates, etc. 2. n [Theatre] advertising material put up outside the theatre. 3. v [Theatre] to give out free tickets (paper) to fill a poor house; thus a 'paper house' is an audience composed almost completely of free admissions.

paper a car, also **roll a car** v [US] [Car salesmen] See **trip a car**.

paper boys n pl [Glass-making] workers who put the trade mark on to the finished glassware.

paper feet n pl [Dog breeding] feet with thin and poorly cushioned pads.

paper jack n [Merchant navy] a captain with qualifications but no experience.

paper market n [Espionage] information generated by journalists, newspaper stringers, writers of 'confidential newsletters', diplomats, researchers, etc. in any country – all of which must be assessed by a CIA station. See also **paper mill**.

paper mill n [Espionage] in the CIA this means any interest group who attempts to further its cause with the intense production of supposedly useful information, usually fabricated, which is sold off to the highest bidder.

paper setting n [Advertising] the type-setting of an advertisement by the printer of the magazine or newspaper in which it will appear. See also **trade setting**.

paper tiger n [Politics] in Chinese communist terminology this is any country, person or weapon that looks outwardly terrifying but is in fact no more dangerous that a tiger made from paper. The term was coined in 1946 by Mao Zedong when he told correspondant Anna Louise Strong 'All reactionaries are paper tigers'.

papery a [Textiles] said of cloth that has been made excessively smooth and thin by **calendering**.

PAR n [Military] acro **Perimeter Acquisition Radar** sited at the former **ABM** base in North Dakota, this is used by the USAF for north-facing space tracking by phased array radars which can spot missiles coming over the Pole at a range of 4600km.

par 1. n [Golf] the standard score in strokes assigned to each hole on a course and as such the score expected, in fair conditions and barring disasters, from a first class player on that course; thus a given hole is 'par three', 'par five' etc. 2. n [Journalism] abbr of **paragraph**.

para a [Medicine] abbr of **paraplegic**.

paradiastole n [Literary criticism] the use of an alternative word, usually ironic or euphemistic, to describe a situation. It often refers to a person's mental or physical state; eg: 'tired and emotional' for 'extremely drunk'.

paradigm 1. n [Science] a general way of seeing the world which dictates to the scientist what kind of scientific work should be done and what kinds of theory will be acceptable. 2. n [Sociology] a school of sociological work, with its own theories, research methods etc.

paraffin budgie n [Oil rigs] a helicopter that serves an oil rig.

parajournalism n [Journalism] a type of unconventional journalism which brought in the personality of the writer, urged greater involvement than was traditional for many reporters, and took liberties with the once sacred facts. See also **new journalism**.

parallel 1. n [Audio] a connection between various electrical devices whereby a single current is split between the various devices. **2.** *n* [*UK*] [*Railways*] a speed limit of 50–55 mph that is set for regular travel between stations on the London underground system. See also **series, shunt 3**.

parallel turn *n* [*Skiing*] a turn in which one keeps one's skis parallel from beginning to end of the movement when turning on a downhill slope back up into the hill.

parallelism *n* [*Computing*] the simultaneous handling by a computer of a large number of calculations.

parameter *n* [*Communications*] a boundary, a limit, a basic factor, a framework; parameter has a number of highly specific, technical and abstruse meanings in mathematics, none of which seem to have been appreciated by those in business, government, communications, media, etc, who have elevated it into one of the most widely used (and abused) current vogue words.

parameter driven software *n* [*Computing*] a scheme whereby a user can specify a number (perhaps 50%) of the attributes he requires in a program; such programs are created with a number of inbuilt variables which can be used or discarded according to the individual whim. Such customisable software provides a cheaper compromise than having an entire program written to one's specific needs.

parametric design *n* [*Architecture*] an architectural school of the mid–1960s which emphasised the analysis, measurement and reconciliation of all those elements which they termed 'parameters' in a building.

paraph *n* [*Printing*] the flourish that follows certain ornate signatures.

parasite **1.** *n* [*Aerospace*] any aircraft which relies on another for propulsion and lift; such an aircraft can ride on the back of its 'parent', or be towed behind it. **2.** *n* [*Politics*] in Marxist terms these are the people without any legitimate occupation of their own who batten on to the efforts of those who do. It was first used to attack absentee landlords but is currently extended to define all those who rebel (in the style of Western youths) against the constraints of socialist states.

parasite drag *n* [*Gliding*] the drag of any surface of a glider that is not productive of lift.

parataxis *n* [*Literary criticism*] a style of writing in which sentences and clauses are ranged one after another without co-ordinating connectives; it is typical of the 'hard-boiled' style of US pulp writing.

parcel **1.** *n* [*Mining*] See **take 6**. **2.** *n* [*UK*] [*Prisons*] rather than remain all night in a cell with a plastic bucket full of excrement, prisoners prefer to wrap it in newspaper and toss the resulting 'parcel' out of the window. **3.** *v* [*Sailing, Ropework*] to bind strands of canvas around a rope before securing it to another rope.

parchment **1.** *n* [*Coffee production*] the dried

endocarp of the coffee bean. **2.** *n* [*Navy*] a rating's service certificate on which his abilities and personality are assessed by the commanding officer of each ship on which he serves.

pardon *n* [*US*] [*Coal-mining*] a side track for coal cars.

parent **1.** *n* [*Computing*] a node A is the parent of node B in a tree, if B is the root of one of the subtrees of the tree rooted at A. See also **tree**. **2.** *n* [*New Therapies*] in transactional analysis (**TA**), this is the judgemental part of one's being. **3.** *n* [*Science*] in nuclear physics this is a nuclide that becomes transformed into another nuclide (known as the daughter) by nuclear disintegration.

parent company *n* [*Commerce*] a company which holds more than 50% of the shares in a subsidiary company.

parent page *n* [*TV*] in teletext paging this is the page which immediately precedes the one that the user has specified as required on the screen.

parergon *n* [*Literary criticism*] a subordinate or secondary piece of writing, an embellishment, often carried out at one's leisure, of one's main work.

pargeting *n* [*Building, Plastering*] the lining of chimney flues with mortar; originally it was the solid decorative plasterwork to be found in some external work.

parish pump *a* [*Politics*] used of parochial or local politicians who are unable or unwilling to extend their knowledge or interests outside their own constricted social and/or geographical limits.

parity *n* [*Military*] a situation in which two hostile nations can offer equal military capability; it would arise especially in the case of a conflict between the US and USSR.

park *n* [*Soccer*] the actual field of play; thus 'keep it on the park' means keep the ball in play, rather than kicking it over the sidelines into touch.

park railing *n* [*Hunting*] any variety of iron fence.

parking *n* [*Finance*] placing one's assets in a safe investment where they can accrue some regular income while surveying the possibility for more spectacular investment.

parking orbit *n* [*Aerospace*] an orbit in which a spacecraft waits prior to moving on, either before landing or before proceeding further on its assigned journey.

parlay *v* [*Gambling*] to exploit something with great success; specifically it means to take a small stake and turn it into substantial winnings; this gambling use has been taken up in risk areas such as business, the stock market, etc.

parney *n, v* [*UK*] [*Market-traders*] water, rain; urination; to pour with rain; to urinate.

parole *n* [*Linguistics*] a term introduced by Ferdinand de Saussure (1857–1913) to denote language as it is spoken by an individual speaker at a given moment. See also **langue**.

P

parr n [Angling] a young salmon after it has got rid of its umbilical sac.

parrot 1. n [Aerospace] See **IFF**. **2.** also **cannel coal** n [Coal-mining] strong, non-banded coal with a satin sheen or wax lustre; such coal has a high volatile content and is readily ignitable.

parrot mouth n [Hunting] the overshot jaw of a hound.

parse v [Computing] in programming this is to resolve a string of characters representing, for example, a program statement, into its elemental parts as defined by, for instance, the program language; it comes from English grammar.

Part I Crimes n pl [US] [Law] major crimes, as defined by the FBI Uniform Crime Reports: aggravated assault, burglary, criminal homicide, rape, larceny, theft, motor vehicle theft, robbery. See also **Part II Crimes**.

Part II Crimes n pl [US] [Law] lesser crimes, as defined by the FBI Uniform Crimes Report; those not included in **Part I Crimes**.

partial tender n [US] [Commerce] a cheap way of gaining control of a company: shareholders are divided into 'first- and second-class' citizens. The top 51% are offered a high price in hard cash to obtain their shares and thus give the purchaser control; the remainder are later offered a package of securities that may (or more likely may not) be worth the same as the cash.

participant observation n [Sociology] a research technique in which the researcher observes a social group of which he/she is also a part; such observation is often on a covert basis.

participative political structure n [Sociology] a democratic society.

participatory art n [Art] art works that are created specifically to encourage the participation of the spectators, eg: **Environmental Art, Cybernetic Art, Happenings, Kinetic Art**.

particular average n [Shipping] an accidental loss on board ship, such as damage by fire or sea water, in which the ship itself is not threatened, merely the cargo; such a loss is borne wholly by the owners of that cargo.

particularity n [Religion] the role of Christ as a reincarnation of God in human form at a particular time and place.

parting n [Metallurgy] in iron-founding this is the plane where the sections of a mould are separated.

parting powder n [Metallurgy] in iron-founding this is the material that is dusted on to a mould to reduce the adherence of the sand to the cooling metal.

partly paid a [Stock market] referring to a security on which part of the issue price has been paid but the remainder has still to be paid, at a specified rate.

parton n [Science] in nuclear physics this is each of the hypothetical point-like constituents of the nucleon which, according to RP Feynman in 1969, explain the way that the nucleon inelastically scatters electrons of very high energy.

party n, v [Sex] sexual intercourse between a prostitute and a client, hence the query 'What kind of party did you fancy . . . ?' Different 'parties' come at different prices.

party line n [Espionage] the official standpoint of an intelligence agency.

party plan n [Commerce] a scheme for selling products by setting up parties – eg: Tupperware parties – at which they are featured. A hostess volunteers to provide a few refreshments, the salesman brings along his wares and afterwards the hostess receives some free gifts or discounted goods as her reward.

partyness n [Politics] this comes from Russian 'partinost' and means the use of the Party and its ideology as a guide and an inspiration in every part of one's daily life – professional, social and recreational.

pasadena, also **el paso** n [Film] two punning references to the idea of 'passing' a deal, ie: turning it down, but still remaining open to further suggestions; it comes from the poker bid of 'pass' in which one skips a round of betting but still remains playing that hand.

PASCAL n [Computing] an algorithmic **high-level language** used for programming which is popular among scientific users, although giving way to COBOL and **FORTRAN** in this field. See also **BASIC, FORTH**.

pass 1. v [US] [Car salesmen] to refuse a deal. **2.** v [Gambling] when the **shooter** in dice makes a winning throw. **3.** v [Pop music] to turn down a deal or a new singer or band. See also **pasadena**. **4.** also **push out** n [TV] See **dump 10**. **5.** n [Metallurgy] a single passage of a steel **bar, billet** or **bloom** through a pair of rolls for the purpose of altering its shape and/or reducing the cross-sectional area. **6.** n [Magic] the secret cutting of a deck of cards. **7.** n [Magic] any form of sleight-of-hand. **8.** excl [Magic] a command, used to embellish a part or the climax of a given **effect**.

pass a dividend v [Finance] the directors of a company do this when they vote against issuing a dividend for the current financial year.

pass instruction n [Computing] See **no-op instruction**.

pass-along n [Economics] the way in which the increased costs to a producer or a creator of a service are passed along to the consumer or purchaser in the form of higher prices, rents, etc.

pass-along readership, also **pass-on readership** n [Advertising] those readers who do not actually buy a given newspaper or magazine but still read someone else's copy and as such are potential targets for the advertising it contains. See also **page traffic**.

passant a [Heraldry] walking along towards the **dexter** with the head in profile and the right forefoot raised.

passenger 1. *n* [*Gambling*] a poor card-player. 2. *n* [*Sport*] any member of a sporting team who is considered not to be playing to capacity, through injury, laziness, deliberate cheating, etc.

passengers *n pl* [*Military*] the multiple warheads that are fired from a **MIRV** bus on a signal from its guidance computer; each missile should explode within 600 ft to 100 ft of its target and either of these figures should be adequate to cause satisfactory destruction.

passer *n* [*Athletics*] in relay races this is the runner who is about to pass on the baton to the next runner.

passive *a* [*Electronics*] said of equipment that is incapable of amplification or power generation.

passive bond *n* [*Commerce, finance*] a bond on which no interest is payable. See also **active bond**.

passive commerce *n* [*Commerce*] goods that are imported or exported by a country which uses ships that are registered in other countries.

passive defence *n* [*Military*] any non-aggressive (unarmed) modes of defence: cover, concealment, subterfuge, dispersal or mobility.

passive safety *n* [*Cars*] safety features that are built into a car but which, unlike **active safety**, only operate after a crash has taken place: seat belts, cushioned fascias, airbags, strengthened construction, etc.

passive smoking *n* [*Medicine*] a situation in which non-smokers inhale cigarette smoke from the atmosphere, despite their own reluctance to smoke.

passive star *n* [*Computing*] a network topology in which the outer nodes connect to a single central node; this central node has no autonomous function, serving merely to make a connection between the other nodes and permit their mutual transmissions. See also **active star, network architecture**.

pass-over *n* [*Aerospace*] that time when a spacecraft passes over a given point.

password hacker *n* [*Computing*] a meddler in a computer room who is not working but merely attempting to pick up scraps of information by fiddling aimlessly with the machines. See also **hacker**.

paste 1. *n* [*Angling*] a bait made from compressed bread and water. 2. *n* [*Cheese-making*] the interior of soft and semi-soft cheeses. 3. *n* [*US*] [*Garment trade*] a second-rate sewing job.

pasteboard *n* [*US*] [*Theatre*] a ticket.

pasteup *n* [*Advertising, Printing*] a printing process whereby the elements of an advertisement, booklet, newspaper page, etc. are assembled and pasted on to a white board (suitably ruled as to column width, etc. when necessary) to show their correct positions.

pastology *n* [*Education, Science*] the study of the past – as opposed to futurology – and the drawing of conclusions regarding the present that are based on that research.

patacca *n* [*UK*] [*Police*] this comes from It. for 'worthless rubbish' and means fake jewellery in general and fake 'Swiss watches' in particular; such watches are also referred to as a 'mug's ticker' or a 'ramped watch' and are popularly peddled by street traders and airline stewards.

patch 1. *v* [*Advertising*] to alter one small element of a layout or a plate. 2. *v* [*Computing*] to make a minute alteration in a program or in the workings of a machine. 3. *v* [*Technology*] to connect up temporarily one electronic device to another; especially one radio or telephone system to another. 4. *n* [*UK*] [*Police*] an area within the jurisdiction of a given police station; an individual's beat. See also **manor**.

patch system *n* [*Social work*] a method of organising local authority social work whereby each geographical area is allocated to one or two social workers, and all referrals that arise within those areas are referred to them.

patchboard *n* [*Computing*] a matrix of sockets that can be interconnected manually, using **patchcords**, to make temporary connections between devices and to connect **peripherals** to computer lines.

patchcord *n* [*Computing*] a cable with a plug at each end for use in connecting the sockets of a **patchboard**.

patcher *n* [*Logging*] in a sawmill this is one who cuts out knots, pitch marks, etc, when preparing panels for sanding.

patera *n* [*Building, Plastering*] any small flower used as an ornament.

path 1. *n* [*Medicine*] abbr of **pathology**. 2. also **pattern** *n* [*Railways*] a schedule which is allotted to or is available to an individual train over a given route.

pathetic fallacy *n* [*Philosophy*] the use of anthropomorphic images and metaphors when considering inanimate objects or nature.

pathopoeia *n* [*Literary criticism*] the deliberate arousing of emotions through writing.

patrial *a* [*UK*] [*Government*] referring to those who have the right to live in the UK; thus 'non-patrial' means the opposite. In many cases the two words appear to stand for 'white' and 'non-white' as far as immigration practice is concerned.

patrimonial *a* [*Politics*] referring to that area immediately subtending a nation's coastal waters which also belongs to that nation, although the shipping and airplanes of other nations may pass through or over that area with impunity. It is measured at approximately 200 miles beyond the edge of the territorial (coastal) waters, which themselves run 12 miles from the coastline.

pattern *n* [*Metallurgy*] in iron-founding this is a model of wood, resin, plaster, metal or another suitable material around which the mould cavity is formed.

P

pattern bargaining *n* [*Industrial relations*] negotiations which bring in examples of settlements between similar groups of workers and their employers as a means of using such precedents to further the satisfactory solution of the current situation.

pattern variable *n* [*Sociology*] a phrase coined by Talcott Parsons as part of his theory that all social action could be found within a range of five main dichotomous patterns of behaviour.

patzer *n* [*Chess*] a poor player, a rabbit; it comes from Ger. 'patzen' meaning 'to bungle'.

paunch *v* [*Shooting*] to disembowel a dead rabbit.

pave paws *n pl* [*Military*] two phased array radars sited in Otis Air National Guard Base, Massachusetts, and Beale Air Force Base, California, which watch for SLBMs; they also help with space tracking. Two further sites are planned for Georgia and Texas.

pavement *n* [*Religion*] the level of the sanctuary, a space at least six feet long, that extends from the lowest step before the altar to the communicants' rail.

pawl *n* [*Weaving*] the lever that fits into the teeth of a ratchet to stop the ratchet from turning backwards.

pawn *v* [*Stock market*] to use one's stocks as security for a bank loan.

PAWOB *n* [*Air travel*] acro **Passenger Arriving Without Baggage** a passenger whose luggage has been mislaid or misdirected during his/her journey.

pax *n* [*Air travel*] this comes from 'passengers' and means the fare paying customers on a flight.

pay on the line *v* [*Business*] to pay bills promptly.

pay or play *n* [*Film*] a contract under which the studio is forced to pay a star or director for their services, whether or not the film for which they have been hired is actually made.

pay pole *n* [*Logging*] a log fit for commercial use.

pay zone *n* [*Oil rigs*] the stratum of rock formation in which oil or gas is found; it comes from gold-miners' 'pay dirt'.

paybob *n* [*Navy*] the senior accountant officer.

payload **1.** *n* [*Military, Aerospace*] the bombs, warheads, etc. carried in a military aircraft; or the capsule, instruments, astronauts etc. carried in a space vehicle. **2.** *n* [*Air travel*] that part of an airliner's load from which the company makes its money; the passengers, cargo and possibly airmail.

payment buyer *n* [*US*] [*Car salesmen*] a customer buying by instalments who is more worried by the monthly payment than the final purchase price.

payoff **1.** *n* [*US*] [*Car salesmen*] the amount a customer still owes on a car. **2.** *n* [*Crime*] any confidence trick whereby the victim is lured into making a large bet or investment by his initial success with a smaller bet or investment; once he

has been persuaded to make that larger investment he will invariably lose it.

payola *n* [*Record business*] the payment of bribes, in cash and commodities, to disc jockeys who would then play certain records more than others and thus ensure their increased sales. It was allegedly wiped out in the 'Payola Scandals' of the late 1950s, but few insiders would really believe that. Thus 'plugola' means the purchased plugging of specific records on the radio; 'royola' means the promise of a share in the royalties of a record that a corrupt DJ has been willing to plug to success.

pay-per-view **1.** *n* [*Video*] the system of video rental whereby a store purchases cassettes wholesale and then rents them to customers. **2.** *n* [*Video*] the system whereby stores rent out videocassettes which they in turn have leased from a central supplier, reimbursing that supplier for each rental. **3.** *n* [*TV*] the system for the distribution of television programmes whereby the consumer pays directly for the programmes viewed, in contrast to 'free' television which is financed by advertising, licence fees, or Government.

payroll vote *n* [*UK*] [*Government*] the votes that are cast in the House of Commons by ministers and Parliamentary private secretaries, all of whose absolute loyalty to the Government is supposedly assumed.

pbs *n pl* [*Science fiction*] abbr of **paperback books**.

PBW *n* [*Military*] abbr of **Particle Beam Weapons** high-energy, sub-atomic particle beams generated by huge nuclear accelerators of hitherto unprecedented power and designed for use as anti-ballistic missile weapons. Supporters of space warfare envisage such platforms dominating the earth from the high altitudes. Space PBWs are the stuff of true science fiction; as far as any development schedule might be considered, they are due to follow the laser weaponry (**SBL**) into the arms factories. Such PBW development as does exist is strictly ground-based.

PC **1.** *n* [*Gambling*] abbr of **percentage** the advantage gained by offering less than the true odds, or by using crooked dice; thus 'percentage dice' means crooked dice which work in the cheater's favour; 'PC game' means a percentage game in which the bank always keeps the advantage by offering less than honest odds; 'percentage tops and bottoms' means a pair of crooked dice, one of which is mis-spotted, usually by having two 2s or two 5s on the same die. **2.** *Lat. abbr* [*Medicine*] medication or treatment to be given after meals; it comes from Lat. 'post cenum' meaning 'after dinner'.

pc *n* [*Navy*] abbr of **polite conversation** an art instilled into officer cadets.

PD–59 *n* [*Military*] Presidential Directive No. 59: President Carter's executive order, signed in mid-1980, which supposedly redefined US strategic doctrine in terms of 'limited options counterforce targeting' and called for the first time on US forces to enable themselves to fight an enduring and protracted nuclear war. For all President Reagan's distaste of his predecessor's efforts, PD–59 remains the basis of much of his own nuclear foreign policy. See also **countervailing strategy**.

PDL *n* [*Computing*] abbr of **Push-Down List** any priority queue, the set of whatever things the operator must do next.

pea *n* [*Aus.*] [*Horse-racing*] the favourite; it refers to the pea which is used in the three-shell game and which signifies the winning shell.

peaceful nuclear technology *n* [*Politics*] any nuclear research or development which ostensibly concentrates on the creation of energy and ignores the military possibilities of enriched uranium; the results of such research projects are termed 'peaceful nuclear devices'.

Peacekeeper *n* [*Military*] the **MX** missile.

peach picker *n* [*US*] [*Road transport*] See **cherry picker 3**.

peacock alley *n* [*US*] [*Hotels*] the main lobby or promenade of fashionable luxury hotels; it originally described that of the Waldorf-Astoria Hotel, New York.

peak *v* [*Custom cars*] to form a point with metalwork; it is often used on air scoops or over headlights.

peak day *n* [*Gas industry*] the twenty-four hour period of greatest total gas send out in any given period under consideration.

peak experience *n* [*New therapies*] a term coined by Abraham Maslow to describe the breakthrough moments of supreme emotional significance that transcend any other levels of perception that may hitherto have been achieved; it is the sensing of life's every nuance with one's entire being.

peak hour, also **peak time** *n* [*TV*] a **daypart** at which time TV viewing figures are at their most concentrated; it runs from approximately 6.30 pm to 10.30 pm allowing for season and daily (the weekends differ) alterations.

peak (hour) pricing *n* [*Utilities*] a proposed price structure for US electricity: charges vary as to the time of day the electricity is consumed; the greater the overall demand, the more the electricity costs the consumer. See also **time-of-day**.

peak shaving **1.** *n* [*Gas industry*] the use of fuels and equipment to generate or manufacture gas to supplement the normal supply of pipeline gas during periods of extremely high demand. **2.** *n* [*Technology*] the storing of energy when demand is low so that it can be used to bolster supplies when demand increases again.

peaker log *n* [*Logging*] the top log on a load of logs. See also **brink log**.

peaking *n* [*US*] [*Politics*] a method of campaigning which seeks to bring every effort to a triumphal crescendo in the day or two prior to the actual election.

peanut gallery *n* [*US*] [*Theatre*] the highest gallery with the cheapest seats and the most vociferous theatre-goers. See also **gods**.

peanut wagon *n* [*US*] [*Road transport*] a small tractor hauling a large **semi-trailer**.

peardrops *n pl* [*Wine-tasting*] an undesirable overtone sometimes noticeable in poorly made white wines of lesser vintages. The wine is probably unstable and in dubious condition, but still drinkable.

pearling *n* [*Surfing*] when the nose of the surfboard dips below the waves during a ride.

pearls *n pl* [*Hunting*] the bony swellings that form a ring around the **burr** or coronet of a stag.

peasant painting *n* [*Art*] the spare-time paintings created by Chinese peasants in the aftermath of the **Cultural Revolution**; they were characterised by technical proficiency and stylistic uniformity.

peavey *n* [*Logging*] a lever, 5ft–7ft long, fitted with a socket and spike and a curved steel hook which works on a bolt; it was invented by Joseph Peavey in 1838, near Bangor, Maine.

pec *n* [*Body-building*] abbr of **pectoral muscles** thus 'lats' means 'lateral muscles', 'trips' means 'triceps'.

peck horn *n* [*Music*] in jazz this is a mellophone or saxophone.

pecker pole *n* [*Logging*] a long, thin log.

peculiar *n* [*Printing*] any character in a type fount that is very rarely used; these are often mathematical or foreign symbols or letters.

PED *n* [*UK*] [*Prisons*] acro **Parole Eligibility Date**.

ped **1.** *n* [*US*] [*Traffic controller*] abbr of **pedestrian**. **2.** *n* [*Agriculture*] an individual natural soil aggregate such as a crumb, prism or block, as opposed to a clod, which is a mass of such peds.

peddler *n* [*Drugs*] a retail dealer in narcotics, as opposed to the **connection**, who works as a wholesaler.

pedestal *n* [*Aerospace*] a raised box, sited between the pilot and co-pilot, which houses many of the aircraft's controls and the **interfaces** between various systems.

pedestrian housewife *n* [*Advertising*] a poster measuring five foot high by three foot four inches wide, consisting of four double-crown sheets and mounted at street level for maximum accessibility to passing shoppers.

peek *n* [*Computing*] in programming this is a high-level language instruction that examines the content of of an absolute memory location (see **absolute address**). See also **pokel**.

peekaboo **1.** *n* [*Computing*] a technique used when data is stored on punched cards: one card is placed on top of the next to ensure that all the

P

punched holes have been sited correctly. **2.** *n* [*Business*] the taking of a number of elements in a business situation and checking whether or not they match up; this comes from the computing use (see **1**).

peekaboo system *n* [*Data processing*] a manual data processing system which uses holes in specific areas of a card to identify given attributes. By placing cards on top of each other it is possible to sort out those with the attribute one wishes to isolate.

peel 1. *v* [*US*] [*Cattlemen*] to skin the hide from cattle. **2.** *v* [*Croquet*] to hit a ball other than one's own through a hoop. **3.** *v* [*Rock climbing*] to fall off a rock face.

peeling *n* [*US*] [*Paper-making*] imperfections in the finished paper caused by a rough finish, or unequal or incorrect treatment of the pulp.

peep *n* [*Espionage*] a specialist in clandestine photography.

peephole optimisation, also **local optimisation** *n* [*Computing*] an attempt to make the running of a program fully time-efficient by exploiting features of the machine's **architecture** so as to remove as far as possible the potential for **local** mishandling. See also **global optimisation, optimisation**.

peever *n* [*UK*] [*Market-traders*] a public-house.

peewee *n* [*Marbles*] the target marble in the game. See also **dib, duck, kimmie, immie, mib**.

peewees 1. *n pl* [*US*] [*Cattlemen*] short-topped boots worn by cowboys. **2.** *n pl* [*Marbles*] marbles under the average size. **3.** *n pl* [*US*] [*Meat trade*] small, stunted lambs or pigs.

peg 1. *v* [*Gambling*] to place a marker which indicates the dealer in a card game or the point in craps. **2.** *v* [*Gambling*] to mark cards surreptitiously during play, by using a drawing pin concealed in a bandage on a finger or thumb. **3.** *v* [*Shooting*] a gundog does this when it seizes squatting game instead of flushing it correctly. **4.** *n* [*Shooting*] the mark of a **stand** in grouse shooting. **5.** *n* [*Cricket*] a stump. **6.** *n* [*UK*] [*Military*] in the British army this is a charge; usually as in 'on a peg' meaning on a charge, under arrest. **7.** also **stick board** *n* [*UK*] [*Railways*] a semaphore signal.

peg back *v* [*Horse-racing*] to overtake or gain on another horse.

peg house *n* [*Sex*] a brothel staffed by male homosexual prostitutes; thus 'peg-boy' is one who frequents a peg house.

peg out *v* [*Croquet*] to end the game by hitting a ball that has already gone through all the hoops against the winning post.

peg prices *n pl* [*Finance*] prices that are held at artificial levels, usually determined by government interference.

pegging *n* [*Audio*] in recording this is a sharp swing in the needle of a voice unit (VU) meter caused by a sudden, loud noise.

peggy 1. *n* [*Navy*] a dockyard messenger, often a partially disabled dockyard worker who runs errands, cleans up and makes tea. **2.** *n* [*Navy*] a ship's mess steward.

pegs *n pl* [*UK*] [*Railways*] signals.

pel *n* [*Photo-typesetting*] abbr of **pixel**.

pelican in her piety *n* [*Heraldry*] a pelican with wings raised, pecking her own breast, with her young feeding on her blood. The myth that the pelican feeds her young on her own blood was originally Egyptian (then possibly referring to a different species) and became an early symbol of mankind's redemption through Christ's sacrifice.

pen *n* [*Sheep-shearing*] a division of a shearing shed; hence it is the actual work of shearing, the group of sheep one is given to sheer. Thus 'penmate' is a shearer who works out of the same pen.

pen and ink *n* [*UK*] [*Market-traders*] pain, punishment, suffering.

penalty book *n* [*Publishing*] a book that is forced on a publisher by an author as part of the contract so that the publisher can publish the book which he actually wants to publish.

penalty killer *n* [*Ice-hockey*] a skilful defensive player who is used especially when a team has a man in the penalty box since his ability will outweigh that deficiency.

pencil round *n* [*Building, Plastering*] a profile, ranging from a light angle to the approximate diameter of an ordinary pencil, which is formed at external angles.

pencil-case *n* [*Book-binding*] the protuberance of loose paper which has not been properly pressed in at the joint of the end paper and the boards.

pendant *n* [*Sailing, Ropework*] a short rope with a thimble spliced into it to which tackle is hooked.

pendulum arbitration *n* [*Industrial relations*] See **flip-flop arbitration**.

Penelope *n* [*Needlework*] a double-thread canvas used for needle tapestry work.

penetrate *v* [*US*] [*Gliding*] to fly rapidly without great loss of altitude, especially through sinking air or against the direction of the wind; the ability to 'penetrate' is a highly valued quality in higher performance planes.

penetration aids *n pl* [*Military*] decoy objects that are released from a missile as it nears its target in order to divert anti-ballistic missiles; they range from dummy warheads to metallic chaff and plastic 'missile' shapes.

penetration pricing *n* [*Commerce*] the setting of a low price to encourage widespread purchasing of a new product.

penetration rate *n* [*Marketing*] the proportion of a target market that buys a new brand at least once.

penguin 1. *n* [*Air Force*] a training machine, with all the details of a real aircraft, except for its flying power, which is used to familiarise novices with the cockpit. **2.** *n* [*Air Force*] a non-flying member of the RAF: ground crew, clerks, etc.

penguin suit *n* [*Aerospace*] an astronaut's space suit; basically it consists of tight-fitting overalls.

penitentiary *n* [*US*] [*Garment trade*] a shop where work is very strictly regulated.

penk *n* [*Angling*] a minnow.

penman *n* [*UK*] [*Police*] a forger.

penny dog *n* [*Mining, Logging*] an assistant foreman.

penny stock *n* [*Stock market*] a common stock which has a value of less than one dollar – thus highly speculative.

pensioneer *v* [*Politics*] to campaign in an election on the basis of a promised rise in the rate of the old age pension.

pentitent *n* [*Geography*] a spike or pinnacle of compact snow or ice, resulting from the ablation of a snow or ice field under the heat of the sun.

people *n* [*Air travel*] the passengers, but not the crew, carried on a flight.

people journalism *n* [*Journalism*] that style of journalism which is dedicated to the celebration of the famous, no matter how transitory and trivial is their success; it is taken from the social section of 'Time' magazine, entitled 'People' and latterly from People magazine, which exists solely on celebrities.

people sniffer *n* [*Military*] a chemically based machine which can 'sniff out' enemy troops in densely overgrown or jungle areas; by analysing the air, it checks for the ammonia odours of human sweat and notes the tiny seismic reverberations of humans walking.

people-related problems *n pl* [*Industrial relations*] any errors in the workplace that stem from human failings – forgetfulness, hangovers, drinking at work, drugs, worry, instability, temper, etc. – rather than the breakdown or malfunction of the machinery.

people's democracy *n* [*Politics*] a political system in which power is regarded as being invested in the masses. Specifically, in Marxist terms it is the intermediate stage between a **bourgeois democracy** and Soviet democracy – 'a dictatorship of the proletariat without Soviet form' – which will develop into full socialism under the auspices of the Soviets and the implementation of the class struggle.

people's detailing *n* [*Architecture*] a style of house-building popular in the UK in the 1950s: devoid of style or taste, it indulged every petty bourgeois obsession with scaled-down grandeur, all imprisoned in super-suburban environments.

PEPE *n* [*Military*] acro **Parallel Element Processing Ensemble** a US army program for linking together the mass of computers required to process, analyse and respond to the information gained from the mass of US surveillance and sensor input. PEPE will co-ordinate between 300–900 minicomputers, all feeding into a massive mainframe machine. The new system will operate at 800 million instructions per second; it is more than adequate to deal with the estimated 12 million instructions per second that are required to track 200 targets, and the 30 million i.p.s. proposed for ballistic missile defense (**BMD**).

pepper *n* [*Skipping*] the speed at which the rope is turned as quickly as possible.

pepper-fogging *n* [*US*] [*Police*] the spraying by police of rioting/demonstrating crowds with tear gas, brand-named Pepper Gas.

pepper's ghost *n* [*Theatre*] a trick used to create a 'ghost' on stage by using an inclined sheet of plate glass on to which the image of an actor can be projected as if 'walking on air'; it was first developed by Prof. John Henry Pepper (1821–1900).

peppery 1. *a* [*Painting*] said of paint in which small and uniform pieces of foreign matter are distributed. See also **seedy**. **2.** *a* [*Wine-tasting*] used to describe a raw harshness due to immature and unsettled components which have yet to marry together properly; it is noticeable in young ports and full red wines.

per diem *n* [*Business, Film*] expenses and allowances which are either paid each day, or on the basis of each day's expenditure.

perceptual mapping *n* [*Marketing*] See **brand mapping**.

perceptual realism *n* [*Art*] the work of Jack Chambers since 1969 which takes the form of realistic paintings, based on colour photographs, and accompanied by abstruse verbal statements; the aim of his work is to create a type of 'pure' visual experience that exists before culture intervenes and clamps pre-ordained assumptions on the spectator's vision.

perch *n* [*Theatre*] a platform on which lights are mounted and from there directed on to the stage.

perched water *n* [*Mining*] water lodged over an impervious stratum of restricted dimensions at a higher level than that of the water table.

perching *n* [*Tanning*] the softening of leather by suspending the hide from a horizontal bar, then scraping it with a circular knife called a moon knife.

percy *n* [*UK*] [*Military*] an officer or an educated NCO or private.

perennial candidate *n* [*US*] [*Politics*] any politician who continually stands for office, but never achieves his/her objective.

perfect *a* [*Antiques*] referring to a level of restoration that approximates perfection but in fact falls below that required of **museum restoration**.

perfect binding 1. *n* [*Book-binding*] a type of thermo-plastic binding often used for paperbacks in which unsewn sheets are glued individually to the spine. **2.** *n* [*Publishing*] a binding process in which the backs of the **signatures** are trimmed and held together with an adhesive; the name refers not to the quality of the process, but to its

P

originator 'The Sheridan Perfect Binder' designed around 1893.

perfect competition 1. *n* [*Economics*] market competition in which all elements of monopoly have been removed and the market price of a commodity is beyond the control of individual buyers and sellers – neither of whom have any preference as to the various units of the commodity that is for sale, nor as to the individuals involved in the transactions. **2.** also **pure competition** *n* [*Business*] See **atomistic competition**.

perfect market *n* [*Economics*] a market situation, either actual or theoretical, from which all adverse factors have been removed.

perfecta *n* [*Gambling*] a combined bet in horse-racing that involves both the first and second horses in a race. See also **exacta, quinella**.

perfects *n pl* [*Gambling*] dice that are true cubes, measured to within the nearest 1/10,000 of an inch.

performance 1. *n* [*Linguistics*] a term coined by Noam Chomsky (born 1928) to define an individual's use of language in given utterances, which often contain aspects that run contrary to that language's basic rules, eg: hesitations, unfinished sentences, grammatical errors, etc. See also **competence 2. 2.** *n* [*Video*] the extent to which a given cassette succeeds in terms of sales and rentals. **3.** *n* [*Video*] a videocassette rental; the premise is that the hire payment is the equivalent of a cinema ticket. The product can be seen by the hirer but it remains the property of the store or manufacturer.

performance art *n* [*Art*] any form of 'artwork' which comprises a variety of forms: dancing, acting, music, film, video, etc. – all of which are intended to execute a prescribed course of actions before an audience.

performance contract *n* [*US*] [*Education*] a contract made with a private education organisation to accept an agreed fee to improve the educational standards of a group of public school pupils.

performer *n* [*Navy*] a sailor who makes a habit of causing trouble.

peri care *n* [*US*] [*Medicine*] the cleaning of the vulva after delivery of a child.

peril point *n* [*Economics*] the point beneath which the lowering of import tariffs can begin to have a seriously harmful effect on native industrial production.

perimeter weighting *n* [*Sport*] the extending, in the manufacture, of the optimum **sweet spot** on a bat or golf club to maximise the area of effective contact with the ball.

period of grace *n* [*Law, Business*] the time allowed to a party in a contract to fulfil those obligations that have been incurred within that contract.

periodic sentence *n* [*Linguistics*] a sentence which holds back the completion of the thought it contains until its end, which comes after a number of subordinate clauses.

periodisation *n* [*Sociology*] the division of historical researches into set periods; these can be based on monarchs or dynasties, modes of production, fashions, etc.

peripherals 1. *n pl* [*Computing*] equipment linked to the central processing unit of a computer which enhances and increases its basic functions: printers, extra disk drives, external hard disks, terminals that connect with other machines, etc. Peripherals may be 'smart' – with some processing ability of their own – or, if bereft of such ability, 'dumb'. **2.** *n pl* [*Public relations*] secondary, provincial, low circulation or low audience media, of only marginal use in a PR campaign.

periphrasis *n* [*Literary criticism*] the use of circumlocutory words and phrases to inflate but not alter a simple concept; typical examples are the use of 'situation' in 'neck-and-neck situation', 'war-fighting situation' etc.

perisher *n* [*Navy*] the periscope course taken by officers hoping to qualify for service in submarines; it comes from a corruption of 'periscope' and the fact that the course, which many fail to pass, is 'perishing hard'.

permanent arms economy *n* [*Politics*] in International Socialist terminology this means the United States of America.

permanent revolution *n* [*Politics*] a theory developed by Leon Trotsky (1879–1940) whereby the security and continuance of the Soviet Revolution depended on there being a series of European revolutions to stand beside it.

permissible dose *n* [*Science*] the amount of radiation that, in the light of present knowledge, can be absorbed by a human being without suffering appreciable bodily injury. Given the advances in knowledge, this dose does appear to be shrinking in direct proportion to the more one learns of the subject.

permission *n* [*Advertising*] the psychological factor which allows a potential consumer to purchase and use an advertised product.

permissive waste *n* [*Law*] the act of deliberately permitting the buildings on an estate to fall into disrepair and decay.

PERRLA *mnem* [*Medicine*] **pupils equal, round, reactive to light and accommodation**.

persecuted minority *n* [*UK*] [*Railways*] labourers who work in the engine sheds.

persille *a* [*Cheese-making*] said of cheeses with internal molds.

persistence *n* [*Computing*] the length of time that the screen of a VDU or cathode ray tube (CRT) holds the images written on it.

person *n* [*Sociology*] in the decade and a half since the burgeoning of the women's liberation movement, the attack on 'male' vocabulary – spokesman, chairman, etc – has led to a widespread use of 'person' in a variety of neologisms – spokesperson, chairperson, etc. Despite the ostensible androgynous nature of these usages, it can usually be assumed that in such awkward contexts, 'person' equals 'woman'.

personal construct theory n [Social work] 'A person's processes are psychologically channelised by the way in which he anticipates events'. (George Kelly, in L. Schrest 'The Psychology of Personal Constructs: George Kelly', 1964.)

personal explanation n [UK] [Politics] a statement made by a Member of the House of Commons to his/her fellow members in an effort to mitigate such conduct as has been declared by them unacceptable on moral, social or criminal grounds.

personal property n [Law] all property that is moveable and may be legally taken from place to place by the owner. See also **real property**.

personal social services 1. n pl [Social work] those social services that are concerned with the needs and problems that inhibit an individual's ideal social functioning, his freedom to develop his personality and to gain his goals through relations with others. 2. n pl [Social work] a list of local authority welfare departments and other allied services that are available through that authority.

personal violation n [US] [Law, Police] rape.

personalisation n [Advertising] the making of the form letter that accompanies unsolicited advertising material sent through the post into a more personal communication by adding 'Dear Mr. X . . .' at the start; it is a process much facilitated by the speed and sophistication of word processing programs.

personality promotion n [Advertising] a version of the **mystery shopper** but aimed not at retailers but at housewives: a representative calls at a house and asks the housewife whether she has certain of a firm's products; if she can produce some, and answer a simple product-related question, she will receive some form of reward.

personalzine n [TV] a fan magazine produced by a single fan as a showcase for his/her own ideas, writings, drawings, etc; it is especially popular among fans of TV's 'Star Trek'.

personnel reaction time n [Military] the time that elapses between receiving a warning of nuclear attack and the implementation of full defensive measures on an airbase, ship, command post, etc.

persuader 1. n [TV] an electrode in the TV tube that deflects the returning beam of scanning electrons into the electron multiplier. 2. n [Printing] a tool used to force type into the forme and to ensure that it is properly spaced and tightened up.

PERT n [Business] acro **Programme Evaluation and Review Technique** a method of controlling and monitoring the progress of long-term projects by analysing each successive step as it is taken – both on the basis of the step seen in isolation, and as it exists in relation to the rest of the project.

perzine n [Science fiction] a magazine produced for the compiler to feature his/her own writings.

PEs n pl [Publishing] abbr of **printer's errors** corrected with no cost to publisher or author.

P.E.S. n [Satellite TV] abbr of **personal earth station**. See **earth station**.

pessimal a [Computing] maximally bad.

pessimism criterion n [Business] See **maximin 1**.

pester v [UK] [Market-traders] to pay.

Pete n [US] [Road transport] a Peterbilt wagon.

peter 1. v [Cards] to play a high card followed by a low one in bridge or whist; it comes from the flying of a Blue Peter flag when a ship is about to set off on its voyage. 2. v [UK] [Market-traders] to cry, to weep. 3. n [UK] [Market-traders] bag, holdall, valise. 4. n [UK] [Police] a safe; thus 'peterman' is a safe-cracker, and by extension 'peter' is the nitroglycerine that is used for breaking into some safes. 5. n [UK] [Prisons] a cell. 6. n [Taxis] pieces of luggage that have to be put in the front of the cab and for which the driver charges extra. 7. (UK), **echo, come-on** (US) n [Cards] in bridge this is a high-low defence which is used as a sign of encouragement to one's partner.

Peter principle n [Business] a term coined in 1969 by Dr. Lawrence Peter; it is the concept that in a large organisation every individual is promoted to one level above his/her actual competence.

peterman n [UK] [Crime] a safe-cracker; it comes from 'peter' meaning safe; it is also possibly derived from the illicit appliances used by some fishermen in the Thames during the 18th century, which in turn derived from the New Testament's 'Peter the Fisherman'.

petro-dollar n [Economics] surplus dollars that are accumulated by oil-exporting nations and which are used for investments in and loans to oil-importing countries; also, when based on UK currency it means petro-sterling.

petticoat n [Archery] the edge of the target.

petticoat government n [UK] [Railways] a refusal by a London Underground railwayman to work night duties; it is presumably dictated in deference to a wife or girlfriend.

PFL n [Audio] abbr of **pre-fade listen** a device used in a recording studio which enables the engineer to ensure that all **faders** are receiving input material correctly.

PGM n [Military] abbr of **precision guided munitions** mass-produced, often lightweight or hand-held armaments such as anti-tank or – aircraft missiles; with increased destructive power and flexibility of use (from air, sea or land), they have vastly increased the vulnerability of many formerly 'impregnable' targets.

phalanx *v* [*Printing*] to stagger the work in a print shop so that more men may have work.

phase 1. *n* [*Computing*] a particular phase of an individual's waking/sleeping cycle during the normal 24–hour cycle, that is especially relevant to those who prefer to work at night and thus 'breakfast' at 7pm. **2.** *n* [*Computing*] 'to change phase the hard way' means to stay awake for a long time in order to enter a different phase of (1).

phase inverter *n* [*Audio*] See **reflex**.

phase zero *n* [*Government*] the inception of a new governmental or bureaucratic programme; nothing has yet happened and it is possible that if the necessary funds, personnel and go-ahead are not available, nothing ever will.

phased withdrawal *n* [*Military*] 'A rout with insufficient means of transportation' and thus one that must proceed slowly, or, euphemistically, in 'phases'.

phasiness *n* [*Audio*] the blurring of stereo sound images when the phase and amplitude components of a system are incompatible.

phenomenological sociology *n* [*Sociology*] a school of sociology, derived from phenomenological philosophy, that works towards the analysis and description of everyday life.

Philadelphia lawyer *n* [*US*] [*Law*] a lawyer of great ability and an expert in exploiting the tiniest legal loophole to the advantage of his client.

philistines *n pl* [*Gambling*] loan sharks who lend money at extra-high interest while offering less time than usual for the repayments.

Phillips curve *n* [*Management*] a graph that plots the percentage of unemployment in a country against the annual rate of increase in workers' wages and which tends to the theory that the greater the inflation the higher the employment and vice versa. It is named after the UK economist Alban Phillips (1914–).

phizgig *n* [*Aus.*] [*Crime*] a police informer.

phonaesthesia *n* [*Linguistics*] the phenomenon whereby certain sounds appear onomatopoeic, and contain a degree of inner meaning, pertaining to the words in which they are found; thus 'st' calls up fixity (stone, stolid, stiff, stern); 'sl' implies a smooth downward movement (slip, slither, slobber, slope); 'gl' implies shininess and lustre (glitter, glister, glow, glare).

phone it in *v* [*Film*] when a studio feels that the poor quality of a script indicates that the writer has not put his best efforts into the work and has instead dictated it off the top of his head without even bothering to make revisions, such a writer is said to have 'phoned it in'.

phone quality, also **audio quality** *n* [*Radio*] an interview or report that has been recorded from a phone line and is thus of less than perfect quality, but will have to be transmitted nonetheless. See also **studio quality**.

phoneme *n* [*Linguistics*] 'the smallest unit of speech that distinguishes one utterance from another in all of the variations that it displays in the speech of a single person or particular dialect as the result of modifying influences (as neighbouring sounds and stress)'. Webster's Third New International Dictionary.

phones *n pl* [*Record business*] phone-out research by a record company who have their staff phone up random individuals to canvass their opinions of certain records that are currently being played on the radio; thus 'good phones' or 'bad phones' describes the overall response thus elicited to a given record.

phoney flags *n pl* [*Merchant navy*] ships registered under flags of convenience in order to avoid heavy taxes in their home countries. See also **Panlibhonco**.

phono, also **phone-out** *n* [*Radio*] an interview conducted over the phone which can either be broadcast live or first transferred on to tape; it is not to be confused with audience-participatory 'phone-in programmes'.

phosphide streak *n* [*Metallurgy*] See **ghost 9**.

phosphor *n* [*Philately*] stamps which have been inked, overprinted or impregnated with phosphorescent or 'fluorescent' substances for use in electronic letter-facing and post-marking machines. Such stamps are also known, as they emit light, as 'luminescent'. The chemical causes stamps to emit rays of a certain wavelength to a scanner which can thus separate first– and second-class mail. This scheme was introduced to the UK in 1958 and is used on all stamps except those of value £1.00 and upwards.

photo eye *n* [*Photography*] See **slave 4**.

photographic threshold *n* [*Photography*] the minimum amount of light that is required to form an image on the exposed photographic emulsion.

photomatic *n* [*Video, Film*] a demonstration copy of a film, TV programme or commercial which employs still photographs of the models, packs, etc; usually such stills are synchronised to a demonstration soundtrack and then the package is videotaped for the actual client to see. See also **animatic**.

photomontage *n* [*Art*] a technique of cutting up and then re-assembling photographs with the intention of creating a new composite image with a meaning other than that of the individual pictures; it was first used to effect by John Heartfield and other Dadaists in Berlin in the 1920s.

photon *n* [*Racquets*] a powerful shot.

photo-realism *n* [*Art*] artworks that depend for their effect on super-detailed portraits which might be colour photographs but for the materials used.

photoresist *n* [*Computing*] photo-sensitive materials that react to light by hardening; photoresists are used in the construction of silicon chips, which are basic to micro-processor construction.

phrase *v* [*Ballet*] to link various movements into a single choreographic sequence.

piano word *n* [*Logology*] a word which is made up only of the letters a,b,c,d,e,f or g – those of a musical octave – and which therefore can be 'played' on an instrument.

pianola hand *n* [*Cards*] in bridge this is any hand that is easy to play; it comes from the pianola, an instrument which incorporated machinery that allowed it to play without human agency.

piccolo **1.** *n* [*Hotels*] a junior page or waiter who is just embarking on his career. **2.** *n* [*US*] [*Music*] a juke box.

pick **1.** *n* [*Basketball*] a permissible block whereby an offensive player can obstruct a defensive opponent so long as his positioning does not interfere with that player's normal movement. **2.** *n* [*Weaving*] a sharp-pointed stick for picking up **warp** threads. **3.** *n* [*Weaving*] a single **shot** of **weft**; it is usually used in industrial weaving.

pick bids off the wall **1.** *v* [*Auctions*] said of an auctioneer who creates an imaginary bidding contest in order to stimulate some real bids from the public. **2.** *v* [*Auctions*] said of an auctioneer who creates a single fake bidder who will force the one actual bidder up to and ideally beyond the reserve price.

pick it up *v* [*Film*] this is an instruction given to an actor by the director, asking him/her to speed up the delivery of lines and the performance of **business**.

pick play *n* [*Lacrosse*] a deliberate third party obstruction by one attack player that causes a marking defender to have to leave another attack player; the pick may be moving or stationary.

pick up **1.** *n* [*Hunting, Shooting*] the collection of game retrieved by a hunting party; thus it is the quantity of game that has been shot on a given day. **2.** *n* [*Metallurgy*] the adhesion to or partial welding of particles of steel from the surface of a tube to the surface of the die during cold **drawing**. **3.** *v* [*US*] [*Marine Corps*] to promote an officer who has previously been passed over.

picker (US), scutcher (UK) *n* [*Textiles*] a machine that processes cotton by opening and cleaning the stock and then winding it on to a continuous **lap** for use on a **card**.

pickety-poke *n* [*Mining*] a drill for use in soft rock.

picking *n* [*Weaving*] See **tease**.

pickle **1.** *v* [*Antiques*] to give an antique finish or appearance to reproductions of furniture, paintings, etc. **2.** *v* [*Antiques*] to give a light finish to a piece of furniture by bleaching or painting and wiping. **3.** *v* [*Military*] US Dept of Defense code for: bombs or missiles have been triggered manually and are aimed at a surface target. **4.** *n* [*Theatre*] a small, elongated spotlight.

pickle stain *n* [*Metallurgy*] discolouration produced by the acid used in the **pickling** process which removes impurities and scale.

Pickle Works *n* [*Espionage*] a nickname for the building occupied by the CIA in Langley, Virginia.

pickled punks *n pl* [*US*] [*Carnival*] the display of bottled foetuses, which are usually advertised as 'The Show of Life' on the tent's awning.

pickling **1.** *n* [*Painting*] the removal of paint or rust by using strong solvents or an alkaline preparation. **2.** *n* [*Metallurgy*] the removing of scale, which develops during hot-rolling, by immersing the product in acid, then washing it; thus over-pickling is the excessive use of acid to remove scale, resulting in a rough, pitted surface.

pick-off *n* [*Baseball*] a play in which the base runner is caught off base by a quick throw from the catcher or pitcher.

picks *n pl* [*Textiles*] the number of threads in an inch of cloth.

pickup **1.** *n* [*Printing*] typeset material which is used repeatedly in successive editions of a paper and which is thus kept set up permanently. **2.** also **shorts** *n* [*US*] [*Railways*] a freight train that stops every few miles to pick up or discard cars.

pick-up **1.** *n* [*Photo-typesetting*] an extra one or more unwanted **pixels** picked up during the **digitising** of a character. **2.** *n* [*Weaving*] a technique of picking up by hand certain **warp** threads other than those lifted by the **heddles**, to form patterns in weaving. **3.** also **placement** *n* [*Public relations*] the use by any of the media of a PR handout.

pick-up man *n* [*UK*] [*Police*] a small-time thief who specialises in stealing from unlocked motorcars, or simply grabbing whatever packages, luggage, handbags, etc. that he notices are momentarily unattended; such a thief works 'at the pickup'.

pickup tube *n* [*TV*] the tube in a TV camera that accepts a visual image and provides an electrical signal which represents that image.

pickups *n pl* [*Film*] films that have been made by one company and then acquired by a second one.

pictology *n* [*Art*] an analytical method of attributing and evaluating paintings; it involves the checking of artworks for a variety of constant factors: spontaneity of line, organisation of surface, contrasts of light and dark and of warm and cold colours, etc.

pictorial rhetoric *n* [*Art*] an identifiable mass-media 'language' developed through certain devices which are used in advertising, picture and graphic layouts; based on the clichés of these layouts, this **language** is used increasingly by 'fine' artists in an attempt to communicate to a wider audience.

picture *n* [*Computing*] in programming this is a description of a character **string** which is used to describe the length and type of data that may be

P

stored within another string, representing a field of a record, etc.

picture black *n* [*TV*] the light level of the darkest element of a TV picture or the picture signal voltage that corresponds to it.

P.I.D. *n* [*US*] [*Medicine*] abbr of **pelvic inflammatory disease** gonnorhea.

pie 1. *n* [*Aus.*] [*Farming*] a 'ring' of wool dealers who agree not bid against each other at wool sales, but wait until afterwards to divide up the wool which has thus been purchased at bargain rates by chosen members of the group. See also **ring 1**. 2. *a* [*Hunting*] a colour of hounds, lighter than tan, with shades from lemon pie to hare pie and badger pie.

piece 1. *n* [*Drugs*] a measure of a powdered narcotic – eg: cocaine, heroin – equalling approximately one ounce. 2. *n* [*Espionage*] in the CIA this is an item of information which, although seemingly unimportant in itself, is required to make clear some other piece of information or to verify some otherwise misleading item of information obtained through means other than espionage. The term comes from the analogy with the pieces of a jigsaw puzzle. 3. *n* [*Metallurgy*] a single length of wire without joints or welds. 4. *n* [*Journalism*] an article in a newspaper or magazine. 5. *n* [*US*] [*Marine Corps*] a gun or artillery piece. 6. *n* [*Textiles*] a finished length of cloth. 7. *n* [*US*] [*Police, Crime*] any form of gun used for murders, hold-ups, robberies, etc.

piece goods *n pl* [*Textiles*] lengths of untailored fabrics, manufactured for cutting into patterns for clothes.

Piece of Business, a *n* [*Advertising*] the client.

piece of manpower *n* [*US*] [*TV*] a description, faintly derogatory, of major network stars: newscasters, anchormen etc.

piece of tin *n* [*US*] [*Carpenters*] a saw.

piecemeal engineering *n* [*Sociology*] a term coined by Sir Karl Popper (born 1902) to describe his idea of the best manner of social reform: the replacement, as in a machine, of individual parts as they wear out, and thus the gradual improvement of the whole, rather than a wholesale operation which involves shutting down one machine and replacing it with another.

pie-chart *n* [*Business*] a graphic device that shows divisions/proportions/shares etc. by drawing a circle and dividing it into relevant segments, like a sliced up pie or cake, viewed from above.

pied d'éléphant *n* [*Mountaineering*] an 'elephant's foot'; this is a padded sack that is used to keep the lower parts of the body warm when the climber is resting or sleeping.

piffing *n* [*Military*] gunnery training which uses rounds of sub-calibre firing; the word derives from the 'pfff' noise such rounds make.

pig 1. *n* [*UK*] [*Circus*] an elephant. 2. *n* [*Metallurgy*] a crude casting of metal convenient for storage, transportation or melting; it refers especially to one of standard size and shape for marketing direct from the smelting furnace. It is so called because a number of pigs lying together supposedly resemble piglets with a sow; thus pig bed is a bed of sand in which iron is cast into pigs. 3. *n* [*Oil rigs, Gas industry*] a piece of equipment that is inserted into a pipeline and is carried along by the flow of oil or gas; it is used for cleaning or to monitor the internal condition of the pipe, or to mark an interface between two different products. 4. *n* [*Politics*] a popular description for the police in particular and members of the Establishment in general; it was coined as early as the 18th century (for policemen), revived by the 1960s radicals, and is still popular in extremist circles. 5. *n* [*US*] [*Railways*] a small iron or steel car pulled by a cable on a narrow-gauge track and used for handling a railway freight car on an incline too steep for a locomotive. 6. *n* [*US*] [*Road transport*] a trailer transported on a flat car. 7. *n* [*US*] [*Road transport*] a tractor with little power. 8. *n* [*Technology*] a container that holds radioactive materials.

pig and whistle *n* [*Merchant navy*] a canteen on a merchant vessel.

pig boiling *n* [*Metallurgy*] See **puddling**.

pig driving *n* [*Banking*] a discredited method, pre-dating computers, of writing up accounts vertically rather than horizontally. Thus all the customers' names are written down the page, then all the debts, then all the dates, and so on. The clerk would only need to make one error in one column and the whole account would be ruined.

pig eyed *a* [*Hunting*] said of a hound with small, mean-looking eyes.

pig iron 1. *n* [*Journalism*] serious or dull news copy. 2. *n* [*US*] [*Paper-making*] a slitting machine used to determine the width of paper.

pig outfit *n* [*US*] [*Police*] a portable drug analysis kit.

pig-board *n* [*Surfing*] a board that has a wide tail and a narrow nose.

pigeon 1. *n* [*Crime*] abbr of **stool pigeon** a police informer. 2. *n* [*Gambling*] the last card dealt in a round of stud poker when that card makes the hand of a winner. 3. *n* [*US*] [*Gambling*] a pari-mutuel ticket that is either counterfeit or has been cancelled. 4. *n* [*Military*] air intercept code for: your base bears X° and is Y miles away.

pigeon drop *n* [*UK*] [*Police*] a form of confidence trick that is launched by dropping a wallet at the feet of a victim; the con-man then informs the **mark** that they can share the cash inside the wallet if he (the mark) puts up some extra money temporarily as a sign of good faith.

pigeon hole *n* [*Printing*] wide spacing between lines.

pigging *n* [*Journalism*] the holding on to scarce telephone lines by members of the press or TV news crews so as to prevent them falling into the hands of a rival.

piggyback 1. *v* [*Medicine*] to add a second fluid intravenous drip bag to the first one. 2. *n* [*US*] [*Road transport*] the transportation of freight by rail and by road. See also **birdy Back, fishy back**.

piggyback entry *n* [*Data security*] making an illegal access to a system by tapping into another, legitimate, user's input.

piggyback form *n* [*Printing*] the fixing of small items of stationery – envelopes, labels, etc – to a continuous roll of paper which is fed through a printer for the addressing of such items.

piggyback legislation *n* [*Politics*] the use of one piece of legislation as a means of passing another, by quietly attaching the latter to the former and trusting that both bills will pass together without comment.

piggyback loading *n* [*US*] [*Railways*] the loading of cars and trucks on to freight-train flatcars; it originated in circus loading since the first wagons to be transported on flatcars were circus trucks and equipment.

piggyback productions *n pl* [*TV, Film*] the employment of a single crew by two clients for the purpose of cutting the costs of location shooting. If a crew is already flying to an expensive location, the clients can share the basic costs and have whatever material they wish shot at the location.

piggyback registration *n* [*US*] [*Stock market*] the sale of a combination of existing shares in a company with those created by a new issue.

piggybacking 1. *n* [*Commerce*] the practice by one firm of marketing another firm's (usually complementary) products in addition to its own (although usually on a far smaller scale). 2. *n* [*Computing*] See **acknowledgement**. 3. *n* [*Film*] the unofficial showing by an exhibitor of an extra film on a weekly programme which should only be showing the film that the distributor wishes to be shown.

piggy-backing *n* [*Military*] the flying of a spy plane on an identical path to that of a legitimate civil flight so as to merge the radar profiles of the two aircraft and thus confuse ground-based spotters.

pigmented *a* [*Cheese-making*] used to describe the surface of a cheese which is suffused with various coloured moulds.

pigs *n pl* [*Navy*] officers.

pigs and bloods *n pl* [*Merchant navy*] officers and passengers seen as a group.

pigtail 1. *n* [*Logging*] a device driven into a log to support a wire or rope. 2. *n* [*US*] [*Road transport*] a cable used to transmit electrical power to the trailer.

pike *n* [*Diving*] a body position, also used in gymnastics, in which the hips are bent, the knees are straight, the head is pressed forward and the hands touch the toes or clasp the legs behind and just above the knees.

pike pole *n* [*Logging*] a long pole with a spike on the end that is used for moving logs in the water.

piker 1. *n* [*Gambling*] a poor sport, a timid gambler. 2. *n* [*Stock market*] a cautious investor, one who will only speculate on a small scale.

pilaster *n* [*Building, Plastering*] a rectangular column, usually placed against a wall.

pilcrow *n* [*Printing*] the paragraph symbol.

pile-jump *v* [*Tiddleywinks*] to play a shot which involves placing at least two winks on top of at least two more, with one's own winks preferably on top and in command.

piling *n* [*Painting*] a defect in quick-drying paint which occurs when it dries so fast that it is not possible to spread it smoothly and a thick, uneven film is the result.

pill *n* [*Weaving*] the formation of small balls of fibre on a fabric.

Pill Avenue *n* [*UK*] [*Taxis*] Harley Street, London W1 (centre of the private medical profession).

pill palace *n* [*US*] [*Medicine*] a hospital's pharmacy.

pill pusher 1. *n* [*US*] [*Medicine*] a pharmacist. 2. *n* [*US*] [*Medicine*] from the hospital doctor's point of view this refers to any general practitioner or a specialist in internal medicine rather than a specialist in a variety of surgical work.

pillar *n* [*Coal-mining*] a block or mass of coal left unworked, usually to act as a support (which may be removed later).

pillar and stall *n* [*Coal-mining*] See **bord and pillar**.

pillars *n pl* [*Glass-making*] columns supporting the roof of a pot furnace, between which the pots are placed.

pill-rolling *n* [*Medicine*] any symptoms of nervous anxiety, especially the constant twitching of fingers as if rolling something between them. See also **Captain Queegs**.

pilot 1. *n* [*Communications*] a single frequency transmitted over a transmission system to indicate or control its characteristics. 2. *n* [*TV*] the test programme of a potential series; it is often somewhat longer than an episode of the intended series and is designed to check whether the format will stand up to exposure.

pilot launch *n* [*Marketing*] a method of test marketing which launches a product on a limited basis in order to iron out the possible problems that might accompany the actual, national-scale, launch.

pimp-crazy *a* [*Sex*] said of any prostitute who continues to suffer at the hands of her pimp, but who keeps returning to the same man.

pimped down *a* [*Sex*] amongst black pimps this means being dressed for the part in 'pimp shades' (dark glasses), 'pimp socks' and a whole wardrobe of flashy, ostentatious garments.

pimple *n* [*UK*] [*Road transport*] a steep hill.

pimples *n pl* [*Table tennis*] short pimples of rubber which allow good control of the ball, but offer little production of spin. See also **long pimples**.

pimp's arrest *n* [*US*] [*Sex, Police*] a revenge taken by a pimp on a girl who decides to leave his employment: he turns her over to the police. This involves no risk to himself and in addition permits him to reclaim the bail money that he has had to have kept posted against the likelihood of her being arrested for soliciting. Once a new girl is found, the bond will have to be posted again.

pin 1. *n* [*Espionage*] a camera with a lens so tiny that it can be hidden in a variety of everyday objects around a room and used for perfect quality surveillance pictures. 2. *a* [*Taxis*] pin position: the first cab on a rank.

pin up *v* [*US*] [*Road transport*] to hook the tractor to the **semi-trailer**.

pinard *n* [*Military*] used in the French Foreign Legion to mean any kind of wine.

pinch 1. *n* [*Billiards*] the pressure of the cue ball against the surface of the table, which is caused by a downward stroke of the cue. 2. *n* [*Industry*] the space between two rolls in a cracking or grinding mill. 3. *n* [*Metallurgy*] a longditudinal overlap in a steel sheet.

pinch hitter *n* [*Baseball*] a specially hard-hitting batter who is brought into the game when his team's fortunes are slumping.

pinch out *n* [*Coal-mining*] See **nip out**.

pinch passing *n* [*Metallurgy*] See **skin passing**.

pinch rod *n* [*Building, Plastering*] two rods/rules used together for the accurate measurement of openings where only internal measurement is possible: they overlap and are expanded to fit the measurement.

pinch-effect *n* [*Audio*] a distortion in reproducing recorded sound through a stereo or mono system when the pick-up stylus makes slight vertical movements at twice the recorded lateral frequency.

pin-down *n* [*Military*] the concept of saturating enemy missile bases with so many warheads that the resultant electro-magnetic confusion will render their outgoing guidance systems useless.

pine in *n* [*US*] [*Lunch counter*] a pineapple soda.

pineapple *n* [*Logging*] a pineapple-shaped roller that forces lumber down on to the straight edge of the roller platform as the lumber is moved towards the planer in the sawmill.

ping 1. *n* [*Navy*] the Asdic officer; it comes from the noise of the machine he operates. 2. *v* [*Theatre*] to speak one's lines softly, with no special emphasis.

pinger *n* [*Military*] an acoustic array carried in an aircraft's cockpit to help in anti-submarine warfare; by extension it is also a nickname for the crewman who actually operates the ASW equipment.

ping-pong 1. *n* [*Military*] a missile that carries a camera rather than a warhead and, after taking its pictures at various pre-determined heights, releases a parachute and lets the camera float back to a pickup point. 2. *n* [*Music*] in West Indian steel bands this is a drum cut about 7in from the top of the barrel, and on which are marked between 26 and 32 notes.

ping-pong diplomacy *n* [*Politics*] those tentative attempts to re-establish diplomatic relations between the US and China where were initiated in 1971 with the sending of a US table-tennis team to the People's Republic.

ping-ponging *n* [*US*] [*Medicine*] the sending of a patient, with no real need for treatment, to a variety of specialists and clinics, all of whom can then claim Medicaid payments for their (pointless) labours. See also **family ganging**.

pink 1. *n* [*Government*] in the Department of Health and Social Security this is a filing card, irrespective of actual colour. 2. *n* [*US*] [*Horseracing*] abbr of **Pinkertons** a race-track security man, usually recruited from the Pinkerton Detective Agency. 3. also **beaver** *n* [*Sex*] close-up shots of the open vagina which are used in hard-core pornography, either on film or in magazines. See also **flap shots**. 4. *a* [*Navy*] secret, confidential; it comes from the colour of the signal pads used for writing such messages.

pink button *n* [*Stock market*] a **jobber's** clerk, who looks after a firm's communications, both inside and outside the Exchange.

pink collar *a* [*Industrial relations*] said of any jobs held by women in cosmetic factories. See also **blue collar, grey collar, white collar workers**.

pink lady 1. *n* [*US*] [*Medicine*] female hospital volunteer, who often wears a pink uniform. See also **candy-stiper**. 2. *n* [*US*] [*Medicine*] phenobarbital elixir, an anti-nausea drink which is coloured pink; it is a pun on the cocktail.

pink noise *n* [*Audio*] random noise that differs from **white noise** in that it has a greater proportion of low frequency components.

pink paper *n* [*UK*] [*Politics*] a parliamentary notice, printed on pink paper, which gives each day or week the details of all papers either presented to Parliament or printed by order of the Government; the first pink papers were issued as an experiment in 1889 and ratified for continual use in 1894.

pink puffer *n* [*US*] [*Medicine*] a thin patient who is suffering from emphysema.

pink sheets *n pl* [*US*] [*Stock market*] daily publication by the US National Quotation Bureau of the prices asked and bid on the **over the counter** market in **equities**.

pink tea assignment *n* [*Journalism*] covering a social event which has little hard news value.

pinkie *n* [*Docks*] a new trainee docker.

pinking *n* [*Cars*] See **knocking 2**.

pinkslip 1. *v* [*US*] [*Entertainment*] to dismiss from a job. **2.** v [*Industrial relations*] to dismiss an employee; it comes from the practice in US colleges of signifying a failure in an examination by notifying the student concerned by a letter on pink paper.

pink-tea picketing n [*Industrial relations*] a small group of pickets who are being unobtrusive; it refers both to the restrained level of the picket ('pink' rather than the totally radical 'red') and the cosy 'tea-party' atmosphere so created.

pinky-cheater n [*US*] [*Medicine*] a sterile finger-stall or glove used by medical staff when making anal or vaginal inspections.

Pinnacle n [*Military*] a US intelligence code; any message flagged 'Pinnacle' must bypass local commanders and be sent directly to the President and Joint Chiefs of Staff.

pinners n pl [*UK*] [*Coal-mining*] a wooden wedge about 1 ft long, which is used to tighten up the wood chocks and wooden trellis work that are used in timbering cavities and holes above tunnels.

pin-party n [*Navy*] the working party on an aircraft carrier that prepares aircraft for takeoff and deals with them once they have returned to the flight deck. See also **grapes**.

pin-splitter n [*Golf*] any shot that lands dead on the pin.

pintail n [*Surfing*] a surfboard which has a pointed rear end.

pip n [*UK*] [*Military*] the stars worn on an officer's epaulettes to distinguish his rank: one for a second lieutenant (see **one-pipper**), two for a first lieutenant, three for a captain.

pipe **1.** n [*Hunting*] a side-tunnel or hole in a fox's earth. **2.** n [*Metallurgy*] an axial cavity within an ingot caused by contraction of the metal while the ingot is cooling. It is also a defect caused by axial cavity in semi-finished or finished products. **3.** n [*US*] [*Journalism*] a story which has a basis of facts but which has been embellished by the reporter to gain it greater prominence and interest. **4.** n [*US*] [*Medicine*] an enema. **5.** n [*UK*] [*Road transport*] the telephone. **6.** n [*TV, Telephony*] a co-axial cable used for transmitting television or telephone signals. **7.** v [*US*] [*Marine Corps*] to see, to notice.

pipe the side v [*Navy*] to escort a person, usually an officer, on board ship, to the accompaniment of the correct tribute (varied as to rank) from the ship's pipes.

pipeline n [*Film*] the schedule of screen projects in production at a studio or company.

pipe-line n [*Surfing*] a large wave, or the hollow of such a wave; it is also that part of a surfing beach where such waves can be found and ridden. See also **tube 4**.

pipe-lining n [*Computing*] the regulation of computing processes whereby one must be concluded before the next can be initiated; using special modules which can operate concurrently, these processes can be considerably speeded up,

and thus vastly increase the operating efficiency of the whole system.

piping n [*Photography*] See **streaking 1**.

pips n pl [*Dog breeding*] the spots above the eyes of most black and tan breeds, including Dobermann, Rottweiler, etc.

piquant **1.** a [*Cheese-making*] a description of a cheese with an exhilarating or appealing sharpness of flavour or aroma. **2.** a [*Wine-tasting*] said of fresh and mouth-watering acidity.

pirate n [*Espionage*] electronic surveillance which uses electricity that has been 'pirated' from a telephone wire, with the permission of the telephone company.

pirate divers n pl [*Merchant navy*] divers who attempt to salvage a wreck without getting the appropriate prior authority from the owner and the Registrar of Wrecks.

piss fir n [*Logging*] a white or lowland fir, so named for its strong odour.

pisscoat **1.** n [*US*] [*Painting*] a thin mixture of undercoating, containing some colour, that is applied to a wall. **2.** n [*US*] [*Painting*] the misty spray or fog that is blown by the wind from a spray gun.

piss-cutter **1.** n [*US*] [*Railways*] a freight train that works long hours without rest time. **2.** also **fore-and-aft cap** n [*US*] [*Marine Corps*] a regulation garrison cap.

pissing post n [*US*] [*Politics*] a politician's home territory and/or power base.

piste n [*Skiing*] a marked and prepared ski run; it comes from Fr. 'piste' meaning 'track'.

piste basher **1.** n [*Skiing*] a tracked vehicle used for grooming the piste for the best skiing. **2.** n [*Skiing*] a skier who only skis on the marked out piste.

pistol n [*Military*] as used by bomb-disposal units this is the trigger that sets off a bomb.

pit **1.** n [*US*] [*Football*] the centre of the line of scrimmage where opposing heavyweight players battle to attack/defend the quarterback; the implication is of the pure animal viciousness of the brute contact. **2.** n [*US*] [*Hotels*] the area of the hotel lobby where guests leave their baggage while they check in. **3.** n [*Oil rigs*] an unroofed sump or tank which holds the **mud** or any other liquid required on the rig. **4.** n [*Stock market*] that area of the market, usually slightly lower than the surrounding area, where the actual dealing and trading takes place.

pit boss, also **pit inspector** n [*Gambling*] a casino official who supervises the operation of one or more gambing tables, watching players and croupiers alike for actual cheating and mere mistakes.

pit jockey n [*Theatre*] a member of the pit orchestra – competent rather than distinguished.

pit lizard n [*Motor-racing*] a woman who devotes herself to the pursuit of motor-racing drivers.

pitch **1.** v [*Drugs*] to sell narcotics in small

amounts; thus as a noun it refers to the dealer who carries on this trade. **2.** v [UK] [Market-traders] to sell by mock-auction. **3.** n [UK] [Market-traders] in a mock-auction this is the crowd that gathers around the stall. **4.** n [Mountaineering] a section of the climb. **5.** n [Clothing] the balanced insertion of the sleeve into the garment that is controlled by following balance marks in the armhole. **6.** n [UK] [Police] the part of a street worked by a prostitute, three-card monte team, illegal street trader, etc.

pitch and catch v [US] [Prisons] to indulge in both homosexual and heterosexual activity.

pitch fly n [Commerce] among legal street traders, this is someone who takes over their **pitch** without permission.

pitchpole v [Sailing] a vessel does this when it is upended completely by heavy seas, and somersaults forward, stern over bow.

pits, also **screaming area** n [US] [Medicine] the medical screening area of a hospital; it is loathed by doctors because of the many insignificant medical maladies that have to be treated here, which they feel are taking up valuable time better spent in the emergency room.

pitting n [Building, Plastering] See **blowing**.

pixel n [Photo-typesetting] abbr of **picture element** a discrete coded unit or element of the **bit-map** mosaic that represents the image area of a letter or other graphic form.

pixie n [Marbles] a mud roll, put in the centre of the ring, upon which the marbles are placed.

pixillation n [TV, Film] a style of stop-motion photography which makes live actors appear to be moving like cartoon figures.

PK **1.** n [US] [Military] abbr of **probability of kill**. this refers to the potential success rate of anti-aircraft batteries (both guns and missiles). **2.** n [Religion] abbr of **preacher's kid**.

placard n [Gliding] a required statement of operation limitations that is permanently fixed where the pilot can see it during flight.

place, in adv [Espionage] referring to the subject or target of an investigation or surveillance who has arrived at a destination where observers are already waiting.

placement n [Public relations] See **pick-up 3**.

place-money **1.** n [Horse-racing] money that is bet on the chance of a horse being placed in a race; if the horse wins, the punter only receives a proprotion of the money he would have received, had the horse won. **2.** n [Horse-racing] the money that is paid out on horses that come first, (when the horse has been backed for a place, not a win) second or third (in the US second only) in a race.

placer **1.** n [Mining] an economically viable mineral deposit which has been concentrated in a sediment by the natural movement of water. **2.** n [Mining] a deposit of sand or gravel that contains gold or other valuable minerals. **3.** n [UK] [Police] the middleman between the thief and the receiver

of the stolen goods (the 'fence'); he negotiates for the thief the 'placing' of the goods with the best possible buyer.

placing n [Stock market] the finding of specific buyers for large quantities of stocks, especially of a new issue.

plain folks n pl [Politics] in propaganda this is the device of promoting one's own side, particularly an individual political candidate, by emphasising his/her down-to-earth, populist charms, and minimising the less attractive characteristics required by the successful politician.

plain text n [Espionage] in cryptography this is uncoded language. See also **en plein**.

plainface n [Building, Plastering] a perfectly flat even surface in plasterwork and external finishes.

plain-laid n [Sailing, Ropework] three-strand, right-handed rope. See also **hard-laid, short-laid**.

plain-sewing n [Sex] the limiting of the services of a homosexual prostitute to mutual masturbation.

Plan, the n [Religion] in Methodism this is a document issued periodically which lists all preachers throughout a circuit for a period of time.

plane **1.** n [Glass-making] melted glass, free from any apparent and visible impurities (especially small bubbles), and thus ready for working. **2.** v [Surfing] to ride a wave with the hands protecting the face by forming a spear shape which thus cuts through the on-coming water.

planing n [Shooting] the action of birds in seeming to 'sail' downwards with still wings.

planishing n [Metallurgy] improving the surface of the metal by the action of the rolls.

plank n [Politics] one of the positions on various topics upon which a campaign is based; a number of planks form the entire **platform**.

planning continuum n [Military] an alternative phrase for military strategy.

planning horizon n [Economics] in socialist countries this refers to those years that have been included in the run of the current economic plan.

plant **1.** v [Journalism, Politics] used of a politician who places certain information with a journalist who, he believes, will publish it as a scoop. The information can be genuine or not, but in either case the politician is essentially using the journalist as a pawn, either for his own interests or for those of his party as a whole. **2.** n [Snooker] a shot in which the white ball is hit against one red ball which in turns hits a further red ball into the pocket; the second ball is never touched by the cue ball.

plant the pole v [US] [Skiing] to set in the pole ahead of one so as to pivot around when making a turn.

planting n [Public relations] the placing of a promotional piece with a desired newspaper or magazine, or the putting of one's client on to a

TV or radio show that will guarantee maximum publicity.

plasma *n* [*Aerospace*] rocket fuel. See also **lox**.

plasma display *n* [*Computing*] any **peripheral** that has a screen on which information can be displayed.

plastering *n* [*Wine trade*] the treatment of wines with gypsum (plaster of Paris) to induce, when absent, the necessary degree of acidity.

plastic **1.** *n* [*UK*] [*Police*] credit cards, bank cards, cheque cards, etc; thus 'on the plastic' means carrying out a variety of frauds with stolen or forged plastic cards. **2.** *a* [*Theatre*] said of any scenery that is three-dimensional, as opposed to **flats**.

plastic fingerprints *n pl* [*Police*] fingerprints that have been left on soft surfaces and as such are easily detectable.

plastic memory *n* [*Science*] a phenomenon found in physics whereby, when certain kinds of plastic are first moulded into a distinct form, then melted so that the form is lost, if they are then allowed to cool, that original form is to a great extent resumed.

plat **1.** *n* [*Real estate*] a surveyor's proposal for the sub-division of a plot of land that is submitted to a local government official in the 'plat book'. **2.** also **plait** *n* [*Sailing, Ropework*] See **sinnet**.

plate **1.** *v* [*Baseball*] to cross the home plate, thus to score a run. **2.** *v* [*Shooting*] to fire a shotgun at a whitewashed steel plate set up some forty yards away in order to check the pattern of the shot. **3.** *n* [*Furriers*] a number of smaller pieces of pelt are sewn together in a plate; a number of plates are then used for a garment. **4.** *n* [*Horse-racing*] a horse shoe; thus 'racing plate' refers to the special shoes that are used for races.

plate, on the *adv* [*Theatre*] working on the lighting switchboard; it refers back to the 'plate', the control panel which operated the gas-powered illuminations of the Victorian theatre.

plate waste *n* [*Navy*] the amount of food left on the plates of sailors after a meal.

plateau *n* [*Video*] the level of sales at which a title settles after its initial sales surge. See also **burn 3**.

plated weight *n* [*UK*] [*Road transport*] the maximum gross weight designated for a vehicle or its axles by its manufacturer.

plater *n* [*Horse-racing*] abbr of **selling plater** a race, and the horses in it, which are of poor quality; all horses in a selling plater are available for purchase once the race has been run.

platform *n* [*Politics*] the whole assembly of principles and promises that make up a political campaign. See also **plank**.

platinum *a* [*Pop music*] a record that has sold 1,000,000 copies is a 'platinum disk'; thus two million sales equals 'double platinum'. See also **gold**.

platoon *v* [*Sport*] said of a sportsman in a variety of team games who specialises in playing in one position or (in US football) one play.

platoon grouping *n* [*Education*] the teaching of a small class of specially selected pupils.

platter *n* [*Computing*] the metallic base of a magnetic hard disk.

plausible denial *n* [*Espionage*] a cover story which should serve to convince any investigator that they are mistaken in their suspicions of an individual or an organisation.

plawt *n* [*UK*] [*Market-traders*] boot, shoe.

play book **1.** *n* [*US*] [*Football*] the book compiled by football coaches which is used as a strategic bible by the whole team, comprising all those various plays which a team will attempt to execute during a match. **2.** *n* [*Business*] the corporation files and databases that contain plans, manuals, charts and all the other details of the company's plans and programmes; it comes from the sporting use (see **1**).

play on velvet *v* [*Gambling*] to play with the money one has already won from the bank or fellow players.

play pussy *v* [*Air Force*] to fly into cloud cover to avoid being discovered by hostile aircraft.

play the piano *v* [*Sheep-shearing*] to run one's fingers over the sheeps' backs to find the easiest and softest to sheer.

play them in (*UK*), **play the first spot** (*US*) *v* [*Theatre*] to be the actors who appear in Act I, scene i of a play.

player **1.** *n* [*US*] [*Medicine*] a patient. **2.** *n* [*Sex*] a pimp; by extension it means anyone who uses brains and wit rather than sweat and strain to make a living, obtain women, drugs, etc. **3.** *n* [*Business*] any major participant – either corporate or individual – in a given business situation; often referring to trade wars, takeovers, etc.

playing the man *n* [*Sport*] the use in contact sports of deliberate violence. It is a reverse of the old sporting credo whereby one 'played the ball, not the man'.

playlist *n* [*Radio*] the pre-specified list of records, usually the Top 40 plus a certain number of old favourites and a few possible contenders for future success, that make up all the music played in a given period, usually lasting a week, on a radio station.

plea minor *n* [*US*] [*Law*] to plead guilty to a minor charge in the hope of having more serious charges dropped.

plea-bargain *n* [*Law*] the process whereby a defendant, or more usually the defence lawyer, can bargain with the court for a reduction of sentence if he/she is willing to plead guilty on some charges, while others will be dropped. It will help to speed up the legal calendar, although the defendant will forfeit the possible advantages of a general 'Not Guilty' plea in front of a jury.

plead *v* [*Law*] to plead guilty, never not guilty.

plead the blood *v* [*Religion*] to invoke the shed blood of Christ, which is necessary for forgiveness and protection.

pleasure bar *n* [*Air travel*] the first class drinking area in large intercontinental jets.

pleasure principle *n* [*Psychology*] a term coined by Sigmund Freud to describe the unconscious, primitive instincts that drive an individual to seek pleasure for its own sake without any regard for the consequences.

plebe *n* [*Military*] at the US military academy at West Point, NY, this is any new candidate in his first year; it has been extended latterly to cover all entrants to US military or naval academies.

plig *n* [*Religion*] a polygamist, especially in the Mormon church.

plods 1. *n pl* [*Politics*] the House of Commons police; it comes from the children's character Mr. Plod the policeman. 2. *n pl* [*Politics*] the staff canteen of the House of Commons which is extensively used by the Commons' police force, among other staff.

plonker *n* [*Navy*] the firing button or trigger on a gun.

plop *n* [*TV*] one frame of pure tone inserted into the **leaders** of each sound track level with '3' on the picture leader, to indicate to the **dubbing mixer** that he or she is picking up each track.

plot 1. *n* [*Air Force*] a group of hostile aircraft as they come up on the radar screen. 2. *n* [*Theatre*] a plan that shows the positions of furniture and props on stage as needed for the various scenes; thus 'lighting plot' is a plan of the lighting as it varies from scene to scene.

plough 1. *n* [*Hunting*] arable country, whether actual ploughed field, or one with crops growing. 2. also **coal plough** *n* [*Coal-mining*] a wedge-shaped steel device which moves up and down the face, shearing off a thin strip of coal from the seam and deflecting it on to a conveyor belt.

PLU *n* [*Sociology*] acro **People Like Us** shorthand description for the peers of the British upper-middle classes, often found as 'not PLU'; it is the descendant of the 'U' and 'non-U' classifications of the 1950s.

pluck 1. *n* [*Glass-making*] any mark left on the surface of rolled glass where the ribbon of glass has temporarily stuck to the rollers. 2. *n* [*Sailing*] a pull or tow from another boat. 3. *v* [*US*] [*Military*] to cashier or retire an officer compulsorily. 4. *v* [*Printing*] said of ink which does not spread properly on the plates and detaches itself in places from the paper – a printing fault.

pluck in *v* [*Merchant navy*] to tow into port.

plug 1. *n* [*Angling*] a lure with one or more hooks attached. 2. *n* [*Angling*] a lure that can be made to dart and dive, popularly chosen for catching pike. 3. *n* [*Horse-racing*] a useless, second-rate horse. 4. *n* [*Media, Public relations*] any form of advertisement, publicity or promotion, which is usually unpaid. 5. *n* [*Philately*] a part of the stamp printing plate inserted or 'plugged into' the main design; it is often used when the design for all denominations remains the same, but different values have to be inserted. 6. *n* [*Publishing*] a book that will not sell well. See also **dog** 1. 7. *n* [*Textiles*] an assembled spool of yarn. 8. *v* [*Oil rigs*] to fill with concrete and abandon a well that is no longer of use, and never likely to become so.

plug compatible *a* [*Computing*] used to describe compatibility between two devices that can be achieved by simple plug and cable connections; it is often used with regard to IBM equipment. Thus a 'plug-compatible manufacturer' is one who produces equipment that can be directly substituted for that of another manufacturer.

plugging, also **poling** *n* [*Glass-making*] a method of stirring and fining glass in a pot with a wooden pole; from this pot come the gases that are created by the high temperature of the melting process.

plug-in architecture *n* [*Architecture*] a style of design that incorporates one basic structure plus a number of secondary structures that can be attached to it as and when the client desires.

plugola *n* [*US*] [*Radio*] money that is paid to broadcasters to mention, in passing, those products whose manufacturers are giving out the bribes. See also **payola**.

plugs *n pl* [*Aerospace*] mass produced uniform sections of fuselage airframe which can be added to or subtracted from commercial airliners as and when the airlines and their bookings require.

plugs pulled out *adv* [*Navy*] said of a submarine that is diving.

plum book *n* [*US*] [*Government*] an official US government publication that lists all those available government posts that a President may fill by his personal appointment. See also **rainbow book**.

plum pudding voyage *n* [*Merchant navy*] when a whaler returns to port with only half a catch; it comes from the way a plum-pudding shrinks while it is being boiled, leaving the pot half empty.

plumb 1. *a* [*Cricket*] a perfectly level wicket; it comes from the accuracy of a plumb line. 2. *adv* [*Cricket*] unarguably dismissed, especially when a batsman is leg-before-wicket.

plumber 1. *n* [*US*] [*Medicine*] a urologist, whose medical speciality is the 'water works'. 2. *n* [*Navy*] the ship's engineer on a small warship. 3. *n* [*Air Force*] an armourer or engineering officer. 4. *n* [*Shoe-making*] See **backer** 1.

plumbing 1. *n* [*Audio*] waveguides and cavities in ultra high frequency equipment. 2. *n* [*Espionage*] literally this means the stopping of **leaks** (in the government and security services); plumbing and the plumbers – those who did the dirty work – came to prominence in the Watergate Scandal of 1972–74 when it was found that the 'zeal' of President Nixon's plumbers had led them

P

into massive instances of breaking the law, ostensibly for the sake of the President.

plummy *a* [*Wine-tasting*] a colour indicating neither youth nor maturity, but something in between.

plumper *n* [*Shoe-making*] See **backer 1**.

plunder-snatchers *n pl* [*UK*] [*Market-traders*] in a mock-auction, these are the customers who are after real bargains, if not free gifts.

plunge, also **dip, pitch** *n* [*Coal-mining*] the inclination of the rock strata to the horizontal.

plural relations, also **separate development** *n* [*Politics*] the euphemism for the South African government's racist policy of apartheid.

pluralism 1. *n* [*Industrial relations*] the die-hard attitude of some trade unionists who declare that the basis of all industrial relations must be 'us vs. them' and that the two sides can never really reach agreement, but merely wish to crush the desires or aspirations of the other. **2.** *n* [*Politics*] a political philosophy which opposes the idea of a single-state authority and desires to give equal powers to all those bodies that represent the various segments of a society.

plus tick *n* [*US*] [*Stock market*] See **uptick**.

plush family *n* [*Theatre*] empty seats in the auditorium, ie: the plush-covered seats that can be seen from the stage.

PM *n* [*Commerce*] abbr of **Push Money** a form of **payola** which is paid to salesmen and retailers if they push a given product harder than other rival brands that they may also stock; PM is often paid on every item or product sold.

P.M. *n* [*Commerce*] abbr of **past merchandise** less fashionable merchandise on which an extra commission is payable to the salesman who can dispose of it.

PMALS *n* [*Military*] acro **Prototype Miniature Air-Launched System** the state-of-art anti-satellite weapon which is currently being tested by the US. Composed of a rocket which is fired from a high-flying aircraft, it travels into space where it targets a hostile satellite then releases a fast-moving projectile, flying at 7500 mph, which destroys the target simply by crashing into it. See also **ASAT, MHIV**

P.M.D. *n* [*US*] [*Medicine*] abbr of **private medical doctor** a private physician who prefers to send allegedly ill patients to the hospital for diagnosis and treatment rather than perform such activities himself; it is one of the few examples of medical jargon aimed at a fellow professional.

pneumatic logic *n* [*Computing*] See **fluid logic**.

PNQ *n* [*UK*] [*Politics*] abbr of **private notice question**.

PO *n* [*UK*] [*Prisons*] acro **Principal Officer**.

P.O. *v phr* [*US*] [*Undertakers*] abbr of **Please Omit flowers** it is included in funeral notices and is an omission bitterly resented by US florists.

poach *v* [*Tennis*] used of a player in doubles who takes a ball which should have been left to the other partner.

poached *a* [*Hunting*] said of ground that has been badly cut up by horses' hooves and is muddy and slippery, often in front of a gateway or jump.

poacher *n* [*Shooting*] See **greedy shot**.

pocher *n* [*Architecture*] this comes from Fr. meaning 'to fill in, to stencil'; it is a type of design in which the external walls and the inner rooms do not correspond, eg: octagonal rooms built within a square exterior. The 'dead space' between the inner and outer walls is 'poché space' and such designs are drawn on a 'poché plan'.

pochette *n* [*Magic*] a small secret pocket used for various **effects**; it comes from Fr. for 'small pocket'. See also **profonde**.

pocket 1. *n* [*US*] [*Football*] a small area in the backfield where the quarterback is heavily protected by his linemen as he prepares to throw the ball. **2.** *n* [*Military*] an area held by friendly troops who are surrounded by hostile forces; thus 'pocket of resistance' is an area of resistance, often held in the face of overwhelming odds and as such destined in the end to be over-run unless reinforced. **3.** *n* [*Oil rigs*] a cavity in a pipeline where dirt or foreign matter (including air) can collect, with the potential of causing damage to the pipe. **4.** *n* [*US*] [*Football*] the space (created by his blockers) into which the quarterback attempts to run, preparatory to throwing the ball to one of his receivers. **5.** *n* [*Bowling*] a space left between two bowling pins. **6.** *v* [*US*] [*Politics*] said of a President or state Governor who vetos a bill in federal or state law by refusing to sign it even though it has been passed by the legislature; the executive simply waits until that legislative session has been adjourned and the bill becomes dead.

pocket codes *n pl* [*Sex*] the homosexual community uses brightly coloured bandanna handkerchiefs to signify to each other a variety of sexual preferences according to colour. These handkerchiefs are kept hanging out of the back trouser pocket and those who prefer the passive role keep them in the right hand pocket while those who prefer the active one use the left.

pocket universe *n* [*Role gaming*] in 'Dungeons and Dragons' this is a small experimental area created by the 'Dungeon Master' to test out possible innovations within the larger world of the whole game.

pocketbook issue *n* [*US*] [*Politics*] those political issues which are most genuinely interesting to the voters, usually concerning how much money they will have in their pockets and how much it will purchase for them; they are more pertinent than the abstract issues of foreign policy, etc.

POCO *n* [*Government*] acro **Political Co-operation** it is used by Common Market (EEC) bureaucrats.

P

pod and boom *n* [*US*] [*Gliding*] a fuselage configuration in which the cockpit area is connected to the tail surfaces by a very narrow tube or similar structural member.

pogey bait marine *n* [*US*] [*Marine Corps*] a sissy, a weakling; it comes from 'pogey bait' which are sweets.

poggler *n* [*Motor trade*] a car that has crashed but has had the damage repaired prior to being put up for sale.

pogo 1. *v* [*Aerospace*] said of a rocket which experiences severe longitudinal vibrations. **2.** *v* [*Cycling*] to lift up the front wheel of one's BMX bike and land on the back one; it comes from the bouncing toy of the same name. **3.** *v* [*Military*] air intercept code for: switch to the preceding communications channel or, if unable to establish communications on that channel, switch to the next channel after it.

Point *n* [*US*] [*Military*] abbr of **West Point** the US Military Academy at West Point, NY.

point 1. *n* [*Angling*] the final 18in approximately of a weighted nylon cast. **2.** *n* [*Book collecting*] any peculiarity concerning a book, the presence of which in, or absence from, a given book, is worthy of comment in a catalogue. **3.** *n* [*Boxing*] that area of the head between the chin and the ears. **4.** *n* [*UK*] [*Buses*] abbr of **point of departure** the stop or depot from which a London Transport bus departs on a scheduled trip and to which it returns to conclude one **rounder**. Inspectors stay at each point to check out the time-keeping of the various buses in service. **5.** *n* [*Economics*] a fractional number used when quoting movements in interests rates (one point = one percent) or in international currency exchange rates (one point = one hundredth part of the lowest denomination of a country's currency). **6.** *n* [*Gambling*] in craps this is the number the **shooter** is required to make on second or subsequent throws of the dice in order to win his/her bet; this number is determined by the shooter's first throw, assuming that it is not 7 or 11 (automatic winners) or 2 or 12 (automatic losers). The shooter may continue throwing until he/she 'makes the point', unless a 7 – craps – is thrown first and the bet is lost. **7.** *n* [*Hunting*] the distance in a straight line between the start of a run and its end. **8.** *n* [*Military*] the man at the spearhead of a patrol that is moving in a V-shaped formation or in single file. **9.** *n* [*Business*] the head of a negotiating or bargaining team; it comes from the military use (see **8**). **10.** *n* [*Politics*] the candidate in a Presidential election who is the current front-runner and as such is most vulnerable to attacks from the media, from his opponents and from disenchanted members of his own party; it comes from the military use (see **8**). **11.** *n* [*Sailing, Ropework*] a decorative, cone-shaped termination on cables and running rigging. **12.** *n* [*Taxis*] the first place in a cab rank.

point defence *n* [*Military*] the close-quarters defence of one's own position at a late stage of a battle when enemy advances have made it impossible for the engagement to be kept at a greater distance.

point of no return *n* [*Aerospace*] a geographical position or a particular time point during a flight when an aircraft's fuel supply becomes too low to enable the aircraft to return safely to its own or another friendly base.

point of tension *n* [*Government*] in international diplomatic negotiations, this is any geographical area of the globe where tension between the powers concerned is potentially at its highest; eg. Angola, Afghanistan, Cambodia and Nicaragua.

point row *n* [*US*] [*Farming*] the short or diagonally placed row in a field that is not square.

point target *n* [*Military*] a target so small – eg: a missile silo – that it requires only a single map co-ordinate for identification.

pointer phrase *n* [*Politics*] in speechwriting this is a phrase included expressly to make sure that the audience appreciates a given point in the speech. See also **applause line**.

pointing 1. *n* [*Cat breeding*] the disposition and colouring of a cat's coat. **2.** *n* [*Furriers*] the process of inserting hairs into pelts to enhance their appearance and increase their sale value; thus one pelt may, after pointing, be sold as that of a different, and costlier, animal. **3.** *n* [*Photo-typesetting*] the addition of isolated **pixels** to the **bit-map** image of a character so as to sharpen the image of the character where necessary. **4.** *n* [*Sculpture*] the marking out in pencil, on a statue, of the rough outline of the finished figure, so that a workman can chisel away the basic shape before the sculptor takes over.

point-of-purchase *n* [*Video*] retail advertising materials used on the site where the product is being sold.

point-of-sale terminal *n* [*Commerce*] a terminal used in an environment, particularly a retail outlet, where a customer pays for goods or services. Such terminals are usually operated by unskilled personnel and are often used simply to read a bar code, translate this into a price and total up the customer's bill.

points 1. *n pl* [*Audio*] the percentage of profit which a dealer needs to carry on a viable business. **2.** *n pl* [*Film*] abbr of **percentage points** that percentage of the gross takings of a film which may be allotted by the company to a star actor, a director or even, occasionally, a writer; thus 'X has points in movie Y'; 'what they give writers instead of money' (Fran Lebowitz, 'Social Studies', 1981). **3.** *n pl* [*Theatre*] those gestures, vocal tricks and similar variations on technique that are used to underline the climax of a single speech or of a complete role. On the whole the 'making of points' is not considered to be within the best standards of acting, but rather the sacrifice of some larger, more subtle effect in return for easy applause.

point-to-point *a* [*Communications*] a connection between two, and only two terminals.

poison 1. *n* [*UK*] [*Police*] the criminal 'antecedents' that are read out in court prior to the sentencing of a criminal who has been found guilty of a new crime; they 'poison' the chances of an otherwise more lenient sentence. **2.** *n* [*Science*] in chemistry this is any substance which destroys or reduces the activity of a catalyst. **3.** *v* [*Technology*] to use various materials – boron, cadmium, etc – in the control rods of nuclear reactors to poison or inhibit the fission reaction and thus ensure that a chain reaction and therefore a nuclear explosion is impossible.

poison at the box office *n* [*Theatre*] a play or any other entertainment that repels rather than attracts paying audiences.

poison pill *n* [*US*] [*Commerce*] a counter to a successful takeover in which the **raider** has already secured a controlling interest: the taken over company immediately offers the remaining shareholders an expensive package of debt securities which would leave the company deeply in debt. To keep his new acquisition solvent, the raider must buy up all these shares immediately, at a very inflated price.

poison shelves *n pl* [*Publishing*] those special shelves reserved in libraries for material considered obscene by the librarian or the local government officials.

poisonous weeds *n pl* [*Politics*] in Chinese communist terminology these are any writings or allied propaganda that attacked Mao Zedong; thus by extension it also refers to the individuals who propagated those attacks.

poke 1. *n* [*Computing*] a **high-level language** instruction that modifies that contents of an absolute memory location (see **absolute address**). See also **peek**. **2.** *n* [*Cricket*] an aimless, tentative shot by a batsman; such shots often lead to the batsman's being caught behind the stumps. **3.** *n* [*Shooting*] the action of a bad shot who aims with the gun, rather than swinging it on to the target; such incompetence usually ensures a miss. **4.** *n* [*TV repair*] an electric shock. **5.** also **bait poke** *n* [*UK*] [*Coal-mining*] an old army bag, usually used to carry food eaten underground, but referring to any small bag.

poke-bouncer *n* [*UK*] [*Market-traders*] one who appears, by sleight of hand, to put money or valuables into a paper bag, and then offers that bag for sale.

poker *v* [*Religion*] when a verger or similar church official escorts a higher church dignitary ceremoniously.

polar bear's pyjamas *n* [*Rug trade*] an exceptionally good piece or rug.

pole *v* [*Baseball*] to hit the ball very hard.

pole wagon, also **pole carrier** *n* [*UK*] [*Road transport*] a long trailer with front and rear ends connected by a long pole instead of the conventional chassis; it is used for carrying long poles, tree trunks, pipes, etc.

polecat *n* [*TV*] a length of alloy tubing which is braced between two walls or between the floor and the ceiling to support a number of lights.

police 1. *v* [*Soccer*] to shadow one's designated opposite number; to mark an opponent intensely. **2.** also **crum up** *v* [*US*] [*Marine Corps*] to tidy up or straighten up either a place or an individual. **3.** also **crum up** *n* [*US*] [*Marine Corps*] a condition of great neatness or cleanliness, either of a place or a person.

police action *n* [*Military, Government*] a military intervention by one nation into the territory of another, justified by the claim that the second nation is breaking international law. More realistically, this occurs when one of the superpowers (or a lesser area power) feels that political or military developments within a nation are such that their own interest in the region is being threatened and that nothing short of sending in troops will preserve that interest.

police positive, also **police special** *n* [*US*] [*Police*] a type of pistol used by policemen and manufactured by the Colt company.

police power *n* [*Sociology*] a concept in US law that implies the extension of government authority in the repression of individual habits and tastes simply because the so-called 'public interest lobby' demands such interference.

policeman 1. *n* [*Ice hockey*] a heavyweight player whose job is to protect his own goal-scorers, supposedly by fair means alone, but usually by violence, fouls and other illegal tactics. **2.** *n* [*Science*] in microchemistry this is a short glass rod with a rubber tip attached to one end, that is used for separating solids from liquids.

policy keyboard *n* [*Business*] a range of policy options open to executives on a decision-making level; the skilled executive should be able to 'play' such a keyboard with the fluency of a concert pianist.

poling *n* [*Glass-making*] See **plugging**.

Polish notation *n* [*Computing*] a form of mathematical notation, invented by the Polish mathematician Jan Lukasiewicz, in which each operator (the symbols which denote the specific mathematical operation to be performed) precedes its operands (the quality or function, usually a number, upon which a mathematical operation is performed): thus, a+b is expressed as +ab, etc. While this system runs against traditional notation, it is a far more accurate representation of the way in which a computer performs its internal mathematics.

polished coffee *n* [*Coffee production*] wet processed mild Arabica coffee from which the **silverskin** has been removed to reveal a glossy surface.

P

political culture *n* [*Sociology*] the concept that the attitudes, beliefs and rules which guide a political system are determined jointly by the history of the system and the experiences of its members; this is used to analyse different national systems on behavioural terms based on sociology and psychology.

political thinking *n* [*Politics*] in Marxist terms, this is a mixture of ideological purity and civic responsibility, each of which should breed the other. On a general level, it is the involvement of the individual or group in the social and political life of the Party and the State.

politician's job *n* [*US*] [*Painting*] a job that needs slow, careful work, and which the painter can justifiably complete at his leisure.

poll the room 1. *v* [*Aerospace*] to demand a consensus opinion from all those involved in monitoring and directing a space flight before launching the vehicle and its astronauts on the next stage of their mission, or when attempting to sort out any technical problem. See also **go/no go**. 2. *v* [*Business*] on the basis of the aerospace use (see 1), this is to make a request to anyone concerned in a situation for help or advice in solving a problem that has arisen within that situation.

polling 1. *n* [*Computing*] the **interrogation** of a number of devices in sequence to facilitate the orderly operation of a large network. 2. *n* [*Computing*] the scanning by a central processing unit of all peripheral terminals and the 'asking' of them whether or not they have any data to offer.

polycentrism *n* [*Politics*] a term coined in 1956 by P. Togliatti (1892–1964); it is the concept that each national communist party should have the right to establish its own autonomous style and that none need pay any more than formal respect to the Soviet model. Thus, by extension, the concept is that there should be more than one centre of power in any political or ideological group, not simply one in Moscow or, for capitalists, in Washington.

polysemy *n* [*Linguistics*] the multiplicity of meanings that can be found in one word.

polywater, also **water II** *n* [*Science*] See **anomalous water**.

POM *n* [*Computing*] acro **Phase Of the Moon** used facetiously when an operator is attempting to explain why a particular computing event turned out as it did, especially when it went wrong.

Pompey *n* [*Navy*] Portsmouth, a major base for the Royal Navy. See also **Guzz**.

pone *n* [*Cards*] the player, usually seated to his/her right, who cuts the cards for the dealer.

pong 1. *v* [*Theatre*] to ad-lib when one has forgotten the actual line. 2. *v* [*Theatre*] to over-emphasise one's lines, to speak more loudly than a line warrants. See also **ping 2**.

ponger *n* [*UK*] [*Circus*] an acrobat.

pongo 1. *n* [*Navy*] a soldier, a Royal Marine. 2. *n* [*UK*] [*Military*] an officer.

pons asinorum *n* [*Philosophy*] a crucial, critical test of comprehension; a problem that proves too difficult for the less intelligent, or the beginner. It is taken from the fifth proposition of the first book of Euclid, and is a scholarly joke referring to the difficulty 'asses' have in 'getting over it'.

Ponsonby Rule *n* [*Government*] this was named after Arthur Ponsonby, 1st Lord Ponsonby (1871–1946) who signed a minute in 1924 that permits the Government to authorise an agreement without Parliamentary approval if the document has been available and Parliament has failed to act upon it within 21 days.

pontoon *n* [*UK*] [*Prisons*] a 21-month jail sentence; it comes from the card game in which a score of 21 makes the optimum hand.

pony 1. *n* [*US*] [*Education*] a revision notebook used for help in college examinations. 2. *n* [*US*] [*Journalism*] a brief bulletin from a news agency which details only the highlights of the day's news. 3. *n* [*Logging*] a small version of heavy sawmill machinery; it is used for light work. 4. *n, a* [*UK*] [*Market-traders*] trash, rubbish; trashy, rubbishy. 5. *n* [*US*] [*Painting*] a brush used for water paints, or for working in cramped areas. 6. *n* [*UK*] [*Police*] £25. 7. *n* [*Theatre*] a small chorus girl who dances and sings in musicals.

pony editor *n* [*Journalism*] a junior editor, often a boy, who gives a brief summary of the day's news, around 100 words, to a string of small-town newspapers. See also **horse editor**.

ponypot *n* [*US*] [*Painting*] a bucket that has a flared top to allow the dipping of extra-wide brushes.

POO 1. *n* [*Aerospace*] acro **Program 0–0 (Zero-Zero)** used when astronauts clear their onboard computer of current data in order to receive new information from Mission Control. 2. *n* [*Business*] acro this comes from the aerospace use (see 1); when an executive is to 'go to POO (Program Zero-Zero)' he/she has to clear out and forget all current assumptions and information regarding a given situation and prepare to absorb such new material as will be necessary to make fresh decisions in a new situation.

poo phoo *n* [*Navy*] impromptu entertainment provided by the crew for a concert in a warship.

poodler *n* [*UK*] [*Road transport*] a small motor vehicle.

pooh-bah *n* [*US*] [*Politics*] this comes from the character in Gilbert & Sullivan's 'The Mikado' (1885); it is an official of great pomposity and self-importance. See also **muckey-muck**.

pool 1. *n* [*Docks*] the register of freelance dockworkers who seek employment. 2. *n, v* [*Journalism*] the putting together of resources and information by a number of otherwise rival journalists (both print and broadcast). It is either because communications home – eg: from a war front –

are so limited that without such co-operation no one will manage to dispatch material successfully, or because local authorities, often military commanders, will not deal with individuals but only issue a regular, general statement, or because the press interest is so great – eg. in a royal wedding – that the object of this concern refuses to attend to each individual journalistic demand and prefers to satisfy all at once.

poor *a* [*Wine-tasting*] not actually bad, but lacking in quality and character.

POP *a* [*Advertising*] acro **Post Office Preferred** a reference to the regulation sizes of envelopes preferred by post office sorters; they should be sent to the company when despatching an order for mail-order goods.

pop **1.** *n* [*Baseball*] a ball hit high into the air, but which does not travel laterally and thus provides a simple catch. **2.** *n* [*US*] [*Theatre*] the traditional name for the stage-door keeper. See also **George 2. 3.** *v* [*Drugs*] to inject a narcotic drug; thus 'skinpop' is to inject under the skin rather than directly into a vein, the practice in general of the novice user; the ones who inject into the vein are 'mainlining'.

pop architecture **1.** *n* [*Architecture*] buildings that are generally popular with the majority of the public. **2.** *n* [*Architecture*] buildings or structures that are symbolically styled, eg: a hamburger restaurant that is built to resemble a hamburger, etc. **3.** *n* [*Architecture*] buildings by professional architects which reflect the fact that they have been influenced by commercial designs as in (**2**). **4.** *n* [*Architecture*] architectural plans for sculptural projects on a vast scale.

pop art *n* [*Art*] the art movement that developed in the 1960s and drew its inspiration from every variety of mass, popular culture, drawing heavily on the 'visual vocabulary' of that culture and its invariably commercial techniques. Subjects were treated impersonally, with no political or moral statements attached to them, and the art often echoed the mass production techniques of industry.

pop off *v* [*Film*] in animation this refers to the sudden disappearance of pictorial information from the screen. See also **pop on**.

pop on *v* [*Film*] in animation this refers to the instantaneous appearance of an image on an existing scene. See also **pop off**.

Pop Warner football *n* [*US*] [*Football*] the under-15 US football league; it was formed in Philadelphia in 1929 and named after the contemporary coach of Temple U.

pop-down *a* [*Computing*] referring to a **menu** which can be accessed at any time and which appears at the top of a user's screen; a highlighted bar can be moved over the various items on the menu and will, as required, access the function indicated by that item.

popeye *n* [*Military*] air intercept code for: I am in cloud, I have reduced visibility.

poplarism *n* [*UK*] [*Politics*] the policy of offering excessively generous social welfare by a local council, often deliberately flying in the face of a national government which is committed to cutting back on such hand-outs. It comes from the activities in 1919 of the Poplar (East London) Labour council which pushed up local rates to unprecedented heights in order to fund a massive programme of council welfare for the needy.

popout *n* [*Surfing*] a poorly made surfboard.

Popperian *a* [*Philosophy*] this comes from the name of Sir Karl Popper (b. 1902) whose most widely known theory states that scientific laws are only justified by the extent of their resistance to falsification; he has constantly attacked those facets of Marxism that act to curtail individual freedom.

popping **1.** *n* [*Painting*] eruptions in the paint which leave craters in the dried surface. **2.** also **pitting** *n* [*Building, Plastering*] See **blowing**.

popping and banging *n* [*Audio*] an unnecessarily high level of noise when someone is speaking into a microphone, specifically on the letters 'p' and 'b'.

popping John *n* [*US*] [*Farming*] a two-cylinder John Deere tractor.

poppy *n* [*UK*] [*Market-traders*] money.

pop-shot **1.** *n* [*Coal-mining*] a shot fired to trim the edges of a blasted area. **2.** *n* [*Coal-mining*] a method of secondary blasting in a quarry.

popular art *n* [*Art*] those best-selling but anonymously produced artworks which have no pretensions to 'fine art', nor are they in any way 'modern' or experimental, but which appeal massively to the great bulk of the non-discerning British public.

population **1.** *n* [*Marketing*] a group of people, selected in some systematic manner, who are used as a sample for market research. **2.** *n* [*Video*] the number of video cassette recorders in a given market.

pop-up **1.** *n* [*Advertising*] See **spectacular**. **2.** *n* [*Military*] See **cold launch**. **3.** also **pop fly** *n* [*Baseball*] a short fly ball that descends inside the infield or just beyond it.

pop-up missile *n* [*Military*] See **snap-up missile**.

porch *n* [*Aerospace*] a small platform that is attached to the outside of a spacecraft's hatch.

porcupine **1.** *n* [*Military*] a proposed, but subsequently abandoned, defence system for the MX missile: the defences would send up a curtain of steel pellets or darts to deflect/detonate incoming Soviet missiles before they destroyed the US silos. **2.** *n* [*Mining*] a drill that has become stuck while boring a hole. **3.** *n* [*Oil rigs*] a cylindrical steel drum with steel bristles protruding from the surface; it is used for scouring and

P

cleaning sediment filled pipelines. See also **pig 3, rabbit 8**.

porcupi~~e~~ provision n [*Business*] See **shark repellent**.

pork 1. n [*Journalism*] material that is either repeated in a number of editions on the same day, or taken from one's day's final edition and included in the early edition of the following day. **2.** n [*US*] [*Politics*] federal government funds that are obtained for a particular person or area by the manipulation of political patronage.

porkbarrel n [*US*] [*Politics*] the state or Federal treasury into which local politicians can 'dip' for funds that they require for their own area and which they can disperse to encourage the spread of their political patronage. Hence the term 'pork-barrelling' which means using state or federal funds to provide local public works and amenities that would otherwise be beyond the budgets of those areas that require them.

pork chop 1. n [*Industrial relations*] a full-time union official who works not for ideological reasons but because he/she has gained the job through patronage, family ties or as a payoff for services rendered. **2.** n [*US*] [*Sociology*] a US black who is willing to accept a position that is inferior to that of his/her white peers.

porkchop n [*US*] [*Printing*] a portrait that measures one-half of a column width, which varies as to the publication.

pork chops n [*US*] [*Navy*] the supply officer.

pork-knockers n pl [*Commerce*] freelance gold and diamond prospectors in Guyana, whose name derives from the staple content of their rations.

pornopatch n [*Publishing*] See **OSS**.

porpoise 1. v [*Aerospace*] when an aircraft shows that it is in trouble by deliberately flying an exaggerated up and down course through the air. **2.** v [*Air travel*] See **balloon 1**. **3.** n [*Navy*] a submarine that is moving through the water like a porpoise: first rising to the surface, then submerging again, and so on.

porpoising n [*Air travel*] repeated dynamic pitching of the aircraft when being ground launched.

porridge 1. n [*UK*] [*Prisons*] one's time in jail, which traditionally refers to the daily ration of porridge served up for breakfast. **2.** n [*UK*] [*Railways*] the sludge taken out of the drains running by the tracks.

Porridge Bowl, the n [*UK*] [*Railways*] the Royal Scot: the London to Edinburgh express.

port 1. n [*Computing*] the conversion of a program running on one manufacturer's system so that it will run on another system. **2.** n [*Computing*] any socket on a machine into which a variety of terminals and other **peripherals** can be plugged. **3.** n [*Glass-making*] a structure leading to and forming an opening in a furnace wall for introducing fuel and combustion air, or for combustion gases to leave the furnace.

portable 1. a [*Computing*] said of a program that can adapt simply to the operating systems of a variety of machines. **2.** a [*Industrial relations*] referring to the concept that rights, privileges, pension plans and the like should be transferred with an employee when he/she moves to a new firm, rather than their being abandoned wholesale and then re-established through a new process of accumulation. Thus 'portability' is a condition whereby employees may effect such transfers without problems or conditions.

portfolio n [*Stock market*] a collection or list of securities held by a single corporation or individual. Thus 'portfolio investment' means the purchasing of securities in a number of companies to build up such a portfolio.

porthole n [*Sheep-shearing*] a low opening on to a ramp along which the shorn sheep move through to the counting-out pen.

porting n [*Computing*] the movement of a system from one machine to another (to which it is attached by a port). See also **port 1**.

portmanteau n [*Angling*] a very large fish.

portrait n [*Advertising*] a page or illustration size in which the dimensions of the height exceed those of the width. See also **landscape 1**.

portrait-page n [*Advertising*] See **mini-page**.

Portsmouth yardstick n [*Yachting*] an internationally applicable table for the handicapping of yacht races; it was developed in 1950 by Mr. Sinbad Z. Milledge (1904–1983) and first used in Portsmouth; the table is now used in sixty-four countries.

pos n [*Journalism*] abbr of **apostrophe** it is commonly used when dictating copy over the telephone.

P.O.S. n [*US*] [*Medicine*] abbr of **piece of shit** patients unable to look after themselves – it is often aimed at alcoholics.

POSDCORB mnem [*Management*] acro **planning, organising, staffing, directing, co-ordinating, reporting and budgeting** the ideal functions of a chief executive; they were devised in 1937 by US public administration expert Luther Gulick (1892–).

posigrade v [*Aerospace*] to use a small rocket which is fired briefly to give forward momentum to a spacecraft or larger rocket.

position 1. v [*Advertising*] to define the fundamental characteristics of a product; what it is, what it does and who it is for. **2.** v [*Marketing*] to market a particular product by targeting one segment of the market and emphasising the extent to which that product is required by that segment; it is the choosing of the right market for the promotion of a new product. **3.** n [*Futures market*] an interest in the market, either **short** or **long** in the form of an **open contract**. **4.** n [*Stock market*] the state of any broker or **jobber's** book, revealing where he stands in the market.

position paper n [*Politics*] a document prepared

to illustrate the position of any national or interest group – government, unions, civil service, etc. – on a currently vital issue; it is a written statement of attitude and/or intention.

positive *a* [*Wine-tasting*] the opposite of **little** and **dumb**: said of a marked and noticeable wine, with definite quality and character.

positive action *n* [*US*] [*Law*] any aggressive action involved in the committing of a crime: assault, rape, murder, etc.

positive carry *n* [*Stock market*] a situation in which the cost of money borrowed to finance securities is less than the profits that these securities yield. See also **negative carry**.

positive control *n* [*Military*] the sending of strategic bombers to a holding position, prior to recalling them to base or ordering them to proceed to their targets in the USSR. See also **fail-safe 3**.

positive discrimination *n* [*Government*] the hiring of members of minority groups, even though their actual qualifications/abilities might not earn them the job in a normal competition. Such hiring is intended to compensate for the inherent problems, especially in education, that such minorities suffer. See also **affirmative action**.

positive labour relations *n* [*Industrial relations*] See **positive personnel practices**.

positive neutrality *n* [*Politics*] the adopting by smaller nations of a posture whereby they establish good and therefore lucrative relations with all major and superpowers, but studiously refuse to become involved in their political rivalries.

positive personnel practices *n pl* [*Industrial relations*] a euphemism for a growing movement, which is mainly based in the US but is spreading to Europe, to outlaw unions, or to undermine and eradicate their presence in the workforce and make it harder for them to recruit new members.

positive policing *n* [*UK*] [*Police*] the concept of active policing during civil disturbances: charging the demonstrators or rioters, using tear gas or rubber bullets, rather than simply, as is traditional, holding the 'thin blue line'.

positive racism *n* [*Politics*] See **reverse bigotry**.

positive response *n* [*Military*] a euphemism, coined during the Vietnam War, for bombing.

positive sum game *n* [*Business*] a variety of 'game' played by economists, bureaucrats, planners, businessmen, etc. in which the result gives a greater number of winners than losers. Such games embrace the workings of multinational corporations, the nuclear energy programme, etc. See also **negative sum game, zero-sum game**.

positivism 1. *n* [*Sociology*] the insistence that science can only deal with observable entities known directly to experience; thus the positivist aims to construct general laws/theories to express the relationship between phenomena. **2.** *n* [*Sociology*] the conviction that the discipline can be

just as scientific as any natural science and thus show a preference for scientific method – measurement, quantification, etc – as against analysis of human motives and intentions. The concept is mainly decried in contemporary sociology.

positivist *n* [*Sociology*] one who espouses positivist (see **positivism**) theories of the social structure. See also **action theory**.

possibilism *n* [*Politics*] a political philosophy that concentrates on the inception of such social and economic reforms as are actually possible, rather than those that are merely utopian. See also **impossibilism**.

possibles *n pl* [*Sport*] when trials are being held to select a representative team, these are the players considered less likely to be chosen out of those available. See also **probables**.

POSSLQ *n* [*US*] [*Sociology*] acro **Persons Of the Opposite Sex Sharing Living Quarters** used by the US Bureau of the Census to describe cohabiting couples who are not married. See also **de facto couple**.

possum belly 1. *n* [*Oil rigs*] a metal box built underneath a truck which carries pipeline repair tools. **2.** *n* [*US*] [*Road transport*] a livestock trailer which transports small animals on a drop frame beneath large ones.

possum sheriff *n* [*US*] [*Police*] a game warden.

possum walk *n* [*US*] [*Iron workers*] a method of walking an I-beam in high iron work: one straddles the upper half of the beam, hugging it with the knees, while placing the feet on the bottom flare of the beam.

post 1. *n* [*Glass-making*] the formed gather of glass prior to its drawing by the hand process. **2.** *n* [*US*] [*Medicine*] abbr of **post mortem** an autopsy; thus 'do a post' means perform an autopsy.

post holder, also **post gatherer** *n* [*Glass-making*] a workman who handles the **punty** in the hand drawing process and gathers the **post**.

post mortem *n* [*Computing*] the analysis of an operation after its execution.

post-art artist *n* [*Art*] the artist as an individual who has transcended the rules, regulations and strictures of any form of 'Art' and who works simply as a perceiver of social realities.

post-attack blackmail *n* [*Military*] a tactic for waging nuclear war which is designed to minimise defensive damage while maximising first strike offensive damage. One's first strike should destroy hostile defences but spare, as yet, the population; the next stage is to threaten that population with annihilation if surrender is not immediate.

postcall analysis *n* [*Commerce*] See **kerbside conference**.

posted *a* [*Merchant navy*] Lloyds' term for a ship that is declared officially missing.

posted price *n* [*Oil industry*] a price for crude petroleum which is used as a reference for the

P

calculation of those taxes and royalties paid by oil companies to oil-producing countries.

poster session n [Science] a meeting of scientists where their work is exhibited in visual displays; the study of these displays is then used as the basis for subsequent conversations and consultations between them.

posterior a [Midwifery] said of a child who is wedged face forward in the birth canal.

posterior probability n [Science] revised estimates of probability based on the incorporation of information that was not available when the initial calculations were made.

post-figurative culture n [Anthropology] a culture in which the old stand as role models for the young. See also **co-operative, pre-figurative culture**.

postfix notation, also **suffix notation** n [Computing] See **reverse Polish notation**.

post-flashing n [Film] a complex process of light exposure used by cameramen to soften the actual colours they are seeing.

post-formalist art n [Art] in contrast to the Formalists who emphasised the formal properties of an art object, post-Formalists emphasise systems instead of objects and procedures over results; their aim is to establish an inter-active relationship with the world.

post-hoc-propter-ergo fallacy n [Philosophy] the error of believing that a situation has been caused directly by something that occurred previously; it occurs especially in the idea of a 'lucky piece' which one carries, a lucky order of putting on one's clothes (common amongst sportsmen) etc.

post-impressionist art n [Art] a school of early 20th century artists who sought to reveal the structural form of a subject without paying absolute attention to its actual appearance.

posting n [Computing] a procedure for adding additional information to an existing record in a database.

post-launch survivability n [Military] the ability of a weapons system to deliver its bombs on target after having penetrated the enemy's defences. See also **pre-launch survivability**.

postman n [Government] a principal officer in the UK Civil Service; it is a word culled from John Le Carré's 'Smiley's People' (1979) and taken into general use.

postman's knock n [Boxing] two successive, hard, blows, usually with the left hand; it comes from the traditional double-rap that announces the mail.

post-modern design n [Architecture] a movement in architectural design that represents a reaction against the tenets of **modernism**. In essence it is a return to the metaphor of the body rather than that of the machine; a return to the belief in the irrationality and emotionality of human beings, which should be incorporated in the buildings they occupy.

post-modernism n [Art] a movement running across the art world that rejects many of the advances and experiments of the 20th century and substitutes a return to certain classical and historical styles and techniques.

post-object art n [Art] See **anti-object art**.

post-production n [Film] all work on a film that follows the completion of **principal photography**: mixing, editing, dubbing, special effects, printing, etc.

post-SIOP n [Military] any time after a full-scale nuclear war has begun and the operational plans have been put into action. See also **SIOP**.

post-stretching, also **post-tensioning** n [Building] the strengthening of pre-stressed concrete by the application of tension to the reinforcing rods after the concrete has set.

post-synchronisation n [Film] the adding of sound, by **dubbing** it on to pictures that have already been shot; such work may be necessary when it has been impossible to shoot – probably while on location – on a completely silent set and thus background noises have to be eliminated and the dialogue re-recorded.

post-traumatic neurosis n [Military] the current euphemism for those stresses that engulf the mind of a soldier whose mind, in the long or short run, has been overwhelmed by the experiences of battle; it is the contemporary successor to 'shell shock' (World War I) and 'battle fatigue' (World War II and Korea).

posture n [Military] a nation's overall military strength and readiness as far as such factors affect its capacity to fight a war.

POT v [UK] [Police] acro **Prevention of Terrorism Act** to arrest a suspect under the provisions of this act.

pot 1. n [Computing] a reserved area in the memory used for accumulating certain data. **2.** n [Glass-making] an oval or round container made of refractory material in which glass is melted. **3.** n [Metallurgy] any crucible in an iron foundry. **4.** n [US] [Medicine] See **crock 4, turkey 8**. **5.** n [Radio] abbr of **potentiometer** the machine which preceded the development of faders and which engineers formerly used when fading out sound on a broadcast; thus 'to pot' is to fade out. **6.** n [Radio] acro **potential out take** the cutting short of a programme; thus 'pot a tape' or 'find a pot' is to choose a suitable moment in a programme for cutting it off; 'pot point' is that moment on a tape which is marked ready for the cut-off; 'tight pot' is a programme so constructed that the pot point must be taken very quickly and accurately so as to maintain the sense of what is transmitted without cutting off speech in mid-sentence or turning sense into nonsense. **7.** n [Film, Video] acro **potential out take** any part of a production considered to be of secondary importance or quality and which can thus be discarded if necessary. **8.** n [US] [Railways] See **dwarf 2**. **9.** n [US] [Stock market] the portion of a stock or bond issue that is withheld from the general market to facilitate institutional sales; thus the phrase 'the pot is clean' means that the reserved portion of the issue has been sold out. **10.** v [Rugby] to score a dropped goal. **11.** v [Tiddly-winks] to play one's wink(s) into the pot; thus double-pot is a strategy whereby both partners on a team attempt to pot all their winks; it is considered a very dangerous strategy, since it takes no account of any opposition counter-measures.

pot ale, also **burnt ale** n [Distilling] the liquor left in the wash still after the first distillation in the pot still process; it is the residue of the **wash** after the extraction by distillation of the **low wines**.

pot lot n [US] [Car salesmen] See **iron lot**.

pot out v [Radio] See **opt out**.

potato patch n [US] [Medicine] See **vegetable garden**.

potato-masher n [Military] a type of grenade, the shape of which vaguely resembles the kitchen implement.

potential survivors n pl [Navy] sailors who have been fully trained in land and sea survival techniques.

pothook n [Printing] a sharp and rather long beginning and termination to a letter, especially in some italic faces.

pot-hunting n [Hunting] coursing when the object is not to test the relative merits of the dogs, but simply to kill a hare.

potlog n [Building, Plastering] a cross-piece in scaffolding, with a tapered end which is embedded into a hole prepared in the fabric of the building.

potlugger, also **potlucker 1.** n [US] [Painting] a member of the union who takes jobs outside the union's area of jurisdiction, thus contravening the union rules. **2.** n [US] [Painting] a painter who moves quickly from job to job, carrying his equip-ment on his car, and looking for quick profits before moving on.

Potomac fever n [US] [Politics] a lust for political power; it is named after the Potomac River which flows through Washington, DC.

pot-out v [Tiddleywinks] to place all six winks of one's colour in the pot and gain a bonus point.

pots n pl [US] [Coal-mining] loose fossiliferous formations, usually petrified tree roots, which are found in the roof of a mine and which often fall on those working beneath.

pot-squop v [Tiddleywinks] a strategy that involves one of two partners attempting to pot his winks, while the other attempts to stop the opponents playing by covering them. See also **Squop**.

poultry dealer n [Sex] a homosexual pimp who specialises in young boys, ie: 'chickens'.

pounce 1. v [Clothing] to smooth the surface of a felt hat with sandpaper. **2.** n [Painting] a method of creating a pattern by pricking it out through a sheet of paper using a sharp instrument; the resulting pattern can then be transferred on to a surface by using the paper as a variety of stencil over and through which one paints. **3.** n [Military] US Dept. of Defense code for: I am in position to intercept the target.

pounded a [UK] [Railways] said of a train which is shunted into a siding to allow other trains to pass by.

pounder n [Glass-making] See **teaser 4**.

pour n [Entertainment] a cocktail party; it comes from the pouring of drinks thereat.

pour on the coal v [US] [Road transport] to accelerate.

poverty trap n [Sociology, Economics] the situ-ation of poor families who receive benefits, whether means-tested or not. When the main provider finds a job these benefits will probably be relinquished but in many cases the family's real income will then drop, since that provider is unable to qualify for a job that earns, after deductions, sufficiently more than the benefits already provided.

powders n pl [US] [Cattlemen] orders from the ranch boss.

power 1. n [US] [Railways] the number and types of locomotives on a train. **2.** n [US] [Railways] the locomotives available at a given time.

power density n [Satellite TV] the total amount of radiated power transmitted by a satellite divided by the band width of the received signal; it is measured in Watts/Herz.

power drinker n [US] [Bars] a notably heavy drinker.

power dump n [Computing] the accidental or deliberate cutting off of all power.

power excursion n [Technology] an accidental runaway condition in a nuclear reactor.

power play n [Ice-hockey] the procedure of offensive play that is designed to capitalise on periods when the opposition are depleted by having a man in their penalty box.

power politics n [Politics] any national or inter-national policymaking based on the assumption that sabre-rattling has a better chance of gaining an objective than peaceful negotiation; the concept is that 'might is right'.

power take-off n [UK] [Road transport] auxiliary drive attached to the vehicle gearbox to direct engine power for working ancillary equip-ment such as hydraulic pumps for tipping gear, lorry mounted cranes, refrigeration units, tail lifts etc.

power typing n [Printing] in word processing this is the repetition of processing applications, eg: typing standard letters.

power user n [Computing] anyone, though more often a firm or department rather than an indi-

P

vidual, who uses their computer intensively and continually.

powerhouse 1. *n* [*Gambling*] a particularly strong hand in a card game. 2. *n* [*UK*] [*Radio*] a radio station licensed to operate at 50KW on its own assigned frequency.

pow-wow *n* [*Entertainment*] See **huddle 3**.

P.P. *n* [*US*] [*Medicine*] abbr of **professional patient** a regular attender at an emergency room – weekly or even daily – who has trivial or imaginary complaints but who apparently cannot resist the hospital atmosphere.

PPBS *n* [*Government*] See **programme budgeting**.

p.p.p. *n* [*US*] [*Medicine*] abbr of **piss poor protoplasm** a debilitated patient who requires extensive medical treatment – often including transfusions – before any surgery or other definitive therapy can be started. See also **p.p.p.p.p.t**.

p.p.p.p.p.t *n* [*US*] [*Medicine*] abbr of **piss-poor protoplasm poorly put together** a patient in generally poor physical state. See also **p.p.p**.

practical *a* [*Film, Theatre, TV*] said of anything used on a set that actually 'works': edible food, smokeable cigarettes, slammable doors, etc. See also **impractical**.

practical politics *n* [*Politics*] a euphemism for expedient politics: cutting both legal and ethical corners to 'get things done'; it is a style that exceeds mere cynicism but falls marginally short of downright dishonesty.

practicum *n* [*Education*] an alternative for 'practical': any learning that comes from experience rather than rote, eg: field work, laboratory experimentation, etc.

prad *n* [*UK*] [*Circus*] a horse; it comes from Dutch 'praad' meaning 'horse', at least since the 18th century.

pragma 1. *n* [*Computing*] a statement in a programming language that is intended to convey information to a particular implementation, and be ignored in any other implementation of the language. 2. *n* [*Computing*] a statement in a programming language that may assist the **compiler** in translating the program into machine code but can be ignored without prejudicing the correct working of the program.

pragmatism *n* [*Politics*] looking at what can be done in politics rather than dreaming of what might be done; practical, rather than utopian, planning. See also **possibilism**.

prairie dog *n* [*Oil rigs*] a small, simple refinery located in a remote area.

praiser *n* [*Entertainment*] a public relations person or a press agent.

pratique *n* [*Shipping*] permission to use a port that is granted to a ship when the master signs a document (the certificate of pratique) stating that the ship has a clean bill of health or, in the case of illness, will obey the quarantine rules.

praxis 1. *n* [*Sociology*] in Marxist terms this means action as opposed to philosophical speculation. 2. *n* [*Sociology*] a Marxist term meaning that the fundamental characteristic of human society is material production to meet basic needs.

prayer card *n* [*UK*] [*Politics*] a card used by a member of the House of Commons to reserve a seat during morning prayers.

prayer warrior *n* [*Religion*] one who prays loud and long for many people and many causes.

prayerbook *n* [*Navy*] a small holystone – the piece of sandstone used to polish the deck.

pre-cleared fire-zone *n* [*Military*] an area in which anything living – both human and animal – is deemed a legitimate target for one's weapons. See also **free-fire zone**.

preem *n, v* [*Entertainment*] the premier of a film, play, show or TV programme or series; to launch a new film, play, etc.

pre-emphasis *n* [*Audio*] the boosting of high frequencies in recording or broadcasting.

pre-emption *n* [*Advertising*] See **accepted pairing**.

pre-emptive strike *n* [*Military*] an attack launched on an enemy who has had no prior warning of its coming; a surprise attack. The implication is less of staging an ambush but of implementing the philosophy 'do it to them before they do it to you'. See also **splendid first strike**.

pre-fade *n* [*Radio*] material that is performed before a programme is actually faded up for transmission – often in a studio discussion or a live concert.

preferential defence *n* [*Military*] a defence plan that concentrates one's defences on certain key areas – military installations, government centres, industrial conglomerations – at the expense of those considered less valuable – population centres with no 'valuable' personnel, etc.

preferential shop *n* [*US*] [*Industrial relations*] a business that gives hiring preference to members of unions.

pre-figurative culture *n* [*Anthropology*] a culture in which the young become role models for their parents, who learn to alter their adult behaviour accordingly. See also **co-figurative, post-figurative culture**.

prefix notation *n* [*Computing*] See **reverse Polish notation**.

pre-flight *v* [*Military*] to run a full check on an aircraft and its weapons systems prior to take-off.

pre-launch survivability *n* [*Military*] the ability of a given weapons system to ride out a pre-emptive, surprise **first strike** and then to retaliate successfully against enemy targets. See also **post-launch survivability**.

pre-med *n* [*Medicine*] abbr of **pre-medication** any medication given prior to an operation or any other major treatment; it is usually some form of sedative or tranquilliser.

premia *n pl* [*Industrial relations*] overtime,

bonuses, incentive payments – any payments over and above the basic pay.

premie n [US] [Medicine] abbr of **premature baby**.

premise v [Business, Government] to take as a basic assumption.

premium 1. n [Futures market] the excess of one futures contract price over another, either within the same financial instrument or not; it is the opposite of discount. 2. n [Marketing] any item of goods offered by a company to its consumers, retailers, wholesalers and salesmen. 3. n [Marketing] any product which is specifically offered either with another product or after the purchase of the first product. 4. n [Stock market] in the case of a new share issue, this is the excess of the market price over the sale price. 5. n [Stock market] the excess of the market price over the nominal value of quoted stocks. 6. n [Stock market] dollar premium: this is the excess over the official rate of exchange which must be paid for investment dollars which are required to purchase securities outside the Sterling Area.

premium pricing n [Commerce] See **prestige pricing**.

premium raid n [Stock market] an attempt by one company to gain a controlling interest in another by offering shareholders an amount in excess of the current price of their shares; like a **dawn raid**, this is a surprise tactic, but it is regulated by stock exchange rules.

pre-need sale n [US] [Undertakers] the purchase, often on credit terms, of a grave prior to one's death. See also **immediate need sale**.

pre-owned a [Motor trade] a euphemism for a second-hand car.

prep v [Film] abbr of **prepare** to promote a new film prior to its release.

prep time n [US] [Railways] abbr of **preparatory time** a period allotted for checking over the operation of a locomotive before it leaves the roundhouse.

preparation n [Skiing] the lowering of the body by bending at the hips, knees and ankles.

preparation room n [US] [Undertakers] the morgue; it is so called because the majority of American corpses are embalmed and made up prior to actual burial.

pre-production n [Film] all work performed on a film prior to the **principal photography:** writing the script, developing the plot, casting, costumes, hiring the director and crew, finding locations, etc. See also **post-production**.

prequel n [Publishing] the idea of capitalising on a best-seller, whose pessimistic author has been foolish enough to kill off the hero or heroine, by having him/her write the story of their adventures prior to the action narrated in the currently popular book; it is an idea that has also been used in TV and films.

prerecruitment development n [Espionage]
in the CIA this is the first stage of recruiting a potential agent; at first one must not ask him to do anything his conscience might dislike, then that conscience is developed until he will perform all necessary tasks without balking.

presence 1. n [Art] the ability of an art work to command its own space; it is a term based firmly on its theatrical origins denoting a performer who can command the stage. 2. n [Audio] the 'live' quality that may be found in, and is required of, optimum recordings of sound; it is obtained by close microphone work and boosting of the upper-middle frequencies (2–5 kHz).

presentation n [Real estate] architectural layout, interior decoration, special features and any other aspects of a property that enhance its saleability over and above the basic facts of its size and geographical location.

presenting problem n [Social work] the problem that the client may well put forward to the social worker as a mask for the real or deeper problem with which the client finds it much more difficult to deal; it is thus a symptom, rather than the problem, which must actually be treated.

preset v [Computing] See **initialise**.

press 1. v [Golf] to put too much effort into a shot. 2. n [Golf] a side-bet that is proposed and/or taken during a game. 3. n [Lacrosse] a defensive tactic which attempts to force opponents to make errors; it may be executed using a player-to-player or zone defence in backfield, midfield or frontfield. The press often involves double-teaming, (see **double team**). 4. n [Psychology] anything in the environment to which a need in the organism responds – either positive or negative.

press availability n [Journalism, Politics] a variety of press conference in which the speaker makes no introductory statement but immediately opens him/herself to questions from the press.

press gang show n [Navy] an officer who is ordered to represent the ship at some tedious civil function on shore.

press roll n [Music] a drum roll produced by pressing the sticks against the drum head.

pressed to the max a [US] [Prisons] used to describe a well-dressed, neat person. See also **clean 9**.

pressie, also **presser** n [UK] [Radio] a press conference.

pressing flesh, also **glad-handing** n [Politics] the endless handshaking, shoulder-squeezing, baby-kissing etc. to which campaigning politicians seem to have to submit in order to endear themselves to the electorate.

pressing off n [Clothing] the final pressing operations performed on a garment after assembly.

pressing rumble n [Audio] vertical undulations or ripples on a record, which are the result of imperfect pressing and which produce low frequency rumbling during play.

pressure cooker n [US] [Medicine] the intensive care unit. See also **MICU, SICU**.

prestige pricing, also **premium pricing** n [Commerce] the practice of setting (artificially) high prices for certain goods which the consumer would not think were up to standard if they were offered cheaply.

prêt n [Military] used in the French Foreign Legion to mean 'pay day'.

prêt-à-porter n [Fashion] off-the-peg clothes, made up in a range of standard sizes and colours.

pre-to-post n [Advertising] the concept that a consumer's attitude to the possibility of purchasing a product alters after he/she has seen it being advertised; it is a basic test intended to determine whether or not advertising actually works.

pretty boy n [US] [Circus] a bouncer, who removes undesirables.

pretty police n [Police] police officers disguised as homosexuals who frequent various centres of homosexual activity in the hope of making arrests for sex-related crimes; despite such 'prettiness', they allegedly fool few of their potential victims.

pretty printer n [Computing] a program that takes a text file and produces a listing or copy of that file in a format that conforms to some set of conventions for textual layout. Pretty printers are usually employed to format the source text of **high-level languages**; the printer can produce a layout which offers a basic illustration of the program structure.

pretzel n [Music] a French horn; thus 'pretzel bender' is a French horn player.

prevail v [Military] taking the current concept of fighting a nuclear war, ie: that it is actually possible to limit and fight one as if one were using conventional weapons and tactics, the US believes that, however appalling the interim casualties and destruction, it will in such a case 'prevail', ie: win.

prevent defense n [US] [Football] a defensive alignment designed to minimise the successful completion of a long forward pass; backs and linebackers are positioned well behind the line of scrimmage.

preventive action n [Espionage] the concept that prevention is better than cure when fighting enemies (or supposed enemies) of the State; thus it is used to justify a variety of illegal activities (**mail cover**, phone-taps, electronic surveillance, **black bag jobs**, etc.) by intelligence agencies.

preventive detention n [Politics] the imprisonment of one's (political) enemies in order to nullify what, if they were free, might have been their effective opposition to one's rule; it is unnecessary for them to have committed any actual crime.

preventive maintenance n [Industry] maintenance work carried out on plant and equipment that is still in running order to ensure that it does not develop any actual faults at a future date.

preventive war n [Military] a war that is fought on the basis of the concept that conflict between two sides is inevitable and that, given this fact, one may as well get on with it as soon as possible and do one's best to win, whatever the horrors and costs involved; the prevention here is of defeat, not of conflict.

previous n [UK] [Police] abbr of **previous convictions**. See also **form 1**.

prexy, also **prez** n [Business] abbr of **president** (of a company).

price scissors n [Economics] the relationship between the prices of agricultural and industrial goods; ideally, agricultural prices should be held down while industrial ones rise in order to provide plenty of cheap food for the workers.

price-lining n [Commerce] the practice of offering a class of goods in a limited number of price categories so that one can optimise total sales throughout the related group.

price-point v [Commerce] to set a bargain price on a given item.

pricey a [US] [Stock market] said of an unrealistically low bid or an unrealistically high offer for a share.

prick v [Shooting] to wound, but not kill, game; the target will probably die later from loss of blood.

prick farrier n [Air Force] a medical officer.

prick up v [Building, Plastering] to **key up** a surface with a wire scratcher in readiness for a floating coat.

pricked 1. a [Angling] said of a fish that has been first hooked and then lost. 2. a [Hunting, Shooting] said of game that has been disabled but not killed by shotgun fire. 3. a [Wine-tasting] said of an unpleasant sharpness due to excess volatile acidity; it is on the way to the final vinegary state.

pricker n [Coal-mining] a non-ferrous tool used to pierce the primer cartridge and place it in the detonator; once the primary explosion has been set off, this in turn fires the major explosion.

pricket n [Deer stalking] See **knobber**.

pricking up coat n [Building, Plastering] the first plaster coat on wood or metal lathing.

prickly a [Wine-tasting] used to describe a sharp-edged, raw, almost effervescent quality on the palate.

priest n [Angling] a weighted club used to kill a fish after it has been landed/boated.

prima facie a [Law] of or concerning evidence that is sufficiently strong to establish the facts of a situation; if the opposing party cannot disprove such evidence, the first party has a 'prima facie case'. It comes from Lat. and means 'at first view'.

primage n [Shipping] See **hat money**.

primal v [New therapies] the central purpose of primal therapy: to relive one's birth. Such a rebirth is generally accompanied by shouts, screams, yells of 'Mummy!' etc.

primal pains n pl [New therapies] 'the central

and universal pains which reside in all neurotics'; the evocation through pain and shouting of one's earliest infantile traumas, which are the source of all one's subsequent pain and thus central to the inner delvings that make up **primal therapy**.

primal therapy n [New therapies] a system of therapy developed by Arthur Janov and expounded in his book 'The Primal Scream'; the basis of such therapy is the reliving of one's birth. Such a rebirth is generally accompanied by shouts, screams, yells of 'Mummy!' etc.

primary n [Electronics] the input winding on a transformer. See also **secondary**.

primary health care n [Social work] the role of the general practitioner, and those nurses, health visitors and other ancillaries who work with him/her, in containing and treating illnesses that are found in the surgery. As the 'primary health worker' who is nearest to the community, the GP has taken on the responsibility of dealing with all the immediate manifestations of illness in his/her area.

primary market n [Futures market] the principal underlying market for a financial instrument.

primary poverty n [Sociology] such extreme poverty that it denies one the chance even to purchase the basic necessities of life.

primary relationship n [Sociology] interpersonal relationships characterised by emotional intensity, total commitment and mutual satisfaction; as opposed to secondary relationships in which the whole person is not involved and which are ephemeral and partial – as between strangers.

primary structure n [Aerospace] those parts of an aircraft the failure of which would seriously endanger the safety of those flying in it.

primate aesthetics n [Art] the study of creativity among apes and chimpanzees, and the analysis of their discernible visual preferences.

prime 1. v [Tobacco] to pick off the ripening tobacco leaves one by one. 2. a [Meat trade] the highest grade of meat.

prime beef n [US] [Air Force] acro the world-wide **Base Engineer Emergency Force** which was created either to act as direct combat support or to assist local forces who are attempting, in peace time, to tackle major natural disasters.

prime bill n [Banking] a bill of exchange which is considered as a first-class credit risk.

prime commercial paper n [Banking, Finance] promissory notes payable in 4–12 months which are issued by major US businesses and sold to the public through brokers. See also **commercial paper**.

prime crew n [Aerospace] the original person or persons who have been trained and briefed to fly a given space mission, as opposed to the 'backup crew', one or more of whom stand ready to take over in the case of illness, accident or similar indisposition.

prime mover n [Military] an extra-large and powerful truck designed to haul weapons, tanks and other heavy military equipment, plus their crews and ammunition.

prime peltries n pl [Furriers] See **firsts 2**. See also **early-caught, late-caught**.

prime rate n [US] [Banking] the interest rate charged by US banks to their most creditworthy customers.

prime time n [TV] the chief **daypart** of the TV day which runs from early to mid-evening viewing and as such is considered the main viewing period in most households; programmes transmitted during prime time are usually low in taste and intellectual demands but highly successful; the advertising rates that accompany them are the most expensive.

primes 1. n pl [Metallurgy] first quality steel sheets. 2. n pl [US] [Meat trade] top-grade cattle, better than choice.

primitive a [Computing] not capable of being broken down into a simpler form; it is said of a basic or fundamental unit.

primitive art 1. n [Art] those artists working in pre-Renaissance Europe, and their works. 2. n [Art] any artist who has not been formally trained, or those who have chosen to imitate such naive styles.

primitives n pl [Photo-typesetting] the simple geometric elements of a design.

Primo n [Clubs] an official in the Royal Antediluvian Order of Buffaloes.

prince of the earth, also **prince of the power of the earth** n [Religion] Satan as he exists prior to Christ's return; see John 12:31.

Prince of Peace n [Religion] Christ as the source of true peace; see Isaiah 9:6.

principal n [Espionage] in the CIA this is an agent runner, the individual who actually receives the required information and passes it on to the home intelligence service. Usually of the same nationality as the agent, he has a cover that permits them to meet without causing suspicion and he will have contacted and recruited him as well as keeping him under operational discipline.

principal photography n [Film] the filming of the main body of the film, rather than the **pre-** and **post-production** phases or the creation of special effects; this main phase of shooting is the equivalent of the period when a film is cited as being 'in production'.

principles of motion economy n pl [Management] See **characteristics of easy movement**.

print 1. n [Electronics] a signal on magnetic tape produced by **print-through**. 2. n [Farming] a pat of butter, moulded into shape.

print to paper v phr [Printing] this is an instruction to the printer to continue making copies until the paper supply is exhausted, rather than specifying a figure for the print run.

printer's pie n [Printing] the spilling of columns

P

of hot metal type into an unrecognisable chaos on the composing room floor; it was originally used for the similar messes of pre-linotype accidents.

printer's waste *n* [*Philately*] any defective, malformed or misprinted stamps which are discarded and usually burnt at the printshop.

print-out *n* [*Computing*] the printing out on paper of a **hard copy** version of whatever the operator has been working on with a particular program – calculations, word-processing, database accumulation, etc.

print-through **1.** *n* [*Electronics*] the accidental transfer of a recorded signal between adjacent layers in a reel of magnetic tape. **2.** *n* [*Printing*] the extent to which the print on one side of a sheet of paper is visible on the other side. See also **see through, show through**. **3.** *n* [*Video, Audio*] a problem that may arise when magnetic tape is wound on to a spool and stored unused for sometime: parts of the signal information may spread through from layer to layer and when the tape is played back these faults will be revealed, eg: as an unexplained echo on an otherwise untainted tape.

prioponic fermentation *n* [*Cheese-making*] the fermentation of hard cheeses that breaks down the fat and releases carbon dioxide gas, producing holes in the cheese.

prioritise *v* [*Government*] to make a subject into a priority for consideration.

priors *n* [*US*] [*Prisons*] a previous record.

prisoners *n pl* [*Salvation Army*] members of the congregation who are 'under conviction of sin.'

prisoner's dilemma *n* [*Game theory*] a variety of game theory, developed by A. W. Tucker at Stanford University in 1950, which concentrates on seeing how trust in an absent person influences one's choices over one's own interests.

prisoner's friend *n* [*Military*] an officer appointed by a court martial to act as a prisoner's defence counsel.

private **1.** *a* [*Communications*] denoting coded, secure or military use of a data transmission system. **2.** *n* [*US*] [*Medicine*] abbr of a **private practitioner** thus 'double-O private' which is a pun on the James Bond 007 books: a supposedly incompetent and certainly expensive private doctor who is 'licensed to kill'.

private business *n* [*Education*] at Eton College this means extra tuition.

Private Case *n* [*Publishing, Libraries*] a collection of books, considered to be pornography, that is held in the British Museum Reading Room (the British Library).

private notice question *n* [*UK*] [*Politics*] questions that may be asked by any member of the House of Commons after the statutory period of daily 'Question Time', and which refer either to matters of urgent public business or to the arrangement of parliamentary business.

private placement *n* [*Stock market*] an issue

placed with a single investor or a limited number of investors, not normally listed in Europe or registered with the SEC in the US.

private treaty *n* [*Real estate*] the placing by an owner of a reserve price on a property and the subsequent asking of interested parties to submit their written bids for consideration; on a pre-set date all these bids are opened and the property goes to the highest bidder; such deals are fully binding in law.

privates *n pl* [*Antiques*] private customers, as opposed to fellow dealers.

privatisation *n* [*Industrial relations, Government*] the hiving off by a government of formerly nationalised industries, either in whole or in part, and the returning of such industries to private ownership.

privative *n* [*Linguistics*] in grammar this indicates the lack or loss of, absence of or negation; the prefixes 'un-' 'non-' and 'a-' and the suffix '-less'.

privilege *n* [*Computing*] this refers to a program user or characterises the type of operation that can be performed; privileged users or programs can perform operations normally restricted to the operating system and can thus affect the overall performance of the system.

privileged instructions *n pl* [*Computing*] instructions that can only be issued when the computer is operating in one of the higher or highest execution states.

privileged sanctuary *n* [*Military*] any military base from which attacks can be made but which for whatever reason remains inviolate itself.

privileges *n pl* [*Stock market, Commodity exchange*] a contract whereby one party secures the right, but not the obligation, to buy from or sell to another party a specified amount of a commodity or a security at a pre-determined price. See also **put, call 2** and **3**.

prize logs *n pl* [*Logging*] logs that arrive at the sorting area without having been marked with a sign of ownership.

p.r.n *Lat. abbr* [*Medicine*] a prescription notation meaning 'when required'.

pro forma invoice *n* [*Commerce*] an invoice sent to a purchaser in advance of the ordered goods so that all necessary paperwork can be completed.

pro-active *a* [*Government*] said of plans that are made in advance, or of pre-emptive reactions.

probabilism *n* [*Philosophy*] the theory that laws, in whatever fields, are not invariant, but state only probabilities and tendencies.

probability theory *n* [*Management*] the use of mathematics to consider models of phenomena that occur in an unpredictable manner, ie: the number of sales made by a firm in a single day, the number of defective units produced by an imperfect machine in one hour, etc.

probables *n pl* [*Sport*] when a trial is held to

select a representative team in a particular sport, these are the players who are considered most likely to be chosen in the end. See also **possibles**.

probate price n [Stock market] See **quarter up price**.

probie n [US] [Medicine] a probationer nurse, so called for the first six months of her training.

probit n [Statistics] the unit which forms the scale into which percentages may be transformed so that data evenly distributed between 0% and 100% become normally distributed with a standard deviation of one probit.

problem board 1. n [Computing] a specially wired, removable panel which can be inserted into the machine as required by different programs. **2.** n [Computing] a control or wiring panel.

problematic n [Sociology] the concept that sociological concepts do not exist separately, but rather in a general relation to each other: the problematic.

procedural language n [Computing] a conventional **high-level language** used on **fourth generation** computers; the essence of such languages is the specification by the programmer of the means necessary to reach a desired goal, rather than looking primarily at the goal itself. See also non-**procedural language**.

procedure 1. n [Computing] the writing of a program which is specifically designed to solve one problem. **2.** also **subroutine** n [Computing] a small program covering a task that needs to be repeated constantly; such a subroutine is built into a main program.

process v [TV, Film] to develop and print reels of film.

process art n [Art] painting or sculpture in which the actual process of creation becomes the subject of the work and the final object is primarily a record of that evolving process.

process theology n [Religion] religious teachings that emphasise the essential gradualism of the workings of God and emphasise His involvement with and love for human destiny rather than His supposed omnipotence – in the face of which there should, in theory, be no such delay in achieving the perfect world.

processing time n [Photo-typesetting] the time that elapses between the calling up of a character from the store and its construction on the typesetter's output device.

procession 1. n [Cricket] the rapid collapse of a number of wickets, so that the incoming and dismissed batsmen form something of a procession across the pitch. **2.** n [Horse-racing] a race in which the winner leaves all rivals to trail in far behind.

prodsport n [Motor racing] abbr of **production sport** a class of sportscar racing, devised in 1973 by Peter Browning, director of the British Racing & Sports Car Club.

produce n [Horse-racing] the offspring of a dam.

producer man n [Glass-making] an operator in charge of supplying gas to the furnaces.

producer's goods n [Economics] goods such as raw materials and tools which satisfy need only indirectly: in the creation of the actual consumer goods that satisfy direct need.

producer's profits n pl [Film] a fictional sum of money from which a notional percentage is offered to a neophyte in the film business; no such profits exist and the only area from which money can be taken is the **gross**.

product n [Record business] what an artist creates: the music and/or the songs.

product initiation n [Marketing] the familiarisation with a product that is undergone by both its salesmen and its consumers.

product initiation training n [Marketing] a course set up to teach salesmen to market their product in the best way.

product life cycle n [Marketing] a cycle of the stages in the market's acceptance of a new product; these stages can be variously analysed at the levels of the product class, the product form or that of the individual brand.

production 1. a [Motor trade] used to describe a model that is made for normal production and subsequent sale to the public, rather than special test models which never run on public roads. **2.** a [US] [Weaving] a production weaver makes many similar copies of the same design for sale at low prices, emphasising the function of the cloth – table mats, dish cloths, etc – over its aesthetics.

production brigade n [Economics] in socialist countries this is a picked team of workers from within a commune or collective who are required to meet a set agricultural production norm; a 'production team' is a smaller version of the brigade.

production editor n [Journalism] See **make-up editor**.

production run n [Computing] the routine execution of a regularly used program, eg: running a magazine subscription list.

productive a [Medicine] used to describe a cough that brings up mucus or sputum into the throat.

productive debt n [Finance] See **living debt**.

productivity bargaining n [Industrial relations] See **restructuring 2**.

product-plus n [Marketing] any element in the product or in its presentation or performance that gives it an advantage over rivals.

Profession n [Theatre] the craft, calling and personnel involved in the theatre; as opposed to the 'Business' or 'Industry', both of which reflect the commercial basis of the film world.

professional foul n [Soccer] a deliberate foul committed on an opponent by a defender who realises that there is no other more subtle or legal way of stopping him from scoring. See also **profit foul**.

P

professor 1. *n* [*Gambling*] See **dean. 2.** *n* [*US*] [*Garment trade*] a notably competent cutter.

proffing *n* [*UK*] [*Military*] the stealing of any unattended pieces of equipment, personal possessions, etc.

profile *n* [*Commerce, Computing*] in computer dating firms this is the person with whom an applicant for a partner is matched.

profit centre 1. *n* [*Business*] an organizational unit of a business enterprise for which data about expenses and revenue are gathered to enhance planning and control. **2.** *n* [*Business*] any highly profitable unit or activity of a business enterprise; a source of profit. **3.** *n* [*Business*] any part of a firm that is considered autonomous as regards manpower, financing, and production and profit targets.

profit foul *n* [*Basketball*] a deliberate foul that stops the opposition scoring an otherwise certain two points. See also **professional foul**.

profonde *n* [*Magic*] a large secret pocket which facilitates a variety of **effects**; it comes from Fr. meaning deep. See also **pochette**.

program 1. *n* [*Computing*] the instructions written by a programmer that are used to control the operations of a computer system along the lines desired by the individual who creates that program. **2.** *v* [*US*] [*Prisons*] to follow all prison rules and perform all prison duties according to the book with the intention of gaining early parole.

program decomposition *n* [*Computing*] the breaking down of a complete program into a number of interconnected modules. See also **architectural design**.

program, not in the *a phr* [*US*] [*Medicine*] senile, confused. See also **ball game, not even in the**.

programmatics *n* [*Computing*] the study of the techniques and the languages of computer programming.

programme *n* [*Alcoholics Anonymous*] the whole philosophy which constitutes AA. The term is also used by similar organisations such as Narcotics Anonymous and other drug or drink dependency units.

programme budgeting, also **PPBS** *n* [*Government*] a method of determining the best way of sharing out resources between various public sector organisations, eg: education, social welfare, medicine, etc. Rather than paying·item by item, the overall programme is funded as a whole.

programme mix *n* [*TV*] a complete portfolio of a TV company's forthcoming productions.

programme music *n* [*Music*] descriptive music, the opposite of **absolute music**, which is intended to convey the impression of specific subjects, topics, objects, etc.

programme pictures, also **programmer, B pictures** *n* [*Film*] exotic, action-packed melodramas with generally little plot and less intellectual content, but with lurid titles and a high turnover at the box office. Such films have been rendered obsolete by the advance of TV and are no longer made, although their contemporary equivalent, the 'made-for-TV' picture, shares many similar production values and standards.

programme year *n* [*TV*] the breakdown of the complete schedules of a TV company running through an entire year from one autumn to the end of the following summer.

programmed art *n* [*Art*] the post–1945 work of Bruno Munari which takes the form of small viewing screens, each of which displays changing combinations of colour and shape; they are produced by small electric motors which turn moveable parts. The programming consists of the artist's choosing the length of a cycle of transformations on a given screen.

programmed management *n* [*Business*] a systematic process whereby a manager is given a developing set of actions and steps by which he may successfully accomplish a series of specified objectives.

progress *v* [*Basketball*] to run with the ball in a given direction.

progressives *n pl* [*Printing*] a set of proofs, which show each plate of a colour set, printed in its appropriate colour and in registered combination.

project *v* [*Alcoholics Anonymous*] said of an AA member who looks forward to a future of absolute and continuing control over any further drinking.

project Blue Book *n* [*US*] [*Air Force*] the official dossier that the USAF maintains on unidentified flying objects.

projected art *n* [*Art*] any art works which require projection equipment for them to be seen; such techniques mean that films and slides can make available far more of an artist's work than could usually be encompassed within a single gallery.

proletarian internationalism *n* [*Politics*] the direct opposite of **cosmopolitanism**: the desperate desire within satellite nations and individuals within them to become more Russian than the Russians; such enthusiasm acts as a useful cloak for Soviet imperialism.

proletarian redemption *n* [*Politics*] in Marxist terms this is the historic mission of the downtrodden workers: the emancipation of themselves and their peers from servitude to capitalism.

proletarian revolutionary line *n* [*Politics*] in Chinese communist terminology up to 1978 this referred to the ideology and policies of Chairman Mao Zedong.

proletarianisation *n* [*Politics*] the gradual loss of control of the means of production by small producers who are swallowed up by big business; instead of inching their way into the ranks of the bourgeoisie, they are forced downwards into those of the proletariat.

proletkult n [Politics] a socialist art form which believes that a factual description of proletarian life is art enough for a revolution; it concentrates on a complete negation of the past and its potential influence, in favour of absolute concentration on the present, particularly insofar as the present represents the basic facts of a worker's life.

proliferation n [Military] the mass production and the possession of nuclear weapons by an increasing number of nations. Such nuclear capability does not need to come directly from the provision of actual weapons by the US or USSR; 'peaceful' nuclear reactors require plutonium and that same plutonium can, and has been, diverted to warlike uses.

PROLOG n [Computing] acro **Programming Logic** a **non-procedural language** which has been developed for use in **expert systems** and **fifth generation** computers.

PROM n [Computing] acro **Programmable Read-Only Memory** a memory that can be programmed by electrical pulses; such PROM chips can be purchased blank and then programmed for specific needs by users who want to implement their own tailor-made programmes; thus 'erasable PROM' means PROM chips that can be erased and re-used.

PROM zapping n [Computing] programming a PROM using a PROM programmer.

promise n [UK] [Police] 'on a promise' means awaiting information, tipoffs, gifts, favours, possibly bribes; if the 'promise' is a woman, then awaiting sex.

promo n [Advertising] abbr of **promotion** any kind of advertising or marketing designed to sell a new product: giveaways, free gifts, foreign trips, press lunches – a vast spectrum of persuasion from the most costly and unique to the cheapest and most obvious.

promotion zone n [Navy] a theoretical area entered into by those officers who have fulfilled the time requirements of their current rank and are waiting for promotion.

prompt n [Commerce] an agreement between a merchant and an importer whereby the importer is allowed a period of time before he must pay for the goods; a prompt note is issued to warn the importer that the payment is finally due.

Prompt Day n [Commodity exchange] the day that payment is due for goods bought at a commodity-exchange auction sale.

proof v [Baking] to age dough for sufficient time so that the yeast within it can cause the dough to rise.

proof department n [Banking] the department within a bank that deals with listing, sorting, checking and otherwise managing all the commercial transactions of that bank.

propagated error n [Computing] an error in one operation that affects data used in a further operation which in turn creates further error throughout much of the data.

proper a [Heraldry] pictured accurately and naturistically, rather than drawn to heraldic convention.

property n [Entertainment] anyone who is regarded as a draw at the box office; they are usually labelled 'hot property'.

property sort n [Computing] a technique for selecting records from a file, all of which satisfy a given criterion.

prophet n [Religion] one who thoroughly understands the Bible. There is no implication of actual prophecy.

proportion, the n [Banking] the relation between the total of the Bank of England's cash reserves of note and coin and the Bank's liabilities to the public in the form of deposits, expressed as a percentage.

proportionality n [Military] the concept that while European forces alone could not do as much damage to the Soviets as could the US, they could still inflict substantial damage, and make the Soviets think twice about attacking Europe. As General de Gaulle put it, the European forces could 'tear off an arm'.

proposition cheat n [Gambling] a cheat who never once gives his opponents/victims even the thought of a win; a cheat who takes a 100% advantage in every game.

proprietories n pl [Espionage] fully functioning commercial firms which combine their daily business activities with providing fronts for a variety of agents to carry out missions, surveillance and allied intelligence work; the staff of these firms, including those who keep to the business side, are all fully employed members of the agency.

props n [Theatre] the Property Manager or Mistress.

pro-rate v [Pool] if a curfew causes a session to end prematurely, the winnings are split proportionately to the winner's lead at the time the game ended.

prospect 1. n [Advertising] anyone sufficiently interested in a salesman or an advertisement to listen to the pitch, watch the TV commercial, read the print, etc. 2. n [Crime] the selected victim or dupe of a pickpocket or con-man. 3. n [Espionage] a potential CIA agent. Prospects can be divided into (a) primary prospects: officers, confidential secretaries, security officers, all of whom can legally remove documents and handle them without exciting suspicion; (b) secondary prospects: file clerks, typists, messengers etc, all of whom do handle documents but cannot take them from the files and would never have access to them outside normal working hours; (c) tertiary prospects: charwomen, handymen, engineers, etc, who have access to the offices where files are kept, but no immediate access to documents, except by

P

chance. **4.** *n* [*Mining*] a mine that has been sunk but has yet to produce any valuable minerals.

prospects *n pl* [*Radio*] a list prepared twice a day by the 'intake editor' (who supervises the various news stories that arrive continually from wire services and reporters) which puts forward those news stories that a station's reporters should be covering for the first time as well as any continuing stories that might require reconsidering in a new light during the day.

prosumer *n* [*Sociology*] those individuals who prefer to perform for themselves such services hitherto performed by specialists and experts, eg: do-it-yourself enthusiasts.

protect *v* [*US*] [*Railways*] to be available for duty; it is used of an extra locomotive kept at the roundhouse in case one of those in service breaks down.

protected bear *n* [*Stock market*] See **covered bear**.

protected field *n* [*Computing*] data on a VDU which cannot be modified by an operator. Thus 'unprotected field' means data on a VDU which can be modified by the operator.

protection **1.** *n* [*Crime*] the extortion of money by gangs or individuals who threaten to break up a shop, club, pub, etc. unless the owner starts paying regular weekly bribes; the only protection involved is that from the gang themselves. **2.** *n* [*Mountaineering*] the quantity and quality of running belays used to make a pitch safe to lead.

protective reaction *n* [*Military*] bombing raids targeted on anti-aircraft installations, which are intended to clear the path for subsequent raids on different targets.

protest *n* [*Banking*] a certificate stating that a bill of exchange has been dishonoured, ie: it has not been paid when it has been properly presented for payment.

protest vote *n* [*Politics*] the casting of one's vote for a candidate who has no chance whatsoever of winning, purely for the purpose of registering one's disgust with the policies, personalities or simply the general efforts of the 'legitimate' parties.

protested bill *n* [*Commerce*] a bill that has not been paid.

protocol *n* [*Computing*] a set of inbuilt rules that govern the flow of information within the machine and between the various components, thus maximising the efficiency of each operation.

proud *a* [*Building*] in brick – or woodwork – this is said of a piece of wood or a row of bricks that stands out from all the others in the same plane.

prove *v* [*Medicine*] in homeopathic practice this is to give a sample of a drug to a healthy person in order to check the symptoms it produces.

provi *n* [*Advertising*] abbr of **promotional video** especially popular in the pop music business.

provinces *n pl* [*Hunting*] any hunting country outside the **Shires** and the Midlands.

provisional stamps *n pl* [*Philately*] stamps which are issued only for temporary use, consisting of overprints and surcharges on existing stamps; the need for such stamps is usually caused by a shortage of some denominations, special commemorations, or changes in a country's name, government or currency which have occurred at short notice.

prowl *v* [*US*] [*Police*] to rob; specifically it means to look over the site of a possible break-in to check out the exits, ease of access, visibility from the street, etc.

prowl rat *n* [*Police*] a mugger who specialises in beating up and stealing from women.

prozine *n* [*Science fiction*] a professionally produced science fiction fan magazine.

prudent man rule *n* [*US*] [*Law*] the standard adopted in various states whereby those entrusted with the power of investing money for others must do so in a prudent, sensible and responsible way, avoiding speculation as far as possible.

prudential ratios *n* [*Banking*] the ratio between a bank's capital resources and its total deposit liabilities; reference to this ratio helps banks, in theory, conduct their business sensibly and carefully.

prune *v* [*Hot rods*] to out-accelerate a rival driver in a race.

prune-picker *n* [*Oil rigs*] a Californian oil rig driller; it comes from the nickname for inhabitants of that state.

pruno *n* [*US*] [*Prisons*] a fermented liquor made from bread, food, fruit scraps and sugar.

pseudandry *n* [*Literary criticism*] the use of a male pen name by a female writer; eg: 'George Eliot' by Mary Ann Evans (1818–90).

pseudepigraphica *n pl* [*Bibliography*] works ascribed to another author, usually quite consciously; originally they referred to spurious works passed off as the writings of biblical prophets.

pseudo-event *n* [*Media*] an event created with no more justification than the desire of those concerned to have their names and pictures in the newspapers or, better still, on TV; it is often arranged by an advertising agency, public relations firm or even, for lack of anything better to fill their space, the media themselves.

pseudo-language *n* [*Computing*] a notation resembling a programming language which is used for program design. The pseudo-language is a substitute for a flow chart – controlling the flow of actions through the program – and unlike a real programming language does not have to be translated into **machine code**.

PSI *n* [*Science*] any psychic phenomenon that cannot be simply dismissed out of hand or explained away through some variety of legitimate science.

PSI-missing *n* [*Parapsychology*] the use of **PSI** in such a way that the target at which the subject is aiming is 'missed' or influenced in a direction contrary to that intended, more frequently than might be expected if only chance were operating. See also **PSI**.

psych 1. *v* [*Cards*] to make a bid in bridge that deliberately misrepresents one's hand in order to deceive one's opponents. **2.** *n* [*Medicine*] abbr of **psychiatric patient**.

psychiatric deluge *n* [*Social work*] the domination of psycho-analytic rather than psychiatric ideas in social work. This began to be noticed in the US shortly after World War II and has since spread to the UK, although the trend is possibly greater in social work writing than in practice.

psychiatric imperialism *n* [*Social work*] the influence of the psychiatric Establishment in the US and the UK who are opposed to such revisionist thinkers on mental health as R. D. Laing, Thomas Szasz, David Cooper, et al.

psychic bid *n* [*Cards*] a bid in bridge that deliberately misrepresents the player's hand in order to deceive the opponents.

psychic compensation *n* [*Economics*] See **psychic income 2.**

psychic income 1. *n* [*Economics*] the non-measurable mental and emotional satisfaction a consumer gleans from an item or service that he/she purchases. **2.** also **psychic compensation** *n* [*Economics*] the non-monetary and non-material satisfactions that ideally accompany an economic or work activity.

psychobabble *n* [*New therapies*] a term coined in 1976 by US writer R. D. Rosen in 'New Times' magazine, and subsequently in his book 'Psychobabble: Fast Talk and Quick Cure in the Era of Feeling' (1977); 'institutionalised garrulousness', 'psychological patter', 'this need to catalogue the ego's condition' – all by-products of the mass of new therapies that offer easy cures for the various maladies that afflict the affluent Western young of the late 20th century.

psychoceramic, also **serum porcelain** *n* [*US*] [*Medicine*] See **crock 4.**

psychodrama *n* [*New therapies*] created around 1937 by J. L. Moreno, this is a type of psychotherapy in which a patient, helped by other patients and a therapist and his/her assistants, acts out his/her traumas and by thus dramatising these problems and fears, hopes to seek out a better way of coming to terms with them, or to eliminate them completely.

psychographics *n* [*Advertising*] a technique of working out the values, attitudes and lifestyles of all sections of the consuming public.

psychological price *n* [*Management*] See **charm price.**

psychological pricing 1. *n* [*Business*] the pricing of a product to enhance its sales appeal or to increase its value to the consumer. **2.** *n* [*Business*] the fraudulent practice of taking an item actually costing 45p, marking it up to 49p and thus convincing a customer that rather than

paying an extra 4p, a saving of 1p has been made on an assumed full price of 50p.

psychologism *n* [*Sociology*] a pejorative term which condemns explanations of the social structure that are given purely in terms of the attributes of individual psychology.

psy-ops, also **psy-war** *n* [*Military*] abbr of **psychological operations, psychological war** active propaganda that uses actions – some friendly, some frightening – rather than words to persuade those at whom it is aimed that it is better to support you than oppose you; it was further characterised during the Vietnam War as the euphemistic 'winning the hearts and minds' of the Vietnamese people.

PTP *n* [*TV*] abbr of **Pre-Transmission Pee** a vital visit to the lavatory, especially needed by anchormen and commentators working on election marathons, royal occasions, etc.

puant *a* [*Cheese-making*] used to describe a family of cheeses from northern France which are characterised by their strong aroma; it comes from Fr. 'puant' meaning stinking.

pub *v* [*Science fiction*] to publish; thus 'pubber' is a publisher.

pubcaster *n* [*US*] [*TV*] abbr of **public broadcaster** any broadcaster working for the US Public Broadcasting Services (PBS), the subscription funded station that has no advertisements and which attempts to offer a slight improvement on the networks' prime time pap.

public art *n* [*Art*] artworks, usually sculptures, that are designed specifically for large public open spaces; such sculptures, unlike their classic and monumental predecessors, tend to be sited at ground level and rather than celebrating some martial hero, are easily accessible to pedestrians and spectators to enjoy at close quarters.

publics 1. *n pl* [*Marketing*] groups of people that can be easily identified as having some special relevance to a business or other organisation: customers, employees, managers, shareholders, etc. **2.** *n pl* [*Public relations*] specific target groups for PR campaigns: blacks, students, teenagers, the stockholders of a certain corporation, the users of a certain video cassette etc.

pudding 1. *n* [*Espionage*] a derogatory reference to the United Nations Organisation, its membership and its efforts. **2.** *n* [*Hunting*] oatmeal or porridge prepared as hounds' food. **3.** *n* [*Navy*] a rope fender that protects small boats.

pudding stone *n* [*Coal-mining*] See **conglomerate.**

puddle *n* [*Rowing*] the circular, rippled disturbance that remains on the surface of the water every time an oar is pulled out at the end of a stroke.

puddler's candles *n pl* [*Metallurgy*] jets of flame produced when carbon monoxide is released from the molten bath in the **puddling** furnace at the boiling stage.

P

puddling *n* [*Metallurgy*] the conversion, with manual or mechanical aid, of a furnace charge of pig iron or cast iron, by means of chemical action, into a weldable mass of malleable iron for subsequent manipulation into the desired dimensions.

puering *n* [*Tanning*] See **bating**.

puff *n* [*Science*] in cytology this is a short swollen region of a polythene chromosome, active in RNA synthesis.

puff pack *n* [*US*] [*Medicine*] See **eggcrate 2**.

puff pipe *n* [*Aerospace*] on vertical take-off aircraft this is a pipe through which compressed air is blown to help stabilise the aircraft.

puffler *n* [*UK*] [*Railways*] a foreman or ganger; it comes originally from mining use.

pug *v* [*Building*] to plug or pack a space with clay or mortar; thus it means to reduce noise. 'Pugging' is the working of clay to make it plastic and workable.

pugg, also **pug** *n* [*Angling*] a third year salmon.

pugging *n* [*Building, Plastering*] plastering, or other insulating material, applied above the ceiling between the joists to assist sound and thermal insulation.

puggled *a* [*UK*] [*Military*] very drunk.

pulaski *n* [*Logging*] a light, single-bit axe with a straight handle, which has a narrow adze-like trenching blade attached to its head.

pull 1. *v* [*Aerospace*] to operate anything, in any way, on an aircraft. 2. *v* [*Sex*] used of a pimp who persuades a prostitute to leave another pimp's **stable** and commence working for him. 3. *n* [*Angling*] the tug when a fish takes a fly or bait. 4. *n* [*Cricket*] a stroke that 'pulls' the ball from the off to the on side. 5. *n* [*Metallurgy*] an irregular transverse crack on the face of an ingot caused when the metal can contract freely when cooling after casting. 6. *n* [*Mining*] the linear advance into the rock face that is achieved after every explosion. 7. *n, v* [*UK*] [*Police*] an arrest; to arrest a suspect. See also **lift 4**. 8. *n* [*Printing, Advertising*] a proof or specimen print taken from a page of type or a block for an illustration.

pull leather *v* [*Rodeo*] used of a rider who grabs the saddle horn to steady himself while riding a bucking bronco; such an act is illegal under the rodeo rules and leads to instant disqualification.

pull the breakers *v* [*UK*] [*TV*] to go on strike; it comes from the action of removing the breakers – the main circuit switches in a studio – which would deprive the production of lights and power.

pull the cork *v* [*Navy*] a submarine does this when it makes an emergency dive.

pull the monkey *v* [*UK*] [*Railways*] to clean out the **cess** drain by pulling a rubber disc (the monkey) through it.

pull the pin *v* [*US*] [*Painting*] to leave the job and get away for the night.

pull the plug *v* [*Stock market*] to withdraw one's support from a share, when this support had previously maintained the share at an artificial level for the purpose of making a deal; thus it means letting the natural price reassert itself.

pull the strings *v* [*UK*] [*Railways*] to release a vacuum brake.

pull-back 1. *n* [*Dancing*] in tap-dancing this is a tap made by the front part of the foot striking the floor while the body is in the air moving backwards. 2. *n* [*Film*] a shot in which the pulling away of the camera gives the illusion that the background is moving gradually further away.

pulled *a* [*Book collecting*] See **shaken**.

pulled wool *n* [*Weaving*] wool that has been pulled by the roots from a dead sheep.

pullers, also **drawers** *n pl* [*UK*] [*Coal-mining*] the men who withdraw the supports behind the face to let the worked-out area collapse, and who advance the **face chain** forward into the new cutting track, keeping up with the advancing movement into the coalface.

pull-out *n* [*Surfing*] the steering of a surfboard over or through the back of a wave in order to bring a ride to an end.

pull-through *n* [*Gambling*] a sleight-of-hand trick that gives the impression of cutting a pack of cards fairly, but in fact replaces the two halves exactly as they were.

pulmon *n* [*Medicine*] an intern specialising in lung problems.

pulpit 1. *n* [*Merchant navy*] a guardrail fitted at the bow or stern of a vessel. 2. *n* [*Sailing*] a tubular metal guard around the bow and/or stern of a yacht. 3. *n* [*Fishing*] a small platform on which a harpooner stands when fishing for swordfish and similar game.

pulsing *n* [*Navy*] a method of sending large supply convoys across the Atlantic from the US; infrequent surges of large numbers (300–500) of ships would be sent across, with as heavy as possible anti-submarine defences to guard them.

pump 1. *v* [*Angling*] to lift and lower a rod after the fish has taken the bait when it is deep in the water; the intention is to move the fish towards the surface. 2. *v* [*Medicine*] to perform external cardiac massage.

pump ship *v* [*Navy*] to urinate.

pumping *n* [*Audio*] an extreme version of **breathing**.

pump-priming *n* [*Business, Government*] the using of Federal funds to stimulate the economy, particularly during a depression or as a **hedge** against accelerating inflation.

punch up 1. *v* [*Theatre*] said of actors who attempt to put more life and 'sparkle' into a performance. 2. *v* [*TV*] to switch any source – telecine, VTR, slides, captions, etc – into the main transmission. 3. *v* [*TV, Film*] to manipulate the colours in a film or in a TV picture to improve contrast, shade, brightness and general effects. 4. *v* [*Fashion*] to make colour dyes brighter in a piece of cloth or fabric.

punched paper n [US] [Theatre] a free admission pass.

puncher 1. n [US] [Coal-mining] a worker who operates a machine that undercuts the coal. 2. n [Logging] the operator of a small logging engine, the 'donkey'.

punching bag n [Boxing] See **chopping block**.

punching it n [Sex] a homosexual hustler's reference to the tedium of his professional encounters with clients, as repetitively dull as punching the time clock in a factory or office.

pundit n [UK] [Gliding] an experienced pilot.

punishing jaws n pl [Dog breeding] jaws sufficiently well-developed to be able, at least in theory, to bring down and kill a prey.

punk 1. n [US] [Circus] any young animal that performs in the circus. 2. n [Logging] a signalman for a logging crew. 3. n [US] [Prisons] a passive, youthful homosexual; the 'girl' who is either used by older prisoners or who attaches himself to a single older man in a 'marriage' which may last the duration of their sentences.

punner n [Building, Concrete workers] a light hand rammer; thus as a verb it means to ram or to pun.

punt n [Stock market] an investment in shares that really have only a minimal chance of proving profitable; it comes from the gambling use, meaning a foolish long shot.

punter 1. n [Antiques] a buyer, possibly a gullible one. 2. n [Crime] the gullible public, anyone outside one's own coterie. 3. n [Sex] the client. See also **john**. 4. n [Crime] among Glasgow gangs, this was a non-gang member who supplied weapons, bought up the proceeds of robberies, and performed similar services. 5. n [Aus.] [Crime] a pickpocket's assistant who distracts the victim's attention while he is being robbed. 6. n [Gambling] anyone who bets on horses, dogs, casino games, football pools, etc; the inference is invariably of an outsider – as opposed to a professional gambler – and so a potential loser; thus 'mug punter' is a particularly gullible better. 7. n [UK] [Market-traders] a member of the general public, especially when he/she is being cheated in some form of confidence game practised at a market, on or off a stall.

punty n [Glass-making] a solid metal rod used for fashioning hot glass; a small button of hot glass is first placed on the end of the rod and this is used as a means of joining on to the larger mass of hot glass which can then be worked.

PUO n [UK] [Medicine] abbr of **pyrexia fever of unknown origin** used on medical certificates and meaning 'The patient has a high temperature, but I don't know why.'

pup 1. n [Commerce] anything worthless; hence the standard English phrase: 'to sell a pup'. 2. n [Logging] the hook on the loading end of a cable. 3. n [UK] [Road transport] a trailer. See also **dangler** 2. 4. n [TV, Film] a small keylight; a

'baby pup' is a smaller version. See also **baby-kicker, inky dinky**. 5. v [Oil rigs] this comes from an abbreviation of **pick up pump**.

pup rounds n pl [Medicine] the information passed by the out-going nursing shift to the incoming shift regarding the various details, problems, etc. that may occur on the ward and on which the new nurses must keep their eyes.

puppy 1. n [Book-binding] a small ball of gelatinous rubber used to remove excess gold from a book cover after finishing or stamping. 2. n [US] [Medicine] the first call for an ambulance crew on the night-shift.

puppy hole n [Education] a pupil room.

puppyfoot n [Gambling] the ace of clubs; it comes from the apparent visual resemblance.

pups n pl [US] [Journalism] those sections of the large Sunday newspapers that are printed in advance of the main (news and sports) sections and are delivered separately around the surburban wholesalers. See also **bulldog**.

purchase n [Sailing, Ropework] an arrangement of blocks and fall in which the standing part and the fall both lead to the same block.

pure competition n [Business] See **atomistic competition**.

pure notation n [Computing] notation that is either exclusively alphabetic or exclusively numeric.

pure play n [US] [Stock market] a company that is almost completely involved in a single line of business and which is thus the ideal subject for an investor who wishes to put money into that business.

purge v [Oil rigs] to clean equipment or pipelines of any potentially dangerous gases or other substances.

purge and merge v [Advertising] to blend two mailing lists by purging those names and addresses that appear in both, retaining only one entry per address, and merging the remaining lists in one definitive version.

purity n [TV] the degree to which colour signals are produced accurately on the screen.

purple [Military] air intercept code for: this unit is suspected of carrying nuclear weapons.

purple airway, also **purple zone** n [Air travel] any route reserved for aircraft carrying members of a royal family.

purpure a [Heraldry] purple.

purr-word n [Linguistics] a term coined by S. I. Hayakawa; it refers to any subjective expression used to signal one's approval. See also **snarl-word**.

pursuivant n [Heraldry] a junior **herald**.

push 1. v [Air travel] an aircraft does this when it gets underway from its ramp position, at which passengers embark and disembark at the airport. 2. n, v [Cricket] a batsman's stroke that merely eases the ball away, with no great force or deliberate direction. 3. n [Logging] a camp boss, an

P

assistant superintendent, a man in charge of a logging crew. **4.** v [*Photography*] to underexpose a film deliberately, then compensate with special methods of development, in order to lose contrast in monochrome and alter balance in colour film.

push and pull n [*Art*] a theory of dynamic pictorial tensions, the 'in' and 'out' forces that can be seen in abstract paintings composed of many patches of colour; the pictorial depth is created not by perspective but by the control of the colour relationships.

push money n [*Commerce*] See **PM**.

push-back clearance n [*Air travel*] permission to move an aircraft on to a runway in preparation for taxiing and takeoff.

pusher **1.** n [*Aerospace*] an aircraft which carries a propeller to the rear of the wings. **2.** n [*Coalmining*] a pneumatic or hydraulic ram which is used to move forward an armoured face conveyor. **3.** n [*Drugs*] a seller of drugs, especially a lowlevel seller who is never involved in bulk purchase or sales. **4.** n [*US*] [*Railways*] a locomotive that helps to start a heavy train or helps another locomotive up a steep gradient. **5.** n [*Theatre*] a stagehand.

pushers n pl [*Politics*] See **expediters**.

push-pull n [*Audio*] a type of circuit in which balanced components are assembled in phase opposition for greater efficiency of output and lower distortion.

pushup stack n [*Computing*] See **queue**. See also **FIFO list**.

puss n [*Coursing*] a hunted hare.

pusser built a [*Navy*] built to Navy specifications; navy through and through. 'Pusser' means 'purser'.

pusser's crab n [*Navy*] a regulation issue boot.

pusser's medal n [*Navy*] food stains down the front of a uniform.

pusser's wagon n [*Navy*] a warship.

pussy n [*UK*] [*Police*] furs; thus a pussy mob is a gang of fur thieves.

pussy posse n [*US*] [*Police*] the Vice Squad in general and those members who specialise in arresting street prostitutes in particular.

pussy pusher n [*Logging*] See **cat skinner**.

put n [*Stock market*] the right to deliver a specific commodity at a certain time for a designated price. See also **call 2 and 3, straddle**.

put a bid on the book v [*Commerce*] to inform an auctioneer that one wishes to bid for an object, to state a limit that one is prepared to pay and then let the auctioneer conduct the bidding for one.

put and call n [*Stock market*] See **call 2 and 3, put**.

put down **1.** v [*Angling*] to frighten the fish, and thus send them far beneath the surface where they are less accessible. **2.** v [*Angling*] to frighten a fish so much that it either swims away or fails to rise.

put down the anchor v [*Navy*] to get married and settle down.

put in the trees v [*US*] [*Car salesmen*] said of a salesman who overcharges a customer.

put on v [*Taxis*] to join the end of a cab-rank.

put on the air, also **put on the dampers** v [*US*] [*Road transport*] See **anchor it**.

put on the farm v [*US*] [*Crime*] in the US Mafia this means to suspend a man temporarily from his activities; it is either as a punishment for some error or to hide him away from the authorities. Such suspensions usually involve some form of 'internal exile' within the US.

put one's hand up v [*UK*] [*Police*] to confess; it comes from the image of answering a question at school.

put the blacksmith on v [*UK*] [*Market-traders*] to lock out.

put the horns on v [*Gambling*] to make any sort of attempt to change one's luck – changing seats at the table, carrying a 'lucky piece', or some other superstitious practice.

put the mouth on v [*Sport, Media*] used by sports commentators who find that they need only mention a player's talent, good form or current luck for some disaster to overtake that player; it comes from the West Indian voodoo practice of 'talking' someone into trouble or ill health.

put the nark on v [*UK*] [*Market-traders*] to put off, to discourage, to put a stop to.

put the Oliver (Twist) on v [*Gambling*] to place an incorrect entry secretly in the betting ledger for the purpose of fraud.

put up **1.** v [*Angling*] to put a fly on a line. **2.** v [*UK*] [*Postal services*] to prepare any items that are due to be posted around a given district – advertising leaflets, etc. **3.** v [*Printing*] an instruction to the printer to put all copy in capitals; thus 'put down' means all copy is to be put into lower case.

put-through n [*Stock market*] a transaction in which a broker arranges the simultaneous purchase and sale of shares. See also **marry**.

putty **1.** n [*Navy*] a soft seabed – a mudflat, sand bank, etc. **2.** n [*Navy*] a ship's painter.

putty nose, also **cherry nose, flesh nose** n [*Dog breeding*] See **dudley**.

PVC n [*Communications*] abbr of **Permanent Virtual Circuit** a connection in a **packet-switching** system which is always open and requires no set-up prior to data transmission.

PVO strany n [*Military*] abbr of **Protivovozdushnoi oborony strany** the Soviet National Air Defence Command; commanded by an air force marshal, the PVO controls 550,000 men, 7,000 warning radars, its own air force of 2,500 aircraft (including eight different grades of interceptors and the Soviet equivalent to **AWACS**, the Moss), more than 10,000 surface-to-air (SAM) missiles and in the Galosh deployment around Moscow, the only active anti-ballistic missile (see **ABM**) system in Russia or the US.

pylon *n* [*Medicine*] a temporary artificial leg without a knee joint.

pylons *n pl* [*Literary criticism*] those poets of the 1930s – Auden, Isherwood, Spender et al – who concentrated on industrial scenes and imagery in their work.

pyramid **1.** *n* [*US*] [*Journalism*] a headline of several lines in length, in which those lines gradually lengthen, one beneath another. **2.** *v* [*Stock market*] to build up one's stock from the profits made on a series of previous successful deals. **3.** *n* [*Government, Business, Military*] any massive project of which the final aim is to reveal to one's rivals, admirers or detractors, just how accomplished and powerful the creator of that project is, rather than to use it for any useful and on-going purpose. The original pyramid in question is the Great Pyramid of the Egyptian King Cheops.

pyramid selling *n* [*Commerce*] the extension of a franchise by the selling not of the product involved, but of further franchises, and these new franchise holders then sell further franchises in their turn, thus creating a hollow pyramid in which there is very little merchandising, but only a great many outlets with no commodities to offer; such 'pyramids' are illegal in the UK.

pyramiding **1.** *n* [*Business*] a means of expanding a business which is based on the use of loans for the purpose of that expansion. **2.** *n* [*Marketing*] a marketing strategy whereby wholesalers buy both goods and a licence to distribute these goods themselves so as to maximise the market spread and penetration, with the profits returning finally to the original sales organisation.

Q and A *n* [*Radio*] abbr of **Question and Answer** any programme item that uses an expert or pundit and a reporter; the inclusion of the expert upgrades the item from merely a random interview to a supposedly informative discussion.

Q boat *n* [*UK*] [*Police*] a 'plain clothes' police car, carrying plain clothes officers, that is used for surveillance purposes; it comes from the Q boats – disguised merchantmen carrying concealed guns – used in World Wars I and II. See also **nondescript**.

Q clearance *n* [*US*] [*Government*] the highest US Government security clearance, which includes access to nuclear weapons secrets.

QC *n* [*Airlines*] abbr of **Quick Change** aircraft that have been constructed to facilitate their speedy and simple alteration from cargo to passenger use and back again as required.

q. 4 h *Lat. abbr* [*Medicine*] a prescription notation meaning 'every 4 hours'.

q.i.d. *Lat. abbr* [*Medicine*] a prescription notation meaning 'four times a day'.

QL *n* [*Computing*] abbr of **Query Language** that section of a database management system which provides facilities for the interrogation of the database. If the database is to be interrogated directly from a terminal, this is performed by the IQL, the interactive query language.

QR *n* [*US*] [*Medicine*] abbr of **Quiet Room** a euphemism for a locked, padded room which is used for otherwise uncontrollable patients who require maximum restraint.

q.s. *Lat. abbr* [*Medicine*] a prescription notation meaning 'as much as required'.

QT *n* [*US*] [*Stock market*] abbr of **questioned trade**. See **don't know**.

quack *n* [*US*] [*Medicine*] a patient who fakes symptoms in order to obtain drugs or a stay in hospital.

quad **1.** *n* [*US*] [*Medicine*] abbr of **quadriplegic** a patient who is deprived of the use of any limb. **2.** *n* [*Science*] a unit of energy equivalent to 10 (to the power 15) British Thermal Units or 10 (to the power 18) Joules.

quadding *n* [*Printing*] the putting of abnormal spaces between words in order to fill out a line. It comes from 'em quad' and 'en quad'; these are pieces of type bearing no face, the size respectively

Q

of one em and one en, which are used to create white space in a line.

quadra *n* [*Medicine*] abbr of **quadriplegic**. See also **para**.

quadriad *n* [*US*] [*Government*] a special group of top Presidential economic advisers: Chairman of the Council of Economic Advisers, Secretary of the Treasury, Director of the Office of Management, Chairman of the Federal Reserve Board. See also **troika**.

quadriliteralism *n* [*Literary criticism*] the use of 'four-letter' words in writing, both literary and pornographic.

quadruple play *n* [*Audio*] magnetic tape that is one quarter the thickness of standard recording tape.

quads *n pl* [*Custom cars*] four headlights, arranged in pairs, either vertically, horizontally or at an angle.

quaint characters *n pl* [*Printing*] See **ligature**.

qualification *n* [*Boxing*] the status of a boxer – his previous record in particular – that qualifies him for possible inclusion in 'Ring' Magazine's Top Ten and similar listings.

qualified *a* [*Sex*] said of an experienced, efficient and profitable prostitute.

qualify *v* [*US*] [*Car salesmen*] to assess whether a customer can actually buy a car and, if so, in what price range.

quality of life commercial *n* [*Advertising*] any advertisement that stresses the potential of a given product to enhance the purchaser's quality of life.

quango *n* [*Government*] acro **Quasi-Autonomous Non-Governmental Organisation** a government body which acts outside the usual Civil Service departments as an ostensibly public organisation, but which is funded by the Exchequer. Quangos can be created and staffed as quickly and as sweepingly as there emerge topics on which there might need to be discussion and subsequent administration.

quantification *n* [*Government*] the reduction of complex problems to simple yes/no solutions by concentrating on statistics and replacing nuances by numbers.

quantify *v* [*Military*] to calculate on a general rather than on a specific level, with the intention, often, of proving a point that might not, if considered in detail, hold up to criticism.

quantity mark *n* [*Printing*] one of two marks used to show whether a syllable is long or short.

quantophrenia *n* [*Sociology*] an obsession, beyond sense or reason, with results that are gleaned from statistics, especially when such figures fail to reflect the more subtle facets of a situation.

quap *n* [*Science*] a hypothetical nuclear particle, consisting of anti-proton and a **quark**.

quark *n* [*Science*] a term coined in 1961 by US physicist Murray Gell-Mann; the proposition is that all subatomic particles are composed of combinations of three fundamental particles: the quarks, named after 'Three quarks for Muster Mark' in James Joyce's 'Finnegans Wake' (1939). The three types were called 'flavours', notably the 'down quark', 'up quark' and 'strange quark'. Subsequent research has revealed three further quarks: the 'charmed quark' or 'charm', the 'bottom quark' or 'beauty' and the 'top quark' or 'truth'. Other theories claim that there may be as many as 18 quarks altogether.

quarter *n* [*UK*] [*Theatre*] a warning call to actors reminding them that there are only fifteen minutes left before the performance starts.

quarter up price *n* [*Stock market*] the price of a security as accepted by the Estate Duty Office in the estimation of death duties; it is normally the bid quotation from the Official List plus one quarter of the difference between that and the offered quotation.

quarterback sneak *n* [*US*] [*Football*] an offensive play in which the quarterback carries the ball; it is supposedly a surprise move. See also **keeper 1**.

quartering 1. *n* [*Heraldry*] any of the four, or more, sections of a shield, that are usually used to display a variety of inherited coats of arms. **2.** *n* [*Industrial relations*] the practice in factories and offices whereby any employee who clocks in to work more than two minutes late, automatically loses a whole 15 minutes pay.

quarters *n pl* [*Shoe-making*] part of the uppers of a shoe that extends from the vamp to the back.

quasi-loan *n* [*Finance*] a loan made by a public or private company which seeks to confer a monetary or other advantage on one of its directors; the company pays a sum to a third party, often in the form of honouring a company credit card in the director's name. Such loans must not exceed £1000 over two months, by which time the company must have been reimbursed.

quasimodo *n* [*Surfing*] riding a surfboard in a crouched position; it comes from the posture of the fictional 'Hunchback of Notre-Dame' in Victor Hugo's 'Notre-Dame de Paris' (1831).

quasi-money *n* [*Finance*] See **near money**.

quaverer *n* [*UK*] [*Market-traders*] a vacillating, dithering customer.

queen bee 1. *n* [*Air Force*] the director of the Women's Royal Air Force. **2.** *n* [*Air Force*] a remote controlled aircraft that is used for target practice.

queenie *n* [*Building, Plastering*] an external angle trowel, available in a variety of profiles to suit the required shape of finish.

queen's hard bargain *n* [*Navy*] a lazy or incompetent seaman who is felt not to be earning his pay.

Queen's Pipe/Queen's Sewer *n* [*Customs*] the furnace and the drain used by HM Customs for the destruction of contraband tobacco (and drugs) and alcohol.

quenched cullet n [*Glass-making*] the making of **cullet** by running molten glass through water.

query language n [*Computing*] a variety of experimental languages which have been constructed to eliminate the problems that non-experts have in communicating with computers and in learning **high-level languages** such as **BASIC** and **COBOL**. The intention is to allow operators to use standard English in instructing the machine and for the machine to understand such commands.

quetch n [*Textiles*] a trough containing a starchy finish which is applied to the cloth by a roller as it passes through the trough.

queue n [*Computing*] a sequence of tasks or messages held in auxiliary storage memory until the machine can start processing them.

quick 1. n [*UK*] [*Railways*] the fast line, reserved for expresses. See also **bowling green, lawn. 2.** also **quickie** n [*Cricket*] a fast bowler.

quick and dirty 1. a [*Government*] referring to cheap, easy, fast, but generally second-rate solutions to problems and methods for disposing of necessary tasks. **2.** n [*Restaurants*] any restaurant or café in which one can get a quick meal, irrespective of quality, cleanliness and similar gourmet standards.

quick asset ratio n [*US*] [*Finance*] See **acid test ratio**.

quick assets n pl [*Commerce*] assets that can be sold off and realised as cash. See also **slow assets**.

quick entry n [*US*] [*Police*] a police raid which dispenses with knocking at the door or offering any other opportunity to the target(s) to escape.

quick money n [*Finance*] money invested in such a way as to make it speedily available for conversion into cash.

quick ratio n [*Management*] See **acid test ratio**.

quick study n [*US*] [*Theatre*] any performer who learns lines quickly and, apparently, effortlessly.

quick thing n [*Hunting*] a very fast hunt.

quickie n [*UK*] [*Road transport*] a return journey made during one night, along a usual trunk route.

quickstick n [*Lacrosse*] a shot made by a player without using a cradle between catching and sending the ball.

quiescent a [*Computing*] referring to a system that is waiting to start operations.

quiescing n [*Computing*] stopping a multi-programmed system by rejecting operations on new jobs and thus giving it nothing further to do.

quiet v [*Audio*] See **squelch**.

quiet air n [*Police*] police radio frequencies that are enjoying a period of relative peace, with few reports of crimes, and thus creating little for officers to do. See also **busy air**.

quiet error n [*Computing*] any error occurring in a system that can be corrected before it spreads

beyond the area of its origin and thus corrupts the rest of the system.

quiet room n [*Medicine*] a euphemism for a padded room; it is used to house uncontrollable patients who require maximum restraint.

quiet time n [*Stock market*] the period between the registration of a new share issue with the Securities and Exchange Commission and the offering of that share issue for sale to the public.

quietening n [*Audio*] a facility built into some radio receivers whereby background noise is automatically suppressed while tuning between stations.

quieting n [*Audio*] the amount (measured in decibels) by which the level of background noise is reduced when a radio tuner is fed with a radio frequency signal of specified voltage.

quill 1. n [*Weaving*] a bobbin with one pointed end from which the yarn unwinds. **2.** (*US*), **pirn** (*UK*) n [*Textiles*] a light, slender, tapered tube upon which weft yarn (filling, US) is wound before weaving.

quilling 1. n [*UK*] [*Railways*] the pre-selection of the luggage of rich passengers by porters who will approach only such passengers in the hope of the best tips. **2.** n [*UK*] [*Railways*] the art of blowing distinctive sounds on the whistle of a steam locomotive. See also **fluffing**.

Quine sentence n [*Linguistics*] a self-referential sentence in which a phrase or clause is preceded by itself, in the form of a quotation; eg: ' "Is a sentence fragment" is a sentence fragment.' It is named after the US philosopher W. V. Quine.

quinella n [*Gambling*] a bet in which a gambler is required to select the first two horses in a race. See also **exacta, perfecta**.

quirk n [*Building, Plastering*] a V-shaped groove that is usually less than a right-angle in section.

quirley n [*Cowboys*] a hand-rolled cigarette.

quoin 1. n [*Building, Plastering*] an external angle in a building. **2.** n [*Printing*] a short wedge used for tightening up the type held in a **form**.

quota n [*UK*] [*TV*] the amount of material not made in the UK (or in Australia or Canada) that is allowed to be transmitted on British television; it is currently 14% of total programming.

quota quickie n [*Film*] a cheap, speedily produced, film made by US companies outside the US. Such films were peddled in the countries of manufacture as 'home-made' films, thus filling the various national quotas for such films; after that the same companies could bring in the 'real' Hollywood films.

quota sample n [*Marketing*] the selection of a market research sample which is based on the collection of individuals with certain required and observable characteristics.

quotation n [*Stock market, Commodity exchange*] the current price of a share or commodity as published in the Official List or the daily press.

quote fact n [*Journalism*] a term coined by

Arthur Herzog; it is a fact which is not a fact in itself, but which gains the status of fact after it has been printed as a quoted opinion in a newspaper or similarly broadcast on television.

R

rabbi 1. *n* [*US*] [*Politics*] a political patron; no religious meaning is involved. **2.** *n* [*Religion*] the piece of cloth or silk, coloured black or purple according to ecclesiastical rank, that is attached to the front of the clerical collar and covers the wearer's chest.

rabbit 1. *n* [*Baseball*] a ball that is notably springy and thus lively in action. **2.** *n* [*UK*] [*Government*] acro **Regional Benefit Investigation Team** Dept. of Employment special teams that were set up to discourage people from claiming benefit; the teams do not detect fraud, but simply make it clear to claimants they feel may be committing fraud that they should take themselves voluntarily off the register. 'The techniques require not so much the dogged pursuit of evidence, but a lightness of touch in being able to confront claimants with a few suspicious facts that will lead the suspect either to declare work or otherwise leave the register.' **3.** *n* [*Computing*] program modifications, usually created by **hackers** and infiltrated into other programs with the deliberate intention of causing chaos within those programs. They are usually aimed at the computing networks of major companies, government agencies, etc. See also **fox**. **4.** *n* [*Gambling*] a timid or cautious player. **5.** *n* [*Gambling*] a sucker, or an inexperienced player. **6.** *n* [*Navy*] any smuggled, stolen or pilfered item. **7.** *n* [*Oil rigs*] a plug put through flow lines for clearing the lines of foreign matter, water and to test for obstructions. **8.** *n* [*Oil rigs*] any obstruction in the pipeline; it is derived from the actual rabbits which bedevilled the early days of laying pipes by making homes inside open pipelines. See also **pig 3, porcupine 3. 9.** *n* [*US*] [*Athletics*] a pacemaker, or a particularly fast member of a running team. **10.** *n* [*UK*] [*Sport*] a weakling, a coward, anyone who fails to pull their weight in the team. **11.** *n* [*Golf*] a poor player, an amateur. **12.** *n* [*Technology*] See **pig 8. 13.** *n* [*Technology*] a container that takes material into a nuclear reactor or any other place where it is to be irradiated; it is powered by hydraulics or air pressure. **14.** also **hare** *n* [*Athletics*] a runner who acts as pacemaker for those who are aiming at world records in a race. **15.** *v* [*UK*] [*Market-traders*] to talk (too much); it comes from rhyming slang 'rabbit and pork' meaning 'talk'.

rabbit hutch, also **rumble box** *n* [*Theatre*] See **thunder box 2**.

rabbits 1. *n pl* [*UK*] [*Buses*] passengers on a London Transport bus. See also **hutch. 2.** *n pl* [*UK*] [*Railways*] travellers who only go small distances, who only take 'a short hop'. **3.** *n pl* [*UK*] [*Railways*] Leicester-Birmingham parcel trains.

rabbling *n* [*Metallurgy*] working with a rabble, the tool used in a furnace to stir the molten metal with **cinder** to assist purification.

race 1. *n* [*Computing*] an undesirable state produced by the poor design of digital circuits in which the output can produce incorrect operations due to minor changes in the relative time of arrival of input impulses. See also **hazard 2. 2.** *n* [*Religion*] the true Christian life.

racetrack, also **multiple protective structure** *n* [*Military*] one of the many schemes proposed for the basing and operating of the **MX** intercontinental ballistic missile. 200 MXs were to be sited on a complex of 15–20 mile looped roads, one per missile. They would move continually along these loops, shuttling between a number of hardened shelters, and conveyed by massive transporter-ejector-loaders, from which they would be fired. The cost of this scheme, coupled with the vast amount of territory which would have to be used, eventually rendered it inoperable and it was abandoned in 1979.

rack 1. *v* [*Building*] to build a brick wall by stopping each course a little short of the one before, so that the end slopes (usually only until the work is finished off square); it comes from 'rake'. **2.** *v*

[*Oil rigs*] to place lengths of drill pipe in a pipe rack or derrick. **3.** *v* [*Photography*] to focus a lens. **4.** *v* [*Film*] to adjust the film in a projector so that the edges of the film do not appear on the screen; if the edges do appear the film is 'out of rack'. **5.** *n* [*Electronics*] a frame or chassis for mounting equipment **6.** *n* [*Hunting*] a passage through a hedge or fence, created by a deer. **7.** *n* [*US*] [*Medicine*] a cardiac board (a hard rigid piece of wood) which is placed underneath a patient who is undergoing pulmonary resuscitation. **8.** *n* [*US*] [*Marine Corps*] a bed or cot. See also **sack 3**.

rack jobber *n* [*Record business*] a wholesaler who specialises in buying records from the manufacturer and selling them to those large stores who display records on racks.

rack, out of *a* [*TV*] said of a film which has slipped in the projector so that individual frames no longer register with the **gate** and frame borders start appearing across the screen.

rack-jobber *n* [*Video*] a concern whose business it is to monitor products on a store's shelves, removing titles that are selling poorly and replacing them with more popular ones.

racks *n pl* [*TV*] a satellite control room off the larger studio **gallery** which is responsible for the technical quality of vision signals from the studio cameras. The term also extends to the personnel involved.

radar alert *n* [*Business*] the close watching, by the senior executives of a company, of the trading pattern of that company's shares; any exceptional activity might indicate that a takeover bid is building up.

radar alley *n* [*US*] [*Road transport*] any length of road which is known for its radar speed traps; specifically it refers to Interstate 90, between Cleveland and New York City.

raddle *n* [*Weaving*] a comblike tool that is clamped on to the treadle loom during the **beaming** process to keep the **warp** threads evenly spread.

radgepot *n* [*UK*] [*Market-traders*] an idiot, a simpleton.

radgy, also **radgified** *a* [*UK*] [*Market-traders*] stupid, simple.

radiating elements *n pl* [*Aerospace*] the electronic 'eyes' that have replaced antennae on multi-function array radar.

radiation system *n* [*Banking*] a simple system for sending a message speedily throughout a bank's network of branches. The message is first telephoned to a limited number of key branches by Head Office; these branches in turn have lists of branches which they must call, and, if necessary, a third level of lists exists at these secondary branches.

radio *v* [*US*] [*Prisons*] to be quiet, or, as an exclamation: 'shut up!'; it comes from the two-way radios carried by prison guards, hence from a warning that a guard is approaching.

radio Christmas *n* [*US*] [*Lunch counter*] tuna salad on toast without lettuce; it comes from 'down' meaning 'toast' (pushed down into the toaster), thus 'tuna down' is punned by 'tune-it-down', hence 'radio'; Christmas is Noel = no L(ettuce).

radio pill *n* [*Medicine*] an electronic circuit that generates a radio frequency, developed in the 1950s by RCA and used in hospitals for internal examinations that could not otherwise be performed without surgery.

radish communism *n* [*Politics*] that statement of communist faith which rings falsely; like the radish, it is red on the outside, but colourless within.

radius *v* [*Custom cars*] to alter wheel arches to accommodate larger diameter tyres, or to do so after the car has been lowered and the tyre space thus decreased.

radon *n* [*Medicine*] a radiologist.

raffredori *n* [*Crime*] this comes from Sicilian meaning 'a chill'; it refers to the increase of police pressure that leads to a temporary cutting back of visible Italian Mafia activity.

raft 1. *n* [*Building, Concrete workers*] a form of load-spreading foundation which is designed to spread the pressure of the structure above it over the complete area of that foundation. **2.** *n* [*UK*] [*Railways*] a given number of wagons being shunted together.

Rag *n* [*UK*] [*Military*] the Army and Navy Club; the nickname was coined around 1858 by Captain William Duff of the 23rd Fusiliers, who called it the 'Rag and Famish'.

rag 1. *n* [*US*] [*Car salesmen*] See **buck 2**. **2.** *n* [*US*] [*Garment trade*] any garment, expecially a cheap dress. **3.** *n* [*UK*] [*Theatre*] any curtain that divides into two and is pulled to the sides, rather than rising and falling as a single sheet.

rag front *n* [*Circus*] a facade or banner made of painted canvas and used to advertise a sideshow in a carnival or circus.

rag order *n* [*UK*] [*Military*] a state of absolute messiness.

rag top *n* [*Motor trade*] a convertible.

ragged setting *n* [*Printing*] the method used to adjust a line to the desired measure when one interword space value is used: additional spaces are added to the right or left of text, as required, giving the page a ragged look. Thus ragged right, ragged left and ragged centre (in which extra spaces are added equally to both sides).

raggie *n* [*Navy*] a mess jacket (obsolete); a friend so close that one would share one's polishing rags with him.

ragging *n* [*Metallurgy*] a depression that is sometimes cut in a **cogging** roll, to prevent the steel skidding in the rolls.

rags *n pl* [*US*] [*Road transport*] bad tyres.

raid the market *v* [*Stock market*] an attempt to destabilise the market and bring down prices.

R

raider 1. *n* [*Business*] anyone who is contemplating making a takeover bid for another company. See also **dawn raid**. 2. *n* [*Stock market*] anyone who attempts to seize control of a company by buying up a controlling interest in its shares. To hamper these raiders, many companies now prohibit such raids until the agreement of the holders of at least 90% of the shares has been obtained.

rail 1. *n* [*Cars*] a drag racer, a dragster; it comes from the extra-long rail-like chassis on which the powerful engine is mounted. 2. *n* [*Pool*] the cushion on a pool table. 3. *n* [*Surfing*] the edge of the surfboard; thus 'rail turn' is a trick turn during which one edge of the board is submerged.

rail lugger *n* [*Horse, Dog-racing*] a horse or dog which prefers to run near the inside rail during a race.

railings *n pl* [*Navy*] See **tatts 2**.

railroad 1. *v* [*US*] [*Painting*] to paint a surface quickly, using long, horizontal strokes. 2. *v* [*Journalism*] to rush vital, immediate, copy straight to the composing room, regardless of the regular – slower – procedure.

railroad service *n* [*Real tennis*] an overhead service delivered by the server when he/she is standing near the wall between the last gallery and the dedans wall.

railroading *n* [*US*] [*Paper-making*] the formation of air pockets between the sheets of paper, causing a bulge which forms parallel lines along the length of the sheet.

rails *n pl* [*Horse-racing*] the fence that forms the boundary of a race-track; thus 'on the rails' means the horse or horses that run nearest to the fence.

rainbow book *n* [*UK*] [*Government*] a book in which the salaries of local councillors and other officials are listed; its pages are in various colours according to the grade and occupation of those concerned.

rainbow shot *n* [*Basketball*] a shot that arches neatly from the player's hand down into the basket.

rainbowing *n* [*US*] [*Cattlemen*] a horse does this when it bucks, bows its back and shakes its head.

rainmaker 1. *n* [*Business*] any businessman, especially a lawyer, who uses his professional and political connections to bring business into a firm. 2. *n* [*Public relations*] a public relations man who brings in the promotion, coverage and publicity just as he promised the client. 3. also **can of corn** *n* [*Baseball*] a high, slow fly ball.

raise *n* [*Coal-mining*] a vertical or steeply inclined shaft which has been driven upwards.

raise a dummy *v* [*UK*] [*Government*] a means of paying benefit in the absence of the pertinent documents; duplicate documents are filed and payment made until the originals turn up.

raise the wind *v* [*Navy*] to find money for some purpose.

rake 1. *n* [*Mining*] a series of beds of clay-band ironstone lying in proximity to one another, thus making a workable ironstone. 2. *n* [*UK*] [*Railways*] a complete set of coaches or trucks, making up one train. 3. *n* [*UK*] [*Railways*] the amount of freight carried in a single journey by a single railway train.

raking *n* [*Building, Plastering*] an inclined feature distorted in some way so that mitres formed by it are upright, or lines continued by it are plumb.

rally 1. *n* [*Stock market*] the upward movement of prices following a decline. 2. *v* [*UK*] [*Theatre*] to increase the dramatic effect of a performance by speeding up dialogue and **business**.

RAM *n* [*Computing*] acro **Random Access Memory** the memory within a machine that allows data to be stored or retrieved in a random fashion in a short time. It is the part of the machine into which one loads programs and where they are held as long as the operator is using them. See also **ROM 2**.

ram *n* [*Education*] at Eton College this refers to the twin columns of oppidan and colleger sixth formers walking into Chapel; thus it also means a charge in column by one side in the Eton Wall Game.

rambler *n* [*US*] [*Real estate*] a single storey house, often a suburban imitation of a ranch-house. See also **rancher**.

ramp 1. *n* [*Building, Plastering*] the meeting of inclined mouldings/surfaces with horizontal/vertical mouldings/surfaces without the aid of **raking** sections. 2. *n* [*Business*] any financial swindle, especially the fraudulent increasing of commodity prices in order to gain profits; thus 'bankers' ramp' is a Labour Party bugbear. The claim was that the banks would engineer a fake economic crisis whenever Parliament was attempting to increase welfare provisions for the needy.

ramp signal *n* [*Audio*] a signal which changes linearly with time.

rampant *a* [*Heraldry*] rearing up, facing the **dexter** with the left hind foot on the ground, and flourishing the other three feet.

ramrod *n* [*Industry*] in various industries this is a foreman or superintendent.

rancher *n* [*US*] [*Real estate*] a ranch-style property sited in the suburbs; thus 'ranchette' is a smaller version of the rancher. See also **rambler**.

ranchplex *n* [*US*] [*Real estate*] a two storey house with no basement.

random *n* [*Printing*] a special frame used to contain type when making up a page.

random art *n* [*Art*] art based on the laws of chance, involving the statistical techniques derived from probability or information theory.

random noise *n* [*Audio*] distortion – heard as a hissing sound through loudspeakers – that is caused by the random distribution of molecular particles in a magnetic tape and the resulting agitation of those particles.

random round n [*Parachuting*] a series of free-fall manoeuvres chosen at random before the jump is made.

random walk theory n [*Stock market*] the stock trading theory that past share movements are of no use in attempting to predict future fluctuations. Share prices move according to random events, none of which can be directly predicted from past patterns.

range n [*Futures market*] the extreme high or low prices recorded over a specific period.

range change n [*UK*] [*Road transport*] a type of gearbox which multiplies a number of standard ratios (ie: 4,6) by 2, giving 8 or 12 gears, by using an attachment to the gearbox. The same original gears are thus used twice, giving a double spread of ratios at progressive intervals. See also **splitter gearbox**.

ranging n [*Shooting*] the action of gun dogs in searching out game by quartering the ground in front of them.

raniks n pl [*Fleet Air Arm*] small faults in an aircraft that cannot be traced to any particular cause.

rank 1. a [*US*] [*Cattlemen*] referring to any animal that is hard to handle. 2. n [*Logging*] a pile of wood, 4ft high by 8ft long and less than 4ft thick. 3. v [*Logging*] to haul and pile regularly.

rap 1. n [*New therapies*] conversations, often within encounter groups, in which one's feelings are laid out, analysed, supported or criticised; thus 'rap session', 'rap group'. The term comes from black slang, through hippie use. 2. n [*US*] [*Police*] a charge made against a suspect; thus 'rap sheet' is a charge sheet. 3. n [*Textiles*] the quantity of fibres in a carding machine; it is a skein 120 yards long.

rapping 1. n [*Metallurgy*] in iron-founding this is the act of loosening a **pattern** from the moulding to permit easy withdrawal. 2. also **jive-talking** n [*Music*] a style of music and entertainment in which the disc jockey talks in rhyming sentences, often with a witty or pointed lyric, against the rhythm track (see **dub**) of various records; thus 'rapper' is one who performs in this way. See also **scratching 2, toasting**.

rapture n [*Religion*] the sudden disappearance of believers from the earth, at God's bidding, during the last few days before Armageddon; see Luke 17:34–35.

rapture of the deep, also **nitrogen narcosis** n [*Diving*] a dazed or light-headed sensation that comes from breathing in heavily nitrogenised compressed air.

rash n [*US*] [*Coal-mining*] a soft and slaty mine bottom.

rashes, also **rashings** 1. n pl [*Coal-mining*] soft carbonaceous shale with streaks of coal. 2. n pl [*Coal-mining*] loose dirt or shaley beds of rock.

rashings n pl [*Coal-mining*] See **rashes**.

rasper n [*Hunting*] a very big fence; to swish at a rasper is to gallop towards one.

rassing n [*UK*] [*Military*] the illegal acquisition of any item; it comes from the RN acronym 'RAS' meaning 'replenishment at sea'.

raster 1. n [*TV*] an unmodulated TV picture that comprises the horizontal lines one sees on the screen. The US employs 525 lines, the UK 625 and France 819. 2. n [*Photo-typesetting*] the raster runs vertically, from top to bottom of the letter. As opposed to the relatively gross resolution of a domestic TV screen, in which the linage remains constant, irrespective of the screen size, the lines on a typesetting raster may vary with the type size. Alternatively, in certain systems, a constant of 5,300 lines per inch is used for all typefaces.

raster burn n [*Computing, TV*] the gradual deterioration of the scanned area of a cathode ray tube as a result of continual use.

rat n [*US*] [*Car salesmen*] See **roach**.

rat hunter n [*US*] [*Medicine*] a patient whose delirium tremens leads him/her to imagine plagues of rats.

rat lines n pl [*Logging*] See **squirrel lines**.

rat pack n [*UK*] [*Military*] dehydrated Arctic rations.

rat row n [*US*] [*Prisons*] an area of a prison set aside for the segregation and safety of prison informers.

ratcatcher n [*Hunting*] informal but acceptable hunting gear: a bowler, a stock, tweed riding coat, breeches and boots.

ratchet jaw n [*Audio*] in Citizen's Band radio this is anyone who talks excessively when other **breakers** are waiting to use the frequency.

rate 1. v [*Hunting*] to scold the hounds. 2. v [*Photography*] to rate a film at a given exposure and speed for the purpose of developing, even if the pictures were actually shot at a different speed.

rate-buster n [*US*] [*Industrial relations*] See **cowboy 1**. See also **job spoiler**.

rat-fucking n [*US*] [*Politics*] the clandestine disruption of an opponent's campaign by a variety of tricks, both legitimate and actually illegal. The term was coined and originated in S. California campus politics where such trickery was developed; many of the Nixon White House's office-holding 'rat-fuckers' learnt their pre-Watergate trade in these universities. See also **dirty tricks**.

rathole 1. n [*Oil rigs*] a narrow hole in the floor of the drilling derrick, which communicates with the cellar deck below. The **kelly** is placed in the rathole when new pieces of pipe are being attached to the **drill string**. 2. n [*Oil rigs*] the extension of a borehole drilled at a reduced diameter. It is a preliminary step that is taken before a drill stem test, which produces the necessary information concerning the rate of oil/gas production that can be expected from that well. 3.

R

R

v [*Oil rigs*] to drill a small hole of lesser diameter at the bottom of a larger one which has already been pushed to its limit.

ratio *n* [*Film*] the ratio of the width of the screen to its height; prior to 1953 this was 4:3 or 1.33:1; current standard screens are between 1.66:1 and 1.85:1; Cinemascope is 2.35:1; VistaVision is shot at 1.33:1 but screened at 2:1.

rationalisation **1.** *n* [*Business*] the cutting back on staff, supplies, etc. to improve on economic position; it is supposedly a means of reducing inefficiency, poor methods, etc, but is equally often used simply as a euphemism for creating redundancies. **2.** *n* [*TV*] the adapting of films made for cinema projection down to the dimensions of the TV screen.

rationality *n* [*Sociology*] the grounds on which a belief is held, rather than the empirical truth of that belief; beliefs which are coherent, not contradictory and which are compatible with experience, are considered rational.

rat-rac *n* [*Skiing*] See **piste basher** 1. It comes from the trade-name of the Swiss firm who invented these machines.

rats *n pl* [*Military*] low-flying enemy raids.

rat-tail *n* [*Metallurgy*] in iron-founding, this is a casting defect that appears as a narrow, irregular indentation.

ratten *v* [*US*] [*Industrial relations*] to compel workers to go on strike by removing their tools and materials.

rattle **1.** *v* [*Hunting*] said of the hounds when they press hard on the fox's trail. **2.** *n* [*Hunting*] the note sounded on the hunting horn at the kill.

rattle, in the *adv* [*Navy*] in confinement, or on the commander's list of defaulters.

red, in the *adv* [*Business*] in debt; it comes from the red ink originally used to note debts on a ledger.

rattle out, also **skittle out** *v* [*Cricket*] to dismiss a side quickly; it comes from the noise of a ball continually hitting the wooden stumps, although this is often only figurative in practice.

rattle the cage *v* [*US*] [*Politics*] a politician is said to do this when he/she attempts to break free of the restraints imposed by his staff.

rattler **1.** *n* [*US*] [*Coal-mining*] a coal cutting machine. **2.** *n* [*Metallurgy*] See **tumbler** 1. **3.** *n* [*UK*] [*Police*] the London Underground railway.

rat-trap **1.** *n* [*Building*] a form of bond in which the bricks are laid on edge and the headers span the whole thickness of the wall, dividing the wall cavity into square spaces. **2.** *n* [*Cycling*] a pedal that features deep serrations to counter any slipping of the shoes.

rave **1.** *v* [*Computing*] to persist in the discussion of a topic. **2.** *v* [*Computing*] to speak with alleged authority about a topic of which one actually knows very little. **3.** *v* [*Computing*] to complain to someone who has no authority to remedy the problem. **4.** *v* [*Computing*] to irritate someone

with one's conversation. **5.** *v* [*Computing*] to preach at someone. **6.** *n* [*Entertainment*] an excellent review.

ravio *n* [*Military*] used in the French Foreign Legion to refer to anything obtained illegally.

raw **1.** *a* [*Computing*] said of data that has not yet been sorted, analysed or assessed. **2.** *a* [*Espionage*] used to describe information that has only recently been collected and has yet to be analysed and otherwise put to some use.

raw data *n* [*Computing*] data still in the state in which it arrives at the computer – unsorted, not yet checked for correctness, nor processed in any other way.

raw feels *n* [*Psychology*] the immediate 'gut reaction' to a stimulus, before that instinctive feeling is refined and modified by one's emotions.

raw jaws, also **cowboy, choirboy** *n* [*Sex*] any hustler who has yet to establish himself in his occupation.

raw public *n* [*Scientology*] the unconverted, non-Scientological mass of the world. See also **wogs**.

rawner *n* [*Angling*] See **baggot**.

rawness *n* [*Wine-tasting*] the harsh taste of an immature wine; rawness does not denote a poor wine, and may well vanish as the wine, destined for greatness, develops with age.

rays *n pl* [*US*] [*Medicine*] X-Rays; it is a medical speciality in which doctors may qualify.

razor gang *n* [*UK*] [*Railways*] a BR investigating committee who make on the spot checks of drivers' and guards' working hours. The **needle noses** only check paperwork, the razor gangs are far harder to deceive; their probes often form the basis for 'economic' redundancies and similar streamlining measures.

razorback *n* [*Circus*] a circus hand; specifically it is one who loads and unloads the wagons.

RD **1.** *n* [*US*] [*Government*] abbr of **Restricted Data** any information about the design, manufacture or use of nuclear weapons. Such information is classified under the US Atomic Energy Act of 1946. This material is never actively classified; the very fact that it falls into this area renders it secret from the moment of its inception. **2.** *n* [*Medicine*] abbr of **real doctor**. See also **LMD**.

RDSS *n* [*Military*] abbr of **Rapidly Deployable Sensor System** a surveillance system, due to become operational by 1990, that is based on a series of buoys holding passive sensors which can be simply and speedily deployed by ships, aircraft or submarines in specific areas during times of crisis. The system was due to reach the last stages of development in 1977 but it was halted before this stage was reached, possibly to incorporate a new advance in sensor technology.

RDT&E *n* [*Military*] abbr of **research, development, test and evaluation** the successive stages of creating a new weapon for military use.

reach *n* [*Marketing*] the proportion of a target

audience that is exposed to an advertisement at least once.

reach and frequency *n* [*Advertising*] the measurement of the penetration of a specific advertisement into its target market. It is the sum of the reach, those viewers who see an advertisement, plus the frequency, the average number of exposures of that advertisement per member of the target audience over a limited period.

reachback *n* [*Business*] the ability of any form of tax shelter to offer deductions at the end of a financial year that reach back to cover the entire taxable year.

reachy *a* [*Dog breeding*] used to describe a long-striding, untiring and highly economical canine action.

react 1. *v* [*Military*] a unit does this when it comes to the aid of another one which is under attack. **2.** *v* [*Stock market*] share prices are said to do this when they fall after they have recently risen. It is the opposite of **rally**; thus 'reaction' means the downward movement of share prices.

reactionary *n* [*Politics*] a politician who wishes to reverse the progress of politics and society and return to an earlier era; it is generally used to condemn conservatives and the right.

read *v* [*Computing*] to put coded data into a machine or to take it out; thus 'read-in' and 'read-out'.

read in *v* [*Espionage*] to read documents, reports and allied information regarding a case in order to familiarise oneself with a mission involving the subject(s) of this information.

read most *n* [*Advertising*] that percentage of the total readership of a print advertisement who claim to have 'read most' of the advertisement in question.

read mostly memory *n* [*Computing*] programmable memory that holds relatively static data; it is sometimes applied to PROM or RAM which has special safeguards to prevent over-writing. See also **PROM, RAM**.

read off *v* [*US*] [*Marine Corps*] to reprimand severely; to publish the findings of a court-martial.

read out *n* [*US*] [*Journalism*] the headline which is put immediately below the main headline (see **banner**) and which refers to the same story.

read/write memory *n* [*Computing*] See **RAM**.

readability formula *n* [*Education*] the writing of (text) books in such a way that the language and concepts involved are suited to the academic abilities of those who will be using them.

read-around ratio *n* [*Computing*] the number of times a particular piece of information can be extracted from the memory and read, without having an adverse effect on those pieces stored next to it.

reader 1. *n* [*Advertising*] an advertisement that is designed to look as similar as possible to the **body copy** of the newspaper in which it appears;

thus it is set in the typeface and style of that paper. **2.** *n* [*Crime*] a sneak thief who specialises in following deliverymen, reading the address on an expensive looking package, then waiting at the address to take the package, claiming deceitfully to be the rightful addressee.

readers *n pl* [*Gambling*] any sort of marked cards that can be 'read' by the initiated card sharp.

reading 1. *n* [*Theatre*] an audition. **2.** *n* [*Theatre*] a performance in which an actor offers his/her particular rendering of a role, especially when dealing with Shakespeare or similar classic works.

reading copy *n* [*Book collecting*] a copy of a book which, being in generally poor condition, is, to the collector, only good enough to read, rather than fulfilling its prime function in his/her eyes: to preserve and show off.

reading notice *n* [*Advertising*] any advertisement that resembles the editorial material in a newspaper. See also **reader**.

ready *n* [*Ropework*] a strand in a rope or cable.

ready cap *n* [*Air Force*] an aircraft that is in a state of readiness for instant take-off.

ready room 1. *n* [*Military, Navy, Air Force*] a room or hangar where items of hardware (especially missiles and other unmanned vehicles) are prepared for use, launching, etc; it is particularly common on warships. **2.** *n* [*Navy*] the briefing room on an aircraft carrier where pilots receive details of their missions.

ready-ied 1. *a* [*UK*] [*Market-traders*] prepared. **2.** *a* [*UK*] [*Market-traders*] bribed; it comes from readies meaning money.

ready-made *n* [*Art*] a term coined by Marcel Duchamp (1888–1967) to describe the Dadaist innovation of taking everyday objects and exhibiting them as bona fide works of art.

real doctor *n* [*Medicine*] a general practitioner in private practice, who sees him/herself as an active, practical physician, rather than a theorist who has never made a housecall. See also **LMD**.

real money *n* [*Economics*] the actual value of the money one possesses, rather than its face value. It is influenced by inflation, recession, international currency fluctuations etc.

real property, also **real estate** *n* [*Law*] land or the things that are attached to or part of it; eg: timber, fences, etc. See also **personal property**.

real television, real radio, etc. *n* [*Media*] See **good 2, sexy**.

real time 1. *n* [*Computing*] the actual time in which something takes place; it refers to any activities that the computer performs in combination with another entity, usually its human operator, which force the computer to restrict the speed of its actions to those of the other party, eg: recognising the keystrokes at the typist's speed, rather than being able to deal with electronic impulses at its own infinitely faster speeds. **2.** *n* [*Military*] information about what is actually

R

happening or what is happening at a near enough time to permit as near as possible an immediate reaction; thus 'in real time' means 'immediately'.

real user 1. *n* [*Computing*] anyone who uses the machine for specific tasks, rather than a **hacker** who works with the machine for the joy of seeing what it can offer. **2.** *n* [*Computing*] anyone who pays for computer time; a commercial user.

real wages *n pl* [*Economics*] the value of wages in the face of inflation; the drop in value and buying power which are set against the ostensible increase in the cash paid per week.

real world 1. *n* [*Computing*] those people who are not involved professionally or academically with the programming or engineering of computers. **2.** *n* [*Computing*] anywhere outside a university. **3.** *n* [*Computing*] the world of the commuter – the nine to five office job – as opposed to the informal, hothouse world of programming and computer design.

realia *n pl* [*Education*] three-dimensional teaching aids, models, etc, which are used in the classroom to relate verbal teaching to actual events.

realisation account *n* [*Banking*] an account maintained either when a business is being wound up or on the dissolution of a partnership.

realism 1. *n* [*Law*] the theory that the law is best discovered by studying actual legal decisions and precedents, rather than statutes and similar legislative acts. **2.** *n* [*Politics*] the philosophy that power is the true subject of politics, and not ideology, civil rights, doctrine or any other issue that must thus be considered as only secondary. **3.** *n* [*Sociology*] the claim that explanations in both natural and social science consist in uncovering the – real – underlying and often invisible mechanisms that connect phenomena causally, not merely in showing that the phenomena are instances of some observed regularity.

reality programming *n* [*TV*] non-fiction TV shows which are based on the exploits of actual persons (or even animals) and which use these to justify a mass of entertainment with a thin coating of information.

realpolitik *n* [*Politics*] politics that depend on practical realities and day to day expediency for their direction; such ideology as there is will always be subordinated to actual needs. On an international level, it is the taking of those steps that benefit oneself and one's plans, rather than one's moral image before the rest of the world.

real-time language *n* [*Computing*] a programming language designed for systems in which the response time of the computer to time stimuli is critical; it refers especially to those programs that control machines in which they must respond at once to any fluctuations and changes in the working. Real-time languages include **Ada**,

Modula, CORAL 66 and RTL–2. See also **real time 1**.

ream *n* [*Glass-making*] a non-homogeneous layer that occurs in the manufacture of flat glass.

reaming *n* [*Metallurgy*] the removal of the ragged inside edge at the ends of cut tubes.

rear admiral 1. *n* [*US*] [*Medicine*] a proctologist (one who specialises in problems concerning the rectum). **2.** *n* [*US*] [*Navy*] a specialist in the treatment of haemorrhoids. **3.** *n* [*US*] [*Navy*] an enema.

rear floater *n* [*Parachuting*] a jumper who hangs on to the outside of an aircraft to enable the rest of the team to get out of the aircraft door.

rear steer, also **self steer** *n* [*UK*] [*Road transport*] the rear axle of a vehicle or trailer which is connected by mechanical or other means to the steering wheels of the vehicle so that the rear wheels turn simultaneously with the front steering wheels; this helps extra-long vehicles negotiate sharp turns. It is less common in the UK but widespread in Europe.

rearing-crew *n* [*Logging*] the crew that brings up the rear of the logging drive, making sure that there are no stray logs left uncollected on the journey to the mill.

rears *n pl* [*Advertising*] the spaces available on the backs of buses for advertising promotions.

reasonable man *n* [*Law*] a theoretical being (there is no 'reasonable woman') created in common law for the purposes of maintaining a yardstick against which human conduct is to be judged and which exists solely within legal judgements and arguments.

reasonableness check *n* [*Computing*] a test for the existence of a gross error.

reasoned amendment *n* [*UK*] [*Politics*] an amendment to a bill already before Parliament which tries to stop any further reading of that bill by proposing a number of alterations which would so change its character as to render it useless to those who first introduced it.

reast *n* [*Real tennis*] a rally of strokes between two players.

reback *v* [*Book collecting*] to give a tattered book a new spine.

re-backed *a* [*Book collecting*] referring to a book which has been given a new spine in a material intended to match that of the front and back covers.

rebar *n* [*US*] [*Iron workers*] a reinforcing rod used to strengthen concrete.

rebirthing *n* [*New therapies*] a term based on Otto Rank's theory of the birth trauma, a therapy devised by Leonard Orr with the aim of '(unravelling) the birth/death cycle and (getting) your prosperity trip together and (getting) you to realise that truth is your guru'. The organisation which propagates rebirthing is named Theta, representing the non-physical and immortal part of the human being.

recall capability *n* [*Military*] the ability to

R

recall one's weapons or forces after having initially set them in motion. Of the three parts of the nuclear **triad**, only bombers can be recalled if the warnings of missile attack prove false – once **ICBMs/SLBMs** have been launched they cannot be brought back.

recase *v* [*Book collecting*] to refix the contents of a book within new covers.

recce *n* [*Film, Video*] a fact-finding trip made to a location or other venue to inspect its suitability for one's purposes; it comes from the army use.

receivables *n pl* [*Business*] money that is currently owing to a company, either for products or for services to clients, and which is categorised between actual assets and bad debts. The steady collection of receivables (and the accumulation of new ones) represents the basis of a good cash flow.

received pronunciation, also **standard English** *n* [*Education*] the neutral, 'correct' pronunciation of English still taught in many schools; it is the English spoken by the middle-classes of South-East England and, from its provenance in these institutions, is also known as 'BBC English' and 'Oxford English'.

receiver aircraft *n* [*Aerospace*] the aircraft in a mid-air fuelling operation that is taking on fuel supplies. See also **giver aircraft**.

recension *n* [*Literary criticism*] the authoritative version of a text that has been established by a process of critical revision and analysis.

recess *n* [*UK*] [*Prisons*] the toilets, sluices.

recessed *a* [*Audio*] used to describe a hollow sound, often produced in designs with phase anomalies or cabinet diffractions, which distort the sound. See also **open 1**.

recitals *n pl* [*Law*] a statement of the events leading up to, or reasons or justification for the signature of, a formal legal document, such as a deed or treaty; each clause usually begins with the word 'Whereas . . .'

reconceptualisation *n* [*Sociology*] looking at a problem in a new way.

reconciliation *n* [*Accounting*] the practice in accountancy of ironing out discrepancies between two statements to produce balanced accounts.

reconditioning *n* [*Forestry*] reducing warping and collapse in timber by heating it in steam for several hours.

reconstructed *a* [*Navy*] said of stale food or left overs which are put together and served again under another name.

record *n* [*UK*] [*Government*] a computer print-out in the Department of Health and Social Security that shows the records of an individual's unemployment benefit payments.

recovery 1. *n* [*Swimming*] the movement of a limb in any swimming style to that position where it can recommence a driving stroke. **2.** *n* [*Futures market*] a rise in prices that follows a decline.

recovery leg *n* [*Athletics*] the leg that, during a race, is not taking the thrust and is thus momentarily in the air.

recreational drugs *n pl* [*Medicine*] drugs used for pleasure rather than for health reasons: cannabis, amphetamine, narcotics, etc; however, the user's concept of 'pleasure' may be somewhat idiosyncratic.

recreational shopping *n* [*Commerce*] the purchasing of luxury goods rather than necessities; thus Bond Street rather than the local supermarket.

rectification *n* [*Politics*] the periodical checking, in China, of the ideological standing of Party members; censures emerging from this range from mere criticism to absolute expulsion from the party.

rectifier *n* [*Audio*] a type of diode designed to produce a DC supply from an AC source.

recto *n* [*Publishing*] each right-hand page, with an uneven **folio** number. See also **verso**.

recursive function theory *n* [*Computing*] the study of what can and what cannot be done by the ideal computer (all limitations of space and time being absolutely irrelevant to the projections).

red alert *n* [*Military*] military communications code for: an attack by hostile aircraft or missiles is in progress.

red bag *n* [*UK*] [*Law*] a Queen's Counsel's brief-bag, made of red material; thus by extension it refers to the Queen's Counsel (QC) him/herself. See also **blue bag**.

red band *n* [*UK*] [*Prisons*] a trusty, who wears a red band on his arm to indicate his status.

red board, also **red eye** *n* [*US*] [*Railways*] a stop signal sited on an overhead signal board.

red book 1. *n* [*US*] [*Advertising*] the 'Standard Directory of Advertising Agencies'. **2.** *n* [*US*] [*Advertising*] the 'Standard Directory of Advertisers'. Both these volumes are bound in red. **3.** *n* [*UK*] [*Government*] a weekly digest of intelligence material prepared for selected UK government officials.

red bourgeoisie *n* [*Sociology*] See **new class**.

red box *n* [*Military*] the special safe, common to submarines, bombers and the launch command centres of missile installations, in which are held the special codes which validate the launching of nuclear weapons.

red button *n* [*Stock market*] Settlement Room clerks who check bargains made by their firms and who wear red buttons in their lapels. See also **pink button**.

red cat theory *n* [*Politics*] the concept in Chinese politics that there are no ideological boundaries that can be set against the acquisition of knowledge; eg: capitalist computer knowledge, etc. is as useful as its communist equivalent. 'It is irrelevant if the cat is red or not, so long as it catches the mouse' (Deng Xiaoping (b. 1904)).

red clause *n* [*Finance*] a clause in a documentary letter of credit that entitles the beneficiary to

R

draw up to 100% of the specified credit amount before shipping documents are presented and even before shipping; it is primarily used in the Australian wool trade. The clause is typed in red on the contract.

red dick *n* [*Navy*] a frankfurter.

red dog *n* [*US*] [*Football*] a defensive movement by linebackers who charge the opposing quarterback in anticipation of the quarterback's throwing a long pass.

red dwarf *n* [*Science*] in astronomy this is an old, relatively cool, star. See also **red giant**.

red fish *n* [*Angling*] a fish that has adopted its spawning livery.

red giant *n* [*Science*] in astronomy this is a large, relatively cool star. See also **red dwarf**.

red goods *n pl* [*Advertising, Commerce*] products that are frequently purchased, speedily consumed, soon replaced in the shop and then purchased again, eg: fresh foods. Red goods rarely offer the seller high profits.

red hat *n* [*UK*] [*Military*] a staff officer; it comes from the red band around his regulation officer's cap.

red herring *n* [*US*] [*Finance*] an advance copy of a prospectus for the issue of securities that must be filed with the Securities Exchange Commission (SEC); on it is written in red 'not a solicitation, for information only'.

red juice *n* [*Baseball*] liquid amphetamine which is used by baseball players for added energy and stamina.

red leaves *n* [*Tobacco*] a grade of tobacco found on the plant immediately above the prized **good leaves**.

red line value *n* [*Aerospace*] in aircraft specifications these are the values on the dials that must never be exceeded if safety procedures are to be maintained.

red noise *n* [*Audio*] a term coined in 1961 by Prof. E.N. Lorenz; it refers to sound that shows a higher variation in the lower frequencies.

red pipe *n* [*US*] [*Medicine*] an artery.

red run *n* [*Skiing*] an intermediate standard **piste**. See also **black run, blue run**.

red stretch *n* [*US*] [*Lunch counter*] a cherry coke.

red tape operation *n* [*Computing*] an operation on data that is required for internal purposes but which has no bearing on the final answer; it comes from the synonym for bureaucratic paperwork.

red telephone *n* [*Law*] a 'hot-line' telephone system linking officials in W. Germany, Switzerland, Austria and Italy, who are attempting to co-ordinate their attacks on and defences against international terrorism.

redball *n* [*US*] [*Railways*] any fast moving train.

redcap *n* [*UK*] [*Military*] a military policeman.

redcoats *n pl* [*US*] [*Entertainment*] British performers.

redd *n* [*Coal-mining*] See **spoil**.

red-eye **1.** *n* [*Air travel*] a flight that takes off late at night and arrives very early in the morning; its passengers emerge with eyes red from lack of sleep. It is used especially of certain internal US routes. **2.** *n* [*Photography*] the phenomenon occurring in colour prints where the subject's eyes seem to have turned red, through gazing directly at the flash.

redhead *n* [*TV, Film*] a variable beam light, around 800W, constructed from glass fibre.

redlight *n* [*US*] [*Circus*] to toss a cheat, thief or similar bad character from a moving train.

red-lining *n* [*Commerce*] the practice among loan firms and building societies of drawing a real or an imaginary red line around certain urban areas – usually the impoverished 'inner city' – to signify that no credit will be allowed to any individual living in those areas, irrespective of actual credit-worthiness, personal records, etc. The result of such red-lining is to accelerate the decline of these areas, thus preparing them for lucrative development plans which may well enrich the red-liners.

red-out *n* [*Aerospace*] the loss of vision that can overcome an individual who is secured to a seat only by a shoulder harness during the time that his aircraft enters a period of powerful and sustained deceleration.

redshirt *v* [*US*] [*Sport*] in US college football this refers to the extension of a star player's usual four-year eligibility by removing him from competitive teams for one of those years. During this period he can practise and develop his skills, and then re-enter the team with these improved abilities, and still only play for the legal total of four years.

red-tag *v* [*Tyre-making*] to reject a tyre by marking it as below-standard.

reductionism *n* [*Sociology*] an explanation that attempts to account for a range of phenomena in terms of one single determining factor; eg: the insistence of some Marxist theories that everything depends on economics.

reductive fallacy *n* [*Philosophy*] mistakenly forming a conclusion that is too simplistic or exclusive by preferring to eliminate complexities that will not fit in with a convenient theory.

redundancy *n* [*Computing*] the use of additional components in a system over and above the minimum required to ensure adequate backup and security functions; thus network redundancy means providing a network with more links than are actually necessary, so that the extras can function as backup in the case of a breakdown.

reed **1.** *n* [*Building, Plastering*] the reverse of **flute**: a convex moulding. **2.** *n* [*Metallurgy*] a local internal discontinuity containing non-metallic matter. **3.** *n* [*Weaving*] the comblike device on a loom through which **warp** threads are threaded to keep them properly spaced during weaving; it acts as a comb for beating in the **weft**.

re-educate **1.** *v* [*Photography*] to bring a depleted flash capacitor back up to full charge prior to using it again. **2.** v [*Politics*] to condition an errant individual into following an ideologically pure line; this process can involve political classes, an indeterminate stay in a prison or labour camp, etc.

reef 1. v [*US*] [*Cattlemen*] to run one's legs backwards and forwards along the horse's sides as one spurs it. **2.** v [*Crime*] to steal; specifically it means to pull up the lining of a victim's pocket in order to remove its contents.

reef effect n [*Oil rigs*] a situation in which the offshore rig provides a useful ecological niche – as does a natural reef – for marine life; it usually increases local fish populations.

reefer 1. n [*UK*] [*Road transport*] a refrigerated vehicle or trailer. **2.** n [*Shipping*] a refrigerated ship.

reeker n [*US*] [*Medicine*] a patient who has an exceptionally unpleasant body odour.

reel 1. n [*Advertising*] a composite reel of film compiled by the directors of commercials in order to display their past achievements to potential new clients. See also **book 1**. **2.** n [*Film*] a set length of 35mm film stock; originally it was 1000ft, but now is either 2000ft or 3000ft.

reeling 1. n [*Metallurgy*] straightening and improving the surface of a round steel **bar** by feeding it between rolls in a direction approximately parallel to the principal axes of the rolls. **2.** n [*Metallurgy*] the straightening of tubes by passing them through inclined rolls.

re-entry 1. n [*Philately*] a double impression, usually of a small portion of the design, that may be found on certain stamps printed by the line-engraved or 'intaglio' method. This duplication occurs when the second application of the transfer roller is not perfectly lined up with the first application and both entries appear on the printed stamp. See also **double strike, double transfer**. **2.** n [*Surfing*] this is when the greater part of the board leaves the wave and then comes back down to continue the wave; this trick makes it appear that the surfer is 'skating' along the wave.

re-evaluation therapy n [*New therapies*] See **co-counselling**.

reeve v [*Sailing, Ropework*] to pass the end of a rope through any hole or opening.

refer back v [*Industrial relations*] a motion, proposed at a union meeting or conference, that the matter under discussion be taken off the agenda so that it can be reconsidered and brought forward at a later date; it is a convenient way of avoiding the discussion of overly controversial topics.

reference 1. v [*Architecture*] to state the overall theme, design or style of a building. **2.** v [*Politics, Business*] to refer to.

reference group n [*Sociology*] a group to whom the individual can and will refer when assessing the validity and acceptability of his/her own atti-

tudes, opinions, beliefs and actions; one need not actually belong to such a group, but simply acknowledge its relevance to one's own position and actions. Normative groups are those which determine an individual's attitudes, comparative groups are those against whose standards one may determine one's own position, although it may be quite different.

reference tube n [*Electronics*] a cold-cathode gas-filled tube which can maintain an accurately fixed voltage across itself for long periods.

reflation n [*Economics*] See **inflation**.

reflectors n pl [*Gambling*] cards that have been marked by making slight indentations on the back.

reflex, also **phase invertor** n [*Audio*] a type of loudspeaker cabinet with an outlet which permits the enclosed air to be tuned to create a resonance effect with the drive unit cone, thus improving low frequencies.

reflexive theory n [*Sociology*] a theory that refers back to itself.

reform v [*Gas industry*] to cause a hydrocarbon to react with steam to produce a combustible gas. See also **crack 2**.

reformism n [*Politics*] in Marxist terms, this refers to minor and gradual changes in the labour movement which tend towards only a limited form of socialism, but which imply the genuine destruction of exploitative capitalism.

refresh 1. v [*Computing*] a signal sent to dynamic **RAM** to enable it maintain its storage contents. **2.** v [*Computing*] referring to the technique of continually energising the phosphor coating of a cathode ray tube to ensure that the display is constantly visible.

refresher n [*UK*] [*Law*] an extra fee paid to barristers for each day a trial over-runs the initial period allotted to it by the Court.

refugee capital 1. n [*Banking*] See **hot money 1**. **2.** n [*Finance*] See **hot money 2, 3** and **4**.

refugees n pl [*Politics*] the original recruits to the Social Democratic Party (SDP): those individuals who were formerly members of the Labour Party (or, rarely, of the Conservative Party). See also **naives**.

Reg n [*UK*] [*Military*] a senior cadet at the Royal Military Academy, Sandhurst. See also **John**.

regenerate v [*Computing*] See **refresh**.

reggin n [*US*] [*Prisons*] a black prisoner.

regie-book n [*Theatre*] a notebook kept by a director in which the current production is detailed, along with ideas, experiments, etc. for its improvement; it comes from Ger. 'Regie-buch' meaning a director's book.

regime 1. n [*Aerospace*] one specific mode of operation, clearly defined and distinguished from any other type of operation by the same device. **2.** n [*US*] [*Crime*] in the US Mafia, this is a division of 40–60 members led by a capo-regime; (see **capo**).

regimental *a* [*UK*] [*Military*] maintaining or following strict discipline, a 'soldier's soldier'.

registrar *n* [*Scientology*] a Scientology salesman, who proselytises and persuades the public to join the cult.

reglet *n* [*Printing*] See **furniture 3**.

regression 1. *n* [*Statistics*] the way in which the variation in one variable is determined by its dependence on another, plus an error factor. **2.** *n* [*Psychology*] the way in which individuals under stress revert to earlier and more impulsive stages of development.

regret criterion *n* [*Business*] See **minimax 1**.

reguardant *a* [*Heraldry*] looking back over the shoulder.

regular *a* [*Science*] in astronomy this is said of a satellite that maintains as near as possible a circular orbit around its planet.

regular eight *n* [*Film*] 8mm film with forty frames per foot.

regulator 1. *n* [*Antiques, Horology*] a clock designed for the clockmaker so that he can govern the timekeeping of his own clocks; it is usually more accurate than general production clocks. The hands are often set on different spindles, with separate dials for the hour and minute mechanisms. **2.** *n* [*Economics*] a means of manipulating the economy between budgets whereby the Chancellor of the Exchequer may alter the going rate of taxation.

rehabilitation *n* [*Military*] See **fattening up 2**.

rehabilitation medicine *n* [*Medicine*] a special branch of health care which concentrates on the severely disabled and attempts to restore them to an independent and dignified place in society.

re-heat *v* [*Aerospace*] to augment the speed of an aircraft by adding afterburners; these use the oxygen that remains in the combustion gases, once they have passed through the turbine, to burn up additional fuel.

reification *n* [*Sociology, Politics*] in Marxist terms, this means the degeneration of the worker's status from that of a human individual into a mere unit of labour, a 'thing'.

rejectionist *n* [*Politics*] any Arab who refuses to recognise the state of Israel; thus 'Rejectionist Front' means those Arab states that subscribe to this view.

rejector *n* [*Audio*] any circuit or filter which rejects or cuts short a particular frequency or band of frequencies.

rejoneo *n* [*Bull-fighting*] the art of fighting the bull from horse-back; thus 'rejoneador' is a mounted bull-fighter who places the 'rejón', a metal-tipped wooden-handled spear, in the bull.

relation *n* [*Computing*] a **flat file**. See also **relational database**.

relational database *n* [*Computing*] a database made up of a number of **relations**. The ability of the database to manipulate these files creates a very flexible data management system.

relative address *n* [*Computing*] an address specified in terms of its relationship to a base **address**.

relative autonomy *n* [*Sociology*] the concept that the state in capitalist societies, although never truly independent, can act with some autonomy; this is permitted by the ruling class as a means of extending its group power.

relative deprivation *n* [*Sociology*] the concept that people mainly experience feelings of deprivation when they compare their own situation unfavourably with that of another person or group.

relativism *n* [*Politics*] in Marxist terms, this is the belief that orders from above may be adapted to one's own view of the local conditions. Thus 'historical relativism' is the concept that there can be no absolute and objective standard of historical truth, since every historian will impose his/her own 'truth' on the available data. 'Ethical relativism' means that everyone creates their own ideas of moral standards and no general guidelines can be determined. 'Cultural relativism' means no absolutes exist whereby a culture may be judged, since one must study too many and too complex a variety of factors for the easy making of such decisions.

relaxation allowance *n* [*Management*] an addition to the payment for basic time for a job that is intended to allow the worker to recover from the physiological and psychological effects of doing the work ('fatigue allowance') and to allow for the attention to personal needs ('personal needs allowance'); the amount of this allowance varies according to the nature of the job.

release 1. *n* [*Music*] in jazz this is a passage of music that serves as a bridge between repetitions of the main melody. **2.** *n* [*Frisbee flying*] See **whelm**.

release copy *n* [*Journalism*] news copy that has been prepared in advance, eg: obituaries, the text of a political speech which has been sent to the paper, etc.

release period *n* [*Travel agents*] a twenty-eight day period between contracting with a hotel for a specified number of rooms and filling those rooms with customers; if the agent fails to fill the quota the empty rooms automatically revert to the hotel.

relevance ratio *n* [*Libraries*] the number of retrieved documents actually required, divided by the total number of documents retrieved in a search, in response to a given question on a given topic.

reliability *n* [*Military*] the predicted percentage of missiles that will reach their target after they have been launched. The reliability of US missiles varies between 75–80%; Soviet missiles vary between 65–75%.

relief tube *n* [*Aerospace*] a crew member's personal urine tube, which usually discharges directly into the air.

religious punishment n [Politics] in post-Revolutionary Iran this refers to a variety of tortures which are applied to the ideologically impure in the name of religion: eg: whipping with chains or rubber hoses, being suspended from the ceiling by one's hands which have been hand-cuffed behind one's back, electric shocks modified by the 'Apollo machine', an iron 'space helmet' which amplifies the victim's screams.

reload n [Crime] the ensnaring of a sucker in a confidence game: the operator lets him win a few small bets prior to persuading him to wager, and naturally lose, his entire bankroll.

relocate v [Business] to move one's business to new premises.

remainder v [Publishing] to sell off at bargain rates those books that will not sell at their full price; this takes place either through normal bookshops or through a 'remainder shop' which specialises in such bargains.

remaindermen n pl [Law] individuals, usually children, whose inherited property has been held by trustees for the enjoyment of a living person, usually their parent, until that person's death, at which time it passes, if they are of full age, to the children.

remanence n [Science] in physics this is residual magnetism.

Rembrandt a [UK] [TV] used to describe a film that is considered to be particularly excellent: thus 'Rembrandt lighting' means the angling of the **key light** at 45° to the subject of the illumination.

remedial art n [Art, Medicine] the art works which are produced by patients in mental institutions as a form of therapy.

Remington raiders n pl [US] [Marine Corps] clerk typists.

remit v [Industrial relations] referring to a method used at Trade Union conferences and meetings in order to bury a resolution without even bothering to vote on it. Such resolutions, for whatever reason, are remitted, ie: referred to the Conference Executive for unspecified 'future' – ie: never – consideration.

remote n [TV, Radio] any programme that is shot or transmitted from outside the studio and broadcast direct to the viewer or listener without passing through studio facilities, ie: an outside broadcast.

remote damage n [Law] damage which arises as a result of a breach of contract, but does not flow directly from the breach; if the loss is too remote from the breach, no compensation will be awarded.

remote sensing n [Military, Espionage] the obtaining of intelligence data by satellite or spy-plane over-flights; these work from high altitudes and use very strong magnifying lenses.

remoulder n [Glass-making] a worker who moulds selected slabs of optical glass into blanks, approximating the dimensions of the finished article.

removables n pl [Aerospace] all items that the flight crew must remove from the outside of a spacecraft prior to take off.

removal bond n [Commerce] a bond that promises to pay any duty that may be payable on those imported goods which must be removed from a Customs' warehouse for manufacturing or for processing prior to re-export.

remuage n [Wine trade] the periodic turning or shaking of bottled wine (especially champagne) to move sediment towards the cork before **disgorgement**.

rencontre n [Science] an organised but informal meeting of scientists.

render v [Sailing, Ropework] to slacken, to ease off.

rendering coat n [Building, Plastering] See **scratch coat**.

rendezvous n [Aerospace] the planned meeting and possibly docking together of two space capsules or other vehicles during a mission in space.

renewal n [Government] usually used in 'urban renewal', this means the development of urban areas, implying that old and/or slum areas have first been demolished.

Renshaw smash n [Tennis] a fast overhead volley; it was named after William Renshaw (1861–1904) and his twin brother Ernest (1861–1899).

rent 1. n [Merchant navy] stewards' usage for tips given by passengers at the end of a voyage. **2.** v [Sex] to obtain money from someone in exchange for homosexual favours.

rent boy, also **renter** n [Sex] a young, male homosexual prostitute who can be 'rented' for one's enjoyment. See also **meat rack**.

renter n [Film] one who organises the distribution of films to the exhibitors who actually show them in the cinemas.

renversement n [Aerospace] any aerobatic manoeuvre in which an aircraft has to reverse direction.

renvoi n [Law] in international law this is a term that denotes the sending, or determination of, a matter to, or according to, the law of a tribunal outside the jurisdiction of the region where the question arose.

rep 1. n [UK] [Military] abbr of **report** it is always modified by a specific description of the subject of that report; thus: 'ammo' means exchange of fire, 'arrest' means insurgents arrested, 'bang' means an explosion, 'baton' means rubber bullets used, 'car' means suspected vehicle, 'cas' means casualties, 'crowd' means rioting mob, 'explo' means explosions, 'find' means the discovery of a cache of arms, ammunition, etc., 'inc' means incident, 'int' meant intelligence, 'shell' means shelling, 'shot' means insurgents are firing at the Army,

R

R

'tug' means vehicle breakdown. **2.** *n* [*UK*] [*Theatre*] abbr of **repertory** the system of playing a series of regularly alternating plays throughout a season, all using the same company. **3.** *n* [*UK*] [*Theatre*] abbr of **repertory** a provincial theatre company; a stock company (US). **4.** *n* [*UK*] [*Theatre*] abbr of **repertoire** all the parts an actor has ever learnt during his/her career.

repack *n* [*Audio*] a component returned as defective to the factory and then sold as new by the store after it has been repaired.

repatriation *n* [*Finance*] the return of the financial assets of an individual or a company from a foreign country to the home country.

repeat buying *n* [*Marketing*] the continual buying of the same selection of familiar brands by an individual.

repeat rate *n* [*Marketing*] those purchasers who have sampled a new product once, and then return to buy it a second and possibly further times.

repeater *n* [*Computing*] a system component which reconstitutes signals into standard voltages, currents and timing.

repeaters 1. *n pl* [*Hotels*] regular visitors to the same hotel. **2.** *n pl* [*Film*] members of the audience who will pay to watch the same film on several occasions.

repeats *n pl* [*TV, Advertising*] See **residuals**.

repêchage *n* [*Sport*] this comes from Fr. meaning 'rescue', giving a second chance': in track sports and rowing races, it is an additional qualifying heat in which the fastest losers of previous heats have a second chance to reach the finals.

repertoire *n* [*Computing*] those instructions that have been specifically prepared for the operation of one 'family' of machines.

replacement theory *n* [*Management*] the working out of the optimum policy for replacing equipment by comparing the discounted costs likely to be incurred under a variety of different arrangements.

replevin *n* [*Law*] the process of recovering personal property that has been wrongly taken or illegally withheld.

replication *n* [*Sociology*] the duplication or repetition of an experiment or piece of research.

reply *n* [*Law*] the final speech of a Counsel in a trial.

reply device *n* [*Marketing*] in mail order merchandising this is the coupon that is attached to the offer that allows the consumer to make a purchase.

reply vehicle *n* [*Marketing*] in mail order merchandising this is the postcard or stamped addressed envelope that accompanies an offer and allows the consumer to make an order.

repo *n* [*Commerce*] abbr of **repossession** the confiscation of goods purchased on hire purchase, for which the monthly repayments are no longer being made; thus 'repo man' is one who collects from defaulting customers.

report from foreign parts *n* [*TV*] a derogatory reference to a kind of documentary for which the sole discernible rationale is the producer's desire to travel.

reporting pay *n* [*Management*] a guaranteed basic wage paid to every worker who turns up for work, unless otherwise told to stay away, whether there is a specific task to be performed or not.

repose block *n* [*US*] [*Undertakers*] the support used for the cadaver's head and shoulders during embalming.

repple depple *n* [*US*] [*Military*] this comes from 'replacement depot': it is a staging point where US troops who have been serving overseas are assembled prior to sailing or flying home.

representational art *n* [*Art*] the painting or sculpturing of figures as far as possible as they appear to the artist's eye.

reprise *n* [*Marketing*] in mail order merchandising this is the restatement of the basic offer in an accompanying letter; it is often placed as a postscript to that letter.

repro 1. *n* [*Antiques*] the expert imitation of an antique piece, especially an item of furniture. **2.** *n* [*Printing*] in offset-litho printing this refers to the strips of typeset copy that are pasted on to boards and then photographed to make a negative from which the material can be printed.

reproduction *n* [*Economics*] in Marxist terms, this is the continuation of the capitalist economy by the regular turning of that economy's product into more capital; thus 'simple reproduction' means reproduction in which the amount of capital remains constant and any surplus is simply used up in other consumption; 'enlarged/expanded reproduction' means the conversion of any surplus into extra means of production.

reproduction of labour power *n* [*Sociology*] the Marxist theory that the capitalist society must ensure the housing, feeding and health care of the workers in order to sustain an endless flow of labour power and thus sustain its own position.

rep-tile, also **reptile** *n* [*Mathematics*] two-dimensional figures, of which two or more can be grouped together to make larger-scale models of themselves.

republican band wagon *n* [*US*] [*Farming*] a manure spreader; conservative farm states vote Republican, manure makes crops grow, so it makes farmers rich and keeps them happy.

repurchase agreement *n* [*Stock market*] an agreement to sell a security at one price and to buy it back at another price at some future date; the difference between the prices makes up in part for the lack of interest charges. The seller thus has the benefit of the cash for the intermediate period.

request man *n* [*Navy*] a sailor who has made a written request to an officer.

res cogitans *n* [*Philosophy*] the concept of man

as a thinking being; it is derived from Descartes 'Cogito ergo sum' ('*Discours de la Méthode*', 1637)

res communis *n* [*Law*] common property.

res extensa *n* [*Philosophy*] a material thing considered as an extended substance, the material cosmos in which humanity exists.

res gestae *n* [*Law*] the facts of a case; it comes from Lat. for 'the things done' and refers especially to evidence that includes spoken words.

res integra *n* [*Law*] a point in law that is covered neither by a previous decision nor a current rule of law and must therefore be decided on principle.

res ipsa loquitor *phr* [*Law*] this comes from Lat. for 'the thing speaks for itself': it is the principle that the proven occurrence of an accident implies the negligence of a defendant, unless he/she can provide another, exonerating excuse.

res judicata *n* [*Law*] any point that has been decided by a competent legal authority.

res non verba *n* [*Philosophy*] material, solid things rather than insubstantial talk.

res nullius *n* [*Law*] property that does not and cannot belong to anyone.

rescue bid *n* [*Cards*] in bridge this is any bid that attempts to save one's partner from a difficult position.

rescue circle *n* [*Religion*] in Spiritualism this is a seance where those who have died are contacted and helped to appreciate that they are no longer alive but are now in the spirit world.

reservation *n* [*US*] [*Politics*] a particular political party; thus 'on the reservation' means maintaining one's party loyalty. See also **reservation, off the**.

reservation, off the *adv* [*US*] [*Politics*] referring to a politician who remains within his/her party but refuses to support the party's nominee for an election.

reserve 1. *v* [*Ceramics*] to leave a pot or similar artefact in its original colour with additional painting or decoration. 2. *n* [*US*] [*Car salesmen*] See **back end** 1. 3. *n* [*Auctions*] abbr of **reserve price** the price put on a lot to which the bidding must rise, if not exceed, before it can be sold; otherwise the lot is withdrawn from the sale. See also **upset price**.

Reserve, the *n* [*Banking*] cash held in the form of coin and notes in the Bank of England.

reserved power *n* [*Law*] any reservation made in contracts, leases, settlements and other binding agreements.

residence *n* [*Espionage*] an intelligence agent (of the KGB) who works in a foreign country and is attached to the local Soviet embassy, invariably disguised under some anodyne title; thus 'residentura' means the intelligence establishment maintained by the KGB in a foreign country.

resident 1. *n* [*Computing*] any program located permanently in the machine's memory. 2. *n* [*Espionage*] a local resident of a country who, while having a very respectable standing as a member of that community, provides an essential link between the CIA **case officer** and his espionage operations. Typically the resident is an expatriate national of the country for which he works, and lives not in the targeted country but in an adjacent one, often doubling as a businessman, retired officer, etc. in order to meet both the case officer and the **principals**.

residual back-up *n* [*US*] [*Traffic controllers*] this occurs as a result of a back-up of traffic which has been cleared; because of its original size, it still takes time for traffic to flow completely efficiently.

residual family *n* [*Social work*] a family who refuses to leave an area, usually one scheduled for slum clearance, despite their standing in the way of an edifice of bureaucratic intentions.

residuals *n pl* [*Entertainment*] any payments made to performers, writers, directors, etc. for the repeat of a play, TV programme, commercial etc.

residuate *v* [*Government*] to maintain a residual profile, ie: to appear as rarely and insignificantly as possible. See also **low profile 2**.

resistance area, also **resistance level** *n* [*Stock market*] a price level that a share reaches in a rising market and at which it stops because of the increased attractiveness of that price to potential sellers.

reslush *n* [*Paper-making*] converting dry or semi-dry paper stock into slush by the addition of water.

resource aggregation *n* [*Commerce*] the calculation of the requirements for each resource for each time period, worked out on a common basis of rules.

resource time *n* [*Commerce*] the length of time a specific resource is required for the performance of a given task.

respiratory toilet *n* [*US*] [*Medicine*] the process of cleaning the lungs by extensive intermittent positive pressure breathing (IPPB) treatments before or after surgery; more generally, it means forcing a patient to cough in order to clear the lungs.

responaut *n* [*Medicine*] a patient who depends upon any sort of artificial breathing aid.

responsibles *n pl* [*UK*] [*Theatre*] small, but important roles in touring or repertory companies; hence by extension, the actors who take such roles.

reassuage *n* [*Cheese-making*] a step in the manufacture of cheese which takes place immediately after salting, in a ventilated room; it comes from Fr. for 'sweating'.

rest 1. *n* [*Banking*] the time, in the calculation of quarterly, half-yearly or annual interest, at which one period ends and another begins. 2. *n* [*Medicine*] in dentistry this is a projecting part of a removable denture that gives its support by lying against a tooth.

Rest, the 1. *n* [*Banking*] the reserve fund of the

R

R

Bank of England; the excess of its assets over its liabilities into which the Bank's profits are paid and from which dividends to proprietors are paid out. **2.** *n* [*Sport*] those players who are considered the next best in a sport after the actual representative team has been picked.

rest position *n* [*Medicine*] in dentistry this is the relative position of the jaws when relaxed.

resting *adv* [*UK*] [*Theatre*] out of work, awaiting new employment. See also **at liberty**.

restrainer *n* [*Photography*] a chemical added to the developer to retard the speed of the chemical process.

restricted *a* [*Government*] said of any documents that may not be revealed to the general public for alleged reasons of national security. See also **classification levels, RD1, FRD, NSI**.

restricted code *n* [*Sociology*] a speech pattern which depends on a form of shorthand, and which assumes that understanding will come from the context rather than from a more elaborate style. See also **elaborated code**.

restructuring 1. *n* [*Business*] the shutting down of individual companies to save money within the larger corporation. **2.** *n* [*Industrial relations*] the alteration of a wage, job or salary structure.

result 1. *n* [*UK*] [*Police*] an arrest, a successful conviction. **2.** *n* [*UK*] [*Crime*] an acquittal. **3.** *n* [*Soccer*] a victory.

result player *n* [*Gambling*] a gambler who specialises in hindsight: telling the other players what they should have done when the result of playing a hand or throwing the dice is already plain to all concerned.

ret *n* [*Printing*] abbr **retro** the reverse side of a sheet of paper.

retail audit, also **shop audit** *n* [*Marketing*] a continuing research programme that uses a panel of retailers to monitor the progress, or lack of it, in a specific line or a single product.

retail banking *n* [*Banking*] the part of banking that deals with the provision of current accounts to individuals. See also **wholesale banking**.

retain *v* [*Soccer*] referring to a system whereby a player may be kept on at a club although his actual contract of employment has expired; no other club may make an offer to buy him and his current club has no obligation either to use or to sell him.

retained *a* [*Education*] said of a backward child; this is one who is unable to keep up with the rest of his/her age-group and must therefore be 'retained' in a lower form for a further year when the others move up.

retaliation *n* [*Military*] a nuclear attack launched by one nation in reply to an earlier attack by another; ie: a second strike. Whether or not they espouse the concept of 'limited' 'winnable' nuclear wars, most nuclear strategists are determined that if the other side starts the battle, then their forces must retain the capability of retaliation.

retaliatory strike *n* [*Military*] See **second strike**.

retarder *n* [*Building, Plastering*] a material added to a mix in order to delay the setting action.

retemper *v* [*Building, Plastering*] See **knock back**.

reticulation *n* [*Building, Plastering*] a net– or mesh-like finish found in artificial masonry; keystones, quoin-stones.

retinal art *n* [*Art*] paintings that are designed to appeal primarily to the eye and which emphasise basic sensuality over any attempts to introduce an intellectual tone into the art.

retire *v* [*Baseball*] to put out a runner, base runner, or side.

retired bill *n* [*Banking*] a bill of exchange which has not been held until maturity either because it has already been paid or because it has been replaced by one or more new bills and the period of credit thus extended.

retirement 1. *n* [*Stock market*] the cancellation of stocks or bonds that have been re-acquired or redeemed. **2.** *n* [*Finance*] the repayment of a debt. **3.** *n* [*Finance*] the removal from service of a fixed asset – plant, machinery, etc. – when it has either reached the end of its useful life or has been sold or traded.

retread *n* [*Military*] this comes from the idea of repairing and re-using otherwise worn-out automobile tyres: it refers to an officer who has retired but is then brought back into the forces for further employment.

retreatism *n* [*Sociology*] the philosophy of dropping out of life and its various trials and tribulations.

retree *n* [*Printing*] a substandard batch of paper.

RETRO *n* [*Aerospace*] an engineer who specialises in the operation of retro-rockets in a spacecraft. See also **FIDE, GUIDO**.

retro 1. *a* [*Entertainment, Art*] abbr of **retrospective** said of a show or exhibition that gathers together the greatest creations of a major figure in the arts, especially those of an artist or filmmaker. **2.** *a* [*Fashion*] abbr of **retrogressive** used to describe clothing styles which look to the past rather than developing towards the future; they hark back to the 'looks' of earlier eras.

retroactive classification *n* [*Government*] the concept that previously unclassified material, especially articles that have already been published and circulated publicly, were in fact secret – because of their topic – and should henceforth be withdrawn from all files and collections and never republished.

retrograde manoeuvre *n* [*Military*] a euphemism for retreat.

retronym *n* [*Linguistics*] an adjective-noun pairing that arises in order to compensate for the appearance of a modern phrase, eg: 'stage play' is caused by the arrival of 'television play', 'hard-backed book' by the development of the 'paper-back', etc.

return 1. *n* [*Theatre*] a critical review. **2.** *n* [*Theatre*] a ticket stub.

Reuben *n* [*US*] [*Lunch counter*] the Reuben sandwich; it contains cheese, corned (salt, UK) beef and sauerkraut; it is usually hot and on rye bread.

re-up *v* [*US*] [*Marine Corps*] to enlist for a further period of service; thus it also means a Marine who has made this decision.

revanchism *n* [*Politics*] the philosophy of desiring revenge for past defeats; it refers especially to the desire to regain territory that was taken under a disadvantageous treaty, which was negotiated after a defeat.

reveal 1 *n* [*Advertising, Business*] the exhibiting for the first time of a new product or service by an agency or a business to the clients, wholesalers or retailers. Such events are often subject to much creative melodrama to intensify the supposed excitement. **2.** *n* [*Building, Plastering*] the surface, usually at right-angles to the face of the main wall, at the side of a door or window opening.

revenge barter 1. *n* [*Politics*] See **counter trade. 2.** also **revenge counter-sales** *n* [*Politics, Commerce*] a deal in which Western traders import goods from Socialist countries and force those countries to accept payment in kind, rather than in the cash that they actually want.

reverse 1. *n* [*Printing, Advertising*] the printing of a picture back to front: left becomes right, right becomes left. **2.** *n* [*Table tennis*] this is when the pimpled rubber surface of the bat is struck with the **pimples** inwards to form a **sandwich**.

reverse angle *n* [*TV, Film*] a shot that represents the opposite point of view from that taken in the previous shot.

reverse arbitrage *n* [*Banking*] borrowing from the market to pay off one's bank overdraft.

reverse bigotry *n* [*Politics*] the use of 'positive racism' to emphasise that a party or politician is absolutely devoid of any bigotry; it is intended to garner the votes of the minority to whom the party or individual is so ostentatiously favourable.

reverse cut 1. *n* [*Lacrosse*] See **back door play. 2.** *n* [*TV, Film*] a **reverse angle** shot that has been poorly executed; such shots are noticeable from the apparent 'jumping backwards' of one performer, or from the fact that a character appears for no reason to have grown by a couple of feet.

reverse discrimination *n* [*Government, Politics*] the deliberate discrimination against members of a dominant group (usually the White Anglo-Saxon Protestants), in order to compensate for previous discrimination against minorities, especially in the allotment of jobs, college places, etc. to members of such minorities, despite the claims of (sometimes better-qualified) WASPs.

reverse engineering *n* [*Technology, Comput-*

ing] the pirating or copying of a machine by stripping it right down to its components and reproducing both its plan and its parts in perfect detail.

reverse kicker *n* [*Journalism*] See **hammer 1.**

reverse out *n* [*Printing, Advertising*] a printing process that makes black appear as white and white as black.

reverse partiality *n* [*Government*] discrimination or bias against a topic, interest group, race, etc.

reverse Polish notation *n* [*Computing*] a form of mathematical notation, invented by the Polish mathematician Jan Lukasiewicz, in which each operator (the symbols which denote the specific mathematical operation to be performed) follows its operands (the quality or function, usually a number, upon which a mathematical operation is to be performed): thus, a+b is expressed as ab+, a+b*c becomes abc*+, etc. While this system runs against traditional notation, it is a far more accurate representation of the way in which a computer performs its internal mathematics. As such, reverse Polish notation forms the basis of the personal computer scientific program, FORTH. See also **FORTH.**

reverse split *n* [*Stock market*] See **consolidation.**

reverse take-over *n* [*Commerce*] the merging of two companies in a process initiated by the smaller one, which makes an offer to purchase a large number of the shares of the target company and pay for them with newly issued shares in its own company. Since the newly issued shares exceed the total previously issued by the small company, and these are now held by shareholders of the large company, the takeover is only in name, since the shareholders of the large company actually have the majority of all the shares.

Reviewer's Basic *n* [*Journalism*] a term coined by Stephen Potter to denote those tactically convenient words that are used by reviewers to hedge their bets, whether modifying an attack or restricting praise (of a friend's book).

revisionism *n* [*Politics*] the attempt, in socialist countries, to 'debase, emasculate (and) destroy Marxism by (the) . . . reconsideration, distortion and denial of its fundamental tenets' (Russian Political Dictionary, 1958); it originated as a policy by Edward Bernstein (1850–1932) who suggested around 1895 that evolution was a better way of creating socialism than revolution. See also **hegemony.**

revolve *n* [*Theatre*] a circular section of the stage that can be revolved to reveal new sets, characters, etc.

revolving credit 1 *n* [*Finance*] the principle which lies behind any fixed-limit credit cards; a credit facility is granted to a specific person whereby he/she may borrow money or buy goods on credit, up to a known initial limit; when credit is requested or goods bought, that limit is reduced

R

by the equivalent value; it can be increased again by the amount of money paid to the granter of the facility, but never to a greater amount than the set limit, (unless that limit is increased). **2.** *n* [*Banking*] a bank credit against which an unlimited amount may be drawn at any time; or a credit against which a limited amount may be drawn at any one time, but with no limit on the amount of individual withdrawals; or a limited total of borrowing that is automatically renewed once it has been paid off.

revolving door *n* [*Law*] any system of justice which is criticised for continually returning a criminal to the society within which he/she operates, rather than delivering custodial sentences.

revolving fund *n* [*Finance*] a stock or accumulation of money from which loans are made and into which repayments of those loans are paid, so that the money supply is maintained and can be circulated in and out of the fund indefinitely.

rework *n* [*Industry*] the cost of materials and labour lost through bad workmanship.

rewrite *v* [*US*] [*Journalism*] to edit a reporter's copy for publication; thus 'rewrite man' is a sub-editor. See also **sub 2** and **3**.

RHINO *adv phr* [*UK*] [*Education*] acro **Really Here In Name Only** the description of a pupil who attends school as required but makes no effort to learn or participate.

rhubarb! *excl* [*Film, TV, Theatre*] the muttering of a crowd of extras who are traditionally told to mutter 'Rhubarb, rhubarb!' over and over again.

rhubarb **1.** *n* [*Baseball*] an argument or slanging match between players, managers and umpires on the field of play. **2.** *n* [*Military*] a low level flight intended to shoot up whatever targets happen to present themselves.

Rhubarb and Custard *n* [*Cricket*] the club tie of the MCC (Marylebone Cricket Club) which is striped in magenta and yellow.

rib *n* [*Coal-mining*] the solid coal exposed at the ends of an advancing face.

Ribah clause *n* [*Banking*] in Middle Eastern countries, despite the disapproval of the Koran, banks, as elsewhere, charge interest on loans to customers. This clause is inserted into loan agreements to ensure that customers cannot cite the Koran in order to justify a refusal to pay this interest.

ribbon **1.** *n* [*Audio*] an electro-acoustic transducer that employs a thin ribbon of aluminium alloy suspended in a magnetic field; it is used in some microphones and high frequency speakers. **2.** *n* [*Computing*] an extra-thick cable connecting a processing unit to a **peripheral**. **3.** *n* [*US*] [*Journalism*] a headline, set in smaller type than the main headline, that runs across the page above that main headline.

ribs, on the *adv* [*UK*] [*Road transport*] See **hook, on the**.

Rice Hotel *n* [*Oil rigs*] a treater used to remove the impurities from crude oil; it is named after the Rice Hotel, Houston because it has so many compartments (rooms).

rich mixture *n* [*Gas industry*] a gas-air mixture in which the air content is insufficient for complete combustion and the resultant combustion products will contain an excess of carbon monoxide. See also **lean mixture**.

Richard Miles *n* [*Law*] a party to a lawsuit whose name is unknown; this is usually the fourth such party, following on John Doe, Richard Roe and John Stiles. See also **John Doe, John Stiles**.

Richard Roe *n* [*Law*] a party to legal proceedings whose real name is unknown; this is usually the second of such parties – the first is generally called Jane or **John Doe**. See also **John Stiles, Richard Miles**.

rick **1.** *n* [*Gambling*] a phoney bet that is made by a bookmaker's accomplice in order to encourage actual **punters** to put their money down; such a bet is never entered in the book-maker's ledger, nor is any money paid in or out. See also **on top**. **2.** *n* [*UK*] [*Market-traders*] in a mock-auction this is the auctioneer's accomplice. See also **gee 2**.

riddle *v* [*UK*] [*Market-traders*] to steal from the till; or to steal the whole day's take.

riddler *n* [*UK*] [*Market-traders*] a dishonest assistant; one who steals from the till.

ride **1.** *n* [*Logging*] the side on which a log rests when being dragged. **2.** *v* [*Music*] in jazz this is to play with an easy, flowing style. **3.** *v* [*Sailing, Ropework*] when one turn settles over another, a rope 'rides' a capstan. **4.** *v* [*TV*] to monitor the levels of sound and vision signals.

ride in *v* [*Horse-riding*] to exercise a horse gently and thus work off any stiffness.

ride on the cushions *v* [*UK*] [*Railways*] used of non-working British Rail employees who ride as passengers. See also **deadheading**.

ride shotgun *v* [*Business*] this comes from the 'Wild West' practice of manning stage-coaches with a shotgun-wielding co-driver who maintained a look-out for bandits and Indians; it means to be ready to tackle any eventuality.

ride the bite *v* [*Tyre-making*] the rubber does this when it moves too slowly through the rolls of the calender machine; this may cause it to overheat and stick to the machinery.

ride the clock *v* [*US*] [*Industrial relations*] 'to leave the plant during working hours without punching your time-card out, so that you will be paid for the whole day. It is usually only shop stewards who have the opportunity to do this: their absence will not be noticed immediately since they are away from their machines most of the time on union activities;' (letter from T.S. Holman, 6-10-81).

ride the gain *v* [*Radio, TV*] to regulate the volume of a programme in order to transmit it properly over the equipment one is using.

ride the point *v* [*US*] [*Railways*] to ride the front end of a head locomotive in a series, or on the first car in a portion of a train.

rideman *n* [*Music*] in jazz this is the leading soloist, who establishes the rhythm.

rider *n* [*Coal-mining*] a thin seam overlaying a thicker seam.

riders *n pl* [*Navy*] non-military personnel carried on submarines.

ridge soaring *n* [*US*] [*Gliding*] flying a glider in rising air currents generated by the wind striking a hill or ridge, and being diverted upwards by the slope of the ground; the plane is lifted on the windward side of the hill and sinks on the leeward.

riding a ball *n* [*US*] [*Car salesmen*] See **ball, out on a**

riding the boards *n* [*US*] [*Advertising*] driving around an area to check on the billboard advertising that one has had erected.

RIF *n* [*Business*] acro **Reduction In Force** the elimination of low priority jobs for the sake of economy; this may not imply the dismissal of the now jobless individual since he/she may, through seniority, be allowed to **bump** a junior employee out of his/her job, even though such a bump would mean a reduction in authority.

riff *v* [*Music*] in jazz this is to play improvised phrases.

riff money *n* [*TV, Film*] money earned through part-time jobs outside one's regular employment; 'pin money'.

riffler *n* [*Paper-making*] a trough through which pulp flows to separate out any foreign bodies which are caught on a series of upright partitions in the trough.

rifle *n* [*Theatre*] a 2.4KW spotlight with an adjustable beam.

rig 1. *n* [*Audio*] the two-way radio set used by Citizen's Band radio broadcasters. 2. *n* [*Audio*] any 'Pirate' radio transmitter that has not been authorised by the Government. 3. *n* [*Logging*] a sawmill. 4. *n* [*UK*] [*Road transport*] a large articulated truck and trailer. The word originated in the US but is increasingly common in the UK, especially after the fad for Citizens' Band Radio.

rig up *v* [*Oil rigs*] to install tools, machinery, fuel, water, supplies, etc. on a rig before drilling begins.

rigged for red *adv* [*US*] [*Navy*] 'night-time' on a USN strategic submarine, when red lights replace the 'daytime' white ones.

rigger 1. also **rig runner** *n* [*Oil rigs*] a rotary drill rig driller. See also **clutcher, swivelneck**. 2. also **rigging man** *n* [*Logging*] a logger who installs or operates the tackle that is used to skid logs from the forest using a power-drawn cable.

rigging 1. *n* [*US*] [*Industrial relations*] any pro-union propaganda material. 2. *n* [*Soccer*] the goal netting. 3. *n* [*Theatre, TV, Film*] all ropes, blocks, pulleys, wires, weights and anything else used for hanging scenery or lights. The catwalk around the top of a studio or stage used by technicians.

right 1. *a* [*Antiques*] any object, painting, artefact, etc. that can be proved to have come from the period, school, studio, etc. that is claimed for it. See also **wrong 2**. 2. *a* [*Surfing*] using the right foot; thus 'left' means using the left foot.

right and left *n* [*Shooting*] the consecutive firing of both barrels of the shotgun, with no perceptible pause between shots, which brings down two birds.

right finger *n* [*UK*] [*Police*] a skilful thief.

right, in it *adv* [*US*] [*Car salesmen*] owing, or having paid, less for a car than it is worth.

right to know *n* [*Journalism*] a journalistic concept, more easily indulged in the US with its Freedom of Information Act, than in the UK with its stringent libel laws, whereby nothing – information, secrecy, evidence in a trial, etc. – may be permitted to resist the enquiries of the press; it matters not that such probing may run contrary to individual rights.

rightism *n* [*Politics*] in socialist countries this is the failure of a Communist Party member to realise that while certain compromises with pure socialism must be made, they are always temporary, tactical and undertaken for a specific objective only; they are never intended to undermine the bases of Communist ideology. See also **leftism, revisionism.**

rights 1. *n pl* [*Hunting*] the **brow, bay** and **tray** antlers of a stag. 2. *n pl* [*Stock market*] anything to which a shareholder is entitled; thus 'rights issue' is an issue of extra shares (usually calculated as a percentage of those already owned) to those who own shares in a company.

rigid vehicle *n* [*UK*] [*Road transport*] a vehicle with a rigid chassis construction.

rigmo *n* [*Undertakers*] abbr of **rigor mortis.**

rim *n* [*US*] [*Journalism*] a semi-circular copy desk in US newspaper offices where the sub-editors sit; thus 'rim man' is a sub-editor. See also **rewrite, slot 4.**

Ring *n* [*Business*] the members of the London Metal Exchange.

ring 1. *n* [*Auctions*] a group of two or more persons – usually, but not always dealers – who agree before the sale not to outbid each other and thus eliminate the competition and keep the price down. After the lot, or lots, have been secured, the members of the ring hold a private auction: the **knock-out** or settlement. The difference between the price obtained in the sale-room and in the knockout is the 'dividend' and it is shared between all members of the ring. 2. *n* [*Communications*] a network designed in the shape of a ring, in which each node is connected to its neighbour on either side. See also **star network.**

ring fence *n* [*Oil Industry*] a procedure whereby taxable profits from oil or gas production cannot

R

be offset against other losses made by the company involved.

ring in one's nose *n* [*Gambling*] to have a ring in one's nose means that one is losing heavily and betting impetuously in an attempt to regain one's losses; acting therefore like an enraged bull.

ring rusty *a* [*Boxing*] used to describe a boxer who is either slow or ungainly, usually after an overlong absence from the ring.

ring the bell *v* [*US*] [*Football*] to smack someone so hard on his helmeted head that the resultant shock-waves running through his skull can cause disorientation, slight concussion and short-term impairment of motor and speech mechanisms.

ring the shed *v* [*Sheep-shearing*] to beat a shedful of rival shearers in a shed.

ring up *v* [*Logging*] to tally up the number of pieces of various lengths, sizes and grades that have been felled; the totals are put next to the various items and then ringed.

ringer 1. *n* [*Aus.*] [*Farming*] the best shearer in a shed. 2. *n* [*Aus.*] [*Farming*] a stockman, a sheep station hand. 3. *n* [*Navy, Air Force*] the rings on an officer's sleeve; thus 'one-ringer' is a sub-lieutenant, or a flying officer; 'two-ringer' is a lieutenant, or a flight lieutenant; 'half-ringer' is a warrant officer, or a pilot officer (both of whose rings are thinner); 'two-and-a-half ringer' is a lieutenant commander, or a squadron leader (who have two 'fat' and one 'thin' rings). See also **pip, one pipper**. 4. *n* [*US*] [*Painting, Carpenters*] a full week's work. 5. *n* [*Police, Crime*] a phony car with fake documents, made of a variety of parts and quite unsound. 6. *n* [*Police, Crime*] a horse or dog, substituted for another in a race; the purpose of the substitution is to make a betting coup, either by losing the race by putting a weak animal in place of a favourite, or by winning by reversing that process. 7. *n* [*Police, Crime*] by extension of (5) and (6) this refers to any genuine-looking fake, especially as in the phrase 'a dead ringer for . . .'

ringerbarry *n* [*UK*] [*Market-traders*] a customer who returns or wishes to exchange goods.

ring-fence 1. *v* [*Economics, Government*] to erect barriers around certain industries or occupations in order to maintain the workforce within that occupation, eg: making miners stay working as miners. Such control is only possible during emergencies such as wartime, and would not otherwise be tolerated. 2. *v* [*Finance*] a method of dealing with tax demands by setting aside a certain item from the rest of a company's accounts for consideration on its own.

ringie *n* [*Aus.*] [*Gambling*] in a game of two-up this is the player who looks after the side-bets made by the ring of non-players.

ringing 1. *n* [*Audio*] distortion in mid and high frequencies; it is due to movement of the speaker after the electrical signal has stopped. See also **doubling 1**. 2. *n* [*UK*] [*Police*] taking two cars – usually half-serviceable wrecks – and combining

them to make a 'new' car which can then be sold by unscrupulous dealers. 3. *n* [*UK*] [*Motor trade*] altering the documentation of a car to improve the chances of selling it.

ringing out *n* [*Futures market*] the practice of periodically settling any outstanding futures contracts before they mature; this is often performed by a third party to those involved in a deal.

rinser *n* [*US*] [*Bars*] a chaser – the glass of water or soda that often accompanies a shot of liquor.

rint *n* [*Government*] abbr of **radiation intelligence** any information concerning radiation, either in nuclear reactors or in military use. See also **comint, elint, humint, sigint, telint**.

riot *v* [*Hunting*] hounds do this when they hunt any animal other than their proper quarry.

RIP 1. *n* [*Photo-typesetting*] acro **raster-image processor** raster scan electronics which 'write' the text from a screen by the deflection of a laser beam across the width of the text page, with the photosensitive material advancing one scan line after each traverse of the beam. 2. *n* [*Printing*] acro **Rest In Proportion** an instruction requiring all elements of a print job to be reduced or enlarged in the same proportion.

rip 1. *n* [*Entertainment*] the musical punctuation of a violent or melodramatic action, or of a line delivered on stage or in a film, by the playing, by the orchestra, of a fast glissando up to a heavily accented note. 2. *n* [*US*] [*Police*] a fine totalling one day's pay.

rip and reader *n* [*US*] [*TV*] a newsreader; it comes from the tearing off of sheets from wire service machines and Telexes.

rip off the orgs *v* [*Scientology*] to steal money from Scientology funds, especially by diverting fees paid for courses into one's own pocket.

Rip van Winkle money *n* [*UK*] [*Railways*] money earned when actually asleep – eg: returning to the depot as a passenger during the night; it is named after the character created by Washington Irving (1783–1859) in 'The Sketchbook' 1820.

ripe *a* [*Wine-tasting*] used to describe a wine at perfect maturity, in full bloom; it has a mellowness which precedes decline.

ripper 1. *n* [*UK*] [*Coal-mining*] a coalface worker who advances the two tunnels at either ends of the coalface, the **tail-gate** and **main gate**. 2. *n* [*US*] [*Crime*] an implement used to 'rip open' safes.

ripper bill *n* [*US*] [*Politics*] any bill brought in by a legislative body that is designed purely to attack and destroy the power base of the opposition.

ripping *n* [*Coal-mining*] See **back ripping**.

ripple 1. *n* [*Audio*] a residual AC voltage left 'on top of' a DC supply; it is often the cause of hum in amplifiers. 2. *n* [*Audio*] small surface undulations on records. 3. *n* [*Video*] an electronically generated effect that makes the video picture appear to ripple across the screen. **4.** *v* [*Military*] to fire a large batch of rockets in a timed sequence; a typical gap might be 0.01 seconds between each individual firing.

rippled attack *n* [*Military*] a strategy whereby one fires off one's missiles in timed salvos (see **ripple 4**) thus hoping to trick the enemy into expending all his defences on the first few salvos, leaving him defenceless against subsequent attacks.

riprap *n* [*Building*] a kind of loose stone used for embankments, small walls, etc.

riptrack *n* [*US*] [*Railways*] a section of the yard reserved for repairing cars.

rise *n* [*Theatre*] the raising of the curtain at the start of a play or act; thus it means the start of the play or act.

riser 1. *n* [*Aerospace*] a vertical take-off and landing (VTOL) aircraft. **2.** *n* [*Flying*] one of the four straps by which a parachute is attached to its wearer. **3.** *n* [*Metallurgy*] in iron founding this is the opening in the mould that reveals when the mould is full of molten metal. **4.** *n* [*Oil rigs*] a pipe used to pump up **mud** and **dirt** during drilling.

risk averse *n* [*US*] [*Stock market*] the assumption that the prudent investor will always choose the investment with the least risk and will always expect the level of return to rise with that of the risk taken.

risk-capital *n* [*Finance*] any funds that are offered for financial or business speculation. See also **venture capital.**

risk-benefit judgement *n* [*Government*] the assessment of whether or not the inherent risks in performing a particular project outweigh the benefits it offers; it is popularly used when considering such controversial plans as the proliferation of nuclear power stations, when the public are urged to make the 'right' risk-benefit judgement.

Risky Shift Effect *n* [*Business*] the phenomenon whereby groups tend to arrive at riskier decisions than do individuals alone; the term was coined in 1967 by psychologists N. Kogan & M.A. Wallach. The effect stems from the premise that when no one person need take responsibility, everyone feels they may therefore gamble; furthermore, those individuals who are prone to gamble exert the greatest influence on the group.

Risley *n* [*Circus*] the juggling of one acrobat by another who is lying on his back and pedalling his feet in the air; it is named after Richard Risley Carlisle, a US acrobat (d. 1874).

RISOP *n* [*Military*] acro the **Russian Single Integrated Operational Plan.**

ritz wrap *n* [*Hairdressing*] a hairstyling device made of fabric-covered wire, which keeps long hair in an elevated style.

rived *a* [*Building*] referring to wood that has been split rather than sawed.

rivelling *n* [*Painting*] the development of wrinkles in paint as it dries.

river *n* [*Publishing*] the irregular streams of white space that can often be found flowing up and down between the lines of printed words on a page.

river dog *n* [*Gas industry*] a device that holds a pipeline on the river bottom.

river hog, also **river pig, river rat** *n* [*Logging*] a logger who supervises the movement of logs downriver to the mill.

rivers *n pl* [*Printing*] See **hounds teeth.**

ROA *n* [*Oil rigs*] abbr of **return on assets** the net profit after tax expressed as a percentage of the total assets invested in an enterprise.

roach, also **rat** *n* [*US*] [*Car salesmen*] a car in very poor condition.

roach back *n* [*Dog breeding*] an arched or convex back caused by vertebral contour of the back.

road *n* [*Entertainment, Commerce*] the circuit of visits, shops, venues, auditoria, clubs and so on that anyone who travels or tours – salesmen, pop bands, etc – must follow.

road apple *n* [*US*] [*Theatre*] a touring actor; it comes from slang for horse droppings found on the road.

road board *n* [*US*] [*Railways*] a list of engineers who work in rotation, normally filling vacant jobs in all classes of services except passenger and yard service.

road company *n* [*US*] [*Theatre*] a touring company.

road crew, also **roadies** *n* [*Pop music*] the technicians and stagehands who accompany a pop band and assemble and prepare the stage, lighting, sound system, instruments, amplification, special effects, etc; thus 'road manager' is the touring manager who takes care of the band's requirements, checks the venues, supervises the road crew, collects the payments, etc.

road helper *n* [*US*] [*Road transport*] a pep-pill.

road hunter *n* [*Hunting*] a hound with the ability to follow a quarry along a road.

road, on the *adv* [*US*] [*Railways*] away from the home terminal.

road out *v* [*Shooting*] gun dogs do this when they work out a scent completely in order to ensure that all game has definitely gone after being flushed out.

road rash *n* [*Skate-boarding*] the bumps, bruises and general wounds accumulated in falling off the skateboard.

Road, the *n* [*Book trade*] Charing Cross Road, London, WC2, home of many second-hand book dealers.

road, up the *adv* [*UK*] [*Road transport*] referring to a trip to Saudi Arabia and back.

roadeo *n* [*US*] [*Road transport*] a gathering of lorry drivers for competitions and exhibition driving, etc.

roader *n* [*Taxis*] a long-distance fare or journey.

roadhead *n* [*Coal-mining*] that part of the face

which forms or is in line with the roadway and which lies between the last permanent support in that roadway and the face.

roadrunner *n* [*Pool*] a pool player who travels around the country making a living from the game.

roadshow *n* [*Film*] the prolonged exhibition of a new film at selected major cinemas, prior to the general release of the film at smaller, local theatres; roadshows offer bookable seats, higher prices and superior locations.

roar, also **bell** *v* [*Deer stalking*] the sound of the red deer at the end of September, preceding the rut.

roarer *n* [*Horse-racing*] a horse that breathes very noisily when moving at its top speed.

roast *v* [*Mining*] to burn or oxidise an ore in order to eliminate the sulphur that has been mixed with the minerals.

robands *n pl* [*Sailing, Ropework*] pronounced 'robbins': these are the lines with which square sails are bent.

robber economy *n* [*Economics*] an economic system that extracts materials from nature without making sure that they are replaced or which uses materials that can be exhausted – coal, oil, etc. – without due care and restraint.

robot art 1. *n* [*Art*] a form of **kinetic art** that makes use of the natural forces and movements of the earth to activate mobiles and to structure light and shadow. 2. *n* [*Art*] sculpture that combines robotic and human forms.

robust 1. *a* [*Cheese-making*] See **earthy** 2. 2. *a* [*Wine-tasting*] **full-bodied**, somewhat immature, but still well-balanced.

robusta *n* [*Coffee production*] Coffea canephora var. robusta, native to Africa and widely cultivated throughout the world for its heavy crops of small beans. See also **arabica**.

robustness *n* [*Computing*] a measure of the ability of a system to recover from error conditions whether generated internally or externally.

rock 1. *v* [*US*] [*Iron workers*] to collect one's unemployment compensation. See also **rocking chair.** 2. *v* [*UK*] [*Market-traders*] to understand. 3. *n* [*Baseball*] a mistake; thus to 'pull a rock' is to make an error. 4. *n* [*Pool*] the cue-ball.

rock and roll *n* [*TV*] the backwards and forwards movements of the various prints and soundtracks during audio dubbing (see **dub**).

rock happy *n* [*US*] [*Marine Corps*] a soldier whose mind is beginning to suffer from serving too long a tour on a remote Pacific Island.

rock hound *n* [*Oil rigs*] a geologist.

rocker 1. *v* [*UK*] [*Market-traders*] to speak, to talk a language. 2. *n* [*UK*] [*Marine Corps*] one of the curving stripes, under the three chevrons indicating the rank of sergeant, which indicates the actual grade of sergeant. 3. *n* [*Surfing*] the curvature that runs through the length of the surfboard.

rocket head *n* [*US*] [*Journalism*] a display-type or boldface headline that uses words from the text below.

rocketer *n* [*Shooting*] a pheasant which flies high and fast towards the shooter.

rockies *n pl* [*Navy*] officers and men of the navy reserve.

rocking *n* [*Mining*] separating gold or similar valuable minerals from ore by washing them in the 'rocker', a short trough that could be shaken until the various materials had separated.

rocking chair *n* [*US*] [*Iron workers*] unemployment compensation.

rocking cockpit *n* [*Aerospace*] a flying simulator that has all the features of a working aircraft (but flight) and which is used for the training of pilots before they start actual flying. See also **cardboard bomber.**

rocks and shoals *n pl* [*US*] [*Marine Corps*] the punitive articles of the Uniform Code of Military Justice.

rocky *a* [*Navy*] referring to officers of the Naval Reserves; it comes from their 'wavy' stripes of rank and their (allegedly) poor sea-legs.

rod *n* [*Cars*] abbr of **hot rod** thus rodder is one who drives a hot rod or custom car.

rod crack *n* [*Metallurgy*] a longitudinal defect in wire rod or wire due to poor rolling.

rodding *n* [*Metallurgy*] the passing of a small plug (often of a specified diameter) through a tube to ensure a smooth bore.

roding *n* [*Sailing, Ropework*] the anchor warp or cable of any small craft; originally it was of a schooner only.

rods *n pl* [*Textiles*] machine needles, made either of wood, rubber or steel.

roger [*Aerospace*] radio code for: I have received and understood your message.

rogue 1. *n* [*Computing*] an aberrant result. 2. *n* [*Computing*] a misplaced item, or an item that is inserted into the machine out of its usual order.

rogue's salute *n* [*Navy*] the salute fired to signal a court martial. See also **one gun salute.**

ROI *n* [*Oil rigs*] abbr of **return on investment** the net profit after tax expressed as a percentage of the total money invested in an enterprise.

roke, also **roak** *n* [*Metallurgy*] a longitudinal surface defect caused when a blow-hole has perforated the surface of the metal and has become oxidised, or when non-metallic matter (see **inclusions**) is present at the surface.

rolag *n* [*Weaving*] the roll of carded wool which is the result of rolling a mass of fibres when they come off the hand **cards**.

role *n* [*Sociology*] the behaviour that an individual chooses to adopt in response to a particular situation.

ROLF *n* [*Coal-mining*] acro **Remotely Operated Longwall Face.**

Rolfing *n* [*New therapies*] the term was named after Ida P. Rolf (1897–1979), who developed a therapy based on 'deep massage'; it was intended to relax mental tensions by dealing with muscular, physical ones.

roll 1. *n* [*Coal-mining*] See **horseback. 2.** also **bank** *n* [*US*] [*Gliding*] the movement of an aircraft round its longitudinal axis. **3.** *n* [*US*] [*Gliding*] one complete revolution of the aircraft around its longitudinal axis. **4.** *v* [*Film*] to start filming, to shoot a scene.

roll a car *v* [*US*] [*Car salesmen*] See **trip a car.**

roll and pleat *n* [*Custom cars*] a form of interior trim pattern; upholstery is applied in lines of padded pleats with a wide, padded roll around the edge; it is often used on seats.

roll and rest *v* [*US*] [*Road transport*] to drive long distances, taking regular breaks.

roll cloud *n* [*US*] [*Gliding*] a rough-looking cloud appearing at low altitude in connection with a **wave**, and usually indicating severe turbulence.

roll cut *n* [*Lacrosse*] an offensive technique in which a player cuts into space after having set a **screen.**

roll dodge *n* [*Lacrosse*] an offensive technique in which a ball player turns through 360° as the defender is passed.

roll out 1. *v* [*Film*] the opposite of '**open broad**': to launch a new film in a series of steady, successive waves, each one taking in more cinemas. **2.** *v* [*Aerospace*] to reveal a new model of aircraft and to fly it in public for the first time. **3.** *v* [*Marketing*] to launch a new product; it comes from the aerospace use, (see **2**).

roll-back *n* [*Economics*] the return of prices to a previous, lower level after regulatory action by a government or corporation.

rolled pan *n* [*Custom cars*] the reworking of the lower front or rear panels, or adding a completely new lower panel, often when the bumpers have been removed; it is part of the effort to create an all-in-one look for the car body.

roller 1. *n* [*Cricket*] a ball that is delivered to look deceptively as if it will spin, but in fact travels in a straight line after pitching. **2.** *n* [*Horse-racing*] a wide strip of webbing that is secured around a horse's body to keep his blanket in place. **3.** *n* [*US*] [*Prisons*] a policeman, a prison guard; it is a reversal of the usual use, ie a mugger or thief, referring especially to the drunken and incapable. **4.** *n* [*Sex*] a pornographic 'blue' film. **5.** *n* [*Shooting*] a deer which, after being shot on a steep hill, falls and rolls so far that its venison is rendered useless for consumption. **6.** *n* [*TV*] the end of programme credits which are printed on a roll of paper that is rotated around a cylinder placed in front of the camera.

roller skate *n* [*UK*] [*Road transport*] a small, light, truck.

rolling back-up *n* [*US*] [*Traffic controllers*] traffic is moving, but so slowly that the end of the back-up is still increasing; it comes from usage in Baltimore, DC.

rolling break-even *n* [*Film*] a method of cutting down announced profits and thus avoiding the payment of **points**, to those who are owed them, by continually increasing a film's advertising budget. This process only works as long as those who are expecting their extra percentage can be kept in ignorance of what is going on.

rolling plan *n* [*Business*] a long-term plan that is subject to revisions in the light of its development; each revision re-projects the plan forward the same period of time that was envisaged in the original plan.

rolling readjustment *n* [*Economics*] a euphemism for any form of economic decline. See also **extended seasonal slump.**

rolling road *n* [*Cars*] a dynamometer or horse-power measuring device turned by the driven wheels of a car; the wheels turn heavy rollers mounted in a pit in the floor and connected to the requisite dials and meters; it is used to help find faults that do not appear in a stationary vehicle.

rolling spider *n* [*TV, Film*] a wheeled device placed underneath an otherwise static object – eg: a camera tripod – to give it useful mobility on a set.

rolling strikes *n pl* [*Industrial relations*] a series of strikes that follow on one after the other in various factories or towns.

rolling title *n* [*Film*] See **creeping title.** See also **crawl 2.**

rolling up *n* [*Printing*] preparing a lithographic plate for printing.

roll-off *n* [*Audio*] the frequency at which a filter, equaliser or tone-control begins to reduce the signal amplitude.

roll-out 1. *n* [*US*] [*Football*] a play in which the quarterback runs out of the space made by his blockers before passing the ball. **2.** *n* [*US*] [*Gliding*] the path of a landing glider after it touches down and before it comes to a full stop.

rollover *n* [*Computing*] the ability of a keyboard to send the correct codes even when two keys have erroneously been depressed together.

roll-over 1. *n* [*Economics*] the extension or transfer of a debt or any other financial transaction. **2.** *n* [*Economics*] the reinvestment of money gained on the maturing of bonds and stocks. **3.** *n* [*Economics*] a new issue of bonds or stocks that replaces one that has just matured.

rolls *n pl* [*Logging*] metal rollers that carry the lumber through the sawmill.

ROM 1. *n* [*Coal-mining*] acro **Run Of Mine** the product of a coalmine before it has been sorted or cleaned. **2.** *n* [*Computing*] acro **Read Only Memory** a permanent store of information within the computer which can only be changed by a particular user, by particular operating conditions or by a particular external process, but not by conventional write processes, ie. simply adding new data. ROM is used to store permanent procedures in the machine, eg: the operating

R

system. See also **PROM, RAM. 3.** *n* [*US*] [*Medicine*] acro **range of motion exercise** the movement of the patient's limbs to their furthest extent; it is carried out by the nurse.

Roman culture *n* [*Sex*] orgies, group sex.

Roman decoy *n* [*Chess*] a piece that is offered up as bait to save a player from succumbing to a hazardous situation.

roman-feuilleton *n* [*Literary criticism*] a novel that was originally published in episodes in a daily paper.

roman-fleuve *n* [*Literary criticism*] a series of novels, each of which exists on its own merits and can be read as such, but which contain some or all of the same characters (possibly a consistent narrator) and thus together create an episodic and even epic chronicle; eg: Balzac's 'La Comédie Humaine', Anthony Powell's 'Dance to the Music of Time' etc.

Romany-charver *n* [*UK*] [*Market-traders*] a gypsy stall-holder.

rook *v* [*UK*] [*Market-traders*] to grumble, to complain.

rookie *n* [*US*] [*Police, Military, Sport*] a novice, a new recruit.

room 1. *n* [*Coal-mining*] a roadway driven through solid coal in **bord and pillar** mining. **2.** *n* [*US*] [*Coal-mining*] a hollowed out space in a mine from which coal has been removed. **3.** *n* [*Entertainment*] the hall, club, auditorium, etc. in which a singer or comedian performs. **4.** *n* [*Tyre-making*] the various departments in the factory, which are not limited to one area or one floor of the factory, but which do deal with specific and separate processes such as making the treads, milling or heating.

room change *n* [*Hotels*] the complete change of bedlinen, towels, etc. that is performed in a hotel room when its occupancy changes.

room for the scissors *n* [*TV, Film*] a few seconds extra running of the camera, after filming the dialogue in a scene, to enable the editor to have sufficient film to make a satisfactory transition to the next scene.

room tone *n* [*Film*] background noises.

rooms *n pl* [*Antiques*] abbr of **auction rooms** hence this also means the sales that are held within them.

room-temperature IQ *n* [*US*] [*Medicine*] extreme stupidity; such an IQ would be around 70.

roorback *n* [*US*] [*Politics*] a lying smear intended to destroy a rival candidate's campaign; it comes from the fictitious 'Travels of Baron Roorback' (1844).

rooster tail *n* [*Surfing*] the curved plume of water thrown up by a surfboard.

root *n* [*Computing*] the single node in a tree which has no **parent**. See also **tree**.

rootless cosmopolite *n* [*Politics*] a Marxist 'code-word' for the Jews. See also **cosmopolitanism**.

roots *n* [*Hunting*] any field of potatoes, beets etc.

ROP, ROM, ROW, ROY *n* [*Advertising*] acro **Run Of Press, Run Of Month, Run Of Week, Run Of Year** the various specifications of time adopted when ordering space for the publication, or broadcasting on radio or TV, of an advertisement; ROP specifies no special conditions, allowing the publisher or station to place the advertisement as it wishes; ROW, ROM and ROY are more specific.

rope *n* [*Military*] a type of anti-radar **chaff** that consists of long strings of metallic foil or wire and which is designed to confuse the guidance systems of anti-aircraft missiles or radar signals.

rope choker *n* [*Oil rigs*] a cable-tool rig driller. See also **jarhead**.

rope soaper *n* [*Textiles*] a machine that washes cloth in the bleaching process by drawing it in longitudinal folds over and under rollers in a washing solution.

roper 1. *n* [*Horse-racing*] a jockey who deliberately hauls on the reins to slow down his mount and thus lose a race, presumably for financial gain. **2.** *n* [*Industrial relations*] a strikebreaker who circulates among his workmates in the hope of persuading some of them to return to work. **3.** *n* [*Police*] a plainclothesman who hides his real identity in the hope of tempting a suspect to give himself away.

ropes *n pl* [*Building, Plastering*] twined strips of **scrims** soaked in measured amounts of plaster.

ropey *a* [*Building, Painting*] said of paint that dries out with a rope-like appearance.

ropeyarn Sunday *n* [*US*] [*Marine Corps*] a weekday afternoon, usually a Wednesday, when drill, instruction, training and work are abandoned in favour of organised or individual recreation.

ROR *phr* [*Medicine*] acro **relationship on the rocks**.

ro-ro ship *n* [*Commerce*] abbr of **roll-on roll-off ship** a merchant ship so designed that tourist or commercial traffic can drive on at the embarkation point and drive off again at the ship's destination.

rort *v* [*Gambling*] a bookmaker does this when he shouts the odds at a race meeting.

ROS *n* [*Medicine*] acro **review of symptoms**

rosalia *n* [*Music*] the identical repetition of a melody in a key one tone higher, keeping the exact interval between the notes.

rose 1. *n* [*Gemstones*] a diamond so small that it can barely be cut, if at all. **2.** *n* [*US*] [*Medicine*] a comatose, extremely weak patient who is expected to die; it comes from the excessively pink colour of the skin and the frailty of the person so described.

rose box, also **strum box** *n* [*Sailing*] a strainer at the end of a suction pump on a bilge pipe.

rose garden n [US] [Medicine] a group of comatose, extremely weak, patients. See also **rose 2.**

rose garden rubbish n [US] [Politics] supposedly ad-libbed, but in fact carefully prepared, Presidential comments for delivery on official occasions, many of which take place in the Rose Garden of the White House.

rose room n [US] [Medicine] a ward set aside for comatose, extremely weak patients, who may be about to die. See also **rose 2.**

rosebud n [US] [Medicine] the opening of the intestine on the abdomen after a colostomy or ileostomy; it is pink, mucous tissue, about one inch wide.

rosettes 1. n pl [Furriers] the 'spots' carried on a leopard's skin. 2. n pl [Dog breeding] small tan patches on either side of the chest above the front legs of basically black dogs.

rosinback, also **rozinback** n [Circus] a bareback rider who uses rosin rubbed into the horse's back to keep his/her footing.

rosin-belly n [Mining] a labourer in a sawmill.

rosy n [Merchant navy] a large scrapbin in the galley of a ship.

ROT n [Radio] acro **Record Of Transmission** recording a live transmission as it is broadcast; it is for archive use and (in IBA companies) to preserve a record against any possible legal action.

rotate 1. v [Air travel] used of a pilot who pulls up the nose of an aircraft that is moving along the runway at the correct speed and thus takes off. 2. v [US] [Military] to take an individual or unit out of front line duty and give them a period of less arduous duty as a respite. 3. v [Sociology] the concept, after a supposedly amicable divorce, of swapping various mutually cherished possessions rather than letting one partner have everything.

rotating patient n [US] [Medicine] See **crock 4.**

rotten squash n [US] [Medicine] brain damage.

rotten stone n [Industry] a soft, decomposed siliceous limestone which is used as a polishing agent.

rotten stop n [Sailing] a light, temporary, lashing put round a sail to hold it in a bundle while it is being hoisted.

rouf n [UK] [Prisons] back slang meaning four; hence a four-year sentence.

rouge n [Gemstones, Glass-making] a red powder made mainly of ferric oxide which is used for polishing gems and glass or as a pigment.

rough 1. n [Advertising] the basic layout of an advertisement which precedes the finished result and which may well be altered several times. 2. a [Wine-tasting] used to describe a coarse, edgy sort of wine which is usually of ordinary quality.

rough hustle v [Pool] to challenge a room full of potential betters by appearing drunker or rougher, and in both cases less competent, than one is, so as to have them pool a large sum against you.

rough it up v [Gambling] to bet heavily and thus intensify the atmosphere and competitiveness of a game.

rough mix n [Record business] the first, basic mixing together of the various recorded tracks to be incorporated in a song or piece of music. See also **rough-cut.**

rough/smooth a [Tennis] the two sides of the stringed portion of a tennis racket; one has protuberant knots and string edges, the other does not; 'tossing' in tennis is replaced by spinning the racket and calling either 'Rough!' or 'Smooth!'

rough-cut n [Film] the first basic assembly of the film with the narrative in order and the soundtrack synchronised. See also **rough mix.**

roughing n [Metallurgy] See **cogging.**

roughneck n [Oil rigs] an unskilled labourer who works on the floor of the drilling rig. See also **roustabout.**

roulette n [Philately] a perforating tool comprising a toothed disc or wheel.

round 1. n [Textiles] a single stitch made by a knitting loom. 2. a [Wine-tasting] used to describe a well-balanced, mature wine.

round fish n [Fishing] a fish that has not been gutted.

round house [Military] US Department of Defense code for: level three (out of five) war readiness.

round, in the adv [Theatre] a performance given in a theatre where the auditorium surrounds the stage, as opposed to forming the **fourth wall** beyond the proscenium arch.

round lot n [US] [Stock market] the basic unit of trading on the New York Stock Exchange; with the exception of some special instances, this means 100 shares of stock or $1000 worth of bonds.

round out v [Gliding] See **flare 3.**

round robin 1. n [Computing] a method of allotting CPU time in a multi-user environment; each user is allotted a small amount of working time – a quantum – which he exhausts and then passes on the CPU access to the next member of the group. 2. n [Gambling] a racing or sporting bet which involves playing all the available two- or three-race or sports combinations on three or more horses or teams.

round the houses adv [UK] [Road transport] engaged in multiple delivery work along a route.

round trip n [Oil rigs] the process which occurs every time a drill bit has to be replaced: the entire **drill string** is removed in approximately 90ft sections, then put back with a new bit on the end.

round turn 1. n [Futures market] the procedure by which an individual's **long** or **short position** is offset by making an opposite transaction, or by accepting or making a delivery to the actual financial instrument. 2. n [US] [Paper-making] See **twitch road.** 3. also **commission** n [Finance] the one-time fee charged by a broker to a customer

R

when a position is liquidated whether by **offset** or delivery.

rounder 1. *n* [*UK*] [*Buses*] abbr of **round trip** a single journey by one London Transport bus to the end of its stated route and back to the **point** of departure. 2. *n* [*US*] [*Railways*] a transient railway worker.

roundover *n* [*US*] [*Gliding*] in a ground launch this is the period just before release, when the rate of climb is diminishing and the glider is resuming a normal gliding attitude.

roundhouse *n* [*US*] [*Railways*] a circular building in which locomotives may be housed, maintained and repaired.

rounds 1. *n pl* [*Commerce*] articles which are naturally or artificially produced in spherical shapes. 2. *n pl* [*Tiddleywinks*] the last five shots for each of the four players after the time-limit has elapsed.

round-tripping 1. *n* [*Baseball*] scoring a home run, and thus making a trip around the bases. 2. *n* [*Finance*] the practice of earning profits by borrowing on one's overdraft and using the money to lend out at interest in the money markets.

rouse, also **rowse** *v* [*Sailing, Ropework*] to pull together on the cable, to haul in slack.

roustabout *n* [*Oil rigs*] a general or manual labourer. See also **roughneck.**

route 1. *n* [*US*] [*Horse-racing*] a long race, ie: anything in excess of one mile. 2. *n* [*Logging*] the total time of operations worked by a logging camp; thus 'long route' means a long stretch of employment on the same job.

route card *n* [*Industry*] a document which accompanies a batch of work during a manufacturing process and which shows the stages in the work that have to be carried out and the various work centres involved.

route 1 *n* [*Lacrosse*] the quickest path to goal.

routine 1. *n* [*Computing*] a short program. 2. *n* [*Theatre*] any rehearsed or prepared act, sequence of actions or lines, or any other short performance.

routine response behaviour *n* [*Marketing*] a buyer's behaviour in routine situations when the brand is known, the choices understood, and the buyer has purchased the product before.

rover 1. *n* [*Croquet*] the final hoop in a game of croquet. 2. *n* [*Video, TV*] the nickname for the Sony Portapack video camera. 3. also **sweeper** *n* [*Lacrosse*] a player who acts as an extra defender with the job of double teaming (see **double team**) or picking off interceptions from errors forced by team-mates.

roverback *n* [*US*] [*Football*] a combination cornerback and linebacker who alternates between the two roles as the situation or play demands.

roving *n* [*Weaving*] the continuous rope of loosely twisted fibres that has been prepared for spinning.

rowntree *n* [*Building*] the shaft of a shovel, pick,

etc; it is so-called from the tube of fruit gums of the same name.

royal 1. *n* [*Deer stalking*] a red deer that has arrived at its twelfth year. 2. *a* [*US*] [*Government*] a security classification that, as of September 1980, superseded 'Top Secret'.

RPDI *n* [*Finance*] abbr of **Real Personal Disposable Income** the total income available to a private individual after tax.

RPFer *n* [*Scientology*] a member of the Rehabilitation Project Force; this is formed from a group of those who are deemed to have transgressed the 'laws' of scientology and who may thus be employed, as virtual slave labour, as workers in and around the cult's offices; 'sentences' to the RPF can last up to three years.

RPG *n* [*Sport, Computing*] abbr of **Role-Playing Games** also called 'Dungeons and Dragons'. These are a variety of fantasy and adventure games which are popular among computer users – although a computer is not vital – and which let the players work out their own complex fates and personalities in a Tolkienesque world of 'sword and sorcery'; all such games derive from the original 'Dungeons and Dragons', created in the US by Gary Gygax in 1974.

RS232 *n* [*Computing*] a standard interface between microcomputers and their **peripherals** which was created by the US Electronic Industries Association. In 1975 the EIA added the RS423 and RS422 interfaces, both of which allow higher data transmission rates.

RSA *n* [*Sociology*] abbr of **Repressive State Apparatus** the directly coercive means whereby the dominant capitalist class maintains control – secret police, repressive legislation, etc. See also **ISA.**

Rth *n* [*Science fiction*] the planet Earth; thus Rthmen are Earthmen.

rub *n* [*Royal Navy*] a loan.

rub down *v* [*Police*] to search a suspect by passing one's hands over his/her body.

rub queen *n* [*Sex*] a male masseur who supplements his income by doubling as a homosexual prostitute.

rubbed *a* [*Book collecting*] said of a book that is weak in its joints or its spine and which will need repair soon, if not immediately.

rubber *n* [*Baseball*] originally it was the home plate; now it is the pitcher's mound.

rubber aircraft *n* [*Aerospace*] an aircraft which is still at a very early stage of its design and thus still sufficiently flexible for major alterations to be feasible in any aspect of that design.

rubber banding *n* [*Computing*] the flexible movement of interconnecting lines used in computer graphics; some machines have a 'cut and paste' facility which will automatically relocate such lines when a drawing is altered. Otherwise the lines must be erased and then redrawn whenever the location is moved.

R

rubber chicken circuit n [US] [Politics] the round of official dinners, fund-raising banquets, campaign meetings and all the other meals that a politician must attend to further his/her own career and at which, almost invariably, the hosts provide one or another version of the same indigestible chicken.

rubber dog n [Book-binding] See **puppy 1.**

rubber duck n [Navy] a heavy rubber inflatable raft, usually with an outboard motor.

rubber heels n pl [UK] [Police] those policemen whose job it is to investigate possible breaches of discipline – accepting bribes, helping in robberies, etc – among their colleagues on the force; it is also a general term for the Special Branch who investigate internal political cases.

rubbernecker n [US] [Traffic controllers] one who spends too much time observing the scenery and as such slows down the traffic flow (this usage is from Texas). In Detroit this is a 'gonker', in Los Angeles, a 'lookie-Lou'.

rubbers n pl [Stock market] shares in companies that produce rubber.

rubbery 1. a [Cheese-making] a pejorative term for cheeses that are overly chewy or elastic in texture. 2. a [Wine-tasting] a description of the taste that is probably due to the presence of mercaptan, a chemical aberration, that is not infrequently found in old white wines due to the breakdown of sulphur.

rubbish 1. n [Shooting] poor, sub-standard deer, which are only fit for the cull. 2. v [Surfing] to tip another surfer off the board.

rubby-dubby n [Fishing] the minced fish – mackerel, pilchards, etc – which is used as a bait for larger fish, especially sharks.

Rudeiment n [Education] in some Roman Catholic schools this is the lowest class of pupils.

ruf mord n [Espionage] this comes from Ger. meaning 'character assassination': it is the blackmailing of diplomats, especially those who work for the United Nations Organisation.

ruff n [Music] a drum beat used in military drumming.

rug n [Entertainment] a hairpiece or toupee.

rug joint n [Gambling] See **carpet joint.**

rugged a [Wine-tasting] See **manly.**

ruggsy a [UK] [Military] used to describe an image cultivated in the British Army, especially in the paratroops, of super-macho toughness, with ultra-short hair, large boots and a tattered T-shirt for the maximum display of muscles.

rug-ranking n [Government] in Canadian bureaucracies this is the establishing of a secretary's pay by linking it to the status of the official for whom she works; it comes from the idea that seniority in an organisation is obvious from the size of the carpet (if any) that is placed in one's office.

Rule forty-three n [UK] [Prisons] solitary confinement for a prisoner's own safety; many sex offenders, informers and other prisoners who would be at risk within the prison's general population either choose, or are assigned, solitary confinement under this rule; they are sometimes known to fellow prisoners as 'the animals' or 'the beasts'.

rule off v [Commerce] to close the books for a day's trading; it comes from the days of ledger accounting.

ruled bin system n [Management] a stock control system whereby stock is kept in a container on which a line is drawn; once the stock falls beneath this line it is time to re-order. See also **last-bag system.**

rule-out n [Journalism] a non-news story which is published on a slow day when there are no important stories; it comes from the style of such stories in which one posits an unlikely event, and then says that subsequent actions ruled out the happening of such an event after all.

ruler n [Computing] in word processing this is the status display line at the top or bottom of the VDU which tells what margins and/or tabulation are currently being used.

Rules, the 1. n pl [Horse-racing] National Hunt Rules. 2. n pl [Horse-racing] the Jockey Club Rules of Racing.

ruling in n [Building, Plastering] the operation of using the appropriate rule to level plaster that is being applied to a flat surface.

ruly English n [Linguistics] a form of English based on a constant, rigid rule; each word has only a single conceptual meaning, and each concept can be described by only a single word.

rumbelow n [Literary criticism] a combination of meaningless syllables.

rumble 1. v [Air travel] said of air crew who steal food and drink from the aircraft's in-flight stores. 2. n [Audio] low frequency distortions transmitted to the pickup, and thus through the speakers, by faults in the turn-table mechanism.

rumble bins n pl [Audio] very large speakers in which the bass is turned up high; they are useful for special effects such as thunder, aircraft taking off, etc.

rumble box n [Theatre] See **thunder box 2.**

rumble strip n [Cars] specially inserted strips of coarse road surface which are intended to alert drivers to a possible hazard on the road ahead.

rumbler n [Metallurgy] in iron-founding this is a rotating container in which castings are loosely packed and which cleans them by tumbling them over and against each other.

rumbling, also **tumbling** n [Painting] a method of painting small objects which would take too long to be painted adequately by hand. A number of the objects are placed in a drum which has been filled with slightly more paint than is estimated will cover all the objects concerned. The drum is then rotated until such time as all the objects have become fully coated with paint.

rum-cul *n* [*UK*] [*Circus*] the manager of a circus; originally this was a manager of a travelling show (around 1860 onwards); it comes from Romany use.

rummage squad *n* [*UK*] [*Government*] an elite squad of H.M. Customs who make random checks on commercial airliners, with particular regard to the possibility of discovering smugglers among the cabin crew. The squad boards the aircraft before the crew have disembarked and searches both their persons and the aircraft with extreme thoroughness.

run **1.** *n* [*Angling*] a pool, usually of fast moving water. **2.** *n* [*Angling*] the taking out of a line by a hooked fish which is attempting to escape the fisherman. **3.** *n* [*Computing*] a particular execution of a task or program by a computer. **4.** *n* [*UK*] [*Government*] a filing cabinet that holds papers and cards on current Department of Health and Social Security cases. **5.** *n* [*US*] [*Meat trade*] the day's receipts from the market. **6.** *n* [*Oil rigs*] the distance drilled during a period of drilling with the same bit. **7.** *n* [*Printing, Publishing*] the total number of copies of a book, magazine, newspaper, etc., printed during a single period of press-work. **8.** *n* [*US*] [*Railways*] a train to which an employee is assigned; the run includes all of a day's trips by that train. **9.** *n* [*Sheepshearing*] a spell of sheep-shearing. **10.** *v* [*TV*] to transmit.

run a board *v* [*US*] [*Railways*] to halt the train beyond a stop signal.

run a flat *v* [*Theatre*] to carry scenery around the stage.

run a team *v* [*Espionage*] to direct and organise a team of agents who are working in the field.

run book *n* [*Computing*] a written file containing all the material needed to document a computer application: flow charts, coding, operating instructions, problem statement, etc.

run down the game *v* [*Sex*] among black pimps, this is when an experienced pimp explains the nuances of the profession to a neophyte.

run gang *n* [*Air travel*] maintenance engineers who make regular checkups on commercial aircraft.

run it by *v* [*New therapies*] to consider a topic; the image is of items being brought out for consideration at an auction or for selection for an art-gallery exhibition.

run, off the *adv* [*US*] [*Military*] out of order; temporarily withdrawn from service.

run out *v* [*Pool*] to shoot all the remaining balls into the pockets without missing.

run over the hill *v* [*US*] [*Marine Corps*] to force an individual either to resign or to seek a transfer.

run ragged, also **rag right** *v* [*Publishing*] to set type without **justifying** each line.

run scared *v* [*Politics*] when a politician ensures against dangerous complacency by campaigning as if his/her opponents were constantly presenting major threats to the chances of victory, even if the opinion polls advise otherwise; thus it means to keep alert and in touch.

run strong *v* [*Gambling*] to operate a crooked casino.

run the rule over *v* [*UK*] [*Police*] to investigate a suspect both in person and by checking any possible record he/she might have.

run the wrong main *v* [*US*] [*Railways*] used of a train when it is running on the track usually used by traffic moving in the opposite direction.

run time *n* [*Computing*] the time in which a **program** is actually executed, as opposed to that involved in loading, compiling or assembling it. See also **elapsed time, execute time.**

run up *v* [*Military*] to have an individual brought up before the Commanding Officer and charged with a breach of service regulations.

runaround *n* [*Printing*] type that is set in a shorter than usual measure so that it will fit down the side of an illustration.

runaway shop *n* [*US*] [*Industrial relations*] a plant that is transferred from one location to another in order to avoid safety or similar trade union regulations, or to prevent trade union activities by recruiting an entirely new, non-union labour force.

rundown *n* [*Baseball*] a play whereby two players attempt to tag a batter who is caught between them.

rundown sheet *n* [*Gambling*] a list of entries and betting odds for the horses in a day's racing.

run-in **1.** *n* [*Audio*] the wide-spread area of the groove that starts a record and on to which the stylus is placed; it is immediately prior to the closely grooved recorded area. **2.** *n* [*UK*] [*Crime*] a place to which stolen goods are driven after a robbery and at which they may be temporarily hidden. See also **slaughter.**

runner **1.** *n* [*Commerce*] in antiques and the second-hand book trade, a freelance dealer. **2.** *n* [*Metallurgy*] in iron-founding this is the component of the casting process which distributes the molten metal throughout the mould. **3.** *n* [*UK*] [*Police*] a suspect who is likely to abscond if let out of jail or allowed bail by the Court; thus 'do a runner' is to abscond. **4.** *n* [*Printing*] letters or figures set in the margin of a page to aid reference; they are especially found beside long poems, giving a regular line count, etc. **5.** *n* [*UK*] [*Prisons*] an escape. **6.** *n* [*US*] [*Prisons*] a trusty, a prisoner given special privileges and who is allowed greater freedom than normal to move around the jail. **7.** *n* [*UK*] [*Railways*] a platform inspector. **8.** *n* [*Shooting*] a bird, usually wounded, which travels fast across the ground without flying.

runners *n pl* [*Merchant navy*] a small crew signed on to look after a ship that is under tow.

running ahead *n* [*US*] [*Stock market*] the illegal practice whereby a broker buys or sells a share for his or her personal account before carrying out a customer's instructions to perform the same transaction.

running cunning *part phr* [*Coursing*] the way in which a greyhound lies off waiting in order to gain an advantage over the rival dog.

running dog *n* [*Politics*] in Chinese communist terminology, 'zougou' is a running dog; thus it means a lackey or subservient figure, one who serves imperialist/capitalist masters. It was adopted by the Western Left to vilify any supporter of capitalism.

running for the exercise *part phr* [*US*] [*Politics*] referring to a candidate whose campaign has no hope of success, so that he is merely going through the motions out of a sense of pride, self-importance, foolhardiness, etc.

running ground *n* [*Coal-mining*] loose ground which will only maintain an excavation if the whole area is substantially supported first.

running head/foot *n* [*Publishing*] any descriptive line which appears at the top or bottom of all or alternate pages, carrying the title, author's name, **folio** or similar information.

running like a dry creek *part phr* [*US*] [*Politics*] referring to a candidate who is not working hard enough and/or is failing to make the level of impact his managers and advisers desire.

running margin *n* [*Finance*] the difference in the interest rates paid and earned by an individual who borrows a sum which he then invests.

running speed *n* [*Film*] the speed at which a film moves through the projector; it is currently 24 frames per second. Silent films were shot at 16fps and it is that difference, rather than any incompetence of their makers, that makes them look jerky on projectors operating at the modern speed.

running wild *a* [*US*] [*Prisons*] said of consecutive sentences. See also **jammed.**

running-off *a* [*US*] [*Medicine*] used to describe a patient suffering from diarrhoea.

run-off *n* [*US*] [*Politics*] if no candidate in an electoral primary contest has gained a proper majority, then a run-off election is held between the two candidates who polled highest; all other runners-up are eliminated and their votes must be re-directed by the electors.

runoff *n* [*US*] [*Stock market*] the printing of the closing prices of a day's trading on the ticker tape at an exchange; if trading has been heavy, the runoff may continue for some time after actual trading has ceased.

run-of-the-loom *n* [*Textiles*] cloth that is shipped to the buyer direct from the loom without

inspection or elimination of defects. See also **run-of-the-mill.**

run-of-the-mill *n* [*Textiles*] second rate cloth which has not been inspected, or which is substandard. See also **run-of-the-loom.**

run-out 1. *n* [*UK*] [*Market-traders*] a market-based confidence trick: an article is offered for £1.00; when the buyer has paid over his cash, but has not yet received the article, he is persuaded to buy another of the same, plus the one he has already bought, for £2.50, plus his original pound-note; ideally this can then be escalated to a third article, plus the first two, plus the £2.50 already handed over, for £5.00. The right con-man given the right **punter** could well go on for ever. **2.** *n* [*UK*] [*Police, Crime*] a mock auction in which worthless material is sold at apparently super-bargain prices and with a great deal of obfuscatory patter and noise; thus 'run-out mob' means those who carry on mock auctions.

runt *n* [*US*] [*Railways*] See **dwarf.**

run-up *n* [*US*] [*Stock market*] the rapid increase in the value of a share or of a commodity.

runway-masher *n* [*Air Force*] a weapon that is geared to destroying hostile airbases and their runways; this is one of the proposed roles for the controversial 'cruise' missile.

ruptured duck 1. *n* [*US*] [*Air Force*] a damaged aircraft. **2.** *n* [*US*] [*Military*] a discharge medal awarded to US servicemen, which bears the motif of the US eagle.

rurp *n* [*Mountaineering*] acro **realised ultimate reality piton** a very small piton.

rush roller *n* [*US*] [*Medicine*] an emergency patient who is taken immediately to the operating room without the usual preparation of a shave, a scrub and an enema.

rushes *n pl* [*Film*] the day's takes, developed that same afternoon or evening and available for immediate consideration by all concerned. See also **dailies.**

Russian coupling *n* [*Logging*] a narrow, unsawn piece of wood that still connects two pieces of a log that has otherwise been sawn through for dividing into smaller lengths.

Russian drag *n* [*Rodeo*] trick riding on a horse: only one foot is in a strap while the rider's head hangs over the side of the horse.

rust out *v* [*Navy*] to retire from the sea.

rustic *a* [*Cheese-making*] See **earthy.**

rusty *a* [*Mining*] oxidised: it is applied especially to gold that will not amalgamate easily.

ryebuck *n* [*Sheep-shearing*] the top shearer, the expert; it comes from Yiddish 'rebbach' meaning 'profit'. See also **gun 4.**

R

S

s *Lat. abbr* [*Medicine*] a prescription notation meaning 'without'.

S and B boys *n pl* [*Sex*] abbr of **sex and breakfast boys** cheap **hustlers** who will barter their sexual services for a meal.

S and D *n* [*Theatre*] abbr of **song and dance**.

S sleep *n* [*Medicine*] abbr of **sychronised sleep** this is the deepest period of one's sleep, taking up some 75% of the sleeping cycle. See also **D sleep**.

S twist *n* [*Weaving*] the twist in yarn that is spun on to a spindle rotating counter-clockwise. See also **Z twist**.

sable *a* [*Heraldry*] black.

SAC *n* [*Military*] acro **Strategic Air Command** established in 1946 as an elite nuclear strike force – its motto is 'Peace Is Our Profession' – SAC currently controls two-thirds of the US **triad:** the strategic bombers and silo-based **ICBMs**. SAC HQ at Offutt Air Force Base near Omaha, Neb. is one of the three **hardened** US command posts from which a nuclear war would be directed.

saccharify *v* [*Distilling*] the process in distilling which takes place during the malting and mashtun stages by which the enzyme diastase turns the starch in the cereals into sugar, ready for the fermenting action of the yeast.

sachem *n* [*US*] [*Politics*] a political leader; it comes from the Algonquin Indian name for a supreme chief; it was first used around 1876.

sack **1.** *v* [*US*] [*Football*] to tackle the quarterback while he is retreating behind the line of scrimmage and is still preparing to pass the ball. **2.** *n* [*Baseball*] any one of the bases. **3.** *n* [*US*] [*Military*] bed or cot. See also **rack**.

sack, in the *adv* [*Drugs*] said of a dealer who has erroneously sold drugs to a federal or state policeman and who is inevitably heading to court and possibly jail.

sack time, also **sack drill** *n* [*US*] [*Marine Corps*] sleep.

sacker *n* [*Baseball*] any member of the fielding team playing on one of the bases; he is usually designated 'second sacker', 'third sacker', etc.

sacred *a* [*Computing*] reserved specifically for the exclusive use of something – a program, operator, etc.

sacred cow **1.** *n* [*Journalism*] a figure who is exempt from criticism, usually the family and friends of the proprietor. **2.** *n* [*Journalism*] copy that must be neither cut nor altered.

sacrifice hit *n* [*Baseball*] a tactical hit that inevitably dismisses the batter, but which advances one of his team from one base to another.

sacrificial pile, also **sacrificial anode** *n* [*Oil rigs*] a ring or slab of metal which is placed on a key part of an underwater structure to protect it from corrosion; the sea attacks the anode rather than the structure.

sadden *v* [*Weaving*] to dull and darken colour in natural dyeing, usually by adding iron **mordant** to the dyebath.

saddle **1.** *n* [*Building, Plastering*] a fibrous plaster back which holds pieces of a reverse mould in position. **2.** *n* [*Ceramics*] a fire-clay bar used to support ceramic ware during firing. **3.** *n* [*Electronics*] an insulating device designed to be fitted round an electric wire or conduit to hold it in place. **4.** *n* [*Gas industry*] a fitted plate, held in place by clamps, straps or welding over a hole which is punched or drilled in a gas main where a branch line or service connection is made. It may also serve to reinforce the pipeline. **5.** *n* [*Medicine*] in dentistry this is the base of the denture which actually holds the artificial teeth. **6.** *n* [*Tyre-making*] hooks on an overhead conveyor belt which carry the **green tyres**. **7.** *v* [*Deer stalking*] to sling the carcase of a recently killed stag across a pony's back.

saddle block *n* [*Medicine*] a technique of anaesthetising the perineal region by an injection in the lower spine.

Sadlers Wells makeup *n* [*UK*] [*Theatre*] makeup used by an impoverished company: plaster from the walls, dirt from beneath the seats.

safe area *n* [*TV*] that part of the TV image which will definitely be seen on a domestic receiver.

safe field *n* [*Cricket*] any player who is considered a particularly good fieldsman.

safe hand, by *adv* [*Navy*] said of classified documents which are to be transported by hand, using trustworthy couriers.

safe harbor 1. *n* [US] [Finance] any financial or accounting measure designed to avoid tax or legal liabilities. **2.** *n* [US] [Finance] a provision in law that excuses liability for a financial misdemeanour if the company concerned can prove a genuine attempt to comply in good faith with the law in question. **3.** *n* [US] [Finance] a means of fighting off a takeover bid whereby the target company purchases a business that is so heavily regulated, eg. a broadcasting company, that the target company no longer presents so alluring a target.

safe house *n* [Espionage] a building used for housing defectors or other sensitive individuals, or for meetings during clandestine operations to give instructions to, or to debrief, an agent. It is also used by secret police for the imprisonment and/or torture of their victims.

safety 1. *n* [Baseball] a safe hit. **2.** *n* [US] [Football] a safety man: a player who plays in the deepest back position on the field. **3.** *n* [US] [Football] the act of carrying the ball into one's own end-zone and the concomitant sacrifice of two points.

safety paper *n* [Printing] specially treated paper which is designed to resist forgery and unauthorised alterations.

safety stock *n* [Economics] See **buffer stock**.

safety valve *n* [US] [Football] a forward-pass play which gives the passer the option of throwing the ball to a secondary or second-choice receiver when the primary or intended receiver is guarded by defenders.

safing *n* [Military] the reducing of (nuclear) weapons from a state of immediate readiness to fire back, to a safe condition, once the emergency that caused their arming has passed.

sag 1. *n* [Cycling] a saddle that has become limp through excessive use or mis-adjustment. **2.** *v* [Lacrosse] used of a defender who moves away from the opponent back towards the goal; this is at right angles to the lateral floating. See **float 12**.

sagger *n* [Ceramics] a box made of fire clay into which delicate ceramic articles are placed while being fired.

sagger bung *n* [Ceramics] a stack of **saggers**.

sail *n* [Navy] the conning tower of a submarine.

sailer *n* [Baseball] a pitched fast ball that takes off, ie: it sails.

sailing *n* [US] [Painting] a painting job that encounters no obstruction or difficulties.

sailor-boy *n* [US] [Painting] a painter who is good at working on a high scaffold.

sailor's disgrace *n* [Navy] the fouled anchor emblem of the Royal Navy.

sailor's knife *n* [Navy] a knife with the point broken off; all points were broken off knives at the start of old voyages so as to stop anyone using them as weapons.

sailor's knot *n* [Sailing, Ropework] any good or unfamiliar knot.

salamander *n* [Building] a small portable stove used to heat buildings still under construction and to ensure that vital materials such as plaster and concrete do not freeze.

salami *n* [Finance] a computer-based bank fraud: the bank's computer is instructed to shave a thin slice – eg: 1p or the odd pence under 10p – from each account held in its files and to credit a specific account, pseudonymously named, with the sums thereby produced.

salami tactics *n pl* [Politics] a term coined in 1952 by Matyas Rakosi, communist premier of Hungary, to explain how the Party cuts out its opponents in slices, by forcing its nominal allies to purge themselves to such an extent that they are soon too weak to stand against the Communists when they make their bid for power.

sale-proof *a* [US] [Car salesmen] said of a car that looks good in the press or TV advertisement, but which does not appeal to a buyer.

sales engineer *n* [Marketing] a salesman who has specialised technical knowledge of the application of the product in question and can back up basic sales techniques with this.

Sallie Mae *n* [US] [Finance] the Student Loan Marketing Association which was established in 1972 to finance loans to college students. See also **Freddie Mac, Ginnie Mae.**

salopettes *n pl* [Skiing] snow-proof, dungaree-type trousers; it comes from Fr. slang for a pair of canvas trousers that are worn over another pair.

SALT I *n* [Military] acro **Strategic Arms Limitations Talks (I)** talks between the superpowers that lasted from 1969 to the signature in 1972 of the Anti-Ballistic Missile Treaty (**ABM Treaty**). Like all such talks, national strategic interest ensured that little real progress in reducing the arms race could be achieved but the feeling in 1972 was that the world was a safer place. SALT I stands in retrospect as the peak achievement of **detente**. See also **SALT II, SALT III.**

SALT II *n* [Military] acro **Strategic Arms Limitations Talks (II)** a series of ultimately inconclusive negotiations that began in Vladivostock in 1974 and ran on to Vienna in 1979. While President Carter and Secretary Brezhnev signed a document which provided for some very broad restrictions on the arms that can be held by each superpower, the US Congress refused to ratify the treaty and it remained in suspension. In effect, the two powers have held to SALT II, but neither side has felt constrained in any way to restrict their research and development of new and more devastating weapons. See also **SALT I, SALT III.**

SALT III *n* [Military] acro **Strategic Arms Limitations Talks part III** the round of arms talks that were scheduled to follow on the SALT II talks which had ended with the unratified agreement

S

of 1979. These talks were intended, inter alia, to consider the problem of intermediate-range weapons based in the European theatre. Although President Reagan promised in 1980 to prepare for new arms negotiations, there were no immediate developments. In the event SALT III as such never materialised. Instead the abortive **INF** and **START** talks were commenced, neither of which managed to achieve any real progress. See also **SALT I, SALT II.**

salt a memo v [US] [Government] a technique for checking for possible leaks in the bureaucracy by altering a memo that goes to a number of individuals/departments by just one word; thus, if a leak does occur, and the document is reproduced, it will be possible to narrow down the culprit to those who received that specific version.

salt a mine v [Mining] to scatter gold or gems around a mine, which in fact has proved worthless or been worked out, in order to convince someone to buy or invest in it.

salt an account, also **salt the books** v [Commerce] to make fictitious entries in a firm's books in order to persuade a potential buyer of that firm that it is worth far more than is actually true. It comes from the practice of 'salting a mine': the dumping of a few genuine diamonds, gold nuggets or whatever the mine was supposed to yield, in the area under consideration, so that the prospective investor would think he was putting money into something other than the actual dud that was being peddled.

salt and pepper n [US] [Police] a two-man police team composed of one white and one black officer.

salt horse n [Navy] an officer of the executive branch who transfers to a specialist branch and thus forfeits his place on the promotion ladder.

salt the route v [US] [Music] to tour one's own juke-box installations, putting in one's own money, to convince the renters that they are highly profitable.

salted weapon n [Military] a nuclear weapon whose explosion will yield more than average levels of radiation. See also **enhanced radiation weapon.**

saltgrit n [UK] [Surfing] the beach, the shore.

salting n [Cheese-making] a step in the manufacture of cheeses which comes after the unmolding of fresh cheeses; it is performed either by hand sprinkling for small soft cheeses, or by immersion in brine for uncooked pressed cheeses.

salting out n [Medicine] a method of abortion in which a saline solution is injected into the uterus in place of the amniotic fluid; this should kill off the foetus within one hour.

saltire n [Heraldry] a broad diagonal cross, St. Andrew's Cross.

salto n [Gymnastics] a somersault; it comes from Ital.

salts, also **salt water** n [Glass-making] See **gall 1.**

salvage operations n [Espionage] the destruction of incriminating evidence.

salvos [Military] air intercept code for I am about to open fire.

sam n [US] [Law] any member of a federal rather than state or local law-enforcement agency, who is working for 'Uncle Sam'.

SAM n [Military] acro **suface-to-air missile** a prefix that is generally restricted to descriptions of Soviet anti-aircraft missiles.

samizdat n [Politics] this comes from Rus. for 'self-publishing'; it is the dissident 'underground press' that works to copy and disseminate otherwise forbidden literature, criticism and other works that are banned in the USSR and its satellites.

samm, also **sammy** v [Tanning] to pile hides together and to ensure that all of them are evenly watered throughout.

SAMOS n [Military] acro **Satellite and Missile Observation System** one of the three military satellite programmes developed in the wake of the Sputnik I launch in 1959, that was intended to initiate a satellite reconnaissance programme. Initially called 'Sentry' the SAMOS programme was launched in January 1961 when a satellite was put into earth orbit for 20 days, radioing detailed inventories of Soviet ICBM sites and general military topography. SAMOS was the first satellite to give detailed information on Russia from remote sensors, instead of relying on U–2 spy overflights, or even **humint** spies working from within the country.

sampling n [Photo-typesetting] the frequency with which an **analog** design is measured to record changes in the design. The more frequent the sampling, the more recorded measurements, and thus the finer the resolution of the digital record available for subsequent processing and output on a typesetter.

sampling frame n [Marketing] the control data for a market research study, specifying targets, limits, structure, etc.

samson n, v [Logging] a stout pole, sometimes notched into the tree stem at one end and braced at the other, which is used to push a small tree manually in the desired direction.

Samson post n [Oil rigs] a post which bears the weight of the walking beam and the **drill string** in a cable-tool rig, or the rod string in a pumping well.

samurai bond n [Stock market] used in Japan for a **bond** issued by a foreign entity, denominated in yen and purchasable by non-residents of Japan.

sanctifier n [Espionage] one of a team of agents engaged in a sanctifying or blackmailing operation against a specific target. See also **set-up 2, skit, sugar and sweetening.**

sanctify v [Espionage] to blackmail a target for the sake of using such blackmail to obtain infor-

S

mation, create a double agent, force a defection, etc.

sanctuary radar n [*Military*] long-range air-defence radar that does not reveal its presence to approaching aircraft and which can thus be neither jammed nor attacked.

sanctuary strategy n [*Military*] the concept of a European nation, most obviously the UK since it is an island, using its nuclear capability to persuade the Soviets to attack a lesser, weaker member of NATO. In essence this implies disloyalty to NATO and opting out of a war to which one is bound by a treaty, but it can be rationalised by the role that the UK has in acting as a staging post for US forces on their way to Europe. The importance of the UK to the US war effort is also seen as a reason for the Soviets to hold back – attack the UK and the US will certainly take steps to defend its 'unsinkable aircraft carrier'. Conversely, the fact of being a US staging post must make the UK a prime target for Soviet missiles, aimed to disable its use as a forward base. See also **second decision centre, trigger theory.**

sand 1. n [*US*] [*Cattlemen*] courage, bravery. 2. n [*US*] [*Prisons*] sugar. 3. v [*Gambling*] to mark the edges of cards by sandpapering them.

sand and spinach n [*Military*] brown and green 'jungle' camouflage.

sandbag 1. v [*Cars*] to drive a car at high speed, especially when competing in and winning a race. 2. v [*Chess*] to lose games intentionally while playing in a tournament so as to diminish one's overall rating and gain a place in a lower section of a subsequent tournament. Thus the 'demoted' player will gain easier victories and probably win a cash prize. 3. n [*Gambling*] a betting situation in poker where two players are locked into raising each other and continue to do this with no consideration for the third player, who is unwilling to drop out, but equally loath to bet so heavily.

sandbagging n [*Motor-racing*] a motor-car and motor-cycle racing stratagem whereby the favourite lets the rest of the field go ahead, confident that when necessary he can regain the lead and win as expected.

sandgropers n pl [*Cricket*] the Western Australia state cricket team. See also **banana benders, crow eaters.**

sandpapering n [*US*] [*Law*] See **horseshedding**.

sandpit n [*UK*] [*TV*] a large-scale map used by TV news and current affairs programmes to illustrate the progress of wars, sites of disasters, etc.

sandwich 1. n [*Building, Concrete workers*] a waterproof layer that is inserted between two layers of concrete. 2. n [*US*] [*Garment trade*] a flaring seam. 3. n [*Table tennis*] a table tennis rubber which consists of sponge and pimpled rubber (**pimples** in or out) which must be stuck with the sponge rubber side next to the bat.

sandwich debenture n [*Banking*] an arrangement between banks and the Industrial & Commercial Finance Corporation when they both lend to the same company: the banks have first call on floating assets, the ICFC has first call on fixed assets.

sandwich play n [*Lacrosse*] See **double team.**

sanfan n [*Politics*] See **three anti.**

sang a [*US*] [*Medicine*] abbr of **sanguinous** a type of drainage where the red blood cells are present. See also **sero.**

sanitation n [*Computing*] the wiping out of sensitive material from memory systems and memory media.

sanitise v [*Espionage*] to remove any embarrassing, incriminating or classified material from documents that are revealed to the public – as under the US Freedom of Information Act – or circulated within government departments where they may be read by 'insecure' people; by extension it is in general use in government/political circles where it refers to the keeping of such 'dirt' away from the public or the media.

sanitised violence n [*TV, Film*] screened violence that is so stylised and so far removed from reality – eg: that on TV's popular 'A Team' – that its effects in creating real, copycat, violence among the viewers can be seen as minimal if any.

sans n [*Printing*] type that has no serifs – the flourishes and adornments on individual letters.

sapling n [*Coursing*] a coursing greyhound whelped on or after January 1st of the same year in which the season of running commenced.

sappy a [*US*] [*Meat trade*] said of lambs which are still carrying milk fat and which are generally marketed at four months of age.

sar n [*Medicine*] acro **senior assistant resident** at a hospital. See also **jar 1.**

saratoga n [*Tobacco*] a box or hamper used to transport the tobacco around the factory during various stages of processing.

sarbut n [*UK*] [*Police*] a term used only in Birmingham, which means a police informer.

satellite 1. n [*Commerce*] an enterprise that sells its products to one or two large firms only and thus finds its fortunes completely tied to those of the major firms in question. 2. n [*Computing*] a computer which forms part of a system but which is much less capable than the mainframe. Situated at a distance from the main system, it works on auxiliary functions such as printing or remote data entry. It is now nearly synonymous with 'terminal'. 3. v [*TV*] to transmit foreign news and other programmes by one of the various communications satellites. See also **bird 5, 6** and **7, feed 5.**

satellites n pl [*Audio*] small speakers that use a sub-woofer.

satisfaction note n [*Commerce*] in insurance

S

this is an acknowledgement by an individual who is claiming repayment from an insurance company, that the repairs to his car after a crash are satisfactory.

satisfaction piece *n [Real estate]* a notice issued to confirm that a mortgage has been fully paid.

satisfiability *n [Computing]* the property exhibited by any well-formed formula or logical expression for which it is possible to assign values to variables in such a way that the formula or expression is true.

satisficing *n [Business]* aiming for a special predetermined level of profits, sales or allied form of business success; the inference is that this level is specific and that one is not merely trying for a general degree of improvement but for a given goal. It is also used in business as a more complex synonym for 'satisfy'.

saturation *n [TV]* a degree of purity in colour signals: the greater the saturation, the more intense the colour.

saturation attack *n [Military]* an attack that is intended to overstretch enemy defences and to destroy as many as possible suspected targets.

saturation noise 1. *n [Computing]* extraneous material that must be removed from data when that data is being used. 2. *n [Computing]* errors that develop in the data that is held in a system. 3. *n [Computing]* random variations in the characteristics of a given entity. 4. *n [Computing]* any disturbance that tends to interfere with the normal operation of a device or system.

Saturday Night Special *n [US] [Medicine]* a patient – often a derelict and/or alcoholic – who appears regularly at the hospital on Saturday night hoping to gain admission and thus a bed and food for the weekend.

Saturday night special 1. *n [Finance]* a takeover tactic in which the buyer attempts to purchase a bulk share in a company's stocks, without warning that company of his move, so that he can attempt to pre-empt any efforts to challenge the bid. See also **dawn raid.** 2. *n [US] [Police, Crime]* a small handgun, often purchased through a mail-order firm, which is carried on, and is often used to satisfy the mindless passion of, a Saturday night; such weapons are responsible for a large proportion of US murders.

saucer *n [Finance]* a saucer shaped line on a graph of share price movements which indicates that a share has reached a low and has since begun to rise.

saucing *n [Tobacco]* See **greasing.**

saunter *[Military]* air intercept code for: fly for the best endurance your aircraft can offer.

sausage board *n [Surfing]* a surfboard that is rounded at both ends.

save *v [Theatre, TV, Film]* See **kill 5.**

save the food! *excl [Film]* an instruction to actors and technicians not to eat prop food, since a shot may have to be taken again.

save-all *n [Industry]* any form of filtering equipment that is used to reclaim pulp, fillers or chemicals from solution.

saw and hammer *n [US] [Carpenters]* a carpenter who carries his own tools to every new job.

saw the baby in half *v phr [Business]* to make a management decision à la Solomon, ie. one which will satisfy neither of two opposing parties and which in the long run may result in the cancellation of a project or plan.

sawdust joint *n [Gambling]* an inferior or unpretentious casino. See also **carpet joint.**

say *n [Shooting]* birds get 'a say' when they are permitted to feed without disturbance.

sbirri *n [Crime]* this comes from Sicilian and means 'the traditional enemy', ie: the police.

SBL *n [Military]* abbr of **Space Based Lasers** current researches are investigating the possibility of laser-equipped space stations acting as ballistic missile defences (**BMD**) and anti-satellite weapons (**ASAT**). Supporters of the militarisation of space, who include President Reagan since his 'Star Wars' speech of March 1983, the USAF's 'spacemen', and a number of conservatives in politics and the academic-military-industrial complex, hope to see a laser-based BMD system which will, they believe, put paid to **assured destruction** for ever. See also **BMD, SDI, star wars.**

scab 1. *n [Glass-making]* See **gall 2.** 2. *n [Industrial relations]* a worker who refuses to join his/her peers when a strike has been called. 3. *n [Metallurgy]* in iron founding this is a casting defect caused by the buckling, cracking and/or breaking up of the sand surface of a mould or core. 4. *n [Metallurgy]* a relatively thin film or tongue of metal that is poorly attached to the surface of the steel.

scab union, also **company union** *n [Industrial relations]* any union which is more inclined to satisfy the demands of the company by whom its members are employed, than those of the workers themselves.

scad *n [Mining]* the gold that remains after ore has been washed.

scagiola *n [Building, Plastering]* an imitation of marble, consisting of a hard plaster which is coloured with powdered dyes.

scale 1. *v [Coal-mining]* to regulate air currents along a roadway. 2. *n [Entertainment]* the regular rate for the job, act, performance, etc; thus to 'pay scale' is to pay the basic rate, as negotiated by the union, without any special rates for VIPs or celebrities. 3. *n [Glass-making]* an imperfection occurring as a small piece of metal oxide or carbon embedded in the glass. 4. *n [Metallurgy]* the black scaly coating of oxide that forms on metal when heated for processing. 5. *n [Logging]* an estimation of the sound timber in a log or group of logs. 6. *n [Mining]* a piece of rock that has broken off or is seen to be ready to break off and fall.

scaler n [*Industrial relations*] the union-negotiated and determined rate for the job.

scaling n [*Computing*] the adjustment of the values used within a computation so that they adapt correctly to the process or equipment being used.

scalings n pl [*Coal-mining*] pieces of rock which break away and fall from the roof or sides of an excavation.

scallop n [*TV*] a distortion of the screen that renders the picture 'wavy'.

scalp v [*Futures market*] to trade for small gains; it usually involves the establishment and liquidation of a **position** within a short time, often on the same day.

scalper 1. n [*US*] [*Stock market*] an investment adviser who buys a security, then recommends it to clients whose purchases push up the price, at which point he sells. 2. n [*US*] [*Theatre*] a ticket tout who buys tickets in bulk and then sells them to desperate customers at several times their real value.

scalp-hunters n pl [*Espionage*] members of the intelligence services who are on the lookout for potential defectors and who will help them to achieve their intention.

scalping n [*Logging*] clearing the vegetation from the surface of an area of land.

scaly a [*US*] [*Painting*] used to describe a building in a very run-down condition which will need a great deal of preparatory work before starting to paint it.

scaly back n [*Navy*] a naval pensioner.

scam n, v [*Crime, Drugs*] any form of trick, swindle, racket or confidence game; specifically it is a large-scale scheme for the importation and selling of illegal drugs.

scamp n [*Advertising*] a rough sketch of the proposed design for an advertisement.

scandal sheet n [*US*] [*Painting*] a comprehensive list of all the extra work – making good, touch-up, etc – that is submitted by the client to the contractor and which must be carried out before he pays over the painters' wages.

Scans n pl [*Sex*] abbr of **Scandinavians** imported, probably smuggled, magazines, books and films of Danish and Swedish pornography; they are supposedly 'harder' than the UK variety and hence more expensive.

scare head n [*Journalism*] a large, boldface, headline, used for sensational or dramatic stories, the content of which may not necessarily be frightening.

scarf 1. n [*Forestry*] a V-shaped incision cut into a trunk during felling which governs the direction in which the tree will fall; thus it also refers to the sloping surface left in the wood by such an incision. 2. n [*UK*] [*Railways*] a foreman who is always 'around the necks' of his men.

scarfing n [*Metallurgy*] the removal of surface defects from ingots or semi-finished products using an oxy-acetylene flame.

Scargillism n [*Politics*] left-wing extremism, typified by the bending, manipulation or simple over-riding of rules to suit one's own dictatorial ends; it comes from Establishment condemnations of Arthur Scargill, President of the National Union of Mineworkers.

scarlet a [*Hunting*] the colour of a red hunting coat; the common term 'pink' is incorrect.

scarlet pimpernel n [*UK*] [*Railways*] a person who can never be found when required; it comes from Baroness Orczy's dare-devil gentleman, created in 1905.

scarper v [*UK*] [*Market-traders*] to run away; go away!

scatback n [*US*] [*Football*] a fast-running backfield player.

scatter 1. v [*Baseball*] when a pitcher keeps the score down and yields only a few hits. 2. n [*Photography*] the internal reflection of a small portion of light. See also **flare 6**.

scattering n [*Photo-typesetting*] the increase in size of the dot on the cathode ray tube (CRT) due to reflection from adjacent grains of phosphor; attempts to reduce this phenomenon by the use of fine-grained phosphor also tend to reduce the intensity of the original spot.

scatter-read n [*Computing*] the ability to take information from a single physical record and then distribute it around several separate locations within the core memory. See also **gather-write**.

scatters n [*Navy*] diarrhoea.

scattershot approach n [*Business*] a method of approaching a problem by taking a wide variety of random, hopeful approaches – like firing a shotgun towards a bird, hoping to catch it in the spreading shot – rather than taking one specific, worked out approach.

scattersite housing, also **scattered site housing** n [*US*] [*Government*] government-sponsored housing that is intended to break up the concentration of the poor in inner-city ghettos, by spreading such projects throughout all areas of the city.

scavenger sale n [*Real estate*] a property that has been put up for sale because the previous tenants failed to keep up their rental or mortgage payments and were evicted.

scavenging n [*Computing*] See **browsing, hacker 2**.

scawp v [*UK*] [*Market-traders*] to strike, to hit.

scenario 1. n [*Sociology, Business*] a corruption of the film use (see 2) which extends its meaning to include any course of action, description of an event, circumstance, happening etc. 2. also **shooting script** n [*Film*] the script from which the film will actually be shot, with the dialogue, the camera angles and all other technical directions included.

S

schedography *n* [*Education*] the writing of notes and information on the backs of envelopes.

scheduled territory *n* [*Economics*] between 1947 and 1972, this referred to any group of countries, usually within the British Commonwealth, whose currencies were linked to sterling; after 1972, only the UK, the Channel Isles and the Isle of Man were regarded as the scheduled territories.

schematic *n* [*Computing*] a diagram of the elements of a system, and the connections between them.

scheme advertising *n* [*Advertising*] See **above the line 1**. See also **theme advertising**.

schermuly *n* [*Navy*] the telling of 'tall' stories; it comes from the Schermuly pistol which was used to 'shoot a line' from one ship to another.

schlepper *n* [*Air travel*] a small cart used at airports; luggage can be secured on it by an elastic strap and thus more easily moved around by its owner; it comes from Yiddish 'schlep' meaning 'to drag'.

schleppers *n pl* [*Entertainment*] this comes from Yiddish 'schlep' meaning to drag, haul, carry; it is the entourage of hangers-on that surround a star performer. See also **gofer, ligger 3**.

schlockbuster *n* [*Video*] a video programme – often of the sex-and-violence **nasty** category – that sells well despite a lack of any ostensible artistic or popular merit; it is based on the movies' 'blockbuster' plus 'shlock' (Yiddish for 'trash').

schmatte, also **schmutter** *n* [*Fashion*] this comes from Yiddish 'schmatte' meaning a rag meaning clothing; the 'rag trade'.

scholium *n* [*Bibliography*] a scholar's learned remark or explanatory comment which is placed in the margin.

school of instruction *n* [*US*] [*Carpenters*] the carpenter's tool box.

schooler *n* [*Angling*] a sea trout.

schoolie *n* [*UK*] [*Military*] a classroom instructor.

schoolmarm *n* [*Logging*] an inverted crotch, usually at the base of a treetrunk, that is often caused by two trunks growing together.

schooner on the rocks *n* [*Navy*] a joint of meat baked with batter and potatoes.

schuss-boom *v* [*Skiing*] to ski at high speed.

scientific management, also **Taylorism** *n* [*Management*] the theories of US engineer Frederick W. Taylor (1856–1915): managers should (1) develop, through scientific analysis and experiment, the optimum means of performing each task; (2) select and train workers to use the best methods; (3) co-operate with workers, and view management and productive work as absolutely equal partners in a single enterprise; Taylor's theories were developed and they formed the foundations of modern attempts at work study.

scientific notation *n* [*Computing*] See **floating point**.

scientism **1.** *n* [*Sociology*] the concept that in the name of science anything can be promoted and accepted: goods, values, services, decisions, etc. **2.** *n* [*Sociology*] the concept that scientific methods are the only methods fit for the study of humanity in any of its forms.

scissor *v* [*Computing*] in computer graphics this is to remove those parts of a display that lie outside a designated area.

scissor cross *n* [*Theatre*] the simultaneous crossing of the stage by two actors, each moving in the opposite direction.

scissor up *v* [*Business*] corporate plagiarism: to cut up and reassemble a variety of concepts, theories and ideas which have not originated in one's own head but which, it is hoped, will please or fool those to whom they are presented.

scissorbill *n* [*US*] [*Industrial relations*] a non-union worker; a worker who has some source of income other than his/her wages.

scissoring *n* [*Computing*] See **windowing**.

scissors play *n* [*Sport*] an offensive tactic, in rugby, hockey or lacrosse, in which two players cut past each other closely at right angles; it may or may not involve the change of ball possession as they pass.

sclaff *n* [*Golf*] a stroke in which the club hits the ground rather than the ball.

scoop **1.** *v* [*Medicine*] to perform a mastectomy. **2.** *n, v* [*Journalism*] an exclusive story or interview gained ahead of, or without the knowledge of one's rivals; thus it also means to gain such an exclusive. See also **beat 2**. **3.** *n* [*Surfing*] the upturned nose of the board. **4.** *n* [*TV*] a 500W light suspended from the ceiling.

scoop the field *v* [*Flying*] See **drag the field**.

scoopy *a* [*Fashion*] said of a garment which is scoop-necked and low cut.

scooter *n* [*UK*] [*Buses*] a small, single-decker, London Transport bus.

scope *v* [*Medicine*] a general medical abbreviation which refers, in a general context, to a variety of medical and surgical instruments and their use on a patient.

scope and sequence *n* [*Education*] the amount of material covered in a syllabus, and the order in which it is presented to the pupils.

scorched earth *n* [*US*] [*Commerce*] methods used by a company which wishes to avoid being taken over; the company sells off the most attractive part of its business, arranges for debts to fall due immediately after a merger, etc. See also **poison pill**.

score **1.** *n* [*Gambling*] the money won in a game or at a casino. **2.** *v* [*Gambling*] to win money by gambling. **3.** *v* [*Gambling*] to win money by cheating. **4.** *v* [*Drugs*] to buy drugs. **5.** *v* [*Hunting*] said of the whole pack when it gives tongue to a strong scent. **6.** also **hit** *v* [*Public relations*] to find a media outlet for a piece of promotion and thus to please the client for whom that piece was designed.

scorer n [*Logging*] one who scores off the outer portion of a tree trunk before the hewer takes over the felling operation.

scorp n [*UK*] [*Military*] abbr of **scorpion** an inhabitant of Gibraltar.

scotch block n [*Coal-mining*] a wedge-shaped block placed beneath the front wheels of a tub or wagon to act as an improvised brake.

Scotchman n [*Sailing, Ropework*] a wooden batten used to protect ropes from chafing.

scotia n [*Building, Plastering*] a common moulding section: two quarter circles, one twice as large as the other.

Scotsman's fifth n [*UK*] [*Road transport*] coasting along, using a mythical gear ratio. See also **Aberdeen booster**.

scour n [*UK*] [*Coal-mining*] See **drivage 1**.

scouring n [*Coal-mining*] a roadway driven through the **goaf**.

scout n [*Oil industry*] an employee hired specifically to keep an eye on the activities of rival companies.

scout up v [*US*] [*Medicine*] to prepare for an operation; it is used of staff rather than patients, who are 'prepped'.

scow n [*US*] [*Road transport*] a low-sided truck or rig used for hauling pipe or steel.

scramble 1. v [*Espionage, Military*] to make a telephone call unintelligible to potential eavesdroppers by using a scrambler to distort the spoken words; only by using equipment to unscramble the resulting electronic noise can the call be understood. 2. v [*Military*] to take off rapidly.

scrambled egg n [*Military*] the gold braid worn on an officer's cap.

scrambled merchandising n [*Commerce*] the offering for sale by a retailer of a line or lines of goods that are not usually carried by that type of shop; ie: Christmas cards at the butchers, etc.

scrambling n [*Satellite TV*] the mixing of audio and visual signals so as to make them incomprehensible to anyone who is unable to decipher them with specific decoding equipment.

scran 1. n, v [*UK*] [*Market-traders*] food; to eat. 2. n [*UK*] [*Military*] food.

scrap n [*Advertising*] a photograph or other illustration that is cut from a magazine or newspaper and used as a guide for a drawing, or for getting a rough idea of how a photo-session should be arranged to obtain the required pictures for a proposed advertisement.

scrap iron n [*US*] [*Prisons*] weights used for exercising in the prison gym.

scrape n [*UK*] [*Military*] a hideout dug 18in deep and covered first with chicken wire and then hessian netting threaded with grass and plants.

scratch 1. v [*Computing*] to delete a work file. 2. v [*Horse-racing*] to withdraw a horse from a race after the period allowed for so doing has expired. 3. v [*Snooker*] to make a stroke that incurs a penalty; specifically it means hitting the cue ball into a pocket. 4. n [*Navy*] the captain's secretary.

scratch coat, also **rendering coat** n [*Building, Plastering*] the first coat of plaster to be applied to the **background**.

scratch comma n [*Printing*] a comma that is formed of a fine, oblique line, rather than the usual curve.

scratch disk n [*Computing*] a blank formatted floppy disk which does not contain data.

scratch hit n [*Baseball*] a hit that is neither an error nor a clean base hit, but one which still allows a batter to reach first base safely.

scratch line n [*Printing*] the line that divides the numerator and the denominator in the printing of a fraction: ¼, ⅛, etc.

scratch paper n [*Gambling*] cards that have been marked with tiny pinpricks within the pattern of the backs.

scratch party n [*US*] [*Hotels*] See **mickey party**.

scratch wig n [*Theatre*] a rough wig used by actors in comic roles.

scratcher n [*Oil rigs*] a wire 'brush' which is inserted into the drill pipe near the bit end to overcome possible mud sticking and to cut through any build-up of dirt.

scratching 1. n [*UK*] [*Dustmen*] scavenging for saleable goods, scrap, etc, left in dustbins or on the street. 2. n [*Music*] the use by the disc jockey of two or three turntables, each holding a different record, to create a composite musical collage; the 'scratching' refers to the movement of the stylus on each of his turntables to a pre-selected spot on the record. 3. n [*Rodeo*] spurring the horse up and down its sides with a constant kicking motion while it bucks; this continuous motion is demanded by rodeo rules.

scratchpad, also **workspace** n [*Computing*] an area of a machine's memory which is reserved for short-term working with, or storage of, material that can then be erased; it is a small, fast and re-usable memory.

screamer 1. n [*Motor trade*] in the second-hand motor trade this is a persistently complaining customer. 2. n [*Golf*] a particularly powerful shot. 3. n [*US*] [*Medicine*] an hysterical patient. 4. n [*Journalism*] a large headline. 5. n [*Printing*] an exclamation mark.

screaming area n [*US*] [*Medicine*] See **pits**.

screech n [*Espionage*] in the CIA this is an ordinary tape recording so speeded up that when played down a telephone line it merely sounds like interference or some form of malfunction on the line; once received it is played at normal speed and the required message is made clear.

screed n [*Building, Plastering*] a narrow band of material or batten used as a guide to ruling off subsequent material to a true and even surface.

screef n [*Forestry*] to turn over land with a mattock or a plough to clear away the undergrowth (possibly to make tree growth easier), to remove traces of a forest fire, etc.

screen 1. *v* [*Ice-hockey*] to obstruct the goalminder's view at the moment when the puck is driven towards his net. **2.** *n* [*Audio*] any form of electronic wrapping or shielding that provides a screen around or between various components, cables, circuits, etc. within a system. **3.** *n* [*Building, Concrete workers*] a large mechanical sieve. **4.** *n* [*Coal-mining*] See **brattice**. **5.** *n* [*US*] [*Football*] a manoeuvre that cuts an opponent off from the play. **6.** *n* [*Sport*] in US football and lacrosse, an offensive technique designed to delay temporarily the progress of an opponent, or to force him/her to move in a path other than that which is desired. **7.** *n* [*Navy*] the superstructure of a warship. **8.** *n* [*US*] [*Painting*] an implement in a can or pot of paint against which the roller can be revolved, to remove excess paint before it is used.

screenplay *n* [*Film*] a film script which contains the plot and dialogue, but no technical instructions. See also **shooting script.**

screenwash *n* [*Advertising, Business*] a light or group of lights used to cast a subtle coloured glow over a screen and the stage in front of it, during a business theatre presentation when no visual material is actually being shown.

screeve *n* [*UK*] [*Market-traders*] a motor-car.

screw 1. *v* [*Cricket*] to put spin on a ball. **2.** *v* [*UK*] [*Crime, Police*] to break and enter; thus 'screwer' is a skilful housebreaker. **3.** *v* [*UK*] [*Market-traders*] to look at. **4.** also **twirl** *n* [*UK*] [*Prisons*] a warder, a prison officer. See also **corned beef, white shirt.**

screwball *n* [*Baseball*] a ball pitched with reverse spin against the natural curve.

screwdriver job *n* [*Industrial relations*] factory work that consists simply of the final assembly of parts manufactured elsewhere and delivered to the factory. It is often the practice of multinational corporations who maximise profits out of such divisions of labour.

screwdriver operation *n* [*Industry*] any semi-skilled task that demands the ability to operate a screwdriver, but little else.

scrieve *v* [*Navy*] said of a naval architect who draws up a ship's lines and plans.

scrim *n* [*Building, Plastering*] hessian material woven in a mesh wide enough to allow plaster to pass through it easily, both to strengthen and to reinforce the joints between the plasterboards.

scrip *n* [*Stock market*] any form of security, especially those in **bearer** form.

scrip issue *n* [*Stock market*] an issue of shares to existing share-holders that is made possible by the **capitalisation** of reserves.

scrivener *n* [*Finance*] a person who, for a fee or commission, places his clients' money as loans to trustworthy borrowers.

scroll *v* [*Computing*] the moving up or down of a 'page' of information on the computer's screen.

scroop *n* [*Textiles*] the rustling sound and crisp feel associated especially with silk which has been treated with weak mineral acid; it can be imparted to other fabrics by a special treatment.

scrub 1. *n* [*Aerospace*] a mission that has been cancelled either before or during the countdown, and prior to the launch. **2.** *n* [*Glass-painting*] a brush used to scrape out lights in a coat of paint. **3.** *n* [*Sport*] a player belonging to a weaker team in a sport; a team composed of such second-rate players. **4.** *v* [*Horse-racing*] said of a jockey who moves his arms and legs during a ride, especially towards the end of a race. **5.** *v* [*Gas industry*] See **wash 3.**

scrubber *n* [*US*] [*Navy*] a mechanism for the disposal of the carbon monoxide created by the continual breathing of the around 150–strong crew of a nuclear submarine.

scrubbing *n* [*Technology*] the removal of certain impurities from either manufactured or natural gas by passing it through an oil spray or bubbling it through an oilbath.

scrubs 1. *n pl* [*US*] [*Hotels*] hotel maids, chambermaids. **2.** *n pl* [*US*] [*Meat trade*] See **mongrels**

scrunge *v* [*Tiddleywinks*] to pot a wink which then bounces out of the pot again.

scudding *n* [*Tanning*] the removal of hair and flesh from the hide prior to tanning.

scuftings *n* [*Coal-mining*] See **gummings.**

scull *n* [*Glass-making*] the glass remaining in a ladle after most of the molten glass has been poured out.

sculling *n* [*Swimming*] a style of swimming based on a very gentle movement on the surface of the water; the swimmer is on his back, the body is stretched out and the hands move up and down at the sides; it comes from the rowing use.

scullion gullies *n pl* [*US*] [*Navy*] moulded plastic trays used in naval messes to facilitate serving portions of food.

scumble *v* [*TV, Film*] to age a set artificially.

scumbling *n* [*Painting*] a painting technique in which portions of the last coat are removed or textured while still wet so as to expose part of the colour underneath.

scut 1. *n* [*US*] [*Medicine*] a patient held in low esteem by the staff. **2.** also **scut work** *n* [*US*] [*Medicine*] all the trivial and/or unpleasant tasks that have to be performed in a hospital – dirty, tedious or both – and are assigned to the junior member of the medical team.

scuttle *n* [*Cars*] the main bulkhead at the base of the windscreen which gives the body part of its torsional stiffness; it is developed from the dashboard of the earliest cars, whose owners grew tired of keeping their knees warm with rugs.

scuttlebutt *n* [*US*] [*Navy, Marine Corps*] gossip, it comes from the original meaning of scuttlebutt: a ship's water cask or drinking fountain, and hence the idle chatter between those men who gathered there for a drink.

scye *n* [*Clothing*] the armhole of a coat, jacket or shirt.

SDI 1. *n* [*Communications*] abbr of **selective dissemination of information** systems, often based on a computer database, which attempt to distribute selections of up-to-date publications on various topics to individuals who have submitted a statement of their particular interests. See also **interest profiles. 2.** *n* [*Military*] abbr of **Strategic Defence Initiative** the current (1987) research programme for a non-nuclear global defence 'umbrella', probably through powerful satellite based laser weaponry and intelligence systems. Despite the overwhelming criticisms from a broad spectrum of US expert opinion, and the almost inconceivable advances in science required, the demands of national pride, coupled with the keenness of the military-industrial-academic complex to capitalise on the vast sums of cash – the basic research costs will top $30 bn. – available will probably ensure that the SDI will become a centrepiece of the arms race for many years. See also **star wars.**

SDS *n* [*Military*] abbr of **Satellite Data System** a USAF communications system specialising in polar communications. Four satellites in a Molniya orbit (a highly elliptical orbit, named after the Soviet satellites that pioneered it, which varies between a perigee of 200 miles from the earth and an apogee of 24,000 miles) move around the earth twice a day, spending half the time over the US, half over Russia.

sea *n* [*Science*] a physical or mathematical space that is filled with particles of a certain kind.

sea bee *n* [*Merchant navy*] a freighter which carries her cargo in containerised lighters.

sea cook *n* [*Navy*] a thoroughly worthless, incompetent person; it comes from the era of universally poor shipboard cooking.

sea dust *n* [*US*] [*Marine Corps*] table salt.

sea floor housekeeping *n* [*Oil rigs*] the regular inspection of the sea bed by a drilling company to remove any potentially harmful debris.

sea gull *n* [*US*] [*Marine Corps*] chicken.

sea lawyer *n* [*Merchant navy*] a shark; since lawyers are 'sharks', sharks must be lawyers.

sea level *n* [*Navy*] the sailor's opinion.

sea mule *n* [*Logging*] a boat on the log pond that is used for pushing and moving logs.

sea of instability *n* [*Science*] in chemistry this is a group of superheavy chemical elements with highly unstable nuclei. See also **island of stability.**

sea price *n* [*Navy*] an inflated price.

sea rig *n* [*Navy*] the working dress of sailors at sea: dungarees or old uniforms.

sea-blessing *n* [*Navy*] oaths, curses, obscenities.

seagull *n* [*US*] [*Navy*] frozen chicken used in shipboard menus.

seal *n* [*Furriers*] usually in fact muskrat or seal-dyed rabbit rather than actual sealskin.

sealed bid auction *n* [*Commerce*] See **blind auction.**

sealed source *n* [*Science, Medicine*] a pellet of radioactive material, sealed into a container which is used in radiography, and radiotherapy.

seals *n pl* [*Glass-making*] See **gems.**

seam *n* [*Metallurgy*] a longitudinal defect that runs transversely across a steel sheet. See also **roke.**

seamer *n* [*Cricket*] a bowler who uses the raised seam that runs round the centre of the ball to make it change direction either in the air or after its impact on the pitch.

SEAQ *n* [*Stock market*] acro **Stock Exchange Automated Quotations** the electronic price display system which forms the basis of trading – computers permitting – on the post-deregulation (**Big Bang**) London Stock Exchange.

Sears Roebuck driller *n* [*Oil rigs*] a second rate driller on an oil rig. See also **Sears Roebuck license.**

Sears Roebuck license *n* [*US*] [*Road transport*] the licence held by a second rate truck driver. See also **Sears Roebuck driller.**

Seasiders *n pl* [*Soccer*] the nickname for Blackpool Association Football Club.

seasonality *n* [*Commerce*] regular variations for sales during different seasons that can be measured consistently over a number of years.

season-cracking *n* [*Metallurgy*] the occurrence of cracks running the length of cold-worked brass or bronze.

seat 1. *n* [*Glass-making*] the position on the floor of the furnace where a pot is placed. **2.** *n* [*US*] [*Stock market*] a place in the membership of the New York Stock Exchange.

seat mile *n* [*Transport*] a statistical figure, usually referring to air travel and denoting a distance of one mile travelled by a single passenger.

seat only sales *n pl* [*Travel agents*] the sale of airplane seats for a flight only, rather than as part of a full holiday package.

Seatainer *n* [*Aus.*] [*Transport*] a container used for the transport of freight by sea. See also **fishy back.**

seatearth, also **seggar, warrant** *n* [*Coalmining*] a bed, representing old soil and thus often containing abundant rootlets, that underlies a coal seam.

seatwork *n* [*Education*] whatever work serves to keep the children at their desks, working and quiet, while the teacher is left free to correct other work, prepare the next lesson etc.

sec check *n* [*Scientology*] a full-scale interrogation of potentially errant members by officers of the Church police.

second 1. *n* [*Mountaineering*] the second climber on a team. **2.** *n* [*Scouts*] the second in command of a patrol of six boy scouts or girl guides

second blessing *n* [*Religion*] among 'born-again'

S

evangelistic, and usually American, Christians, this is the experience of God's grace that follows one's conversion and which enables one to live a spiritual life; practical examples of such a blessing include the 'gift of tongues' and similar apparent miracles.

second bottom n [Gold-mining] a second level of gold-bearing material that may be found by boring beneath the level which had previously been seen as the lowest place where gold could be mined.

second coming type n [US] [Journalism] the largest, blackest headline type, presumably that which will be used when the Messiah returns.

second cut n [Sheep-shearing] the blow of the shearers that removes a badly cut fleece and thus also the piece of sub-standard or short wool that is produced by such a cut.

second cuts n pl [Weaving] short fibres in a fleece that result from shearing the fibres twice in the same area.

second decision centre n [Military] the concept that the use of nuclear weapons might be decided upon by a British Government independently; this naturally assumes some limits on the traditional US-European consultative mechanisms and targeting plans. The overall aim is supposedly to complicate the calculations of an aggressor when deciding whether or not to launch a nuclear attack and to make it clear that while the US might be reluctant to fire, the UK would not be. Such a scheme has the charm of allowing the UK an independent force, while being touted as benefiting NATO.

second degree arson n [US] [Law] the burning of buildings other than dwellings.

second echelons n pl [Military] troops and their equipment, aircraft, runways and command centres, that are not near the front line and which would be used in the follow up to a successful attack.

second front, also **split page** n [US] [Journalism] the first page of the second section of the paper.

second generation n [Computing] those computers designed after 1955 and which are characterised by both vacuum tube (valve) and discrete transistor logic. They used magnetic core memory. They also took advantage of improving standards in magnetic tape and the first developments of on-line storage as well as a wider range of input-output equipment. See also **first, third – fifth generation.**

second greaser n [Navy] the Second Mate.

second hand n [Textiles] a worker who supervises several other workers.

second horse n [Hunting] a spare horse used in a hunt; such horses are ridden slowly behind the hunt by a groom, then handed over to the huntsman at some pre-arranged point.

second horseman n [Hunting] a groom who rides one of the second or spare horses in a hunt; such horses are ridden slowly behind the hunt, then handed over to the huntsman at some pre-arranged point.

second level carrier n [Air Travel] local or regional airline services. See also **third level carrier**

second mate n [Navy] a generous measure of liquor – 'four fingers' – supposedly as poured by a traditional Second Mate.

second order threat n [Military] some theoretical military struggle, posited perhaps 20 years in the future, which continually justifies vast government expenditure on creating an ever-larger military machine.

second paragraph paralysis n [TV] the inability of many documentaries to capitalise in the subsequent material on the viewer's interest which has been captured by an exciting opening sequence.

second round n [Finance] in venture capital investment this is the stage of development that comes after the start-up money and precedes the **mezzanine level.**

second strike n [Military] the retaliatory attack by whichever of the superpowers has already been hit by a (possibly **pre-emptive**) **first strike.**

second strike capability n [Military] the ability of a military power to launch a retaliatory attack on its enemy, after surviving a hostile **first strike.**

second strike counterforce capability n [Military] the ability to launch a retaliatory strike, after suffering a **first strike**, against the enemy's forces; essentially it is a more specific version of a general second strike and one which, given its supposed 'sparing' of hostile populations, would not be used. Once one side had suffered the effect of a full nuclear attack, the question of where one sent one's retaliation, were it feasible, would probably be academic.

second unit n [Film] a subsidiary film crew – director, cameraman, technicians, etc. – who deal with location work, stunts, special effects, etc.

second working n [Coal-mining] the partial or total extraction of pillars in **bord and pillar** mining. See also **first working.**

Second world n [Politics] all the nations of the 'developed world' with the exception of the two superpowers themselves

secondary 1. n [Audio] the output wrapping of a transformer. See also **primary. 2.** n [US] [Football] the defensive backfield. **3.** a [Geology] referring to any mineral that is not an original constituent of its host rock, but which has been formed by the movement or alteration of the original constituents.

secondary action n [Industrial relations] various actions taken by workers who are not actually party to a strike but who wish to demon-

S

strate solidarity: blacking, secondary picketing, sympathy strikes, etc.

secondary battery n [Electronics] any device that uses electromagnetic induction, especially a transformer.

secondary evidence n [UK] [Law] evidence, not generally liked but accepted if necessary by the courts, which indicates that while it is at present unavailable, other, and better, evidence does exist.

secondary industry n [Economics, Industry] any industry that concerns itself with transforming into saleable items the basic materials provided by a primary industry.

secondary poverty n [Sociology] poverty which is due to individual inefficiency or a waste of resources rather than to basic lack of such resources.

secondary radar n [Military, Air travel] radar signals that are transmitted automatically by an aircraft in response to signals reaching it from ground-based radar.

secondary recovery n [Oil industry] the use of special engineering techniques to recover oil supplies from sources that have already been heavily drained.

secondary worker n [Management] a part-time worker.

second-class paper n [Finance] bills of exchange, promissory notes and cheques drawn on, accepted, endorsed or guaranteed by persons whose financial probity is not generally acclaimed. See also **first-class paper**.

second guesser 1. n [US] [Baseball] any spectator who either during the game or after it criticizes events in such a way as to imply that he knows more than those actually involved. 2. n [Horse-racing] a tipster.

secondman n [UK] [Railways] the assistant to the driver who still rides in diesel trains, ostensibly to handle any emergency, but, in the opinion of many critics, simply as an expensive companion. Phrases to describe the second man – which quietly acknowledge this superfluity – include: the land surveyor, the view finder, sleeping partner, silent partner, estate agent, riding shotgun.

second-order theorizing n [Science] making theories about theories.

seconds n [Building, Plastering] the retarded second coat of plaster which is applied over the **firstings** so that the two coats are bonded together.

secrecy system n [Communications] any system which protects electronic communications by encoding or scrambling the clear speech as it is transmitted.

secret dovetail n [Carpenters] a dovetailed angle in which dovetails are used but which cannot be seen on the surface of the wood.

secret list n [Military, Industry] documentation concerning special, usually military, research projects or developments which must be kept secret from potential espionage. See also **skunk works**.

sectarianism 1. n [Politics] the activities of evangelical Christian sects in the USSR, in defiance of state-approved atheism. 2. n [Politics] referring, in China, to the activities of those who wish to opt out of the worker-peasant class and set themselves up as a **new class** of elitist bourgeoisie.

section 1. n [Metallurgy] any metal bar with a cross-section that is more complex than the basic square, round or flat. 2. n [Computing] the division of a program into self-contained parts. 3. v [Custom cars] to modify a car body by cutting a regular width strip all round the car and then welding the resulting halves back together again; it is the most difficult style of customising.

section eight 1. n [US] [Military] a soldier who qualifies as mentally broken down and who may thus be discharged on health grounds. 2. v [US] [Military] to discharge from the military forces on grounds of mental instability.

sectional n [Furniture] a piece of furniture that is made up of a number of sections and which can be used either as a single unit or in its various parts.

sector 1. v [Computing] to divide up a **floppy** or hard **disk** in order to facilitate the storage and retrieval of data. 2. n [Computing] a sub-division of a track on a **floppy** or hard **disk** or a block of data that has been placed on that sub-division of the track. 3. n [Linguistics] the position in a sentence normally occupied by one of the basic units which make up that sentence.

sector analysis n [Linguistics] the analysis of sentences by considering the basic units that those sentences comprise and the positions those units occupy. See also **sector**.

secular n [Economics, Statistics] referring to a fluctuation or trend that persists regularly over an unlimited period and is neither short-term nor periodic.

secure 1. v [US] [Marine Corps] to stop an activity. 2. a [Military, Espionage] referring to communications systems which are made as immune as possible – either through the technology itself or through the codes used to transmit information – from electronic tampering, eavesdropping or other forms of clandestine interception.

secure telephone n [Espionage] a telephone used for high-level classified conversations and which, for the purposes of normal investigation, exists outside the regular telephone system.

security n [Stock market] a general term that includes all stock market investments.

security assistance n [Military] American financial and material aid that is offered specifically for the creation/arming/training of the forces of potential allies. See also **MAAG**.

S

security blanket *n* [*Government*] any wide-ranging measures designed to stifle information on, or access to, a topic or event and to promote as comprehensive as possible a state of security, against either espionage or physical attack.

security dilemma *n* [*Politics*] the driving force behind the arms race: since one power fears the weapons of the other it adds to its own arsenal, believing that only by this attempt to gain the advantage, which the first power promotes as a purely defensive measure, can it maintain its own security. The second power can only see this increase in weapons as offensive, and thus reverses the situation, pulling ahead once more in the arms race, once again claiming that its new systems are purely defensive. The first power, seeing this, chooses to believe that its opponent is really building up for an attack and then reinforces its already modernised arsenal.

security dollar *n* [*Economics*] See **switch dollar.**

see *v* [*Music*] to read music.

see off the new ball *v* [*Cricket*] when a batsman, either one of the openers if they are not dismissed, or whichever batsmen are together when the second new ball is taken after 85 overs have been bowled, bats until the shine (and thus greater potential speed) of the ball has been knocked off by its being hit.

see through *n* [*Printing*] the extent to which an image on an underlying sheet of paper can be seen through the sheet above it. See also **show through.**

seed 1. *n* [*Medicine*] a small container designed to hold radioactive material which has to be placed inside the body during radiotherapy. **2.** *n* [*Chemistry*] in the crystallization process this is a small amount of the desired substance that is placed in a liquid in order to provide a nucleus for subsequent crystal growth. **3.** *n* [*Glass-making*] small bubbles in glass. **4.** *n* [*US*] [*Tobacco*] any variety of tobacco which is grown in the US.

seed money *n* [*Economics*] the investment of money that is intended to generate a further, and supposedly greater flow of money, in the form of donations, investments or whatever. See also **front-end money.**

seediness *n* [*Painting*] an accumulation of small particles that is a defect in lacquer or varnish.

seeding *n* [*Cheese-making*] the reincorporation of yeast, molds and **ferments** into pasteurised milk so that a balanced cheese may result.

seeds 1. *n pl* [*US*] [*Farming*] hog melts. **2.** *n pl* [*US*] [*Painting*] roughness on a varnished surface that has to be removed by sanding.

seedy *a* [*Painting*] said of paint which, during its storage, has developed deposits of small bits of foreign matter. See also **peppery 1.**

seek frost *n* [*Military*] See **seek igloo.**

seek igloo, seek frost *n* [*Military*] high-powered distant early warning systems which are being built to replace the obsolete DEW (Distant Early Warning) and Pinetree Lines that run across N. America and Canada.

seek talk *n* [*Military*] UHF communicators for the USAF which will be impervious to enemy attempts at electronic interference and jamming; it is currently under development in the US.

seek time *n* [*Computing*] the time in which random access memory (**RAM**) can retrieve a piece of data from storage either on a **floppy** or hard **disk.**

see-safe 1. *n* [*Commerce*] an agreement to sell goods on sale or return. **2.** *n* [*Commerce*] a variation of whereby the customer returns for credit any goods still unsold at the end of a specified period. In both cases the supplier sees that his customer is safe, ie, does not lose money.

seg 1. *n* [*TV*] **segment** one programme of a series. **2.** *n* [*Shoe-making*] a metal stud used to strengthen the heel or toe of a boot or shoe, or to protect it from wear.

seggar *n* [*Coal-mining*] See **seatearth.**

segment 1. *n* [*TV*] See **seg. 2.** *n* [*Linguistics*] a unit that forms part of a flow of speech, or, more rarely, of text. **3.** *n* [*Computing*] a part of a complete specific routine, which can be stored in the internal memory and which contains the coding necessary to call in and transfer control to other segments.

segregation *n* [*Metallurgy*] a non-uniform distribution, with concentrations of certain constituents and/or impurities, that arises during freezing and generally persists through subsequent operations.

segue *n* [*TV, Radio*] pronounced 'segwee', this is bridging transition in sound, an aural mix.

seignorage *n* [*Finance*] the profit made by a government from the manufacture and issue of coins.

seize 1. *v* [*Communications*] to take control of a channel in order to transmit data. **2.** *v* [*Sailing, Ropework*] to fasten two pieces of rope together or to fasten a rope to something else by binding with twine, etc.

seizing *n* [*Sailing, Ropework*] a lashing of spun yarn or **small stuff.**

seizure stick, also **mouth gag** *n* [*US*] [*Medicine*] a padded stick which is used to stop a patient swallowing his/her tongue during a convulsion.

select out *v* [*Government*] a euphemism for dismissing someone from a job.

selection *n* [*Forestry*] a system whereby there is a continuous selection of trees from the entire area of the forest with a view to selling them.

selection pressure *n* [*Biology*] the difference in birth and death rates that affect the way in which a population adapts genetically.

selection rule *n* [*Science*] in physics this is one of a number of rules which define, within certain limits, which quantum transitions can occur within an atom or molecule and which are forbidden.

selective abstract *n* [*Libraries*] an abstract prepared by a librarian for a specific user which contains only those parts of an article which will be relevant to that user. See also **auto, evaluative, general, indicative, informative, slanted abstract.**

selective ordnance *n* [*Military*] a euphemism for napalm; the precise 'selectivity' that this modern version of 'Greek fire' offers the bombing pilot has never been explained.

selectivity 1. *n* [*Audio*] the discrimination of a radio receiver between two adjacent broadcast signals. **2.** *n* [*Audio*] sharpness of tuning in mechanical, acoustic or circuit devices. **3.** *n* [*Social work*] the concept that, irrespective of status or income, those who most require services are those who most definitely should receive them. See also **universalism.**

selenodesy *n* [*Astronomy*] the study of the shape and features of the moon; it comes from Gk. 'selene' meaning moon and 'geodesy'.

self steer *n* [*UK*] [*Road transport*] See **rear steer.**

self will run riot *phr* [*Alcoholics Anonymous*] trying too hard to control one's own destiny.

self-actualisation, also **self-realisation** *n* [*New therapies*] the appreciation by an individual of his/her own potential and the full and creative development of that potential; this is the essential aim, in many cases, of the various 'new therapies' which are available to those who feel they have 'lost' themselves.

self-absorption *n* [*Science*] in physics this is the absorption of radioactivity by the material emitting it.

self-alienation *n* [*Sociology*] in Marxist terms, this is the **alienation** which occurs within oneself. The obsession with earning and possessing money is the supreme example of self-alienation, since it reduces all human qualities to the level of quantitive values of exchange.

self-balancing *n* [*Accounting*] a situation in which the debit side of the accountable items is equal to the credit side; thus 'self-balancing ledger' is a personal ledger that contains a control account.

self-adapting process *n* [*Computing*] a system that is able to adjust its performance characteristics according to its environment and according to perceived relationships between input and output signals.

self-blimped *a* [*Film*] said of a camera which requires no additional housing since its own covering already minimises noise.

self-dealing 1. *n* [*Finance*] the borrowing from, or lending to, a company by an individual who owns that company. **2.** *n* [*Finance*] the use of a charitable foundation as a form of unofficial bank which can make its funds available for loans to some of its more influential contributors.

self-exciting *a* [*Audio*] referrring to a radio sender in which the oscillator determinating the frequency also generates the radio-frequency power.

self-generating, also **self-motivating** *a* [*Business*] referring to an executive who is able to spur him/herself on to tackling the tasks that need to be faced and who generates new ideas for the firm in which he/she works; a live wire. See also **self-starter.**

self-hunting *a* [*Shooting*] said of a gun-dog which goes off foraging in fields and hedgerows for game, irrespective of its master's commands; this is deemed extremely bad, since it may lead, among other things, to cattle and sheep worrying.

self-learning process *n* [*Computing*] See **self-adapting process.**

self-liquidating *a* [*Finance*] said of a loan which is repayable in a short time from the profits made out of selling the product for which the loan was obtained.

self-liquidator *n* [*Advertising*] an offer which, although very attractively priced, still covers the cost to the advertiser.

self-noise *n* [*Navy*] the noise produced by a ship as it passes through the water, as opposed to the noise of the ocean itself. See also **signature 2.**

self-quencher *n* [*Electronics*] See **squegger.**

self-shielding *a* [*Science*] See **self-absorption.**

self-starter *n* [*Business*] an executive who provides his/her own motivation and ideas for the job in hand. See also **self-generating.**

self-twist *n* [*Textiles*] a method of spinning in which the yarn is twisted by the side-to-side movement of a roller.

sell up *v* [*Commerce*] to persuade a customer to take a more expensive item than the one which was the object of his/her initial interest on entering the shop.

sell on close *v* [*Futures market*] to sell at the end of a trading session at a price within the opening **range;** thus to 'sell on opening' is to sell at the start of a trading session and within the opening range.

sell on the good news *v* [*US*] [*Stock market*] to sell stocks immediately after the company by whom they are issued announces some good news; the premise behind this is that such a stock will reach its peak price once those who hear this news have bought it.

sell out *v* [*Futures market*] to cover, **offset** or **close out** a **long position.** See also **buy in.**

sell-in 1. *n* [*Marketing*] the process of selling the goods to the retail trade, prior to the sale to the public. **2.** *n* [*Video*] the number of videocassettes that wholesalers can sell to stores.

selling against the box *n* [*Stock market*] this is when a large shareholder wishes to shield the selling of some shares from the rest of the market; he sells **short** and delivers borrowed certificates

S

rather than the shares he actually holds in his (theoretical) strong box.

sell-through n [Video] a title that is sold to the customer rather than one that is rented: the bulk of titles, given the predominant rental market, are never sell-throughs.

Selsdon man n [UK] [Politics] a theoretical British Conservative politician whose activities were modelled on the policies developed at a meeting of the Party's leaders at the Selsdon Park Hotel in Surrey in January 1970; the reference is to the hotel and to the fraudulent Piltdown Man.

selvedge n [Mining] a thin band of clay found in a vein of minerals.

semantic differential n [Marketing] the list of adjectival choices, eg: 'excellent' through to 'poor', etc, which is often used when questioning individuals in market research.

semantics n [Military, Politics] a euphemism for 'words', eg: 'I am not going to debate semantics with you' means 1. 'I am not going to argue', and 2. 'I am not going to reveal the unpleasant/inadmissible facts behind my hypocritical and inaccurate statement'.

semaphore n [Computing] a method to ensure the synchronisation of co-operating processes; it is used to avoid interference occuring when two processes simultaneously attempt to use a resource. It was introduced in 1965 by Dutch scientist Edsger Dijkstra.

seme 1. n [Linguistics] a sign. 2. n [Linguistics] the smallest unit of linguistic meaning.

sememe n [Linguistics] See **seme**.

semi 1. n [Oil rigs] abbr of **semi-submersible** a floating drilling platform that is supported by underwater pontoons; it is usually used for exploration purposes only. It is better equipped for deeper waters than **jack-ups** because of its greater size, storage and endurance capacity. 2. a [Weaving] the second classification in the grading of wool fleece.

semi-active n [Military] abbr of **semi-active homing** a missile guidance system whereby the vehicle is directed by a signal that emanates from elsewhere and is reflected off the target towards which the vehicle is flying.

semi-display n [Printing] a style of advertising layout that falls between the run-on and fully displayed styles.

semi-main n [US] [Sport] See **repêchage**.

seminar n [UK] [Government] a Cabinet-level committee, dealing with economic policy, that was instituted by James Callaghan in 1979 and consists of the Prime Minister, the Governor of the Bank of England and a few extremely senior economic advisors.

semiotics, also **semiology** n [Sociology, Linguistics] the study of signs and, in sociology, the means of analysing messages, both verbal and non-verbal. Semiotics uses three concepts: the **signifier**, the **signified** and the **sign;** the latter denotes the relationship between the first two. It is possible to go beyond the immediate impact of the sign and ask questions concerning the wider meanings and social functions of the codes and myths that such signs prompt.

semi-trailer n [UK] [Road transport] a trailer drawn by a tractive vehicle where a proportion of the weight of the trailer is superimposed on the tractive unit.

semon n [Linguistics] an elementary semantic feature. See also **seme**.

send v [Radio] See **feed 5**.

send back v [Cricket] to dismiss a batsman, who is thus 'sent back' to the pavilion.

send down v [UK] [Law, Police] a judge does this when he sentences a guilty man/woman to a term of imprisonment; it refers to the flight of steps that leads down from the dock to the cells at the Central Criminal Court in London. See also **steps, up the**.

send-out n [Gas industry] total gas produced, purchased, or not withdrawn from underground storage within a specified interval, measured at the point(s) of production and/or purchase and/or withdrawal, and adjusted for changes in local storage quality; it comprises gas sales, exchange, deliveries, gas used by the supplier and unaccounted-for gas.

senhouse n [Sailing] this comes from Senhouse slip; it is a short length of chain, of the same strength as the anchor chain, which is used to secure the end of a cable.

senior n [TV, Film] a 5KW incandescent, focusing spotlight.

senior security n [Finance] any securities which take precedence in claims on the assets and earnings of a company.

senior statesmen n pl [Navy] a committee of senior petty officers who represent the lower deck on matters of messing, etc.

sensate a [Sociology] according to the theories of P.A. Sorokin this describes a form of culture in which the paramount objective is the satisfaction of material needs and desires; it is the opposite of an idealistic culture.

sense v [Computing] to determine the condition or content of a signal or storage location.

sensible heat n [Oil rigs] the amount of heat required to raise or lower the temperature of a substance without a change of state occurring.

sensing n [Military] the observation of the point of burst or impact of a shell or shot with reference to its proximity, or lack of it, to the target.

sensitive a [Espionage, Government] said of files so utterly secret (and potentially damaging either to a government or its intelligence service) that they can never be released from the premises of the intelligence service itself. Such files often contain material that is not of much interest to foreign governments, but, since it lists a mass of scandals and errors in high places, would be infinitely more fascinating to the public from whom the files are deliberately withheld.

sensitive payments *n pl* [*Business*] bribes offered by US companies to foreign governments in return for bulk orders of their goods.

sensitivity *n* [*Audio*] the measure of the signal level required at an input level to produce a stated output level; the lower the necessary input, the higher the sensitivity.

sensitivity training *n* [*New therapies*] a form of group therapy in which the participants are working towards deeper understanding of themselves.

sensuous *a* [*Wine-tasting*] rich, smooth, with an opulent flavour and texture.

sentinel 1. *n* [*Computing*] a marker that indicates the beginning or end of a section of information accessed by a program. 2. *n* [*Medicine*] **sentinel pile** an external haemorrhoid situated at the lower end of an anal fissure.

separate 1. *n* [*Audio*] any self-contained, free-standing component of a stereo sound system. 2. *v* [*US*] [*Military*] to discharge a member of the US armed forces.

separate development *n* [*Politics*] See **plural relations.**

separation 1. *n* [*US*] [*Military*] resignation or dismissal from the armed forces; this also applies to those leaving a university or more general employment. 2. *n* [*Photography*] one of a number (not less than three) of monochrome reproductions of a coloured picture, each in a different colour, that can be combined to create the full-colour image.

septic verbs *n pl* [*Literary*] a term coined by A. P. Herbert to refer to that class of verbs which stem from adding a verb-ending to a noun; they are usually found in bureaucracies, military forces, etc, and are epitomised by the locutions of Gen. Alexander Haig.

sequence dancing *n* [*Dancing*] in ballroom dancing these are the dances in which the steps must be taken in a specified order; in such a dance all couples are taking the same steps at the same time.

sequence shot *n* [*Film*] a whole scene filmed in a single, unbroken shot.

sequential *a* [*TV*] referring to the usual method of scanning a TV image, whereby all the lines are traversed in the same direction, with a rapid return by the scanning spot to the top of the screen when a single scan has been completed.

sercon *n* [*Science fiction*] this comes from serious plus constructive; it is a type of fan magazine which rejects the jokier, superficial aspects of the genre.

sergeant major 1. *n* [*US*] [*Military*] coffee with cream or with milk and sugar. 2. *n* [*UK*] [*Military*] strong sweet tea or tea with a dash of rum.

serging *n* [*Clothing*] the stitching by a machine of the edge of a garment to prevent fraying.

serial *n* [*Journalism*] a running story, which maintains its newsworthiness for several days or longer.

serial art *n* [*Art*] the production of a series of pictures as variations on a single theme, rather than attempting in each painting to create a definitive, one-off masterpiece.

serialism *n* [*Philosophy, Physics*] the concept put forward by J. W. Dunne (1875–1949) in his book 'Experiment With Time' (1927); we exist in a Serial Universe in which time rotates around an axis rather than proceeding endlessly from the far past to the distant future. Using this theory, Dunne was able to account for the phenomenon of the apparent precognition that occurs in dreams and the common feeling that one has 'been here before'.

series *n* [*UK*] [*Railways*] a speed limit of 25 mph established for certain parts of the London underground system. See also **shunt 3, parallel.**

sero [*US*] [*Medicine*] abbr of **serology, serous** a type of drainage in which the red blood cells are not present. See also **sang.**

serum porcelain *n* [*US*] [*Medicine*] See **crock 4.**

servante *n* [*Magic*] a secret shelf; it comes from Fr. for a butler's tray, a dumb waiter.

server *n* [*Computing*] a node on a network that offers a specific service to all network users; eg: a printer server for printing services, a file server for file storage, a communication server for communications to other media, etc.

service 1. *n* [*Sailing, Ropework*] thin rope bound round standing rigging for protection against wear and weather; thus serving board and serving mallet are tools for putting on and tightening the service. 2. *n* [*US*] [*Undertakers*] all the arrangements surrounding a death – transport, embalming, engaging the clergyman, insurance, taxes, licences, posting an obituary notice, etc – that add up to complete care of the corpse and stage-managing of the funeral.

service ceiling *n* [*Aerospace*] the practical upper limit of steady, level flight.

service class *n* [*Sociology*] the class position of certain higher-level, non-manual groups such as business managers, professionals employed by institutions – rather than self-employed and public officials who exercise power and expertise on behalf of corporate bodies or the capitalist class.

service crimes *n pl* [*Sociology*] crimes that have no apparent victim, but are merely against a state's laws: prostitution, gambling, drug abuse. Such crimes are not reported to the police since both 'criminals' and 'victims' may be said to benefit from them.

service delivery *n* [*Social work*] the concept of social work as a group of separate but interconnected services which must be delivered to those

S

S

requiring them by competent people in an efficient and useful manner.

service module n [Aerospace] a separable section of a spacecraft, such as that which holds the engine, the crew capsule, etc.

service routines n pl [Computing] the collection of programs and subroutines that are incorporated in all computer systems, and which provide a variety of useful functions, including file copying and deleting, text preparation, program cross-referencing, etc.

services n pl [Military] technical experts – medical, ordnance, communications, etc. – who advise staff officers on topics falling within their own area of expertise.

servicing n [Public relations] making material available to media in the hope that they will pick it up for publication.

servitor n [Glass-making] the second man in a team or **chair** who adds feet or legs to glassware when necessary and who 'serves' the foreman.

session n [Stock market] a working day at the Stock Exchange.

sessional indemnity n [Can.] [Government] the fee paid to a member of a legislative assembly in Canada.

set 1. n [Psychology] the mental state one occupies, that is governed by a variety of emotions, preconceptions and expectations. 2. n [Bell-ringing] the inverted position of a bell, with its mouth upwards and a little beyond the point of balance, when it is poised to turn and ring. 3. n [Carpenters] the distance that the blade of a plane projects from the **sole**. 4. n [UK] [Buses] an accident involving a London Transport bus. 5. n [Coal-mining] See **journey** 1. 6. n [US] [Garment trade] a team of operator, baster and finisher who between them turn out a finished garment. 7. n [Logging] a pair of workers who actually fell the trees. See also **faller**. 8. n [UK] [Railways] a driver and a fireman. 9. n [UK] [Surfing] a number of waves in sequence.

set a tub v [Distilling] to fill a large vat with yeasted mash which will then ferment into 'beer', which in turn will be pumped into stills where it distills into **high wines**

set of books n [Business] a new company that started from an idea and is based on the investment of **venture capital.**

set off v [Printing] the wet ink on a newly printed sheet of paper does this when it marks the underside of the sheet placed in the pile immediately above it.

set theory n [Mathematics] that branch of mathematics which deals with sets, regardless of their individual makeup, but which permits the general discussion of the set as a concept.

set up 1. n [Police, Drugs] the arrest of a drugs dealer, often on information received by the police. 2. v [Football] the quarterback does this when he drops back from the line of scrimmage and prepares to throw a forward pass. 3. v [Sailing, Ropework] to tighten rigging at the **lanyards** with a tackle.

set-aside n [US] [Government] anything – food supplies, vehicles, various commodities – that is reserved by the Government for a special purpose; originally it meant supplies for the military but now covers material or crops used to aid poorer nations, etc.

set-back n [Architecture] in the building of skyscrapers this is the method whereby after a certain level, the higher storeys are successively setback a certain distance from the line of the lower floors; such set-backs are included both for design purposes and as a precaution against suicides.

se-tenant a [Philately] adjoining stamps, printed on the same sheet, which differ from each other – in value, design, etc. or in that one is overprinted, surcharged or whatever and the other is not; they are found particularly in stamp booklets. It comes from Fr. meaning 'joined together'.

set-off n [Philately] a form of reversed print, caused by laying a sheet of stamps on another printed sheet which has been insufficiently dried, resulting in a 'transfer' of the design images in reverse on to the gummed underside of the top sheet.

sett n [Weaving] the number of **warp ends** per inch.

setter-up n [Skittles] See **sticker-up.**

setting out the stool n [Building, Plastering] the manner in which a plasterer makes his preliminary assessment of the job in hand and sets about the sequence of necessary operations; such an assessment is indicative of his skill and experience – or otherwise!

settlement price n [Futures market] the daily price at which the Clearing House clears all received trades; the settlement of each day's trading is based upon the closing **range** of that day's trading; settlement prices are used to determine both **margin calls** and invoice prices for deliveries.

Settlement, The n [Stock market] See **Account Day.**

settling Sam n [US] [Police] a prosecutor who will accept any kind of sentence, however diminished, on a guilty plea, rather than fight a not guilty plea through a trial.

settlings n [Oil rigs] See **basic sediment.**

set-up 1. n [Film] a completed set that is ready for the filming of a shot, scene or sequence; the background, props and camera are all in place, only the actors are needed for filming to begin. 2. n [Espionage] the trap into which a potential blackmail victim will be drawn by a team of **sanctifiers**, eg: a bedroom with a hidden camera and/or tape. 3. n [US] [TV] a shot of the reporter who is about to deliver a news report – which is usually in the form of a voice-over retailing his report while the viewers see only the pictures accompanying his text. **4.** *n* [*Boxing*] a fighter who can be defeated easily since, it is presumed, he has already been set up to lose. **5.** *n* [*US*] [*Bars*] in unlicensed premises this is the glass, ice, mixer, lemon slice and similar items that are provided to customers who bring their own drink. **6.** *n* [*Shooting*] the arrangement of guns, decoys and other relevant items for the shooting of wildfowl.

seven beller *n* [*Navy*] a cup of tea.

seven guarantees *n pl* [*Politics*] in Chinese Communist terms these are the guarantees of a minimum standard of living in the better communes: 1. food, 2. clothes, 3. medical care, 4. housing, 5. maternity pay, 6. marriage allowance, 7. burial allowance.

seven sisters 1. *n pl* [*Commerce*] the seven largest international oil companies: British Petroleum, Exxon, Gulf, Mobil, Royal Dutch Shell, Standard Oil of California, Texaco (as of 1979). **2.** *n pl* [*US*] [*Education*] the women's equivalent of the male Ivy League: the seven oldest established and most reputable women's colleges: Barnard, Bryn Mawr, Mount Holyoke, Radcliffe, Smith, Vassar and Wellesley.

seven tenths rule *n* [*Military*] based on the fact that many isotopes have very short lives, this is the estimation that seven hours after a nuclear explosion the amount of radiation will be only a tenth of the amount that it was immediately after the explosion.

seven-eight-two gear *n* [*US*] [*Marine Corps*] basic field kit including rifle, bayonet, canvas shelter, first aid kit, eating utensils, field pack, cartridge belt, leggings, bedding, poncho, etc.; it comes from the number of the form that specifies this equipment.

seven-pointer *n* [*Deer-stalking*] a red deer in its eighth year.

Seventh Avenue *n* [*US*] [*Garment trade*] the centre of the US garment trade: Seventh Avenue, NYC, the Wall Street or Broadway of the garment trade. It was recently renamed 'Fashion Avenue' by the New York City government, but is so called only by the tourists.

several fishery *n* [*Angling*] owning the fishing rights but not the adjacent land.

severe *n* [*Mountaineering*] a taxing, and thus challenging, climb or route up a mountain or a rockface.

severe *a* [*Wine-tasting*] used to describe a wine with a **hard** taste, unyielding and probably immature.

severe damage *n* [*Military*] as categorised by US bombing analysts, this is the reduction of a target to dust; thus 'light damage' means reduction to rubble; 'moderate damage' means reduction to gravel.

sewel, also **sewin** *n* [*Shooting*] anything hung up to scare deer or to prevent them from entering a place; a scarecrow.

sewelling *n* [*Shooting*] a method of persuading pheasants to fly by moving a card bedecked with coloured rags and feathers about 2ft. above ground level.

sewer rats *n pl* [*UK*] [*Railways*] drivers on London's underground trains. See also **earthworms.**

sewer trout *n* [*US*] [*Prisons*] any form of fish served to prisoners.

sewing-machine perforation *n* [*Philately*] in some countries bereft of any more sophisticated methods, stamps were perforated by household sewing machines which produced a rough but serviceable perforation.

sexism *n* [*Sociology*] discrimination and prejudice based on sex, usually biased against women; it is the stereotyping of women into 'mother', 'mistress', 'typist', etc.

sexploitation *n* [*Film*] any film, although not necessarily hard- or soft-core pornography, that depends for its appeal to the audience on its maker's unashamed and deliberate exploitation of its sexual content and of the alleged sexiness of its (female) star.

sextuple play *n* [*Audio*] magnetic tape one sixth of the thickness of standard recording tape.

sexual counsels *n pl* [*UK*] [*Railways*] Sectional Councils: high level negotiating committees.

sexy *n* [*Journalism*] in print and broadcast media this means any newsworthy event, especially those involving war, disaster, death or anything suitably violent and/or shocking; it was coined by the Sunday Times 'Insight' team in the early 1960s.

sferics *n pl* [*Communications*] this comes from atmospherics; they are the reports of the positions of thunderstorms, based on the atmospherics which such storms give out.

sfumato *n* [*Art*] a technique of softening outlines by permitting tones and colours to blend into one another; thus it refers to the modified outlines and tones created in this manner.

shack 1. *v* [*US*] [*Coal-mining*] to absent oneself from work or, if at work, to neglect one's duties. **2.** *n* [*UK*] [*Market-traders*] a vagrant, a tramp. **3.** *n* [*Oil rigs*] a cabin on the corner of the rig floor which houses the driller and the controls needed to control the drilling machinery.

shad-bellies *n pl* [*Hunting*] a type of scarlet hunting-coat with a high-cut front, common at one time in the **shires.**

shade *v* [*Finance*] to make a minimal or a gradual reduction in a price or value, or to fall very slightly in price or value.

shade fishing *n* [*Angling*] See **dapping.**

shade ticket *n* [*Textiles*] a temporary label sewn on to a piece of cut cloth, identifying it with the bolt from which it was cut; this ensures that a complete garment can be made from the same shade of cloth.

shading *n* [*Gambling*] a method of marking cards

S

by delicately shading in certain areas of the backs of suitably patterned cards.

shadow 1. *n* [*Communications*] any situation in which reception of a signal is distorted or diminished by an obstacle. 2. *n* [*UK*] [*Politics*] those members of the Opposition who are appointed to the 'Shadow Cabinet'; these are the non-executive parallel roles to those of the actual Ministers who are currently in government. 3. *v* [*Ice-hockey*] to follow an opponent wherever he goes on the ice; it is quite legal so long as there is no interference.

shadow calendar *n* [*US*] [*Stock market*] securities issues which have been registered with the Securities and Exchange Commission, but for which no date has yet been announced on which they will be offered to the public.

shadow director *n* [*Commerce*] as defined (for the first time) in the Companies Act (1980) this is: 'a person in accordance with whose directions or instructions the directors of a company are accustomed to act. He is to be treated . . . as a genuine director of the company, unless the directors are accustomed so to act by reason only that they do so on advice given by him in a professional capacity.'

shadow gazer *n* [*US*] [*Medicine*] a radiologist.

shadow price *n* [*Commerce*] the true marginal value of a commodity, which may differ from the market price.

shadowmask *n* [*TV*] the perforated mask, sited immediately behind a TV screen, which is used to separate the electron beams that produce the colours red, green and blue.

shaft alley *n* [*Navy*] rumours, gossip; it comes from the supposed conversations of men working in the shaft-alley, the passage extending from the engine room to the stern that contains the propeller shaft and its bearings.

shaft pillar *n* [*Coal-mining*] a portion of the coal that is deliberately left unworked so that it may provide a support for the roof of the working.

shaftman *n* [*S. Wales*] [*Coal-mining*] a **cage** operator.

shafty *n* [*US*] [*Bars*] a customer who will not tip.

shag 1. *n* [*Logging*] the brakeman on a logging railroad. 2. *n* [*US*] [*Road transport*] a small trailer used for city deliveries/pickups.

shake *n* [*Logging*] a crack in the stem of a tree, caused by frost or excessive bending in a strong wind.

shake the tree *v* [*Espionage*] the CIA do this when they make it known to potentially dissatisfied Soviet bloc individuals, through a variety of clandestine and overt means, that their defection would be both feasible and welcome.

shake-down *n* [*Transport*] the initial flights or sailings of new airplanes or ships that are designed to test out the air– or seaworthiness of the machinery and equipment and to give their putative crews some on-the-spot training.

shakedown *n* [*Crime, Drugs*] a confidence trick whereby the addict attempts to convince a dealer that he has hidden some drugs in a dealer's home and that, unless the dealer hands over a large quantity of free drugs at once, he, the addict, will inform the police of the dealer's address.

shaken, also **loose, pulled** *a* [*Book collecting*] said of a book the contents of which are loose within the covers, but not actually detached; this obviously diminishes its value.

shake-out *n* [*Stock market*] any unforeseen and noticeable event on the Exchange, eg: a sudden fall in share prices or the sudden sale of a particular stock.

shaker screen, also **shale shaker** *n* [*Oil rigs*] a sieve on to which the **mud** is pumped after it has carried **dirt** out of the well bore; the dirt is abandoned, and the mud recycled for further use.

shakes *n* [*Fleet Air Arm*] the bosun's mate who is responsible for waking air crew on an aircraft carrier; a lower deck man is not permitted to shake an officer awake, since this equals laying a hand – illegally – upon a senior rank.

shaking out *n* [*Metallurgy*] See **knocking out.**

shakings *n pl* [*Sailing, Ropework*] odds and ends of rope, once used for making oakum.

shale shaker *n* [*Oil rigs*] See **shaker screen.**

sham hole *n* [*Clothing*] a counterfeit buttonhole, often found on the sleeves of suit jackets, that is made by putting in a double row of stitching.

shamateurism *n* [*Sport*] the accepting of money by a player who is ostensibly an amateur and thus supposedly unattracted by such payments. In the event those athletes who are sufficiently popular for promoters to use their names to attract large crowds, often find their 'expenses' payments substantially higher than might have genuinely been required. See also **appearance money, boot money.**

shanghai *v* [*US*] [*Marine Corps*] to get rid of an incompetent and/or genuinely unpopular individual by effecting his impromptu or involuntary transfer to another posting.

shank 1. *v* [*Golf*] to hit the ball with the neck of the club. 2. *n* [*US*] [*Prisons*] a knife, usually manufactured from ersatz materials, and vital to survival in the prison. 3. *n* [*Shoe-making*] the portion of the underside of the shoe that lies beneath the arch of the foot – the narrow part between the heel and the sole. 4. *n* [*Angling*] a line of pots attached to a rope and used in shallow water to catch crabs, lobsters, whelks, etc.

shanty 1. [*US*] [*Circus*] chief electrician; it comes from chandelier. 2. also **library** [*UK*] [*Railways*] the engineman's restroom where orders are awaited from the supervisor.

shape *n* [*Cards*] in bridge this is the distribution of the suits in a hand.

shape memory *n* [*Science*] the property that is possessed by certain alloys which can recover their original shape even after they have been heated and squashed, twisted or otherwise deformed out of that shape.

shaped canvases *n pl* [*Art*] See **colour field painting.**

shaped noise *n* [*Audio*] a specially selected and shaped spectrum of **white noise** that is used for testing purposes.

shapes 1. *n pl* [*Gambling*] dice that have been altered in such a way as to make them less than perfect cubes. **2.** *n pl* [*Stock market*] where one purchase is satisfied by a number of sales, or vice versa, the part deliveries are known as shapes. **3.** *n pl* [*Tobacco*] cigars that are tapered at both ends.

share 1. *v* [*Sociology*] in a variety of therapeutic and self-help groups, such as Alcoholics Anonymous and **est,** this is the public confession of one's innermost angsts and agonies; it is a concept and a word taken directly from the traditional, evangelistic 'holy roller' churches, and the Moral Re-Armament movement. **2.** *n* [*TV*] the rating of a TV audience that assesses the percentage of sets actually in use and watching a specific show; a 30% share is considered (by the US networks) to be the minimum feasible for a programme to survive on the air.

shareware *n* [*Computing*] a system of software design and distribution whereby copies of a program are sent out to certain selected individuals who are then encouraged to make copies and give them out. Satisfied users – who receive basic instructions on the disk – can send a set fee to the program's author, who will then send a proper manual, updates, etc.

shark repellent *n* [*Business*] any measure taken by a company to ward off unwanted takeover bids, including a **poison pill** provision, the threatened borrowing of a vast sum of **dear money**, making one's own takeovers to create an excessively large company which a **raider** does not want, etc. See also **golden parachute, scorched-earth policy.**

shark watcher *n* [*Finance*] a firm that specialises in keeping a watch on the market to check for any signs of an approaching takeover bid, many of which may be prepared surreptitiously so as not to alert the target company.

sharp *a* [*Wine-tasting*] used to describe a degree of acidity between **piquant** and **pricked**; it is a stage beyond that of being attractively refreshing.

sharp coat *n* [*Painting*] a coat of white lead in oil which has been liberally thinned with turpentine; when used for coating new plaster this coat is known as 'sharp colour'.

sharp sand *n* [*Metallurgy*] in iron founding this is clay-free sand composed of silica or quartz grains.

sharps *n pl* [*Medicine*] discarded blades and needles that have been used in an operation.

sharpshooter 1. *n* [*US*] [*Cattlemen*] a cattle buyer who works neither to feed the cattle up for subsequent sale, nor on commission, but simply to buy up small numbers of cattle that will be sold for a profit. **2.** *n* [*US*] [*Law*] a lawyer who concentrates on exploiting loopholes in the law and thus secures the acquittal of otherwise apparently guilty plaintiffs.

shash *n* [*TV*] the flickering 'snowstorm' that can appear on a TV screen, caused by a lack of a proper vision signal.

shaving *n* [*Custom cars*] the removal of all trim from a car, as in dechroming (see **dechrome**) but also removing the door handles as well as badges, etc.

shaving crew *n* [*US*] [*Logging*] the workers who plane wood in the sawmill.

SHE economy *n* [*Economics*] abbr of **sane, humane and ecological economy** which would 'put people before things, recognizing that people's energies and skills are important renewable resources.' See also **black economy.**

she stuff *n* [*US*] [*Cattlemen*] female cattle.

sheaf *n* [*Libraries*] a catalogue recorded on individual slips filed together in loose-leaf binders.

sheared terminal *n* [*Printing*] a curved line that is ended by a straight line.

sheariness *n* [*Painting*] variations in the gloss or sheen of a coat of paint that ought to be regular.

shears *n pl* [*Sailing, Ropework*] two spars lashed together at the top and guyed; they are used for raising heavy weights.

shed 1. *n* [*UK*] [*Government*] a filing cabinet containing file cards which refer to papers that have been transferred to another Department of Health and Social Security office. **2.** *n* [*Weaving*] the space, made by raising certain **warp** threads and lowering others, through which the **weft** passes. **3.** *n* [*Science*] a unit of area of nuclear cross-section equal to 10 to the power of – 24 barn or 10 to the power of – 48 square centimetres; it is the smallest area of nuclear measurement used in sub-atomic physics. See also **barn.**

shedder *n* [*Angling*] See **baggot.**

sheep *n* [*Parapsychology*] a believer in parapsychology and allied phenomena. See also **goat 3.**

sheep dipping *n* [*Espionage*] the use of clandestine operations of a military instrument – either equipment or personnel – usually under civilian cover. The placing of individuals within (subversive) groups for the purpose of surveillance of those groups.

sheep herder *n* [*US*] [*Road transport*] a driver whose ability is questioned.

sheepherder *n* [*Logging*] an inexperienced logger.

sheet 1. *n* [*Advertising*] the basic size of a single-sheet poster: 28in by 42in. **2.** *n* [*Sailing, Ropework*] a rope used to trim the lower corner of a sail; thus sheet home, sheet flat means to haul the sheet taut. **3.** *n* [*UK*] [*Road transport*] a tarpaulin that covers a load. **4.** *v* [*UK*] [*Road transport*] to cover one's load with a tarpaulin.

sheetlines *n pl* [*Military*] See **neatlines.**

S

Sheffield composition n [Metallurgy] See compo 3.

sheftsvo n [Government, Politics] the Soviet equivalent of 'empire-building'; it is the use of patronage and influence for their personal advantage by party bosses and other senior officials.

shelf life n [Commerce] the time that any perishable item will remain fresh; the maximum shelf-life is now marked on most items by a 'sell-by' date.

shelf module, off the n [Business] any form of mass-produced and widely applicable business presentation, eg: how to make a sale, deal with a difficult customer, use a word processor, etc. Such modules can be rented as required.

shelf, off the adv [Aerospace] referring to an aircraft which has been fully developed to military requirements and standards and is available for manufacture and procurement without the need for any further modifications.

shelf-talker n [Commerce] a small point-of-sale device, with promotional copy printed on it, which is fixed to the shelf in a supermarket next to the product which is to be boosted.

shell 1. n [Glass-making] a small flake of glass chipped from an edge by a sharp blow. 2. n [Sailing, Ropework] the carcase of a **block**, before any ropes have been threaded through it. 3. n [Skiing] the rigid outer casing of a modern ski-boot. 4. n [Textiles] the part of a loom in which a reed, the device which spaces the **warp** yarns evenly, is fitted. 5. n [Science] a set of electrons that forms one of a number of concentric structures around the nucleus of an atom; specifically it is a set of electrons all having the same principle quantum number. 6. also **sliver** n [Metallurgy] a relatively thin film or tongue of metal that is poorly attached to the surface of the steel.

shell company 1. n [Business] a company which exists on paper but not in fact and which is used for illegal reasons – eg: tax avoidance – rather than for actual legitimate trading. 2. n [Business] a company that is registered for the purpose of its name, and is then made available for sale to anyone who requires a ready-made company.

shell model n [Science] a theoretical description of a nuclear structure in which the nucleus is supposed to consist of nucleons arranged as **shells**.

shell scheme n [Marketing] the standard design of the individual display booth which is provided by the organisers of a trade exhibition.

shellback n [Navy] a veteran sailor.

shelling off n [Textiles] this is when the filling (the **weft**) flies off the bobbin.

shells n pl [US] [Meat trade] old, thin cows.

shelly 1. a [Dog breeding] said of general inadequacy of measurements, usually regarding chest or leg bones. 2. a [Furriers] used to describe a pelt that is unduly stiff or of a parchment-like quality, rather than desirably pliable. 3. a [Horse-racing] said of hooves that are scaly and brittle and resemble seashells.

sheltered 1. a [Economics] said of trades and industries, and the commodities in which they deal, which need not face competition. 2. a [Economics] offering relief or exemption from tax.

shelves n pl [Audio] parts of the frequency response curve that are found between peaks.

sheoke net n [Merchant navy] a net that is rigged below the gangway to catch any drunken seamen returning and falling off; it comes from 'sheoke' meaning cheap, raw spirits.

shepherd's crook n [Angling] a desirable result of casting a dry fly, when the fly, line and cast rest on the water in the shape of a crook.

Sherman statement n [US] [Politics] a final and absolutely irrevocable statement that a politician is not about to run as a candidate in a forthcoming election. It comes from the statement by General William Tecumseh Sherman in 1884: 'I will not accept if nominated, and will not serve if elected.'

sherpas n pl [Government] a team of bureaucrats, assistants and advisors to those participating in an international conference, who prepare the agenda, statements, etc. to save the ministers, heads of states, etc. valuable time at the actual conference; like the Himalayan guides after whom they are called, they help on the way to the 'summit'.

Sherwood forest n [Navy] the rows of missile tubes on a Polaris submarine – these tubes are painted green.

shice n [UK] [Market-traders] nothing; for free.

Shice McGregor n [UK] [Market-traders] the personification of an unprofitable trading day.

shift 1. n [Gambling] See **hop** 3. 2. n [Ice-hockey] a span of several minutes during which a player or **line** is on the ice without a respite.

shift the cut v [Gambling] to return the two halves of a supposedly cut pack to their original position in the deck, without any other player noticing.

shift units v [Record business] to sell records through retail outlets.

shifter n [Linguistics] a word that is understood only in its context.

shikar n [Shooting] either big or small game.

shill 1. n [Crime] in a game of **three-card monte** this is a decoy player, allied to the promoters of the game, who pretends to 'bet' and is allowed to 'win'; his successes are intended to encourage the genuine public to join the game. 2. n [Gambling] a house player who is employed to encourage the public players to join in the betting.

shilling on n [Horse-racing] any small bet wagered on a race.

shim n [Industry] a tapered piece of wood, metal or stone inserted into spaces for levelling purposes or to take up wear.

shimmy n [Transport] an oscillation or vibration

in the wheels of a car or undercarriage of an aircraft that is usually caused by an uneven surface; thus 'shimmy damper' is a device that can be fitted to minimise the problem.

shine n [Cricket] the newness, and thus the greater speed with which a ball should travel; hence a batsman scoring freely will 'knock the shine off' the ball.

shiner 1. n [Gambling] a small mirror, often concealed in a ring or on a coin, that is used to reflect the faces of the cards as they are dealt face-down around the table. 2. n [Window-cleaning] a window-cleaner. 3. n [Paper-making] a shining particle on the surface of finished paper that indicates some tiny mineral impurity.

shingling n [Metallurgy] hammering or squeezing a ball of hot metal to form a puddled **bloom** or **billet** for subsequent rolling in the forge.

shinplaster n [US] [Stock market] a worthless promissory note.

ship n [Aerospace] any aircraft.

ship gold v [Record business] said of a record when it amasses over 500,000 orders from retailers before it has even been released for sale.

ship one's killick v [Navy] to be promoted from able seaman to leading seaman. See also **hookey**.

ship one's swab v [Navy] to be promoted from midshipman to sub-lieutenant.

ship over v [US] [Marine Corps] to re-enlist. See also **re-up**.

ship's derrick, under adv [Shipping] a term used in a bill of lading contract to imply that the shipowner's responsibility for a consignment of goods ends when they have been placed on deck in such a way that the consignee or his agent can have them unloaded using the ship's derrick or some other suitable equipment.

ship's husband n [Shipping] a person, usually one of the joint owners of a ship, who has been appointed by the other owners to manage the affairs and the use of that ship.

ship's protest n [Shipping] See **captain's protest**.

ship's rail, at phr [Shipping] See **ship's derrick, under**.

ship's voice n [Navy] the ship's bell.

shires n pl [Hunting] the focus of British hunting: Leicestershire, Rutland (before its incorporation), Warwickshire, Northamptonshire and part of Lincolnshire; shire packs are the Pytchley, Quorn, Fernie, Belvoir and Cottesmore.

shirley 1. n [Photography] any picture of a model. 2. n [Photography] standardised test negatives used for colour balance; they are derived from (1) since facial tones are ideal for checking such balance.

shirring n [Clothing] a type of gathering which is done by using multineedle chain stitch machines which use elastic thread.

shirt fronts n [Real estate] the false fronts

attached to units of a housing development in which the majority of internal materials are cheap and building standards are second-rate, but which can be sold to the unsuspecting and gullible as prime property.

shirtsleeve environment n [Aerospace] the ideal environment of a high-flying aircraft or a spacecraft: special clothing can be dispensed with and human efficiency maximised by the wearing of normal garments which do not impair movement and bodily flexibility.

shish kebab n [Science] in some flowing polymer solutions, this is a fibrous crystalline structure which is made up of many plate crystallites – the kebabs – all growing outwards from a long ribbon or rod – the shish.

shit on a shingle n [US] [Marine Corps] corned beef hash on toast. See also **horse cock**.

shit or bust shot n [Ten pin bowling] a shot aimed at removing both the extreme left and right pins, when no others are standing, by hitting one and causing it to bounce across to knock down the other.

shiv n [Sailing, Ropework] the grooved wheel of a **block**; originally it was shiver.

shive n [Paper-making] an impurity in finished paper that is seen as a dark particle which has remained after insufficient processing of the raw materials.

shivering n [Pottery] the peeling and splitting of the glaze.

shock room 1. n [US] [Medicine] a room where a patient is given electroshock therapy (EST). 2. n [US] [Medicine] that part of the emergency room where trauma and arrest cases receive shock treatment.

shock treatment n [US] [Car salesmen] a very low estimate of the value of a customer's trade-in; it is the customer who is shocked.

shock worker n [USSR] [Industry] a Soviet term of approbation for any worker who voluntarily exceeds the production norms. Such workers were formed into brigades and used to conquer urgent or especially demanding projects. See also **stakhanovite**.

shocky n [US] [Medicine] a sudden drop in blood pressure that may occur during an operation.

shoe 1. n [Glass-making] a clay vessel, in the shape of a crucible, which is laid horizontally at the side of a pot mouth for heating the ends of blowing irons. 2. n [Oil rigs] a valve set at the bottom of a **conductor casing** through which, when the drill bore reaches an oil-bearing formation, a special concrete mix is pumped to achieve a bond between the hole and the formation.

shoemaker n [US] [Bars] a clumsy bar-tender.

shoes n pl [Espionage] false documents.

shoeshiner n [US] [Garment trade] an inefficient presser who puts an unwanted shine on to the garments with which he deals.

S

shoestring catch n [Baseball] a ball that is caught on a level with the top of the fielder's boots.

shome n [Commerce] this comes from 'show me'; it is a customer who wants to look but never buys.

shoofly n [US] [Police] a police officer who is more interested in trapping his own men in possible errors than in arresting criminals

shoo-fly 1. n [US] [Railways] a temporary railway track constructed for use while the main track is undergoing repair; also 'shoo-fly finger'. 2. n [US] [Printing] in certain flat-bed presses this is a set of narrow strips which lift the edge of the paper sheet off the cylinder ready for delivery. 3. n [Needlework] a simple, traditional patchwork design.

shoo-in 1. n [US] [Horse-racing] a guaranteed winner; it comes from the fraudulent practice of jockeys getting together before a race to decide which horse will win, so that all the rest can then 'shoo it in' past the post. 2. n [US] [Politics] a certain winner in an election; it comes from the horse-racing term. See 1.

shook 1. n [Cooperage] a set of the trimmed staves that are required for a single barrel and are bound together as a unit. 2. n [Industry] a bundle of the tops, bottoms, sides and ends required, and ready, to make boxes.

shoot 1. n [Advertising] a photographic session, especially when on location rather than in a studio. 2. n [Oil industry] the seismic mapping of an area when prospecting for oil, by sending waves of energy through the earth's crust and using special microphones – geophones – to measure reflection and thus depth. 3. v [Coal-mining] to remove rock by air blasting. 4. v [US] [Painting] to use a paint sprayer to cover a surface. 5. v [Cards] in bridge this is to play abnormally in an attempt to reach top scores in a tournament. 6. v [Oil rigs] to increase the flow of oil or gas from a well by detonating an explosive charge in the well.

shoot a letdown v [Air travel] the crew of a commercial airliner do this when they perform the regular approach and landing procedure.

shoot an avalanche v [US] [Skiing] to release an avalanche deliberately by shooting – in order to prevent an accident.

shoot around v [TV, Film] to shoot a scene, even though one of the actors involved in it is missing; the absentee's lines and shots can be added later and edited into the film as necessary.

shoot 'em up n [TV] a particularly violent TV programme.

shoot off v [TV] to site a camera so that part of the studio is visible in the shot.

shoot one, soda back phr [US] [Bars] a bourbon, neat, with a soda on the side.

shoot the line v [Angling] to allow a quantity of the line, held in the hand, to run out through the rings with the forward motion of the rod.

shooter 1. n [US] [Bars] a straight shot of liquor, swallowed at a single gulp. 2. n [Cricket] any ball that is delivered at speed and which keeps low, 'shooting' along the ground. 3. n [Gambling] the player who is currently throwing the dice in craps. 4. n [Marbles] the favourite marble which is shot by the player, as distinguished from the mass of **baits**.

shooters n pl [New therapies] miniature orgone boxes, designed by Wilhelm Reich.

shooting ratio n [Film] the ratio of all the film shot to the amount used for the finished film.

shooting script n [Film] a film script which contains the plot, dialogue and all the necessary technical instructions for the cameraman to shoot it. See also **screenplay**.

shoot-look-shoot capability n [Military] the ability to attack an enemy, assess the consequences of that attack and their counter-attack, and then plan and execute further strikes.

shop 1. n [Espionage] an intelligence agency. 2. n [Glass-making] a team or gang of men working from one pot furnace, or from one machine in a blowing or pressing process. 3. n [Stock market] the South African gold market. 4. n [UK] [Theatre] a theatrical engagement; thus 'seasonal shop' means working the summer (or other season) only.

shop a car v [US] [Car salesmen] to take a car that has not sold on the lot from dealer to dealer to see how good a price can be obtained.

shop audit n [Marketing] See **retail audit**.

shop the trade v [Commerce] to confer with rival salespeople or stores on the progress and pricing of certain lines of goods.

shopper 1. n [Advertising, Journalism] a local publication that resembles a newspaper in its design but which contains approximately 90% advertising to 10% editorial and which, on the basis of that revenue, can be distributed free to all the households in an area. 2. n [Sex] a man who enjoys checking over the available **hustlers** but only looks and rarely 'buys', since no-one is ever 'Mr. Right'.

shopping n [Billiards] potting one's opponent's ball; the sense is one of betrayal since it comes from the slang 'shop' meaning to inform on (to the police).

shopping goods n pl [Management] high-priced consumer goods which are purchased only after careful consideration of available alternatives, the checking of the best price and the comparing of a variety of competing shops. See also **convenience goods 1**.

shopping list credit, also **shopping bag credit** n [UK] [Finance] a very large loan from one country to another, whereby the central bank to whom the loan is made allocates portions of the loan in the form of credits to a variety of buyers of UK goods.

shorn n [Aerospace, Navy] acro **short range navigation** a system of radar-based navigation whereby a ship or aircraft uses the bearings taken on two widely-spaced ground stations to calculate its own position. See also **loran**.

short 1. *a* [*Cycling*] when assessing a time trial, this refers to a time marginally under the figure stated; thus 'short 59' means a fraction under fifty-nine minutes. See also **long** 1. 2. *a* [*Drugs*] said of a measure of drugs that is smaller than the dealer claimed it would be. 3. *a* [*Futures market*] referring to one who has sold a futures contract to establish a market position and who has not yet closed out this short position through an offsetting purchase. See also **long** 2. 4. *a* [*US*] [*Prisons*] having only a short period of one's sentence left to run. 5. *a* [*Stock market*] said of a **jobber** who is holding a **bear** position, having bought more stock than he has sold. See also **long** 2. 6. *a* [*Stock market*] said of Government stocks which have a life of less than five years. 7. *n* [*Film*] a film, usually non-fiction, that is less than 3000ft or runs for under 34 mins. 8. *n* [*Metallurgy*] the residue remaining when a coil of narrow strip steel is cut into lengths of specified dimensions.

short con *n* [*US*] [*Crime*] a quick, simple confidence trick, which can be worked by one operator, needs little or no equipment or preparation (apart from the con-man's expertise) and will bring in relatively small profits. See also **big con**.

short doors *n pl* [*TV*] small adjustable flaps attached to the sides of a light. See also **barn doors**.

short end *n* [*Stock market*] the section of an Exchange which deals in short-term stocks.

short eyes *n* [*US*] [*Prisons*] a child molester. See also **nonce**.

short finals *n* [*Air travel*] the last point of approach to a landing, usually defined as commencing at an airport's inner ground marker.

short hedge *n* [*Futures market*] a **hedge** against a rise in interest rates. See also **long hedge**.

short lighting *n* [*Photography*] in portrait photography this is the placing of the main light so that it illuminates the side of the face away from the camera; is useful in 'thinning down' otherwise plump features.

short ringup *n* [*Commerce, Crime*] the ringing up on a cash register of a lower price than that actually paid by the customer; the clerk then pockets the difference.

short run *n* [*Metallurgy*] in iron-founding this is a casting which is incomplete because insufficient molten metal was poured into the mould.

short selling *n* [*Futures market*] selling something that is probably not owned by the seller with the idea of buying it back quickly at a lower price.

short squeeze *n* [*Futures market*] a situation in which a lack of supply tends to force prices upwards.

short strokes *n* [*US*] [*Bars*] a customer who will not tip.

short ton *n* [*Commerce*] a weight of 2,000 lbs. See also **long ton**.

shortcake *v* [*Gambling*] to give someone short change.

shortening tabs *n pl* [*UK*] [*Road transport*] flaps fitted with eyelets some distance away from the edge of a tarpaulin so that a driver can **sheet** a smaller load without having excess tarpaulin.

shortenings *n pl* [*Banking*] the inexplicable, but common, shortfall in large cash deposits, eg: the loss of a single £5 note in a bundle of £20,000.

short-handed *a* [*Ice-hockey*] said of a team which has fewer players on the ice than its opponents, due to one or more suffering a penalty; it is also said of a goal that is scored during this situation.

short haul *a* [*Travel agents*] used to describe journeys within the UK and Europe. See also **long-haul**.

shorting *n* [*US*] [*Medicine*] delivering fewer pills than have been prescribed for a patient, but still charging the full price for the prescription; it comes from 'short-change', 'short-weight'.

short-laid *a* [*Sailing, Ropework*] See **hard-laid**. See also **plain-laid**.

short-money game *n* [*Sex*] See **cop and blow**.

short-pants division *n* [*US*] [*Police*] a juvenile court and its officers.

shorts 1. *n* [*US*] [*Railways*] See **pickup**. 2. *n pl* [*Tobacco*] varieties of filler tobacco used in the making of some types of cigar. 3. *n pl* [*Tobacco*] tobacco leaves that are under 18in long; they are usually used to tie up **hands** of larger leaves.

shortstop *n* [*Pool*] a player one degree below the top rank of ability; it comes from baseball use.

shortstops *n pl* [*Gambling*] bettors who have little money available for risking.

shot 1. *n* [*US*] [*Bars*] the amount of liquor that shoots straight out of the bottle with one twist of the wrist; an expert bartender should pour about one-and-a-half ounces in every shot. 2. *n* [*Glassmaking*] See **slug** 12. 3. *n* [*Weaving*] the single passage of a **weft** thread through the **shed**. 4. *a* [*Furriers*] used to describe a fur that is marred by a wound of any type – single shot or buckshot.

shot down *a* [*Gliding*] unable to stay in flight and forced to land; the assumption is that the conditions rather than the pilot were to blame.

shot lengths *n pl* [*TV, Film, Video*] a general term for the various distances a camera may be from the subject to be filmed. The most common of these, assessed in relation to a human figure, are: BCU: big close-up (the face, concentrating only on eyes, mouth and nose); CU: close-up (the whole head plus neck and top of shoulders); MCU: medium close-up (head, shoulders and upper torso); MS: medium shot (figure from the waist up); MLS: medium long shot (three-quarters of the figure); LS: long shot (the full length of the figure, head to foot); VLS: very long shot (the full length of the figure covering only 50% of the frame

S

size); ELS: extremely long shot (the figure is seen in the distance).

shot of cable n [*Sailing, Ropework*] two lengths of cable – each usually 120 fathoms long – spliced together to make one length.

shotgun 1. n [*US*] [*Football*] an offensive formation in which the quarterback lines up directly behind the centre in order to receive a direct snap from the line. 2. v [*Government, Business*] to relay a message as widely as possible over all available frequencies and through all channels; it comes from the image of a shotgun blast.

should cost technique n [*US*] [*Military*] a method whereby the Pentagon attempts to impose economic strictures on the costing of defence projects by establishing at the outset a figure that such projects 'should cost'; if this figure, assessed within the Pentagon, contradicts the estimates put forward by the actual manufacturers, these estimates have to be altered to fit the Pentagon's wishes.

shoulder 1. n [*Air travel*] the time of the year when traffic is sluggish and bookings slump. 2. n [*Air travel*] the time of the day when the rush of take-offs and landings slows for a while. See also **noon balloon.** 3. n [*Audio*] the top edge of the groove in a record. 4. n [*Shoe-making*] the half-sole, a sole for the front part of the shoe only. 5. n [*Skiing*] See **shovel.** 6. n [*UK*] [*Surfing*] that part of the wave that is rideable by surfers. 7. n [*Surfing*] the calm portion of a wave breaking on the beach.

shoulder arms v [*Cricket*] a batsman does this when he raises his bat out of the way of a ball which he has decided will not hit the stumps and at which he does not wish to play.

shoulder tap n [*Computing*] a technique that enables one processor to communicate with another.

shoulder time n [*Marketing*] the time which immediately precedes or follows peak-time TV viewing, shopping, etc.

shoulder-pod n [*Photography*] a camera support that uses the operator's shoulder.

shout 1. n [*UK*] [*Fire brigade*] an emergency call, phoned into the station and printed out on the teleprinter for immediate response. 2. n [*Journalism*] exclamation mark. See also **astonisher, screamer 5.**

shoutline n [*Publishing*] the headline of a **blurb** on the back of a book, often proclaiming 'The Novel That . . .' etc.

shouts n pl [*UK*] [*Police*] radio alerts that are broadcast to patrolling police vehicles, usually in response to 999 emergency calls.

shovel, also **shoulder** n [*Skiing*] the front of the ski, where it is widest.

shovel nose n [*Cars*] a full width nose fitted to some racing cars; the object is to shroud the front wheels and thus create some **downforce.**

show 1. v [*Gambling*] to throw in one's hand

during a card game. 2. n [*Coal-mining*] a concentration of flammable gas that is just strong enough to form a visible cap above the flame of a safety lamp. 3. n [*US*] [*Horse-racing*] the third place in a race, after 'win' and 'place'. 4. n [*Logging*] the area of the woods where the logging operations are carried out. 5. n [*Oil rigs*] an indication of gas or oil from an exploratory well.

show copy n [*Advertising, Film, Video*] the final version – of a commercial, a film, a tape or similar production – which is shown to the audience for which it has been created. See also **show print.**

show print n [*TV*] the final print of a programme that is selected for transmission.

show through n [*Printing*] the degree to which an image on the reverse side of a sheet of paper can be seen on the front. See also **see through.**

showboat n [*UK*] [*Road transport*] a large, eight-wheeled van.

showcase 1. v [*Film*] to release a film in many cinemas across the country; this level of release follows **first-run.** 2. n [*US*] [*Theatre*] a production that is designed to display the talents of all concerned for agents, producers, etc; such productions often pay very poorly, if at all.

showing a [*US*] [*Railways*] said of a job that is vacant, without a regular man.

show-out n [*UK*] [*Police*] a nod, or any other sign of acknowledgement, made by a police informer when he is meeting his police contact in a public place.

showreel n [*Advertising*] See **reel 1.**

show-up n [*US*] [*Police*] a police identification parade.

shpos n [*US*] [*Medicine*] abbr of **sub-human piece of shit** the most derogatory dismissal of a patient. See also **GOMER, toad 2.**

shrimp boat n [*Air travel*] a small plastic chip which is placed next to an electronic blip on the radar screen by an air traffic controller and which helps keep track of the various aircraft for whose safety that controller is responsible.

shrimps n pl [*UK*] [*Railways*] tamping machines which are used to clean ballast and return it to the track; the plenitude of cranks and pistons apparently resembles a shrimp. See also **waltzing matilda.**

shrinkage n [*Commerce*] a retail trade euphemism for shoplifting; many stores assume an annual level of shrinkage and if this drops it may equally well reflect an overall decline in trade just as much as an increase in security operations. See also **browsing.**

shroud 1. n [*Rug trade*] a funeral shroud; the implication is that a rug costs so much and is probably worth so little that, rather than sell it, the dealer will end up – financially and literally – using it as a shroud. 2. n [*Custom cars*] a hood, usually around the number plate, which is moulded into the bodywork and painted the body colour. 3. n [*Engineering*] a circular band attached

S

around the rotor of a turbine, or a flange on the tip of a turbine rotor blade. **4.** *n* [*Aerospace*] a temporary covering for a rocket or part of a rocket, especially one that streamlines and protects its **payload** during launch. **5.** *n* [*US*] [*Garment trade*] a cheap dress.

shroud-laid *a* [*Rope-making*] used to describe rope composed of four strands wound right-handed around a **heart**.

shrouds *n pl* [*Sailing, Ropework*] lower standing rigging that leads from the **channels** to the **tops**.

shtick, also **shtik, schtick** *n* [*Entertainment*] the basic elements of an entertainer's performance, especially of the style adopted by a comedian. The implication is of tried and tested material on a variety of topics that can be trotted out at will to please an audience; thus to 'do shtick' means to perform such material.

Shubert alley *n* [*US*] [*Theatre*] a popular gathering for New York actors; it is a short, narrow private street that runs between W44th and W45th Streets, off Times Square. It is named after the family of theatrical producers and managers whose office is in the Sam Shubert Theater, the stage door of which opens into the alley.

shuffler *n* [*UK*] [*Market-traders*] a tramp, a victim.

shunt 1. *n* [*Audio*] any component or circuit connected across another component or circuit. **2.** *n* [*Motor-racing*] a crash. **3.** *n* [*UK*] [*Railways*] the minimum speed limit for London underground trains. See also **parallel 2, series. 4.** *n* [*Medicine*] a natural or artifical route from a vein to an artery whereby blood may bypass a capillary bed; it is also the passage of blood along such a route.

shunter *n* [*Stock market*] a broker who transacts business with provincial exchanges and attempts to make his profits on the difference in prices between the various markets.

shushy *n* [*UK*] [*Market-traders*] a chicken.

shut down *v* [*Custom cars, Drag racing*] to beat a challenger over a quarter-mile race.

shut in *a* [*Oil industry*] said of oil or gas production capacity that is available but is not being used.

shut-out *n* [*Cards*] in bridge this is a bid that is intended to discourage the opposition from bidding.

shutout 1. *n* [*Baseball*] a complete game in which one team is held without scoring. **2.** *v* [*Baseball*] to achieve (1).

shutter *v* [*Entertainment*] to close the show, to 'put up the shutters'.

shuttering *n* [*Building, Concrete workers*] See **falsework**.

shuttle diplomacy *n* [*Government*] negotiations between two or more countries conducted by a mediator who flies frequently back and forth between the various parties to the dispute; it was first highlighted by the efforts of Dr. Henry Kiss-

inger to unravel the Middle Eastern imbroglio, around 1974.

SI *n* [*Government*] acro **Special Intelligence** it is collected by **sigint** and kept apart from other military intelligence.

siamese twins *n pl* [*UK*] [*Railways*] trade union and negotiating secretaries in discussion.

siamesed *a* [*Cars*] said of two-into-one inlet or exhaust ports, or exhaust pipes.

Sibe *n* [*Bird-watching*] a Siberian bird.

sibling, also **brother, sister** *n* [*Computing*] either of two nodes in a tree that are both the children of the same **parent**. See also **tree**.

SICBM *n* [*Military*] acro **Small Intercontinental Ballistic Missile** any one of a variety of small ICBMs – 'little guys' or 'mini-missiles' – that the US is attempting to develop in face of the difficulties in finding a suitable basing mode for the **MX** and the increasing vulnerability of existing static silos in the face of super-accurate delivery systems. See also **Midgetman**.

sick 1. [*Military*] air intercept code for: equipment indicated is operating at less than 100% efficiency. **2.** *a* [*Wine-tasting*] diseased, out of condition.

sick bay tiffy *n* [*Navy*] a sick berth attendant; tiffy is an abbreviation of artificer.

sick horse *n* [*US*] [*Road transport*] a tractor in poor mechanical condition.

sick seam *n* [*Sailing*] in sailmaking this is a seam in which worn stitches are giving way.

sick-in *n* [*Industrial relations*] a form of industrial action whereby a number of workers fail to appear on the job under the pretext of their all being ill.

sick-out *n* [*Industrial relations*] in order to avoid the legal penalties that may accompany an actual strike, a union organises mass absences – officially through 'sickness' – of the employees.

SICU *n* [*US*] [*Medicine*] acro **Surgical Intensive Care Unit**.

side 1. *n* [*Logging*] a crew of men including **fallers, buckers, riggers**, loaders and all others who work with the yarding **donkey. 2.** *n* [*US*] [*Theatre*] a script prepared for an individual actor in which only his/her speeches, entrances, exits and cues are listed.

side pipes *n pl* [*Custom cars*] visible, often chromed, exhaust pipes which, unlike open **lake pipes**, do have silencers.

side raves *n pl* [*UK*] [*Road transport*] very low sides to a platform vehicle or trailer to assist in restraining the load from sideways movements while on the trailer.

side winder *n* [*UK*] [*Railways*] starting the diesel engine by using a start button located on the side of the train.

sidebar 1. *n* [*Journalism*] a piece designed to accompany a larger one and run next to it on the page; such a piece expands one or more points in the main feature with extra information, illustrations, etc. **2.** *n* [*Film*] any form of secondary event, eg: a retrospective screening at a film

S

festival as opposed to the competitive section; it comes from the journalistic use (see **1**).

side-bearings *n pl* [*Photo-typesetting*] the amount of white space left between the characters when set on a line. Such spacing can be altered as required by the typesetting program.

sidecut *n* [*Skiing*] the arc that is formed along the length of a ski – which is wide at the **shoulder**, narrow at the **waist** and flares out again at the **tail** – and which determines the ski's turning characteristics.

sidehead *n* [*Journalism*] a sub-heading in the text set **flush** left.

side-head *n* [*Printing, Journalism*] See **sidebar**.

siderod *n* [*Logging*] the boss of a logging team in the woods.

side-slipping *n* [*Skiing*] slipping sideways down a slope.

side-stepping *n* [*Photo-typesetting*] a technique of deflecting the cathode ray tube (CRT) beam a measured distance of 90° to the tangent of a curve at any point of the image; this permits the contour of a character to be reinforced.

side-suit *n* [*Cards*] in bridge this is any suit other than trumps.

sidetracking *n* [*Oil rigs*] the creation of a new section of well bore to avoid impenetrable debris, straighten holes, etc; it comes from sidetrack drilling.

sidewheeler *n* [*Baseball*] a left-handed or side-arm pitcher.

sideways market *n* [*US*] [*Stock market*] horizontal price movement; it is a market in which there is virtually no share movement outside a narrow and relatively stable range.

siege *n* [*Glass-making*] the floor of a tank or pot furnace.

siege blocks *n pl* [*Glass-making*] blocks made of refractory material which are used to form the bottom of a tank furnace.

siesta *n* [*Chess*] a variety of gambit that is an extension of the popular Ruy Lopez opening; it is named after its appearance at a tournament in the town of Siesta, Italy.

sieve *n* [*US*] [*Medicine*] an intern in the emergency room who allows too many non-emergency patients in for treatment and thus increases an already excessive workload.

sieve map *n* [*Cartography*] a map that employs a basic image upon which a number of overlays can be placed to show additional information and features.

sifting **1.** *n* [*Computing*] the translation by a machine of one **high-level language** into another. **2.** *n* [*Computing*] a method of internal sorting within a machine whereby one set of records are moved round to make room for the insertion of a further set.

sigalert *n* [*US*] [*Traffic controllers*] slow moving traffic that is not quite a jam, but which is still too slow to allow easy flow; it is named after Lloyd

Sigmund, a traffic broadcaster of the 1960s and is used in Los Angeles, California. See also **rolling back-up**, **slow and go**.

sight **1.** *n* [*Gambling*] in poker this is the show of hands which one player may demand when he cannot match or surpass another's bet, but has bet all the chips or cash that he owns. **2.** *n* [*Commerce*] in the jewellery trade this is the sale of packets of uncut diamonds; those held in London take place ten times a year.

sights *n pl* [*Billiards*] diamonds sited around the table edge.

sightseers *n pl* [*UK*] [*Crime, Police*] See **hedge 2**.

sigint *n* [*Military*] abbr of **signals intelligence** intelligence that is derived from the processing of electronic intelligence and communications intelligence sources. See also **comint**, **elint**, **humint**, **telint**.

sigla *n pl* [*Book collecting*] editorial designations of the various versions of a literary text that are often used when preparing a specific edition of that text.

sign *n* [*Sociology, Linguistics*] in **semiotics** this is the association of the signifier and the signified. Signs are divided into iconic – those relatively free of social mediation – and arbitrary – those more dependent on such mediation. Signs can also function as myths and as codes and may not only associate an object with a concept but also with the feelings that that object engenders within us. See also **signified**, **signifier**.

signature **1.** *n* [*Military*] the 'blip' that appears on a radar screen and signifies the presence of some object. **2.** *n* [*Navy*] the sound made by a submarine propeller which can be picked up by undersea surveillance devices. **3.** *n* [*Publishing*] a printed sheet folded one or more times so that when trimmed at the top, outside and bottom it will resemble a small unbound pamphlet; most signatures are folded four times to produce 32 pages and a suitable number of these are bound together to form the finished book.

significance *n* [*Statistics*] the level at, or the extent to which, a result has some statistical significance.

significant quantity *n* [*Science*] the amount of enriched Uranium–235 that is required to make an atomic bomb.

signified *n* [*Sociology, Linguistics*] in **semiotics** this is a mental concept indicated by the signifier. See also **sign**, **signifier**.

signifier *n* [*Sociology, Linguistics*] in **semiotics** this is a physical object, a word or picture of some kind. See also **signified**, **sign**.

signify *v* [*US*] [*Prisons*] to create trouble deliberately, often by setting off a round of ritualised verbal insults between two prisoners. See also **wolf ticket 2**.

signing *part* [*Government*] abbr of **signing on** claiming unemployment benefit.

signpost writing *n* [*Literary criticism*] writing that is filled with directional modifiers such as 'above-mentioned', 'heretofore', etc.

silent salesman *n* [*Marketing*] any point-of-sale material embodying display and attention-getting contents and used as a merchandising technique; includes the actual packaging of the product.

silent Swamper *n* [*Logging*] a mythical figure resident in the woods who is, according to loggers, the being responsible for the sudden and unpredictable fall of otherwise untouched timber.

silk 1. *n* [*Photography*] a sheet of white material, not necessarily silk, which is stretched on a frame and used to reduce the harshness of lighting on a subject. 2. *n* [*Gemstones*] a silky lustre found in certain rubies and sapphires due to certain microscopic crystals; it is considered to be a defect. 3. *n* [*UK*] [*Law*] a Queen's Counsel.

silk label *n* [*Textiles*] a label sewn on to a textile – garments, bedding, towels, etc – to give a description of the material used.

silked *a* [*Book collecting*] said of a book in which the leaves are so fragile, or need so much repair, that they have been faced on both sides with a thin, transparent textile or fabric.

silks *n* [*Horse-racing*] the blouse or jacket worn by a jockey and which displays the owner's colours. See also **blouse**.

silky *a* [*Wine-tasting*] firm, yet with a distinctly soft texture on the palate; a characteristic of the best dessert wines.

sill *n* [*Glass-making*] the floor of a **port**.

silly *a* [*Cricket*] describing various fielding positions found near and usually slightly in front of the batsman; the inference (OED 1897) is that the fieldsman is foolish to expose himself so close to the batsman.

silly nick *n* [*Cricket*] See **Chinese cut**.

silly season *n* [*Journalism*] the period, essentially and traditionally the summer holiday season, when **hard news** seems to vanish and the front pages and the TV and radio news bulletins are filled with trivia and absurdities. See also **closed period**.

silo operator *n* [*US*] [*Theatre*] the owner of a summer theatre, so-called because such seasonally opened theatres tend to be in the corn-belt states of the US Midwest.

Silver Age *n* [*Literary criticism*] Russian literature and art created at the start of the Twentieth century and continued until the Revolution; it is the successor to the Golden Age of the 19th century.

silver bullets *n pl* [*UK*] [*Railways*] London Transport aluminium coated underground stock.

silver handshake *n* [*Business*] a relatively small payment given either on retirement from a job or as compensation for one's dismissal. See also **golden handshake**.

silver tux *n* [*Aerospace*] a special variety of astronaut suit. See also **Apollo suit**.

silverskin *n* [*Coffee production*] the dried seed coat of the coffee bean which has a silvery/coppery appearance.

similar trees *n pl* [*Computing*] **trees** that have the same structure or shape.

simolivac *n* [*Aerospace*] abbr of **silicon molten in a vacuum** a synthetic 'moon rock', with some of the same properties as the real thing, that is manufactured by earth scientists.

simple *a* [*Wine-tasting*] better than **ordinary**; a straightforward, uncomplicated wine.

simple labour *n* [*Economics*] in Marxist terms this is the basic unskilled labour of the lowest level of productivity.

simple pimp *n* [*Sex*] in the world of black pimps this is a pimp who has reached his limits, and one who will never attain the pimp's main aim – to progress to higher things.

simple toilers *n pl* [*Politics*] See **broad masses**.

simple vows *n pl* [*Religion*] the vows taken by members of a religious order at an early stage in their enrolment and from which they may later be released. See also **solemn vows**.

simplex *n* [*Computing*] communications that are sent down a data line in one direction only. See also **duplex 1**.

Simpson's rule *n* [*Mathematics*] a rule created in 1743 by Thomas Simpson (1710–1761) for estimating the area under a curve where the values of the odd number ordinates, including those at the limits, are known; the approximate area is given by the sum of the first and last ordinates, double all the other odd ordinates, and quadruple all the even ordinates, multiplied by one third of the distance between adjacent ordinates.

simul *n* [*Chess*] an exhibition match in which one player takes on a number of opponents in simultaneous games.

simulcast *n* [*Radio, TV*] abbr of **simultaneous broadcast** the broadcasting of an event – usually a concert of either classical or pop music – in which TV supplies the live pictures and stereo FM radio supplies the sound to go with them.

sin bin *n* [*Education*] any remedial class or institution that is designed to deal with children whose persistent trouble-making at school defeats normal methods of control.

sin bosun *n* [*US*] [*Navy*] the ship's chaplain.

sindonology *n* [*Theology, Archaeology*] the study of the Holy Shroud of Turin, in which allegedly the remains of Jesus Christ were wrapped after the Crucifixion.

sinewy *a* [*Wine-tasting*] lean, lacking in **fat**, but still muscular.

singer's node *n* [*Medicine*] a small pale swelling on a vocal cord that is seen in singers (particularly tenors and sopranos) but also in others who use their voices above the average.

singing *n* [*Communications*] extraneous sounds caused by unwanted oscillations on the communications line.

S

singing point n [Communications] the maximum gain that a telephone repeater can have without being liable to self-oscillation in the circuit and the onset of sub-standard communications.

single 1. n [Baseball] a hit that permits the batter to reach first base. See also **double 1**. 2. n [Hunting] the tail of the red deer. 3. n [Metallurgy] a piece or section of sheet metal over one thirty-second of an inch thick. 4. n [TV, film] a shot of a single character only. 5. n [US] [Theatre] an artist who works alone in an act; it is usually in vaudeville/variety shows.

single bond n [Commerce, finance] a bond to which no extra conditions are attached regarding payment. See also **double bond**.

single capacity n [Stock market] a dealing situation in which a firm commits itself either to the role of principal or **agent**, but never both. This system was customary in the Stock Exchange prior to the deregulatory processes of the **Big Bang** of October 1986. See also **dual capacity**.

single clad a [TV, film] said of scenery that is designed and built to be viewed from one side only.

single entry n [Libraries] a cataloguing system which has no cross-references and thus lists each title at one place in the catalogue only.

single sticks n pl [Navy] signal flags used for hand semaphoring.

single-o n [Sex] a freelance homosexual prostitute; it comes from the carnival term for an act that is good enough to stand by itself in the promotional billing.

singles n [Weaving] thread that is a single ply.

single-stroking n [Industrial relations, Journalism] the concept that a print union (the National Graphical Association in the UK), which was formerly responsible for all typesetting on linotype (hot metal) machines, will permit journalists and the advertising departments of newspapers to set copy directly on to computerised terminals after the installation of such modern equipment.

singleton 1. n [Book collecting] a single leaf, where a pair might be expected; such a leaf is probably the survivor of a pair from which the other has been cut, or it can be a solitary, extra leaf. 2. n [Espionage] an agent who operates by him/herself.

sing-song theory n [Linguistics] the theory proposed by O. Jespersen that all languages originally evolved from primitive singing.

singularism n [Philosophy] the belief that explains the phenomena of the universe from a single principle.

singularity n [Science] a hypothetical point in space so distorted by gravity that nothing can escape being crushed into infinite density and microscopic volume; a black hole.

sinister 1. n [Heraldry] the left-hand side of the coat-of-arms from the wearer's point of view; for the on-looker it is the right-hand side. See also **dexter**. 2. n [Heraldry] oriented in the opposite direction to the usual.

sink 1. n [Computing] a point of data usage in a communications network. 2. n [Metallurgy] the reduction of the diameter of a tube during drawing. 3. n [Printing] a part of the area of a printing plate that is too low to print properly. 4. n [Science] any place where, or process whereby, energy is removed from a system or a specific device is removed from a system, and either stored or destroyed.

sink the wind v [Hunting] said of a fox which passes beneath the line of scent.

sink tree n [Computing] the set of all paths to a destination in a communcations network. See also **data**, **sink**, **sink 1**.

sinkage n [Publishing] the insertion of extra space between the normal top margin of a page and the first line of type.

sinkbox n [Hunting] See **battery 7**.

sinker 1. n [Baseball] a pitched ball that suddenly descends from a straight course as it nears the batter. 2. n [Building] a narrow wire nail. 3. n [Coal-mining] a heavy drill used in sinking a mineshaft. 4. n [Logging] a log that is too heavy to float on the log pond. 5. n [US] [Stock market] any bond held in a sinking fund.

sinking n [Art] a dull spot on the surface of an oil painting caused by the absorption of the pigments by the ground on which they are painted; it is also the process whereby pigments are absorbed by the ground.

sinking fund n [Banking] a fund which is created by setting aside certain sums at regular intervals for investment outside a business in order to provide for the repayment of an asset, or the repayment of a liability which will fall due at a known future date.

sinnet n [Sailing, Ropework] braided cord.

SINS n [Navy] acro **Ship's Inertial Navigation System** used on board nuclear submarines, the system requires neither radio transmitting or receiving and thus helps prevent detection by hostile forces.

SIOP n [Military] acro **Single Integrated Operational Plan** the top secret range of interlocking contingency plans under which the US (and the UK) would fight a nuclear war. The first SIOP was issued in 1960, as an amalgam of the various strategic bombing plans evolved by the **SAC** in the 1950s, and has been modified continually since. The current plan is SIOP–6, issued on October 1st, 1983; as well as its basic function – the mass targeting of almost every sector of Soviet life that might be seen as contributory to the war and/or industrial effort – there is the concept, first elaborated in the previous plan – 5D, issued in 1980 – that any future nuclear war has to be seen as possibly limited and thus 'winnable'.

siphoning n [TV] the transmission by a cable television station of a programme originally available on a network direct broadcast; in the US there are 'anti-siphoning laws' to prevent pay cable channels gaining exclusive rights to programmes, especially sportscasts and films, which would otherwise be available on network television.

sippers n [Navy] a sip of rum, often taken from a shipmate's tot, as a reward for some service or as a celebration.

sister n [Computing] See **sibling**. See also **tree**.

sister company n [Commerce] one of two or more companies within a group or organisation.

Sister Dora n [Medicine] a type of nurse's cap, tied under the chin with a butterfly bow, and named after Sister Dorothy Pattison (1832–78).

sister strands n pl [Sailing, Ropework] where there are two opposed sets of strands, these are the related members of each set.

sisters n pl [Espionage] See **ladies 2**.

sit 1. n [Commerce] the salesman's first face-to-face meeting with a client. 2. n [Merchant navy] a berth.

sit down v [Golf] the ball does this when it lands on the green and stops without rolling any further.

sit flat v [Aerospace] said of a spacecraft when it is in the correct orbit with all equipment functioning as it should be.

sit position v [Military] to collect strategic information in one of the many US installations around the world that conducts electronic surveillance. See also **comint, elint, humint, sigint, telint**.

sit on the splice v [Cricket] to score very slowly; the image is of the batsman leaning on the splice, which joins the handle of the bat to its blade, rather than actually striking the ball with it.

sit spin n [Skating] See **jackson haines**.

sit up and beg n [Cycling] a heavy, old-fashioned bicycle, with an upright posture, high handlebars, etc.

sitcom n [TV] abbr of **situation comedy** a programme, usually screened as a series, which takes a specific group of characters in a particular background and uses their (mis-)adventures and mutual interaction as the source of a continuing comedy, eg: 'Dad's Army', 'Hi-De-Hi', 'All In The Family', 'Sergeant Bilko', etc.

sitrep n [Military] abbr of **situation report**.

sitter, also **dolly** n [Cricket] an extremely easy catch. See also **gaper**.

sitting 1. n [New age] meditating. 2. a [Hunting, Shooting] said of an easy target, sitting conveniently in front of one's gun.

sitting by Nellie part phr [Management] learning to do a job by watching someone else do it.

situation 1. n [Film] See **location 2. 2.** n [Sociology] a redundant descriptive word, often found in combination with **on-going** and meaning anything that is continuing to happen, or with some noun as a qualifier, eg: penalty situation (sport), riot situation (police), etc.

situation comedy n [TV] See **sitcom**.

situation ethics n [Philosophy] the belief that ethics and morality can and must alter according to an over-riding external situation that puts pressure on such ethics in their 'pure' form.

situation morality n [Philosophy] See **situation ethics**.

situationism n [Politics] a set of revolutionary beliefs proposed and espoused by members of the French movement 'Situationiste Internationale' and its followers from the 1950s to the 1970s. These beliefs centred on a fight against a modern society in which the rise of technology and science had reduced the individual to one more commodity, subject to massive cultural repression and impotent in the face of the all-embracing industrial world. Situationists chose to attack that world, especially in its faceless bureaucracy and international homogeneity. Situationist philosophy underpinned much of the ideology that emerged in the 'Evénements' of 1968.

situations n pl [Film] the cinemas where films are exhibited.

situs 1. n [US] [Law] a work site occupied by two or more employers. 2. n [US] [Law] the place to which a property is deemed to belong for the purposes of law and for taxation.

sitzmark n [Skiing] the impression left in the snow by a skier who has fallen down backwards; it is also the act of so falling; it comes from Ger. 'sitzen' meaning to sit.

six n [Horticulture] a large flower-pot, six of which can be made from one cast of clay. See also **sixteen, sixty**.

six banger n [US] [Car salesmen] a six-cylinder car.

six foot n [UK] [Railways] the space between standard tracks; it is actually 6ft 5in plus.

six in the gate n [TV, Film] ready for filming; when the number 6 appears in the camera's **gate**, the film is ready to be used for shooting the scene.

SIX teams n pl [Espionage] acro **Sabotage, Intelligence and Experiment** small groups of agents who are sent on missions for the purposes of 'SIX'.

six-ace flats n pl [Gambling] crooked dice used by cheats.

six-by-six n [Military] a six-wheel truck with six-wheel drive.

sixie from Dixie n [Gambling] in craps dice, the point of six.

six-sheet 1. v [Theatre, film] to exaggerate, to lie. 2. v [Theatre, film] to promote a show or film with an excess of ballyhoo and advertising; both uses come from the 'six-sheet': the largest size of theatrical or circus poster.

sixteen n [Horticulture] a medium-sized flower-

S

pot, sixteen of which can be made from one cast of clay. See also **six**, **sixty**.

sixteen bells *n* [*Navy*] struck at midnight on December 31st to herald the New Year; merchant ships strike thirty-two bells.

sixty *n* [*Horticulture*] a small-sized flower-pot, sixty of which can be made from one cast of clay. See also **six**, **sixteen**.

sixty mess *n* [*Navy*] a mess set aside for sailors suffering from venereal disease.

sizing 1. *n* [*Computing*] preparing an estimate of the likely size of a program or software system. 2. *n* [*Weaving*] a starchy solution into which yarn can be dipped to protect it during the weaving process.

sizzle seller *n* [*Commerce*] a product that is sold on its image rather than on its content; it comes from selling the sizzle, rather than the steak.

skate 1. *n* [*Navy*] a sailor who refuses to accept discipline. 2. *n* [*Navy*] See **bird 3**.

skating *n* [*US*] [*Car salesman*] the practice of surreptitiously taking over another salesman's customer in order to claim the full commission.

skating force *n* [*Audio*] the inward bias on a pick-up arm caused by offset geometry and the friction between the record's grooves and the stylus.

skaz *n* [*Literary criticism*] in Russian literature this is a first person narrative in which the author takes on a specific persona other than his/her own.

skeds *n pl* [*TV*] a corruption/abbreviation of schedules.

skeg *n* [*UK*] [*Surfing*] the fin that is found on the underside of a surfboard, helping the surfer to maintain balance and direction.

skein *n* [*US*] [*TV*] a series that is made by one of the **webs** – the major US networks – rather than by an independent production company.

skel *n* [*US*] [*Bars*] abbr of **skeleton** a customer who does not tip.

skeleton 1. *n* [*Chess*] the dispostion of one player's pawns in any position of play. 2. *n* [*Printing*] a face, using only extremely thin lines.

skeleton account *n* [*Accounting*] See **T account**.

skeleton army *n* [*Salvation Army*] in the formative years of the S.A. these were the groups of people antagonistic to its aims who attempted to undermine its activities.

skeleton car *n* [*Logging*] a piece of railway rolling stock made up of two sets of four wheels joined by a piece of heavy timber; on this timber are set steel struts which carry the logs.

skeleton drill *n* [*Military*] in the training of officers these are drill parades in which a far smaller number of men than would actually be required form a 'battalion', on whom the officers can practise their commands.

skeleton forme *n* [*Printing*] reusable typographical parts – **quoins**, **furniture**, etc. – that are used in printing; everything required to print a page but the set metal type itself.

skeleton tie-up *n* [*Weaving*] the tie-up in which each treadle is tied to only one shaft or harness.

skell *n* [*US*] [*Subways*] a New York Transit Police term for a down-and-out vagrant, possibly insane, who lives in the New York subway system.

skelp *n* [*Metallurgy*] hot rolled steel strip with slightly bevelled or square edges which is used to make welded tubes.

skew 1. *n* [*TV, Video*] the vertical breakup of the top of the picture that is found on poor video recordings; it is caused by maladjusted tape tension. 2. *n* [*Statistics*] a graph that is asymmetrical, or a number of statistical returns that show an asymmetrical distribution about the mean.

skewbacks, also **springers** *n pl* [*Glassmaking*] specially shaped blocks that support the roof of a furnace.

skewer *n* [*Chess*] an attack on a straight line; as the opponent is forced to move one piece out of the way, it automatically reveals the secondary piece, which has always been the intended target, to the full force of the attack.

ski bunny, also **snow bunny** *n* [*US*] [*Skiing*] a novice skier, usually female.

ski stopper *n* [*Skiing*] a ski brake comprising two prongs which spring open when a boot is released from a binding to prevent the ski running away downhill after it has become detached.

skid 1. *v* [*US*] [*Gliding*] to perform a turn in an aircraft using too much rudder input and not enough aileron input. 2. *n* [*US*] [*Gliding*] a wooden or metal plate attached underneath the nose of a glider to absorb friction from the runway or ground on landing. 3. *v* [*Gliding*] a glider does this when it makes sideways motions with the wings level; or, in a turn, when it makes motions away from the low wing. See also **slip 3**. 4. *n* [*Oil rigs*] abbr of **skid beam** used to **skid the rig**.

skid artist *n* [*UK*] [*Police*] a skilful getaway driver.

skid level *n* [*Oil rigs*] the ground level, or deck of the offshore platform on which the rig platform stands, with the **cellar**, **shaker screen**, **slush tank** etc.

skid one's rig *v* [*Oil rigs*] to surpass, to outperform.

skid the rig *v* [*Oil rigs*] to move the rig from one hole to another with as little dismantling of equipment as possible.

skids *n pl* [*Publishing*] wooden or metal pallets on which newly bound copies of a book are stored and transported.

skim *n* [*Gambling*] the retention of a portion of the profits of a casino and not declaring them to the tax authorities; this money is sent out of the country to foreign banks which will **launder** it before it is returned to the country of origin; hence the practice of 'skimming'.

skimboard *n* [*Surfing*] a type of board used for riding in shallow water.

skimmer *n* [*Oil rigs*] an anti-pollution device – like a large vacuum cleaner – which sucks waste oil from the surface of the sea.

skimmers *n pl* [*US*] [*Navy*] surface shipping.

skimming 1. *n* [*Business*] a pricing policy designed to maximise profit margins by launching a product at an artificially high price and then, as it grows in appeal, gradually dropping that price so as to saturate the market. **2.** *n* [*Crime*] the use of profits from an illegal operation, eg: drug trafficking, to establish a legitimate business for the channelling of such profits and to provide a front for future illegal activities. **3.** *n* [*US*] [*Medicine*] the practice in health insurance programmes, that are based on prepayment or which have a capitation basis, of seeking to enrol only the healthiest of clients, or those exhibiting the minimum of risk, so as to control costs and payments. **4.** *n* [*US*] [*Medicine*] the practice in health insurance programmes of denying members the services they have paid for as a way of holding down costs.

skimmish *v* [*UK*] [*Market-traders*] to drink heavily; thus 'skimmisher' is a heavy drinker; 'skimmished' means very drunk.

skin 1. *v* [*Custom cars*] See **panelling. 2.** *n* [*Electronics*] the outer or surface layers of a conductor in which alternating current is concentrated at high frequencies. **3.** *n* [*Gemstones*] the outer layer of a pearl. **4.** *n* [*Hot rods*] a tyre.

skin effect *n* [*Electronics*] the tendency of an alternating current of high frequency to flow through the outer layers only of a conductor, causing an increase in effective resistance. See also **skin**.

skin flicks *n pl* [*US*] [*Medicine*] slides illustrating a variety of skin diseases that are used to teach dermatology. See also **skin game**.

skin game *n* [*US*] [*Medicine*] dermatology. See also **skin flicks**.

skin passing *n* [*Metallurgy*] a light cold rolling of annealled, normalized or hot rolled sheet or strip steel. This operation is designed to resist any deformation of the product on subsequent manipulation.

skin the cat *v* [*Gymnastics*] to perform an exercise in which the feet and legs are passed between the arms while one hangs by the hands from a horizontal bar, thus drawing the body up and over the bar.

skinning *n* [*Military*] the disarming of a person or of a weapon.

skinning out bag *n* [*Merchant navy*] a bag kept packed ready for emergencies; it contains the seaman's survival kit.

skins 1. *n pl* [*US*] [*Transport*] tyres. **2.** *n pl* [*US*] [*Meat trade*] thin, low-grade hogs. **3.** *n pl* [*Skiing*] fabric stretched over the soles of skis allowing them to slide forward but not backwards; they were originally made of seal skin. **4.** *n pl* [*Theatre*] tights.

skinshow *n* [*Fashion*] a revealing garment with either a plunging neckline, a short skirt or both.

skintle *v* [*Building*] to build in a deliberately uneven manner to create a supposedly 'quaint' effect in the bricks.

skip 1. *n* [*Building*] a small spot left unworked when painting, planing wood, etc. **2.** *n* [*Gambling*] abbr of a **skip straight** in poker; this means five alternate cards in sequence; such a run is twice as hard to get as a normal, consecutive straight, and the odds against it are 423–1. **3.** *n* [*Audio*] a dead area in radio reception which occurs between the points where the signal has proceeded beyond a certain distance from the transmitting station and before it begins to be reflected back from the upper atmosphere and becomes audible again. **4.** *n* [*UK*] [*Postal services*] a container into which mail is placed in the sorting office. **5.** *v* [*Hotels*] to leave without paying one's bill.

skip effect *n* [*Radio*] the long distance reflection of radio waves from the ionosphere.

ski-pack *n* [*Travel agents*] a package holiday, aimed at skiers, in which travel, board and lodging at the resort and the hire of ski equipment are all offered at an inclusive price.

skipper *n* [*US*] [*Hotels*] a hotel guest who leaves without paying the bill and who cannot be traced at the address given on registering.

skippers *n pl* [*US*] [*Painting*] See **catface**.

skirt 1. *v* [*Weaving*] to remove the short, dirty fibres from around the edges of a fleece. **2.** *n* [*Food processing*] the small globules of ice-cream that appear at the base of a scoop of ice-cream and which are considered as over-serving and waste by the retail trade. **3.** *n* [*Aerospace*] the lower portion of a parachute's canopy. **4.** *n* [*Engineering*] a portion of a vehicle or aircraft that is designed to protect the underside or the wheels; it is found in aircraft, motor cars, hovercraft, etc. **5.** *n* [*Engineering*] the lower part of the curved surface of a piston in a piston engine, below the grooves for the piston rings. **6.** *n* [*Statistics*] the lower sloping portions of a peak or rise on a graph.

skirter *n* [*Hunting*] a hound that cuts corners in pursuing the fox, rather than following the exact line.

skish *n* [*Angling*] a competition in which anglers use a standard bait to cast twice at each of ten targets.

skit *n* [*Espionage*] a faked event that makes the entrapment of a blackmail victim even more plausible; it is a 'police raid' or the entry of an 'outraged husband' – when neither police nor husband are genuine – in order to convince the victim that his problems are quite as they seem and that accepting the demands of the **sanctifiers** is the only sensible course.

skittle pot, also **cannon pot** *n* [*Glass-making*] a pot for melting small quantities of glass in a

S

furnace which usually contains pots of a normal size.

skive *v* [*Industry*] to cut off in thin slices, eg. leather or rubber.

skoob *n* [*Art*] this comes from the reverse of the word 'books'; it is a quantity of books assembled deliberately for subsequent (public) burning. Such burnings were created by the artist John Latham, who concentrated on art books, as a statement against what he considered was an excessive proliferation of and respect for the printed word.

skookum *a* [*Logging*] referring to anything strong; or generally praiseworthy; it comes from Chinook.

skull 1. *v* [*Golf*] to hit the ball too far above its centre. 2. also **take** *v* [*Film*] to make an exaggerated physical reaction to a line, gesture or event. 3. *n* [*Metallurgy*] in iron founding this is a film of metal or dross which remains in the ladle after the mass of molten metal has been poured into the mould. 4. *n* [*UK*] [*Road transport*] a passenger. 5. *n* [*US*] [*Theatre*] an admission pass.

skull ball *n* [*Cricket*] See **beamer**.

skull practice *n* [*Sport*] a pre-match pep-talk and final strategy session conducted by the team coach.

skull session 1. *n* [*Government, Business*] this comes from sporting usage and means a meeting for consultation, discussion and general interchange of ideas and strategies. See also **brainstorming**. 2. *n* [*Sociology*] general intellectual sparring and mutual mental therapy between members of the intelligentsia.

skunk *n* [*US*] [*Navy*] any unidentified surface craft.

skunk wagon *n* [*US*] [*Police*] a black-and-white patrol car.

skunk works *n* [*US*] [*Military*] a small team of highly trained experts who are given a project by the managers of their firm (and often by the Pentagon) and told to get on with it. They suffer minimal interference and, like the animal in question, are left alone by the curious; this freedom allows them greater latitude and less government intervention than most defence contractors. The best known 'Skunk Works' is run in California by Lockheed, makers of the U–2 and SR–71 'Blackbird' spy planes; their engineers coined the word when designing the F–80 jet fighter in 1940.

sky *n* [*UK*] [*Market-traders*] pocket; it comes from rhyming slang sky-rocket.

sky artist *n* [*Navy*] a naval psychiatrist.

sky hook, also **bathook** *n* [*Mountaineering*] a hook which can be attached to the smallest of projections and to which an etrier – a set of small, portable steps – can in turn be attached.

sky pan *n* [*TV*] See **scoop 4**.

skybound *a* [*Logging*] said of a tree that is unable to fall because of the density of surrounding timber.

skyhook 1. *v* [*Coal-mining*] to reinforce a mine ceiling by inserting bolts vertically into the secure rock above. 2. *n* [*Mountaineering*] a hook fixed into a rock face on to which ropes may be attached to facilitate the climb.

skying *n* [*Textiles*] the passing of cotton cloth through air in order to oxidise the reduced indigo used in dyeing.

skylights *n pl* [*Navy*] holes in the polar ice canopy through which a nuclear submarine is able to surface. See also **friendly ice**, **hostile ice**.

skyline *n* [*Journalism*] a headline that runs above the newspaper's logo on the front page.

skyrigger *n* [*Logging*] a logger whose task is to attach the **high-line** to the felled trees.

slab 1. *v* [*US*] [*Coal-mining*] to cut a passage way into the side of a **pillar** either to gain easier access past it, or to obtain some of the coal which constitutes that pillar. 2. *n* [*Logging*] a piece cut from the outside of a log when it is being prepared for sawing into planks, etc. 3. *n* [*Architecture*] a rectangular block of pre-cast concrete that is often used in building high-rise blocks; a single slab might form a ceiling, another a wall. 4. *n* [*Architecture*] a styleless, unattractive, high-rise building, possibly constructed from (3). 5. *a* [*Printing, Type-faces*] used to describe a square, sectioned face, especially in its serifs; eg. a 'Wild West' face.

slack 1. *n* [*New therapies*] in **co-counselling** this is a period of about 60 minutes during which the counsellor listens to the client; they then swop roles for a similar period and then exchange notes. 2. *n* [*UK*] [*Railways*] a depression in the rail level. 3. *n* [*Management*] in **critical path analysis**, this is the length of time during which an event can be delayed without delaying the completion of the overall objective.

slack bobs *n pl* [*Education*] at Eton College, a small number of boys who need neither row nor play cricket, but are allowed to play tennis.

slack capacity *n* [*Air travel*] a situation in which there are too many available aircraft and too few passengers to fill them.

slack fill *n* [*Marketing*] the filling of containers or packets in such a way that despite the splendour of the packaging, they actually contain more air than advertised product.

slag *n* [*UK*] [*Market-traders*] a loafer, a layabout.

slain in the spirit *a* [*Religion*] so overcome with the Holy Spirit that one collapses on the floor.

slaister *v* [*Art*] to paint or colour in an inferior, vulgar manner; it comes from the original meaning of eating in a slobbering manner.

slamming 1. *n* [*Gambling*] a fast game with plenty of heavy betting. 2. *n* [*Gambling*] cheating.

slan *n* [*Science fiction*] a being of superior intelligence and power; it comes from AE Van Vogt's 'Slan'.

slan shack *n* [*Science fiction*] anywhere that

more than two science fiction fans live; it may be a commune of the like-minded.

slang n [UK] [Market-traders] a licence, a permit.

slanger, also **slat** n [Angling] See **kelt**.

slanted abstract n [Libraries] an abstract which deliberately emphasises the aspects of a document that will appeal to a specific user or users. See also **auto, evaluative, general, indicative, informative, selective abstract**.

slap n [UK] [Theatre] make-up.

slap shot n [Ice-hockey] a shot delivered by swinging the stick against the puck, like a golf shot, rather than flicking it with the wrists.

slapdab n [Building, Plastering] a 'cowboy' plasterer.

slash n [Logging] branches, bark, tops, chunks, cull logs, uprooted stumps and anything else that remains on the ground after an area of woods has undergone logging.

slash print n [TV] a black and white print of a colour programme which is used for dubbing. See **dub**.

slash sheet n [US] [Computing, Government] a government-designed and distributed specification list for the procurement of officially accepted parts for data transmission systems.

slasher 1. n [Brick-making] an implement that uses an iron blade to prod or slash the clay from which the bricks are made, in order to detect stones. 2. n [US] [Crime] a thief who specialises in robbing from fashion wholesalers where he slashes open the canvas covers that protect the garments and steals as many as he can. 3. n [Logging] a worker who cleans up the debris after logging operations. 4. n [Logging] a machine used in saw-mills or pulp mills to saw logs into short pieces. 5. n [Textiles] a machine that lays the fibres of warp yarn parallel and coats the yarn with size to strengthen it against the strain of weaving.

slashers n pl [Film] a genre of film in which victims, almost invariably women, are slashed with razors, hatchets, knives, and similar weapons; this is possibly a sub-conscious backlash against the allegedly 'castrating' advances of feminism.

slat n [Skiing] the ski itself.

slatch n [Sailing, Ropework] the loose or slack part of the rope.

slate 1. n [US] [Politics] a list of political candidates; the implication is that, like words on a schoolroom slate, the names written on it can easily be erased and replaced. 2. n [Entertainment] a schedule. 3. n [TV] a brief marking shot of the **clapperboard** that is placed at the start of a take.

slate bull n [Stock market] stock that is retained for a long period without making a profit.

slather and whack v [Navy] to work carelessly with little thought for the safety of others.

slaughter n [UK] [Police] a place where villains can hide recently stolen goods.

slave 1. n [Computing] a large processor that works within a **master-slave system**. 2. n [Video] a video cassette or disk recorder that is used, often in very large numbers, by duplicators to make copies of a master-tape. Since this must be done in **real time** the multiplicity of slaves is vital. 3. n [Video, TV] any machine that is controlled by another machine. 4. n [Photography] a small auxiliary flash unit used in a studio. 5. n [Sailing] a sail jib; it is a jib slightly larger than the storm jib that is kept in almost permanent employment.

SLBM n [Military] abbr of **Submarine-Launched Ballistic Missile** the submarine version of the heavyweight silo-based ICBM. These long-range missiles include the Polaris, Poseidon, and Trident C–4. Given the elusiveness of the submarine, SLBMs, and the submarines on which they are carried, represent the most awe-inspiring examples of destructive nuclear power.

SLCM n [Military] acro **Sea Launched Cruise Missile**. See also **ALCM, cruise 2, glockem**.

Sleaford Tech n [UK] [Air force] a derogatory reference to RAF Cranwell, the service's main training centre near Sleaford, Lincolnshire.

sleazy a [Textiles] said of cloth that is thin, lacking in firmness, or open-meshed.

sledging n [Cricket] abbr of **sledgehammering** this comes from the phrase 'subtle as a sledgehammer' – it refers to the practice, especially prevalent in Australia, of the fielding side aiming continuous and aggressive insults at the batsmen during the match. The intent is to intimidate or to provoke a loss of concentration.

sleek n [Glass-making] a fine elongated mark with smooth boundaries that is found on polished glass.

sleep n [Crime] a sentence from six months to two years.

sleeper 1. n [Farming] an unbranded calf which has had a notch cut in its ear. 2. n [Architecture] a horizontal beam placed on or near the ground to act as support for a floor or superstructure. 3. n [Architecture] a heavy strip of wood set in a concrete floor to enable a wooden floor to be nailed on top of the concrete base. 4. n [US] [Bars] any amount of money larger than the average tip that is left on the bar; since the bartender does not know if this actually is a tip, it is left available to the customer until his/her drinking is finished. 5. n [Bowling] a pin that cannot easily be seen because it is sited behind another pin. 6. n [Business] a share apparently overlooked by investors and therefore selling too low in respect to the market as a whole. 7. n [Business] an apathetic, lazy and unambitious executive who is interested neither in his/her own progress nor in that of the firm. 8. n [Espionage] See **mole**. 9. n [Gambling] money that has been wagered on a gambling table or roulette layout and then forgotten by the player who put it there. 10. n [Horse-racing] an appar-

S

ently lackadaisical horse that suddenly 'wakes up' and wins a race. **11.** n [*Media, Entertainment*] a book, play, film, TV programme or any other form of entertainment that creates no major stir on its launch, but which slowly builds up its appeal until after a while, perhaps as long as a year, it becomes immensely popular and lucrative. **12.** n [*US*] [*Politics*] an amendment placed secretly on a bill, which will pass into law with that bill, but the effect of which is separate from that of the main bill; thus it is a bill whose real effects are not fully appreciated when it is passed, but become apparent when it starts to operate.

sleeper brand n [*US*] [*Cattlemen*] an unrecorded and unknown brand found on cattle.

sleeper team n [*US*] [*Road transport*] team of two men who take turns in driving over long distances.

sleepers n pl [*UK*] [*Coal-mining*] like the sleepers on surface railways these are the heavy wooden batons placed at regular intervals under the tracks.

sleeping beauty n [*Business*] any company that has the potential, as yet unnoticed, to become a target for a takeover bid.

sleeping policeman n [*Cars*] an artificial bump in the road intended to slow down a car and keep speeds at a low level; it was first introduced under the UK Road Traffic Act, 1974.

sleeve **1.** n [*Gas industry*] a piece of pipe that covers and reinforces joints in the pipeline. **2.** n [*Gas industry*] a tubular case inserted in a prepared hole in a structure for the reception of an installation or service pipe.

sley v [*Weaving*] to thread the **reed**.

slice of life spot n [*Advertising*] any advertisement that bases its appeal on creating an atmosphere of 'real life', rather than of unattainable glamour. See also **TCK**.

slick **1.** n [*US*] [*Agriculture*] an unbranded range animal. **2.** n [*Journalism, Printing*] a magazine printed on smooth, often shiny paper; it is the opposite of the cheaper 'pulp' magazines, produced on inferior stock. See also **glossy 1**. **3.** n [*Industry*] any implement used for producing a smooth surface, eg. on the floor or on the sand in a mould. **4.** n [*Motor-racing*] a smooth, treadless tyre used for racing on dry tracks.

slick tech n [*Architecture, Design*] See **high tech**.

slickenside n [*Mining*] a polished and striated surface on a fault plane.

slick-licker n [*Oil industry*] a machine used to remove oil slicks from water.

Slick-Six n [*Military*] SLC–6: Space Launch Complex Six, sited at Vandenburg Air Force Base, California; it was originally built by the USAF for launching its (now aborted) Manned Orbiting Laboratory, and is now under development as a launch pad for the space shuttle (the National Space Transportation System).

slickum n [*Military*] **Sea-Launched Cruise Missile (SLCM)** a variety of the Tomahawk **cruise** missile – the BGM–109 – that can be used aboard both surface ships and submarines. Highly accurate, with a range of 2,500 km, the SLCM has been deployed since 1983. See also **ALCM**, **glockem**.

slide **1.** n [*Navy*] butter; thus slide and glitter is butter and marmalade on toast. **2.** n [*Mining*] a fault that intersects a number of beds at an acute angle. **3.** v [*Surfing*] to ride across the face of a wave; thus it is also a wave that can be surfed in this manner.

slide culture n [*Art*] the way in which once any event is reduced to a slidemounted colour photograph – often for educational purposes – that event, no matter how terrifying, awe-inspiring, extraordinary or otherwise alien to every day experience it might be, is rendered anodyne, of interest only as a photograph, rather than as the portrait of an important event.

slider n [*Baseball*] a fast pitch that breaks away from its original path.

sliding fifth wheel n [*UK*] [*Road transport*] a fifth-wheel plate mounted on a tractive unit, which can be moved forwards and backwards to accommodate different lengths of trailers.

slime n [*Industry*] a sediment, high in gold, silver and other precious metals, that is produced in electrolysis tanks during the refining of copper.

slimwear n [*Sex*] a euphemism used in fetishist magazines for latex and rubber garments.

slinger n [*UK*] [*Military*] bread soaked in tea.

slingshot n [*Aerospace*] the use of a planet's gravitational pull to alter the course and increase the speed of a passing spacecraft.

slinks n [*UK*] [*Market-traders*] a loafer, good-for-nothing; often as in 'slinks and slags'.

slip **1.** v [*Air travel*] to change crew; thus 'slipstops' are those places where an aircraft stops to change its crew. **2.** v [*Alcoholics Anonymous*] to take the first drink after a period of successful sobriety. **3.** v [*Gliding*] when a glider makes a sideways motion towards the lowered wing. See also **skid 3**. **4.** n [*Aerospace, Shipping*] the difference between the pitch of a propeller on a ship or aircraft and the distance it travels through water or air in one rotation. **5.** n [*Electronics*] the degree to which the speed of an electric motor falls short of the speed of the rotation of the magnetic flux inside it.

slip edition n [*Journalism*] a special edition of a newspaper, usually carrying extra items of local importance.

slip sheet n [*Printing*] a sheet interleaved between newly printed sheets to prevent smudging or adhesion.

slippage **1.** [*Gambling*] the amount of money staked on a single betting slip. **2.** [*US*] [*Politics*] the gradual collapse of a lead that had been assessed by opinion pollsters; it is a problem that tends to occur as polling day nears.

slipper **1.** n [*US*] [*Cattlemen*] a smooth horseshoe, without cleats or calks. **2.** n [UK] [Medicine] the urine bottle given to male patients.

slips 1. n [US] [Coal-mining] the grain in a coal seam. **2.** n pl [Mining] small faults found in the rock strata.

slips! excl [Marbles] cried when one's marble slips when shooting; it entitles the player to a free throw.

slip-skid ball n [Gliding] the inclinometer: a ball in a fluid-filled, curved, glass tube, which indicates whether the aircraft is slipping or skidding.

slipstream v [Motor-racing] to take advantage of the low-pressure area created behind a fast-moving car by driving within that area and thus avoiding wind-resistance.

slipstreaming n [Motor-racing] See **drafting 2.**

slit n [Coal-mining] a small connecting roadway.

slit, on the adv [UK] [Police] used of airport thieves who slit open mailbags and luggage in the hope of finding a lucrative reward.

slitter n [Glass-making] a worker who removes unwanted material from slabs of optical glass prior to their being remoulded into lens blanks.

sliver n [Weaving] an industrial term for wool carded and ready for spinning yarn.

slop 1. n [Distilling] waste products created during distilling; it is used for distiller's dry feed which helps fatten livestock. **2.** n [US] [Printing] typeset material that is left over after all pages have been filled. **3.** v [US] [Marine Corps] to consume fast and plentifully; thus 'slop up' is to eat to excess, 'slop down' is to drink to excess.

slop out v [UK] [Prisons] to empty one's latrine bucket in the morning, to collect fresh water, etc.

slop artist n [US] [Painting] a second-rate painter who is more interested in the quantity of the work than in its quality.

slop chute n [US] [Marine Corps] any local tavern, civilian or military.

slop oil n [Oil industry] substandard petroleum by-products.

slop wagon n [US] [Road transport] See **ghost 6.**

sloper n [Oil rigs] a variety of valve used on an oil-rig. See also **nipple.**

slops chest n [Merchant navy] a chest containing spare clothing and gear.

slot 1. n [Aerospace] a specific orbit in outer space. **2.** n [US] [Football] a gap in the defence line, usually between the end and the tackle. **3.** n [Ice-hockey] the area immediately in front of the opposition goal that an offensive player seeks to occupy. **4.** n [US] [Journalism] the inside of the semi-circular copy desk in a newspaper office; thus 'in the slot' means the seat where the copy chief sits, supervising the sub-editors who sit around the **rim. 5.** n [TV] a transmission segment, often referring to the breaks for advertising. **6.** n [Hunting, Shooting] the track of a deer, or the foot that makes the track. **7.** v [Hunting] to track a deer by following its footprints. **8.** v [Soccer] to kick the ball accurately through a narrow space between two or more opponents or between the goal-keeper and the goal post.

slot, down the adv [UK] [Railways] said of a slow train that has to be diverted out of the path of an oncoming express.

slot man n [US] [Journalism] a news editor or chief sub-editor. See also **slot 4.**

slot time n [Air travel] for air traffic controllers this is a specific time within which an aircraft must become airborne; if this slot is missed, a new one must be arranged, and this will mean further delay.

slough, also slough up v [Gambling] to close up (a game).

slough pig n [Logging] a man who rafts logs in a boom.

slow a [Photography] referring to any photographic process – exposure, developing – that requires a longer than average timescale.

slow and go n [US] [Traffic controllers] traffic is moving so slowly that the jam will keep increasing; it is used in Denver, Col. See also **rolling back-up, sigalert.**

slow assets n pl [Commerce] assets that cannot be sold off for cash.

slow pass n [Cards] in bridge this is the decision to call 'pass' that is reached only after a long, portentous period of alleged thought; such a hiatus is supposed to bluff one's opponents into thinking that one has a strong hand without actually revealing anything by a bid and is considered unethical play.

slow rubber n [Table tennis] rubber chosen by defensive players who like to deaden the pace of the ball. See also **fast rubber.**

sloyd n [Woodwork] a single-bladed knife used for trimming, carving or slicing.

SLSI n [Electronics] abbr of **Super Large Scale Integration** of fabrication technology that can put in excess of 100,000 **gates** on a single chip. See also **LSI, MSI, SSI, VLSI.**

slubber-doffer n [US] [Textiles] a worker who removes full bobbins from slubber frames (on the slubber machines which process raw cotton).

sludge 1. n [Medicine] a clump of agglutinated red blood cells. **2.** n [Oil industry] the residue that is created in the treatment of petroleum with sulphuric acid.

sludging n [Medicine] the aggregation of blood cells into jelly-like masses and the subsequent blocking of good circulation.

slug 1. n [Electronics] a metal cylinder fitted round the core of an electromagnetic relay to control the speeds of opening and closing. **2.** n [Electronics] an adjustable magnetic core used to vary the inductance of a coil containing it. **3.** n [Science] in nuclear engineering this is a rod or bar of nuclear fuel. **4.** n [Engineering] a unit of mass equal to 32.1740 lb.; this is the mass of a body that accelerates at one foot per second per second when acted on by a force of one pound. **5.** *n* [*Film*] a strip of film – blank or carrying an image – that is used as a **leader**. **6.** *n* [*Gas industry*] the liquid that separates naturally, by condensation from natural gas; before the gas reaches the treatment plant the slug is removed from an undersea pipeline by the operation of a **pig**. **7.** *n* [*Gemstones*] an irregularly shaped freshwater pearl. **8.** *n* [*Pharmaceuticals*] a large, flat-faced disk that is used in the mixing of the ingredients of medicinal pills and tablets. **9.** *n* [*Printing*] a line of type or a blank line set on a Linotype machine; thus 'slug machine' is a Linotype machine. **10.** *n* [*Printing*] a scratch or tear on a negative or a plate. **11.** *n* [*UK*] [*Radio*] the name of a story; this slug is used to identify any story that runs through one, or more, day's broadcasting. All material pertaining to that story will be labelled with the same slug as well as the name of the reporter who **voiced** the tape. **12.** also **shot** *n* [*Glass-making*] an imperfection in fibre glass that occurs when any non-fibrous glass appears in a product.

slug catcher *n* [*Gas industry*] an arrangement of pipes designed to remove the **slug** liquids that have been removed from the pipeline; the catcher creates a pressure drop in the incoming gas line and thus allows the slugs of heavier hydrocarbons to accumulate and be diverted from the gas.

sluice-gate price *n* [*Economics*] under Common Market (EC) regulations this is the quarterly imposition of minimum prices for agricultural products which are imported into the EC from non-member states; if goods are imported below these prices, the importer must pay an additional levy.

slum 1. *n* [*Circus, Carnival*] cheap items given away as prizes at a carnival, circus or fair. **2.** *n* [*US*] [*Marine Corps*] beef stew. **3.** *v* [*Sheep-shearing*] to shear as fast as possible, concentrating on the easier sheep, with the degree of carelessness that such speed tends to entail. See also **gun**.

slumber room *n* [*US*] [*Undertakers*] the room in an undertakers' where the corpse is laid out, embalmed, made up and surrounded by flowers, preparatory to burial or cremation.

slumpflation *n* [*Economics*] See **stagflation**. See also **inflation**.

slush tank *n* [*Oil rigs*] a container that holds the liquid **mud** or slush used for lubricating or flushing the **drill string**.

slur 1. *n* [*Printing*] extended or deformed dots, found especially in the terminations of some old faces in the letters, f, a, etc. **2.** *n* [*Printing*] a fault caused by a lateral movement during the impression of the paper on the inked typeface.

slurvian *n* [*Linguistics*] a term coined by John Davenport for those carelessly slurred speech forms that most people use to a greater or lesser extent; eg: 'y'know', 'doncha', 'wanna' etc.

slush 1. *v* [*Coal-mining*] to scrape up waste

material with a rope-hauled bucket or system of boxes. **2.** *n* [*US*] [*Paper-making*] pulp, which has been chemically treated and which is ready for manufacturing into paper and cardboard. **3.** *n* [*Publishing*] unsolicited manuscripts, which very rarely make their way into becoming published books. **4.** *n* [*Oil rigs*] See **mud 3**.

slush fund 1. *n* [*Politics*] any illicit political financing; it is the collection of money that is not openly declared as part of one's permitted level of campaign funding; it is money which may be used for paying off members of one's campaign staff whose activities (as in the Watergate scandal) one would prefer kept from public knowledge. **2.** *n* [*UK*] [*Military, Navy*] any fund established amongst soldiers or sailors to buy extra luxuries; it comes from the 19th century Royal Naval tradition of selling the 'slush' or fat collected after salt beef has been boiled.

slush pump, also **mud pump** *n* [*Oil rigs*] a multi-stage piston pump which circulates the **mud** at the required pressure and density.

slusher *n* [*Mining*] a mechanical device for loading or packing broken material that consists of a bucket attached to ropes running between two drums; it is drawn by those ropes through the pile of material.

slushy *n* [*US*] [*Navy*] a ship's cook.

SMA *n* [*Military*] abbr of **standard metropolitan area** a figure used for the calculations of the numbers of deaths in a variety of levels of nuclear attack; the US, for instance, has 53 SMAs.

smack it about! *excl* [*Navy*] an exhortation to sailors to work hard; it comes from the smacking of paintbrushes against the sides of a ship.

small stuff *n* [*Sailing, Ropework*] rope that is under 1in in circumference.

smalls 1. *n pl* [*Coal-mining*] coal with no minimum size, but with a maximum of 50mm as its upper limit. **2.** *n pl* [*Printing, Advertising*] the small advertisements run the 'Classified' section that are usually printed in 6pt. or even smaller type.

smart *a* [*Technology*] said of any technological advance that involves the use of computers.

smart card *n* [*Banking*] a plastic card, the size of a credit card, which can be used as an 'electronic cheque book'; the card holds a processor and a memory for processing payments to a **point-of-sale terminal.**

smart weapons *n pl* [*Military*] any form of precision guided munitions (**PGM**), especially those with built-in computers, variable radar frequencies, anti-jamming devices and similar means of homing in accurately on a target and eluding all the defences, electronic and conventional, that may be encountered.

smartening *n* [*Computing*] the introduction of computers into any hitherto non-technological area of life, eg: banking, supermarket checkouts, etc.

smartlet *n* [*Military*] a small fragmentation bomb with its own guidance system.

smasher *n* [*Publishing*] one who operates a power press that creases the folds of the **signatures** of books prior to their being bound.

smear **1.** *n* [*Aerospace*] bad radio reception due to the transmission of another message on top of the one which one wishes to hear. **2.** *n* [*US*] [*Garment trade*] a careless pressing job. **3.** *n* [*Glass-making*] a surface crack, especially on the neck of a bottle. **4.** *n* [*US*] [*Lunch counter*] a pat of butter.

Smersh *n* [*Espionage*] a department of the Russian secret service – it comes from Rus. for 'Death to spies' – but (pace James Bond) was used only from 1942–46; during this period its responsibilities included: 1. military counter-espionage; 2. political supervision of the armed forces at home; 3. political supervision of Russian forces operating abroad; 4. the elimination of any dissidence within Russia; 5. the re-education (see **re-educate**) of those who had been 'tainted' by a spell out of Russia, ie: fighting in World War II.

smoke **1.** *v* [*US*] [*Road transport*] to pass another vehicle. **2.** *n* [*Espionage*] disinformation.

smoke-filled room *n* [*Politics*] the concept of a group of influential political patrons meeting together in the early hours, wreathed in smoke and alcohol fumes, to decide on a party's presidential candidate and then to scheme towards his being nominated. It comes from the statement by Ohio Republican Harry Daugherty, who backed Warren G. Harding for the Presidency in 1920: 'the convention will be deadlocked, and after the other candidates have gone their limit, some twelve or fifteen men, worn out and bleary-eyed from lack of sleep, will sit down about two o'clock in the morning, around a table in a smoke-filled room in some hotel and decide the nomination.'

smoke-oh *n* [*Navy*] a break, for tea, a cigarette, etc.; it is also found amongst sheep-shearers.

Smokey Sams *n pl* [*Air Force*] fake ground-to-air missile defences used for testing the accuracy/ability of RAF fighter pilots and aircraft.

smoking *n* [*Angling*] the mist rising above the water.

smoko *n* [*Merchant navy*] a short break in work for seamen to smoke or have a cup of coffee.

smoky *a* [*Wine-tasting*] used to describe a characteristic subtle overtone found in some white wine districts. See also **flinty.**

smolt *n* [*Angling*] a young salmon or sea trout going out to sea for the first time.

smooth **1.** *a* [*Audio*] used to describe a seamless blend of high and low frequency components in which neither extreme is favoured. **2.** *v* [*Statistics*] to iron out the irregularities and fluctuations in a graph by removing such material from one's calculations.

smoothing *n* [*Audio*] the removal of alternating current **ripple** from a direct current supply – it is performed by **rectifiers.**

smooth-mouthed *a* [*Horse-racing*] referring to a horse that has worn teeth without cusps; this is a condition found in those aged more than seven or eight years.

smother **1.** *n* [*UK*] [*Market-traders*] quality material, top-class goods. **2.** *n* [*UK*] [*Market-traders*] an overcoat.

SMT money *n* [*Banking*] money invested in the securities and money markets by the Securities Management Trust Ltd, a wholly-owned subsidiary of the Bank of England which works on behalf of and at the request of clients of the Bank.

smudge *n* [*Sex*] still pornographic photographs, or the magazines that contain them.

smudger *n* [*UK*] [*Railways*] an engine cleaner.

smudgy *n* [*Merchant navy*] the ship's cook; it comes from Ger. 'smutje'.

smuggler's eye *n* [*Government*] the alleged ability possessed by experienced members of H. M. Customs to spot the smugglers among the rest of the innocent passengers who file past them at airports and other entries to the UK.

smut **1.** *n* [*Agriculture*] a fungoid disease that attacks a variety of plants and grasses. **2.** *n* [*Angling*] a tiny fly of the 'diptera' family; fish who takes such bait are 'smutting'. **3.** *n* [*Coal-mining*] a thin band of soft, inferior coal. **4.** *n* [*Dog breeding*] the encroachment of tan colouring into the blue coat areas of such breeds as the Australian Silky Terrier and the Australian Terrier. **5.** *n* [*Dog breeding*] in the British Bulldog this is a whole colour except for a black mask or muzzle.

smutting *n* [*Angling*] the action of fish in taking minute black flies. See also **curse.**

snabbo *n* [*US*] [*Hotels*] the hotel lobby.

snag *n* [*Logging*] a dead, standing, tree 20 ft. or more high.

snagger *n* [*Sheep-shearing*] an incompetent, slow or inexperienced sheep-shearer.

snagging *n* [*Angling*] intentional foul hooking with a **treble** when fishing for pike.

snags, also **snorkers** *n pl* [*Navy*] sausages.

snake **1.** *v* [*Logging*] to move a log with snaking movements. **2.** *v* [*Coal-mining*] to move an armoured flexible conveyor forward, section by section, without dismantling it, by using power-operated rams. **3.** *n* [*Economics*] a system of jointly floated currencies established in 1972 by the then member countries of the Common Market (EC); their exchange rates are allowed to fluctuate against each other as well as, within a wider margin, against those of non-EC countries. **4.** *n* [*UK*] [*Fire brigade*] the hose. **5.** *n* [*Oil rigs*] a driller; it comes from a formation so dense that only a snake could get through it. **6.** *n* [*Aus.*] [*Military*] a sergeant. **7.** *n* [*US*] [*Railways*] a switchman, who works in the **yard** uncoupling cars and changing points; it is possibly because his job takes him over/under/around trains and

S

their rolling stock. **8.** also **plumber's snake** *n* [*Plumbing*] a long, flexible rod that is forced through drains or pipes to remove obstructions.

snake in the tunnel *n* [*Economics*] a decision by the EC countries to hold the 'snake' (the European Monetary System, whereby the exchange rates of member countries fluctuate against each other within agreed limits) to a limit of 2.25% (1.125% either side of parity relative to each other) fluctuation within the 'tunnel' set up by the IMF. In 1971 the IMF established the dollar as the middle rate around which all currencies fluctuate. The IMF tunnel extends to a fluctuation of 4.5%.

snakecheck *n* [*Politics*] the checking of any public speech or statement to ensure that nothing gets through that might rebound adversely on the speaker; it comes from the idea of checking a sleeping bag for any unwelcome snakes before using it.

snake-eyes *n* [*Gambling*] a throw of double 1.

snakes *n pl* [*Oil rigs*] tools which have been buried in a well which has caved in.

snakes' honeymoon *n* [*Merchant navy*] a tangle of ropes.

snap **1.** *v* [*Pool*] to recognise a **hustler**, or his hustle (the schemes he uses to lure the gullible to the table). **2.** *n* [*US*] [*Football*] the act of passing the ball by the centre to the quarterback that initiates each offensive play. **3.** *n* [*Radio*] flash news on a teleprinter or agency wire. **4.** *n* [*UK*] [*Railways*] food; thus snap tin is a container in which food is brought to work; both originate in mining use. See also **jock.**

snap fishing *n* [*Angling*] live bait fishing for pike with tackle arranged for **striking** (see **strike**) as soon as the fish takes the bait.

snapback timing *n* [*Industry*] See **flyback timing.**

snapper **1.** *n* [*US*] [*Coal-mining*] one who couples and uncouples mine cars. **2.** *n* [*Entertainment*] a comedian's punch-line. **3.** *n* [*US*] [*Painting*] a painter who takes on ('snaps up') extra work even though he is already employed on a job by a contractor.

snapping time *n* [*Mining*] a brief period of rest; presumably it comes from 'snap' meaning food.

snapshot *n* [*Computing*] a printout of the state of a program during the running of that program; snapshots are useful when attempting to isolate **bugs** in the program.

snap-up missile *n* [*Military*] an air-to-air missile that is capable of hitting a target far higher in the sky than is the aircraft which served as its launch platform.

snare pictures *n pl* [*Art*] the name given to his own work by Daniel Spoerri: accumulations of objects, eg: those remaining on a table after a meal, which are 'snared', ie: affixed to boards, hung on walls and presented as 'art'.

snarf *v* [*Computing*] to grab; specifically it is to remove, a large document or file for the purpose of using it with/without its owner's permission.

snarl-word *n* [*Linguistics*] a term coined by S. I. Hayakawa to cover those words which imply one's dislike; it is the verbal equivalent of a snarl. See also **purr-word.**

snatch **1.** *v* [*Angling*] to **foul hook** intentionally. **2.** *v* [*Espionage*] in the CIA this is an illegal arrest, without warrant or caution. **3.** *n* [*Angling*] an illegal method of hooking fish that involves a weighted triangular frame lowered on a hand-line by a poacher. **4.** *n* [*US*] [*TV*] See **bite 2.**

snatch-crop *n* [*Agriculture*] a crop that is grown for quick profits, regardless of the strain this may put on the future productivity of the soil.

snatcher **1.** *n* [*Angling*] a man who snatches when casting. **2.** *n* [*Angling*] See **tailer 1. 3.** *n* [*UK*] [*Buses*] a London Transport bus that arrives too soon behind its predecessor along the route and 'snatches' its passengers.

sneak **1.** *n* [*Film*] abbr of **sneak preview** the first showing of an as yet unreleased picture to an audience chosen at random and who are expecting to see a different film. They are issued questionnaires and from the answers to these the studio hopes to calculate the success/failure of the film and possibly tinker with it accordingly before proper distribution. **2.** *v* [*Gambling*] to run a game without the knowledge or protection of either the police or the local villains.

sneak path *n* [*Electronics*] an unwanted electrical path in a circuit.

sneakie *n* [*Espionage*] a clandestine device – any hidden microphones, cameras, electronic gadgetry, etc – which provides a variety of technical intelligence.

sneaking deacon *n* [*US*] [*Police*] a married officer who has affairs with other women.

sneeze guard *n* [*Catering*] the plastic or glass shield that is used in salad bars, patisseries, etc. to protect the fresh food.

snifters *n pl* [*Merchant navy*] big seas, especially near Cape Horn.

sniggle *v* [*Angling*] to fish for eels with the worm on a needle instead of a hook.

snip *n* [*UK*] [*Railways*] a ticket collector; it comes from his basic function.

snipe **1.** *v* [*Logging*] to round off the end of a log in order to make it skid more efficiently. **2.** *n* [*US*] [*Navy*] engine room staff in a submarine. **3.** *n* [*US*] [*Politics*] a political poster that is affixed to any 'free space' – walls, telegraph poles, etc. – for which, unlike privately owned billboards, the candidate need not pay. **4.** *n* [*US*] [*Merchant navy*] one of a group of workers on board ship.

snippet journalism *n* [*Journalism*] the broadcasting or writing of serious information, eg: news, current affairs, in small, easily assimilable chunks that act as a series of headlines but actually convey few useful facts.

snitchering n [Angling] jerking out eels with the roughened blade of a sickle lashed to a pole.

snob n [Sheep-shearing] see **cobbler**; the original slang meaning of 'snob' was cobbler or shoe-maker.

snob zoning n [US] [Government] the use of zoning requirements – eg: specifying that each house shall have one acre of land – to ensure that only a certain, rich, class of owners will be able to live in an area; it is popularly used in the suburbs to bar the poor from infiltration.

SNOBOL n [Computing] acro **String Orientated Symbolic Language** a programming language created specifically for dealing with complex strings of symbols.

snobs n [UK] [Military] a bootmaker. It comes from the original meaning (pre-19th century) of 'snob': a cobbler.

snooger n [Marbles] a near miss.

snoot n [TV] a conical attachment that can be fitted to a light in order to concentrate the beam.

snorrer n [UK] [Market-traders] a difficult customer; possibly it comes from Yid. 'schnorrer' meaning a thief.

snorter n [Cricket] a fast, dangerous ball; one that can trouble, or even hurt, a batsman.

snot-agate n [Marbles] a glass agate streaked with white.

snottie n [Navy] a midshipman; allegedly it comes from the habit that such junior seamen have of wiping their noses on their sleeves; thus 'snottie nurse' is the lieutenant who is assigned to super-vise the midshipmen.

snow 1. n [Mining] a shower of small particles from the tunnel ceiling which indicates that a cave-in is imminent. 2. n [Video, TV] random interference that causes 'blizzard' effects on a screen.

snow boat n [US] [Skiing] a boat-like rescue sled; it is usually made of aluminium.

Snow Man n [Military] US Dept. of Defense level seven war readiness.

snowball n [Gambling] in bingo this is a cash prize which accumulates over successive games as long as no player manages to complete their card successfully.

snowballing n [US] [Stock market] a process by which the activation of stop orders in a sharply moving market, either upwards or downwards, causes an increase in pressure on the direction of that market, thus triggering more orders, causing more pressure, and so on. See also **gather in the stops.**

snowbird 1. n [US] [Traffic controllers] a stalled and disabled vehicle on an icy roadway; it is used in Minneapolis. 2. n [US] [Industry] migrant workers who move to the southern states during the cold northern winters. 3. n [US] [Travel agents] New Yorkers and other Northerners who take their holidays in Florida and thus avoid the chilly northern winters.

snowdrop n [US] [Military] a military policeman.

snow-eater n [Meteorology] a warm wind that causes the rapid melting of snow.

snowflake curve n [Mathematics] a mathematical curve with sixfold symmetry that was discovered in 1904 by the Swedish mathematician Helge von Koch and which resembles the traditional shape of a snowflake.

snowflakes n pl [Metallurgy] internal ruptures within the steel which, when exposed by frac-turing, appear as bright, crystalline areas, almost circular in form.

snowman n [Archaeology] a technique of clay modelling that resembles, in its pinching of the clay into the body shape and subsequent adding on of various small pellets to represent arms and legs, a child's making of a snowman.

snowplough v [Skiing] a method of slowing down or stopping often used by novice skiers; the points of the skis come together as the **tails** form the wide wedge of a 'V'. See also **stern 1.**

snowshoe feet n [Dog breeding] the specialised feet of the arctic breeds; they are oval, firm and compact with strong toes and tough, deeply cushioned pads; the webbing between the toes is strongly developed and helps the dogs in hauling heavy loads over harsh terrain.

snub v [Sailing, Ropework] to check a line, gener-ally with a round turn on a post or pin.

snubbing n [Oil rigs] the process of running pipe or casing into the well while the well is exerting pressure on the surface equipment.

snuff-bottle, also **snuff-box** n [UK] [Market-traders] anything that 'snuffs' one: it can be shocking, depressing, economically or physically damaging.

snuffler n [UK] [Market-traders] a veterinary surgeon; it comes from his function in 'snuffing' (putting down) animals.

soak n [Computing] a method of detecting program or system errors by running the machine under operating conditions and keeping a detailed watch on its performance. See also **soaksite.**

soaker n [Oil industry] a tank in which oil vapours are separated into petroleum (from the lighter vapours) and tar (from the heavier ones).

soaksite n [Commerce] any site used by distribu-tors of a new product for the assessment, through a variety of tests, observations, etc., of the appeal of that product.

soap 1. n [US] [Carpenters] overtime. 2. n [Espionage] this comes from so-pe (sodium penta-thol); it is a mixture of sodium pentathol (a truth serum but simultaneously a depressant) and a form of amphetamine to induce articulate confessions from a subject so dosed up. 3. n [US] [Medicine] **Subject, Objective, Assessment, Plan** the basic guidelines used for working out the optimum methods of treatment for the care of a particular patient.

S

soap and flannel n [Navy] bread and cheese.

soap and towel n [UK] [Railways] a meal of bread and cheese.

soap opera n [TV] long-running domestic series, set in a variety of supposedly 'average' homes, families and environments, which are broadcast on TV and radio in the morning, afternoon and early evening. The form and the nickname were initiated on US radio in the 1920s by 'The Goldbergs', sponsored by the detergent manufacturers Proctor & Gamble, who used the programme to sell their soaps. See also **carbolic soap operas, horse opera.**

soapbox derby syndrome n [US] [Medicine] a rapidly progressing illness; ie: the patient is 'going downhill fast'.

soarboard n [Aerospace] a board on which were recorded, at its height, the various achievements of the US Space programme.

SOB adv [Medicine] acro **short of breath.**

sob snatch n [UK] [Police] a particular kind of crime that is committed in airports, railway stations and similar places associated with travel; as the weeping passenger puts down his/her luggage to embrace loved ones, the thief grabs the luggage and vanishes with it into the crowds.

SOC n [UK] [TV, Radio] acro **Standard Out Cue** the stating by a reporter of his/her name and dateline to sign off a report.

social accounting n [Commerce] the cost sustained by a company in complying with environmental, safety, health and similar socially beneficial requirements which influence its activities.

social action n [Sociology] deliberate action that results in changes in society at large or in the restructuring of the institutions that compose it.

social atoms n pl [New therapies] in **psychodrama**, these are the significant human influences upon one's early life – parents, siblings, perhaps a special teacher.

social character n [Sociology] the selective learned system of feeling and acting that develops in each individual as a result of experiencing the community into which he/she is born and grows up.

social closure n [Sociology] the action of a social group in limiting access to rewards (usually economic) to members of the group and thus closing access to outsiders and maintaining its own dominant position. This philosophy divides into strategies of exclusion: confirming the closing of ranks, and usurpation: the attempt to break into the advantaged group.

social distance n [Sociology] the physical distance between individuals that each finds acceptable in social situations.

social Darwinism n [Politics] a society arranged on Darwinian lines, ie: the survival of the fittest (nation, individual, social class) and the subservience or elimination of the weakest.

social distance n [Sociology] the perceived feelings of social distance or separation between social groups.

social fact n [Sociology] social phenomena that are external to the individual yet constrain his/her actions; eg: the legal system.

social imperialism n [Politics] a term originally coined by Lenin to attack those Social Democrats and others who refused to join the Russian Revolution because they were more concerned with fighting the World War; more recently it was used by the Chinese to attack all aspects of Soviet Communism.

social marketing n [Marketing] the application of marketing techniques to non-commercial activities, especially community and welfare interests; it is an effort to prove that marketing has its uses outside the merely commercial sphere. See also **societal marketing concept.**

social physics n [Sociology] the science of social phenomena which is subject to certain invariable natural laws.

social racism n [Politics, Sociology] implicit racism that is not expressed openly in word or action, but exists all the time in the basic fabric of a nation's life, thus ensuring that racial minorities – Indians and blacks in particular in the UK – form an accepted, but never declared, second-class citizenry.

social reproduction 1. n [Sociology] the reproduction over generations of people's social organization. **2.** n [Sociology] in Marxism this is the reproduction of **labour power.**

social safety net n [Politics] long-range programmes of basic income security, typified in the US New Deal or UK Welfare State, that are made available to the economically needy.

social space n [Sociology] the 'space', as seen in terms of the different social position, or different level of freedom of action, that is perceived as existing between one person and another.

social statics n [Sociology] a branch of **social physics** that deals with fundamental laws of the social structure in question and the equilibrium of forces in a stable society.

socialisation n [Social work] the learning of the processes of living within a society or social group; the adoption of appropriate rules within accepted norms.

socialism ex cathedra n [Politics] See **academic socialism.**

socialism with a human face n [Politics] journalistic shorthand for the ill-fated 'Prague spring' of liberalisation in Czechoslovakia in 1968 under Alexander Dubcek.

socialist realism n [Art] the socialist creative method that is obligatory for artists and writers; in essence all concerned should be committed to extolling and strengthening the Communist status quo in every vestige of their work, and in accordance with the Party line. 'Realism' in this context means the reflection of 'reality' as defined by its revolutionary development.

societal marketing concept n [Marketing] a view of marketing's role that concentrates not merely on short-term desires but on the long-term welfare of the consumer.

sociobiology n [Sociology] a concept created by E. O. Wilson in an attempt to explain the social organization of animals, including man, by reference to biological characteristics.

sociodrama n [Sociology] events, usually rituals or games, that have taken on a particular symbolic significance for certain social groups or for society at large, eg: the World Cup, royal events, etc.

sociogram n [Sociology] a visual presentation of relationships which provides a pictorial view of certain sociological data.

sociography n [Sociology] an empirical method of sociological analysis that uses both qualitative and quantitative data.

sociogroup n [Sociology] a group of people who associate for any reason over and above personal preference: jobs, blood relationships, etc.

sociolect n [Sociology] a variety of language that is characteristic of the social background or status of its user.

sociologism n [Sociology] the tendency to ascribe a sociological basis to all phenomena and academic disciplines.

sociology of development n [Sociology] the analysis of the social and political effects of the industrialisation of the Third World.

sociometry n [Sociology] an attempt to study small-group relations by using **sociograms.**

socio-technical systems n [Sociology] the concept, invented at the Tavistock Institute of Human Relations, that industry can only work well if the social needs of employees and the technical needs of production can be met simultaneously.

socio-technics n [Sociology] the term used in Communist countries as a substitute for the West's 'sociology', which is a discipline that the Party does not accept.

sock 1. n [Flying] abbr of **wind sock** a cloth cone, open at both ends, with the larger end held rigid and mounted on a tall pole; it is used on airfields to determine the direction of the wind. **2.** n [Golf] a soft protective covering used by golfers to protect the heads of their wooden clubs. **3.** n [US] [Painting] a hood used by painters to protect themselves from noxious fumes when using a spraygun. **4.** n [US] [Painting] the cover – made of foam or fabric – of a paint roller (which actually rolls the paint on). **5.** also **socko, sokko** a [Entertainment] extremely successful, wonderful, etc.

socked in adv [Aerospace] referring to an airfield which is shut to flying because of poor visibility.

socks n pl [Dog breeding, Horses] white markings on coloured animals involving the lower portions of the legs up to the knee; those that reach higher than normal – up to the forearms – are termed stockings.

SOF phr [Film] acro **sound on film** a notation explaining that the sound track has been recorded simultaneously with the filming, rather than being **dubbed** on later.

SOFAR n [Military] acro **Sound Fixing And Ranging** the measurement, at a number of distant listening stations, of the sound waves emanating from an underwater explosion in order to determine its exact position.

soffia vento n [Crime] this comes from Sicilian for 'the wind is blowing'; in the Italian Mafia it means 'the heat's on', the police are becoming over-active.

soffit n [Building, Plastering] the underside of a beam or ceiling.

soft 1. a [Audio, Computing] in sound recording, this is said of magnetic materials that become strong magnets when placed in a magnetic field, but which lose that magnetism once the field is removed. The read/write heads of magnetic recorders must be made from soft magnetic material. See also **hard 1. 2.** a [Cheese-making] a pejorative term to describe an insufficiently drained or excessively runny cheese; it is nothing to do with soft cheese as such; it comes from Fr. 'mou' meaning 'soft'. **3.** a [Flying] said of the airplane's controls when they are not responding speedily and 'crisply' to the pilot's touch. **4.** a [Military] undefended; specifically it means lacking the special hardening (see **harden**) measures that, to an increasingly limited extent, can shield installations, individuals and weapons systems from nuclear attack. **5.** a [Coal-mining] used to describe second-rate, inferior coal, usually bituminous or brown coal. **6.** a [TV] out of focus; thus an incompetent cameraman is known as 'soft for hard', on the analogy of '**day for night**'.

soft arbitrage n [Banking] switching between market and bank facilities to take advantage of differentials in interest rates; it also means borrowing from banks while still retaining easily realisable money market investments. See also **round-tripping.**

soft boot n [Computing] a **bootstrap** command executed under program control rather than by any physical action by the operator. See also **hard boot.**

soft brick n [Building] a brick that has been underburned because of its position in the kiln during the firing process.

soft copy n [Computing] a non-endurable form of data output, eg: the information currently available on a VDU. See also **hard copy.**

soft crash n [Computing] brief interruptions in data processing or message transmission.

soft currency 1. n [Economics] a currency that is not soundly backed, nor can it easily be converted into foreign currencies, except under restrictions or at a punitive discount. **2.** *n* [*Economics*] a currency that cannot be converted into gold nor heavily backed by a gold reserve; it is thus typically low, unstable and depreciating in value. **3.** *n* [*Economics*] a currency that is available to borrowers in ample supply and at low interest rates.

soft dollars **1.** *n pl* [*Economics*] the portion of an investment that can be taken as an income tax deduction. **2.** *n pl* [*Economics*] the commissions received by a US brokerage house for performing transactions for their clients. See also **hard dollars.**

soft facility dispersal *n* [*Government*] a secondary, backup, records centre which is sited some way from the building holding the original records; this facility is not protected from explosion and is sited above ground.

soft focus *n* [*Film*] a diffused effect that is used for shooting 'romantic' scenes and other 'atmospheric' effects.

soft funding *n* [*Government*] government schemes that cannot rely on an endless flow of funds; thus for a variety of reasons – the scheme is not working, it is no longer fashionable – the funds are cut off and the project must be abandoned unfinished. See also **hard funding.**

soft gaming *n* [*Gambling*] that form of casino gaming whereby the house hires out seats at a given table rather than taking a cut of each pot; it was originally introduced as an attraction for women players, but its lack of profit (for the casino) has diminished its popularity. It is usually found in games of poker, baccarat and kalooki (a form of gin rummy).

soft goods *n pl* [*Textiles*] woollen goods which are soft to the touch and loosely woven; woollens are constructed of yarns in which the wool has been carded but not combed, and then spun. They are manufactured from shorter wool stock or blends of other fibres; the nap shows but the yarn is barely visible. See also **hard goods.**

soft keyboard *n* [*Computing*] a keyboard in which any of the functions ostensibly allotted to the keys can be altered as the user wishes by program control.

soft landing **1.** *n* [*Aerospace*] the landing of a spacecraft either on a planet or back on Earth without causing any damage to itself. **2.** *n* [*Economics*] the slowing down of the rate of economic growth without simultaneously causing a recession or high unemployment.

soft loan *n* [*Economics*] a low interest/long term or a no-interest loan granted by a developed country to a developing or Third World nation.

soft market *n* [*Stock market*] a market in which either prices are falling or the volume of buyers is decreasing.

soft money **1.** *n* [*Economics*] paper money, as distinct from coin. **2.** *n* [*US*] [*Education*] college funds that come from uncertain, variable sources: gifts from alumni, grants from foundations, temporary government schemes, etc. See also **hard money.**

soft news *n* [*Journalism*] news stories that lack immediacy; it is the treatment of news as another, slightly less amusing, but still primarily entertaining medium in which, therefore, the informational content must be kept to a minimum while its personalities must be played up like one more variety of TV celebrity. See also **hard news, informational entertainment.**

soft ordnance *n* [*Military*] a euphemism for napalm.

soft paper *n* [*Photography*] photographic paper that produces low contrast. See also **hard paper.**

soft pedal *v* [*Politics*] to play down the importance of a particular issue, both to the public and in the way it is treated internally.

soft player **1.** *n* [*Gambling*] an inexperienced player. **2.** *n* [*Gambling*] a player who is overwhelmed by winning substantially.

soft policing *n* [*Government, Police*] a style of policing deliberately adapted to minimise the potential sources of conflict in deprived inner-city areas. This style, with its emphasis on turning the blind eye rather than prosecuting every minor offence is as much criticised for condoning 'no-go areas' as it is praised for improving police-community relations.

soft rock *n* [*Pop music*] See **AC 2.**

soft science *n* [*Science*] any of the social or behavioural sciences: psychology, sociology, etc.

soft selling, also **low pressure selling** *n* [*Commerce*] concentrating on winning confidence and respect from a customer over a long-term period rather than concentrating one's efforts on one immediate order.

soft spot *n* [*US*] [*Stock market*] stocks or groups of stocks that fail to respond to the general upwards movement of an otherwise strong market.

soft target *n* [*Military*] an undefended target: missile silos, military installations and above all civilian centres that have not been given adequate defences to withstand a nuclear attack. The increasing accuracy of nuclear weapons means that more and more hitherto near-impregnable targets – military command centres, etc. – have been rendered soft as well.

soft technology *n* [*Science*] See **AT.**

soft temper *n* [*Metallurgy*] steel strip that has been annealed (heated and then cooled for the purposes of further manipulation) prior to undergoing hardening processes.

soft values *n pl* [*Market research*] the attributes of a product that appeal to those feelings which are considered soft – nourishment, maternal instincts, physical affection, etc. See also **hard values.**

soft-copy *n* [*Photo-typesetting*] a transient image of text or a graphic as viewed on a cathode ray

S

tube or **VDU**, as opposed to printed material. See also **hard copy**.

soft-sectoring *n* [*Computing*] a fast method of finding the start of **sectors** on **floppy disks** in which program instructions are used to identify sectors, rather than the slower, punched-hole system of **hard-sectoring**.

software **1.** *n* [*Computing*] the programs which give instructions to the **hardware** and which actually make it work, without which the machine is still effectively a 'dumb', albeit immensely complex collection of electronics; these packages have been worked out in advance to take advantage of the ability of the machine to perform a wide variety of tasks – word processing, calculations, spreadsheets, database management, etc. **2.** *n* [*Military, Aerospace*] the plans, designs and operating instructions of aircraft, weapons systems, rockets, etc.

software rot *n* [*Computing*] the gradual decline in the efficiency of pre-packaged software which can cease to function if left unused for too long.

soil **1.** *v* [*Hunting*] when a stag takes to water; the place where he takes to water is the 'soiling place'. See also **break soil**. **2.** *n* [*Engineering*] any fragmented material found at or near the surface of the earth, regardless of its suitability for plant growth.

soil sickness *n* [*Agriculture*] a condition in which soil is no longer capable of supporting the growth of healthy crops.

soil wash *n* [*Agriculture*] the movement of soil by the flow of ground water.

sola *n* [*Banking, Finance*] a bill of exchange or of lading that has been issued without any copies; it comes from Lat. 'solus' meaning 'alone'.

soldier **1.** *n* [*Building*] a brick that is placed on its end in a wall, its narrow side exposed. **2.** *n* [*US*] [*Crime*] in the US Mafia this is a rank and file member of a **family**; all soldiers are employed by a family and will fight for that family during feuds. **3.** *n* [*US*] [*Painting*] a spot formed when paint dries unevenly. **4.** *n* [*Royal Marines*] an officer. **5.** *n* [*Carpenters*] a heavy vertical timber or metal strut that is used to support the sides of an excavation. See also **waling**.

soldier blocks *n pl* [*Glass-making*] blocks of refractory material which extend more than the full depth of the glass in a furnace.

soldiering *n* [*Industrial relations*] time-wasting, 'coming the old soldier'.

soldiers *n pl* [*US*] [*Coal-mining*] posts supporting the roof of the mine.

soldier's wind *n* [*Navy*] a following wind which requires no complexities of steering.

sole **1.** *n* [*Mining*] the floor of the working. **2.** *n* [*Carpenters*] the smooth metal base of a plane, through which the blade protrudes.

solid **1.** *a* [*Wine-tasting*] used to describe an undeveloped wine, packed with alcohol, acidity and tannin. **2.** *a* [*Printing, Typesetting*] used to describe a block of copy with no spaces between the lines.

solid, in the **1.** *adv* [*Coal-mining*] referring to coal that is still part of the seam and which has yet to be dug out. **2.** *adv* [*UK*] [*Road transport*] referring to material due to be carted from a site and which has yet to be excavated or dug up; such material will take up a greater volume, and thus cost more, than that which has already been dug up. See also **loose, in the**.

solid suit *n* [*Cards*] in bridge this is a suit of such length and strength as to be almost sure of winning every trick in a hand.

solid stowing *n* [*Coal-mining*] the practice of filling up discarded workings with solid material, usually spoil from previous mining.

solid, working off the *n* [*Coal-mining*] the extraction of coal that is limited to a single free face.

solidarism *n* [*Economics*] the economic concept that every individual has certain financial obligations to those members of society who are less well off.

solid-mouth *n* [*US*] [*Meat trade*] a young ewe, with all its teeth; it is the opposite of the older 'broken-mouth'.

solo *v* [*Mountaineering*] to climb without a partner.

solon *n* [*Show business*] a pundit, an expert, anyone 'in the know'; it comes from Solon (lived 6th century BC), the founder of the Athenian democracy, and a staple of the US elementary civics curriculum.

solus **1.** *n* [*Oil industry*] a garage or petrol station that sells the products of one company only. **2.** also **island copy** *n* [*Advertising*] an advertisement entirely surrounded by either editorial matter or the margin.

son *n* [*Computing*] See **child**. See also **tree**.

son file *n* [*Computing*] in an series of file updates this is the most recent update of the master or **father file**. See also **grandfather file**.

sondage *n* [*Archeology*] a deep trench dug to investigate the stratigraphy of a site; it comes from Fr. 'sondage' meaning 'sounding, borehole'.

sonic throttling *n* [*Cars*] supersonic air flow.

sonic writing *n* [*Literary criticism*] the unwitting misspelling of words which sound identical to the correct words.

son-of-a-bitch with slides *n* [*US*] [*Medicine*] a guest speaker lecturing on his or her speciality at a medical meeting.

SOOB *phr* [*Medicine*] acro **sit out of bed**.

soogee *n* [*Navy*] soft soap, used for cleaning a ship's paintwork.

sophiology *n* [*Theology*] the doctrine of Divine Wisdom, which explains the relations between God and the world.

sophisticated *a* [*Book collecting*] said of a book that has in some way been made to appear more valuable and/or collectible than it really is; a fake.

S

sophistication *n* [*Printing*] the alteration of a literary text in the process of copying or printing.

sophomore *n* [*US*] [*Horse-racing*] a three-year old horse.

sore-shin *n* [*Tobacco*] a disease of the tobacco plant that starts at the root and spreads upwards.

sortie *n* [*Photography*] a series of aerial photographs taken during a single flight.

sortkey *n* [*Computing*] the information, sited in a record of information, that is to be compared in a sorting process. For example, an employee's name in a database which can be used to set such names in alphabetical order, etc.

s.o.s *Lat. abbr* [*Medicine*] a prescription notation meaning 'if necessary'.

SOS *n* [*US*] [*Marines*] abbr of **shit on a shingle**.

SOSUS *n* [*Military*] acro **Sound Surveillance System** the backbone of the USN open-ocean sensing system; passive underwater listening devices – hydrophones – are permanently fixed on the continental shelves of the US and its allies; the information elicited from these devices is sent to shore stations by cables. SOSUS was installed in 1960 and undergoes continuous improvements. When conditions are favourable it can spot a submarine anywhere in the ocean and pinpoint it to a 60 mile radius. It can also intereact with ASW aircraft and escort surveillance ships.

soudure *n* [*Cheese-making*] that period when the feed of animals is changed, so the milk thus produced may alter, and with it the quality of the cheeses.

souls *n pl* [*Air travel*] all those carried on a flight, including both crew and passengers.

sound 1. *v* [*Angling*] when the fish, once hooked, swims down to the sea bed. 2. *n* [*Espionage*] aural surveillance of a blackmail operation to ensure that not only are any verbal blunders fully recorded, but that if a subject becomes obstreperous, suitable force can be brought in to calm him down. 3. *a* [*Wine-tasting*] used to describe clear and bright appearance, with a clean **bouquet** and flavour; it is the essential quality for any wine pertaining to excellence.

sound bite *n* [*TV*] a brief audio segment inserted into a filmed report used on television news.

sound off 1. *v* [*Navy*] to play a particular bugle call through the ship's public address system. 2. *v* [*US*] [*Navy*] communications code for: reply to my message.

sound op *n* [*Advertising, Business*] abbr of **sound operator** the person who sets up and operates the sound equipment at a business theatre presentation.

sound-bite, also **sound cut** *n* [*US*] [*TV*] a piece of news reporting in which the reporter is actually on-camera while delivering the story.

sound-law *n* [*Linguistics*] a rule governing the regular occurrence of a phonetic change in the history of a language or a language family.

sound-orientated *a* [*Government*] said of an official who prefers to hear a report rather than read one.

sounds *n pl* [*Angling*] the entrails of a fish.

soup 1. *n* [*Anthropology*] the primordial mix of amino acids, purine, pyrimidine and phosphate from which life supposedly began. 2. *n* [*Building, Concrete workers*] an excessively wet concrete or mortar mix that is used for construction. 3. *n* [*Film, Photography*] fluid used in film laboratories for developing purposes. 4. *n* [*Flying*] dense fog or cloud formations. 5. *n* [*Oil rigs*] nitro-glycerine. 6. *n* [*Science*] the waste products of a chemical process. 7. *n* [*Surfing*] the froth formed by waves breaking on the beach.

soupe *n* [*Military*] used in the French Foreign Legion to mean any form of food.

soupy *n* [*US*] [*Military*] mess call.

sour 1. *a* [*Music*] out of tune. 2. *a* [*Cheese-making*] describing a cheese with excessive acidity. 3. *a* [*Oil rigs*] bearing a high sulphur content; thus 'sour crude', 'sour gas', etc. See also **sweet**.

source code, also **source program** *n* [*Computing*] a program which has been written in a **high-level language** and which has to be translated into **object** or **machine code** for the machine to run it.

source credibility *n* [*Marketing*] the degree of trust placed in a source of communications.

source-criticism *n* [*Theology*] the analysis and study of the sources used by the authors of the biblical texts.

source language *n* [*Computing*] See **source code**.

South *n* [*Politics*] those nations of the world which are generally seen as less wealthy and less developed than the average and which tend to be found in the Southern hemisphere. See also **North**.

South Bank *a* [*Theology*] concerning the theories proposed in the book 'Honest to God' by the Bishop of Southwark, John Robinson, and adopted by many Anglicans during the 1960s; they attempted to bring traditional Christianity more in line with contemporary society, its attitudes, beliefs and needs.

sovereign lending *n* [*Banking*] lending by banks and consortia in the European money markets to national governments.

Soviet man *n* [*Politics*] See **new Communist man**.

sow *n* [*Metallurgy*] in iron-founding this is the iron flowing in the main runner which conducts molten metal to moulds used for pig iron.

space *n* [*New therapies*] '**where you're at**'; the mental position that one has adopted, one's attitude towards the world one lives in and the way in which one deals with that world.

space and bronze deal *n* [*US*] [*Undertakers*] the **pre-need** sale of both a grave and a coffin to a potential customer by a door-to-door salesman.

space gun *n* [*Aerospace*] a handheld instrument

that propels the astronaut while he/she is working outside the capsule.

space, on *a* [*Journalism*] said of payments to free-lance writers that are based on the amount of copy published, rather than on a retainer which is paid out irrespective of work printed. See also **linage 2**.

space opera *n* [*TV*] a television series based on adventures in space, eg: 'Star Trek'. See also **horse opera**.

space stage *n* [*Theatre*] a technique of modern stage lighting in which only the area of the stage on which significant action is being performed is lit, while the rest remains in darkness.

space-case *n* [*US*] [*Subways*] New York transit police term for people who get themselves jammed between the side of the train and the platform.

spaceframe *n* [*Cars*] a chassis made from a web of steel tubes which preceded the **monocoque** style of building Grand Prix cars.

spaceman economy *n* [*Economics*] economical planning based on a finite universe with limited resources, like that of an enclosed spaceship. Such an economy looks to recycling and conservation of the available resources, accepting the real limits of what the earth can supply. See also **cowboy economy**.

spacemen *n pl* [*Military*] those members of the US military who advocate and develop concepts of 'space power', the fighting of wars with space based weapons and satellites. Spacemen believe in the great military potential of space, even to the extent that ultimate power over the earth may be gained through developments there. See also **star wars**.

spackle *n* [*US*] [*Painting*] a paste used to repair holes or cracks in plasterboard.

spad *n* [*Mining, Building*] a pole with a spike at one end and a hole at the other which is used to stick in the ground and support a plumb line for surveying, marking and measuring activities.

SPADATS *n* [*Military*] acro **Space Detection and Tracking Stations** used by **NORAD** to process some 10,500 inputs per day from world-wide sensors that track every object in space, including satellites, rocket and allied debris and, in the event, hostile missiles. Such objects are estimated at roughly 10,000 by the end of 1985. The heart of the SPADATS system is the USAF's 'Spacetrack', with its pair of massive radars at Eglin Air Force Base Fla., and Shemya Is. in the Aleutians. The system is also fed by the USN NAVSPASUR (tracking satellites across the southern states).

spade 1. *n* [*Golf*] an alternative name for the No. 6 iron. 2. *n* [*UK*] [*Railways*] a metallic connector put into the back of a relay, near its base, which can break the circuit as required. 3. *n* [*Shoe-making*] See **flare 7**.

SPADOC *n* [*Military*] acro **Space Defence Operations Center** the nerve centre of all NORAD-controlled surveillance and weapons systems that monitors every aspect of the network. See also **NORAD, SPADATS**.

spaghetti 1. *n* [*Aerospace*] the complex masses of electrical, hydraulic and other cables running through an aircraft. 2. *n* [*Aerospace*] the coloured piping that is slipped over wires and which serves to identify one from another. 3. *n* [*Audio*] the mass of wires that connect the various parts of a stereo system. 4. *n* [*Tyre-making*] See **noodles**.

Spaghetti Western *n* [*Film*] a genre of cowboy films; they were mainly products of the 1960s, and were made by Italians (especially the director Sergio Leone); they are long on 'atmosphere' and minimal on dialogue and often star US actors, notably Clint Eastwood and Lee Van Cleef.

spake *n* [*Coal-mining*] See **paddy 1**.

spallation *n* [*Science*] the detachment of a number of nucleons or small nuclei from a larger nucleus, often as a result of the striking of the nucleus by a high-energy neutron.

spam in a can *n* [*Aerospace*] a derogatory self-description of the early astronauts; former test pilots, they were disgusted that computerised, non-orbital space flights would render them powerless passengers with no responsibility for, or manual control of, the vehicle.

span of control *n* [*Management*] in Business Studies this is the area of activity, ie. the number of functions or subordinates or similar responsibilities which accrue to a single individual in a company.

spandrel *n* [*Building, Plastering*] a three-sided area, the sides of which may be curved, that is formed between features.

spandrels *n pl* [*Antiques, Horology*] the corner pieces on the clock dial.

spangles *n pl* [*Logging*] knots in the wood.

Spanish practices, also **Spanish customs** *n pl* [*UK*] [*Press*] fraudulent but generally accepted practices amongst Fleet Street print unions whereby a number of non-existent 'employees' exist purely for the purpose of obtaining wages, but are never seen to perform actual work.

spanker *n* [*Air travel*] an aircraft in first class condition and excellently maintained, especially as regards fuel economy.

spar 1. *n* [*Building, Plastering*] white and light-coloured stone chippings. 2. *n* [*Oil industry*] a floating storage and loading terminal that is anchored over a submarine wellhead; it provides both large oil tanks and various service facilities.

spar tree *n* [*Logging*] a large self-propelled crane which carries a variety of sheaves and cables and is used to haul the felled timber; it comes from the original spar tree which was an actual piece of timber, similarly equipped.

sparaciu *n* [*Crime*] in the Italian Mafia this means a prison warder; it comes from Sicilian for 'asparagus'.

spare *n* [*Skittles, Ten-pin bowling*] the knocking

down of all nine pins with the first two balls thrown; gaining a spare means that all nine pins are re-spotted and the player throws again at the full set.

spare parts dependency n [*Politics*] the selling of sophisticated weaponry by major powers to lesser ones in the knowledge that the weaponry is so complex that the buyer will continually be dependent on the expertise and spare parts – and thus the good will – that the seller can provide, if the buyer wishes to capitalise on this high technology.

sparger n [*Oil rigs*] a sprinkling device; it is usually one that distributes gas or air in liquids.

sparkle n [*Film*] white spots or speckles that may occasionally appear on projected film; they are usually caused if there is dirt on the negative which has been used to make that particular print of the film.

sparks n [*TV, Film*] an electrician. See also **juicer**.

sparrow n [*UK*] [*Dustmen*] the shareout at the end of a day's work of any spare cash – gained from tips (usually bribes to take extra rubbish away), the sale of valuable goods found thrown away, etc.

sparrow bill maker n [*Industry*] the maker of wrought iron nails from iron rods.

sparrow-pecking n [*Building, Plastering*] a key for plastering that is formed on a smooth dense background with a special bit in a mechanical hammer.

spasm war n [*Military*] a conflict in which both sides abandon themselves to uncontrolled reflex attacks; goals, aims, plans and any other modifications are rendered irrelevant in the gut-directed mania; it is the final rung on Kahn's **escalation ladder**.

spats n pl [*Aerospace*] See **pants 4**.

speak v [*Hunting*] said of a hound when it gives tongue, indicating that it has struck the **line** or found the scent.

speaker support n [*Advertising, Business*] any form of slide-based material that is used by the speaker at a business presentation.

spear 1. n [*Angling*] a spike that can be fixed to the rod and inserted in the ground. 2. n [*US*] [*Paper-making*] a piece of wood used to cut paper. 3. v [*AUS*] [*Football*] to make an illegal tackle on a player by upending him and throwing him on to the ground headfirst.

spearing 1. n [*US*] [*Car salesmen*] the practice of gathering customers by first spotting and then tracing their licence-plate number. 2. n [*Ice-hockey*] using one's stick as a weapon with which to attack – usually by jabbing or slashing – one's opponents. 3. n [*US*] [*Football*] butting one's opponent with the helmet.

spec n [*US*] [*Circus*] abbr of **spectacle** the opening number of the circus performance or the grand entry of the troupe.

special 1. n [*US*] [*Car salesmen*] a car that is advertised, but not automatically at a reduced price. 2. n [*Theatre*] a spotlight which illuminates that part of the stage where something special happens, eg: a door, window, etc.

special activities n pl [*Government*] this is used as a euphemism for Special Intelligence (**SI**) when hiding such activities within larger budgets.

special beef n [*Catering*] in Chinese restaurants this is dog meat.

special character n [*Computing*] a graphic character that is neither a letter, a number nor a space character.

special class n [*Education*] a remedial class for backward pupils.

special drawing rights n pl [*Economics*] a special scheme whereby members of the International Monetary Fund (IMF) are able to draw on that fund according to their investment in it.

special orders n pl [*US*] [*Railways*] train orders delivered over the radio.

special programmes, also **special update programmes** n [*Government*] See **special activities**.

special situation n [*Business*] an exceptional corporate position or prospect that offers unusual opportunities for capital gains.

speciating n [*Ecology*] the creation of new species of plant or vegetable.

species being n [*Politics, Philosophy*] a Marxist term derived from the Ger. 'Gattungswesen' (coined by P. C. Reinhard in 1797) which denotes man's objective consciousness of life and the mastery of the world through work, which differentiate human beings from all other species; thus man is considered with regard to these qualities.

speciesism n [*Politics, Ecology*] the discrimination by man against other species – animals, fish, etc. – on account of humanity's supposed superiority.

specific n [*Medicine*] abbr of **specific disease** it is often used in front of a patient as a euphemism for an 'unmentionable disease', eg: syphilis.

specific element n [*Biology*] the second part of the Latin name that is given to a species in the binomial system of nomenclature: the first name determines the genus, the second deals with the species within that genus.

specificity 1. n [*Libraries*] the extent to which a cataloguing system permits a precise reference to be made to the subject of a document which is to be processed. 2. n [*Libraries*] a measure expressing the ratio of non-relevant documents not retrieved in a search to the total number of non-relevant documents on file. See also **exhaustivity**.

speck v [*Mining*] to search for gold or opals on the surface.

specking n [*Ceramics*] the discoloration of pottery through contamination of the glaze; this effect may be achieved deliberately for decorative purposes.

specs 1. *n pl* [*Building*] abbr of **specifications** the detailed instructions issued to a builder by the architect or the client and on the basis of which he carries out the work required. 2. *n pl* [*Show business*] abbr of **specials, spectators, spectaculars**, depending on context.

spectacles *n pl* [*Dog breeding*] circular, light-coloured areas around the eyes of a Keeshond.

spectacular *n* [*Advertising*] in mail order merchandising this is three-dimensional material that jumps out when its envelope is opened.

spectail *n* [*US*] [*Stock market*] a portmanteau term for a broker-dealer who combines work as a retail broker with that as a dealer and speculator.

speech code *n* [*Cryptology*] a simple verbal code created by the regular substitution of secret words for the usual ones.

speech island *n* [*Linguistics*] a small area, inhabited by speakers of a language or dialect, that is isolated from the general language or dialect spoken by those inhabiting the surrounding area.

speech, the *n* [*Politics*] the one basic campaign speech a politician needs, with all the necessary points included, rhetoric well-presented and any other vital ingredients in place. This speech, altered only as to town, state of the weather, localised references and possible topical jokes, can be delivered by a candidate at any stage and in any arena on a campaign tour.

speed *n* [*Photography*] the light sensitivity of film emulsion.

speed! *excl* [*Film*] a call to the director by the sound man to indicate that the sound recording equipment is operating correctly.

speed shop *n* [*Cars*] any garage which specialises in supplying hot-rod drivers and in helping to maintain their vehicles.

speed, up to *a* [*US*] [*Politics*] said of a politician who has the current facts and information at his/her fingertips; 'on the ball'.

speeders *n pl* [*Industrial relations*] See **pacers**.

speed-to-fly *n* [*Gliding*] the indicated airspeed which produces the flattest glide in any convection situation.

spent fish *n* [*Angling*] a fish that has spawned.

speranzari *v* [*Crime*] in the Italian Mafia this means to escape abroad to avoid arrest; it comes from Sicilian for 'to gain hope'.

spew *n* [*Glass-making*] an imperfection in light bulbs or valves that occurs as localised finely divided extraneous material or small bubbles.

spider 1. *n* [*Industry*] one of a variety of contrivances which have radiating arms or members; it includes a frame for strengthening a core or mould in founding, a casting forming the hub and spokes to which the rim of a wheel or pulley is secured, a machine element consisting of a ring with outward projections, etc. 2. *n* [*Logging*] a small metal tool that tests the setting of the cutting teeth in a saw. 3. *n* [*US*] [*Painting*] a motorised cradle or platform that can be raised and lowered mechanically. 4. *n* [*UK*] [*Railways*] a flat box with signal wires radiating from it like the legs of a spider. 5. *n* [*TV, Film*] a folding metal brace that holds a camera tripod firmly on shiny surfaces; thus 'rolling spider' is a wheeled device fitted under the tripod, sometimes on tracks, to increase the flexibility of camera movements.

spider box *n* [*TV, Film*] a junction box to which are connected a number of lights.

spider hole *n* [*Military*] a camouflaged foxhole. See also **scrape**.

spiderdeck *n* [*Oil rigs*] a substructure beneath the main deck of a semi-submersible drilling unit; the deck is suspended beneath the rig floor and gives access to the top of the equipment under the rotary table.

spiderman *n* [*Merchant navy*] a rigger on an offshore oilrig.

spieler 1. *n* [*UK*] [*Police*] an illegal gambling house; a gambler. 2. *n* [*US*] [*Police*] an inside man who helps operate a large-scale confidence trick, the **big con**. 3. *n* [*US*] [*Radio*] a radio announcer.

spiff 1. *n* [*Commerce*] a commission on articles sold; it was originally paid only in drapers shops to the assistants. 2. *n* [*Commerce*] unfashionable merchandise on which an extra commission is payable if the salesmen can dispose of it. See also **P.M.**

spike 1. *n* [*Electronics*] a sharp, short-duration voltage peak. 2. *n* [*Futures market*] a rapid, sharp price increase. 3. *n* [*Theatre*] a mark on the stage that denotes the exact place for a piece of furniture or other prop. 4. *v* [*Journalism*] to reject a story for publication or transmission. 5. *v* [*US*] [*Football*] used of a player who has scored a touchdown, when he expresses his pleasure by hurling the ball, point-down, on to the pitch and thus bouncing it high in the air. 6. *v* [*Military*] to programme two warheads to explode as nearly as possible at the same moment over the same target; this simultaneous explosion will multiply the destructive effects by a factor of far more than simply one plus one. 7. *v* [*Science*] to enrich a nuclear reactor or its fuel with a particular isotope.

spike a temp *v* [*US*] [*Medicine*] said of a patient who shows a sudden increase in temperature; it comes from the inverted sharp 'V' that appears on the temperature chart.

spike, on (*US*), **on its dead** (*UK*) *adv* [*Theatre*] referring to scenery, furniture or props that are arranged correctly on their various marks, ready for a performance or a scene to begin.

spiking *n* [*Clothing*] a method of ensuring that fine materials are laid out correctly ready for cutting by attaching one edge to a row of spikes running along an edge of the table; the table top can be tilted to hang the material, then tilted back to the horizontal for cutting.

spiky *a* [*Religion*] referring to a particularly ritualistic or ultra-High Church Anglican.

spiling *n* [*Coal-mining*] the driving in of supports ahead of the face when mining through running ground.

spill 1. *n* [*Metallurgy*] See **scab 3**. 2. *n* [*Aus.*] [*Politics*] the vacating of other posts in a government that follows a major change in one office.

spilling *n* [*Aerospace*] the action of causing air to escape from a parachute, and also the escape of such air; it is caused either by side-slipping in the descent or by the instability of the parachute.

spims *n* [*Commerce*] See **spiff**.

spin *n* [*UK*] [*Prisons*] an unexpected search, either of one's person or of one's cell.

spin a car *v* [*US*] [*Car salesmen*] See **clock a car**.

spin a drum *v* [*UK*] [*Police*] to search the house of a suspected person.

spinach *n* [*Architecture, Design*] excessive and distasteful ornamentation and frills in any form of design, from housing to aircraft.

spine *n* [*Printing*] the central portion of the letter S.

spingularu *n* [*Crime*] in the Italian Mafia this means a petty thief, a category of villainy outlawed by the Mafia; it comes from Sicilian for 'grubber up of cigarette ends'.

spinning 1. *n* [*Angling*] fishing with revolving bait. 2. *n* [*Building, Plastering*] 'running' circular fibrous plasterwork, when the running mould is pivoted so that the moulding revolves around it.

spin-off 1. *v* [*Commerce*] to distribute stock in a new company to shareholders of the parent company. 2. *v* [*Commerce*] to create a new company by the distribution of stock as in (1).

spin-spin *a* [*Science*] referring to the interaction between two or more particles both of which possess spin.

spin-timed *a* [*Radio*] used to describe a rough but speedy method of timing a piece of tape by running it through a tape recorder on 'spool' or 'fast forward'; this is a highly inaccurate method of timing, and the producer must be warned of its use, in case the tape runs out early.

spiralism *n* [*Sociology*] career and residential mobility as seen in one who strives for success under the tenets of modern industrial society.

spiralist *n* [*Sociology*] a typical upwardly mobile career businessman who is willing to move frequently both in geography and status to keep his status improving. See also **burgher**.

spiritual dryness *n* [*Religion*] a period of one's life when the spiritual life seems desolate and lifeless.

spit *n* [*Customs*] an instrument used by Customs officers to probe and examine cargo for contraband.

spit and spy *n* [*UK*] [*Government*] SSPI(T) and

SSPI(E): two Department of Health and Social Security forms that deal with statutory sick pay.

spit cup *n* [*US*] [*Bars*] the glass of water that accompanies the actual drink bought by a **mixer**. Every sip of alcohol is followed by one of water, but in fact the alcohol is spat out into the water glass which prevents the woman from becoming drunk, while her victim grows ever more so.

spit sock *n* [*Audio*] the foam cover that is often placed over microphones to deaden extraneous noise both in the room or made by the speaker him/herself.

spitball *v* [*Government, Business*] to speculate, to guess wildly; it comes from the fact that the veteran baseball players who threw the (now outlawed) spitball often had little idea of how those pitches would turn out.

Spithead pheasant *n* [*Navy*] a bloater or a kipper.

spitting [*Military*] US Department of Defense code for: I am laying sonar buoys and will be out of contact for a while as I am flying at very low levels.

spitting around *n* [*Mining*] lighting the fuses to set off explosive charges.

spittoon *n* [*US*] [*Paper-making*] an incorrectly formed paper cup.

splash 1. *n* [*US*] [*Bars*] soda in the glass, with the ice and the liquor; it is the opposite of **back**. 2. *n* [*Dog breeding*] an irregularly shaped white mark anywhere on the body. 3. *n* [*Journalism*] the front-page lead story in an edition of a newspaper; thus 'splash-sub' is the sub-editor whose sole job is to write that story, altering it as and when necessary in each edition. 4. *n* [*US*] [*Drugs*] amphetamines. 5. *n* [*Military*] a code word sent to an observer five seconds prior to the supposed explosion of a missile on target. 6. *v* [*Military*] to shoot down a hostile aircraft over water with a sea-to-air missile. 7. *v* [*Military*] the code for: target destruction verified by radar or visual source.

splashover effect *n* [*Sociology*] the concept that once an area is given over to pornography and prostitution, there inevitably develop concomitant upsurges in crimes such as robbery, assault and mugging.

splat *n* [*Computing*] a name for the symbol '*'.

splatter movies *n* [*Film*] a genre of ultra-violent films, coined as a name by director George Romero, such as the 'Texas Chainsaw Massacre' in which the main action/appeal is the covering of the screen in blood. See also **nasties**.

splatterdash *n* [*Building, Plastering*] a slurry of sand plus cement, sometimes with a bonding additive, that is stippled on to the surface of a **background** to form a rough **key** for later work.

splayed *a* [*Printing*] said of a letter M in which the outer strokes are not vertical.

splendid first strike *n* [*Military*] a pre-emptive first strike that destroys the enemy's forces before he can activate them and so should provide the aggressor with an outright victory.

spline 1. *n* [*Building, Plastering*] a wood lath used for reinforcement of fibrous plaster casts. **2.** *n* [*Design*] a flexible strip used by draughtsmen to guide them when drawing curves. **3.** *n* [*Mathematics*] a polynomial function used to approximate a curve with a high degree of smoothness. **4.** *n* [*Photo-typesetting*] the arc-and-vector or spiral **algorithms** that are used in electronic curve fitting to record a character outline digitally.

splint coal, also **splent coal** *n* [*Coal-mining*] hard coal with a dull lustre, which breaks off unevenly.

split 1. *n* [*Coal-mining*] a coal seam separated from another seam by a thick parting. **2.** *n* [*Coal-mining*] any of the air currents in a mine formed by dividing a larger current.

split bit *n* [*US*] [*Prisons*] an indeterminate prison sentence, offering the inmate a minimum and a maximum period to be served, dependant on parole. See also **flat bit**.

split half *a* [*Statistics*] referring to a technique for checking the accuracy of information by splitting supposedly homogenous results into two portions and then testing them again to confirm that they are indeed identical.

split page *n* [*US*] [*Journalism*] See **second front**.

split roll *n* [*Croquet*] a shot in which two balls are sent equal distances in different directions.

split run *n* [*Advertising*] the use of slightly different advertisements in different editions of the same paper; it is often used for different areas of the same town; alternatively both versions are used in alternative copies of the same edition to ensure a good mix throughout the distribution area. See also **split test**.

split test *n* [*Advertising*] the slicing of a mailing list into two or more parts in order to send to each group a different style of mail order advertising for the same product and then to compare the response as regards each type. See also **split run**.

split ticket *n* [*US*] [*Politics*] a vote cast by a voter who has no regard for party candidates.

split the wicket *v* [*Pool*] to shoot the ball into the dead centre of a pocket without touching the sides as it drops in.

split-down *n* [*US*] [*Stock market*] the reduction of the number of shares into which the ownership of a company is divided.

splithead *n* [*Building, Plastering*] an adjustable metal tripod, with a channelled clamp, that is used to provide a convenient portable system of low-level scaffolding.

splits *n* [*Tennis*] a covert agreement between finalists in a professional competition whereby they decide to split the prize money for winner and runner-up equally between them, irrespective of who actually wins on the day.

splitter *n* [*Taxonomy*] a taxonomist who used

meticulous differences as a basis for classifying species and types. See also **lumper 1**.

splitter gearbox *n* [*UK*] [*Road transport*] a means of increasing the number of gear ratios available from a standard gearbox by splitting each full gear in half to give progressive but narrowly spaced steps across the ratio range. See also **range change**.

splosh it on *v* [*Gambling*] to bet heavily with a book-maker.

splurge *n* [*Advertising, Journalism*] a large, showy and ostentatious advertisement; it is often an 'advertising feature' running to several pages.

spoil *n* [*Coal-mining*] any waste material extracted during mining operations.

spoil heap *n* [*Coal-mining*] a tip that consists mainly of solid wastes. See also **lagoon 1**.

spoil the market *v* [*Stock market*] to force a sudden rise or fall in the price of a security by making a large number of deals in that stock at one time, rather than spreading them out over a period.

spoiler 1. *n* [*US*] [*Politics*] a candidate who knows he/she cannot win, but is still determined to stand, simply to divert some votes from a rival, and thus ensure that that rival is also unable to win. Thus 'spoiler party' is a third party that cannot win office alone, but is determined to ruin the chances of one of the major parties and help see it defeated at an election. **2.** *n* [*Cars*] a structure placed on a motor vehicle which is intended to reduce lift and thus increase the pressure on the wheels when the vehicle is moving at speed. It was originally seen only on racing cars, which achieve speeds requiring such a modification, but is now a component of family saloons as well. **3.** *n* [*Boxing*] a boxer who attempts to compensate for his actual inferiority by aiming to break up the pattern and flow of his opponent's style and thus possibly beat him.

spoilers 1. *n pl* [*Aerospace*] speed brakes: panels on top of the wings which block the airflow and speed up the rate at which an aircraft can descend; the most powerful spoilers are 'lift dumpers'. **2.** *n pl* [*Gliding*] devices which disturb the airflow across the wing in order to reduce lift and to increase drag. See also **spoiler 2**.

sponge *v* [*Horse-racing*] to insert a piece of sponge into a horse's nostril prior to a race; this will impair the animal's breathing and, feloniously, thus influence the outcome of the race.

sponge word *n* [*Linguistics*] a word so over-used and misused that it loses all real meaning; eg: 'parameter', 'scenario', 'interface', etc.

sponges *n pl* [*Technology*] temporary employees hired by a nuclear energy plant to perform certain tasks where there is a risk of radiation poisoning.

sponsor *n* [*Alcoholics Anonymous*] a fellow member of AA who will help one maintain sobriety.

sponsored mobility *n* [*Sociology, Education*] in

an educational system this is any selective system which divides the brighter from their contemporaries and thus puts them in line for higher-level occupations in later life.

spontaneity 1. *n* [*New therapies*] 'the response a person makes which contains some degree of adequacy to a new situation or novelty to an old one' (J. L. Moreno 'Who Shall Survive', 1934). **2.** *n* [*Politics*] in Marxist terms this is the belief that both the emancipation of the proletariat and the collapse of capitalism will come through spontaneous demonstrations of worker solidarity.

spontaneous architecture *n* [*Architecture*] any buildings or enclosures that are erected by members of the public who ignore architects and governmental planning regulations and put up exactly what they want.

spoof 1. *v* [*Computing*] to make a deliberate attempt to cause a user or resource to perform an incorrect action. **2.** *v* [*Computing*] in data communications this refers to a technique that enables a multiplicity of computers to deal with a variety of terminals. It is achieved by software emulators running on microprocessors in the channel interfaces which make the network appear to the terminal as its own type of computer, and the terminals appear to the computer as its own type of terminal. **3.** *v* [*Military*] to copy a hostile identification of friend or foe (**IFF**) code in order to confuse the enemy. **4.** *v* [*UK*] [*Military*] to plant misleading or totally false information for the purposes of fooling the enemy.

spoofer [*Military*] US Department of Defense code for: contact is employing electronic and/or tactical deception methods.

spook 1. *n* [*Espionage*] a member of an intelligence agency, specifically the CIA; it comes from the original recruits to the pre-CIA OSS (a World War II security group) who, like their opposite numbers in the UK, were primarily recruited from the Establishment. In the case of many OSS men, it was from Yale University's 'Skull and Bones' club, an exclusive, secret student club. **2.** *n* [*US*] [*Medicine*] a psychiatrist. See also **wig picker**.

spooky *a* [*Surfing*] referring to a dangerous or intimidating wave.

spooling *n* [*Computing*] acro **Simultaneous Peripheral Operation On-Line** the ability, while accessing a database, to store all fetched information in a local memory buffer, from which it may be recalled for subsequent use, or dumped to a disk or printer.

spoon 1. *n* [*Building*] a slender iron bar, tapered at one end, which is used to insert rivets into hollow metal posts. **2.** *n* [*Surfing*] a surfboard with a noticeable upturn at its nose. **3.** *n* [*Drugs*] a measure of narcotic drugs: approximately 2 gms. **4.** *n* [*Golf*] the traditional name for a No. 3 wood. **5.** *n* [*Ice-skating*] the track left in the ice by a poorly-executed figure-skating turn. **6.** *v* [*Cricket*]

to hit the ball high into the air, usually no great distance, and thus usually offer an easy catch.

sporadic E *n* [*Audio*] intermittent reflections of radio waves due to periods of heavy ionisation in the E-layer of the ionosphere (a layer approximately 65 miles above the earth, which reflects radio waves); it affects reception above 40mHz.

spot 1. *v* [*Aerospace*] to form up aircraft on the deck of a carrier, preparatory to launching them by catapult. **2.** *n* [*US*] [*Circus*] a leopard. **3.** *n* [*Radio*] the length and position of an advertisement. **4.** *n* [*TV*] the spot of light which results from an electronic beam hitting the screen of a cathode ray tube and which traces out the TV picture.

spot a car *v* [*US*] [*Railways*] to put a car in a given place for future convenience in loading or unloading.

spot coverage *n* [*Media*] on the spot live broadcasting or reporting.

spot effect *n* [*Radio*] a special effect created 'on the spot' – in the studio.

spot market *n* [*Futures market*] a commodities market in which those products in which one is dealing are actually available for immediate sale for cash. See also **forward market**.

spot news *n* [*Journalism*] events occurring shortly before publication of the paper, as opposed to the less immediate **features**.

spot the body *v* [*US*] [*Road transport*] to park the trailer.

spot-plague *n* [*Literary criticism*] a prose style that relies on an excess of full-stops, rather than using commas, semi-colons, etc.

spotting *n* [*Photography*] cleaning up the white marks on a print left by dirt in the enlarger; this is done by applying spotting dye to them.

spousal support *n* [*Social work*] a synonym for alimony.

spouse fares *n pl* [*Air travel*] a scheme whereby when one partner flies at full fare – probably on company expenses – their husband or wife can get a 50% reduction.

spout *n* [*Hunting*] a rabbit's earth.

sprag 1. *v* [*Merchant navy*] to adjust machinery or equipment in order to deceive an inspector or a commercial competitor. **2.** also **locker** *n* [*Coal-mining*] a wooden or iron bar that can be pushed through the spokes of a tub to act as a rudimentary brake.

sprang *n* [*Weaving*] a braiding or plaiting technique in which the ends of the threads are held in a fixed position and progressive twists are held in place by temporary rods.

sprauncy *a* [*Antiques*] used to describe a flashy, ostentatious, usually expensive item for sale.

spray *n* [*Espionage*] an invisible electronic substance which can be sprayed on to an object and which will then act as a directional transmitter to monitor a subject over limited distances.

spread 1. *n* [*Futures market*] the simultaneous

S

purchase and sale of futures contracts for the same instrument for delivery in different months, or the simultaneous purchase and sale of futures in different, but related instruments, for delivery in the same or different months. **2.** *n* [*Gemstones*] in diamond cutting, this is the width of a stone considered in proportion to its depth. **3.** *n* [*Billiards*] the rebound of the cue ball from the object ball when this causes it to deviate considerably from its previous course. **4.** *n* [*Cards*] in bridge this is a hand which the declarer can show as proof of his/her ability to win all thirteen tricks. **5.** *n* [*Publishing*] two facing pages of a book viewed as a whole. **6.** *n* [*Oil rigs*] the total assemblage of men, equipment and materials that are required for a job, eg: laying a pipeline. **7.** *n* [*TV*] a programme which increases its running time during the production schedule. **8.** also **top** *n* [*Journalism*] a major story of some length. **9.** *n* [*Journalism*] an important story which has various related **sidebars** printed adjacent to it.

Spread Eagle *n* [*Ten-pin bowling*] a split where the 2–3–4–6–7–10 pins are left standing. See also **baby split, bucket, Cincinnati.**

spread the broads *v* [*UK*] [*Police*] to cheat at cards; specifically it means to perform the 'three-card trick'; thus 'broad tosser' is anyone who works the three-card trick, and 'broad tossing mob' is a gang of confidence men who specialise in this swindle.

spread-eagle *n* [*Stock exchange*] an operation by which a broker agrees to buy shares of stock within a specified time at a specified price, and sells the option of buying the same stock within the same time at a higher price.

spread-eaglism *n* [*Politics*] ultra-nationalism, the US equivalent of British jingoism.

spreader **1.** *n* [*Meat trade*] a short stick inserted in the breast of a hog carcass to prevent the meat curling during the freezing process. **2.** *n* [*Weaving*] see **raddle.**

spreadover *n* [*Industrial relations*] staggered hours or split shifts.

sprig *n* [*Cricket*] a stud used to increase the grip of one's cricket-boots.

spring **1.** *n* [*Shoe-making*] the curvature of the instep of a boot or shoe. **2.** *n* [*Shoe-making*] the rise of the toe of the last above the ground line. **3.** also **flush** *v* [*Shooting*] to cause birds to take flight.

springboard *n* [*Logging*] a platform on which a logger stands while sawing and chopping the tree prior to felling.

springer **1.** *n* [*Angling*] a spring salmon, which enters the river from the sea in spring. **2.** *n* [*Navy*] a physical training instructor. **3.** *n* [*US*] [*Meat trade*] a spring lamb; a cow about to calve. **4.** *n* [*Food processing*] a can of food that bulges excessively at one or both ends; such bulging is caused by improper exhausting of air from the can before

it is sealed, or by bacterial or chemical growths. See also **flipper, swelter.**

springers *n* [*Glass-making*] See **skewbacks.**

springing *n* [*Mining*] a method of quarry blasting whereby a series of charges are fired in a borehole in order to open up a chamber.

springy **1.** *a* [*Furriers*] a fur of poor quality, usually **late-caught**; very poor quality pelts are 'overspringy'. **2.** also **supple** *a* [*Cheese-making*] used to describe a cheese, usually semi-soft, which has just the right degree of resilient and pliable texture; the cheese is bendable but not **rubbery.**

sprint *n* [*Horse-racing*] a short race, under a mile.

sprints *n pl* [*Cycling*] racing wheels.

sprod, also **slob trout** *n* [*Angling*] sea trout.

sprog *n* [*UK*] [*Military*] a recruit, trainee or novice; it is also used of junior policemen.

sprue **1.** *n* [*Metallurgy*] in iron founding this is the main passage, running vertically, which allows metal to enter the mould from the ladle via the pouring basin. **2.** *n* [*Metallurgy*] the waste material that accumulates in this passage (see 1). The same definitions are applicable to the plastics industry.

sprung *a* [*Cricket*] said of a bat, when the handle has lost its essential springy resilience.

SPSS *n* [*Sociology*] abbr of **Statistical Package for the Social Sciences** the most widely used computer programme for the analysis of research data in sociology.

spud **1.** *n* [*Logging*] a tool used to remove bark from the logs. **2.** *n* [*Mining*] a means of marking an underground surveying station, by using a flat spike which has been pierced to take a plumbline. **3.** *n* [*Tobacco*] a tobacco-cutting knife. **4.** *n* [*TV, Film*] the pole that is fitted into a **turtle** in order to connect it to a light. **5.** *n* [*Plumbing*] a short length of pipe used to connect two components, eg: a valve and a radiator in a central heating system; it is also a projection from a fitting to which a pipe may be attached.

spud can *n* [*Oil rigs*] a truss-reinforced and stiffened shell structure which can be sunk into a soft sea-bed and used as the base of a platform that rises above the surface.

spud in *v* [*Oil rigs*] to start any activity on the rig; originally it meant to commence the actual drilling.

spud tank *n* [*Oil rigs*] large tanks that are attached to the legs of a **jack-up** rig and which can be inflated to add buoyancy and to spread the 'footprint' area of the rig.

spud-basher *n* [*UK*] [*Road transport*] a lorry carrying a load of potatoes.

spudder *n* [*Oil rigs*] a small drilling rig used to start the drilling of a well.

spudding in *n* [*Oil rigs*] the process of starting to drill a well by making a hole in the earth or sea bed, using a large-diameter bit.

spur *n* [*Printing*] a line that extends or completes an arm or serif.

S

sputnik *n* [*TV*] a 2KW focussing lamp.

sputter *v* [*Science*] to remove atoms of a metal from a cathode by bombarding it with fast positive ions.

squab **1.** *n* [*Cars*] the part of the seat upon which one sits. **2.** *n* [*Cars*] the back of the seat, against which one rests.

squabble *v* [*Printing*] said of type which becomes twisted.

squad *n* [*Espionage*] the team of musclemen and surveillance experts who provide backup for the **ladies** who are actually involved at first hand in **sanctifying** the target of a political blackmail operation. See also **lion-tamer, peep, sound 2**.

squad bay *n* [*US*] [*Marine Corps*] barracks for junior NCOs and privates.

squame *n* [*Medicine*] a small flake of dead tissue that falls from the skin in certain illnesses.

square **1.** *n* [*Book-binding*] the portion of the cover of a bound book that projects beyond the edges of the leaves. **2.** *n* [*Sex*] the various urban centres where **hustlers** gather: Times Square (New York), Pershing Square (Los Angeles), Union Square (San Francisco), etc. **3.** *v* [*Soccer*] to pass the ball across the pitch, especially towards the centre.

square away **1.** *v* [*US*] [*Marine Corps*] to arrange one's possessions, bedding and spare kit in the prescribed military manner. **2.** *v* [*US*] [*Marine Corps*] to make sure that those under one's command are correctly disciplined; this comes from (1).

square business *n* [*US*] [*Prisons*] the truth.

square groupers *n pl* [*Drugs*] wrapped bales of marijuana that are tossed into the sea by smugglers and then picked up at pre-determined points by those who take them inshore; they supposedly resemble aberrant grouper fish.

square number *n* [*Navy*] an easy posting in a shore establishment.

square rig **1.** *n* [*Navy*] the traditional garments worn by seamen, especially as portrayed on stage, in illustrations, etc: jumper, flannels, jean collar and bell-bottomed trousers. **2.** *n* [*US*] [*Navy*] a double-breasted uniform.

square tail *n* [*Angling*] sea trout.

square wheeler *n* [*Motor trade*] in the second-hand trade, this is a car that will not sell and which stands on the forecourt without attracting the attention of any buyer.

squash rot *n* [*US*] [*Medicine*] the state of being a human vegetable; in the US 'squash' means 'marrow, pumpkin'. See also **gork 2**.

squat *n* [*Cars*] the tendency of the rear of a car to move downwards during acceleration.

squatter *n* [*Cricket*] a ball that remains low after it hits the pitch. See also **shooter 2**.

squaw hitch *n* [*Logging*] the bite of the piece of wire rope that is tied around a log to drag it away.

squawk **1.** *n* [*Air travel*] in air traffic control this is a four-figure number that is used to identify each aircraft that appears on the traffic controller's radar screen. **2.** *n* [*Military*] a transponder that identifies an aircraft on a radar screen.

squawk book *n* [*Air travel*] a book kept by commercial airline maintenance engineers in which are entered all those faults, occurring within a fleet of aircraft, that must be dealt with.

squawkbox *n* [*TV*] a two-way communicator used to connect the control room with the studio floor.

squawker *n* [*Gambling*] a poor loser.

squeaker *n* [*US*] [*Sport*] any game won by a very small margin; a close game.

squeal **1.** *n* [*US*] [*Police*] a call for police assistance or investigation. **2.** *n* [*US*] [*Police*] a report of a case currently under investigation.

squeal line *n* [*Video*] a telephone number, maintained by an industry or governmental agency, which a retailer can phone and use to inform against any competitor allegedly dealing in a pirated product.

squealer *n* [*US*] [*Road transport*] the tachograph which makes an automatic record of the driving distance, stops, speed and other factors during a trip; thus it makes it harder for the driver to manipulate his **lie sheet**.

squeegee *n* [*US*] [*Hotels*] in a New York City hotel this is a guest who comes from out of town.

squeegee arrangement *n* [*Stock market*] an agreement whereby one guarantees to back a security within a stated time at a loss.

squeeze **1.** *v* [*Audio*] to remove as much as possible of the treble and bass tones from a recorded track, leaving the kind of sound that one hears over a telephone; thus speech recorded on squeezed tracks is sometimes known as a 'telephone voice'. **2.** *n* [*US*] [*Bars*] a twist of lime. See also **twist 1**. **3.** *n* [*Building, Plastering*] an impression taken in clay or similar material of a plaster mould in situ. **4.** *n* [*Oil rigs*] an operation to insert cement, under pressure, between the casing and the well bore at a given depth. **5.** *n* [*Tyre-making*] the placing of one rubber or fabric on to another. **6.** *n* [*Cards*] in bridge this is a tactic designed to force one's opponent to discard or make vulnerable an otherwise winning card.

squeeze and freeze *n* [*Economics*] government measures to control wages (squeeze) and hold down prices (freeze).

squeeze play *n* [*Baseball*] a **bunt** attempted or executed so as to bring a runner on third base safely back to the home plate.

squeeze the shorts *v* [*Stock market*] to force those who have sold **short** to pay high prices in order to cover their deliveries.

squeezer *n* [*Coal-mining*] See **grips**.

squegger *n* [*Electronics*] an oscillator whose oscillations build up to a certain amplitude and then cease for a time before beginning again; thus as a verb it is 'to squeg'.

squegging *n* [*Audio*] a variety of high frequency

S

oscillation in which there is a build-up to a high amplitude then a sudden period of quiescence, followed by a further build-up of high frequency oscillation, then quiescence again and so on.

squelch, also **quiet** v [Audio] to reduce the volume of a radio signal in the absence of a sufficiently clear transmission.

squib n [Journalism] a brief item of news.

squibs n pl [Film] artificially controlled explosions that are used to simulate 'bullet hits'.

squid 1. n [Science] a super-sensitive device that is used to measure magnetic fields. 2. n [Aerospace] a parachute that is stable, with the inflow to the canopy equalling the outflow, and only partially extended; it comes from its resemblance to the marine creature. 3. also **cereb, grub, pencil geek, spider, wonk** n [US] [Education] a very dedicated hard worker.

squidge-off n [Tiddleywinks] the playing of one wink per player towards the pot to determine who starts the game.

squidger n [Tiddleywinks] a circular plastic counter – between 1 and 2 inches in diameter – that is used to pot smaller winks; hence 'squidging', 'to squidge'.

squire n [Deer-stalking] a young stag that attaches himself like an esquire to his 'knight', the fully grown old stag.

squirrel cage 1. n [US] [Painting] a small, motorised platform, with handrails for safety, that is used for painting very high steelwork. 2. n [Tyre-making] a large slatted roll in the drying room around which the dipped fabric travels as it dries. 3. n [Weaving] a **swift** that is a vertical stand with two free-turning and adjustable cylindrical cages around which the skein is placed.

squirrel lines, also **rat lines** n pl [Logging] short sections of light line that are used to move the position of the heavier line.

squirrel the tech v [Scientology] to misinterpret Church doctrine; it is a major heresy.

squish 1. n [Engineering] in certain internal combustion engines this is the forced radial flow of mixture into the combustion chamber as the piston moves towards the cylinder head as it finishes a single stroke. 2. n [Cars] the action of squeezing the air/petrol mixture in a cylinder head, which is aimed at reducing the possibility of **knocking**.

squitter n [Communications] random pulses produced by a **transponder** in the absence of interrogating signals.

squop v [Tiddleywinks] to cover one's opponent's wink with one's own. Thus 'double-squop' is a strategy whereby both partners attempt to cover their opponents' winks; 'squopped-up' means in a position where all one's winks are covered and no shot can be played.

SRAM n [Military] abbr of **Short Range Attack Missile** air-to-ground missiles designed to destroy hostile ground defences. They are carried by B–

52 and F–111 strategic bombers in addition to their warheads. Some 1150 SRAMs are deployed on US aircraft, each capable of delivering a 200KT warhead over a range of 50–140 miles, travelling at 2,000 mph and employing inertial guidance and terrain clearance sensing systems.

SRBM n [Military] abbr of **Short-range Ballistic Missiles** a variety of land-based ballistic missiles, none of which have a range in excess of 900km. The US and NATO deploy the Pershing 1A, Lance and Honest John missiles; the Soviets have SS–12, SS–22, SS–21, SS–23, Frog 7 and SS–1. Such weapons are reasonably mobile and if the range is shortened, can double for medium range missiles in dealing with most of the same targets. The SS–12 and SS–22 can hit 85% of the targets in NATO that are assigned to the SS–20 once it has been moved forward into a Warsaw Pact country for launching. The US Pershing II, which can similarly substitute for Tomahawk (**cruise**) is viewed with equal misgivings by the USSR.

SRO 1. n [US] [Theatre] **Standing Room Only** a completely full theatre; thus used as a verb it means to fill the theatre, and as an adjective it denotes success. 2. n [Stock market] abbr of **Self Regulatory Organisation** a British financial organisation that conducts its own affairs, including the disciplining of its members, as specified in the Financial Services Bill (1986).

S-S a [Military] abbr of **Surface-to-Surface** the overall designation of Soviet ground- or sea-launched missiles. These are further modified by the addition of – N– for naval weapons and – X– for experimental missiles.

SSBN n [Military] abbr of **ship, submersible, ballistic, nuclear** a nuclear powered ballistic missile submarine.

SSI n [Computing] abbr of **Small-Scale Integration** integration technology that allows the placing of 100 or less transistors on a single chip. See also **LSI, VLSI**.

SSSPk n [Military] abbr of **single shot probability of kill** a calculable formula for assessing the percentage likelihood that a single warhead delivered as one part of a **MIRVed** missile will hit and destroy its target.

stab 1. a [US] [Industrial relations] referring to anything that has been negotiated; thus 'stab wages' are the negotiated daily rate for a job. 2. n [Medicine] an individual who has been wounded in a knife fight. 3. n [TV] See **sting** 5. 4. v [Oil rigs] to insert the threaded end of a pipe or rod into the coupling at the end of another pipe or rod.

stabber n [Oil rigs] one who joins up two lengths of pipe. See also **stab** 4.

stabbing board n [Oil rigs] a board on which a **stabber** stands to manipulate the lengths of pipe he is joining together.

stability of cadres n [Politics] in Communist countries this was a method whereby a single official found it hard to establish his/her own network of patronage, dependent on promoting or demoting their juniors, since Party officials, once elected, were confirmed in office for life, rather than finding themselves subject to the whims and favouritism of local or national bosses. With the accession of Deng Xiaoping in China and Gorbachov in the USSR, this stability, itself long a producer of corruption and complacency, has been largely undermined in the interests of replacing the inept with the, theoretically, efficient.

stable *n* [*UK*] [*Coal-mining*] the **tail gate** area of the face.   *n* [*Coal-mining*] the space excavated to form a short step, at right angles to the face, from which a coal-cutter or power loader can start its run.   *n* [*Sex*] the prostitutes who all work for the same pimp.   *n* [*Espionage*] this comes from the commercial sex use (see); those women who are employed by intelligence services to work as 'Mata Haris' and extract information by means of political blackmail. See also **ladies**.   *n* [*Boxing*] a gymnasium where a group of boxers train.   *n* [*Boxing*] a group of boxers working for the same manager.

stable knit *n* [*Textiles*] any knitted garment which is assumed to be incapable of anything other than minor stretching, eg: double-knits.

stable machine *n* [*UK*] [*Coal-mining*] a small coal-cutting machine that cuts at the **tail gate** end of the coalface; an area of coal is cut at this end of the face to provide a buttock or jib for the larger coal-cutter to attack.

stack *v* [*Aerospace*] to assemble a multi-stage launch vehicle.   *n* [*Air travel*] a 'queue' of aircraft, all ranged at 1000ft. distances above each other, circling an airport and awaiting their various permissions to land.   *n* [*Computing*] a structure in which all accesses, insertions and removals are made at one end of the sequence, designated the top. All use of the stack is thus conducted on a last-in-first-out basis. See also **LIF** .

stack offence *n* [*Lacrosse*] a high risk, but very effective, attack tactic in which the numbers of people in attack are boosted; it is susceptible to a fast break by the opposition if it fails to result in a goal.

stacked head *n* [*Audio*] a head in a tape recorder in which the gaps that correspond to the tracks in multi-channel recording are sited one above another.

stacking *n* [*Air travel*] See **holding pattern**.

staff bead *n* [*Building, Plastering*] a moulding section: three quarters of a circle in profile.

staff status *n* [*Industrial relations*] See **harmonisation**.

stag *n* [*Deer-stalking*] a red deer in its sixth and seventh years.   *n* [*Stock market*] an insider who applies for a new issue before it is generally available and is still on special offer; he then sells

his shares four or five days later when dealings commence and the price has risen considerably.

stage *n* [*US*] [*Painting*] a platform from which external surfaces are painted.

stage line *n* [*Athletics*] See **leg line**.

stage loader *n* [*UK*] [*Coal-mining*] the control panel in the **main gate** containing all controls, VDUs, and telephones to monitor the face; it carries the iron scraper chain which takes coal to the gate belt and out of the pit.

stage manager *n* [*Sex*] a pimp who runs a **stable** of male homosexual prostitutes.

stage mother *n* [*US*] [*Medicine*] a parent who coaches her ailing child in its symptoms and then tells the nursing staff which tests and treatment they should be giving the child, irrespective of her actual knowledge of the case.

stages theory *n* [*Government*] the concept that underdeveloped countries follow the same industrial path already taken by advanced countries. It starts with textiles and footwear, and develops through shipbuilding, engineering, iron and steel, automobiles, aircraft to chemicals and electronics. It is criticised on the grounds that under-development is not a historical stage but a continuing consequence of the world economy.

stag ation, also **slump ation** *n* [*Economics*] a stagnant economy allied to rising unemployment and growing inflation. See also **in ation**.

stagger *n* [*TV*] the first complete rehearsal of a television drama.

staggered terms *n pl* [*US*] [*Commerce*] a means of making things difficult for the new chairman who has just taken over a company, whereby directors are not all elected at the same time, but come up only gradually for re-election. Thus it takes longer than might be desired for the company to be recreated in a new image.

stagger tuning *n* [*Electronics*] the broadening of the overall frequency response in an amplifier by tuning its different stages to slightly different frequencies.

staggie *n* [*Deer-stalking*] a red deer in its fourth and fifth years.

staghorn *n* [*Navy*] a metal bollard with two horizontal arms.

staging *n* [*Drag racing*] the procedure immediately preceding a competitive run; it usually includes warming the tyres to optimum operating heat. See also **burn out**.

stagnation point *n* [*Aerospace*] a point on the leading edge of a moving aerofoil at which the air is at rest relative to the aerofoil.

stain painting *n* [*Art*] See **colour   d painting**.

staircase *n* [*Electronics*] a voltage that alters in equal steps to a maximum or minimum value.

stair stepping *n* [*Photo-typesetting*] a staircase effect produced when diagonal lines of an image cross either vertical or horizontal lines of a raster scan; thus any line approaching an angle of 45°

appears as a series of steps, as the raster is increased by one increment.

stairway to the stars n [UK] [Railways] a signal ladder; in foggy weather the fireman can climb the ladder to check the position of the signal.

stake horse n [Pool] a player's financial backer who stakes him in his games and takes a percentage of his winnings.

staker n [Coal-mining] a strut used for anchoring a stationary piece of machinery.

stakhanovite n [Economics] in socialist countries this is a 'storm-shock worker' who regularly exceeds any labour norms and is seen by the leadership as an outstanding figure. It comes from one Alexei Stakhanov, a Ukrainian miner, who in 1935 began increasing his output by the skilled organisation of a group of subordinate workers; for this he was allowed incentive payments and as such alienated many of the rank and file workers. He is now canonised for ever as a Hero of Soviet Labour.

staking n [Tanning] See **crutching, perching**.

stale a [UK] [Railways] said of an overdue freight train; it comes from the perishable goods that might thus go off. See also **stinker 2**.

stale cheque n [Banking] a cheque which has not been presented for payment within six months of the date on which it was originally drawn and as such is no longer valid.

stale fish n [Angling] a migratory fish which has been some time up the river.

Stalin's organs n [Military] a term originally coined in World War II for a rapid-firing Soviet missile-launcher which sounded like an organ and looked like a bunch of phalluses; it was revived more recently to describe the Russian-made 122–BM–21 rocket launcher, which is especially popular in Africa.

stalking n [Taxis] the illegal practice of some cab-drivers who keep their meter on 'Hired' in order to avoid fares they feel will be short and thus unprofitable; they only light the 'For Hire' sign when they believe the fare will be expensive. See also **high-flagging**.

stalky a [Wine-tasting] reminiscent of the smell of damp twigs; it is recognisable in young wines and can come from excessive contact with grape stalks during fermentation.

stall 1. n [UK] [Coal-mining] the underground face unit with adjoining **main** and **tail-gates**; it is the area where the **fillers** are actually cutting out the coal. 2. n [US] [Railways] a track within a roundhouse where a locomotive is stored. 3. v [UK] [Surfing] to slow down to enable the wave to catch you up.

stamp v [Coal-mining] to make a hole in the strata for setting a support or anchor for the conveyor.

stamps n [Navy] a person of no importance.

stand 1. n [Advertising] a poster that fills a whole billboard: 24 sheets. 2. n [Cricket] a lengthy and often vital batting partnership during an innings; it comes from military use. 3. n [Oil rigs] an additional length of pipe which is added to the **drill string** as the bit moves deeper downwards into the earth or seabed. 4. n [Shooting] the selected place that each **gun** takes up when waiting for **driven** birds. 5. v [Antiques] to cost; as in 'standing at . . . (sum)'. 6. v [Cycling] to stop a fixed wheel cycle by sudden and forceful pressure on the pedals (such a bicycle has no brakes).

stand in the doorway v [US] [Politics] to take a dramatic and possibly vote-winning stance on an issue about which one may well be able to do very little.

stand on velvet v [Stock market] to succeed in one's speculations.

stand up v [Religion] to get to one's feet during a meeting to acknowledge formally one's conversion to the faith.

stand-alone n [Computing] a piece of a computing system that can stand alone and perform its tasks without needing to be linked to any other machine.

standard American n [Cards] in bridge this is the most common method of bidding among American players.

standard deviation n [Sociology] the measurement of the distribution of data around the mean value, as expressed in the equation: $\sigma/N = \sqrt{\Sigma x^2}$.

standard money n [Finance] the main unit of currency that is used in a country.

standard play n [Audio] magnetic recording tape that has the standard thickness of 2mm.

standards n pl [Building, Plastering] the tubular uprights which provide vertical rigidity in a scaffolding system.

standards and practices n pl [US] [TV] the morals and ethics department of a major network; it checks that the network adheres to all Federal regulations.

stand-first n [Journalism] the first paragraph in a newspaper story. See also **A-matter**.

standfirst n [Journalism] introductory matter which stands separately on the page from the actual story that it introduces.

standing 1. a [Textiles] said of a colour which is still wet and has not been assimilated by the cloth which is being dyed. 2. n [Law] a position from which one has the right to prosecute a claim or seek legal redress; thus it is the right of claim or redress itself.

standing bed n [US] [Medicine] a freshly made bed that is awaiting a new patient.

standing credit situation n [Banking] a loan or overdraft.

standing knot n [Sailing, Ropework] any knot that is considered to be of a semi-permanent nature.

stand-off a [Military] usually as in 'stand-off

S

missile'; this is said of a missile that can be fired at its target from long range – it is often carried on a fighter or bomber aircraft – and thus permits the firer to escape retaliation.

standpattism *n* [*US*] [*Politics*] a philosophy that advocates holding fast to one's political position come what may; such a position tends towards a reactionary attitude.

stands *n pl* [*UK*] [*Stock market*] the raised seats in which stock exchange **waiters** sit and from which they maintain communications between the various firms that trade on the Exchange.

standstill agreement *n* [*Finance*] an agreement between two countries, one of which cannot pay a debt owed to the other, whereby the debtor country is allowed an extension of time to pay.

stand-up paintings *n pl* [*Art*] See **combine paintings**.

stanza **1.** *n* [*TV*] a segment (see **seg**) of a weekly TV series. **2.** *n* [*Film*] a week's performances at a cinema. **3.** *n* [*US*] [*Sport*] a period of a game or a match.

staple *n* [*Weaving*] a length of unstretched wool fibre.

star **1.** *n* [*Boxing*] the top level of referees who are used for championship and international fights. **2.** *n* [*Parachuting*] a free fall formation; it comes from the shape formed in the air. See also **doughnut 6, zipper 2**. **3.** *n* [*UK*] [*Prisons*] abbr of a **star prisoner** a prisoner who has never been jailed before.

star network *n* [*Computing*] a simple network design in which every node is connected to a single, central control station. The main advantage of such a network is its simplicity; the disadvantages stem from having only one controller: if this fails the whole system is wrecked; if a circuit fails between a node and the control there is no alternate path, and the costs of linking more distant nodes to the control will be high; the speed of the whole system is limited to that of the central unit. See also **active star, network 1, passive star**.

star rank *n* [*Military*] officers whose official vehicles are painted with stars to denote their rank: field marshal (5 stars), general (4 stars), lieutenant general (3 stars), major general (2 stars), brigadier (1 star).

star wars *n pl* [*US*] [*Military*] all space-based missile defences, especially laser weapons that are aimed both at earth targets and at rival defences in space orbit.

stare decisis *n* [*Law*] the policy of standing by legal precedents established in prior judicial decisions; it comes from Lat. for 'to stand by what has been decided'.

star-drag *n* [*Angling*] an adjustable tension device, based on a star-shaped nut, that is built into certain reels used in deep-sea game fishing.

star-bright *a* [*Wine-tasting*] referring to a wine (or cider) that is absolutely clear and free of any

sediment; such a property is not an automatic guarantee of excellence and many great wines possess a degree of sediment.

stargazer *n* [*US*] [*Cattlemen*] a horse that carries its head unnaturally high, possibly after suffering from a roughly handled bit during training.

staring coat *n* [*Hunting*] the coat of an out-of-condition or ill hound; the hair looks dull rather than shiny.

starrer *n* [*Film*] a film which features a star performer; thus 'John Wayne starrer' etc.

stars *n pl* [*Marketing*] highly successful, profitable products, which have established themselves in the marketplace.

START *n* [*Military*] acro **Strategic Arms Reduction Talks** the arms talks with which the US and USSR replaced the series of **SALT** meetings between 1981 and 1983. Nothing practical came of the talks, which foundered on the superpowers' inability to accept each other's terms of reference. The Reagan Administration could not overcome its fundamental reservations about negotiations per se and they became a continuing series of propaganda announcements. The talks were further undermined by the appearance of the Strategic Defence Initiative (**SDI**) and collapsed in late 1983.

start *v* [*Sailing, Ropework*] to slacken off, to ease the strain.

starter **1.** *n* [*Cheese-making*] the culture of milk bacteria that is used to increase **lactic** acid and set off the process of flavour development; cheese producers are very careful in the selection of the right starter which is vital in creating the finished product. **2.** *n* [*US*] [*Sport*] in a variety of American team sports in which multiple substitution is accepted, this is one of those players who actually takes the field at the beginning of a game.

starter home *n* [*Real estate*] a basic house with few amenities but a reasonably low price; it is the first house a young couple are likely to buy.

start-up *n* [*Finance*] in **venture capital** investment, this is the first stage at which finance will be injected into a new venture; by extension, it is also the company that is launching itself on the basis of that investment.

startup *n* [*Video*] the opening of a new homevideo retail store.

starvation, also **constipation** [*Computing*] a form of **deadly embrace**, in which the computer is unable to proceed properly with its allotted tasks due to insufficient input; this is usually caused by the machine's inability to gain access to a particular source.

starve *v* [*Religion*] to deprive someone of spiritual food.

starved *a* [*Painting*] See **hungry**.

stasis *n* [*Psychoanalysis*] in the theories of Wilhelm Reich this is a hypothetical accumulation of unused or repressed sexual energy.

stat *adv* [*US*] [*Medicine*] abbr this comes from Lat.

'statim' meaning 'immediately'; thus the command 'stat!' means do something at once.

state 1. *n* [*Navy*] a daily report on the state of a ship's fuel, water and provisions level. **2.** *n* [*Printing*] any change made in the text of a book; such changes may take place at the publisher's, the printer's or the binder's, or even between the sending out of review copies and the actual publication date. For book collectors, the optimum text is in original or 'First State'.

state capitalism *n* [*Politics*] in Marxist terms this is a country that combines some nationalism with some free enterprise.

state chicken [*Military*] US Dept. of Defense code for: my fuel state requires recovery, a tanker, or my plane being diverted to an airfield closer by. See also **state lamb**.

state lamb [*Military*] US Dept. of Defense code for: I do not have enough fuel to make the required intercept and then to make my way back to the carrier. See also **state chicken**.

state monopoly capitalism *n* [*Economics*] in Marxist terms this is an alliance between monopoly capital and a substantial state presence in the operation of a nation's economy; it is seen generally as a capitalist smokescreen behind which profits can be raised and the struggling proletariat suppressed.

state of the art *a* [*Technology, Design*] referring to the current level of scientific or technological advance in an industry, especially in electronics, computers, etc.; thus 'state of the art contract' is a contract for construction, design, etc. that calls for those techniques currently in use.

state of the whole people *n* [*Politics*] the official designation of the Soviet Union since the 22nd Congress of the Communist Party in 1961; by extension it stands for the ideal state, devoid of a vestige of class antagonism, and for the socialism that can only exist fully when the 'exploiting classes' have been eliminated.

state tiger [*Military*] US Dept. of Defense code for: I have sufficient fuel to return to the carrier; my mission has been successfully accomplished.

stateless currency *n* [*Finance*] money and credit which have no specific government to administer them but which simply fuel the random ups and downs of the financial market.

statement *n* [*Computing*] the unit from which a **high-level language** is constructed; a program is a series of statements. See also **declaration**.

static Marxists *n pl* [*Politics*] a derogatory term that accuses many communists of a dogmatic adherence to the letter of the Marxist law and of ignoring its more subtle spirit.

statics *n* [*Economics*] an area of economic theory that deals with the forces and conditions that exist during a state of equilibrium in an economic system, without considering any changes over a period of time.

station 1. *n* [*Air travel*] an airport. **2.** *n* [*UK*]

[*Catering*] a group or set of tables, under the responsibility of a number of waiters. **3.** *n* [*Cycling*] the position on a track where race competitors start. **4.** *n* [*Dog breeding*] the height at the withers as compared to leg length from the point of the elbow to ground. If the latter exceeds the former, the dog is 'of high station'; if the measurements are reversed, the dog is 'of low station'. **5.** *n* [*Espionage*] a small group of CIA personnel, attached, usually under misleading but apparently authentic titles, to US embassies around the world. Stations are run by a 'station chief' who runs his personnel, liaises with the US ambassador and ensures the smooth functioning of any CIA operation in his area of interest.

station head waiter *n* [*UK*] [*Catering*] a senior ranked waiter in a high class restaurant; he is in charge of a **station** and is responsible for seating customers, taking orders, dealing with complaints and maintaining as high a level of service as possible.

station march *n* [*TV*] the opening identifying theme tune that is broadcast when a TV station comes on the air at the start of a day's transmissions.

station time, also **local time** *n* [*US*] [*TV*] a period in the TV day that is reserved for the affiliates to show their own programmes or syndicated shows; no network shows are transmitted.

station-keep *v* [*Military*] to fly in formation.

statism *n* [*Economics*] a controlled, rigidly planned economy.

stats *n pl* [*Scientology*] abbr of **statistics** Church membership figures.

Statue of Liberty *n* [*US*] [*Football*] an offensive play in which the quarterback holds the ball up, as if to throw it, and a back circles behind to take the ball from him and then attempt to advance it by rushing.

status *n* [*Sociology*] the position an individual holds in the social system: parent, child, etc.

status anxiety *n* [*Sociology, Psychology*] fears concerning one's social status, especially as regards the possibility of losing it.

status crystallisation *n* [*Sociology*] consistency in the individual's statuses throughout the system; eg: the well-educated person in the high status, well-paid job. See also **status inconsistency 1.**

status deprivation *n* [*Sociology*] a person whose unpopularity stems from the image he/she offers to others.

status grouping *n* [*Sociology*] social networks of those who share similar social prestige, whether respected or otherwise.

status inconsistency 1. *n* [*Sociology*] the fact that individuals may occupy inconsistent statuses in multi-dimensional systems of stratification: eg: the well-educated person in a menial job. See also **status crystallisation. 2.** *n* [*Sociology*] an individual who is not quite sure where he/she stands either socially or emotionally; an emotional adolescent.

status offender *n* [*US*] [*Law*] any child or adolescent who is placed 'in care' because he/she is too unruly or disobedient to remain living at home; such an individual has broken no laws that would bring them before a court, but has achieved too unruly a status to remain at large.

status passage *n* [*Sociology*] the transitional periods that bond one variety of human existence, eg: bachelorhood, with another, eg: marriage.

statute-barred *a* [*Law*] unenforceable by legal action because the statute of limitations has come into force due to the time that elapsed before a case could be brought.

statutory undertaker *n* [*Management*] a person (and company) authorised by statute to provide public utilities, such as gas, electricity, railways, canals, etc.

staving *n* [*Metallurgy*] the thickening or altering of the shape of the ends of tubes by means of end pressure. When this process causes additional thickness to accrue on the tube it is 'external upset' if on the outside of the tube and 'internal upset' if on the inside.

stay with the money *v* [*Film*] a comment/instruction made by the director to the cameraman, telling him to concentrate on filming whichever star on the set is the biggest box office draw.

stayer *n* [*Sport*] in a variety of sports – horseracing, cycling, running – this is a competitor (either human or animal) who can last the pace of a long-distance race, rather than succeed only in a sprint.

stays *n* [*Sailing, Ropework*] standing rigging, that is secured at both ends.

steady-state *a* [*Science*] in astronomy, this is the theory that at any time the universe, when considered on a large scale, is essentially unchanging; thus 'steady-stater' is one who espouses such a theory.

steady-state economy *n* [*Economics*] See **spaceman economy**.

steal 1. *v* [*Baseball*] when a base runner advances one base by moving at the instant that the pitcher is winding up and throwing the ball; the base is stolen by this move 'behind the pitcher's back'; the runner's teammate remains safely at bat. A stolen base does not require the batter to have hit the ball or been **walked**, nor has there to have been a **wild** pitch, passed ball or defensive error. 2. *v* [*Basketball*] a player does this when he takes possession of the ball from an opponent.

steals *n pl* [*Printing*] arrow-shaped marks that appear on the surface as a result of foreign matter accumulating behind the **doctor**.

stealth 1. *n* [*Military*] a development programme which is attempting to create a new technology that will enable military ships, submarines and airplanes to avoid hostile radar scanners. 2. *n* [*Military*] the Advanced Technology Bomber

(ATB); based on stealth technology, this as yet unproven aircraft has a redesigned tail, high-mounted engines, heat-suppression devices and a carefully shaped airframe, in which radar-reflecting 'corners' are eliminated as far as possible, thus deflecting radar beams to the side rather than sending them straight back to their source.

steam nigger *n* [*Logging*] See **nigger**.

steam pig *n* [*UK*] [*Railways*] an all-purpose description of anybody or anything not immediately definable.

steamer *n* [*UK*] [*Market-traders*] a fool, a sucker; it comes from rhyming slang 'steam tug' meaning 'mug'.

steamy *a* [*Golf*] referring to a short putt, or a putt that passes right over or through the green.

steel beach picnic *n* [*US*] [*Navy*] on US aircraft carriers these are exercises that are performed on the deck when regular flights have to be suspended.

steel-collar worker *n* [*Industry*] a robot used in a manufacturing industry. See also **blue collar, white collar workers**.

steep *a* [*Dog breeding*] used in relation to **angulation**; steep angulation means that the dog lacks sufficiently wide angles of articulation at the joints.

steeple cast *n* [*Angling*] a cast that begins upwards rather than backwards, in order to avoid any obstacles that are behind the caster.

steepler *n* [*Cricket*] a shot which is hit very high into the air but over no great distance and which tends to be caught; thus it is also the catch itself. See also **skier**.

steer guy *n* [*Pool*] a knowledgable pool watcher, who guides an out-of-town player to lucrative action, taking a percentage of the profits for his efforts.

steerer *n* [*Gambling*] an individual who persuades people to come to an illegal gambling game; thus 'steer game' is an illegal game to which **punters** are steered.

steering *n* [*US*] [*Medicine*] sending patients to a specific pharmacy, usually one that has some link – often in the form of financial kickbacks – to the Medicaid **mill**.

steever *n* [*UK*] [*Market-traders*] 5p, a shilling.

stem 1. *v* [*Skiing*] to move the heels apart while the tips of the skis remain close together. See also **snowplough**. 2. *n* [*Oil rigs*] abbr of **drill stem** in percussion drilling this is a heavy metal rod used immediately above the bit to provide added weight. 3. *n* [*Oil rigs*] abbr of **drill stem** in rotary drilling this is the entire drilling column.

stemming *n* [*Mining*] inert material that is packed between the explosive charge and the outer end of the shothole.

stemwinder *n* [*US*] [*Politics*] an orator or speaker who can arouse crowds to enthusiasm.

stenton, also **air slit, breakthrough, cross-cut** *n* [*Coal-mining*] a connecting roadway between two adjacent roadways, that is often used for ventilation.

step deal *n* [*Film*] a contract for a script which is paid in pieces; every time the writer and his/her ideas surmount a new hurdle and produce a more finished version of the script, another portion of the fee is paid out.

step on *v* [*Drugs*] to adulterate drugs.

step on (someone's) lines *v* [*US*] [*Theatre*] to start one's own speech before another actor has finished his.

step on the laughs *v* [*Entertainment*] a fault found in a nervous comedian: he/she tells a string of jokes so quickly that the audience dare not laugh at one for fear of missing the next.

step out well, also **out step well** *n* [*Oil rigs*] a well drilled beyond the proven limits of a field to see whether those limits can in fact be extended yet further.

step wedge *n* [*Photography*] a line of contiguous rectangles each of a uniform neutral shade, and becoming progressively darker from white/light-grey at one end to black/dark-grey at the other.

step-frame *n* [*UK*] [*Road transport*] a low type of platform trailer, with a step part-way along the platform resulting in the front of the platform being higher than the rear. See also **low-loader**.

step-frame trailer *n* [*UK*] [*Road transport*] a trailer with a stepped frame, to reduce the height of the load platform.

step-head *n* [*US*] [*Journalism*] a headline composed of successively indented lines.

stepping-stone hypothesis *n* [*Drugs*] the concept that marijuana use automatically leads one towards heroin addiction. See also **domino theory 1**.

steps, up the *adv* [*UK*] [*Police*] on trial; it comes from the steps that lead straight up to the dock from the cells beneath the London Central Criminal Court (the Old Bailey).

sterile *a* [*Military*] referring to any weapons systems that are foreign manufactured and untraceable to the country of their origin; such weapons are ideal for clandestine sales to a favoured, but possibly non-aligned country by the power who has first obtained them from source.

steriles *n* [*Coal-mining*] See **dirt 1**.

sterilise 1. *v* [*Espionage*] to 'clean up' any formerly sensitive document that may have been released into the public domain and thus ensure that it no longer contains classified information. 2. *v* [*Military*] to destroy all human and animal habitation, plus all crops and edible foodstuffs in order to create a wasteland in which it is impossible for an enemy to survive.

sterility money *n* [*Military*] extra pay that is given to submariners who risk the danger of 'leaky' nuclear reactors on board their vessel.

stew *n* [*Mining*] nitroglycerin.

stewed *a* [*Wine-tasting*] said of a somewhat ill-defined nose, that is not as good as it should be.

stewmer *n* [*UK*] [*Market-traders*] a difficult customer; an ill-behaved child.

stfnal *a* [*Science fiction*] abbr of **science fictional**.

stforever [*Science fiction*] a signature used to terminate a letter to a fellow fan.

stick 1. *n* [*US*] [*Bars*] the tap, originally made of wood but now rarely either wooden or even stick-shaped, that is used to draw measures of draught beer. 2. *n* [*Gambling*] See **shill 2**. 3. *n* [*Aerospace*] a group of parachutists jumping in quick succession. 4. *n* [*Military*] a number of bombs dropped in succession from the same aircraft. 5. *n* [*US*] [*Gliding*] a control handle that governs the ailerons (roll control) and elevator (pitch control) in a glider; it usually projects from the cockpit floor, but is sometimes mounted at one side of the pilot. 6. *n* [*Journalism*] one line of typeset matter. 7. *n* [*Journalism*] a column of newsprint. 8. *n* [*Navy*] the mast. 9. *n* [*US*] [*Paper-making*] a double roll of wall-paper. 10. *n* [*Sex*] in black pimp terms this is a prostitute. 11. *n* [*Skiing*] a ski pole. 12. *n* [*Golf*] a golf club. 13. *n* [*Surfing*] a surfboard. 14. *n* [*Tobacco*] the horizontal lath on which the bunches of tobacco leaves are hung for drying. 15. *v* [*Industry*] to run or plane mouldings in a machine, rather than working by hand.

stick and rudder man *n* [*US*] [*Air Force*] a 'natural pilot', one who seems born to fly.

stick board *n* [*UK*] [*Railways*] See **peg 7**.

stick daddy 1. *n* [*US*] [*Police*] a policeman – married or single – who pursues women. 2. *n* [*US*] [*Police*] a woman who pursues policemen out of sexual interest, a police 'groupie'.

stick him on! *excl* [*UK*] [*Police*] an instruction to the desk sergeant to draw up a charge against a suspect and enter it on the charge sheet.

stick thermal *n* [*US*] [*Gliding*] a misleading reading on a **vario** which appears to indicate rising air but which is only a momentary upwards zoom of the glider caused by an involuntary movement of the **stick**.

stick time *n* [*Aerospace*] flying time for test and space pilots.

stickbait *n* [*Angling*] caddis fly larvae used for bait.

sticker 1. *n* [*US*] [*Garment trade*] a garment that sells slowly. 2. *n* [*Horse-racing*] a sharp projection on a horseshoe, that is designed to give the animal a better grip on a muddy, wet track. 3. *n* [*Industrial relations*] a worker who shows no interest in promotion. 4. *n* [*Journalism*] one who adds inserts to the regular run of a newspaper or magazine. 5. *n* [*Logging*] a cable in which the wires have rusted through or otherwise worn out. 6. *n* [*Marbles*] the target marble in the game. See also **common, dib, duck, Kimmie, immie, mib**. 7. *n* [*Meat trade*] a slaughterhouse worker who sticks a knife into the necks of cattle, sheep or hogs to sever the jugular vein. 8. *n* [*Meat trade*] one who kills poultry by thrusting a knife through the roof of the mouth into the brain. 9. *n* [*Woodwork*] a stick

S

of wood used in stacks of lumber to differentiate separate courses of boards.

sticker-up, also **setter-up** *n* [*Skittles*] the individual who sets up the skittles after each **hand**.

stickies *n pl* [*Politics*] in Northern Ireland this is the official branch of the Irish Republican Army (as opposed to the Provisionals); it comes from the sticky backs of the Easter seals that are used by Catholics.

stickman 1. *n* [*Crime*] a member of a pickpocket gang who takes the freshly stolen goods from the **dipper** so that in the case of any problems, the dipper can be searched with impunity. 2. *n* [*Gambling*] one who supervises the play in a dice game.

stick-out *n* [*Horse-racing*] a horse that appears to be a certain winner.

sticks 1. *n pl* [*US*] [*Car salesmen*] furniture that is taken as collateral for a loan. 2. *n pl* [*US*] [*Skiing*] a pair of skis. 3. *n pl* [*Horse-racing*] jumps used on a race-course; thus 'to go over the sticks' is to run in a jumping race.

sticks and whistles *n pl* [*UK*] [*Prisons*] the regular parade held before a new shift of warders begin their duty; they are all checked for their truncheon and whistle, given any special information on a particular individual or development, etc.

sticks, between the *adv* [*Soccer*] playing as a goalkeeper.

sticky deal *n* [*US*] [*Stock market*] a new issue of securities that the underwriter fears may be hard to sell.

sticky dog, also **glue pot** *n* [*Cricket*] See **sticky wicket**.

sticky prices *n pl* [*Stock market*] steady prices that change only rarely.

sticky tops, also **sticky coal** *n* [*Coal-mining*] coal that sticks firmly to the roof.

sticky wicket *n* [*Cricket*] a damp, soft wicket that provides particular problems for a batsman. The 'sticky' vanished from first-class cricket for several years during which all pitches were covered at night, but the rules were reversed in 1987 and presumably these wickets, susceptible to overnight rain, will reappear.

stiff 1. *v* [*Antiques*] to remove the oil of a French polish with a rubber. 2. *n v* [*Film*] a film that fails; thus as a verb, when a film fails. 3. *n v* [*Record business*] a record that will not sell; thus, as a verb, when a record fails to sell. 4. also **dead** *a* [*Golf*] said of a shot that has stopped so close to the hole that it is impossible to miss the putt. 5. *n* [*Hotels*] any customer who departs without leaving any tips. 6. *n* [*UK*] [*Prisons*] an illicit, presumably smuggled communication. 7. also **stiffener** *n* [*Auctions*] an individual who enters a **knock-out** to push along the bidding but who has no intention of making the actual purchase. 8. *n* [*Soccer*] a member of the second eleven or the reserves.

stiffening *n* [*Shipping*] ballast placed in the bottom of a ship to give it stability.

stiffie *n* [*UK*] [*Road transport*] a passenger who simply sits tight while the driver does the work.

stiffs *n pl* [*US*] [*Police, Prisons*] shackles connected by a solid metal bar, thus making movement of the hands almost impossible.

stifle *n* [*Dog breeding*] the knee joint.

stile *n* [*Building*] a vertical side piece of a door or window frame.

stiles *n pl* [*Building, Plastering*] cross-members of decorative arch/beam **soffits**.

still hunting *n* [*Shooting*] See **ghooming**.

stilyag *n* [*Sociology*] in Russia this is a type of unpopular youth who enjoys US and Western music and clothes; a tearaway.

sting 1. *n* [*Crime*] the successful carrying out of a scheme by a confidence man or gang. 2. *n* [*Meat trade*] an electric shock of 250V that is used to stun smaller animals such as pigs and lambs. 3. *n* [*Radio*] one of a variety of brief (around 10 secs.) station identification themes used for weather, news, a particular programme or presenter. 4. *n* [*Sex*] this comes from the basic criminal use (see 1); it is when a **hustler**, as part of his need for self-esteem, feels that he has fooled a client, although the client may actually have obtained what he knowingly paid for. 5. also **stab** *n* [*TV*] any short burst of music used as a station identification, a link between programmes, etc. 6. *n* [*TV*] a short burst of music, even a single note, used for dramatic punctuation in a programme.

stinger 1. *n* [*US*] [*Journalism*] See **kicker** 3. 2. *n* [*Logging*] the part of a truck that extends beyond the trailer wheels. 3. *n* [*Oil rigs*] the boom, mounted on a lay-barge, which is used to lay an underwater pipeline on the seabed between the rig and the land. 4. *n* [*US*] [*Prisons*] a home-made electrical gadget used for boiling up water in one's cell.

sting-out *n* [*Glass-making*] combustion gases or flames issuing from openings in furnace walls.

stinker 1. *n* [*Navy*] a sudden squall at sea. 2. *n* [*UK*] [*Railways*] wagons delayed several days in the marshalling yards; if they are carrying perishable goods, these might be going bad. See also **stale**.

stinker bean *n* [*Coffee production*] a coffee bean which gives off an unpleasant odour when cut open.

stinkpot *n* [*Sailing*] a motor-propelled boat.

stinky-pinky *n* [*Logology*] any noun that is coupled with a rhyming adjective; eg: 'obese niece', etc.

stipe *n* [*Horse-racing*] abbr of **stipendiary magistrate** the person who licences a meeting; thus it is anyone engaged professionally at a race-meeting.

stir up the animals *v* [*US*] [*Politics*] to set in motion any sort of controversy which can only have a negative effect on one's campaign or career.

stirrup 1. *n* [*Building*] a U-shaped steel bar that is used to reinforce concrete beams and girders. **2.** *n* [*Sailing, Ropework*] the strap or pennant that suspends a footrope, which is used for climbing rigging.

stitch up *v* [*UK*] [*Police*] said of the police when, in criminal eyes, they fabricate evidence which is produced in court to ensure a conviction. See also **fit up**.

stitched *a* [*Printing*] referring to magazines, pamphlets or small books in which the signatures are stapled rather than bound together.

stitching *n* [*Tyre-making*] pressing together the layers of rubberised fabric that make up the tyre.

stithe, also **stythe** *n* [*Mining*] See **blackdamp**.

stobing *n* [*Video, TV*] a visually disturbing effect created on the screen when the **raster** lines and the patterns or colours of scenery or clothing clash; the offending article appears to shimmer.

stochastic process *n* [*Business*] any process is 'stochastic' if it includes random variables. In business terms the word is used for a process such as the forming of a queue, where the variables are the demand – the formation of that queue by the customers – and the supply – the speed and efficiency with which they can be served or otherwise attended to.

stochastic simulation *n* [*Business*] any variety of research that comes down to the trial and error testing of a number of random variables in order to assess the possible effects of a policy or a plan.

stock 1. *n* [*Film, TV*] raw, unexposed film. **2.** *n* [*Tyre-making*] either the natural or synthetic rubber that is used at all stages of the tyre-making process. **3.** also **stuff** *n* [*US*] [*Paper-making*] pulp.

stock cheque *n* [*Finance*] a special type of demand used by a stockbroker in one country to pay for securities bought in another country.

stock company *n* [*US*] [*Theatre*] See **rep 3**.

stock head *n* [*US*] [*Journalism*] a headline kept for repeated use, usually one announcing a regular section of the paper, eg. Review Section, etc.

stock shot *n* [*Film*] a shot or sequence that can be hired from a library or taken from archives, rather than requiring the crew to go to the expense and effort of setting up the particular scene; it is usually employed when the director needs a plane landing, train departing, etc. See also **library shot 1**.

Stockholm syndrome *n* [*Sociology*] the phenomenon noticed in kidnaps, hijacks or any other situation in which hostages are taken and held for some time; after a certain period the hostage, rather than hating or fearing his/her captor, starts to ally with them and even feels some degree of affection, in the face of the police/army or other authorities who are waiting for them to give up. It was first noted in a bank robbery in Stockholm in 1973.

stock-out *n* [*Business*] a situation in which a particular item is not in stock and customers' demands cannot be met.

stockpile energy *n* [*Military*] the sum of the total nuclear energy currently available for use in a global conflict: one stockpile equals 40,000,000,000,000 tons or 1.3 Beach (see **beach energy**).

Stocks, The *n* [*Stock market*] perpetual annuities: the part of the UK National Debt that consists of stocks which have no fixed date for redemption or payment.

stockturn *n* [*Commerce*] the rate at which stock is sold and replaced.

stockwork *n* [*Mining*] a network of numerous intersecting small veins of ore, or a solid mass of ore that is irregular in shape and much thicker than the adjacent tabular deposits.

stomp *n* [*Art*] a cigar-sized roll of grey paper that is used by artists to blend or soften the effects of charcoal or pastels.

stoke *v* [*Surfing*] to excite, to thrill; it is usually found in 'stoke out'.

stoma *n* [*Medicine*] a permanent opening made into a hollow organ.

stomp a rock *v* [*US*] [*Coal-mining*] See **bobbie a rock**.

stone 1. *n* [*Glass-making*] an imperfection occurring as a crystalline inclusion in the glass. **2.** *n* [*Printing*] the smooth steel or iron table on which newspaper pages are composed; it was originally made of marble.

stone a pool *v* [*Angling*] to throw in stones to drive salmon towards a required spot.

stone sub, also **stone editor** *n* [*Journalism*] See **make-up editor**.

stoneman *n* [*UK*] [*Coal-mining*] See **ripper 1**.

stonewall *v* [*Politics*] used of a politician (or any public figure, especially a civil servant) who presents a resolutely obdurate front to critics and questioners, whether political, journalistic or public. Coined in the UK around 1876, the term was more recently used to describe President Nixon's adamant stance during the Watergate Affair of 1972–74.

stonie *n* [*Marbles*] a pottery-like marble, very smooth and heavy, that is used mainly as a **shooter**.

stonking *n* [*UK*] [*Military*] extremely heavy, accurate and thus unpleasant shelling.

stoop *v* [*Coal-mining*] to remove a **pillar**.

stoop and room *n* [*Coal-mining*] See **bord and pillar**.

stooper *n* [*Gambling*] one who searches racetrack stands in the hope of finding an erroneously discarded winning ticket.

stop 1. *n* [*US*] [*Circus*] a clown number performed as the clowns move around the circus ring; as various acts come on, the clowns halt their progress. **2.** *n* [*Cryptography*] a character in a code that represents a punctuation mark. **3.** *n* [*Dog*

S

breeding] a depression in the topline of the head, situated almost centrally between the eyes, at the junction of the frontal bones of the skull with those of the upper jaw and nose bones. **4.** *v* [*Sailing, Ropework*] to **seize** or **whip** temporarily.

stop a stock *v* [*Stock market*] to agree to postpone the sale or purchase of a stock while holding its price at that at which the deal was originally made.

stop down *v* [*Photography*] to reduce the setting of the lens aperture to produce a smaller opening.

stop list *n* [*Libraries*] a list of words or terms, or roots of words, which are not considered sufficiently significant for them to be indexed; eg: prepositions, conjunctions, definite and indefinite articles, etc.

stop motion *n* [*Film*] the single frame exposure of a film that permits the rearrangement of models, etc. for 'trick shots' of miniature 'monsters', 'space ships' and other creations that cannot move themselves.

stop squawk [*Military*] air intercept code for 'turn off the **IFF** transponder monitor'.

stope *n* [*Mining*] a working either above or below the level where the majority of the ore is mined.

stoper *n* [*Coal-mining*] a light, percussive drill which incorporates a pneumatic cylinder that gives support and thrust when drilling steeply upwards.

stop-go *n* [*Economics*] a British economic policy that alternates between economic expansion and contraction; it is generally considered a bad one, since the continuous changes never allow the economy to establish itself properly.

stoping *n* [*Mining*] breaking the ore above or below a level.

stoploss order *n* [*Futures market*] an order to buy or sell a commodity when a specific price has been reached.

stopper **1.** *n* [*Computing*] the highest memory location in any system. **2.** *n* [*Soccer*] a large, powerful member of the defence whose job is to stop attacks by the opposing forwards, usually through tackling them. **3.** *n* [*Sailing, Ropework*] a short rope or cable with a knot at one end and a hook or shackle at the other that is used for securing a cable to the deck.

stops *n pl* [*Shooting*] men specially posted on the flanks of a beat to ensure that game does not break out.

stopword *n* [*Computing*] a word which is automatically omitted from or treated less fully in a concordance or index that has been created by a computer; such words are usually those occurring most frequently in a language or a specific text.

store and forward *n* [*Computing*] a method in data communications in which information is passed from node to node in a network, pausing at each node until sufficient resources – bandwidth, buffer pools, etc – are available for the information to move on to the next node. This infor-

mation moves as a message or a **packet**. See also **hop 1**.

story art *n* [*Art*] an art movement that flourished in the early 1970s and which used a combination of photographs, drawings, tape recordings, texts and models to put over the story it wished to tell.

story stock *n* [*US*] [*Stock market*] stock that is made more attractive to investors by the creation of a 'story' which underlines its unique properties, the excellence of the company's executives, etc.

storyboard *n* [*Advertising*] the original, two-dimensional rough plan for a filmed advertisement, depicted in a series of mocked-up 'stills', usually with the proposed script inserted where relevant, which trace the 'story' that runs through that advertisement and upon which the filming can be based. Such stills are assembled on one or more cards and can be shown to clients, film directors, and allied interested parties before proceeding with the actual, and more expensive, photography.

stoting *n* [*Clothing*] hand stitching that draws together two edges of cut material.

stouch *n* [*Navy*] a boxing tournament on board ship; it may also mean an engagement with the enemy.

stove *v* [*Aerospace*] to bake on a primary coat of epoxy resin to harden parts of a fuselage.

stowbord *n* [*Coal-mining*] an old roadway used for stowage of waste material and **dirt**.

straddle **1.** *n* [*Stock market*] an option which gives the right of a **put and call**. **2.** *n* [*Stock market*] the condition of being **long** in one market and **short** in another.

straggling *n* [*Science*] a spread of the various attributes of charged particles about a mean value as a result of collisions experienced during their passage through matter.

straight **1.** *n* [*US*] [*Coal-mining*] coal that has not yet been screened as to size. **2.** also **tailor-made** *n* [*UK*] [*Prisons*] See **civvy**. **3.** *a* [*Sex*] said of anything heterosexual and above the age of consent: a prostitute, a client, pornographic pictures or films, etc.

straight job *n* [*US*] [*Road transport*] a truck with the body built on to the chassis; a single-unit truck.

straight line, also **straight wire with gain** *n* [*Audio*] a circuit with a spartan-simple design which is supposed to increase the quality of sound due to the deliberate excision of inessential components.

straight of bowl *n* [*Printing*] the stem of the letter against which the bowl appears; it is found in b,p,d, q.

straight re-buy *n* [*Marketing*] See **routine response behaviour**.

straight standup *n* [*US*] [*TV*] the delivery of a news report by a reporter who is facing squarely into the camera.

straight ticket *n* [*US*] [*Politics*] the list of candidates nominated by a party for an election; thus 'to vote the straight ticket' is to vote for all those nominated candidates.

straight twenty *n* [*US*] [*Painting*] a long, single ladder of 20ft in length.

straight-arm *v* [*US*] [*Football*] to ward off a tackler by extending a stiff arm and pushing him away.

straightener *n* [*UK*] [*Police*] a bribe; thus to 'straighten' means to bribe successfully.

straight-line responsibility *n* [*Politics, Business*] hierarchical relationships; the relationship between a superior and his/her subordinates; the image is of lines on an organisational chart. See also **dotted line responsibility**.

straights 1. *n pl* [*Tobacco*] cigars that have not been tapered. **2.** also **flats** *n pl* [*Cycling*] very short, flat handlebars without any turns at the end; they are often used in winter racing.

straight-sell house *n* [*US*] [*Car salesmen*] a dealership in which one salesman handles the complete transaction, with the sales manager's final approval. See also **system house**.

strand *n* [*Sailing, Ropework*] two or more yarns twisted together for making a rope.

stranded *a* [*Logging*] said of a cable in which strands are defective.

stranded rope *n* [*Sailing, Ropework*] a rope with one badly worn or chafed strand.

strange *a* [*Wine-tasting*] untypical, not having the expected smell or taste.

strange quark *n* [*Science*] the third quark, so called because the particles within it were seen to act in a strange way; such quarks possess the property of 'strangeness'. See also **quark**.

strangeness *n* [*Science*] See **strange quark**.

stranger *n* [*Religion*] a member of the Christian faith; see 1 Peter 2.11.

stranger group *n* [*Management*] in group training – the study of group dynamics – this is a group that consists of people who did not know each other previously. See also **cousins group, family group**.

strangle *v* [*Horse-racing*] to restrain a horse from winning by pulling back on the reins.

strangle the parrot *v* [*Aerospace*] to turn off the **IFF** transponder.

strap *n* [*Journalism*] a subsidiary headline placed above the main headline.

strap-down *a* [*Aerospace*] referring to an inertial guidance system in which the gyroscopes are fixed to the vehicle rather than working from gimbals.

strap-on *n* [*Aerospace*] a booster rocket that is mounted on the outside of the main rocket, from which it can be jettisoned after use.

strap-up *n* [*Merchant navy*] extra, unpaid duties on board a passenger liner.

strapwork *n* [*Building, Plastering*] Tudor ceiling ornamentation featuring strap-like panel moulding.

strategic *a* [*Military*] possessing the capability or intent to fight a nuclear war.

strategic architecture *n* [*Military*] the overall construct of nuclear war strategies, involving command, control and intelligence (C^3I), arms and troop dispositions, the targetting of hostile centres (military and civilian), etc.

strategic balance *n* [*Military*] the comparative strengths of the two superpowers and of their allies and satellites. See also **balance of terror**.

strategic bombing *n* [*Military*] using strategic bombers to attack targets in the USSR or the US.

strategic connectivity, also **connectivity** *n* [*Military*] the improvement of the command and control of nuclear forces to ensure that in the event of an actual nuclear conflict, despite its magnitude and potential chaos, the **war-fighting** plans would proceed as scheduled.

strategic doctrines *n pl* [*Military*] a variety of theories on the best way to maintain **deterrence** and, if that fails, to wage a nuclear war. See also SIOP.

strategic nuclear weapons *n pl* [*Military*] any missiles capable of reaching targets inside the Soviet Union or the continental US; these were originally limited to ICBMs, but the increased range of **SLBMs** and of intermediate range weapons sited in Europe, has greatly expanded the arsenal of such missiles, and made it harder to draw a line between them and strictly **tactical** nuclear weapons.

strategic submarines *n pl* [*Military*] submarines that act as weapons platforms for the launching of nuclear missiles, rather than as fighting ships themselves. See also **hunter-killer**.

strategic superiority *n* [*Military*] 'the ability to control a process of deliberate escalation in pursuit of acceptable terms of war termination. The United States would have a politically relevant measure of strategic superiority if it could escalate out of a gathering military disaster in Europe, reasonably confident that the Soviet Union would be unable or unwilling to match or overmatch the American escalation. It follows that the United States has a fundamental foreign policy requirement that its strategic nuclear forces provide credible limited first strike options.' Colin S. Gray, Director of National Security Studies at the Hudson Institute, 1978.

strategic triad *n* [*Military*] the tripartite military alliance which determines the military planning and strategy of both superpowers. Influenced by geography, national obsessions, technological developments, the demands of the respective military-industrial complexes and inter-service rivalries, the two triads differ in their composition. The US triad, in order of precedence, comprises the Navy's missiles, SLBMs carried on strategic submarines; the USAF's missiles, carried by ICBMs based in their silos, and the USAF fleet of strategic bombers. The US Army,

S

which has never really maintained its presence in the triad, is attempting to stake its claim with the Pershing II missile, supposedly capable of hitting Moscow if launched from W. Germany. The Soviet triad is dominated by the Strategic Rocket Forces, whose 1,398 silo-based missiles total some 75% of the total USSR strategic strength (US ICBMs represent only 25% of the national forces).

strategic warning *n* [*Military*] a prior warning of imminent nuclear warfare that can be appreciated months or at least weeks before the crisis which precipitated the warning becomes insupportable and one side launches a first strike.

strategic withdrawal *n* [*Military*] any level of defeat, from an ordered withdrawal that does have some degree of plan, to a simple, panic-stricken rout; the level of real order depends on the degree of euphemism which the censors choose to impose.

stratification *n* [*Sociology*] the formation and establishment of different levels of social and cultural life that result from differences in occupation and in political, ethnic and economic influences.

Strat-X *n* [*Military*] the study of the potential direction of US nuclear arms planning that was instituted by the Pentagon in 1966 and carried out between 1966–68 by the Institute of Defense Analysis. The overall brief was to discover the ideal successors to the then current strategic arsenal, either through creating new technology or developing that which existed. The decisions taken through Strat-X led variously to the **MX** missile, and the **Trident** missile system with its submarine launcher.

straw house *n* [*UK*] [*Circus*] a full house; so many people want to see the show that straw bales have to be used for extra seating.

straw man *n* [*Real estate*] someone under whose name a broker illegally purchases one of his own listed properties for himself.

straw poll *n* [*Politics*] originally this was a quick poll of the nearest voters, often taken among those just emerging from a polling station, simply to gain a broad view of the voting trend; lately it has become the definitive professional poll that is based on a largescale, but still random sample.

strawhat *n* [*US*] [*Theatre*] a summer theatre; thus the 'strawhat circuit' refers to theatres which open only in the summer and offer venues to touring companies.

strawline *n* [*Logging*] a lightweight wire rope used to haul heavier cables into place.

stray *n* [*Radio*] atmospheric interference.

streaking **1.** *n* [*Photography*] the partial fogging of film that is caused when light is allowed to leak into the film while it is in the camera. **2.** *n* [*TV*] horizontal distortions on a TV screen.

stream *n* [*Computing*] a flow of data which moves for a relatively long duration and at a constant rate.

streamer **1.** *n* [*Journalism*] a multi-column headline which runs at the top of a page but does not necessarily extend over the full width of that page. See also **banner**. **2.** *n* [*Angling*] a fly with feathers attached that simulates a small fish; thus it also refers to the feathers used in such a fly.

street book *n* [*Futures market*] a daily record kept by futures traders of all their transactions.

street credibility *n* [*Sociology*] a popular phrase that was used originally in the rock business and is now popular in any of the industries that cater for the young consumer, including pop music, magazine publishing, fashion and clothing, etc. It is a contemporary variation on the adoration of youth as youth in the 1960s, the belief that the 'artist' must relate genuinely to the 'people', ie: the working class youth of the streets and housing estates who are the consumers of such goods and whose tastes must be monitored and as far as possible satisfied.

street dealings *n pl* [*Stock market*] See **after-hours dealings**.

street furniture *n* [*Architecture*] lampposts, seats, rubbish bins, bollards, crash barriers, etc.

street jewellery *n* [*Antiques*] old enamelled advertising signs that were formerly attached to the walls of buildings, etc., and are now considered worthy of collecting.

street money *n* [*US*] [*Politics*] See **walking around money**.

street name *n* [*US*] [*Stock market*] securities that are held in the name of the broker rather than in that of a customer, thus facilitating their transfer in a sale; the street is Wall Street.

strength, on the *a* [*Royal Marines*] married.

stress interview *n* [*Management*] a selection interview in which the interviewer deliberately behaves aggressively in order to discover how the candidate performs under stress.

stretch **1.** *n* [*Metallurgy*] a specified length of pipe comprising two or more lengths jointed together. **2.** *n* [*Prisons*] a sentence of one year. **3.** *n* [*Baseball*] the action taken by a baseball pitcher in raising his arms above his head preparatory to pitching the ball. **4.** also **stretch-out** *n* [*Entertainment*] an extra-long, multi-seat limousine favoured by actual and aspirant show business celebrities.

stretch 'em out *v* [*US*] [*Railways*] to pull cars in a train tight before accelerating.

stretch one *n* [*US*] [*Lunch counter*] a Coca-Cola.

stretch one and make it pucker *n* [*US*] [*Lunch counter*] a lemon coke.

stretch printing *n* [*Film*] a technical process intended to make silent films – which were run at 16 or 20 frames per second – adaptable for use on modern equipment that runs at 24 fps. To achieve this, each frame is printed twice and this manages to eliminate many, but still not all, of the jerky movements that stem from the technical inconsistencies.

stretched *a* [*Custom cars*] said of panels that have been lengthened or widened; it is applied to wings that have been made longer and thus sleeker, as well as to a roof which has been altered to accommodate **chopping**.

stretcher 1. *n* [*Weaving*] a tool used to hold fabric out to its full width during the weaving process. 2. also **tail fly** *n* [*Angling*] the last fly of a wet cast.

stretcher match *n* [*Wrestling*] a bout with no rounds, no time-outs, no stopping for injuries; such a bout only stops when one of the participants is removed from the ring on a stretcher.

stretch-out 1. *n* [*Industry, Commerce*] the slackening of production schedules in order to save money – a set quantity of goods will be produced over a longer period than originally promised. 2. *n* [*Industry, Commerce*] the postponement of the date for fulfilling contracts, orders, etc.

strides *n pl* [*UK*] [*Market-traders*] trousers, pants, knickers.

strike 1. *v* [*Angling*] a sharp jerk to drive a hook into the fish's flesh. 2. *n* [*Cricket*] the right to receive the next ball bowled; hence the more usual phrase 'on strike' meaning awaiting the next ball. 3. *n* [*US*] [*Football*] a forward pass thrown directly into the hands of the receiver. 4. *n* [*Mining*] the horizontal course of a stratum of rock, coal, mineral ore, etc. 5. *n* [*Baseball*] a pitch within the strike zone at which a batter does not swing, or at which he swings and misses, or hits into foul territory; three strikes put out a batter. 6. *n* [*Weaving*] the penetration of dye into a fibre.

strike for *v* [*Navy*] to learn the trade of; it is usually in pursuit of a higher rank.

strike in *v* [*Music*] in bagpiping this is to thump the bag and start the reeds sounding.

strike out *n* [*US*] [*Medicine*] a patient who has fallen into a coma or who is dead; it comes from baseball usage. See also **hit 4**.

strike rate *n* [*Commerce*] the success rate of a salesman, measured by the percentage of clients who have been approached and are then willing to place an order.

strike suit *n* [*Business*] the practice whereby a minor shareholder in a corporation instigates a suit against that corporation; if the plan works, the corporation will buy out his/her shares at whatever price is desired, merely to deprive him/her of the right to pursue such a suit.

strike the set *v* [*TV, Film, Theatre*] to dismantle the scenery.

striker 1. *n* [*US*] [*Navy*] an unqualified sailor studying for a rating or promotion. 2. *n* [*US*] [*Marine Corps*] an apprentice who is attempting to learn a military speciality. 3. *n* [*US*] [*Marine Corps*] on a ship this is an individual Marine assigned to the operation and maintenance of a specific gun. 4. *n* [*Shipping*] an engineer's apprentice on a steam boat. 5. *n* [*Theatre*] a stagehand. See also **strike the set. 6**. *n* [*US*] [*Road transport*]

a truck driver's apprentice; it comes from nautical use (see **1**).

strikethrough *n* [*Printing*] a print on the reverse side of a sheet that shows through to the front.

striking *n* [*Building, Concrete workers*] the release or lowering of the **centring** that supports the drying concrete.

striking a blow for freedom *n* [*US*] [*Politics*] an ironic code used by politicians for a pleasant chat over a few drinks in the privacy of one's office.

striking price *n* [*Stock market*] the price at which the holder of an option has the right to make a purchase or a sale. When a new issue of shares is made, the issuing house works out the lowest price at which the issue will be fully subscribed; this sets the 'striking price'.

string 1. *n* [*Computing*] any linear sequence of elements, eg. alphanumeric characters. See also **word. 2**. *n* [*US*] [*Railways*] See **cut of cars. 3**. *n* [*Sex*] See **stable 3. 4**. *n* [*Mathematics*] a sequence of symbols or linguistic elements in a specific order. **5**. *n* [*Sport*] a fixed number of turns at a game or in a competition. **6**. *n* [*Sport*] a series of similar results (victories or losses) in the same game or competition. **7**. *n* [*Billiards*] a baulk-line.

string months *n pl* [*Oil rigs*] the length of a drilling season, calculated from the number of months the rig was actually making a hole; it comes from **drill string**.

stringer 1 *n* [*Coal-mining*] a narrow mineralised veinlet, often of a simpler minerology than major veins. 2. *n* [*Coal-mining*] a thin layer of coal at the top or bottom of a seam, but separated from it by material similar to that comprising the main roof or floor. 3. *n* [*Journalism*] a freelance correspondent for a newspaper, based either abroad or certainly some way away from the paper's national headquarters; his/her local expertise and contacts give him/her an on-the-spot usefulness which surpasses that which would be gained from dispatching a reporter from the home office; such stringers often work fulltime for their local paper, radio or TV station. 4. *n* [*Engineering*] a long, horizontal member that is used to support, or tie together, a bridge. 5. *n* [*Aerospace*] a span built into an aircraft's wing, designed to give lateral stiffness to the ribs; it is also a longitudinal member running the length of the fuselage, designed to reinforce and strengthen the skin of the aircraft and to maximise the load-bearing capacity.

stringy *a* [*Wine-tasting*] a skinnier version of **sinewy**, another description that can best be related to the physical attribute it reflects.

strip 1. *v* [*Angling*] to squeeze the eggs or semen (milt) from a fish. 2. *v* [*Gas industry*] to remove heavy hydrocarbon fractions from gas for recovery and sale. 3. *v* [*Oil industry*] to separate crude oil or gas into fractions, or to extract and recover a light fraction from a mixture. 4. also **strip in** *v*

S

[*Printing*] in lithographic printing this is to mount copy in the correct position on a sheet prior to making the plate from which printing can take place. **5.** *v* [*US*] [*Road transport*] to unload a truck. **6.** *n* [*Metallurgy*] a rolled piece of steel that is the same thickness as sheet steel but relatively longer and narrower. **7.** *n* [*Philately*] three or more stamps joined in a single row, horizontal or vertical. **8.** *n* [*Tobacco*] the part of the leaf which remains after the stem vein has been removed. **9.** *n* [*US*] [*TV*] a show that is scheduled for transmission at the same time every day; it comes from the similar regularity and positioning of newspaper comic strips.

strip the reel *v* [*Angling*] said of a fish which **runs** with all the line.

stripe *n* [*US*] [*Circus*] a tiger.

stripes *n pl* [*UK*] [*Prisons*] the yellow stripes sewn on to a prisoner's uniform to denote one or more previous escape attempts.

stripey *n* [*Navy*] a sailor who holds three good conduct badges, signifying twelve years service.

striping the lot *n* [*Commerce*] the painting of the parking lot at a new shopping mall with extra-wide spaces for the positioning of cars; this gives the impression of the mall attracting more customers than it really does, and when business genuinely picks up, the lot can be repainted with narrower spaces.

stripper **1.** *n* [*US*] [*Meat trade*] See **canner**. **2.** *n* [*Oil rigs*] a well from which production has dwindled almost to nothing; it is possibly on an analogy with a cow whose yield of milk has declined severely. **3.** *n* [*Oil industry*] a still that is used for breaking down petroleum products into their fractions.

stripping **1.** *n* [*Building, Concrete workers*] the removal of the **shuttering** that holds the drying concrete in place. **2.** *n* [*Communications*] the extraction of the essential data contained in a message by discarding the **header** and the **tail** from the message **envelope**.

stripping in *n* [*Publishing*] the process, in photocomposition, of assembling the necessary pieces of film to produce the finished page.

stroke *n* [*New therapies*] in transactional analysis (**TA**) this is the basic unit of social intercourse: the giving to another of that emotional stimulus for which they are searching.

stroke books *n pl* [*Sex*] pornographic novels or magazines produced and used simply for masturbation; thus 'stroke house' is a cinema that shows only pornographic films.

stroke out *v* [*Medicine*] to suffer a stroke (a cerebro-vascular accident or CVA).

stroke play *n* [*Cricket*] stylish, elegant play featuring copybook strokes made by a superlative batsman.

stroked out *a* [*US*] [*Medicine*] said of a patient who is suffering from decreased consciousness and muscular disability following cerebral bleeding (a stroke).

stroker *n* [*US*] [*Medicine*] a patient suffering from a stroke.

stroking *n* [*Cars*] increasing the cubic capacity of an engine by lengthening the throw of the crankshaft and thus the stroke of the pistons.

strong *a* [*Sex*] said of hard-core pornography. See also **adult 1**.

strong force, also **strong interaction** *n* [*Science*] the force that causes neutrons and protons to bind together in an atom; it is the strongest force known in nature.

strong square *n* [*Chess*] a square that is well forward on the board, is secure from attack and firmly under the player's control.

strongers *n* [*Navy*] a compound cleaning mixture, made up of a variety of caustic elements such as spirits of salts, acids, etc.

structural *a* [*Sociology, Psychology*] in a variety of social sciences and various disciplines, which concentrate on the analysis of social, mental or linguistic organisation, this refers to those aspects of a system that depend or stem from its structure and formal laws, rather than its actual function.

structural adjustment loan *n* [*Finance*] a euphemistic term used by the World Bank for bailing out the economies of poor or bankrupt nations.

structural crisis *n* [*Government*] used in the Common Market (EC) to denote a problem that occurs when too much money has been spent in one area of EC interest, to the detriment of other areas, equally in need of funds.

structural funds *n pl* [*Government*] money distributed by the Common Market (EC) to alleviate unemployment in areas hit by the recession.

structural grammar *n* [*Linguistics*] a grammatical system intended to explain the working of a language in terms of the functions of its components, and their relations to each other, without dealing with the actual meanings of those components.

structural integration *n* [*New therapies*] See **Rolfing**.

structural semantics *n* [*Linguistics*] the study of the relations in the meanings of a number of single words or of groups of words.

structural unemployment *n* [*Economics*] unemployment that results from changes in the structure of the economy: new technology, population shifts, foreign economic influences, etc.

structuralism **1.** *n* [*Sociology*] a sociological perspective based on the concept of social structure and the view that society comes before individuals. **2.** *n* [*Sociology*] for the school of Levi-Strauss (1908–) this is the theory that there are a set of social structures which are unobservable but which generate observable social phenomena.

struggle – criticism – transformation *n*

[*Politics*] this comes from the Chinese 'Tou – p'I – Kai': the three steps that were to be carried out in all parts of Chinese society during the **Cultural Revolution**: 1. the identification of and struggle against the **capitalist roaders**; 2. the criticism and self-criticism of all those involved in the movement; 3. the transformation of all organisations, methods, plans and systems into revolutionary socialism.

strum box *n* [*Sailing*] See **rose box**.

stub 1. *n* [*Computing*] a substitute component that is used temporarily in a program so that progress can be made in testing or compiling the program until the actual component is available. 2. *n* [*Logging*] a standing section of a tree, 20ft or less in height. See also **snag**. 3. *n* [*Printing*] a short, or rounded serif.

stub party *n* [*Theatre, Music*] a reception following a first night or a concert.

stuck *a* [*Angling*] referring to the playing of a fish after it has been hooked.

stud *n* [*Metallurgy*] See **chaplet**.

stud duck *n* [*Oil rigs*] a top man, the boss of a drill rig.

student *n* [*US*] [*Railways*] a new employee who has not fully qualified for the job.

studentisation *n* [*Statistics*] the standardisation of hitherto complicated statistics by dividing throughout by their estimated standard deviation.

studhorse *n* [*Printing*] anything set in large, black type; it dates from the pre-automobile era when horse-breeders' advertising was a large source of income for a printer; breeders liked the large, bold faces.

studhorse type *n* [*US*] [*Journalism*] the largest, boldest, blackest headline type.

studio quality *n* [*Radio*] material that has been recorded under controlled conditions in a studio, rather than an outside broadcast. See also **phone quality**.

studwork *n* [*Building, Plastering*] a wood or metal framework for plasterboard or lath attachment, that is mainly used for forming partitions.

stuff 1. *v* [*US*] [*Car salesmen*] to exert maximum pressure on a customer to persuade him to buy. 2. *n* [*US*] [*Cattlemen*] an all-embracing term for the stock that is reared and controlled by a ranch and its employees.

stuff and other stuff *n* [*Science*] a mixture of energy-producing particles: pions, baryons, photons, etc.

stuffer *n* [*Marketing*] a piece of publicity matter intended for general distribution with other material such as outgoing mail or goods.

stuffing 1. *n* [*Tanning*] impregnating leather with mixtures of oil, fats and waxes, either manually or mechanically. 2. also **checker bricks** *n* [*Glassmaking*] pieces of refractory material that are used to fill the regenerator which heats air passing through the furnace.

stump *n,v* [*US*] [*Politics*] the campaign trail; to campaign in the open air. Both uses imply the candidate's standing on a tree stump addressing an audience of local people out in the country.

stump shot *n* [*Logging*] the splinters that are left in the stump and the butt end of a tree after it has been felled.

stump word *n* [*Literary criticism*] a shortened word that has become common in general speech, eg. 'veggies', 'phone', 'cab', etc.

stumpage 1. *n* [*Logging*] the value of the timber, assessed while it stands uncut in the woods; thus it is also the timber itself. 2. *n* [*US*] [*Papermaking*] pulpwood that is still standing, prior to being felled for the papermill.

stunt box *n* [*Communications*] a device which controls the non-printing functions of a teleprinter terminal.

stunting *n* [*US*] [*Football*] a predetermined movement by defensive players at or near the line of scrimmage prior to the **snap**.

sturdy *a* [*Wine-tasting*] said of a fairly **full-bodied** and immature wine; substantial.

style *a* [*Commerce*] when this is appended to a description in an auction-room catalogue, the buyer is being told politely that the auctioneers feel that the piece is not genuine, only a reproduction.

sub 1. *n* [*Oil rigs*] a length of drill pipe shorter than standard; it is used for supporting pieces of equipment. Thus 'kelly sub' is a length of pipe supporting the **kelly**. 2. *n* [*Journalism*] abbr of **sub-editor** thus 'chief sub' is the chief sub-editor. 3. *v* [*Journalism*] abbr of **sub-edit** to edit copy for publication. 4. *v* [*Tiddleywinks*] to play one's wink inadvertently under an opponent's wink or pile; it comes from submarine.

subbotnik *n* [*Economics*] in the USSR this is a day's work performed voluntarily and outside normal working hours, usually on Subbota (Saturday). The practice was originated in 1919 to help with the building of the Moscow-Kazak railway; it is felt that all the proceeds of such work must be donated to charity.

subdeck *n* [*Journalism*] a subsidiary headline that runs beneath the main headline. See also **strap**.

sub-dwarf *n* [*Science*] a star which, in its luminosity, falls slightly below the main sequence of stars, notably **dwarfs**.

subemployment *n* [*Economics*] any form of inadequate employment, including actual unemployment and part-time or full-time employment, that fails to provide the worker with a proper living wage.

subject *n* [*Stock market*] an offer or bid from the market which has been made to more than one broker and which is considered 'subject' rather than 'firm'; thus it may not be available unless one of those brokers accepts it immediately.

subjective probabilities *n* *pl* [*Business*] euphemism for educated guesswork.

submarginal land *n* [*Economics*] land so unproductive that it is not worth cultivating. See also **marginal land**.

submarine *n* [*US*] [*Prisons*] a plastic bag placed over a prisoner's head to induce fainting or choking.

submarines, go on the *v* [*UK*] [*Buses*] to work any London Transport route that takes the Blackwall or Rotherhithe tunnels beneath the Thames.

suboptimal *a* [*Market research*] less than ideal.

suboptimisation 1. *n* [*Business*] a compromise solution which means that neither of the contesting parties will have things all their own way. **2.** *n* [*Business*] the achievement of optimum working in one area of an organisation or company without regard for the possibly deleterious effect this may have on the rest of the organisation.

subpoena *n* [*Law*] a document that orders a person to be present in court under penalty of fine or imprisonment for refusing/failing to do so; it comes from Lat. for 'under a penalty'.

subroutine *n* [*Computing*] See **procedure 2**.

subscription *n* [*Publishing*] the initial order for a book that is made by individual booksellers from a publisher's salesmen; by adding up the subscription a publisher can make a reasonable estimation of the first print run that the book will require.

subsidiarity *n* [*Business, Government*] the concept that headquarters staff do not perform any tasks than cannot equally well be performed by the subsidiary branch who were requesting help in the first place; it comes from the Roman Catholic precept that the Vatican should not interfere in those matters best dealt with on a local level. It is currently popular among Common Market (EC) officials who wish to restrict their activities to those which can best be performed by the EC as an entity, and avoid those which can best be left to individual member states.

substitute money *n* [*Finance*] See **near money**.

substitution 1. *n* [*Commerce*] the phenomenon of a consumer rejecting a product that has gone up in price and turning to something cheaper as a replacement. **2.** *n* [*Industrial relations*] the use by employers of job creation schemes, and the government grants that go with them, to hire cheap, young labour and thus deprive senior, experienced but unemployed workers of the chance of getting a job.

subtopia *n* [*Architecture*] a fantasy world projected by optimistic architects that combines surburbia with utopia.

subtractive mixture *n* [*Weaving*] a colour theory based on subtracting rays from white light, the total subtraction of which leaves no colour, ie: black. See also **additive mixture**.

sub-underwriter *n* [*Stock market*] one who underwrites part of a share issue (or other liability) that has already been underwritten as a whole unit by someone else.

subway rider *n* [*US*] [*Medicine*] a patient who attends the emergency room with only a trivial complaint in order to qualify for the free subway fare to take them home.

sub-woofer *n* [*Audio*] an extra bass loudspeaker either added to the system or which is part of the system – in both cases it is used to extend the low frequency response.

success stories *n pl* [*Public relations*] stories that are planted around the media to point out how successfully a client's product has already been used by a variety of individuals or firms; the intention is to use this pseudo-advertising to encourage others to try the product.

sucker head *n* [*US*] [*Journalism*] See **scarehead**.

sucker list *n* [*US*] [*Stock market*] a list of potential investors that is used by unscrupulous or even fraudulent peddlers of dubious stocks and shares.

sucker operations *n pl* [*Espionage*] the giving of covert support by the CIA to international trade associations, student movements, newspapers and magazines, especially those that seemed left-wing but remained anti-Communist; subsequent to the decision in 1967 to bar such funding, these relationships were still maintained, but by methods that avoided offending 'the public conscience'.

sucker punch *n* [*Boxing*] a blow that takes advantage of a momentary lapse of concentration by an opponent, who should have seen it coming. See also **telegraph 1**.

suction *n* [*Building, Plastering*] the water absorption of a **background**.

SUDS *n* [*New therapies*] acro **Subjective Units of Disturbance Scale** the noticing by a noisy individual of how upsetting it can be when someone else starts shouting at him or her.

sudser *n* [*TV*] See **soap opera**.

suede shoe operator *n* [*Business*] a high-flying entrepreneur or salesman who is flashy and smart, both visually and verbally, although the suede shoes of the 1950s have been replaced by Gucci loafers; the inference is of a high-pressure operator for whom ethics take a distant second place to the closing of a major deal.

sufferance *n* [*Shipping, Commerce*] permission granted by the Customs, by a bill of sufferance, to land potentially dutiable goods without producing detailed entry papers; such goods are open to Customs inspection at any time.

suffix notation *n* [*Computing*] See **reverse Polish notation**.

sugar *n* [*Glass-making*] minute crystalline lumps produced on the surface of lead crystal glass by faulty acid polishing.

sugar and sweetening *n* [*Espionage*] the various alluring inducements offered to a target by a team of **sanctifiers** who aim to entrap him in a compromising position.

sugar coated pills *n pl* [*Navy*] unpleasant missions with a reward for success.

sugarbagging *n* [*Wrestling*] the tossing of an opponent on to the canvas as if he were a bag of sugar; the usual result is a vicious jarring of the vertebrae.

sugary *a* [*Glass-making*] used of the roughness that may occur along the cut edge of a piece of glass.

suggestion selling *n* [*Marketing*] a style of selling whereby the customer is persuaded to feel that he had chosen to buy of his own volition, rather than that he had been manipulated by the salesman.

sui *n* [*Chess*] See **sui-mate**.

suicide box *n* [*US*] [*Road transport*] a shelf or rack used for sleeping inside the truck's cab; it is supposedly dangerous.

suicide clause *n* [*Insurance*] a clause written into a life insurance policy that releases the insurer from liability if the person insured commits suicide within a specified period.

suicide connection *n* [*Science*] a technique employed when one wishes to reverse the motion of very large electric motors; eg: from full speed forward to full speed reverse in three seconds.

suicide squad *n* [*US*] [*Football*] the team that defends the player who kicks off, and who thus incur extreme violence from their opponents.

suicide squeeze *n* [*Baseball*] the action of the runner on third base who runs for home base the moment the ball is pitched.

suicide suits *n pl* [*Navy*] diving suits.

sui-mate *n* [*Chess*] the equivalent of self-mate, a situation in which one player forces the other to mate him.

suint *n* [*Weaving*] the secretion from the sweat glands of the sheep that combines with the wool grease to form the **yolk**.

suitcase magician *n* [*Magic*] a travelling magician who works **casuals** and whose act and props are contained in his luggage.

suitcase rancher *n* [*US*] [*Cattlemen*] an absentee rancher, whose visits to the range are accompanied by his suitcase.

suitcasing *n* [*US*] [*Crime*] the handing over of bribes in such large amounts that a suitcase is required to hold all the currency involved. See also **attaché-casing**.

suite *n* [*Computing*] a suite of programs: a collection of separate, but integrated programs which are run consecutively in the performance of one major task. The various items of **bundled software** – database, word processing, spreadsheet, etc. – that are produced by the same company and given away with a particular machine are sometimes known as a 'suite'.

sulker *n* [*Rodeo*] an unreliable, unpredictable and thus potentially dangerous horse.

sulling *n* [*Metallurgy*] allowing a reddish brown coating of hydrated oxide to form on rods or wire by keeping the surface wet after **pickling**.

sum-and-difference *n* [*Audio*] two types of signal derived from a normal pair of stereo signals: one is made up of the sum of the two signals, the other of the difference between them; on discs, the two qualities are represented respectively by lateral and vertical modulation components.

summer stock *n* [*US*] [*Theatre*] a second-rate company who takes old favourite plays on tour throughout the summer season.

summer valley *n* [*Gas industry*] the depression that occurs during the summer months in the load curve of a gas distribution system or pipeline, or in the production of natural gas.

Sumner *n* [*Sailing*] this comes from Sumner's position line; it is a method of finding one's position on the surface of the earth by combining dead reckoning with astronomical observation. It was named after the US shipmaster Thomas H. Sumner (1807–76), who discovered his navigational aid in 1837.

sump *n* [*Coal-mining*] See **cut**.

sump in *v* [*Coal-mining*] to break into the solid coal prior to cutting along the face.

sumpsimus *n* [*Literary criticism*] the use of the strictly correct form, rather than the more popular, time-honoured, but less correct form. It is the promotion of language as a social institution against speech in individual usage. See also **mumpsimus**.

sun gun *n* [*TV*] a small, battery operated, portable lamp.

sun outage *n* [*Communications*] in satellite communications this is a period during which the system functions below par because of the relative position of the satellite and the sun. See also **outage**.

sun-belt socialists *n pl* [*Politics*] the current (1985) group of leftish-inclined Prime Ministers of Portugal, Spain, Italy, France and Greece, all Mediterranean countries.

sunburner *n* [*Glass-making*] an excessive local thickness in some part of a mouth-blown glass article.

sundown *v* [*Medicine*] to experience night-time hallucinations because of strange surroundings; it is a problem that particularly afflicts old people taken into a hospital or geriatric home.

sundowner 1. *n* [*US*] [*Medicine*] a patient who is quiet during the daylight hours, but who loses control and becomes noisy and agitated after dark; these are usually senile patients. See also **sundown. 2.** *n* [*Navy*] a bullying and unreasonable officer; such officers will only grant leave until sunset.

sundowners *n pl* [*TV repair*] repairmen who take on extra work.

sunk up *a* [*TV*] said of properly synchronised

sound and vision; it is a corruption of 'synch(ron-ised) up'.

sunlighting *n* [*Management*] holding a full-time job after retirement. See also **moonlight**.

sunnambula, la *n* [*Crime*] in the Italian Mafia this means the 'sleepwalker', ie. the law and its guardians.

sunned *a* [*Book collecting*] a book which has been regularly and cleanly faded, by the sun on library shelves, rather than food stains, coffee-cup rings, etc.

sunray *n* [*UK*] [*Military*] in British Army radio code this is the commander of a unit or formation. See also **actual 1**.

sunrise *n* [*Journalism*] See **lobster shift 1**.

sunrise industry *n* [*Commerce*] the new, successful styles of manufacturing industries, upon which the economic sun is supposedly rising; they involve the manufacture and use of high-technology electronics, with robots, microchips, and sophisticated automation. See also **sunset industry**.

sun-seeker *n* [*Aerospace*] a photo-electric device used in spacecraft and satellites which maintains its orientation regarding the sun and can be used to guide instruments and aid navigation.

sunset industry *n* [*Commerce*] the old staples of the 19th century Industrial Revolution upon which, in their accelerating decline, the economic sun is setting: steel, shipbuilding, textiles and other traditional trades. The decline in such trades – or their increasing monopolisation by the lower-paid workers of the Third World – is creating massive unemployment and many Western governments are forced to invest in the sunset industries, against all economic sense, both to sustain jobs and to maintain electoral support. See also **sunrise industry**.

sunset law *n* [*US*] [*Government*] a law that requires all US government agencies, commissions and programmes to undergo a regular re-assessment to check on their continuing usefulness and efficiency.

sunset provision *n* [*US*] [*Law*] a condition in a law or regulation that states the expiry date of that provision, unless specifically reinstated by a further law.

sunshine *n* [*US*] [*Painting*] petrol or oil in a paint mixture.

sunshine law *n* [*US*] [*Government*] a law that obliges all US government bodies – national, state, city and federal – to conduct their regular business in public.

sunshine miner *n* [*US*] [*Coal-mining*] a worker in a strip mine or open-cast mine, rather than one who works underground.

sunshine network *n* [*Computing*] the sharing of computer facilities on an international basis; when the user in one time zone is asleep, the machine is free for the partner for whom it is daytime, and vice versa.

sunshine notice *n* [*US*] [*Communications*] a notice issued by the Federal Communications Commission (FCC) stating that members of the public may attend its regulatory proceedings.

suntans *n pl* [*US*] [*Military*] lightweight summer uniforms, especially the trousers, worn by US military personnel.

super **1.** *n* [*US*] [*Theatre*] abbr of **supernumerary** an extra or a walk-on, sometimes not even a professional actor. **2.** *v* [*US*] [*TV*] abbr of to **superimpose** either a caption or some form of special effect.

supercomputer *n* [*Computing*] a class of extremely powerful computers, capable of in excess of 10 megaflops (**flops**) and thus used for massive mathematical calculations requiring this high speed and substantial storage capacity. See also **number cruncher**.

superdynamism *n* [*Film*] a term coined by monster-creator Ray Harryhausen for his individually created method of animating his range of rubber monsters.

superfecta *n* [*Gambling*] a bet that forecasts the correct running order of the first four horses in a race. See also **exacta, perfecta, quinella, trifecta**.

superficial *a* [*Wine-tasting*] used to describe a wine that lacks depth or aftertaste.

super-foot **1.** *n* [*Timber trade*] a square foot of timber of a given thickness, eg. 2in. **2.** *n* [*Timber trade*] when applied to standing timber, this is a unit equal to one twelfth of a cubic foot.

superfounts *n pl* [*Photo-typesetting*] master images that are held on disk by the users; they are of a lower resolution than the macrofounts held by the designers, but like them can be used to generate a variety of typestyles. See also **macrofounts**.

supergiant *n* [*Science*] a very large star of the brightest luminosity, surpassing even a **giant**.

supergraphics *n pl* [*Art*] outsized abstract designs used to cover the interiors and exteriors of shops, offices, restaurants and homes; they work as a cheap and attractive way of enlivening otherwise mundane architecture.

superheavy *n* [*Science*] in nuclear physics, this is an element with an atomic mass or atomic number greater than those of the naturally occurring elements; thus it is an element having an atomic number of 110 or more.

supermobile *n* [*Business*] a high-flying young executive who moves from firm to firm, continually obtaining new jobs through his/her excellence. It is applied especially to those favoured recruits who are seen by a firm as worthy of training and grooming for the most senior positions and who will enjoy all the favours on offer, prior to spurning every entreaty, not to mention the rage of those who have invested a great deal of money/time in them, and moving on.

supernuke *n* [*Technology*] an adviser at a nuclear energy plant.

superordinate *n* [*Management*] a superior; it is the reverse of a 'subordinate'.

supers *n pl* [*Advertising*] abbr of **superimpositions** messages written across the television screen to boost the verbal message of the commercial.

superset *n* [*Weightlifting*] a set of exercises for one group of muscles which are followed by a set for an opposing group.

supersite *n* [*Advertising*] a large, tailor-made poster or display, often hand-printed or cut so as to create a 'three dimensional' effect.

superstructure *n* [*Sociology*] those social forms, other than the economy (the base), which usually comprise institutions such as the state, the family and the kinds of ideology within a society. In Marxist theory, the character of the superstructure is determined by that of the base. See also **base**.

supervisor 1. *n* [*Computing*] the permanently resident section of an operating system that co-ordinates the use of the physical resources within a computing system and maintains the flow of processor unit operation. 2. also **monitor** *n* [*Computing*] See **operating system**.

superwater *n* [*Science*] See **anomalous water**.

superzapping *n* [*Data security*] operations which misuse the computer access program in order to bypass normal security arrangements and make illegal alterations to programs and/or data.

supp *n* [*Advertising*] abbr of **supplementary spot** an extra commercial booking in addition to an agency's regular order that is given discount rates.

supple *a* [*Wine-tasting*] used to describe a combination of sap, vigour and a lively, healthy flavour.

supply-side economics *n* [*Economics*] the economic standpoint which advocates monetary restraint, reduction in the role of the government in the economy, and a cut in the tax rate to stimulate investment and increase the production of goods and services. It is claimed as new, but its roots can be seen in the work of the early 18th century French and Italian Physiocrats, who attempted to create tax structures that would liberate business enterprise and later in the claim by Jean-Baptiste say that 'Supply creates its own demand'. See also **demand-side economics**.

support *n* [*Pop music*] abbr of **support group** any of the groups playing at a concert lower down the bill than the main attraction; such bands are rarely famous and often receive a less than enthusiastic response from the fans.

support buying *n* [*Commerce*] the buying of a commodity, a currency, or stocks and shares with the intention of forcing prices up.

supporters *n pl* [*Heraldry*] beasts or human figures standing on either side of a shield; eg: the British lion and unicorn.

suppressive *n* [*Scientology*] a cult member who has been branded as a law-breaker, anti-ideologue or generally evil.

surcharge 1. *n* [*Engineering*] the part of the load that is above the horizontal plane containing the top of a retaining wall. 2. *n* [*Engineering*] a load placed on top of uncompacted material in order to compress it.

surf *n* [*UK*] [*Theatre*] an actor or technician who works in the theatre at night but takes another job in the daytime.

surf and turf *n* [*Restaurant*] seafood and beefsteak served as a single course; it is also a proprietory chain of restaurants in the US.

surf port *n* [*Shipping*] a port at which ships cannot tie up and thus they must be loaded/unloaded by barges which commute between them and the quay.

surface bargaining *n* [*Commerce*] bargaining carried out for its form rather than its content; it is used especially when the bargaining is deliberately aimed – as in certain stages of industrial disputes – at sabotaging the very negotiations of which it is a part.

surface burst *n* [*Military*] See **ground burst**.

surface raiders *n pl* [*UK*] [*Railways*] Southern Region electric trains.

surface-ripened *a* [*Cheese-making*] referring to cheeses that ripen from the outside inwards, as a result of the application of mold, the spores of various fungi, yeast or bacteria to the surface.

surfer's knob, also **surfer's knot** *n* [*Surfing*] a bump on the knee or instep that is characteristic of continual surfing.

surge 1. *n* [*Navy*] the ability of a navy to put all its nuclear submarines to sea at once in response to a crisis. 2. *v* [*Sailing, Ropework*] to slacken up suddenly on a tackle.

surgical soup, also **surgical liquids** *n* [*US*] [*Medicine*] the first food, usually broth, that is fed to a patient after surgery.

surgical strike *n* [*Military*] an attack, often without a declaration of war or even a prior warning, that is made to deal with a specific target; eg: the Israeli destruction of Iraq's nuclear plant in 1981.

surplus *v* [*Government*] to dismiss, to fire.

surreptitious entry *n* [*Espionage*] the breaking and entering into a house by members of an intelligence agency; such activity is of course illegal, but agencies rationalise it as a necessary part of the struggle against their country's enemies.

surrogates *n pl* [*US*] [*Politics*] celebrities and similar VIPs who undertake personal appearances on behalf of the candidate of their choice, thus garnering possible support, saving the candidate a number of appearances, and co-incidentally gaining themselves some publicity.

SURTASS *n* [*Military*] acro **Surveillance Towed Array Sensor System** this surveillance system was made operational in 1980 and uses

S

arrayed sonar sensors that are towed slowly through the oceans by tuna clipper-type boats. Data is broadcast from the towing ship to a satellite and thence to a shore station for analysis and processing. The complete SURTASS fleet will comprise 18 arrays, complete with towing ships, code-named T-AGOS and AGOS (air-to-ground ocean surveillance).

survey 1. *n, v* [US] [Marine Corps] the regular checking of military equipment to see whether it needs to be repaired or even discarded. 2. *n, v* [US] [Marine Corps] by extension from (1) it is a discharge on medical grounds. 3. *n* [US] [Marine Corps] second helpings of food in the messhall.

survey line *n* [Medicine] in dentistry this is a line scribed on the cast of a tooth to mark the place of greatest diameter for the insertion of a denture.

surveyor *n* [Medicine] in dentistry this is an instrument used to survey various features occurring on a cast of teeth.

survivability *n* [Military] the ability to survive a full-scale attack or war, especially one involving nuclear weapons.

survivable weapons *n pl* [Military] weapons that can endure a nuclear first strike and be launched in a retaliatory second strike.

susie *n* [UK] [Road transport] the air supply coupling pipe between the tractive unit and the semi-trailer. See also **glad hands**.

suspended painting *n* [Art] canvases without stretchers which are re-hung from walls or ceilings, then draped, pleated or twisted to create sculptural forms.

suspense file *n* [Computing] a file that is designed in such a way that its contents are produced at the times when they become relevant to the compiler, eg: on the dates of payment of a direct debit through a bank, etc.

sustaining programme *n* [US] [TV, Radio] a programme broadcast by a station which takes up any time not sold to sponsors.

swab jockey *n* [US] [Marine Corps] a derogatory term for a USN sailor.

swabbing *n* [Oil rigs] inward fluid flow caused by pulling equipment out of a fluid-filled bore-hole.

swabs *n pl* [Navy] the gold epaulettes worn on an officer's ceremonial uniform.

SWAG *n* [Science] acro **Scientific Wild-Assed Guess** a cynical acronym used by scientists intending to baffle the uninitiated, eg: 'the SWAG methodology'.

swag *v* [Sailing, Ropework] the centre of a horizontal rope does this when it sags downwards.

swag and plunder *n* [UK] [Market-traders] in a mock-auction these are cheap and shoddy goods.

swaging *n* [Metallurgy] reducing the diameter, usually for short distances, at the ends of tubes.

swallow *n* [Sailing, Ropework] the mortice between the two cheeks of a block.

swallow the anchor 1. *v* [Navy] to retire from the Navy. 2. *v* [Navy] to malinger.

swamp *v* [Logging] to clear an area of undergrowth and similar obstructions prior to starting work on an area of the woods.

swamper 1. *n* [Logging] one who clears roads through virgin woods. 2. *n* [US] [Road transport] See **digger**. 3. *n* [US] [Road transport] a helper who rides with the driver, but does not drive. 4. *n* [US] [Road transport] a person who helps unload produce trucks. 5. *n* [US] [Catering] a cook's assistant; it is also a bar-tender's helper etc.

swampy back *n* [Dog breeding] a form of hollow back; other forms include slack back, soft back, saddle back, sway back.

swan neck *n* [UK] [Road transport] the front of a trailer which has a very low platform height, but which needs a much higher coupling point to attach it to the drawing unit; it is so called after its alleged resemblance to a swan- or goose-neck.

swap fund *n* [US] [Stock market] a fund which investors enter by exchanging securities directly for shares in that fund, obtaining a diversified portfolio without selling stock, and thus avoiding the payment of capital gains tax when these securities are sold.

swapping *n* [Computing] this is used in time-sharing computer systems to combine the needs of various users: information is written from the main memory to a backing store during periods when it is not in use and can be read back into main memory when required. Thus various jobs can be swapped in and out of main memory as needed.

swapzine *n* [Science fiction] a magazine that is not sold, but swapped or traded for another.

swarf 1. *n* [Industry] any fine waste produced by a machining operation; it is usually in the form of strips or ribbons. 2. *n* [Audio] the material cut out of a gramophone record when the groove is made.

swarm *v* [Oil rigs] the pipes in a derrick do this when they go out of control. See also **hayrack**.

swarmjet *n* [Military] a defence concept for protecting US missile bases, especially those of the **MX** missile. Thousands of small rockets would be launched along the corridor through which it could be calculated that attacking Soviet missiles must fly; the rockets ought to destroy at least some of the incoming weapons.

swart gevaar *n* [Politics] this comes from Afrikaans 'zwart' meaning 'black' plus 'gevaar' meaning 'danger'; it refers to the concept held by many white South Africans of the danger posed to the Western way of life by the existence of the black races. It is the Afrikaaner version of the 'yellow peril'.

swash *a* [Printing, Typesetting] said of exaggerated or extended typefaces.

sway *v* [Sailing, Ropework] to haul vertically on a rope, especially when hoisting upper yards.

swealing n [*Metallurgy*] wash heating: raising the surface temperature of a heated ingot or **bloom** immediately prior to rolling so that a fluid scale is formed which will remove defects.

swearing contest n [*US*] [*Law*] a routine legal contest with cut-and-dried evidence and solid witnesses for either party; the winner will be the side who can 'swear' their evidence most convincingly.

sweat box n [*UK*] [*Railways*] a swing-jack or aligning jack, the operation of which needs a good deal of human energy.

sweat boxes n pl [*UK*] [*Prisons*] the individual compartments in the van which conveys prisoners between court and prison. See also **meat wagon 1**.

sweat equity 1. n [*Business*] the effort that goes into a project – planning, selling to the customer, etc. – rather than the actual investment of cash. 2. n [*Business*] the share or interest in a building that is given to a tenant who has helped with the building's maintenance or renovation.

sweat out v [*Building, Plastering*] said of water which appears on a finished surface.

sweat serve v [*Table tennis*] to serve a ball deliberately covered with moisture that has usually been gained by wiping the hand across a sweaty forehead. This will cause the ball to skid rather than grip the bat and both fool the opponent as to the extent of spin on the ball, and make the ball harder to control and return. It is considered illegal, like baseball's outlawed 'spitball'.

sweat-hog n [*US*] [*Education*] a difficult or backward student who has to be given special instruction in school.

sweating 1. n [*Painting*] the exudation of oil matter from supposedly dry coats of paint. 2. n [*Painting*] the development of gloss in dry paint or varnish which has been rendered dull and matt by rubbing or 'flatting' down. 3. n [*Industry*] the joining of metal parts by heating solder so that it runs between those parts. 4. n [*Oil industry*] a petroleum refining process in which liquid and amorphous wax are separated from solid crystalline wax by the gradual application of heat. 5. n [*Tanning*] the heating of dampened hides to help loosen hair or wool.

swede n [*Logging*] a machine with rollers which catches the ends of the boards as they go by and switches them to another sawing table.

swedish fiddle 1. n [*Logging*] a special bow saw used for cutting wood pulp. 2. n [*Logging*] a crosscut saw.

Sweeney n [*UK*] [*Police*] the Flying Squad; this comes from rhyming slang 'Sweeney Todd'.

sweep 1. v [*Espionage*] in the CIA this is to use electronic instruments to check that a building or room contains no clandestine eavesdropping devices or bombs. 2. n [*Metallurgy*] controlled dishing, making a **pack** of sheets concave, in order to ensure a flat product after annealing.

sweeper 1. n [*Lacrosse*] See **rover**. 2. n [*Soccer*] a player who acts as the last line of defence other than the goal-keeper, especially in 'sweeping' up long balls hit forward by the opposition. 3. n [*Espionage*] an electronic device used to detect clandestine recording or listening apparatus; thus it is also the individual who operates the device.

sweeps n pl [*US*] [*TV*] special Nielsen TV audience ratings that are prepared for November, February and May; diaries are kept by chosen viewers and Nielsen subscribers can thus obtain a detailed viewing pattern for every station in the US. The months chosen are those traditionally selected by the networks for the release of what they hope will be their potential blockbusters.

sweet a [*Oil rigs*] bearing a low sulphur content; thus 'sweet crude', 'sweet gas', etc. See also **cow 3**.

sweet crude n [*Oil rigs*] See **sweet**.

sweet gas n [*Gas industry*] natural gas that has only minor impurities and which can therefore be used with purification.

sweet glass n [*Glass-making*] glass that is easily workable.

sweet savagery n [*Publishing*] a genre of romantic fiction in which helpings of sex and violence are added to the usual menu of historical or contemporary amorous fantasy. It comes from 'Sweet Savage Love' by Rosemary Rogers, although the first attempt at the genre was 'The Flame and the Flower' by Kathleen Woodiwiss (1971). See also **confessionals, gay gothics, hysterical historicals**.

sweet spot n [*Sport*] the point on a cricket bat, tennis racket, golf club and similar implements, at which it makes the most effective contact with the ball.

sweeten v [*Music*] to add instrumentation, often strings, to build up the 'feel' of a record.

sweetener n [*Finance*] any special bonuses that are added to a project in order to tempt investors or potential customers.

sweetening n [*Oil industry*] chemical processes which remove the foul odours from various petroleum products and substitute compounds that have very little or no odour.

sweetheart n [*Navy*] a small portable radio set, used by beach parties.

sweetheart contract n [*Industrial relations*] any labour contract that is heavily in favour of the employer. See also **yellow-dog contract**.

sweetheart deal n [*Stock market*] a deal in which shares are allotted to a client on the basis of favouritism rather than simple business relations.

sweetman n [*Sex*] a pimp who lives off the efforts of a single girl.

swell 1. n [*Metallurgy*] in iron-founding this is a casting defect that appears as a distortion on the face of the casting when the moulding has failed to withstand the pressure of the metal or has not been rammed into place properly. **2.** *n* [*UK*] [*Surfing*] clean waves, as opposed to wind **chop**.

sweller *n* [*Food processing*] a can of food that bulges excessively at one or both ends through spoilage; all swellers must be discarded except those containing molasses which naturally expands inside the can when in a warm climate. See also **flipper, springer 3**.

swept circle *n* [*UK*] [*Road transport*] the outermost arc covered by the vehicle's bodywork while moving in a circle.

SWIFT *n* [*Banking*] acro **Society for Worldwide Interbank Financial Telecommunication** an international system, registered in Brussels and used by 800 banks in 26 countries for the speedy computer-based transfer of assets, sending of messages and payments and all allied inter-bank transactions.

swift 1. *n* [*Metallurgy*] a rotating device on which coils of wire are placed for unwinding. **2.** *n* [*Weaving*] a tool for holding different sizes of skeins of yarn for unwinding. **3.** *v* [*Sailing, Ropework*] to bring two **stays** or **shrouds** together with a rope.

swift 'un *n* [*UK*] [*Police*] an arrest for 'loitering as a suspected person'.

swifter 1. *n* [*Sailing, Ropework*] the forward lower **shroud;** it is the rope that holds the ends of the capstan bars in place. **2.** *n* [*Theatre*] a taut steel wire along which objects or people can slide or 'fly' across the stage.

swig off *v* [*Sailing, Ropework*] to pull on the centre of a taut rope at right angles to the **fall**.

swilly *n* [*Coal-mining*] a portion of the roadway floor that has longitudinal concavity. See also **brow 1**.

swim 1. *v* [*Computing*] in computer graphics, this is said of display elements when they move around their usual positions in an undesirable manner. **2.** *v* [*Angling*] to swim a bait: to allow the bait to drift with the current. **3.** *n* [*Angling*] a place where one can swim (see **3**) a bait for coarse fish. **4.** *n* [*Angling*] a place where fish may be expected to lie.

swing 1. *n* [*Banking, Commerce*] the movement of an account from one figure to another; the more an account swings, the healthier a company's trading position must be. **2.** *n* [*Cards*] in bridge this is the difference between the total scores of two teams of two pairs playing the same deal at two tables, each team having north-south positions at one table and east-west at the other. **3.** *n* [*Logging*] a donkey engine which relays logs from the woods to the loading points. **4.** *v* [*UK*] [*Railways*] to switch a set of points to a new position. **5.** *v* [*Sex*] when couples meet for wife and husband swapping parties; the euphemism is used in the magazines that advertise such delights.

swing boy, swing girl *n* [*US*] [*Theatre*] a chorus dancer or singer who has learned all the other chorus parts and can fill in whenever needed.

swing clearance *n* [*UK*] [*Road transport*] the clear arc swept by the front corners of a trailer when turning, in relation to the towing vehicle.

swing credits *n pl* [*Commerce*] the allowance between East and West trading partners of a credit (of between 5–20%) to cover seasonal trading fluctuations and the possible excess of imports over exports; on the whole these credits tend to benefit the Eastern (socialist) countries.

swing shift *n* [*Industrial relations*] variable shift hours that are worked to maintain a factory's production rate.

swing voter *n* [*Politics*] a voter who has no particular party allegiance and is just as likely to prefer a personality to a policy; such voters often provide the real imponderables in an election and can swing the result one way or the other.

swing with *v* [*New therapies*] to accept, to tolerate, to participate.

swing-by *n* [*Aerospace*] an interplanetary mission in which a spacecraft uses the gravitational pull of a planet near which it passes for changing course.

swinger 1. *n* [*Audio*] any record in which the central hole is not perfectly positioned and thus causes the pickup to oscillate in the groove as the disk rotates. **2.** *n* [*Glass-making*] a worker who helps decant the full ladle of molten glass on to the **marver** table. **3.** *n* [*UK*] [*Railways*] a coach that is additional to a train's normal complement.

swirl *n* [*Cars*] the rotational movement, usually around the cylinder axis, of the incoming mixture of fuel and air, that is induced by tangential ports and possibly also an inlet valve which has been shrouded to guide the swirl direction; it is used to improve air/fuel mixing and thus the engine's combustion.

swish *v* [*Basketball*] to drop the ball cleanly into the basket without it hitting the metal ring.

Swiss *a* [*Chess, Cards*] referring to chess or (usually) bridge tournaments using the Swiss system; it is used of a partial round-robin all-play-all system which combines knockout and full round-robin in which each player or team is matched in each round against an opponent with a similar score, but no two opponents may meet more than once.

swish pan *n* [*TV, Film*] See **whip pan**.

swiss float *n* [*Building, Plastering*] a double-handed float.

switch 1. *v* [*US*] [*Car salesmen*] to divert a customer's interest from the car he initially wants to buy, to the one the salesman wishes to sell him. See also **bait and switch**. **2.** *n* [*Deer-stalking*] a stag which grows an abnormal pair of antlers above the brow line.

switch board *n* [*US*] [*Railways*] a roster of men on **yard** duties.

switch dealing *n* [*Commerce*] the agreement by

S

a Western country that it will take Socialist products which it neither wants nor needs in exchange for goods that it is selling to that country. Such excess Eastern European products are then sold to a variety of specialist agents, usually based in Switzerland, who buy them for up to 45% discount and then offload them as and where they can. See also **revenge barter 2**.

switch dollar n [Economics] the switch dollar and the switch dollar market exist to circumvent the controls on investment in foreign securities by UK residents. Direct investment projects may be financed either by borrowing abroad or by using the non-sterling currency proceeds of the sale of foreign securities. Such funds, in whatever currency they may be, are expressed as switch dollars, security dollars or investment dollars.

switch hands v [Lacrosse] to change the top hand on the stick to increase manoeuvrability, especially when closely guarded by the defence on one side of the body.

switch hitter n [Baseball] a batter whose batting stance varies according to the pitcher he faces; eg: one who bats left-handed against a right-handed pitcher and vice versa.

switch selling n [Commerce] a technique of personal selling in which (1) a prospective customer responds to an advertisement that has concentrated on the low cost of a product; (2) a salesman calls and demonstrates an obviously cheap and poorly-made commodity; (3) when the customer complains, the salesman then produces the expensive (often excessively so) version that is of a far higher quality and, if the plan works, he sells this to the customer. A variation on this technique is for the salesman to claim that while there is an enormous waiting list for the advertised (and cheap) model, which he has therefore been unable to bring, the expensive one, which he has with him, can be produced immediately.

switch trading n [Commerce] international commodity trading that is paid for in other commodities, services, benefits or some variety of barter instead of cash.

switchback v [Chess] to return to one's original position at the end of a sequence of play.

switched star n [TV] a system of cable TV distribution whereby a main cable serves a series of junctions which in turn connect the individual subscribers to that cable. This system is particularly useful for the development of information services, in which the subscriber can interact with the cable, sending his/her own messages back up the line. See also **tree and branch**.

switcher 1. n [Politics] a voter who is nominally registered with one party, but who may equally well vote for its rivals at an election. 2. n [US] [TV] a vision mixer.

switching n [Futures market] liquidating an existing position while simultaneously rein-

stating that position for another month on the same financial instrument.

swivel neck n [Oil rigs] a rotary drill rig driller. See also **clutcher rigger**.

swoop 1. v [Parachuting] to dive down quickly. 2. v [UK] [Prisons] to wander round the prison picking up discarded cigarette ends for rolling into 'new' cigarettes of one's own.

sword 1. n [Religion] the bible; see Hebrews 4:12. 2. n [Weaving] the vertical side members of the **beater** on a treadle loom.

sylvester n [Coal-mining] a hand-operated rack and lever pulling device, used mainly for withdrawing supports.

symbiotic marketing n [Marketing] the alliance of the resources of two or more independent firms with the intention of maximising the joint marketing potential so created.

symbolic a [Computing] referring to programs which use alphanumeric symbols to represent the locations and operations of the machine.

symbolic delivery n [Commerce, Law] the passing of documents pertaining to goods (rather than the actual goods) which confer the title in those goods to the individual who now holds the documents.

symbolic interaction n [Sociology] the shared use of common symbols in human communications.

symbolic interactionism n [Sociology] the study of the relationship between the individual and society as a process of symbolic communications between social actors; thus society itself is the product of infinite transactions of social actors.

symmetricals n pl [Theatre] padded tights used by actors, dancers, acrobats, etc.

sympathetic action n [Industrial relations] support from another union or unions for the union which is actually involved in a dispute.

sync a [TV, Film] abbr of **synchronised** said of film and sound that have been filmed and recorded simultaneously.

synchronicity n [Psychology] a term coined by C. G. Jung (1875–1961) to describe the phenomenon of events which coincide in time and which seem to have a meaningful relationship but for which one cannot in fact discover a causal connection.

syncopation n [Logology] the removal of a letter from within a word to leave a different word.

syndicate v [Horse-racing] to sell a horse to a syndicate of owners.

syndicate, the n [UK] [Railways] a union negotiating committee. See also **college of knowledge**.

synectics n [Business] the conscious, preconscious and subconscious states that are present in any creative act. The word was registered as a proprietary term in the US in 1966 and usually refers to a method of problem-solving used in many corporations, advertising agencies and similar businesses; it is aimed at discovering new concepts, techniques, products and solutions.

synergetics *n* [*Design*] the culminating concept of the design philosophy of R. Buckminster Fuller: 'the behaviour of whole systems unpredicted by the behaviour of their parts taken separately'.

synergy *n* [*Business*] the belief that backs many takeovers and mergers; it is that the new combined version of the two firms will create a more perfect commercial entity than they could achieve as individual companies.

syntax *n* [*Computing*] a set of rules common to **high-level languages** which explain how commands in those languages may be used and fitted together in such a way that the program will work.

synthetic *a* [*Aerospace*] referring to any exercises, training programmes, etc. which are conducted on the ground but which simulate exactly what happens in actual flight.

synthetic incentive *n* [*Economics*] in socialist economies this is an incentive that is offered to all workers in a factory and is based on the overall production rate rather than on the singling out of any individuals.

syphon *n* [*Glass-making*] a block of refractory material used in the construction of the bath that is used in a tank furnace.

system house *n* [*US*] [*Car salesmen*] a dealership that uses several salesmen to make a single deal. See also **straight-sell house**.

System I, System II, System III, System IV *n* [*Management*] four management systems developed by US social scientist Rensis Likert (1903–1981); I is 'exploitative-authoritative', II is 'benevolent-authoritative', III is 'consultative', IV is 'participating group'.

systemic painting *n* [*Art*] painting that uses a single image or pictorial device, repeated over and over again in a variety of colours over a series of canvases, demanding from the viewer a search for 'variety within conspicuous unity'.

systems bargaining *n* [*Military*] the preservation, during an **escalation** towards nuclear war, of precedents that reduce the likelihood of further escalation, and which place thresholds in the way of an **eruption** into war.

systems engineering *n* [*Military*] the organisation of the building and installation of a complicated new piece of military hardware.

systems furniture *n* [*Business*] office furniture designed to accommodate the hardware of the modern electronic/computerised office.

systems hackers *n pl* [*Computing*] engineers and programmers who work to develop new computer systems.

systems theory *n* [*Computing*] the study of computer systems as a phenomenon, in order to find characteristics common to all systems, or to all of a class of systems. Such theories can be developed for their own sake or for the application of ideas within certain disciplines or problem areas.

systems theory *n* [*Sociology*] this is a theory that developed from attempts to establish parallels between physiological systems in medical science and social systems in the social sciences; the theory is that every social system has four sub-systems, corresponding to functional imperatives – adaptation, goal-attainment, integration and latency or pattern maintenance (AGIL) – and that any system must deal with these four problems to continue surviving.

T

T *n* [*Basketball*] abbr of **technical foul** thus 'to get the T' means to have a technical foul awarded against you. 'T' is a technical foul for which a number of free throws can be awarded; 't' means a technical foul for which only one free throw is awarded.

T account *n* [*Accounting*] the standard form of account used in double-entry book-keeping; the name of the account is written across the top of the ledger page and a vertical line splits the page beneath it into credit and debit columns.

T and A theme *n* [*Entertainment*] abbr of **Tits**

and Ass (**Arse**, *UK*) **theme** any show that depends on scantily clad (chorus) girls for its over-riding appeal.

T formation *n* [*US*] [*Football*] an offensive backfield formation in the shape of a T, so that the quarterback, just behind the centre, is in turn ahead of two more backs who are stationed in a rank parallel to the line scrimmage.

T man 1. *n* [*Drugs*] abbr of **top man** a large scale smuggler and distributor of drugs. 2. *n* [*Drugs*] abbr of **Treasury Man** a Bureau of Narcotics agent.

T test *n* [*Marketing*] a statistical test to determine the difference between two average values.

ta tzu-pao, also **tatzepao, ta-tzu-pao** *n* [*Politics*] See **big character poster**.

TA *n* [*New therapies*] acro **Transactional Analysis** a form of psychotherapy, created by Eric Berne and Thomas Harris, which concentrates on analysing individual episodes of social interaction by breaking down each individual into a tripartite entity containing 1. the Parent, 2. the Child, 3. the Adult (as in Freud's superego, id and ego).

tab 1. *v* [*UK*] [*Military*] in the British Army (para-troops) this means to carry a 130lb. pack plus weapons for long distances, over difficult terrain, in atrocious conditions; after this hike it is assumed that the troops will be fit and ready to fight whatever battle comes their way. See also **yomping**. 2. *n* [*Entertainment*] the bill, or the overall costs of a production. 3. *n* [*Journalism*] abbr of **tabloid** a tabloid newspaper, or a tabloid insert inside a **broadsheet** newspaper. 4. *n* [*Theatre*] abbr of **tableau curtain** any curtain that rises in festoons or splits down the middle, rather than rising as one large sheet.

tab show *n* [*Theatre*] a short version of a musical, usually performed by a touring company; it comes from tabloid show.

tabard *n* [*Heraldry*] a herald's coat, showing the arms of his lord.

Tabasco sauce *n* [*Oil rigs*] acid that is used to break down a limestone formation.

tabby *n* [*Weaving*] a balanced plain weave, or a plain-weave **shed**.

table 1. *n* [*Computing*] a collection of data that is stored in memory and is readily available for reference. 2. *n* [*Cards*] in bridge this is the hand held by dummy.

Table A *n* [*Commerce*] a series of model articles for a limited company as specified in the Companies Acts since 1948. New companies can either adopt Table A wholesale, use their own modified version, or write their own unique articles.

table hand *n* [*Sheep-shearing*] a woolshed oper-ative who helps the fleece-picker to skirt and roll the fleeces.

table top *n* [*Advertising*] a still-life shot of the product or its ingredients that are featured in a print or TV advertisement; no people are included. See also **backshot**.

tableau *n* [*Art*] a form of sculpture which employs life-sized figures and real accessories/props that are all frozen together in a 'real-life' scene; usually the spectator stands outside the tableau, but some are created as actual rooms into which one may walk.

table-hand *n* [*Printing*] a bindery assistant.

table-top 1. *n* [*Cycling*] in BMX cycling this is a large obstacle with a flat top. 2. *v* [*Cycling*] in BMX cycling this is to jump and lay the bike and oneself horizontal to the ground.

tabling *n* [*Sailing, Ropework*] the wide hem at the edges of a sail, to which the heavy, edging boltrope is sewn.

tabloid *n* [*Journalism*] a newspaper page size equivalent to half that of a full-size rotary press plate; it is used in the UK for the popular press, notably the Sun, Mirror and Star. See also **broadsheet**.

tabnab *n* [*Navy*] in the Royal Navy, this is a cake, bun or savoury snack.

TACAMO *n* [*Military*] acro **Take Charge And Move Out** a world-wide network of high-powered communications stations and a fleet of fourteen (to be increased to eighteen) specially equipped Lockheed C–130 transports which fly in relays twenty-four hours a day and which are used to pass on messages to the US fleet of strategic submarines by reeling out a 5.5 mile long antenna for VLF communications. The planes are also equipped with satellite UHF communications. One aircraft patrols the Pacific, the other the Atlantic.

TACAN *n* [*Military*] acro **Tactical Air Navigation** a navigational system that is based on the taking of bearings from a ground beacon to provide information on direction and distance.

tachisme *n* [*Art*] the European equivalent of the US **action painting** that was developed and popu-larised in the 1950s; artists sought spontaneity and intuitive style by dripping or throwing paint on to canvases.

tachy *n* [*US*] [*Medicine*] abbr of **tachycardia** an abnormally fast heartbeat of 100+ beats per minute. See also **Brady**.

tack *n* [*US*] [*Road transport*] abbr of **tachograph** See **squealer**.

tack-up *n* [*Theatre*] a poster on heavy card, approximately 20 in by 24 in, which is used to advertise a current performance.

tacky *n* [*Table tennis*] a soft rubber produced with a high coefficient of friction, causing the ball to stick to the bat and allowing the player to put heavy spin on the ball.

tactical loading *n* [*Military*] the loading of a transport vehicle whereby priority is given to the tactical (ie: actual combat) needs rather than to administrative ones; in practice this tends to mean lighter loads, concentrating on weapons and

T

ammunition rather than on more general supplies. See also **administrative loading**.

tactical nuclear weapon *n* [*Military*] a short or intermediate range nuclear weapon which, unless fired from European bases near the USSR borders, could not penetrate targets within the Soviet Union.

tactical vandalism *n* [*US*] [*Crime*] vandalism that is committed in order to advance some cause, rather than simply breaking or destroying property.

tactical warning *n* [*Military*] an alert prior to a nuclear war that comes only days, hours or even minutes before that war breaks out. See also **strategic warning**.

tactile *a* [*Wine-tasting*] used to describe any wine that provokes a response which can be sensed physically.

tactile sculpture 1. *n* [*Art*] sculptures produced with the intention that the blind should be able to appreciate them. **2.** *n* [*Art*] sculptures that are produced to be touched and handled by the spectator.

tag 1. *n* [*TV*] the closing line of dialogue in a TV programme. **2.** *n* [*Business*] the price, account or bill. See also **tab. 3.** *v* [*Baseball*] to put out a runner moving between bases by touching him with the ball or with the gloved hand holding the ball. **4.** also **tap** *v* [*Entertainment*] to appoint to a job.

tag axle *n* [*Road transport*] a non-powered set of wheels attached to a truck or trailer to bear the extra weight of long or heavy loads.

tagging *n* [*Metallurgy*] tapering one end of a bar, rod, tube or wire prior to drawing or stretching it through a hole of specified diameter.

taglocks *n pl* [*Weaving*] the short, dirty ends of a fleece.

tags *n pl* [*US*] [*Medicine*] the remains of tonsils that are left in the patient's throat after an operation.

tail 1. *n* [*Angling*] the downstream end of a pool. See also **neck 1. 2.** *n* [*Communications*] a set of codes appended to a message that indicate its termination. **3.** *n* [*Cricket*] the lower end of the batting order, usually composed of the wicket-keeper and an assortment of specialist bowlers; thus 'the tail wagged' means the lesser batsmen did far better than they might have been expected to. **4.** *n* [*Insurance*] the interval between the receipt of a premium payment and the payment of any claim on the policy. **5.** *n* [*US*] [*Government*] the difference between the lowest competitive bid made for US Treasury bills and the average bid for such paper. **6.** *n* [*US*] [*Finance*] in underwriting, the decimal places that follow a round number of dollars in a competitive bid for shares. **7.** *n* [*Journalism*] the bottom of a page. **8.** *n* [*Printing*] the bottom edge of a book. See also **head 3. 9.** *n* [*Skiing*] See **heel 3. 10.** *n* [*UK*] [*Surfing*] the back 12in of the surfboard. **11.** *n*

[*Theatre*] smaller parts that are listed at the 'tail' of the cast-list in a programme; it is similar to the cricketing use (see 3). **12.** (*UK*), **pigtail** (*US*) *n* [*Theatre*] a short piece of cable used for stage electrics.

tail crew *n* [*Logging*] the men who anchor the large wire rope used in logging to the tractor.

tail fly *n* [*Angling*] See **stretcher 2**.

tail off *v* [*Logging*] to take lumber from the end of the processing machine.

tail out *a* [*Radio*] said of a taped interview in which the tape has not been rewound and thus the start of the interview is at the wrong end of the tape.

tail wag *n* [*UK*] [*Railways*] the swaying motion of the last coach in a train.

tailback *n* [*US*] [*Football*] the player stationed furthest from the offensive line.

tailboard artist *n* [*US*] [*Road transport*] anyone who thinks he is the perfect driver.

tailer 1. *n* [*Angling*] a weapon forming a wire noose that is used for landing salmon; it is intended to save **kelts** from injury. **2.** *n* [*Sailing*] in offshore yachting this is the crew member who tails the sails.

tail-gate *n* [*UK*] [*Coal-mining*] the supply tunnel down which all materials used in the operation of the face must pass; half of the men travel to the face down this gate as well, the others using the **main gate**. Air usually travels up the **main gate**, across the **stall** and out along the tail-gate.

tailgate *v* [*US*] [*Road transport*] to drive too closely behind the vehicle in front.

tailgating *n* [*US*] [*Stock market*] the unethical practice of a broker who uses his client's expertise and the effect of his purchasing power to make a purchase of the same security – which is presumably increased in price because of the client's buying – for his or her personal gain.

tailings 1. *n pl* [*US*] [*Cattlemen*] stragglers in a herd of cattle. **2.** *n* [*Mining*] a mixture of waste materials and water that results from the extraction of valuable materials from ore.

tailism *n* [*Politics*] in Marxist terms, this is the political error of framing one's policy to accommodate the wishes of the masses and thus permitting the passive tail to wag a head that should be actively revolutionary.

tail-lift *n* [*UK*] [*Road transport*] a hydraulically or electrically operated loading platform that is fitted to the rear of a vehicle body to help in loading/unloading heavy objects.

tailor *v* [*Shooting*] to wound game but not to kill it cleanly.

tailor-made 1. *n* [*Advertising*] any promotion that has been especially designed for use in a single shop or by a single chain of stores. **2.** *n* [*UK*] [*Prisons*] See **civvy**.

take 1. *v* [*Angling*] to kill a fish. **2.** *n* [*Hunting*] in stag hunting this is the successful conclusion of the run, whether or not the animal is actually killed. **3.** n [*Printing*] a single portion of a story which is given to a compositor at any one time, and the type that he sets from it. **4.** n [*Printing*] a unit of text which may vary as to size but which will relate to the overall typesetting job in question. **5.** n [*TV, Film*] a continuous section of film photographed at one time, usually covering one scene or one part of a scene in a film; given that the director may not be satisfied with the quality of the acting or dialogue, or the actors may have forgotten lines or **business**, there are usually a number of takes per scene. The best takes, or even parts of takes, are amalgamated in the editing process. **6.** also **holding, taking** n [*Mining*] a mineral bearing area in which a mine can operate successfully.

take a dive, also **go in the tank, the water** v [*Boxing*] when a fighter loses a bout deliberately, usually by faking his own knock-out and falling to the canvas despite sustaining no real injury.

take a geographical v [*Medicine*] referring to the belief shared by a number of anti-drug or drink therapies, specifically Alcoholics Anonymous and Narcotics Anonymous, that a major geographical move – of town, country, job, house, or even of husband or wife – will help considerably in cutting down one's alcohol or drug abuse.

take a meeting v [*Film*] to hold a meeting; Hollywood executives and their staff invariably 'take' meetings rather than call them, hold them or merely 'meet'. The inference is that meetings, like phonecalls, are something one only accepts when there is no more pressing business.

take a walk v [*US*] [*Politics*] to leave one's party after an irrevocable argument.

take camera v [*Film*] an actor does this when he turns towards the camera.

take felt v [*Navy*] to retire from active service, and thus the wearing of a uniform, and to be given a desk job at the Ministry of Defence; it is the Royal Navy's equivalent of the Army's 'bowler-hatted'.

take in v [*Stock market*] to accept stocks or securities as security for a loan and thus carry over a sale until the next **settlement**.

take one v [*UK*] [*Police*] said of a policeman who accepts a bribe. See also **straightener**.

take out **1.** n [*US*] [*Horse-racing*] the tax deducted from one's winnings on a horse-race. **2.** v [*Military*] to kill a person or destroy a weapon, building or other target.

take part v [*Religion*] to give oral testimony of one's faith during a meeting.

take report v [*US*] [*Medicine*] said of a nurse, arriving to start a shift, who takes note of all the necessary details that concern patients on her ward: admissions, deaths, specific treatments for certain patients, etc. Thus 'to give report' is when the outgoing nurse passes on these details.

take the Fifth v [*Politics*] to plead the Fifth Amendment of the US Constitution: 'no person shall be compelled in any criminal case to be a witness against himself to avoid self-incrimination'. It was a procedure often used in the face of Senator McCarthy's anti-Communist witch-hunts of the early 1950s and latterly has become the refuge of those alleged members of the US Mafia facing embarrassing investigation.

take the knock v [*Motor trade*] to sell a car at a loss.

take up quarters v [*Angling*] used of trout when they prepare for their evening rise.

takeaways n pl [*Industrial relations*] the union term for **givebacks** which is more usually used from a management perspective.

taken to see the cups adv [*UK*] [*Police*] up before the superintendent, probably for a reprimand; such cups – for sporting and similar prowess – as a station might have won, are displayed in the superintendent's room.

takeout **1.** n [*Real estate*] a long-term mortgage taken out to finance the expenses of a short-term construction project. **2.** n [*Finance*] securities: the withdrawal of cash from a brokerage account which stands in profit.

take-out **1.** n [*US*] [*TV*] a longer than average news report, broadcast with the news, but incorporating a great deal more research and general work that the average short news item; it is a feature within the news format. **2.** n [*Sport*] in bowls or curling this is the knocking of one's opponent's wood or stone away from the jack.

take-up **1.** n [*Sailing, Ropework*] the amount of rope used in making a knot, splice or **sinnet**. **2.** n [*Social work*] the receiving by an individual of some welfare benefit to which he/she is entitled; by no means all those who could claim such benefits do so, and the actual 'take-up rate' is the percentage of those who do claim against those who should. **3.** n [*Stock market*] the action of paying in cash for stock originally bought on the **margin**.

takeup n [*Weaving*] the extra length that is taken up by the undulation of the yarn over and under the threads.

takings n pl [*US*] [*Garment trade*] the raw materials for dress-making that are bought from textile mills.

tale n [*Commerce*] a number, as opposed to a quantity assessed by weight or volume.

talent n [*TV, Film, Advertising*] actors, models, etc; any human performers who are employed in these occupations.

talent money n [*Soccer*] bonuses paid over and above basic wages to successful players in the leading clubs. See also **boot money**.

talisman n [*Stock market*] acro **Transfer Accounting Lodgement for Investors, Stock Management for Jobbers** a central pooling system, established in 1979, for the purchase and sale of listed securities. This system is highly beneficial to smaller firms, giving them a relatively cheap entrée into an expensive business.

talk game *v* [*Sex*] said of a group of black pimps when they gossip about their profession.

talkies *n pl* [*UK*] [*Railways*] a meeting of trade unions and management.

talking heads 1. *n pl* [*Advertising*] a derisive name given to commercials which consist of a pitchman extolling the virtues of a product. As with the TV use of the phrase, the screen is filled with a continual head-and-shoulders shot of the speaker. **2.** *n pl* [*TV*] anyone seen talking, rather than moving, usually in a head-and-shoulders close-up shot; talking heads programmes tend to ignore the dynamic visual opportunities of the medium and remain static and often didactic.

tally, also **motty** *n* [*Coal-mining*] a tag attached to a mining car which bears the name of the man responsible for filling it.

tallyband, also **tally-ribbon** *n* [*Navy*] the band worn around a sailor's cap on which is written the name of his ship.

tally-ho! [*Military*] air intercept code for: target sighted, contact will follow. It comes from the RAF use in World War II, that in turn was taken from fox-hunting, to announce that hostile aircraft had been seen and a dogfight was about to commence.

talon 1. *n* [*Finance*] the part of a bond that remains after the interest **coupon** has been clipped off and cashed in. **2.** *n* [*Cards*] the portion of the pack which remains after the hands have been dealt.

tamizdat *n* [*Publishing*] this comes from Rus. 'tam' meaning 'there' plus 'izdat' (an abbreviation of 'izdat el stvo') meaning 'publishing house'; it refers to Russian writings that are originally published abroad and then smuggled back into the USSR for clandestine distribution. See also **samizdat**.

tamping *n* [*Building, Plastering*] in the formation of floor **screeds**, this is the technique of consolidating the surface by ramming the material with a straight edge, bearing off from wooden battens.

tan *v* [*Photography*] to harden gelatin chemically in proportion to the amount of exposure.

tandem axle *n* [*UK*] [*Road transport*] two axles of a vehicle, located close together and usually having a linked suspension system.

tangible personal property *n* [*Law*] clothes, furniture, crops, minerals, etc. See also **intangible personal property**.

tank 1. *n* [*UK*] [*Buses*] See **tub**. **2.** *n* [*US*] [*Car salesmen*] See **big iron**. **3.** *n* [*Film*] a pool kept at a film studio for use when filming action at sea or when using models of ships. **4.** *n* [*Painting*] an acid bath in which metal is immersed. **5.** *v* [*Tennis*] when a player deliberately loses a match; it comes from the boxing use. See also **tanker**.

tank, in the *adv* [*US*] [*Stock market*] used of prices when they drop rapidly.

tank farm *n* [*Oil industry*] a collection of tanks used for the large-scale storage of oil.

tanker *n* [*Boxing*] a cheating boxer, who deliberately loses his fights and **goes in the tank** for bribes.

tankey *n* [*Navy*] a navigator's assistant; originally he was responsible for the state of the ship's water supplies.

tannin *n* [*Wine-tasting*] an essential preservation derived from grape skins during fermentation; part of the maturation process consists of the breaking down of tannin in the wine. It is more prevalent in red than in white wines since in white the grape skins are removed before fermentation.

tantivy *n* [*Hunting*] a full gallop; its origin is obscure (OED); possibly it echoes the pounding horses' hooves.

TAP *n* [*Advertising*] acro **Total Audience Package** a specification used when buying space on networked radio; the advertisement should be broadcast across the network to obtain the largest possible audience.

tap 1. *v* [*Glass-making*] to remove excess slag from the floor of a pot furnace. **2.** *v* [*Glass-making*] to drain a furnace. **3.** *v* [*UK*] [*Market-traders*] to ask a person for a loan. See also **mung 4**. **4.** *v* [*Entertainment*] See **tag 4**. **5.** *n* [*Finance*] government securities which are issued in unlimited quantities and can be obtained at any time. Such bonds are offered at a fixed price and yield and the intent is to sell out the issue at once; if this is not achieved, the 'tap' of supply is turned on and off as required. **6.** *n* [*Phonetics*] a single momentary contact between vocal organs in the production of a speech sound and thus the sound produced by such a contact. **7.** *n* [*Stock market*] a security for which sales consistently come from one source; in particular it is a government issue where the departments are gradually liquidating their holdings to the public.

tap stock *n* [*UK*] [*Stock market*] a UK Government bond issued through the Government Broker at a stated price; the flow of such shares to the market can be adjusted, like a tap, in order to influence the market in **gilts**.

tape, also **stripe** *n* [*UK*] [*Military*] the chevrons worn by non-commissioned officers in the British Army to distinguish their rank.

tapo *n* [*Science fiction*] an error on a taped message; it is a pun on the traditional print journalism **typo**.

tapper 1. *n* [*UK*] [*Market-traders*] a borrower. **2.** *n* [*UK*] [*Railways*] a carriage and wagon examiner, who moves down a train, tapping the wheels with a special hammer.

tapping *n* [*Metallurgy*] cutting the internal screw thread into the end of a tube.

tappy *n* [*Tennis*] a poor serve or an underhit drive.

tar baby *n* [*Mining*] a man who lubricates hoisting cables.

tare weight *n* [*UK*] [*Road transport*] the weight of the vehicle in road-going condition, including the driver and any passenger, prior to loading. See also **kerb weight 2**.

target 1. *n* [*Electronics*] the point on the cathode ray tube that is struck by the electron beam in order to 'write' on the screen. **2.** *n* [*Espionage*] a victim specially selected to be the target of a blackmailing scheme in order to extract from him/her such information as is required.

target company *n* [*Commerce*] a company which has been selected for a take-over bid by another company.

target language *n* [*Computing*] the **machine code** into which the **source language** must be translated to make it 'intelligible' to the machine.

target of opportunity 1. *n* [*Espionage*] any source of information that has not been categorised as a specific target, but which becomes vulnerable to access by agents and is thus employed for such uses as it offers them. **2.** *n* [*Military*] a target that is not on the prepared orders with which attacking aircraft are briefed prior to making an attack, but which emerges during the progress of that attack and which is reported to the pilots concerned by ground control. Such a target is attacked by the planes in addition to their primary targets before they return home.

target population *n* [*Commerce*] a section of the population – or even the whole population – which it is desired to reach by some form of communication, especially an advertising campaign.

target pricing *n* [*Economics*] in socialist economies this is the use of flexible pricing – both up and down – to achieve desired social objectives and to further a current economic plan; people's purchasing power is deliberately channelled to consume surpluses and to ignore scarcity.

target response *n* [*Military*] the effect on troops, **materiel** and civilians of the blast, heat, flash and fallout from a nuclear explosion.

target servicing 1. *n* [*Military*] attacking a target with either conventional or nuclear weapons. **2.** *n* [*Military*] the provision by military planners of worthwhile targets with either troops or weapons in place.

target weighting *n* [*Advertising*] the weighting of advertising expenditure according to the relevant demographic analysis.

targeted action *n* [*Politics*] a terrorist assassination that is deliberately intended to gain publicity for a cause.

task *v* [*Military, Government*] to commit an agency, a service or an individual to a task; it is often researching and reporting on a project.

task closure *n* [*Business*] the ability to carry a job or assignment right through to its completion; it is the office equivalent of the salesman's closing a sale.

task method *n* [*Advertising*] a method of calculating the budget for an advertising campaign by relating it to the aims of that campaign rather than using a budget worked out on a more general basis. See also **affordable method**.

task people *n* [*Espionage*] active intelligence agents of various nationalities.

tasseling, also **tossling** *n* [*US*] [*Farming*] the stage of growth in which the corn develops tassels.

tassels *n pl* [*Sheep-shearing*] greasy locks of wool left on the legs or brisket of a sheep.

taste 1. *n* [*Computing*] the quality of a program. This tends to vary according to the simplicity of that program; the more fiddling the program becomes, the poorer its quality is likely to be. Thus 'tasty', 'tasteful', and 'tastefulness'. **2.** *n* [*Drugs*] a sample of drugs. **3.** *n* [*Drugs*] a small amount. **4.** *n* [*US*] [*Theatre*] a share or percentage of the profits from a show.

taster *n* [*TV*] a short trailer or **teaser** on the BBC for a future programme that is to be broadcast either that night or at a later date.

tasty *a* [*UK*] [*Police*] referring to a villain who has already amassed an appreciable amount of criminal **form**.

tat 1. *n* [*TV, Theatre*] costumes, especially old ones; thus 'tatbox' is a container for the tat. **2.** *n* [*TV, Theatre*] by extension from (1) it also means a poor performance. **3.** *n* [*Tea-planting*] in tea-drying this is a tray or shelf, often made from hessian, on which green tea leaves are spread out to dry.

ta-ta theory *n* [*Linguistics*] a theory that language developed as an attempt by the vocal organs to imitate the gestures of the body.

tats *n pl* [*Religion*] at theological colleges these are ecclesiastical paraphernalia.

tatt *n* [*US*] [*Crime*] a form of confidence trick played with a dice: the confidence man engages his victim at a bar, pretends to have 'found' a dice lying on the floor, then suggests they 'roll for drinks'. The victim is allowed to win the first, small bets, but is then systematically divested of his cash; the drinks that he is continually urged to take help mask the trickster's efforts.

tattle-tale *n* [*US*] [*Road transport*] See **squealer**.

tatts 1. *n pl* [*Gambling*] dice. **2.** also **railings** *n pl* [*Navy*] false teeth, dentures.

Taurus *n* [*Stock market*] a computerised transfer and registration system which is designed to eliminate paper share certificates and is scheduled for introduction on the London Stock Exchange in 1989.

taut *a* [*Wine-tasting*] somewhat **severe**, unyielding, probably immature.

tautliner, also **curtain sider** *n* [*UK*] [*Road transport*] an articulated trailer with canvas as opposed to rigid metal sides – it is used for easy loading; the canvas can be made so tight that it is nearly as rigid as metal.

tautonym *n* [*Logology*] a word made up of a repetition of two identical parts, eg: tom-tom.

T

tawing n [*Tanning*] the tanning of light leathers, eg. glove kid, with an alum mixture.

tax holiday n [*Commerce*] a period during which an enterprise is exempted from tax on its profits – it is allowed as an incentive to the establishment of new businesses.

taxi squad n [*US*] [*Football*] those players who train with the team but are not chosen for the matches; this allegedly dates from the practice of one owner who employed his non-playing footballers to staff his fleet of taxi-cabs.

taxing n [*UK*] [*Prisons*] in Borstals this is the collection of 'protection money' by the larger, older prisoners, who threaten the younger, weaker ones with violence.

taxonomy n [*Sociology*] the classification of phenomena, as opposed to their explanation.

Taylorism n [*Management*] See **scientific management**.

T-bone v [*Motor racing*] said of a car which hits another amidships at an angle of 90° after the first car has skidded and slewed across the course.

TC adv [*Advertising*] abbr of **Till Cancelled** a specification used when buying advertising space which instructs the newspaper, radio or TV station to continue running an advertisement until given further instructions.

T.C.J. a [*Sociology*] abbr of **Twentieth Century Jewish** it is used by British upper classes to denote a style of furniture, often from Maples or similar emporia, that is seen as beloved of parvenu taste, supposedly a Jewish monopoly.

TCK n [*Advertising*] abbr of **two cunts in a kitchen** agency shorthand for a television advertisement, usually for instant coffee, breakfast cereal, floor cleaner, etc., in which a couple of 'housewives' are chatting, in an allegedly 'real-life situation', about the merits of the product that is being promoted.

TE bread n [*Sex*] abbr of **Top Eliminator Money** the homosexual **hustler**'s dream of the one client who will enable him to give up selling himself; it comes from the boxing term for the fight that eliminates all but the top challengers for a title.

tea and buns all round n [*Fleet Air Arm*] an operation in which success is assured.

tea gardens n [*UK*] [*Railways*] a marshalling yard at Somers Town, London NW1, which is built on the site of a former tea garden.

teacher n [*Oil rigs*] a driller.

teaching situation n [*Education*] the classroom.

TEAL AMBER n [*Military*] a proposed satellite-based surveillance system which uses a TV camera to 'stare' at an area of space and register the passage of anything that moves across it and immediately to spot orbital characteristics, comparing these with previous sightings. TEAL AMBER will be so sensitive that it will be able, weather conditions permitting, to spot an object

no larger than a dinner-plate up to 40,000 miles distant.

team ministry n [*Religion*] a group of clergymen, under the leadership of a team rector, who jointly administer a number of parishes. See also **group ministry**.

team-handed a [*UK*] [*Police*] said of a gang of thieves or a posse of police.

tear n [*Glass-making*] an open crack on the surface of glassware or glass tubing.

teardown n [*Industry*] the complete dismantling of a piece of machinery.

tearing n [*TV*] a distortion in the on-screen image that is produced by a lack of sweep synchronisation.

tears, also **teardrops** n pl [*Painting*] the effect of overly viscous paint which runs down a surface, rather than covering it smoothly. See also **curtain 2**.

tear-up n [*Gambling*] a means of convicting a suspicious victim that he has not been cheated out of his money (although he certainly has); the cheat acts affronted and ostentatiously tears up the cheque he has just been paid in front of the victim who has just written it; in fact he has palmed the real one and torn up a fake and so leaves quickly to cash the real cheque, before his victim realises what has happened.

tease v [*Weaving*] to pull fibres apart by hand in preparation for carding or spinning.

teasel 1. v [*Textiles*] to create a nap on cloth by drawing all the free fibres in one direction. 2. n [*Textiles*] the instrument with projecting wire burrs that creates the **nap**.

teaser 1. n [*Angling*] a fish-shaped wooden lure (without a hook) that is towed 50 to 100 yards behind the boat. 2. n [*Sailing*] a knotted rope's end. 3. n [*Electricity*] the winding or transformer that is connected to the middle of the other transformer in a T connection. 4. n [*Film*] a poster which lures the public into a film without offering any but the barest details. 5. n [*Radio, TV*] a trailer which promotes a future attraction, for transmission either that day or in the near future. 6. also **pounder** n [*Glass-making*] an operator who maintains the correct furnace temperature for the melting of glass; it comes from Fr. 'tiseur'. 7. (*US*), **proscenium border** (*UK*) n [*US*] [*Theatre*] a short, horizontal curtain or **flat** that is used to mark the **flies** and frame the top of the inner stage opening, just behind the proscenium arch and in front of the **tormentors**.

tea-wagon n [*Film*] the sound-mixer's console.

technical market n [*Stock market*] a market in which unnatural price levels are being maintained through speculation or manipulation.

technical surveillance n [*Espionage*] any form of information-gathering that depends on wire taps, hidden microphones, etc.

technical trespass n [*Espionage, Government*] the breaking and entering into premises by a member of the US Government, usually an FBI agent. No warrant or proper permission is ever obtained for such incursions, but they are always justified by expedient need.

technofear, also **technophobia** n [Sociology] the (unnatural) fear of the advances in, or the complexities of, technology; eg: the inability of many individuals to break down a personal barrier against the use of computers.

technofreak n [Sociology] an enthusiast, probably a fanatic, for the latest advances in technology, either in general or as regards a specific discipline or piece of machinery.

technological determinism n [Sociology] the notion that social change is produced by major changes in productive technique – the cotton gin, the spinning jenny, etc. – and that social changes are only caused by the technology, rather than running in parallel.

technologism n [Sociology] the belief that society should be governed on technological principles.

technology assessment n [Sociology] the assessment of the impact of technological developments on society.

technology transfer n [Politics] the transfer of the latest technology or technological information from developed countries to those that are less developed.

technostructure n [Sociology] those individuals in a society who control its technology.

TECO n [Computing] acro **Text Editor and Corrector** a **peripheral**, first developed at the Massachusetts Institute of Technology (MIT), which is now used for on-screen editing in many computers.

teem v [Glass-making] to pour molten glass from the ladle.

teeth arms n pl [Military] those parts of the military services that actually engage the enemy in battle: armour, infantry, etc.

teeth-to-tail ratio n [Military] the ratio of actual combat troops to those required in support; the closer one is to fighting on one's home territory, the smaller this ratio needs to be. Hence Germany, if fighting in Europe, will need far less support than the US, since the US are 5000 miles from home.

TEL n [Military] acro **transporter-erector-launcher** a six-axle, 24–wheel vehicle, weighing 670,000lb, that is used to carry the **MX** missile, which itself weighs 190,000lb, and its **modesty shield**.

tel quel rate, also **t.q. rate** n [Banking] the effective exchange rate at which someone offers to pay in one currency to purchase a particular financial document which represents an entitlement to payment in a foreign currency; it comes from Fr. for 'such as it is'. It is also a rate used by banks when buying a foreign currency bill of exchange which has some time to run before becoming due for payment.

tele n [New therapies] a term coined by Jacob L. Moreno to describe one aspect of his psychodramas: 'a feeling that holds individuals into one another, the cement that holds groups together' (J. L. Moreno 'Group Psychotherapy', 1945).

telecine n [TV] a system of transferring filmed material on to videotape for transmission as part of a TV programme.

telecon 1. n [Military, Business] abbr of **teletype** plus **conference** a secure device developed by the US military for the transmission of messages over long distances, using either radio, satellites or underwater cable and usually displaying such messages on a terminal screen. **2.** n [Business] a conference between a number of businessmen, all in different offices and/or cities, that is conducted through teletypes or computer networks; it comes from the military use (see **1**).

telegraph 1. v [Boxing] a boxer does this when he shows exactly which punch he is throwing, thus making defence or avoidance simple for his opponent. **2.** v [Gambling] to reveal unintentionally the fact that one is about to make a cheating move. **3.** v [Gambling] in poker this is to reveal, by some involuntary but noticeable movement, gesture or tic, that one is either bluffing, holds a vital card, or has some other lucrative secret at one's disposal.

telemark n [Skiing] a swing turn that is used to change direction or to stop abruptly; it comes from Telemark, an administrative area of southern Norway.

teleology n [Sociology] sociological explanations which try to explain social processes, especially those of social change, by reference to the end-state towards which they are supposedly working, or the ultimate function they are said to serve.

telepic n [TV] a feature-length film funded by a network for first screening on television.

telepuppet n [Aerospace] a machine under remote control which is intended to erect space platforms.

teleroman n [Can] [TV] a French-Canadian **soap opera**.

telescope n [TV] a device that uses a series of retractable tubes to suspend studio lighting at different heights.

telescope word n [Linguistics] See **brunch word**.

television cut off n [Film] the area of the image that will appear on a TV screen when a feature film is being transmitted.

television mask n [TV, Film] a mask that is used to judge how much of a cinema film's image will appear when reduced to the proportions of a TV screen.

television safe action area n [Film, TV] See **television cut off**.

telint n [Military] abbr of **telemetry intelligence**

T

all information gathered through tracking and listening in to USSR missile tests. See also **comint, elint, humint, sigint.**

tell box n [*Distilling*] a meter that measures the rate of flow and quantity of whisky production; it also records the proof.

telling n [*Military*] the communicating of air surveillance and other tactical data between the commander and various subordinate facilities.

telop n [*US*] [*TV*] the projection on to the screen of the pictures that accompany a news story, while the reporter reads a script off-camera.

temper 1. n [*Metallurgy*] the mechanical condition of steel strip as controlled by heat treatment and cold rolling; this extends through degrees of hardness from soft to hard temper. **2.** n [*Metallurgy*] the percentage increase in the length of steel sheet after cold rolling.

template n [*Oil rigs*] a frame anchored to the sea floor to which in turn the rig itself may be secured.

temple n [*Weaving*] See **stretcher 1.**

temps n [*Ballet*] one of a number of movements in which there is no transfer of weight from one foot to another.

ten cents on accuracy n [*Parachuting*] used to refer to the landing ten centimetres only away from the chosen target, usually a small disc.

ten foot n [*UK*] [*Railways*] the space that divides the two inner tracks of a four-track line.

ten foot rule n [*Ice-hockey*] a rule that prohibits any player from standing within ten feet of the two players engaged in a face-off.

ten great relationships n [*Politics*] a relatively right-wing speech which Mao Zedong wrote in 1956 but kept suppressed until it was published after his death in 1976; the speech emphasised the importance of economic common sense over ideological purity and the need for the efficient marshalling of resources, rather than the imposition of plans which owed more to political than productive imperatives.

ten great years n pl [*Politics*] in China this was the first decade – from 1949 to 1959 – of the communist revolution.

ten (in one) 1. n [*Carnival*] a large circus or carnival. **2.** n [*Carnival*] a tent sideshow that holds ten performers, especially freaks and grotesques.

ten minute rule n [*UK*] [*Politics*] in the House of Commons this is a standing order which allows the brief discussion of a motion for permission to introduce a new bill; no speech in the discussion may exceed ten minutes in length.

Ten, the, also **top ten** n [*US*] [*Law*] the FBI's list of the Ten Most Wanted criminals in the US.

ten wheel bob-tail load n [*US*] [*Road transport*] a short trailer which takes a load of ten pallets.

ten-A (10–A) n [*Navy*] the punishment meted out to sailors in a warship, originally called 'the black list'; sailors were woken early, ate meals on the upper deck supervised by the ship's police, worked during normal mealtimes and were deprived of their rum ration.

tender a [*US*] [*Coal-mining*] said of a roof that is considered potentially dangerous.

tender v [*Futures market*] to deliver against futures.

tender loving care n [*UK*] [*Medicine*] the stopping of the provision of active medical care to terminally ill geriatrics, and the permitting or (with an overdose of tranquilisers or barbiturates) hastening of death; this benign description also covers the treatment of all cases where current medical practice can do little to help.

tender wool n [*Weaving*] an industrial term for wool that breaks easily.

tendon n [*Engineering*] a steel rod or wire that is stretched while in liquid concrete; this will pre-stress it while the concrete sets.

Ten-F n [*US*] [*Medicine*] a stereotypical gall bladder patient who is a 'fat, fair, fecund, fortyish, flatulent female with foul, floating faeces'.

tenner n [*TV, Film*] a 10KW incandescent focussing lamp.

tennis-match sort n [*Computing*] a variety of **bubble sort** in which sort passes are made in alternating directions.

tenor n [*Banking*] the length of time it takes for a bill of exchange or promissory note to reach maturity.

tensile architecture n [*Architecture*] any structure that is held rigid by cables or rods.

tension relief n [*Sex*] masturbation; this is one of the extra services that can be obtained at a so-called 'massage parlour' for a payment somewhat greater than that required for the basic massage.

tensioners n pl [*UK*] [*Road transport*] See **chains and dogs.**

tentacle n [*Military*] a detachment of signals personnel, with its own radio and transport.

tents n pl [*US*] [*Garment trade*] large sizes of dresses.

ten/two n [*Espionage*] intelligence code for a hired assassin who has been contracted to work for an intelligence agency.

TERCOM n [*Military*] acro **Terrain Contour Matching** a sensor system that acts as the 'eyes' of a **cruise** missile and backs up the in-built inertial guidance system. TERCOM follows a computerised map of the route to the target with virtually 100% accuracy. The sensor also watches the ground below, giving cruise the ability to 'hug' the contours it overflies. In flight TERCOM continually compares its map, which is programmed into each missile according to its target, and the path the flight is actually taking; any discrepancies are automatically corrected and instructions executed by the missile's automatic pilot.

term bank n [*Computing*] abbr of **terminological data bank** a database – such as this dictionary – that is devoted to storing terms used in specialised vocabularies. Such banks can be called upon for the compilation of glossaries, word lists and multi-lingual translations of specialist terminologies.

term shares *n pl* [*Finance*] money deposited with a building society under an agreement that it cannot be withdrawn for a number of years; such money earns a higher than normal rate of interest as an inducement to make the deposit.

terminal market *n* [*Commerce*] a market that deals in **futures**.

terminate with extreme prejudice *v* [*Espionage*] to assassinate; it is usually with the suggestion that the target is a major political figure or even a head of state.

termination capability *n* [*Military*] the ability of a nation or nations to bring a nuclear war to an end.

termor *n* [*Law*] one who holds an estate for life, or for a specified term of years.

tern *n* [*Medicine*] abbr of **intern**.

terpers *n* [*Entertainment*] a corruption of 'terpsichore' that means 'singers', as in 'Tokyo Terpers Triade Towards Topless Taboo' (Variety 13–10–82).

terra firma *adv* [*UK*] [*Railways*] off the track at trap points.

Terrace, the *n* [*Taxis*] the London cabby's name for Paddington Station; it comes from its external architecture.

territorial justice *n* [*Social work*] the distribution of resources within an area in proportion to the needs of that area.

tertiary care *n* [*Medicine*] medical services that are provided by various specialist units: neuro-surgery, heart transplants, etc.

test a meeting *v* [*Religion*] to invite those present at a meeting to **stand up**.

testimony *n* [*Religion*] the Christian faith.

tête de cuvée *n* [*Wine trade*] the premier vineyard of an area surrounding a particular village; it comes from Fr. for 'head of the vatful'.

tête-bêche *n* [*Philately*] a joined pair of stamps in which one is upside-down in relation to the other; it comes from Fr. for 'head to foot', 'head to tail'.

TEWT *n* [*UK*] [*Military*] acro **Tactical Exercise Without Troops** an exercise used for the training of junior officers.

Texas leaguer *n* [*Baseball*] a short **fly ball** that drops in the outfield for a hit, permitting the batter to advance safely one base.

textile *n* [*Naturism*] anyone who is not a naturist and prefers to wear clothes.

textuality *n* [*Literary criticism*] the transformation of the common language of a civilisation into the language of a work of literature which belongs to that civilisation.

textura *n* [*Printing*] this comes from Lat. meaning 'texture'; it is one of a group of typefaces found in the earliest printed books. Textura faces have narrow angular letters and strong vertical emphasis.

TF *adv* [*Advertising*] abbr of **'Til Forbid**. See **TC**.

T-group training *n* [*Business*] a system of human relations training for business executives which emphasises inter-personal events and the relationships that evolve through the establishment of a formal training group and letting those involved begin to communicate; the hope is that the lessons learnt in the group will be taken back and used in the office.

that play, also **Harry Lauder, the Caledonian tragedy, the comedy of Glamis, the Scottish play, the unmentionable** *n* [*UK*] [*Theatre*] a variety of nicknames that subscribe to the British theatrical superstition that Shakespeare's 'Macbeth' should never be mentioned by name inside a theatre.

that's nominal *v phr* [*Aerospace*] there are no problems, ie; not within the nominated guidelines for a flight or mission.

Theatre *n* [*Theatre*] the dropping of any article, definite or indefinite, as in 'Film', implies the whole topic of the theatre as an art form as opposed to a public entertainment; it also refers to the intellectual opinions, discussions and developments that stem from it, rather than the plays or personalities that otherwise form the staples of theatrical conversation.

theatre armaments *n pl* [*Military*] short-range weapons – both conventional and nuclear – that are designed for use by troops engaged in a face-to-face battle.

theatre nuclear forces *n pl* [*Military*] battlefield troops armed with short-range **theatre armaments**.

theatre of chance *n* [*Theatre*] a theatrical style that plays with words, delivering them at random, out of sequence and with no discernible script or narrative.

theatre of cruelty *n* [*Theatre*] a form of theatre based on the theories of Antonin Artaud (1886–1948); the audience is deliberately provoked, the actors subordinate plot and narrative to harsh physical and sensual rituals and the overall intention is for all involved to undergo a savage and shocking experience.

theatre of fact *n* [*Theatre*] plays that are essentially contemporary documentaries, based on the dramatic representation of current events and often using actual public statements, speeches and documents to provide their script.

theatre of involvement *n* [*Theatre*] any performance which blends audience and actors and creates an experience that, whatever else it does, defies the conceptions of the bourgeois theatre and, in theory, changes the way one lives.

theatre of panic *n* [*Theatre*] a term coined by Fernando Arrabal (1932–1983) to define a genre of theatre that combined bad taste, rustic energy,

T

awful tragedy and great fun; all of these deliberate contrasts were intended to promote a feeling of overall instability amongst the audience.

theatre of protest *n* [*Theatre*] any performance, in or out of the traditional theatre, that was intended to make a social statement and, it was hoped, influence the spectators to positive political action.

theatre of the absurd *n* [*Theatre*] a form of theatre that concentrates on the absurdity of the human condition, as epitomised by the work of Samuel Beckett, Eugene Ionesco, et al.

theatre of the mind *n* [*Theatre*] a popular theatrical style of the 1960s in which performances drew heavily on light shows, slides and other effects in an attempt to recreate the experience of taking LSD.

theatre of the streets *n* [*Theatre*] a form of the **theatre of protest** which concentrated on giving its 'performances' in the street and in the form of a confrontation with the Establishment and its mores.

theatrical *a* [*Film*] referring to any film that is designed for commercial exhibition in mass market cinemas.

thematics *n* [*Philately*] a popular method of collecting stamps on a particular theme, usually pictorial. See also **topical**.

theme advertising *n* [*Advertising*] See **above the line**. See also **scheme advertising**.

theme scarf *n* [*Fashion*] any form of colour-coordinated fashion accessory – scarf, bag, hat, gloves, etc.

theodicy *n* [*Sociology*] the justification, in religion, of divine justice, despite the presence of evil, and thus, by extension, the legitimising of social inequality and injustice.

theology *n* [*Media*] at the British Broadcasting Corporation (BBC) this is the nickname given to the internal organisation of the corporation and the concomitant politicking that is carried on at senior level.

theory *n* [*Computing*] any idea, plan, set of rules, etc.

theory X *n* [*Industrial relations*] developed by Douglas MacGregor in 'The Human Side of Enterprise' (1960), this is a management concept based on the categorisation of people as basically lazy, inept and needing a firm, coercive hand to keep them working. See also **theory Y, theory Z**.

theory Y *n* [*Industrial relations*] developed by Douglas McGregor in 'The Human Side of Enterprise' (1960), this is a management concept based on the theory that people are naturally productive and merely need the right kind of guidance from a concerned, involved and participative manager. See also **theory X, theory Z**.

theory Z *n* [*Industrial relations*] a management concept developed beyond MacGregor's **theories X and Y** which targets the future management style that will be required to deal with, and

include, people whose concerns are not merely with their own firm but with a wider range of social and ethical considerations which were ignored by the managers of earlier corporations. See also **theory X, theory Y**.

theory-laden *a* [*Sociology*] used to describe a proposition or empirical finding that will only make sense in the context of a given theory, and which is thus already influenced by the theory it is meant to back up. See also **theory-neutral**.

theory-neutral *a* [*Sociology*] used to describe a proposition or empirical finding that makes sense even in the absence of any supporting theory, and which will stand up on its own account. See also **theory-laden**.

therapeutic segregation *n* [*US*] [*Prisons*] a solitary confinement cell; prisons that contain such cells are sometimes known as 'therapeutic correctional communities'.

therapeutic window *n* [*Medicine*] the maximum effectiveness of a medication at the precise dosage range; it is used especially with reference to those medications used in psychiatry.

therblig *n* [*Management*] one of 17 basic elements of body movement used by humans while working. They were originally tabulated by US engineer Frank Gilbreth (1868–1924); 'therblig' is a reverse of his surname. It is now used in work study and micromotion analysis.

there's work down *v phr* [*Gambling*] the announcement by one player that an unspecified fellow player is cheating.

thermal death point *n* [*Biology*] the lowest point, which varies as to the specific circumstances, at which a micro-organism can be killed.

thermal imaging *n* [*Science*] the technique of using the heat given off by objects or substances to produce an image of them.

thermal noise *n* [*Electronics*] the noise created by the random thermal movement of electrons.

thermal runaway *n* [*Electronics*] a dramatic or destructive rise in the temperature of a transistor caused by an increase in its temperature which in turn causes an increase in the current passing through it or vice versa.

thesp *n* [*Theatre*] abbr of **thespian** an actor.

theta pinch *n* [*Technology*] the rapid compression of a magnetic field which surrounds plasma (highly ionised gas) to produce a controlled fusion reaction in a nuclear reactor.

thetan *n* [*Scientology*] the human spirit, the creative potential of which is the subject of scientology.

thick chart syndrome *n* [*US*] [*Medicine*] a patient with multiple admissions and many outpatient attendances whose medical file has grown increasingly huge.

thick film *n* [*Electronics*] a method of creating integrated circuits in which the components are mounted and interconnected on a ceramic substrate (the material upon which the circuit is fabricated). See also **thin film**.

thick space *n* [*Printing*] a third of an em space used in separating words. See also **thin space**.

thief 1. *n* [*Distilling*] a hollow metal instrument that is used to take samples from a barrel of whisky by using atmospheric pressure. 2. *v* [*Oil rigs*] to take a sample of oil from a tank.

thief vault *n* [*Gymnastics*] a vault over a piece of gymnastic apparatus that is executed from a one-foot take-off and in which both feet are thrust forward and over and the hands are placed on the apparatus as the body passes over it.

thieves' kitchen *n* [*UK*] [*Taxis*] the Stock Exchange.

thimble 1. *n* [*Building*] a metal joint for fixing a lead pipe to stoneware. 2. *n* [*Sailing, Ropework*] a ring of metal, with a concave groove, around which a rope is secured and which thus forms an **eye**, grommet etc.

thin film *n* [*Electronics*] a method of creating integrated circuits in which thin layers of material are deposited on an insulating base in a vacuum. See also **thick film**.

thin red line *n* [*UK*] [*Railways*] a jam sandwich.

thin route *n* [*Air travel*] an intercontinental air route that is only lightly used by traffic.

thin window display *n* [*Printing*] in word processing this is a single display of 15–32 characters which prompts an operator to display a section of text. See also **marching display**.

thin space *n* [*Printing*] a fifth of an em space used in separating words. See also **thick space**.

thing *n* [*New therapies*] See **bag 3**.

thingism *n* [*Literary criticism*] See **chosisme**.

think-piece *n* [*Journalism*] a general article, concentrating on background information, expert (or otherwise) opinion and analysis and similar examples of soft news.

third coat *n* [*US*] [*Painting*] the last coat applied to a surface; this is not the actual third coat – there can be many more applied before the job is complete.

third degree arson *n* [*US*] [*Law*] the burning of property other than buildings.

third force *n* [*Politics*] any political group that can be seen as setting up a buffer between the superstates of the US and USSR.

third generation *n* [*Computing*] machines designed after 1960 and which exhibit the characteristics of integrated families of machines, as typified by the IBM 360, which would be introduced by manufacturers in groups of at least three, architecturally similar but different in price and performance. This era saw the introduction of high-performance printers, multiprogramming, the true integration of communications technology and computers, employing on-line and data-entry terminals, the use of large on-line storage and larger fixed disks and removable disk packs. The third generation saw the virtual end of

punched card and punched paper tape as primary input/output media. See also **first, second, fourth, fifth generation**.

third level carrier *n* [*Air travel*] feeder or commuter services which, like suburban commuter railways, operate in and out of one major airport. See also **second level carrier**.

third man (in the ring) *n* [*Boxing*] the referee; the official magazine of boxing referees is 'The Third Man'.

third market *n* [*Commerce*] the market in listed stocks which are not traded on a stock exchange. See also **fourth market, counter, over the**.

third party credibility *n* [*Public relations*] a PR method whereby the target audience is persuaded of the truth of a client's claim on hearing the supposedly unbiased evidence of a third party – neither the PR nor the client – that supports that claim; it is a far more subtle means of convincing the sceptical than is direct advertising.

third room *n* [*UK*] [*Diplomacy*] the junior members of a Foreign Office department; originally there existed only one Third Room, but with the expansion of the F.O. there are now several physical rooms, though only the one general category.

Third World 1. *n* [*Politics*] the non-aligned nations of Africa and Asia. 2. *n* [*Politics*] the under-developed, or developing, nations, although Third World is often replaced by **South**.

third world briefcase *n* [*Commerce*] in the audio retail trade, these are the combination radio and stereophonic cassette players which tend to be favoured by otherwise impoverished black youths.

thirds *n pl* [*Industry*] items that contain major imperfections of workmanship.

thirling *n* [*Mining*] See **holing**.

thirst after righteousness *n* [*Navy*] the first drink in the wardroom that follows a church service.

thirty *n* [*Journalism*] usually written as '30' and typed at the end of a piece; it is the shorthand indication that there is no more copy to come on that piece. See also **fourteen (14)**.

thirty day boy *n* [*Sex*] a homosexual **hustler** who enjoys sex every day of the month and who thus turns his enthusiasms into cash.

thirty minutes *n* [*US*] [*Theatre*] a call to indicate to actors that the performance commences in half an hour. See also **half, the**.

Thirty Rock *n* [*US*] [*TV*] 30, Rockefeller Plaza, New York: the headquarters of NBC-TV.

thirty-eight, also **34½, 37½** *n* [*Sex*] supposedly half of 69 (soixante-neuf): mutual oral genital stimulation but, as practised by homosexual **hustlers** only the client actually ejaculates.

thirty-four 1. *n* [*US*] [*Shoe trade*] an indication that a line is sold out. 2. *n* [*US*] [*Shoe trade*] an indication to another salesman that he should go away and 'stop interfering with my customer'.

T

thirty-miler, also **forty-miler** *n* [*US*] [*Circus*] a circus veteran; thirty or forty miles was the traditional journey between venues.

thirty-ninth street *a* [*US*] [*Garment trade*] referring to an excellent milliner; 39th Street, New York City, is the centre of the US millinery trade.

thish *n* [*Science fiction*] the current – this – issue of a fan magazine.

Thomas *n* [*Medicine*] this is named after H. O. Thomas (1834–91), an English surgeon who invented a splint for immobilising the hip; the splint consists of a soft ring encircling the thigh from which two rigid rods extend on either side of the leg and meet beyond the foot.

thorazine shuffle *n* [*US*] [*Medicine*] the characteristic slow, foot-dragging gait seen in psychiatric patients who are on a long-term course of major tranquilisers.

thoroughfoot *n* [*Sailing, Ropework*] a tangle in a tackle due to a block's turning around its rope.

thought-cliché *n* [*Sociology*] a variety of concepts, usually received ideas that have little basis other than in their popular acceptance, which may be considered as less important than easily assimilated clichés.

thought-forms *n pl* [*Theology*] the combination of pre-suppositions, imagery, vocabulary and allied attitudes current at a given time or place, and which define the way in which thinking on a particular system of belief is orchestrated.

thought-world *n pl* [*Psychology*] the opinions, attitudes, emotions, beliefs and similar determinants that, taken together, define the way in which a particular people at a particular place and/or time see the world.

thrashing *n* [*Computing*] a malfunction that occurs in a **virtual memory** system when an excessive proportion of CPU time is spent in moving data between main and auxiliary storage. This means that the machine's resources are diverted to this movement instead of actually referencing the pages of data.

threaded tree *n* [*Computing*] a tree in which additional pointers have been added to the basic tree to assist in the scanning of the overall structure. See also **tree**.

threat assessment conference *n* [*Military*] a check, of maximum three minutes duration, in which US commanders assess incoming missile threats and determine the immediate response; with current USSR missiles, this leaves nineteen minutes before impact.

threat azimuth *n* [*Military*] a missile launch that appears to have been fired on a threatening path, rather than merely as a test.

threat fan *n* [*Military*] a missile launch from the USSR that is assessed as being targeted on the US or one of its allies.

three anti *n* [*Politics*] in China this is a campaign to attack corruption, waste and excessive bureaucracy within the government and the Party; it comes from Chinese 'san' meaning three plus 'fan' meaning against.

three As *n pl* [*UK*] [*Medicine*] the traditional code practised by Harley Street consultants, defining the attributes best loved by their patients: availability, affability, ability.

three Cs *n pl* [*US*] [*Skiing*] courtesy, control and conditioning: the necessary attributes of US ski patrols.

three greens [*Aerospace*] radio code for: the landing gear is down and locked into position. It comes from the three green lights which indicate this to the pilot.

three heart rule *n* [*US*] [*Military*] anyone wounded three times, and thus gaining three Purple Hearts during the same tour of duty, is automatically taken out of the combat zone.

three honest and four stricts *n pl* [*Government*] a Chinese communist campaign for law and order in the late 1960s and early 1970s: 1. honest people, 2. honest words, 3. honest deeds plus 1. strict demands, 2. strict organisation, 3. strict behaviour, 4. strict discipline.

three ill winds *n pl* [*Government*] in China this was the post-revolutionary attack on the 'Eight-Legged Essay', the ultra-complex and massively dogmatic regulations that dominated the government before 1949; the ill winds were 1. sectarianism, 2. subjectivism, 3. excessive formalism – all three of which were to be absent from the new style of government.

three magic weapons *n pl* [*Politics*] the three stages of seizure of power by the proletariat as defined by Mao Zedong: 1. the formation of a united workers' front, 2. the armed struggle of the Party's armed units, 3. the construction of the Party which would consolidate worker power under the aegis of Communist doctrine.

three on a post [*US*] [*Car salesmen*] a gear shift attached to the steering wheel and having three gears. See also **four on the floor**.

three togethers *n pl* [*Military*] the principles of the Chinese People's Liberation Army (PLA): 1. work together, 2. eat together, 3. live together.

three twelves *n* [*US*] [*Farming*] a plough consisting of three twelve-inch plough-shares; thus any similar numerical reference, eg. four fourteens, two fourteens, etc.

three worlds theory *n* [*Politics*] a pamphlet published in China in 1977 entitled: 'Chairman Mao's Theory of the Differentiation of the Three Worlds as a Major Contribution to Marxism-Leninism': 1. the superpowers, US, USSR; 2. the economically developed nations, West and East Europe, Canada, Australia, New Zealand and Japan; 3. Africa, Asia and South America. In Mao's ideal plan (2) and (3) should ally to defeat both members of (1).

three-bin system *n* [*Management*] a variation on the two-bin system of stock control; here a third bin is kept aside as a safety stock to back up the other two. See also **last-bag system**.

three-card monte n [UK] [Police] the three-card trick, 'find the lady'; it is a popular sleight-of-hand confidence trick practised in the street.

three-D problem n [Military] the assessing of targets for missiles on the basis of Detection, Discrimination and Destruction.

three-D system n [Management] a theory of managerial styles developed around 1970 by William J. Reddin, citing three separate dimensions: tasks orientation, relationships orientation, effectiveness.

three-decker n [Sex] a three way sexual 'party': one man sodomises another man who is engaged in heterosexual intercourse with a woman.

three-eighths n [Weaving] the third category in the blood system of grading wool.

three-eye league n [US] [Politics] a hypothetical club to which membership is gained by any politician who has visited the homes of the US's three most powerful minorities: Israel, Italy and Ireland.

three-four defense n [US] [Football] a variation on the standard defensive line-up, using three instead of four defensive linemen, and four instead of three linebackers.

three-H enema n [US] [Medicine] a particularly virulent enema: 'high, hot and a hell of a lot'.

three-in-one alliance n [Politics] the triumvirate that was destined to rule China once the **Cultural Revolution** had run its course: 1. the old cadres, 2. the activists who had risen from the people during the Cultural Revolution, 3. the People's Liberation Army (PLA); a blend of all three would form revolutionary committees and take over all aspects of government in China.

three-legged riding n [US] [Cattlemen] riding with a tight rein and thus pulling hard on the bit in the horse's mouth.

three-masted schooner n [Aus.] [Billiards] this is when the three balls are in a direct line, with the opponent's ball standing exactly between the cue ball and the red. See also **line-up 1**.

three-ply organisation n [Business] the concept that an organisation is constructed from three inter-related 'plies': 1. ideational, dealing with the long-range view from a philosophical and ideological standpoint; 2. synergistic, dealing with a variety of specialist areas such as planning, analysis, research, etc; 3. process, involving the technology and operation of the organisation.

three-sheet 1. v [Theatre] to exaggerate, to lie, to boast; it comes from the idea of a large advertising poster. 2. v [Theatre] to stand around in the lobby after one's performance and chat to the departing audience; to show off. 3. v [Theatre] to have the leading role in a play.

three-sheeting n [Theatre] keeping on one's make-up after the show; it comes from the carnival term for putting one poster on top of another and from **three-sheet 2**.

three-sixty n [UK] [Surfing] a complete 360° turn on the face of the wave.

three-toed sloth n [US] [Medicine] a slow-thinking, slow-talking and slow-acting patient, eg: a degenerated alcoholic.

three-two-two system n [Management] a rapidly rotating shift system, popular in Europe, under which each group of workers changes from working one type of shift to another three times each week (3 days one type, 2 days a second, 2 days a third) with a 24-hour break at each change. See also **continental shift system**.

three-way girl n [Sex] a prostitute who is willing to offer all her orifices separately or simultaneously to one or more clients.

threshold 1. n [UK] [Industrial relations] the concept of tying wage increases to the cost of living index and thus automatically raising the former when the latter reaches certain levels. 2. n [Wine-tasting] the level at which a particular smell or taste can be perceived; thresholds naturally vary according to the taster. 3. n [Aerospace] the start of the landing area on a runway.

threshold worker 1. n [US] [Industrial relations] an experienced worker who is only on the threshold of gaining any expertise in his job. 2. n [Management] a newly hired worker who has not been previously employed.

thribble v [Theatre, Film, TV] to be vague about one's lines when acting.

thrifts n pl [US] [Finance] the federal savings and loan associations and the savings banks as a group.

throat 1. n [Building, Plastering] the sunken bed or horizontal member of the **drip** section of a cornice. 2. [US] [Education] abbr of **cutthroat** a dedicatedly hard-working student, willing to do anything (to anyone) to gain top marks. 3. n [Glass-making] the submerged channel through which glass passes from the melting end to the working end of the glass furnace. Thus, 'straight throat' is a throat on the same level as the melting end; 'dropped throat' is a throat, the bottom of which lies below the bottom level of the melting end; 'throat cheeks' are the side blocks of the throat passage; 'throat cover' is the blocks forming the roof of the throat. 4. n [TV] the gap left in one wall of a set to permit access to the camera.

throat edge n [Shoe-making] the point where the vamp of a shoe meets the upper.

throttle, at the adv [US] [Railways] in the engineer's seat while the locomotive is running.

Throttlebottom n [US] [Politics] shorthand for an incompetent, laughable Vice President; it comes from the George S. Kaufman/Morrie Ryskind political satire 'Of Thee I Sing' (1931), in which the supremely ludicrous Vice-President was named Alexander Throttlebottom.

through and through n [Logging] a board with edges that still have bark on them.

through the gate 1. adv [US] [Air Force] said of a lift-off which has been successfully achieved. 2. adv [Cricket] to be bowled 'through the gate' is to be bowled by the ball passing through the gap between bat and pad and then hitting the wicket. A batsman thus dismissed has been 'gated'.

through-deck n [Navy] a flight deck that runs the full length of a ship, thus 'through-deck cruiser' is a lightly armed aircraft carrier.

throughput n [Computing] the total amount of work done by a computer in a period of time.

throw 1. n [Film] the distance between a projector and the screen on to which it projects. 2. n [Film] the distance between a light and the area it can illuminate most effectively. 3. n [Mining] the amount of vertical displacement caused by a fault.

throw a colour off v [US] [Painting] to add a number of tints to a basic colour to create a unique shade; thus if repainting is needed, only the original contractor will know how to make up that colour again and so he will have to be rehired.

throw a cop v [Gambling] See **fairbank 1** and **2**.

throw a tree, also **trip a tree** v [Logging] to use wedges to topple over a tree that is being felled.

throw their tongues v [Hunting] hounds do this when they announce the presence of a fox by baying.

throwaway n [Athletics] in pole-vaulting this is the tossing aside of the pole as one clears the bar, so that it does not knock down the bar by its forward momentum.

throw-out n [Book-binding] a leaf, usually bearing some form of illustration, bound in at one edge and designed to fit the book when folded.

throw-outs n pl [US] [Meat trade] animals eliminated from the market due to a variety of defects.

throw-weight n [Military] the total weight of what can be carried by a missile over a particular range. It covers the weight of the 'business end' of a rocket, including armaments and the guidance system that will deliver it on target once the launch vehicle has boosted the missile to the apogee of a ballistic trajectory and all the other stages of the missile have been discarded. In older missiles, the throw-weight was merely the warhead itself; modern **MIRV**ed missiles create a throw-weight that includes all the warheads, the post-boost vehicle (the 'bus'), plus all necessary guidance systems and electronic counter-measures and any other propulsion or penetration aids. Unlike single-warhead missiles, most of this throw-weight neither lands on nor explodes on the target.

thrums n pl [Sailing, Ropework] short pieces of yarn used to protect from chafing.

thrust stage n [Theatre] a stage which has the audience seated on three sides, the thrust being a runway that extends out from the usual front of the stage.

thruster 1. n [Business] an ambitious, go-getting, high-flying executive. See also **sleeper 7**. 2. n [Hunting] an unpopular rider to hounds, whose reckless bravery is outweighed by his obnoxious, over-forceful personality.

thud 1. n [Military] an air crash, especially when the aircraft is shot down by anti-aircraft fire. 2. n [Military] by extension from (1) this is the F–105 Thunderchief fighter, which was very susceptible to North Vietnamese surface-to-air (SAM) missiles.

thumbnail n [UK] [Printing] a portrait measured across 50% of the column width.

thumbsucker 1. n [Journalism] an essay in a newspaper or magazine which ruminates in a leisurely manner on some topic or another; occasionally it is the writer who specialises in such pieces. 2. n [Media] any media pundit who deliberates upon a topic and then delivers a suitably learned opinion. 3. also **backgrounder** n [Politics] press conferences or interviews which are offered to the media by politicians, often of very senior rank, so that detailed information on government plans and attitudes can be revealed. It is always with the proviso that none of the facts can ever be attributed to anyone but 'a senior Whitehall source' and the like.

thunder and lightning n [Angling] a variety of artificial fly.

thunder box 1. n [UK] [Railways] a water closet. 2. also **thunder run, thunder roller** n [Theatre] a box in which iron balls can be rolled up and down as a means of creating artificial 'thunder' during a performance.

tick, also **point** n [Futures market] the minimum alteration – either up or down – of a price.

tick up v [Banking] to make a series of last-report checks, varying as to banks and methods of accounting, to find any possible errors in the bank's trading day.

ticket 1. n [UK] [Police] a search warrant or arrest warrant. 2. n [US] [Politics] a list of candidates for one of the parties. See also **slate 1**. 3. n [US] [Prisons] a disciplinary report which is included in one's **jacket**. 4. n [Stock market] a slip prepared by the buying broker to identify his purchase. This slip is passed to the selling broker either via the Settlement Department or through the **jobbers**; thus 'ticket day' is the second day of the settlement, and the one on which tickets must be passed. See also **name day**.

tickets n pl [Entertainment] a play, music, concert, pop band, film, etc. which has box office potential; eg: 'Rambo has tickets'. See also **legs 1**.

tick-hunter n [Bird-watching] an excitable, ardent bird-watcher, keen to tick off, on a list, every bird he sees. See also **lister, twitcher**.

tickle 1. n [Gambling] a reasonable win. 2. n [UK]

[*Police*] a successful crime – 'a nice little tickle' – or a worthwhile arrest.

tickler *n* [*Navy*] a hand-rolled cigarette.

tickler file *n* [*Computing*] See **suspense file**.

tickling *n* [*Angling*] a method of poaching which involves tickling the fish's belly and then pulling it from the water.

ticks *n pl* [*Dog-breeding*] very small areas of hair that are different in colour from the dog's basic ground colour; they are distributed throughout the coat, usually as dark spots on light/white ground.

tick-tock *n* [*US*] [*Journalism*] a piece that details the chronological background to any major announcement or event.

t.i.d. *Lat. abbr* [*Medicine*] a prescription notation meaning 'three times a day'.

tiddley *a* [*Navy*] smart; thus a 'tiddley suit' is the sailor's best uniform.

tie breaker *n* [*Computing*] a device that resolves the conflict when two CPUs attempt simultaneously to access the same **peripheral**.

tie down 1. *v* [*US*] [*Painting*] to paint over a dirty wall surface with one coat of paint that barely covers it and then immediately cover this with a finishing coat. 2. *v, n* [*US*] [*Gliding*] to park a glider outdoors and to fasten it securely to the ground to prevent potential damage from high winds. Thus 'tie down' is the site where the aircraft is secured; 'tie down line' is the place at an airport where a number of tiedowns are sited; 'tie down flight' is the last flight of the day, before the aircraft is tied down.

tie flies *v* [*Angling*] to make artificial flies.

tie iron *v* [*US*] [*Iron workers*] to join iron bars with wire using any of the prescribed methods.

tie on *v* [*US*] [*Railways*] to connect a locomotive with a number of cars or a train.

tie up 1. *v* [*Boxing*] a boxer does this when he temporarily stops his opponent's assault by holding on to his arms; such obstruction will be stopped by the referee. 2. *v* [*US*] [*Railways*] to complete a run by leaving the locomotive at the roundhouse.

tie-in 1. *n* [*Publishing, Advertising*] two PR or advertising campaigns that are linked by a theme common to both, eg: when a TV programme or film is linked to a line of toys, clothing, etc. 2. *n* [*Oil industry*] a connection between two pipelines or sections of pipeline.

tie-line 1. *n* [*Telephony*] a line that connects two private branch exchanges. 2. *n* [*Oil industry*] a pipeline or transmission line that connects two distribution systems or two parts of the same system.

tie-off *n* [*Mountaineering*] a method of reducing the leverage on a piton, which has not been fully inserted, by tying a short loop of rope to the piton blade, close to the rockface.

tie-up *n* [*Weaving*] the arrangement of ties made between the treadles and the **heddle** shafts.

tiger *n* [*UK*] [*Railways*] a diesel locomotive; it comes allegedly from its 'roar of power'.

tiger country *n* [*Golf*] an area of particularly dense rough.

tiger suit *n* [*Military*] jungle fatigues, supposedly reminiscent of a tiger's stripes.

tiger team *n* [*US*] [*Government*] a team of specialists chosen for their expertise in tackling a particularly difficult problem in their field.

tight back *n* [*Book-binding*] a book cover which is stuck directly on to the spine.

tight day 1. *n* [*Journalism*] a day with an excess of important news and/or advertising, all of which must be squeezed into the paper. 2. *n* [*Journalism*] a day when a lack of advertising means printing a smaller than average paper.

tight paper *n* [*Journalism*] a day on which there is more copy than space available; drastic cutting is inevitable.

tight rate *n* [*Management*] a piecework rate so low that the worker is hard put to earn a living wage.

tight well 1. *n* [*Oil rigs*] a well the existence of which is deliberately withheld from public knowledge. 2. *n* [*Oil rigs*] a well which has caved in and buried the drilling tools. See also **snakes**.

TIHNYTO *phr* [*TV*] acro **Things I Have Not Yet Thought Of** the final item on a budget proposal; it is more formally known as 'contingencies.'

tilt 1. *n* [*Film*] the upwards or downwards movement of the camera. 2. *n* [*UK*] [*Road transport*] a lorry or trailer with an open body covered by canvas sides and top, usually supported by metal or wooden stays which can be removed for ease of loading.

timber beast *n* [*Logging*] a logger.

time *n* [*Merchant navy*] the period of apprenticeship served in the merchant navy by a cadet officer.

time bargain *n* [*Stock market*] an agreement to contract business at a given time.

time bomb *n* [*Computing*] a program 'hidden' within a computer's existing memory; at a specific time this program will be executed, either **crashing** the whole computer or erasing important files and in either case subsequently deleting itself to prevent any detection. See also **Trojan Horse**.

time deposit *n* [*US*] [*Banking*] a sum which is deposited in a bank on interest and which may not be withdrawn prior to a pre-set maturity date.

time dilation *n* [*Science*] the apparent slowing down of the passage of time in a frame of reference that is moving relative to the observer.

time equals minus infinity *n* [*Computing*] a **hacker's** term meaning as long ago as anyone can remember.

time frame *n* [*Business*] a fake technicality borrowed from science by businessmen who simply mean 'length of time'.

time line *n* [*Aerospace*] the duration of a flight.

time off the cuff *n* [*Industrial relations*] the recording by piece workers of a greater time spent on one job than was actually worked, in order to accumulate some extra time in which to tackle a harder job which they could not so easily accomplish within the allotted hours.

time out *n* [*Computing*] a time interval that allows certain operations to take place.

time preference *n* [*Economics*] a preference for present as opposed to future consumption.

time sensitive target *n* [*Military*] a target that remains vulnerable only if it can be destroyed before it can leave the ground, eg: aircraft and missiles.

time sharing *n* [*Computing*] the simultaneous use of the same computer by two operators, each of whom works from his/her own remote terminal. The machine actually works by shuttling between the two jobs, but its speed is so great that as far as the two operators are concerned, they are effectively working at the same time.

time slice *n* [*Computing*] a predefined period of time, the quantum, which is allocated to a specific task in a time-shared system. All tasks receive slices in rotation until they are completed, thus ensuring that all users have a fair share of the machine. See also **time sharing**.

time urgent target *n* [*Military*] See **time sensitive target**.

timelength *n* [*Advertising*] the length of a radio or television commercial spot.

time-of-day *n* [*US*] [*Utilities*] a proposed price structure for US electricity; charges vary according to the time of day the electricity is consumed: the greater the overall demand, the more the electricity costs the consumer. See also **peak pricing**.

time-sampling *n* [*Statistics*] the collection of data or observations at certain times, or at intervals within certain periods of time.

time-slip *v* [*US*] [*Railways*] to claim a day's pay by reporting a rule infraction; it is usually because of some infringement of job demarcation.

timespan of discretion *n* [*Management*] the maximum time for which the holder of a specified job would normally work on a task without being reviewed or checked by his superiors.

t.i.n. *Lat. abbr* [*Medicine*] a prescription notation meaning 'three times a night'.

tin 1. *n* [*Weaving*] stannous chloride, a **mordant**. **2.** *n* [*Squash*] the strip of metal fitted along the bottom of the front wall of the court, which resounds when the ball hits it, thus ensuring that the players know that it is out of play.

tin beard *n* [*Theatre*] a badly adjusted and made up crêpe hair beard.

tin can *n* [*US*] [*Navy*] a destroyer.

tin, on the *adv* [*US*] [*Police*] using one's 'tin' – the official badge – to gain free admission, meals and other favours.

tin pants *n pl* [*Logging*] heavy trousers which loggers use in the rainy season; they are often coated with paraffin to increase resistance to rain.

tin soldier *n* [*Sex*] a voyeuristic male, often from the professional middle classes, who has no interest in active sex for himself, but who enjoys volunteering to act as a prostitute's 'slave' (if masochistic) or companion.

tincture *n* [*Heraldry*] one of the colours used in heraldry; it is divided into metals, colours and furs.

tinfish *n* [*Navy*] See **kipper 3**.

tingalairy, also **wimbler** *n* [*UK*] [*Railways*] a hand-operated auger; it originated in the Western Region.

tins *n pl* [*Cricket*] the rectangular metal pieces, each bearing a single number, which are used on manually operated scoreboards in small grounds.

Tins, the *n pl* [*UK*] [*Military*] a nickname for the Household Cavalry; it comes from their cuirasses.

tip *n* [*Military*] the warhead, whether nuclear or conventional, of a ballistic missile.

tip in *v* [*Book-binding*] to attach a single leaf of a book, usually an illustration, to the neighbouring leaf, using a thin line of paste.

tip roll *n* [*US*] [*Skiing*] a stunt which is the equivalent to turning a cartwheel; the skier pivots on the poles and the ski tips.

tipper *n* [*UK*] [*Railways*] a relay, controlling a set of points. This is defined by the letters TIPR. See also **ulcer 1, whizzer 2**.

tipple *n* [*US*] [*Coal-mining*] a building in which coal undergoes sorting, screening, crushing and similar processing.

tippler *n* [*Coal-mining*] a machine that tips coal wagons and tubs.

tippy wool *n* [*Weaving*] an industrial term for brittle, dry fibres in a wool fleece.

tiptop *n* [*Angling*] a line guide on a fishing rod.

tissue *n* [*Horse-racing*] a racing form used by bookmakers and other racing professionals.

tissue committee *n* [*US*] [*Medicine*] a hospital committee that evaluates all surgical operations performed at the hospital on the basis of agreement between the pre-operative, post-operative and pathological diagnoses, and on the acceptance of the procedures used to reach such diagnoses; thus 'tissue review' is the report of this committee.

tit *n* [*TV*] any button on any machine used in the studio or control box.

tit shooters *n pl* [*Shooting*] novice and incompetent shooters; it was orginally coined in Col. Peter Hawker's 'Instructions to Young Shooters' (19th cent.) and comes either from the small bird or from the shooters being, as it were, barely weaned. See also **foreshore cowboys**.

Titanic-clause *n* [*Law*] a clause that may be inserted in a will, that deals with the possible situation in which (as happened to many of those who died when the SS Titanic sank in 1912) both the testator and his/her spouse die in the same disaster.

tite *a* [*TV*] abbr of **tight** it is used on shooting scripts.

tizzy, also **tizzy-snatcher** *n* [*Navy*] an assistant paymaster; it comes from Cockney slang 'tizzy' meaning 'sixpence'.

TKVO, also **TKO, K/O** *v* [*US*] [*Medicine*] abbr of **to keep vein open**.

tlc *n* [*Medicine*] abbr See **tender loving care**.

TLU *n* [*Computing*] abbr of **table look-up** a method of searching for an unknown quantity by looking first for a related known quality in a table. See also **hashing**.

TO 1. *v* [*US*] [*Car salesmen*] abbr of to **turn over** a customer from one salesman to another. 2. *n* [*US*] [*Shoe trade*] abbr of **Turn Over** a difficult customer who is to be turned over to another clerk who may have better luck. 3. also **PO** *n* [*US*] [*Medicine*] abbr of **telephone** or **'phone order** delivered over the telephone by a physician. See also **VO 1**.

TO man *n* [*US*] [*Car salesmen*] a good **closer**.

toad 1. *n* [*US*] [*Car salesmen*] See **buck**. 2. [*Medicine*] abbr of **trashy old derelict** a derogatory nickname for a patient, especially a tramp. See also **GOMER, shpos**.

toasting *n* [*Music*] the practice of West Indian disc jockeys who add their own lyrics, often witty and/or relevant to current affairs, to a background of the bass line of a reggae song that can also be found with its own, different, set of lyrics; thus a 'toaster' is the disc jockey who performs this style. See also **scratching 2**.

toasting fork *n* [*UK*] [*Railways*] a tool for isolating the engines from the transmission of a diesel car; it is so called from the shape.

tober *n* [*UK*] [*Circus*] the circus field, in which the big top is erected; it comes from Romany 'tober' meaning 'road'.

tobogganning *n* [*Military*] a manoeuvre to facilitate the mid-air refuelling of military aircraft from tankers; to compensate for the difference between the speeds of the two aircraft both must dive from 20,000ft to 10,000ft to increase their joint velocity.

Toby *n* [*US*] [*Theatre*] a stock comic character, the boisterous, blundering yokel type; thus 'Toby play' is a show revolving around such a character.

toby 1. *n* [*UK*] [*Police*] a police division. See also **manor, patch**. 2. *n* [*Angling*] a type of lure used in spinning.

toe in, toe out *adv* [*Cars*] 'toe in' means a very slight inclination of the front wheels towards each other, if viewed from above; 'toe out' means the opposite. Both are used to counteract the tendency in certain drives for the wheels to splay outwards or inwards.

toe rake *n* [*Skating*] a set of teeth set at the front of the blade of a skate.

toeboard *n* [*Building, Plastering*] a protective board fitted around the perimeter of a scaffolding work platform to prevent tools or materials from accidentally falling off.

toehold purchase *n* [*Business*] the initial purchase of anything less than 5% of the shares of a target company in a takeover bid – this can be carried out without any formal statement. Once the 5% total has been reached the buyer must inform the Securities and Exchange Commission, the appropriate stock exchange and the target company of its intentions.

toe-hole *n* [*Mining*] a horizontal or upwards-angled shothole placed at the foot of a quarry face.

toenail *v* [*Logging*] to drive in a nail at an angle.

toe-rag *n* [*UK*] [*Market-traders*] rubbish, trash, unsaleable goods.

TOEs *n pl* [*Science*] abbr of **Theories Of Everything** a development of grand universal theories, which will account, if particle physicists are successful in their current researches, for all known forces. See also **GUTs**.

together *adv* [*New therapies*] in a state of calmness, efficiency, self-awareness, mental and emotional stability.

toggle *n* [*Electronics*] any device that has two stable states, eg: a switch.

toggling *n* [*Tanning*] the tying together of hides or skins to facilitate moving them from process to process in the tannery.

toil and doil *n* [*UK*] [*TV*] acro **Time Off in Lieu, Days Off in Lieu** a system whereby instead of taking overtime payments for working extra hours, employees can choose to take off extra days or hours in compensation, depending on how much time they are owed.

token *n* [*Linguistics*] in semiotics this is a particular and individual sign; it is the opposite of **type**.

token economy *n* [*Psychiatry*] a system of treating behavioural disorders in which rewards, in the form of tokens – exchangeable for goods or privileges – can either be issued for good behaviour or withheld as a punishment for deviant activities.

token estimate *n* [*UK*] [*Government*] a provisional statement of a sum of money that is placed before Parliament in order to permit discussion to proceed.

token vote *n* [*UK*] [*Government*] a vote of money that is based on a **token estimate**.

tokenism *n* [*Sociology*] the use by governments, the media, business and many other areas of essentially white, male society, of a few blacks, women, members of minority or handicapped groups for cosmetic 'token' purposes; such variations on the 'visible negro' pander to a growing agitation, but do little or nothing to alter the continuing realities of the status quo.

tole *n* [*Military*] used in the French Foreign Legion to mean the regimental prison.

tolkach *n* [*Government*] the unofficial but fully acknowledged system of 'string-pulling' and short

T

cuts that every Russian attempts to manipulate in order to accelerate or even bypass Soviet bureaucracy.

tom 1. *n* [*UK*] [*Police*] this comes from rhyming slang 'tom foolery' meaning 'jewelry'. 2. *n* [*UK*] [*Sex, Police*] a prostitute. When street prostitution was still legal in London, the girls were divided into 'toms', high-class prostitutes who worked in Mayfair, and 'edies', rougher girls who worked the East End, the railway stations and 'the Baze' (Bayswater Road).

Tom Collins *n* [*Navy*] no choice at all; Collins was supposedly an 18th century 'Captain of the Heads (Latrines)'.

tom patrol *n* [*UK*] [*Police*] a special patrol that formerly existed to arrest street prostitutes. See also **pussy posse**.

Tom Swifties *n* [*Logology*] sentences in which the aim is to make a pun on an adverb or adverbial phrase; thus ' "I work at the quarry," said Tom stonily'. The vogue for stickers declaring 'Runners do it speedily' etc. stems from this game. The term was coined by Edward Stratmeyer around 1920 in a series of books featuring a character, Tom Swift, who used such sentences.

tomahawk 1. *n* [*US*] [*Carpenters*] See **knocker** 3. 2. *n* [*US*] [*Painting*] a brush shaped like a hatchet which is used to reach difficult places.

tombstone 1. *n* [*Commerce*] a list of underwriters advertised as acting in connection with a new share issue; this list, when in print, makes a solid block of type which may be seen to resemble a tombstone. 2. *n* [*US*] [*Journalism*] two boldface headlines (in large black type) positioned next to each other on the page.

tombstone ads *n pl* [*Business*] any advertisement placed in a print medium for the purposes of fulfilling contractual obligations rather than attempting to sell a product; eg: many grocery manufacturers offers discounts to retailers who will run such an advertisement, which is usually no more than the retailer's name and address, plus a list of product names.

tommy *n* [*UK*] [*Railways*] a small shunting disc ground signal.

ton 1. *n* [*Antiques*] one hundred pounds sterling. 2. *n* [*Cricket*] the score of 100 runs. 3. *n* [*US*] [*Finance*] $100,000,000.

tone language *n* [*Linguistics*] a language which uses variations in pitch as well as different consonants and vowels to distinguish the meanings of words; eg: Chinese.

tone on tone *a* [*Textiles*] referring to designs that are composed of toning rather than contrasting shades of colour.

tone track *n* [*Film*] a recording of random background noise that is used to provide the right atmosphere for a film. See also **room tone**.

tongs *n pl* [*Oil rigs*] hydraulically operated grabs that are used to hold sections of pipe during screwing or unscrewing operations.

tongue 1. *n* [*Glass-making*] a dividing wall between the air and gas uptakes in tank furnace ports. 2. *n* [*Glass-making*] a dividing wall at the base of a chimney stack.

tool *n* [*Oil rigs*] any piece of equipment which is not plant or the rig itself.

tool-dresser *n* [*Oil rigs*] See **roustabout**.

toolie *n* [*Oil rigs*] See **roustabout**.

toolpusher *n* [*Oil rigs*] the supervisor in charge of the drilling rig and ancillary equipment.

tools *n pl* [*Industrial relations*] normal work as an engineering craftsman, as opposed to office work on the local or national union executive; thus to 'go back to the tools' is to return to a job after leaving such a post, or losing an election to obtain one.

tooth *n* [*Painting*] dry paint that has a relatively coarse pigment and which therefore provides a good 'grip' for the next coat that is painted over it.

tooth carpenter *n* [*US*] [*Medicine*] a dentist.

toothy *n* [*Navy*] the ship's dentist.

top 1. *v* [*Logging*] to remove the upper portion of a standing tree with a power saw. 2. *n* [*Journalism*] See **spread** 8. 3. *n* [*Sailing, Ropework*] a ropemaking tool, with grooves for the strands, which **lays** the rope after the strands have been twisted. 4. *n* [*Weaving*] a continuous coil of combed fibres in the commercial preparation of wool or hair for spinning. 5. *n* [*Sport*] abbr of **top of the innings** the start of a team's innings at bat in cricket or baseball. 6. *n* [*TV*] the most important story of a news programme. 7. *n* [*Cards*] in bridge this is either of the two highest cards in a suit. 8. *n* [*Cards*] the best score made in the play of a particular hand. 9. *n* [*US*] [*Military*] abbr of **top sergeant**.

top and tail 1. *n* [*Advertising, Business*] in business theatre, when the same presentation is being made at a variety of venues, the speaker and the crew acclimatise themselves to each new stage, lighting rig, etc. by an abbreviated 'top and tail' rehearsal in which the basic elements of the presentation are checked over, while missing out the bulk of the programme. 2. *n* [*Rugby*] an illegal and dangerous tackle whereby one opponent grabs a player's knees from one angle, while another gets the chest from a different angle and together they corkscrew their victim on to the ground. See also **crashback**. 3. *v* [*UK*] [*Radio*] to prepare a tape for transmission by fixing green and red leaders respectively to the start and finish of the tape.

top banana *n* [*Entertainment*] the comedian in a burlesque show who gets the top billing.

top board *n* [*Chess*] the leading player of a team competing in a tournament.

top cutter *n* [*US*] [*Military*] top sergeant.

top hand *n* [*US*] [*Cattlemen*] a cowboy who is also a first-rate ranch-hand.

top hat *n* [*UK*] [*Police*] a regulation police helmet.

top hat pensions *n pl* [*Industrial relations*] special pension plans offered to retiring senior management that feature extremely large annual payments, usually linked to the cost of living, plus a lump sum 'golden handshake' payment at the time of the actual retirement. See also **cloth cap pensions**.

top man **1.** *n* [*Glass-making*] a worker in a glass producing plant who attends to poking and charging with coal. **2.** *n* [*UK*] [*Market-traders*] a mock-auctioneer. **3.** also **breaker** *n* [*Building*] in demolition gangs this is the man who stands on top of the wall and smashes down the courses of bricks.

top of the line *n* [*Commerce*] the brand leader, a position gained either through cost, efficiency, sales appeal or any other outstanding characteristic.

top on *adv* [*Cricket*] said of a ball which has a heavy topspin applied.

top out **1.** *v* [*Stock market*] a share is reckoned to have done this when it has reached a high, stable price at which level it may well remain for some time. **2.** *v* [*US*] [*Cattlemen*] to begin breaking a horse; some of the fight is taken out of the animal, but it is not yet fully broken.

top plate *n* [*US*] [*Carpenters*] a heavy beam at the top of a house frame to which the rafters are attached.

top quark *n* [*Science*] a quark that may have a mass thirteen times that of the proton. See also **quark**.

top shot *n* [*TV, Film, Video*] a camera shot that is taken from overhead.

top soldier *n* [*US*] [*Military*] top sergeant.

top speed *n* [*Cars*] the average speed of two runs in opposite directions, so that wind and gradient cancel each other out; it is not simply the fastest a car can go on a downhill slope with a following wind.

top up for Mum and Dad *v* [*Air travel*] to take on extra fuel when flying to an airport that is known to present various problems in landing and take-off. Thus the crew ensure that there is enough reserve fuel for them to take the plane, if necessary, to an alternative safe destination.

topcast *v* [*Entertainment*] to cast the lead role in a production.

top-cut *n* [*Audio*] the reduction of treble or high frequencies.

top-down development, also **top-down method** *n* [*Computing*] a method of designing a system or computer program starting with a simple structure, then refining each component as required until the whole complex, detailed structure has been achieved. See also **bottom-up method**.

top-dyeing *n* [*Weaving*] dyeing a colour over already-dyed wool.

top-hat pension *n* [*Insurance*] an endowment policy taken out by a firm on the life of an excep-tionally valuable employee that will give him an extra pension on retirement.

topic *n* [*Stock market*] acro **Teletext Output of Price Information** the Stock Exchange viewdata price distribution service.

topic A *n* [*US*] [*Journalism, Politics*] the major topic of current interest in the media on a given day or over a given period; it is of paramount importance that a politician should acquaint him/herself with every available detail on this topic.

topical *n* [*Philately*] the American term for a collection based on a single, if wide-ranging, pictorial theme. See also **thematics**.

topless radio *n* [*Radio*] radio programmes in which listeners are invited to call in and chat about their personal sexual proclivities and problems to a studio host and one or two experts – sex therapists, doctors, newspaper advice columnists, etc.

topline **1.** *n* [*Dog breeding*] the dog's entire upper profile starting at the ears and ending at the tail. **2.** *v* [*Entertainment*] to star in a show; it comes from one's position on the bill or in the programme.

topper **1.** *n* [*Business*] in a company, especially an entertainment one, this is the chief executive. **2.** *n* [*US*] [*Military*] top sergeant.

toppy *a* [*Stock market*] in money-trading this refers to a market that is high and unstable.

tops and bottoms *n pl* [*Aus.*] [*Navy*] a derogatory Australian term for sailors in the Royal Navy who allegedly never washed more than their faces and feet.

topside **1.** *n* [*Clothing*] the front section of trousers, extending from the trousers bottom to the waistband, and between the inside and outside seams. **2.** *n* [*Oil rigs*] any place that is above the ground or ground level; it now mainly refers to the parts of an offshore rig that stand above the water. **3.** *n* [*Meteorology*] that part of the ionosphere above the height at which there is the greatest concentration of free electrons, approximately 300 km.

topsides *n* [*Navy*] above the waterline of a ship.

top-slicing **1.** *n* [*Economics*] the tax payable on unit-linked single-premium bonds when such bonds are converted into cash. **2.** *n* [*Economics*] a method of assessing income tax or surtax chargeable on a lump sum by averaging it out over the years during which it has built up and then taxing it accordingly on a per annum basis. **3.** *n* [*Mining*] a method of working in which slices of ore 12in thick are mined from the top of the ore body, working downwards.

topspin **1.** *n* [*Film*] a film that has bite, meaning, effectiveness, edge; in tennis the topspin shot 'bites' into the surface of the court. **2.** *n* [*Journalism*] 'the artificial additive and colouring newspapers employ to make a story appetising'; such colouring often stretches or even invents

T

facts, embellishes and manufactures quotes and generally has little bearing on the simple truth. **3.** *n* [*TV*] the aspect of a show that maintains the audience's interest from one scene to the next.

topstain *n* [*Printing*] the colour applied to the top edges of the pages.

top-table theory *n* [*Politics*] the belief that only by maintaining a nuclear arsenal can the UK justify its increasingly parlous position as a great power. Otherwise France, the actual dominant military force in Europe, would oust her.

torista *n* [*Bullfighting*] a bullfighting enthusiast who is more interested in the performance of the bull than of the torero who kills it.

tormentor *n* [*US*] [*Theatre*] one of a pair of narrow curtains or **flats** placed just behind the **teaser** and used to frame the sides of the inner proscenium opening and to mark off-stage space at the sides.

torpedo *n* [*US*] [*Railways*] an explosive device fastened to the rail which can warn an approaching train to reduce speed.

torps *n* [*Navy*] the Torpedo Officer.

tort *n* [*Law*] a wrongful act committed against an individual or a private organisation; it is the opposite of crime which is a wrongful act committed against society as a whole.

tortillon *n* [*Art*] a small **stomp** about the size of a pencil.

torus *n* [*Building, Plastering*] a moulding section: a half-circle on a flat base.

tosher *n* [*UK*] [*Market-traders*] a market stall; the site for a stall or a stall-holder's caravan; the rent for the stall or site.

total institution *n* [*Sociology*] any place of residence where individuals are cut off from society for a considerable period of time and together lead a monastic, enclosed and formally administered life; eg: prison, mental hospital, monastery, boarding school, etc.

total theatre 1. *n* [*Theatre*] theatre that aims to extract total involvement from both its performers and its audience. **2.** *n* [*Theatre*] theatre that draws upon the widest possible range of techniques and styles to create a required dramatic effect.

Tottenham pudding *n* [*UK*] [*Agriculture*] a mixture of sterilised kitchen waste used for poultry or pig feed.

touch 1. *v* [*Angling*] to feel a fish for an instant on the hook. **2.** *v* [*Hunting*] to blow the horn.

touch base with *v* [*Film*] to make a phone call to someone.

touch signature *n* [*US*] [*Banking*] the fingerprinting check that is made on customers who wish to cash travellers' cheques in America, but who are not presenting a passport as proof of identification.

touche *n* [*Furriers*] the process of eliminating defects, especially bald or pale spots on the pelt,

by touching them up with powders and dyes; it comes from Fr. 'toucher' meaning 'to touch'.

touch-up time *n* [*TV*] the final adjustments to an actor's make-up prior to an actual **take**.

tough 1. *a* [*US*] [*Farming*] said of crops that are tough and hard to pick. **2.** *a* [*Wine-tasting*] used to describe a **full-bodied** wine of overpowering immaturity and an excess of **tannin**; it may well turn out excellent in due course.

tough pitch *n* [*Metallurgy*] commercially pure copper in which the amount of cuprous oxide has been reduced to a point where maximum brittleness is achieved.

tourist guide *n* [*New therapies*] in a **psychodrama** group, this is the therapist or expert who leads the group.

tout *n* [*Politics*] a term used in the Irish Republican Army (IRA) for an informer.

toutery *n* [*Film*] a public relations and/or publicity firm.

tow *n* [*Industry*] a bundle of twisted fibres, either natural or man-made, that is used in both textiles and electronics.

tow cards *n pl* [*Weaving*] hand **cards** used for preparing heavier fibres – jute, flax or hemp – and thus using heavier wire in the brushes.

tow truck *n* [*Medicine*] a special lift used to move a non-ambulatory patient out of bed.

tower 1. *n* [*US*] [*Railways*] the signal box. **2.** *v* [*Shooting*] said of a bird which soars almost perpendicularly after being shot; it then plummets vertically downwards and is usually found lying on its back. Towering occurs when birds – shot in the throat, windpipe or lung – suffer a haemorrhage.

towerman *n* [*US*] [*Painting*] a painter who prefers to work on high buildings or steel structures.

town clearing *n* [*Banking*] the clearing within the same day of cheques in excess of £10,000 that are drawn on or paid into banks within 'Town' – the City of London; such cheques do not need to be sent to the Central Clearing House. Town Clearing has been largely replaced since 1983 by **CHAPS**.

toy boy *n* [*Sex*] a junior gigolo who is taken as a lover by an older woman. He is invariably attractive; she is, at least, rich.

toys *n pl* [*Sex*] the accoutrements of sado-masochistic games: whips, chains, leather, plastic or rubber clothing, gags, spurs, high boots, uniforms, etc.

TPR *n* [*Medicine*] abbr of **Temperature, Pulse, Respiration** the three **vital signs** exhibited by a patient and for which a nurse or doctor must always check.

trace 1. *n* [*Electronics*] the luminous line or pattern that appears on the screen of a cathode-ray tube. **2.** *n* [*Mathematics*] the sum of the elements in the principal diagonal of a matrix.

tracing *n* [*Audio*] the accuracy with which the

pick-up is capable of following the geometry of recorded modulations.

track 1. *n* [*Cars*] the distance between the wheels of a car, measured laterally. **2.** *n* [*Computing*] the channel of a **floppy disk** on which data is stored. **3.** *n* [*Cricket*] the actual wicket along which the bowler bowls, 22 yards in length; thus one can have a 'fast track' or a 'slow track'. **4.** *n* [*Aerospace*] the line on a map that represents an aircraft's path between take-off and destination. **5.** *n* [*Aerospace*] the plane in which the blades of a correctly-operating propeller will rotate.

track system *n* [*Management*] a method of escalating payments for professional employees. A salary is set, by comparison with rates paid in peer organisations, for the senior jobs. It is assumed that an executive will gradually find promotion within the firm. To match this his salary is increased at regular intervals that should parallel his climb through the executive ranks.

track, up the *n* [*UK*] [*Road transport*] a journey down a regular trunk route. See also **road, up the**.

trackability *n* [*Audio*] the ability with which a pickup can track recorded material of high amplitude and velocity; the lower the playing weight on the pickup required, the greater the trackability.

tracking 1. *n* [*Audio*] the ability with which the pickup follows the movements – caused by the rotation of the turntable – of the recorded modulations. **2.** *n* [*Cars*] misalignment of the front wheels of a car, or unsymmetrical **toe-in** or **toe-out**; these cause uneven tyre wear and a tendency to wander off to one side.

tracking shot *n* [*Film*] any shot in which the camera moves backwards or forwards, following the action; these shots can be handheld, but the camera is usually mounted on specially rigged tracks.

trade 1. *n* [*Horse-racing*] the professional backers of horses, rather than **punters**. **2.** *n* [*Navy*] a somewhat derogatory, snobbish term for submariners that was used, in imitation of the upper-class disdain for tradesmen, by officers on surface shipping; it has largely been discarded since World War II. **3.** [*Espionage*] the British Secret Service.

trade binding *n* [*Publishing*] the normal binding in which a publisher issues the book for public sale, rather than special bindings for libraries, collectors, etc.

trade down *v* [*Commerce*] a firm does this when it introduces a range of commodities that aim at a lower segment of the market than had hitherto been considered.

trade paperback *n* [*Publishing*] a large format paperback, often a facsimile of the hardback edition, but in soft covers and selling at an intermediate price between the usual hardback and paperback ranges.

trade setting *n* [*Advertising*] the typesetting of advertising copy by a professional firm, which produces high-quality material and then sends it to the relevant newspaper or periodical for which the advertisement is scheduled.

tradeable *a* [*Antiques*] said of an item which can be sold within the trade, to a fellow dealer.

tradecraft *n* [*Espionage*] the various skills involved in the intelligence and counter-intelligence professions.

trade-off *n* [*Business*] a method of assessing the best alternative ways of achieving an objective.

trades *n pl* [*Film, Record business*] the trade papers: Variety, the Stage, Cashbox, Billboard, etc.

trading post *n* [*Stock market*] a post or position on the floor of an exchange where the stocks assigned to that location are traded.

traffic analysis *n* [*Cryptography*] a method of obtaining information by the systematic analysis of patterns of communication rather than by actually deciphering the information itself.

traffic builder *n* [*Marketing*] any in-store promotion – usually in a supermarket or other self-service shop – that is designed to stimulate the traffic of customers through the store.

traffic control *n* [*Computing*] the control of input and output in the hardware and software operations of a computer to achieve an orderly and accurate system.

trafficability *n* [*Military*] the extent to which a particular terrain will bear military traffic, and the type of traffic which it will bear.

traffic-cast *n, v* [*US*] [*Traffic controllers*] a broadcast detailing the current state of traffic flow/congestion; thus a 'traffic-caster' is the radio/TV reporter responsible for such reports.

trail 1. *v* [*Radio*] to advertise the future attractions of the station. **2.** *v* [*Bowls*] to use one's shot to force the jack further up the field.

trail hog *n* [*US*] [*Skiing*] a skier who takes up all the space on a narrow trail.

trail printer *n* [*Printing*] in word processing this is a printer that is shared between a number of work stations.

trailer *n* [*Lacrosse*] the player backing up the ball player as she advances through the midfield towards the goal and who is available to receive a pass if required.

train bombing *n* [*Military*] bombs dropped in a sequence, punctuated by short, regular intervals.

train smash *n* [*Merchant navy*] canned tomatoes.

train spot *n* [*Advertising*] an advertisement on a card which is displayed in a British Rail train. See also **car card 2**.

train-in *v* [*US*] [*Marine Corps*] to end a drill or exercise.

trainman *n* [*US*] [*Railways*] a member of the train crew whose duties do not involve the engine: the brakeman, switchman and conductor. See also **engineman**.

trainwreck *n* [*US*] [*Medicine*] a patient who is very ill, is suffering from several problems simultaneously and is comatose.

Trakehner *n* [*Horse-riding*] in cross-country eventing this is a fence comprising a ditch spanned by rails in the centre; it comes from the name of the Trakehnen stud in Germany.

tram *n* [*S. Wales*] [*Coal-mining*] one truck of the underground train that conveys miners and materials.

trammer *n* [*Coal-mining*] a person who moves tubs of coal from the face to a gathering point convenient for the underground haulage tracks.

tramp **1.** *n* [*Cars*] a condition where the driven wheels tramp up and down under wheelspin. **2.** *v* [*UK*] [*Road transport*] to transport goods to a variety of destinations which differ according to the load; the irregularity of such routes is not popular among drivers.

tramp's lagging *n* [*UK*] [*Prisons*] a sentence of two weeks.

tranche **1.** *n* [*Finance*] an instalment of a loan. **2.** *n* [*Finance*] a block of bonds or government stock.

transaction **1.** *n* [*Computing*] any event that requires a record to be generated within the computer's system. **2.** *n* [*Management*] See **arms length bargain**. See also **arms length price**. **3.** *n* [*New therapies*] in transactional analysis (**TA**) this is an exchange of **strokes**, ie: the fulfilment of 'stimulus hunger', eg: applause given to an actor.

transfer *n* [*Politics*] a device whereby a propagandist carries over the authority, prestige and sanction of something that is already respected, and implies that it belongs equally to something that he wishes to become similarly respected. Thus national flags become tangible symbols of the nation, and their mistreatment can arouse hostility.

transfer to the ECU *v* [*Medicine*] to die, ie: to transfer to the 'External Care Unit'.

transfer to the Nth + 1 floor *v* [*Medicine*] to die; 'N' denotes the top floor of the hospital. See also **transfer to the ECU**.

transference *n* (*Psychoanalysis*) the emotional relationship of the patient to his/her analyst. From 'Übertragung', coined by Freud in 1895, it denotes the transfer to the patient of powerful but long forgotten emotions (often from childhood) which had originally been directed at some other person or thing, and since repressed.

transformation *n* [*New therapies*] in **est**, this is the actual experience of undergoing est as a therapy.

transhumance *n* [*Agriculture*] the seasonal movement of livestock between summer and winter feeding grounds.

transience *n* [*Audio*] sudden changes of state occurring in sound, eg: plucked strings, beaten drums, etc.

transire *n* [*Shipping*] a customs document which permits a coasting ship to move from port to port in the same country.

transition *v* [*Business, Technology*] to change, to move from one mode or activity to another.

transitivism *n* [*Psychiatry*] a mental state in which the patient attributes his own feelings or experiences to others.

translator *n* [*Computing*] a program which converts a program written in one language into another. See also **compiler**.

translocation *n* [*Naturalists*] the moving of an apparently threatened species of wild animal to a new and hopefully more secure home.

transom, over the *adv* [*Publishing*] a book that comes into a publisher's office 'over the transom' is an unsolicited manuscript.

transparency *n* [*Business*] the inability to assess whether or not a particular company is being subsidised.

transparency of information *n* [*Government*] a phrase used by Common Market (EC) bureaucrats; it refers to the clear labelling of commodities.

transparent **1.** *a* [*Computing*] used to describe a process or procedure which is invoked by a user without him/her being aware of its existence. See also **virtual**. **2.** *a* [*Communications*] said of a network or facility that allows signals to pass through it unchanged. **3.** *a* [*Audio*] said of reproduced sound that is clear and has no distortions, and offers each element distinctly and separately. **4.** *a* [*Linguistics*] referring to a word or sentence that is obvious in structure and meaning, or to a phonological rule which can be extrapolated from every occurrence of a linguistic phenomenon.

transponder *n* [*Satellite TV*] the system on board a satellite that receives the signal broadcasts from the earth and rebroadcasts them back to earth.

transportation car *n* [*Motor trade*] a car that simply takes one from A to B, offering no special gimmicks, frills or any other sales allure beyond that basic usefulness.

transputer *n* [*Computing*] this comes from 'transistor' plus 'computer'; it is a 'computer on a chip', ie. a single microchip on which are incorporated all the functions of an entire microprocessor, including the memory. The potential of this miniaturisation is to multiply to a vast extent the power of the machine in which such chips are installed.

trans-SIOP *adv* [*Military*] during the performance of the Single Integrated Operational Plan (**SIOP**), ie: during a nuclear war.

transtage *n* [*Aerospace*] the final stage of a multi-stage rocket that can be restarted in order to make changes in the orbit or the flight path.

trap **1.** *n* [*Geology, Oil industry*] an underground rock formation in which deposits of oil or gas are found. **2.** *n* [*Audio*] a circuit used to block or divert signals of a specific frequency, and especially to reduce interference in a receiver tuned to a nearby frequency. **3.** *n* [*Computing*] See **interrupt**. **4.** *n* [*US*] [*Football*] a rushing play using the strategy to create an opening in the opposition defence; an opposition player is allowed to penetrate the offensive formation, he is then blocked sideways and the gap this leaves is exploited by the ball-carrier.

trap door *n* [*Computing*] a means of entering a system by using the identity and password of a legitimate user and then accessing, altering or even destroying, files. Once within the system, the illegal user can create a new and de facto legitimate identity which can be used for infinite entries into the system in the future.

trap-door *n* [*Espionage*] a clue, usually based on the discovery of secret information, that enables cryptographers to break an otherwise highly complex code.

trapeze *n* [*Sailing*] in dinghies this is a sliding support used by the crew for outboard balancing when they lay up to windward.

trash 1. *v* [*UK*] [*Market-traders*] to frighten, to terrify. See also **trasher**. **2.** *n* [*Tobacco*] leaves of the tobacco plant immediately above the lowest, bottom leaves.

trasher *n* [*UK*] [*Market-traders*] any form of thriller – film, TV, paperback. See also **trash**.

trauma truck *n* [*US*] [*Medicine*] an ambulance.

travaux préparatoires *n pl* [*Diplomacy*] this comes from Fr. for preparatory works; it means the preliminary discussions and the allied paperwork, drafting, etc. that precede the formulation and signing of an international agreement or treaty, or domestic legislation.

travel 1. *v* [*Theatre*] to convey costumes, props, etc from one place to another. **2.** *v* [*Publishing*] when a sales representative takes books from one place, presumably a bookshop, to another in order to promote and sell them.

travelled blood *n* [*Medicine*] blood that has spurted from a severed artery.

traveller 1. *n* [*Textiles*] a reciprocating arm on a winding machine that distributes thread evenly along a spool. **2.** *n* [*Theatre, TV*] a curtain that runs along a sliding track. **3.** *n* [*Industry*] a craftsman's tool that is used for measuring circumferences, especially the circumference of wheels.

travelling road *n* [*Coal-mining*] a roadway along which miners travel to and from their working places.

travelling roadblock *n* [*US*] [*Road transport*] See **peanut wagon**.

travelling salesman *n* [*Sex*] a **hustler** who obtains his clients by posing as a hitch-hiker, albeit without luggage or a real destination

travelling salesman problem *n* [*Mathematics*] based on the perambulations of a salesman, this is a problem that seeks to determine the shortest route which will pass once only

through each of a series of points and then return to its starting point.

travisher *n* [*Carpenters*] a carpenter's shaver which is used to finish off the smoothing of chair seats.

tray 1. *n* [*Road transport*] the part of a truck on which goods are carried. **2.** *n* [*Radio*] local atmospheric disturbances caused by small activity within thunderclouds. See also **click**.

treacle-stick *n* [*UK*] [*Market-traders*] social security; once one starts going 'on' the dole, one cannot extract onself.

treading in the turf *part phr* [*Polo*] the half-time break between polo chukkas during which the crowd walk over the torn-up pitch and press back divots of disturbed turf.

treads *n pl* [*TV*] any steps that are built into the set.

treasure chest *n* [*US*] [*Painting*] a tool kit.

treasury call *n* [*UK*] [*Theatre*] pay day in the theatre, usually Friday afternoon. See also **ghost 7**.

treatment *n* [*Film*] the first attempt to expand a basic idea for a script into an actual narrative form with rough sequences, the outlines of dialogue, possible camera angles, etc.

treble, also **triangle** *n* [*Angling*] three hooks soldered or welded together.

tree *n* [*Computing*] a data structure incorporating a series of connected nodes. One node, the **root**, is the starting point of all paths; the **leaves** represent the termination of those paths. No path from root to leaf ever passes through a single node more than once.

tree and branch *n* [*TV*] a proposed method of installing cable TV in the UK, whereby a main coaxial cable would be laid under roads (the tree) and each subscribing household would take a subsidiary cable (the branch) into their own TV.

tree walking *n* [*Computing*] a path through a **tree** in which every node is visited once.

treff *n* [*Espionage*] in CIA use this means a clandestine meeting place; it comes from Ger. 'treffen'.

trench *n* [*Oil rigs*] a branch pipe used to remove **mud** and **dirt** from the well bore.

trepan 1. *v* [*Engineering*] to cut a groove or hole in some material using a crown or similar saw. **2.** *v* [*Engineering*] to cut a hole and remove the core of the material from that hole.

trey *n* [*Deer-stalking*] the third branch of a stag's antler.

triad 1. *n* [*Marketing*] a test of selection – usually from three products, one of which is markedly different from the others – that is used in market research. **2.** *n* [*Military*] See **strategic triad**. **3.** *n* [*TV*] the triangular grouping of red, green and blue phosphor dots on the screen of a **shadow-mask** tube.

triage *n* [*Government*] this comes from the medical term for dividing the wounded into three groups according to the severity of their wounds;

it is the principle or policy of allocating limited resources – eg: food – on the basis of urgency or expediency, rather than on humanitarian or moral principles.

triangular pass *n* [*Lacrosse*] See **give and go**.

triangular trade *n* [*Commerce*] a system of trading whereby one country pays for its imports from another by using the profit made on its exports to a third.

tri-axle *n* [*UK*] [*Road transport*] three axles of a vehicle or trailer in line at right angles to the chassis frame.

tribble *n* [*Science fiction*] anything, especially living, with no apparent purpose, of no consequence; it originated in a 'Star Trek' episode: 'The Trouble with Tribbles'.

tribology *n* [*Technology*] a branch of science and technology that concentrates on the interaction of surfaces in relative motion and on matters that arise from this motion, eg: friction, wear, lubrication, etc.

tribulation *n* [*Religion*] a period of intense persecution for Christians that will signal the imminence of the Second Coming.

trice *v* [*Sailing, Ropework*] to haul up with a single rope or **whip**.

trice up *v* [*Merchant navy*] to move something out of the way.

trick 1. *n* [*Merchant navy*] a watch on a merchant ship. 2. *n* [*UK*] [*Police*] a turn of duty involving an unpleasant, tedious job. 3. *n* [*Sex*] a client for any prostitute, heterosexual or homosexual; thus to 'turn a trick' is to service a client, the implication being that the prostitute is conning the client, making him pay for what a 'real man' could have for free.

trickle diversions *n pl* [*Government, Business*] the gradual growth, within a system, of problems that develop so slowly and in so limited, albeit continuous, a way, that they are overlooked in the context of the general activity (see **noise level**) until too much damage has been done for anything less than radical repair to be needed.

trickledown *n* [*Economics*] the theory that the profits generated by giving government aid to major corporations will eventually permeate through to lesser business and even to the consumer.

tricks *n* [*UK*] [*Market-traders*] a rage, a bad temper.

Trident *n* [*Military*] the latest generation of UK nuclear missiles and their accompanying weapon platforms: the Trident submarines. The Trident I C–4 missile is currently deployed on both Poseidon and Trident vessels, but it is to be replaced by the massively powerful Trident II D–5 version. With this missile, boosted by a variety of **state of the art** high technology to an accuracy of only 30 feet from its specified target, sea-launched nuclear weapons will offer the true long-range strategic

threat that has previously been limited to silo-based **ICBM**s.

trier *n* [*Foods*] a shallow scoop that is used to extract samples of various foods, eg: sugar, bacon, etc.

trifecta, also **triple** *n* [*Gambling*] a bet in which the bettor must select the first three horses in a race, in the exact order in which they finish. See also **exacta**, **perfecta**, **quinella**.

trigger point *n* [*US*] [*Economics*] the point, when a price level reaches a particular stage, that price controls are imposed or re-imposed.

trigger pricing *n* [*Commerce*] the keeping open of old and obsolete facilities, eg. steel plants that offer employment but are in fact economically useless, by holding the price of their products well above that which would be charged, were they produced in new, cost-efficient facilities.

trigger theory *n* [*Military*] the concept that, if such a situation were feasible, the early use of nuclear weapons by a small power would act as a trigger or catalyst on the subsequent development of superpower relations in the crisis; ie: once even small nuclear weapons had been used, how could the superpowers keep from unleashing a full-scale war?

triglyph *n* [*Building, Plastering*] a block with three vertical channels (glyphs) cut in; it is a distinguishing feature of Doric friezes.

trim 1. *a* [*UK*] [*Surfing*] describing a surfboard that is moving in a straight line at maximum speed. 2. *n* [*Film, TV*] a short piece of film or videotape that is discarded during editing. 3. *v* [*TV, film*] to change the carbon rods in an arc light; it comes from the traditional trimming of a candle wick.

trim out *v* [*US*] [*Painting*] to paint large areas of a surface, leaving only the sills and the woodwork for completion.

trim size *n* [*Publishing*] the final dimensions of a page after its edges have been trimmed.

trimmer 1. *n* [*Audio*] a small adjustable capacitor, usually pre-set to trim radio frequency circuits. 2. also **bailer** *n* [*Cricket*] a ball that barely glances against the bails in passing, but does so firmly enough to dislodge one and thus take the wicket.

trimmers *n pl* [*Mining*] shots fired at the peripheral wedges of excavations, in order to define the limits of the excavation.

trims 1. *n pl* [*Gambling*] cards that have been doctored by the trimming of some along one edge and others along another. 2. *n pl* [*TV*] short pieces of film that are hung in **bins** in film editing rooms; they have initially been discarded in editing but may still be required. Thus 'small trims' and 'tiny trims' mean pieces of 20 frames or less in length.

trip a car *v* [*US*] [*Car salesmen*] to draw up the final papers to transfer the ownership of the car from the dealership to the customer.

trip a tree *v* [*Logging*] See **throw a tree**.

tripe *n* [*US*] [*Meat trade*] a stunted, aged steer,

sutiable only for canning. See also **bowwow**, **canner**.

tripe man *n* [*Tobacco*] an employee who handles the filler tobacco.

tripehound *n* [*Greyhound racing*] a consistently disappointing dog; it comes from derogatory slang meaning 'mongrel'.

triping *n* [*Coal-mining*] coal that has been brought up to the pit-head but has yet to be cleaned or graded.

triple *n* [*Baseball*] a hit that permits a batter to reach third base safely. See also **double 1**, **single 1**.

Triple A *a* [*Finance*] said of a company that is considered to be of unimpeachable reputation and potential profitability.

triple A *n* [*Military*] anti-aircraft artillery.

triple alliance *n* [*UK*] [*Industrial relations*] the traditional trade union alliance between railwaymen, coal-miners and transport workers; concerted action by these unions has the potential of paralysing the national economy, although of late varieties of self-interest appear to have undermined its effectiveness.

triple hat *v* [*Espionage*] used when the same agent undertakes a variety of assignments at the same time; he/she 'wears several hats'.

triple play *n* [*Audio*] magnetic tape one third the thickness of standard recording tape.

triple threat *n* [*Film*] any individual who is proficient in three capacities, eg: writing, producing and directing, and thus threatens anyone who is talented only in one. See also **hyphenates 2**.

triple-cream *n* [*Cheese-making*] the legal definition of a cheese which contains more than 75% butterfat.

tripling *n* [*Sex*] the inviting in, by a husband or wife, of a third party, usually another woman, for group sex or swinging (see **swing**).

tripoli *n* [*Industry*] an abrasive substance, high in silicates, that is used for buffing wheels to facilitate polishing.

tripwire force *n* [*Military*] those troops who are stationed on a hostile border as the first line of defence; such troops are deemed expendable and their role is not to stop an invasion, merely to hold it up long enough for the major part of the defences to be activated.

tripwire position *n* [*Military*] the area – usually on a border with a hostile power – in which **tripwire forces** are stationed.

triumphalism *n* [*Religion*] the sense of pride (and even ostentation) that certain of the devout feel in the achievements, and particularly the moral rightness, of their church.

troika *n* [*US*] [*Government*] a special group of economic advisors to the President; they are the Chairman of the Council of Economic Advisers, the Secretary of the Treasury, the Director of the Office of Management. See also **quadriad**.

Trojan horse 1. *n* [*Computing*] an entry point placed in a computer system by an invader of that system. The regular users of the system will be unaware of the entry which can be used to break down data security, destroy or alter files, or for computer fraud and theft. See also **time bomb**. **2.** *n* [*Computing*] a program deliberately inserted into a system in order to destroy data, scramble files, etc. **3.** *n* [*Computing*] an unexpected or malicious side-effect of a program that usually works as required.

troll *v* [*Angling*] to trail a fly or bait behind a boat.

Trollope ploy *n* [*Diplomacy*] the deliberate misinterpretation of foreign situations in order to act on that one which appears most advantageous to one's own interests; it comes from a novel by Anthony Trollope (1815–82), in which the heroine consciously decides to interpret a mere squeeze of her hand as an ardent proposal of marriage.

trombone *n* [*Film*] an extendable support with which lights can be attached to the ceiling or walls of a set.

tromboning *n* [*TV*] the excessive use of the zoom lens on a camera.

tromp and stomp *n* [*US*] [*Marine Corps*] the morning inspection, which is followed by close-order drill.

tronc *n* [*Catering*] the communal deposit of tips. All tips are added together over a night's work, then shared out between the waiting staff after the restaurant has closed; from Fr. meaning 'church collecting box'.

troops 1. *n pl* [*US*] [*Politics*] the lower echelons of party workers who perform the mundane, menial tasks that never make any headlines but may well 'get out the vote'. **2.** *n pl* [*Politics*] to the Catholic population of Northern Ireland this means the British Army. See also **Army**.

troppo *n* [*Navy*] any form of abnormal behaviour attributed to service in the tropics.

trossing *n* [*UK*] [*Postal services*] walking; it comes from 'stroll' or 'trot'.

trot 1. *v* [*Auctions*] to bid up the price, especially by making a spurious or false bid simply to force other bidders higher. **2.** *n* [*Sailing*] a multiple mooring for small boats or yachts. **3.** *n* [*Education*] summary, outline or translation used by students.

trot, on the *adv* [*UK*] [*Police*] on the run.

Trotskyism 1. *n* [*Politics*] the concept advanced by Leon Trotsky (1879–1940) that his rival Stalin had turned the Russian Revolution into a bureaucratic tyranny. **2.** *n* [*Politics*] the phase of the Revolution in which Trotsky was still attempting to rival Stalin for supreme power, a battle that Trotsky lost. **3.** *n* [*Politics*] in modern Communist Party ideology, this is any form of anti-Party heresy that stands outside the Party line. **4.** *n* [*Politics*] in the UK this is blanket shorthand for any party of the extreme left, eg: Militant.

Trotslot *n* [*TV*] any programme, usually on current affairs, that attacks the prevailing Establishment position and is thus considered, perhaps ironically, to be fomenting red revolution.

trotting *n* [*Auctions*] the tactic used by a **ring** of dealers who will force an outsider, who refuses to let them have a particular lot, to bid up to an absurdly high figure, at which point the counter-bidding dealer drops out, leaving the amateur with an inflated bill.

trouble unit *n* [*Telephony*] a figure assessed for a telephone circuit which predicts the likely possibility of breakdown on that circuit over a specified period.

trough *n* [*Theatre*] a long metal container which holds stage lights.

trouncer *n* [*UK*] [*Road transport*] the driver's assistant, especially a drayman's mate on a brewery lorry. He is so called because the early assistants had the task, in the days before tarmacked roads, of 'trouncing' or manhandling the dray over potholes and similar obstructions.

trousers, also **pants, culottes, breeches 1.** *n pl* [*Dog breeding*] the fringes of longish hair on the posterior borders of some breeds. **2.** *n pl* [*Dog breeding*] the ridge-like pattern of longer than usual hair in short-coated breeds at the junction of inner and outer thighs.

trout fishing *n* [*Sex*] the searching by a young **hustler** for a rich older man who will keep him in (temporary) luxury.

truck acts *n pl* [*UK*] [*Industrial relations*] a series of acts passed in the UK between 1831 and 1940 which protected all those workers to whom they now apply – all manual labourers other than domestic servants – from abuse in the payment of their wages.

truck system *n* [*Industrial relations*] the system, now largely outlawed, of paying wages in kind rather than in cash.

trucklot *n* [*US*] [*Commerce*] a quantity of goods that will fill a truck and which are sold as such at a lower rate than a smaller quantity.

trudgen *n* [*Swimming*] a swimming style that combines the crawl and the breast-stroke – each arm comes out of the water alternately, makes a low circular movement in front of the head, then thrusts back into the water; the legs make a frog-like movement; it is named after its inventor.

true *a* [*Cycling*] perfectly adjusted; thus 'to true up' is to adjust one's cycle to perfection.

true believer *n* [*US*] [*Politics*] two ways of describing political supporters: as used by one member of a party this describes a fellow enthusiast; as used by an enemy of a party it attacks one of its fanatical supporters.

true crimes *n pl* [*Crime, Sociology*] those major crimes on which many sociologists feel the police should concentrate their efforts, rather than worrying about soft drugs, etc. They are aggravated assault, burglary, murder, rape, robbery and grand theft.

trufan *n* [*TV*] a dedicated fan of TV's science

fiction series 'Star Trek'; for the real fan one's allegiance must only be to 'Star Trek' and not to any other programme, science fiction or not.

trumpet 1. *n* [*Dog breeding*] the dog's temple; a slight depression or hollow situated on either side of the skull just behind the eye socket. **2.** *n* [*Metallurgy*] a vertical tube, lined with refractory material, that has a bell mouth; metal is poured through this tube into runners for uphill casting.

trumping *n* [*Education*] at Oxford University this is a system of admissions whereby those accepted as commoners at the college of their first choice can be trumped away by the offer of a scholarship at the college of their second choice.

trunk *n* [*Computing*] a set of linking components that join one part of a computer to another; it is the equivalent of the micro-computer's **bus**, but applied to larger machines.

trunk hunting *n* [*Telephony*] a procedure in an automatic exchange whereby the incoming call is switched to the next number in sequence if the original number called is engaged.

trunky *n* [*Navy*] the chief electrical artificer, whose duties include attending to the wiring and trunking in the ship.

truss *n* [*Building, Plastering*] a rectangular block, **enriched** or **plainface**, which acts as a support to a feature.

truth *n* [*Science*] the property of a **top quark**. See also **beauty, charm, quark, strange quark**.

truth squad 1. *n* [*Government*] members of government agencies who defend controversial positions in public by appearing at press conferences or protest meetings as a group in order to push the government point of view, often while posing as disinterested, but 'concerned' citizens. **2.** *n* [*US*] [*Politics*] a special team of opposition experts who follow a candidate around his/her campaign tour and attempt to unsettle the smooth running of that tour by producing facts and figures which are deliberately aimed at discrediting the various statements and promises made by the candidate.

truth table *n* [*Computing*] in logic operations this is a means of describing the functions of a logical operation, or a circuit containing logic units.

truth-in-lending *n* [*US*] [*Finance*] the legal requirement that any bank must explain fully all the details of any loan scheme which it operates.

try gun *n* [*Shooting*] a gun which can be adjusted to fit any shooter.

try it out on the dog *v phr* [*US*] [*Theatre*] to try out a new play by giving it a variety of previews on towns and cities outside New York; thus 'dog house' is a preview audience, 'dog show' is a preview, 'dog town' is a town used for such a preview.

Ts, also **tops** *n* [*Gambling*] See **busters**.

tub, also **tank** *n* [*UK*] [*Buses*] a London Transport bus.

tub goods *n pl* [*Textiles*] any goods, especially

summer-wear, that are designed to withstand constant washing.

tube 1. *v* [*US*] [*Medicine*] to die; it comes from slang 'to go down the tubes'. See also **box out, flatline. 2.** *v* [*Tyre-making*] to use the tuber machine to produce the outer component of the finished tyre, the tread, which consists of the **cap** and the sidewall. **3.** *n* [*New therapies*] a derogatory term used by an **est** instructor to insult those undergoing a weekend's indoctrination; the implication is that, devoid of any real personality, they are capable only of eating and, at the other end of the tube, excreting. **4.** [*UK*] [*Surfing*] a hollow curl in the wave that forms into a rideable cylinder of water.

Tube alloys *n* [*Science*] the secret code name for the British Department of Scientific and Industrial Research, formed in 1940 in order to develop an atomic bomb.

tube artillery *n* [*Military*] any weapon which has a barrel, rather than one which is delivered by missile or rocket, eg: a howitzer, mortar or field gun.

tubism *n* [*Art*] by analogy with Cubism this is a style developed by Fernand Léger (1881–1955), which concentrated on cyclindrical and other mechanistic forms.

tubs *n pl* [*Cycling*] racing tyres.

tuck *n* [*Tobacco*] the end of the cigar which is to be lit. See also **nip 1**.

tuck up *v* [*Antiques*] to defraud, to sell a fake to someone.

tucked up 1. *adv* [*Cricket*] used of a batsman who is forced to play defensively, making cramped, awkward strokes. **2.** *adv* [*UK*] [*Police*] said of a situation that is fully under control. **3.** *adv* [*UK*] [*Police*] referring to a target under successful surveillance. **4.** *adv* [*UK*] [*Police*] referring to a suspect who is safely arrested.

tuff *n* [*Mining*] compacted fine volcanic ash and dust.

tufted, also **diamond tufted** *a* [*Custom cars*] used to describe an upholstery design in which the stitching is in a diamond pattern with a button at each corner of the diamond.

tufters *v pl* [*Hunting*] the hounds which hunt the red and fallow deer.

tug 1. *n* [*US*] [*Gliding*] the powered aircraft which tows the glider into the air. **2.** *n* [*UK*] [*Police*] an arrest, usually as in 'to give a tug'.

tuggies *n pl* [*UK*] [*Market traders*] clothing.

tuism *n* [*Linguistics*] the use of the second person instead of the first, especially when musing on oneself and generally referring to one's soul or consciousness. See also **illeism, nosism**.

tumbler 1. *n* [*Metallurgy*] a machine which cleans castings by placing them in a cylinder, together with various abrasive materials, and then rotating the cylinder until the castings are clean. **2.** *n* [*US*] [*Paper-making*] a machine which cleans mud and dirt from pulp logs by using high-

pressure sprays. **3.** *n* [*Window-cleaning*] an inexperienced or incompetent window-cleaner.

tumbling *n* [*Painting*] See **rumbling**.

tun *n* [*UK*] [*Market-traders*] one hundred.

tuner *n* [*Theatre*] a musical.

tunnel *n* [*Economics*] the restricted area of currency fluctuation in which the EC **snake** is supposed to move.

tunnel mouth *n* [*UK*] [*Railways*] anyone lacking a number of teeth.

tunnelling *n* [*Custom cars*] the sinking of any external feature – headlights, rear lights, aerials, etc – into the bodywork; it is often confused with **frenching**.

tup 1. *n* [*Metallurgy*] in iron-founding this is a heavy ball used to smash up scrap metal castings prior to melting them down for further use. **2.** *v* [*UK*] [*Market-traders*] to strike with the head, to butt – both popular methods of ending an argument swiftly and decisively.

tuple *n* [*Computing*] a related set of values.

turd beater 1. *n* [*US*] [*Painting*] in wallpapering this is a stick or paddle used to stir the paste. **2.** *n* [*US*] [*Printing*] an old, worn-out brush.

turf *v* [*US*] [*Medicine*] to get rid of or pass on an unwanted patient from one ward to another one or to a special surgical unit; a turf is usually preceded by a **buff**, which legitimises the turf, but if that is inadequate, the patient returns to the original ward as a **bounce**.

Turing machine *n* [*Computing*] a notional computer, designed by the English mathematician Alan Turing (1912–54), which could perform a variety of simple tasks – writing, reading and shifting operations – in accordance with a prescribed set of rules.

Turing Test *n* [*Computing*] this was named after Alan Turing, a pioneer of UK computing. The test – for aritifical intelligence – is based on the notion that if a person interacting with a computer is unable to tell the difference between such a dialogue and a conversation between two people then the machine is 'acting intelligently'. The subtleties of human dialogue make this a poor test, but popular scientific use makes 'He hasn't passed his Turing Test' refer to an individual who is less than human, lacks a sense of humour, etc.

turkey 1. *n* [*Bowling*] three successive strikes. **2.** *n* [*Business*] anything that fails to perform as required: a business, an investment, a stock, a product line, etc. **3.** *n* [*Drugs*] fake drugs, sold as the real thing; specifically it is a capsule which contains not the required narcotic, but chalk dust or sugar. **4.** *n* [*Entertainment*] a film, TV programme, record, etc. that flops. **5.** *n* [*Forestry*] a pack carried by an itinerant logger. **6.** *n* [*US*] [*Gliding*] a pilot of poor ability; it comes from general slang use. **7.** *n* [*US*] [*Painting*] See **treasure chest. 8.** *n* [*US*] [*Medicine*] any patient with a trivial complaint. **9.** *n* [*US*] [*Medicine*] any

T

patient whom doctors do not feel is a genuine case, but in fact a malingerer. See also **bounce 3**, **meet'em and street'em**. 10. *n* a patient who has been mishandled by a hospital. 11. *n* [*Navy*] See **bootneck**.

turkey-basting *n* [*Medicine, Sex*] a means of aritifical insemination preferred by some lesbians. A number of male homosexuals ejaculate into a common receptacle; the sperm so produced and mixed is used for insemination by the putative mother.

turk's head *n* [*Shooting*] a woollen mop attached to a cleaning rod and used for oiling shotgun barrels.

turn 1. *v* [*Angling*] to cause a fish to change direction. 2. *v* [*Drugs*] said of a dealer who agrees to sell drugs to an addict. 3. *v* [*Soccer*] to pass an opponent by forcing him to change direction and putting him off-balance. 4. *n* [*Logging*] a unit of logs sent to the yard; it is as large a load as can be transported in a single round trip on the skidder carriage which moves them. 5. *n* [*Stock market*] the difference between the **bid** and the price offered by the **jobber**; the **jobber's turn** is the same as the gross profit that he makes on a security when he buys and sells equal amounts at the bid and the offered prices.

turn around *v* [*Espionage*] to persuade an enemy agent to start working for one's own side.

turn over 1. *v* [*Angling*] to hook a salmon, have it come to the surface and then lose it. 2. *v* [*UK*] [*Police*] to search the home of a suspect, usually by making a destructive mess; literally turning everything over. 3. *n* [*US*] [*Prisons*] to denounce a fellow inmate to the authorities. See also **drop a dime**, **flip 4**. 4. *n* [*Printing*] to carry a letter or part of a word over to the next line.

turn over the covers *v* [*Business*] to look into both sides of a problem.

turn round 1. *v* [*UK*] [*Radio*] to have a tape ready for use; edited, timed and running forwards. 2. *v* [*Transport*] to prepare a ship or aircraft for its return journey.

turnaround 1. *n* [*Aerospace*] the readying of the launch pad and all the other vital facilities that are needed for the successful launching of a spacecraft. 2. *n* [*Film*] a situation in which a studio abandons a project and gives its producer a set time – usually twelve months – to find another buyer who is interested in it; in the meantime the studio retains its rights in the project.

turnaway *a* [*Commerce*] referring to trade or business that is so successful that customers have to be turned away; it is used especially of restaurants or show business.

turnback *n* [*US*] [*Police*] a procedure whereby drug smugglers arrested at the Mexico-US border by US agents are offered the choice of becoming narcotics agents/informers themselves or being turned over to the Mexican authorities.

Turners *n pl* [*Medicine*] hermaphrodites who are in fact essentially women, with just a few male characteristics. They are individuals who would be completely female but for the lack of an X chromosome. See also **Klinefelters**.

turning box, also **hand lathe** *n* [*Building, Plastering*] a box or frame within a profile and metal spindle that is used to form plaster ballisters or similar features.

turning pitch *n* [*Cricket*] a pitch on which the ball will turn or change direction.

turnkey 1. *a* [*Business, Technology*] referring to any piece of technology or manufacturing that is delivered to a customer ready for use; the maker or seller has provided a stock system or unit, the client takes his recommendation at face value and merely accepts delivery of the product, requiring only to 'turn a key' to set things in motion. Turnkey deals extend from an entire office-block or factory through to a single piece of equipment. 2. *n* [*Commerce*] a commercial or industrial contract involving several suppliers of specialist skills which are to be subcontracted by the main supplier.

turnkey contract *n* [*Commerce*] the commissioning by a client of a specialist to arrange the design and construction of a specific, complex project; all decisions are left to the specialist and when the project is completed and paid for, all the client need do is 'turn a key' and set everything in satisfactory motion.

turnkey reactors *n pl* [*Technology*] tailor-made 'off the peg' nuclear reactors made in one country – usually the US – and sold around the world to interested parties.

turnkey system *n* [*Computing*] a system which has been designed, assembled and checked by its manufacturer, double-checked by the retailer, and is then turned over to the user who needs only to turn a real or metaphorical key for the system to be ready for immediate use.

turnout *n* [*Coal-mining*] the means of splitting a single track into two tracks.

turnover 1. *n* [*Audio*] the frequency at which an audio system undergoes a change in the mode of its operation. 2. *n* [*Business*] the hiring and firing of staff. 3. *n* [*Sport*] in a variety of ball-games, especially US football and lacrosse, this is a change in team possession forced by defensive harassment or offensive error. 4. *n* [*Printing*] an extension of printed matter beyond the space allotted; it is also the last line of a paragraph which does not extend to the full measure.

turns *n pl* [*Video*] the number of times per year a retailer or distributor can hope to sell out an entire inventory of video products; the optimum profitable number is seven or eight.

turntable hit *n* [*Record business*] a record that is regularly played on the radio and in jukeboxes, but is not actually bought in the stores and thus cannot be counted in the charts.

turps *n* [*Navy*] any kind of alcohol.

turtle *n* [*TV*] a three-legged floor stand into which a lamp, connected by a **spud** can be fitted.

turtles *n pl* [*UK*] [*Police*] this comes from rhyming slang 'turtle doves' meaning 'gloves' meaning the gloves used by a housebreaker to mask his fingerprints.

tush hog *n* [*Pool*] a spectator who tries to intimidate a player through threats of violence.

tutti frutti communism *n* [*Politics*] the Italian communist party's joking description of its home-grown variation on the Soviet party line, after N.S. Khruschev had advocated in 1956 that the various European Communist parties should take individual roads towards the generally desired socialist millenium.

tuxedo unionism *n* [*US*] [*Industrial relations*] the lifestyle and attitudes which take over a senior trade unionist or 'labour statesman' whose rank has made him or her forget the mass of union members in favour of the delights of participation in higher politics and negotiations with top business executives.

TV-Q *n* [*US*] [*TV*] an assessment of the popularity of a TV performer. Two areas are measured: the familiarity rating (who recognises the performer's face?) and the Q-rating (who likes that face?) and together they make up the TV-Q rating.

T.V.R.O. *n* [*Satellite TV*] abbr of **television receive only** a type of **earth station**.

twank *n* [*Sex*] See **jims**.

tweak **1.** *v* [*Advertising*] to fine-tune a campaign; to make certain adjustments in its presentation or promotion that do not alter the essential direction of the campaign, but simply improve certain possibly weak spots. **2.** *v* [*Computing*] to fine-tune the machine.

tweaker **1.** *n* [*TV*] a small screwdriver used by electricians or carpenters. **2.** *n* [*Cricket*] a bowler who spins the ball; thus it is also the ball delivered in this way.

tweedler *n* [*UK*] [*Police*] a stolen or faulty vehicle which is offered for sale as a genuine, fully functional article.

tweedling *n* [*UK*] [*Police*] the selling of stolen property, of shoddy or worthless goods, or of property that does not even exist but for which money can be obtained in advance from the gullible.

tweel blocks **1.** *n pl* [*Glass-making*] blocks of refractory material placed in front of a newly set pot. **2.** *n pl* [*Glass-making*] blocks of refractory material used to control the flow of glass in forming machine canals.

tweeter *n* [*Audio*] the part of the loudspeaker that produces high-frequency sound waves. See also **woofer**.

twelve and twelve *n* [*Alcoholics Anonymous, Narcotics Anonymous*] the twelve steps and the twelve traditions upon which AA and NA are founded and to which members are assumed to subscribe.

twentieth century cut *n* [*Gemstones*] a method of diamond-cutting in which the number of facets – eighty or eighty-eight – is greater than that found in brilliant-cutting; the facets are also arranged in a different manner.

twenty-five *n* [*US*] [*Marine Corps*] a communications man; it comes from his military occupational speciality (**MOS**) number, 2500.

twenty-four/twenty-four **(24/24)** *n* [*US*] [*Prisons*] all day; twenty-four hours out of the twenty-four.

twewe *n* [*Film, TV*] the brand-name of a viewfinder, manufactured in Germany, with which the director can assess the same shot as will be seen through the camera lens.

twice-laid stuff *n* [*Sailing, Ropework*] See **nettles, sinnets**.

twiddle **1.** *n* [*Computing*] a small and insignificant alteration to a program; such a change often serves to fix one major problem but may simultaneously create several lesser ones. **2.** *v* [*Computing*] to change something in a small way.

twiddler *n* [*Table tennis*] a player using a **combination bat** who turns it between shots in an attempt to confuse his opponent.

twig *a* [*Boxing*] fit, cheerful and ready for the fight.

twiggy *a* [*Wine-tasting*] See **stalky**.

twilight shift *n* [*Industrial relations*] a three- to four-hour early evening shift, often worked by married women employed in light industrial plants, or by those who are **moonlighting** elsewhere.

twilight zone *n* [*UK*] [*Railways*] the period of time spent awaiting one's promotion.

twin paradox *n* [*Science*] in relativity theory this is the concept that if one of a pair of twins makes a journey at high speed and then returns, he will have aged less than the twin who has stayed behind.

twin steer *n* [*UK*] [*Road transport*] See **Chinese six**.

twinkle *n* [*Advertising, Business*] in business theatre this is a very fast change of slides between two projectors; it is used to create an illusion of movement, a waving hand, etc.

twin-screw *n* [*US*] [*Road transport*] a tractor with two powered rear axles.

twinset *n* [*Diving*] a two-bottle aqualung.

twirl *n* [*UK*] [*Prisons*] See **screw 2**. See also **corned beef, white shirt**.

twist **1.** *n* [*US*] [*Bars*] a twist of lemon. See also **squeeze 2**. **2.** *v* [*Insurance*] a salesman does this when he persuades an individual to change his/her policy from one company to another.

twister *n* [*Insurance*] an insurance salesman who specialises in persuading those who hold policies with another company to change those policies to his/her own company.

twisting **1.** *n* [*Insurance*] persuading a policy holder to alter a current policy or to take out a new one for no reason other than that the salesman wishes to earn the extra commission on the sale. **2.** n [*Banking*] shifting a long-term debt to a short-term one, or vice versa, so that one can take advantage of the changing interest rates involved. **3.** n [*Stock market*] persuading a client to indulge in deals the only real purpose of which is to generate commissions for the broker.

twist-lock n [*UK*] [*Road transport*] a metal fastener, built into the platform of a vehicle or trailer and strengthened by attachment to the chassis itself, which fits into the holes of an **ISO** container and clamps it securely to the vehicle. The operator needs merely to lift and twist the fastener to secure the container firmly.

twist-off n [*Oil-rigs*] the breaking off of the rotary drill while in the hole as a result of torsional stress.

twitch 1. n [*Bird-watching*] a trip to see a rarity, the sight of which will render the enthusiast a **twitcher**. Special rare species are considered 'twitchable'. 'Twitcher' was allegedly coined around 1955 by R.E. Emmett, to describe a well-known enthusiast Howard Medhurst at the moment of sighting. See also **dude. 2.** n [*Golf*] a nervous problem that afflicts players when putting. See also **yips. 3.** n [*Navy*] a physical and mental complaint that emerges during the last stages of a cruise on board a nuclear submarine; the symptoms are loss of appetite and vague feelings of incompetency.

twitch factor n [*Air travel*] a decrease in the efficiency of members of a commercial aircraft's crew, especially that of the pilot, through fear of the mounting pressure of the workload.

twitch road n [*US*] [*Paper-making*] a small, rough road cut through the wood to facilitate logging operations.

twitched a [*US*] [*Paper-making*] referring to logs that have been hauled to the main track from which they are dragged or transported to the mill.

twitcher 1. n [*Building, Plastering*] a square scoop trowel that is used in the finishing of internal angle work or at setting coat stage. **2.** n [*Bird-watching*] a bird-watching enthusiast who pursues new species and 'twitches' with delight on sighting one. See also **lister.**

two blocks a [*Navy*] utterly dissatisfied; it comes from two blocks on a tackle crashing together.

two carbon abuser n [*US*] [*Medicine*] an alcoholic. It comes from the formula for alcohol: C_2H_6O.

two crows for a banker phr [*UK*] [*Railways*] a whistle code used between an engine and the second **banker** engine, when they wish to announce they are ready to depart.

two key lockout n [*Computing*] a device which halts further keyboard action after two keys have erroneously been pressed together. See also **two key roll over.**

two key rollover n [*Computing*] a device which allows both keystrokes to be interpreted correctly,

even though the two have erroneously been pressed together. See also **two key lockout**.

two lines n [*Politics*] in Chinese terminology this is the clash between the bourgeois line and the proletarian line; individuals may change but the basic division never alters: the bourgeoisie wish to suppress the revolution, while the masses, epitomised in the Maoist poster 'Bombard the Headquarters', yearn to smash once and for all the bourgeoisie and the **capitalist roaders**.

two lines and a spit n [*Theatre*] See **cough and a spit**.

two lunger n [*US*] [*Farming*] any two cylinder engine.

two man rule n [*Military*] the rule operated by the US Strategic Air Command (**SAC**), in order to ensure as far as possible that one individual cannot trigger off nuclear war 'by mistake' or through an excess of drink, drugs, nervous tension or misplaced patriotism. This rule extends through all phases of nuclear weapons handling – from guarding them in storage to arming and actually firing them. The Soviet forces, for similar reasons, employ four man crews.

two weeks under, one week out phr [*US*] [*Theatre*] a clause in a contract which gives the theatre owner the right to have a show closed within one week, if the gross box office take drops below a pre-set figure for two consecutive weeks.

two-bagger n [*Baseball*] a hit that enables the batter to reach second base easily.

two-bin system n [*Management*] See **last-bag system**.

two-block 1. v [*US*] [*Marine Corps*] to hoist a flag or pennant to a ship's yardarm. **2.** v [*US*] [*Marine Corps*] to straighten up one's fieldscarf and position it neatly in the centre of one's uniform.

two-dollar broker n [*US*] [*Stock market*] a floor broker who carries out transactions for other brokers who do not have the time to perform them for themselves; such brokers once received a flat fee of $2.00 but now obtain a graduated commission.

twofer n [*US*] [*Theatre*] a ticket that allows the purchaser to buy 'two for' the price of one.

twofers n [*Entertainment*] abbr of **two-for-the price of one** a special box office offer that gives two tickets to a show for the price of one.

two-four-six n [*TV*] small wooden blocks, glued together like a set of stairs, each 2in high, that are used by **grips** to lay and strengthen the camera tracks. See also **paganini**.

twoing up n [*UK*] [*Prisons*] putting two prisoners in a cell originally designed for one; such prisoners are 'twoed-up'. Thus 'three-up' and 'four-up'. See also **double-ceiling**.

two-line whip n [*UK*] [*Politics*] a notice of forthcoming parliamentary business which is distributed to MPs and in which the text is underlined twice. This denotes less urgency than the absolute demands of the three-line whip.

two-oh-one file *n* [*Espionage, Government*] a special biographical file compiled by the CIA on any individual in whom the agency is interested, either as a potential ally or as a possible or certain enemy. Such a file is particularly detailed as to social life, friendships, sexual predilections, weaknesses, etc.

two-star *a* [*US*] [*Military*] referring to a rear-admiral or a major-general; it comes from the two stars worn on the shoulder straps of these senior officers.

two-tailed test *n* [*Parapsychology*] statistical analysis in which it has not been specified whether the direction of the statistic being tested is expected to be positive or negative, but the expectation includes either possibility. See also **one-tailed test**.

two-tier bargaining *n* [*Industrial relations*] a situation in which national pay agreements with a union are subsequently backed up by local branch agreements which give further wage concessions to those branches, in addition to the original deal.

two-tone *n* [*UK*] [*Fire brigade*] the siren; it comes from its sound.

two-up *n* [*Cycling*] two cyclists competing in a team time-trial.

two-way man *n* [*Sex*] a **hustler** who will take a passive role in sex, possibily for pleasure rather than the usual trade. See also **three-way girl**.

two-way player *n* [*Ice-hockey*] See **honest player**.

Two-Way Street *n* [*Military*] a US initiative to liberalise the US/European arms trade, by developing US projects under licence in European countries.

tympanum *n* [*Building, Plastering*] the triangular centre section of a pediment that is enclosed by the horizontal and two **raking** mouldings.

typamatic *a* [*Computing*] said of keyboard characters that can be held down for the automatic repetition of the character being depressed until such time as the key is released.

type 1. *n* [*Military*] used in the French Foreign Legion to mean an eccentric legionnaire. **2.** *n* [*Linguistics*] in semiotics this is a sign representing a category or set of instances, as opposed to the individual **tokens** which are examples of the category.

typewriter word *n* [*Logology*] a word that can be typed on a single line of typewriter keys, eg: (second line) 'halfs'.

typey *a* [*Agriculture*] said of domestic animals that, as far as possible, exhibit to perfection the representative characteristics of their breed.

typification *n* [*Sociology*] the way in which people classify the world around them and the things within it by noting typical features.

typo 1. *n* [*Printing*] a spelling error found in printed matter. **2.** *n* [*Publishing*] abbr of **typographical error**.

tyre kicker *n* [*Business*] anyone who is charged with inspecting a project and does so only in the most superficial manner. Such negligence can stem either from genuine incompetence, or from the fact that it is more important for a particular person to be seen looking over a project than for him/her to know exactly what they are looking for.

tyre scrub *n* [*Cars*] the friction generated between tyres and the road surface when the car is cornering.

tyrolean *n* [*Building, Plastering*] a machine-applied external finish where the resultant surface has a honey-combed or cellular texture.

U

ubi sunt *v phr* [*Literary criticism*] this comes from Lat. for 'where are they?'; it denotes a style of writing in which the motif is regret for the decline or absence of things past; it is found particularly in Mediaeval works.

uckers *n* [*Navy*] a board game that resembles ludo, played by the Royal Navy

ufocal *n* [*Science*] the optimum location for the possible sighting of unidentified flying objects; it comes from 'UFO'.

uglies n [*Diving*] See **bends**.

ugly American n [*Politics*] a derogatory description of a type of American who uses foreign 'aid' programmes to exploit, alienate and destabilise the country in which such a programme is operating. It comes from the novel 'The Ugly American' by William J. Lederer and Eugene Burdick (1959), but the phrase is a misinterpretation of that novel, in which a physically unattractive American belies his ugliness by helping the country to which he is posted.

ujamaa n [*Politics*] this comes from Swahili 'jamaa' meaning family, thus brotherhood; it is the form of socialism that was introduced into Tanzania in the 1960s by President Nyerere; it was centred on village co-operatives based on equality of opportunity and self-help.

ULCC n [*Oil rigs*] abbr of **ultra-large crude carrier** an ocean-going oil tanker of more than 300,000 metric tons deadweight. See also **VLCC**.

ulcer 1. n [*UK*] [*Railways*] a points relay marked by the letters ULSR. See also **tipper, whizzer 2.** **2.** n [*TV*] a light diffuser made out of a board from which various portions have been cut out and which is placed in front of a light.

ullage 1. n [*Commerce*] the amount of which the contents of any vessel containing liquid falls short of the full measure, due to evaporation or leakage. **2.** n [*Commerce*] the actual contents of a vessel at the time of importation – it is used by Customs to calculate a specific duty. **3.** n [*Commerce*] the spillage when beer is served in a public house.

ultimate painting n [*Art*] a series of paintings – 'The Black Paintings' – produced by Ad Reinhardt between 1960 and 1967 and which he termed the 'ultimate abstract paintings'.

ultra n [*Printing*] the ultimate degree: of weight, extension, height, etc, in any design.

ultrafiche n [*Technology*] a microfiche, or the documents held on it, in which material is reduced by a factor of 100 or more.

UMA n [*Industrial relations*] acro **Union Membership Agreement** a closed shop.

umbilical n [*Aerospace*] a large multiple cable connection between ground control and a spacecraft which delivers all necessary supplies and communications right up to the moment of lift-off when it is jettisoned.

umbrella 1. n [*TV*] a reflector, shaped like an umbrella, that is placed behind a light. **2.** also **veil** n [*Dog breeding*] that portion of a dog's forelock which hangs straight down over the eyes and at least partially covers them.

umbrella brigade n [*UK*] [*Police*] a Metropolitan Police nickname for the Special Branch, which deals with the internal security of the UK.

umbrella defence n [*US*] [*Football*] a defensive alignment in which the backfield is positioned to resemble the shape of an open umbrella.

umbrella field n [*Cricket*] an arrangement of fielders, usually in the slips or otherwise close to the batsman, which resembles the shape of an open umbrella.

umbrella swift n [*Weaving*] a **swift** made of umbrella-like ribs that unfold to accommodate different-sized skeins of yarn.

umpties n pl [*UK*] [*Medicine*] abbr of **units of medical time** the overtime worked by NHS senior registrars; such overtime can boost their (1985) basic income of £15,000 by £2,500.

unacceptable damage n [*Military*] the concept that the damage which one's own nation would suffer in a projected **second strike** might be too great to consider launching a **first strike** against the enemy.

unblock v [*Bird-watching*] to see a rarity that no-one else has noticed and thus to get even with a fellow-enthusiast who has seen a rarity you have missed. See also **gripped off**.

unbundle v [*Business*] to separate the costs of the various operations carried out in one business or project into their separate entities.

unbundling n [*Computing*] the selling to consumers of software separately from hardware. See also **bundled software**.

unc n [*Merchant navy*] a nickname for a steward; it comes from 'uncle'.

uncertainty n [*Business*] a business risk that cannot be measured and the outcome of which cannot be predicted or insured against: it is a non-insurable risk.

uncharmed a [*Science*] referring to **quarks** and similar particles that do not possess **charm**.

uncle 1. n [*Theatre*] a theatrical backer. See also **angel 4. 2.** n [*Film*] a film agent.

unclean fish n [*Angling*] a fish that is about to spawn, or which has recently spawned.

uncorrected cybernetic machinery n [*New therapies*] in **est**, this is the human mind in the random, unplanned state in which it exists prior to undergoing the transformation of est therapy.

under the gun adv [*Gambling*] said of a situation in draw or stud poker where a player must make some kind of decision as to betting or leaving the round before the general play can continue.

under the rule adv [*US*] [*Stock market*] said of any deal on the New York Stock Exchange that has not been closed out by the dealer who initiated it and which therefore has to be concluded by an official of the exchange.

under wraps adv [*Horse-racing*] said of a horse who is restrained from running at his best. It is possibly done with the intention of disguising his true form prior to a more important race, and thus giving his owner and others in the know the opportunity of attempting a betting coup.

under-achiever n [*Education*] any pupil who appears to be less competent than he/she ought to be for his/her age, development, etc. See also **over-achiever**.

under-boss n [*US*] [*Crime*] in the US Mafia this

is the 'sotto capo', the man who is second in command of a **family**.

underchosen *a* [*Sociology*] individuals who, according to statistical research, are found to be chosen as companions, fellow-workers, etc., significantly less frequently than are others in the same survey.

underclass *n* [*Sociology*] the absolute lowest level of all the classes, usually seen as members of various **disadvantaged** and minority groups.

underclub *v* [*Golf*] to choose a club which does not strike the ball in the manner, and to the distance, which one desired.

undercount *n* [*Statistics*] an incomplete enumeration of figures; the amount by which the number enumerated in a census falls short of the actual number in the group.

undercut *n* [*Logging*] the notch cut into a tree which determines the way it will fall.

underfill *n* [*Metallurgy*] a cross-section that has not filled up the roll **pass** so that the product is inaccurate in both shape and dimensions. See also **overfill**.

underflow *v* [*Computing*] said of an arithmetical operation which becomes too small for the equipment intended to store it.

undergraduate *n* [*Aerospace*] any member of an air crew who has not yet qualified in his speciality; it is used especially for a trainee pilot who has not yet 'gained his wings'.

undergrip *n* [*Mountaineering*] See **under-hold**.

under-hold *n* [*Mountaineering*] a climbing hold used to maintain one's balance, in which the hand grasps a downward edge or point from beneath with the palm upwards.

underkill *n* [*Military*] the inability of one's forces to defeat a particular enemy.

underlead *v* [*Cards*] in bridge this is to lead a low card when one holds a higher one of the same suit.

underline *n* [*US*] [*Journalism*] a caption to a picture or illustration.

underneath *n* [*Radio*] a record that continues to play softly while a disc jockey uses it as a music background to an announcement.

undersides *n pl* [*Clothing*] the back section of trousers, extending from the trousers bottom to the waistband, and between the inside and side seams.

under-square *n* [*Cars*] See **longstroke**.

under-strapper *n* [*UK*] [*Railways*] the second in command of a station or a depot.

undertaker's job *n* [*Horse-racing, Greyhound racing*] an animal that was never meant to win a race; thus by extension this means an idea or suggestion that was always pointless.

undifferentiated marketing *n* [*Marketing*] See **market aggregation**.

undue influence *n* [*Law*] the improper exercise of influence over the mind of another person (though without any threat or use of violence) to persuade them to act against their will. See also **duress**.

unfair house, also **unfair shop** *n* [*Industrial relations*] an employer who offers pay and/or conditions of work that fall below the standards generally accepted in the same industry or in any industries in the locality.

unhair *v* [*Furriers*] to remove by machine the long, gleaming 'guard-hairs' that are found – acting as sensors and water-shedding devices – on most pelts.

unhook *v* [*Navy*] to pilfer or to borrow without permission.

unilateral statement *n* [*Government*] in diplomatic negotiations this is a statement made by one side only, following discussions which have ended in stalemate and from which there can be no hope of a joint statement or a common understanding.

union catalogue *n* [*Libraries*] a catalogue that combines details on the holdings of a number of different libraries.

union hall *n* [*Sex*] an answering service that is used by homosexual 'call-boys'.

union list *n* [*Libraries*] See **union catalogue**.

unionateness *n* [*Sociology*] the measure of the commitment of an employees' collective organisation to the principles and ideology of trade unionism.

unipolar *a* [*Psychiatry*] said of a psychiatric disorder which is characterised by depressive but not manic disorders.

unit *n* [*US*] [*Railway*] a single locomotive.

unit pricing *n* [*Commerce*] a method of pricing which shows both the price per pound, ounce or any other standard measure and, on that scale, the price charged for the actual item that is being purchased.

unit train *n* [*US*] [*Railways*] a train which transports only one commodity, at special rates, and between two particular points.

unitary approach, also **unitary model** *n* [*Social work*] the concept that, for all its different areas of interest, social work is an all-embracing phenomenon and should be viewed as such, as an overall manifestation of the management of social learning.

unitisation *n* [*Oil industry*] the joint development by a number of companies of an oilfield which extends into territory owned by each of them.

unitised handling *n* [*Commerce*] the transport of goods by container.

universal *n* [*Linguistics*] any of the universal attributes of natural languages based on a variety of basic rules and features.

universal donor *n* [*Medicine*] anyone whose blood group is O; it comes from the earlier belief that O type blood was compatible with any of the other groups.

universalism *n* [*Social work*] the principle of

U

running social services in such a way that all contribute equally and are thus entitled to draw equal benefit; it is the opposite of selectivity.

universe *n* [*Marketing*] those individuals who make up a sample for the purposes of market research. See also **population**.

univocalic *n* [*Logology*] any form of writing that uses only one of the five vowels; eg: 'Persevere, ye perfect men, Ever keep the precepts ten', W. T. Dobson 'Literary Frivolities' (1880).

unkennel *v* [*Hunting*] to move a fox when hunting with hounds.

unk-unks *n pl* [*Aerospace*] abbr of **unknown-unknowns** those phenomena which are doubly unknown, ie: in the first place it is not known whether they exist, and assuming they do exist, no-one would have any means of identifying them.

unlock *n* [*Computing*] an operation by which a process indicates that it has completed its access to a resource. See also **lock**.

unofficial classification *n* [*Government*] a method of countering journalistic enquiries whereby a government official claims that the requested piece of information has been classified as secret, when in fact it has not.

unpack *v* [*Computing*] to recover the original data from its packed format. See also **packing**.

unpin *v* [*Chess*] to release a piece that has hitherto been pinned in one position.

unpleasure *n* [*Psychiatry*] the opposite of pleasure; it is epitomised by a sense of pain, unhappiness and frustration which develops when the instinctual impulses of the ego are blocked.

unpractical *n* [*Theatre*] any prop or item of stage furniture that cannot actually be used on the stage but exists only for its visual effect. See also **impractical**, **practical**.

unrecovered *a* [*Film*] referring to a film that has failed, ie: it has failed to recover its initial costs.

unscheduled engine removal *n* [*Aerospace*] any unexpected engine failure or other repairs undertaken outside normal working hours.

unsocial hours *n pl* [*Industrial relations*] any working hours that do not correspond to those of one's peers and which thus destroy one's social life: split shifts, overtime, weekend or night work, etc.

unweighting *n* [*Skiing*] reducing the weight on the skis by body movements, and thus reducing the friction between the skis and the snow.

unwhipped *a* [*UK*] [*Politics*] referring to a politician who is not subject to a party whip or influenced by the policies of a single party.

up **1.** *adv* [*US*] [*Bars*] abbr of **'straight up'** meaning 'without ice'. **2.** *adv* [*Cycling*] ahead of schedule in a time trial, or leading an opponent in a pursuit race. **3.** *adv* [*Horse-racing*] used when identifying the jockey who is riding a particular horse; thus 'Horse X, Lester Piggott up'. **4.** *adv* [*Computing*] in good working order; it is the opposite of **down**. **5.** *v* [*Computing*] to create a

working version of an otherwise malfunctioning machine; to mend or to start up.

up above *n* [*US*] [*Police*] in New York City this is any part of Manhattan above 42nd Street. See also **down below**.

up/down **1.** *adv* [*UK*] [*Railways*] said of lines going towards or away from London. **2.** *adv* [*UK*] [*Railways*] said of the two operating modes of a relay that control a set of points.

up front *n* [*Film*] money that is paid in advance – to actors, directors, technicians, etc.

up quark *n* [*Science*] a quark which supposedly possesses an 'upward spin'. See also **quark**.

up through *n* [*Parapsychology*] the guessing of symbols on a pack of cards, working through from bottom to top. See also **down through**.

up time *n* [*Computing*] the time during which a computer is functioning. See also **down time 2**.

up-and-under *n* [*Rugby*] a high kick which is intended to give the attacking players time to run up and either catch the ball themselves or threaten whichever opponent catches or attempts to catch it.

upcut *v* [*Media, Advertising*] to cut material out of a TV or radio programme in order to fit in more commercials.

update **1.** *v* [*TV, Radio*] to bring a news item up to date. **2.** *n* [*TV, Radio*] an additional item referring to or added to an earlier news story which brings that story up to date.

up-front *a* [*Finance*] said of rates of interest with a very high rate, up to 50% payable in the first year of a loan, and a lower rate, around 5%, in each of the later years; it is designed to allow the borrower to gain the maximum tax deduction in the first year.

upfront *a* [*New therapies*] honest, revealing, vulnerable, emotionally unguarded, confessing one's deepest feeling.

upgrade **1.** *v* [*Air travel*] to put a passenger, who has paid only the economy fare, into a higher class when there are no seats available in the class to which the ticket applies. **2.** *v* [*Business*] the fraudulent practice of substituting a product of lower quality for one of higher quality in order to gain a greater profit.

upgrading *n* [*US*] [*Medicine*] billing patients, and thus their Medicaid medical insurance, for services that have not actually been provided.

uphills *n pl* [*Gambling*] dice that have been loaded to produce high or 'up' numbers.

uplift *n* [*Oil rigs*] the amount of oil that can be recovered annually from a well before taxes have to be paid.

uplink *n* [*Satellite TV*] an earth to satellite transmit link; this is the communications channel used to get the TV picture up to the satellite before broadcasting it back to earth; it usually operates on 6 Gigaherz (1GHz = 1 billion cycles/sec.) waveband. See also **downlink**.

upload *v* [*Electronics, Military*] to send fresh

information and instructions to an orbiting satellite by a ground based computer and transmission system.

upmarketing *n* [*Marketing*] See **creaming**.

upper *n* [*Logging*] a superior grade of timber or log.

upper-case *a* [*Publishing*] said of capital letters which were originally kept in the upper case of the typesetter's type case; it is the opposite of lower-case uncapitalised letters.

UPS *n* [*Espionage*] acro **Uncontested Physical Searches** illegal break-ins by members of intelligence agencies for the purpose of extracting otherwise unobtainable information. See also **black boy job**.

upscale 1. *v* [*Advertising*] to make larger, to reproduce in a larger, though still similar version. See also **downscale 1. 2.** *a* [*Advertising*] said of a higher income or one that is higher than that previously mentioned, although not necessarily rich.

upset price *n* [*Auctions*] the price which the bidding for a lot must either equal or surpass if a sale is to be made; if the bids fail to reach this price, the lot is withdrawn. See also **reserve 3**.

upside *n* [*Stock market*] the future.

upside potential *n* [*US*] [*Stock market*] the amount of upward movement that may be expected in the price of a stock or commodity.

upstage *adv* [*Theatre*] a stage direction that implies 'behind' either a person or an item of stage furniture. See also **above 3, below, downstage**.

upstart *n* [*Gymnastics*] a series of movements on the horizontal, parallel or asymmetrical bars by which the gymnast swings to a position with the body supported by the arms above the bars; it is often found at the start of a routine.

upstairs 1. *adv* [*Aerospace*] in the air, in flight; thus 'to go upstairs' is to take off, to climb to a higher altitude. **2.** *n* [*Navy*] the surface of the sea as regarded by submariners.

upstairs market *n* [*US*] [*Stock market*] deals that are carried out within the broker-dealer's firm but not on the actual floor of the exchange. See also **off-board**.

upstream loans *n pl* [*Finance*] loans given by subsidiary companies to their parent company when that parent has an insufficiently strong credit rating to obtain money elsewhere.

upthreat *v* [*Military*] to increase the aggressiveness of one's military posture vis-à-vis the enemy.

upthrow *n* [*Mining*] the amount, measured vertically, of the upward displacement in beds of rock that is caused by a fault.

uptick *n* [*Business*] an upswing in trading.

uptight *a* [*New therapies*] 'a word used to describe an individual experiencing anything from mild uneasiness to a clinical depression', (R.D. Rosen 'Psychobabble' 1977).

upward compatible *a* [*Computing*] said of a machine that can do everything that the previous model of its type could do, plus some exciting extras; it is a phrase used by enthusiastic computer salesmen.

ur- *pref* [*Arts*] this comes from Ger. for 'original', 'earliest' and, prefixed to a variety of words, often refers to the more serious areas of the arts, denoting purity or originality. See also **echt**.

urban ecology *n* [*Sociology*] created by the **Chicago School**, this is the concept that the city is as much an environment as any found in nature and can thus be studied in a similar manner. The dominant force in the city is competition, and this creates the divisions of social groups within the city, each of which, like animals in nature, adapt to their own separately defined, but still mutually interdependent environment. The crucial assumption of the theory is that city life is governed by natural, impersonal forces and cannot be influenced by planning.

urban managerialism *n* [*Sociology*] the role of various urban managers – council house officials, building society managers, etc – in distributing the resources at their disposal, and the values and ideologies which determine their decisions.

urbanisation *n* [*Sociology*] the growth in the proportion of a country's population that lives in cities.

US country team *n* [*Espionage*] the senior US co-ordinating team which supervises all intelligence operations in a foreign country and which consists of the ambassador, or his equivalent, plus the heads of any US intelligence departments or agencies that are represented in that country.

usage pull *n* [*Marketing*] the proportionate change in the usage of a product between those who are familiar with the advertising of a product and those who are not.

usance *n* [*Banking, Commerce*] the usual period at which foreign bills of exchange are drawn between two countries; such periods have been created by long custom.

use immunity *n* [*US*] [*Law*] a method whereby prosecutors can circumscribe the immunities offered by the Fifth Amendment (see **take the Fifth**), by offering a witness immunity from any subsequent prosecution that might otherwise arise from the self-incriminating facts which would inevitably emerge in the testimony that such a witness would provide.

use the user *v phr* [*Advertising*] a promotional scheme which offers a **premium** to those consumers who are able to persuade fellow consumers to start purchasing/using a particular product.

use them or lose them *v phr* [*Military*] the concept in nuclear **war-fighting** that a commander should fire his missiles, even in an uncertain situation, rather than wait and risk having them destroyed uselessly in their silos.

used *a* [*Book collecting*] said of a book in a state of repair that is slightly poorer than a **reading copy** but better than a **working copy**.

U

useful load *n* [*Gliding*] the difference between gross weight and empty weight.

user *n* [*Computing*] a gullible programmer who believes whatever he is told, rather than troubling to find out things for himself; it is a derogatory allusion to the average, non-programming user, who has to take what the salesman/manual/engineer states very much at face value.

user time *n* [*Computing*] the time a human user, rather than the machine, requires to perform a task with a computer.

user-friendly *a* [*Computing*] said of a machine which is supposedly geared to the needs and abilities of the average non-professional, inexpert user – eg: in an office – who wants to benefit from the machine's potential without delving into its technology.

USP *n* [*Advertising*] acro **Unique Selling Proposition**, a term coined in the 1950s by US advertising executive Rosser Reeves; it is the advertising process whereby one accentuates whatever attributes one's product possesses that its many apparently similar rivals do not have or their agencies have neglected to highlight in their campaigns.

usual *n* [*Science fiction*] the price of a fan magazine; thus magazines are advertised as 'available for the usual'.

utility *a* [*Design*] used to describe plain, economically priced furniture, made in sturdy, practical materials. 'Utility' design was created between 1941 and 1951 when the UK Government, in order to make the best use of scarce labour and raw materials, imposed a degree of state control on the production of furniture, textiles, clothes and some household goods.

utility meats *n* [*Catering*] offal.

utility operative *n* [*Espionage*] a **principal** in the CIA who is removed from actual espionage and given the task of extracting, perfectly legally, such information about the target – both human and inanimate – that can be obtained through non-classified sources; it is a request that would only alert rival intelligence services if a known or suspected CIA officer showed an interest.

utilised capacity *n* [*Industry*] the amount produced by a plant that is not in full operation. See also **installed capacity**.

utter *v* [*Law*] to publish, to put into circulation.

V

v & v *n* [*Computing*] abbr of **Verification and Validation** the complete range of checks that are performed on a system to ascertain its efficiency.

v, the *n* [*Cricket*] the area of the field that falls between the positions of mid-on and mid-off.

va banque *v* [*Gambling*] in chemin-de-fer and baccarat this is to take a bet against the whole of the bank's stake.

vagnari lu pizzu *v* [*Crime*] in the Italian Mafia this comes from the Sicilian 'to dip one's beak', meaning to take a rake-off or commission, on **laundering** money, selling stolen goods, smuggling drugs, etc.

vair *a* [*Heraldry*] having alternative pelts of blue and white.

VAL index *n* [*Sociology, Business*] abbr of **values and lifestyles index** this was developed in the 1970s at Stanford Research Institute to offer a graded stratification of consumer lifestyles. From the bottom, the nine areas include: poverty stricken sustainers; elderly survivors; belongers; I-am-mes; emulators; achievers; integrators (top 2%).

valentine *n* [*TV*] a soft light, or either 1KW or 2KW.

vales *n pl* [*Merchant navy*] promissory notes or IOUs issued by a merchant captain for the purchase of provisions in a foreign port.

validation codes *n pl* [*Military*] codes which authenticate the nuclear control order issued by the President and which assure missile launch officers that there really is a war on.

valorisation 1. *n* [*Commerce*] the fixing and maintaining of an artificial price for a commodity through government action; it is usually through the addition of subsidies. **2.** *n* [*Science*] in chemistry this is the converting of one element or substance into another, more generally useful one. **3.** *n* [*Sociology*] currently used in sociology meaning 'to value (for)'.

value analysis *n* [*Management, Business*] the systematic and critical assessment of the design and costs of a project in relation to its realised value.

value billing *n* [*Public relations*] the charging of a client on the basis of the actual results achieved by a PR campaign in planting material successfully and generally boosting an image as required, rather than using a set tariff charged by the month.

value calling *n* [*Cards*] in bridge this is a system of estimating bids which is based on the scoring values of the four suits.

value engineering *n* [*Engineering*] the modification of engineering design on the basis of results found by **value analysis**.

value freedom *n* [*Sociology*] a series of professional standards in sociology: 1. sociology can successfully exclude ideology and non-scientific assumption from research; 2. sociologists should not make evaluative judgements from empirical evidence; 3. value judgements should only stem from the researcher's own competence; 4. sociologists are indifferent to the moral implications of their findings; 5. sociologists should make their own values open and clear; 6. sociologists should not advocate any particular values.

value neutrality *n* [*Sociology*] the notion that social science is not competent to pronounce on social values because there remains a gap between logical, empirical findings and moral actions; thus the sociologist should make his/her values clear and should not, as a teacher, attempt to dictate the values of students.

value theory *n* [*Politics*] the Marxist labour theory of value.

value-loaded *a* [*Sociology*] weighted or biased in favour of certain values.

value-relevance *n* [*Sociology*] the distinction between value-judgement and value-interpretation; this acts in three ways: (1) the philological interpretation that establishes the meaning of written documents and texts, (2) ethical interpretation in assigning value to an object of inquiry, (3) the rational interpretation in which a meaningful relationship is sought between phenomena in terms of casual analysis.

vamp **1.** *n* [*Shoe-making*] the part of the upper of a shoe that covers the instep and, if the shoe has no separate tip, the toes. **2.** *v* [*Theatre*] to improvise, especially when using either makeshift or homemade props and costumes, through poverty or an unforeseen emergency. **3.** *v* [*Music*] to play a short (2 or 4 bar) chord sequence – usually on the piano – over and over, as an introduction to the melody.

vamping *n* [*Entertainment*] the extension of a series or programme until a required actor or actress has worked out a current contract and can then start work for the new company, which will then halt that series and start new work with the new member.

vampire, also **vulture** *n* [*US*] [*Medicine*] anyone who works in a hospital laboratory.

VAN *n* [*Communications*] acro **Value Added Networks** basic telecommunications networks or facilities to which some additional service has been added.

van *n* [*Aerospace*] air-conditioned, towed vehicles that are used as temporary bases for any major engineering operations which have to be performed away from a proper workshop, eg: the stripping down, checking and reassembly of a large engine.

van- *pref* [*Marbles*] prefixed to any of the cries, this cry nullifies them and stops the shooter from gaining a bonus throw or any other special privilege; thus 'van-burns!', 'van-slips!', 'van-dubbs!', etc.

van-dragging *n* [*UK*] [*Police*] See **jump-up**.

vandyke print *n* [*Printing*] a print made from a tracing, which has brown lines on a white background or vice versa; it comes from the deep brown pigment 'Vandyke brown'.

vangs *n pl* [*Sailing, Ropework*] ropes with which to trim the peak of a spencer or spanker (a fore-and-aft sail set with a gaff).

vanguard art *n* [*Art*] See **avant-grade art**.

vanguardism **1.** *n* [*Politics*] in Marxist terms, this is the need for a highly disciplined communist party, led by professional revolutionaries who stand as the vanguard of working class aspirations. **2.** *n* [*Politics*] used negatively this refers to the leftist **adventurism** of an elitist few who fought the masses and concentrate on glorifying themselves as 'revolutionary heroes'.

vanilla *a* [*Computing*] standard, run of the mill, ordinary. See also **flavour 1**.

vanity surgery *n* [*Medicine*] plastic surgery carried out purely for cosmetic purposes, eg: straightening or shortening a nose, removing unsightly warts or facial hair, etc.

vardo *n* [*UK*] [*Market-traders*] a gypsy caravan.

vardy *n* [*UK*] [*Market-traders*] opinion, attitude, point of view.

variance **1.** *n* [*Law*] an official dispensation from a building regulation. **2.** *n* [*Economics*] the difference between actual and expected figures – costs, profits, outputs, etc. – in any economic or statistical analysis. **3.** *n* [*Statistics*] the average of the squares of the deviations of a set of quantities.

variety *n* [*Philately*] a stamp that differs in some visual detail of its manufacture from the normal issue; it is usually caused by a fault during the printing process. Varieties range from barely noticeable (and thus marginally valuable) to major (and highly prized) mistakes – eg: the

V

failure to print the Queen's head on a UK stamp, etc. See also **error, flaw**.

variety meats *n pl* [*Catering*] in Chinese restaurants this is a euphemism for offal.

vario *n* [*US*] [*Gliding*] abbr of **variometer** the instrument that indicates whether a glider is flying through rising or sinking air.

variorum *n* [*Bibliography*] an edition of a work that contains notes and comments by a number of scholars, and offers all textual variations.

varmint *n* [*Hunting*] the fox.

VDU *n* [*Computing*] abbr of **video display unit** the screen on which a computer user can see word processing, spread sheets, calculations, graphics and other visual displays of the program that is being run. See also **CRT**.

veepee *n* [*Business*] this comes from VP which stands for 'vice president'.

veer *v* [*Sailing, Ropework*] to slacken and pay out gradually.

vegetable garden *n* [*US*] [*Medicine*] a ward filled with patients, suffering from serious brain damage, who are unable to care for themselves; such patients are vegetables, potatoes, carrots, cucumbers, etc.

vegging *n* [*UK*] [*Catering*] the serving of vegetables which is the main task of a commis or trainee waiter.

vehicle *n* [*Painting*] the liquid portion of a paint, in which the pigment is 'carried'.

veil *n* [*Dog breeding*] See **umbrella**.

veiled *a* [*Audio*] suffering from audible distortions. See also **clean 3**.

vein *n* [*Metallurgy*] in iron-founding this is a wafer of metal projecting from the casting at any position other than where the halves of the mould have been separated. See also **overfill**.

vela *n* [*Military*] the general designation for any nuclear explosion detection programme, whether space- or ground-based.

velocity of circulation *n* [*Economics*] the speed with which money passes from person to person in an economy.

velvet *n* [*Hunting, Shooting*] the network of arteries which covers and nourishes the growing horns of a stag; extremely delicate, it will bleed easily if knocked.

vend *n* [*Mining*] the saleable product of a mine.

venereal noun *n* [*Literary criticism*] a collective noun which means a group or gathering of various animals; it comes from venery, or hunting.

vent 1. *n* [*Tyre-making*] the excess rubber which protrudes from the sides of a finished tyre and which will be trimmed off by the vent trimmer machine. **2.** *n* [*Theatre*] abbr of **ventriloquist**.

ventilator *n* [*Theatre*] a play that is so appallingly bad that the bulk of the audience leave long before the end and their seats are thus filled only with fresh air.

venture capital *n* [*Finance*] funds used for the funding of **venture capitalism**.

venture capitalism 1. *n* [*Finance*] the investment of long-term capital in ventures that are particularly prone to risk; such ventures usually involve new ideas, relatively untried individuals and their business ideas, etc. **2.** *n* [*Finance*] the provision by persons, other than the proprietors, of the financial backing for a new undertaking.

venturi *n* [*Cars*] a streamlined constriction or 'throat' in the entrance duct of a carburettor; due to basic physical laws the increased air pressure this causes will enrich the air/fuel mixture and improve the combustion.

Venus hair stone *n* [*Gemstones*] See **cupid's darts**.

verbal 1. *n* [*UK*] [*Police*] talk, conversation, specifically a confession. **2.** *v* [*UK*] [*Police*] used to describe the manufacture by police of a spurious confession which is then read out in court in all its incriminating detail.

verbals *n pl* [*Drug addicts*] at Broadway Lodge Clinic these are corrective public statements about oneself delivered in group therapy.

verbiage *n* [*Education*] any written matter; no derogatory reference is intended.

verification *n* [*Military*] the checking by one partner in a treaty that the other partner is keeping to the terms of that treaty. As far as nuclear arms control is considered, verification is carried out by the spy satellites of each superpower. Verification is vital to the continued success of deterrence; a statement by the Arms Control and Disarmament Agency (**ACDA**) in 1980 noted 'The deterrent value of verification depends to a considerable extent upon the potential violator being ignorant of the exact capability of the intelligence techniques used to monitor his compliance with an agreement', but did add that 'verification contributes to mutual trust among the parties.'

verismo *n* [*Literary criticism*] the emphasis in art or literature on 'real life', including the less appealing aspects; eg: hard-boiled or kitchen sink styles of writing.

verist sculpture *n* [*Art*] the three-dimensional, sculptured equivalent of **photo-realism**; such sculptures are created by taking casts from the human body in fibreglass and polyester resin.

verkrampte *n* [*Politics*] the extreme right wing of the South African National Party. Diehard supporters of apartheid, they continue to fight with increasing foolhardiness against any concessions or compromises in the white South African way of life. The term comes from Afrikaans for 'cramped'.

verligte *n* [*Politics*] the liberal wing of the South African National Party. Still staunchly white supremacist, they are increasingly willing to accept a variety of necessary compromises and concessions to an increasingly militant black majority population. The term comes from Afrikaans for 'enlightened'.

vermiculate *a* [*Cheese-making*] said of grooves in the rind which resemble tracks made by worms.

vernacular *a* [*Architecture*] used to describe the indigenous style of architecture to be found in an area; it is relatively unsophisticated but is considered to be of great virtue and is seen as the surviving representative of some form of ideal age.

verso *n* [*Publishing*] the left hand page, bearing even numbering. See also **recto**.

verstehen *n* [*Sociology*] a process of empathy, followed by introspection, through which it is considered that one individual may come to appreciate the reasons for the behaviour of another individual; it comes from Ger. for 'to understand'.

vert *a* [*Heraldry*] green.

vertical circulation *n* [*Publishing*] a business publication which is edited to appeal to all levels of that business or profession.

vertical integration *n* [*Business*] a process whereby a company expands by taking over other firms who are in the same type of business, but which work at other levels of the production process: suppliers, distributors, etc. See also **horizontal integration**.

vertical linkage *n* [*Espionage*] the formation of secure intelligence cells in which each individual involved knows only his/her own role and that of the two other individuals, immediately 'above' and 'below' in the organisation.

vertical market *n* [*Economics*] a market that includes all potential purchasers in a particular occupation or industry.

vertical proliferation *n* [*Military*] the upward spread of the numbers of nuclear weapons held by those nations who already have some degree of nuclear arsenal.

vertical publication *n* [*Publishing*] the production of books for a small, specialist audience rather than for the mass market. See also **horizontal publication**.

vertical unions *n pl* [*Industrial relations*] industrial unions. See also **horizontal unions**.

very good *a* [*Book collecting*] the second category of a dealer's description: a book with minimal faults, usually just slight wear.

vesting *n* [*Industrial relations*] the gradual accumulation by long-service employees of the various benefits offered by the firm for which they work.

vesting date *n* [*Law*] the date on which a new law comes into force and those empowered to enforce it receive their new powers.

vest-pocket magician *n* [*Magic*] See **close-up worker**. See also **mental worker**.

veterinarian *n* [*US*] [*Medicine*] a doctor who considers his patients to have no more intelligence than a 'dumb animal'. See also **botanist**, **geologist**.

VFR *n* [*Air travel*] abbr of **Visiting Friends and Relations** a note added to the relevant names on a passenger list to point out the family or friends of the cabin crew, or employees of the airline, who are travelling on the flight. VFRs have no special fare reductions but aged grandmothers and young children do tend to get some extra personal attention from the cabin crew.

VHSI *n* [*Electronics*] abbr of **very high speed integrated circuits** ultra high speed, high density circuits, concentrating on chips measuring only 5–7 microns (millionths of a metre) wide, that are central to military-based electronics developments.

via affirmativa *n* [*Theology*] an approach to God which is based on the belief that it is possible to make positive statements about his nature. See also **via negativa**.

via negativa *n* [*Theology*] an approach to God which is based on the belief that his nature completely transcends human understanding; to make such an approach the soul must abandon all rational conceptions and sense perceptions. See also **via affirmativa**.

vicar *n* [*UK*] [*Government*] an assistant secretary in the civil service; it is derived from John Le Carré's 'Smiley's People' (1979, televised 1982) and taken into general, 'real' use. See also **mole**.

vicious abstraction *n* [*Philosophy*] the abstraction of one quality or term from a thing or concept at the expense of the other qualities or terms which are part of its make-up.

vicious cycle *n* [*Economics*] a cycle of events that leads gradually to the decline of a national currency.

vid lit *n* [*TV*] abbr of **video literature** programmes such as 'Edward and Mrs. Simpson', 'Jennie', etc., which are in fact lavish costume dramas, are based loosely on historical events but focus more on the glamorous personalities involved than the issues which make up the real background.

vidclip *n* [*Film*] excerpts from a film or TV programme that are used for promotion.

videotex *n* [*Communications*] a variety of video broadcasts linking the public and a central computer, including viewdata, teletext, interactive video, home banking, shopping, etc.

vidkids *n pl* [*Entertainment*] industry shorthand for the youthful addicts of computerised arcade video games which are played either at the arcade or on the versions reprocessed for the home computer.

viff *n* [*Military*] acro **vectoring in forward flight** thus as a verb, to vector in flight; this means to change direction abruptly as a result of a change in the direction of the engine thrust.

vigilance men *n pl* [*Industrial relations*] union investigators who visit factories to check up on any possible management abuses and/or work grievances and who then report back to the union

V

headquarters prior to considering what action should be taken.

vignette 1. *n* [*Advertising*] any illustration, photograph or camera shot with deliberately 'atmospheric' fuzzed edges. **2.** *n* [*Advertising*] a TV commercial made up of short scenes, each of them different and often humorous, which all tell ultra-short stories featuring the product as the leading 'character'. **3.** *n* [*TV*] a mask that is placed in front of the camera and which thus only allows a selected portion of the view to be photographed.

vigorish 1. also **the vig** *n* [*Gambling*] the percentage taken by an operator who stands as 'the bank' in a gambling game; it is either a straight fee taken as a percentage of all winnings, or a hidden levy that is taken automatically through the mechanics of the game. **2.** *n* [*Finance*] the interest charged on a loan.

vigorous *a* [*Wine-tasting*] used to describe a lively, healthy, positive flavour associated with youthful development.

villuta *n* [*Crime*] in the Italian Mafia this comes from Sicilian for 'velvet' and means a prostitute.

vinyl *n* [*Pop business*] a record, or records; it comes from the material of which they are made.

violate *v* [*US*] [*Railways*] to exceed the maximum speed limit.

violets *n pl* [*Navy*] onions.

violin piece *n* [*US*] [*Journalism*] the lead story, especially in magazines; it is the piece that 'sets the tone' for a publication.

virgin *n* [*Navy*] the Petty Officer's mess, which was originally part of the seaman's mess, screened off for privacy.

virgin medium *n* [*Computing*] anything related to the computer that is as yet completely untouched: a brand-new **floppy disk**, a roll of fresh paper tape, etc.

virgin tape *n* [*Audio*] brand-new, absolutely untouched recording tape, fresh from the manufacturer.

virgin wool *n* [*Weaving*] wool fibre converted into yarn or fabric for the first time.

virtual *a* [*Computing*] said of any computing facility that does not physically exist, but is offered to a user or system as if it really did. See also **transparent 1**.

virtual memory *n* [*Computing*] a system designed to overcome the limitations of a machine's actual hardware by temporarily redefining the memory to accept programs that, usually, would require computers of infinitely greater power. The distinction between the internal memory and the disk drive is set aside; the computer then 'reads' the large program as a number of small, and thus accessible, segments. It runs the program by taking on such segments as it can handle and then, after use, replacing them with the next one required. It was originated in 1960 by Honeywell and IBM.

virtual storage *n* [*Computing*] a large notional main store is made available to the user by mapping virtual **addresses** on to actual addresses in auxiliary storage.

virus *n* [*Computing*] an illicit command or commands that in turn generate a train of similar commands, all of which gradually incapacitate a system in a way which cannot be controlled once it has been set in motion. Such viruses are often introduced into the large public computing systems by external **hackers** who enter the system at one mode and program in commands which affect the larger system. See also **logic time bomb, Trojan horse 2**.

visible *a* [*Economics*] referring to actual goods which are imported or exported; it is the opposite of 'invisible', which refers to services rendered or received and for which money is charged.

visible negro *n* [*US*] [*Business*] any black employee who is deliberately placed in the forefront of a firm, rather than being, as is more usual, hidden away as a janitor, maintenance man or nightwatchman, in order to convince anyone who cares that the firm offers equal opportunity to all races. See also **tokenism**.

visit *n* [*Dog breeding*] the introduction of a bitch to a dog for mating.

visual *n* [*US*] [*Politics*] any event that offers the potential for the candidate to be photographed in an ostensibly flattering manner: kissing babies, welcoming war heroes, etc. This is generally known in the UK as a 'photo opportunity'.

visual interaction *n* [*Photo-typesetting*] the editing of the **bit-map** of a character on the screen so that the operator can keep track of the changes as they are made.

vital signs *n pl* [*Medicine*] See **vitals**.

visualiser *n* [*Advertising*] a commercial artist who designs the layouts of the advertisements.

vital statistics form *n* [*US*] [*Undertakers*] a death certificate.

vitals *n pl* [*US*] [*Medicine*] the three 'vital signs' that can help determine the state of a patient's health: temperature, respiration and pulse. See also **TPR**.

VLCC *n* [*Oil rigs*] abbr of **very large crude carrier** an ocean going oil tanker of 200,000 to 300,000 metric tons deadweight. See also **ULCC**.

VLSI [*Computing, Technology*] abbr of **Very Large Scale Integration** the fabrication technology which makes it possible to produce chips with more than 1000 **gates** on each one.

VO 1. *n* [*US*] [*Medicine*] **voice order** delivered in person by a physician. See also **TO**. **2.** *n* [*UK*] [*Prisons*] abbr of **Visiting Order** an official chit that must be sent out by a prisoner (other than those on remand) to request the admission of his/her family or friends for a visit.

Vo-Ag *a* [*US*] [*Education*] abbr of **Vocational Agriculture** agriculture taught as a course to those who wish to take it up as their occupation.

V

vocabulary *n* [*Art*] a set of artistic forms, techniques and movements available to an individual.

voice 1. *n* [*UK*] [*Politics*] a vote given vocally in Parliament. **2.** *v* [*Radio*] to make a report or to conduct an interview over the air; thus a reporter 'voices' a story. See also **voicer**.

voice messaging *n* [*Business*] the current sophisticated version of inter-office communications, combining computerised 'electronic mail' with an advanced telephone answering tape machine.

voice wrap *n* [*TV*] the use of the newscaster's voice to introduce a news item which is then narrated by a reporter. See also **telop**.

voice-over *n* [*TV, Advertising*] any words that are broadcast over pictures – either on a news or sports report, a documentary or, in advertising, over the pictures of the product – by a commentator or speaker who is not on screen.

voicer *n* [*Radio*] a taped programme item – either on cassette or reel-to-reel tape – on which only the reporter is heard speaking. Such a piece has no **actuality**; it can be the regurgitation of a piece of wire service copy of which the reporter is personally ignorant. Court reports, foreign reports or opinion pieces are also classifed as voicers.

voicing *n* [*Music*] in jazz this is the blend of the various instruments in an ensemble, the harmonisation.

voids *n pl* [*Building, Plastering*] the spaces in a material occupied by air, water or both.

volatile storage *n* [*Computing*] a computer memory in which the stored information is destroyed once the power supply to the machine is turned off.

voluntarism 1. *n* [*Industrial relations*] a policy that has been mutually agreed to both unions and management regarding the ideal way of conducting industrial relations: the law should not intervene directly in the process of collective bargaining. The main threats to voluntarism have been the various incomes policies that have emerged from a succession of British governments. **2.** *n* [*Sociology*] sociological theories based on the intentions and motives of actors who thus act 'voluntarily' and not as 'determined' by the social structure.

volute *n* [*Building, Plastering*] the spiral feature found in Ionic, Corinthian or composite capitals.

Von Neumann *a* [*Computing*] used to describe the **architecture** of a conventional (**first to** fourth generation) computer. Von Neumann architecture is typified by (a) a single computing element which incorporates processor, communications and memory; (b) linear organisation of fixed memory cells; (c) one level address space of cells; (d) low level machine language; (e) sequential, centralised control of computation; (f) primitive input/output capability. Among a number of other advances, the **fifth generation** machines are the first to discard the Von Neumann architecture.

vorlauf *v* [*US*] [*Skiing*] to be the forerunner of the race; to go over a race circuit to demonstrate the layout of the track and give an idea of the time it may take.

Vostro account *n* [*Banking*] an account maintained abroad by a bank in the currency of the country where the account is held. See also **nostro accounts**.

vote bank *n* [*Politics*] in India this is a group of people who can be relied upon to deliver their votes as a single block in favour of the same party.

vote on account *v* [*Politics, Economics*] a resolution at the close of a financial year to assign a sum of money to a government department as an advance payment before its full annual budget has been voted into law.

voting system *n* [*Military*] a security system designed to prevent 'accidental' nuclear war: bomber and missile silo crews must obtain coded correlation of launch plans from an outside source, without which codes they are unable to remove the locks on their weapons. This system has not been applied to submarines, whose captains alone possess the power to control their missiles. See also **two-man rule**.

voucher *n* [*Advertising*] a free copy of any print medium which is sent to an advertising agency and/or an advertiser to show that a commissioned advertisement was actually published as and when required.

vox pop *n* [*Radio, TV*] abbr of '**vox populi**' Lat. meaning 'the voice of the people'; these are interviews conducted with men and women in the street in order to elicit their views on whatever topic the broadcaster may care to throw at them.

vulgar Marxism *n* [*Politics*] simplified or misinterpreted Marxism, a caricature of the whole ideology; it is often the production of the naive, the ultra-left or any other socialist fanatic.

V

W

W **1.** *n* [*UK*] [*Police*] abbr of **warrant** an authorisation for a policeman to search a house or arrest an individual. **2.** *n* [*Air travel*] an aircraft flight schedule: the plane flies to its destination and then makes a further detour to an intermediate destination before returning to its base to pick up more outgoing passengers; the flight thus resembles the letter W.

wabash *n* [*US*] [*Railways*] See **cornfield meet**.

wads *n pl* [*Building, Plastering*] pieces of **scrim** soaked in measured amounts of plaster and used in the making or fixing of fibrous plaster casts.

WAF *adv* [*Book collecting*] acro **with all faults** a proviso issued by dealers who send out books from a catalogue by post; the collector undertakes to accept the book as found, given the honest description in a catalogue.

wafer *n* [*Computing*] the thin slice of silicon from which a semi-conductor chip is made.

wafer fab *n* [*Technology*] a factory where silicon chips are assembled.

waffle *v* [*Racquets*] to hit another player in the face, leaving a 'waffle' imprint from the impact of the strings on his/her flesh.

waffler *n* [*Coal-mining*] a mobile cutter, used mainly for driving **headings**, which uses its cutting chain both for cutting and loading.

waft *n* [*Frisbee flying*] the floating motion of a frisbee in mid-flight; it is the fifth of nine flight modes.

wafty *a* [*UK*] [*Market-traders*] of poor quality, second-rate.

wage drift *n* [*Economics*] a gradual, unplanned escalation of national wage levels when individual companies choose to offer higher increases than government policy has recommended.

wage stop *n* [*Economics*] the principle held in the UK that those who are unemployed ought not to receive more in welfare benefits than they would in wages were they employed.

wage-push inflation *n* [*Economics*] inflation that results from too many, and too substantial, increases in wages.

wagon-wheel effect *n* [*Film*] the apparent reverse motion of a spoked wheel when filmed; this is caused by the blend of the time between spoke movement and camera shutter openings and causes a stroboscopic effect.

wagtail **1.** *n* [*Angling*] a form of **spinning** bait. **2.** *n* [*Carpentry*] a parting strip used in the construction of a sash window.

WAHF *v phr* [*Science fiction*] abbr of **we also heard from** this is appended to a list of names whose letters cannot be included in the **loccol**.

wahine *n* [*Surfing*] this comes from Hawaiian for 'woman' and means a female surfer.

waist *n* [*Skiing*] the narrowest part of the ski, between the **shoulder** and the **tail**.

wait condition *n* [*Computing*] a situation during which the processor suspends operations until it receives a specific external signal that tells it to continue.

wait in front *v* [*Horse-racing*] to be in the lead.

wait list *n* [*Air travel*] a standby ticket, usually indicated by the abbreviation 'WL' on the ticket.

wait out *v* [*Baseball*] said of a batter who forces a pitcher to throw a maximum number of pitches in the hope of getting to first base 'on balls', ie after three pitches have failed to cross home base, and at which, as such, the batter need not attempt a hit.

waiter **1.** *n* [*Chess*] a **waiting problem**. **2.** *n* [*UK*] [*Stock market*] a uniformed attendant at the Stock Exchange; it is derived from the waiters working at the original 18th century coffee house where the Stock Exchange first began its affairs.

waiting problem *n* [*Chess*] any situation in which White's first move leads to checkmate after every reply essayed by Black and as a result of the move which is that reply.

waiting slop *n* [*US*] [*Lunch counter*] working on the grill in a cheap lunch counter or diner.

waiting time **1.** *n* [*Computing*] the time that elapses between calling up data from memory and the transfer of that data to the control unit. **2.** *n* [*Industry*] in work study this is the period of time for which an operator is available for production but is restricted from working.

wake-up, also **get-up** *n* [*US*] [*Prisons*] one's last day in prison: one wakes/gets up in prison but goes to bed free.

waldo *n* [*Technology*] this is named after Waldo

F. Jones, an inventor created by science fiction writer Robert Heinlein in 'Astounding Science Fiction' magazine in 1942; it is a device for handling or manipulating objects by remote control.

waling n [Carpentry] a heavy horizontal timber or metal strut that is used to support the **soldiers** that run up the sides of an excavation.

walk 1. v [Cricket] said of a batsman who knows he is out – especially to a catch by the wicketkeeper or slips – and leaves the wicket before the umpire needs answer an appeal; it is supposedly the epitome of cricketing sportsmanship. 2. v [Baseball] the batter can do this when a pitcher throws three foul balls; the batter does not have to play at these and is instead allowed to advance to first base. 3. v [Military] to swing a (machine-) gun across a target, leaving a trail of bullets across it. 4. v [US] [Car salesmen] said of a customer who leaves the lot without buying. 5. n [Aerospace] the steady orbiting of a spacecraft around a star or planet.

walk a flat v [Theatre] to carry a **flat** in an upright position; to walk a flat up/down means to raise or lower a flat by hand.

walk back the cat v [Politics] in international negotiations this is to retreat from a hard-line position to one in which more compromises may have to be accepted.

walk the train v [US] [Railways] to make a thorough inspection of the air pipes and braking system on a train.

walk through n [Computing] the review of a software system performed by a specialist team who check the design and the performance of the system. One member of the team 'walks through' the logic of the system prior to opening a debate among the entire group.

walk to v [US] [Lunch counter] to take away.

walk up v [Shooting] the **guns** do this when they walk in line and in silence towards the game, in order to **flush** partridges, etc; beaters may walk between the guns. See also **driving**.

walkaround n [US] [Circus] a clown number performed while the clown is moving around the ring.

walkie-lookie n [TV] See **creepie-peepie**.

walkie-talkie n [Tyre-making] a transporting device that operates on the factory floor; it is essentially just a truck or tractor.

walk-in defector n [Espionage] a defector who turns him/herself over to the chosen nation and brings along secrets or similar information as the 'price' of gaining political asylum. Such a defector has probably not been wooed by an intelligence agency, but has decided to make the move reasonably spontaneously.

walking n [Aerospace] the advancing of an aircraft's throttles in asymmetric steps, eg: left, right, left, right, etc.

walking around money n [US] [Politics] money paid to those precinct workers who knock on doors and ring at bells in order to help their candidate's campaign, and generally help to 'get out the vote'; such payments are not wholly legal, but neither do they constitute a major breach of electoral ethics.

walking gentleman, walking lady n [Theatre] an extra, a walk-on, a bit part.

walk-on 1. n [Theatre] a very small speaking role. See also **cough and a spit**. 2. n [US] [Sport] a team member who has no regular status.

walks department n [Banking] a department in a clearing bank which deals with cheques drawn on non-clearing banks that are presented by messengers or clerks from those banks, generally within the City.

walk-through 1. n [Theatre] a rehearsal without costumes but with the **business** that accompanies the dialogue. 2. n [Theatre] a very small part, a **walk-on**.

walk-up 1. n [Horse-racing] the walking of racehorses up to the starting line or tape, as opposed to their being placed in starting stalls. 2. n [Real estate] any building that has more than two floors but does not offer a lift.

wall! excl [Computing] an interjection that implies confusion; a request for more information.

wall 1. n [US] [Medicine] an intern in the emergency room who keeps the workload down to genuine emergencies by refusing to admit any but the most important of cases; it is the opposite of a **sieve**. 2. n [Surfing] the steep face of a wave just before it breaks.

Wall Street n [Finance] a general term that embraces the whole of the New York's financial district. See also **Lombard Street**.

wallflower n [Stock market] any share that is no longer popular with investors.

wallop n [Painting] any washable distemper, but it was originally only the proprietary brand 'Walpamur'.

wallpaper 1. n [Music] piped music that is played in lifts, hotel lobbies, down phones; Muzak. 2. n [US] [TV] stock footage, eg: the White House, the Pentagon, which serves as a background picture for any general story that concerns its subject.

walnut storage disease n [US] [Medicine] obsessive, squirrel-like hoarding by a senile patient.

Walter Plinge n [UK] [Theatre] an imaginary pseudonym used by an actor who takes two roles in the same production; it possibly originated around 1870 to honour the stagestruck landlord of a pub opposite the Theatre Royal, Drury Lane, who was generous in his credit and was rewarded by being given a benefit performance in his honour. Another theory is cited in a letter (1981) from Norman A. Punt, FRCS Ed: 'invented in a pub off the Strand by H. O. Nicholson, brother of my old friend Nora Nicholson, who died in 1973 after 60 years on the stage.' See also **George Spelvin**.

W

waltzing matilda *n* [*UK*] [*Railways*] a machine used to clean ballast and return it to the track; its jerky, eccentric movements appear to some people as a crazy dance. See also **shrimps**.

WAN *n* [*Computing*] acro **Wide-Area Network** a communications network, similar to a local-area network (**LAN**), but spread over a larger geographical area, taking in whole states, counties or even countries.

wand *n* [*Computing, Commerce*] See **optical wand**.

wane *n* [*Frisbee flying*] the sixth of nine flying modes: the frisbee begins to enter the second half the flight.

wangan *n* this comes from Algonquin meaning 'trap'; literally it means 'that into which something falls'.

wangan 1. *n* [*Logging*] debts owed by loggers at the company store. 2. *n* [*Logging*] a shelter equipped for office and accommodation (including sleeping) that is often mounted on wheels or caterpillar tracks and dragged around the woods as needed. 3. *n* [*Logging*] the equipment a pulp cutter needs, including tools, food and water, when working in a remote area of the woods.

wangle *v* [*UK*] [*Taxis*] to learn the routes and rules involved in driving a London cab. See also **the Knowledge**.

wango *n* [*Government*] acro **wholly autonomous non-governmental organisation** usually international organisations to which Britain contributes on a formula based on the gross national product or under a treaty agreement; the largest is the UN (current contribution 20m). Outside the regulations of normal government accountancy, and often playing on First World guilt as regards Third World poverty, wangos thrive on subsidy without accountability. See also **quango**.

want *n* [*Coal-mining*] an area of a coal seam which is missing, due to the presence of a fault, a **washout**, **horse** etc.

wap *n* [*Metallurgy*] a single turn in a coil.

war babies *n pl* [*US*] [*Stock market*] shares in those companies which work mainly as defence contractors for the US military.

war brides *n pl* [*US*] [*Stock market*] See **war babies**.

war of resolution *n* [*Military*] a term coined by Herman Kahn (1922–) to denote a contest in which all restraints are abandoned in a 'naked matching of resolve with resolve in an exchange of exemplary attacks and reprisals' or, as he adds, 'a drive towards a showdown' in which presumably there will be a result, a victor and a loser.

ward *n* [*Religion*] in the Mormon church this is an adminstrative division of the congregation.

Ward X *n* [*Medicine*] a euphemism for the hospital morgue.

warehouse to warehouse *phr* [*Insurance*] referring to a clause in cargo insurance policies which guarantee that insurance cover is provided throughout the whole time of transit.

warehousing 1. *n* [*Finance*] the use of money invested in an insurance company or unit trust to purchase shares which would otherwise have dropped sharply in price. Such purchases can be used to start a clandestine attempt to obtain sufficient shares to make a takeover bid. See also **concert party, dawn raid**. 2. *n* [*Finance*] the spreading of share purchases through a group of buyers either acting as a consortium or as nominees for a single person – either method is used to initiate a takeover bid without alerting the target company. See also **concert party, dawn raid**. 3. *n* [*US*] [*TV*] the rerunning of successful series by independent TV stations while the same shows are still proving successful on a network **first run** basis.

war-fighting *n* [*Military*] usually as in 'nuclear war-fighting capability' this means actually launching an attack, rather than merely rattling nuclear sabres.

wargame *v* [*Military*] to experiment with a variety of putative 'battles', 'attacks', 'nuclear strikes', etc, with the intention of developing a strategy that might have to be tested in a real war.

wargasm *n* [*Military*] a term coined by Herman Kahn in a series of briefings delivered to the US military in the late 1950s: 'in which some war-plan proposals were referred to as "orgastic spasms of destruction". During one of these briefings I said to the audience "You people do not have a war-plan, you have a war-gasm". These expressions were put forward with no particular reference to their sexual implications, but some of my colleagues, more conversant with Freudian concepts . . . than I, argue that the term "spasm war" is more accurate and descriptive than one might think . . .'

warm *a* [*Industry*] in constant readiness to respond to new developments, production plans, etc.; it refers directly to the machinery itself.

warm boot *n* [*Computing*] the restarting of the operating system of a computer without turning off the machine.

warm standby *n* [*Computing, Communications*] a backup system which is kept in readiness for operational use within a few seconds of the failure of the primary system. See also **cold standby, hot standby**.

warm the bell *v* [*Navy*] to finish watch duties before time; old sailors thought that warming the bell with their hands would make it strike sooner and thus end their watch early.

warmbody device *n* [*Data security*] any device that can measure some characteristic unique to an individual and check it against pre-recorded identification information, stored on the computer itself or on a credit card or **smart card**. See also **earprint**.

W

warmed-up 1. *a* [*US*] [*Cattlemen*] referring to cattle that are beginning to fatten up. 2. *a* [*US*] [*Meat trade*] said of cattle that are beginning to show the effects of fattening.

warm-up *n* [*Sex*] the washing by a prostitute of either sex of a client's penis prior to sex.

warning red *n* [*Military*] code/radio signal for: a hostile attack is either imminent or actually in progress.

warp 1. *v* [*Sailing, Ropework*] to shift a vessel by means of towing or hauling on hawsers. 2. *n* [*Weaving*] the group of parallel threads that are held in tension during the weaving process. 3. *n* [*Frisbee flying*] the eighth of nine flying modes; it is any turn in direction made by the moving frisbee.

warrant *n* [*Coal-mining*] See **seatearth**.

warrantless investigation *n* [*Espionage*] See **technical trespass**.

warranty *n* [*Law*] a statement of fact, as opposed to a statement of opinion or advertisement; it is made by the seller of the goods and the buyer can legally rely on it.

Warrington *n* [*Carpenters*] a cross-peen joiner's hammer; it comes from the name of the Cheshire town.

warrior *n* [*Mining*] an excavating drill.

warry *a* [*UK*] [*Military*] See **ruggsy**.

wart *n* [*Journalism*] an incident or anecdote, reported in a story or profile, which reflects discredit, in a flattering, humanising way, on the subject.

warwick *n* [*Coal-mining*] a safety device that comprises a long bar pivoted from the roof, which can be dropped down or placed in the path of a runaway vehicle.

was *n* [*Frisbee flying*] the final, ninth, flying mode; it is the catching of the frisbee by the receiving player.

wash 1. *n* [*US*] [*Garment trade*] speedy but second-rate pressing. 2. *n* [*Distilling*] the liquid obtained by fermenting **wort** with yeast. 3. *v* [*Gas industry*] to remove impurities from gas or vapour by passing the gas through water or another liquid which retains or dissolves the impurity. 4. *v* [*Sports*] in mah-jongg this is to shuffle the tiles at the conclusion of a round, prior to building a new wall.

wash sale *n* [*Stock market*] an illegal deal between two brokers who arrange a fake 'sale' and thus create an illusory market price for a share; it is used for purposes of tax evasion.

washboard *n* [*Glass-making*] ripples or waves, usually horizontal, found on the surface of glassware.

washed *a* [*Cheese-making*] washed rind cheeses are **surface-ripened** cheeses which have been 'washed' or brushed with brine, beer, brandy, marc, etc.

washed in the blood *a* [*Religion*] freed from one's sins by acknowledging Christ's sacrifice for mankind.

washing 1. *n* [*Coffee production*] a technical process which removes by water all traces of the mucilagenous metacarp from the surface of the **parchment**. 2. *n* [*Cheese-making*] a process in cheese-making whereby the developing cheese is 'washed' or brushed with brine, beer, brandy, marc, etc.

washing machine *n* [*Crime*] any system or individual bank or financial institution where money gained illegally can be rendered legal by **laundering** it through that system or institution.

wash-line *n* [*Journalism*] a column of gossip and social news and trivia.

washout *n* [*Coal-mining*] local thinning of a coal seam due to erosion during or shortly after its formation.

wash-up *n* [*Navy*] a conference that takes place after a military/naval operation in which the operation is discussed and its success, failure, short- and long-term effects, etc. are analysed.

wastage *n* [*Industrial relations*] the reduction of manpower that is achieved simply by leaving vacant the jobs of those employees who resign or retire from a company.

waste 1. *v* [*Horse-racing*] said of a jockey who loses weight. 2. *v* [*Military*] to kill; the implication is of savagery, of 'laying waste' a people and their homes. 3. *n* [*Frisbee flying*] the seventh of nine flying modes; it is the downward descent towards the catcher.

wasting assets *n pl* [*Commerce*] those assets that are gradually used up by their very nature: oil in a well, coal in a mine, etc.

wasty wool *n* [*Weaving*] an industrial description of weak, tangled wool that will be wasted during spinning.

watch list *n* [*Espionage*] a list of special words that is programmed into a computer which is used in analysing intelligence; the list helps it sort out specific material from a mass of otherwise undifferentiated material.

watchman *n* [*Printing*] a piece of cardboard inserted between lines of metal type in order to point out an error in the setting.

watchpot *n* [*Government*] a back-formation from 'a pot that needs to be watched'; it was coined, like so many similar terms, by Alexander Haig when he was US Secretary of State; thus 'Lebanon is a Mid-East watchpot'.

water course *n* [*Oil rigs*] a wide, rounded shape of drill bit. See also **fishtail 5, Mother Hubbard**.

water hammer *n* [*Oil rigs*] the energy developed when fluid in motion is stopped abruptly.

water haul *n* [*Journalism*] unsuccessful research, or unsuccessful attempts to obtain an interview or to make useful capital from an interview or story.

water landing *n* [*Aerospace*] landing in the sea or ocean; 'ditching'.

W

water note n [UK] [Coal-mining] a note permitting men working in pre-agreed levels of water to work shorter shifts.

water the garden, the vegetables v [US] [Medicine] to change the glucose drips that provide the sole method of feeding for those patients whose brain damage precludes any other sustenance. See also **vegetable garden**.

watered stock 1. n [Stock market] stock in a company that has increased its issued capital to a level that far exceeds the value of its tangible assets. **2.** n [Stock market] shares in a company that has increased its issued capital on paper but has not obtained any actual cash to back it up. **3.** n [Stock market] loan stock in a company that has increased its loan capital but has not made provision to pay the additional interest.

waterhole n [Science] a part of the electromagnetic spectrum that is reasonably free from interference and which, it is felt, would be that waveband most likely to pick up signals from extra-terrestrial beings who wished to contact Earth.

water-laid 1. a [Sailing, Ropework] said of three strand, left-laid rope. **2.** a [Sailing, Ropework] used to describe rope that has been moistened with water rather than oil in its making; it is also called 'white rope'. **3.** a [Sailing, Ropework] said of cable-laid rope, which supposedly absorbs less water than hawser-laid rope.

watermelon 1. n [Oil rigs] the weight placed on a rod line to keep it from unthreading the winch when the rod is released. **2.** n [Oil rigs] the weight on a heat-exchanger that is used on gas-lift wells to prevent the gas choke from freezing.

watery a [Wine-tasting] lacking fruitiness, **extract**, low in alcohol and acidity.

wave n [US] [Gliding] a large-scale phenomenon of rising and falling air currents caused by a strong prevailing wind striking a high ridge or mountain. Given a strong wind and a large mountain chain, the effect can be magnified, creating very high waves; the record, set by Paul Bikle, was 46,267ft. (14,102m).

wave-off n [Aerospace] a signal – either from a man on the ground or sent by radio from the control tower – which instructs an incoming aircraft that it must not land.

wavy navy n [Navy] officers of the RNVR (Royal Naval Volunteer Reserve) whose stripes of rank are wavy, rather than straight as in the regular service.

wax n [Frisbee flying] the third of nine flying modes; the frisbee increases its angle of climb during the first part of the flight.

wax his tail v [US] [Air Force] to lock in on a hostile aircraft's tail during a dogfight, from which position one's heat-seeking air-to-air missiles should guarantee his destruction.

waxworks n pl [US] [Politics] the main guests at a political dinner who have to sit on a raised platform and try to hide their boredom behind expressions of frozen enthusiasm which seem to originate in Madame Tussaud's exhibition.

WDWN in NAD phr [Medicine] abbr of **well-developed, well-nourished, in no acute distress**.

weaponeering n [Military] the process of assessing exactly which type and calibre of weapons are needed to cause the required damage to a range of specified targets.

weapons system n [Military] the military equivalent of the machine; it involves a weapons platform (ship, plane, etc), a weapon (gun, missile, etc) and a means of command and communication; plus the human support – scientists to invent, engineers to maintain and service, soldiers to use, workers to build, etc. It was developed by the USAF in the 1950s as a deliberate parallel to civilian 'management systems'.

weapons tight [Military] an order given to air defence units when friendly as well as hostile forces are flying in the area: no weapons are to engage targets unless they are identified with 100% accuracy as enemy aircraft.

wearable n [US] [Weaving] a garment intended to be worn; thus its intrinsic artistic value is diminished by its function.

weasel 1. n [Gas industry] a proprietory yarn-swellant manufactured by ICI; it is injected into gas-distribution mains to swell the yarn packing with which many lead/yarn joints are constructed and so minimise leakage. **2.** n [Advertising] an intentionally (and thus illegal) misleading statement that is inserted into the claims made by the text or script of an advertisement. **3.** n [Military] a light cargo and personnel carrier. **4.** also **weezle** v [UK] [Railways] to extract tips from passengers; it is used by porters and carriage staff.

weather mark n [Sailing] a mark on a racing course towards which boats sail into the wind.

weather window n [Oil industry] the period, usually short, that is available to offshore oil rigs, when the weather is sufficiently calm, to permit a variety of maintenance and supply operations to be carried out safely.

weathercock n [Aerospace] the tendency of an aircraft or missile to turn slightly in the same direction as the wind.

weather-dodger n [Navy] a screen on the bridge of a ship which protects its occupants from adverse weather.

weave n [Lacrosse] a zig-zag run by the ball player when chased by the defence, that is intended to upset the stride pattern and attempted tackle of the defence; each change of direction should coincide with a lift of the defender's stick.

weave problems n pl [Sociology] problems that cannot be solved in isolation, but which are related and dependent on several or many inter-

W

linked situations, each of which must be considered in its due turn.

web 1. *n* [*Building*] the vertical plate or portion that connects and strengthens the upper and lower parts of a girder or rail. **2.** *n* [*Coal-mining*] the width of a slice or cut of coal that is removed from the face by a power loader in one cycle of operation. **3.** *n* [*Industry*] the socket of a tool or implement that receives the handle. **4.** *n* [*US*] [*Paper-making*] a continuous sheet of paper manufactured or actually being manufactured on a paper machine. **5.** *n* [*Printing*] a reel of paper used on a newspaper or similar printing press. **6.** *n* [*Weaving*] the woven fabric. **7.** *n* [*Weaving*] See **batt**.

webs *n pl* [*US*] [*TV*] the major US broadcasting networks: ABC, CBS, NBC.

wedding 1. *n* [*Mining*] a collision in the mine between a number of buckets or trucks. **2.** *n* [*Printing*] strong, fine-textured, smooth, dull writing paper, suitable for wedding invitations.

wedge 1. *n* [*Golf*] the traditional name for the No.10 iron. **2.** *n* [*Medicine*] a piece of bone removed (eg from a foot) to correct a deformity or malposition. **3.** *n* [*Frisbee flying*] the second of nine flying modes; the frisbee, after release from the hand, begins spinning and moving away from the thrower.

wedge up *v* [*UK*] [*Prisons*] to barricade oneself behind one's cell door, either to register a protest or to set up a (temporary) defence against a beating from the prison officers.

wedged 1. *a* [*Computing*] referring to a machine that is 'locked up' unable to proceed further with its calculations or with the running of a program. See also **deadly embrace**. **2.** *a* [*US*] [*Theatre*] stranded without money in a hotel far from New York and with one's baggage held as security against the unpaid bill.

wedgie *n* [*Motor trade*] an Austin Princess motorcar; it comes from the shape of the body.

weed 1. *n* [*UK*] [*Crime*] in a fairground this is the 'official' pilfering from the till by the person running a stall. The owner accepts this, as long as the sums involved stay at a reasonable level; if they exceed this level a second person is put on the stall and by demanding his share of the weed, penalises the original thief by taking 50% of the basic permitted sum. **2.** *n* [*Navy*] a sailor's grievance. **3.** *v* [*Computing*] to remove unwanted items from a file. **4.** *v* [*Sailing, Ropework*] to clear rigging and cable of any stops, rope yarns, etc. **5.** *v* [*Angling*] a trout does this when it buries itself in weeds when hooked.

weeded *a* [*Angling*] said of a fish that is hiding among the weeds.

weeder *n* [*UK*] [*Government*] a civil service official responsible for sorting out classified material before it is placed in the Public Record Office.

weeding 1. *n* [*UK*] [*Crime*] stealing from one's employer. **2.** *n* [*UK*] [*Crime*] stealing from a place where a crime has already been committed recently.

weekend bride *n* [*US*] [*Hotels*] a woman staying with a man who is not her husband.

weekly *n* [*Film*] a weekly wage.

weenie, also **gnurd, gome, tool** *n* [*US*] [*Education*] See **squid 2**.

weep *n* [*Public relations*] a sob story told by a desperate PR man, usually a press agent, who claims to a columnist that if a certain story is not placed, his client will certainly fire him and his family, or worse still, the PR man himself will suffer untold miseries.

weeper *n* [*Building*] a hole built into masonry to provide for drainage.

weeping *n* [*Cheese-making*] the sign of excellence in a true Swiss Emmental or Gruyere, when the holes in the cheese are shining with butterfat.

weft, also **filling, woof** *n* [*Weaving*] the independent thread that is woven across the **warp** threads in such a way as to join them together and make a fabric.

weigh off *v* [*UK*] [*Law*] to sentence a prisoner who has been found 'Guilty' in court.

weight *n* [*Drugs*] one pound weight (1 lb.), usually applied to hashish or marijuana.

weighting *n* [*Marketing*] the adjustment of **raw** data by assigning definite proportionate values, varying as to the assigned degree of importance, to the various aspects of the data under consideration.

weigh-up *n* [*UK*] [*Market-traders*] an assessment of a customer's eagerness and/or ability to buy (and whether he can be successfully cheated).

welcome sleeves *n pl* [*US*] [*Medicine*] cloth bindings that restrain a child's hands from touching the face or head and which put the bound-up arms into a 'welcoming' gesture.

welfarism *n* [*US*] [*Sociology*] the principles and policies associated with a welfare state.

well *n* [*Frisbee flying*] the third of nine flying modes; it is the climb to a desired height.

well drink *n* [*US*] [*Bars*] the house liquor; a customer fails to specify a brand of liquor but asks 'What have you got in the well?'

we'll let you know *v phr* [*Theatre*] See **come back Tuesday**.

well-behaved *a* [*Computing*] referring to computer programs which will work on the operating systems of a variety of machines.

well-end *a* [*Sex*] abbr of **well-endowed** used as part of the description of themselves that is provided by **hustlers** who look for trade through contact magazines and wish to point out that they have a large penis.

well-firmed *a* [*Theatre*] used to describe a part that has been thoroughly memorised.

wellhead cost *n* [*Oil industry*] the cost of bringing oil or gas to the surface, before any extra

W

W

costs for transport, refining, taxes, etc. have been added.

wellness *n* [*New therapies*] the state of positive physical and mental well-being that is more than simply not being ill.

welly, give it some *v* [*Hot rods*] to accelerate.

Weltanschauung *n* [*Sociology*] this comes from Ger. for 'world view'; it is an individual's conception of, and relation to, the world in which he/she lives.

West Coast Sound *n* [*Audio*] a genre of speaker design, attributed to Californian designers; it is characterised by exaggerated mid-bass output and middle frequency presence. See also **East Coast Sound**.

western *n* [*Tennis*] a method of gripping the racket whereby the palm of the hand is under the handle.

wet 1. *a* [*US*] [*Meat trade*] said of a cow that has milk in the udder. **2.** *a* [*Chemistry*] referring to chemical tests which involve solvents or other liquids. **3.** *a* [*Gas industry*] referring to natural gas which contains significant amounts of the vapour of higher hydro-carbons.

wet affair, also **wet stuff** *n* [*Espionage*] an assassination; it is the KGB equivalent of **wet work**.

wet down *v* [*US*] [*Marine Corps*] to hold a (drunken) party to celebrate one's promotion.

wet edge *n* [*Painting*] an edge of a coat of paint which has not yet dried and which is still workable.

wet end *n* [*US*] [*Paper-making*] the part of the paper-making machine where the pulp begins to form the **web**.

wet finger perspective *n* [*Business*] a superficial assessment of a situation: only the tip of one finger has been dipped in to 'try the temperature', instead of rolling up one's sleeves and plunging one's hands in properly.

wet herd *n* [*US*] [*Cattlemen*] a herd composed completely of cows.

wet lease *n* [*Air travel*] the leasing of an aircraft in which the owner contracts to supply a crew and, in some cases, the fuel for the flight(s). See also **dry lease**.

wet leasing *n* [*Air travel*] the renting out of aircraft, complete with crews, engineering and other support services.

wet pan *n* [*Industry*] a large revolving metal pan containing two heavy milling wheels which crush and mix clay with water. See also **dry pan**.

wet rent *n* [*Business*] a levy paid by the publican of a tied public house to the brewery, based on the amount of that brewery's beer that he sells.

wet sell *n* [*Business*] a business deal which is helped along by the increasing drunkenness of both participants, presumably over lunch.

wet ship *n* [*Navy*] a ship with a reputation for hard drinking.

wet spinning *n* [*Textiles*] the spinning of natural fibres which are still wet after being run through a water bath.

wet stuff *n* [*US*] [*Cattlemen*] cows that are currently giving milk.

wet thumb *n* [*Commerce*] a fish farmer's term for proficiency and success in breeding fish commercially; it is based on the model of the gardener's 'green fingers'.

wet time *n* [*Building trade*] periods during which work cannot be carried out due to poor weather conditions.

wet tree *n* [*Oil rigs*] a sub-sea wellhead where the equipment is left exposed to the sea. See also **dry tree**.

wet wing *a* [*Aerospace*] referring to aircraft which have been designed with integral fuel tanks in the wings.

wet work *n* [*Espionage*] an assassination carried out for political purposes.

wets 1. *n pl* [*Cars*] racing tyres which are used for a wet track. **2.** *n* [*UK*] [*Politics*] those members of the Conservative party who disagree with Prime Minister Margaret Thatcher's hard-line **monetarist** economic policies and complain that their main result has been the creation of increased unemployment and wide-spread social suffering. Mrs Thatcher categorised all such weaklings as 'wet', implying both the schoolchild's derogatory sneer and a 'dilution' by such rebels of her policies.

wetted *a* [*Aerospace*] said of an aircraft surface that is in contact with the moving airflow.

wetted area *n* [*Gliding*] the external surface of a glider; the smaller the wetted area (as in the latest designs) the less the **parasite drag**.

wetware *n* [*Computing*] any organic intelligence involved with a computer, particularly the human brain, which is neither **hardware** nor **software**.

wet-white *n* [*Theatre*] white liquid make-up, as used by clowns.

whale *n* [*US*] [*Medicine*] a grossly obese patient. See also **blimp 1**.

whales *n pl* [*Navy*] tinned sardines.

whammer *n* [*Mountaineering*] a type of piton hammer.

wham-whams *n pl* [*US*] [*Prisons*] See **zoo-zoos**.

whangdoodle *n* [*US*] [*Cattlemen*] a cattle brand made of a group of interlocking wings, but with no central flying figure.

what-if games, also **whif games** *n pl* [*Business*] planning experimentation which uses 'games' in which those involved ask 'What if . . . ?' and attempt to follow through their various queries to a useful solution. Such games have been made more complex and sophisticated by the inclusion of a correctly programmed computer.

wheel *n* [*Cycling*] any particularly narrow victory in a race. See also **half-a-wheel**.

wheel, on a *adv* [*Cycling*] slipstreaming the rider directly in front during a race.

wheel sucker *n* [*Cycling*] a rider who uses the slipstream of another to conserve energy.

wheelhorse *n* [*US*] [*Politics*] a loyal, hard-working party supporter whose efforts during the campaign – stuffing envelopes, getting out the vote, etc. – are unlikely to be rewarded by a real stake in the party hierarchy.

wheelie *n* [*Cycling*] in BMX cycling this is riding on the back wheel only; it is equally beloved of motorcyclists.

whelm *n* [*Frisbee flying*] the first of nine stages of frisbee flight.

where list *n* [*Publishing*] a list printed next to a graph or diagram giving such detail as is required to understand its illustrative symbols and/or letters.

where you're at *n* [*New therapies*] one's state of being: emotional, psychological, and given the context, regarding one's opinions on any given topic. Like many such phrases (see **bag 3** etc) it is derived from the drug-obsessed hippie era of the late 1960s.

whey *n* [*Cheese-making*] the water part or serum of the milk which remains when the **curd** has been removed after separation.

whif games *n pl* [*Business*] See **what-if games**.

whiff *n* [*Golf*] a stroke that misses the ball; it is also used as a verb meaning to play such a shot.

whip 1. *v* [*Sailing, Ropework*] to bind the end of a rope to prevent fraying. 2. *n* [*Printing*] in manual typesetting this is an exceptionally fast compositor.

whip pan *n* [*TV*] the rotation of a TV camera in one complete 360° circle; it is often used in films to denote the action that is moving from one place to another but still occurring at the same time.

whip the water, also **thrash the water** *v* [*Angling*] to continue fishing indifferently.

whiparound *n* [*US*] [*TV*] a shot that moves horizontally around a desk of newsreaders while the **anchor man** introduces them all in one continuous breath.

whipper *n* [*US*] [*Paper-making*] a device which beats and cleans the **felt** in a paper-making machine.

whipping side *n* [*Sheep-shearing*] the last side of a sheep to be shorn; the stroke employed resembles that of a downward crack of a whip.

whipsaw 1. *v* [*Industrial relations*] used to describe a bargaining process in which unions start by 'picking off' those companies which can least afford to fight a wage claim. Once these deals have been made, the union takes them to the harder-line employers and presents them as faits accomplis, satisfactory bargains which these other companies should have no option but to accept as the models for their own deals. 2. *v* [*US*] [*Politics*] used to describe an illegal and corrupt procedure whereby an apparently susceptible but actually hard-nosed politician will collect bribes from individuals representing both sides of an issue and then deliver his favours only to one, or even to neither of them. 3. *v* [*Stock market*] to manipulate the market so as to cause a rival to buy high and sell low.

whipstock *n* [*Mining*] a deflection wedge; it is a wedge shaped tool which ensures that the bit moves in the required direction along the borehole.

whirl *n* [*Athletics*] the rotation of the body when tossing the discus, throwing the hammer, putting the shot, etc.

whirley bird *n* [*Computing*] disk-pack equipment.

whisker, also **cat's whisker** *n* [*Electronics*] a wire used to form a rectifying contact with the surface of a semi-conductor.

whisker pole *n* [*Navy*] a short bearing out spar used in smaller yachts and sailing dinghies to extend the jib and thus gain some of the advantage given to larger vessels that use a spinnaker.

whiskers 1. *n* [*Drugs*] a popular nickname among dealers for a Federal narcotics agent, or the entire agency. 2. *n* [*Science*] in chemistry this is a mono-crystalline fibre composite used to reinforce cement, resin and silver amalgam.

whiskey, also **whiskey stick** *n* [*US*] [*Carpenters*] a plumb-line or spirit level.

whiskey seats *n pl* [*Theatre*] seats on the aisle, popular both with critics, who need to get out before the rush and phone in their copy, and with those who like to escape to the bar when the action palls.

whistle punk *n* [*Logging*] See **punk 2**.

whistle-blower *n* [*Politics*] a government employee who is unable to bear the evidence of duplicity, incompetence, corruption or misman-agement that he sees around him and decides to inform the press, and thus the public, of what he has hitherto managed to accept. Similar revelations by corporate employees make them also 'whistle-blowers'.

whistler 1. *n* [*Audio*] a form of radio interference that sounds like a whistle which is falling in pitch; it is generated by the effect of lightning on radio waves. 2. *n* [*Metallurgy*] in iron-founding this is a smaller version of a **riser** that is primarily used to relieve pressure in the mould cavity.

whistlestop *v* [*US*] [*Politics*] to campaign by touring local communities in a specially chartered train.

white *n* [*Printing*] any part of the page that does not carry printing.

white alert *n* [*Military*] the all-clear signal.

White Alice *n* [*Military*] See **Alice**.

white arms *n pl* [*Fencing*] any light, pointed or cutting weapon: a sword, bayonet, lance, etc.

white book *n* [*US*] [*Government*] an official government report bound in white. See also **blue book 3**.

white coal *n* [*Industry*] water when used as a source of electric power, rather than coal.

white coat rule *n* [*Advertising*] the prohibition of the use in advertising of real doctors, or actors made up to resemble them, on the principle that the public's natural trust in the medical profession could be used to sell second-rate products.

white collar mercenaries *n pl* [*Military*] US advisors whose work involves training the armies of potential allies. See also **MAAG**.

white collar workers *n pl* [*Industrial relations*] staff employees, non-manual labourers, clerks, etc. See also **blue collar, pink collar**.

white dial, also **painted dial** *n* [*Antiques, Horology*] from about 1770 these began to replace the traditional brass dials; they consist of an iron plate enamelled with several coats of furnace-hardened paint (not necessarily white) with the numbers and **spandrels** painted on.

white dwarf *n* [*Science*] a whitish star of high surface temperature and low intrinsic brightness; its mass is approximately that of the sun but its size is far smaller, thus its density is enormous.

white flight *n* [*Sociology*] the flight of urban whites from the decaying inner cities of US towns, which is still greater than the volume of those who are returning to **blockbust** such areas.

white gas *n* [*US*] [*Oil industry*] petrol that contains no lead.

white goods 1. *n pl* [*Commerce*] fridges, freezers, washing machines, dishwashers, etc. See also **brown goods**. 2. *n pl* [*Commerce*] household linens, towels, etc.

white grease *n* [*Food*] lard considered unfit for human consumption and used industrially. See also **yellow grease**.

white hole *n* [*Science*] a hypothetical source of matter and energy that is posited as the 'other end' of a **black hole** and as such expelling into space all the matter and energy which has been sucked into a black hole.

white hope *n* [*UK*] [*Railways*] a steam locomotive fitter, caked in grease.

white knight *n* [*Commerce*] a third firm, more acceptable to the one under threat of takeover, who is encouraged by that firm to challenge the original **raider**.

white label *n* [*Pop music*] a pre-release copy of a record, perfect in every aspect except that the company's coloured and printed label has yet to be affixed to it; such copies are sent out for review to journalists, radio stations, etc.

white land *n* [*Government*] land which has been left unshaded on those local maps that delineate ownership, development, demolition, etc; thus it is land which is as yet untouched and has not become subject to any planning decision.

white letter *n* [*Printing*] an early name for Roman faces to distinguish them from **black letter** or Gothic faces.

white level *n* [*TV*] the maximum value of video signal voltage, ie: the brightest spot on the TV display. See also **black level**.

white line *n* [*Sailing, Ropework*] cordage that has not been tarred.

white noise *n* [*Audio*] See **acoustic perfume**.

white oil *n* [*Oil industry*] any of a variety of lubricants prepared from a high-boiling petroleum distillate and used for machinery in the food and textile industries and in the preparation of medicines and pharmaceuticals.

white out 1. *v* [*Printing*] to create more white space on a page by inserting more spacing **leads**. 2. *v* [*Printing*] to paint out unwanted areas of type or illustration using Tipp-Ex or a similar proprietary substance.

white paper 1. *n* [*Government*] an official statement of government policy and the background information which helped create that policy. See also **blue book 3, green paper**. 2. *n* [*Journalism*] space sold to advertisers; it is left blank by the make-up department when designing the day's dummy.

white pickling *n* [*Metallurgy*] the second **pickling** of a steel sheet after annealing, prior to tin coating.

white radio *n* [*Espionage*] propaganda radio that makes no secret of its origins, eg: Radio Free Europe, which bombards the Warsaw Pact countries with pro-US material. See also **black radio**.

white room 1. *n* [*Aerospace*] a special building used for the storage of unused space capsules. 2. *n* [*Aerospace*] a room kept surgically clean and purged of all dust and other foreign bodies and used for the assembly of those delicate mechanisms which are used in space flight.

white shirt *n* [*UK*] [*Prisons*] a senior prison officer. They wear white shirts, as do senior policemen, as opposed to the blue shirts of their juniors. See also **screw 4**.

white sour *n* [*Textiles*] the treatment of a textile with dilute hydrochloric or sulphuric acid to bleach and clean it.

white space skid *n* [*Communications*] the acceleration of printing that is achieved on some data transmission terminals whereby the printer skids across white spaces, rather than typing out a number of individual blank characters.

white suits *n pl* [*Military*] the civilian employees of a contractor who work on a military air base or similar establishment to service the hardware supplied to the military by that contractor. See also **blue suits**.

white wash *n* [*Glass-making*] See **gall 1**.

white weeks *n pl* [*Skiing*] an off-season period, especially in Italy, at which time skiing facilities – lift passes, accommodation, etc. – are less expensive than usual.

white writing *n* [*Literary criticism*] See **zero degree writing**.

whitecoat *n* [*UK*] [*Police*] the senior examiner of the Police Public Carriage Office – the official body responsible for examining London taxi-

W

drivers in their **Knowledge** of London. See also **browncoat**.

Whitehouse factor n [UK] [Government] the belief in the UK civil service that some standards of 'morality' must be imposed on people's freedom of choice regarding their entertainments; it comes from the name of Mrs Mary Whitehouse, a self-appointed censor of the British media.

white-knuckle sobriety n [Drug addicts] at Broadway Lodge Clinic this means the pointless temporary abstention from drugs through will-power but lacking the solid base of deeper psychological motivation.

white-out n [Flying] zero visibility caused by fog or heavy snow.

whiteprint n [Printing] a variety of blueprint in which the image appears in black on a white background.

whites n pl [US] [Marine Corps] a Marine officer's uniform.

whitewalls n pl [US] [Marine Corps] the regulation super-short Marine haircut in which the hair is cropped on top and shaved high up the back and sides.

whitewash v [Sport] in certain sports this is to defeat an opponent so completely that one loses no games, rubbers or any other portion of the encounter.

whitey n [Pool] the cue-ball.

whiz v [Antiques, Auctions] to age artificially; it is often used of coins; it comes from slang 'whiz' meaning pickpocket.

whizzer 1. n [UK] [Police] a pickpocket; thus 'the whiz' means the craft of picking pockets. 2. n [UK] [Railways] a relay, controlling the points, that is identified by the letters WZR. See also **tipper**, **ulcer** 1. 3. n [Industry] one who works a machine which spins felt hat bodies in order to remove excess water from the material. 4. n [US] [Wrestling] an arm lock that traps one's arm against the opponent's body from a position behind the opponent.

who is it really? v phr [New therapies] in **primal therapy** this is a basic trigger for the release of a patient's inner emotions and **deep** feeling; the patient is making some statement that attacks the therapist, who replies 'Who is it really?'. The repetition of this question is supposed eventually to force the patient to make the connections that will lead to the primal experience.

who is this man, and why is he telling me all this? phr [TV] the stock critical response of an executive when faced with his first sight of a new documentary.

who-are-you n [Communications] a transmission control character that is sent down a communications line to initiate data transmission; the receiver should send back some form of identification to confirm readiness to take and send messages.

whole back n [Clothing] a garment back cut in one piece, not two or more as is common in tailored garments.

whole child concept n [Education] the belief that one must understand the child not merely in the classroom but at play as well as at work, and in the home as well as at school, if that child is to gain the full benefits of being taught.

whole number rule n [Science] an empirical law that the atomic weights of the elements are mostly close to being whole numbers.

whole working n [Coal-mining] See **first working**.

wholesale banking n [Banking] the part of banking that deals with the provision of large loans to business and institutional borrowers. See also **retail banking**.

wholism n [New therapies] See **holism**.

whoops, also **whoopsie** n [Cycling] in BMX cycling this is overcoming a couple of small jumps or similar obstacles placed close together.

whorfian a [Linguistics, Philosophy] this comes from the name of the US linguist Banjamin Lee Whorf (1897–1941); it refers to the Whorfian hypothesis which states that one's perception of the world is influenced or determined by the structure of one's native language.

wickets n pl [Theatre, Film] turnstiles, ticket offices, box offices.

wide open a [Boxing] referring to a fighter who is useless at defending himself.

widen v [US] [Railways] to increase the speed of the train by moving the throttle.

widow n [Printing] an example of poor typography in which a single word is left isolated on a line by itself at the end of a paragraph.

widow maker n [Logging] a limb from a fallen tree which has become lodged in the branches of a standing tree and which suddenly falls, possibly causing death or injury.

widow-and-orphan stock n [US] [Stock market] extremely stable stock that pays high dividends to investors.

widows and orphans n [UK] [Railways] the foolish practice of walking down the track with one's back to the oncoming traffic; this is likely to bereave one's family.

wig v [UK] [Market-traders] to eavesdrop; thus 'wigger' is one who eavesdrops. It comes from **earwig**.

wig picker n [US] [Medicine] a psychiatrist. See also **spook** 2.

wiggle v [Navy] to semaphore with the hands.

wiggle seat n [US] [Police] a special lie detector that can be fitted to a seat and which will measure the bodily reactions of a subject sitting in it when answering certain crucial questions.

wiggler n [Angling] a form of wobble bait, ie: bait that wobbles in the water.

wigwag n [Tyre-making] a machine that feeds the strips of rubber through various processes, especially through the calender or mill; at a steady rate; wigwags are divided into feed and let-off wigwags depending on their position before or after the mill.

wild 1. *n* [*Baseball*] a pitcher consistently incapable of throwing **strikes. 2.** *a* [*Baseball*] said of a ball thrown beyond the reach of an intended receiver.

wild garlic *a* [*Wine-tasting*] used to describe a faint whiff that denotes the presence of sorbic acid.

wild line *n* [*TV, Film*] an extra line of dialogue that is recorded out of context and which can be cut in later to replace one that was delivered badly or simply used as an extra line of dialogue.

wild track, also **non sync** *n* [*TV, Film*] a tape of random sounds, not synchronised with any action, which can be used as and where necessary for aural atmosphere.

wild well *n* [*Oil rigs*] a rig that has run out of control and is bleeding oil or gas from its borehole.

wildcat *n* [*Oil rigs*] an exploration well drilled without knowledge of the contents of the underlying rock formation.

Wilkie *n* [*Horse-racing*] a race-card; this comes from rhyming slang 'Wilkie Bard' meaning a card.

willie *n* [*Espionage*] 'This is the jargon for a person, often a newspaperman, who is used by real agents to pass on secret information and perform other subversive services without knowing it', (letter from Chapman Pincher, The Times, April 1981).

Wilson *n* [*US*] [*Shoe trade*] when taking an inventory the person counting says 'Wilson' to indicate that there are no more styles in a given size.

wimbler *n* [*UK*] [*Railways*] See **tingalairy**.

WIMEX *n* [*Military*] abbr of **WorldWide Military Command and Control System** the network of computers, warning sensors, command posts and communications used by the US President and his commanders to run the US military forces around the world.

wimps *n* [*Computing*] acro **window, mouse and pointer-directed systems** these are pointer systems, operated by a **mouse**, which facilitate the use of windows and similar displays on PC screens.

win *n* [*Computing*] a program that runs smoothly and encounters no unexpected snags.

Winchester *n* [*Computing*] the hard disk memory, capable of holding millions of bytes (megabytes) of information and offering concurrently faster retrieval times than **floppy disks**. It is named after the IBM 3030 computer, whose nickname comes from the Winchester 3030 gauge rifle, which it resembled in speed and accuracy.

wind 1. *n* [*Boxing*] the solar plexus; thus touch wind means to hit the opponent in the solar plexus. **2.** *v* [*Film*] wind up; to bring filming to a close.

wind chop *n* [*UK*] [*Surfing*] surf generated by local high winds.

wind jammer *n* [*UK*] [*Railways*] a blockage in the airpipe of a diesel engine.

wind rose 1. *n* [*Meteorology*] a diagram showing, for one place, the frequency, strength and direction of winds from those directions that have been plotted. **2.** [*Meteorology*] a diagram showing the average occurrence of other meteorological phenomena – rainfall, sunshine, etc – as well as the recorded winds for a given point. (Both of these stem from the 'compass rose': the diagrammatic compass which includes all the cardinal and lesser points.)

wind shadow *n* [*Gliding*] an area of calm in the lee of windbreaks such as hills, buildings and rows of trees. Such spots, when sunny, are likely sources of thermals on windy days.

wind up *v* [*Baseball*] when a pitcher makes preliminary movements of the arms and legs prior to delivering his pitch.

windbag-blower *n* [*UK*] [*Market-traders*] a market-based confidence trick: the seller fills a number of packets with a cheap staple object (collar studs, safety pins, etc); he then ostentatiously puts more valuable objects into some packets, jumbles them all up and offers them for sale. His accomplices in the crowd pay up at once and all apparently get the 'lucky' packs; the **punters** then offer their money – they are rarely so fortunate.

windbill *n* [*Finance*] an **accommodation bill** that is accepted without consideration by the drawee in order to oblige the drawer.

windjammer *n* [*US*] [*Circus*] a musician.

windmill *v* [*Swimming*] a method of swimming whereby the swimmer is on his back, the legs thrash the water alternately and the arms come up straight from the sides.

window 1. *n* [*Espionage*] any means, often through anonymous tipoffs or general gossip, that enable security officers to gain information regarding their own employees in the CIA. **2.** [*Finance*] in the money market this is the supply of cash made available by a central bank to the banking system by methods other than the usual one. Thus 'open the window' and 'close the window' refer to the making available or shutting down of these alternative methods of supply. **3.** [*Furriers*] a hairless patch on a pelt or fur. **4.** [*Gemstones*] a small polished facet on the surface of a rough gemstone which permits examination of the interior. **5.** [*Military*] strips of foil and wire that are dropped from an aircraft or missile, or shot into the air from a ship, in order to confuse radar scanners or the guidance systems of **smart** missiles. See also **chaff. 6.** [*Statistics*] a range of acceptable values on either side of a variable; a standard deviation. **7.** also **clearance** [*Video*] the time between a product's release in one medium and its release in another.

window jump *n* [*US*] [*Skiing*] a kind of ski jump or stunt in which the skier supports himself on

W

the poles, swings the skis between them, and then turns the skis in the air.

window of opportunity n [Politics] any situation, often temporary and spontaneously created, which can be used for one's own benefit. One side's window of opportunity often coincides with another's **window of vulnerability**.

window of vulnerability n [Military] a term coined by General Edward Rowney, the Joint Chiefs of Staff representative at the **SALT II** talks in 1980. The result of the agreement reached between Carter and Brezhnev, with constraints on missile launchers and a freeze on warhead per type of missile, was that the Russians emerged with an approximate 5:2 advantage in **ICBMs** and in ballistic missile **throw-weight**. To the general, this meant an unacceptable strategic imbalance and potential vulnerability for the US, since through this 'window', the Soviets could and would take devastating advantage. This 'window', a descendant of various 'gaps', has been used to justify much current US weapons development.

window, out of the adv [UK] [Law] utterly absurd, completely ludicrous; over the top (**OTT**).

window people n [Business] those members of a Japanese company who have failed in the corporate struggle; they maintain their jobs but achieve no promotion and thus spend their days gazing impotently out of the office window.

window rate n [Finance] the fluctuating rate of interest charged on loans, mortgages, etc. that is paid by the customer to a metaphorical 'teller' at a 'window'.

window-dressing n [Finance] a deceitful method of making a business seem more attractive by deliberately hiding its shortcomings and manipulating its accounts.

windowing, also **scissoring** n [Computing] the processing of the stored data of a large image so that a part of it can be shown on the screen; the entire image can be seen by scrolling the screen as desired.

windows n pl [Computing] a rectangular area on a VDU, inside which part of an image or file can be displayed. A screen can incorporate a number of windows revealing a number of files or images simultaneously. Windows can expand or contract and 'move' about the screen. Data can be moved from one window to another. See also **wimps**.

window's open v phr [Gambling] a comment made by one player to inform the others that an inept and obvious cheat is at work.

wind-up n [Salvation Army] the climax of a SA service, with the congregation marching round the hall, clapping their hands, singing hymns and waving flags.

windup n [TV] a signal from the studio floor manager – a winding motion with one or both hands – which tells a performer or speaker to speed up his/her delivery and draw it to a close.

wing 1. n [Printing] the upper extension of a script or ornamental typeface. 2. v [Theatre] to fasten one's script to one of the wing flats or some other part of the scenery when one has failed to learn it properly and thus needs to make an occasional reference to it during the performance; thus 'to wing it' is to make one's way through a performance more by luck than judgement (a phrase which has passed into general slang).

winger n [Merchant navy] a steward on a cruise liner.

wings n pl [Horse-riding] in show-jumping these are the small triangular flags which are set at either end of a fence to indicate its length.

wink 1. n [Management] an interval of 0.03 seconds (0.0005 minutes) that is used in method study research for the visual analysis of the performance of a task. 2. [Tiddleywinks] the counter used in tiddleywinks; two of $3/32$in thick and $7/8$in in diameter, plus four of $1/16$in thick and $5/8$in in diam.

winkie n [US] [Fire brigade] a volunteer fireman.

winning n [Coal-mining] the various operations involved in breaking the coal from the seam and loading it for transport underground.

winter book n [Horse-racing] a book-maker's early appraisal of the odds for races in the season to come.

winze n [Coal-mining] a vertical shaft that connects two or more levels of a mine, but which has no access to the surface.

wipe n [Film, TV] an optical device used for quick changes of scene; a line appears at one edge of the screen and moves across the picture, obliterating the old picture as it 'pulls' the new one with it.

wipe out v [Surfing] when a surfer is thrown off the board by a wave he/she cannot manage to ride.

wipes n [US] [Cattlemen] the cowboy's neckerchief which is used for a multitude of purposes.

wire 1. n [Angling] the hook. 2. [US] [Gambling] the finish line at a race-course. 3. [US] [Gambling] a signal used between two card cheats working in the same game. 4. [US] [Gambling] in poker, a 'wired hand' is a hand that holds a pair, of which one card is visible and the other is face down on the table. 5. [Paper-making] a mesh of parallel or woven wire on which the wet **web** paper is formed from the pulp and on which it can drain.

wire edges n pl [Logging] partial separations of the grain in a piece of wood; it is caused by dull knives or improper seasoning.

wire house n [Business] a major national or international brokerage house whose offices are linked by some form of electronic communications system to maximise business efficiency. Many smaller firms have such links, but the term still refers to the original era when only the very large firms had such technology.

wire stripping n [Journalism] the removal of **head** and **tail** codes from wire service agency messages to obtain the copy required for use.

W

wired *adv* [*Gambling*] See **back to back 1**.

wired for sound *adv* [*Film*] referring to an extra or walk-on who has a very few lines to speak.

wireman 1. *n* [*Journalism*] a journalist who works for one of the wire-service agencies, eg: UPI, AP, etc. **2.** *n* [*Espionage*] one who specialises in the use of electronic surveillance devices.

wires, under the *adv* [*UK*] [*Railways*] referring to trains that are powered by overhead electrification.

WISC *n* [*Military*] acro **Warning System Controller** the officer in charge of an installation for tracking incoming missiles.

wishbone 1. *n* [*Cars*] an A-shaped link, resembling a wishbone in a chicken, in an independent suspension system. **2.** [*US*] [*Football*] a variation of the **T formation** in which two deep backs are lined up behind a third in the rough shape of a wishbone. **3.** [*US*] [*Football*] a play in which, unusually, the half-backs line up further from the line of scrimmage than does the fullback.

witch-doctor 1. *n* [*US*] [*Medicine*] a specialist in internal medicine. **2.** *n* [*UK*] [*Military*] a psychiatrist.

withdrawal of enthusiasm campaign *n* [*US*] [*Government*] a bureaucratic euphemism for a boycott.

withered *a* [*Wine-tasting*] used to describe an old, tired-out wine, lacking fruit and 'flesh' as it grows old.

withhold target *n* [*Military*] a reserve nuclear target, not to be attacked unless specifically indicated; the US **SIOP** war plan has a number of such targets in addition to the primary range.

without the blessing *adv* [*US*] [*Bars*] said of a shot of liquor without a water or soda chaser.

wizard 1. *n* [*Computing*] a person who understands the most complex problems and can **debug** any problems that may occur in the machine. **2.** *n* [*Computing*] a person whose expertise gains him certain privileges as far as concerns the operation of his firm's or college's computers.

WMP *phr* [*Navy*] abbr of **with much pleasure** a signal for accepting an invitation. See also **NCD**.

WNL *phr* [*Medicine*] abbr of **within normal limits** also defined as 'we never looked' or 'we never listened', when referring to an inadequate examination of a patient.

W.O.B. *n* [*Journalism*] acro **white on black** printing which reverses the normal black on white format.

wobble *n* [*Audio*] a collective term for both **wow** and **flutter**.

wobbler 1. [*Angling*] a lure that wobbles, rather than spins. **2.** [*Industry*] a projection on a roll that is used in a rolling mill by which it may be turned.

wobblyscope 1. *n* [*TV*] hand-held camerawork. **2.** *n* [*TV*] in a derogative usage it means badly executed hand-held camerawork.

wobbulator *n* [*Audio*] a device that produces a

signal which varies rapidly and continually between two frequencies.

wocs *v* [*Oil rigs*] it comes from an abbreviation of 'waiting on cement to set'.

wogs *n pl* [*Scientology*] those members of the world population who have so far resisted the cult. See also **raw public**.

wolf ticket, sell a 1. *v* [*US*] [*Prisons*] to boast, to lie, to talk nonsense. **2.** *v* [*US*] [*Prisons*] to create trouble deliberately, often by setting off a round of ritualised verbal insults between two prisoners. See also **signify**.

wolf trap *n* [*Aerospace*] a device that reports on the possibility of the existence of microbial lifeforms on other planets; it sucks in samples of soil and air and immerses them in nutrient solutions. It is named after Dr. Wolf Vishniac.

wolf tree *n* [*Logging*] a large, old tree that inhibits the growth of new trees around it.

wolly *n* [*UK*] [*Police*] a uniformed policeman, especially a young and inexperienced constable.

wonk *n* [*Navy*] an inexperienced or inefficient sailor, especially a novice midshipman.

wood *n* [*Wine-tasting*] a distinct and desirable odour derived from ageing in wooden casks.

wood down *v* [*Logging*] to put as many as possible logs on to a single truck.

wood family *n* [*Theatre*] empty seats in the theatre. See also **plush family**.

woodchuck *n* [*US*] [*Road transport*] a driver with low seniority.

wooden bomb *n* [*Military*] the hypothetical concept of a perfect weapon: absolutely reliable, carrying an infinite shelf life and requiring no special surveillance, storage or handling.

wooden head *n* [*US*] [*Journalism*] See **flat head**.

wooden logs *n* [*Logging*] seasoned timber.

woodie *n* [*Surfing*] an old wood-panelled station wagon popularly used by surfers to carry themselves and their boards.

woodpecker *n* [*Military*] the development by Soviet scientists, sometime since 1977, of a high-powered radar beam that follows the earth's curvature and thus removes the advantage hitherto enjoyed by hostile bombers of being able to penetrate beneath the radar scan. See also **OTH, OTH-B radar**.

woodpusher *n* [*Chess*] an inferior player who knows the moves but lacks finesse or skill.

woodshed *v* [*Music*] to rehearse, especially in private; it comes from the image of a musician retiring to the woodshed in his/her garden to practise in peace.

woodshedding 1. *n* [*Music*] rehearsing alone (as it were, out in the woodshed). **2.** *n* [*Music*] learning a piece of music without benefit of a written score, but by listening to it repeatedly until it can be copied exactly. **3.** *n* [*Music*] in barbershop quartets these are improvised singing sessions, often after-hours and similar to rock or jazz music 'jam sessions'.

woodwork 1. *n* [*Cricket*] the stumps and bails. 2. *n* [*Football*] the frame of the goal, although this is no longer invariably made of wood.

woody *a* [*Wine-tasting*] used to describe an undesirable taste that comes from keeping wine too long in the cask.

woof *n* [*Weaving*] See **weft**.

woofer *n* [*Audio*] the part of a loudspeaker that produces low-frequency sound waves. See also **tweeter**.

wool *n* [*Glass-making*] spun glass, formed by steam-blowing.

woollybacks *n pl* [*Industrial relations*] non-militant workers who may be members of a union but who still allow the employers to treat them like woolly-backed sheep.

Woolworth *n* [*Ten-pin bowling*] a split where the 5 and 10 pins are left standing; it comes from the nickel and dime (10) store. See also **baby split, bucket, Cincinnati**.

Woolworth weapons *n pl* [*Military, Espionage*] small, simply manufactured, short-life arms and other killing weapons; they are cheap, expendable and ideal for close-in combat, assassination and other quiet but deadly tasks.

woppitzer *n* [*Gambling*] a **kibbitzer** who has bad breath or body odour as well as a propensity to comment on a game in which he is not playing.

word *n* [*Computing*] a fixed number of **bits**, varying as to the overall capacity of the machine, but always representing the maximum number of bits that a machine can handle at any one time. The majority of current (1985) office microcomputers operate on a 16–bit word. See also **string 1**.

word geography *n* [*Linguistics*] the study of the regional distribution of words and phrases.

word problem *n* [*Mathematics*] the problem of working out whether two different products are equal, or whether two sequences of operations are equivalent.

word-engineering *n* [*Government*] the doctoring of information so that the public learn only such facts as those who are handing out the information – the government, the military, scientific and bureaucratic agencies, etc – wish to have revealed. Such 'engineering' involves suppression, alteration, censorship and outright falsification. See also **managed news**.

word-method *n* [*Education*] a method of teaching reading in which pupils are taught to recognise whole words before they are taught the letters or syllables which make them up.

wordies *n* [*Theatre*] a script.

words *n pl* [*Science*] in DNA research these are any of the three-letter combinations – eg: UGA (uracil-guanine-adenine) – that represent the nucleotide triplets or codons in the genetic code.

word-salad *n* [*Medicine*] a sign of advanced schizophrenia in which the patient's speech is a mixture of unintelligible and random words and phrases.

work 1. *v* [*Sailing, Ropework*] to draw up and mould a knot. 2. *v* [*Cricket*] used of a bowler who manipulates the ball in such a way that it turns or spins in the desired manner on touching the pitch. 3. *v* [*Cricket*] when a batsman aims the ball towards a given spot, often between two defensive fieldsmen. 4. *n* [*Cricket*] the combination of finger and wrist action with which a bowler makes the ball swing or spin in the air. 5. *n* [*Gambling*] crooked cards or dice.

work and back *n* [*Printing*] See **sheet work**.

work and tumble *n* [*Printing*] a method of printing and the second side of a sheet of paper from the same form as the first.

work flow *n* [*Industry*] the sequence of processes through which a piece of work passes from its initiation to its completion.

work for Jesus *v* [*US*] [*Industrial relations*] to put in extra work without asking for extra pay.

work in a few rips *v* [*Sex*] said of a homosexual **hustler** who sodomises his client.

work one's bolt *v* [*US*] [*Marine Corps*] to resort to extraordinary measures – legal or otherwise – to achieve a desired end.

work over 1. *v* [*US*] [*Marine Corps*] to lay heavy fire on a target. 2. [*US*] [*Marine Corps*] to reprimand severely.

work print *n* [*Film*] the first print that an editor considers; it contains all those takes which are to be used, to one extent or another, in the **final** cut. The effects have been prepared and the soundtrack is roughly synchronised.

work the come-in *v* [*US*] [*Circus*] clowns do this when they warm up the audience prior to the appearance of the first big top act.

work the fly *v* [*Angling*] to keep the fly moving.

work the hole *v* [*US*] [*Police*] used of a mugger who specialises in attacking drunks on the subway in New York.

work the house *v* [*US*] [*Circus*] to sell popcorn, peanuts, etc, to work up the audience's thirst before one produces trays of drinks and ices.

work through *v* [*Social work*] to discuss a controversial or difficult subject in the hope that gradually a solution can be found by talking about the problem and working out the best way of dealing with it.

work train *v* [*US*] [*Railways*] to work on special duties, including spraying chemicals to control weeds, operating snow ploughs, etc.

work up 1. *v* [*US*] [*Medicine*] to perform a series of routine diagnostic procedures: X-rays, blood tests, ECG, enema, bowel run, etc. 2. *n* [*Printing*] a smudge on the paper caused when a piece of spacing material works loose in the forme and thus smears the work.

work with the cramps *v* [*Sex*] said of a **hustler** who accepts the pain of being sodomised, providing the money is sufficient.

W

workaround *n* [*Aerospace*] a back up; an alternative method available to astronauts and ground control who can 'work around' the failure of an instrument or mechanism and save the mission from being abandoned completely.

worker *n* [*Religion*] See **messenger 2**.

workerist *a* [*Politics*] referring to middle class left-wingers who attempt to submerge their backgrounds in the obsessive assumption of working class accents, eating and entertainment habits, and similar ideological subterfuges.

workfare *n* [*Government*] this comes from work plus welfare; it is a policy whereby those in receipt of welfare benefits must do some work in exchange for those benefits.

working 1. *n* [*Free-masonry*] the performance of a Masonic rite or ritual. **2.** *n* [*US*] [*Coal-mining*] the movement of the roof of a mine passage as it collapses in a cave-in; hence the warning cry 'She's working!'.

working copy *n* [*Book collecting*] a copy of a book or some other document which has been annotated by someone working on its contents.

working girl, also **working broad, working chick** *n* [*Sex*] a prostitute.

working the fence *n* [*Politics*] the campaign of a politician who ensures that it centres on a great deal of personal contact with the voters. See also **fence mending**.

workover *n* [*Oil rigs*] the process whereby a completed (see **completion**) production well is subsequently re-entered and any necessary cleaning, repair and maintenance carried out.

workspace 1. *n* [*Computing*] a block of locations within main memory that are used for temporary storage of data during processing. **2.** [*Computing*] See **scratchpad**.

worm 1. *v* [*Sailing, Ropework*] to fill the seams of a rope with spun yarn, marline or fishline. **2.** *n* [*Oil rigs*] a new and inexperienced worker on a drill rig. **3.** *n* [*Distilling*] a coiled copper tube of decreasing diameter that is attached to the head of the Pot Still (essentially a huge copper kettle) and kept cold in a bath of continuously running water; in it the vapours from the still condense. Fed by the still, the worm feeds the receiving vessel with the condensed distillate.

worm fly *n* [*Angling*] a dark Palmer fly mounted in tandem with two bodies and two hooks, but only one eye; it is good for tempting trout that are eating caterpillars sheltered by overhanging trees or bushes.

wormburner *n* [*Shooting*] in live pigeon shooting this is a pigeon which has been released from the trap and which goes off very fast and very low, supposedly singeing the worms.

wormhole *n* [*Science*] a hypothetical corridor in space connecting **black holes** and **white holes**.

worry *v* [*Hunting*] hounds do this when they kill the fox.

worsted *n* [*Textiles*] a fine, soft woollen yarn used for knitting and embroidery, in which the fibres are arranged in parallel.

wort *n* [*Distilling*] the liquid drawn off the mash-tun in which the malted and unmalted cereals have been mashed with warm water. Wort contains all the sugars of the malt and certain secondary constituents; after cooling it is passed to the fermentation vats.

wortle *n* [*Metallurgy*] a small plate used for wire drawing, containing a series of tapered holes in a straight line.

would you take *n* [*US*] [*Car salesmen*] a sales technique in which the salesman sounds out what the customer would be willing to take for his trade-in.

WOW *phr* [*Oil rigs*] abbr of **waiting on weather**.

wow 1. *n* [*Audio*] in sound recording this is a low frequency noise usually caused by variations in the speed of the system's mechanical components. See also **flutter 1**. **2.** *n* [*Audio, Video*] slow variations of running speed that affect audio tape and videotape recorders.

WPA *n* [*Insurance, Shipping*] abbr of **With Particular Average** a policy that protects goods in transit, covering the loss of individual parcels or of partial quantities.

wrap *n v* [*TV, Film*] the end of a day's shooting, often announced as 'It's a wrap!'; thus it also means to end the day's shooting.

wrap party *n* [*TV, Film*] a party held to celebrate the conclusion of filming. See also **wrap**.

wraparound 1. *n* [*Computing*] a procedure whereby a linear sequence of memory locations is treated cyclically and when the last has been counted or occupied, the first is automatically returned to. **2.** *n* [*US*] [*TV*] a general term for a news item in which an **anchor man** introduces the piece, the reporter concerned, either live or on tape and with or without accompanying pictures, then reads the story, and finally the anchorman rounds it off before moving on to the next item. **3.** *n* [*Publishing*] a book cover made from a single sheet of material. **4.** *n* [*Publishing*] a jacket design that extends all the way around both front and back covers, including the spine. **5.** *n* [*US*] [*Business*] a mortgage which continues when the property is sold; the repayments to the original lender, plus additional funds for the purchase, are paid by a new lender, who holds the mortgage of the new occupier. **6.** *n* [*US*] [*Business*] a tax-deferral scheme whereby the interest on certain investments can be invested in the premiums for an annuity.

wrappers *n* [*Tobacco*] the best and highest priced tobacco at an auction.

wrap-up *n* [*US*] [*Politics*] the standard, predictable climax that winds up a touring candidate's regular speech; experienced campaign staff and media people soon learn to recognise the wrap-up and start moving towards their transport as soon as they hear it.

W

wrench *n* [*Coursing*] this occurs when a hare turns at anything less than a right-angle, when under pressure.

wring it out *v* [*Aerospace*] to fly in an ostentatious manner that deliberately pushes the aircraft to the limits of its performance specifications.

wrist *n* [*Dog breeding*] the carpus: the joint between the forearm and knee joint (pastern) on the front legs.

write *v* [*Computing*] to store information in a machine's memory, either in the form of a tape or a **floppy** or **hard disk**. See also **read**.

write down/write up *v* [*Business*] to reduce or increase the paper value of certain assets for the purpose of including them in the company accounts.

write-in candidate *n* [*US*] [*Politics*] a candidate whose name has not been included on the printed ballot-paper and who has thus to be written into the blank space provided by those voters who wish to offer their support. Thus 'write-in vote' refers to the votes registered by those who wrote in their favoured candidate and eschewed those offered by the main parties.

write-protect *v* [*Computing*] to protect a disk from accidental erasure by making sure that it is impossible – usually by covering the notch on a **floppy disk** – to write over the material it holds.

writer *n* [*Navy*] a clerical rating in a warship.

writing speed *n* [*Video*] the speed of the tape past the head of a VTR when the speed of the head itself is taken into account.

writing-speed *n* [*Electronics*] the maximum speed at which an electron beam can scan the screen of a cathode-ray tube and can still be recorded on the screen or on photographic film.

wrong **1.** *a* [*Antiques*] said of a fake or forged antique, painting, artefact, etc **2.** *a* [*Antiques*] used to describe any thing that does not belong to the period that is claimed for it, although not necessarily a fake as such. See also **right 1**.

wrong foot *v* [*Tennis*] to direct a shot so as to catch an opponent off balance and out of position.

wrong post *n* [*Banking*] the placing of a debit or credit to the wrong account.

wrong set *n* [*Film*] a comment by the director that announces that filming has finished on the current set and that the actors and crew should move on to start work on the next one.

wrong 'un *n* [*Cricket*] See **bosie**.

wrongfont *n* [*Printing*] a piece of type which is different to all that which surrounds it on the page.

WWMCCS *n* [*Military*] abbr of **World-Wide Military Command and Control System**. See **WIMEX**.

wye *n* [*Plumbing*] a short pipe with a branch joining it at an acute angle.

wylocks *n pl* [*UK*] [*Market-traders*] children.

WYSIWYG **1.** *phr* [*Business*] abbr of **What You See Is What You Get** the description of the product matches its capabilities; there are no hidden extras. **2.** *phr* [*Computing*] referring to word processing programs, the copy as typed on to the screen will be the copy that appears on paper; such programs probably include on-screen italics, underlining, boldface, etc.

x *pref* [*US*] [*Air Force*] the regular prefix that designates experimental aircraft.

x height, also **z height** *n* [*Printing*] the height of the body of all lower case letters, excluding ascenders and descenders.

Xmas tree, also **Christmas tree** *n* [*UK*] [*Railways*] a multiple aspect signal which has gone wrong and is flashing green, red and amber in rapid succession.

xmas-tree sort *n* [*Computing*] a method used in internal portions of an overall sort; successfully sorted parts of the larger unit are set aside for incorporation into the full sort at a later stage.

X-movie *n* [*Espionage*] a potential **lady** or **sister** who lacks the necessary subtlety and other attributes that would make her the perfect member of a **sanctifying** team.

Y

Y *pref* [*US*] [*Air Force*] the regular prefix used to denote a prototype aircraft.

yackoop *n* [*Shooting*] a space between the screens of a duck decoy through which a dog may jump.

yagi *n* [*Audio*] abbr of **Yagi aerial** a highly directional aerial developed in 1928 by the Japanese electrical engineer Hidetsugu Yagi (born 1886) which transmits VHF and UHF waves within a narrow frequency band.

yak *n* [*UK*] [*Market-traders*] a watch.

Yank *n* [*Bird-watching*] an American bird.

yankee bond *n* [*Stock market*] a bond issued by non-US entities trading in the US stock market and registered with the SEC.

yankee white *a* [*US*] [*Government*] referring to super-WASP characteristics that are allegedly sought out when choosing very high-risk workers in the national security areas of the US; supposedly they are more loyal than other groups.

YAP *n* [*Sociology*] abbr of **young aspiring professional**. See also **YUP**.

yappy *n* [*UK*] [*Market-traders*] a fool, an idiot.

yard **1.** *n* [*Banking*] one thousand millions, 1,000,000,000; it comes from 'a milliard'. **2.** *n* [*US*] [*Railways*] a system of tracks and sidings within a railway terminal that is used for the shunting, storage, maintenance and making up of trains. **3.** *n* [*US*] [*Coal-mining*] a wide space in the main roadway where mine cars can be switched and changed; it comes from conventional railroad marshalling yards. **4.** *v* [*Logging*] to accumulate logs in a yard.

yardbird **1.** *n* [*US*] [*Military*] a recruit or newly enlisted serviceman. **2.** *n* [*US*] [*Military*] a serviceman assigned to menial tasks and fatigues. **3.** also **yard jockey** *n* [*US*] [*Road transport*] See **hostler 2**.

yashmak *n* [*TV*] a type of diffuser that covers only the lower half of a lamp; it comes from the mask that covers all but the eyes of a devout Muslim woman.

YAVIS *n* [*Psychology*] acro **Young, Attractive, Verbal, Intelligent, Successful** those patients who are allegedly preferred by analysts to the less charming and less articulate but possibly more genuinely needy cases.

yearling *n* [*Stock market*] a stock issued by British municipal authorities, maturing within a year.

year-on-year *a* [*Economics*] referring to statistics which compare current figures with those of twelve months earlier.

yeasty *a* [*Wine-tasting*] used to describe a smell of ferments, alive or dead; it is a sure sign of impending secondary fermentation.

yell *n* [*Theatre*] a tremendous joke; it comes from the response that such a joke ought to obtain from the audience.

yellow alert *n* [*Military*] an alert that prepares troops for a state of initial war readiness. See also **red alert, white alert**.

yellow book *n* [*Government*] an official report of government affairs in various European countries.

yellow books *n pl* [*Government*] official government documents that are bound together and published in yellow-bound books by the French government; they are the equivalent of the British **blue books**.

yellow card *v* [*US*] [*Theatre*] a touring theatrical company does this when it requests the local labour unions to supply stagehands as and when they are needed.

yellow goods *n pl* [*Commerce*] products that are bought only rarely and which offer high profits to the retailer: cars, stereo equipment, computers, ect. See also **brown goods, red goods**.

yellow grease *n* [*Food*] an inedible fat obtained from the parts of hogs not used for making lard, from condemned animals or from refuse fat – it is used for lubrication. See also **white grease**.

yellow in the middle *n* [*US*] [*Railways*] See **diverging approach**.

yellow peril *n* [*Navy*] smoked haddock.

yellow room *n* [*Electronics*] the area of a silicon foundry in which the actual chips are assembled.

yellow sheets *n pl* [*US*] [*Stock market*] daily publications of the National Quotation Bureau that list details of the **over-the-counter** market in corporate bonds. See also **pink sheets**.

yellow union *n* [*Industrial relations*] See **scab union**.

yellow unions *n pl* [*Industrial relations*] company unions which have no real interest in representing the workers, but merely pander to the employer. It comes from a strike held in 1887 by miners at Montceau-les-mines in France; the company **scabs**, themselves union members, met, preparatory to breaking the strike, in a hall where they covered the windows in yellow paper to frustrate interested onlookers.

yellow-backs *n pl* [*Sex*] hard-core picture-books with only a token story-line.

yellowcake *n* [*Military*] uranium oxide which is used in the manufacture of nuclear weapons.

yellow-dog contract *n* [*Industrial relations*] a contract in which the employer offers a job only on condition that the worker will relinquish any current membership of a union and will not attempt subsequently to join a union or to encourage union activity in the plant. Such contracts are almost universally illegal.

yellow-dog democrat *n* [*US*] [*Politics*] a die-hard Democratic loyalist; it is only used to imply praise.

yellow-dog fund *n* [*Industrial relations*] a fund set aside for bribery and corruption or for paying off those who perform any distasteful task; such funds are illegal.

yellowhammer 1. *n* [*US*] [*Meat trade*] small common-bred cattle bred in the southern states. **2.** *n* [*Oil rigs*] an Ohio oil rig driller; it comes from the nickname of the inhabitants of the state.

yhuk *n* [*UK*] [*Surfing*] a distasteful person; it comes from the exclamation 'yuk!'.

yield 1. *n* [*Military*] the force of a nuclear explosion, expressed in the number of tons of TNT which would have been required to create an equivalent explosion. **2.** *v* [*Religion*] to give in or be receptive to the Holy Spirit; it is used particularly by a large group to an individual who is on the verge of acknowledging his/her belief.

yield gap *n* [*Finance*] the excess rate of return provided by long-term or undated Government stocks over ordinary stocks.

yield to weight ratio *n* [*Military*] the assessment of the force of a nuclear explosion by comparing the force of that explosion to the size of the bomb that caused it.

yip *v* [*Golf*] to hit the ball poorly when putting.

yips *n pl* [*Golf*] nervous fumbling and twitching that ruin one's concentration and one's swing.

yock *n* [*UK*] [*Market-traders*] an eye.

yoga art *n* [*Art*] a type of Indian art which uses 'nuclear' or 'power' diagrams as an aid to yoga meditation.

yogg *n* [*UK*] [*Market-traders*] a domestic fire, the hearth, etc.

yoking *n* [*Mining*] See **wedding** 1.

yolk *n* [*Weaving*] the combination of wool grease and **suint** in a fleece.

yomping *n* [*UK*] [*Military*] a Royal Marine term for marching with weapons and a 120lb. pack across appalling terrain in extremely hostile conditions, on the premise that once this ultimate in route marches is concluded, the troops will be prepared to fight a battle at the other end. Possibly it comes from a Norwegian word used by skiers to describe the crossing of obstacles.

yorer *n* [*UK*] [*Market-traders*] an egg.

yorker 1. *n* [*Cricket*] a ball pitched well up to the batsman, that is aimed at the blockhole or at the base of the stumps, and is intended to slip beneath the raised bat unless speedy evasive action can be taken. **2.** [*US*] [*Meat trade*] a hog weighing 160–190 lb; it is a popular choice among New York City butchers.

Yorkshire gallop *n* [*Horse-racing*] any trial race, irrespective of length or venue.

You bee owe *n* [*UK*] [*Government*] a pun on 'U.B.O.': the unemployment benefit office, labour exchange, 'job centre'.

young 1. *a* [*US*] [*Railways*] referring to a relatively inexperienced employee. **2.** also **youthful** *a* [*Wine-tasting*] used to describe a positive, attractive feature: fresh, immature, with youthful acidity.

yours *a* [*Finance*] used by dealers on the foreign exchange market to indicate that they are the sellers of the currency in question.

yo-yo 1. *v* [*Business*] said of a company which contracts alternately for large and for very small orders from the same supplier with the intention of keeping him off balance. The deliberate destabilisation of the business relationship is emphasised on a personal level – the client appears satisfied or unhappy at random, with no apparent reason for either emotion. The net result of such tactics is to win negotiating points in highly competitive businesses by putting a supplier into economic and emotional dependence on his client. **2.** *phr* [*TV*] acro **you're on your own** a genre of investigative programme in which one public and/or controversial figure is placed alone beneath the lights and is questioned at length and in detail by a panel of knowledgable experts and journalists who sit in the cool and quiet, just outside those lights.

yoyo mode *n* [*Computing*] a state in which a fault system alternates rapidly between being **up** and **down**, moving from one mode to the other and then back again for no apparent reason.

yo-yo stock *n* [*Stock market*] a stock that fluctuates from high to low prices with no apparent stable pattern emerging.

YP *n* [*UK*] [*Prisons*] abbr of **young prisoner**.

yrast *a* [*Science*] referring to any level of nuclear energy that is the lowest for some value of the spin.

yump *n* [*Cars, Rallying*] the action of a car flying through the air, or the sharp bump or crest that initiates the flight; it comes from the Scandinavian pronunciation of 'jump'. As stars of the rally circuit, their descriptions take pre-eminence.

Y

yumpsville *n* [*Film*] the unsophisticated rural and small town audience whose favourite films are a mix of sex and violence and in which it is advisable to keep the intellectual stimulus and dialogue down to a minimum.

YUP 1. *n* [*Sociology*] abbr of **young urban professional**. See also **YPA**. **2.** *n* [*Sociology*] abbr of **young upwardly-mobile professional**; generally found as 'yuppy' or 'yuppie'.

Z

z height *n* [*Printing*] See **x height**.

Z twist *n* [*Weaving*] the twist in yarn spun on a clockwise rotating spindle. See also **S twist**.

Z zones *n pl* [*Military*] in 1958 the UK government issued details of 'the provisional scheme for the control of the public under fallout conditions'. Belts of radioactivity following a nuclear explosion were divided into W, X, Y, and Z zones, with the radiation increasing in intensity in each successive zone and the possibility of survival, shelter or rescue becoming decreasingly likely. In an all-out attack on the UK, Z zones would include the destroyed urban centres, which are generally known to have been 'written off' by those who assess the chances of existence for anyone after a nuclear war.

zap 1. *v* [*Computing*] to use special equipment to erase the programmable read-only memory (see **PROM**). **2.** *v* [*US*] [*Medicine*] to administer electric shock treatment to a patient. **3.** *v* [*Military*] to attack, to kill. **4.** *v* [*Parachuting*] to land more than five metres from the target and thus to fail to score in a competition.

zareba *n* [*Navy*] the protective armour surrounding a gun turret.

Z'd frame *n* [*Custom cars*] a chassis modification which involves cutting the rear frame rails and then rewelding them in a stretched Z to lower the car. See also **C'd frame**.

zebra 1. *n* [*US*] [*Football*] an umpire; it comes from the black and white vertically striped shirts worn by the officials. **2.** *n* [*US*] [*Medicine*] any obscure diagnosis.

zephyr haul *n* [*US*] [*Road transport*] See **balloon freight**.

zero 1. *v* [*Computing*] to erase, to discard all data from a memory. **2.** *v* [*Computing*] to set to zero. **3.** *v* [*Military*] to set the sights of a weapon.

zero degree writing *n* [*Literary criticism*] a style of dispassionate writing pioneered by certain French novelists in which the normal attempts to evoke emotions, involvement and similar engagement with the story being told, by using metaphor, imagery, characterisation and the like, are rigorously excluded from the text.

zero delay *n* [*US*] [*TV*] the showing by **affiliates** of taped network shows just one week after they have been taped, ie: as soon as they have been distributed to the affiliate stations.

zero delta *n* [*Medicine*] no change (in a patient's condition).

zero downtick, also **zero-minus tick** *n* [*Stock market*] a sale of shares that takes place at the same price as that of the previous sale, but at a lower price than the last different price.

zero life *v* [*Aerospace*] to restore a formerly worn out aircraft to so excellent a condition that it can be rated as brand new, with zero previous wear and tear.

zero option *n* [*Military*] this originated as the 'Null Losung' (zero solution) by German Chancellor Helmut Schmidt in 1981 and was briefly espoused by President Reagan as a bargaining chip in the **INF talks**: if the USSR would scrap their medium range SS–20 missiles, then the US would not deploy **cruise**. This idea, more a propaganda ploy than a real policy, did not survive the talks but was revived in a variety of Soviet proposals during 1986–87.

zero uptick, also **zero-plus tick** *n* [*Stock market*] a sale of shares that takes place at the same price as existed at the last sale, but at a higher price than the last different price registered for those shares.

zero-balance *a* [*Banking*] referring to a bank account that is operating with no running balance and into which no more funds are transferred than are required to meet the drawings that are made on it.

zero-base budgeting, also **zero-line budgeting** n [*Government, Business*] the starting of every economic year with a budget which calls on all programmes, projects, and similar schemes that require funding, to justify their continuing claims on such funds. Under such a scheme nothing is sacred and anything may be discarded if it is unable to prove its efficiency and worthiness.

zero-basing n [*Economics*] the re-assessment of all current budgets by taking each project or requirement and checking it in detail from first principles onwards. The aim is to cut away the dead wood that has accrued to the project as it has progressed.

zero-coupon n [*Finance*] a bond that carries no interest but which is issued below its redemption price.

zero-energy a [*Science*] referring to a small nuclear reactor that develops so little power that no cooling and only minimal shielding are required to control its radio-activity.

zero-length a [*Aerospace*] said of a rocket launcher which is no longer than the rocket that it supports.

zero-minus tick n [*Stock market*] see **zero downtick**.

zero-norm n [*Economics*] during a period of pay restraint, this is the establishment of a norm of 0% for otherwise automatic annual pay increases.

zero-plus tick n [*Stock market*] See **zero uptick**.

zero-sum game 1. n [*Business*] a game theory conflict in which the advantage that accrues to one party is exactly equal to the disadvantage suffered by the other party. Such a 'game' works as a model for rivalries in a trade market, although it is naturally modified when that market is expanding. 2. n [*Politics*] a political or diplomatic confrontation in which there is no compromise; if one side wins, then the other side must lose; there is no feasible saving of face.

zero-zero 1. n [*Gliding*] ceiling and visibility are both 0. 2. n [*Military*] a nuclear weapons moratorium in which neither superpower would increase their nuclear arsenals; this was a short-lived concept that emerged during the **INF talks** of 1981–83 and did not survive their demise. See also **zero option**.

zero-zero seat n [*Aerospace*] an ejector seat which works safely at ground level (zero height) and when the aircraft is stationary (zero speed).

zest n [*New therapies*] in **co-counselling** this means the naturally positive and optimistic feelings experienced by a human being.

zestful a [*Wine-tasting*] used to describe a lively, crisply flavoured wine.

zing n [*Wine-tasting*] an exciting, refreshing attribute in a wine.

zinger n [*Politics*] a punchline at the end of a speech, or any line within a speech, that comes across with particular force and emotional impact; it comes from the similar use in show-business, especially by comedians.

zipper 1. n [*Military*] a combat air patrol that flies either at dawn or at dusk. 2. n [*Parachuting*] a freefall formation; it comes from the shape formed by the jumpers. See also **doughnut 6, star 2**.

zippers n pl [*US*] [*Football*] the permanent scars which disfigure the bodies of many US footballers after years of tough contact play.

zobbs n pl [*Fleet Air Arm*] hand signals made by a pilot.

zombie 1. n [*Gambling*] a gambler who betrays no emotions either when winning or losing. 2. n [*Gambling*] a horse that seems to have no appetite for racing.

zone centre n [*Telephony*] an exchange that acts as a switching service for a number of other exchanges.

zone of transition n [*Sociology*] the area immediately adjacent to the city centre in which older housing is being replaced by expanding businesses, offices, hotels, etc. Until this development is complete, the housing stock is allowed to decline while landlords await optimum prices. It is generally known as the inner city. See also **concentric zone theory**.

zone therapy n [*Medicine*] a therapeutic technique in which parts of the feet are massaged in accordance with their connection to various parts of the body.

zoo n [*US*] [*Marine Corps*] any jungle or jungle area.

zoo plane n [*Journalism, Politics*] the second of the two aircraft which convey a candidate, his entourage and the media around a Presidential campaign. The zoo plane is so named both because it is used by the TV techicians ('animals'), and also because it offers a generally more relaxed and enjoyable atmosphere in which to travel, than the reverential, earnest world of the plane in which the candidate himself travels.

zoom n [*TV, Film, Video*] any type of lens, whether for still or motion pictures, that has a variable length of focus; on film and video cameras this can be altered while shooting is actually in progress.

zoom bags n pl flying suits worn by fighter pilots.

zoo-zoos, also **wham-whams** n pl [*US*] [*Prisons*] confectionery purchased from automatic vending machines in the prison.

zugzwang n [*Chess*] the moving of a chess piece when under duress, rather than choosing the move one wishes.

zulu n [*Aerospace*] the aeronautical name for Greenwich Mean Time (GMT); it is so called since Greenwich is sited on 0° (zero degrees) longitude.

Z

Appendix A

Suffixes

-diplomacy *n* [*Politics*] volleyball-, baseball-, table-tennis-; these are all variations on **ping-pong diplomacy**, and all refer to the use of international sporting fixtures to make initial contact where previously there had been no official relations between (usually Western and Communist) nations. The terms are descendants of gunboat- (19th century), dollar- (early 20th), and shirtsleeve diplomacy (early 20th). See also **ping-pong diplomacy**.

-ed [*Medicine*] a popular suffix that is added to various medical instruments/procedures to render them slang; thus 'scoped' means to have undergone gastroscopy; 'bronked' mean 'bronchoscopy'; 'cathed' means 'catheterised', etc.

-gate *n* [*Media*] a scandal that features charges of cover-up and deliberate obfuscation by those determined to protect themselves. It comes from the US Watergate Affair, 1974, which brought down Richard Nixon. Famous '-gates' include Koreagate (the alleged bribery of US congressman by S. Korean officials, 1977), Muldergate (the corrupt espionage practices of S. African official Konnie Mulder, 1979), Lancegate (the various problems of US Government official Bert Lance, 1977), Volgagate (Russian bureaucrats), Winegate (a wine-labelling scandal), etc.

-intensive *a* [*Language*] an all-purpose suffix used for the embellishment of otherwise simpler concepts; eg. labour-intensive (laborious), capital-intensive (requiring heavy investment), brain-intensive (intellectually demanding), etc.

Appendix B

US restaurant number codes

2½ a small glass of milk.
5 a large glass of milk.
13 white bread; this is a coded warning indicating that the owner or manager is nearby.
14 a special order.
19 a banana split.
21 a limeade.
22 a customer's bill has not been paid.
23 'go away; leave me alone, I am working'.
30 'the restaurant is about to close'.
33 red a cherry Coke.

41 a lemonade or a small glass of milk.
48½ 'someone has been fired'.
51 hot chocolate.
55 a glass of root beer.
66 an empty bowl or glass; dirty dishes in general.
81 a large glass of water.
86 sold out or unavailable.
87½ 'look at the pretty girl'.
95 'a customer is trying to walk out without paying'.
99 'look out, the manager is coming'.

Sources

Books

Abercrombie, Nicholas et al., *The Penguin Dictionary of Sociology*, Penguin Books, Hardmondsworth, 1984.

Adams, Ramon F., *Western Words*, 2nd edn, University of Oklahoma Press, Norman, Oklahoma, 1968.

Alexander, Shana, *Very Much a Lady*, Little, Brown, Boston, 1983.

Androuet, Paul, *Guide du Fromage*, Omnibus Press, London, 1973.

Arlen, Michael, *The Camera Age*, Farrar, Straus & Giroux, New York, 1981.

Armstrong, Brian, *The Glossary of TV Terms*, Barrie & Jenkins, London, 1976.

Ashley, C. W., *The Ashley Book of Knots*, 1944, rev. edn, Faber & Faber, London, 1981.

Atyeo, Donald L., *Blood and Guts: Violence in Sports*, Paddington Press, London, 1979.

Augarde, T., *The Oxford Guide to Word Games*, Oxford University Press, Oxford, 1984.

Avis, F. C., *The Sportsman's Glossary*, Souvenir Books, London, 1960.

Avis, F. C., *Typeface Terminology*, Souvenir Books, London, 1965.

Baker, Sidney, *The Australian Language*, 2nd edn, Currawong Publishing, Sydney, Australia, 1966.

Bannock, Graham, Baxter, R. E., and Rees, Raj, *The Penguin Dictionary of Economics*, 2nd edn, Penguin Books, Harmondsworth, 1980.

Barnhart, Clarence L., Steinmetz, Sol, and Barnhart, Robert K., *A Dictionary of New English*, Longman, London, 1973.

Barnhart, Clarence L., Steinmetz, Sol, and Barnhart, Robert K., *The Second Barnhart Dictionary of New English*, Barnhart/Harper & Row, New York, 1980.

Barr, A. & York, P., *The Sloane Ranger Handbook*, Ebury Press, London, 1982.

Barron's Dictionary of Finance and Investment Terms, Barron's, Woodbury, New York, 1985.

Bennett, R. & Watson, J., *Philatelic Terms Illustrated*, 2nd edn, Stanley Gibbons Publications, London, 1978.

Berrey, Lester V., and Van Den Bark, Melvin, *American Thesaurus of Slang*, 2nd edn, Harrap, London, 1954.

Bonavia, David, *The Chinese*, Penguin Books, Harmondsworth, 1982.

Bowman, W. P., and Ball, R. H., *Theatre Language*, Theatre Arts Books, New York, 1961.

Boycott, Rosie, *Batty, Bloomers and Boycott*, Hutchinson, London, 1982.

Brander, Michael, *Dictionary of Sporting Terms*, A. & C. Black, London, 1968.

Brewer's Dictionary of Phrase and Fable, 2nd rev. edn, Cassell, London, 1981.

British Gas, *Glossary*, 1981.

British Surfing Association Handbook, 1981.

British Standards Institute glossaries.

Broadbent, Michael, *Pocket Guide to Wine-Tasting*, Mitchell Beazley, London, 1979.

Brown, Rachael, *The Weaving, Spinning & Dyeing Book*, 2nd edn, Routledge & Kegan Paul, London, 1983.

Bullock, Alan, and Stallybrass, Oliver (eds), *The Fontana Dictionary of Modern Thought*, Fontana/Collins, London, 1977.

Bullock, Alan & Woodings, R. B., *Fontana Dictionary of Modern Thinkers*, Fontana, London, 1983.

Butterfield, John, Parker, Philip and Honigmann, David, *What Is Dungeons and Dragons?*, Penguin Books, Harmondsworth, 1982.

Calder, Nigel, *Nuclear Nightmares*, Penguin Books, Harmondsworth, 1980.

Campbell, C., *War Facts Now*, Fontana Paperbacks, London, 1982.

Caputo, Philip, *A Rumour of War*, Arrow Books, London, 1978.

Clare, Anthony W., and Thompson, Sally, *Let's Talk About Me*, BBC Publications, London, 1981.

Clark, Al, *Raymond Chandler in Hollywood*, Proteus, London, 1982.

Clinton, Michael, *A Hunting We Will Go*, n.d.

Cockburn, Andrew, *The Threat*, New English Library, London, 1983.

Cohen, Dr. Sidney, *The Drug Dilemma*, McGraw-Hill, New York, 1976.

Coleridge, Nicholas, *Shooting Stars*, Heinemann, London, 1984.

Collinson, W. E., *Contemporary English*, B. G. Teubner, Leipzig and Berlin, 1927.

Commercial Vehicle Buyer's Guide, 1981.

Complete CB Slang Dictionary, 9th edn, Merit Publications, N. Miami, Fla., 1980.

Conway, Carle, *The Joy of Soaring*, The Soaring Society of America Inc., 1969.

Copeland, Miles, *The Real Spy World*, Weidenfeld & Nicolson, London, 1974.

Cornwall, Hugo, *The Hacker's Handbook*, Century, London, 1985.

Counihan, Martin, *A Dictionary of Energy*, Routledge & Kegan Paul, London, 1981.

Cox, Barry, Shirley, John, Short, Martin, *The Fall of Scotland Yard*, Penguin Books, Harmondsworth, 1977.

Crouse, Timothy, *The Boys on the Bus*, Ballantine Books, New York, 1973.

Davies, Peter, *Davies' Dictionary of Golfing Terms*, Simon & Schuster, New York, 1980.

De Sola, Ralph, *Crime Dictionary*, Facts on File, New York, 1982.

Deighton, Len, *Funeral in Berlin*, Hodder & Stoughton, 1964.

Derrida, Jacques, *Dissemination*, Editions du Seuil, Paris, 1972.

Dickson, Paul, *Words*, Arena Books, London, 1983.

Dictionary of Computing, Oxford University Press, Oxford, 1983.

Douglass, David & Krieger, Krieger, *A Miner's Life*, Routledge & Kegan Paul, London, 1983.

Driver, Christopher, *The British at Table*, Chatto & Windus, London, 1983.

Dunne, John Gregory, *Gone Hollywood*, E. P. Dutton, New York, 1976.

Dunne, John Gregory, *Sneak*, E. P. Dutton, New York, 1969.

Dunne, John Gregory, *Stunts*, E. P. Dutton, New York, 1976.

Dunne, John Gregory, *Tinsel*, E. P. Dutton, New York, 1974.

English Table Tennis Association, *Glossary*, 1982.

Ensrud, B., *The Pocket Guide to Cheese*, Muller, London, 1981.

Faust, Bernice, *Women, Sex and Pornography*, Penguin Books, Harmondsworth, 1980.

Federal Writers Project (New York), 'Lexicon of Trade Jargon', unpub. MS, in Library of Congress, 1939.

The Flier's Handbook, Pan Books, London, 1978.

Ford, Daniel, *The Button*, George Allen & Unwin, London, 1985.

Franklyn, Julian, *Rhyming Slang*, 2nd edn, Routledge & Kegan Paul, London 1981.

Fraser, Edward, and Gibbons, John, *Soldier and Sailor Words and Phrases*, George Routledge & Sons, London, 1925.

Freed, David, and Lane, Mark, *Executive Action*, Charisma Books, London, 1973.

French, D. & Saward, H., *A Dictionary of Management*, rev. edn, Pan Books, London, 1984.

Garrison, Paul, *Gliders: How To Build & Fly Them*, Drake Pubs, New York, 1978.

Goldman, Albert, *Elvis*, Allen Lane, London, 1981.

Gowers, Sir Ernest, *The Complete Plain Words*, 2nd edn, Penguin Books, Harmondsworth, 1973.

Grambs, David, *Literary Companion Dictionary*, Routledge & Kegan Paul, London, 1985.

Granada Television, *Some Technical Terms and Slang*, Granada Television, Manchester, n.d.

Granville, Wilfrid, *A Dictionary of Theatrical Terms*, André Deutsch, London, 1952.

Green, Jonathon, *The IT Book of Drugs*, Knullar Publications, London, 1971.

Greener, Michael, *The Penguin Dictionary of Commerce*, Penguin Books, Harmondsworth, 1979.

Gunston, Bill (ed.), *Jane's Dictionary of Aerospace Terms*, Macdonald & Jane's, London, 1980.

Halliwell, Leslie, *Halliwell's Filmgoer's Companion*, 5th edn, Granada Publishing, London, 1976.

Hamilton, J. Dundas, *Stockbroking Today*, Macmillan, London, 1968.

Hare, C. E., *The Language of Field Sports*, Country Life Books, London, 1949.

Hart, N. A. & Stapleton, J., *Glossary of Marketing Terms*, 2nd edn, Heinemann, London, 1981.

Harwood, M., *The Language of Photography*, Star Books, London, 1981.

Hayward, Brigadier P. C. H. (ed.), *Jane's Dictionary of Military Terms*, Maconald & Jane's, London, 1975.

Heinl, Captain Robert D., *The Marine Officer's Guide*, Naval Institute Press, Annapolis, Md., 1977.

Herr, Michael, *Dispatches*, Pan Books, London, 1977.

Hilgartner, Stephen, Bell, Richard C., and O'Connor, Rory, *Nukespeak: The Selling of Nuclear Technology in America*, Sierra Club Books, San Francisco, 1982.

Hodgkinson, H., *Doubletalk: The Language of Communism*, George Allen & Unwin, London, 1955.

Howard, Philip, *New Words for Old*, Hamish Hamilton, London, 1977.

Howard, Philip, *Weasel Words*, Hamish Hamilton, London, 1979.

Howard Philip, *Words Fail Me*, Hamish Hamilton, London, 1980.

Howe, R. W., *Weapons*, Sphere Books, London, 1980.

Hudson, Kenneth, *Dictionary of Diseased English*, Macmillan, London, 1977.

Hudson, Kenneth, *The Language of Modern Politics*, Macmillan, London, 1978.

Hudson, Kenneth, *The Jargon of the Professions*, Macmillan, London, 1978.

Hutt, Allen, *The Changing Newspaper*, Gordon Fraser, London, 1973.

International Confederation of Free Trade Unions, *Glossary of Trade Union Terms*, ICFTU, Brussels, 1972.

Jarrett, Dennis, *Good Computing Book for Beginners*, ECC Publications, London, 1980.

Jenkins, Dan, *Semi Tough*, Star Books, London, 1972.

Johannsen, Hanno, and Page, G. Terry, *International Dictionary of Management*, Kogan Page, London, 1975.

Johnson, Hugh, *Wine*, Mitchell Beazley, London, 1974.

Jones, Jack, and Morris, Max, *A–Z of Trades Unionism and Industrial Relations*, Heinemann, London, 1982.

Kaldor, Mary, *The Baroque Arsenal*, Andre Deutsch, London, 1982.

Kaplan, Donald M., and Schwerner, Armand, *The Domesday Dictionary*, Jonathan Cape, London, 1964.

Karas, Thomas, *The New High Ground*, New English Library, London, 1983.

Kempner, Thomas (ed.), *A Handbook of Management*, 3rd edn, Penguin Books, Harmondsworth, 1980.

Kennedy, William, *Billy Phelan's Greatest Game*, Penguin Books,

Harmondsworth, 1978.

Kidder, Tracy, *Soul of a New Machine*, Allen Lane, London, 1982.

Laffin, John, *The French Foreign Legion*, Dent, London, 1974.

Landig, Victor, *Basic Principles of the Funeral Service*, 1956.

Lasch, Christopher, *The Culture of Narcissism*, Sphere Books, London, 1979.

Lee, William (William Burroughs), *Junkie*, Ace Books, New York, 1953.

LeSure, James, *Guide to Pedaguese*, Harper & Row, New York, 1965.

Lind, L. *Sea Jargon*, Patrick Stephens, Cambridge, 1982.

Longman Concise Dictionary of Business English, Longman, London, 1985.

Maas, Peter, *The Valachi Papers*, G. P. Putnam's Sons, New York, 1968.

MacArthur, P., *Industrial Relations Terms*, Ashridge Management College, Berkhamsted, 1976.

McFadden, Cyra, *The Serial*, Pan Books, London, 1978.

Machlin, Milt, *The Gossip Wars*, Star Books, London, 1981.

McKenna, F., *A Glossary of Railwayman's Talk*, Ruskin College, Oxford, 1970.

Macmillan Dictionary of Data Communications, Macmillan Press, London, 1985.

Macmillan Dictionary of Information Technology, Macmillan Press, London, 1982.

McShane, Frank (ed.), *The Selected Letters of Raymond Chandler*, Jonathan Cape, London 1981.

Mager, N. H., and S. K., *The Morrow Book of New Words*, William Morrow, New York, 1982.

Mars, G. & Nicod, M., *The World of Waiters*, Allen & Unwin, London, 1984.

Maurer, David W., *The Language of the Underworld*, collected and edited by Allan W. Futrell and Charles B. Wordell, University Press of Kentucky, Lexington, Ky, 1981.

Maurer, David W., and Vogel, Victor H., *Narcotics and Narcotic Addiction*, 4th edn, Charles C. Thomas, Springfield, Ill., 1973.

Mencken, H. L., *The American Language*, Alfred Knopf, New York, 1936, Supplements 1945, 1948.

Michaels, Leonard, and Ricks, Christopher, *The State of the Language*, University of California Press, Berkeley, Calif., 1980.

Miller, Don Ethan, *The Book of Jargon*, Macmillan, New York, 1981.

Miller, Tony, and George, Patricia, *Cut! Print!*, O'Hara Publications, Los Angeles, Calif., 1972.

Milner, Christina and Richard, *Black Players*, Michael Joseph, London, 1973.

Milton, David, Milton, Nancy and Schurman, Franz (eds), *People's China 1966–72*, Penguin Books, Harmondsworth 1977.

Mitford, Jessica, *The American Way of Death*, Hutchinson, London, 1963.

Motor Magazine, *ABC Glossary*, 1980.

Moynahan, Brian, *Airport International*, Pan Books, London, 1978.

Mueller, Robert K., *Buzzwords: A Guide to the Language of Leadership*, Van Nostrand Reinhold, New York, 1974.

Nemmers, E. E., *Dictionary of Economics and Business*, Littlefield, Adams, Totowa, N.J., 1978.

Newman, G. F., *Sir, You Bastard*, Sphere Books, London, 1970.

Newman, G. F., *You Nice Bastard*, Sphere Books, London, 1972.

Newman, G. F., *You Flash Bastard*, Sphere Books, London, 1974.

Ogilvy, David, *Ogilvy on Advertising*, Pan Books, London, 1983.

Oliver, Gordon, *Marketing Today*, Prentice-Hall, Englewood, Cliffs, N.J., 1980.

Oxford Companion to Sports, Oxford University Press, Oxford.

The Oxford English Dictionary, 12 vols and Supplement, 1933; Supplements A-G (1972), H–N (1976), O-Scz (1982), Se-Z (1986), Oxford University Press, Oxford.

Palmer, Joseph (ed.), *Jane's Dictionary of Naval Terms*, Macdonald & Jane's, London, 1975.

Partridge, Eric, *A Dictionary of the Underworld*, 3rd edn, Routledge & Kegan Paul, London, 1968.

Partridge, Eric, *Slang, Yesterday and Today*, 4th edn, Routledge & Kegan Paul, London, 1970.

Partridge, Eric, *A Dictionary of Slang and Unconventional English*, 7th edn (two vols), Routledge & Kegan Paul, London, 1970.

Partridge, Eric, *A Dictionary of Slang and Unconventional English*, 8th edn, Routledge & Kegan Paul, London, 1984.

Pegg, B. F. & Stagg, W. D., *Plastering: A Craftsman's Encyclopedia*, Crosby Lockwood, London, 1976.

Pei, M., *Words in Sheep's Clothing*, George Allen & Unwin, London, 1970.

Perry, F. E., *Dictionary of Banking*, 2nd edn, MacDonald & Evans, 1983.

Phillips Petroleum, *Glossary*, Phillips Petroleum, London, 1981.

Plate, Thomas, and Darvi, Andrea, *Secret Police: The Inside Story of a Terror Network*, Robert Hale, London, 1982.

Powis, David, *The Signs of Crime*, McGraw-Hill (UK), London, 1977.

Prenis, John, *The Language of Computers*, Star Books, London, 1981.

Pringle, Peter, and Arkin, William, *SIOP*, Sphere Books, London, 1983.

Public Affairs Bureau, Washington, D.C., *A Dictionary of US Military Terms*, 1963.

Rawson, Hugh, *A Dictionary of Euphemisms and Other Doubletalk*, Macdonald, London, 1983.

Reader's Digest, *Success With Words*, Reader's Digest, New York, 1983.

Rodgers, Bruce, *The Queen's Vernacular*, Blond & Briggs, London, 1972.

Root, Waverley, *Food*, Simon & Schuster, New York, 1980.

Rosen, R. D., *Psychobabble*, Wildwood House, London, 1977.

Roth, Philip, *The Great American Novel*, Jonathan Cape, London, 1973.

Safire, William, *Safire's Dictionary of Politics*, rev. edn, Ballantine Books, New York, 1978.

Safire, William, *On Language*, Avon Books, New York, 1980.

Safire, William, *What's the Good Word*, Times Books, New York, 1982.

Safire, William, *I Stand Corrected*, Times Books, New York, 1984.

Sampson, Anthony, *The Changing Anatomy of Britain*, Hodder & Stoughton, London, 1982.

Santoli, Al, *Everything We Had*, Ballantine Books, New York, 1981.

Scarne, J., *Complete Guide to Gambling*, Simon & Schuster, New York, 1967.

Schulberg, Budd, *The Harder They Fall*, The Bodley Head, London, 1949.

Sciascia, Leonardo, *Mafia Vendetta*, Jonathan Cape, London, 1963.

Scotch Whisky: Questions & Answers, Scotch Whisky Association, Edinburgh, 1981.

Scruton, Roger, *A Dictionary of Political Thought*, Pan Books, London, 1982.

Sheppard, H., *Railway Slang*, Dillington House, Somerset, 1964.

Shem, Samuel, *The House of God*, Corgi Paperbacks, London, 1978.

Sipra, Harold, *Canine Terminology*. Harper & Row, New York, 1982.

6,000 Words: A Supplement to Webster's Third New International Dictionary, G. and C. Merriam, Springfield, Mass., 1976.

Soaring Flight Manual, Jeppeson Sanderson Inc., Englewood, Col., 1980.

Spencer, Donald D., *Computer Dictionary for Everyone*, Charles Scribner's Sons, New York, 1979.

Stephenson, Michael & Weal, John, *Nuclear Dictionary*, Longman, London, 1985.

St Maur, Suzan, *The A-Z of Video and Audio-Visual Jargon*, Routledge & Kegan Paul, London, 1986.

Sunday Times 'Insight' Team, *The Falklands War*, Sphere Books, London, 1982.

Talbott, Strobe, *Deadly Gambits*, Alfred Knopf, New York, 1984.

Tatchell, Peter, *The Battle for Bermondsey*, Heretic Books, London, 1983.

Taylor, J. B., *Plastering*, Godwin, London, 1970.

Timms, N. and R., *Dictionary of Social Welfare*, Routledge & Kegan Paul, London, 1982.

Toffler, Alvin, *The Third Wave*, Collins, London, 1980.

Uris, Leon, *Battle Cry*, Panther Books, London, 1953.

Versand, K., *The Polyglot's Lexicon*, Links Books, London, 1973.

Vogue Glossary of Fabrics, Condé Nast, London, 1985.

Walker, John A., *Glossary of Art, Architecture and Design since 1945*, 2nd rev. edn, Clive Bingley, London, 1977.

Wasey Campbell Ewald, Ltd., *Ad Jargon Dictionary*, Wasey Campbell Ewald, London, 1980.

Waterhouse, Keith, *Daily Mirror Style*, Mirror Books, London, 1981.

Webb, James, *Fields of Fire*, Granada Publishing, St Albans, Herts, 1978.

Webster's Third New International Dictionary, G. Bell & Sons, London, 1966.

Wentworth, Harold and Flexner, Stuart Berg, *Dictionary of American Slang*, 2nd supplemented edn, Thomas Y. Crowell, New York, 1975.

Whitaker, Ben, *The Police in Society*, Methuen, London, 1980.

Whiteside, T., 'The Blockbuster Complex', *New Yorker*, New York, 1981.

Wilczynski, Josef, *An Encyclopedia of Marxism, Socialism and Communism*, Macmillan, London, 1981.

Witherow, John, and Bishop, Patrick, *The Winter War*, Quartet Books, London, 1982.

Wodehouse, P. G., *The Clicking of Cuthbert*, Herbert Jenkins, London, 1922.

Wodehouse, P. G., *The Heart of a Goof*, Herbert Jenkins, London, 1926.

Wolfe, Tom, *The Right Stuff*, Farrar, Straus & Giroux, New York, 1979.

Wynn, Dilys, *Murder Ink*, Workman Publishing, New York, 1977.

Zuckermann, Solly (Lord), *Nuclear Illusion and Reality*, Collins, London, 1982.

Newspapers, Magazines, Broadcast Media

Newspapers: *Daily Express; Daily Herald; Daily Telegraph; Evening News; Guardian; Independent; New York Times* (US); *Observer; Standard; Sunday Times; Times; Today; Variety* (US); *Yorkshire Post.*

Magazines: *American Journal of Nursing* (US); *American Speech Magazine* (US); *Army* (US); *Byte Magazine* (US); *Collier's* (US); *Electronics Magazine; Electronics Weekly; Esquire* (US); *Esso Magazine; Futurist; HiFi Choice; Hi-Fi News & Record Review* (1978); *Hot Rod & Custom Magazine; International Video Yearbook* (1981); *Listener; Lore & Language; Marine Corps Gazette* (US); *Melody Maker; New Musical Express; New Statesman; Newsweek* (US); *New Times* (US); *New York* (US); *New York Review of Books* (US); *New York Times Magazine* (US); *Omni; Personal Computer World; Practical Computer; Practical Computing; Private Eye; Professional Printer Magazine; Psychology Today* (US); *Quill* (US); *Rolling Stone* (US); *Spectator; Streetlife; Television Magazine; Time* (US); *Travel News; Travel Trade Gazette; Tropic Magazine; Verbatim.*

Broadcast Media: BBC Radio 3; BBC–1 TV; BBC–2 TV; Channel–4 TV; Granada TV; Satellite TV News.